Speakers and Lecturers: How to Find Them

A Directory of Booking Agents, Lecture Bureaus, Companies, Professional and Trade Associations, Universities, and Other Groups which Organize and Schedule Engagements for Lecturers and Public Speakers on All Subjects, with Details about Speakers, Subjects, and Arrangements

Paul Wasserman
Managing Editor

Jacqueline R. Bernero
Associate Editor

Gale Research Company • Book Tower • Detroit, Michigan 48226 • 1979

Editorial Staff Manager: Effie Knight

Editorial Assistants: Laurence P. Fiedler, Jr., Margaret W. Fiedler, Elizabeth Kaszubski, Marek Kaszubski

Library of Congress Cataloging in Publication Data

Wasserman, Paul.
Speakers and lecturers.

Includes indexes.
1. Lectures and lecturing--United States--Directories.
I. Bernero, Jacqueline, joint author. II. Title.
PN4007.W3 808.5'1'02573 78-26025
ISBN 0-8103-0392-2

Table of Contents

PREFACE v
ORGANIZATION OF THE VOLUME vi
HOW TO USE THIS BOOK vii

Section I

SPEAKERS AND LECTURERS: HOW TO FIND THEM 1

Section II

SPEAKER INDEX 135

Section III

LECTURE TITLES AND KEYWORD INDEX 165

Section IV

GEOGRAPHIC INDEX 369

Section V

LIST OF SUBJECT HEADINGS 381
SUBJECT INDEX 384

PREFACE

Meetings in the United States which make use of speakers drawn from outside the convening organization undoubtedly run into the tens of thousands. The need for informed, knowledgeable, and lively lecturers is universal, but up to now there has not been a single, comprehensive book which brings together in one source information about agencies which handle speakers in all subject and geographical areas.

SPEAKERS AND LECTURERS: HOW TO FIND THEM seeks to fill this gap. It provides up-to-date, concise, and accurate details useful to program planners who require information about sources of speakers, as well as about the speakers themselves. It places the widest possible range of possibilities before persons responsible for arranging for speakers.

Sources of speakers covered in this volume are: Commercial lecture booking agencies; college and university speakers bureaus; companies which offer their employees as speakers; government agencies which provide speakers; and professional societies and trade associations which have speakers bureaus.

LISTINGS BASED UPON QUESTIONNAIRES

In order to assure the accuracy and currentness of each listing, the information published here has been taken from questionnaires completed by the organizations themselves, to whom the editors are very grateful. The descriptive material in listings is not intended as an evaluation or judgment of the organizations or of their speakers, and inclusion of an organization or individual is not an endorsement.

Anyone who is considering using a bureau or engaging a speaker is urged to contact previous users of the organization's services or officers of groups before which the prospective speaker has appeared; it is common for bureaus and speakers to offer such references, particularly if their fees are substantial.

USES AND INDEXES

The several ways in which this book may be used will depend upon the particular needs of its user. In some instances, speakers are available for modest or no fees, and this may be a criterion of choice. Some organizations will want to draw speakers from a particular region, while other groups may wish to bring before their audiences nationally and internationally prominent authorities. The volume is organized in such a way as to provide assistance with any of these requirements.

The organization of the work is basically by speaker bureau or lecture-arranging agency. In addition there are extensive indexes to the content, including indexes to more than 4,200 speakers and lecturers. Also included is a keyword approach to the content of their lectures, as well as a thorough-going subject index to all of the topics dealt with by these speakers. A geographic index facilitates locating speaker bureaus and booking agencies in the different regions and local areas.

The editors appreciate the help of Linda Stemmy, who typed the manuscript. Recognition must also be given to Gayle Batty for the meticulous effort of preparing the subject index.

Comments and suggestions of possible new entries will receive careful attention in the preparation of succeeding editions of this work.

ORGANIZATION OF THE VOLUME

The work is divided into five sections:

SECTION I, SPEAKERS AND LECTURERS: HOW TO FIND THEM is an alphabetical listing of the Speaker and Lecture Bureaus which form the basic content of this work. Under each entry number there is provided the following details whenever available:

> Name, Address and Description of Speakers Bureau sponsoring speakers - Speakers arranged alphabetically followed by their code number in parentheses - Titles of lectures arranged alphabetically under each speaker - Subjects covered arranged alphabetically under each speaker.

SECTION II, SPEAKER INDEX is an alphabetical listing of all lecturers mentioned in the book, followed by the entry numbers for the Speakers Bureaus and then the speaker code numbers in parentheses under which they are listed in Section I, Speakers and Lecturers: How to Find Them.

SECTION III, LECTURE TITLES AND KEYWORD INDEX arranges the titles alphabetically and by keyword providing entry numbers and speaker code numbers in parentheses for each to facilitate their look-up in the main body of the text, Section I, Speakers and Lecturers: How to Find Them.

SECTION IV, GEOGRAPHIC INDEX arranges Speakers Bureaus by state and city, followed by their entry numbers referring to their listings in Section I, Speakers and Lecturers: How to Find Them.

SECTION V, SUBJECT INDEX is a detailed and comprehensive list of subjects on which lecturers speak. The entry numbers and speaker code numbers given here refer back to the Speakers Bureau listings in Section I, Speakers and Lecturers: How to Find Them.

To facilitate identification of speakers in the indexes, each speaker is referred to by a code number. The number consists of the entry number, followed by a number in parentheses indicating the speaker's numbered sequential position in the Bureau's listing. For example, the citation 210(2) would refer to the second speaker listed in entry 210.

If the Speakers Bureau has identified subjects only, the entry number for the Bureau is used, and the citation does not include a number in parentheses.

HOW TO USE THIS BOOK

1. To locate a specific Speakers Bureau:

   Turn directly to the listings in Section I, SPEAKERS AND LECTURERS: HOW TO FIND THEM, where the Speakers Bureaus are arranged alphabetically. Each entry has also been assigned an entry number, as in the following illustration:

   ★ 205 ★
   UNITED STATES INTERNATIONAL COMMUNICATIONS AGENCY

   Listings in this section include Bureau name, address, telephone number, details of the general program, and information about speakers, topics, and terms and arrangements for lectures.

2. To locate a specific speaker:

   Turn to Section II, SPEAKER INDEX. This alphabet lists all the speakers and lecturers covered in the volume. The speaker's name is followed by the entry number for the Speakers Bureau or Bureaus which arrange for the speaker's services, and by the code number for the speaker, as in the following illustration:

   Lundgren, Jon C. 226(1)

   Turn to the entry number (in this example [226]) in Section I, SPEAKERS AND LECTURERS: HOW TO FIND THEM, where the Speakers Bureau is listed alphabetically. The speaker will be listed with his code number [(1)]:

   Example: ★ 226 ★
   WISCONSIN ELECTRIC POWER COMPANY

   Speaker: Jon C. Lundgren (1)

3. To locate topics or titles on which speakers are available:

   Turn to Section III, LECTURE TITLES AND KEYWORD INDEX. Titles and keywords for all the lectures listed in the volume are arranged alphabetically. Following the title or keyword, the entry number for the Speakers Bureau is given, followed by the code number for the speaker when a specific lecturer has been identified, as in the following illustrations:

   Doing Business in Saudi Arabia 210(2)
   Business in Saudi Arabia. Doing 210(2)
   Saudi Arabia Doing Business in 210(2)

   Turn to the entry number (in this example [210]) in Section I, SPEAKERS AND LECTURERS: HOW TO FIND THEM, where the Speakers Bureau is listed alphabetically. The lecture title will be listed following the name of the speaker [(2)].

   Example: ★ 210 ★
   UNITED TELECOMMUNICATIONS, INC.

   Speaker: R.V. Ward. Title: Doing Business in Saudi Arabia (2)

4. To locate Speakers Bureaus included in this volume according to their location:

   Turn to Section IV, GEOGRAPHIC INDEX, where Speakers Bureaus are listed under state and then city, followed by their entry number, as in the following illustration:

   COLORADO

   Lakewood

   Concerns of People, Inc. 39

Turn to the entry number (in this example [39]) in Section I, SPEAKERS AND LECTURERS: HOW TO FIND THEM, where the Speakers Bureau is listed alphabetically.

5. To locate Speakers Bureaus and their lecturers according to the broad general subjects in which they specialize:

   Turn to Section V, SUBJECT INDEX, and check under the subject being sought. Under each subject are listed the Speakers Bureau and its entry number, followed by speaker(s) and code number(s), as in the following illustration:

   FINANCIAL MANAGEMENT

   Dial Corporation 48
   Glazer, Edward (1)

   Turn to the entry number (in this example [48]) in Section I, SPEAKERS AND LECTURERS: HOW TO FIND THEM, where the Speakers Bureau is listed alphabetically.

   Example: ★ 48 ★
   DIAL CORPORATION

   Speaker: Edward Glazer. Title: Speak up for Credit (1)

SECTION I

SPEAKERS AND LECTURERS: HOW TO FIND THEM

This section contains an alphabetical listing of the speaker and lecture bureaus which form the basic content of this work. In each numbered entry the following details are provided, whenever available:

Name, address and description of speakers bureau sponsoring speakers - Speakers arranged alphabetically followed by their code number - Titles of lectures arranged alphabetically under each speaker - Subjects covered arranged alphabetically under each speaker.

A

★ 1 ★
THE AHMADIYYA MOVEMENT IN ISLAM, INC.
2141 Leroy Place, N.W.
Washington, D. C. 20008 (202) 232-3737

Speakers are available to lecture on The Ahmadiyya Movement in Islam.

Speaker: Yahya Sharif Abdullah. Titles: From Judaism to Islam; Fundamental Principles of Islam; Jesus in the Quran; New World Order of Islam (1)
Speaker: Imam Masud Ahmad. Titles: Ahmadiyyat or the True Islam; Islam and the World Peace; Islam as Religion of Humanity; Islam Versus Christianity; Islamic Conception of God; Islamic Morals; Muhammad the Liberator of Woman (2)
Speaker: Mubashir Ahmad. Titles: Existence of God; Islamic Conception of Caliphat; Islamic Conception of Purpose of Life (3)
Speaker: Rashid Ahmad. Titles: Islam the Final Religion for Mankind; Life After Death; A Man Relationship With God (4)
Speaker: Qazi M. Barkatullah. Titles: Jesus as Precursor of The Holy Prophet Muhammad; The Promised Messiah and the Signs of the Time; Unity Versus Trinity (5)
Speaker: Bashir Ahmad Bhatti. Titles: The Basic Principles of Islam; In Defense of the Holy Quran; Proofs of the Existence of God (6)
Speaker: Hasan Hakeem. Titles: Ahmadiyyat or The True Islam; Islam the Only Solution for the World Problems; Islam Versus Christianity (7)
Speaker: Imam Ata Ullah Kaleem. Titles: The Appearance of the Promised Messiah and the Promised Mahdi; A Glimpse into the Life and Teachings of Muhammad; Islamic Conception of God; Islamic Worship; Jesus in The Holy Quran; Life After Death; Muhammad in the Bible; Prayer and its Effectiveness; Salvation; The Second Advent of Christ and its Fulfillment; A Short Sketch of Islam (8)
Speaker: Daud Abdul Malik. Titles: Discovery of Soloman Gold Mines; Islam in Africa; Proofs Concerning Jesus' Survival from Death on the Cross (9)
Speaker: Saeed Ahmad Malik. Titles: Peculiarities of Islam; Kingdom of God and Secret of Adam's Slip; Why I Believe in Ahmadiyyat (10)
Speaker: Khalil Ahmad Nasir. Titles: Ahmadiyyat the True Islam; Islam and the World Problems; Islamic View Point on Any Aspect of Man's life; The Object of Man's Creation and the Means of its Attainment (11)
Speaker: Munawar Saeed. Titles: The Holy Prophet Muhammad as an Examplar; Islamic Prayer; The Principles of Islam (12)
Speaker: A. Muzaffar Ahmad Zafr. Titles: Equality and Brotherhood in Islam; The Holy Prophet Muhammad as Benefactor of Humanity; Islam my Best Choice (13)

★ 2 ★
AMERICAN COLLECTORS ASSOCIATION, INC.
4040 West 70th Street
Post Office Box 35106
Minneapolis, Minnesota 55435 (612) 926-6547

Members of the Association speak to different types of audiences on topics related to consumer credit and collections, directed both to the credit grantor and the credit user. Expenses and an honorarium are expected to be paid.

★ 3 ★
AMERICAN GRADUATE SCHOOL OF INTERNATIONAL MANAGEMENT
Thunderbird Campus
Glendale, Arizona 85306 (602) 938-7000

Arranges for speakers who are academics and/or business executives turned professors, to lecture on a wide range of topical areas. Fees range from $200 to $500, plus expenses.

Speaker: R. Duane Hall. Titles: Advertising/ Promotion Around the World; Helpful Hints for Hopeful Heroes (1)
Speaker: Akihisa Kumayama. Title: Development and use of Chinese Alphabet (2)
Speaker: Robert McMahon. Titles: Bank Marketing Storing and Selling Dollar; The Checkless Society (3)
Speaker: Robert T. Moran. Titles: Doing Business in Saudi Arabia; The Management of Change (4)
Speaker: Issa Peters. Titles: After Lebanon, What Next?; Middle East Oil in a Revolutionary Age (5)
Speaker: Helmut R. Roessler. Titles: The German Manager; Social Insurance in Germany (6)
Speaker: Jorge H. Valdivieso. Title: The Law of the Sea (7)
Speaker: George M. Wattles. Titles: An Escape from Poor Postal Service; Freedom versus Security (8)

★ 4 ★
AMERICAN INSTITUTE FOR EXPLORATION
1809 Nichols Road
Kalamazoo, Michigan 49007 (616) 381-8237

Speakers lecture on travel-adventure and field sciences, wildlife studies and environmental action. Fees vary with speaker and length of program.

Speaker: Ruthann Allen. Titles: Exploring the Aleutians; Flying Free (1)
Speaker: John Alley. Titles: Nepal Photo Diary; Photographing Nature (2)
Speaker: Ted P. Bank II. Titles: Exploring Backdoor to Siberia; How Man Came to the New World; Humor in Exploration; Living with the Eskimos; Sense and Nonsense About Race (3)
Speaker: Herman Kitchen. Titles: The Bald Eagle - National Symbol; In Search of the Santa Maria; Wildlife Filming and Conservation (4)
Speaker: Peter Lipsio. Title: Romance of Undersea Archaeology (5)
Speaker: Jay Ellis Ransom. Titles: Alaskan Adventures; The Aleut-Eskimos; Hunting for Gems and Fossils (6)
Speaker: Richard Williams. Titles: Biofeedback; Experiences with Mind Control; Exploring the Unconscious (7)

★ 5 ★

AMERICAN MONTESSORI SOCIETY
150 Fifth Avenue
New York, New York 10011 (212) 924-3209

Speakers are prepared to lecture on all phases of the Montessori curriculum. Fees vary.

Subjects: Child Psychology; Class Management; Dance and Movement; Day Care Programs; Nutrition

★ 6 ★

THE AMERICAN PARTY
100 River Road
Pigeon Forge, Tennessee 37863 (615) 453-6111

Speakers are available to lecture on topics related to the platform of The American Party.

Speaker: Tom Anderson. Subjects: The Constitution; Defense; Economics; Foreign Aid; God (1)
Speaker: Percy Greaves. Subject: Economics (2)
Speaker: Rufus Shackelford. Subjects: The Constitution; Defense; Economics; Foreign Aid; God (3)

★ 7 ★

AMERICAN POLYGRAPH ASSOCIATION
3105 Gumwood Drive
Hyattsville, Maryland 20783 (301) 779-5530

An organization of professionals who use the polygraph as a lie detector instrument as part of their work. Principal officers of the association are available for public lectures on the ways in which the polygraph is designed for effective use. Fees vary. Expenses are expected to be paid.

Speaker: Walter F. Atwood. Subject: Polygraph (1)
Speaker: Raymond J. Weir, Jr. Subject: Polygraph (2)

★ 8 ★

AMERICAN PROFESSIONAL PRACTICE ASSOCIATION
292 Madison Avenue
New York, New York 10017 (212) 949-5960

Lecturers are prepared to speak to local, state and nationally recognized medical and dental groups about almost any area relating to practice management, retirement planning, estate planning, wills and trusts, and other economic topics relating to the business side of a doctor's practice. When a speaker can be provided locally, there is no charge to a recognized medical or dental group. When a nationally known figure is involved, travel expenses and a modest honorarium are charged.

Speaker: Ralph T. Biddle. Title: All Aspects of Practice Management (1)
Speaker: Edmund G. Brown, Sr. Title: A Former Governor Looks At Health Programs (2)
Speaker: Wesley W. Hall, Sr. Title: Early and Current Economic Education of Young Doctors (3)
Speaker: Eugene J. Keogh. Title: The Need for Retirement Planning (4)
Speaker: Max L. Lewis. Title: Estate Planning for Doctors and Their Spouses (5)
Speaker: Eugene McCarthy. Title: The Rising Cost of Health Care (6)
Speaker: John W. Savage, Jr. Title: The Need for Doctors to Get Involved in Politics (7)
Speaker: Henry Schick. Title: Deferred Compensation Plans for Doctors (8)
Speaker: Arnold Slavet. Title: Professional Corporations and the Doctor (9)
Speaker: Barry Ross Weiner. Title: Estate Planning for Doctors (10)

★ 9 ★

AMERICAN RADIO RELAY LEAGUE
225 Main Street
Newington, Connecticut 06111 (203) 666-1541

Speakers seek to promote ham radio use throughout the United States and Canada. Fees vary.

Speaker: Peter O'Dell. Title: Interference to Your Television (1)

★ 10 ★
THE AMERICAN SUNBATHING ASSOCIATION, INC.
810 North Mills Avenue
Orlando, Florida 32803 (305) 896-8141

Speakers offer lectures to educate the public on nudism.

Speakers: Betty Jane Bond (1); Nate Kates (2); Roland R. Senecal (3)

★ 11 ★
AMERICAN TEILHARD ASSOCIATION FOR THE FUTURE OF MAN
867 Madison Avenue
New York, New York 10021 (212) 861-3240

The association sponsors lectures dealing both with the thought of the French Jesuit paleontologist Pierre Teilhard de Chardin and the many issues relating to the direction, purpose and meaning of life. Fees and other arrangements are made with the individual speakers.

Speaker: Thomas Berry. Title: Changing Religious-Cultural Ideas (1)
Speaker: Anne Brennan. Title: Teilhard and the Feminine (2)
Speaker: Beatrice Bruteau. Title: Teilhard and Philosophy (3)
Speaker: Evert Cousins. Title: Religion and the Future (4)
Speaker: Robert Francoeus. Title: Teilhard and New Biology (5)
Speaker: Donald Gray. Title: Teilhard's Religious Ideas (6)
Speaker: Alice Knight. Title: Episcopal Church Groups (7)
Speaker: R. Wayne Kraft. Title: Teilhard and Science (8)
Speaker: Margaret Lynch. Title: Inspirations (9)

★ 12 ★
AMERICANS UNITED
8120 Fenton Street
Silver Spring, Maryland 20910 (301) 589-3707

Speakers specialize in matters dealing with separation of church and state relations. Expenses of lecturers are paid by organizations sponsoring the lectures.

Speakers: E. Mallary Binns (1); Edd Doerr (2); E. Don Giddens (3); Andrew Leigh Gunn (4); Adelle Holloman (5); Richard F. McFarland (6); Albert J. Menendez (7); James W. Respess (8); Gioele Settembrini (9)
Titles: Freedom's Unfinished Tasks; The Future of Church Tax Exemptions; The Myth of Humanism in the Public Schools; Public Utility Invisible Taxes for Religion; Religion and Public Education; Religious Kidnapping and Deprogramming; Religious Liberty and Our Third Century; Should Government Support Church Colleges?; Tax Support for Sectarian Schools?; Transcendental Meditation in Public Schools

★ 13 ★
ANCIENT ARTS OF THE FUTURE
210 Main Street
Evanston, Illinois 60202 (312) 869-6999

Presents lectures on palmistry, acupuncture, astrology and psychic awareness. Fee is $500 plus expenses.

Speaker: Justin Pomeroy. Subjects: Acupuncture; Palmistry (1)
Speaker: Marcella Ruble Rook. Subjects: Astrology; Psychic Awareness (2)

★ 14 ★
ASIAN SPEAKERS BUREAU
86 Riverside Drive
New York, New York 10024 (212) 799-2600

Provides expert speakers who deal with Far Eastern affairs and with the political, economic and cultural issues of this part of the world. Fees vary. Detailed information supplied upon request.

Speakers: Anthony Bouscaren (1); Teh-Kuang Chang (2); Duk-Shin Choi (3); Chow Ching-Wen (4); Richard G. Ciccolella (5); Joseph N.P. Dang (6); Raymond de Jaegher (7); Saiji Hasegawa (8); Michael Jala (9); Walter H. Judd (10); Masahide Kanayama (11); Watana Keovimol (12); Hyung I. Kim (13); Myong Whai Kim (14); Anthony Kubek (15); Han Lih-Wu (16); John S. McCain, Jr. (17); Robert Morris (18); Andrew C. Nahm (19); Stephan C.Y. Pan (20); Chung Soo Park (21); Stefan T. Possony (22); David N. Rowe (23); Phyllis Schlafly (24); Pauline N. Van Tho (25)

★ 15 ★

ASSOCIATED FILM ARTISTS
6391 Vicanna Drive
San Jose, California 95129 (408) 257-0880

Experts narrate details about different countries and cultures while showing films of these regions. Fees vary.

Speaker: Chris Borden. Titles: Afghanistan; Bali; Faces of France; Iran; Ireland; Micronesia, America's Pacific Paradise; Nepal; Portugal; Switzerland (1)
Speaker: Clay Francisco. Titles: Argentina; Brazil; Czechoslovakia and Ukraine; Greece; Israel: Then and Now; Morocco: Cities, Seas, Sahara; The Russian Experience (2)
Speaker: John Jay. Titles: Ski Down the Years; Switzerland in Winter; Winter Holidays in the Americas; Winter Magic Around the World (3)
Speaker: Ed Lark. Titles: Ceylon; Germany; Hawaii; Norway; San Francisco; Scotland and Wales; Taiwan; Vanishing Old West (4)
Speaker: Ken Wolfgang. Titles: Austria; In Search of Singapore; India; Legendary Siam; Soul of Japan (5)

★ 16 ★

AUBURN UNIVERSITY
Speakers Bureau
Auburn, Alabama 36830 (205) 826-4075

Lecturers are available to speak on a wide variety of topics of general and specific interest to civic clubs and organizations in the state of Alabama and in towns near the border in Georgia. There are no fees.

Speaker: Murray C. Adams. Titles: Arts in Society; Community Power; Power in Interpersonal Relationships (1)
Speaker: Raymond S. Askew. Titles: Community Recreation Facilities; A Look at Energy Research; Solid Wastes and Their Management - Garbage or Gold? (2)
Speaker: Kenneth M. Autrey. Title: U.S. Food Abundance in a Hungry World (3)
Speaker: Wilford S. Bailey. Titles: Biomedical Research; Veterinary Medical Education; Veterinary Parasitology (4)
Speaker: Ben B. Barnes. Title: The Computer's Role on the University Campus (5)
Speaker: Mary E. Barry. Titles: Consumer Product Safety; International Trade With China; Is the Sales Person Dead? (6)
Speaker: Gene A. Bramlett. Titles: Economic or Community Development; Quality of Life; University Extension or Public Service (7)
Speaker: Robert N. Brewer. Title: Solar Energy to Heat Farm Buildings (8)
Speaker: David B. Brown. Title: Highway and Traffic Safety (9)
Speaker: Mary Quinn Burkhart. Titles: Career Development for Women; The Continuing Education Program (10)
Speaker: Chester C. Carroll. Titles: The Social Responsibility of Engineers and Research Scientists; What Research Means to the University (11)
Speaker: A. Ray Cavender. Titles: Cooperative Extension Programs; Community Resource Development (12)
Speaker: Samuel Terry Coker. Titles: Drug Abuse; Poison Prevention; Poisonous Plants; Silent Killer - Hypertension (13)
Speaker: Donald E. Davis. Title: Pesticides, Pollution and Politics (14)
Speaker: Neil O. Davis. Title: The Newspaper and the Bicentennial (15)
Speaker: Norman D. Davis. Title: Mushrooms of Alabama (16)
Speaker: Robert D. Davis. Titles: Stock Market Speculation; Winemaking (17)
Speaker: J.W. Duncan. Titles: Aerobics, the Art of Keeping Physically Fit; Personnel Administration in the Public Schools; Soviet Espionage in North America (18)
Speaker: Charles P. Edmonds III. Titles: Managing a Personal Budget in Today's Economy; Using Credit (19)
Speaker: Charles N. Fortenberry. Titles: Programs of the Present Congress; Trends and Changes in Southern Politics (20)
Speaker: James F. Foy. Titles: Development of the University Student; The Spiritual Revival on the University Campus; Student Life on the University Campus; Student Participation in University Policy Making; Values of Today's College Student (21)
Speaker: Harry Frank. Titles: Adult Competency Education versus Traditional Courses; Career Education for Adults (22)
Speaker: W. Harold Grant. Titles: Are Students Today Better Prepared for a College Education?; College Students: How Have They Changed?; Professors and Their Impact on Students (23)
Speaker: B. Eugene Griessman. Titles: The Future of the South; Race Relations; The Southern Experience (24)
Speaker: Charles A. Gross. Title: Energy Conservation (25)
Speaker: David M. Hall. Title: History of Alabama Counties (26)
Speaker: Sherman D. Hanna. Title: Consumer Affairs Legislation (27)
Speaker: Ian R. Hardin. Titles: Flame Retardant Textiles; Man-Environment Relations (28)

Speaker: A. Cleveland Harrison. Titles: The Role of the University Theatre; Theatre in the Community (29)

Speaker: Kirby L. Hayes. Titles: Contraceptives for Population Control; The World Food Situation; World Populations and Their Trends (30)

Speaker: James Hendrick. Title: Saving Energy While Increasing Agriculture Production (31)

Speaker: Charles J. Hiers. Titles: How to Train A Professional Artist; Japanese Art History; Printmaking (32)

Speaker: Earl B. Higgins. Titles: College Student Growth; Community Development; Development of Minority and Underprivileged Children (33)

Speaker: Walter B. Hitchcock, Jr. Titles: The Achievement of Nationality in American Literature; The Writing Crisis (34)

Speaker: Norma G. Hodson. Titles: The Emotionally Disturbed Child and Family; Marriage and Family Relations; Marriage Counseling (35)

Speaker: George R. Horton. Titles: American Transportation Problems; Cooperation Between the University and the Business Community; Facing Employment with a College Degree (36)

Speaker: Donald R. House. Titles: Government Policy and the Economy; Inflation: Causes and Cures (37)

Speaker: Milford Kenneth Howard. Title: Care of the Athlete (38)

Speaker: Dale L. Huffman. Titles: Meat in a Hungry World; New Technology in the Meat Industry (39)

Speaker: J. David Irwin. Titles: Careers in Engineering; Engineering (40)

Speaker: Wartan A. Jemian. Titles: Chamber Music; Modern Materials Science (41)

Speaker: Stephen R. Jenkins. Titles: Officiating High School Football; Water, Water Everywhere--and Not a Drop to Drink (42)

Speaker: Gerald W. Johnson. Titles: Human Relations Motivation; State and Local Government (43)

Speaker: Albert F. Killian. Titles: The Alabama National Guard; Antique Automobiles (44)

Speaker: Nelson B. King. Titles: Animal Diseases and the Resultant Food Loss; Food and Agriculture Organization of the United Nations (45)

Speaker: Gary W. Kiteley. Titles: Expansion of the Auburn Airport; General Aviation and the Community Airport (46)

Speaker: John W. Kuykendall. Title: Status of Religion in America (47)

Speaker: Ben T. Lanham. Titles: Administration and Colleges Today; Plans and Problems of Education in the Seventies (48)

Speaker: Worth Lanier. Title: Project H.E.L.P. (Health Education Learning Program) (49)

Speaker: Alfred M. Leppert. Title: Energy from Garbage (50)

Speaker: W. David Lewis. Titles: Science Fiction; Technology and Religion; Technology and the Future of the South (51)

Speaker: Taylor D. Littleton. Title: The Nature of Undergraduate Education (52)

Speaker: R.T. Lovell. Titles: Growing Fish to Increase World Protein Supply; Human Nutrition in Developing Countries (53)

Speaker: R. Warren McCord. Titles: Community and Regional Planning and Development; Land Use Planning (54)

Speaker: Malcolm C. McMillan. Titles: Alabama Government; Governors of Alabama; Yesterday's Birmingham (55)

Speaker: John Stokes Martin. Titles: Public School Curriculum; Trends in Educational Administration (56)

Speaker: Mark E. Meadows. Titles: College Students: How Have They Changed?; Improving Personal Effectiveness Through Facilitative Communication (57)

Speaker: William W. Morgan. Title: How to Improve Safety in the Home (58)

Speaker: Daniel J. Nelson. Title: Relationship of the United States to the United Nations (59)

Speaker: David S. Newton. Titles: Health Care Services; Pharmacy Services (60)

Speaker: Joan Stidham Nist. Titles: The Bicentennial of Children; Roman Grandeur (61)

Speaker: Awbrey G. Norris. Titles: Career Opportunities in the Military; Computer-Assisted Instruction; The Military Budget; The New Military (62)

Speaker: Henry P. Orr. Titles: Flower Arranging; Landscape Gardening; Landscape Plant Materials (63)

Speaker: Lillian Unger Pancheri. Titles: Ethical and Social Problems in Medicine; Quilts and Quilting (64)

Speaker: Patrick F. Pendergast. Title: Criminal Justice (65)

Speaker: Donald Y. Perkins. Title: The Scope of Horticulture Research and Teaching (66)

Speaker: Phyllis P. Phillips. Title: Speech and Language Disorders (67)

Speaker: Charles B. Roberts. Titles: Alabama's Student Financial Assistance Program; The Cost of a College Education (68)

Speaker: B.T. Robertson. Title: Veterinary Findings Which May Lead to Human Cures (69)

Speaker: R. Dennis Rouse. Title: One Hundred Years of Agricultural Research (70)

Speaker: Kenneth S. Rymal. Titles: Food Composition, Food Safety and Food Fermentations; Home Canning and Freezing (71)

Speaker: Charles G. Schroeder. Titles: College Student Growth; Getting Back to Nature; The Wilderness Experience (72)

Speaker: Alan John Shields. Title: Halfway Houses (73)

Speaker: Jack Simms. Titles: How the News is Collected; The Sports Explosion (74)

Speaker: J. Michael Sprott. Titles: Alabama Agriculture; Alabama Cooperative Extension Service (75)
Speaker: Eugene E. Stanaland. Title: Economic Conditions (76)
Speaker: Jon J. Tanja. Titles: The Emerging Clinical Role of the Pharmacist; The Use of Intravenous Fluids (77)
Speaker: Wilbur A. Tincher. Titles: Academic Credit for Work Experience; Adult Contemporary Education versus Traditional Courses; Are Students Today Better Prepared for a College Education? (78)
Speaker: Thomas M. Tole. Title: Investments and Today's Economy (79)
Speaker: Reginald I. Vachon. Titles: Energy Alternatives; Energy Conservation; How You Can Save Energy in the Home; Legal Problems to Avoid in Everyday Life (80)
Speaker: Lidia M. Vallarino. Titles: Community Mental Health; Humanism in the Classroom; The Indian Subcontinent - Bangladesh, Pakistan, India; Law with University Students; Psychology of Women (81)
Speaker: Frank Vandegrift. Titles: Career Planning for Young People; Total Education Through Cooperative Education (82)
Speaker: John C. Walden. Titles: Legal Aspects of Education; The Politics of Education (83)
Speaker: Richard W. Warner, Jr. Titles: Drug Abuse Prevention; Helping Your Child Become High on Life (84)
Speaker: John D. Weete. Title: Earthy Odors in Drinking Water (85)
Speaker: Ed Wegener. Titles: The Role and Responsibility of Public Television; Twenty Years of Educational Television (86)
Speaker: J. Herbert White. Titles: The Responsibilities of Public Institutions to the Taxpaying Public; Speak Out for Higher Education (87)
Speaker: Louis Edward White. Titles: Bringing About Change in a Bureaucracy; Life-Long Education (88)
Speaker: Stanley P. Wilson. Titles: Agricultural Research; Food Production and World Population (89)
Speaker: Richard M. Wingard. Titles: Data Processing in Pre-Costing Meals; Institutional Food Services (90)
Speaker: Joseph H. Yeager. Titles: Agriculture Outlook; Farm Real Estate Value Trends; Significance of Agriculture and Agribusiness on the Economy (91)

B

★ 17 ★
BALD HEADED MEN OF AMERICA
211 North King Avenue
Post Office Box 'Bald'
Dunn, North Carolina 28334 (919) 892-7365

The organization's founder is available for humorous public speaking engagements on baldness. A minimum fee of $100 plus travel expenses and lodging is required.

Speaker: John T. Capps. Title: The Bare Facts (1)

★ 18 ★
BALTIMORE FEDERAL SAVINGS AND LOAN ASSOCIATION
Fayette and St. Paul Streets
Baltimore, Maryland 21202 (301) 685-7000

Lecturers are provided to speak to organizations, clubs, churches, civic and community groups, and business firms on money, retirement and other financially related matters. There are no fees.

Speaker: T. Frank Sheehan. Titles: Dedicated Dollars; Direct Deposit of Social Security Checks; Energy-Saving Homes for Profit and Comfort; The Extra Mile; Tax-Deferred Individual Retirement Accounts; Tax-Deferred Keogh Retirement Accounts (1)

★ 19 ★
BEECH AIRCRAFT CORPORATION
9709 East Central
Wichita, Kansas 67201 (316) 681-7603

Arranges for lectures by company officials at state and national conventions of non-aviation groups. No fees.

Speaker: Marvin B. Small. Title: General Aviation Benefits the Nation (1)

★ 20 ★
BETHLEHEM STEEL CORPORATION
Bethlehem, Pennsylvania 18016 (215) 694-3131

The company sponsors lectures to different types of groups on a variety of business and public affairs subjects of current interest. No fees are charged.

Titles: Balancing the Scales; Big Business; Fuel for the Future; The King-Size Clean-Up; Laughing Matters; Steel Imports; The Steel Industry; Understanding Profits

★ 21 ★
BLACKMAN AND RABER LIMITED
545 Fifth Avenue
New York, New York 10017 (212) 986-1420

Speakers are provided for engagements to talk with groups about topics relating to sports and athletic events. Fees vary.

★ 22 ★
BURNS SPORTS CELEBRITY SERVICE, INC.
One IBM Plaza, Suite 3615
Chicago, Illinois 60611 (312) 321-1650

A booking agency specializing in arranging for speakers drawn from the ranks of sports celebrities in many athletic fields.

★ 23 ★
BUSINESS COMMUNICATION COUNCIL
1441 Kapiolani Boulevard, Suite 1505
Honolulu, Hawaii 96814 (808) 941-7722

Fifty business executives and middle managers comprise the speakers bureau. They lecture on economic topics and on their own business operations.

Titles: Advertising and Promotion; Attitudes about Business; Bankruptcies; Basic Economic Concepts; Business/Government Relations; Careers in Accounting and Finance; Collective Bargaining in Private Industry; Employee Benefit Programs; Energy Conservation; Financial Planning and Management; Free Enterprise; General Sales and Marketing; How a Career in Business Can Bring Personal Fulfillment in Life; How Businesses are Financed; How Industries Affect Hawaii's Economy; How Industries Market Their Products/Services; How to Increase Your Motivation Level; How to Make Your Career More Exciting and Meaningful; How to Start a Business; Investments; Job Opportunities in Industries; Management/Leadership; Safety Programs and Administration; Sales Management; Social Responsibilities of Business; Taxation; Utility Regulation; What is Profit?; Why do People Misunderstand Business?

C

★ 24 ★
C.A.L.M. - CHILD ABUSE LISTENING MEDIATION, INC.
Post Office Box 718
Santa Barbara, California 93102 (805) 966-9762

Speakers are available to lecture on child abuse.

Speaker: David A. Root. Subject: Child Abuse (1)
Speaker: Joan Selman. Subject: Child Abuse (2)

★ 25 ★
CAL-LAND IMPROVEMENT CONTRACTORS
2033 West Sierra
Fresno, California 93711 (209) 439-9448

Arranges for speakers to discuss safety and soil and water conservation. The fee is $165.

Speaker: Stary Gange. Title: Tomorrow Be A Great Day (1)

★ 26 ★
UNIVERSITY OF CALGARY
2920 24th Avenue, N.W.
Calgary, Alberta T2N 1N4, Canada (403) 284-5726

Speakers are available to lecture on a wide range of topics to service clubs, professional organizations and schools. No fees other than a reimbursement of travel and hotel accommodations.

★ 27 ★
UNIVERSITY OF CALIFORNIA, IRVINE
Speakers Bureau
Irvine, California 92717 (714) 833-6922

Faculty and staff members lecture on topics of educational, cultural and community interest. Some speakers may require an honorarium or travel expenses.

Administration and Business

Speaker: Paul Bernstein. Title: Experimenting with Democratic Management in Business (1)
Speaker: Ramon Curiel. Titles: Affirmative Action and the Chicano, Women's Employment Rights and Opportunities; A Historical Overview of Equal Employment Opportunity and Affirmative Action Laws and Regulations, The Employment Interview (2)
Speaker: Joseph F. DiMento. Title: Environmental Law and Management (3)
Speaker: Mason L. Hill. Title: Energy and Petroleum Resources, Earthquakes - Prediction, Control, and Nuclear Power Plants (4)
Speaker: Eloise E. Kloke. Title: Making the Wheels Turn (5)
Speaker: Robert E. Lovett. Title: The Challenge of Choice (6)
Speaker: James K. McCann. Title: Organizational Transactional Analysis (7)
Speaker: Len Miller. Title: Overcoming Obstacles to Achieve Productivity in Business (8)
Speaker: William W. Wadman. Titles: The Nuclear Power Option in Perspective; Radiation, Radioactivity and the Public Health; Radiation Safety at a University Campus; Vanadium - Tattletale of Environmental Polluters (9)

Arts, Letters, and Science

Speaker: Richard Frank. Title: Medieval Rome - The New Social History (10)
Speaker: Lucia Guerra-Cunningham. Title: Chile - Its History and Its Culture (11)
Speaker: Franklin Potter. Title: Dramatic Demonstrations in Physics for Young and Old (12)
Speaker: Carl Reinhart. Title: Sailing (13)
Speaker: Eloy Rodriguez. Title: Medicinal Flowering Plants of South America (14)
Speaker: Tracy D. Terrell. Title: A Natural Approach to Foreign Language Teaching (15)
Speaker: Virginia Trimble. Title: Cosmology - Man's Place in the Universe (16)
Speaker: Howard G. Tucker. Titles: Mathematical Statistics and/or Probability; Professional Opportunities in Mathematics (17)
Speaker: Helen H. Weil. Titles: Language as Living Symbols of a Culture; Male-Female Roles in Russian Culture as Reflected in 19th and 20th Century Literature (18)

Education - The University

Speaker: Alfred Bork. Title: The Future of Education (19)
Speaker: John C. Hoy. Titles: Higher Education and the World of Work; Meeting the Educational Consumer Interest; Where Have All the Rebels Gone? (20)
Speaker: Robert S. Lawrence. Title: Changing Attitudes of University Students (21)
Speaker: Juel Lee. Title: Student Financial Aid (22)
Speaker: Sylvia G. Lenhoff. Title: Educational Opportunities in the University of California (23)
Speaker: Harvey Williams. Title: Career Planning for the 1980's (24)

Health and Medicine

Speaker: Warren Bostick. Titles: National Health Insurance; Rising Cost of Medical Care; So You Want to Get Into Medical School (25)
Speaker: Earle A. Davis, Jr. Title: Anatomy of the Brain or of the Visual System (26)
Speaker: Cindy Eddleman. Title: Health Sciences Careers (27)
Speaker: Arthur I. Goldstein. Title: Prenatal Detection of Birth Defects (28)
Speaker: Richard Hochschild. Title: A Vitamin Formula to Counter Aging (29)
Speaker: Deryck R. Kent. Title: The Medical and Psychological Aspects of Adolescent Pregnancy (30)
Speaker: Robert I. Kohut. Title: Dizziness (31)
Speaker: Sylvia G. Lenhoff. Title: Planning for Developmentally Disabled (32)
Speaker: Harold S. Novey. Titles: Allergies; New Hope for Asthma Sufferers (33)
Speaker: Ravi Prakash. Titles: Acute Myocardinal Infarction; Echocardiography (34)
Speaker: Lubomir J. Valenta. Title: When Should You Consult an Endocrinologist? (35)
Speaker: Robert W. White. Titles: Issues in the Delivery of Health Care; The UCI Medical Center (36)

Human Issues

Speaker: Arnold Binder. Title: Juvenile Delinquency as a Persistent Social Problem (37)
Speaker: Joseph F. DiMento. Title: Teaching About Social Change (38)
Speaker: Al Hollinden. Title: Research Program of the UCI Institute of Transportation (39)
Speaker: John C. Hoy. Title: The Presidency and the Media (40)
Speaker: Eloise E. Kloke. Title: Call Me Ms. (41)

Social Issues

Speaker: Howard M. Lenhoff. Titles: Minority Groups - A General Picture, A Visit with Soviet Dissidents; Modern Israel (42)
Speaker: Sylvia G. Lenhoff. Title: Russia, the Refusedniks and Human Rights (43)
Speaker: R.W. Novaco. Titles: Aggression; Stress (44)
Speaker: Michael J. Price. Title: Gestalt Therapy (45)
Speaker: Helen H. Weil. Title: Soviet Underground Humor (46)
Speaker: Helen D. Wildman. Title: Cuna Women - Mola Artists of San Blas (47)

★ 28 ★
CALIFORNIA POLYTECHNIC STATE UNIVERSITY
San Luis Obispo, California 93407 (805) 546-2246

Faculty lecturers cover a wide range of topics in the fields of their expertise.

Subjects: Agriculture; Architecture; Business; Child Development; Communications; Engineering; Home Economics; Sciences

★ 29 ★

CALIFORNIA STATE UNIVERSITY, FULLERTON
Fullerton, California 92634 (714) 870-2417

Lecturers are provided to speak on topics of popular and timely interest. Fees vary.

Africa

Speaker: Giles T. Brown. Title: Africa - An Emerging Giant (1)
Speaker: Miriam S. Cox. Title: Africa - In Myth and Folktale (2)
Speaker: George J. Giacumakis. Title: North African Affairs (3)
Speaker: Frank B. Kalupa. Title: Footloose Family - Azusa to Marrakech (4)
Speaker: Alan S. Kaye. Titles: Travel in Africa; Safari in Africa (5)
Speaker: Boaz N. Namasaka. Titles: Christianity in Africa - Women and Their Societies; The Jew - Afro-American and African (6)
Speaker: Mougo Nyaggah. Titles: African Cultures and Societies; African History; The Importance of Family in African Societies; Portugal and Her African Territories; Race Conflict in Africa; South Africa - Fire Next Time; West Africa: The American Black Homeland?; Women in Africa: Liberated or Oppressed?; Youth in Africa (7)
Speaker: Barbara A. Weightman. Title: Botswana Safari (8)

Art

Speaker: Darryl J. Curran. Title: Los Angeles Contemporary Photography Premeditated Fantasy (9)
Speaker: Irma E. Desenberg. Titles: Art in Orange County; Current State of the Arts; Specific Art Interest of a Group (10)
Speaker: D. Richard Odle. Titles: An Artist's Eye of Russia; Seven Days around Austria (11)
Speaker: Otto J. Sadovszky. Title: The Scythian Frozen Tombs of Siberia (12)
Speaker: James A. Santucci. Title: Art and Architecture in South India (13)

Asia

Speaker: Giles T. Brown. Title: Mongolian Puzzle (14)
Speaker: Miriam S. Cox. Title: The Oriental: Myth and Folklore (15)
Speaker: Alan S. Kaye. Title: Travel in Asia (16)
Speaker: D. Richard Odle. Title: An Artist's Eye of Russia (17)
Speaker: Lawrence R. Przekop. Title: Educational Development in Nepal (18)
Speaker: Naimuddin Qureshi. Titles: The Origin of the California Indians; The Social and Cultural Facts about Pakistan (19)
Speaker: Otto J. Sadovszky. Title: The Scythian Frozen Tombs of Siberia (20)
Speaker: James A. Santucci. Title: The Ancient Indian Sacrifice (21)
Speaker: Barbara A. Weightman. Title: Afghanistan Adventure (22)

Cal State Fullerton

Speaker: Joseph E. Butterworth. Title: Engineering Careers (23)
Speaker: James M. Colletto. Titles: Administration of the Intercollegiate Football Program; Football at Cal State Fullerton (24)
Speaker: Issa I. Fasheh. Title: Use of Microforms at the Cal State Fullerton Library (25)
Speaker: Richard Gilman. Title: The New Information Systems Degree Program in the Cal State Fullerton School of Business (26)
Speaker: Shirley M. Grant. Title: Cal State Fullerton (27)
Speaker: C. Eugene Jones. Titles: The Fullerton Arboretum; Heritage House (28)
Speaker: Joanne L. Lynn. Title: What Good is a Major in English? (29)
Speaker: William J. Reeves. Title: College Students - Where Their Heads Are At (30)
Speaker: Otto J. Sadovszky. Title: How to Prepare for College (31)
Speaker: David L. Walkington. Title: Science and Engineering at Cal State Fullerton (32)

Communications

Speaker: Kenward L. Atkin. Titles: Advertising Management; Consumer Behavior; Media Strategy (33)
Speaker: Richard Gilman. Title: What Do You Mean I Can't Communicate? (34)
Speaker: Teresa M. Hynes. Titles: Communication Technology; Women in Communication (35)
Speaker: Raynolds Johnson. Titles: Current Issues in Mass Media; Mass Communications in Modern Society; Public Relations (36)
Speaker: Frank B. Kalupa. Title: Public Relations (37)
Speaker: Alan S. Kaye. Title: Photographing Exotic Places (38)
Speaker: Norman R. Nager. Titles: Disaster Public Relations; Institutional Public Relations; Public Relations by Objective; Public Relations in Crisis (39)
Speaker: Rick D. Pullen. Title: Ethics and the Press (40)
Speaker: Naimuddin Qureshi. Title: Dissemination of Information (41)
Speaker: Ted C. Smythe. Titles: Agenda Setting;

Communications (continued)
Don't Blame the Mass Media; When the Mass Media Are Irresponsible (42)
Speaker: Miriam C. Tait. Titles: Family Mime; Mime in Elementary and Secondary Education; Theater - Space - and the Actor (43)
Speaker: Geoffry D. White. Title: Assertion Training (44)
Speaker: Guthrie Worth. Title: Management by Objectives (45)
Speaker: Allen M. Zeltzer. Titles: Media - What's It All About?; Radio - My Time is Your Time (46)

Current Local, State, National and World Affairs

Speaker: Bayard H. Brattstrom. Titles: The Politics of Ecology; The Population Explosion (47)
Speaker: Giles T. Brown. Titles: Africa - An Emerging Giant; Middle East Checkerboard; Mongolian Puzzle; Our Plundered Planet (48)
Speaker: W. Garrett Capune. Titles: Our Police Problems; Racism Explained; Sex Offenses; Why Rehabilitate Prisoners? (49)
Speaker: William E. Coffer. Title: American Indian Contemporary Issues (50)
Speaker: Roger R. Dittman. Titles: Nuclear Power; Nuclear Weapon Strategy (51)
Speaker: Arthur D. Earick. Titles: Behind the Headlines; Urban Renewal (52)
Speaker: George J. Giacumakis. Title: International Affairs (53)
Speaker: Christopher R. Hulse. Title: The Future of Man (54)
Speaker: Raynolds Johnson. Titles: Current Issues in Mass Media; Mass Communications in Modern Society; Public Relations (55)
Speaker: Karl H. Kahrs. Titles: European Security and Detentes; West German Politics (56)
Speaker: Alan S. Kaye. Title: Islam in the World Today (57)
Speaker: Jess A. Lopez. Title: Methods of Entering Police Departments (58)
Speaker: Robert B. McLaren. Titles: The Family - Conflicts and Resolutions; Trends in Higher Education (59)
Speaker: Boaz N. Namasaka. Titles: Civil Rights Laws; The Jew - Afro-American and African (60)
Speaker: June Salz Pollak. Title: Collective Bargaining in Higher Education (61)
Speaker: Lorraine E. Prinsky. Title: Juvenile Justice in California (62)
Speaker: Naimuddin Qureshi. Title: The Role of the United Nations in World Affairs (63)
Speaker: Nancy R. Reckinger. Titles: What Alternatives Do You Have in Secondary Public Schools?; What is Fundamental Basic Education; What Needs Reforming? (64)
Speaker: Otto J. Sadovszky. Title: Life Behind the Iron Curtain and in the Soviet Union (65)
Speaker: Alan L. Saltzstein. Title: Equal Employment Compliance in Municipal Governments (66)
Speaker: Ted C. Smythe. Titles: Agenda Setting; Don't Blame Mass Media (67)
Speaker: George E. Triplett. Titles: A Humorous Look at Education; A Humorous Look at Politics; A Serious Look at Education; A Serious Look at Politics (68)

Ecology

Speaker: Bayard H. Brattstrom. Titles: Environmental Awareness; The Politics of Ecology; The Population Explosion (69)
Speaker: Giles T. Brown. Title: Our Plundered Planet (70)
Speaker: Michael H. Horn. Titles: Deep-Sea Biology; Food from the Sea (71)
Speaker: Fred M. Johnson. Title: Energy (72)
Speaker: Albert M. Liston. Title: Environmental Quality and the Problem of Economic Growth (73)
Speaker: Imre Sutton. Titles: Law and Environment; Property and Ecology (74)
Speaker: Barry Thomas. Titles: Australian Wildlife; Tucker Wildlife Sanctuary (75)

Economics and Business

Speaker: Basil E. Gala. Title: To Invest or Not to Invest (76)
Speaker: Richard Gilman. Titles: Time-Phased-Order-Planning for Wholesalers; What Do You Mean I Can't Communicate?; Which Computer if Any? (77)
Speaker: Raynolds Johnson. Title: Public Relations (78)
Speaker: Albert M. Liston. Title: Environmental Quality and the Problem of Economic Growth (79)
Speaker: Donald H. Mann. Titles: Advertising; Capitalism (80)
Speaker: Peter M. Mlynaryk. Titles: California Economic Forecast; Current Business Review; Economic Forecast; Energy Trends and Directions; Real Estate Market Activity (81)
Speaker: Boaz N. Namasaka. Title: The Afro-American in the U.S. Constitution (82)
Speaker: Rolf Winterfelt. Title: Small Business Administration; Small Business Subjects (83)
Speaker: Guthrie Worth. Titles: Consumer Behavior; How to Know When You Are Doing a Good Job; Improving Productivity in Marketing Operations; Management by Objectives; Marketing Objectives (84)

Education

Speaker: Frank M. Bagrash. Title: Vision in Children (85)
Speaker: C. Ian Bailey. Title: The New Physical Education (86)

Education (continued)

Speaker: William E. Coffer. Title: American Indian Education (87)

Speaker: Gerald F. Corey. Titles: Humanistic Education; Problems of Adolescents (88)

Speaker: Arthur D. Earick. Title: Geography as a Profession (89)

Speaker: Morton C. Fierman. Titles: Challenge in Education; Ideas on Education in the Thought of A. J. Heschel; Ideas on Education in the Thought of Martin Buber; Jewish Education and Moral Implications; Tasks for Teachers (90)

Speaker: George J. Giacumakis. Titles: Education; Religion and the Academic World (91)

Speaker: Richard Gilman. Title: The Information Systems Degree Program in the Cal State Fullerton School of Business (92)

Speaker: Shirley L. Hill. Titles: Parents - How to Help Your Child Succeed in School; What's Happening in Early Childhood? (93)

Speaker: Raynolds Johnson. Titles: Public Relations; Who Controls Education? (94)

Speaker: Jacqueline M. Kiraithe. Titles: Bilingual Education in California; Language Acquisition and Bilingual Children; Reading Programs (95)

Speaker: Hans H. Leder. Title: An Anthropological Look at American Education (96)

Speaker: Joanne L. Lynn. Title: What Good is a Major in English? (97)

Speaker: Miles D. McCarthy. Title: Getting into the Health Professions (98)

Speaker: Robert B. McLaren. Titles: The Family - Conflicts and Resolutions; Trends in Higher Education (99)

Speaker: Lawrence R. Przekop. Titles: Educational Development in Nepal; The Science Teacher and Educational Technology (100)

Speaker: Nancy R. Reckinger: Titles: What Alternatives Do You Have in Secondary Public Schools?; What is Fundamental Basic Education? What Needs Reforming? (101)

Speaker: Otto J. Sadovszky. Titles: Existentialism and the Modern Youth; How to Prepare for College (102)

Speaker: Miriam A. Tait. Titles: Family Mime; Mime in Elementary and Secondary Education; Movement Therapy (103)

Speaker: George E. Triplett. Titles: The Future of Education; A Humorous Look at Education; A Serious Look at Education (104)

Speaker: Clarence E. Tygart. Title: Today's University Facility (105)

Speaker: David L. Walkington. Title: Museum and Youth Science Center of North Orange County (106)

Engineering

Speaker: Joseph E. Butterworth. Title: Engineering Careers (107)

Speaker: Eugene B. Hunt. Title: Cal State Fullerton Engineering Program (108)

Speaker: Fred M. Johnson. Title: Energy, Where Art Thou? (109)

Speaker: Edward F. Sowell. Title: Prospects for Solar Energy (110)

Speaker: David L. Walkington. Titles: Careers in Science and Engineering; International Science and Engineering Fair; Minorities and Women in Science and Engineering; Science and Engineering at Cal State Fullerton (111)

Speaker: Guthrie Worth. Titles: How to Know When You Are Doing a Good Job; Improving Productivity in Marketing Operations; Management by Objectives (112)

Ethics

Speaker: Natalie Barish. Titles: Ethics and Genetic Research; Genetic Counseling; Genetics and Future of Man; Society and Genetics (113)

Speaker: Morton C. Fierman. Titles: The Impact of the Prophets of Israel upon Religious Ideas; Jewish Education and Its Moral Implications (114)

Speaker: Raynolds Johnson. Title: Current Issues in Mass Media (115)

Speaker: Robert B. McLaren. Title: An Ontology of Values (116)

Speaker: Rick D. Pullen. Title: Ethics and the Press (117)

Speaker: J. Michael Russell. Titles: Sartre and Man's Search for a Missing God; Sartre's Theory of Sexuality (118)

Speaker: Ted C. Smythe. Title: When the Mass Media Are Irresponsible, What Can We Do? (119)

Europe

Speaker: Roger R. Dittman. Title: Self-Management of Science in Jugoslavija (120)

Speaker: Karl H. Kahrs. Title: European Security and Detentes (121)

Speaker: Frank B. Kalupa. Title: Footloose Family - Azusa to Marrakech (122)

Speaker: Hans H. Leder. Title: The Portuguese Peasant in Europe and America (123)

Speaker: Joanne L. Lynn. Title: The Landscape of Greek Mythology (124)

Speaker: Marcial Prado. Title: Spain after Franco (125)

Speaker: William D. Truesdell. Titles: Monasticism; Monasticism and... (126)

Speaker: Elena V. Tumas. Titles: Aspect of the 19th Century Russian Literature; East European Culture; A. Solzhenitzyn and the Russian Writers' Tradition; Soviet Society in M. Zoshchenko's Writings (127)

Far East

Speaker: Alan S. Kaye. Title: Travel in the Far East (128)

Far East (continued)

Speaker: James A. Santucci. Titles: The Ancient Indian Sacrifice; Art and Architecture in South India; Buddhism in South and Southeast Asia (129)

General Interest

Speaker: C. Ian Bailey. Titles: The New Physical Education; Sport in Society (130)

Speaker: Natalie Barish. Titles: Ethics and Genetic Research; Genetic Counseling; Genetics and Future of Man; Genetics and Mental Retardation; Society and Genetics (131)

Speaker: Bayard H. Brattstrom. Titles: Being a Human Teacher; Environmental Awareness - An Approach to Learning and Self; The Politics of Ecology; The Population Explosion (132)

Speaker: W. Garrett Capune. Titles: Our Police Problems - Whose Fault?; Racism Explained; Sex Offenses; Why Rehabilitate Prisoners? (133)

Speaker: Miriam S. Cox. Title: A Poem is Born (134)

Speaker: Arthur D. Earick. Titles: Geography Behind the Headlines; Planning for Travel; Urban Renewal for Better Living (135)

Speaker: Basil E. Gala. Titles: Mysterious Laws of Chance and Fortune; Profile of a Leader; Security Systems for Home and Office (136)

Speaker: Richard Gilman. Titles: The Information Systems Degree Program in the Cal State Fullerton School of Business; What Do You Mean I Can't Communicate? (137)

Speaker: Eric S. Hanauer. Title: Wreck Diving (138)

Speaker: Arthur A. Hansen. Titles: Japanese American Evacuation During World War II; The Mormons in Mexico; Orange County History; Richard M. Nixon's Early Years (139)

Speaker: Michael H. Horn. Titles: Deep-Sea Biology; Food from the Sea (140)

Speaker: Christopher R. Hulse. Titles: Can We Control the Future of Man?; The Culture of Poverty and Political Cultures in Hawaii; Ethnicity and Culture Changes of Modern Hawaiians; Theories of Man (141)

Speaker: Teresa M. Hynes. Titles: Communication Technology; Women in Communication (142)

Speaker: C. Eugene Jones. Titles: The Fullerton Arboretum; Heritage House (143)

Speaker: Jess A. Lopez. Titles: Alternative Methods of Entering Police Department; California State University Police Departments (144)

Speaker: Joanne M. Lynn. Title: Serial Careers for Women (145)

Speaker: Michael L. McPherson. Title: The Critical Treatment of Women Dramatists in America (146)

Speaker: Boaz N. Namasaka. Title: Civil Rights Laws (147)

Speaker: D. Richard Odle. Titles: An Artist's Eye of Russia; Seven Days around Austria (148)

Speaker: Tai K. Oh. Title: Japanese Management (149)

Speaker: Fraser Powlison. Title: Divorce: Disaster or Opportunity? (150)

Speaker: Marcial Prado. Title: Spain after Franco (151)

Speaker: John A. Ryan. Titles: Earthquakes; Southern California Weather; Viking on Mars (152)

Speaker: Melvin D. Sims. Titles: Assassination, Riot, Public Violence; Basketball; Black Slang; Blacks in Sports; Crime in Society; Disco and Soul Dance; Oral Interviewing (153)

Speaker: Preston Stedman. Title: Having Fun Fund-Raising (154)

Speaker: Clarence E. Tygart. Titles: Effects of Work on Health; Today's University Students; Today's University Facility; Will Religion Survive? (155)

Speaker: James F. Woodward. Title: Science versus Religion (156)

Speaker: Guthrie Worth. Title: Consumer Behavior (157)

Geography and Anthropology

Speaker: William E. Coffer. Titles: American Indian and the U.S. Government; American Indian Contemporary Issues; American Indian History; American Indian Tribalism (158)

Speaker: Arthur D. Earick. Titles: Geography as a Profession; Geography Behind the Headlines; Planning for Travel Pleasure; Urban Renewal for Better Living (159)

Speaker: Arthur A. Hansen. Titles: The Mormons in Mexico; Orange County History (160)

Speaker: Christopher R. Hulse. Titles: Can We Control the Future of Man?; The Culture of Poverty and Political Culture in Hawaii; Ethnicity and Culture Changes of Modern Hawaiians; Theories of Man (161)

Speaker: Helen M. Jaskowski. Title: American Indian Poetry (162)

Speaker: Alan S. Kaye. Titles: Jews and Arabs; Travel in Africa; Travel in Asia; Travel in the Middle East (163)

Speaker: Hans H. Leder. Titles: Anthropological Look at American Education; The Portuguese Peasant in Europe and America; Soul and the Search for Identity (164)

Speaker: Otto J. Sadovszky. Titles: Daily Life of the California Indian; The Origin of the California Indians; The Scythian Frozen Tombs of Siberia (165)

Speaker: Imre Sutton. Titles: Indian Land Rights; Indian Reservations and the States (166)

Speaker: Barbara A. Weightman. Titles: Afghanistan Adventure; Botswana Safari; A Visit to the Amazon (167)

Speaker: Corinne S. Wood. Title: A Prehistoric View of Women (168)

Health

Speaker: Frank M. Bagrash. Title: Vision in Children (169)

Speaker: Natalie Barish. Titles: Genetic

Health (continued)

Counseling; Genetics and Future of Man; Genetics of Mental Retardation; Society and Genetics (170)

Speaker: Beverly Wills Davenport. Title: Drugs in Society (171)

Speaker: Calvin A. Davenport. Title: Biology of Venereal Disease (172)

Speaker: Basil E. Gala. Title: Computers in Medicine (173)

Speaker: Miles D. McCarthy. Titles: Getting into the Health Professions; Human Sexuality (174)

Speaker: Miriam A. Tait. Title: Movement Therapy (175)

Speaker: Clarence E. Tygart. Title: Effects of Work on Health (176)

History (other than U.S.)

Speaker: Roger R. Dittman. Title: The Copernican Revolution (177)

Speaker: Charles A. Frazee. Titles: Byzantine Emperors; The Christian Church in the Fifth Century; Origins of Christian Monasticism (178)

Speaker: George J. Giacumakis. Titles: Middle Eastern Conflicts; North African Affairs (179)

Speaker: Mougo Nyaggah. Title: African History (180)

Speaker: Naimuddin Qureshi. Title: The Social and Cultural Facts about Pakistan (181)

Speaker: Madeline F. Schatz. Title: Women in Music (182)

Speaker: William D. Truesdell. Titles: Monasticism; Monasticism and... (183)

Speaker: James F. Woodward. Title: Science versus Religion (184)

Humor

Speaker: Miriam S. Cox. Titles: American Folk Heroes; Folklore Americana (185)

Speaker: Fred M. Johnson. Titles: Adventures of a Man of Science; Lasers--Medical Applications; New Cosmology; Voyage into Space (186)

Speaker: Miriam A. Tait. Titles: Family Mime; Mime in Elementary and Secondary Education (187)

Speaker: George E. Triplett. Titles: A Humorous Look at Education; A Humorous Look at Politics (188)

Speaker: Elena V. Tumas. Title: Soviet Society in M. Zoshchenko's Writings (189)

Latin America

Speaker: Barbara A. Weightman. Title: A Visit to the Amazon (190)

Law

Speaker: Thomas M. Apke. Titles: Consumer Protection; Landlord-Tenant Law (191)

Speaker: William E. Coffer. Title: American Indian Contemporary Issues (192)

Speaker: Jess A. Lopez. Title: California State University Police Departments (193)

Speaker: Boaz N. Namasaka. Titles: The Afro-American in the U.S. Constitution; Civil Rights Laws (194)

Speaker: Imre Sutton. Titles: Indian Land Rights; Indian Reservations and the States; Law and Environment; Property and Ecology (195)

Libraries and Books

Speaker: Issa I. Fasheh. Titles: Arab Libraries in Jordan; Microforms at the Cal State Fullerton Library (196)

Speaker: Joanne L. Lynn. Titles: Children's Books Only Grownups Should be Allowed to Read; The Landscape of Greek Mythology (197)

Speaker: Naimuddin Qureshi. Title: The Role of Books and Libraries in Society (198)

Speaker: William D. Truesdell. Titles: Monasticism; Monasticism and ... (199)

Literature and Language

Speaker: Miriam S. Cox. Titles: Africa - In Myth and Folktale; Alice in Wonderland Revisited; American Folk Heroes; Delight - Keynote in Literature for Children; Folklore Americana; Greece - In Myth and Folklore; The Hodja - Folk Hero of Turkey; The Oriental - Myth and Folklore; A Poem is Born; Storytelling - Antidote for Television (200)

Speaker: David H. Evans. Title: American Folklore (201)

Speaker: Helen M. Jaskoski. Title: Lives of American Women in Autobiography (202)

Speaker: Alan S. Kaye. Titles: The Arabic Language Today; Phonetics and Language Learning; What a Linguist Does (203)

Speaker: Jacqueline M. Kiraithe. Titles: Bilinigual Education in California; An Essential Component in Bilingual Education; Language Acquisition and Bilingual Children (204)

Speaker: Joanne L. Lynn. Titles: Children's Books Only Grownups Should be Allowed to Read; Is Literacy Obsolete?; The Landscape of Greek Mythology (205)

Speaker: Willis E. McNelly. Title: The Future and Science Fiction (206)

Speaker: June Salz Pollak. Title: D.H. Lawrence (207)

Speaker: Marcial Prado. Titles: Spanish Dialects in the World; Spanish Pronouns; Spanish Slang (208)

Speaker: Otto J. Sadovszky. Title: The Origin of the English Language (209)

Speaker: Clarence E. Schneider. Title: Transformational Grammar and Literature (210)

Speaker: Melvin D. Sims. Titles: Black Slang; Oral Interviewing (211)

Speaker: William D. Truesdell. Titles: Monasticism; Monasticism and... (212)

Speaker: Elena V. Tumas. Titles: The Aspect of the 19th Century Russian Literature; East European Culture; Literature and Society; A Solzhenitzyn and the Russian Writers' Tradition; Soviet Society in M. Zoshchenko's Writings (213)

Mathematics

Speaker: Vuryl J. Klassen. Title: Mathematics in Gambling (214)

Middle East

Speaker: Giles T. Brown. Title: Middle East Checkerboard (215)
Speaker: Issa I. Fasheh. Title: A Tour through the Holy Land (216)
Speaker: George J. Giacumakis. Titles: Ancient New East; International Affairs; Middle East Conflicts; North African Affairs (217)
Speaker: Alan S. Kaye. Titles: The Arabic Language Today; The Glorious Koran; Islam in the World Today; Jews and Arabs; Travel in the Middle East (218)
Speaker: Boaz N. Namasaka. Titles: Christianity in Africa; The Jew - Afro-American and African (219)

Music

Speaker: David H. Evans. Titles: American Folk Music; Black Folk Music in the South (220)
Speaker: Nors S. Josephson. Titles: The Music of Charles Ives; The Music of Leos Janacek (221)
Speaker: Madeline F. Schatz. Titles: I Hate Music; Women in Music (222)
Speaker: Melvin D. Sims. Title: Disco and Soul Dance (223)

Near East

Speaker: Giles T. Brown. Title: Middle East Checkerboard (224)
Speaker: Issa I. Fasheh. Titles: Arab Libraries in Jordan; A Tour through the Holy Land (225)
Speaker: George J. Giacumakis. Titles: Ancient New East; International Affairs; Middle Eastern Conflicts; Near Eastern Archaeology; North African Affairs (226)
Speaker: Nors S. Josephson. Title: Egypt - Old and New (227)
Speaker: Alan S. Kaye. Titles: The Glorious Koran; Islam in the World Today; Travel in the Middle East (228)

Philosophy, Psychology, Religion

Speaker: Frank M. Bagrash. Titles: Vision in Children; Visual Perception and the Real World (229)
Speaker: William E. Coffer. Title: American Indian Tribalism (230)
Speaker: Gerald F. Corey. Titles: Counseling and Psychotherapy; Marriage Counseling; Problems of Adolescents; Therapeutic and Encounter Groups (231)
Speaker: Roger R. Dittman. Titles: Challenges to the Logical-Empirical School of Philosophy; The Copernican Revolution (232)
Speaker: Morton C. Fierman. Titles: Education in the Thought of A.J. Heschel; Education in the Thought of Martin Buber; Jewish Education and its Moral Implications (233)
Speaker: Charles A. Frazee. Titles: Byzantine Emperors; The Christian Church in the Fifth Century; Origins of Christian Monasticism (234)
Speaker: George J. Giacumakis. Title: Religion and the Academic World (235)
Speaker: Fred M. Johnson. Title: Energy (236)
Speaker: Alan S. Kaye. Titles: The Glorious Koran; Islam in the World Today; The Linguistic Study of the Bible (237)
Speaker: Hans H. Leder. Title: Soul and the Search for Identity (238)
Speaker: Carol U. Lindquist. Titles: Becoming Assertive - Between Mouse and Monster; Working Mothers - Are You Helping or Hurting Your Child? (239)
Speaker: Richard A. McFarland. Title: Biofeed-back and Self-Control (240)
Speaker: Robert B. McLaren. Titles: An Ontology of Values; The Science-Religion Dialogue (241)
Speaker: Boaz N. Namasaka. Titles: Black Psychology; Christianity in Africa (242)
Speaker: June Salz Pollak. Title: D.H. Lawrence (243)
Speaker: Fraser Powlison. Title: Divorce - Disaster or Opportunity? (244)
Speaker: J. Michael Russell. Titles: Gestalt Therapy and Sartrian Theory; Sartre and Man's Search for a Missing God; Sartre's Theory of Sexuality; Some Philosophical Assumptions of Psychotherapy (245)
Speaker: Otto J. Sadovszky. Title: Existentialism and the Modern Youth (246)
Speaker: James A. Santucci. Titles: The Ancient Indian Sacrifice; Buddhism (247)
Speaker: William D. Truesdell. Titles: Monasticism; Monasticism and... (248)
Speaker: Clarence E. Tygart. Title: Will Religion Survive? (249)
Speaker: Arthur W. Webber. Titles: How to Relax and Live Longer; Understanding Sexual Dysfunction (250)
Speaker: Marjorie Weinzweig. Titles: Identity and Authenticity; Philosophy and Women's Liberation (251)
Speaker: Geoffry D. White. Titles: Assertion Training; Enhancing Marital Happiness; Enhancing Sexual Pleasure; Sex Counseling for Couples; Sex Counseling for Single Adults (252)
Speaker: Guthrie Worth. Title: Consumer Behavior (253)

Political Science

Speaker: William E. Coffer. Title: American Indian and the U.S. Government (254)
Speaker: Roger R. Dittman. Titles: Changes in Nuclear Weapon Strategy; Funding of Research; Nuclear Power - Boom or Bust?; Self-Management of Science in Jugoslavija (255)

Political Science (continued)

Speaker: Gary L. Guertner. Titles: Can Nuclear Weapons be Controlled?; The Soviet-American Arms Race; U.S. Defense Policies (256)

Speaker: Christopher R. Hulse. Titles: The Culture of Poverty and Political Culture in Hawaii; Ethnicity and Culture Changes of Modern Hawaiians (257)

Speaker: Raynolds Johnson. Title: Public Relations (258)

Speaker: Karl H. Kahrs. Titles: European Security and Detentes; West German Politics after the 1976 Elections (259)

Speaker: Albert M. Liston. Titles: Environmental Quality and the Problem of Economic Growth; The Ombudsman (260)

Speaker: Boaz N. Namasaka. Title: The Black and Compromises in American History (261)

Speaker: Alan L. Saltzstein. Titles: Equal Employment Compliance in Municipal Governments; Public Administration as a Career (262)

Speaker: George E. Triplett. Titles: A Humorous Look at Politics; A Serious Look at Politics (263)

Science

Speaker: Frank M. Bagrash. Title: Visual Perception and the Real World (264)

Speaker: Natalie Barish. Titles: Ethics and Genetic Research; Genetics of Mental Retardation (265)

Speaker: Bayard H. Brattstrom. Titles: The Politics of Ecology; The Population Explosion (266)

Speaker: Calvin A. Davenport. Title: Biology of Venereal Disease (267)

Speaker: Roger R. Dittman. Titles: Challenges to the Logical-Empirical School of Philosophy; Changes in Nuclear Weapon Strategy; The Copernican Revolution; Funding of Research; Nuclear Power - Boom or Bust?, Self-Management of Science in Jugoslavija (268)

Speaker: George J. Giacumakis. Title: Near Eastern Archaeology (269)

Speaker: Eric S. Hanauer. Title: Undersea Life of Southern California (270)

Speaker: Michael H. Horn. Titles: Deep-Sea Biology; Food from the Sea (271)

Speaker: Fred M. Johnson. Titles: Adventures of a Man of Science; Energy; Lasers; New Cosmology; Voyage into Space (272)

Speaker: C. Eugene Jones. Titles: The Fullerton Arboretum; Plant Sex (273)

Speaker: Miles D. McCarthy; Titles: Getting into the Health Professions; Human Sexuality (274)

Speaker: Robert B. McLaren. Title: The Science-Religion Dialogue (275)

Speaker: John A. Ryan. Titles: Earthquakes; Southern California Weather; Viking on Mars (276)

Speaker: Barry Thomas. Titles: Australian Wildlife; Tucker Wildlife Sanctuary (277)

Speaker: David L. Walkington. Titles: Careers in Science and Engineering; International Science and Engineering Fair; Minorities and Women in Science and Engineering; Museum and Youth Science Center; Science and Engineering (278)

Speaker: James F. Woodward. Title: Science versus Religion (279)

Sociology

Speaker: John W. Bedell. Titles: Alcoholism in America; The American Child (280)

Speaker: Tony Bell. Titles: Bereavement, Grief and Mourning; Changing Attitudes toward Death and Dying; Death in Modern and Premodern Societies; Dignified Death; Kubler-Ross Revisited; Widowhood (281)

Speaker: Jonathan J. Brower. Titles: Deviance - Society's Whipping Boy; Myths in the World of Sport; Sport - Social Stresses and Strains (282)

Speaker: William E. Coffer. Titles: American Indian Contemporary Issues; American Indian Tribalism (283)

Speaker: Christopher R. Hulse. Titles: The Culture of Poverty and Political Culture in Hawaii; Ethnicity and Culture Changes of Modern Hawaiians; Theories of Man (284)

Speaker: Teresa M. Hynes. Titles: Communication Technology; Women in Communication (285)

Speaker: Boaz N. Nanjundappa. Title: Christianity in Africa (286)

Speaker: G. Nanjundappa. Title: Population Problems (287)

Speaker: Lorraine E. Prinsky. Title: Juvenile Justice in California (288)

Speaker: Otto J. Sadovszky. Title: Life Behind the Iron Curtain and in the Soviet Union (289)

Speaker: Elena V. Tumas. Titles: East European Culture; Literature and Society (290)

Speaker: Clarence E. Tygart. Titles: Effects of Work on Health; Today's University Facility; Today's University Students; Will Religion Survive? (291)

Soviet Union

Speaker: Gary L. Guertner. Titles: Can Nuclear Weapons be Controlled?; The Soviet-American Arms Race; U.S. Defense Policies (292)

Speaker: D. Richard Odle. Title: An Artist's Eye of Russia (293)

Speaker: Otto J. Sadovszky. Title: Life Behind the Iron Curtain and in the Soviet Union (294)

Speaker: Elena V. Tumas. Titles: A. Solzhenitzyn and the Russian Writers' Tradition; Soviet Society in M. Zoshchenko's Writings (295)

Speaker: Michael Yessis. Titles: Comparison of U.S. - U.S.S.R. Training for the Olympics; Sport in the Soviet Union (296)

Speech

Speaker: Jacqueline M. Kiraithe. Titles: ESL - An Essential Component in Bilingual Education; Language Acquisition and Bilingual Children (297)

Speaker: Otto J. Sadovszky. Title: The Origin of the English Language (298)

Sports

Speaker: C. Ian Bailey. Titles: The New Physical Education; Sport in Society (299)
Speaker: Jonathan J. Brower. Titles: Myths in the World of Sport; Sport - Social Stresses and Strains (300)
Speaker: James M. Colletto. Titles: Administration of an Intercollegiate Football Program; Football (301)
Speaker: Eric S. Hanauer. Titles: Baja California Dive Trip; Undersea Life in Southern California; Wreck Diving (302)
Speaker: Naimuddin Qureshi. Title: Introduction to Cricket and Field Hockey (303)
Speaker: Melvin D. Sims. Titles: Basketball; Blacks in Sports (304)
Speaker: Ronald L. Witchey. Titles: Biomechanics of Sport; Biomechanics of Tennis; Doubles and Singles Strategy in Tennis; What Research Tells Us about the Decathlon (305)
Speaker: Michael Yessis. Titles: Comparison of U.S. - U.S.S.R. Training for the Olympics; How to Improve Your Game; Sport in the Soviet Union (306)

Taxes

Speaker: Burton L. Graubert. Title: Tax Planning for the Individual and Small Businessman (307)

Theater and Television

Speaker: Teresa M. Hynes. Titles: Communication Technology - Past, Present and Future; Women in Communication (308)
Speaker: Michael L. McPherson. Title: The Critical Treatment of Women Dramatists in America (309)
Speaker: Jack H. Mewett. Title: Broadcasting in Great Britain (310)
Speaker: D. Richard Odle. Titles: An Artist's Eye of Russia; Theater at Cal State Fullerton (311)
Speaker: Ted C. Smythe. Titles: Agenda Setting - Why We Think about What We Think About; Don't Blame the Mass Media; When Mass Media Are Irresponsible, What Can We Do? (312)
Speaker: Miriam A. Tait. Titles: Family Mime; Theater--Space--and the Actor (313)

Travel

Speaker: Arthur D. Earick. Title: Planning Travel Pleasure (314)
Speaker: Issa I. Fasheh. Title: A Tour through the Holy Land (315)
Speaker: Eric S. Hanauer. Title: Baja California Dive Trip (316)
Speaker: Nors S. Josephson. Titles: Classical Greece; Egypt--Old and New (317)
Speaker: Frank B. Kalupa. Title: Footloose Family - Azusa to Marrakech (318)
Speaker: Alan S. Kaye. Titles: Large Cities of the World; On Safari in Africa; Photographing Exotic Places; Travel in Africa; Travel in Asia; Travel in the Far East; Travel in the Middle East (319)
Speaker: Joanne L. Lynn. Title: The Landscape of Greek Mythology (320)
Speaker: Robert B. McLaren. Title: Four Seasons in Europe (321)
Speaker: D. Richard Odle. Titles: An Artist's Eye of Russia; Seven Days around Austria (322)
Speaker: Marcial Prado. Title: Spain after Franco (323)
Speaker: Barry Thomas. Titles: Australian Wildlife; Tucker Wildlife Sanctuary (324)
Speaker: Barbara A. Weightman. Titles: Afghanistan Adventure; Botswana Safari; A Visit to the Amazon (325)
Speaker: Marjorie S. Weinzweig. Title: Impressions of Australia (326)
Speaker: Allen M. Zeltzer. Titles: Bicycling in Europe (327)

United Nations

Speaker: Alan S. Kaye. Title: What is an Underdeveloped Country? (328)
Speaker: Boaz N. Namasaka. Title: The Jew - Afro-American and African (329)
Speaker: Naimuddin Qureshi. Title: The Role of the United Nations in World Affairs (330)

United States and U.S. History

Speaker: William E. Coffer. Title: American Indian History (331)
Speaker: Miriam S. Cox. Title: Folklore Americana (332)
Speaker: Arthur A. Hansen. Titles: Japanese American Evacuation during World War II; Orange County History; Richard M. Nixon's Early Years (333)
Speaker: Christopher R. Hulse. Title: Can We Control the Future of Man? (334)
Speaker: Teresa M. Hynes. Titles: Communication Technology - Past, Present and Future; Women in Communication (335)
Speaker: Helen M. Jaskowski. Title: Her Own Words - Lives of American Women in Autobiography (336)
Speaker: Boaz N. Namasaka. Titles: The Afro-American in the U.S. Constitution; The Black and Compromises in American History; Black Psychology - The Afro-American Woman in American History; Civil Rights Laws; The Jew - Afro-American and African (337)
Speaker: Ronald D. Rietveld. Titles: Abraham Lincoln and the Emancipation of American Blacks; Did Lincoln Aides Abet His Assassin?; The Lincoln-Rutledge Romance - Hoax or Reality? Lincoln's Use and Abuse of America's Founding Fathers; Was Abraham Lincoln a Christian? (338)
Speaker: Otto J. Sadovszky. Titles: Daily Life of the California Indian; The Origin of the California Indians (339)

Youth

Speaker: John W. Bedell. Title: The American Child (340)
Speaker: Arthur D. Earick. Title: Geography as a Profession (341)
Speaker: Shirley L. Hill. Titles: Parents - How to Help Your Child Succeed in School; What's Happening in Early Childhood? (342)
Speaker: Carol U. Lindquist. Titles: Becoming Assertive - Between Mouse and Monster; Working Mothers - Are You Helping or Hurting Your Child? (343)
Speaker: Jess A. Lopez. Title: Alternative Methods of Entering Police Departments (344)
Speaker: Robert B. McLaren. Title: The Family - Conflicts and Resolutions (345)
Speaker: Lorraine E. Prinsky. Title: Juvenile Justice in California (346)
Speaker: Nancy R. Reckinger. Titles: RISE - What Needs Reforming? Why? How Do You Get Involved?; What Alternatives Do You Have in Secondary Public Schools?; What is Fundamental Basic Education? (347)
Speaker: William J. Reeves. Title: College Students - Where Their Heads Are At (348)
Speaker: Otto J. Sadovszky. Titles: Existentialism and the Modern Youth; How to Prepare for College (349)
Speaker: Melvin D. Sims. Title: Crime in Society (350)
Speaker: Clarence E. Tygart. Title: Today's University Students (351)
Speaker: David L. Walkington. Titles: International Science and Engineering Fair; Museum and Youth Science Center of North Orange County (352)

★ 30 ★
CALUMET AREA FOUNDATION FOR MEDICAL CARE, INC.
2825 Jewett Street
Highland, Indiana 46322 (219) 923-8614

Arranges for speakers to lecture on the socio-economic aspects of medical care, alternative medical care delivery systems and research into medical economics. Reimbursement of fees and an honorarium is expected.

Speaker: Charles C. Shoemaker. Titles: Current Problems in Medical Politics; Incursions Into the Private Delivery System of Government Projects (1)

★ 31 ★
CARNEGIE-MELLON UNIVERSITY
500 Forbes Avenue
Pittsburgh, Pennsylvania 15213 (412) 621-2600

Faculty members lecture on many subjects based upon their expert knowledge and subject backgrounds. Fees vary.

Accounting

Speaker: Robert S. Kaplan. Titles: Accounting for Inflation; Effects of Financial Data on Stock and Bond Markets (1)

Aggression Control

Speaker: Kenneth E. Moyer. Title: Techniques of Aggression Control (2)

Architectural History

Speaker: Franklin Toker. Titles: Gothic Architecture; Various Architects and Movements of the 19th Century (3)

Art

Speaker: David Carrier. Title: Art Today (4)
Speaker: Bernard Keisch. Title: Art and the Atom (5)

Basic Cell Biology

Speaker: Robert Goldman. Title: Differences in Normal and Cancer Cells (6)

Behavior

Speaker: Kenneth E. Moyer. Title: The Law of Effect (7)

Biological Control

Speaker: Bernard D. Coleman. Title: Biological Control of Plant and Animal Pests (8)

Carnegie-Mellon University

Speaker: Earl J. Birdy. Title: Intramural Athletics at Carnegie-Mellon (9)
Speaker: Kenneth Service. Title: Carnegie-Mellon University (10)

Chemical Engineering

Speaker: Edward L. Cussier; Titles: Membrane Separations; Predicting Texture; Rate Processes in Bile (11)

Cinema

Speaker: Concetta Greenfield. Titles: American and European Cinema; Cinema Today (12)

Cities

Speaker: Joel A. Tarr. Titles: Perspectives on Pollution; The Quality of Life in the American City (13)

Civil Liberties

Speaker: Thomas M. Kerr. Titles: Civil Liberties; Civil Rights; U.S. Bill of Rights (14)

College Financial Aid

Speaker: Walter C. Cathie. Titles: Financial Aid - How, When, Where; No Need Athletic and Academic Scholarships (15)
Speaker: William F. Elliott. Title: College Admissions and Financial Aid (16)

Computers

Speaker: Dwight M. Bauman. Title: Civic Applications of Computers (17)

Speaker: Ronald L. Krutz. Title: Computer-on-a-Chip (18)

Speaker: John W. McCredie. Title: Trends in Information Processing Systems (19)

Death

Speaker: Richard Schulz. Title: The Process of Dying (20)

Ecology

Speaker: Bernard D. Coleman. Title: Ways Mathematics Can Help with Ecological Problems (21)

Emergency Housing

Speaker: Charles Goodspeed. Title: Post Disaster Housing in Developing Countries (22)

Energy

Speaker: Tobias W.T. Burnett. Titles: Cost of Imported Oil; Our Energy Situation (23)

Eye

Speaker: Wlodzimierz M. Kozak. Titles: Electric Signs of Diabetic Retinopathy; Oscillations in the Eye and Brain; Subjective Color Sensations (24)

Federal Fiscal Policy

Speaker: John P. Crecine. Title: Federal Fiscal and Budgetary Policy Processes (25)

Foreign Students

Speaker: Concetta Greenfield. Title: Foreign Students in the U.S.A. (26)

Lobbying

Speaker: Dennis Schatzman. Title: Lobbying in State and Local Government (27)

Middle Ages

Speaker: Franklin Toker. Titles: Medieval Archeology; Medieval Cities; Medieval Living Patterns (28)

Music Composition

Speaker: Byron McCulloh. Title: Meet the Composer (29)

Nuclear Power

Speaker: Tobias W.T. Burnett. Titles: The Effects of Nuclear Radiation; The Human Costs of Regulatory Delays; Nuclear Safety and Risks in Perspective; Nuclear Waste Disposal (30)

Pittsburgh

Speaker: David Demarest. Titles: Out of this Furnace; Pedestrian Pittsburgh (31)

Speaker: Joel A. Tarr. Title: The Evolution of Pittsburgh (32)

Product Safety and Liability

Speaker: Alvin S. Weinstein. Titles: Perspectives in Product Liability; Perspectives in Product Safety (33)

Public Policy

Speaker: John P. Crecine. Title: Educational Programs in Public Policy (34)

Public Relations

Speaker: Dennis Schatzman. Title: Community Public Relations (35)

Speaker: Kenneth Service. Title: The Practice of Public Relations (36)

Self-Consciousness

Speaker: Michael F. Scheier. Title: Self-Consciousness - Private and Public (37)

Social Security

Speaker: Robert S. Kaplan. Title: Social Security - Current Problems and Prospects for Reform (38)

Sports

Speaker: Earl J. Birdy. Titles: College Football Officiating; Intramural Athletics (39)

Transportation

Speaker: Dwight M. Baumann; Titles: Paratransit; Regulation of Transportation; Taxies (40)

★ 32 ★

CENTER FOR SOUTHERN FOLKLORE
1216 Peabody Avenue
Post Office Box 4081
Memphis, Tennessee 38104 (901) 726-4205

A non-profit organization designed to document the rapidly disappearing folk traditions of the South. The directors and staff conduct programs at regional and national meetings, conferences and workshops for teachers, folklorists, filmmakers, students, librarians, historians, and similar groups through lectures and the demonstrations of films and publications. Fees vary.

★ 33 ★

CHAMPION SPARK PLUG COMPANY (Highway Safety Team)
900 Upton Avenue
Post Office Box 910
Toledo, Ohio 43661 (419) 535-2567

Professional race drivers are available to lecture on safe driving. No fees.

Speakers: Fred Agabashian (1); Tom Bigelow (2); Duane Carter, Jr. (3); Wally Dallenbach (4); Jerry Grant (5); Bob Harkey (6); Brett Lunger (7); Benny Parsons (8) Johnny Parsons (9); Tom Sneva (10); Bill Vukovich (11)
Title: Highway Safety is No Accident

★ 34 ★
CHEMETRON CORPORATION
111 East Wacker Drive
Chicago, Illinois 60601 (312) 565-5000

The company provides speakers in the areas of industrial and medical gas, welding, piping components and valves, fire protection, chemicals, pigments for coloring, medical products, x-ray equipment, food processing equipment, microwave ovens (institutional), and railway products. No gratuity required, however, the speaker would expect to be compensated for travel and lodging expenses.

Speaker: L. David Moore. Titles: The Contributions of the Chemical Industry to Midwestern United States Economies; Federal Regulation; Federal Regulation and Its Excesses; Profits and Their Importance to the Economy. (1)
Speaker: Harold E. Whatley. Title: Profits--Business/Government Relationship (2)

★ 35 ★
CHEVRON U.S.A. INC.
225 Bush Street
San Francisco, California 94104 (415) 894-4086

Speakers lecture with the objective of promoting greater knowledge and understanding of the company, its policies, activities and the oil industry in general. No fees.

Titles: Alternate Energy; Energy Economics; Environment and Conservation; General Energy Outlook; Offshore Exploration and Production; Petroleum Operations

★ 36 ★
CHILDBIRTH WITHOUT PAIN EDUCATION ASSOCIATION
20134 Snowden
Detroit, Michigan 48235 (313) 345-9850

Lectures and discussion groups are conducted by the executive director and the members of education committees working with medical and lay groups as well as supervised school audiences and covering subjects related to material and childbirth, parenting and like topics. Fees range from $25 to $50.

Speaker: Flora Hommel. Titles: The Contribution of Psychoprophylactic Childbirth to the Era of Feminism; The History of the Lamaze Method in the United States; Home Birth, Hospital Birth and Alternatives to Both; Major Causes of Pain in Childbirth and Methods for Combating Them (1)

★ 37 ★
COE COLLEGE
Cedar Rapids, Iowa 52402 (319) 398-1600

Some thirty-five faculty and administrators are available to lecture on topics of interest to academic and cultural groups.

★ 38 ★
COMMODITY EXCHANGE, INC.
Four World Trade Center
New York, New York 10048 (212) 938-2900

The Commodity Exchange, Inc. offers its Speakers Bureau as a public service to meet requests for speakers from business, financial and professional organizations and educators. Lecturers are drawn from the officers of the Exchange and various members of its Board of Governors. No fees.

Titles: Commodity Trading; Function and Operation of a Major Futures Trading Facility; Metals Futures Contracts in Gold, Silver, and Copper

★ 39 ★
CONCERNS OF PEOPLE, INC.
Post Office Box 15577
Lakewood, Colorado 80215 (303) 237-6844

Speakers are available to lecture on a wide range of topics of human concern and interest.

★ 40 ★
JAMES A.H. CONRAD
3529 1/2 Broadway
Chicago, Illinois 60657 (312) 528-9360

Provides lectures and conducts seminars in the field of antiques. Fee is $250 and expenses.

Speaker: James Conrad. Subjects: Furniture; General Antiques; Silver (1)

★ 41 ★

CONSOLIDATED EDISON COMPANY OF NEW YORK, INC.
Four Irving Place
New York, New York 10003 (212) 460-6919

Speakers are made available to schools, senior citizens' organizations, professional, social and community groups to lecture on all aspects of energy and environment.

Subjects: Career Suggestions; Con Edison; Consumer Education; Electricity; Energy Conservation; Energy History and Research; Natural Gas; Protecting our Environment

CONSORTIUM ON PEACE RESEARCH, EDUCATION AND DEVELOPMENT
See: Gustavus Adolphus College

★ 42 ★

THE CONTEMPORARY FORUM
2528a West Jerome Street
Chicago, Illinois 60645 (312) 764-4383

Speakers present lectures on every facet of the contemporary scene.

The Arts

Speakers: Suzanne Benton (1); Bernie Casey (2); Rob Cuscaden (3); Alonzo Davis (4); Joshua Hoffman (5); Dale Messick (6); Jean Mary Morman (7); Turtel Onli (8); Don Seiden (9); Joseph Young (10)

Civil Liberties - Law - Community Affairs - Polls - Labor - Government - Politics - Penology - Activists

Speakers: Imamu Amiri Baraka (11); Willie Barrow (12); George Gallup (13); Sanford Gottlieb (14); Charles Hamilton (15); Lowell Jones (16); William Kunstler (17); Sidney Lens (18); Eugene McCarthy (19); Newton Minow (20); Calvin Morris (21); Chuck Stone (22); I.F. Stone (23); Thomas Todd (24); Jill Volner (25); Marvin Ziporyn (26)

Critics - Book Reviews - Films - Theater

Speakers: Ed Bullins (27); Walter Burrell (28); Del Close (29); William Derl-Davis (30); Michael Jutza (31); Tom Palazzolo (32); Dorothy Samachson (33); James Shiflett (34); Piri Thomas (35)

Journalism - Communications - Mass Media - Editor/Publisher

Speakers: Frank Beaman (36); Lerone Bennett, Jr. (37); Merri Dee (38); Ouida Lindsey (39); Bob Logan (40); Dale McCarren (41); Norman Mark (42); Newton Minow (43); Askia Muhammad (44); Ethel Payne (45); Nido Qubein (46); Barbara Reynolds (47); Clete Steward (48); Chuck Stone (49); I.F. Stone (50); Studs Terkel (51)

Literature - Poetry - Playwriting

Speakers: Imamu Amiri Baraka (52); Lerone Bennett, Jr. (53); Harry G. Black (54); Henry Blakely (55); Gwendolyn Brooks (56); Claude Brown (57); Ed Bullins (58); Paul Carroll (59); Bernie Casey (60); Ralph Ellison (61); Hauling Nieh Engle (62); Paul Engle (63); Mari Evans (64); Grant Gard (65); Sam Greenlee (66); Samuel Hazo (67); Elizabeth Janeway (68); June Jordan (69); George Kent (70); James Kilgore (71); John Killens (72); Audre Lorde (73); Mary McBride (74); Haki Madhubuti (75); D.H. Melhem (76); Ned O'Gorman (77); Eugene Perkins (78); Harry Mark Petrakis (79); Dudley Randall (80); Barbara Reynolds (81); Carolyn Rodgers (82); Sonia Sanchez (83); Studs Terkel (84); Piri Thomas (85); Bryan Walters (86); John Wolfe (87)

Psychiatry - Mental Health - Drugs - Youth

Speakers: Joyce Brothers (88); Claude Brown (89); James Comer (90); Ned O'Gorman (91); Eugene Perkins (92); Mari Piers (93); Don Seiden (94); Miriam Uni (95); Marvin Ziporyn (96)

Sports

Speakers: Johnny Bench (97); Curt Gowdy (98); Billy Kidd (99); Jack Kramer (100); Jim McKay (101); Carol Mann (102); Jeannie Morris (103); Johnny Morris (104); Jesse Owens (105); Ara Parseghian (106); Bob Richards (107); Bill Russell (108); Johnny Rutherford (109); Jimmy "The Greek" Snyder (110); Bart Starr (111); Roger Staubach (112); Fran Tarkenton (113)

Unknown - Gestalt - Psychic Development - Parapsychology - Astrology

Speakers: Ruth Berger (114); Katherine DeJersey (115); Joseph DeLouise (116); Uri Geller (117); Roy Mackal (118); Morda (119); David Techter (120); Alfred Webre (121); Frank Young (122)

Urbanology - Sociology - Social Psychology - Human Rights - Economics - Religion - National and International Affairs

Speakers: Jean Palmer Akers (123); Willie Barrow (124); Claude Brown (125); Pierre DeVise (126); Erwin France (127); Jack Grossman (128); Charles Hamilton (129); Vincent Harding (130); Bill Hayden (131); Christopher J. Hegarty (132); Robert Holderby (133); Eliot Janeway (134); Lowell Jones (135); William Kuntsler (136); William Leahy (137); Sidney Lens (138); Ouida Lindsey (139); Helena Lopata (140); Richard Lopata (141); Robert Marx (142); Richard Peterson (143); William Radke (144); Milton Rosenberg (145); William Sadler (146); I.F. Stone (147)

Women

Speakers: Heather Booth (148); Gloria Cobb (149);

Brenda Eichelberger (150); Mari Evans (151); Elizabeth Janeway (152); Ethel Payne (153); Charlotte Rosner (154); Sonia Sanchez (155); Joyce Schrager (156); June Sochen (157)

★ 43 ★
LEO CROWDER PRODUCTIONS, INC.
5310 Radnor Road
Indianapolis, Indiana 46226 (317) 547-4886

A booking agency for professional entertainment which maintains a roster of public speakers available for engagements with groups on a wide range of topics.

D

★ 44 ★
DATA COURIER, INC.
620 South Fifth Street
Louisville, Kentucky 40202 (502) 582-4111

Speakers will visit with any group of information or library specialists or subject-related personnel with regard to modern information delivery and access, specifically online delivery and access of data bases in the sciences and business management. Fees are negotiable.

Speakers: Dennis Auld (1); Gregory Payne (2); Jo Susa (3); Loene Trubkin (4)
Title: Information Access in Science and Business

★ 45 ★
DAWN BIBLE STUDENTS ASSOCIATION
199 Railroad Avenue
East Rutherford, New Jersey 07073 (201) 438-6421

Traveling lecturers are available to speak to religious groups. Expenses are expected to be paid.

Speaker: Edward E. Fay. Title: The World's Only Hope (1)
Speaker: Kenneth M. Nail. Title: Why Not Live Forever (2)
Speaker: Felix S. Wassmann. Title: Israel in History and Prophecy (3)

★ 46 ★
DELTA NU ALPHA TRANSPORTATION FRATERNITY
15017 Detroit Avenue
Cleveland, Ohio 44107 (216) 521-6626

Speakers are available to lecture to transportation organizations and related civic organizations with the purpose of promoting greater knowledge of traffic and transportation. No fees.

Speakers: Richard A. Brown (1); Pat Calabro (2); Michael Cohen (3); Roy L. Hamlin (4); Peter W. Riola (5)
Title: Transportation, Education and Self-Development Concepts

★ 47 ★
DETROIT EDISON
2000 Second Avenue
Detroit, Michigan 48226 (313) 237-9205

Lecturers are available to speak to clubs, organizations and educational groups on energy and energy-related topics. No fees.

Titles: Energy Challenge; Energy Options for Food Production; The Great Ice Storm; It's Your Energy - Use It Wisely; Western Coal Project

★ 48 ★
DIAL CORPORATION
207 Ninth Street
Des Moines, Iowa 50307 (515) 243-2131

Lectures deal with the use of credit in contemporary life.

Speaker: Edward Glazer. Title: Speak up for Credit (1)

★ 49 ★
DIRECTORS GUILD OF AMERICA
Special Projects, Speakers Referral Service
7950 Sunset Boulevard
Hollywood, California 90046 (213) 653-8052

More than 400 director members of the Guild are available to lecture, conduct workshops, teach or serve as artists-in-residence. While the majority reside in the New York City or Los Angeles areas, directors from eighteen other states, Canada and Europe are also available. Teaching and interactive situations rather than celebrity appearances are encouraged. The Special Projects Office attempts to match organizational needs, budget and program format to its cross-index of potential speakers and their accomplishments. These choices are discussed with the institution and when a name or list of names is agreed upon, the individual directors are approached for their availability. Fees begin at $300 for directors of television and non-fiction films; $500 for feature film directors. Fees vary depending upon whether a seminar, formal lecture, informal sessions over several days, or some combination of them is requested. If the institution desires a director of celebrity stature for a large general audience, a fee schedule comparable to that of commercial lecture bureaus is used; restricted teaching situations involving lesser-known directors are encouraged with lower scales. The Guild requests that first-class air travel be provided for the speaker along with accommodations and other amenities usually

accorded an honored guest.

Speakers: Rudy E. Abel (1); Edward Abroms (2); Perry Miller Adato (3); William Affleck (4); Dominick Albi (5); Lewis Allen (6); Louis Antonio (7); Jack Arnold (8); Gerald Auerbach (9); Larry Auerbach (10); Annette Bachner (11); John Badham (12); Ed Bailey (13); James F. Baker (14); Muriel Balash (15); John K. Ball (16); Joel N. Banow (17); Charles L. Barbee (18); Allen Baron (19); Paul Bartel (20); Gordon Barto (21); Saul Bass (22); Rudolph Behlmer (23); Richard Benedict (24); Richard Bennett (25); Stuart Berg (26); Frank Bianco (27); Bruce Bilson (28); Robert Birnbaum (29); Eli Bleich (30); Robert Bleyer (31); Arthur Bloom (32); Lee Bobker (33); Peter Bonerz (34); Paul Bosner (35); Aram Boyajian (36); David Bradley (37); Charles Braverman (38); Robert Braverman (39); Buddy Bregman (40); Charles W. Broun, Jr. (41); Himan Brown (42); Michael Brown (43); James Buckley (44); Thomas Burrows (45); Robert Butler (46); Jo Anna Cameron (47); Eric Camiel (48); Robert Carlisle (49); Martin Carr (50); Gilbert Cates (51); Zeida Cecilia-Mendez (52); Everett Chambers (53); John Champion (54); Martin Charnin (55); Robert Chenault (56); Stephan Chodorov (57); Chris Christenberry (58); Byron Chudnow (59); Bob Clampett (60); James Coane (61); John Coleman (62); Richard Colla (63); Gunther Collins (64); Nicholas Cominos (65); Hal Cooper (66); Norman Corwin (67); Barry Crane (68); Thomas Craven (69); Neill Cross (70); George Cukor (71); Tad Danielewski (72); Marc Daniels (73); Herbert Danska (74); Martin Davidson (75); Nicholas De Marco (76); Andre De Toth (77); Peter Deyell (78); Mark Dillon (79); Edward Dmytryk (80); Lawrence Dobkin (81); Walter Doniger (82); Clive Donner (83); James Drake (84); Cal Dunn (85); Nat Eisenberg (86); Gustave Eisenmann (87); Barry Elliott (88); Howard Enders (89); Roger Englander (90); Richard Erdman (91); John Erman (92); Harry Essex (93); Jerry Evans (94); James Faichney (95); Paul Falkenberg (96); E. Robert Fiedler (97); Albert Fiore (98); Richard Fleischer (99); John Florea (100); Louis Ford (101); Richard Foster (102); Ken Fouts (103); John Frankenheimer (104); Wendall Franklin (105); Victor French (106); Daniel Freudenberger (107); Kim Friedman (108); Robert Friend (109); Alexander Frisbie (110); Frank Furino (111); Louise Tiranoff Gaddis (112); Timothy Galfas (113); Michael Gargiulo (114); Lee Garmes (115); Ray Garner (116); Tay Garnett (117); Lila Garrett (118); Mike Gavin (119); Bruce Geddes (120); Bill Gibson (121); Theodore Goetz (122); Murray Golden (123); Peter Goldfarb (124); Allen Gomez (125); Mark Goode (126); Sol Goodnoff (127); Michael Gottlieb (128); Walter Grauman (129); Warren Gray (130); William Greaves (131); Norman Hall (132); Louis Harris (133); Anthony Harvey (134); Richard Harwood (135); Jeffrey Hayden (136); Timothy Hayes (137); Bob Henry (138); Stuart Hersh (139); Larry Higgs (140); Jack Hill (141); Bernard Hirschenson (142); Martin Hoade (143); Victoria Hochberg (144); Gary Hoffman (145); Finley C. Hunt Jr. (146); Peter Hyams (147); James Ivory (148); Henry Jaglom (149); Lamont Johnson (150); Eugene Jones (151); Ron Joy (152); Nathan Juran (153); Jay Kacin (154); Jeremy Kagan (155); Konstantin Kalser (156); Michael Kane (157); Jonathan Kaplan (158); Sheldon Kaplan (159); Mort Kasman (160); Max Katz (161); Jerome Kaufman (162); Donald Keeslar (163); Harry Keller (164); Ken Kennedy (165); Durnford King (166); Michael Kitei (167); Randal Kleisar (168); Herbert Kline (169); Dennis Knife (170); John Korty (171); Julian Krainin (172); Stanley Kramer (173); Frank Kratochvil (174); John Kuehn (175); Buzz Kulik (176); Morton Lachman (177); Harvey Laidman (178); Paul Landres (179); Andrew Laszlo (180); Stan Lathan (181); Arnold Laven (182); Louie Lawless (183); Anton Leader (184); Reginald LeBorg (185); Francis Lederer (186); Alan Lee (187); Thomas Leetch (188); Robert Leland (189); Sheldon Leonard (190); Irving Lerner (191); Joseph Lerner (192); Mervyn LeRoy (193); William Levey (194); Leonard Levin (195); Peter Levin (196); Joseph Lewis (197); Kenneth Licata (198); Jason Lindsey (199); Nancy Littlefield (200); Lynne Littman (201); Doc Livingston (202); J.D. Lobue (203); Jerry London (204); Nate Long (205); Stanley Losak (206); Ernest Losso (207); Ross Lowell (208); Ted Lowry (209); Arthur Lubin (210); Dean Lyras (211); Robert McCahon (212); Sean McClory (213); Joseph McDonough (214); Andrew McLaglen (215); Jay McMullen (216); Hugh McPhillips (217); Martin Magner (218); Rouben Mamoulian (219); Hans Mandell (220); Harvey Mandlin (221); Thomas Mangravite (222); Joseph Mankiewicz (223); Daniel Mann (224); Alex March (225); Frank Marrero (226); Garry Marshall (227); Ross Martin (228); Sobey Martin (229); Andrew Marton (230); Paul Maslansky (231); Mark Massari (232); Ronald Maxwell (233); Gerald Mayer (234); Harold Mayer (235); Ira Mazer (236); John Meiklejohn (237); Niels Melo (238); Newton Meltzer (239); Anthony Messuri (240); Marvin Mews (241); Jay Michaels (242); Richard Michaels (243); John Milius (244); J. Philip Miller (245); Richard Milton (246); W. Peter Miner (247); Bruce Minnix (248); A.J. Pete Miranda (249); Robert J. Mitchell (250); David Monahan (251); Hollingsworth Morse (252); Alfred Muller (253); Warren Murray (254); John Myhers (255); Robert Myhrum (256); William Neff (257); David Nelson (258); Ralph Nelson (259); Jeffrey Newby (260); William Newton (261); Alexander Nicol (262); Leo O'Farrell (263); Jack Ofield (264); Phil Olsman (265); Wyott Ordung (266); Bruce Paltrow (267); Jerry Paris (268); Francine Parker (269); Richard Patterson (270); Mario Pellegrini (271); William Peters (272); Russell Petranto (273); John Peyser (274); Lee Philips (275); Ronald Phillips (276); Ernest Pintoff (277); James Polakof (278); Peter Poor (279); Ted Post (280); Rick Potter (281); Otto Preminger (282); Richard Pyle (283); Alan Rafkin (284);

William Rainbolt (285); Maurice Rapf (286); Irving Rapper (287); Harry Rasky (288); Walter Reisch (289); Gene Reynolds (290); Frederic Rheinstein (291); Ron Richards (292); Charles Rickey (293); Gordon Rigsby (294); Willard Robbins (295); John Robins (296); Chris Robinson (297); Albert Rogell (298); Doug Rogers (299); Thomas Rook (300); Herbert Ross (301); Marvin Rothenberg (302); Jose Luis Ruiz (303); Phil Ruskin (304); Sidney Salkow (305); Denis Sanders (306); Jay Sandrich (307); David Saperstein (308); Joseph Sargent (309); Ronald Satlof (310); Vincent Scarza (311); George Schaefer (312); Thomas Scheuer (313); Alan Schneider (314); Richard Schneider (315); Max Schindler (316); Allen Schwartz (317); John Sedwick (318); Jules Seidman (319); Steve Sekely (320); Leo Seltzer (321); Anatole K. Semenchuk (322); Mel Shavelson (323); Jack Shea (324); Barry Shear (325); James Sheldon (326); Joshua Shelley (327); Vincent Sherman (328); Pat Shields (329); Lee Sholem (330); George Sidney (331); Marvin Silbersher (332); Elliot Silverstein (333); Edward Simmons (334); Jack Simon (335); Alexander Singer (336); Robert Slatzer (337); Sanford Spillman (338); Michael Stearns (339); Robert Steel (340); Donald Stern (341); Steven Stern (342); Victor Stoloff (343); Andrew Stone (344); Ezra Stone (345); Jon Stone (346); Herbert Strock (347); Joseph Stuart (348); Arthur Swerdloff (349); William Tannebring (350); David Tapper (351) Jud Taylor (352); J. Lee Thompson (353); Fred Thorne (354); Philip Thornton (355); Kevin Tighe (356); Norman Toback (357); Marice Tobias (358); Leo Trachtenberg (359); Shepard Traube (360); John Trent (361); Carl Tubbs (362); Harold Tulchin (363); Stephen Verona (364); Louis Volpicelli (365); Duhhaine Waeker (366); Warren Wallace (367); Charles Walters (368); Albert Wasserman (369); Mark Waxman (370); Nicholas Webster (371); Don Weis (372); Brice Weisman (373); Reinald Werrenrath (374); Leo Hap Weyman (375); Sam White (376); Gordon Wiles (377); Oscar Williams (378); Paul Williams (379); Nelson Brock Winkless (380); Jorn Winther (381); Lori Wintner (382); Robert Wise (383); Edmond Witalis (384); Art Wolff (385); John Wray (386); Robert Wynn (387); Harold Yates (388); Michael Zinberg (389); Albert Zugsmith (390); Frank Zuniga (391)

★ 50 ★
DISCLOSURE INC.
4827 Rugby Avenue
Bethesda, Maryland 20014 (301) 951-0100

This firm sponsors lectures about the reports American companies are required to make available at regular intervals to the United States government and the sources of information relating to this topic. There are no fees.

Speaker: Steven Goldspiel. Title: The Value and Uses of Financial Reports Filed by American Corporations With the Securities and Exchange Commission (1)

★ 51 ★
DOUGLAS MANAGEMENT
1215 Wylie Road
Norman, Oklahoma 73069 (405) 321-1200

Neil Douglas narrates about different countries and cultures while showing films of these regions. Fees range from $450 to $1200.

Speaker: Neil Douglas. Titles: America - The Greatness That is Ours; Austria for all Seasons; The Bold New Germany; The Magnificent Fury of Alaska; The Most Exciting Road Through Europe; Norway - The Bold Vikings; The Russia Few Ever Get to See; Turkey - Yesterday's Tomorrow (1)

★ 52 ★
DREW UNIVERSITY
Madison, New Jersey 07940 (201) 377-3000

Lecturers are available to speak to church and civic organizations on various subjects ranging from art to zoology. Speakers require an honorarium of $25 - $50 plus travel expenses where significant distances are involved.

Speaker: Robert K. Ackerman. Subjects: Religious Fundamentalism; The South (1)
Speaker: E.G. Stanley Baker. Subjects: Biology; College Curricula; Premedical Education (2)
Speaker: Paul Barry. Subjects: New Jersey Shakespeare Festival; Professional Theatre (3)
Speaker: Lucille F. Becker. Subject: French Literature (4)
Speaker: Lester Berenbroick. Subjects: Church Music; Hymnology (5)
Speaker: Jacqueline Berke. Subjects: Arab-Israeli Conflict; Contemporary Writing (6)
Speaker: John W. Bicknell. Subjects: Being an American; Human Relations; Literature (7)
Speaker: George N. Bistis. Subjects: Biology; Botany (8)
Speaker: Harold A. Brack. Subjects: Communication; Religion (9)
Speaker: Robert J. Bull. Subject: Archaeology (10)
Speaker: Vivian A. Bull. Subjects: Economics; The Palestinian Problem (11)
Speaker: Louise F. Bush. Subjects: College Students; Marine Biology (12)
Speaker: Robert L. Chapman. Subjects: Dictionaries; English (13)
Speaker: Edward W. Chillak. Subjects: Education; Mathematics (14)
Speaker: Thomas R. Christofferson. Subject: France (15)
Speaker: Lillian T. Cochran. Subjects: Population; Spain (16)
Speaker: Ilona C. Coombs. Subject: French Literature (17)
Speaker: John W. Copeland. Subjects: Civil Disobedience; Ethnics; Morality (18)

SPEAKERS AND LECTURERS

Speaker: Charles Courtney. Subjects: Human Rights; Religion (19)
Speaker: David A. Cowell. Subjects: Civil Rights; Middle East; United Nations (20)
Speaker: H. Jerome Cranmer. Subject: Current Economics (21)
Speaker: Martyvonne Dehoney. Subjects: Art; Sculpture (22)
Speaker: Peter De Jong. Subjects: Ethnics; Religion; Science; Theology (23)
Speaker: Robert De Veer. Subjects: College Admissions; Latin America; Peace Corps (24)
Speaker: Lala Kalyan Dey. Subject: Religion (25)
Speaker: Edward A. Domber. Subject: Learning and Motivation (26)
Speaker: Darrell J. Doughty. Subject: Religion and Society (27)
Speaker: Richard H. Eiter. Subject: The Soviet Union (28)
Speaker: Robert L. Fenstermacher. Subject: Radio Astronomy (29)
Speaker: Carlos Fuentes. Subjects: Cuba and Communism; Latin America (30)
Speaker: Norma Gilbert. Subject: Marriage (31)
Speaker: Joanna Bowen Gillespie. Subjects: Education; Family; Women (32)
Speaker: David Graybeal. Subjects: Church and Society; The Family (33)
Speaker: Sidney Greenblatt. Subject: China (34)
Speaker: Bernard Greenspan. Subject: Mathematics (35)
Speaker: Lydia Hailparn. Subject: Music (36)
Speaker: Neill Q. Hamilton. Subjects: Church Renewal; Japan; New Testament; Prayer and Meditation (37)
Speaker: Paul Hardin. Subjects: Higher Education; The Law (38)
Speaker: David E. Harper. Subject: Physical Education (39)
Speaker: Bruce Hilton. Subject: Bioethics (40)
Speaker: Peter R. Jennings. Subjects: Asia; Latin America; Third World Hunger (41)
Speaker: Barent Johnson. Subjects: Education; Philosophy; Theology (42)
Speaker: Arthur Jones. Subjects: American Literature; Libraries (43)
Speaker: Donald Jones. Subjects: Ethics; Politics; Religion (44)
Speaker: John Knox, Jr. Subjects: Philosophy, Religion (45)
Speaker: Edwina G. Lawler. Subjects: German Literature; Philosophy (46)
Speaker: J. Perry Leavell. Subject: History (47)
Speaker: Alfred McClung Lee. Subjects: The Conflict in Northern Ireland; The Family; Propaganda (48)
Speaker: Theodore Chace Linn. Subject: Church and Society (49)
Speaker: J. Mark Lono. Subjects: Drew University; Higher Education; Public Relations (48)
Speaker: W. Scott McDonald, Jr. Subjects: Civil Engineering; Management Information; Planning (51)
Speaker: Afework A. Mascio. Subjects: Ethiopia; Microbiology; Public Health in Developing Nations (52)
Speaker: Eleanor C. Mason. Subject: Women's Physical Education (53)
Speaker: Julius Mastro. Subjects: Local Government; Political Science (54)
Speaker: James A. Metzler. Subject: Computers (55)
Speaker: James Miller. Subject: Chemistry (56)
Speaker: James W. Mills. Subjects: Counselling; Student Life (57)
Speaker: John Mulder. Subject: English Literature (58)
Speaker: James J. Nagle. Subjects: Environmental Crisis; Genetics; Population (59)
Speaker: Gregory Nelson. Subjects: Chemistry; Television (60)
Speaker: Frank V. Occhiogrosso. Subject: Shakespeare (61)
Speaker: Thomas Clark Oden. Subjects: Church; Ethics; Theology (62)
Speaker: James M. O'Kane. Subject: Social Problems (63)
Speaker: Nadine Ollman. Subject: Literary Criticism (64)
Speaker: John F. Ollom. Subjects: Religion; Science (65)
Speaker: James H. Pain. Subjects: Eastern Orthodoxy; Religion (66)
Speaker: Philip M. Peek. Subjects: African Art; Folklore; Nigeria (67)
Speaker: Joy Phillips. Subjects: Biology; Women in Science (68)
Speaker: Leland Wells Pollock. Subjects: Environmental Sciences; Marine Biology (69)
Speaker: Paul G. Properzio. Subject: Greco-Roman World (70)
Speaker: James G. Ranck. Subjects: Psychiatry; Psychology; Religion (71)
Speaker: John A. Reeves. Subject: Physical Education (72)
Speaker: Paul A. Reimann. Subject: Old Testament (73)
Speaker: Kurt W. Remmers. Subjects: Audio-visual Education (74)
Speaker: Richard S. Rhone. Subjects: International Politics; United Nations (75)
Speaker: Charles L. Rice. Subjects: Literature; New Zealand; Religion; South Africa (76)
Speaker: Russell E. Richey. Subject: American Christianity (77)
Speaker: Neal Riemer. Subject: Political Philosophy (78)
Speaker: Robert Michael Rodes, Jr. Subjects: Asia; Political Science (79)
Speaker: Harole Clark Rohrs. Subject: Zoology (80)
Speaker: Kenneth E. Rowe. Subject: Church History (81)

Speaker: Michael Daniel Ryan. Subjects: Religion; Theology (82)
Speaker: Karl M. Salathe. Subjects: Education in Europe; England; Fund Raising (83)
Speaker: John M. Schabacker. Subject: Germany (84)
Speaker: Donald A. Scott. Subject: Chemistry (85)
Speaker: Donald R. Siebert. Subject: Laser Applications (86)
Speaker: Douglas W. Simon. Subjects: American Foreign Policy; International Relations; Political Violence; United Nations (87)
Speaker: Calvin L. Skaggs. Subjects: Contemporary Literature; Film (88)
Speaker: Ralph B. Smith. Subject: Buildings and Grounds Management (89)
Speaker: Joan Elizabeth Steiner. Subjects: Contemporary Issues; Literature (90)
Speaker: William Stroker. Subjects: Biblical Studies; Christian History (91)
Speaker: Shirley Sugarman. Subjects: Psychology; Religion (92)
Speaker: Nelson S.T. Thayer. Subjects: Psychology; Religion (93)
Speaker: Bard Thompson. Subjects: Graduate Studies; Religion (94)
Speaker: James Varner. Subjects: Black America; Social Problems (95)
Speaker: John T. Von Der Heide, Jr. Subjects: European History; Modern Asia (96)
Speaker: Joan S. Weimer. Subjects: Women in Brazil; Women in Egypt; Women's Movement (97)
Speaker: Roger W. Wescott. Subject: Anthropology (98)
Speaker: Charles J. Wetzel. Subjects: History; Peace Corps (99)
Speaker: Frank Wolf. Subjects: Africa; Politics (100)
Speaker: Florence M. Zuck. Subject: Botany (101)
Speaker: Robert K. Zuck. Subject: Botany (102)

★ 53 ★

DUKE UNIVERSITY
Office of Special Events
614 Chapel Drive
Durham, North Carolina 27706 (919) 684-3747

Provides speakers drawn from the university community who lecture on a wide range of contemporary topics. Fees vary.

★ 54 ★

DUQUESNE UNIVERSITY
Special Events Office
Administration Building #406
Pittsburgh, Pennsylvania 15219 (412) 434-6052

Lecturers are offered to tri-state groups and organizations on subjects as diverse as hypnotism and international economics. Fees vary.

Ecology

Titles: Air Pollution; Clean and Cheap Energy; The Environmental Crisis; Fight for Clean Air; Human Ecology; Is There an Energy Crisis?; Modern Ecological Questions; Smoke in the Air Isn't Good for the Economy; Ten Years from Now?; Too Many People!; Water Pollution

Economics, Law and Finance

Titles: Accounting; Can Legislation Improve Consumer Welfare?; Defense Spending; Economics and Politics of Local Government; Economics of Pro and College Sports; Economic Shortages; The Economics of Taxes; Estate Planning; Federal Taxation; Getting More for Your Money; Government Expenditures and the Economy; Government Regulations in Economics and Business; High International Finance; Improving Schools; Inter-Relationships With Law and Society; International Economics; Land Use; Law; Making Out a Will; Making Sense of the Doomsdayers; Mass Transit; Motivating for Profit; National Health Insurance; Planning and Control; Problems in Inflation; Red China, Laos, Thailand and the Golden Triangle; Rising Health Care Costs; The Roles of Unions in Business; Tax Reform; Techniques of Urban Planning; Trust Funds; Unemployment Problems; Welfare Reform

Education and Youth

Titles: The Black Community Competing Academically; Conflict and Confrontation in our Schools; Education for Social Change; Education for the 70's; The Educational Crisis; Educational Lobbying; Effective Guidance Does Make a Difference!; Financial Aid for Students in Post-Secondary Education; General College Admissions; The Impact of Duquesne University and Alumni On the Pittsburgh Area; The Impact of Guidance On Personality; A Proposal for Improvement in American Education; ROTC On the College Campus; The Role of Private Higher Education in Pennsylvania; Role of the Catholic School in the United States: Sex and the College Student; Sex Education; Talent Waste - the Moral Crisis of Our Times; The Teenage Problem - The Adult!; The Youth Culture, Drugs and Revolution; Youth in Conflict

Fine Arts

Titles: Contemporary Music in Poland; Contemporary Themes in Drama; Contemporary Themes in Fiction; Contemporary Themes in Poetry; The Duquesne Tamburitzan Institute of Folk Art; The Duquesne University Tamburitzans; Historical Periods in Music; Individual Musical Composers and Their Works; The Kodaly Approach to Music Teaching; Music in the Community; Musical Composers; Mythology - Form and Meaning in our Times; The Role of Music in Education;

Fine Arts (continued)

Styles of Music; What It Means to Understand Music;

History, Government and Politics

Titles: Ancient Greece and Rome; The Angola Crisis; Commentaries and Observations on the Bicentennial; Communist Ideologies; Decisions of the Supreme Court in Constructing the Constitution; The Defense Establishment; Detente; Ethnic Communities in the Pittsburgh Area; Ethnic Politics; Folklore in History; How Dark Were the Dark Ages?; Issues in the Middle East; Medieval; Political Assassinations - The Kennedys and King; Politics in Eastern Europe; Politics in the U.S.S.R.; Problems and Issues in Local Government; ROTC - The Political Pressures; The Role of Women in History; Soviet Foreign Policies; Urban Politics; World and American History

Science and Medicine

Titles: Abortion; Ambulatory Pharmaceutical Services; Antimicrobial Agents; The Biochemistry of a Cell; A Biologist Looks at Evolution 100 Years After the Publication of The Origin Of The Species; Biology; Childbirth; A Clinical Approach to Out-Patient Pharmacy Services; Clinical Toxicology; Cutaneous Reactions to Cosmetics and Topical Pharmaceutics; Drug Abuse; Drug Addiction - The Physiological and Pharmacological Aspects; Drug Blood Levels; Drug Induced Modification of Diagnostics; Enzymes - Life's Key Chemicals; The Evolution of a Clinical Pharmacy Service; Facts People Should Know About Alcohol Intoxication; Industrial Applications of Radioisotopes; Interactions Between Drugs and Food; The Legal and Medical Aspects of Organ Transplants; Medical Malpractice; Medical Microbiology; Medicinal Plant Alkaloids; Medicinal Plant Glycosides; Microbiology; Narcotic Deaths; Patient Susceptibility to Adverse Drug Reactions; The Pharmacy Clinic - Outgrow of the Clinical Pharmacy; Physiology; Poisonous Plants of Pennsylvania; Practice of a Clinical Pharmacy; Pregnancy; Prescription Drug Interactions; Prolonged Release Dosage Forms; Quick Chemical Tests in Toxicology; A Reappraisal of Organic Form with Respect to Time and Space; The Role of Toxicology in Death Investigations; Selection and Purchase of Generics; Structure of a Protein; Vitamins; The Why and How of Ambulatory Pharmaceutical Services; The Wonders of the Human Body

Theology, Philosophy and Personal Development

Titles: Are You a Mystic?; Censorship and Pornography; Contemplative Prayer in a Busy World; A Critique on Both Sides of Abortion Legislation; The Equality of Women; Euthanasia; Existentialism; The Guru and Spiritual Growth; Issues in Contemporary Theology; The Many Possibilities of Man; Meditation - The Christian Tradition; Morality and Law; Non-Violence and the Gandhi Experience; Religion and the College Student; Religion in the Modern World; A Theology of Change in the Modern World; What's the Fuss About Meditation?; World Religions - Buddhists, Confucianists, Taoists, Maoists, Jews, Christians and Muslims

E

★ 55 ★

EARLHAM COLLEGE
Richmond, Indiana 47374 (317) 962-6561 ext. 416

Faculty members and their wives are available to lecture to local organizations and schools on subjects of their expertise. No fees expected other than transportation expenses.

★ 56 ★

EAST CAROLINA UNIVERSITY
Division of Continuing Education, Speakers Bureau
Greenville, North Carolina 27834 (919) 757-6143

Offers speakers to church, school, civic and business groups on subjects and themes adapted to suit the specific purposes of the interested group.

Anthropology and Sociology

Speaker: Margaret S. Bond. Title: Ancient MesoAmerica (1)

Speaker: Robert Louis Bunger, Jr. Titles: Africa - An Overview; The Afro-Americans and African Culture; River People - The Pokomo of Kenya (2)

Speaker: Thomas H. Johnson. Title: Education for Human Sexuality (3)

Speaker: Y.H. Kim. Title: Changing Race Relations in America (4)

Speaker: David Knox. Titles: Behavior Modification and You; Keeping Happiness in Your Marriage; The Meaning of Love; Your Questions Answered on Love, Sex, and Marriage (5)

Speaker: Martin E. McGuire. Titles: Social Change in the Middle East; South America - Prospects for Development (6)

Speaker: Mel Markowski. Title: Child Discipline, Cohabitation, Patterns of Family Interaction (7)

Speaker: Karl Rodabaugh. Title: Race Relations in the South (8)

Art and Theatre

Speaker: Lloyd Benjamin. Titles: The Art of the Netherlands from the 15th to the 17th Century; Art Treasures in Western Europe; The Survey of Medieval Art (9)
Speaker: Emily Farnham. Titles: Cubism - Major Route of Modern Painting, Sculpture and Architecture; 18th Century English Painting (10)
Speaker: Art Haney. Title: Ceramics in the Public School System (11)
Speaker: Edgar Loessin. Title: Theatre (12)
Speaker: Edward Reep. Titles: Evolution of the Art Form; Genesis of Landscape Painting; The History of Watercolor Painting; The Reality of Art; The Talent Myth Exploded (13)
Speaker: William Stephenson. Title: Popcorn and the Piety of Celluloid Sin (14)

Business and Economics

Speaker: Ralph E. Birchard. Title: The Middle East in the United States Energy Picture (15)
Speaker: Marshall Colcord. Title: Accounting (16)
Speaker: Umesh C. Gulati. Titles: Food, Fuel and Fertility; Foreign Economic Aid; Inflation and Unemployment; Wage-Price Controls (17)
Speaker: Oscar Moore. Title: North Carolina's Changing Position in the Tobacco Economy (18)
Speaker: Roswell M. Piper. Titles: American Business - The Next Fifty Years; Education for Business; Environment and Business (19)
Speaker: Jim Rees. Title: Effective Conference Participation and Leadership (20)
Speaker: Jack Thornton. Title: The Birth Dearth (21)
Speaker: Bruce Wardrep. Title: The Role of the Community in Land Resource Planning (22)
Speaker: Louis H. Zincone, Jr. Titles: The Changing Relationship of Business to Other Areas of the Social Structure; Fiscal and Monetary Policies (23)

Eastern North Carolina: Heritage, Values and Future

Speaker: Ralph Birchard. Title: The Economic Impact of Students of East Carolina University on Business in Greenville, North Carolina (24)
Speaker: Trenton Davis. Title: Environmental Services in Eastern North Carolina (25)
Speaker: Frank W. Eller. Title: From the Land of the Phamlysoun (26)
Speaker: William W. Hankins. Title: The Development of the East Carolina University Campus (27)
Speaker: Edgar Hooks. Title: History of Recreation, Physical Education, and Leisure Activities in Eastern North Carolina (28)
Speaker: Clifford B. Knight. Titles: Energy - The Tip of the Iceberg; The Future of Eastern North Carolina Waterways; How Much is Too Much (29)
Speaker: Donald R. Lennon. Title: Colonial Town Life in Eastern North Carolina (30)
Speaker: Martin McGuire. Title: Social Changes in Eastern North Carolina (31)
Speaker: Bodo Nischan. Title: Religious Roots of Eastern North Carolinians (32)
Speaker: Michael P. O'Conner. Title: The Outer Banks and Man (33)
Speaker: Herbert Paschal. Titles: The Sound Society of Colonial North Carolina; The Tuscarora Indians in North Carolina (34)
Speaker: Charles L. Price. Title: Railroad Travel in Eastern North Carolina (35)
Speaker: F. David Sanders. Titles: Ovid Pierce on What the Present Can Learn From the Past; Ovid Pierce's The Wedding Guest; Ovid Pierce's View of Eastern North Carolina (36)
Speaker: Ralph Steele. Title: Prophets of Profit (37)
Speaker: Richard A. Stephenson. Titles: Coastal and Marine Resources in Eastern North Carolina; Eastern North Carolina - The Year 2000; Eastern North Carolina's Relative Location; Population on the Physical Environment in Eastern North Carolina (38)
Speaker: Charles E. Stevens. Title: Music of the 18th Century America (39)
Speaker: Edith Webber. Title: Adventures and Errands on the Original Horseless Carriage (40)
Speaker: Thomas A. Williams. Title: Tales of the Tobacco Country (41)

Education

Speaker: Thomas A. Chambliss. Titles: Education of the Disadvantaged; Teaching as a Profession; Trends in Methodology (42)
Speaker: Patricia Dunn. Title: Value Clarifying Strategies (43)
Speaker: Ruth G. Fleming. Title: Opportunity in the Two-Year College (44)
Speaker: Betsy Harper. Title: Cooperative Education (45)
Speaker: Furney K. James. Title: Placement of Students in Jobs (46)
Speaker: Thomas H. Johnson. Title: Education for Human Sexuality (47)
Speaker: Douglas R. Jones. Titles: Administration at the High School or Elementary School Levels; Disadvantaged Children; Elementary Education; Grouping Within the Schools; Modern Elementary Math (48)
Speaker: Y.H. Kim. Title: Problems in School Integration (49)
Speaker: Gene D. Lanier. Titles: Intellectual Freedom; Multi-Media Concepts and New Approaches to Learning (50)
Speaker: Rosina C. Lao. Title: Achievement Motivation (51)
Speaker: Donald Lawler. Title: The Road Not Taken (52)

Education (continued)

Speaker: Frederick C. Lewis. Titles: Dialectical Differences in Children; Language and Speech Disorders in Children; Normal Language Development; Speech and Language Difficulties in Adults (53)

Speaker: Peter Mueller-Roemer. Title: A Comparison of the German and American Education Systems (54)

Speaker: Robert A. Muzzarelli. Titles: Hearing Disorders; Management of Speech Disorders in Public Schools; Speech and Hearing Disorders (55)

Speaker: Jim Rees. Title: Four Dimensions of Communication (56)

Speaker: John Thomas Richards. Titles: Early Childhood Education; Mental Retardation; Special Education (57)

Speaker: Ralph Steele. Title: Think About Not Thinking (58)

Speaker: Thomas A. Williams. Title: How to Prepare Your Child for Success (59)

English and Literature

Speaker: Nicole Aronson. Title: Great Names in French Literature (60)

Speaker: Ira Baker. Title: Elizabeth Timothy - America's First Woman Editor (61)

Speaker: Anita Brehm. Title: A Handful of Earth (62)

Speaker: Nell C. Everett. Titles: The Historical Origin of Mother Goose Rhymes; Nonsense Poetry; Selecting Good Literature for Children (63)

Speaker: Donald Lawler. Titles: Science Fiction and the Future; Science Fiction - The New Methodology (64)

Speaker: James R. Wright. Titles: Articulatory Phonetics; Career Opportunities in Linguistics; Linguistics; Phonology, Morphology, Syntax of English; Transformational Grammar (65)

Environment

Speaker: Vincent J. Bellis. Title: Ecological Problems in North Carolina (66)

Speaker: Trenton Davis. Titles: Environmental Pollution; Environmental Services in North Carolina (67)

Speaker: Lokenath Debnath. Title: Oceans (68)

Speaker: Grover W. Everett. Titles: Air Pollution; Water Pollution (69)

Speaker: Clifford B. Knight. Titles: How Do We Go From Here?; Too Much Of a Good Thing (70)

Speaker: Y.J. Lao. Titles: The Chemical Environment; Energy and Pollution (71)

Speaker: Michael P. O'Conner. Title: The Outer Banks and Man (72)

Speaker: Richard Padgett. Title: Man and His Environment (73)

Speaker: Roswell Piper. Title: Environment and Business (74)

Speaker: Prem P. Seghal. Title: Environmental Education (75)

Health, Safety and Athletics

Speaker: Rod Compton. Titles: Cryokinetic Therapy in Athletics; Drugs and Athletics, Uses and Abuses; Sports Medicine, A Young and Growing Profession (76)

Speaker: Sheldon C. Downes. Titles: Architectural Barriers; Community Rehabilitation; Greenville and the Medical Rehabilitation Community (77)

Speaker: Robert S. Fulghum. Titles: Anaerobic Bacteria in Disease; Anaerobic Bacteriology in the Clinical Laboratory (78)

Speaker: George Hamilton. Titles: Care of the Hand Injured Patient; Physical Therapy as a Career; Rehabilitation - Putting People in Motion (79)

Speaker: Edgar W. Hooks. Titles: Conservation of Human Resources; Physiological Efficiency in Technological Societies; Urban Living Problems Related to Health (80)

Speaker: Thomas H. Johnson. Titles: Drug Misuse and Abuse, More and More Leisure (81)

Speaker: N.M. Jorgensen. Titles: Alcohol Education; Athletics (82)

Speaker: Lionel Kendrick. Titles: Drug Abuse; Drug Abuse - A Course for Parents and Teachers (83)

Speaker: Alfred King. Title: Traffic Safety Programs (84)

Speaker: John Schlick. Title: Traffic Safety Programs (85)

Speaker: Ray Sharf. Titles: Competitive Swimming; Water Safety (86)

Speaker: Clarence Stasavich. Titles: Athletics; Athletics in Education; Winning (87)

Speaker: Ralph Steele. Title: Scalpel, Forceps, and Seawater (88)

Speaker: Mary Susan Templeton. Titles: Helping the Physically Handicapped Child to Grow in Contemporary Society; Physical Rehabilitation Needs of the Geriatric (89)

History

Speaker: Nicole Aronson. Title: Great Names in French History (90)

Speaker: Robert J. Gowen. Title: America and the Vietnam War (91)

Speaker: Umesh C. Gulati. Titles: The History of Bangladesh; History of India and Pakistan (92)

Speaker: Anthony J. Papalas. Titles: Morality and the Fall of Rome; The Trojan War: Myth or History? (93)

Speaker: Fred Ragan. Title: Freedom of Speech and Press (94)

The Home

Speaker: Diane Carroll. Titles: Better Management of Time; Lighting in the Home (95)

The Home (continued)

Speaker: Pat Hurley. Titles: Historical Furniture Styles; Home Furnishings; Selecting a Home (96)
Speaker: Bruce Wardrep. Title: Home Buying and Selling for the Layperson (97)

Miscellaneous

Speaker: J.W. Batten. Titles: Humorous; Space Science (98)
Speaker: James Chantrill. Title: The Government Printing Office and You (99)
Speaker: Frank W. Eller. Title: Notes on Home Gardens (100)
Speaker: W.W. Hankins. Titles: Campus Planning - Luxury or Necessity?; Introdution to Urban and Regional Planning; The Planning Process - The Planner and the Public (101)
Speaker: William A. Shires. Titles: Ethics of News Media; Newspapering, Today and Yesterday; Public Relations (102)
Speaker: Howard Sugg. Titles: Arms, Disarmament, and Security; Environmental Problems; International Relations (103)
Speaker: Robert Ussery. Title: Making Soap (104)
Speaker: Thomas A. Williams. Title: The Mysterious World of the Mind (105)

Music

Speaker: Lokenath Debnath. Title: Mathematics and Music (106)
Speaker: Charles Moore. Titles: Choral Music in a Time of Affluence; Music of the Churches in Change; Singing as Recreation (107)
Speaker: Everett Pittman. Titles: Comprehensive Musicianship; Music of the Avant-Garde (108)
Speaker: William E. Stephenson. Title: Magical Movie Music (109)
Speaker: Charles Stevens. Titles: Moravian Music - A Valuable American Heritage; Music of 18th Century America (110)

Other Cultures and Societies

Speaker: Nicole Aronson. Title: Everyday Life in France (111)
Speaker: Michael F. Bassman. Title: Eastern Europe Today (112)
Speaker: Ralph Birchard. Title: Background of the Ethiopian Situation (113)
Speaker: Robert Louis Bunger. Titles: Africa - An Overview; The Afro-Americans and African Culture; River People - The Pokomo of Kenya (114)
Speaker: Grace Ellenburg. Title: Contemporary France (115)
Speaker: Frank W. Eller. Title: Observations on Russia, Alaska, or New Mexico (116)
Speaker: Robert J. Gowen. Title: The Agony of Modern China (117)
Speaker: Umesh C. Gulati. Title: Social and Economic Problems of India and Pakistan (118)
Speaker: Usha T. Gulati. Titles: The Caste System in India; Fashions and Customs in India; Role of Women in India (119)
Speaker: Edward P. Leahy. Title: Brazil; Chile; West Indies (120)
Speaker: Nancy Mayberry. Titles: Aspects of Bilingualism in Canada; Our Neighbors to the North (121)
Speaker: Anthony J. Papalas. Title: Greece Today (122)
Speaker: Avtar Singh. Titles: Family Life in Asia and the United States; Growth and Development in Southern Asia; Religious Traditions of India (123)
Speaker: Vernon Smith. Title: The Cyprus Dilemma (124)

Physical Sciences and Mathematics

Speaker: Lokenath Debnath. Titles: Mathematics - The Queen and Servant; Wave Phenomena (125)
Speaker: Tennala A. Gross. Titles: The Changing Role of Women; The Computer - Friend or Enemy; Mathematics as a Tool (126)
Speaker: F. Milam Johnson. Title: How Computers Affect You (127)
Speaker: Terence E. McEnally, Jr. Title: Polarized Light (128)
Speaker: Peter Mueller-Roemer. Titles: Can There Be Anything New in Mathematics; Causality and Quantum Physics; Does Nature Obey Mathematical Laws?; Philosophical Aspects of Mathematics (129)
Speaker: Tom C. Sayetta. Titles: Einstein's Theory of Relativity; The Eye, Light, and Illusions; The Laser; Probability and Gambling (130)

Politics

Speaker: Janice Hardison Faulkner. Titles: Political Parties in North Carolina and the United States; Women in Political Life (131)
Speaker: Edith Webber. Title: The Equal Rights Amendment (132)

Psychology

Speaker: Patricia Dunn. Title: Normal Gratifications of Grief (133)
Speaker: William F. Grossnickle. Titles: The Apathetic Bystander; Communications; Leadership and Productivity; The Use of Tests (134)
Speaker: Rosina C. Lao. Titles: Introduction to Achievement Motivation; Three Processes of Attitude Change (135)
Speaker: Clinton R. Prewett. Titles: Community Psychology; Educational Leadership; Human Relations in Business; Human Relations in Education; Organizational Effectiveness (136)

Religion and History

Speaker: Dawyer D. Gross. Titles: Philosophy of Religion; Recent Developments in Religion; The World's Religions (137)

Speaker: N.M. Jorgensen. Titles: History and Doctrine of the Mormon Church; Man - His Origin, Purpose, Destiny (138)

Speaker: Bodo Nischan. Titles: Church History; German Culture and Politics; German History (139)

Speaker: Avtar Singh. Title: Religious Traditions in India (140)

Speaker: Henry Wanderman. Title: Judaism (141)

Social Welfare

Speaker: H.G. Moeller. Titles: Corrections in the Community; The Jail as a Community Corrections Center; The Prison, Its Problems and Prospects (142)

★ 57 ★

EASTERN ILLINOIS UNIVERSITY
Charleston, Illinois 61920 (217) 581-2820

More than ninety faculty members are prepared to lecture on subjects in which they are specialists to community organizations, meetings, and conferences. The matter of honorariums or expenses lies between the speaker and the sponsoring organization.

Speaker: Eulalee L. Anderson. Titles: Brazil; Comparative Education; Women In Other Cultures (1)

Speaker: Dennis Aten. Titles: Handicapped Children; Strains of the Lower Extremities; Therapeutic Exercise (2)

Speaker: Ferrel Atkins. Titles: Rocky Mountain Yesterdays; Windows to Wilderness (3)

Speaker: John Beall. Titles: Contemporary Trends in Music; Creativity in Music; Electronic Music (4)

Speaker: Benjamin L. Brooks. Titles: The Law and the Handicapped; Parents' Rights (5)

Speaker: David Buchanan. Titles: Chemistry of Smell; A Chemist's View of the Energy Crisis; Scientific Truth - Knowledge or Certainty (6)

Speaker: William A. Butler. Title: Physics (7)

Speaker: Bob Butts. Titles: Alternative Life Styles; Communication in Marriage; Death and Dying; Women in Society (8)

Speaker: Robert P. Chen. Title: Taiwan (9)

Speaker: Donald G. Christ. Titles: Developing Alternative Funding Sources; Long Range Educational Planning; The Ombudsman in Public Education; Regional Delivery of Educational Services; Soviet Education; The State Office and Public Education (10)

Speaker: Wayne Coleman. Titles: Acceptable Quality Control; Industrial Technology; Metric Conversion (11)

Speaker: Lewis H. Coon. Title: Going Metric - In Business, Industry, Stores, and Schools (12)

Speaker: William J. Crane. Titles: Psychology Testing?; Role Playing and Defense Mechanisms; What Does Your Child Get Out of School?; Where Do The Students Go? (13)

Speaker: A. Douglas Davis. Title: Physics (14)

Speaker: Ruth Dow. Titles: Changing Societal Roles - Today and Tomorrow; Managing Your Time; Nutrition - It's Your Choice; Quality of Life - Options and Opportunities; Stretching Your Food Dollar (15)

Speaker: Leonard Durham. Titles: Effects of Thermal Pollution on Rivers; Management of Fishes (16)

Speaker: David C. Dutler. Titles: The Changing Trends in Intramurals; Intramural Recreational Activities for Everyone; Programming, Organizing and Administering Intramurals (17)

Speaker: William F. Egloff. Titles: Handling Conflict; Interpersonal Relations; Market Targets (18)

Speaker: John R. Faust. Titles: Contemporary Issues in American Foreign Policy; Future Control of the Oceans; United States Relations With the Third World; United States Relations With the United Nations; World Hunger (19)

Speaker: Karen Ferguson. Titles: Cell Membranes and Heroin; Cholesterol; Women in Science (20)

Speaker: John Flynn. Titles: Financial Aids; Scholarships (21)

Speaker: John P. Ford. Titles: Glacial Geology of Coles County, Illinois; Mission to Earth (22)

Speaker: Lucina P. Gabbard. Title: The New Stars of British Drama (23)

Speaker: Ronald E. Gholson. Titles: The Future and Education; Secondary School Student Activities; Viable Alternatives in Social Studies (24)

Speaker: John R. Griffith. Titles: Energy Allocation; Energy Conservation; Energy Development; Environmental Preservation (25)

Speaker: George Hackler. Titles: Adult-Continuing Education; Continuing Education and You; Life-Long Learning (26)

Speaker: Kenneth E. Hadwiger. Titles: Barefoot Sailing Charters; Communication; Graduate Education (27)

Speaker: Lavern M. Hamand. Titles: Antietam - America's Bloodiest Day; Beef-Buffalo-Barbed Wire; Lincoln the Man Not Myth; Mary Todd Lincoln; Our Greatest General: R.E. Lee (28)

Speaker: Burton E. Hardin. Titles: French Horn Performance; Multitrack Recording Techniques; Violin Making (29)

Speaker: Edith R. Hedges. Titles: Food and Nutrition Beliefs; Nutrition for Modern 49'ers; Nutrition for the Two of You; The Ups and Downs of Weight Control (30)

Speaker: Paul Henry. Title: University Residential Living (31)

Speaker: Joseph Heumann. Titles: American Film; Contemporary Film; Film and Television as an Industrial Process; Social Consequences of Television; Television, Media Criticism (32)

Speaker: Billy J. Heyduck. Titles: Ceramics; History of Ceramics (33)

Speaker: William M. Hillner. Titles: Classroom Management; Effect of the Family Upon Children; Mental Health; Parenting, A Difficult Job (34)

Speaker: Dan Hockman. Titles: American Colonial History; Continuing Education (35)

Speaker: Charles A. Hollister. Title: Public Law Matters (36)

Speaker: Stephan M. Horak. Titles: From Autocracy to Totalitarianism; Nationalism and Human Rights in the Soviet Union; Russia - Past and Present; Soviet Foreign Policy (37)

Speaker: Vaughn Jaenike. Titles: The Arts and Quality of Life; The Arts to the People and of the People; Community Resources for Better Living (38)

Speaker: George Hilton Jones. Title: Margery the Medium (39)

Speaker: Rhoderick E. Key. Title: What the Music Department Has to Offer East Central Illinois (40)

Speaker: William G. Kirk. Titles: The Art of Asserting Yourself; The Art of Self Disclosure; How to Create a Disturbed Child; Marriage - Vocation or Avocation (41)

Speaker: Ronald Kogen. Titles: American Jazz; The American Symphony Orchestra; The Violin - History, Development and Literature (42)

Speaker: Paul Krause. Title: National Parks of the Southwest; A Park Ranger in South Dakota (43)

Speaker: June Krutza. Titles: Contemporary Ceramics; England; Japan; Japanese Folk Craft Pottery; Japanese Gardens; Oriental Art; Scotland (44)

Speaker: Clay Ladd. Titles: Psychological Self-Help; Teaching Personally Useful Psychology (45)

Speaker: Donald P. Lauda. Titles: Education and the Future; Technology and the Future; Technology and Values (46)

Speaker: Dorothy M. Lawson. Titles: Career Education and the Elementary School; Career Education and the Junior High School; The Career Education Movement; The Community and the Classroom; Using Community Resources (47)

Speaker: Ronald Leathers. Titles: Grammar of the English Sentence; Illinois Teacher Certification; Organizing the English Curriculum (48)

Speaker: Peter R. Leigh II. Titles: How County Government in Illinois Could be Improved; Major Problems in our Criminal Justice System; A Review of Various Types of City Government; What is the State Legislature Doing Which Affects the Ordinary Citizen? (49)

Speaker: Michael B. Leyden. Titles: A Look at Elementary School Science; Piaget - Some Ideas on Efficient Learning; Science Never Tasted Like This (50)

Speaker: Phillip Lindberg. Titles: Campus Facilities; Campus Facilities and the Successful Program; How to Plan a Conference (51)

Speaker: John Linn. Titles: Art History; Understanding Chinese Painting (52)

Speaker: W.S. Lowell. Title: The U.S. Naval Academy (53)

Speaker: Fred MacLaren. Titles: The Latest Reading Controversy; Sexism in Reading Materials; Speed Reading (54)

Speaker: Gerhard C. Matzner. Titles: Legal Duties and Responsibilities of Boards of Education; The Schools in Illinois: How We Pay for Them; The Teacher, The Pupil and the Law (55)

Speaker: David J. Maurer. Titles: Big Government - When it Began; The Cold War; The Golden Twenties; Organizing the Small Museum (56)

Speaker: B.F. McClerren. Titles: Barriers to Communication; Communication is Impossible; Responsible Communication (57)

Speaker: Gene McFarland. Titles: Forming a Rifle, Pistol, or Shotgun Class; Successful Shotgun Shooting (58)

Speaker: Edward O. Moll. Titles: Malaysian Turtles; Malaysian Wildlife; The Web of Pollution (59)

Speaker: Mike Mullally. Titles: Athletics and Education; Athletics and the Student Athlete; Recruiting the Student Athlete (60)

Speaker: Ahmad Murad. Titles: The Arab-Israeli Conflict; How to Achieve Peace in the Middle East; The International Economic Situation; The New International Economic Order; Politics and Economics of the Arab World (61)

Speaker: Louise Murray. Titles: Africa - Tawny Lion of Tomorrow; Canada and Its Changing World; Modern Trends in Children's Literature; Myth, Magic, and Reality; A New Look at the Old Jerusalem; The Power of Poetry; Reading - The Magic Art (62)

Speaker: James E. Nicely. Titles: Prevention of Speech and Language Problems; Rehabilitative Services for Children and Adults with and/or Hearing Problems (63)

Speaker: Carol Noland. Titles: Choosing the Proper Contraceptive; Sex Education for Parents; What I Learned as a Widow about Consumer Education (64)

Speaker: John T. North. Titles: Collective Bargaining - The Good and the Bad; The Survival of Public Education (65)

Speaker: Sharon Pearson. Titles: Expository Writing - A Necessary Skill; What We Can Do About Johnny's Writing (66)

Speaker: Jack C. Rang. Titles: The Arts? Who Needs Them?; The Golden Age of Radio (67)

Speaker: Jane Reed. Title: Camping and Backpacking for the Beginner (68)
Speaker: Jack J. Richardson. Titles: The Drug Scene; Drug Use and Abuse; Human Erosion and Human Conservation (69)
Speaker: Donald L. Rogers. Titles: Matching Models in Education; Metrics for the Layman; Motivation In the Classroom (70)
Speaker: Robert E. Saltmarsh. Titles: Assertiveness Training; Critical Skills for Effective Life Making; Enrichment of Marriage Relationships; Gestalt Therapy; The Human Potential Movement (71)
Speaker: Carol Sanders. Titles: Career Development and Subject Matter Concepts; Career Education Program Development; Involving the Community in Career Education Programs (72)
Speaker: Claud D. Sanders. Title: Career - Planning and Job Hunting; Motivation (73)
Speaker: J.W. Sanders. Titles: Motivational Aspects of Sports Participation; Sociology of Sport; Sport Officiating (74)
Speaker: Wolfgang Schlauch. Titles: Berlin - the Eternal Crisis; East-West Relations; European Unity; Modern Germany (75)
Speaker: Gene W. Scholes. Titles: Designing Effective Instruction; Effective Media; Instructional Problems (76)
Speaker: Frederick R. Schram. Titles: Ancient Egypt; The Fossils of Mazon Creek; Human Evolution (77)
Speaker: Phillip M. Settle. Title: Folk Arts (78)
Speaker: Kathlene Shank. Titles: Creative Writing in the Classroom; The Future of Elementary Education; Stimulating Children to Write Poetry; Teaching More Creatively in Reading and Language Arts; Title Ideas; Using Language Experience (79)
Speaker: H.S. Sharaway. Titles: Informative Systems for Instruction, Administration and Research; Yoga, Health and Fitness (80)
Speaker: Robert V. Shuff. Titles: Alaska - Its Schools and People; Community Education and Life-Long Learning; Schools in an Era of Contraction (81)
Speaker: Carl Shull. Titles: Folklore and Edibility of Wild Plants; Folklore and Legend of Birds in Art; Indian Culture and Art; Sports and Art (82)
Speaker: Sue C. Sparks. Title: Meeting College Costs (83)
Speaker: Gayle Gilbert Strader. Titles: Consumerism Today; Energy Consumer Problems; Metrics for Consumers; Recycling Clothing (84)
Speaker: Kenneth Sutton. Titles: Alternative Education; Contemporary Philosophy and Education; The Future of Working; The Meanings of Lifelong Learning; Mistakes We Make About the Aged; Teaching the Culturally Different; What Work Should Mean (85)
Speaker: Mary Ruth Swope. Title: Nutrition and You (86)
Speaker: Henry A. Taitt. Titles: Life Elsewhere in the Universe; The Use of Hobbies in the Teaching of Physics (87)
Speaker: Dan Thornburgh. Titles: Journalism; The Press and First Amendment; Your Newspaper Needs You (88)
Speaker: Larry Thorsen. Titles: Contemporary French Government and Politics; United States Energy Policy (89)
Speaker: Wayne L. Thurman. Titles: Myself as Seen in My Voice; Speech Problems (90)
Speaker: Charles Titus. Titles: Alumni and Eastern Illinois University; Forgotten Hero of the War of 1812; An Historical Look at Jesus Christ; Our National Anthem; The Spirit of '76; Why an Alumni Program? (91)
Speaker: Leyla Peck Waddell. Titles: The Alexandrian Library; A Bibliophile View of the Bible; Egypt; England; France; Lebanon; The Preservation of Historic Buildings; The Renaissance in France; Scandinavia; U.S.S.R. (92)
Speaker: Peter Wetterlind. Titles: Build Your Own Information System; Data Systems for Higher Education; An Eclectic Enrollment Projection Model; Talking to the Computer in its Language (93)
Speaker: Steve Whitley. Titles: Aspects of Environmental Biology; The Environmental Protection Agency; Environmental Quality and the American Way of Life; Pollution and You; Water Quality (94)
Speaker: Rebecca Smith Wild. Titles: Bornese Festival For the Dead; Japanese Rage for Order; Japanese Women's Lib; Martin Ritt, Latter-Day Son of Ben (95)
Speaker: Glenn D. Williams. Titles: Dixie Darlings of the Cloak and Dagger; Don't Take Yourself Too Seriously; Gettysburg, The Valley Campaign; Professional Excellence; Wisdom - A Many Splendored Thing (96)
Speaker: Robert C. Wiseman. Titles: Creating With Media; Media in Education (97)

★ 58 ★

ESPERANTO LEAGUE FOR NORTH AMERICA
6451 Barnaby Street, N.IW.
Washington, D.C. 20015 (202) 362-3963

Speakers are available to lecture in most parts of the United States on Esperanto, the international language, its use, purposes and historical development. Generally no fees.

Speaker: William R. Harmon. Title: The Status of Esperanto in The Orient (1)
Speaker: E. James Lieberman. Title: Esperanto After Ninety Years (2)
Speaker: Jonathan R. Pool. Title: Esperanto and the Right to Communicate (3)

Speaker: Humphrey Tonkin. Title: Esperanto in the World Today (4)

F

★ 59 ★
FAME LIMITED
880 Black Mountain Road
Hillsborough, California 94010 (415) 343-1001

Arranges engagements with clubs, colleges, universities and private sponsors throughout the Western States for speakers, all of whom narrate in conjunction with travel documentary and film material. Fees range from $350 - $750.

Speaker: Ken Armstrong. Titles: Amazing Korea; Bewitching Thailand; Brawny Australia!; Hong Kong and Macao; Outback Australia! (1)
Speaker: Jens Bjerre. Titles: China After Mao; China Today; New Guinea Expedition; Soul of India (2)
Speaker: Willis Butler. Titles: Alaska; Hong Kong; Switzerland Today; Turkey (3)
Speaker: Ralph Gerstle. Titles: Colombia - Andes to the Amazon; Guatemala and Yucatan; Sri Lanka (4)
Speaker: Irving M. Johnson. Titles: Great Sailing Adventures; Yankee Sails Inland; Yankee Sails Scandinavia; Yankee Sails the Mediterranean; Yankee Sails the Nile; Yankee Sails the Trade Wind Islands (5)
Speaker: Dewitt Jones. Titles: John Muir's High Sierra; Robert Frost's New England (6)
Speaker: Doug Jones. Titles: Broadway, U.S.A.; Egypt - Gift of the Nile; Hawaiian Adventure; Magic of Venice; Paris of the Parisians; Royal London (7)
Speaker: Martin Litton. Title: Grand Canyon (8)
Speaker: Bill Madsen. Titles: Bonnie Scotland; Dakar to Timbuctu; Ireland; Rare Jewels of the Mediterranean; Wonderful Mexico (9)
Speakers: Matthew and Sherilyn Mentes. Titles: Bonjour, France!; California's Mission Trail; Greece - Islands to the Mountains; Hungary; Poland (10)
Speaker: Frank Nichols. Titles: Colorado; Portugal; Surprising Switzerland (11)
Speaker: Harry Pederson. Titles: Bahamas - Top to Bottom; Four Fathom World; Village Beneath the Sea (12)
Speaker: Dick Reddy. Titles: Austria; Germany; Mark Twain in Italy; Mark Twain in Switzerland; Russia; Swedish Summer (13)
Speaker: John Roberts. Titles: Caribbean Paradise; Delightful Denmark; Holland and the Amazing Dutch; Magnificent Austria; The Majestic Rhine; New England - Cradle of America; The New Norway; Puerto Rico; Switzerland (14)
Speaker: Bob Roney. Title: Yosemite and the High Sierra (15)
Speaker: Bill Stockdale. Titles: All Aboard for Siberia!; Australia by Camper; Backroads, U.S.A.; The Holy Lands; Israel - The Holy Land; Pathways through England (16)
Speaker: Charles Taylor. Titles: America the Beautiful; The Biblelands; The Great Trans-Canada Train Ride; There'll Always be an England (17)
Speaker: Theodore Walker. Titles: Alaska Wilderness Lake; Sea and Shore of Baja (18)

★ 60 ★
FEDERAL RESERVE BANK OF RICHMOND
Bank and Public Relations Department
Post Office Box 27622
Richmond, Virginia 23261 (804) 649-3611

Speakers are available to lecture on such topics as central banking, monetary policy, and economic forecasts. No charges or fees for speakers.

★ 61 ★
FEDERAL RESERVE BANK OF SAN FRANCISCO
400 Sansome Street
San Francisco, California 94120 (415) 544-2191

The Federal Reserve Bank of San Francisco maintains a Speakers Bureau consisting of officers, economists, managers and key staff members. Speakers will discuss the business outlook, monetary policy, functions and purposes of the Federal Reserve system, housing and construction trends, the electronic funds transfer, the check and money payments system, currency operations, and the role of the Federal Reserve. Speakers are provided at no cost to organizations.

★ 62 ★
FEMINIST KARATE UNION
101 Nickerson Street, Building A, Suite 250
Seattle, Washington 98119 (206) 282-0177

Speakers are available for talks, discussion, workshops and seminars covering a variety of topics. Demonstration teams are also available. Speakers fees are $100 plus travel expenses.

Speaker: Py Bateman. Titles: Rape Intervention; Rape Prevention; Self Protection for Senior Citizens; Women's Self Defense; Women's Sport Karate (1)

Speaker: Suzanne Mitten. Titles: Rape Intervention; Rape Prevention; Women's Self Defense (2)
Speaker: Kathy Reid. Titles: Rape Intervention; Rape Prevention; Women's Self Defense (3)

★ 63 ★
FIRST FEDERAL OF BROWARD
301 East Las Olas Boulevard
Fort Lauderdale, Florida 33302 (305) 763-1121 ext. 373

Provides speakers to lecture on subjects pertaining to business and finance. No fees.

Subjects: Advertising; The Economy; Marketing; Public Relations; Sales Motivation; Savings and Mortgage; Women in Business

★ 64 ★
FLORIDA A&M UNIVERSITY
Office of University Relations
Box 368
Tallahassee, Florida 32307 (904) 599-3413

Some fifty-three speakers are available to lecture on a variety of subjects to community, civic, and social organizations in the Tallahassee area. No fees.

★ 65 ★
FLORIDA ASSOCIATION OF REALTORS
Post Office Box 1231
Orlando, Florida 32802 (305) 849-0443

Speakers are prepared to lecture on many real estate topics to groups and organizations in the state of Florida. No fees other than reimbursement of expenses.

Speaker: Marlene M. Alexander. Titles: Appraising; Condominiums; Economic Outlook; Forecasting and Research; Market Feasibility; Mobile Homes (1)
Speaker: Theo D. Baars, Jr. Titles: Ethics; Motivation (2)
Speaker: Clyde M. Banks. Titles: Commercial Property; Condominiums; Investment Real Estate (3)
Speaker: Parker C. Banzhaf. Titles: Civic Participation; Economics of Real Estate; Ethics (4)
Speaker: Thomas J. Bermingham. Titles: Closing; Ethics; Property Management; Real Estate Law Applications (5)
Speaker: Blanche Boardman. Titles: Advertising; Closing; Communication; Ethics; Public Relations; Qualifying; Salesmanship; Salesmen Training (6)
Speaker: Betty Jane Boone. Titles: Closing; Ethics; Investment Real Estate; Listing; Qualifying; Salesmanship; Showing (7)
Speaker: Robert H. Bossen. Titles: Closing; Listing; Office Management; Presenting Offer and Counter-offer; Prospecting; Qualifying; Salesmanship; Showing (8)
Speaker: Otto L. Cantrall. Titles: Closing; Ethics; Finance; Listing; Office Management; Qualifying; Salesmanship; Salesmen Training; Showing (9)
Speaker: J.E. Carroll. Titles: Appraising; Ethics; Independent Contractor Status; Multiple Listing; Realtor Associate Program; Realtor Associate Relations (10)
Speaker: J. Rodney Clark. Titles: Closing; Franchising; Listing; Office Management; Overcoming Objections; Qualifying; Salesmanship; Salesmen Training (11)
Speaker: F.P. Concannon. Titles: Building For Your Own Account; Exchanging; Investment Real Estate; Listing; Office Management; Salesmanship; Salesmen Training; Syndication (12)
Speaker: Peter O. Dalton. Titles: Listing; Qualifying; Salesmanship; Salesmen Training (13)
Speaker: Horace C. Danforth. Titles: Closing; Economics of Real Estate; Ethics; Finance; Listing; Qualifying; Salesmanship; Showing (14)
Speaker: Carlos Dominguez, Jr. Titles: Closing; Construction; Economics of Real Estate; Ethics; Listing; Office Management; 100% Commission Concept; Qualifying; Salesmanship; Salesmen Training; Showing (15)
Speaker: J. Wayne Falbey. Titles: Closing; Condominiums; Investment Real Estate; Protecting Title to Realty; Realtor Attorney Liaison; Syndication (16)
Speaker: Karl S. Fantle. Titles: Advertising; Appraising; Commercial Property; Ethics; Investment Real Estate; Listing; Property Management; Salesmen Training (17)
Speaker: Reid D. Farrell. Titles: Closing; Economics of Real Estate; Ethics; Finance; Guaranteed Trade Sales Plan; Salesmen Training (18)
Speaker: Joe Fearnley. Titles: Economics of Real Estate; Investment Real Estate; Office Management; Salesmanship; Salesmen Training; Syndication (19)
Speaker: Robert J. Frost, III. Titles: Closing; The Lazy Man's Trip to the Bank or Real Estate, the Profession of Happy People; Listing; Motivation of People for Profits; Salesmanship; Salesmen Training; Showing; Women in Real Estate - Equal at Last (20)
Speaker: G. Fritz Gale. Titles: Listing; Negotiating the Sale (21)

Speaker: Jack German. Titles: Advertising; Appraising; Closing; Commercial Property; Ethics; Finance; Listing; Public Relations; Qualifying; Real Estate Law (22)

Speaker: Jim Graham. Titles: Investment Real Estate; Real Estate Auctions; Salesmen Training (23)

Speaker: Errol L. Greene. Titles: Closing; Ethics; Listing; Protection of Private Property Rights; Qualifying; Salesmanship; Showing; Syndication (24)

Speaker: Robert Hannan. Titles: Commercial Property; Exchanging (Commercial and Residential); Home Trade-in Program; Investment Real Estate (25)

Speaker: Mac D. Heavener, Jr. Titles: Advertising; Appraising; Closing; Finance; Listing; Qualifying; Salesmanship; Showing (26)

Speaker: Jerrold R. Hinton. Titles: Residential Developments; Surveying; Tennis-oriented Developments (27)

Speaker: Henry Hoche. Titles: Office Management; Persuasion and Motivation; Property Management; Salesmanship; Salesmen Training (28)

Speaker: John Hogan. Titles: Dealing With a Newcomer Buyer; Investment Real Estate; Listing; Showing (29)

Speaker: Walter V. Horn. Titles: Closing; Ethics; Listing; Public Relations; Qualifying; Salesmanship; Salesmen Training; Showing (30)

Speaker: Max Hudson. Titles: Ethics; Finance; Franchising; Listing; Motivational Aspects of Real Estate; Qualifying; Salesmanship; Salesmen Training (31)

Speaker: Alan W. Jacobson. Titles: Closing; Financing; Listings; Office Management, Operation and Forms; Qualifying; Salesmanship and Communication; Salesmen Training; Showing; Telephone Techniques; Time Planning and Goal Setting (32)

Speaker: Ernest A. Jones: Titles: Appraising; Closing; Construction; Ethics; Public Relations; Realtor Attorney Relationships (33)

Speaker: Robert W. Kirk. Titles: Appraising; Commercial Property; Economics of Real Estate; Finance; Groves, Ranches, Farms; Investment Real Estate (34)

Speaker: Sidney Konigsburg. Titles: Finance; National United States Economy; Property Management (35)

Speaker: Maggie S. Lassetter. Titles: Education in Real Estate; Ethics; Human Relations; Personality Development; Real Estate License Law; Realtor Associate Relations (36)

Speaker: Paul Walton Ledridge. Titles: Appraising; Construction; Ethics; Listing; Salesmanship; Showing (37)

Speaker: George M. Linville. Titles: Advertising; Closing; Ethics; Listing; Office Management; Public Relations; Qualifying; Salesmanship (38)

Speaker: Frank Lynn. Titles: Advertising; Closing; Ethics; Listing; Public Relations; Salesmanship; Salesmen Training; Showing (39)

Speaker: Albert A. McCoy. Titles: Appraising; Closing; Listing; Qualifying (40)

Speaker: George E. McCullough. Titles: Elements in Properly Preparing a Real Estate Sales Contract; Exchanging; Listings; Public Relations; Qualifying the Seller and His Property (41)

Speaker: Claudette E. McIntosh. Titles: Closing; Ethics; Listing; Motivation - Youth in Real Estate; Public Relations; Qualifying; Salesmanship; Salesmen Training (42)

Speaker: Frank H. Martens. Titles: Appraising; Education and Board Education Programs; Ethics; Exchanging; Investment Real Estate; Property Management; Salesmanship; Salesmen Training (43)

Speaker: Steven A. Moore. Titles: Advertising; Buying Motivations; Closing; Overcoming Objections; Prospecting; Qualifying; Salesmanship; Salesmen Training; Time Control (44)

Speaker: Lilyb Moskal. Titles: Advertising; Listing; Public Relations; Salesmanship; Salesmen Training; Self-Motivation (45)

Speaker: Madora Moutz. Titles: Advertising; Civic Participation; Creative Selling; Ethics; Orientation; Public Relations; Residential Merchandising; Sales Meetings (46)

Speaker: W.B. Moutz. Titles: Creative Selling; Ethics; Listings; Merchandising; Office Operations; Salesmen Training (47)

Speaker: Richard A. Newstreet. Titles: Closing; Condominiums; Listing; Office Management; Qualifying; Salesmanship; Salesmen Training; Showing (48)

Speaker: D. William Overton. Titles: Appraising; Condominiums; Finance; Investment Real Estate (49)

Speaker: William P. Pardue. Titles: Appraising; Commercial Property; Condominiums; Economics of Real Estate; Investment Real Estate (50)

Speaker: Phillip Pickens. Titles: Appraising; Economics of Real Estate; Ethics; Real Estate License Law (51)

Speaker: John E. Pierce. Titles: Advertising; Listing; Office Management; Qualifying; Salesmanship; Salesmen Training; Showing (52)

Speaker: Jack Pyms. Titles: Commercial Property; Ethics; Exchanging; Mobile Homes and Parks; Office Management; Salesmanship; Salesmen Training; Syndication (53)

Speaker: Monroe G. Randol. Titles: Advertising; Commercial Property; Economics of Real Estate; Ethics; Exchanging; Finance; Franchising; Guaranteed Sales (54)

Speaker: John F. Ring. Titles: Commercial Property; Condominiums; Ethics; Investment Real Estate; Listing; Property Management; Public Relations; Salesmen Training (55)

Speaker: Mack Robison. Titles: Commercial Property; Construction; Country Boy Approach; Economics of Real Estate; Ethics; Investment Real Estate; Public Relations (56)
Speaker: Frank W. Schieber. Titles: Commercial Property; Franchising; Investment Real Estate; Syndication (57)
Speaker: Ted C. Slack. Titles: Appraising; Commercial Property; Economics of Real Estate; Investment Real Estate (58)
Speaker: L. B. Slater. Titles: Appraising; Economics of Real Estate; Ethics; Listing; Public Relations; Qualifying (59)
Speaker: Ver Lynn Sprague. Titles: Closing; Inspirational and After Dinner Assignments; Public Relations; Qualifying; Salesmanship; Salesmen Training (60)
Speaker: William H. Stemper, Sr. Titles: Appraising; Closing and Negotiating the Sale; Commercial Property and Investment; Exchanging; Finance; Investment Real Estate; Listing; Salesmanship; Syndication; Tax Depreciation and Shelter (61)
Speaker: Phillip A. Thomas. Titles: Commercial Property; Condominiums; Economics of Real Estate; Industrial Real Estate; Investment Real Estate (62)
Speaker: Henry L. Van Brackle. Titles: Closing; Listing; Office Management; Public Relations; Qualifying; Salesmanship; Salesmen Training; Showing (63)
Speaker: E. Lee Varnadore. Titles: Closing; Finance; Listing; Office Management; Qualifying; Salesmanship; Salesmen Training; Showing (64)
Speaker: Robert L. Ward. Titles: Commercial Property; Economics of Real Estate; Ethics; Exchanging; Finance; Investment Real Estate; Syndication (65)
Speaker: Paul W. Waters. Titles: Commercial Property; Economics of Real Estate; Ethics; Finance; Investment Real Estate; Motivation; Public Relations (66)
Speaker: W.J. Wegman. Titles: Commercial Property; Economics of Real Estate; Investment Real Estate; Listing (67)
Speaker: Olin R. Wilcox. Titles: Advertising; Ethics; Listing; Office Management; Public Relations; Qualifying; Salesmanship; Salesmen Training (68)
Speaker: James T. Wilson. Titles: Computer Applications to Real Estate Marketing; Economics of Real Estate; Exchanging; Investment Real Estate (69)
Speaker: Dorothy M. Yates. Titles: Advertising; Closing; Ethics; Office Management; Salesmen Training; Showing (70)

★ 66 ★
FLORIDA POWER AND LIGHT
Post Office Box 013100
Miami, Florida 33101 (305) 552-3884

More than two hundred speakers are available to lecture on current activities in the utility industry. No fees.

Titles: Energy Alternatives; How Energy Wise Are You; Nuclear - The Viable Alternative; Why You Pay What You Pay; Yesterday's Fuel Tomorrow

★ 67 ★
FOOD PROCESSING MACHINERY AND SUPPLIES ASSOCIATION
1828 L Street, N.W., Suite 700
Washington, D.C. 20036 (202) 833-5770

The Association maintains a speakers bureau consisting of member firm officials who are prepared to lecture on subjects in which they and their companies have special competency. In the details which follow, speakers are identified by the title of their speeches, their company affiliations and telephone numbers are provided so that contact can be made directly with them. The Association can provide additional information on other related subject area presentations.

Speaker: Kenneth E. Alpers, Eric C. Baum and Associates, Inc., (312) 527-2570. Title: How Productivity Can be Enhanced in the Food Processing Industry (1)
Speaker: Eric C. Baum, Eric C. Baum and Associates, Inc., (312) 527-2570. Title: Increasing Productivity Through Employee Motivation (2)
Speaker: Rich Baumann, Kay-Ray, Inc., (312) 259-5600. Title: Moisture Measurement and Control (3)
Speaker: Body Guard, Inc., (614) 291-7601. Title: Food Plant Noise Control (4)
Speaker: J. David Bourke, Robbins and Myers, Inc., Moyno Pump Division (513) 327-3543. Title: Flow Characteristics of Solids - Liquid Mixtures in Pumps and Piping (5)
Speaker: Louis J. Busalacchi, Hughes Company, Inc., (414) 623-2000. Title: Sweet Corn, Green Beans, Cherry, Bright Stack and Filling Equipment (6)
Speaker: Peter K. Butler, Benthos, Inc., (617) 563-5917. Title: Taptone Quality Inspection Systems (7)
Speaker: R.B. Clarke, Baldor (501) 646-4711. Title: Electric Motors - Energy Efficiency (8)
Speaker: Lee M. Clegg, Solbern Corporation (201) 227-3030. Title: Overcoming Problems in Slack Fill (9)

Speaker: Robert W. Coughlin, Pneumatic Scale Corporation (617) 328-6100. Title: Bottling and Packaging Foods and Beverages (10)
Speaker: David A. Ehrhardt, Electro-Coatings, Inc., (415) 376-5161. Title: Corrosion Resistant Plating for Processing Equipment (11)
Speaker: Dennis G. Flynn, Hughes Company, Inc., (414) 623-2000. Title: Sweet Corn, Green Beans, Cherry, Bright Stack and Filling Equipment (12)
Speaker: L. Gilde, Technological Resources, Inc., (609) 964-5603. Title: Land Treatment of Food Plant Waste Water (13)
Speaker: Craig Hogan, Key Electro Sonic (503) 938-5556. Title: French Fries Made From Riced Potatoes (14)
Speaker: W.C. Hollingsworth, Hayssen Manufacturing Company (414) 458-2111. Title: Gas Flushing Horizontal Form, Fill and Seal Packaging (15)
Speaker: D.L. Houmes, Hayssen Manufacturing Company (414) 458-2111. Title: Training Machine Operators (16)
Speaker: Richard S. Hunter, Hunter Associates Laboratory, Inc., (703) 591-5310. Title: Optical Causes of Color in Foods (17)
Speaker: Raymond P. Jones, Ladish Company (414) 694-5511. Titles: Aseptic Processing; Automated Flow Control Systems; Batch Weigh Systems; Blending; Central Cleaning; Designing Piping Systems; Pumps for Food Processing; Sanitary Design (18)
Speaker: Gary Lewis, Kay-Ray, Inc., (312) 259-5600. Title: Nuclear Density, Level and Belt Scale Process Gauges (19)
Speaker: M.T. Ligett, Hayssen Manufacturing Company (414) 458-2111. Title: State of the Art (20)
Speaker: Larry E. Maley, Anacon Inc., (713) 777-2392. Titles: Measurement of Moisture in Dehydrated Food Products, Grain and Other Moisture Measurements in Food Processing; Measurement of Soluble Solids in Food Processing (21)
Speaker: Robert T. Manwaring, Hycor Corporation (312) 473-3700. Title: Removal of Suspended Solids From Industrial Waste Water (22)
Speaker: John M. Michalec, PTE Corporation (408) 735-8900. Title: Fluid Drive Systems (23)
Speaker: P.E. Nelson, Bishopric Products, Company (513) 641-0500. Title: Aseptic Bulk Storage and Transportation (24)
Speaker: S. Rechtsteiner, Bishopric Products, Company (513) 641-0500. Title: Aseptic Bulk Storage and Transportation (25)
Speaker: Bruce Root, Keystone Seed Company, Inc., (414) 886-0907. Title: Development, Production and Processing of Vegetable Seeds Used in the Food Processing Industry (26)
Speaker: Robert D. Saunders, Jr., (305) 395-5126. Title: Development, Production and Processing of Vegetable Seeds Used in the Food Processing Industry (27)
Speaker: C.B. Schultz, Ralphs-Pugh Company, Inc., (707) 745-6363. Title: V-Trough Carriers and PVC Rollers and Pulleys (28)

★ 68 ★
FOOD SHOPPERS UNION
2847 South 13 Street
Milwaukee, Wisconsin 53215 (414) 383-1047

Goals are to improve communication between consumers, retailers, agriculture and government on food questions and consumerism. Lectures are prepared for the particular audience. Fees: Lecture fee plus expenses, subject to negotiation.

Speaker: Joan E. Prochnow. Subject: Consumerism (1)

★ 69 ★
MARTIN A. FORREST
51 Church Street
Boston, Massachusetts 02116 (617) 542-2479

Professional adventurers present travel lectures.

Speaker: Norman Baker. Titles: The Epic Voyages of Ra; Operation Tigris (1)
Speaker: Jens Bjerre. Titles: Bangladesh and India; Bushmen of Kalahari; China After Mao; The Last Cannibals (2)
Speaker: Jean Louis DuBois. Titles: The Amazon; Megreb - Land of the Setting Sun (3)
Speaker: Dewitt Jones. Titles: John Muir's High Sierra; The New England of Robert Frost (4)
Speaker: Michael Kefford. Titles: The Drama of Nuptse; Nepal; Soldiers on Everest (5)
Speaker: Richard Kern. Titles: Florida - Cypress Sanctuary-Fisheating Creek; The Great Smokey Mountains; Hidden Worlds of Florida's Big Cypress Swamp (6)
Speaker: George Lange. Titles: Colombia - From the Spanish Main to the Amazon; Venezuela - Land of Natural Wonders (7)
Speaker: Martin Litton. Titles: Grand Canyon by Dory; Wild Rivers of the West (8)
Speaker: Kal Muller. Titles: The Huichol - Tribe of the Sacred Cactus; People of New Hebrides (9)
Speaker: Frank Mundus. Titles: Master Hunters of the Deep; Shark-Folklore and Reality (10)
Speaker: John Paling. Titles: Frontiers of Wildlife Photography; Secrets of the Wildlife World; The World That the Eye Cannot See (11)
Speaker: Roger Payne. Title: Among Wild Whales (12)

Speaker: Tom Sterling. Titles: The Marsh - A Quiet Mystery; Newfoundland (13)
Speaker: Theodore Walker. Titles: Alaska Wilderness Lake; Great American Deserts; The Sea and Shore of Baja (14)
Speaker: Stanton Waterman. Titles: Chambers of the Sea; The Hidden Sea; Making Sea Movies (15)

★ 70 ★
FREE SOUTHERN THEATER
1328 Dryades Street
New Orleans, Louisiana 70113 (504) 581-5091

The producing director of the theater group is available for lectures. Fee is $200 plus travel and accommodations.

Speaker: John O'Neal. Title: Theater Art and the Struggle Against Oppression (1)

★ 71 ★
RICHARD FULTON INC.
850 Seventh Avenue
New York, New York 10019 (212) 582-4099

Offers lecture services and speakers in a wide range of topical areas. Details are available upon request.

Arts

Speakers: Clive Barnes (1); Judith Crist (2); Vincent Canby (3); Barbaralee Diamonstein (4); Mel Gussow (5); Leonard Harris (6); Marvin Kitman (7); Stewart Klein (8); Hilton Kramer (9); Leonard Probst (10)

Communications

Speakers: Martin Agronsky (11); Mary Albert (12); Rona Barrett (13); Chris Borgen (14); Ben Bradlee (15); Patrick Buchanan (16); Stan Burns (17); Mort Crim (18); Paul Duke (19); Douglas Edwards (20); Bergen Evans (21); Barry Farber (22); John Henry Faulk (23); Joan Fontaine (24); Joe Franklin (25); Nick Gage (26); Ralph Ginzburg (27); Sidney J. Harris (28); Skitch Henderson (29); Sy Hersh (30); Brit Hume (31); Don Imus (32); Tom Jarriel (33); Marvin Kalb (34); Douglas Kiker (35); Gene Klavin (36); Lee Leonard (37); Max Lerner (38); Irving R. Levine (39); Peter Lisagor (40); Rod MacLeish (41); Robert MacNeil (42); Marjorie Margolis (43); Bruce Morrow (44); Jack Newfield (45); Edwin Newman (46); Gil Noble (47); Jack Perkins (48); Gabe Pressman (49); Sally Quinn (50); Harry Reasoner (51); Geraldo Rivera (52); Carl Rowen (53); Ray Scherer (54); Moses Schonfeld (55); Walter Scott (56); Carl Stern (57); Carl Stokes (58); John Cameron Swayze (59); Bob Teague (60); Lowell Thomas (61); Melba Tolliver (62); Liz Trotta (63); Garrick Utley (64); Harriet Van Horne (65); Less Whitten (66); Sidney Zion (67)

Economics

Speakers: Peter Brennan (68); Victor Gotbaum (69); Eliot Janeway (70); Arthur Kemp (71); Irving A. Levine (72); Marshall Loeb (73); Arthur M. Okun (74); Laurence J. Peter (75); Franz Pick (76); Albert Shanker (77); Robert Townsend (78); Al Ullman (79)

Education

Speakers: John Barth (80); Bruno Bettelheim (81); Mary Calderone (82); George A. Friedman (83); Alice Ginott (84); Nathan Glazer (85); Nathan Hare (86); Fred Hechinger (87); Peter Janssen (88); Christopher Jencks (89); Max Rafferty (90); Robert Rimmer (91); Charles Silberman (92); Harold Taylor (93)

Environment

Speakers: B. Bruce Briggs (94); Frank Field (95); Morris Fishbein (96); Kahn-Tineta Horn (97); Leon Jaroff (98); Seymour M. Lipset (99); Ashley Montagu (100); Shorty Powers (101); I. I. Rabi (102); Charles Robbins (103); Ted Sorensen (104); Studs Terkel (105); Stewart Udall (106)

Film

Speakers: Vincent Canby (107); Shirley Clarke (108); Judith Crist (109); Sam Greenlee (110); Elia Kazan (111); Jonas Mekas (112); Ernest Pintoff (113); Otto Preminger (114); Andrew Sarris (115); Budd Schulberg (116)

Government

Speakers: Ralph Abernathy (117); Carl Albert (118); Herbert Aptheker (119); Lerone Bennett (120); Lloyd Bentsen (121); Nathaniel Branden (122); James Buckley (123); Yvonne Burke (124); Robert Byrd (125); Kenneth B. Clark (126); O. Edmund Clubb (127); Alan Cranston (128); John C. Culver (129); Ronald V. Dellums (130); Robert Dole (131); Mervyn Dymally (132); Charles Evers (133); James Farmer (134); Joel Fort (135); George Gallup (136); Leonard Garment (137); Kenneth A. Gibson (138); Charles Goodel (139); Mike Gravel (140); Charles Hamilton (141); Fred Harris (142); Mark Hatfield (143); Dorothy J. Height (144); Jesse Jackson (145); Samuel Lubell (146); Eugene McCarthy (147); Lester Maddox (148); Mike Mansfield (149); William E. Miller (150); Hans Morgenthau (151); Robert Moses (152); Bess Myerson (153); Gaylord Nelson (154); John Pastore (155); Kevin Phillips (156); Dean Rusk (157); James R. Schlesinger (158); William Shockley (159); Adlai Stevenson (160); John Stoessinger (161); Strom Thurmond (162); Robert F. Wagner (163)

Management/Motivation

Speakers: Leo Cherne (164); Fred Herman (165); Sam Hunter (166); Arthur Kemp (167); Charles Lapp (168); Kenneth McFarland (169); Cavett Robert (170); Merryle Rukeyser (171); Arthur Secord (172); Herb True (173); Chuck Vance (174); Heartsill Wilson (175)

Mid East

Speakers: Martin Abend (176); Frank Gervasi (177); Meyer Levin (178); Allan Pollack (179); Alvin Rosenfeld (180)

Poetry - Literature

Speakers: Claude Brown (181); James T. Farrell (182); Leslie Fiedler (183); Gerold Frank (184); Allen Ginsberg (185); Herb Gold (186); June Jordan (187); Alfred Kazin (188); John Killens (189); Kenneth Koch (190); Maxine Kumin (191); Don L. Lee (192); Denise Levertov (193); Jessica Mitford (194); Anais Nin (195); John Rechy (196); Leo Rosten (197); Norman Rosten (198); Adela Roger St. John (199); Isaac B. Singer (200); W.D. Snodgrass (201); Tom Wolfe (202)

Sports - Athletics

Speakers: Mel Allen (203); Roone Arledge (204); Dick Barnett (205); Duffy Daugherty (206); Walt Frazier (207); Marty Glickman (208); Curt Gowdy (209); Rocky Graziano (210); Red Holzman (211); Paul Hornung (212); Alex Karras (213); Lee Leonard (214); Jim McKay (215); Larry Merchant (216); Archie Moore (217); George Plimpton (218); Bobby Riggs (219); Oscar Robertson (220); Dick Schaap (221); Chris Schenkel (222); Ray Scott (223); Bart Starr (224); Bob Teague (225); Jack Whitaker (226)

G

★ 72 ★

GEORGIA FEDERAL SAVINGS AND LOAN ASSOCIATION
20 Marietta Street, N.W.
Atlanta, Georgia 30303 (404) 577-4151

Provides speakers to garden clubs and other civic and community groups. The speakers lecture on a variety of topics including home loan financing, savings and investments, retirement programs, advertising and marketing, research and economics. There are no fees.

Speakers: Mrs. Donald Hastings (1); Edith Henderson (2); Barbara Simcock (3); Troy Keeble (4)

★ 73 ★

GEORGIA-PACIFIC CORPORATION
900 S.W. Fifth Avenue
Portland, Oregon 97204 (503) 222-5561

Speakers are available to lecture on environmental problems, plywood, lumber, pulp and paper, chemicals, and timber management. No fees.

Titles: Chemicals; Environmental Problems; Lumber; Plywood; Pulp and Paper; Timber Management

★ 74 ★

GETTY OIL COMPANY
3810 Wilshire Boulevard, Suite 1310
Los Angeles, California 90010 (213) 381-7151

Speakers are provided for local, civic, social, educational, and political organizations to lecture on topics associated with the petroleum industry. No fees.

Titles: Future of Free Enterprise for Local, Civic, Social, Educational and Political Organizations; Natural Gas Shortages; Offshore Drilling

★ 75 ★

GLENDALE FEDERAL SAVINGS AND LOAN ASSOCIATION
401 North Brand Boulevard
Glendale, California 91209 (213) 956-4616

Dr. Carlson is made available to clubs and community groups for speaking engagements on many contemporary topics. No fees.

Speaker: Kenneth A. Carlson. Titles: Drinking From Old Wells; For Better or Worse; Four Things We Must Learn; Getting the Most From the Best; Great Stories I Have Heard; How to Live With Courage; Little Foxes That Nibble Your Vines; The Miracle of Being You; The Person These Times Demand; Putting Christmas Where it Counts; Religion and Medicine; Three Ways to Manage Your Life; View From a Police Car; What America Means to Me; What the Church Must Be; What You Need to Know About Yourself (1)

★ 76 ★

THE GOODYEAR TIRE AND RUBBER COMPANY
Public Relations Department
Akron, Ohio 44316 (216) 794-2121

Offers the lecture service of a prominent speaker who discusses timely issues before businesses and educational groups from coast to coast. No fees.

Speaker: W.R. Bryan. Titles: Are You a Processionary Caterpillar?; Head 'em Off at the Gap; Instant Turmoil; Profit is a Six Letter Word; Still the Last, Best Hope (1)

★ 77 ★
THE GREEN CIRCLE PROGRAM, INC.
801 Market Street
Philadelphia, Pennsylvania 19105 (215) 922-1639

Develops and implements programs for elementary school through adult audiences. Lecture programs are developed for senior citizens, abusive parents, school personnel, and handicapped individuals. Fees range from $25 to $150.

Speaker: Nancy Gitomer. Titles: Developing a Positive Sense of Self Worth; Human Relations Education (1)

★ 78 ★
GUSTAVUS ADOLPHUS COLLEGE
Consortium on Peace Research, Education and Development
Saint Peter, Minnesota 56082 (507) 931-4300 ext. 500

Lectures are offered on peace education for teachers and community groups. Fees range between $50 and $300.

H

★ 79 ★
HANDWEAVERS GUILD OF AMERICA
65 La Salle Road
Post Office Box 7-374
West Hartford, Connecticut 06107 (203) 233-5124

The listings of this organization offer details about lecturers available and the subject matter they cover. The Guild does not recommend or endorse any particular speakers since individual group needs vary. Arrangements must be made directly with the lecturers whose addresses are provided in the listings. Fees, transportation and housing expenses and other arrangements will vary and are arrived at through correspondence. For further details or additional speaker suggestions write to: Verda Elliott, 28873 Leamington, Farmington Hills, Michigan 48108.

Speaker: Susan Aaron-Taylor, 843 St. Louis, Ferndale, Michigan 48220. Titles: Basketry, Traditional and Contemporary; Quilting, Traditional and Contemporary; Retrospective of Own and Students' Work (1)

Speaker: Rita J. Adrosko, Division of Textiles, Smithsonian Institute, Washington, D.C. 20560. Titles: A General View of Textiles in America; Looms (2)

Speaker: Marthann Alexander, 701 Alden Road, Muncie, Indiana 47304. Titles: Hand Spinning; Two Harness Techniques; Weaving on Small Devices (3)

Speaker: Jeorgia Anderson, 434 Tenth Avenue, San Francisco, California 94121. Titles: Basketry Techniques; Blueprint on Fabric; Photo Imagery on Fabric with Photo Silkscreen; Printing on Photosensitized Fabrics (4)

Speaker: Joan F. Austin, 708 J Avenue, National City, California 92050. Titles: Basketry, Historical Introduction, Contemporary Investigations, Process, Structure and Motivation; Fiber, People, Places (5)

Speaker: Mary Baker, One Harrington Road, Brighton 6, BN1 GRE Sussex, England. Titles: Cloth Structure, Double Cloth; Wall Hangings, 3-D Structures; Working on Paper (6)

Speaker: Rose S. Bank, Three Roselawn Terrace, Pittsburgh, Pennsylvania 15213. Title: Double Weaves. Samplers and Tapestry (7)

Speaker: Clotilde Barret, 624 Peakview Road, Boulder, Colorado 80302. Titles: Interrelationships of Non-loom Techniques; Multiple Harness Fabric Design; Rug Weaving; Textile Techniques of Ethnic Groups and Contemporary Adaptations; Vertical Loom for Navajo (8)

Speaker: Nancy Belfer, Upton 401, State University College, 1300 Elmwood Avenue, Buffalo, New York 14222. Titles: Batik and Tie-dye Techniques; Design in Stitch and Applique; Frame Loom Tapestry Weaving (9)

Speaker: Rosalind K. Berlin, 414 1/2 Court Street, Saginaw, Michigan 48602. Titles: Designing Circular Weave Clothing; Weaving for My Home; Weaving Stuffed Forms (10)

Speaker: Eleanor Best, 7130 Eastwick Lane, Indianapolis, Indiana 46256. Title: Harness Weaving (11)

Speaker: Edna Blackburn, Albion Hills Farm School, Rural Route 3, Caledon East, Ontario, Canada. Title: Spinning, Dyeing, Weaving, Sheep Raising (12)

Speaker: Edwina Bringle, 2220 Belvedere, Charlotte, North Carolina 28205. Titles: Double Weave with Weighted Warps; Dyeing; Spinning (13)

Speaker: Lois Ziff Brooks, 606 North Sierra Drive, Beverly Hills, California 90210. Titles: African Textiles; Batik, Tie-dye, Commercial Dyes for the Handcraft Person; Indigo Dyeing; Starch Paste Resist on Textiles (14)

Speaker: Janice C. Brown, 2246 Rugby Terrace, Post Office Box 87306, College Park, Georgia 30337. Title: Spinning and Vegetable Dyeing (15)

Speaker: Jan Burhen, Box 84, Burton, Washington 98013. Title: Loom Shaped Garments (16)

Speaker: Jane Busse, 7545 Fourwinds Drive, Cincinnati, Ohio 45242. Titles: Art Weaves - The Weaver Controlled Weaves; Rug Weaving; 3-Dimensional Weaving (17)

Speaker: Adele Cahlander, 3522 Knox Avenue North, Minneapolis, Minnesota 55412. Titles: Art and Techniques of Bolivian Highland Weaving; Bolivian Fabrics and Contemporary Adaptations (18)

Speaker: Ted Carson, Handcraft Wools, Box 378, Streetsville, Ontario, L5M 2B9, Canada. Titles: Fibers - History, Function, Identification; Handspinning and Chemical Dyeing (19)

Speaker: Grace Carter, Route 5, Box 360, Hood River, Oregon 97031. Titles: Primitive Spinners - Spindles and/or Distaffs from Greece, Turkey, and Yugoslavia; Spin-offs from the Sheep-raising Business and the Wool-raising Game; Vegetable Dyeing (20)

Speaker: Robert Cawood, 551 Church Street, Toronto, Ontario, Canada. Titles: Double Cloths; Hangings; Warping Without Cross (21)

Speaker: Doloria Chapin, 2178 Pompey-Fabius Road, Rural Delivery 1, Fabius, New York 13063. Titles: Distaffs; Plying, Doubling, Cabling, Fancy Designer Yarns; Spinning - Techniques, Trends (22)

Speaker: Eleanor Chase, 101 Woodland Road, Easton Pennsylvania 18042. Titles: Have You Tried This? (name drafting); M's & O's; A Profile Draft (23)

Speaker: Hilary Chetwynd, Spindle Hoo, Itchen Stoke, Alresford, Hampshire, England. Titles: Leno Weaves Using Doups; Making a Warp and Setting up a Loom; Use of Color in Weaving, Design and Pattern Weaving (24)

Speaker: Doris and Ted Clement, Hemlock Hill, Macedon, New York 14502. Titles: Color - Physical and Psychological Investigation; Hammocks as Made by the Cuna Indians of the San Blas Islands and the Mayans of Yucatan; The Mola Blouse - Origin, Symbolism and Development (25)

Speaker: Martha E. Constandse, 22 Hall Road, Briarcliff Manor, New York 10510. Titles: Designs in Guatemalan Weaving; Inca Designs in Weaving (26)

Speaker: Louise Todd Cope, c/o American Crafts Council, New York, New York 10019. Titles: Explorations of Fiber in Miniature; Fiber, the Body, and the Senses; Layering, Transparency and Lace; Potentials of Fleece; Textile Recycling (27)

Speaker: Leslie Correll, 415 Hudson Street, Oakland, California 94618. Titles: Body Adornment; Jewelry and Body Adornment from Non-Western Perspective; Pattern Making and Clothing Construction and Theory; Psychology of Clothing and Dress - Historical, Folk and Traditional (28)

Speaker: Lucille Coutts, 2505 Walnut Avenue, Manhattan Beach, California 90266. Titles: Basketry Workshops Making Christmas Ornaments, Using Thrums; Color; Fiber Techniques in Weaving; Layered Weaving; Making Wearables; Needlelace; Warp-Weighted Twining (29)

Speaker: Libby Crawford, 18235 Holcomb Road, Grand Haven, Michigan 49417. Titles: Bound Weaves; Double Weave; Knotted Baskets; Put a Little Weaving in Your Home (interiors); Summer and Winter Bags; X More Weaving Months 'Til Christmas (30)

Speaker: Clara H. Creager, 75 West College Avenue, Westerville, Ohio 43081. Titles: Unconventional Ways of Using Your Loom; Variations on a Weave; Weaving as a Life Style (31)

Speaker: Candace Crockett, Star Route Box 5, Woodside, California 94062. Titles: Cardweaving; Contemporary Loom-Woven Hangings; Designing for Textiles; Garments - Our Immediate Environment (32)

Speaker: Ruth Pearson Culbertson, Post Office, Box 33, Monmouth, Oregon 97361. Titles: Dimensional Fiber Forms; Dye Techniques; Ethnic Cloth and Costume as Design; Function and Fantasy; Inventive Wearables; Selected, neglected Textile Techniques (33)

Speaker: Mary Frances Davidson, Route 3, Gatlinburg, Tennessee 37738. Title: Vegetable Dyeing (34)

Speaker: Esther Warner Dendel, 236 East 16th Street, Costa Mesa, California 92627. Titles: African Fabric Crafts; Ancient Textile Techniques for Today; Design Approaches to Tapestry; Nature as Source; Sculptural Twining (35)

Speaker: Susan C. Druding, Post Office Box 2904, Oakland, California 94618. Titles: Basketry; Commercial Dye; Dye Theory; Ethnic Baskets; Fibers; Ikat; Indigo Natural Dyeing; Leaf Printing; Spinning; Textile History (36)

Speaker: Joan B. Eicher, College of Human Ecology, Michigan State University, East Lansing, Michigan 48824. Titles: Nigerian and African Dress; Nigerian Handcrafted Textiles (37)

Speaker: Verda Elliott, 28873 Leamington, Farmington Hills, Michigan 48018. Titles: Contemporary Sprang; Designing and Weaving With Supplementary Warps; Rug Techniques - Creatively Used; Weaving Straw Ornaments in the Scandinavian Manner (38)

Speaker: Lois Ericson, Box 349, Tahoe City, California 95730. Titles: Bags and Handsome Ethnic Clothing; Basketry; Contemporary Tapestry Techniques; Crochet; Designing; Knotting; Netting (39)

Speaker: Jonda Friel, Post Office Box 1141, Tahoe City, California 95730. Titles: Fingerweaving; Hungarian Weaving; Knotless Netting; Layered Weaving; Mandalas; Planning a 3-D Project (40)

Speaker: Gordon W. Frost, 24642 Walnut Street, Newhall, California 91321. Title: Guatemala, Its Textile Arts (41)

Speaker: Brigita Fuhrmann, 43 North Hoosac Road, Williamstown, Massachusetts 02167. Title: Bobbin Lace, Needle Lace, Embroidery (42)

Speaker: Fred and Nita Gerber, 31 Amsden Road, Box 1355, Ormond Beach, Florida 32074. Title: Weaving, Spinning and Dyeing (43)

Speaker: Ruth Ginsberg-Place, 157 Warren Avenue, Boston, Massachusetts 02116. Titles: Tapestry Weaving, History and Design; Weaving Aesthetics; The Woven Image - My Development as a Tapestry Weaver (44)

Speaker: Ronald Goodman, 1852 Columbia Road, N.W., Apartment 201, Washington, D.C. 20009. Titles: Fabric Decoration; Fabric Processes in Rural India; Textiles; Viewpoint India (45)

Speaker: Beverly Gordon, Rural Delivery 1, Box 73, Housatonic, Massachusetts 01236. Titles: Explorations of the Role Fiber Has in Our Lives; Shaker Textiles, Dyeing, Soft Art (46)

Speaker: Lida G. Gordon, Louisville School of Art, 100 Park Road, Anchorage, Kentucky 40223. Titles: Basketry Techniques; Braiding - Plaiting; Crochet; Relief Surfaces; Soft Sculpture; Wrapping (47)

Speaker: Esther Gotthoffer, 2507 Washington Circle, Cincinnati, Ohio 45215. Titles: Art Weaves; Design and Color; Double Weave; Macrame; Rugs; Tapestry; Textiles of Guatemala; Wallhangings (48)

Speaker: Margareta Grandin-Nettles, Textile Studios, Inc., 121 Union Street, North Adams, Massachusetts 02147. Titles: Design; Rugs; Tapestry, Traditional and Contemporary; Wallhangings (49)

Speaker: Susan Grant, Ma Goodness Handspun Yarns, Four High Street, Box 142, Mauricetown, New Jersey 08329. Titles: Building Simple Looms; Cherokee Finger Weaving; Four Harness Weaving; Frame Looms; Hammock Twining; Inkle Looms; My Life and Hard Times as a Weaving Woman; Natural Dyes; Spinning (50)

Speaker: Persis Grayson, 4520 Old Stage Road, Kingsport, Tennessee 37664. Titles: Advanced Spinning; Crafts of the Southern Highlands; Hand Spinning - All Kinds of Fibers (51)

Speaker: Evelyn M. Gulick, 10301 Sierra Vista Avenue, LaMesa, California 92041. Titles: Contemporary Use of Primitive Knotless Netting; Theory and Use of Multilayer Weaving on Eight Harness Looms (52)

Speaker: Sallie T. Guy, Route 6, Box 217, Murray, Kentucky 42071. Titles: Basic Theory; Braids, Fringes and Joining Stitches; Color; Creating the Contemporary From the Traditional; Creative Fabric Designing; Leftover Warp; Off-Loom Techniques (53)

Speaker: Joanne A. Hall, 1514 Sixth Street, Los Osos, California 93402. Titles: Mexican Tapestry Weaving; Spinning and Natural Dyeing of Wool (54)

Speaker: Ted Hallman, 2301 Cedar Street, Berkeley, California 94708. Titles: Drafting for Creative Insight; Textile Constructions; The Weaver as Designer (55)

Speaker: Arthur A. Hart, Idaho Historical Museum, 610 North Julia Davis Drive, Boise, Idaho 83706. Title: Indian Arts and Crafts (56)

Speaker: Ellen Hauptli, 1030 Colusa Avenue, Berkeley, California 94707. Title: Ethnic Costume (57)

Speaker: Kathleen M. Henry, 616 West Church, Champaign, Illinois 61820. Titles: Natural Dyes, Quilting, Spinning (58)

Speaker: C. Norman Hicks, 4383 Piedmont Drive, San Diego, California 92107. Titles: Saxony Wheel, Walking Wheel, Navajo Spindle, Large Orifice Spinners; Selection and Preparation of Fleeces for Hand Spinning; Wool Spinning on Drop Spindle (59)

Speaker: Mary Lou Higgins, 4210 Briggs Avenue, Erie, Pennsylvania 16504. Titles: Creative Crochet and Double Weave; Weaving as an Art Form; Weaving in the Round; Woven Clothes Assembled by Crochet or Knots (60)

Speaker: Mary Bausch Hinman, c/o Living Designs, 313 South Murphy Avenue, Sunnyvale, California 94086. Titles: Design; Navajo Carding and Spinning, Along With Rugs and Navajo Dye Plants; Navajo Weaving; Rugs (61)

Speaker: Juanita Hofstrom, Route 2, Milner Road, Clinton, Wisconsin 53525. Titles: Double Weave; Ikat Warps; Spinning With Spindle and Wheel; Weaving With a Simple Loom (62)

Speaker: Ruth Holroyd, 20 Old Farm Circle, Pittsford, New York 14534. Titles: Ancient Peruvian Textiles; Basic Techniques; Cloth Analysis; Double Weave; Drafting; Drawdowns; Lenos (63)

Speaker: Margaret F. Howard, 128 West Queen Lane, Philadelphia, Pennsylvania 19144. Titles: Drafting Methods; Introduction to Weaving and Drafting; Weave Planning (64)

Speaker: Jan Janeiro, 2023 Clemens Road, Oakland, California 94602. Titles: Double Weaves; Ikat; The Navajo Blanket; Peruvian Needle Knitting; Peruvian Textiles (65)

Speaker: Phyllis M. Janis, 425 Garden City Drive, Monroeville, Pennsylvania 15146. Titles: Card Weaving; Fiber Arts; Inkle Weaving; Macrame (66)

Speaker: Jeanetta L. Jones, 265 Western Avenue, Westfield, Massachusetts 01085. Title: Embroidery Weaves (67)

Speaker: Urban Jupena, 1516 Chicago Boulevard, Detroit, Michigan 48206. Titles: Frame Loom Workshop; Sculptural Shaped Rugs; Tapestry Techniques; Warp and Weft Ikat (68)

Speaker: Edith Karlin, Six Laurel Way, Sea Cliff, New York 11579. Titles: Double Weave and Hand Manipulated Double Weave Tapestry; Rug Techniques; Weaver Controlled and Loom Controlled Lace Weaves (69)

Speaker: Glen Kaufman, Department of Art,

University of Georgia, Athens, Georgia 30602. Titles: Contemporary Activity; Historic Fabrics; Woven and/or Non-Woven Structures (70)

Speaker: Bucky King, Box 371, Buffalo Star Route, Sheridan, Wyoming 82801. Titles: American Indian Textiles; Clay and Fiber; Contemporary Weaving; Lace; Metal Thread Work; Mixed Stitchery; Mixed Textile Techniques; Stitchery on the Loom; 3-D Weaving (71)

Speaker: Sheila Klein, 851 Sneeoosh Road, La Conner, Washington 98257. Titles: Contemporary Clothing Construction; Yarn Design (72)

Speaker: Jon W. Kowalek, Director, Tacoma Museum of Art, 12th and Pacific Avenue, Tacoma, Washington 98402. Titles: Contemporary Crafts in America; Place of Crafts in a Museum (73)

Speaker: Julienne Hallen Krasnoff, Beech House, Valley Road, Glen Cove, New York 11542. Titles: Double Weave - Four Harness Tapestry; 48 Techniques for Beginners; Variations on a Theme (74)

Speaker: Hans Krondahl, Textile Studio Inc., Windsor Mill, 121 Union Street, North Adams, Massachusetts 01247. Titles: Applique; Color and Design; Ecclesiastical Design; Fiber Paintings; Modern Swedish Tapestries; Pictorial Stitchery; Rugs and Rya; Tapestry Weaving; Woven Portraits (75)

Speaker: Connie La Lena, 2851 Roab B 1/2, Grand Junction, Colorado 81501. Titles: Ancient and Modern Southwest Indian Spinning, Dyeing; Basic Weaving; Color and Design; Spinning; Tapestry Techniques; Weave Design (76)

Speaker: Max L. Lenderman, 120 Alpine Drive, Rochester, New York 14618. Titles: Basketry; Crochet; Double Weave; Learning to See in Nature and Relate to Your Weaving; Multiple Layer Weaving (77)

Speaker: Michelle Lester, 361 West 36th Street, 12th Floor, New York, New York 10018. Titles: Color Theory and Yarn Dyeing; Contemporary and Traditional Tapestry; Drafting - Analysis and Design of Weaves; Rug Design and Rug Weaving (78)

Speaker: Mimi Levinson, 1730 Alta Vista Way, San Diego, California 92109. Titles: Batik, Dye Painting; Body Covers; Mixed Media Weaving; Trials of a Woman Artist (79)

Speaker: Savetta L. Livingston, 523 North Granados Avenue, Solana Beach, California 92705. Titles: Back-Strap Loom; Braids, Tassels and Fringes; Osage Braid; Small Appliance Weaving (80)

Speaker: Patricia M. Lyster, 74 Bancroft Avenue, Reading, Massachusetts 01867. Titles: Application of Historical Motifs in Weaving; Color in Weaving; Drafting; Ecclesiastical Weaving; Twill (81)

Speaker: Lois and Walter McBride, 2738 Elmwood Drive, S.E., Grand Rapids, Michigan 49506. Titles: Creative Stitchery; Design - Background for the Crafts; Design - Inspiration From Nature; Nature Through the Eye of a Needle (82)

Speaker: Copeland H. Marks, 57 Montague Street, Brooklyn, New York 11201. Title: Contemporary National Dress of Mayan Indians of Guatemala - Historical Interpretation and Future of the Tradition (83)

Speaker: Grace Marvin, 2750 Weston Ridge; Cincinnati Ohio 45239. Titles: Applique and Quilting; Color in Weaving; Double Weave; Embroidery Weaves; Fashion Fabrics; Sampling Techniques; Stitchery-Crewel or Contemporary(84)

Speaker: Joanne Mattera, 29 South Manning Boulevard, Albany, New York 12203. Titles: Exploring Weaving on Primitive Looms; Natural Dyeing; Navajo Weaving; Off-Loom Weaving; Rug Weaving; Tapestry Weaving (85)

Speaker: Dona Z. Meilach, 3991 Crown Point Drive, San Diego, California 92109. Titles: Basketry; Fiber Happenings; Three-Dimensional Macrame; Weaving Off-Loom (86)

Speaker: Marilyn Meltzer, 5830 Marlborough Avenue, Pittsburgh, Pennsylvania 15217. Titles: How to Design, Weave and Construct a Variety of Chairs, Swings, Hammocks; Structuring Woven Furnishings (87)

Speaker: Theo Moorman, Stonebarrow, Painswick, Gloucester, England. Titles: Design; Moorman Technique; Wall Hangings (88)

Speaker: Mable Morrow, 1114 Taos Highway, Santa Fe, New Mexico 87501. Titles: Comprehensive Exhibits; Design, Textiles; Dyeing With Natural Dyes; Loose Warp Weaving; Navajo Weaving; Pueblo Embroidery; Rawhide; Spinning (89)

Speaker: Jacquetta Nisbet, 3000 Webster Street, San Francisco, California 94123. Titles: Ancient American Indian Weaving Techniques and Contemporary Uses; Light Forms; Navajo and Hopi Bar Weaves; Peruvian Pebble Weave; Unusual Inkle Weaves; Weft Brocades (90)

Speaker: Judith G. Noble, 1218 North 46, Seattle, Washington 98103. Titles: Navajo Weaving; Yarn Design for Hand Spinners; Spinning (91)

Speaker: Walter G. Nottingham, Rural Route 1, Box 26, River Falls, Wisconsin 54022. Titles: Baskets of the World; Crocheted Tapestries and Sculpture; Manipulation of Fabric; Navajo Weaving; Ritual Objects in Fiber; Weaving Today (92)

Speaker: Janet Nyquist, 33 Fiddlers Lane, Newtonville, New York 12128. Titles: Fundamentals of Drafting and Designing Fabrics; Multiple Harness Weaving; Speed Warping; Three Basic Weaves (93)

Speaker: Marjorie O'Shaughnessy, 2126 Skyline Place, Bartlesville, Oklahoma 74003. Titles: Color and Weave Effect Method of Designing; Designing Within a Rectangle; Gaining Design Vertically in Weaving; Special Methods of Treadling; Three Bronson Weaves With Variations (94)

Speaker: Sallie O'Sullivan, Headford Cottage, Avoca Avenue, Blockrock Co., Dublin, Ireland. Titles:

Color and Weaving; Creative Weaving and Wall Hangings; Design and the Textile Arts; Drafting and Loom Controlled Pattern Development; Loom Controlled Color and Structure (95)

Speaker: Hal Painter, Star Route, Chiloquin, Oregon 97624. Titles: Design and Color; How to Arrive at Selling Prices; Plant Material Wall Hangings; Tapestry Techniques (96)

Speaker: Norma Papish, 6405 Whittier Court, Bethesda, Maryland 20034. Title: The Excitement of Embroidery (97)

Speaker: Joan Michaels-Paque, 4455 North Frederick Avenue, Shorewood, Wisconsin 53211. Titles: Basketry; Braiding; Creative Designing With Concepts or Ideas; Fiber-fabric Experimental and Sculptural Techniques; Finger Weaving; Knotting; Needle Laces; Quilting; Stitchery; Twining (98)

Speaker: Karen Pauli, 515 North Spring Avenue, LaGrange Park, Illinois 60525. Titles: History, Folklore and Processes of Spinning; Repair, Care, and Maintenance of Antique Spinning Wheels (99)

Speaker: Mary Pendleton, Post Office, Box 233, 407 Jordan Road, Sedona, Arizona 86336. Title: Navajo and Hopi Weaving Techniques (100)

Speaker: Beth Pennington, 1993 West Liberty, Ann Arbor, Michigan 48103. Titles: Candle Dipping; Hand Spinning; Historic Spinning Wheels; Natural Dyeing; Soap Making (101)

Speaker: Louise Piranian, 2612 Englave Drive, Ann Arbor, Michigan 48103. Title: Acid Dyes for Wool (102)

Speaker: Libby Platus, 1359 Holmby Avenue, Los Angeles, California 90024. Titles: Architectural Commissions; Architectural Fiber Sculpture; Basketry; Crochet; Cross-Tension Knotting; Knotless Netting; Public Art (103)

Speaker: Sylvia Pocock, 1225 Elmridge Avenue, Baltimore, Maryland 21229. Titles: Boundweave; Double Weave; Theory and Designing; 3-D Drafting (104)

Speaker: Marjorie F. Pohlmann, 320 Prospect Avenue South, Minneapolis, Minnesota 55419. Titles: Fabrics for Workshops; How to Visualize Ideas Before Weaving; Weaving on Paper; Working on Commission (105)

Speaker: Yvonne Porcella, 3619 Shoemake Avenue, Modesto, California 95351. Titles: Color and Design; Dress Design; Joy of Creating; Multiple Approach to Form and Fiber Fashion; Nail Frame Weaving; Pin Warp (106)

Speaker: Sally Posner, Box 327, Canyon Dam, California 95923. Titles: Beginning 4-H Weaving; Children's Weaving; Frame Loom Tapestry; Inkle Weaving; Natural Dyeing; Rug Weaves; South American Pick-up Weaves; Teaching Weaving on a Zero Budget; Weaving With Natural Materials (107)

Speaker: Richard M. Proctor, Associate Professor of Art, School of Art, University of Washington, Seattle, Washington 98195. Titles: Achieving Texture in Tapestry Weaving; Advanced Batik; Color and Design for Weavers; Combined Resist Dyeing Techniques; Man Made Dyes; Pattern in Design and the Crafts (108)

Speaker: Victoria Rabinowe, 821 Canyon Road, Santa Fe, New Mexico 87501. Titles: Costume Design; Explorations in Tubular Weave; Innovative Dyeing and Spinning Techniques (109)

Speaker: Gale Ray, All Saints School, Vicksburg, Mississippi 39180. Titles: Backstrap Weaving; Basic Techniques; Meso American Indians and Weaving; Spinning; Tapestry Weaving (110)

Speaker: Mrs. Curtis Reed, 331 Blackhawk Road, Beavers Falls, Pennsylvania 15010. Titles: Early American Dyeing; Herbs for Dyes, Fragrances, Culinary (111)

Speaker: Else Regensteiner, 1416 East 55th Street, Chicago, Illinois 60615. Titles: Contemporary Trends in Weaving; Inspiration for Weaving From Nature and the Arts; Tapestry - Tradition and Innovation; Wall Hangings; Weaving in Other Countries (112)

Speaker: Zenaide Reiss, Box 328, Ocean Beach, New York 11770. Titles: Backstrap Looms; Bound Weave; Card Weaving; Color - What it Can do for You; Double Weave; Finger Weaving; Gauze Weaves; Tapestry and Tapestry Looms; Twining; Warp Weighted Looms; Warping and Beaming (113)

Speaker: Mary Elinor Riccardi, 2906 Brandemere Drive, Tallahassee, Florida 32302. Title: Advanced Loom-Controlled Weaves (114)

Speaker: Jon Eric Riis, Art Department, Georgia State University, 33 Gilmer Street, Atlanta, Georgia 30303. Titles: Basketry; Ikat; Weaving of Tribal India (115)

Speaker: Irma F. Robinson, 1019 N.E. 62nd Street, Seattle, Washington 98115. Title: Color in Weaving (116)

Speaker: Marianne S. Rodwell, 114 West Brown Deer Road, Milwaukee, Wisconsin 53217. Titles: Designing; Folk Art Stitchery; Inlay; Tapestry; Trips to South America, Central America, Mexico and Greece (117)

Speaker: Joy M. Rushfelt, 9845 Overbrook Court, Leawood, Kansas 66206. Titles: Basic Weaving Techniques; Commission Weaving for Corporate Building; Contemporary Tapestry; Design for Weaving; Double, Multilayered Weaves; Non-Loom Techniques; Rug Techniques (118)

Speaker: Joan Russell, 2831 Espy Avenue, Pittsburgh, Pennsylvania 15216. Titles: Dimensional Tapestry Using Double Weave; Patterns, a Contemporary View (119)

Speaker: Cindy Sager, 6311 Thornhill Drive, Oakland, California 94611. Titles: Ethnic Applique; History of Printed Textiles; Quilting, East to West (120)

Speaker: Joan Reid Saltzman, 2605 Haste Street, #107, Berkeley, California 94704. Titles: Beginning Weaving; Ornamental Braiding; Pattern Drafting for Four-Harness Looms; Pattern Drafting for Multi-Harness Looms (121)

Speaker: Philis Alvic Schroeder, 1622 Miller Avenue, Murray, Kentucky 42071. Titles: Colonial Coverlets; Drafting for an Art Form; Multi-Harness Weaving (122)

Speaker: Joseph E. Senungetuk, Sheldon Jackson College, Box 379, Sitka, Arkansas 99835. Titles: Eskimo Arts and Culture; Wood Block Printing in Alaska (123)

Speaker: Stephen D. Shawley, Post Office Box 698, Kamiah, Idaho 83536. Title: Life and Culture of North American Indians (124)

Speaker: Susan L. Shimkunas, 1821 Sherwood Court, Santa Rosa, California 95405. Titles: Basketmaking; Ecclesiastical Vestments; Maskmaking; Seminole Patchwork (125)

Speaker: Allen P. Slickpoo, Sr., Box 311, Kamiah, Idaho 83536. Title: American Indian History, Legends and Culture (126)

Speaker: Lee Erlin Snow, 430 South Burnside Avenue, Apartment 11-L, Los Angeles, California 90036. Titles: Creative Canvas Work; Creative Stitchery; Sculptural Crochet; Weaving Off-Loom - Board or Frame Set Ups (127)

Speaker: Mel Someroski, 628 East Summit, Kent, Ohio 44240. Titles: The Arts and Crafts of Ceylon; Color and Design; Fiber Activities for Public Places; Weaving and Enameling Technique; The Weaving of Ceylon; The Weaving of Sikkim (128)

Speaker: Elsa M. Sreenivasam, 1805 West 21st Terrace, Lawrence, Kansas 66045. Titles: Batik; Dyes and Pigments; Fiber Forms and Small Loom Techniques; Photographic Images on Fabric; Soft Sculpture; Textile Printing and Dyeing as an Art Form; Tie-Dye (129)

Speaker: Lotus Stack, 4804 12th Street South, Minneapolis, Minnesota 55417. Titles: Dyeing for Weavers; Novelty Yarns, Their Creation and Use; A Practical Guide to Working With Home-Spun; Special Projects for Two Harness Looms (130)

Speaker: Judith Stein; 733 Stannage Street #1, Albany, California 94706. Titles: Indian Textiles; Patolas; Split-Ply Twining; Western Indian Camel Girths (131)

Speaker: Merle H. Sykora, 416 Fifth Street South, Saint Cloud, Minnesota 56301. Titles: Design in Nature and Weaving; Double Gang Weaving on Eight Harnesses; Liturgical Design Conceptualizing; Mock Tapestry; Weft Faced Loom Controlled Patterning (132)

Speakers: Sylvia and Harold Tacker, Post Office Box 292, Kirkland, Washington 98033. Titles: Band Weaving; Techniques for Inkle Bands; Warp and Weft Twining (133)

Speaker: Janet Roush Taylor, 203 Highland Avenue, Kent, Ohio 44240. Titles: Color and Design; Navajo Weaving (134)

Speaker: Mary Temple, 1011 Cottage Place, Saint Paul, Minnesota 55112. Titles: Contemporary Basketry as Functional or Sculptural Forms; Rigid Heddle Frame Loom (135)

Speaker: Roger K. Thomason, 1230 Greenbrier, Denton, Texas 76201. Titles: Contemporary Textiles; Fashion Fabrics; Loom-Designed Garments; Macrame (136)

Speaker: Margaret Thompson, 683 Santa Cruz Avenue, Salinas, California 93901. Titles: Stuffed/Quilted 3-Dimensional Tapestries; Wool Rag Rugs (137)

Speaker: Stephen Thurston, 2672 North Halsted Street, Chicago, Illinois 60614. Titles: Basketry; Card-weaving; Double and Quadruple Weaves; Fiber Magic; Functional Sculpture in Fiber; Shaped Garments; Tapestry (138)

Speaker: Winifred M. Tonken, 2591 Richland Avenue, San Jose, California 95125. Titles: Bound Weave; Color; Double Weave; Lace; Leno; Pattern; Pick-up; Supplementary Warps; Texture; Twill (139)

Speaker: Naomi Whiting Towner, 1410 South Oak Street, Bloomington, Illinois 61701. Titles: Critiques; Double Weaving; Experimental Weaving; Free-form Wall Hangings; Gang Weaving; Manipulated Tensions; Multi-Harness Weaving; Nature as a Source for Design and Color; Non-Loom Techniques; Supplementary Warps; Tapestry; Weave Formation (140)

Speaker: Merta Sue Trumble, 1600 Hillridge, Ann Arbor, Michigan 48103. Title: Acid Dyes for Wool (141)

Speaker: Alta R. Turner, Ten Valhalla Way, Verona, New Jersey 07044. Titles: Finger Weaving; Pueblo and Navajo Weaving; Woodland Indian and Ancient Peruvian (142)

Speaker: David B. Van Dommelen, 1981 Highland Drive, State College, Pennsylvania 16801. Title: Decorative Wall Hangings (143)

Speaker: Lydia Van Gelder, 758 Sucher Lane, Santa Rosa, California 95401. Titles: Bobbin Lace, Traditional and Contemporary; Ikat, Shibori and Tritik, Using Commercial Dyes; Spinning and Natural Dyeing (144)

Speaker: Leslie C. Voiers, Route 121, Post Office Box 30, Cambridgeport, Vermont 05144. Titles: Beginning Weaving; Coiling; Double Weave; How to Teach Weaving; Overshot and What You Can do With It; Peruvian Pick-up; Structural Design in Free Crochet (145)

Speaker: Irene Waller, 249 Hagley Road, Ebgbaston, Birmingham B16 9RS, England. Titles: Designing in Fiber, Yarn, Fabric; Embroidery; Fiber and Yarn Manipulation; Knotting; Spinning; Tatting; Weaving; Working on Commission (146)

Speaker: Marie Walling, 4409 Bakman Avenue, North Hollywood, California 91602. Titles:

Chain Warping; Clasped Warp and Weft; Expanded Honeycomb; Garments Made on Loom; Lace Weaving the Easy Way; Painted Warp; Sectional Warping (147)

Speaker: Ken Weaver, 309 Vincent Drive, Athens, Georgia 30001. Titles: Commission Weaving; Weaving as Art in Interior Design; Workshops on Rep Weaving (148)

Speaker: Palmy Weigle, Oliver Road, Bedford, New York 10506. Titles: Dyeing Wool With Natural Materials; Off-Loom Weaving Techniques (149)

Speaker: Sigrid Weltge, 37 West Southampton Avenue, Philadelphia, Pennsylvania 19118. Titles: Bag Workshops; Influence of the Bauhaus on Contemporary Crafts; Off-Loom Weaving; Pillow Workshops; Textile History; 3-D Workshops (150)

Speaker: Virginia West, Westwood Rural Free Delivery #7, Baltimore, Maryland 21208. Titles: Fashion Fabrics; Finishing Touches for Handwoven Fabrics; Forms in Fiber; The International Scene in Fiber; Techniques of Basketry (151)

Speaker: Carol D. Westfall, 40 Edgewood Avenue, Nutley, New Jersey 07110. Titles: Batik; Earth Fibers; Plaiting; Soft Skins Dyeing (152)

Speaker: Jean Wilson, 949 Overlake Drive East, Bellevue, Washington 98004. Titles: Pile Weaves; Plain Weave Tapestry Techniques; Weaving With Yarn and Words (153)

Speaker: Barbara Wittenberg, 17640 Westland, Southfield, Michigan 48075. Titles: Basketry; Fiber; Nature-Abstractions in Fiber Forms (154)

Speaker: Jackie Wollenberg, 20 Terrace Walk, Berkeley, California 94707. Titles: Card Weaving - Techniques and Design; The Warp Weighted Loom; Warp Weighting (155)

Speaker: Phyllis Yacopino, 1220 East 38th Street, Eugene, Oregon 97405. Titles: Greek Traditions of Textiles; The Imagination and Textile Design; Innovative Natural Dye Experimentation With Mordants; Natural Lichen Dyeing (156)

Speaker: Kathleen L. Zien, 5246 West School Street, Chicago, Illinois 60641. Titles: Beginning Four-Harness Loom Weaving; Children's Workshop in Knotless Netting, Basic Basketry, Wrapping (157)

Speaker: Nell Znamierowski, 448 East 88th Street, New York, New York 10029. Title: Color, Design and the Contemporary Scene (158)

Speaker: Mary Ann Zotto-Beltz, 46010 Nine Mile Road, Northville, Michigan 48167. Titles: Basketry; Design, Color, and Texture in Weaving; Garments; Inkle Band and Card Weaving; Marketing Your Work; Tapestry; Weft Face Rugs (159)

★ 80 ★
HARDWOOD PLYWOOD MANUFACTURERS ASSOCIATION
Post Office Box 6246
Arlington, Virginia 22206 (703) 671-6262

This association provides speakers to lecture on hardwood plywood manufacturing. No fees.

Speaker: William J. Groah, Jr. Title: Technical Aspects of Hardwood Plywood, and Veneer (1)

Speaker: Clark E. McDonald. Titles: Flamespread Testing and Structural Testing; Laminated Hardwood Block Flooring; Prefinished Hardwood Plywood; The Use, Manufacturing, and Marketing of Hardwood, Plywood, and Veneer (2)

★ 81 ★
BOB HARRINGTON
Box 2408
New Orleans, Louisiana 70176 (504) 581-4357

A speaker who offers inspirational lectures on a wide range of topics ranging from religion to humor to personal development. Fees are $2,000 for week nights and $3,000 for Sundays.

Speaker: Bob Harrington. Titles: I Like Me; It's Fun Being Successful; It's Fun Making Money; Think - Act Now (1)

★ 82 ★
THE HERITAGE FOUNDATION
513 C Street, N.W.
Washington, D.C. 20002 (202) 546-4400

The Foundation is a research institution dedicated to the principles of free competitive enterprise, limited government, individual liberty, and a strong national defense. Speakers provide programs which are timely and useful to policy makers and the interested public.

★ 83 ★
CHARLES HUTAFF
Speakers and Entertainment Bureau
243 Bradley Road
Bay Village, Ohio 44140 (216) 871-8500

Some twenty-five speakers present lectures to service clubs, women's groups, business organizations, school groups and college groups on a variety of topics. Fees range from $150 to $2,500.

Speaker: Doug Adair. Title: Television and You (1)
Speaker: Don Cockroft. Title: Sports and Christian Athletes (2)
Speaker: James Doney. Title: Adventure Road (3)
Speaker: Tom Field. Title: World Brotherhood (4)
Speaker: Ed Fisher. Titles: The Heart of the Circle is a Square; You Talk, I'll Listen, for a Change (5)
Speaker: Dorothy Fuldheim. Titles: Reminiscences of a News Analyst; The World at the Moment (6)
Speaker: Patrick L. Gerity. Title: Police and Politics (7)
Speaker: Dick Goddard. Title: Six Inches of Partly Cloudy (8)
Speaker: Bub Guest. Title: On the Sunny Side of the Street (9)
Speaker: Janet Henry. Title: Funny Thing Happened on the Way... (10)
Speaker: William Hickey. Title: Television - Is It Really That Bad? (11)
Speaker: Brian Hodgkinson. Title: Penalty of Permissiveness (12)
Speaker: A.L. Jones. Title: Energy and Morality (13)
Speaker: Harry Jones. Title: Baseball is a Funny Game...But this is Ridiculous (14)
Speaker: Earl Neff. Title: Flying Saucers--Fact or Fiction (15)
Speaker: Dick Schafrath. Title: Eye-Ball to Eye-Ball (16)
Speaker: Louise Winslow. Title: The Art and Craft of Threads (17)

I

★ 84 ★
INSTITUTE FOR SCIENTIFIC INFORMATION
325 Chestnut Street
Philadelphia, Pennsylvania 19106 (215) 923-3300

Lecturers are prepared to speak primarily to librarians and faculty members in the science and social science fields on the types of services this Institute has to offer. No charge.

Speaker: Diane Hoffman. Titles: How to Use Current Abstracts of Chemistry, Index Chemicus, and the Chemical Substructure Index; How to Use the Science Citation Index; How to Use the Social Sciences Citation Index (1)

★ 85 ★
INTERCOLLEGIATE STUDIES INSTITUTE, INC.
14 South Bryn Mawr Avenue
Bryn Mawr, Pennsylvania 19010 (215) 525-7501

Speakers are made available to lecture at colleges and universities. They are drawn from the ranks of distinguished scholars who are notably competent in their disciplines, sensitive to the social problems of the day and aware of the intellectual needs of students. Schedule of fees provided upon request.

Speaker: Martin Anderson. Titles: The Draft vs. An All-Volunteer Armed Force; Social Problems in Economics and Urban Policy; The Social Responsibilities of the Corporations; Urban Renewal (1)
Speaker: Yale Brozen. Titles: Are United States Manufacturing Industries Monopolized?; Capitalism and the Ghetto; Is Government the Source of Monopoly?; Minimum Wage Laws - Cure for or a Cause of Poverty?; Private Alternatives to Government Programs; The Role of Open Markets in Coordinating and Directing Economic Activity (2)
Speaker: Philip M. Crane. Titles: Blessings of Liberty; Contemporary Social Issues; Education for What?; Should the University be Saved? (3)
Speaker: Harold Demsetz. Titles: Capitalism and the Public Interest; Problems of Social Planning; Solving Social Problems Through the Market; What is Capitalism? (4)
Speaker: Gottfried Dietze. Titles: American and German Government; Problems of Civil Rights; Problems of Constitutional Government and Modern Democracy; Problems of Federalism; Problems of Higher Education (5)
Speaker: Lev E. Dobriansky. Titles: Ferment in the Soviet Empire; The Politics of Trading with Communist Countries; The Vulnerable Russians (6)
Speaker: James E. Dornan, Jr. Titles: The Conservative Tradition and Foreign Policy; Liberalism and the Tragedy of American Foreign Policy; The Origins of the American Tradition in Foreign Affairs; The Quest for Purpose in Contemporary American Foreign Policy (7)
Speaker: Milorad M. Drachkovitch. Titles: Does the New Left Represent the Greening of America?; Marxism; The Present Situation of the International Communist Movement; Radical Movements (8)
Speaker: M. Stanton Evans. Titles: American Constitutional Foundations; The Future of Conservatism; The New Left and the New Right; The Politics of Surrender; The Religious Roots of Liberty (9)
Speaker: Roger A. Freeman. Titles: The Alchemists in Our Public Schools; Crisis in American Education; National Priorities in the Decade Ahead; The Wayward Welfare State; Why Don't They Stop Inflation? (10)
Speaker: Jerzy Hauptmann. Titles: American Politics and Political Philosophy; Citizenship in an Ideological Environment - Thrust or Trick; The Dream of a Utopia in Government Structure; Life in the Community - Challenge or Check; Politics on the International Scene - Sovereignty

and Suppression; The Search for Utopia through Government Action (11)

Speaker: Will Herberg. Titles: Alienation, Dissent, and the Intellectual; America's Negro Problem in Historical Perspective; Liberalism and Conservatism in Historical Perspective; New Winds - The Decline of Liberalism and the Rise of Conservatism; Religion and Culture in Present-Day America; Social Change, Revolution, and the Politics of Benign Neglect; Unities and Tension in Mid-Twentieth Century America; What is the Moral Crisis of Our Time?; What is the New Morality? (12)

Speaker: Harry V. Jaffa. Titles: The American Political Tradition; Equality and Liberty in American Politics; The Meaning of the Declaration of Independence (13)

Speaker: Arthur Kemp. Titles: The Economics of Rights - Property and Personal; How to Square the Ideological Circle; Inflation - Can It Be Controlled?; The International Monetary Structure - An Eternal Crisis?; Paternalism, Economics, and the Welfare State; The Political Economy of the Medical Profession; Prices and Production in Variant Economic Systems (14)

Speaker: William R. Kintner. Titles: Communist Ideology and Strategy; Communist Organization and Tactics; Contemporary Problems in International Relations; The Impact of Technology on International Relations; U.S. Foreign Policy and U.S. Governmental Machinery for Carrying it Out; U.S. National Security Policy (15)

Speaker: Russell Kirk. Titles: Academic Freedom and Academic License; American Conservatives in the Middle of the Journey; Fanatic Ideologies in Our Midst; Protest, Revolution, and the Permanent Things; Reviving the Moral Imagination; Toward a Wiser Foreign Policy (16)

Speaker: Anthony Kubek. Titles: Communist China and the Modern World; Realities of American Foreign Policy; Taiwan and Communist China; The United States Role in Vietnam (17)

Speaker: Erik Von Kuehnelt-Leddihn. Titles: Africa Today; An Alien Look at America's Faith; America-Europe - The Great Misunderstanding; The Church in an Age of Confusion; Colonialism - Myth and Reality; Eros, Sex and Marriage; The Future of Democracy; Neo-Conservatism and Neo-Liberalism; Political Problems of Asia; Student Unrest in Four Continents; The U.S.S.R. and Soviet Man Today; What's Right - What's Wrong with America (18)

Speaker: Henry G. Manne. Titles: The Consumerism Boomerang; An Economic Analysis of Large Corporations; The Economics and Politics of Government Regulation of Business; The Full Disclosure Myth; Regulation of Securities Markets; A Response to Modern Corporate Critics (19)

Speaker: William Oliver Martin. Titles: The Contemporary Corruption of Language; The Death of Liberalism; Dissent and the Intellectual; Is All Truth and Morality Relative?; The New Atheism and Its Tactics; Philosophical Truth and the Meaning of Ideology; Truth, Objectivity, and Some Interesting Facts about the Nature of Knowledge (20)

Speaker: Frank S. Meyer. Titles: Anarchism, Nihilism, and the New Left; The Crisis in American Education; The Future of Conservatism in Post-Liberal America; Trends in U.S. Foreign Policy; Viet Nam and Its Consequences; What is Conservatism? (21)

Speaker: H.E. Michl. Titles: The Agricultural Price Support Program; Can Government Stabilize the Economy?; International Trade in the Seventies; Minimum Wage Law and the Poor; Wage and Price Controls - Do They Work? (22)

Speaker: Thomas Molnar. Titles: Conservatism and Intelligence; The Counter-Revolution; The Gnostic Tradition and its Varieties; Marxism and its Revolutionists; The New Left; The Restoration of Philosophy; Tradition and Social Change (23)

Speaker: Gerhart Niemeyer. Titles: Communism, Its Ideology and Morphology; The New Left; The Reconstruction of Political Theory; Religion and Politics (24)

Speaker: Edmund A. Opitz. Titles: The Freedom Nobody Wants; God and Political Freedom; The Importance of Scholarship to Society; Let's Not Save the World; The Limits of Majority Rule; Painting Government into a Corner; Religion and Capitalism; Two Ideas of Equality; The War on Poverty - A Critical View (25)

Speaker: William H. Peterson. Titles: How to Work Harder and Get Less - Or, Let Uncle Sam Do It; Who Killed the Ice Man - Or, An Answer to Ralph Nader and Consumerism; Why Your Dollar Continues to Buy Less - With or Without Wage-Price Controls (26)

Speaker: Sylvester Petro. Titles: Freedom and the Common Law Tradition; The Labor Policy of the Free Society; Property and Freedom - The Remarkable Identity (27)

Speaker: Robert L. Pfaltzgraff, Jr. Titles: Arms Control and Disarmament; The Emerging U.S.; The International System in the 1970's; The United States and European Security; United States Foreign Policy (28)

Speaker: Stefan T. Possony. Titles: American Strategy in Foreign Policy; Geostrategic Problems; Middle East - Dangers and Opportunities; Sino-Soviet Conflict; South East Asia Today; Soviet Affairs (29)

Speaker: Benjamin A. Rogge. Titles: Capitalism, Racism and Poverty; Consumerism - Threat to the Consumer; The Long Run Outlook for the American Economy; The Myth of Monopoly (30)

Speaker: Joseph Schiebel. Titles: Big Power Confrontation in the Middle East; The Future of

Soviet-American Relations; The Operational Significance of Marxist-Leninist Ideology in the 1970's; Sources and Goals of Soviet Foreign Policy; Soviet Strategy in the Middle East; The Soviet Union and Germany - History and Prospects; The Soviet Union and the Third World (31)

Speaker: Peter J. Stanlis. Titles: Burke and Rousseau; Edmund Burke and Revolution; Edmund Burke's Conception of History; The Idea of Progress Today; Irving Babbitt - The Humanist as Critic of Contemporary Society; Robert Frost - Individualistic Democrat (32)

Speaker: Stephen J. Tonsor. Titles: Education in the 1970's; The Idea of a Catholic University; Science, Technology and the Cultural Revolution; Why Moderates, Conservatives, and Catholics are Excluded from Campus; Youth Movements in History (33)

Speaker: Gordon Tullock. Titles: The Cost of Transfers; The Economics of Revolution (34)

Speaker: Ernest Van Den Haag. Titles: How Come Less Poverty and More Welfare?; Law, Order and Justice; Love, Spontaneity and Enduring Values; Pornography and Censorship; Riots - Causes and Remedies; Students vs. Universities; Utopianism, Sex and Reality; Violence in a Democratic Society; Women's Liberation and Sexual Roles (35)

Speaker: Eliseo Vivas. Titles: Dostoevsky's Grand Inquisitor, Slavery and Freedom; Is the Good Life Possible Today?; Marcuse and The Hell of the Affluent Society; Moral Relativism and Its Alternatives; Myths of Today; Science and Happiness (36)

Speaker: Eric Voegelin. Titles: Gnosticism and Politics; The University and the Order of Society; Utopia (37)

Speaker: James W. Wiggins. Titles: Discrimination, A Universal Imperative; Irrefragable Man; The New Luddites; Population - Explosion and Implosion; Relativism and Its Limits; Sodom and Tomorrow (38)

Speaker: Francis G. Wilson. Titles: American and European Conservatism - The Vital Link; The Case for Conservatism; Rediscovering the American Political Tradition (39)

Speaker: Donald A. Zoll. Titles: Authority and Aristocracy; The Death of Liberalism; The Fallacy of Libertarianism; The Nature and Future of Tory Radicalism; Order, Freedom, Law and Political Institutions; Reason and Rebellion; The Relevance of Conservatism in an Age of Ideology; The Rule of Law and the Rule of Lawyers; Varieties of the American Political Right (40)

★ 86 ★

INTERNATIONAL ENTERTAINMENT BUREAU
3612 North Washington Boulevard
Indianapolis, Indiana 46205 (317) 926-7566

A full service bureau arranging speakers and personalities for public appearances with the general public, companies, associations, political parties, governmental organizations, educational institutions, unions, and other types of entertainment consumers.

Speaker: Herb True. Titles: The Comedy of Love; Humor Power; Psychological Small Change (1)

★ 87 ★

INTERNATIONAL INDUSTRIAL TELEVISION ASSOCIATION
26 South Street
New Providence, New Jersey 07974 (305) 279-1792

Maintains a speakers' bureau and plans to issue a catalog of speakers available for conferences and other meetings.

★ 88 ★

INTERNATIONAL NARCOTIC ENFORCEMENT OFFICERS ASSOCIATION
112 State Street, Suite 1310
Albany, New York 12207 (518) 463-6232

Presents lectures on the prevention of drug abuse. An honorarium and expenses are expected to be paid.

Speaker: John J. Bellizzi. Titles: Drug Abuse; Hospital Drug Security; Medical Professionals in Drug Abuse; Methadone (1)

★ 89 ★

INTERNATIONAL PLATFORM ASSOCIATION
2564 Berkshire Road
Cleveland Heights, Ohio 44106 (216) 932-0505

This organization is the principal professional association of lecturers in the United States. Its membership is drawn from the political, entertainment, scholarly and media world and the organization has been in existence for almost 150 years. As the most important international body of those interested in oratory and the spoken word, its annual program of workships for its members includes a who's who of well known public speakers drawn from every field of human activity.

★ 90 ★
INTERNATIONAL WAGES FOR HOUSEWORK CAMPAIGN - CANADA
Post Office Box 38
Station E
Toronto, Ontario M5T 2L7, Canada (416) 466-7457

Speakers sponsor lectures on the women's right to be paid for housework. Fee is $200 per lecture plus travelling expenses and lodging.

Speaker: Judith Ramirez. Titles: The Economic Status of Women in the Home; How Wagelessness in the Home Effects Women's Options for Fertility; The Place of Immigrant Women in the Hierarchy of Wages (1)

★ 91 ★
IOWA MOUNTAINEERS, INC.
30 Prospect Place
Iowa City, Iowa 52240 (319) 337-7163

Presents travel adventure film-lectures to the people of Eastern Iowa. Fees vary according to lecturer and topic.

Speakers: John Booth (1); Edward Brigham, Jr. (2); Don Cooper (3); John Ebert (4); C.P. Lyons (5); James Metcalf (6); Stan Midgley (7); Curtis Nagel (8); Ken Richter (9); Charles Taylor (10); Gene Wiancke (11)

J

★ 92 ★
JERSEY CENTRAL POWER AND LIGHT COMPANY
Madison Avenue at Punchbowl Road
Morristown, New Jersey 07960 (201) 539-6111

Speakers offer lectures on energy and energy related topics to civic groups, special interest groups, and members of the Morristown community. No fees.

Speakers: L. Duckworth, Jr. (1); R.K. Fullagar (2); K. Goddard (3); R.A. Golden (4); R.W. Kane (5); R.A. Keleher (6); J. Knubel (7); E.F. Lord (8); H.K. Mayer (9); G.F. Metzgar (10); P.L. Shearin (11); E.J. Stominski (12); E. Vieweg (13); R.D. Waldman (14); J.E. Walsh (15); M.B. Welden (16)

★ 93 ★
JEWS FOR JESUS
Post Office Box 3558
San Rafael, California 94902 (415) 457-7822

Speakers are prepared to discuss how and why Jewish people have a belief in Jesus. Fees vary.

Speaker: Mitch Glaser. Title: What We Believe (1)
Speaker: Amy Rabinovitz. Title: Why I, A Jew, Believe in Jesus (2)
Speaker: Moishe Rosen. Title: Christ in the Passover (3)
Speaker: Tuvya Zaretsky. Title: How to Be a Jew for Jesus (4)

★ 94 ★
CARL M. JOHNSON
116 South Michigan Avenue
Chicago, Illinois 60603 (312) 372-4188

Offers services of speakers on unusual topics. Fees variable, details furnished upon request.

Speaker: Carole M. Baron. Title: Handwriting Analysis as a Science (1)
Speaker: Irene Hughes. Title: The Psychic World (2)
Speaker: Ted Phillips. Title: UFOs and Their Landing Sites (3)

K

★ 95 ★
KANSAS STATE UNIVERSITY
Institute of Nuclear Materials Management, Inc.
Seaton Hall
Manhattan, Kansas 66506 (913) 532-5837

The organization offers a speaker who is prepared to lecture on nuclear safety.

Speaker: G. Robert Keepin. Subject: Nuclear Safety (1)

★ 96 ★
KANSAS WESLEYAN UNIVERSITY
South Santa Fe at Claflin
Salina, Kansas 67401 (913) 827-5541

The Community Lecture Series features speakers of a statewide interest on topics of interest to people in .e community.

Subjects: Agriculture; Politics; Religion

★ 97 ★
KEEDICK LECTURE BUREAU, INC.
475 Fifth Avenue
New York, New York 10017 (212) 683-5627

Arranges for speakers to lecture on such topics as literature, science, exploration, the arts, national, and international affairs. Fees range from $300 up.

Speaker: Cleveland Amory. Titles: Curmudgeon At Large; The Yankees (1)
Speaker: Worth H. Bagley. Title: Foreign Policy and the Power Balance (2)
Speaker: Jerry Baker. Titles: I Never Met a Houseplant I Didn't Like; Plants Are Like People (3)
Speaker: Charles Bartlett. Titles: The Look From Washington; Where Do We Go From Here? (4)
Speaker: Marvella Bayh. Titles: A Dream Deferred; The Washington Whirl - 15 Years of Change (5)
Speaker: Polly Bergen. Title: Just For Us Girls (6)
Speaker: Barbara Brown. Title: Unlocking the Mind-Bodies (7)
Speaker: John Cairney. Title: The Robert Burns Story (8)
Speaker: Joe Callaway. Title: The American Dream...In Politics, Poetry and Humor (9)
Speaker: Frank Cappiello. Title: The Post-Election Economy (10)
Speaker: Kitty Carlisle. Titles: Everyone Plays a Part; First Person Singular (11)
Speaker: Winston Churchill. Title: Could the West Fall Without a Shot Being Fired? (12)
Speaker: Norman Cousins. Titles: Environment for Survival; World Report (13)
Speaker: John Charles Daly. Title: An Orbital View of the Current Scene (14)
Speaker: Clive David. Title: Party Planning Par Excellence (15)
Speaker: Olivia de Havilland. Title: From the City of Stars to the City of Light (16)
Speaker: Fitzhugh J. Dodson. Titles: Confessions of a Psychologist Father; How to Parent (17)
Speaker: Angier Biddle Duke. Title: The American Image Abroad (18)
Speaker: Mrs. Angier Biddle Duke. Titles: The Making of an American Image; The Quality of Life (19)
Speaker: Richard Eder. Title: Abroad in the Theatre (20)
Speaker: Robert Farr. Title: How to Protect Yourself Against White Collar Crimes (21)
Speaker: Eileen Ford. Title: The More Beautiful You (22)
Speaker: Norman Garbo. Titles: The Psychology of Love; Pull Up An Easel (23)
Speaker: Lawrence E. Gichner. Titles: Adventures in Attics; Hunting Antiques Around the World (24)
Speaker: Ruth Gordon. Title: How to Have Fun (25)
Speaker: Robert L. Green. Title: Creating Your Own Image and Lifestyle (26)
Speaker: Philippe Halsman. Title: Photographic Insights (27)
Speaker: Betty Jo Hawkens. Titles: Miracles in Monologue; Sarah Bernhardt (28)
Speaker: Peter Lind Hayes. Titles: For Amusement Only (29)
Speaker: Joyce Hifler. Title: Think on These Things (30)
Speaker: Marjorie Holmes. Titles: Two From Galilee; Which Is the Real You? (31)
Speaker: Marion Javits. Title: A Woman's Place in the Business World (32)
Speaker: Irene Kampen. Titles: More About Everything; Of Cabbages and Kings and Things (33)
Speaker: Garson Kanin. Title: It Takes a Long Time to Become Young (34)
Speaker: Ruth Sheldon Knowles. Title: Americas Oil Famine (35)
Speaker: Frances Lang Koltun. Title: Collecting - The Pleasant Way to Become Wealthy (36)
Speaker: Bill Lignante. Title: The Life of a Courtroom Artist (37)
Speaker: Jon Morrow Lindbergh. Titles: Man Dives Deep; The Oceans - Conservation or Exploitation (38)
Speaker: Henry Cabot Lodge. Titles: National Outlook; Prospects for Mankind (39)
Speaker: Nila Magidoff. Titles: Everyday Life in the Soviet Union; My Discovery of America (40)
Speaker: Leila Martin. Title: We've Come A Long Way Baby (41)
Speaker: Thomas Patrick Melady. Titles: Africa - U.S. Relations; The U.N. Must Face Up to Its Responsibilities (42)
Speaker: Leland Miles. Titles: Americans Are People; What Is a Classic? (43)
Speaker: Lord Montagu. Titles: How to Live In A Stately Home and Make Money; Is British Aristocracy Decadent? (44)
Speaker: Robin Moore. Titles: The Corrupt Society; How Soon Will the Arabs Own America ? (45)
Speaker: Leo Narducci. Title: Fashion Designing (46)
Speaker: Beverly Norris. Title: Carl Sandburg, Here and Now (47)
Speaker: Clarence Norris. Title: Our Freedoms and How to Fight for Them (48)
Speaker: Rufus Norris. Title: Carl Sandburg, Here and Now (49)
Speaker: John Peer Nugent. Titles: African Crisis - Blacks vs. Whites; The Darkening Continent (50)
Speaker: Ulick O'Connor. Titles: The Irish Literacy Renaissance; The Last of the Bucks (51)
Speaker: Willem L. Oltmans. Titles: Europe After Helsinki; The Far East Revisited; The USSR in 1990 (52)
Speaker: Charles Osgood. Title: The Lighter Side of the News (53)

Speaker: David Atlee Phillips. Titles: The CIA - A Peculiar Service; Latin America Today (54)
Speaker: George Plimpton. Title: An Amateur Among the Pros (55)
Speaker: Rex Reed. Title: Rex Reed at the Movies (56)
Speaker: Jack Reynolds. Titles: Asia Today and Tomorrow; China and The New Regime (57)
Speaker: Princess Rudivoravan. Title: East and West Can Meet (58)
Speaker: Richard D. Rush. Title: Getting a Greater Return on Your Money (59)
Speaker: Ralph Salerno. Titles: Organized Crime; The Question of Legalized Gambling (60)
Speaker: Bill Schustik. Titles: New England and the Sea; Schustik's Variety of Songs (61)
Speaker: Walter Sullivan. Titles: Continents in Motion; The New Vikings (62)
Speaker: Gloria Swanson. Title: Look Back in Laughter (63)
Speaker: Lowell Thomas. Title: Lowell Thomas Remembers (64)
Speaker: Jim Thorne. Title: Mysteries of Inner Space (65)
Speaker: Gloria Vanderbilt. Title: The Art Spirit (66)
Speaker: Carleton Varney. Title: The You Look (67)
Speaker: Barbara Ward. Title: The Economy (68)
Speaker: Allen Weinstein. Titles: The Hiss Case and the FBI Files; On Dealing With the FBI (69)
Speaker: June Weir. Title: The Four Ws of Fashion (70)
Speaker: Anne Wilson. Titles: Anne Wilson Speaks Contempo; The Ballet Story; Modern American Ballet (71)
Speaker: Bob Wright. Title: Musical Theatre Cavalcade (72)
Speaker: Alexandra York. Title: Natural Beauty (73)
Speaker: Elmo Zumwalt. Titles: Morality in Government; Russia's Challenge to Our Naval Supremacy; Strategic Arms Limitation (74)
Speaker: Mouza Coutelais-du-Roche' Zumwalt. Title: The Life of a Public Wife in Washington (75)

L

★ 98 ★

THE HATTIE LARLHAM FOUNDATION, INC.
9772 Diagonal Road
Mantua, Ohio 44255 (216) 274-2272

Lecturers are available to present the Hattie Larlham story through slide presentations and discussions at clubs, churches, and organizations. The Foundation specializes in the care of severely and profoundly mentally and physically disabled infants and young children. No fees.

Speakers: Gina M. Dreussi (1); Jean McNicholas (2); William A. Schenk (3)
Title: The Hattie Larlham Story

★ 99 ★

THE LEARNING EXCHANGE
Post Office Box 920
Evanston, Illinois 60204 (312) 864-4136

This not-for-profit educational and recreational listing and referral service, puts individuals in touch with one another to teach, learn or share over 3,000 subjects including arts and crafts, foreign languages, music, academic subjects, and sports. Its officials are available for speaking engagements on the work of the organization. Fee is $50 plus travel and lodging expenses.

Speakers: G. Dennis Conroy (1); Edward R. Dobmeyer (2); Diane Reiko Kinishi (3)
Title: The Learning Exchange

★ 100 ★

LECTURE SERVICES, INC.
155 Greenway South
Forest Hills, New York 11375 (212) 263-9246

Maintains a list of speakers available to lecture on various topics related to travel, foreign cultures and international themes. Fees vary.

Speaker: John H. Furbay. Titles: Business in a Jet Age; Dawn in the Dark Continent; Global Minds for a Global World; Let's Join the Human Race; The Middle East Unveiled; Only a Day to Anywhere; The Shape of Things to Come (1)
Speaker: Phillip Geary. Titles: People are People; Silver Bridges; Travel in the Jet Age (2)

★ 101 ★

FRAN LEE FOUNDATION INC.
15 West 81st Street
New York, New York 10024 (212) 873-5507

Fran Lee, founder of the organization lectures on numerous topics ranging from consumer affairs to medical research. Fees vary.

Speaker: Fran Lee (1)

★ 102 ★

THE LEIGH BUREAU
1185 Avenue of the Americas
New York, New York 10030 (212) 869-8430

Provides speakers to lecture on a wide variety of topics.

Speaker: Russell Baker. Title: Russell Baker's Witty World (1)
Speaker: Art Buchwald. Title: Buchwald at Large! (2)
Speaker: Lindley Clark. Titles: The Economy Over the Next Five Years; The Role of Confidence in Business (3)
Speaker: Joe Culligan. Titles: Creative Communicating; How to Kill Stress Before It Kills You (4)
Speaker: Nancy Dickerson. Title: Nancy Dickerson's Washington (5)
Speaker: John Diebold. Titles: Corporation of 2001; Future of Private Enterprise (6)
Speaker: Peter Duchin. Title: The Musical World of Peter Duchin (7)
Speaker: Robert Ellsworth. Title: Where Are We Headed in the Arms Race? Is the U.S. Falling Behind? (8)
Speaker: Nora Ephron. Title: Some Funny Things About Women (9)
Speaker: Rowland Evans. Title: The New Administration - What Washington Plans for U.S. Business (10)
Speaker: Clifton Fadiman. Titles: Mass-Communications; The Prospect Before Us; A Techno Society? (11)
Speaker: Arthur Goldberg. Titles: Can We Afford Liberty?; A Constitutional/Moral Foreign Policy (12)
Speaker: Alex Haley. Title: Roots, a Saga of Black History (13)
Speaker: Richard C. Hottelet. Titles: America's Role in World Affairs; The UN and World Peace (14)
Speaker: Nicholas Johnson. Titles: Deregulating America; Improving TV; Shaping a Future Life Style (15)
Speaker: James J. Kilpatrick. Title: Washington Wonderland (16)
Speaker: James Lavenson. Titles: Management By Walking Around; Think Strawberries (17)
Speaker: Jack Linkletter. Titles: Have You Had Your Annual Shake-Up?; How to Sell Almost Anything to Almost Anyone; How to Understand and Be Understood (18)
Speaker: Stanley Marcus. Titles: Building a Corporate Image; Can Free Enterprise Survive Success?; The Care and Cultivation of Collectors; Minding the Store (19)
Speaker: Leon C. Martel. Titles: The Next 200 Years; Prospects for Mankind (20)
Speaker: Robert Novak. Title: The New Administration - What Washington Plans for U.S. Business (21)
Speaker: Vance Packard. Titles: Changing Life Styles; Exploding Technology - A New Way of Life; A Nation of Strangers (22)
Speaker: Esther Peterson. Titles: Consumerism As a Marketing Plan; Equal But Different; In the Public Interest (23)
Speaker: Gerard Piel. Titles: Genetic Engineering: Life in Our Hands; A Round Trip to 2000 A.D.; What Energy Crisis? (24)
Speaker: Vincent Price. Titles: Appreciation of Great Art; Great American Eccentrics; Three American Voices; Villains Still Pursue Me (25)
Speaker: Donald Rumsfeld. Titles: America's Status in the World Today; Leadership and the Outlook for America; Washington Outlook (26)
Speaker: Harrison Salisbury. Titles: America's Stake in Asia; Freedom and Responsibilities of the Press; What's Ahead for America (27)
Speaker: John Scali. Titles: John Scali's Europe; Role of the UN in the Middle East (28)
Speaker: Daniel Schorr. Titles: Politics and Education; The Public's Right to Know; The Role of the Intelligence Community (29)
Speaker: Hugh Sidey. Titles: Implications of a New Administration; Nature of Leadership (30)
Speaker: Leonard Silk. Titles: Economic Outlook; Ethics and Profits (31)
Speaker: Hedrick Smith. Title: The Russians (32)
Speaker: Joel Stern. Titles: Planning for the Future; What Counts in Business?; Why Americans Are Losing Faith in Free Enterprise (33)
Speaker: J.F. terHorst. Title: The Press and the People (34)
Speaker: Lionel Tiger. Titles: Aggression, Violence and Human Nature; Effects of Human Biology on Behavior; Individuals in the Corporate Society (35)
Speaker: Alvin Toffler. Titles: The Coming Political Upheaval; The Corporation of the Future; Learning for Tomorrow (36)

★ 103 ★

ANN LEWIS PROGRAM SERVICE
97 Port Washington Boulevard
Roslyn, New York 11576 (516) 627-0054

This agency arranges for lecturers to appear before clubs, schools, colleges and other audiences drawing upon a very wide range of topics and popular speakers. Fees vary.

Speaker: Joseph J. Fahey. Titles: The Challenge of Building Peace; Mahatma Ghandi and Martin Luther King (1)

Speaker: Sheridan H. Garth. Title: A Swing Over Today's World Headlines (2)
Speaker: Douglas Hannan. Titles: American Antiques; Antiques for Investment (3)
Speaker: Rowland M. Myers. Title: The Romance of Words (4)
Speaker: Lewis Owen. Titles: Aaron Burr, Rascal Patriot; Early American Crafts; Road to Revolution (5)
Speaker: Roland W. Robbins. Titles: Hidden America; The Road to Ruins and Restorations; Yankee Country (6)

M

★ 104 ★
MAHGO ENTERPRISES, INC.
185 East 85th Street
New York, New York 10028 (212) 427-4444

Represents exclusively prominent figures from the world of athletics who are available for lecture engagements.

★ 105 ★
MARQUETTE UNIVERSITY
Public Relations Department
1834 West Wisconsin Avenue
Milwaukee, Wisconsin 53233 (414) 224-7448

Faculty experts are made available to local and regional groups in order to address audiences on topics related to their subject specialties. Some speakers do not charge a fee for their service. For those who do charge, the fees are flexible, depending on time, locality and nature of the group.

Anthropology

Speaker: Alice B. Kehoe. Titles: Anthropology in General; Archaeology (Prehistory) - Early Man of North America; Modern American Indians (1)

Biology

Speaker: James B. Courtright. Titles: Animal and Plant Genetic Improvement; Biochemistry; Genetic Engineering; Human Genetics (2)
Speaker: Bela E. Piacsek. Titles: Aging and Hormones; Population Control; Sex Education; Sexual Maturation (3)

Business and Computers

Speaker: Ralph E. Brownlee. Titles: Modern Marketing; Truth in Advertising (4)
Speaker: Richard A. Kaimann. Titles: Data Processing Feasibility; The Management of Data Processing; Management Planning, Computing in Business and Computing in Education; Management Science, Effective Management (5)
Speaker: Gene R. Laczniak. Titles: The American Enterprise System; Business and Ecology; Business and Its Environment; Business and the Arts; Business Ethics; Legal Aspects of Business (6)
Speaker: Michael J. Piasecki. Titles: Choosing the Form of Business; 1976 Tax Reform Bill; Other Federal Income Tax Topics; Payroll Taxes; Recordkeeping (7)
Speaker: Richard K. Robinson. Titles: Marketing Management - Product Management; Marketing Research and Information Systems; Transit Marketing (8)
Speaker: James W. Schreier. Titles: General Management; Personnel - 1776-2076 (9)
Speaker: James P. Trebby. Titles: Accounting; Finance (10)
Speaker: Noel T. Wood. Title: Personnel Management and Administration (11)

Communications

Speaker: Alfred J. Sokolnicki. Titles: Essentials of Effective Personal Communication; People are My Business (12)
Speaker: Joseph M. Staudacher. Titles: How to Become a More Interesting Conversationalist; Human Relations; Interpersonal Communication; Listening is Money--Both Ways; Public Speaking is Easy; Put Some Wind in Your Sails; Remembering Names--A Demonstration; Saving Time in Running Meetings; What Your Voice Reveals About You (13)
Speaker: Thomas B. Taft. Titles: Effective Communication Strategies; Utilizing Media in Patient Education (14)
Speaker: William T. Tracy. Title: Communication as a Management Tool (15)

Culture

Speaker: Carolyn Asp. Titles: Greek or Roman Literature; Greek or Roman Religion; Love and Death in Literature; Shakespeare (16)
Speaker: Frederick E. Brenk. Titles: Greece; Rome (17)
Speaker: Louis Cartz. Title: Gemstones (18)
Speaker: Leo M. Jones. Titles: Journey to the Iris; Technique for Enjoying Art; What Makes America Laugh (19)
Speaker: Sadanand G. Manoli. Titles: East and West; India and the Orient (20)
Speaker: Donald L. Metz. Title: Impact of Social Sciences on Cultural Values (21)

Speaker: Robin C. Mitchell. Titles: Melville; Melville and Hawthorne, A Timely Friendship; Steinbeck's First and Last Love - The Arthurian Legends (22)

Speaker: Hagop S. Pambookian. Titles: Journey Through Biblical Lebanon; The People of Ararat: The Armenians and Their Contributions (23)

Speaker: Michael J. Price. Title: Multi-media Presentation of Educational Theatre (24)

Speaker: Mark Siegchrist. Title: Romantic and Victorian Literature (25)

Speaker: James P. Siettman. Titles: For God's Sake, Laugh; A Lost Art: Reading Aloud; The Musical: America's Contribution to Theatre (26)

Speaker: Alfred J. Sokolnicki. Titles: Polish Contributions to American and World Culture; Polish Culture; Talks on American Culture (27)

Dentistry

Speaker: Virendra B. Dhuru. Titles: Dental Materials; Modern Trends in Dentistry; Stress Analysis in Dental Research (28)

Speaker: Sadanand G. Manoli. Title: Dentistry and Health (29)

Speaker: Ronald Pruhs. Titles: Child Management in Dental Office; Controversies in Pulp Therapy; Modern Pediatric Dentistry (30)

Speaker: Don L. Williams. Titles: Anxiety Control; Behavioral Sciences in Dentistry (31)

Economics

Speaker: Nyle Kardatzke. Titles: Central Economic Planning: Organization Versus Order; The Economics of Minimal Government; More Than You Ever Wanted to Know About Economics and Had the Sense Not to Ask; The Simple Economics of--- (32)

Education

Speaker: Louis Cartz. Title: The University in France and England (33)

Speaker: Robert J. DeRoche. Titles: Adult Education: You're Never Too Old; Career Planning; College Programs for Underachievers; Transition from High School to College; Your Human Potential: You Can Achieve!; (34)

Speaker: Dennis J. Doherty. Title: Liberal Arts Education Today (35)

Speaker: Adrian Dupuis. Titles: Existentialism and Education; Humanism vs. Behaviorism in Education; Issues in Education; Modern Philosophies (in Education) (36)

Speaker: Linda Fehrer. Title: High School Student Recruitment (37)

Speaker: Leo B. Flynn. Titles: Financial Assistance is Available for Higher Education; Independent Private Education as an Alternative; Preparing for Higher Education (38)

Speaker: Sarah Ann Ford. Titles: Student Activity Professionals Response to Non-Traditional Students; Student Development Programs for Black Students at Predominantly White Institutions (39)

Speaker: Jack B. Greene. Title: Physics as a Career (40)

Speaker: Marc F. Griesbach. Title: Why Catholic Universities? (41)

Speaker: Jeffrey S. Kaiser. Titles: Accountability; Administrative Mindedness; Educational Administration (42)

Speaker: M. Rosalie Klein. Title: Nursing Education (43)

Speaker: Arthur Mayberry. Title: The Educational Opportunity Program (44)

Speaker: Linda Milson. Titles: Medical Technology--Professional Information; Medical Technology--Recruitment (45)

Speaker: Robin C. Mitchell. Titles: English and the College Freshman; The "Johnny Can't Write" Debate (46)

Speaker: Robert B. Nordberg. Titles: Catholic Education; Guidance and Counseling; Philosophy of Education; Theories of Learning (47)

Speaker: Hagop S. Pambookian. Title: Teacher Evaluation and Improvement of Instruction (48)

Speaker: Gloria Rechlicz. Titles: The Balance of Research and Teaching in Nursing Education; Faculty Participation in University Governance; Medico-Moral Legal Ethics in Nursing; The Model Code of Procedures for Academic Freedom (49)

Speaker: James L. Sankovitz. Titles: Financing Postsecondary Education; From Classroom to Community; Government Support for Independent Colleges and Universities (50)

Speaker: William T. Tracy. Titles: Administering Through People; The Administrator and the School Board; The Role of the Board in Catholic Education (51)

Speaker: Diane M. Washbush. Title: Recruitment--Medical Technology (52)

Finance

Speaker: Barbara Szyszko. Titles: How to Research Foundation Grants; Philanthropic Foundations in Wisconsin (53)

Government

Speaker: Richard M. Brown. Titles: America's Overseas Information; Deep Throat, the Mystery of Watergate; The Dominican Crisis; The First Amendment - Is it Working (54)

Speaker: John R. Johannes. Titles: American Government and Politics; Congress; Elections; Political Parties; The Presidency; Voters and Voting (55)

Speaker: Ramon A. Klitzke. Titles: Administrative

Law; Antitrust Law; Law School Study; Local Government; Patent, Trademark and Copyright Law; Social Welfare Law (56)

Speaker: John K.C. Oh. Titles: The End of Pax Americana in Asia; The Future of the American Role in Asia; New Patterns of Asian Politics; Religious-Political Movements in Asia (57)

Speaker: Roger A. Olsen. Title: Election of the President (58)

Speaker: Athan Theoharis. Titles: Civil Liberties During the Cold War Years; The FBI; The Presidency and the Intelligence Community (59)

History

Speaker: John F. Berens. Titles: The American Revolution Considered as a Religious Revival; The First Un-Americans; Was the American Revolution Caused by a Conspiracy? (60)

Speaker: John P. Donnelly. Title: The Peasant in the Art of Peter Bruegel (61)

Marquette University

Speaker: Roger A. Olsen. Title: Student Judicial Boards at Marquette (62)

Speaker: William N. Robersen. Title: Marquette University Today (63)

Speaker: James L. Sankovitz. Title: Marquette University Impact on Milwaukee (64)

Media

Speaker: Craig G. Allen. Titles: Cable TV; The Educator and the Media (65)

Speaker: James W. Arnold. Titles: Critical Judgments on Art or Morality; Social Significance of Movies and Television (66)

Speaker: David J. Foran. Titles: News Media and Public Relations - Friendly Adversaries; Turmoil to Tranquility (67)

Speaker: Marian Pehowski. Titles: Magazines and American Life; News in the Soviet Union; News to and from the Two Chinas; So You Want to Be a Writer; Soviet Humor; Telling It Like It Is--and Isn't; Who Reads What in Japan (68)

Speaker: James T. Tiedge. Titles: The Modern Mass Media Myth; The Ratings Game; Support Televised Violence or I'll Kill You (69)

Military

Speaker: Ronald J. Denny. Titles: Air Navigation; Anti-submarine Warfare; Nautical Navigation; Naval ROTC (70)

Speaker: J. Michael Dunn. Titles: NROTC; Naval Weapons (71)

Speaker: Richard E. Maresco. Title: NROTC (72)

Speaker: Richard S. Park. Titles: NROTC; Naval Ships Engineering (73)

Speaker: Adrian G. Traas. Titles: Corps of Engineers, History and Current Roles; Reserve Officers Training Corps; Voluntary Army (74)

Speaker: Noel T. Wood. Titles: The Navy; The Navy ROTC; Sea Power; Submarines (75)

Modern Life

Speaker: Dennis J. Doherty. Titles: Abortion; Amnesty; Conscientious and Selective Objection; Divorce and Remarriage; Just War (76)

Speaker: Virginia Dotson. Titles: Assertiveness Training; How to Run a Meeting Effectively; Human Potential; Parapsychology; Personality/Leadership; Transactional Analysis (77)

Speaker: David Hartz. Title: Goal Setting: Exercises to Increase Awareness of Oneself (78)

Speaker: Roger A. Olsen. Title: Programming a Successful Event or Activity (79)

Speaker: Hagop S. Pambookian. Title: Motivation in One's Life; Who Am I? (80)

Speaker: Therese Pelt. Titles: Dynamics of Weight Control; Leadership; Program Planning; Students and Activities (81)

Speaker: Margi Peterson. Titles: Assertive Training; Leadership Development; Problem-Solving (82)

Speaker: Marva A. Richards. Title: Assertiveness Training (83)

Speaker: James W. Schreier. Titles: Drug Problems in Organizations; Entrepreneurs: Male and Female (84)

Speaker: James P. Siettmann. Titles: The How and Why of Conducting a Meeting; Programs of Readings for Special Occasions; TV or Not TV and Your Family (85)

Speaker: Jane D. Swan. Titles: Assertiveness Training; Women and Higher Education (86)

Speaker: Alfred P. Szews. Titles: Consumer Product Safety Commission; Consumer Safety; Electrical Safety; Product Safety (87)

Speaker: Dennis K. White. Titles: Assertive Training; Preventive Approaches to Alcohol and Drug Abuse (88)

Philosophy

Speaker: Margaret T. Crepeau. Titles: Philosophy of Suffering; Self-Disclosure--A View of Self (89)

Speaker: Marc F. Griesbach. Titles: Beauty is Not in the Eye of the Beholder; The New Morality Argument; The Worth of Philosophy (90)

Speaker: Thomas L. Prendergast. Title: Life After Death--Some Philosophical Considerations (91)

Physical and Mental

Speaker: Daniel Cotrone. Title: Death and Dying (92)

Speaker: Margaret T. Crepeau. Titles: Conflict; Laughter and Tears as Communication (93)

Speaker: Rita T. McDonald. Titles: Child Development; Mental Health (94)

Speaker: Margaret Anne Schlientz. Titles: Charismatic Renewal; Clinical Specialization; Emergency Psychiatric Measures; Healing; Management of Patient Care; Psychiatric Concepts; Psychiatric Nursing (95)

Speaker: Alice Semrad. Title: Clinical Laboratory Sciences (96)

Speaker: Terry Tobin. Title: Various Aspects of Childbearing (97)

Speaker: Nick J. Topetzes. Titles: Helping Children Reach Their Potential; Personality and Mental Health; Seeing Through Johnny So as to See Johnny Through; Understanding Your Child; What Makes a Person Tick (98)

Psychology

Speaker: James J. Blascovich. Titles: Environment and Behavior; Gambling Behavior; Risk Taking Behavior (99)

Speaker: Raymond J. McCall. Titles: Communication of Feeling; Psychological Effectiveness; Psychology of Alcoholism; Psychology of Drug Abuse; Psychology of Obesity; Psychology of Sexual Deviation; Psychosomatic Disorders (100)

Speaker: Rita T. McDonald. Title: Abnormal Psychology (101)

Speaker: M.Y. Quereshi. Titles: Cross-cultural Studies of Stereotypes; Future Trends in Psychology; Psychological Testing in Education and Industry; Psychology of Obesity (102)

Speaker: Anees E. Sheikh. Titles: Effects of Different Kinds of Child-Rearing Practices; Effects of Television on Children; Psychology of Prejudice; The Role of the Father in Child Development (103)

Religion

Speaker: Dennis J. Doherty. Titles: Ecclesiastical Authority; Genetic Counseling and Genetic Engineering; Medical Ethics; The New Morality; The Sacrament of Matrimony; The Sacrament of Penance, its Development and Renewal; Sexual Ethics; Theology of Sin; Today's Crisis of Faith (104)

Speaker: Elizabeth Dreyer. Titles: Ministry to the University; Prayer and Spirituality; Scriptural Prayer; Spiritual Direction (105)

Speaker: Keith J. Egan. Titles: Doing Theology in the Parish; Images of Christ; Mysticism; Prayer and Poetry; T.S. Eliot and the Religious Search; To Believe is to Pray; What is Prayer (106)

Speaker: Joseph T. Lienhard. Titles: The Beginnings of Religious Life; The Fathers of the Church; The History of the Early Church; Monasticism in the Early Church; The Sacrament of Penance in the Early Church; Spirituality of the Fathers (107)

Speaker: Donald L. Metz. Title: Sociology of Religion (108)

Speaker: George Muschalek. Titles: Christ as Man and God; The Christian Meaning of Being Man; The Experience of God Within Christian Faith (109)

Speaker: Lawrence M. Rich. Titles: The Berrigans and American Catholicism; Oral Interpretation and the Liturgy; Religion and the Movies (110)

Speaker: Richard R. Roach. Titles: Christian Ethics; Roman Catholic Moral Theology (111)

Sports

Speaker: Kevin Byrne. Titles: Marquette Athletics; Money in College Athletics; Warrior Basketball (112)

Speaker: Robert J. DeRoche. Title: Ice Hockey (113)

Speaker: J. Michael Dunn. Titles: Intramural Programing; Lifetime Individual Sports; Officiating and Professionalism; Outdoor Recreational Activities; President's Council on Physical Fitness; Sports Clubs; Team Handball (114)

Speaker: Robert H. Fitts. Titles: Exercise; Fatigue; The Marathon; Muscle Function (115)

Technology

Speaker: Mamdouh Bakr. Titles: Facilities Planning; Industrial Engineering; Management of Innovation and Change; Metric System and Conversion; Transit Management; Work Design (116)

Speaker: Warren J. Deshotels. Titles: Education for Present and Future Technology; Scientific Investigators; Solar Energy (117)

Speaker: James D. Horgan. Title: Technology and Human Values (118)

Speaker: Thomas K. Ishii. Titles: Lasers and Their Applications; Microwave Oven Safety; Microwaves and Their Applications; Police Traffic Radar Speed Measurement (119)

Speaker: Raymond J. Kipp. Titles: Industrial Wastewater Control; Wastewater Treatment; Water Pollution (120)

Speaker: Chai Hong Yoo. Titles: Earthquake Resistant Design of Highways; Highway Bridge Structures (121)

Speaker: Ronald E. Zupko. Title: Metric System (122)

Women

Speaker: Carolyn Asp. Title: Women in Literature (123)

Speaker: Betty J. Gabryshak. Title: Women in the Navy (124)

Speaker: Marva A. Richards. Titles: Rape;

Women's Consciousness Raising (125)
Speaker: Catherine Shiely. Title: Women's Athletics (126)
Speaker: Jane D. Swan. Titles: Breast Cancer; Eliminating Cancer (127)

★ 106 ★
UNIVERSITY OF MARYLAND
Office of Campus Activities
College Park, Maryland 20742 (301) 454-5605

The University is in the process of forming a speakers' bureau. Lecturers will be available to discuss educational, cultural, and social issues.

Subjects: Agriculture; Animals; Arts and Crafts; Behavorial and Social Science; Business and/or Management; Careers; Clothing and Textiles; Communications; Criminology and Law; Education; Engineering; Entertainment; Fine Arts; Foods and Nutrition; Forestry; Government and Politics; Health Care and Education; History; Hobbies and Practical Skills; Individual, Family and Community Development; Inter Cultural and Ethnic Studies; Languages; Leadership and Organization; Life and Physical Sciences; Literature; Mathematics; Physical Education; Recreation; Theology, Philosophy, and Religion; Travel; University

★ 107 ★
MASSACHUSETTS BAR ASSOCIATION
One Center Plaza
Boston, Massachusetts 02108 (617) 523-4529

Maintains a list of approximately one hundred attorneys. The lawyers speak on a wide range of subjects relating to the legal profession to schools and civic organizations. No fees.

Subjects: Civil Rights; Consumer Protection; Court Reform; Criminal Justice; Custody and Divorce; Labor Relations; Landlord-Tenant Problems; Legal Careers; Legislative Process; Malpractice; Real Estate Law; Rights to Privacy; Sex Discrimination; Tax Law; Wills

★ 108 ★
MEDITATION INSTITUTE
330 North 121st Street
Wauwatosa, Wisconsin 53226 (414) 475-1656

Offers a relaxation demonstration and through lectures shows people how to use the basic aspects of meditation and other mind exercises to relax. Fees vary from $25 for a short talk where little or no travel time is required to $500 plus expenses for a more extensive out of town presentation.

Speakers: Pamela Everix (1); William F. Schwartz (2)
Title: Meditation and Its Practical Application

★ 109 ★
MEDTRONIC, INC.
3055 Old Highway Eight
Post Office Box 1453
Minneapolis, Minnesota 55440 (612) 574-3548

Provides speakers to lecture to civic organizations, schools, fraternal groups, nursing and old people's homes in the Minneapolis-Saint Paul area on pacemakers and the history of this medical device. There are no fees.

Subject: Pacemakers

★ 110 ★
MEMPHIS STATE UNIVERSITY
Goodwyn Institute
Memphis, Tennessee 38152 (901) 454-2512

Lectures offered are concentrated on illustrated travel films. No fees.

Speaker: John N. Booth. Title: Spotlight on Spain (1)
Speaker: Ted Bumiller. Title: The Many Faces of France (2)
Speaker: Sid Dodson. Title: Focus on Finland (3)
Speaker: Ralph Franklin. Title: The Canyon (4)
Speaker: Ralph Gerstle. Title: Colombia (5)
Speaker: Jonathan Hagar. Title: Immortal Poland (6)
Speaker: Howard Meyers. Title: Shadow and Splendor (7)
Speaker: William Moore. Title: Fabulous Rio - Portrait of Brazil (8)
Speaker: Frank Nichols. Title: Colorado - Where the West Comes Alive (9)
Speaker: Alton Parrott. Title: The Road to Mandalay (10)
Speaker: Lucia Perrigo. Title: Shadow and Splendor (11)
Speaker: John Roberts. Title: Puerto Rico (12)

★ 111 ★
MEN'S FASHION ASSOCIATION OF AMERICA
1290 Avenue of the Americas
New York, New York 10019 (212) 581-8210

Speakers are available to address educational audiences on any facet of the mens wear industry. In addition to the lecturers listed below, other members of the Association are also possible speakers in different regions of the country. No charges other than reimbursal for expenses and transportation costs.

Speakers: Norman Karr (1); Chip Tolbert (2)
Title: The Male Fashion Scene

★ 112 ★
MID WEST PROGRAM SERVICE, INC.
9729 Lee Boulevard
Leawood, Kansas 66206 (913) 648-1308

Provides speakers to lecture on various topics to business organizations, professional groups, civic and service clubs, social clubs, and college audiences. Fees vary.

Speaker: Martin Agronsky. Title: Newscasting (1)
Speaker: Jack Anderson. Title: News in Washington (2)
Speaker: Robert Ardrey. Titles: Man: The Final Hunter; Territory - The Imperative; Why Do We Kill Each Other? (3)
Speaker: Murray Banks. Title: What to Do Until the Psychiatrist Comes (4)
Speaker: Joe Batten. Title: The Nuts and Bolts of Success (5)
Speaker: Cathrina Bauby. Title: Many Faces of Cathy (6)
Speaker: Birch Bayh. Title: Politics (7)
Speaker: Betty Beale. Title: No Seats - No Fun (8)
Speaker: Edward Beasley. Title: From Archie Bunker to Fred Sanford (9)
Speaker: Dan Bellus. Title: Probable Causes of Success (10)
Speaker: Paula Bishop. Title: Tattle Tales About First Ladies (11)
Speaker: James Blakely. Title: Livin' on Love and Laughter (12)
Speaker: Joe Blatchford. Title: The American Presidency (13)
Speaker: Michael Braude. Title: Profit - An All-American Word (14)
Speaker: David S. Broder. Title: American Politics (15)
Speaker: Joyce Brothers. Title: People and Their Problems (16)
Speaker: Lester R. Brown. Title: World Food Problems (17)
Speaker: Monte Burch. Title: Wildlife (18)
Speaker: Ethel Burge. Titles: Charisma - Everybody Has It; Poise Aplenty (19)
Speaker: Pat Buttram. Titles: The Great Western Movie Scene; Sense and Nonsense (20)
Speaker: Earl Butz. Title: Food Crisis - Fact or Fiction? (21)
Speaker: John N. Christianson. Title: Management by Motivation (22)
Speaker: Alan Cimberg. Title: Management (23)
Speaker: Gary K. Clarke. Title: Zoology (24)
Speaker: Ron Cook. Title: What A Man on the Moon Means for You (25)
Speaker: Jean-Michel Cousteau. Titles: Sharks - Past and Present; Underwater Jungle Law (26)
Speaker: Richard Crabb. Title: The Impossible Dreams (27)
Speaker: Sam Dash. Title: America's Goal - Justice Through Law (28)
Speaker: Robert DeFlores. Title: The Big Band Era (29)
Speaker: R.E. Delaney. Title: Give Up or Get Involved (30)
Speaker: Dave Diles. Title: Toy Department of Life (31)
Speaker: E. Grey Dimond. Title: China: New, Old, Ancient (32)
Speaker: Mary Clark Dimond. Titles: Children in China; Women in Modern China (33)
Speaker: Jeane Dixon. Title: A Gift of Prophecy (34)
Speaker: Robert Dole. Title: Politics (35)
Speaker: Paul Duke. Title: Newscasting (36)
Speaker: Harold Ensley. Titles: Keep Your Bait in the Water; There Is No Easy Way (37)
Speaker: Ronald J. Fields. Title: Life and Times of W.C. Fields (38)
Speaker: Mig Figi. Title: Your Greatest Sense - Your Sense of Humor (39)
Speaker: Joan Fontaine. Title: The Golden Years of Hollywood (40)
Speaker: Grant Gard. Title: We Create Our Own Problems (41)
Speaker: Clyde Gentry. Title: Be Alive Inside and Out (42)
Speaker: Bill Glass. Title: Get In the Game (43)
Speaker: Curt Gowdy. Title: Looking At Sports From the Broadcasting Booth (44)
Speaker: Maury Graham. Title: The Open Road (45)
Speaker: Mike Gravel. Title: Politics (46)
Speaker: Joe Griffith. Title: How Long Has This Been Going On? (47)
Speaker: Martha W. Griffiths. Title: The Issues Nobody Likes to Talk About (48)
Speaker: James Gunn. Title: Science Fiction (49)

Speaker: Tennyson Guyer. Title: This Miracle Called America (50)
Speaker: Peter Hackes. Title: News and Information Services (51)
Speaker: Tom Haggai. Title: Values for Living (52)
Speaker: Laurence Hall. Title: Humor - A Business Asset (53)
Speaker: Amy Harris. Title: Are You Achieving More and Enjoying it Less? (54)
Speaker: Sydney Harris. Title: Strictly Personal (55)
Speaker: Thomas Anthony Harris. Title: I'm Okay - You're Okay (56)
Speaker: Gary Hart. Title: Politics (57)
Speaker: Paul Harvey. Title: Newscasting (58)
Speaker: Floyd Haskell. Title: Politics (59)
Speaker: Timothy Hays. Title: Marriage, Middle Age and Other Perils (60)
Speaker: Fred Herman. Titles: Creative Persuasion; Planned Selling (61)
Speaker: Ross Hersey. Title: The King of the Shaggy Dog Story (62)
Speaker: Newt Hielscher. Title: A Good Laugh and Something to Think About (63)
Speaker: Joe Higgins. Title: College - Is There Life After College? (64)
Speaker: Art Holst. Title: A Pro on the Go (65)
Speaker: David Hoy. Title: ESP (66)
Speaker: Cecil Hunter. Title: How to Pulverize an Audience With Laughter (67)
Speaker: Allan Hurst. Titles: Leadership of Man; Motivating Human Behavior (68)
Speaker: Don Hutson. Title: The Business Boom of the Seventies (69)
Speaker: Eliot Janeway. Title: Survival in the Seventies (70)
Speaker: Elizabeth Janeway. Title: Living With Crisis (71)
Speaker: Charles Jarvis. Title: Open Wide And Laugh (72)
Speaker: Donald C. Johanson. Title: When Man First Walked Erect (73)
Speaker: Mildred Johnson. Title: Ask Yourself (74)
Speaker: Herb Kaplow. Title: Newscasting (75)
Speaker: Bel Kaufman. Title: Don't Flunk the Teacher (76)
Speaker: Judith Keith. Title: I Haven't a Thing to Wear (77)
Speaker: Joan Corrier Kemper. Title: Goal Setting - A Means to Self Improvement (78)
Speaker: Garry Kinder. Title: How to Be a Star Salesman (79)
Speaker: Jack Kinder. Title: How to Sell Successfully (80)
Speaker: Irving R. Levine. Title: Newscasting (81)
Speaker: Art Linkletter. Title: Drug Abuse and Disaster (82)
Speaker: Jack Linkletter. Title: A New Day - A New Way (83)
Speaker: Curtis R. McClinton, Jr. Title: Minorities in Business (84)
Speaker: Kenneth McFarland. Title: America's Opportunity (85)
Speaker: Jim McKay. Title: The Wide World of Sports (86)
Speaker: Catherine Mackin. Title: Newscasting (87)
Speaker: Jacquelyn Mayer. Title: The Crown and the Shadow (88)
Speaker: Dave Melton. Title: How Parents Can Change Our Schools (89)
Speaker: Edward A. Milligan. Title: New Insights Into Indian Affairs (90)
Speaker: Clark Mollenhoff. Title: Newscasting (91)
Speaker: Richard L.D. Morse. Title: Consumer Rights and Responsibilities (92)
Speaker: Von Nash. Title: Motivation (93)
Speaker: Gaylord Nelson. Title: Politics (94)
Speaker: George Nigh. Title: What We Can Do Together (95)
Speaker: R.L. Noran. Title: Journey to the Depths of the Human Mind (96)
Speaker: Harry E. Olson, Jr. Title: Take Charge of Yourself (97)
Speaker: Ike Pappas. Title: Newscasting (98)
Speaker: Ruth Stafford Peale. Titles: Bloom Where You are Planted; Today's Woman (99)
Speaker: Charles Plumb. Titles: Resources Unlimited; You've Got a Lot Going for You (100)
Speaker: Ed Podolak. Title: Sports vs. Business (101)
Speaker: William Proxmire. Title: Politics (102)
Speaker: Fred H. Pryor. Title: Managing in Changing Times (103)
Speaker: Nido Qubein. Title: Awaken Your Sleeping Giant (104)
Speaker: Jennings Randolph. Title: Politics (105)
Speaker: Ronald Reagan. Title: Politics (106)
Speaker: Bruce Rice. Title: The Great World of Sports (107)
Speaker: Bob Richards. Title: There Is Genius in the Average Man (108)
Speaker: Jane Richardson. Title: Regal India (109)
Speaker: Will Rogers, Jr. Title: The Life and Times of My Father (110)
Speaker: Andrew A. Rooney. Title: Mr. Rooney Goes to Washington (111)
Speaker: Harold Russell. Title: The Handicapped (112)
Speaker: Phyllis Schlafly. Title: What's Wrong With Equal Rights for Women? (113)
Speaker: David L. Schmidt. Title: Management (114)
Speaker: Robert E. Shepherd. Title: Don't Just

Stand There - Worry (115)
Speaker: Joe Spear. Title: Newscasting (116)
Speaker: Robert W. Spitzer. Title: World Food Problems (117)
Speaker: Bill Stiles. Title: What's Going on in There? (118)
Speaker: Stuart Struever. Title: Cache in the Cornfield (119)
Speaker: Cody Sweet. Title: Body Language (120)
Speaker: Carl Terzian. Title: The American Way (121)
Speaker: Nick Thimmesch. Title: Newscasting (122)
Speaker: Strom Thurmond. Title: Politics (123)
Speaker: Francis Tritt. Titles: Is Your Leadership Showing?; Personal Management in Selling (124)
Speaker: Herb True. Title: What Makes a Leader? (125)
Speaker: William Turner. Title: The Noble Art of Being Average (126)
Speaker: Richard Valeriani. Title: Newscasting (127)
Speaker: Marilyn Van Derbur. Title: Motivation in Education (128)
Speaker: Everett D. Watson. Title: Motivation - Success and You (129)
Speaker: Somers H. White. Title: How to Sell Twice as Much in Half the Time (130)
Speaker: Les Whitten. Title: Newscasting (131)
Speaker: Charles Wilkinson. Title: The Winning Attitude (132)
Speaker: Charles Willey. Title: You Can't Do Business With an Empty Wagon (133)
Speaker: Justin Wilson. Title: Hunting With Justin Wilson (134)
Speaker: Carl Winters. Title: The Businessman's Glory Road (135)
Speaker: John Wolfe. Title: Sell Like an Ace - Live Like a King (136)
Speaker: John Wooden. Title: Motivation (137)
Speaker: Zig Ziglar. Title: See You at the Top (138)

★ 113 ★
THE GILBERT MILLER AGENCY
8350 North Kimball Avenue
Skokie, Illinois 60076 (312) 674-3630

Well known figures from the world of sports and public events are offered as lecturers to speak to organizations of all kinds. Fees range from $1500 to $2500 plus transportation and expense charges.

Speaker: Curt Gowdy. Titles: Baseball; Basketball; Broadcasting; Fishing; Football (1)
Speaker: Jimmy Piersall. Titles: Drinking; Drugs; Mental Health; Smoking; Sports (2)
Speaker: Lendon H. Smith. Titles: Behavior and Diet; How to Win Without Cheating; An Odd Thing Happened on the Way to the Office; A Pediatrician Straightens Out the World (3)

★ 114 ★
MIXTER ARTIST MANAGEMENT
172 Whitman Avenue
West Hartford, Connecticut 06107 (203) 521-8010

Lecturers present talks on a variety of topics. Fees range from $500 to $2400 plus expenses.

Speaker: Steve Dacri. Title: Magic (1)
Speaker: John Kolisch. Title: Phenomena of the Mind - Mentalism and Hypnotism (2)
Speaker: Hunter S. Thompson. Title: American Politics and Craziness (3)
Speaker: Heddie Tracy, Sr. Title: Alcoholism (4)

★ 115 ★
MONSANTO COMPANY
800 North Lindbergh Boulevard
Saint Louis, Missouri 63166 (314) 964-5418

Monsanto employees from the research, manufacturing, marketing and management areas are provided to lecture on the role of chemicals in improving the quality of life. Speakers are provided free of charge.

Subjects: Agricultural Production; Chemical Risks and Benefits; Natural Foods; Product Testing

★ 116 ★
MORALITY IN MEDIA, INC.
487 Park Avenue
New York, New York 10022 (212) 752-7611

Speakers will discuss the problem of obscenity and the problem of gratuitous sex and violence on television and the solutions to these problems. Fee is $750 plus transportation expenses.

Speaker: Jack Chernus. Titles: Gratuitous Sex and Violence on TV; Obscenity Problem and Obscenity Law (1)
Speaker: John Douglas. Titles: Gratuitous Sex and Violence on TV; Obscenity Problem and Obscenity Law (2)
Speaker: Irving Gavrin. Title: Obscenity Problem and Obscenity Law (3)
Speaker: Morton A. Hill. Title: Obscenity Problem and Obscenity Law (4)

Speaker: Paul Murphy. Title: Obscenity Problem and Obscenity Law (5)
Speaker: Stephen E. Shapiro. Titles: Gratuitous Sex and Violence on TV; Obscenity Problem and Obscenity Law (6)
Speaker: Constantine Volatis. Title: Obscenity Problem and Obscenity Law (7)

★ 117 ★
MURRAY STATE UNIVERSITY
Murray, Kentucky 42071 (502) 762-3011

Some one hundred speakers from the university community are provided to lecture on numerous timely topics. No fees.

Agriculture

Speaker: Durwood Beatty. Titles: Harmful Plants in the Environment; Weed Control Around the Home (1)
Speaker: William N. Cherry. Titles: Agriculture as it Relates to Industry; Agriculture is More Than Agriculture; Farmers in a Changing World (2)
Speaker: Harry L. Conley. Title: Organophosphate Pesticides and Food Production (3)
Speaker: Harold E. Eversmeyer. Title: Vocational Education in Agriculture (4)
Speaker: Roger L. Macha. Titles: Backyard Fruit Production; Botanical Gardens - Arboretums in North America; Garden Flowers - Varieties and Culture; Home Gardening with Vegetables (5)
Speaker: Gilbert L. Mathis. Title: Agricultural Economics (6)
Speaker: Amos Tackett. Titles: Fine Turf; Floral Design; Gardens; Landscaping; Lawn Care (7)
Speaker: James T. Thompson. Titles: Adult Farmer Classes; World Food Situation (8)

Anthropology

Speaker: William P. McHugh. Title: Prehistoric Cultural Adaptations in Saharan Africa (9)

Art

Speaker: Michael A. Brun. Titles: Discussion of Personal Art Work; Poetry Reading with Illustrative Slides (10)
Speaker: Robert Head. Titles: Art of Various Parts of the World; Comparative Art Forms; Technical and Conceptual Approaches to Drawing (11)
Speaker: Richard G. Jackson. Title: Children's Art (12)

Biology

Speaker: Harold E. Eversmeyer. Title: Common Plant Diseases and Man (13)

Business

Speaker: Marvin Albin. Titles: Banking Relations with Regulatory Agencies; Planning Business Education for the Future; Production Standards and Work Measurement in the Office (14)
Speaker: R.B. Barton. Titles: Alcoholism - A Business Problem; Business - Society's Scapegoat; Profits - Spoils or Just Rewards (15)
Speaker: Maurice Clabaugh. Titles: Consumer Attacks on the Auto Industry; Consumerism - Cognitive Dissonance Restated (16)
Speaker: John W. DeVine. Titles: Economic Literacy; Transportation Innovations; Women's Role in Business and Education (17)
Speaker: Howard C. Giles. Title: Concepts of Public Choice (18)
Speaker: Thomas F. Holcomb. Titles: Job Success: What It Takes to Make It; Occupational Stress: The Elements which Contribute to Stress on the Job (19)
Speaker: Lloyd B. Jacks. Title: Social Competencies and Job Success (20)
Speaker: Roy V. Kirk. Titles: Management Education at MSU; Managerial Values and Organizational Effectiveness (21)
Speaker: John Lindauer. Title: The National Economy (22)
Speaker: Gilbert L. Mathis. Titles: Comparative Economic Systems; The Economic Outlook; International Economics (23)
Speaker: Howard F. Newell. Titles: The American Economy Today: Current Policy, Future Implications; Is Poverty in the United States Increasing or Decreasing? (24)
Speaker: William B. Seale. Titles: Advertising; Marketing; Selling (25)
Speaker: James T. Thompson. Titles: The Causes and Effects of Inflation; Government Economic Policy (26)
Speaker: Faye C. Wells. Title: Certified Professional Secretary Examination (27)
Speaker: Jane Freeman Wells. Titles: Advertising and Vulnerability of Man; Authority, Its Use and Abuse; The Woman's Role in Business (28)

Ecology, Environment, Pollution

Speaker: Michael A. Brun. Title: Muhlenberg County, Kentucky - Its Strip Mining Industry (29)
Speaker: Harold E. Eversmeyer. Title: Ecology of North America (30)
Speaker: William P. McHugh. Title: Environmental Impact Studies and Archaeological Research (31)

Speaker: James P. Matthai. Titles: Air Conservation; Soil; Water (32)

Speaker: Michael G. Miller. Title: Environment (33)

Speaker: Howard F. Newell. Title: The Economics of Environmental Quality (34)

Speaker: James T. Thompson. Titles: The Economic Aspects of Pollution; The Economic Aspects of the Energy Crisis (35)

Education

Speaker: Robert F. Aslup. Titles: Reading and Language Arts in the Open School; Teaching and Reading Skills in the Elementary Schools; Using the Diagnostic Approach to the Teaching of Reading (36)

Speaker: Lewis Bossing. Titles: Behavior Modification in Normal School Settings; Classroom Management (37)

Speaker: Richard R. Childress. Title: Professional Negotiations in the Public Sector (38)

Speaker: Ken S. Dean. Titles: Carkhuff Learning and Counseling Models for Teachers; Interpersonal Communication; Teacher Modeling Behavior in the Physical, Intellectual and Emotional Domains (39)

Speaker: John W. DeVine. Titles: Economic Literacy; The Role of Vocational Education (40)

Speaker: Franklin G. Fitch. Titles: Audio-Visual Education; Interpersonal Relationships in School Administration; Methods of Instructing in Secondary Education (41)

Speaker: Wilson Gantt. Title: Today's College Student - Who Is He? (42)

Speaker: Thomas F. Holcomb. Titles: The Art of Parenting; Everybody is Somebody: The Self-Concept; Peopling: Humanizing the Educational Process (43)

Speaker: Ben Humphreys. Titles: Characteristics of a Helping Relationship; Student-Centered Teaching (44)

Speaker: Bobby G. Malone. Titles: Human Relationships - Component of Teacher Preparation; The Parents' Role in the Education of a Young Child; Questioning Skills of Teachers (45)

Speaker: S.M. Matarazzo. Titles: Financing Capital Outlay for Schools; Integration-Busing; Leadership; Liability and the Administrator; Liability and the Guidance Counselor; Liability and the School Nurse; Liability and the Teacher; Liability and the Vocational Teacher; School Board Liability; Students' Rights and Due Process (46)

Speaker: Gilbert L. Mathis. Title: Economics of Education (47)

Speaker: Sandra A. May. Titles: Art, Music, and Cooking Activities for the Classroom Teacher; Encouraging Children's School Success; Helping Children to Be More Creative - Ways Parents and Teachers Can Encourage Creativity; Language Arts and Math Activities for Teachers - Nursery - 4th Grade; Opening Up the Classroom - Activities and Suggestions for Individualizing and Informalizing Education; A Positive Approach to Discipline Problems - Effective Ways Parents Can Deal with and Understand Young Children (48)

Speaker: Hugh A. Noffsinger. Titles: Collective Bargaining in Education; Goals and Objectives of Education; School Organization and Administration (49)

Speaker: Garth F. Petrie. Titles: Individualized - Personalized Education; Non-Verbal Communication - The Subconscious Language; Rating Your School; Setting Limits for Children (50)

Speaker: Bill Price. Titles: Providing Structure in the Unstructured Classroom; A Realistic and Humanistic Approach to Classroom Discipline (51)

Speaker: Robert W. Rowan. Titles: Issues in Testing; Research into the ACT (52)

Speaker: Donald Rye. Title: Welfare Rolls of Country Clubs (53)

Speaker: Thomas P. Sholar. Titles: Education; Recreation (54)

Speaker: Vernon E. Shown. Title: Improving Teacher-Student Relationship (55)

Speaker: June Warden Smith. Titles: Children's Literature; History and Methods of Kindergarten; Language Arts and Related Activities (56)

Speaker: Joan Stranahan. Title: Alternatives in Public Schools (57)

Speaker: John Taylor. Titles: Discipline in the School Setting; Innovation Practices for Improving the Instructional Staff in the Elementary and Secondary Schools; Non-Verbal Communication: A Program Dealing with the Many Aspects of this Overlooked Part of Communications; Value Clarification in the Educational Setting (58)

Speaker: Charles H. Tolley. Title: The Community College Program (59)

Speaker: Wayne M. Williams. Titles: The Learning Process; Student Teaching in Teacher Education (60)

English

Speaker: Gordon J. Loberger. Titles: Contemporary Standards for Grammatical Correctness; The Nature of Language - How it Influences Our Behavior, Our Conceptions, Our View of Self and Others, How It Functions (61)

Geography

Speaker: Ivan S. Lubachko. Title: The U.S.S.R.: Land and People (62)

Speaker: James P. Matthai. Titles: Geography of the Middle East; Geography of the Soviet Union (63)

SPEAKERS AND LECTURERS

History

Speaker: Wayne T. Beasley. Titles: Ancient Religions and Philosophies; French Revolution and Napoleon; Today's Isms (64)

Speaker: James W. Biggs. Titles: Leadership in a Democracy; The Role of Persuasion in a Democracy; Values of Free Speech in a Democracy (65)

Speaker: Robert L. Burke. Titles: Current Issues in American Foreign Policy; John F. Kennedy and the Civil Rights Movement; Why Vietnam? (66)

Speaker: Harvey L. Elder. Titles: The Siege of Vicksburg; West Kentucky in the War Between the States (67)

Speaker: Gene J. Garfield. Titles: Current Public Policies and Problems; United States Foreign Policy: Emphasis of the United States in Asia (68)

Speaker: James W. Hammock, Jr. Titles: Governor Isaac Shelby and the War of 1812; Love and War: The Courtship of a Civil War Belle; Reclaiming the Past with Tape Recorders; The Second Awakening as a Turning Point in Kentucky Religious History, 1780-1805 (69)

Speaker: James M. Kline. Title: Kentuckyhenge: Stonehenge Revisited (70)

Speaker: Hughie G. Lawson. Title: Witchcraft at Salem: An Overview of the Witchcraft Trials at Salem, Massachusetts (71)

Speaker: Ivan S. Lubachko. Titles: Education in the U.S.S.R.; The U.S.S.R.: Land and People (72)

Speaker: Don M. Pace. Titles: The History of Livingston County; What Happened to Our Inalienable Rights? (73)

Speaker: Walter D. Sagrera. Titles: French Revolution; Mussolini; Napoleon; Renaissance (74)

Speaker: Edwin C. Strohecker. Titles: Collecting Children's Books; History of American Juvenile Periodicals; History of Children's Literature; The Pennsylvania Dutch: The Land of the Hex Sign (75)

Speaker: Robert Valentine. Title: The Bicentennial Orators (76)

Speaker: J. Riley Venza. Titles: The American Revolution; Hamilton and Jefferson: Comparison and Contrast of Philosophies (77)

Home Economics

Speaker: Alice Koenecke. Title: Trends in Home Economics (78)

Speaker: Alta V. Presson. Titles: Nutrition and Activity for the Overweight; Nutrition for the Family (79)

Industrial Technology

Speaker: George T. Lilly. Titles: Careers in Teaching Industrial Arts; Choosing a Career or Vocation; Preparing for Employment in Today's World (80)

Speaker: Paul K. Lynn. Titles: Industrial Education: Careers, Opportunities, and Offerings; Plastics Technology: History, Importance and Fundamentals (81)

Speaker: Eugene M. Schanbacker. Titles: The Metric System, Its Impact and Its Implementation; Technical Drawing: The Universal Graphic Language (82)

Journalism and Radio-Television

Speaker: Carl J. Denbow. Title: The First Amendment: An Unqualified Right to Be Unfair? (83)

Speaker: Robert Howard. Titles: Bias in Television News; The Development of Mass Communication; Ethical Problems in Broadcasting; Fairness Doctrine and Equal Time; The Proper Relationship Between Broadcast Journalists and the Government (84)

Speaker: Robert H. McGaughey III. Titles: Advertising - Why We Buy What We Do; Philosophical Background of Freedom of Press; Putting Together the Campus Newspaper (85)

Speaker: William Ray Mofield. Titles: Broadcasting's Fairness Doctrine; The Operation of Radio and Television Stations (86)

Linguistics

Speaker: Howard H. Keller. Titles: Comparative Linguistics; Linguistics and Language Teaching (87)

Literature

Speaker: Kent Forrester. Titles: 18th Century Literature; Science Fiction: What It's All About (88)

Speaker: Jean Lorrah. Titles: Chaucer's England; Dracula Meets the New Woman (89)

Speaker: Michael G. Miller. Title: Recent American Literature (90)

Speaker: Robert Valentine. Title: Life and Humor of Mark Twain (91)

Mathematics

Speaker: Harvey L. Elder. Titles: The Metric System; Motivation in the Teaching of Mathematics; Our Number System; Programs in Mathematics at Murray State University; What is Calculus? (92)

Speaker: Jack D. Wilson. Titles: An Introduction to Convexity; Intuitive Topology; The Tower of Hanoi (93)

Medical

Speaker: Alta V. Presson. Title: Diet Therapy for Sick People (94)

Music

Speaker: David Nelson. Titles: Public School String Programs; String Quartet - For School Demonstrations and Performances (95)

Occult

Speaker: Jean Lorrah. Titles: ESP Through the Tarot; Palmistry: Your Life Is in Your Hands (96)

Philosophy

Speaker: Frederick L. Kumar. Titles: Buddhist Notion of Liberation; Illumination and Zen; Indian Culture - Marriage Customs, Holidays and Festivals; Mrs. Gandhi and Indian Democracy; The Notion of Person in Existentialism; Oriental Philosophy; Phenomenology and God; Vedanta Concept of Salvation (Moksha) (97)

Speaker: Wayne Sheeks. Titles: Modern and Contemporary Philosophies; On the Nature of Truth, Goodness, and Beauty; Plantonism (98)

Political Science

Speaker: Wayne T. Beasley. Title: Todays Isms (99)

Speaker: Jack B. Johnson. Titles: Changing Trends and Directions in America; Social Benefits and Costs in Developing Rural Areas; Social Welfare; Strategies for Changing that Work (100)

Speaker: Howard H. Keller. Title: The Soviet Union Today (101)

Speaker: Charles O'Neil. Titles: The Present Brazilian Regime; The United States and Latin America: The Latin View (102)

Speaker: Joseph L. Rose. Titles: Do You Want to Know about Latin America; Public Policy; They Are Your Civil Liberties, Your Civil Rights (103)

Speaker: Farouk F. Umar. Titles: American Government's Issues and Problems: Democracy; Arab-Israeli Conflict: Its Origin and Analysis of Present Situation; Government and Politics of the Middle East; International Relations: Observations, Comments and Analysis (104)

Speaker: J. Riley Venza. Title: A Cultural and Political Analysis of Mexico (105)

Speaker: Steven L. West. Titles: The Fourth Branch of Government; Packaging Our Elected Officials; The Political Decision; The Politics of Nuclear Energy (106)

Psychology

Speaker: R.B. Barton. Title: Alcoholism - A Business Problem (107)

Speaker: Thomas F. Holcomb. Title: Mental Health for Daily Living (108)

Speaker: Tom Muehleman. Titles: Behavior Modification; Smoking - Can I Quit? (109)

Speaker: Joan Stranahan. Titles: Competition vs. Cooperation; Humanism - What is it?; Life Management Skills (110)

Speaker: Machree A. Ward. Title: Psychology of Normal Human Growth and Development (111)

Public Affairs

Speaker: James W. Biggs. Titles: Leadership in a Democracy; The Role of Persuasion in a Democracy; Values of Free Speech in a Democracy (112)

Speaker: Robert L. Burke. Title: Current Issues in American Foreign Policy (113)

Speaker: William E. Freeman. Titles: Investments; Tourism in West Kentucky (114)

Speaker: Vernon W. Gantt. Titles: Interpersonal Relations; Words are Meaningless (115)

Speaker: Gene J. Garfield. Title: Current Public Policies and Problems (116)

Speaker: Jack B. Johnson. Titles: Social Benefits and Costs in Developing Rural Areas; Social Welfare (117)

Speaker: Don M. Pace. Title: What Happened to Our Inalienable Rights? (118)

Speaker: Joseph L. Rose. Titles: Kentucky; Public Policy; Your Civil Rights (119)

Speaker: Vernon E. Shown. Titles: Better Employer-Employee Relationship; Improving Teacher-Student Relationship (120)

Recreation

Speaker: William E. Freeman. Titles: Investments; Tourism in West Kentucky - Present Status and Future Prospects (121)

Speaker: Roger L. Macha. Titles: Backyard Fruit Production; Botanical Gardens; Garden Flowers; Home Gardening with Vegetables (122)

Speaker: William O. Presson. Title: Physical Education (123)

Speaker: Joseph L. Rose. Title: Did You Know That...? (124)

Speaker: Thomas P. Sholar. Title: Recreation (125)

Speaker: Amos Tackett. Titles: Fine Turf; Floral Design; Gardens; Landscaping; Lawn Care (126)

Regional Services

Speaker: Wilson Gantt. Title: Today's College Student (127)

Speaker: Lloyd P. Jacks. Titles: Conducting Business Meetings; Use of Parliamentary Procedure (128)
Speaker: William Ray Mofield. Titles: Broadcasting's Fairness Doctrine; Projects and Programs for Community Development (129)
Speaker: Billy J. Puckett. Title: Evolution of Antique Firearms (130)

Special Education

Speaker: Billie Downing. Titles: The Child with Behavior and Learning Problems; Educational Approaches to Mental Handicap; Learning Disabilities; Mainstreaming: Pros and Cons; Mental Retardation (131)
Speaker: James L. Fitch. Titles: Child and Multiple Handicaps; The Handicapped Child; What it Means to Have a Hearing Loss (132)
Speaker: Jon Hufnagle. Titles: Communications in the Brain Damaged Adult; The Exceptional Child in Today's Society; Speech after Cancer of the Larynx (133)
Speaker: Yancy Watkins. Titles: MSU's Right to Read Program; Motivation - A Key to Learning; Reading and MSU (134)

Speech

Speaker: Jerry W. Mayes. Titles: Communication Now...More Than Ever; How Free is Free Speech; Is There a Conflict Between Higher Education and Religion?; The Need for Speech Training (135)
Speaker: Robert Valentine. Title: What You Say is What You Get; You Can't Not Communicate (136)

Travel

Speaker: Lloyd P. Jacks. Title: Europe 1975 (137)
Speaker: Suzanne M. Keeslar. Titles: Culture Shock; The French: How We Differ; French Impressionist Art; The French: What We Have in Common; Highlights of The Louvre; How to Plan an Affordable Trip to Europe; Paris, That Beloved Monster; Travelogue of Western Europe; A Visit to the Jeu de Paume-Impressionist Museum (138)
Speaker: Howard H. Keller. Title: The Soviet Union Today (139)
Speaker: Alice Koenecke. Title: Guatemala - Land of Eternal Spring (140)
Speaker: Ivan S. Lubachko. Title: The U.S.S.R. (141)
Speaker: Eugene M. Schanbacker. Titles: Ethiopia, the Country and Her People; Wildlife and Game Preserves of East Africa (142)

N

★ 118 ★
NCR CORPORATION
1700 South Patterson Boulevard
Dayton, Ohio 45479 (513) 449-3551

Lectures are presented on achieving success in our free enterprise system. The fee is $500 and travel expenses.

Speaker: Ira M. Hayes. Title: Keeping Pace With Tomorrow (1)

★ 119 ★
NAREMCO SERVICES, INC.
60 East 42nd Street, Suite 1714
New York, New York 10017 (212) 697-0290

Speakers promote the preservation of business records for corporate memory and business histories. Fees are negotiable.

Speaker: Robert A. Shiff. Titles: Administrative Management and Office Support Systems; Clients; Information Retrieval; Records Management; Word Processing, Text-Editing, and Secretarial Support; Work Measurement and Work Simplification (1)

★ 120 ★
NATIONAL ASSOCIATION OF FLEET ADMINISTRATORS, INC.
295 Madison Avenue
New York, New York 10017 (212) 689-3200

Maintains a speakers bureau of members who are available to speak on various aspects of automotive fleet operations.

Subject: Automotive Fleet Operations
Titles: Cost Control; Efficiency; Leasing; Management; Safety; Vehicle Selection

★ 121 ★
NATIONAL ASSOCIATION OF HOUSING COOPERATIVES
1828 L Street, N.W., Suite 1100
Washington, D.C. 20036 (202) 872-0550

Provides speakers who discuss all aspects of co-operative housing development and management. Fees vary.

★ 122 ★
NATIONAL ASSOCIATION OF PARENTS AND PROFESSIONALS FOR SAFE ALTERNATIVES IN CHILDBIRTH (NAPSAC)
Marble Hill, Missouri 63764

Sponsors lecturers who are prepared to speak on natural childbirth. Fees are an honorarium of $150 and travel expenses.

Speaker: Mayer Eisenstein. Title: The Practicing Physician in Homebirth (1)
Speaker: Janet Epstein. Title: Homebirths and the Nurse Midwife (2)
Speaker: Lewis Mehl. Title: Scientific Studies on Homebirth and Other Alternatives (3)
Speaker: David Stewart. Title: Homebirth: The Way of the Future (4)
Speaker: Genna Withrow. Title: The Lay Midwife in Today's Society (5)

★ 123 ★
NATIONAL ASSOCIATION OF SUGGESTION SYSTEMS
435 North Michigan Avenue, Suite 2112
Chicago, Illinois 60611 (312) 644-0075

Lecturers are available to speak on all aspects of the operation of formalized suggestion systems in government or industry. Some speakers require a fee. Speakers expect reimbursement for travel expenses and accommodations.

Speakers: Paul M. Bailey (1); Robert E. Bonville (2); J. Alan Carter (3); James J. Dennard (4); John A. Flagge (5); Charles H. Foos (6); Leo J. Kirk (7); Walter M. Kleinmann, Jr. (8); Francis C. Knautz (9); James L. McVittie (10); H. Bruce Palmer (11); Frank Perry (12); Herman W. Seinwerth (13); Herbert F. Shain (14); Alvin B. Shoalts (15); Robert E. Slough, Jr. (16); Andrew E. Smith (17); Harold G. Walker (18); J. Robert Watts (19)

★ 124 ★
NATIONAL CABLE TELEVISION ASSOCIATION
918 16th Street, N.W.
Washington, D.C. 20006 (202) 457-6700

This Association provides speakers who lecture on cable television to clubs, groups, and organizations.

Speaker: Robert L. Schmidt. Title: Cable Television: 30 Years of Innovation and Service (1)
Speaker: Thomas E. Wheeler. Title: Cable, Broadcasting and Ma Bell (2)

★ 125 ★
NATIONAL COMMITTEE FOR RESPONSIBLE PATRIOTISM
Commodore Hotel
109 East 42nd Street
New York, New York 10017 (212) 684-0640

Provides lectures on the free enterprise system in America to organizations and school groups. Fees vary.

Speaker: Charles Wiley. Titles: The Threat to Our Survival; What's Right With America (1)

★ 126 ★
NATIONAL FARMERS ORGANIZATION
720 Davis Avenue
Corning, Iowa 50841 (515) 322-3131

Lecturers are available to discuss the preservation of the family farm system. No fees other than actual expenses incurred.

Speakers: Oren Lee Staley (1); DeVon Woodland (2)
Title: The Family Farm System

★ 127 ★
NATIONAL LIBERTY CORPORATION
Valley Forge, Pennsylvania 19481 (215) 648-5616

This insurance marketing firm sponsors lectures on insurance at colleges and universities. There are no fees, but expenses are charged in some situations.

Speaker: Gerald F. Beavan. Title: Direct Response Marketing of Insurance (1)

★ 128 ★
NATIONAL MICROGRAPHICS ASSOCIATION
8728 Colesville Road
Silver Spring, Maryland 20910 (301) 587-8444

The Association's Speakers Bureau has approximately fifty speakers who lecture on various topics in the micrographic field. Speakers often combine engagements with business trips and thus do not charge a fee. There are others who lecture or prepare a half day or full day seminar who require both an honorarium and travel expenses.

★ 129 ★

NATIONAL ORGANIZATION FOR NON-PARENTS
806 Reisterstown Road
Baltimore, Maryland 21208 (301) 484-7433

Speakers offer lectures on non-parenthood to schools and organizations. Honoraria are accepted.

Speakers: Carole Goldman (1); Jean Hosman (2); Kenneth Hunter (3); Gail McKirdy (4)
Title: Non-parenthood

★ 130 ★

NATIONAL PREMIUM SALES EXECUTIVES, INC.
1600 Route 22
Union, New Jersey 07083 (201) 687-3090

Offers speakers, seminars and panel discussions and audiovisual presentations, to business and educational groups on the subject of the incentive marketing field. There are no fees. Business expenses are charged to groups of more than one hundred people.

Speakers: Jack Albertson (1); Philip Anoff (2); Maurcy Ball (3); Chuck Blazer (4); James Bowers (5); Timothy Carroll (6); Calvin Cobb (7); John Daly (8); Edmund David (9); William Dean (10); Robert Dewalt (11); Philip Driscoll (12); Paul Elias (13); Dean Fitch (14); Gary Ganim (15); Lewis Halper (16); L.H. Harris (17); Jon Hultman (18); Irv Kiem (19) George Kling (20); Alan Klitzner (21); John Kochenbach (22); Lee Leonard (23); James McReynolds (24); Stan Mindlin (25); John Morley (26); John North (27); Charles Peacock (28); Sheryl Rosenfield (29); Neil Rowe (30); Robert Sanford (31); Clifford Smith (32); Robert Stelle (33); Harlan Strong (34); Roy Thomas (35); William Ward (36)
Title: Techniques of the Incentive Marketing Field

★ 131 ★

NATIONAL RIGHT TO WORK COMMITTEE
8316 Arlington Boulevard, Suite 600
Fairfax, Virginia 22038 (703) 573-8550

Provides speakers and film presentations about the right to work to civic and fraternal groups throughout the United States. The Committee asks that travel and hotel expenses be provided by the group sponsoring the speech.

Speaker: Charles W. Bailey. Title: Right to Work - Supported by Facts, Figures and the American People (1)
Speaker: Andrew Hare. Title: Right to Work - Capitol Hill Perspective (2)
Speaker: Reed Larson. Title: Right to Work - A National Concern (3)
Speaker: Susan Staub. Title: Right to Work - Forcing Public Employees into Unwanted Labor Unions (4)

★ 132 ★

NATIONAL SCHOOL SUPPLY AND EQUIPMENT ASSOCIATION
1500 Wilson Boulevard
Arlington, Virginia 22209 (703) 524-8819

Provides speakers to lecture on a variety of timely topics.

Speaker: Kenneth M. Book. Title: The Cause and Effect of Education's Nervous Future (1)
Speaker: Don Bresnan. Title: Provocative Contractual Questions for School Purchasers (2)
Speaker: E.J. Fleming III. Title: Speak Up for Education (3)
Speaker: Kay Fredericks. Title: The Role of Instructional Materials in Education (4)
Speaker: R.J. Girdler, Jr. Title: The Low Bid Syndrome (5)
Speaker: James W. Long. Title: Your School Distributor Does It All (6)
Speaker: John Pace. Title: Distribution - A Vital Link for Education (7)
Speaker: William J. Payne. Title: Playground Equipment Safety (8)
Speaker: O.L. Petty, Jr. Title: Why Business Supports All Levels of Education (9)
Speaker: E.W. Schmelzel. Title: The Ten Most Asked Purchasing Questions (10)
Speaker: Frank E. Smith. Title: The Status of Education as Viewed by Business (11)
Speaker: Max L. Smith. Title: The Principal of Profit (12)
Speaker: Guy V. Sweet. Title: The Safety-Maintenance - Common Sense Equation (13)

★ 133 ★
NATIONAL SOLID WASTE MANAGEMENT ASSOCIATION
1120 Connecticut Avenue, N.W., Suite 930
Washington, D.C. 20036 (202) 659-4613

Provides speakers to lecture on topics related to waste management. Fees are variable.

Speaker: Richard L. Hanneman. Title: Waste Management (1)
Speaker: Michael Hill. Title: General Public Policy Issues (2)
Speaker: Charles A. Johnson. Title: Sanitary Landfills, Resource Recovery, and Handling of Hazardous Waste (3)
Speaker: Phil Nowers. Title: Refuse Collection, Solid Wastes' Handling Equipment (4)
Speaker: Eugene J. Wingerter. Title: Waste Management (5)

★ 134 ★
NATIONAL SPEAKERS' AND PSYCHICS' REGISTRY
2814 New Spring Road, N.W.
Atlanta, Georgia 30339 (404) 435-0010

Makes available speakers who lecture on parapsychology and other unusual topics. Fees range from $300 to $5000.

Speaker: Christopher Bird. Title: The Secret Life of Plants (1)
Speaker: Martin Ebon. Title: Exorcism: Fact or Fiction (2)
Speaker: R. Buckminster Fuller. Title: Towards a New World (3)
Speaker: Uri Geller. Title: Parapsychology (4)
Speaker: John Ott. Title: Health and Light (5)
Speaker: Brad Steiger. Title: The Starmaidens and Numerous Others (6)

★ 135 ★
NATIONAL SPEAKERS BUREAU, INC.
222 Wisconsin Avenue
Lake Forest, Illinois 60045 (312) 295-1122

This agency maintains a large roster of speakers who are offered to address all types of organizations, associations, academic audiences, women's clubs, fraternal orders and convention groups. Fees are available on request.

Speaker: Martin Agronsky. Title: The State of our Nation (1)
Speaker: Jack Anderson. Titles: The New Spirit in Investigating Reporting; The Washington Merry-Go-Round (2)
Speaker: James Arch. Title: Success is a State of Mind (3)
Speaker: Gordon Barnes. Title: Weather-or Whether? (4)
Speaker: Joe Batten. Titles: The ABC's of Decision-Making; Tough-Minded Management (5)
Speaker: Fred Bergsten. Title: 2000 Young American Leaders (6)
Speaker: George Blanda. Title: Being an Eternal Quarterback (7)
Speaker: David Brinkley. Title: Newscasting (8)
Speaker: Joyce Brothers. Title: Human Interactions (9)
Speaker: William F. Buckley. Title: News and The World Today (10)
Speaker: Joe Cappo. Titles: The Consumer End of Business; The Sins of Advertising (11)
Speaker: John Chancellor. Title: Presidential Documentaries (12)
Speaker: James J. Cribbin. Title: Management of the Future (13)
Speaker: R.E. Delaney. Title: What's Right With America (14)
Speaker: Jeane Dixon. Title: A Gift of Prophecy (15)
Speaker: James Dornoff. Title: The Power of Enthusiasm (16)
Speaker: Hugh Downs. Title: Communication and Environment (17)
Speaker: Douglas Edwards. Title: Newscasting (18)
Speaker: Julius Fast. Title: Body Language (19)
Speaker: Pauline Frederick. Title: Professional Journalism (20)
Speaker: George Gallup. Title: Urban Problems (21)
Speaker: Georgie Ann Geyer. Title: The Latin American Revolution (22)
Speaker: Virginia Graham. Title: Consumer Affairs (23)
Speaker: W. Phillip Gramm. Title: The Economy (24)
Speaker: Peter Hackes. Title: Everything You Wanted to Know About Washington But Didn't Know Who to Ask (25)
Speaker: Sidney J. Harris. Title: Newscasting (26)
Speaker: Paul Harvey. Title: The Uncommon Man (27)
Speaker: Henry Heimlich. Title: The Heimlich Maneuver (28)
Speaker: Fred Herman. Title: Management by Action - The Manager's Role (29)
Speaker: J. Allen Hynek. Title: UFOs (30)
Speaker: Eliot Janeway. Title: What is Ahead America? (31)
Speaker: Dennis Johnson. Title: The Front Line

and The Bottom Line (32)
Speaker: Earl Johnson. Title: Beyond Management by Objectives (33)
Speaker: Charles Jones. Title: Life is Tremendous (34)
Speaker: Herb Kaplow. Title: Newscasting (35)
Speaker: Douglas Kiker. Title: Covering the Convention Circuit (36)
Speaker: Carol Kleiman. Title: The Housewife's Dilemma (37)
Speaker: Charles Kuralt. Title: Newscasting (38)
Speaker: Irving R. Levine. Title: How Today's Economy Affects Your Future (39)
Speaker: Art Linkletter. Title: Youth-Oriented Problems (40)
Speaker: Elmer W. Lower. Title: Behind the Scenes in Television News (41)
Speaker: Kenneth McFarland. Title: Selling America to Americans (42)
Speaker: Catherine Mackin. Title: Newscasting (43)
Speaker: Paul Micali. Title: The Five Basic Methods of Salesmanship (44)
Speaker: George Murphy. Title: The Hollywood Story - Experience in Communications (45)
Speaker: Bess Myerson. Title: Consumer Affairs (46)
Speaker: Earl Nightingale. Title: Our Changing World (47)
Speaker: Len O'Connor. Title: Len O'Connor Reports (48)
Speaker: Harry Olson. Title: Reach Beyond Your Grasp (49)
Speaker: Laurence J. Peter. Title: Competence in Spite of Theory (50)
Speaker: J. Lewis Powell. Title: Cave Man To Space Man (51)
Speaker: Frank Reynolds. Title: Newscasting (52)
Speaker: Bob Richards. Title: There's Genius in the Average Man (53)
Speaker: William F. Rickenbacker. Title: The Rickenbacker Papers (54)
Speaker: Pierre A. Rinfret. Title: The Economy (55)
Speaker: Walter Schirra. Title: Technology From Space (56)
Speaker: Whitt Schultz. Title: The Goldmine Between Your Ears (57)
Speaker: Mike Vance. Title: Why Businesses Fail: Why People Fail (58)
Speaker: Heartsill Wilson. Title: Stand Up America (59)

★ 136 ★

NATIONAL WATER WELL ASSOCIATION
500 West Wilson Bridge Road
Worthington, Ohio 43085 (614) 846-9355

National Water Well Association staff members are prepared to offer lectures on topics related to the water well industry. No fees other than travel expenses and hotel accommodations.

Aids to Better Business

Speaker: Kathy Butcher. Titles: Education in the Ground Water Industry: What You Didn't Learn at Daddy's Knee; Hassle-Free Meeting Planning: Fact or Fiction (1)
Speaker: Max Clay. Title: Safety Program For Drilling Contractors (2)
Speaker: Harold W. Heiss, Jr. Title: The Mathematics of the Well Drilling Industry (3)
Speaker: Wayne McLaughlin. Titles: Accidents Can Kill Businesses as Well as People; Trade Associations - A Business Asset Not Listed on Your Balance Sheet (4)
Speaker: Anita Bacco Stanley. Title: How to Advertise Your Company (5)
Speaker: Donald Tosi. Title: The Psychology of Selling (6)

Business Management

Speaker: Pat B. Alcorn. Titles: Are You Losing Money in Inventory; Cash Flow Planning; Collections in Following with the Squeaky Wheel Principle; Efficient Handling of Accounts Receivable; Introduction of the Basic Bookkeeping System; Now That You Can Run a Drilling Rig, Can You Run a Drilling Business?; Trials, Tribulations and Joys of Family Owned Business; Working With Your CPA, Banker and Attorney (7)
Speaker: Max Clay. Title: Basic Insurance Needs of the Small and Medium Size Drilling Contractor (8)
Speaker: Laurence E. Sturtz. Title: Problems of the Businessman: A Lawyer's View (9)
Speaker: Donald Tosi. Title: Management by Objectives (10)
Speaker: Karen Zag. Title: Introduction of the Basic Bookkeeping System (11)

Ground Water Geology/Hydrology

Speaker: Tyler E. Gass. Title: Land Subsidence; Using Fracture Traces to Locate Water Wells (12)
Speaker: Joel Hunt. Title: Glacial Deposition of Aquifers and Other Interesting Landforms (13)
Speaker: Jay H. Lehr. Titles: Ground Water Flow in Living Color; Ground Water Pollution Control; How a Water Witch Drowns in a Dry Hole (14)

Speaker: Gail Branscome Palmer. Title: A Brief Introduction to the History of the Earth (15)

Potpourri

Speaker: Roslyn B. Albert. Titles: Everyone Can Take a Pleasing Photograph; How Public Relations Can Benefit You (16)
Speaker: Kathy Butcher. Title: Culinary Creativity (17)
Speaker: Joel Hunt. Title: Whitewater Rafting in West Virginia (18)
Speaker: Jay H. Lehr. Title: Is Our Representative Democratic Government a Reality or an Alice in Wonderland Fantasy (19)
Speaker: Wayne McLaughlin. Titles: National Water Works Association Today; The Trials and Tribulations of Association Work (20)
Speaker: Judy May. Title: Estate Planning for Women (21)
Speaker: Gail Branscome Palmer. Titles: Geology and Hydrology Careers for Women; Water Conservation in the Home (22)
Speaker: Anita Bacco Stanley. Titles: How to Read More Effectively; The Relaxation Response: How to Use Mental Relaxation Techniques to Enrich Your Life (23)
Speaker: Donald Tosi. Title: The ABC's of Personally Controlling Stress at Home and at Work (24)

Water Well Technology

Speaker: Tyler E. Gass. Titles: Don't Let the Bugs Get the Best of You; Everything You Ever Wanted to Know About Plastic Well Casing... But Were Afraid to Ask; The Ground Water Source Heat Pump; The Impact of Abandoned Wells on Ground Water; Well Maintenance and Rehabilitation (25)
Speaker: Harold W. Heiss, Jr. Titles: Hydraulic Ram; Your State's Drilling Regulations in Plain Talk (26)
Speaker: Jay H. Lehr. Title: How to Use the Manual of Water Well Construction Standards (27)
Speaker: Judy May. Title: Metric Conversion and the Water Well Industry (28)

★ 137 ★
NETWORK AGAINST PSYCHIATRIC ASSAULT
558 Capp Street
San Francisco, California 94110 (415) 285-6353

Seeks to educate the public on forced psychiatric treatment. Average fee is $20.

★ 138 ★
NEW YORK MERCANTILE EXCHANGE
Four World Trade Center
New York, New York 10048 (212) 938-2222

Speakers are drawn from the officers of the Exchange who lecture on topics which relate to the purposes and activities of the commodity markets carried out under the auspices of the Exchange. No fees.

Speaker: Allen C. Abrahams. Title: International Economics and Trade (1)
Speaker: Melvin Falis. Title: Commodity Futures Regulation (2)
Speaker: Howard Gabler. Title: Management of Commodity Futures Trading Activities (3)
Speaker: Richard Levine. Title: Management of Commodity Futures Trading Activities (4)

★ 139 ★
NEWSWEEK, INC.
444 Madison Avenue
New York, New York 10022 (212) 350-2684

Newsweek occasionally makes available the magazine's reporters, writers, editors and management staff to speak to university audiences.

Subjects: Arts; Education; Energy; International Affairs; Justice; Life/Style; Medicine; National Politics; Religion; Science; Sports

★ 140 ★
NO-LOAD MUTUAL FUND ASSOCIATION
Valley Forge, Pennsylvania 19481 (215) 783-7600

Provides speakers in major cities of the United States to lecture on No-Load Mutual Funds. No fees.

Speaker: G. Richmond McFarland. Titles: How to Get the Most for Your Invested Money; Kinds of No-Load Mutual Funds; Services Offered by No-Load Mutual Funds (1)

★ 141 ★
NORTH CAROLINA NATIONAL BANK
Post Office Box 120
Charlotte, North Carolina 28255 (704) 374-5682

Bank officers are available to speak on banking and the economy throughout North Carolina. There are no fees.

Subjects: Banking; Economy

★ 142 ★

NORTHEASTERN ILLINOIS UNIVERSITY
5500 North Saint Louis Avenue
Chicago, Illinois 60625 (312) 583-4050

Faculty members present lectures on various topics to organizations in the Chicago area. Fees vary.

Speaker: Charles M. Barber. Titles: Comparative Revolutions; Free Institutions vs. Fascism; 20th Century Germany; Western Civilization; World in the 20th Century (1)
Speaker: Joseph C. Beaver. Titles: Bird Songs; Dialects; Poetic Meters; Proper Language; Social Levels of Language (2)
Speaker: Louis Becker. Titles: Computer Science; Jewish History; Jewish Literature; Physics (3)
Speaker: Mary A. Bell. Titles: Curriculum Planning; Guidance and Counseling; Mainstreaming; Parent's Groups; Resource Rooms (4)
Speaker: Sherman Beverly, Jr. Titles: Oral History Techniques; Teaching Research Methods to Elementary School Children; Utilization of Local History in Education (5)
Speaker: Gary Bevington. Titles: The Balkans; Foreign Language Pedagogy; Linguistics (6)
Speaker: Sophie K. Black. Titles: Books; Libraries (7)
Speaker: Jill K. Bohlin. Title: Fashion Merchandising (8)
Speaker: Mary W. Bowers. Titles: Remedial Reading; Research; Testing (9)
Speaker: Vern Braun. Titles: Antiques; Extensions and Continuing Education; Fishing (10)
Speaker: Harry A. Broadd. Titles: Art Appreciation; Art History (11)
Speaker: Bernard J. Brommel. Titles: Communications; History (12)
Speaker: Mary Louise Burger. Titles: Child Development; Children's Literature; Cognition; Creative Activities; Curriculum for Early Childhood; Day Care; Learning Centers; Mathematics for Young Children; Piaget (13)
Speaker: Josiane Caron. Titles: Anthropology of Haiti; Child Care; Minority Women; Organizing Women; Racism and Sexism; Single Parenthood; Unmarried Motherhood; Women Services (14)
Speaker: Roger H. Charlier. Titles: Non-polluting Energy Sources; Save the Environment; The Sea and Us (15)
Speaker: Ronald Combs. Titles: Opera as a Contemporary Art Form; Opera History (16)
Speaker: Margo Crawford. Titles: Afro-American History and Culture; Black Liberation Movements; Black Women in America (17)
Speaker: Daniel Creely. Titles: Fishing; Jogging; Physical Fitness; Weight Training (18)
Speaker: Frank W. Dobbs. Titles: Chemistry of the Universe; Science and It's Ethical Impact (19)
Speaker: Marion Etten. Titles: Health Subjects; Nursing; Nutrition; Physical Fitness (20)
Speaker: Ahmed A. Fareed. Titles: Curriculum Development; Diagnosis and Treatment of Reading Disabilities; Educational Measurement; Intelligence Testing; Planning, Administering and Evaluating Reading Programs; Reading Measurement; Reading Problems at the Elementary and Secondary Schools; Reading Skills (21)
Speaker: Reynold Feldman. Titles: American Literature and Culture; Hawaii; Indonesia; Mysticism/Non-Western Philosophy; Non-Traditional Higher Education; West Germany (22)
Speaker: Ferydoon Firoozi. Titles: Baha'i Faith; Middle East; Money and Banking (23)
Speaker: Frederick O. Flener. Title: Metric Education (24)
Speaker: Joyce Ann Flory. Titles: Advertising; Business and Professional Speaking; Communication Between the Sexes; Discussion Techniques; Interpersonal Communication; Interviewing; Male Liberation; Non-Verbal Communication; Persuasion; Public Speaking; Television and the Mass Media; Women's Right (25)
Speaker: Mary Ann Fowler. Titles: Dog Obedience; Elementary School Mathematics; Metric System (26)
Speaker: Duke Frederick. Titles: Abraham Lincoln; The American Presidency; The Civil War; Guerilla Warfare; Popular Literature; Reconstruction (27)
Speaker: Philip R. Garrett. Titles: Animal Training; Behavior Modification; Child Management (28)
Speaker: Melvin R. George. Titles: Censorship Matters; Collection Development; Library Buildings; Library Management (29)
Speaker: Peri P. Georgiou. Titles: Aesthetic Education; Developing Reading Centers; Early Childhood Education in Art, Music and Children's Literature; Instructional Materials for Developing Skill Areas; Science for Young Children; Teaching Reading to Young Children (30)
Speaker: R.L. Gilbert. Titles: Astronomy; Evolution of the Universe; History and Philosophy of Science; Scuba Diving; Space Travel; Stars (31)
Speaker: Jean Gillies. Title: Madison Avenue Mannequins (32)
Speaker: C. Edward Gilpatric. Titles: Adult and Non-traditional Education; The Future of Higher Education; Politics of Education; Public Administration; Urban Politics (33)

Speaker: Rodrigo C. Gonzalez. Titles: Mexico - Culture and Civilization; Paris - Culture and Civilization; Traveling Through Europe (34)

Speaker: Clarice L. Hallberg. Title: Interdisciplinary Method of Teaching Art (35)

Speaker: Jane S. Hawley. Titles: Educational Materials Development; English Education; In-Service Training of Teachers; Journalism Education; Secondary Education; Teacher Training (36)

Speaker: Richard Hesler. Titles: Alternative Theatre in Chicago; Non-Verbal Aspects of Human Communication (37)

Speaker: Marge Munn Hobley. Titles: Ballet; Choreography; Jazz; Modern Dance (38)

Speaker: Frank C. Hostetler. Titles: Camping; Community Health; First Aid; Health Education; Planning; Safety Education; Sex Education; Teaching Techniques; Values Clarification (39)

Speaker: Randolph H. Hudson. Title: Academic Programs and Aspirations (40)

Speaker: Asad Husain. Titles: International Relations; Middle East and South Asia; Reading and Writing; Religion of Islam (41)

Speaker: Hilary I. Iregbulem. Titles: Collective Bargaining; Personnel Management; Public Administration (42)

Speaker: William Itkin. Titles: Creativity; Divergent Thinking (43)

Speaker: Charles J. Jackson. Titles: Career Centers; Career Development; Career Education; Careers; Drugs; Guidance and Counseling; Mental Health (44)

Speaker: Claire M. Jacobs. Titles: Child Development; Early Education and Intervention; Parent-Child Relationship; Parenting; Preventative Mental Health (45)

Speaker: Violet Johnson. Titles: Coaching; Gymnastics; Judging (46)

Speaker: Arnold P. Jones, Jr. Titles: Affirmative Action; Bridge; Motivation; Special Learning Problems of the Black Child (47)

Speaker: Lucy J. Kamau. Titles: African Affairs; American Race Track Culture; Medical Anthropology; Squatter Settlements in Africa (48)

Speaker: Raymond Kasper. Titles: Baseball; Baseball Coaching; Fencing (49)

Speaker: Harry Kiang. Titles: China; Urban Land Use Planning (50)

Speaker: James A. Kokoris. Titles: American Capitalism; Comparative Economic Systems; Consumer Economics; Economic Development of Japan and China; International Economics (51)

Speaker: Mary L. Kooyumjian. Title: Gifted and Talented Children (52)

Speaker: Jules Lerner. Titles: Biochemical Genetics; Human Genetics (53)

Speaker: Ely Liebow. Titles: Detective Fiction; Sherlock Holmes; Yiddish Literature (54)

Speaker: Margaret R. Lindman. Titles: Greece; The Orient (55)

Speaker: Jose E. Lopez. Titles: Alternative Education and Freirian Model; General Brazilian History; Neo-colonialism and the Third World; Puerto Rican Migration; Puerto Rican Nationalism; Theories of Imperialism (56)

Speaker: James A. Lucas. Titles: Choral Music; Folk Music; Medieval and Renaissance Music; Orchestral Music; The Role of Men in the Women's Movement (57)

Speaker: James MacDonald. Title: Human Evolution (58)

Speaker: Carol D. Mardell. Titles: Dial (A Screening Test); Learning Disabilities; Pre-school Children with Special Needs (59)

Speaker: Betty Meyer. Title: Beginning Gymnastics and Tumbling (60)

Speaker: Gertrude Meyers. Titles: Educating the Adolescent with Special Problems; Parents of Handicapped Children and Solutions (61)

Speaker: Hugh S. Moorhead. Titles: On Aging and Dying; Sex Past and Future (62)

Speaker: Joseph C. Morton. Titles: American Revolution; Benjamin Franklin; Colonial America; Early American Presidents (63)

Speaker: John J. Murphy. Titles: American Politics; Congress; Intelligence Agencies; Presidents; Voting Behavior (64)

Speaker: Charles Nissim-Sabat. Titles: Astronomy; Cosmology; General Relativity; The Impact of Technology on Society; Nuclear Physics; Unionism in Higher Education (65)

Speaker: Bettye J. Parker. Titles: Afro-American Literary Criticism; Afro-American Literature; Afro-American Oral History; Afro-American Women Writers; Creative Writing; Modern Afrikan Literature; Non-traditional Education (66)

Speaker: Charles R. Pastors. Titles: Chicago Politics; Constitutional Law; Illinois Legislature (67)

Speaker: Angelina Pedroso. Titles: Bilingual Education; Cuban History; Role of the Latino Women in the United States (68)

Speaker: William J. Pizzi. Titles: Behavioral Pharmacology; Brain Research; Drug Abuse; General Aviation (69)

Speaker: Richard Reichhardt. Titles: Mathematical Models; Mathematics and Computers - Future Trends; Operations Research; Teaching with Computers (70)

Speaker: Stanley R. Renas. Titles: Communication; Discrimination Against the Older Worker; Economics; Management; Marketing; Motivation (71)

Speaker: Steven A. Riess. Title: Professional Baseball and American Culture (72)

Speaker: Richard J. Robertson. Titles: Community Psychology; Group Dynamics; Group Therapy;

Human Systems; Psychotherapy; Rehabilitation Theory (73)
Speaker: Edward A. Robinson. Titles: Acting; Afro-American Literature; Directing Theatre Groups; Drama; English Education; Multi-Cultural Education; Radio and Television Announcing and Script Writing; Secondary Teacher Education (74)
Speaker: Ronald A. Saiet. Titles: Education and Technology; Multi-Image Production Techniques (75)
Speaker: Leopold B. Segedin. Titles: Art Concepts; Art History; Contemporary Art (76)
Speaker: Charles W. Shabica. Title: Lake Michigan (77)
Speaker: Gregory H. Singleton. Titles: American Society; Computers and Society; Effects of the Economy on Work and Play; The Family in Historical Perspective; The Politics of Abortion; Quantitative Methods in the Social Sciences; Religion; Social History (78)
Speaker: Melvyn A. Skvarla. Titles: Frank Lloyd Wright; History of Chicago Architecture and Preservation; Library Design; Mies van der Rohe; School Site Location and Theory (79)
Speaker: June Sochen. Titles: U.S. Cultural History; Women in America; Women in Film (80)
Speaker: Mohan K. Sood. Titles: Economic and Political Aspects of India; Energy and Mineral Resources; Energy-Environment; Indian Scene; Indian Way of Life; Philosophy of India; Rocks and Minerals (81)
Speaker: Nancy A. Spencer. Title: Archaeology (82)
Speaker: Humphrey Stevens. Titles: Curriculum; Educational Television and Commercial Television (83)
Speaker: Sandra Styer. Titles: Child Development; Early Childhood Education; Literature for Young Children; Moral Judgment Development; Sex-role Development (84)
Speaker: Patricia A. Szymczak. Title: Hawaii (85)
Speaker: Neal Tremble. Title: Adult Physical Fitness (86)
Speaker: Edward C. Uliassi. Title: Career Education; Education in the Social Sciences (87)
Speaker: Hansa D. Upadhyay. Titles: Earthquakes and the Prediction; Origin of Mountains; Plate Tectonics and Our Restless Earth (88)
Speaker: Kusol Varophas. Titles: Guerilla Warfare; Political, Cultural, Social and Economic Aspects of Southeast Asia (89)
Speaker: Rudolfo E. Vilaro. Titles: Bilingual Education; Teaching Language Arts, Reading, Mathematics and Science to Bilingual Classes in the Elementary Grades (90)
Speaker: Francis X. Vogel. Title: School Organization (91)
Speaker: Robert Walker. Titles: Communication; Media Sexploitation - Bad Ads; Performing Arts (92)
Speaker: William M. Walsh. Titles: Child Counseling; Family Therapy; General Counseling and Guidance; Group Counseling; Individual Counseling; Psycho-Educational Assessment (93)
Speaker: Gussie M. Ware. Title: Flannel Board Usage (94)
Speaker: Ulestine Watson. Titles: Adult Education; Competency-based Degree Programs; Graduate School Admissions; Law School/Business School Admissions; Non-traditional Education (95)
Speaker: Floyd J. Wiercinski. Titles: Biology; Muscle Contractions; Research; Ultrasonics (96)
Speaker: Marvin Willerman. Title: Conflict in Schools (97)
Speaker: Robert Elie Zegger. Titles: French Writers and Opinions on England; Heroes in History; London Through the Centuries; Lord Byron and Greece; Paris; Popular Recreation and Reform in the 19th Century England and France; Provence (98)

★ 143 ★
NORTHWEST MINING ASSOCIATION
West 1020 Riverside Avenue
Spokane, Washington 99201 (509) 624-1158

Provides speakers to lecture on topics related to mining and economics. There are no fees.

Speaker: Russell Babcock. Title: Thrill of Discovery (1)
Speaker: John C. Balla. Title: The World of Copper (2)
Speaker: Frank H. Blair, Jr. Title: Is Mining Important to You? (3)
Speaker: Russell Chadwick. Title: Down to Earth (4)
Speaker: Ernest H. Gilmour. Title: Soviet Union (5)
Speaker: D.E. Hintzman. Title: Land Use Planning and Mineral Potential (6)
Speaker: John B. Hite. Title: The Homestake Mine (7)
Speaker: M.A. Kaufman. Title: The United States Energy Crisis (8)
Speaker: Wallace McGregor. Titles: The Impending Mineral Crisis; Twenty Years of Change in Alaskan Exploration (9)
Speaker: Eldon Pattee. Title: Wilderness Studies of the Bureau of Mines in the Western States (10)
Speaker: David A. Robbins. Title : Minerals and Mountains (11)

Speaker: Eberhard A. Schmidt. Title: What Does it Take to Find a Mine? (12)
Speaker: Jackie E. Stephens. Title: Costs and Adventures of the Modern Day Prospector (13)
Speaker: Albert E. Weissenborn. Title: Geology of Northeastern Washington and the Spokane Area (14)
Speaker: W.J. Whinnen. Title: Diamonds, Ecology and Conservation (15)
Speaker: Keith Whiting. Title: The Ungava Venture (16)

O

★ 144 ★
OHIO BELL TELEPHONE COMPANY
100 Erieview Plaza, Room 1152
Cleveland, Ohio 44120 (216) 822-2125

Presents talks on subjects ranging from the history of the telephone to the development of the laser. Talks are available to groups and organizations, high school level and above. No fees.

Entertaining Talks

Titles: Buckeye Q; Your Voice Is You

Informative Talks

Titles: The Art of Communicating With Lasers and Lightwaves; Caveman to Spaceman; Cleveland; For Humans Only; Hello, Ohio!; The Longest Bridge; Services for the Handicapped; Slippery Wire and Other Telephone Stuff; Solving the Maze; Terror by Telephone; The World Direct to You; The World's Biggest Computer

Issue - Oriented Talks

Titles: The Bell System: A Viewpoint; In Pursuit of a Dream; One Bell System - It Works; Opening the Doors; Profitability; Use Your Phone for all It's Worth

P

★ 145 ★
PABST BREWING COMPANY
917 West Juneau Avenue
Milwaukee, Wisconsin 53201 (414) 271-0230

Lecturers are provided to speak on the history, marketing, and advertising of malt beverages. No fees.

Speakers: N.P. Allerup (1); R.J. Ratcheson (2); A.J. Winograd (3)
Title: Story of Pabst History, Marketing and Advertising

★ 146 ★
PACIFIC UNION COLLEGE
Angwin, California 94508 (707) 965-6304

Makes available speakers to lecture on a wide range of topics. Travel expenses are expected to be paid.

★ 147 ★
PACKAGE DESIGNERS COUNCIL
Post Office Box 3753
Grand Central Station
New York, New York 10017 (212) 682-1980

The Council maintains a Speaker's Bureau, filling requests from business groups and associations for speakers to lecture on the packaging industry. An honorarium is expected to be paid.

Speakers: May Bender (1); Jack Blyth (2); Morison Cousins (3); Si Friedman (4); Frank Gianninoto (5); Wilfred Goldshmidt (6); Ed Kozlowski (7); Richard Overlock (8); Jack Schecterson (9); Joseph Selame (10); Irv Werbin (11)
Title: Packaging Design and Corporate Graphics

★ 148 ★
GEORGE PEABODY COLLEGE FOR TEACHERS
21st Avenue, South at Edgehill
Nashville, Tennessee 37203 (615) 327-8024

Lecturers are provided to speak on all aspects of education. In most cases there are no fees.

★ 149 ★
PEARL HARBOR SURVIVORS ASSOCIATION, INC.
8920 S.E. Clay Street
Portland, Oregon 97216 (503) 253-1691

Offers speakers who lecture on the need "to keep America alert by remembering Pearl Harbor". Expenses are expected to be paid.

★ 150 ★

PENNSYLVANIA ELECTRIC COMPANY
1001 Broad Street
Johnstown, Pennsylvania 15907 (814) 536-6611

Speakers will discuss the many facets of the engineering processes required to provide customers with reliable and adequate supplies of electric energy.

Speaker: James E. Davidson. Title: Power Cable Specifications (1)
Speaker: John F. Furst. Titles: Electric Thermal Storage; Energy in the Future (2)
Speaker: David H. Fyock. Titles: Energy Alternatives for the Future; Environmental Systems (3)
Speaker: Cynthia D. Good. Titles: Environmental Standards for Generating Station Operations; Sewage Treatment; Water Quality Control (4)
Speaker: John B. Middleton. Title: Forestry as Adapted to a Power Company (5)
Speaker: Richard E. Orris. Title: OSHA Requirements and Safety Measures in the Electric Industry (6)
Speaker: W. Richard Rossman. Title: Tree Trimming and Right-of-Way Management (7)
Speaker: Alfred A. Slowik. Title: Air Quality Monitoring: Air Pollution Control (8)
Speaker: Robert R. Spaulding. Titles: Load Management Opportunities; Research and Development in Co-generation (9)
Speaker: Jerome S. Stephens, Jr. Title: Utility Rate Cases (10)
Speaker: James H. Tice. Titles: Coal Cleaning Systems; Electric Generation at a Fossil-Fuel Steam Electric Plant; Environmental Protection Systems (11)
Speaker: Charles L. Tremel. Title: Planning the Distribution System (12)
Speaker: Robert C. Yeager. Title: Protective Relaying (13)

★ 151 ★

THE PENNSYLVANIA STATE UNIVERSITY
Department of Public Information and Relations
312 Old Main
University Park, Pennsylvania 16802 (814) 865-2501

Speakers are available to lecture on a wide range of topics to civic, church, scholastic, service and professional organizations throughout Pennsylvania. No fees.

Administration

Speaker: William W. Asbury. Titles: Affirmative Action at The Pennsylvania State University; Business Practices and Employee Benefits; Federal Laws, Regulations, and Executive Orders; How to Recognize Affirmative Action Complaints; Understanding Affirmative Action for the Disabled (1)
Speaker: George W. Bierly. Titles: Associate Degree - A Historical Perspective; Engineering Education: U.S. and U.S.S.R.; The Wilkes-Barre Campus, Service from Mining to Biomedical Technology (2)
Speaker: John W. Black. Title: Alumni Affairs (3)
Speaker: William J. David. Title: The Hazleton Campus of Penn State (4)
Speaker: James R. Dungan. Titles: Building Plastic Model Aircraft; University Planning (5)
Speaker: Kenneth E. Hershberger. Titles: Penn State's Many Faces; University Park: Its Lure to Young and Old (6)
Speaker: Otis B. Morse, IV. Titles: Life in an Education Factory; The University in Your Backyard (7)
Speaker: Kenneth P. Mortimer. Titles: Academic Administration; Academic Governance; Collective Bargaining; Faculty Affairs (8)
Speaker: Robert A. Patterson. Titles: Audits; Banking; Budget Development; Fiscal Planning; Hospital Operations; Investment Control; Labor Negotiations; University Operations (9)
Speaker: Harry Prystowsky. Title: The Milton S. Hershey Medical Center (10)
Speaker: D.M. Seward. Titles: Discovering Single Blessedness; Four Decades of College Students; How to Travel; The New Woman in a New World; Women in the Peoples' Republic of China (11)
Speaker: Robert L. Shuman. Title: Partners in Progress (12)
Speaker: August H. Simonsen. Titles: Geology of Pittsburgh Area; Local Geologic Features; Penn State McKeesport Campus (13)
Speaker: Robert L. Smith. Titles: Altoona Campus - Facilities and Services; Altoona Campus - History and Growth; Basic Industrial Resources of Blair County (14)
Speaker: Judith P. Snyder. Titles: The Admissions Game; Making Plans for College (15)
Speaker: John D. Vairo. Title: The Delaware County Campus - Its Mission and History (16)

Aging

Speaker: Harry J. Berman. Titles: Aging: Realities and Myths; How to Lie With Statistics (17)
Speaker: Joe Fleishman. Titles: Aging; Physiological Psychology; Rehabilitation Psychology - Coping (18)

Agriculture

Speaker: James M. Beattie. Titles: How Shall We Feed Them?; A New Commitment to Agriculture (19)

Speaker: Mae D. Bleiler. Title: Berks County 4-H Youth Programs (20)

Speaker: Robert L. Cunningham. Titles: Land Use for Agriculture; Soil; Soil Conservation (21)

Speaker: James E. Haldeman. Titles: The Future of Agriculture in Berks County; Pennsylvania Agriculture (22)

Speaker: Thomas B. King. Titles: Extension's Role in Today's Agriculture; Land Use Issues and Concerns (23)

Speaker: Walter I. Thomas. Titles: Agricultural Research; Food and Food Production Research (24)

Speaker: Herbert A. Wetzel. Titles: Farming in the Dark; Home Lawn Care; The Home Vegetable Garden; Ornamentals Around the Home (25)

Arts and Architecture

Speaker: James W. Beach. Titles: Extant Wood Screens in Devonshire; Noise is Pollution; Word Painting in the Music of Byrd (26)

Speaker: Zeljko Kujundzic. Titles: Contemporary Trends in Art; The Indians of British Columbia; Integration of Science and Art; Latin American Renaissance; Survey of Art of the American Indians of Southwest (27)

Speaker: Fredric Leeds. Titles: Early French Gothic Art; French Gastronomy (28)

Speaker: Walton J. Lord. Titles: The Architecture of Colonial Philadelphia; Frank Lloyd Wright's Own Homes - The Two Taliesins; Isfahan is Half the World - Its Art and Architecture; Music (29)

Speaker: Robert W. Ott. Titles: The Aesthetic Education of the Child; Arts Education in Today's Society; The Arts in Schools Today; Back to the Basics with the Arts; The Museum as Educator (30)

Speaker: Emma S. Rocco. Titles: Architecture: An Edifice of Sound; Women in Art: Portrayed and Portrayers; Women in Music: Sung and Unsung (31)

Speaker: Alice M. Schwartz. Titles: The Arts in Elementary Schools; Educational Television in the Arts; Fibers and Textiles (32)

Aviation

Speaker: Barnes W. McCormick. Titles: Aviation; Design and Construction of Airplanes; Flying; Helicopters (33)

Speaker: Hubert C. Smith. Titles: Aerospace Engineering as a Profession; Aerospace Engineering at Penn State; Aviation in Our Society; Opportunities in Aviation (34)

Business/Management

Speaker: David L. Ambruster. Titles: Breaking the Time Trap Barriers; Invent Your Own Future; Manage Your Time Effectively (35)

Speaker: Harold W. Aurand. Title: Labor and Industry in Anthracite Mining (36)

Speaker: Robert J. Brown. Titles: Current Economic Situation; Methods of Financial Management for a Business (37)

Speaker: Alec Calamidas. Titles: The Art of Motivating People; Control Your Time at All Times; The Effects of Loneliness to Organizations; How Can Education Become Meaningful and a Lifetime Reward?; How Communities Can Improve the Quality of Education; How to Cope with Stress; How to Reduce the Chances of Obsolescence; Identify Frustrations to Enhance Productivity; Learn to Live a Fuller and More Rewarding Life; What Young Adults Should Know to Better Their Chances of Success (38)

Speaker: Samuel C. DeWald. Titles: The Effective Manager; Handling the Stress of Life; How to Manage by Objectives; Managing Your Time (39)

Speaker: Samuel S. Dubin. Titles: Continuing Professional Education: Its Importance; Keeping Up-to-Date; Motivation for the Older Professional; Motivational Approach to Updating; Professional Obsolescence (40)

Speaker: James T. Elder. Titles: The Nonverbal Side of Sales; The Power of One; A Visit with Rev. John Witherspoon; Your Body is Shouting at Me (41)

Speaker: Thomas G. Fox. Titles: Is a High Level of Unemployment Really Necessary?; National Economic Issues (42)

Speaker: Harold L. Gilmore. Titles: Management in Developing Nations; Organizational Behavior and Motivation; Quality Assurance; Social Responsibility and Management Ethics (43)

Speaker: B. Wayne Kelly. Titles: Federal and Pennsylvania Income Tax; Tax Inferred and Exempt Income (44)

Speaker: Eugene Kozik. Titles: Data Management Systems; Do Engineers Make Good Managers?; Systems Engineering (45)

Speaker: Blake D. Lewis, Jr. Titles: Effective Leadership; Management by Objectives; Motivation of Self and Others; Performance Appraisal; Transactional Analysis (46)

Speaker: Robert H. McCormick. Titles: Energy Savings by Preventive Maintenance; How the Pennsylvania Technical Assistance Program Can Help You; Transferring Technology (47)

Speaker: H. Lee Mathews. Titles: Changing Cultural Values Impact on Business; Corporate

Planning; Personal Time Management (48)
Speaker: Peter B. Meyer. Titles: The Community Economic Development - Dependence or Autonomy?; The Community in the Corporate State; Economic Crises; Is Growth Still Possible - and Desirable?; Small is Beautiful (49)
Speaker: Robert E. Monahan. Titles: Economics in One Easy Lesson; How to Read a Financial Statement; Income Taxes and How They Affect You (50)
Speaker: Nicholas Skimbo. Title: The Free Enterprise System (51)

Careers

Speaker: Robert E. Carnahan. Titles: Blue Collar Worker (52)
Speaker: Joseph E. Dandois. Title: Careers in Engineering Technology (53)
Speaker: Kenneth R. Graham. Titles: Career Planning/Job Search for College Students (54)
Speaker: Josephine F. Hatalla. Titles: The Collegiate Experience; Occupational Outlook; Penn State Curriculums (55)
Speaker: Doris J. Meyers. Titles: A Majority in the Minority (56)
Speaker: Dawn Stegenga Prince. Titles: Do You Hear Me?; Employment Interviewing (57)
Speaker: Louis E. Ridgley, Jr. Titles: The Black Experience; Career Education Components; Interpersonal Competence Skills (58)
Speaker: Sally S. Small. Titles: Berks Campus Has a New Library Building; Careers in Library Service (59)
Speaker: Richard G. Swails. Titles: Career Development and Placement Service; Employment Trends for the College Graduate (60)

Communications and Journalism

Speaker: Priscilla H. Allison. Titles: Body Language and Other Nonverbal Languages; Don't Eat Your Neighbor's Salad; Girls, Ladies, Women, or Persons? (61)
Speaker: Frank Anthony. Title: Perception (62)
Speaker: Woodrow Bierly. Title: For Your Information (63)
Speaker: William E. Campbell, Jr. Titles: News of Penn State; Penn State's Commonwealth Campus System (64)
Speaker: Marion M. Odell Carr. Titles: I.A. Richards' and Kenneth Burke's Theories of Metaphor; Synergetic Models of Communication; United Nations Association and You (65)
Speaker: Joe Douglas Carter. Titles: Copyright Law as It Applies to Instructional TV; History and Current Status of Instructional TV at Penn State; Instructional TV as a Teaching Tool; TV Production Techniques (66)
Speaker: Arthur Ciervo. Titles: How to Manage Your Time; Run for Your Life; What Penn State Does for You; What Public Relations Can Do for You; What's Wrong with the Press? (67)
Speaker: Anthony R. Curtis. Titles: Amateur C.B. Radio; Broadcasting and Broadcast Journalism; Magazine Journalism; Newspapers, Reporting, Editing, Ethics; Professional and Hobby Printing (68)
Speaker: Terry Denbow. Title: When the Muckrakers Took on College Football (69)
Speaker: Michael Felack. Titles: Communication and Word Power; The Power of Radio (70)
Speaker: William H. Folwell, III. Titles: Meeting Management; Nuts and Bolts of Photography; Tell and Show your Story (71)
Speaker: Lynn Martin Haskin. Titles: The American Woman; Career Opportunities in the Media; We Are What We Watch; Women in the Media (72)
Speaker: Heinz K. Henisch. Titles: Beginnings of Photography; Early Photography in Eastern Europe; How Scientists Communicate - If and When They Do!; Non-crystalline Solids; The Non-objective Image; Ohm's Law: Is It Enforceable?; Painterly Photography and Photographic Painting; The Role of Interdisciplinary Research in Universities; The Scientific Detection of Art Forgeries (73)
Speaker: Lantz A. Hoffman. Title: And Who Shall Censor the Censors? (74)
Speaker: Harry D. Lehew. Titles: Developing More Effective Campaigns; How to Buy Communications Vehicles; The Obligation of Industry and the Role of Internships in Advertising Education (75)
Speaker: Ross B. Lehman. Titles: How One Writes a Town-Gown Column; Today's Alumni - No Raccoon-Coat Set (76)
Speaker: Frank Mansuy. Title: The Media Behind the News (77)
Speaker: Cathy S. Mester. Titles: Communication in Small Groups; Ministerial Rhetoric (78)
Speaker: Sharman Stanic Mullen. Titles: Communications in a Multidisciplinary Setting; Concept to Bookshelf: Editor's Perspective; The Creative Potential in Technical Editing; Fiction of Technical Writing; Mechanics of Technical Reports/Proposals (79)
Speaker: Cable Neuhaus. Title: The Six O'Clock News (80)
Speaker: Harold J. O'Brien. Titles: Homo Sapiens Characteristics Causing Communications Problems; Industrial and Management Communications; Why Don't They Listen? (81)
Speaker: Dawn Stegenga Prince. Title: Do You Hear Me? (82)
Speaker: John D. Sias. Titles: The American Cancer Society; Do You Mean to Tell Me You

Are Still Smoking?; The Panama Crisis; Speaking about Speaking (83)

Speaker: Claire H. Sink. Titles: Effective Newspaper Publicity; Producing Attractive Newsletters; Public Relations for Your Organization (84)

Speaker: Shirley A. Snyder. Title: No! No! No! Censorship: Past, Present, Future (85)

Speaker: Anita H. Thies. Titles: City Room to Corporate Office; Journalism Ethics: Scoops to Scandals; Public Relations: Getting to the Media (86)

Speaker: Roger J. Waun. Titles: The Cautious Communicator: American Politicians; Nonverbal Communication: The Silent Messages; Television Advertising Techniques (87)

Education

Speaker: John W. Beatty. Titles: Parents' Role in Career Decision Making; Rape: Victims of Crises; Yoga - A Journey to Inner Peace; Yoga Psychology (88)

Speaker: John E. Brugel. Titles: Do Students Still Need Private Philanthropy?; Dollars for Scholars (89)

Speaker: Glenn G. Carter. Titles: Maximizing Your Career Options; The Pennsylvania State University - Is It for You?; Trends in College Going; Why College? (90)

Speaker: Carol Cartwright. Titles: Directions in Early Childhood Education; Working with Young Handicapped Children (91)

Speaker: Richard A. Clouser. Title: Communication and the Deaf (92)

Speaker: Joseph J. Costa. Titles: Is the Family Still Basic?; Officiating Sports; Parents and Reading; Something Must Be Wrong (93)

Speaker: Mary M. DuPuis. Titles: Censorship: What Should Children Read?; Have We Come a Long Way?; How Can Your Community Support Reading?; How to Get Your Child to Read a Book (94)

Speaker: Donald E. Evans. Title: Partners in Progress - Cooperative Education (95)

Speaker: Tom Frank. Titles: Hearing Disorders; Hearing Disorders of the Aged; Speech Perception; Who Needs a Hearing Aid? (96)

Speaker: Joseph E. Gilmour, Jr. Titles: The Development of Post-Secondary Education Programs; Furniture Refinishing Techniques (97)

Speaker: Gordon C. Godbey. Titles: Adult Education; Compulsory Adult Education by 1984?; Liberalizing Adult Vocational Education; Some Major Issues in Adult Education (98)

Speaker: Leslie P. Greenhill. Titles: The Improvement of Instruction at Penn State; Instructional Services (99)

Speaker: Michael A. Grella. Titles: Censorship in the Schools - A Threat to Freedom?; Learning Disabilities - Fact or Fancy?; Public Education - Promise or Ruin?; What Should the Schools Teach?; Why Johnny Still Can't Read (100)

Speaker: Stanley O. Ikenberry. Titles: Penn State and the Future; People, Quality, and Priorities; What Should the Public Expect from Our Colleges and Universities (101)

Speaker: Robert C. Klomp. Title: Today's Need for Continuing Education (102)

Speaker: Edward K. Kraybill. Titles: Distinguishing Features of American Higher Education; How to Choose a Vocation; New Life Through Higher Education; Problem-Solving Techniques; The University Comes to the Student (103)

Speaker: Wilbur K. Kraybill. Title: On Making a Good Academic Decision (104)

Speaker: Benjamin A. Lane. Titles: Affirmation in Contemporary Poetry; Cocurricular Education - Beyond the Classroom; College Life: The Student and the Void; Landlord or Educator: The Resident Hall Dilemma (105)

Speaker: Louis F. Milakofsky. Title: Should You Trust Your School Board? (106)

Speaker: Craig A. Millar. Titles: Foreign Student Education Implications for Pennsylvania; Student Leadership Development: A Participative Strategy (107)

Speaker: Raymond Murphy. Title: Penn State Students (108)

Speaker: Murry R. Nelson. Titles: History of Social Studies in Schools; Salish Indian Basketry - Techniques and Purposes (109)

Speaker: Robert T. Oliver. Titles: America and the World: Cross-Cultural Communication; Education: Whatever Happened to the Ivory Tower?; Foreign Affairs: What Happened to Our Investment in Korea?; Foreign Affairs: What the Diplomats Are Doing and Why (110)

Speaker: David O. Ongiri. Titles: The Black Family and Black Youth; Education Abroad; Modern Africa; Open Education; Transracial Adoption (111)

Speaker: Harold W. Perkins. Titles: The Capital "You"; Partners in Progress - Berks County and the Berks Campus of Penn State; Tuning Education to 2000 A.D. (112)

Speaker: Marian A. Quick. Titles: Educating Hearing Impaired; Hearing Impaired; How Penn State Serves Hearing Impaired (113)

Speaker: Marietta R. Raneri. Titles: Plight of the Woman Writer: Historical View; Writing Deficiencies: Need for Remediation (114)

Speaker: Byron M. Robinson. Title: Be Curious: Practice Learning! (115)

Speaker: John J. Romano. Titles: Academic Advising in Colleges and Universities; The Liberal Arts as Preparation for an Uncertain Future (116)

Speaker: Robert Schanker. Titles: The Need for Continuing Education; Penn State Services to the

Community (117)

Speaker: John M. Shemick. Titles: Industrial Arts in the Modern School; Korea: The Land of Industrial Revolution; Peace Corps: The Modern Adventure (118)

Speaker: M. John Smith. Title: Lifelong Learning (119)

Speaker: James South. Titles: Changing Higher Education; College Students; Where Do Students Learn? (120)

Speaker: Frank Swetz. Titles: Education and the Social Revolution in China; Modern Math: What Went Wrong?; Teaching Children Mathematics (121)

Speaker: W.J. Zimmerman. Titles: Adult Education in the United States; Analyzing Business Training Needs; History and Development of the Land Grant Colleges (122)

Energy

Speaker: Thomas F. Barone. Titles: Alternative Energy Sources; Energy Conservation; PENNTAP Can Help (123)

Speaker: Edwin Biederman, Jr. Titles: Oil and Gas Exploration (U.S.); Technology Transfer - PENNTAP (124)

Speaker: William E. Chasko. Titles: Engineering Careers; Latest Energy Developments; New Materials and Processes (125)

Speaker: Stanley F. Gilman. Title: Solar Energy Utilization for Heating and Cooling Buildings (126)

Speaker: John F. Houlihan. Titles: Energy - Where Will It Come From?; Hydrogen from the Sun (127)

Speaker: Richard G. Johnston. Titles: Caves and Caving in Pennsylvania; The Disposal of Nuclear Power Plant Waste (128)

Speaker: Edward H. Klevans. Titles: Controlled Fusion; Why Nuclear Energy? (129)

Speaker: Gregory J. McCarthy. Title: Problems and Solutions in Radioactive Waste Management (130)

Speaker: Arthur J. Marsicano. Titles: The Energy Crisis; The Engineering Team; U.S.A. - Science and Technology (131)

Speaker: Nunzio J. Palladino. Titles: Energy for the Future; Safety of Nuclear Power Plants; Selecting a Career in Engineering; Trends in Engineering Education (132)

Speaker: Forrest J. Remick. Titles: The Moral Question of Nuclear Power; Nuclear Energy Regulation (133)

Speaker: George Schenck. Titles: Economics of Scale and Choice of Technology; Energy Needs, Economic Choices, and Coal Beneficiation; Population, the Food Chain, and Chemical Fertilizers (134)

Speaker: Carl W. Sherman. Titles: Oil and Gas Conservation and Regulation - State and Federal; The Oil and Gas Industry - Drilling and Production; The Oil and Gas Industry - Supply and Demand; Underground Gas Storage (135)

Speaker: Robert Stefanko. Titles: Modern Coal Mining; Solving the U.S. Energy Dilemma; Thriving in Spite of Paraplegia (136)

Speaker: Warren F. Witzig. Title: Nuclear Power: Problems and Promise (137)

Engineering

Speaker: J.L. Duda. Titles: Engineering on the Last Frontier; Enchanced Oil Recovery in Pennsylvania (138)

Speaker: Paul Ebaugh. Titles: The Administration of Research on Campus; Engineering Research at Penn State; Remote Sensing of Earth Resources (139)

Speaker: Edward M. Elias. Titles: Engineering Technology; Higher Education; Management (140)

Speaker: John C. Johnson. Titles: The Noise in Your Community; Technology Transfer from Universities to Society (141)

Speaker: Mary J. Kummer. Title: Opportunities for Women in Engineering (142)

Speaker: Blaine R. Parkin. Title: Research at the Garfield Thomas Water Tunnel (143)

Speaker: Duane R. Prosser. Title: Engineering - The Challenge of the Future (144)

Speaker: Gerhard Reethof. Titles: How to Design Machines to be Reliable and Safe; Noise Control in Machinery (145)

Speaker: Denton A. Steffy. Title: Mechanical Engineering Technology (146)

Speaker: Jack Stein. Titles: Error Correcting Codes; Lasers; Microprocessors; Reliability (147)

Speaker: Luis Henry Summers. Titles: Intentional Communities; Operational Gaming; User Oriented Planning Methodologies (148)

Speaker: Merwin L. Weed. Titles: Engineering and Engineering Technology at Penn State; Faith vs. Science; The Metric System Now or Later (149)

Environment

Speaker: Terry A. Ferrar. Titles: Energy Facility Siting; Energy Parks; Environmental and Energy Policy (150)

Speaker: Herbert Grossman. Titles: Effect of Ionizing Radiation on Bryophytes; Genetic Engineering; Pollution: Are We Through Yet? (151)

Speaker: C.J. Hillson. Title: Seaweed Utilization (152)

Speaker: Abbas Labbauf. Titles: Health in the Occupational Environment; The Impact of Environmental Hazardous Agents on Women; The Protection of Workers; Public Awareness of Environmental Problems (153)

Speaker: John A. Lieb. Titles: Acid Mine Drainage; The Ohio River Valley Sanitary Water Commission (154)

Speaker: H. Panofsky. Titles: Air Pollution Meteorology; Clear Air Turbulence; Threats to the Ozone Layer (155)

Speaker: K.K.S. Pillay. Titles: Mercury Pollution; Nature's Pollution Almanac; Neutron Activation Analysis; Nuclear Methods in Criminal Investigations (156)

Speaker: Michael A. Santulli. Titles: Technology and Human Values; Transition in the Arts in America (157)

Speaker: William E. Sharpe. Title: Water Conservation (158)

Speaker: Wilmer C. Stowe. Titles: Coastal Wetlands; The Microscopic World; The Sea Our Salvation? (159)

Speaker: John J. Zavodni. Titles: Citizen Involvement in Pollution Control; How Many People Can We Feed?; The Need for Sex Ecucation (160)

Family and Counseling

Speaker: Edward S. Beck. Titles: Counseling for Attitudes and Values; Counseling the Non-traditional Student; Drug and Alcohol Abuse; Uses of Counseling Groups and Techniques; Volunteerism and Training (161)

Speaker: Jay Breckenridge. Title: Village Life in the Philippines (162)

Speaker: Robert E. Brown. Titles: Adolescence; Personality (163)

Speaker: Jane E. Cooper. Titles: Ethical Implications of Advances in Biology; Genetic Counseling; Genetic Engineering and the Future of Man (164)

Speaker: Larry R. Eckroat. Title: Prenatal Diagnosis of Genetic Counseling (165)

Speaker: Colien Hefferan. Titles: Income Tax and the Distributing of Income; Money and Retirement; Two Earner Families - How They Spend and Save (166)

Speaker: Joan D. Mandle. Titles: The Changing American Family; Women and Social Change; Women's Liberation Movement; Youth and Families: Conflict and Resolution (167)

Speaker: Ivan W. Moyer, Jr. Titles: Fact or Inference: For Those Who Jump to Conclusions (168)

Speaker: Henry O. Patterson. Titles: Compulsory Parenthood Education; The Death of the Lecture: Using the Personalized System of Instruction in Higher Education; The Psychology of Dreaming; The Psychology of Sleep (169)

Speaker: James L. Perine. Titles: The Death of the White Liberal; Storm and Stress: Adolescence Revisited (170)

Speaker: Mary Rieck. Title: The Expanded Nutrition Education Program in Pennsylvania (171)

Speaker: James E. Van Horn. Titles: Children, Discipline, and Parents; Have You Listened Lately?; Parents - First Teachers of Children (172)

Food

Speaker: Daniel Y.C. Fung. Titles: Automation in Microbiology; Communications with Internationals; Food Poisoning - Facts and Prevention; Internationals in State College and Penn State (173)

Speaker: Glenn Gerhard. Title: Nutrition and Health Foods (174)

Speaker: Glenn R. Kean. Titles: Consumers Talk; Do You Really Want Cheap Meat? (175)

Speaker: Leon R. Kneebone. Titles: The Commercial Mushroom Industry; Edible Fungi (176)

Speaker: Manfred Kroger. Titles: Environmental Pollution and Food; Food Additives; Food Regulations and Food Laws; Foods of the Future; How Safe Is Your Food?; Naturally Occurring Toxic Substances in Food; Raising Food Consciousness; Technology and the Food We Eat; Yogurt (177)

Speaker: Gerald D. Kuhn. Titles: Controlling Microbiological Food Hazards at Home; Food Additives; Preserving your Home-Produced Foods (178)

Speaker: Monty J. Montjar. Title: Food Additives (179)

Speaker: Fay B. Strickler. Titles: Improve Your Quality of Living; Preserving Food in Your Home (180)

Speaker: Walter I. Thomas. Titles: Food and Food-Related Research in Agriculture; Research in the Agricultural Experiment Station (181)

Speaker: John H. Ziegler. Titles: Future Trends in Meat; Lamb Carcass and Its Cuts; The Meat We Eat; Penn State Rockview Beef Project; Pork Carcass and Its Cuts (182)

Geography

Speaker: Ronald Abler. Titles: Communication, Transportation, and Settlement Pattern; The Postal Service and Its Problems; Telephone Industry and Telecommunication Policy (183)

Speaker: Wilbur Zelinsky. Titles: The Cultural Region and General Cultural Geography of the U.S.A.; Distribution Trends of America's Population (184)

Gifts and Endowments

Speaker: A. William Engel, Jr. Titles: From Lettuce Seed to Fifty Million Dollars; Giving Is Old but New to P.S.U.; Private Giving for the Public Good; Why Private Support for Penn State? (185)

Speaker: Herbert K. Kraybill. Titles: The Four Diamonds Fund; The Milton S. Hershey Medical Center (186)

Speaker: Charles Lupton. Titles: The Humorous Side of Athletics; Planning a Deferred Gift for the University; Private Giving to Penn State (187)

Speaker: George Moellenbrock, Jr. Titles: Annual Giving; Creative Direct Mail for Fund Raising (188)

Government

Speaker: Henry S. Albinski. Titles: Australian Politics and Foreign Policy; Canadian Politics and Foreign Policy; Problems of Political Development; Southeast Asia (189)

Speaker: Robert J. Bresler. Titles: Ideology of the Executive State; Politics After Watergate; Presidential Politics; Prospects for Arms Control (190)

Speaker: Newton O. Catell. Title: Penn State and the U.S. Congress (191)

Speaker: Stephen J. Cimbala. Titles: American Foreign Policy; International Relations; Military Affairs (192)

Speaker: Stuart D. Goldman. Titles: Contemporary International Relations; Contemporary Japan; The Sino-Soviet Conflict and the United States (193)

Speaker: Arthur E. Goldschmidt, Jr. Titles: The Current Situation in the Middle East; Middle East Studies at Penn State (194)

Speaker: Luis F. Gonzalez-Cruz. Title: The Cuban Revolution (195)

Speaker: Robert LaPorte, Jr. Titles: The Dynamics of International Development: Alleviating World Poverty; Organizing and Managing U.S. Foreign Policy; United States and Asia; United States and Latin America; United States Foreign Assistance Administration (196)

Speaker: James McAree. Titles: England is Closing; India and the United States; The United States and Canada Today (197)

Speaker: Eugene W. Miller, Jr. Title: Communism and Fascism (198)

Speaker: Joseph Puthenpurayil. Title: India, Its Religions, Political Systems and Culture (199)

Speaker: Marthamae C. Schlow. Titles: Freedom of or from Religion?; Strangers in Paradise - Foreign Students; You've Come a Long Way, Baby (200)

Speaker: Marshall E. Wilcher. Title: The Non-military Aspects of NATO (201)

Speaker: Georgine Yatron. Title: Relationship Between Puerto Rico and the United States (202)

Health and Recreation

Speaker: Peter J. Behrens. Titles: The Mind - The Last Frontier; Penn State - Something for Everyone; The Psychology of Stress (203)

Speaker: John M. Caporali. Titles: Coaching of Basketball; Enjoying Fitness and Conditioning; Jogging Fundamentals (204)

Speaker: Richard Caputo. Titles: Jogging; Personal Defense for Women; Physical Fitness (205)

Speaker: Frederick G. Ferguson. Title: Use of Animals for Biomedical Research (206)

Speaker: Willis M. Frankhouser, Jr. Titles: I.Q. and You; Mind over Body (207)

Speaker: Edward E. Hunt, Jr. Titles: Anthropology and Dentistry: Teeth and Civilization; Fertility and Longevity of Wild Chimpanzees; Obesity and Health (208)

Speaker: Richard C. Nelson. Titles: Analysis of Sports Skills; Biomechanics of Human Movement; Improving Your Athletic Skills; Sports Research at Penn State (209)

Speaker: Alfred R. Pray. Titles: Clocks and Watches; The Japanese Game of Go (210)

Speaker: Paul Todd. Titles: Cancer Research; Genetic Manipulation; Origin of Life (211)

Speaker: J. Robert Wirag. Titles: Alcohol, Drinking Behavior, and College Students (212)

History

Speaker: Charles D. Ameringer. Titles: The Panama Canal Treaty Talks; The United States and Latin America: How Do We View One Another?; Venezuela: The Democratic Revolution (213)

Speaker: Michael Barton. Titles: The American Character; The American Conscience; Contemporary Trends in Anthropology; The History of American Psychiatry; The Morals of Civil War Soldiers (214)

Speaker: A. Daniel Frankforter. Titles: American Religious Institutions; Ancient and Medieval European History; Ancient History; Medieval Feminism (215)

Speaker: George W. Franz. Titles: Colonial Pennsylvania; Martin Van Buren; Revolutionary Pennsylvania (216)

Speaker: Cyril E. Griffith. Titles: African History; Afro-American History; Pan-Africanism (217)

Speaker: Robert E. Hauser. Title: African Culture and Its Transplantation to the New World (218)

Speaker: J. Lorell Price. Titles: Is the Party Over?; Your American History I.Q. (219)

Speaker: Gerald Reyburn. Titles: Survival Within by Doing Without; Vikings - Iceland, Greenland, Newfoundland (220)

Speaker: Leonard R. Riforgiato. Titles: America as a Secularized Religious Faith; The Imperial Presidency; Youth in American History (221)

Speaker: George D. Wolf. Titles: American National Politics; The Capitol Campus; Great Americans - Lincoln, the Master Politician; Great Americans - Washington; Pennsylvania Politics (Governor William W. Scranton) (222)

Labor

Speaker: Mark L. Brown. Title: Labor Relations Today (223)

Speaker: Donald E. Kennedy. Titles: Labor History; Labor Studies (224)

Land Use

Speaker: Hays B. Gamble. Titles: Farmland; Is My Land Your Land?; Pollution is Great (Growth, Resources, Economics, Affluence, Technology) (225)

Speaker: Irving Hand. Title: State, Regional, and Community Planning (226)

Law

Speaker: Richard H. Fulmer. Title: The Politics of Punishment (227)

Speaker: John N. Grode. Titles: Architectural Barriers to the Handicapped and Aged; Education of Handicapped Individuals; Housing - A Problem for the Handicapped; Legal Rights of Mentally/Physically Handicapped Individuals; Transportation Barriers to the Handicapped and Aged (228)

Speaker: Stephen P. LaGoy. Titles: The Criminal Justice System; Discretion in Our System of Justice; Plea Bargaining: A Barter System of Justice (229)

Speaker: Bill Solley. Titles: Criminal Justice Education through Berks Campus; The Criminal Justice System (230)

Literature

Speaker: James D. Adams. Titles: American Literature between the Great Wars; Palatable Writing Experiences (231)

Speaker: John E. Freed. Titles: American Literature; Contemporary Literature (232)

Speaker: Ana M. Garcia. Titles: The Character of Don Juan in Western Literature; Cuba (233)

Speaker: Robert J. Graham. Titles: Children's Literature and Film; Contemporary Novelists You Should Know; Women in American Literature (234)

Speaker: Paul T. Hopper. Titles: Civil Disobedience; German (and Scandinavian) Educational System; Ideas in Science Fiction; Linguistics and Literature; On Being a Translator (235)

Speaker: Evelyn Hovanec. Titles: The Future Promises and Perils; Literature/Lore of Bituminous Mining; Myth and Literature: Selected Topics (236)

Speaker: Harrison T. Meserole. Titles: The Earliest American Fiction; The Mystery of Edgar Allan Poe; Orchids as Windowsill Plants; Shakespeare in America (237)

Speaker: R. Alan Price. Title: Edith Wharton: American Woman Novelist (238)

Speaker: David R. Simboli. Title: English as a Third Language (239)

Speaker: Michael K. Simmons. Title: American Literature (240)

Speaker: Jane M. Singh. Titles: Racism in Children's Literature; Sexism in Children's Literature (241)

Speaker: Mary Smith. Titles: It's a Man's World, Too; Your Slip is Showing (242)

Speaker: Lawrence R. Suhre. Titles: Bitter Bierce; Black Humor: Humor of the Bruised Sensitivities; A Diabolical Duo: Ambrose Bierce and Mark Twain; A Swinger of Birches; What's So Funny? (243)

Speaker: John C. Tamplin. Title: Poetry: Music of the Spheres (244)

Speaker: Daniel Walden. Titles: Saul Bellow, Novelist; Technology in Literature (245)

Speaker: Stanley Weintraub. Title: Biography and Truth (246)

Mathematics

Speaker: Nicholas S. Ford. Titles: Games and Puzzles in Elementary Topology; Graph Theory and the Bridges of Konigsberg; The Map Coloring Problems (247)

Speaker: Anton Glaser. Titles: Metrication: Too Important to Leave to the Expert; Metrics for Everyday Life; S.I. Metrics vs. Old Metrics; Sensible Ways to Teach Metrics (248)

Speaker: Henry I. Herring. Title: Sucker Bait - The Gambling Odds (249)

Speaker: Roland E. Larson. Title: Elementary School - Mathematics Can Be Fun (250)

Speaker: Vedula N. Murty. Titles: Quality of Statistical Data; United Nations Technical Assistance in Statistics (251)

Speaker: Anthony A. Salvia. Titles: Careers in Mathematics; Statistics/Probability - How to Lie with Statistics (252)

Minerals

Speaker: Gordon Bowjer. Title: Conservation of Raw Materials (253)

Speaker: John C. Frey. Titles: Interdisciplinary Research Management and Evaluation; Natural Resource Management (254)

Speaker: Robert Newnham. Title: Gemstones (255)

Nursing

Speaker: Janet A. Williamson. Titles: Decanal Roel; Graduate Education; Issues in Nursing Education (256)

Pennsylvania

Speaker: Irwin Richman. Titles: Early American Medicine; Lady Radicals in American History; Pennsylvania Architecture; Pennsylvania 1776 (257)

Religion

Speaker: Keith M. Hagenbuch. Titles: A Christian and Modern Science; Why I Am a Christian (258)

Speaker: William O. Williamson. Titles: The Mystique of Materials; Occultism in the Ancient World; Spiritualism - Fact or Fancy? (259)

Safety

Speaker: William C. Arble. Titles: Fire Prevention; Fire Safety (260)

Speaker: Lynn A. Carpenter. Title: Shocking Experience to Avoid (261)

Speaker: William L. Harkness. Titles: Nuclear Radiation and Infant Mortality; Statistics and Infant Mortality; Statistics, Society, and Public Policy (262)

Speaker: Charles E. Suloff. Titles: Pennsylvania Agriculture; Tractor Safety on the Farm; What Is a Cooperative? (263)

Science

Speaker: Ruth Botdorf. Titles: Around the World in Slides; Chemistry and Food; Michelangelo Inspires After 500 Years; Pearls of the Orient (264)

Speaker: Jack Chapin. Title: Chemical Technology: Opportunity for Women (265)

Speaker: Richard G. Cunningham. Titles: Accreditation of Engineering Education Degree Programs; Engineering Education: Future Trends; Research Organization; Role of Research in the University (266)

Speaker: Stanley D. Furrow. Title: Glass Blowing (267)

Speaker: Roland H. Good, Jr. Title: Physics as an Art Form (268)

Speaker: Robert Jennings Heinsohn. Titles: Science, Technology, and Society; Understanding Technology (269)

Speaker: Richard H. McKinstry. Title: Psychology of Laughter (270)

Speaker: Kiyoe Mizusawa. Titles: Japanese Art; Japanese Culture and Society; Psychology (271)

Speaker: Rustum Roy. Titles: Making Radioactive Wastes Safe; Science, Technology, and Society; Technology and Human Values (272)

Speaker: Edward S.J. Tomezsko. Title: Science and Human Value (273)

Speaker: David L. Wallach. Titles: Careers in Physics; Theories of the Origin of the Moon (274)

Sports

Speaker: Paul B. Agate. Titles: America's First Olympic Team and Athletes; Differences in Ancient and Modern Olympic Games; History of the Ancient Olympic Games; Olympic Games: Arena of World Problems (275)

Speaker: Dorothy V. Harris. Titles: Behavior in Sport; How Sport Involvement Socializes Individuals; Masculinity-Femininity and Sport Participation; Why People Play; Women and Sport (276)

Speaker: Richard L. Henry. Title: Basketball and Athletics (277)

Speaker: Herbert Lauffer. Titles: Physical Education Activities; Soccer; Tennis (278)

Speaker: Sayers J. Miller, Jr. Titles: The Care and Prevention of Athletic Injuries; A Career in Athletic Training; The National Athletic Injury/Illness Reporting System (279)

Speaker: Chauncey A. Morehouse. Titles: Evaluation of Sports Equipment; Standards for Sports Equipment and Facilities (280)

Speaker: John Morris. Title: Athletic Programs at Penn State (281)

Speaker: Ed Onorato. Titles: Football; Weight Control; Wrestling (282)

Speaker: John W. Powell. Titles: Athletic Injury; Drugs in Sports; Injury Prevention for the Athlete; Sports Injury Research: Data Interpretation (283)

Speaker: Clarence H. Stoner. Title: Baseball and/or Athletics (284)

Speaker: Roger Sweeting. Titles: Athletics at Behrend College; Competitive Athletics; Intercollegiate Athletics; Physical Fitness for Adults (285)

Speaker: G. Thomas Tait. Titles: Hypnosis in Athletics and Physical Education; Power Volleyball the Penn State Way (286)

Technical Assistance

Speaker: H. LeRoy Marlow. Title: Penn State's Management Development Services (287)

Speaker: Donna S. Queeney. Title: Transferring Technology PENNTAP Style (288)

Theatre

Speaker: Ellis Grove. Titles: The Form and Physical Comedy; The Line of Laughter; Sound Comedy: In the Beginning (289)

Transportation

Speaker: Y. Chan. Titles: Land Use Forecasting; Traffic Forecasting; Transportation and Land Use; Transportation in Hong Kong; Transportation Planning; Transportation Systems Analysis; Transportation Technology; The United States Domestic Airline Industry (290)
Speaker: Sabir H. Dahir. Titles: Bituminous Pavements for Highways and Airports; Middle East Problems and the U.S.A.; The Palestine Problem - Prospects for Peace; Pavement Skid Resistance for Safe Travel; Portland Cement Concrete as a Major Construction Material (291)
Speaker: Thomas D. Larson. Title: Transportation in Pennsylvania (292)
Speaker: Bert J. McCauley. Title: Getting the Most from Transportation Technology (293)
Speaker: Russell A. Reed. Title: The Rise and Fall of the Model-T Ford, 1909-1927 (294)
Speaker: H.E. Weber. Titles: Engines for Power or Vehicular Transportation; Turbine Type Engines; Wave Engines - A Different Concept in Engines (295)

Travel

Speaker: Winifred Dickinson. Titles: Leningrad and the Environs of Lake Baikal and Irkutsk; To Russia with Love (296)
Speaker: Stuart Erwin. Title: European Travel and Culture (297)
Speaker: Catherine M. Lynch. Titles: In Search of Jane Austen; Youth Hosteling in Europe (298)
Speaker: William L. Perry. Titles: Trinidad, Tropical Island; A Visit to the Philippines (299)
Speaker: Francis Pierucci. Title: European Travel Relative to Spanish and Italian Culture (300)
Speaker: Marjorie E. Ward. Title: Antarctic Adventure (301)
Speaker: Stam M. Zervanos. Titles: The Desert Pigs of Arizona; Wolf Research in Alaska (302)

Weather

Speaker: Alistair B. Fraser. Title: Mirages (303)

Wildlife and Forestry

Speaker: Peter W. Fletcher. Titles: Aerial Photos in Resource Management; Canoeing; Forest Recreation; Scenic Rivers; Water Conservation with Water-Saving Devices (304)
Speaker: Ronald R. Keiper. Title: The Wild Ponies of Assateague Island (305)
Speaker: James S. Lindzey. Titles: The Black Bear of Pennsylvania; Our Wildlife in a Changing World (306)
Speaker: Donald McKinstry. Titles: Reptile Collecting; Venom in Harmless Snakes (307)
Speaker: Edward Masteller. Titles: Insects; Natural Areas of Erie County; Streams of Erie County; Wild Flowers (308)
Speaker: Michael Ondik. Titles: Basic Principles of Wildlife Management and Conservation; Birds of Prey (Hawks and Owls); White Tail Deer (309)
Speaker: Edgar H. Palpant. Titles: Collection of Tree Seeds in the Rocky Mountains; Mass Production of Genetically Superior Trees (310)

★ 152 ★
PHILADELPHIA ELECTRIC SPEAKERS BUREAU
Consumer Affairs Division
2301 Market Street, S13-1
Philadelphia, Pennsylvania 19101 (215) 841-4116

Some two hundred Philadelphia Electric employees present programs on energy matters, consumer information, and company operations. No fees.

Titles: Consumer Tips; Electrical Safety - Safety House; Energy Alternatives; Energy - Going... Going...Gone; Franklin to Fusion; Kaleidoscope of Energy; Miracle of Electricity; More Power to You; Nature's Way - Nuclear Power; Today's Man and the Environment; Today's Woman and the Environment

★ 153 ★
PINKERTON'S INC.
100 Church Street
New York, New York 10007 (212) 285-4800

Lecturers speak on protection and investigation at various types of industries and institutions. No fees charged.

Subjects: Investigative Work; Security

★ 154 ★
PODIUM MANAGEMENT ASSOCIATES, INC.
75 East 55th Street
New York, New York 10022 (212) 752-4653

Represents speakers in areas from arts to the sciences, business, communications and the media. Lectures are arranged which are suited to the individual needs of sponsoring organizations.

Fees range from $500 to $3500 plus transportation expenses.

Speaker: Marian Anderson. Title: My Life and Music (1)
Speaker: Timothy Beard. Titles: American Indian and Black Genealogy; How to Find Your Family Roots; Popular Ancestors (2)
Speaker: Robert Brown. Title: Twentieth Century American Mercenary (3)
Speaker: Ed Bullins. Title: The Black Playwright in America (4)
Speaker: William Davis. Titles: Can Capitalism Survive?; It's No Sin to be Rich; The Monarchy (5)
Speaker: Borden Deal. Titles: The Creative Process and the Collective Unconscious; The New South, Today and Tomorrow (6)
Speaker: David Dick. Titles: The Carter Administration; The New South: Born Again (7)
Speaker: Douglas Edwards. Title: What's Right About America (8)
Speaker: Frank Gifford. Title: Football Seen by a Former Pro (9)
Speaker: Arthur Godfrey. Title: The Life and Times of Arthur Godfrey (10)
Speaker: Roger Grimsby. Title: Eyewitness to the Modern Time (11)
Speaker: Hans Holzer. Titles: ESP and You; The Occult Scene of the 70's; Possession and Exorcism; Scientific Evidence for Ghosts and Psychic Photography; The Truth about Witchcraft (12)
Speaker: Jim Jensen. Title: The Impact of Electronic Journalism (13)
Speaker: Michael Korda. Titles: Power In Our Society; Women and Power (14)
Speaker: Charles Kuralt. Title: The America Behind the Headlines (15)
Speaker: Maxine Marx. Title: Marxes Are the Craziest People (16)
Speaker: Frederick Ordway. Titles: Earth Resources; Exploration of the Solar System; Future and Applications of Science and Technology; History of Astronautics; Intelligence in the Universe; 2001: A Space Odyssey - Its Making and Meaning (17)
Speaker: Jan Peerce. Title: The World of Music (18)
Speaker: Nicholas Ray. Title: Film-making (19)
Speaker: Buddy Rich. Title: Music and My Life (20)
Speaker: Will Rogers, Jr. Titles: The Rights of the American Indian; The World of Will Rogers (21)
Speaker: Wolfgang Roth. Titles: Brecht and His Theatre; Designing for Theatre and Opera; Opera In the United States and Europe; Pre-Hitler German Kabarett and Its Influence (22)
Speaker: Anna Russell. Title: The Music World (23)
Speaker: Mary Stuart. Title: What It's Like to be Queen of the Daytime Dramas (24)
Speaker: Piri Thomas. Title: Growing Up in the Ghetto (25)
Speaker: Av Weston. Titles: Politics and the Media; Television Journalism (26)
Speaker: William Wilson. Titles: Human Rights Violations; International Law (27)

★ 155 ★

THE "PRIDE IN AMERICA" COMPANY
176 Warwick Drive
Pittsburgh, Pennsylvania 15241 (412) 831-9600

Offers the services of the proprietor of the firm as a public speaker on a pro- America, pro- individual liberty, pro- personal freedom and responsibility platform.

Speaker: George F. Cahill. Subjects: America; Freedom; Liberty (1)

★ 156 ★

PROGRAM CORPORATION OF AMERICA
234 North Central Avenue
Hartsdale, New York 10530 (914) 428-5840

Offers lecture services and speakers in a wide range of topical areas.

Speakers: Shana Alexander (1); Jack Anderson (2); F. Lee Bailey (3); Clive Barnes (4); Melvin Belli (5); Polly Bergen (6); Charles Berlitz (7); Bruno Bettelheim (8); Frank Blair (9); Mel Blanc (10); David Brinkley (11); Joyce Brothers (12); Patrick Buchanan (13); Earl Butz (14); Liz Carpenter (15); Alex Comfort (16); Jean Michel Cousteau (17); Judith Crist (18); Jeane Dixon (19); Hugh Downs (20); Douglas Edwards (21); John Eisenhower (22); Sam Ervin (23); Geraldine Fitzgerald (24); Arlene Francis (25); Pauline Frederick (26); David Frye (27); George Gallup (28); Uri Geller (29); Curt Gowdy (30); Paul Harvey (31); Barbara Howar (32); Bruce Jenner (33); Sam Levinson (34); Art Linkletter (35); Eugene McCarthy (36); Jim McKay (37); Ashley Montagu (38); Marabel Morgan (39); Bess Myerson (40); Joe Namath (41); Jesse Owens (42); Laurence J. Peter (43); Dan Rather (44); Ronald Reagan (45); Geraldo Rivera (46); Hughes Rudd (47); Mark Russell (48); Morley Safer (49); Mort Sahl (50); Jonas Salk (51); Jimmy "the Greek" Snyder (52); Ted Sorensen (53); Robert Taft, Jr. (54); Mike Wallace (55); William Westmoreland (56); Les Whitten (57); Earl Wilson (58); John Wooden (59)

★ 157 ★
PUBLIC CITIZEN VISITORS CENTER
1200 15th Street, N.W.
Washington, D.C. 20005 (202) 659-9053

Arranges lectures on a wide variety of topics for all groups. An honorarium is expected to be paid.

Speaker: Mike Horrocks. Subject: Consumer Affairs (1)

★ 158 ★
PUBLIC SERVICE ELECTRIC AND GAS COMPANY
80 Park Place
Newark, New Jersey 07101 (201) 430-5863

Offers programs on subjects related to the nation's energy problems. No fees.

Titles: Alternate Sources of Energy; Environmental Concerns; Fuel Shortages

★ 159 ★
UNIVERSITY OF PUGET SOUND
1500 North Warner
Tacoma, Washington 98416 (206) 756-3100

Provides speakers to lecture on a wide range of topics. No fees.

Speaker: Robert G. Albertson. Titles: Defining America - Biblical Themes; Eve 'n Adam; The Values that Use Us (1)
Speaker: Gordon Alcorn. Titles: Birds; Conservation; Wild Plants (2)
Speaker: Paul Anton. Titles: Alternative Futures; Corporate Social Responsibility; Future of Small Business Enterprise in the United States (3)
Speaker: William Baarsma. Titles: Campaigns and Candidates; Governmental Budgeting for the City of Tacoma; Political Decision-Making (4)
Speaker: F. Carlton Ball. Titles: Art in Nature; Design Inspiration - Nature and Pottery (5)
Speaker: Suzanne W. Barnett. Titles: Asian Studies in the Liberal Arts Setting; Chinese History (6)
Speaker: Barry Bauska. Titles: Poetry Readings; The Well Travelled Student (7)
Speaker: James E. Beaver. Titles: The Decline of the Law; Evidence and the Law (8)
Speaker: Jeffry A. Bernstein. Title: Federal Income Taxation (9)
Speaker: J. Raymond Berry. Title: Readers Theatre (10)
Speaker: Keith O. Berry. Titles: Crime and Science; Forensic Science: Utilization of Physical Evidence; The Scientist as an Expert Witness (11)
Speaker: Jeffrey Bland. Titles: Arsenic and the Tacoma Smelter; Ethics in a Technological Era; Nutrition for the Future (12)
Speaker: Mitchell Bloom. Titles: Forestry Techniques; Management Information Systems; Program Evaluation Methods (13)
Speaker: Dawn Bowman. Titles: Cardiovascular Fitness; Women in Sport (14)
Speaker: Doulgas M. Branson. Title: Corporations and Modern Society (15)
Speaker: David Brubaker. Titles: American History; Urban History and History of the American West (16)
Speaker: Shelby J. Clayson. Titles: Exercise; Physical Therapy (17)
Speaker: Bill Colby. Titles: Contemporary Art; Contemporary Printing; Design in the Arts and Crafts; Jurying an Art Exhibit; Oriental Art (18)
Speaker: Ralph E. Corkrum. Titles: Shakespeare's Histories; William Faulkner: Prose Poet; Works of Contemporary Fiction (19)
Speaker: Zdenko F. Danes. Titles: Communism; Czechoslovakia; Earth's Interior (20)
Speaker: Lawrence E. Ebert. Title: Similarities Between 20th Century Art and Music (21)
Speaker: Sheldon S. Frankel. Titles: Personal Injury Law; Taxation (22)
Speaker: LaVerne Goman. Titles: Book Reviews; Children Literature; Comic Books; Fairy Tales; Folk Literature; Libraries; School Libraries (23)
Speaker: Tim Hansen. Titles: Contemporary Literature; Indian Fishing Rights; The Liberation of the White Male Professional (24)
Speaker: Norman L. Heimgartner. Titles: Developmental Levels of Children; Developmental Levels of Deaf Children; Mainstreaming in Special Education (25)
Speaker: Mary Lou Henderson. Titles: Multidisciplinary Approach to Treatment and Evaluation; Normal Gross and Fine Motor Development; Perceptual Motor Development; Reflexive Development (26)
Speaker: Ilona Herlinger. Title: Dramatic Readings (27)
Speaker: William G. Hobson. Titles: Marxism and Human Alienation; Prisons: Rehabilitation or Punishment? (28)
Speaker: Richard E. Hodges. Titles: How Children Learn Language; Language and Reading; Language and Spelling; Trends in Elementary Education (29)
Speaker: Barbara Hoffman. Title: Art and Law (30)
Speaker: Margo Holm. Titles: Helping the Family Adapt to a Disability; Occupational Therapeutic Activities; Occupational Therapy in the Community; Occupational Therapy Yesterday, Today and Tomorrow (31)

Speaker: Milton Hoyt. Titles: The Federal Government and Indian Education; Security vs. Liberty; Teaching Moral Values in the Public Schools (32)
Speaker: Charles A. Ibsen. Titles: The Marital Relationship; Sociology of the Family (33)
Speaker: Ernest L. Karlstrom. Titles: Future Developments of Point Defiance Park - The People Speak; Marine Biology of South Puget Sound; Northwest Trek, a Closer Biological View (34)
Speaker: Stephen T. Kerr. Titles: Fifty Million Consumers; Two Different Worlds: United States and Soviet Education Compared (35)
Speaker: Jai-Kyup Kim. Titles: Contemporary Problems of American Foreign Policy; The Future Role of United States Government in Asia; Military Aid and Foreign Policy; National Security Problems Involving Japan and Korea (36)
Speaker: Grace L. Kirchner. Title: Psychotherapy with Families, Individuals and Groups (37)
Speaker: J. Stewart Lowther. Titles: Aerial Views of Washington Geology; Fossils; Geology of Lower Puget Sound; Plants of the Past; Pollen Grains and Geologic History (38)
Speaker: John McCulstion. Title: Contemporary American Ceramics (39)
Speaker: Jacquie Martin. Titles: Avant-Garde Theater; The Literature of Existentialism; Negritude: Black and White Aspects; The Rebel in Literature; Science on the Stage (40)
Speaker: Keith A. Maxwell. Titles: Environmental Law; Law and Society; Trans-Racial Adoption (41)
Speaker: Bruce F. Meyers. Title: Law Schools (42)
Speaker: Steve J. Moreland. Titles: Child Abuse and Neglect; Mental Retardation; Mental Retardation as a Social Disease (43)
Speaker: Jeffrey W. Morse. Title: Genetic Engineering: The Full Scope (44)
Speaker: George R. Nock. Titles: Capital Punishment; Criminal Law; Criminal Procedure (45)
Speaker: William Oltman. Titles: Community Property; Estate Planning; Trusts; Wills (46)
Speaker: Joe Peyton. Title: Physical Education and Athletics (47)
Speaker: John W. Phillips. Titles: Biblical Scenes of the Holy Land; Communication; Fathers are Parents Too; Keeping Your Marriage Alive and Growing; Sex as a Family Affair (48)
Speaker: Beverly Pierson. Titles: Bacteria in Hot Springs; Microbial Ecology; Photosynthetic Bacteria (49)
Speaker: Roy J. Polley. Titles: Auditing 2000 A.D.; Changing Trends in Accounting Education; Financial Accounting (50)
Speaker: Darrell Reeck. Titles: Disneyland: Entertainment or a New American Religion?; What's Happening in Southern Africa? (51)
Speaker: Hamlin Robinson. Titles: Economic Relationships; Problems of Development in the Less Developed Countries (52)
Speaker: John W. Robinson. Titles: Financing Public Education in Washington; How Effective are Our Public Schools?; Open Concept Schools - What are They?; Voluntary Armed Forces - Will it Work? (53)
Speaker: Ramon Roussin. Titles: Creative Drama: A Basic Skill for Living; Creative Writing: A Basic Skill for Living; Reading is Caring and Communicating, Too; What is Literacy? (54)
Speaker: Kenneth Rousslang. Titles: Cryogenics; Luminescence Phenomena; Protein Folding and Conformation Studies (55)
Speaker: Thomas V. Rowland. Titles: Aqueous Solution Chemistry; Nuclear Magnetic Resonance Techniques (56)
Speaker: M. Harvey Segall. Titles: Management Information Systems; Managerial Accounting (57)
Speaker: Joseph A. Sinclitico. Titles: Arbitration; Legal Education (58)
Speaker: James R. Slater. Title: Trees, Ferns, and Wildflowers of Washington (59)
Speaker: Carol L. Sloman. Titles: Communication and Better Relationships; Communication and Good Management; Communication and Human Relations; Conflict in Interpersonal Relationships; Non-Sexist Marriage; The Subtleties of Sex Discrimination (60)
Speaker: David Smith. Title: 19th Century English Prisons (61)
Speaker: Thomas F. Somerville. Titles: Directing, Designing and Lighting for Theatre; Effects of Television on Society; The Role and Place of Theatre in the Public Community (62)
Speaker: John A. Strait. Titles: Criminal Law and Justice; Criminal Related Areas (63)
Speaker: Michael Veseth. Titles: Economic Policy; Inflation; Revenue Sharing; Tax Policies, Property Tax, Tax Reform (64)
Speaker: Esther Wagner. Titles: Book Reviews; Contemporary Fiction and Non-Fiction; Great Letter-writers; Problems and Hopes in Contemporary Ireland; Quality of Life in the Irish Republic; Trends among Irish Youth and Irish Women (65)
Speaker: Robert Waldo. Titles: Applied General Systems Theory; Management by Objectives; The School of Business and Public Administration (66)
Speaker: Paul Wallrof. Titles: Athletics; Physical Fitness; Working With Young People (67)
Speaker: Steven M. Weber. Title: The Sleep and Dream Mechanisms of the Brain (68)
Speaker: Roberta A. Wilson. Titles: Conditioning for a Lifetime; The Role of Women in Athletics (69)
Speaker: Pamela Yorks. Titles: Costa Rica -

Tropical Plants; Native Wildflowers of the West Coast; The Pollination of Flowers (70)

Q

★ 160 ★
QUEEN'S UNIVERSITY
Kingston, Ontario, Canada (613) 547-2880

Offers speakers who are available to lecture on a variety of subjects to organizations, associations, and institutions. Travel expenses are expected to be paid by the sponsor.

Speaker: Vivian Abrahams. Subjects: Brain; Physiology (1)
Speaker: George Andrew. Subjects: Aging; Heart; Physical Fitness (2)
Speaker: Diego Bastianutti. Subjects: Immigration; Modern Languages (3)
Speaker: Ivan Beck. Subject: Drugs (4)
Speaker: Charles Bird. Subjects: Hormones; Physiology (5)
Speaker: Chris Chapler. Subject: Physiology (6)
Speaker: Miguel Chiong. Subject: Heart (7)
Speaker: Robert de Pencier. Subject: Technology (8)
Speaker: Peter Doris. Subjects: Physiology; Surgery (9)
Speaker: Donald Jennings. Subjects: Heart; Physiology (10)
Speaker: Jacob Kraicer. Subjects: Endocrinology; Physiology (11)
Speaker: Denis Lywood. Subject: Biomedical Engineering (12)
Speaker: Gerald Marks. Subject: Drugs (13)
Speaker: John Milligan. Subjects: Physiology; Research (14)
Speaker: Kanju Nakatsu. Subjects: Drugs; Education; Research (15)
Speaker: Roderick Robertson. Subject: Theatre (16)
Speaker: Robert Semple. Subject: Environment (17)
Speaker: Seon Shin. Subject: Physiology (18)
Speaker: Duncan Sinclair. Subjects: Education; Sociology; Universities (19)
Speaker: John Wiginton. Subjects: Computers; Finance (20)
Speaker: Terry Willett. Subjects: Military; Sociology (21)

★ 161 ★
QUEST ASSOCIATES
167 High Top Circle West
Hamden, Connecticut 06514 (203) 397-0678

Presents lectures on ghosts and witches. Fees are $650 plus expenses.

Speakers: Ed Warren (1); Lorraine Warren (2)
Title: Ghosts, Witches

R

★ 162 ★
RAINIER NATIONAL BANK
Post Office Box 3966
Seattle, Washington 98124 (206) 621-4287

Speakers are available to lecture on financial and business topics. No fees other than reimbursement of travel expenses.

Titles: Affirmative Action; Corporate Communications; Employee Relations; Women in Business

★ 163 ★
RAP AND ASSOCIATES
Route 1
Foreston, Minnesota 56330 (612) 983-6750

Speakers lecture on alternative energy systems, their design, application, and socio-economic consequences. Fees vary.

Speaker: Tom Abeles. Titles: Biomass Conversion; Integrated Energy Systems; Management and Analysis of Energy Systems (1)
Speaker: Robert Pauls. Titles: Decentralized Energy Production; Integrated Energy Dwellings; Self-sufficient Energy Systems for Rural and Urban Dwellings and Small Businesses (2)
Speaker: Al Rutan. Titles: Integrated Farmstead Energy Systems; Small Scale Methane Production (3)

★ 164 ★
REID INTERIORS
20575 Erie Road
Rocky River, Ohio 44116 (216) 333-6657

Provides lectures on interior design and related areas to clubs and organizations. Fees range from $50 to $100.

Speaker: J. Lawrence. Titles: Architecture; Art; Interior Designer (1)
Speaker: Charlotte Reid. Titles: Antiques; Decoupage; Exotic Plants; Fabrics - Carpeting and Wallcoverings; Interior Design; Repousse; Wood Refinishing (2)

★ 165 ★
R. J. REYNOLDS TOBACCO COMPANY
401 West Main Street
Winston-Salem, North Carolina
27102 (919) 748-2061

Some sixty speakers are made available to colleges, universities and other groups. Subjects cover a wide range of topics from energy conservation, to marketing, to sales, to agricultural research. There is no fee.

★ 166 ★
NED ROESLER
Elk Creek Road
Rural Delivery 2
Delhi, New York 13753 (607) 746-3924

Presents talks on long distance backpacking in North America. Fees range from $250 to $400 plus travel expenses.

Speaker: Ned Roesler. Titles: Long Distance Backpacking in Alaska; Long Distance Backpacking in Jasper National Park; Long Distance Backpacking on the Pacific Crest Trail (1)

★ 167 ★
THEODORE ROOSEVELT ASSOCIATION
Post Office Box 720
Oyster Bay, New York 11771 (516) 922-7777

Speakers are available to lecture on the ideals of Theodore Roosevelt and to spread knowledge of his character and career. No fee is charges.

Speaker: John A. Gable. Title: Theodore Roosevelt (1)
Speaker: Mrs. Harold Kraft. Title: Sagamore Hill (2)

S

★ 168 ★
SAINT CLOUD STATE UNIVERSITY
Saint Cloud, Minnesota (612) 255-3151

Faculty members offer lectures on significant issues to various organizations. Fees vary.

Speaker: Kenneth A. Ames. Titles: Philosophical Considerations in Education; Philosophy as a Base for Counseling (1)
Speaker: Arlynn L. Anderson. Title: Men's Gymnastics: From High School to the Olympics (2)
Speaker: Garry G. Anderson. Titles: The Geology of Minnesota; The Geology of Various Western United States National Parks; The Glacial Geology of Minnesota (3)
Speaker: Julie Andrzejewski. Titles: Feminism; Hunger in the United States; Sexism; The Sexually Disenfranchized; Social Change Skills (4)
Speaker: Gary E. Bartlett. Titles: Club Sports; The College Center (5)
Speaker: L.R. Bjorklund. Titles: Construction Technology Education; Industrial Technology Education; Man and Modern Industrial Technology; Manufacturing Technology Education (6)
Speaker: Charles J. Boltuck. Titles: Behavior Modification; Child Management; Solving Family Problems; Training Paraprofessionals in Psychology (7)
Speaker: Chester Buckley. Title: Techniques of Portrait Artistry (8)
Speaker: Mary B. Craik. Titles: Images of Women in Advertising; Sexism in Language; Socialization of Women (9)
Speaker: R. John De Santo. Titles: Censorship and the Press; High School Journalism; Internships; Mass Communications; Mass Communications Law; The Presidents and the Press; Radio/Television News; School/Community Public Relations (10)
Speaker: Alan J. Downes. Titles: Americans Are Not Born Stupid; Assertiveness and Manipulation; Practical Decision-Making; Some of My Best Friends are Racists; Where the Future Comes From; Who Controls You? (11)
Speaker: Tom Eveslage. Titles: Community Communication; Freedom of the Scholastic Press; Student Rights (12)

Speaker: Wayland L. Ezell. Titles: Evolution and the Bible; Plant Biology; The Role of Plant Taxonomist; Studies in Plant Evolution (13)
Speaker: George A. Farrah. Titles: Evaluation and Research; School Administration; School Curriculum (14)
Speaker: Dennis C. Fields. Titles: Curriculum Design; Educational or Instructional Television; Graphics and Graphic Methods; Instructional Development; Systems Analysis in Curriculum Development; Visual Literacy (15)
Speaker: Ruel Fischmann. Titles: Photography; The Right to Punishment; The Underground Film (16)
Speaker: Arthur F. Grachek. Titles: Leadership in Small Group Communication; Listening, then Speaking; The Persuasive Speaker; Problem-Solving and Decision-Making; Speaking with a Conversational Quality (17)
Speaker: Charles J. Graham. Titles: American Higher Education in the 1970's; Do Colleges Educate?; Saint Cloud State University Today and Tomorrow (18)
Speaker: James J. Grunerud. Titles: The Student and the Law; The Teacher and the Law (19)
Speaker: Nestor Guimaraes. Title: M.I.S. and Data Processing (20)
Speaker: Owen Hagen. Titles: Education and the Future; Europe on 84 Students a Day; Humanizing Education in the 70's and Beyond; Life-Long Learning; The Process of Curriculum Change (21)
Speaker: Delaine Halberg. Titles: Elective Studies: Planning Your Own Degree; The Old Lady in Tennis Shoes Syndrome; Why Life-Long Education? (22)
Speaker: Patrice Hoffman Halton. Titles: Assertiveness Training; Birth Control; Female Sexuality; Rape (23)
Speaker: Reid Hans. Title: Coaching Philosophy (24)
Speaker: David J. Hellwig. Titles: Blacks as Immigrants: The Myth of the Bootstrap; Latin America: A Racial Paradise? Minority Studies: Beyond Tokenism; Some Other Country's History (25)
Speaker: Priscilla J. Herbison. Titles: Appalachian People and Literature; Changing Family Life; Child Welfare; Current Political Issues; Paradox of a Forgotten Land; West Virginia (26)
Speaker: James M. Highsmith. Title: Antitrust Section of the Attorney General's Office (27)
Speaker: Patricia Hoffman. Titles: Counseling with College Students; Interest, Intelligence and Personality Tests (28)
Speaker: Theophanis Hortis. Titles: Air Pollution; Alcohol and Traffic Accidents; Drug Use, Abuse; Environmental Microbiology; Food Additives; Health Quackery; Hospital Disinfection; The Infectious Process; Water Pollution (29)
Speaker: David C. Johnson. Titles: Cross-Cultural Studies of Drinking Behavior; The New Ethnicity in America; The New Immigrants in Europe (30)
Speaker: James C. Johnson. Title: Transportation (31)
Speaker: Milford Johnson. Titles: Rotary; Scouting; Student Financial Aid (32)
Speaker: John M. Kelly. Titles: Adult Exercise; Exercise and Weight Control; Role of Exercise in Our Society; Training and Conditioning Young People (33)
Speaker: Robert D. Kendall. Titles: Drama as a Sermonic Alternative to Monologue Preaching; First Person Monologues; Lectures on Social/Political/Ethical/Theological Topics (34)
Speaker: Keith A. Kennedy. Title: The Metric System in Your Future (35)
Speaker: Douglas A. Kleiber. Titles: Adjustment to Leisure; Psychology of Sport (36)
Speaker: Keith M. Knutson. Titles: Green Scum on Lakes; Pollution Problems; Toxic Algae and Cattle Kills (37)
Speaker: Walter G. Larson. Titles: Careers and Career Choices; The Choice is Yours; Do You Have What It Takes to Be a Teacher?; How to Put Your Best Foot Forward; Student Profile (38)
Speaker: Jonathan Lawson. Titles: Persuasive Writing; Rural Poetry; Written Communication (39)
Speaker: A.A. Lease. Titles: Commencement Speeches; Industrial Education; Technology (40)
Speaker: Guy Levilain. Titles: African Literature in French; Economics of Racism and Poverty; French Caribbean Literature; NATO and Southern Africa; The Negritude Movement from 1930 to Today; The Third World; Vietnamese Poetry; The Vietnamese Revolution (41)
Speaker: Harold Lieberman. Titles: Citizenship in a Democratic Society; The Knowledge Most Worth Having; Population Change and the American Future; Social Impact of Technology (42)
Speaker: Harold A. Lofgreen. Titles: Economics and Environmental Quality Control; Economics of Regional Planning; Perspectives on the Current State of the Economy (43)
Speaker: Russell D. Madsen. Titles: Records Management; Tax Return (44)
Speaker: James G. Marmas. Titles: The College of Business; Economic Education; The Function of Consumers in our Economy; Personal Finance; Social Responsibility of Business (45)
Speaker: Meredith A. Medler. Titles: The Reformation of the Sixteenth Century; Women in History; The Women's Movement (46)
Speaker: Gerald C. Mertens. Titles: Behavior Modification; Child Management; E.S.P.;

Ethics of Behavior Control; The Future; Magic Shows; Religion and Psychology; Self Control (47)

Speaker: Joan D. Miller. Title: Adopting Foreign Children (48)

Speaker: Martin Miller. Titles: Organized Crime; The Professional Criminal; Reform of the Prison; Victimology; White Collar Crime (49)

Speaker: Terry Montgomery. Titles: The Direction of Higher Education; Impact of Mass Media on Values; Politics and Higher Education; Techniques of Public Relations; Television and Public Opinion Formation (50)

Speaker: J. Brent Norlem. Titles: The Role of the Student Press in Its School and Community; Will the Public Schools Be the Death of English? Your Organization Can Have an Effective Newspaper (51)

Speaker: William H. Nunn. Titles: Human Relations and Communications; Japan; Japanese Studies; A Japanese Village; A Latern Festival (52)

Speaker: Don H. Otto. Titles: Creating with a Movie Camera; The English Curriculum; English Teaching Methods; Everyday Problems in Writing; Good Books for Home Reading Programs; Writing Reports in Business and Government (53)

Speaker: Alfred A. Pabst. Title: The SCS Denmark Study Program (54)

Speaker: Thomas C. Park. Titles: Comparative Education; Current Issues in Education; Korean Culture; Oriental Languages (55)

Speaker: Max Partch. Titles: Adventures with Birds; A Natural History of Central Minnesota; Searching for Prairies, Forests and Bogs; Wild Flowers and their Habitats (56)

Speaker: James F. Paull. Titles: Federal Judicial Appointments; Innovative Method of Forecasting Community Needs (57)

Speaker: John Peck. Title: Why We Need Zero Population Growth (58)

Speaker: Jim Pehler. Titles: Building an Advertising Program for the Media; Radio; Television (59)

Speaker: John N. Phillips. Titles: Man as Atlas; On Being a Rational Animal Today (60)

Speaker: Mary H. Phillips. Titles: European Travel on a Budget; A Visit to English Infant Schools (61)

Speaker: Rose K. Reha. Titles: Barriers to Women in Management; Women as Bosses (62)

Speaker: Douglas F. Risberg. Titles: Developing Moral Reasoning for Children and Professionals; Intergroup Relations (63)

Speaker: Eugene Rosenthal. Titles: Behavior Modification in Business and Industry; Behavior Modification of the Retarded; Behavioral Teratology; Effect of Environmental Pollutants on Behavior; Exploring Warmth; Recreational Behavior Modification (64)

Speaker: Howard Ray Rowland. Titles: Effective Public Relations; Modern Denmark; Saint Cloud State University; Western Europe Today; What is Important? (65)

Speaker: Dale Schwerdtfeger. Titles: Japanese and/or Chinese Family; Locating Self in Society; The Meaning of Japan for Americans; Minority Group Relations; Modern Japanese Lifestyles; Sex and Society; Social and Technological Change in Japan; Social Change: The Individual and the Community (66)

Speaker: Allen Stensland. Titles: Consumerism; Consumerism and the Aged; Death and Grief; The High Cost of Money; Problems of the Aged (67)

Speaker: Alf A. Swenson. Title: Areas of Risk, Management and Insurance (68)

Speaker: Merle H. Sykora. Titles: Interior Design; Nature Fibers (69)

Speaker: Terry Wagenius. Titles: Antique Clocks; Clock Collecting and Repair (70)

Speaker: Robert Waxlax. Titles: Expectations for College Athletes in Running; Long-Distance Running; Psychology of Sport; Sport and Society; Track and Field (71)

Speaker: Homer E. Williamson. Titles: Minnesota Politics; Public Administration; Urban Politics (72)

Speaker: Jeffrey Wise. Titles: How to Enrich Your Marriage; Marital Communication; Preparing for Marriage; Self Awareness; Sexuality (73)

Speaker: Dorothy Wollin. Titles: Environmental Psychology; Group Processes; Relating to People (74)

★ 169 ★

SANTA BARBARA COUNCIL FOR THE RETARDED
136 East Figueroa Street
Santa Barbara, California 93101 (805) 963-8984

Provides speakers to lecture on the needs of the mentally retarded. Fees are $100 and expenses.

Speaker: Sanford Gerber. Title: Helping Developmentally Disabled Infants Learn (1)

Speaker: Ulrich W. Gulje, Sr. Title: Organization and Functions of ARC (Ass'ns for Retarded) (2)

Speaker: Sidney Ottman. Title: Educational System for Mentally Retarded (3)

★ 170 ★
SHOE SUPPLIERS OF AMERICA
601 Washington Street
Lynn, Massachusetts 01901 (617) 598-9853

Speakers are prepared to discuss the shoe industry.

Titles: Shoe Manufacturing; Shoe Production

★ 171 ★
SIMON FRASER UNIVERSITY
Burnaby, British Columbia V5A 1S6, Canada (604) 291-4323

Arranges for lecturers to speak on various topics to clubs, schools, special interest groups, and other organizations in the Vancouver area. No fees.

Canada and the World

Speaker: Heribert Adam. Title: Southern Africa (1)
Speaker: Michael Eliot Hurst. Titles: The Growth of Technocratic Society; The New China; The Soviet Union; The Swedish Road to Capitalism; Yugoslavia (2)
Speaker: A.P. Kup. Titles: African History; Current Affairs in Africa (3)
Speaker: Karl Peter. Title: The Hutterites of the Western Plain (4)
Speaker: Stanley Roberts. Title: Is the CRTC Running Your Life? (5)
Speaker: Turgut Var. Title: The Cyprus Crisis (6)

Economics and Commerce

Speaker: Denes Devenyl. Titles: Creative Engineering; Creative Management; Maintenance Management; Management by Doubt (7)
Speaker: Herbert G. Grubel. Titles: The British Columbia Milk-Marketing Board Rip-Off; Unemployment Insurance and the Rate of Unemployment (8)
Speaker: Arthur Guthrie. Titles: The Impact of Computers on the Accounting Profession; Management in Inflationary Times; Manager-Computer Interaction; Metrification; Problems in Management Information System Implementation (9)
Speaker: George C. Hoyt. Titles: Human Problems in Northern Communities; Northern Development; Northern Industry (10)
Speaker: Kenji Okuda. Titles: Canadian Foreign Aid; Economic Development; Lesotho (11)
Speaker: Theodor D. Sterling. Title: The Computer Ombudsman Service of Vancouver (12)
Speaker: Turgut Var. Titles: Accounting in Economic Development; Accounting Uniformity; Tourism; Tourism in British Columbia's Economy (13)

Education

Speaker: Kenneth Conlbear. Title: Three Months with Grey Owl (14)
Speaker: Dennis Foth. Titles: Adult Education; The Part-time Student; Recurrent Education (15)
Speaker: Perry L. Franklin. Titles: How to Remember What You Read; Learning to Read; What is Speed Reading and Does it Work? (16)
Speaker: Roger Gehlbach. Titles: Early Childhood Education; Educational Innovations (17)
Speaker: Milton McClaren. Titles: Continuing and Adult Education; New Directions in Continuing Education (18)
Speaker: Sheila O'Connell. Titles: Age for Learning to Read; Preventing Reading Difficulties; Valuing Children's Books; Ways of Studying Children's Books (19)
Speaker: Leone Prock. Titles: Evaluation and Education; Learning Disabilities (20)
Speaker: John V. Trivett. Titles: How Children Learn; The Subordination of Teaching to Learning; Teacher Training at Simon Fraser; The Teaching of Mathematics; The Teaching of Reading (21)

Fitness, Sport and the Human Body

Speaker: E.D. Allen. Title: Athletics and Academics (22)
Speaker: Eric Banister. Titles: Can Exercise Help Your Heart?; How Science Produces Good Athletes (23)
Speaker: N.M.G. Bhakthan. Title: Hormones and Human Reproduction (24)
Speaker: W. Lorne Davies. Title: Sport - 1970s Style (25)
Speaker: Allan J. Davison. Titles: Appetite Regulatory Mechanisms in Obesity; Food Pharmacology (26)
Speaker: Martin Hendy. Title: Physical Recreation and Education for Leisure (27)
Speaker: William Ross. Titles: Growth and Development in Young Athletes; The Unisex Phantom (28)
Speaker: Margaret Savage. Titles: Sport Psychology; Women in Sports (29)
Speaker: Hal Werner. Titles: Fitness for Your Future; Track and Field Techniques (30)

Science

Speaker: Tom Bennett. Title: Space Research (31)
Speaker: John Cochran. Title: The Evolution of the Radio (32)
Speaker: Albert Curzon. Titles: The Electron Microscope; In Praise of Science (33)
Speaker: B.L. Funt. Titles: Science in the Economy; Short Stories about Long Molecules (34)

Speaker: Ronald Harrop. Titles: Contradictions in Mathematics; Logic and Truth Tables; What is Computability? (35)
Speaker: Dave Huntley. Title: What Science Can Do for Archaeology (36)
Speaker: Milton McClaren. Titles: The Environment; Environmental Education; Long-Range Planning for our Environment; Outdoor Recreation and Conservation (37)
Speaker: Jack D. Nance. Title: Becoming Human; Reconstructing the Human Past (38)
Speaker: Peter Oloffs. Titles: Fate and Behavior of Pesticides in the Environment; The Health Effects of Pesticides; Pesticides (39)
Speaker: Leigh Hunt Palmer. Titles: The Physics of Low Temperature; The Physics of Music; The Physics of the Laser (40)
Speaker: R.A. Rockerble. Title: Laboratory Medicine (41)
Speaker: Abby Schwarz. Titles: Fish Behavior; Marine Biology (42)
Speaker: Harold Wienberg. Titles: Biofeedback; The Biomedical Revolution; Electrical Potentials of the Brain and their Relation to Behavior (43)

Social Science

Speaker: Bruce Alexander. Title: Heroin Addiction and the Family (44)
Speaker: Anneliese Altmann. Title: Causes for Communication Gaps (45)
Speaker: Richard DeArmond. Titles: The Relationship of Languages and Mind; The Slavic Languages; The Study of Linguistics (46)
Speaker: Denes Devenyl. Titles: Creative Photography; Photography as Self-Expression; Photography in Education (47)
Speaker: Michael Eliot Hurst. Titles: Cars, Chaos and Capitalism; Homosexuality; The New Cities (48)
Speaker: John Hutchinson. Title: The History of Public Health and Social Welfare (49)
Speaker: Brian D. Kaneen. Title: Language and Human Rights (50)
Speaker: Bernard Lyman. Titles: Feelings and Imagery in the Selection of Food; Improving Self-awareness; Observing the World Around Us (51)
Speaker: Sheila O'Connell. Title: Canadian Realistic Fiction for Children (52)
Speaker: R.A. Rockerble. Title: Alcohol and Drugs of Abuse (53)
Speaker: Abby Schwarz. Titles: Feminism; Women; Women in Science (54)
Speaker: Jon Wheatley. Titles: Humanities Research; Philosophy and Ordinary Life (55)
Speaker: Anthony Wilden. Titles: Competition and Cooperation; Pornography and Propaganda (56)

University Affairs

Speaker: George C. Hoyt. Title: Simon Fraser's MBA Program (57)
Speaker: Stanley Roberts. Titles: The 1976 Student is a Flashback!; University Programs in Interior British Columbia (58)
Speaker: George Suart. Title: Past Problems and Future Aspirations (59)
Speaker: Jon Wheatley. Titles: The Future of Universities; The University (60)

★ 172 ★

SOCIALIST PARTY, USA
135 West Wells #325
Milwaukee, Wisconsin 53203 (414) 276-0773

Speakers are provided to lecture on electoral, environmental, labor and community affairs. No fees other than travel and housing expenses.

Speaker: Diane Drufenbrock. Titles: Community Organizing; Cooperative Living (1)
Speaker: David Gil. Titles: Alternative Social Institutions; Equality; Social Policy and Philosophy (2)
Speaker: William Hart. Titles: Indian Affairs; State Politics (3)
Speaker: Beatrice Hermann. Titles: American Indian Affairs; Socialist-Feminism (4)
Speaker: Rick Kissell. Titles: International Affairs; Party History; State Politics (5)
Speaker: David McReynolds. Titles: The Left - Old and New; Peace and Disarmament (6)
Speaker: Edward Marcus. Title: Aging and Agism in the United States (7)
Speaker: H.L. Mitchell. Titles: Socialism and the New Deal; Southern Tenant Farmers Union (8)
Speaker: Linda Randolf. Title: Cooperative Enterprises (9)
Speaker: Ann Rosenhaft. Title: Welfare Reform (10)
Speaker: Tom Spiro. Titles: International Affairs; Political Organizing (11)
Speaker: Frank P. Zeidler. Titles: City Planning; Labor Relations; Urban Affairs (12)
Speaker: Scott Zierten. Title: Labor and the Environment (13)

★ 173 ★

SOHIO SPEAKERS BUREAU
The Standard Oil Company Ohio
1760 Guildhall Building
Cleveland, Ohio 44115 (216) 575-5554

Speakers are available to lecture on topics of personal interest and on topics of energy and energy-related matters. No fees.

Speakers: Jack Akers (1); Sam Baker (2); Lawrence C. Ball (3); Daniel P. Barnard (4); Kenneth E. Blower (5); Betty A. Caldwell (6); Jon Curtis (7); Marvin Danziger (8); John M. Dempster (9); Diane G. Farrington (10); Stuart W. Feils (11); Robert E. Garman (12); Jeanette Grasselli (13); Raymond H. Klein (14); John J. Klement (15); Herbert D. Knudsen (16); John H. Lehman (17); Horace B. Loomis (18); Wallace N. Martel (19); Jack S. Ott (20); William J. Pruitt (21); Roger A. Reeves (22); Richard L. Riedel (23); Don C. Roberson (24); Herbert H. Rolland (25); Richard D. Schieman (26); Edwin H. Scott (27); Warner E. Scovill (28); Marcia K. Snavely (29); Robert W. Snyder (30); Norman W. Standish (31); M. Edward Stewart (32); Leonard W. Swett (33); Walter R. Tuuri (34); Frank Veatch (35); Lynn E. Wolfram (36); Dale L. Wunderle (37)

★ 174 ★

UNIVERSITY OF SOUTHWESTERN LOUISIANA
East University Avenue
Lafayette, Louisiana 70504 (318) 233-3850

Faculty members offer lectures on some two hundred fifty topics. There are no fees.

Speaker: Clayton J. Arceneaux. Titles: Communication among People; The Community Junior College versus the Vocational Technical School; Developmental Process in Humans; Guidance; Students; Teaching and Learning in a Free Society; Teaching Black Students; Teaching the Disadvantaged Pupil (1)

Speaker: J. Robert Barry. Title: Vegetable Gardening (2)

Speaker: William T. Bass. Title: USL Conference Center-Alumni Ownership (3)

Speaker: William C. Beckman. Titles: Fisheries; Food and Agricultural Organizations; United Nations (4)

Speaker: Glenn F. Bender. Title: Socrates and the Unwritten Philosophy (5)

Speaker: Doris B. Bentley. Titles: The Programs in Business Education; The Programs in Office Administration (6)

Speaker: Dolores C. Bess. Title: Nursing (7)

Speaker: Frances P. Billeaud. Titles: Communication Problems of Children and Adults; Normal Development of Speech and Language Skills (8)

Speaker: Charles W. Blair. Titles: How to Handle Anxiety and Tension; Meaningfulness in the Process of Life; Problems of University Students (9)

Speaker: Dwayne D. Blumberg. Title: The Purpose of a University (10)

Speaker: Delta T. Bonnette. Title: Computers and Our Lives (11)

Speaker: Richard M. Bonnette. Titles: Alcohol and the Driving Task; Alcohol and the Human Body; The Art of Driving Defensively (12)

Speaker: Sarah C. Brabant. Titles: Culture Conflict in the Classroom; Women's Issues (13)

Speaker: Carl A. Brasseaux. Titles: Acadian Education; General Lafayette's Visit to Louisiana; Steamboats on the Teche (14)

Speaker: Joan A. Cain. Titles: Foreign Languages; The Role of Women in Today's World (15)

Speaker: David A. Cameron. Titles: Physical Education; Why Your Elementary School Needs Physical Education (16)

Speaker: E. Everett Caradine. Titles: Collective Bargaining; Federal Labor Relations; Government and Business; Louisiana Workmen's Compensation; Public Finance; The State of the Economy; Union Growth and Development (17)

Speaker: Jane Ellen Carstens. Titles: Children's Literature; Early American Children's Books; History of Children's Literature (18)

Speaker: Glenn R. Conrad. Titles: The Acadians; Archival Holdings; Aspects of Louisiana Architecture; Colonial Louisiana; Editing Scholarly Works; The History of New Iberia; Individuals of Local Prominence; Louisiana Courthouses; The National Register for Historic Places; The Teche Country (19)

Speaker: Carroll Cordes. Title: Louisiana's Wildlife Resources (20)

Speaker: Don Cornwall. Titles: Government Fiscal Policy; Inflation (21)

Speaker: Richard C. Cusimano. Titles: Lost Worlds and Ancient Astronauts; Prehistoric Man and Evolution (22)

Speaker: Wayne D. Dominick. Titles: Computerized Data Management; Computerized Information System Environment (23)

Speaker: Mary H. Ducharme. Titles: Cardiopulmonary Resuscitation; Elementary Health Education; First Aid (24)

Speaker: Robert J. Ducharme. Title: Elementary Education (25)

Speaker: Edmond A. Dugas. Title: Physical Education (26)

Speaker: Byrdie E. Eason. Titles: Cardiac Rehabilitation; Child Growth and Development; Exercise for the Aging; Exercise Physiology; Physical Fitness (27)

Speaker: Dennis Ehrhart. Titles: National Land Use Legislation; Planning (28)

Speaker: Herbert V. Fackler. Titles: Contemporary Poetry; Creative Writing; Irish Literature (29)

Speaker: Emilio Garcia. Title: Seashells and Shell Collecting (30)

Speaker: Jeanette Gardiner. Titles: Child Development Associate Program; Early Childhood Education; Implications for the Future (31)
Speaker: Irby J. Gaudet, Jr. Titles: Childhood Behavior Management; General Psychology; Group Dyamics (32)
Speaker: Robert J. Gentry. Titles: Contemporary German; German Attitudes (33)
Speaker: Jon L. Gibson. Title: Indians and Archaeology (34)
Speaker: Donald A. Gill. Title: Louisiana Place Names (35)
Speaker: Edward B. Goellner. Titles: Audiovisual Instruction; East Africa (36)
Speaker: Philip R. Goyert, Jr. Titles: The Architects Role in the Built Environment; Historic Preservation; Washington, Louisiana (37)
Speaker: Joe L. Green. Titles: Earl Long and Louisiana Education; Huey Long and Louisiana Education; The Longs and Louisiana Education (38)
Speaker: Edward G. Grimsal, Jr. Title: Energy and the Future (39)
Speaker: Charles F. Hamsa. Titles: The Acadian Village; Amateur Wine and Beer Making; Inflation and Its Effects; Join a Civic Club (40)
Speaker: Frank L. Hanley. Titles: Chinese Export Porcelain; The Mexican Retablo and Related Folk Art; The Past Preserved for the Present; Piano Sonority and the Poetic Impulse of Debussy and Ravel; The 17th and 18th Century Italian Creche Figure (41)
Speaker: Particia A. Harris. Titles: Deviant Behavior; Social Issues; Womens Issues (42)
Speaker: Rex Hauser. Titles: Computers and Management; Cost and Decision Making; Information Systems; Management Attributes (43)
Speaker: J. Norman Heard. Titles: The Around-the-World Tropical Gardens; Mentally Retarded Citizens of Acadiana (44)
Speaker: Jefferson T. Hennessey. Title: Trampoline (45)
Speaker: Walter E. Hill. Title: Recombinant DNA Molecule Research (46)
Speaker: Brenda Castille Hobbs. Titles: Special Education; Speech and Hearing Therapy Services (47)
Speaker: Stewart Hoch. Titles: Acting; Contemporary Theatre; Directing; Improvisation; Theatre (48)
Speaker: Bruce B. Holmes, Jr. Titles: Continuous Progress Schools; Elementary Education; Elementary Math and Science; Professional Teacher Organizations; Southern Association Accreditation Teaching Profession (49)
Speaker: Stephen R. Hotard. Titles: Adjustment; Behavioral Management of Children (50)
Speaker: David C. Johnson. Titles: Geography-Past Connotations vs. Current Trends; Land Use within Cities; The Pattern of Cities - Understanding Their Locations; Population Measurement; Population Problem; Population Trends; Why Do Cities Exist? (51)
Speaker: Paul E. Joubert. Title: Crime and Punishment (52)
Speaker: Edmund D. Keiser, Jr. Titles: Amphibians and Reptiles of Louisiana; Poisonous Snakes of Louisiana; Research in the Atchafalaya Basin; Science and Religion; Science in Louisiana Secondary Schools (53)
Speaker: Heather C. Kelly. Titles: The Equal Rights Amendment; Textiles, Apparel and the Consumer; Women in Education and the Community (54)
Speaker: Robert T. Kirkpatrick. Titles: Altered States of Consciousness; Existentialism; Metaphysics; Mysticism; Zen Buddhism (55)
Speaker: George R. Kneller. Title: Person-to-Person Communication (56)
Speaker: Jeanne T. Kreamer. Titles: Children's Literature; Meducational Media; Student Evaluation of Instruction (57)
Speaker: John F. Kunkle. Titles: Bilingual Education; Foreign Languages; Foreign Language Skills (58)
Speaker: Donn M. Kurtz, II. Titles: Local Politics; Politics of Africa; Politics of Asia; Politics of the Middle East; State Politics (59)
Speaker: Marie Louise Lacaze. Title: The Certified Professional Secretary (60)
Speaker: Dickie Ladousa. Titles: Centrifugal Casting; Chasing and Repousse Techniques (61)
Speaker: B. Geraldine Lambert. Titles: Adjustment Problems; Career Development; General Psychology; Human Relationships (62)
Speaker: James J. Lapoint. Titles: Consumer Finance; Economics; Inflation/Recession; Personal Budgeting; Spending Money Wisely; State of the Economy (63)
Speaker: Sherry Lebas. Titles: Aerobic Dancing; Exercises for the Office; Figure Control for Women; Self-Defense for Women (64)
Speaker: Theodore G. Lewis. Title: The Household Computer (65)
Speaker: Marguerite R. Lyle. Titles: Give a Speech in One Easy Lesson; How We Communicate; Listening: Do We (66)
Speaker: Conrad McKnight. Title: Reading Mathematics (67)
Speaker: Margaret McMillan. Title: Water Safety (68)
Speaker: Wilmer MacNair. Titles: The Contraception Controversy; Population Control; Population Problems; The Relations of Protestantism and Catholicism; Sociology; Theology (69)
Speaker: David P. Manuel. Titles: Crime and Economic Conditions; Economic Growth; Energy Economics; Foreign Trade; Inflation; National Economic Policy; Poverty in Louisiana; Public

Finances; Unemployment; Urban Poverty in Louisiana (70)
Speaker: Glenn Menard. Titles: Student Programming; The Student Union (71)
Speaker: Jeremy Millet. Titles: American National Policy; American Political Ideas; American Revolution; Economic Freedom and Civil Liberty; Liberty; The Second American Revolution (72)
Speaker: Wayne E. Moeller. Title: Antiques (73)
Speaker: Joseph F. Moffat. Title: Louisiana Transportation Systems (74)
Speaker: Muriel K. Moreland. Title: Contemporary Dance (75)
Speaker: John R. Morella. Titles: Education for Socio-Economic Middleclass Children; The Exceptional Child; The High School Counselor; Managenent of Children; Psychological Tests; Psychology of Sex (76)
Speaker: Jean Mouton. Titles: Children's Books; Materials Center (77)
Speaker: Allan R. Ohaver. Titles: Reading; Speed Reading; Your Child Has a Reading Problem (78)
Speaker: James R. Oliver. Titles: The Application of Computers; Chess by Mail; Conversion to the Metric System; Education for All; The Future of Higher Education in Louisiana; Human Relations Problems Still Facing Us; Opening Up Systems of Government; Unusual Photographs; The Use of Computers in State Government; What is Ham Radio?; Why Boy Scouts (79)
Speaker: Harold Peterson. Title: General History (80)
Speaker: Charles W. Purcell. Titles: Air Force Flying Career; Air Force ROTC Program; Air Force School Systems; Air Force Teaching Methods; General Air Force; Undergraduate Pilot Training (81)
Speaker: William C. Rense. Titles: Bangkok; Camping, Backpacking and Hiking; East Africa; Greece; Hong Kong; India; Iran; Japan; Nepal; Turkey (82)
Speaker: Lawrence Rice. Titles: The American Revolution; Education for the Future; The Historian as Social Commentator (83)
Speaker: Patricia V. Rickels. Title: Education of the Gifted (84)
Speaker: Gladys H. Robinette. Titles: Clinical Supervision; Community School Relationships; Trends in the Elementary School (85)
Speaker: Walter R. Robinette. Titles: Professional Education; Student Teaching; Teacher Education (86)
Speaker: Fred E. Rugg. Title: Oil and You (87)
Speaker: Allen H. St. Martin. Titles: Problems Faced by First Time College Freshmen; Service Functions of USL; USL Academic Offerings; USL Service Programs; USL Scholarship Programs (88)
Speaker: John V. Vigorito. Titles: Buddhist Conception of Man; Marx's Critique of Capitalism; University Relations with the Community; What is Philosophy? (89)
Speaker: Walter C. Vodraska. Titles: Energy Conservation in Traffic Operations and Highway Design; Energy Conservation in Transportation; Historic Civil Engineering Land Marks (90)
Speaker: Robert M. Webb. Titles: East Africa; Ghana; Liberal Arts in Vocational Education; Man's Environment; Southeast Asia; World Campus Afloat (91)
Speaker: Yvonne Webb. Titles: Love Charms of 29 Countries; Voodoo and Superstititious Influences (92)
Speaker: Barron Wells. Title: Better Business Communications (93)
Speaker: Jan Werner. Titles: Assertiveness Training; Stress and Personal Adjustment; Tension and Anxiety Reduction; Values Clarification; Women's Awareness (94)
Speaker: Ronald White. Title: Education of the Gifted (95)
Speaker: Alfred B. Williams. Titles: Business Communication; Business Education; Office Administration (96)
Speaker: Robert L. Young. Titles: Engineering; Engineering Technology; Technical Training (97)

SPEAKERS AND ENTERTAINMENT BUREAU
See: Charles Hutaff

★ 175 ★
SPEAKERS BUREAU OF AMERICA, INC.
1735 DeSales Street, N.W. #500
Washington, D.C. 20036 (202) 347-0872

Offers speakers who lecture on a variety of critical issues. Fees are negotiable.

Speaker: Allan C. Brownfeld. Titles: Communism; The Middle East; South Africa (1)
Speaker: Leslie Masimini. Title: Fighting for Freedom in South Africa (2)
Speaker: Thomas Sowell. Title: Race and Economics (3)
Speaker: Nick Thimmesch. Titles: Jimmy Carter; The Middle East (4)
Speaker: Walter Williams. Title: Economic Freedom (5)

★ 176 ★
THE SPEAKER'S BUREAU OF PHILADELPHIA
226 West Rittenhouse Square
Philadelphia, Pennsylvania 19103 (215) 732-8158

More than three hundred speakers are provided to lecture on many different topics. Fees vary.

Speaker: Lynn Abraham. Title: The Courts (1)
Speaker: Gerard Adams. Title: Economics (2)
Speaker: Alene Ammond. Title: Public Involvement in Government (3)
Speaker: Jack Anderson. Title: Media (4)
Speaker: Richie Ashburn. Title: Media (5)
Speaker: Birch Bayh. Title: The Constitution (6)
Speaker: Steve Bell. Title: World Affairs (7)
Speaker: Jules Bergman. Title: Science (8)
Speaker: Ginger Berk. Title: Enhancing Your Features (9)
Speaker: Freida Pastor Berkowitz. Title: Musical Nicknames (10)
Speaker: Clara Bernard. Title: Today's Problems (11)
Speaker: Carl Bernstein. Title: Watergate (12)
Speaker: Ralph Bernstein. Title: Associated Press (13)
Speaker: Diane Betzendahl. Title: Media (14)
Speaker: Charles Bierbauer. Title: Changing Nature of America (15)
Speaker: Tobyann Boonin. Title: Education (16)
Speaker: Bob Bradley. Title: Media (17)
Speaker: Glenn Brenner. Title: Sportscasting (18)
Speaker: David Brinkley. Titles: National Affairs; World Affairs (19)
Speaker: Ida Brodsky. Title: Raising Children (20)
Speaker: Tom Brokaw. Title: The Political Scene (21)
Speaker: Joyce Brothers. Title: Psychology (22)
Speaker: Reginald Bryant. Title: Minorities (23)
Speaker: Liz Carpenter. Title: The Washington Scene (24)
Speaker: Sara Kay Cohen. Title: Marriage and Family Therapy (25)
Speaker: Charles C. Cole. Titles: Future of the Independent College; The Potential of Women (26)
Speaker: Dolores Cooper. Title: Travel (27)
Speaker: Mort Crim. Titles: Media; Motivation; Religion (28)
Speaker: Dennis Cunningham. Titles: Film; Theatre (29)
Speaker: Gunter David. Title: Media (30)
Speaker: La Deva Davis. Titles: Home Economics; Nutrition (31)
Speaker: Rose De Wolf. Title: Media (32)
Speaker: Paul Duke. Title: The Washington Scene (33)
Speaker: Joan Durham. Title: Psychic Phenomena (34)
Speaker: Douglas Edwards. Title: World Affairs (35)
Speaker: Sam Ervin. Title: The Constitution (36)
Speaker: Don Fair. Title: Crime (37)
Speaker: Frances Farenthold. Title: Politics (38)
Speaker: Larry Fields. Title: The Media (39)
Speaker: Arnold Finkel. Title: The Art World (40)
Speaker: Frank Ford. Title: Media (41)
Speaker: Steve Gary. Title: Sports (42)
Speaker: Cheryl Ginn. Title: The Human Intrigue and Electronic Journalism Phenomenon (43)
Speaker: Virginia Graham. Title: Consumer Affairs (44)
Speaker: Peter Hackes. Titles: Atomic Energy; Environmental Problems; Federal Aviation Commission (45)
Speaker: Trudy Haynes. Titles: Culture; Entertainment; Theatre (46)
Speaker: Jack Helsel. Title: Media (47)
Speaker: Don Henderson. Title: Sportscasting (48)
Speaker: Murray Horwitz. Title: Acting (49)
Speaker: Barbara Howar. Title: The Washington Scene (50)
Speaker: Lynn Hubschman. Title: Family Living (51)
Speaker: James Humes. Title: The Washington Scene (52)
Speaker: Henry Jackson. Title: Democratic Party (53)
Speaker: Eugene Jaffe. Title: Economics (54)
Speaker: Jack Jones. Title: Media (55)
Speaker: Tom Katen. Title: The Assassination of John F. Kennedy (56)
Speaker: Jerry Kramer. Title: Motivation (57)
Speaker: Bill Kuster. Title: Weather (58)
Speaker: Jay Lamont. Title: Real Estate (59)
Speaker: Deborah Lawson. Title: Pets (60)
Speaker: Len Lear. Titles: Consumer Fraud; Crime (61)
Speaker: Sam Lehrer. Title: Criminal Justice in America (62)
Speaker: Ted Leitner. Title: Sportscasting (63)
Speaker: Maury Levy. Title: Journalism (64)
Speaker: Steve Levy. Title: Sportscasting (65)
Speaker: Claude Lewis. Titles: Minorities; News Media (66)
Speaker: Elizabeth Lodge. Title: Tracing Your Family History (67)
Speaker: Joseph Lord. Title: Legal Affairs (68)
Speaker: Arline Lotman. Title: The Future is Here (69)
Speaker: Lynn Lowenthal. Titles: Health; Nutrition (70)
Speaker: Catherine Mackin. Title: Politics (71)
Speaker: Mike Mallow. Title: The Media (72)
Speaker: Marciarose. Title: People in the News (73)

Speaker: Leo Marshall. Title: Aviation (74)
Speaker: Carmen Martucci. Title: Fitness for Busy Executives (75)
Speaker: Jean Mayer. Title: Food and Health (76)
Speaker: Al Meltzer. Title: Sports (77)
Speaker: Bernard Meltzer. Titles: Media; Real Estate (78)
Speaker: Andrea Mitchell. Titles: Government; Politics (79)
Speaker: Ashley Montagu. Title: Anthropology (80)
Speaker: Edmund Muskie. Titles: Awareness; Environment; Government; Meditation; Relaxation; Sensitivity; Weight Control (81)
Speaker: Alma Nelson. Titles: Nutrition; Yoga (82)
Speaker: George Packard. Title: Media (83)
Speaker: Michael Pakenham. Titles: Public Affairs; Wine (84)
Speaker: Norman Vincent Peale. Title: Religion (85)
Speaker: Ralph Penza. Title: Media (86)
Speaker: Bonnie Perry. Title: Consumer Attitudes (87)
Speaker: Malcolm Poindexter. Title: Media (88)
Speaker: Nido Qubein. Title: Motivation (89)
Speaker: Matt Quinn. Title: Media (90)
Speaker: Dan Rather. Title: Media (91)
Speaker: Orien Reid. Titles: Consumer Protection; Marketing (92)
Speaker: Lisa A. Richette. Title: Child Abuse (93)
Speaker: Robin Roberts. Title: Baseball Hall of Fame (94)
Speaker: Frank Rocco. Title: Hypnosis (95)
Speaker: Carol Saline. Title: Media (96)
Speaker: Penny Sarama. Title: Psychic Phenomena (97)
Speaker: Jessica Savitch. Titles: Media; Changing Lifestyles; In Pursuit of Excellence; Your Image (98)
Speaker: John Scheuer. Title: Money Management (99)
Speaker: Arthur Schlesinger. Title: Media (100)
Speaker: Maxine Schnall. Title: Media (101)
Speaker: Ken Schreffler. Title: How Television and Film Stars are Made and Promoted (102)
Speaker: Loretta Schwartz. Titles: Hunger; Nursing Home Abuses; Unwanted Children (103)
Speaker: Marci Shatzman. Title: Consumer Dilemma (104)
Speaker: Arnold Shay. Title: Concentration Camps (105)
Speaker: Fulton J. Sheen. Title: Religion (106)
Speaker: Dick Sheeran. Title: Media (107)
Speaker: Estelle Colwin Snellenburg. Title: The Art of Assemblage (108)
Speaker: Leroy Snyder. Title: Life in China (109)
Speaker: Tillie Spetgang. Title: Media (110)
Speaker: Carl Stern. Title: Law (111)
Speaker: Samantha Stevenson. Title: Sports (112)
Speaker: Cody Sweet. Title: Body Language (113)
Speaker: Elaine Tait. Title: Fashion (114)
Speaker: Bill Toffel. Title: Television and Radio (115)
Speaker: Marilyn Van Derbur. Title: Motivation (116)
Speaker: Lou Wagner. Title: Fishing (117)
Speaker: Ruth Wall. Title: Awareness (118)
Speaker: Bill Webber. Title: Media (119)
Speaker: Valerie Willard. Title: Psychic Phenomena (120)
Speaker: Tom Woodeshick. Title: Sports (121)
Speaker: Bill Woodruff. Title: Motivation (122)
Speaker: Bob Woodward. Title: Watergate (123)
Speaker: John Wydra. Title: Media (124)
Speaker: Marian Zabrowsky. Title: Soap Operas (125)

★ 177 ★

SPEAKERS UNLIMITED
Post Office Box 27225
Columbus, Ohio 43227 (614) 864-3707

This agency presents lecturers who specialize in the areas of sales, motivation, and management. Fees vary.

Speakers: Bob Albin (1); Neil Armstrong (2); F. Lee Bailey (3); Dan Baker (4); Murray Banks (5); Joe Batten (6); Cathrina Bauby (7); Jay Beecroft (8); Dan Bellus (9); Howard Bonnell (10); Ty Boyd (11); Sandy Breighner (12); Joyce Brothers (13); Ron Brown (14); Nick Carter (15); Alan Cimberg (16); Jeff Coats (17); Bob Conklin (18); Lloyd Cullen (19); Merlyn Cundiff (20); Rita Davenport (21); Hallie Dewey (22); James Dornoff (23); Mack Douglas (24); Tom Duro (25); Cecil Edge (26); Douglas Edwards (27); Mig Figi (28); Ray Foster (29); D. Michael Frank (30); John Furbay (31); Joe Gandolfo (32); Grant Gard (33); Dick Gardner (34); Dick Gariepy (35); Willie Gayle (36); Joe Girard (37); Bill Glass (38); Kip Glasscock (39); Bill Gove (40); John Grogan (41); Eldon Gunter (42); Tennyson Guyer (43); Tom Haggai (44); Mark Victor Hansen (45); Paul Harvey (46); Roy Hatten (47); Ira M. Hayes (48); Christopher J. (49); Porter Henry (50); Fred Herman (51); George Herpel (52); Peg Higginbotham (53); G. Worthington Hipple (54); Art Holst (55); Tom Hopkins (56); Don Hutson (57); Charles Jarvis (58); Mildred Johnson (59); Charles Jones (60); Barbara Jordan (61); Zenn Kaufman (62); Joe Klock (63); Jerry Kramer (64); Hal Krause (65); Joe Lahart (66);

Ann Landers (67); Noah Langdale (68); Charles Lapp (69); Ken Lewis (70); Mona Ling (71); Art Linkletter (72); Don Lonie (73); Jerry Lucas (74); John Lumbleau (75); Kenneth McFarland (76); Clint McGhee (77); Og Mandino (78); Morris Massey (79); Ray Monsalvatge (80); Red Motley (81); Charles K. Murdock (82); Jim Newman (83); Earl Nightingale (84); Thom Norman (85); Jim Nussbaum (86); Jesse Owens (87); Ara Parseghian (88); Lester Pazol (89); Norman Vincent Peale (90); Mike Pekarek (91); Joe Powell (92); Ernie Prichard (93); Nido Qubein (94); John Ralston (95); Ken Reyhons (96); Bob Richards (97); Bobby Richardson (98); Cavett Robert (99); Eden Ryl (100); Jack Schiff (101); David Schwartz (102); Jack Schwartz (103); Arthur Secord (104); Dick Semaan (105); Robert Staight (106); Carl Stevens (107); Dave Stone (108); Bruce Summa (109); Suzy Sutton (110); Cody Sweet (111); Donald Arthur Thoren (112); Lewis Timberlake (113); Phil Tornabene (114); Herb True (115); Marilyn Van Derbur (116); Mike Vance (117); Dennis Waitley (118); Dorothy M. Walters (119); Somers H. White (120); Charles Willey (121); Sy Willing (122); Heartsill Wilson (123); Larry Wilson (124); Carl Winters (125); John Wolfe (126); John Wooden (127); Dave Yoho (128); Judge Ziglar (129); Zig Ziglar (130)

★ 178 ★
SPOKESPEOPLE
One Thomas Circle #304
Washington, D.C. 20005 (202) 347-7178

Spokespeople is the national speaker's bureau of the People's Party. Speakers are available to lecture on various topics. Fees are variable.

Speaker: Kayren Hudiburgh. Titles: How Collective Living Breaks Down the Isolation and Alienation of Today's World; How Food Co-ops and Community Stores Can be Used for Political Organizing; How to Spread Feminist and Socialist Ideas Through Electoral Politics (1)
Speaker: Sue Lenaerts. Title: Anti-rape Organizing (2)
Speaker: Kay McGlachlin. Title: Sex and Politics (3)
Speaker: David McReynolds. Title: Non-violence (4)
Speaker: Benjamin Spock. Titles: Child Care; The Need for Fundamental Political Changes in America; Contemporary Social Problems (5)

★ 179 ★
PATRICIA STEVENS MODEL AND MERCHANDISING AGENCY
4638 J.C. Nichols Parkway
Kansas City, Missouri 64112 (816) 531-5866

Provides lecturers to speak on fashion and self-improvement. Fees range from $200 to $300 plus travel expenses and hotel accommodations.

Speaker: Melissa Stevens. Title: Beauty Tips (1)
Speaker: Patricia Stevens. Title: Femininity and Liberated Women (2)

★ 180 ★
SUCCESS LEADERS SPEAKERS SERVICE
3121 Maple Drive, N.E., Suite 1
Atlanta, Georgia 30305 (404) 261-1122

Supplies some four hundred lecturers who speak at management conferences, sales seminars, meetings, and conventions of all kinds. Fees range from $300 to $5000 plus travel and expenses.

Speaker: Arnold G. Abrams. Title: Verbal, Vocal and Visual Cues to Better Job Performance (1)
Speaker: Bill Adams. Title: The Nuts, Guts, and Feathers of Selling (2)
Speaker: Howard M. Anderson. Title: Effective Time Management (3)
Speaker: James Arch. Title: How to Deal Successfully with People (4)
Speaker: Guy B. Arthur, Jr. Title: Coaching (5)
Speaker: Satya Pal Asija. Title: Criminal Information (6)
Speaker: Bob Bale. Title: Real Estate (7)
Speaker: Ronald Bates. Title: Industrial Psychology and Relations (8)
Speaker: Hal J. Batten. Title: Motivation and Communications (9)
Speaker: Joe Batten. Title: Tough Minded Business (10)
Speaker: Cathrina Bauby. Title: O.K. Let's Talk About It (11)
Speaker: Joe Bauer. Title: Mass Media (12)
Speaker: Dan Bellus. Title: People Business (13)
Speaker: Millard Bennett. Title: Successful Communications and Effective Speaking (14)
Speaker: Edwin C. Bliss. Title: Getting Things Done (15)
Speaker: Edwin E. Bobrow. Title: How to Make Big Money as an Independent Sales Agent (16)
Speaker: Lee Boyan. Title: "Living It" in Business (17)
Speaker: Arnold Brekke. Title: Agriculture (18)

Speaker: Earl D. Brodie. Title: How Businessmen Can Help Themselves (19)
Speaker: Frank M. Butrick. Title: How to Buy a Company - For Next to Nothing (20)
Speaker: Lew H. Byrd. Title: Marketing (21)
Speaker: Robert W. Carney. Title: Human Relations (22)
Speaker: Arnold Carter. Title: Sales Presentations (23)
Speaker: C.L. Carter. Title: Management Training and Development (24)
Speaker: Robert N. Carter. Title: Human Relations (25)
Speaker: W.C. Christians. Title: Industry (26)
Speaker: John N. Christianson. Title: Sales (27)
Speaker: Alan Cimberg. Title: Salesmanship (28)
Speaker: Ray K. Clark. Title: Commodities in Economics (29)
Speaker: William A. Clennan. Title: Think and Remember (30)
Speaker: Peggy Cleveland. Title: Telephone Techniques (31)
Speaker: Jeff Coats. Title: Transactional Analysis (32)
Speaker: LaVarne Cobb. Title: Ways to Attain Health, Wealth, Happiness, Success and Prosperity (33)
Speaker: Thomas K. Connellan. Title: Cost Containment (34)
Speaker: William J. Cook, Jr. Title: Motivation (35)
Speaker: Lloyd G. Cooper. Title: Human Resources Development (36)
Speaker: John D. Corrigan. Title: Management (37)
Speaker: Robert W. Croskery. Title: Counseling Executives (38)
Speaker: Lloyd Cullen. Title: Real Estate (39)
Speaker: Wayne Dehoney. Title: Personal Motivation (40)
Speaker: Hallie Dewey. Title: How to Do a Better Job (41)
Speaker: Bobby G. Dollar. Title: Educational Affairs (42)
Speaker: James Dornoff. Title: Successful Selling (43)
Speaker: Rose Dorrance. Title: The Career Woman (44)
Speaker: Mack Douglas. Title: How to Make a Habit of Succeeding (45)
Speaker: Merrill E. Douglass. Title: How to Control the Time of Your Life (46)
Speaker: Samuel S. Dubin. Title: Professional Obsolescence (47)
Speaker: Marion Claude Duncan. Title: What You See is What You Get (48)
Speaker: William R. Eggert. Title: Motivational Management (49)
Speaker: Robert Evans. Title: Producing Films (50)
Speaker: Art Fettig. Title: Enjoying Your Work (51)
Speaker: Dorothy K. Fierst. Title: Management (52)
Speaker: Henry Flarsheim. Title: Sales and Marketing (53)
Speaker: Cort R. Flint. Title: Broadcasting (54)
Speaker: Ray Foster. Title: Sales Management (55)
Speaker: D. Michael Frank. Title: Motivation (56)
Speaker: Jo Frazier. Title: Politics (57)
Speaker: Ralph W. Frost. Title: Travel (58)
Speaker: John H. Furbay. Title: The Changing World (59)
Speaker: Dick Gardner. Title: Salesmanship (60)
Speaker: Dick Gariepy. Title: Management (61)
Speaker: James E. Gates. Title: Economics (62)
Speaker: Les Giblin. Title: Salesmanship (63)
Speaker: Frank Goodwin. Title: Sales Management (64)
Speaker: Jack Gren. Title: Communication (65)
Speaker: Robert J. Griffin. Title: Alcoholism in Business (66)
Speaker: James N. Griffith. Title: Humor (67)
Speaker: Peter Hackes. Title: The Washington Scene (68)
Speaker: Alvin R. Haerr. Title: Management (69)
Speaker: Walter B. Hailey, Jr. Title: Positive Thinking (70)
Speaker: William H. Hale, Jr. Title: Human Awareness (71)
Speaker: Woodie Hall. Title: Salesmanship (72)
Speaker: George Halsted. Title: Communications (73)
Speaker: Mark Victor Hansen. Title: Management (74)
Speaker: William Franklin Harrington. Title: Business Affairs (75)
Speaker: Dorothy Lipp Harris. Title: Communications and Human Behavior (76)
Speaker: Philip R. Harris. Title: Management and Organization (77)
Speaker: Lillian K. Harrison. Title: Renaissance 2000 - You Are What You Value (78)
Speaker: Ira M. Hayes. Title: Achieving Success in the Free Enterprise System (79)
Speaker: Robert Hays. Title: Training Programs (80)
Speaker: Christopher J. Hegarty. Title: Effective Sales Management (81)
Speaker: Fred Herman. Title: Salesmanship (82)
Speaker: Ross Hersey. Title: Business (83)
Speaker: David Hoy. Title: ESP (84)
Speaker: Leonard C. Hudson. Title: Management

and Motivation (85)
Speaker: Russell J. Humphries. Title: Licensed Private Investigative Security-Consulting (86)
Speaker: Don Hutson. Title: Management (87)
Speaker: Gene Jakubek. Title: Family Counseling (88)
Speaker: Robert H. Jansen. Title: Proven Ideas for Profitable Selling (89)
Speaker: Joan Jewett. Title: Self-Improvement (90)
Speaker: Bill Johnson. Title: Marketing (91)
Speaker: Mildred Johnson. Title: Sales Management (92)
Speaker: L. Bevel Jones. Title: Athletics (93)
Speaker: Adiel Moncrief Jordan. Title: The Clerical-Collar Mind (94)
Speaker: DuPree Jordan, Jr. Title: Management (95)
Speaker: Anita Norris Josey. Title: Psychic Phenomena (96)
Speaker: Bruce Karstedt. Title: Success and Motivation (97)
Speaker: Ron Kauffman. Title: Communications (98)
Speaker: Zenn Kaufman. Title: Showmanship (99)
Speaker: Kenneth C. Kellar. Title: Community Affairs (100)
Speaker: Ed S. Koschel. Title: Sales and Marketing (101)
Speaker: William W. Lancaster. Title: Management (102)
Speaker: Charles Lapp. Title: Sales Management (103)
Speaker: Donald Lawrence. Title: Communications (104)
Speaker: John W. Lee. Title: Management (105)
Speaker: Peter D. Letterese. Title: Sales and Management Personnel (106)
Speaker: John E. Linder. Title: The Free Enterprise System (107)
Speaker: Clarence W. Lokey. Title: Personal Counseling (108)
Speaker: Harry Lorayne. Title: Memory Training (109)
Speaker: Fred E. Luchs. Title: Youth (110)
Speaker: Harold R. McAlindon. Title: Health Care (111)
Speaker: John J. McCarty. Title: Management (112)
Speaker: William J. McGrane. Title: Human Behavior (113)
Speaker: Robert N. McMurry. Title: Employee Selection (114)
Speaker: John H. McQuaing. Title: Motivation (115)
Speaker: King MacRury. Title: Management (116)
Speaker: Jules A. Marine. Title: Sales and Motivation (117)
Speaker: W. Lee Martin. Title: Communications (118)
Speaker: Roger Masquelier. Title: Management (119)
Speaker: Paul Micali. Title: Sales Training (120)
Speaker: L.C. Michelon. Title: Economics (121)
Speaker: Ray Monsalvatge. Title: Psychology (122)
Speaker: Robert L. Montgomery. Title: Management Communications (123)
Speaker: George I. Morrisey. Title: Management (124)
Speaker: Richard M. Mundt. Title: Motivation (125)
Speaker: Victor Muravin. Title: Communism (126)
Speaker: Charles K. Murdock. Title: Community Affairs (127)
Speaker: John R. Murphy. Title: Journalism (128)
Speaker: Herbert Nettleton. Title: Multi-Media (129)
Speaker: Andrew J. Noland. Title: Management and Attitude (130)
Speaker: R.L. Noran. Title: ESP (131)
Speaker: Thom Norman. Title: Sales and Management (132)
Speaker: Gordon Owen. Title: Human Relations (133)
Speaker: Joe Panichello. Title: Motivation (134)
Speaker: Winston K. Pendleton. Title: Public Relations (135)
Speaker: Morris I. Pickus. Title: Management (136)
Speaker: Al Pollard. Title: Public Relations (137)
Speaker: J. Lewis Powell. Title: Executive Speaking (138)
Speaker: Miles Powell. Title: Selling Can be Fun (139)
Speaker: Sterling Price. Title: Positive Thinking (140)
Speaker: Nido Qubein. Title: Christian Youth (141)
Speaker: John Ralston. Title: Think Positively (142)
Speaker: Erwin Rausch. Title: Educational Materials (143)
Speaker: Paul Reilly. Title: Communications (144)
Speaker: Gilbert P. Richardson. Title: Religious Subversion of Foreign Policy (145)
Speaker: Cavett Robert. Title: Human Engineering and Motivation (146)
Speaker: Henri Saint-Laurent. Title: Sales Training (147)
Speaker: Robert J. Samp. Title: Survival and

Length of Life (148)
Speaker: Lawrence E. Schlesinger. Title: Psychology (149)
Speaker: Whitt Schieltz. Title: Creative Education (150)
Speaker: David Schwartz. Title: The Magic of Thinking Big (151)
Speaker: Bjorn Secher. Title: Personal Development (152)
Speaker: William Lee Self. Title: Communications (153)
Speaker: Dick Semaan. Title: Success (154)
Speaker: Dorothy Shaffer. Title: Nonverbal Communication (155)
Speaker: Don Sheehan. Title: Marketing (156)
Speaker: J.E.B. Shi. Title: Marketing (157)
Speaker: E. Ralph Sims. Title: Management (158)
Speaker: Leonard J. Smith. Title: Behavior (159)
Speaker: Reginald Snyder. Title: Success (160)
Speaker: Eugene D. Sollo. Title: Marketing (161)
Speaker: Ray Sonnenberg. Title: Success in Business (162)
Speaker: Robert Staight. Title: Sales (163)
Speaker: Donald Stewart. Title: Memory Techniques (164)
Speaker: Suzanne Stewart. Title: Crisis: Challenge to Change (165)
Speaker: Judy Ford Stokes. Title: Food Management (166)
Speaker: Louis Stokes. Title: Politics (167)
Speaker: McNeill Stokes. Title: Labor Law (168)
Speaker: John W. Stone. Title: Business Administration (169)
Speaker: Rolland Storey. Title: Marketing (170)
Speaker: A.G. Strickland. Title: Management (171)
Speaker: Paul Sturgeon. Title: Salesmanship (172)
Speaker: Suzy Sutton. Title: Communication Skills (173)
Speaker: James L. Swab. Title: Management (174)
Speaker: Cody Sweet. Title: Non-verbal Communications (175)
Speaker: Maxine Taylor. Title: Astrology (176)
Speaker: Carl Terzian. Title: Public Relations (177)
Speaker: M. Donald Thomas. Title: Sales Management (178)
Speaker: Donald Arthur Thoren. Title: Employee Relations (179)
Speaker: Dave C. Tripp. Title: Vocational Guidance (180)
Speaker: Frances Tritt. Title: Management (181)
Speaker: Miriam Uni. Title: Human Behavior (182)
Speaker: Paul Kenneth Vonk. Title: The American Ideals of a Christian Capitalist Democracy (183)
Speaker: Les Waas. Title: Advertising (184)
Speaker: E. Jerry Walker. Title: Religion (185)
Speaker: Dorothy M. Walters. Title: Selling Power of a Woman (186)
Speaker: Frederick J. Walters. Title: Business (187)
Speaker: David L. Ward. Title: Management (188)
Speaker: Robert D. Weber. Title: Management (189)
Speaker: Charles T. Wellborn. Title: Management Training (190)
Speaker: Somers H. White. Title: Management (191)
Speaker: Leo G. Wilsman. Title: Moving and Transportation (192)
Speaker: James O. Winter. Title: Motivation (193)
Speaker: Carl Winters. Title: Crime (194)
Speaker: Dwayne R. Woerpel. Title: Leadership Training (195)
Speaker: John Wolfe. Title: Sales Training (196)
Speaker: Bill Woodruff. Title: Management (197)
Speaker: Martha Yates. Title: Coping (198)
Speaker: Thomas Daniels Yawkey. Title: Childhood Education (199)
Speaker: Dave Yoho. Title: Salesmanship (200)
Speaker: Judge Ziglar. Title: Salesmanship (201)
Speaker: Zig Ziglar. Title: Salesmanship (202)

T

★ 181 ★
TEMPLE UNIVERSITY
Broad Street and Montgomery Avenue
Philadelphia, Pennsylvania 19122 (215) 787-1283

Two hundred lecturers are provided to speak to the citizens of the Delaware Valley on a wide variety of topics. Travel expenses are expected to be paid.

Athletics and Recreation

Speaker: Bonnie Averbach. Titles: Color Cubes; Coloring Applied to Solitaire Games; Mathematical Games; Mathematical Recreations (1)
Speaker: Marian T. Barone. Titles: The Blind or Handicapped Student; The Coaching of Diving; The Olympic Games 30 Years Ago (2)
Speaker: Leroy W. Dubeck. Title: Chess (3)
Speaker: Samuel Kotz. Title: Mathematics in Games of Chance (4)
Speaker: Robert Leahy. Titles: Scuba Diving; Scuba Lifesaving (5)
Speaker: Barbara D. Lockhart. Titles: Education Amendment of 1972; Olympics; Women in Sport (6)

Speaker: Elmer L. Offenbacher. Title: Physics of Ice Skating (7)
Speaker: Florence V. Shankman. Title: Games and Activities to Liven up Reading (8)
Speaker: James M. Shea. Title: Jogging (9)
Speaker: Thomas H. Slook. Titles: Sailing to Win Races; The Science of Sailing (10)
Speaker: Marianne Torbert. Titles: Elementary Physical Education; Humanistic Physical Education; Meeting Children's Needs; Motor Development (11)
Speaker: Delores T. Williams. Titles: The Future of Work and Leisure; Recreation in a Modern Society (12)

Biology

Speaker: Richard C. Adelman. Title: Biology of Aging (13)
Speaker: F. David Aker. Title: Willing One's Body to Science (14)
Speaker: Harry D. Karpeles. Title: Aging in Our Society (15)
Speaker: Mildred L. Kistenmacher. Title: Genetics (16)
Speaker: Harold Meyer. Title: Adolescence (17)
Speaker: Richard L. Miller. Titles: Basic Research in the United States; A Biologist in East Africa; Fertilization; Marine Biology; Nuclear Power (18)
Speaker: M.C. Niu. Title: Genetic Engineering (19)
Speaker: Dorothy B. Platt. Titles: Darwin's Islands; Human Genetics; Human Reproduction; Test Tube Babies (20)
Speaker: Rita Smith. Title: Effects of Colonization (21)
Speaker: Elizabeth G. Tiffany. Title: Human Development (22)
Speaker: Gail Tower. Title: Development in the First Year of Life (23)
Speaker: Elliott White. Titles: Biology and Politics; Genetic Diversity and Political Life (24)

Black Culture

Speaker: Odeyo O. Ayaga. Titles: Africa and the United States; Black Studies and Liberal Arts Education; Contemporary Africa Culture; Contemporary Africa Politics; Pan-Africanism (25)
Speaker: Harry A. Bailey, Jr. Title: Centrifugalism in Black Politics (26)
Speaker: Barbara L. Hampton. Titles: African Music and Culture; Afro-American Music (27)
Speaker: Clement T. Keto. Titles: African History; Apartheid; Change in South Africa; United States and Human Rights (28)
Speaker: Emma Lapsansky. Titles: Afro-American Thought; Philadelphia Black Community (29)
Speaker: Audrey S. Pittman. Title: Black Family, Black Experience (30)
Speaker: Rita Smith. Titles: Black Family; Black Psychology; Black Woman; Ecology; Mental Health; Physiological Effects of Colonization; Social and Psychological Effects of Colonization (31)

Business

Speaker: Harry A. Bailey, Jr. Title: Corporate Accountability in America (32)
Speaker: Vladimir N. Bandera. Titles: The Incredible Bread Machine; Will the Sheiks Buy America? (33)
Speaker: Douglas Bennett. Title: Multinational Corporations in the Food Business (34)
Speaker: Jack L. Gross. Title: Small Business Management (35)
Speaker: Franklin S. Houston. Title: Marketing for Non-profit Institutions and Public Agencies (36)
Speaker: Jay Lamont. Titles: How and Where to Buy a Home; Real Estate Investments; The Real Estate Professional of the 1980's; Real Estate Today; Super Tax Shelters (37)
Speaker: Jerome I. Leventhal. Title: Distributive Education (38)
Speaker: Roger A. McCain. Titles: Kelsonian Economics; Worker Self-Management (39)
Speaker: Robert J. Myers. Title: Social Security (40)
Speaker: Walter H. Powell. Titles: Management; Personnel Management and Motivation; Public Sector Labor Relations (41)
Speaker: George F. Rohrlich. Titles: Conceptual Problems in Economics; Economic Development; Economic Motivations; Economic Security and Public Policy (42)
Speaker: Albert Schild. Title: Mathematics in the World of Business (43)
Speaker: H. Wayne Snider. Titles: The Automobile Accident Problem; Medical Malpractice Insurance; Product Liability Crisis; Risk Management (44)
Speaker: Donald L. Walters. Title: Understanding School District Budgets (45)
Speaker: Walter E. Williams. Titles: Economics of Discrimination; Law and Race (46)
Speaker: Samuel M. Wilson. Titles: An Integrative Approach to Technology; Management's Ethical Dilemma; Performance Evaluation (47)
Speaker: Seymour L. Wolfbein. Titles: Economic Forecasting; Employment and Unemployment; Manpower (48)

Careers and Career Planning

Speaker: Jean L. Brodey. Titles: Career Change and Development; Careers in Communications; Careers for Women (49)

Speaker: Patricia L. Dengler. Titles: Career Opportunities by College or Major; Career Opportunities for College Graduates; Career Planning (50)

Speaker: Frank L. Friedman. Titles: Cooperative Study and Internships in Higher Education; New Techniques of Computer Programming (51)

Speaker: Nancy E. Gilpin. Titles: Career Planning; Career Planning for Women; Careers in Education; Careers in Journalism (52)

Speaker: William C. Gutman. Titles: Career Opportunities by College or Major Career Planning; Career Opportunities for College Graduates (53)

Speaker: Lisa N. Heyman. Title: Criminal Justice System (54)

Speaker: Marvin Hirshfeld. Titles: Distributive Education; Vocational Student Organizations; Vocational Students Can Go to College (55)

Speaker: Inderjit Jaipaul. Titles: Supervision of Social Workers, Volunteers and Human Service Workers; Supervisors in Health and Social Welfare Agencies (56)

Speaker: Harry D. Karpeles. Title: Careers in the Health Care Field (57)

Speaker: Andrew J. Kutney. Title: Careers in Campus Security (58)

Speaker: Marthe LaVallee-Williams. Title: The Unity of Language Study (59)

Speaker: Calvin Leifer. Title: Careers in Dental Research (60)

Speaker: Jerome I. Leventhal. Titles: Career Education; Career Education for Career Planning; Distributive Education (61)

Speaker: Richard L. Miller. Title: Marine Biology (62)

Speaker: Amos C. Rivell. Title: Vocational Education (63)

Speaker: Bonita S. Rosenberg. Title: Careers in Medical Technology (64)

Speaker: James P. Smith, Jr. Titles: Make Your Job Satisfying; Mid-Life Career Change; Vocational and Job Satisfaction (65)

Speaker: Lee Transier. Title: Volunteerism in Action (66)

Communications

Speaker: Jean L. Brodey. Title: Careers in Communications (67)

Speaker: John De Mott. Titles: Ethics and the News Media; Free Press and Fair Trial; A Newsman's Sermon; The People's Right to Know; Your Community's Newspaper (68)

Speaker: Donald J. Fork. Title: Audiovisual Production (69)

Speaker: Minaruth Galey. Title: Cable Television for Education; Community Role of Cable Television; Educational Media; Educational Television (70)

Speaker: Nancy E. Gilpin. Title: Careers in Journalism (71)

Speaker: William F. Grady. Title: Educational Communications Media (72)

Speaker: John P. Hayes. Title: Men's Magazines (73)

Speaker: Marthe LaVallee-Williams. Title: Cinema (74)

Speaker: Robin E. Lawrason. Titles: Individualized Learning Strategies of Materials; Media in Teaching and Learning (75)

Speaker: Nikos Metallinos. Titles: Asymmetry of the Screen; Television Aesthetics (76)

Design and the Arts

Speaker: Sara A. Chapman. Titles: The Arts; Dance; Dance Education; Movement Education? (77)

Speaker: George L. Claflen, Jr. Titles: The Architecture of Alvar Aalto; The Architecture of Frank Lloyd Wright; Choosing an Architect; Housing Design; Neighborhood Design; Urban Design (78)

Speaker: Raymond J. Cormier. Titles: Early Irish Christian Art; Early Pagan Celtic Art; West Coast Jazz (79)

Speaker: Abraham A. Davidson. Titles: American Art; Jewish Art; Modern Art (80)

Speaker: Caroline Drummond. Title: Classical Greek Drama (81)

Speaker: Edrie Ferdun. Title: Dance, Bodies and People in Process (82)

Speaker: Glenn B. Geer. Title: Landscape Graphics (83)

Speaker: Barbara L. Hampton. Title: African Music and Culture; Afro-American Music (84)

Speaker: Dennis S. Lebofsky. Title: Opera (85)

Speaker: Nikos Metallinos. Title: Greek Folk Dancing (86)

Speaker: Norbert M. Samuelson. Title: Synagogue Architecture (87)

Speaker: Bradley H. Smith. Titles: Attitudes and Aptitude in the Arts; Frames of Reference (88)

Education

Speaker: Richard A. Adamsky. Titles: Mastery Learning; Research in Education; Teacher Education (89)

Speaker: Odeyo O. Ayaga. Title: Black Studies and Liberal Arts Education (90)

Speaker: Marian T. Barone. Title: The Blind or Handicapped Student (91)

Speaker: Sara A. Chapman. Titles: Are the Arts Interrelated in Your School?; Dance Education in the Schools; Movement Education? (92)

Speaker: William W. Cutler, III. Title: Minorities and Public Education; Oral History and Teaching (93)

Speaker: Caroline Drummond. Title: Education for Improved Communication (94)
Speaker: Leroy W. Dubeck. Title: American Association of University Professors (95)
Speaker: Jonathan First. Title: The Jewish Faith and Jewish Educational Opportunities (96)
Speaker: Donald J. Fork. Titles: Audiovisual Production Techniques; Instructional Technology; Learning Resource Centers; Multisensory Communication; Visual Literacy (97)
Speaker: Minaruth Galey. Titles: Cable Television; Educational Media; Educational Television; Individualizing Instruction (98)
Speaker: Nancy E. Gilpin. Title: Careers in Education (99)
Speaker: William F. Grady. Title: Educational Communications Media (100)
Speaker: John H. Hartsook. Title: Instruction in Spanish (101)
Speaker: Robert H. Holtzman. Titles: Church-State Issue in Public Education; The Educational Philosopher's Role Today; Moral Education; Professionalization of Teaching (102)
Speaker: Donald Humphreys. Title: Individualized Learning (103)
Speaker: Jon H. Hunt. Titles: Educational Accountability; Mainstreaming the Disadvantaged; Vocational Education (104)
Speaker: Linda R. Jensen. Titles: Creativity in Elementary School Math; Diagnosis and Evaluation of Gifted Children; Math for the Pre-School Child (105)
Speaker: Marjorie Seddon Johnson. Title: Reading (106)
Speaker: Roy A. Kress. Titles: Parents and the Reading Program; Reading Difficulties in Children (107)
Speaker: Eleanor Ladd. Title: Balancing the Parameters of a Reading Program (108)
Speaker: Marthe LaVallee-Williams. Titles: Faculty Union and Higher Education; Women and Higher Education (109)
Speaker: Robin E. Lawrason. Titles: The Demystification of Education Technology; Individualized Learning Strategies of Materials; Interpersonal Communication and the Learning Process; Media in Teaching and Learning; Teaching Staff or Faculty (110)
Speaker: Robert Leahy. Titles: Adult Education; Continuing Education; Higher Education and Continuing Education (111)
Speaker: Dennis S. Lebofsky. Title: Running a Secular Jewish School (112)
Speaker: Patricia M. Legos. Titles: Health Education for Elementary Teachers; Major Areas of Health Education; Teacher Behavior; Values Clarification in Health Education (113)
Speaker: Calvin Leifer. Title: Research in Dental Education (114)
Speaker: Jerome I. Leventhal. Titles: Career Education; Career Education for Career Planning; Cooperative Education; Distributive Education; Humanizing Instruction; Vocational Education (115)
Speaker: Robert E. McCollum. Titles: Basic Skills; Educational Quality Assessment; Needs Assessment for Schools (116)
Speaker: Jane E. Paalborg. Title: Current Mathematics Trends and Programs (117)
Speaker: Barbara Pavan. Titles: The Elementary Principal; Nongradedness; Open Education: U.S.A. and Great Britain; Team Teaching; Trends in Elementary Education (118)
Speaker: Reed Payne. Titles: Child Advocacy; Mainstreaming; Serving Handicapped Children (119)
Speaker: Amos C. Rivell. Title: Vocational Education (120)
Speaker: Jill C. Rosenman. Title: Reading Disability (121)
Speaker: Adele F. Schrag. Titles: Approach for Teaching and Learning; Teacher Education; What Does the Research Tell Us? (122)
Speaker: Florence V. Shankman. Titles: Liven up Reading; Parents and the Reading Program; Reading Success; Study Skills; Teaching Reading (123)
Speaker: Bradley H. Smith. Title: Search and Discovery (124)
Speaker: Eugene H. Stivers. Title: Transference in Everyday Life (125)
Speaker: Ken Thurman. Titles: Behavior Modification; Current Trends in Special Education; Disabled Populations; Exceptional Development (126)
Speaker: Elizabeth G. Tiffany. Title: Occupational Therapy (127)
Speaker: Lee Transier. Title: Continuing Education (128)
Speaker: Robert L. Walter. Title: Teachers and Collective Bargaining (129)
Speaker: Donald L. Walters. Titles: Research in Education; Understanding School District Budgets (130)

Geography and Geology

Speaker: David J. Cuff. Titles: Population Growth; The Oil Sands of Alberta; The Realities of Oil and Gas Supply (131)
Speaker: Glenn B. Geer. Titles: Fountains in the Landscape; The Home Landscape; Landscape Graphics; The Philadelphia Landscape; Sundials (132)
Speaker: Donald Humphreys. Title: The Birth and Death of a Lake (133)
Speaker: Lane J. Johnson. Titles: Megalopolis; The Metropolitan Organization of American Space; Sinclair's Model (134)

Speaker: Rita Smith. Title: Physiological Effects of Colonization (135)
Speaker: Erwin C. Surrency. Title: Preserve the Environment (136)
Speaker: Gene C. Ulmer. Titles: The Energy Crisis; Geology of Philadelphia; Geothermal Energy; Mineral Wealth of South Africa; Volcanoes (137)

Literature and Poetry

Speaker: Raymond J. Cormier. Title: The Medieval French Hero (138)
Speaker: Caroline Drummond. Title: Classical Greek Drama (139)
Speaker: John P. Hayes. Title: James A. Michener (140)
Speaker: Roger A. McCain. Title: Science Fiction and Utopias (141)
Speaker: Nikos Metallinos. Title: Research in Greek Folklore (142)
Speaker: J. Mitchell Morse. Title: James Joyce (143)
Speaker: Anne D. Roos. Titles: Literature for Children; Poetry (144)
Speaker: Jaqueline Shachter. Titles: Children's Authors; Children's Literature; Profiles in Literature (145)
Speaker: Eugene H. Stivers. Titles: The Making of Americans; Psychological Liberation (146)
Speaker: Fredrick Trautmann. Titles: Charles Dickens; Harriet Beecher Stowe (147)

Mathematics

Speaker: Bonnie Averbach. Titles: Color Cubes; Coloring; Mathematical Games; Mathematical Recreations (148)
Speaker: Emil Grosswald. Titles: Classical Problems; Number Theory?; Questions (149)
Speaker: Linda R. Jensen. Titles: Creativity in Elementary School Math; Math for the Pre-School Child (150)
Speaker: Samuel Kotz. Title: Mathematics in Games of Chance (151)
Speaker: Jane E. Paalborg. Titles: Mathematics Appreciation; Mathematics Trends and Programs (152)
Speaker: Albert Schild. Titles: Mathematics in the Modern World; Mathematics in the World of Business; The New Mathematics (153)
Speaker: Thomas H. Slook. Titles: Designing an Analog Computer; Mathematics vs. the Modern Computer (154)

Medicine and Health Care

Speaker: Ernest Baran. Titles: Biomedical Engineering; Electrodiagnosis; Evoked Electro-spinograms; Human Myotatic Reflex; Rehabilitation Medicine; Single Fiber Electromyography (155)
Speaker: Gopal K. Batra. Titles: Occupational Lung Disease; Respiratory Diseases; Smoking and the Lung (156)
Speaker: William H. Binns, Jr. Title: Children's Dentistry (157)
Speaker: Mary Louise Cote. Titles: Kidney Disease in Children; Kidney Transplants in Children; Women in Medicine (158)
Speaker: Peter H. Doukas. Title: Drugs of Abuse and Their Action (159)
Speaker: George E. Ehrlich. Title: Rheumatic Diseases (160)
Speaker: Allen Fred Fielding. Titles: Correction of Facial Deformities; Impacted Teeth; Oral Surgery (161)
Speaker: Anthony Fugaro. Titles: Anesthesia; Anesthetic Agents; Cardiopulmonary Resuscitation; Mystery of Anesthesia (162)
Speaker: Ronald F. Gautieri. Titles: Birth Defects; Poisons (163)
Speaker: Allen R. Geiwitz. Titles: Anti-convulsants and Epilepsy; Drug Treatment of the Mentally Retarded; Psychotherapeutics (164)
Speaker: Dorothea D. Glass. Titles: Rehabilitation; Sexuality of the Disabled (165)
Speaker: Richard Golder. Title: Nutrition and Diet (166)
Speaker: David M. Goodner. Titles: Modern Obstetrical Care; Prenatal Genetic Diagnosis (167)
Speaker: Earl Greenwald. Title: Pelvic Cancer (168)
Speaker: Eugene M. Hoenig. Titles: Electron Microscopy of Nervous System; Photomicrography; Structure of Brain in Diseased States (169)
Speaker: Harry D. Karpeles. Titles: Aging in Our Society; Careers in the Health Care Field; Consumerism in Health; The Health Care Revolution (170)
Speaker: A. Richard Kendall. Titles: Diagnosis of Renal Masses; Prostate Carcinoma Testicle; Urinary Infections in the Child (171)
Speaker: Nancy Kenepp. Title: Anesthesia (172)
Speaker: Mildred L. Kistenmacher. Titles: Genetic Counseling; Genetics; Prenatal Diagnosis (173)
Speaker: Harold Lantz. Titles: Complete Dentures; Fractional Dentures; Geriatric Dentistry; Implant Dentures; Prosthetic Measures (174)
Speaker: Calvin Leifer. Titles: Dental Research; Role of Research in Dental Education; Tumors of Salivary Glands; Ultrastructure of Salivary Glands (175)
Speaker: Ruth Ellen Levine. Titles: Ethnicity and Culture; Health Care; Rehabilitation Services; Supervision Techniques (176)
Speaker: Joan G. Liebler. Title: Patient Records in Drug Abuse and Alcoholism (177)
Speaker: Prabhakar D. Lotlikar. Titles: Environment and Cancer; Food Additives (178)

Speaker: James G. McElligott. Title: Brain Research (179)
Speaker: Nathaniel Mayer. Title: Rehabilitation Engineering (180)
Speaker: Harold Meyer. Title: Adolescence (181)
Speaker: Arthur S. Miller. Titles: Oral Cancer; Teaching Pathology (182)
Speaker: Alex M. Mohnac. Titles: Early Oral Cancer Detection; Facial Deformities (183)
Speaker: Bruce G. Morton. Titles: Eating Low on the Food Chain; Environmental Health Hazards; Philadelphia; Positive Health Behavior (184)
Speaker: Elaine O. Patrikas. Titles: Health Information System; Health Records Administration; Patients' Access to Medical Records (185)
Speaker: Charles F. Peterson. Titles: Are You a Drug Abuser?; How to Choose Your Pharmacist; How to Talk to Your Child about Drugs (186)
Speaker: Robert L. Pollack. Title: Modern Nutrition for Everyday Living (187)
Speaker: Mordecai M. Popovtzer. Title: Osteoporosis (188)
Speaker: Glenda D. Price. Titles: Allied Health; Medical Technology (189)
Speaker: F.A. Reichle. Titles: Current Trends in Portal Hypertension; Diabetic Ischemic (190)
Speaker: Bonita S. Rosenberg. Title: Medical Technology (191)
Speaker: Dolores Korman Sloviter. Title: Law and the Elderly (192)
Speaker: H. Wayne Snider. Title: Medical Malpractice Insurance (193)
Speaker: Paschal M. Spagna. Titles: Cardiac Pacemakers; Coronary Artery By-Pass Surgery; New Advances in Open Heart Surgery (194)
Speaker: Gail Tower. Titles: Cerebral Palsy; The Nervous System (195)
Speaker: Murray M. Tuckerman. Titles: Consumerism: Choosing Health Care Professionals; Consumerism: You and Your Medicine Chest (196)
Speaker: Salvatore Turco. Titles: Hospital Pharmacy; Parenteral Therapy (197)
Speaker: Theodore Villafana. Titles: New Radiological Imaging Devices; Radiation Safety in Medical Procedures (198)
Speaker: Stephen S. Washburne. Title: Organic Chemistry (199)
Speaker: Stanley L. Wendkos. Titles: Physical Therapy; Rehabilitation (200)

Modern Living

Speaker: Ernestyne James Adams. Title: The Older, Disadvantaged College Student (201)
Speaker: Harry A. Bailey, Jr. Title: Political Power in America (202)
Speaker: Vladimir N. Bandera. Titles: The Incredible Bread Machine; Will the Sheiks Buy America? (203)
Speaker: Ranan B. Banerji. Titles: Can Computers Do Everything?; Limitations on Complexity of Computation; Playing Games with Computers; State of the Art in Mechanized Intelligence; What Makes Computers Tick? (204)
Speaker: Gopal K. Batra. Title: Smoking and the Lung (205)
Speaker: Kenneth E. Burnham. Title: The New Religious Groups (206)
Speaker: George L. Claflen, Jr. Title: Choosing an Architect (207)
Speaker: Raymond J. Cormier. Title: The New Spirituality (208)
Speaker: David J. Cuff. Title: The Realities of Oil and Gas Supply (209)
Speaker: Abraham A. Davidson. Title: Modern Art (210)
Speaker: John De Mott. Titles: Ethics; Free Press vs. Fair Trial; The Right of Privacy; Your Community's Newspaper? (211)
Speaker: Peter H. Doukas. Title: Drugs of Abuse and Their Action (212)
Speaker: Leroy W. Dubeck. Title: UFO's (213)
Speaker: Frank L. Friedman. Titles: Computer Programming; Portability of Computer Programs (214)
Speaker: Minaruth Galey. Titles: Community Role of Cable Television; Educational Television (215)
Speaker: Ronald F. Gautieri. Titles: Drug-Induced Birth Defects; Misuse of Drugs; Poisons around the House (216)
Speaker: Glenn B. Geer. Title: The Home Landscape (217)
Speaker: Henry Goehl. Title: Social Dialects (218)
Speaker: Jack L. Gross. Title: Small Business Management (219)
Speaker: Lisa N. Heyman. Title: The Criminal Justice Field (220)
Speaker: Eleanore S. Isard. Titles: Abuse: Child and Woman; Human Sexuality; The Middle Years of Womanhood; Separation (221)
Speaker: Lane J. Johnson. Title: Megalopolis (222)
Speaker: Harry D. Karpeles. Title: Aging in Our Society (223)
Speaker: Andrew J. Kutney. Title: Rape Prevention (224)
Speaker: Jay Lamont. Titles: Buy a Home Today; The Real Estate Professional (225)
Speaker: Dennis S. Lebofsky. Title: How to Talk Like a Philadelphian (226)
Speaker: Patricia M. Legos. Titles: Human Sexuality; Major Areas of Health Education (227)
Speaker: Ruth Ellen Levine. Title: Ethnicity and Culture (228)

Speaker: Howard Liddle. Title: Marital/Family Relationships (229)
Speaker: Prabhakar D. Lotlikar. Titles: Environment and Cancer; Food Additives (230)
Speaker: Roger A. McCain. Titles: Futurology; Science Fiction and Utopias (231)
Speaker: Nikos Metallinos. Title: Television Aesthetics (232)
Speaker: Robert Miller. Title: Current Events (233)
Speaker: J. Mitchell Morse. Title: Racial, Religious and Sexual Prejudice (234)
Speaker: Elaine O. Patrikas. Title: Patients' Access to Medical Records (235)
Speaker: Charles F. Peterson. Titles: Are You a Drug Abuser?; Talk to Your Child about Drugs (236)
Speaker: Margaret M. Rappaport. Title: Changes in the American Family (237)
Speaker: Dennis A. Rubini. Titles: Homosexuality, Marriage and the Family; Pornography; Sexual Minorities in America (238)
Speaker: Norbert M. Samuelson. Title: Trends in Jewish Thought (239)
Speaker: Arthur Schmidt. Title: Urban Society and the Future (240)
Speaker: Dolores Korman Sloviter. Title: Law and the Elderly (241)
Speaker: Rita Smith. Titles: Helplessness; Race, Heredity and I.Q.; Racism (242)
Speaker: H. Wayne Snider. Title: Automobile Accident Problem (243)
Speaker: David A. Soskis. Titles: International Terrorism; Terrorists, Hostages and Victims (244)
Speaker: Ira M. Steisel. Titles: The Meaning of the I.Q.; A Successful Weight Reduction Program (245)
Speaker: Eugene H. Stivers. Title: Challenges of the Life Cycle (246)
Speaker: Gail Tower. Titles: Education for Childbirth; The Single Parent Adoptive Experience (247)
Speaker: Lee Transier. Titles: The Mass Society; Volunteerism in Action (248)
Speaker: Murray M. Tuckerman. Titles: Consumerism: Choosing Health Care Professionals; Consumerism: What's in Our Food?; Consumerism: You and Your Medicine Chest (249)
Speaker: Gene C. Ulmer. Title: The Energy Crisis: Real and Unreal (250)
Speaker: Ilona Ulmer. Titles: Breast Feeding; Natural Childbirth (251)
Speaker: Frances Vandivier. Title: Services for Families and Children (252)
Speaker: Stephen S. Washburne. Title: The Energy Crisis (253)
Speaker: Conrad Weiler. Title: Neighborhoods and City Recycling (254)
Speaker: Walter E. Williams. Title: Law and Race (255)

The Nation

Speaker: Ernestyne James Adams. Title: The American Melting Pot (256)
Speaker: Odeyo O. Ayaga. Title: Africa and the United States (257)
Speaker: Harry A. Bailey, Jr. Titles: Centrifugalism in Black Politics; Corporate Accountability in America; Political Power in America; The Post-Watergate Presidency (258)
Speaker: Douglas Bennett. Title: The Founding Fathers (259)
Speaker: George L. Claflen, Jr. Title: Urban Design in San Francisco (260)
Speaker: William W. Cutler, III. Title: Concept of Public in American Education (261)
Speaker: Herbert Ershkowitz. Titles: American Politics; Free Masonry in 19th Century America; Jewish Image in the American Mind, 1607-1900; 19th Century City (262)
Speaker: Jeffry Galper. Title: Socialism and America (263)
Speaker: Mark H. Haller. Titles: Historical Development of American Cities; Organized Crime; Urban Crime and Police (264)
Speaker: Waldo Heinrichs. Titles: American Foreign Policy; American Relations with China and Japan; Isolationism; Pearl Harbor (265)
Speaker: Lane J. Johnson. Title: Presidential Voting Patterns (266)
Speaker: Clement T. Keto. Titles: African History to Americans; The United States and Human Rights in Southern Africa (267)
Speaker: Emma Lapsansky. Title: The American Home (268)
Speaker: Robert Miller. Titles: Current Events; United States History (269)
Speaker: Shumpei Okamoto. Title: Japanese-American Relations (270)
Speaker: Dolores Korman Sloviter. Title: Law and the Elderly (271)
Speaker: Eugene H. Stivers. Title: Gertrude Stein's The Making of Americans (272)
Speaker: James A. Strazzella. Titles: Criminal Justice; Criminal Law; Criminal Procedure (273)
Speaker: Erwin C. Surrency. Titles: American Law and Institutions; Judicial Administration (274)
Speaker: Conrad Weiler. Titles: Neighborhood Government and Organization; The Neighborhood Movement in American Politics; Neighborhoods and City Recycling; Neighborhoods, Housing and Community Development (275)

Physics

Speaker: Leroy W. Dubeck. Title: UFO's (276)
Speaker: Jerrold Franklin. Titles: Elementary Particles; The Structure of the Proton (277)

Speaker: Leonard Muldawer. Title: Seeing the Invisible (278)
Speaker: Elmer L. Offenbacher. Titles: Outstanding Jewish Scientists; The Physics of Ice; Physics of Ice Skating (279)
Speaker: Howard L. Poss. Titles: Astronomy and Astrology; The Universe According to Modern Astronomy (280)

Psychology and Behavior

Speaker: Ronald Baenninger. Titles: African Animal Behavior; Aggressive Behavior; Humans and Other Animals (281)
Speaker: William Hetznecker. Titles: Mental Health Consultation; Psychosocial Problems of Children and Adolescents; Talking with Children (282)
Speaker: Boris Iglewicz. Title: Surveys in a Group Environment (283)
Speaker: Eleanore S. Isard. Titles: Human Sexuality; The Middle Years of Womanhood; Separation-Loss-Grief: Renewal (284)
Speaker: Louise Kidder. Titles: Community and Individual Responses to Crime (285)
Speaker: Patricia M. Legos. Titles: Human Sexuality; Teacher Behavior (286)
Speaker: Howard Liddle. Titles: Family Counseling/Family Therapy; Marital Counseling/ Marital Therapy; Marital/Family Relationships; The Training of Counselors (287)
Speaker: Roger A. McCain. Title: Libertarian Socialist and Democratic Socialist Ideas (288)
Speaker: Richard J. Malnati. Titles: Counseling and Working with the Aged; Improving Human Relationships; Individual and Group Therapy; Individual or Group Psychotherapy; The Problems of Children (289)
Speaker: Martin B. Millison. Title: Social Behavior at Shopping Centers (290)
Speaker: Herbert Rappaport. Titles: The African Medicine Man and Western Psychotherapy; Existential Psychoanalysis; Psychological Perspectives on the American Family; Psychotherapy in American Society (291)
Speaker: Margaret M. Rappaport. Titles: Changes in the American Family; Discovering the Child; Parenting with Versatility, Vibrancy and Values; The Personal Revolution; Self-Esteem Exercises for Adults (292)
Speaker: Norbert M. Samuelson. Titles: The Arab-Israeli Conflict; The Rise of the Modern State of Israel (293)
Speaker: Rita Smith. Titles: Black Psychology; Mental Health and the Black Community; Race, Heredity and I.Q.; Social and Psychological Effects of Colonization (294)
Speaker: David A. Soskis. Title: Terrorists, Hostages and Victims (295)
Speaker: Ira M. Steisel. Titles: Behavior Modification; The Meaning of the I.Q.; Successful Weight Reduction Program (296)
Speaker: Eugene H. Stivers. Title: Challenges of the Life Cycle (297)
Speaker: Fredrick Trautmann. Title: Anarchism (298)
Speaker: Samuel M. Wilson. Title: Performance Evaluation (299)
Speaker: Bibhuti S. Yadav. Title: Philosophy and Psychology of Yoga (300)

Religion

Speaker: Abraham A. Davidson. Title: Jewish Art (301)
Speaker: Jonathan First. Title: The Jewish Faith and Jewish Educational Opportunities (302)
Speaker: Robert H. Holtzman. Title: Church-State Issue in Public Education (303)
Speaker: Dennis S. Lebofsky. Title: Running a Secular Jewish School (304)
Speaker: J. Mitchell Morse. Title: Racial, Religious and Sexual Prejudice (305)
Speaker: Norbert M. Samuelson. Titles: The Arab-Israeli Conflict; External Influences on Synagogue Architecture; Jewish-Christian Dialogue; Modern Trends in Jewish Thought; The Rise of the Modern State of Israel; When Arabs and Jews Were Friends (306)
Speaker: Bibhuti S. Yadav. Titles: Buddhism; Hinduism; Yoga (307)

Social Welfare

Speaker: Ernestyne James Adams. Titles: The Older, Disadvantaged College Student; Social Welfare (308)
Speaker: Jeffry Galper. Titles: The People's Fund of Philadelphia; Political Implications of Social Services; Political Implications of Social Work (309)
Speaker: Howard Liddle. Titles: Family Counseling/Family Therapy; Marital Counseling/ Marital Therapy; Marital/Family Relationships; The Training of Counselors (310)
Speaker: Audrey S. Pittman. Title: Child Welfare (311)
Speaker: Dolores Korman Sloviter. Title: Law and the Elderly (312)
Speaker: Frances Vandivier. Titles: Child Care; Developmental Disabilities; Services for Families and Children (313)

Speech and Hearing

Speaker: Henry Goehl. Titles: Can Chimps Learn Human Language?; Child Language Disorders; Language and Mind; Language and Thinking; Social Dialects (314)

Speaker: Marthe LaVallee-Williams. Title: New Directions in Language Study (315)
Speaker: Robin E. Lawrason. Title: Interpersonal Communication and the Learning Process (316)
Speaker: Dennis S. Lebofsky. Titles: How to Talk like a Philadelphian; The King's English or the Mayor's? (317)
Speaker: Jean Lovrinic. Titles: Hearing; Hearing Loss; Noise on Hearing (318)
Speaker: Harry J. Sheldon. Titles: Language Arts and the Study Skills; Language Development in Young Children; Listening (319)

Women

Speaker: Jean L. Brodey. Title: Careers for Women (320)
Speaker: Mary Louise Cote. Title: Women in Medicine (321)
Speaker: Nancy E. Gilpin. Title: Career Planning for Women (322)
Speaker: Eleanore S. Isard. Titles: Abuse; The Middle Years of Womanhood (323)
Speaker: Louise Kidder. Title: Psychology of Women (324)
Speaker: Andrew J. Kutney. Title: Rape Prevention (325)
Speaker: Marthe LaVallee-Williams. Title: Women and Higher Education (326)
Speaker: Barbara D. Lockhart. Title: Women in Sport (327)
Speaker: Rita Smith. Title: Black Woman (328)
Speaker: Ilona Ulmer. Title: Natural Childbirth (329)
Speaker: Bibhuti S. Yadav. Title: Woman (330)

The World

Speaker: Odeyo O. Ayaga. Titles: Africa and the United States; Contemporary Africa: Culture; Contemporary Africa: Politics; Pan-Africanism (331)
Speaker: Vladimir N. Bandera. Titles: The Incredible Bread Machine; Will the Sheiks Buy America? (332)
Speaker: Gopal K. Batra. Titles: Culture and Civilization of India; Poverty and Unemployment (333)
Speaker: Douglas Bennett. Title: Multinational Corporations in the Food Business (334)
Speaker: George L. Claflen, Jr. Title: Urban Spaces of Europe (335)
Speaker: David J. Cuff. Titles: The Oil Sands of Alberta; Population Growth (336)
Speaker: Waldo Heinrichs. Titles: American Foreign Policy; American Relations with China and Japan (337)
Speaker: Clement T. Keto. Titles: Apartheid; Change in South Africa (338)
Speaker: Benjamin Lev. Title: The Middle East in War and Peace (339)
Speaker: Richard L. Miller. Title: A Biologist in East Africa (340)
Speaker: M.C. Niu. Title: Current Affairs in People's Republic of China (341)
Speaker: Shumpei Okamoto. Titles: Japan; Japanese-American Relations (342)
Speaker: Norbert M. Samuelson. Titles: The Rise of the Modern State of Israel; When Arabs and Jews Were Friends (343)
Speaker: Arthur Schmidt. Title: Modern Latin America (344)
Speaker: David A. Soskis. Titles: International Terrorism; Terrorism in the Middle East Conflict (345)
Speaker: Erwin C. Surrency. Title: Preserve the Environment on an International Scale (346)
Speaker: Gene C. Ulmer. Title: Mineral Wealth of South Africa (347)

★ 182 ★

TIME LIFE AND LEE, INC.
Post Office Box 1603
Crawfordville, Florida 32327 (904) 926-3970

Provides speakers to lecture on the subject of time and how to make the most of it.

Speakers: Duey Blackwell (1); Michael Henderson (2); John W. Lee (3)
Titles: Delegation; Hour Power; Make Today Count; Managing Other People Time; Time Out

★ 183 ★

TIN RESEARCH INSTITUTE, INC.
483 West Sixth Avenue
Columbus, Ohio 43201 (614) 424-6200

Speakers are provided to lecture on all aspects of tin. There are no fees.

Speakers: John M. Bihl (1); William B. Hampshire (2); Joseph B. Long (3)
Subject: Tin

★ 184 ★

THE TOBACCO INSTITUTE
1776 K Street, N.W., #1200
Washington, D.C. 20006 (202) 457-4862

Speakers present the industry's side on the many allegations made concerning the use of tobacco.

Travel expenses are expected to be paid.

Speakers: Anne Browder (1); Connie M. Drath (2); William F. Dwyer (3); Walker Merryman (4)
Title: Cigarette Controversy

★ 185 ★
TOOL AND DIE INSTITUTE
777 Busse Highway
Park Ridge, Illinois 60068 (312) 825-1120

Speakers present lectures on the tool and die industry.

★ 186 ★
TRANS WORLD AIRLINES
605 Third Avenue
New York, New York 10016 (212) 557-8333

Speakers present talks on the changing world of travel. There are no fees.

Subject: Travel

★ 187 ★
TUNA RESEARCH FOUNDATION, INC.
1101 17th Street, N.W., Suite 607
Washington, D.C. 20036 (202) 296-4630

Lecturers are provided to speak on various topics to civic groups and school audiences. Travel expenses are expected to be paid.

Speaker: Harold F. Kierce. Title: Food and Nutrition (1)
Speaker: Anthony J. Kimmick. Title: Law of the Sea (2)
Speaker: John P. Mulligan. Title: Marine Mammals (3)
Speaker: Anthony V. Nizetich. Titles: Environmental Issues; Industry (4)

U

★ 188 ★
UNION COLLEGE
Schenectady, New York 12308 (518) 370-6000

Speakers are available to lecture on a variety of topics.

★ 189 ★
UNION ELECTRIC SPEAKERS FORUM
Post Office Box 149, Code 100
Saint Louis, Missouri 63166 (314) 621-3222 Ext. 2798

The Union Electric Company Speakers Forum program is conducted as a service to the community and as a way of communicating information on energy-related topics and general interest subjects. There are no fees charged.

American Heritage and Free Enterprise

Titles: The Excitement of America; Patriotism; Practical Politics; Red, White and Blue

Electricity and the Power Industry

Titles: Economics of Union Electric's Operations; Energy Efficiency; Interconnected Electric Systems; A New Kind of Power; Nuclear Power; Regional Power Planning; The Union Electric System

Gardening

Titles: Gardening Problems; Lawn Care; Roses; Safe Use of Pesticides; Tree Maintenance; Tree Planting; Zoysia Lawn Management

Human Relations and Communications

Titles: The Challenge of Leadership; Communications is Understanding; Eye of the Beholder; Group Dynamics; The Managerial Grid

Safety

Titles: Electric Power and Common Sense; The Smith System of Driving

★ 190 ★
UNIQUE PROGRAMS, INC.
450 Santa Clara Avenue
Oakland, California 94610 (415) 451-5550

Arranges lectures and specialized programs for organizations, associations and conventions. Fees vary according to subject, length of program, administrative and promotional costs and travel.

UNITED STATES ARMS CONTROL AND DISARMAMENT AGENCY
See: United States Department of State - Arms Control and Disarmament Agency

UNITED STATES BUREAU OF INDIAN AFFAIRS
See: United States Department of the Interior
Bureau of Indian Affairs

UNITED STATES COAST GUARD
See: United States Department of Transportation
United States Coast Guard

★ 191 ★
UNITED STATES CONSUMER PRODUCT SAFETY COMMISSION
1750 K Street, N.W.
Washington, D.C. 20207 (202) 634-7700

Speakers are available to discuss product safety topics and related subjects with organizations and groups requesting a lecturer.

★ 192 ★
UNITED STATES DEPARTMENT OF AGRICULTURE
14th and Independence Avenue
Washington, D.C. 20250 (202) 447-5247

Officials, specialists, and scientists are prepared to address audiences on topics which relate to the work of the Department of Agriculture and its specific agencies such as the Agricultural Research Service, Soil Conservation Service, Forest Service, etc. From time to time the Secretary of Agriculture and the various assistant secretaries are also available. No fees.

★ 193 ★
UNITED STATES DEPARTMENT OF DEFENSE
The Pentagon
Washington, D.C. 20301 (202) 545-6700

Provides speakers to inform the public about defense-related matters by developing, understanding and stimulating patriotic spirit. There are no fees.

★ 194 ★
UNITED STATES DEPARTMENT OF DEFENSE
Department of the Air Force
Air Force Speakers Branch
Hq USAF (SAF/OICD)
Washington, D.C. 20330 (202) 697-6205

Speakers are made available to lecture on Air Force related topics to private organizations and community groups.

★ 195 ★
UNITED STATES DEPARTMENT OF DEFENSE
Department of the Army
Public Affairs Office
Washington, D.C. 20310 (202) 697-5720/1683

Offers services of speakers on any Army-related topics. Army speakers are not permitted to accept honorariums. Normally, if the speaker is located within 100 miles of the speaking site, and can complete a round trip in one day, there is no charge to the sponsor.

★ 196 ★
UNITED STATES DEPARTMENT OF DEFENSE
Department of the Navy
Office of Information
Washington, D.C. 20350 (202) 694-8205

Speakers from this branch of the military service are available to lecture to interested audiences on subjects related to the role and mission of the Navy.

★ 197 ★
UNITED STATES DEPARTMENT OF DEFENSE
United States Marine Corps
Division of Information, Headquarters
Washington, D.C. 20380 (202) 694-1046

Lecturers are available to speak on the Marine Corps to groups and organizations.

★ 198 ★
UNITED STATES DEPARTMENT OF HEALTH, EDUCATION AND WELFARE
Public Health Service
Food and Drug Administration
5600 Fishers Lane
Rockville, Maryland 20852 (301) 443-5006

Provides speakers to discuss the current policies of the Food and Drug Administration with interested groups. No fees.

★ 199 ★
UNITED STATES DEPARTMENT OF HEALTH, EDUCATION AND WELFARE
Social Security Administration
200 Independence Avenue, S.W.
Washington, D.C. 20201 (202) 245-6221

Speakers are provided by this agency who are matched with the special interests of the group or audience requesting the lecturer. Topics generally relate to the social security and retirement system of the United States and the range of benefits available to the public. There are no fees.

★ 200 ★
UNITED STATES DEPARTMENT OF STATE
Arms Control and Disarmament Agency
320 21st Street, N.W.
Washington, D.C. 20451 (202) 632-0392

Seeks to inform the public about the government's efforts to control the level of nuclear and conventional weapons and to move in the direction of actual reductions in existing stockpiles. No fees.

★ 201 ★
UNITED STATES DEPARTMENT OF STATE
Foreign Service Institute
Office of Programs
Washington, D.C. 20520 (202) 632-1710

Speakers are available to lecture on foreign policy to campus, civic, business, religious, and ethnic groups. No fees.

UNITED STATES DEPARTMENT OF THE AIR FORCE
See: United States Department of Defense
Department of the Air Force

UNITED STATES DEPARTMENT OF THE ARMY
See: United States Department of Defense
Department of the Army

★ 202 ★
UNITED STATES DEPARTMENT OF THE INTERIOR
Bureau of Indian Affairs
1951 Constitution Avenue, N.W.
Washington, D.C. 20245 (202) 343-7445

Provides speakers to discuss topics related to the United States Indians. No fees.

UNITED STATES DEPARTMENT OF THE NAVY
See: United States Department of Defense
Department of the Navy

★ 203 ★
UNITED STATES DEPARTMENT OF TRANSPORTATION
United States Coast Guard
Community Relations Branch G-APA3/83
Washington, D.C. 20590 (202) 426-1587

Makes available speakers to lecture on topics concerning the missions of the United States Coast Guard. Speakers vary according to locale. Ranking officers of the Coast Guard are used to lecture to national organizations. There are no fees. A sixty day advance notice is preferred.

★ 204 ★
UNITED STATES ENVIRONMENTAL PROTECTION AGENCY
401 M Street, S.W.
Washington, D.C. 20460 (202) 426-4188

Speakers will discuss environmental issues before national, regional, and local organizations and groups. Fees, honoraria, and reimbursement of travel expenses are accepted for the United States Environmental Protection Agency Scholarship Fund.

Titles: Air and Water Pollution Control; Chemicals and Toxic Substances; Energy and the Environment; Enforcement of Pollution Control Laws; Environmental Radiation; Health Effects of Environmental Pollutants; Industrial and Municipal Wastewater Treatment; International Environmental Programs; Noise Pollution; Pesticides Regulation

UNITED STATES FOOD AND DRUG ADMINISTRATION
See: United States Department of Health, Education and Welfare
Public Health Service
Food and Drug Administration

UNITED STATES FOREIGN SERVICE INSTITUTE
See: United States Department of State
Foreign Service Institute

★ 205 ★
UNITED STATES INTERNATIONAL COMMUNICATIONS AGENCY
1750 Pennsylvania Avenue, N.W.
Washington, D.C. 20547 (202) 724-9099

Speakers will discuss a wide range of foreign affairs topics. No fees.

Titles: The Conduct of United States Information and Cultural Programs in Particular Regions of the World or in Individual Countries; Cross-Cultural Communications; Foreign Attitudes Concerning the United States; Modern Communications Technology; Public Diplomacy in the Foreign Policy Process; The United States Foreign Information and Cultural Program Today; The Voice of America and International Broadcasting

★ 206 ★
UNITED STATES INTERSTATE COMMERCE COMMISSION
Public Information Office
Washington, D.C. 20423 (202) 275-7252

Officials of the Commission are prepared to discuss the Commission's organizations, operations, procedures and regulations with interested groups. No fees.

UNITED STATES MARINE CORPS
See: United States Department of Defense
United States Marine Corps

★ 207 ★
UNITED STATES NATIONAL TRANSPORTATION SAFETY BOARD
Director of Public Affairs
Washington, D.C. 20594 (202) 426-8787

Lectures are provided on subjects relating to the Board's organizations, functions, activities, procedures, and regulations. There are no fees.

★ 208 ★
UNITED STATES POSTAL SERVICE
475 L'Enfant Plaza West, S.W.
Washington, D.C. 20260 (202) 245-4000

The Bureau schedules speakers as appropriate at public forums in the interest of the Postal Service and the public. Postal Service speakers do not accept fees or gratuities when representing the United States Postal Service.

UNITED STATES SOCIAL SECURITY ADMINISTRATION
See: United States Department of Health, Education and Welfare
Social Security Administration

★ 209 ★
UNITED STATES TRADEMARK ASSOCIATION
Six East 45th Street
New York, New York 10017 (212) 986-5880

Provides speakers on trademarks - the brand names and symbols of products and services to groups and organizations. Generally, if we are able to furnish a speaker in the area of the meeting/lecture, etc. there is no charge. Expenses might be requested if any are involved.

Titles: How Trademarks are Protected and Abused; How Trademarks are Selected; The Role of Trademarks in Advertising and Marketing on Domestic and Foreign Levels; What Trademarks Are; Why Trademarks Matter

★ 210 ★
UNITED TELECOMMUNICATIONS, INC.
Post Office Box 11315
Kansas City, Missouri 64112 (913) 384-7345

Speakers are available to lecture on a wide range of topics. No fees.

Speaker: J.F. McCarthy. Title: The Energy Question (1)
Speaker: R.V. Ward. Title: Doing Business in Saudi Arabia (2)

UNIVERSITY OF....
See: Main Element of Name

★ 211 ★
UNIVERSITY SPEAKERS BUREAU
Post Office Box 175
East Sandwich, Massachusetts
02537 (617) 888-1280

Sponsors lectures and workshops on a variety of timely topics. Fees are variable.

Speaker: Harvey A. Bender. Titles: Genes and Society; Prenatal Diagnosis of Genetic Defects (1)
Speaker: Sidney Callahan. Titles: Man/Woman Relationship; The New Women; The Once and Future Family; Sexual Revolution (2)
Speaker: Robert T. Francoeur. Titles: The Re-creation of Sex; Sex, Monogamy and the Freedom of Choice; Social Sex and the Work Ethic (3)
Speaker: Rosemary Haughton. Titles: Christian Options in a Disintegrating Culture; Community for Our Time; Educating Christians (4)
Speaker: Karen Laub Novak. Titles: The Artist's Way of Life; The Inner Way; Journeys to the Unconscious; Zen and the Artist (5)
Speaker: Michael Novak. Titles: The Awareness of God; Building a New America; The New Ethnicity; Sports as a Religion (6)

V

★ 212 ★
B. L. VAUGHAN AND ASSOCIATES
2613 Via Cordova
Carrollton, Texas 75006 (214) 242-6070

Lectures and seminars are conducted on non-verbal communication. Lecture fees are $500 plus expenses.

Speaker: B.L. Vaughan. Titles: A Greater Understanding of People Through Face and Body Language; How to Increase Your Psychic Abilities Through Face Language; Human Awareness Through Face Language (1)

★ 213 ★
VIEWPOINT SPEAKERS BUREAU
(A Division of Pathfinder Press)
410 West Street
New York, New York 10014 (212) 741-0690

Provides speakers to lecture on controversial, social, and political issues. Fees range from $300 to $1500.

Speaker: Leonard Boudin. Title: From Pentagon Papers to Cointelpro (1)
Speaker: Maceo Dixon. Title: The Fight for School Desegregation (2)
Speaker: Philip Foner. Title: The Great Labor Uprising of 1877 (3)
Speaker: Ed Heisler. Title: The Struggle for Union Democracy (4)
Speaker: Cindy Jaquith. Titles: The Attacks on Women's Rights; Feminism and Socialism (5)
Speaker: Linda Jenness. Title: Women's Liberation in Spain (6)
Speaker: Malik Miah. Title: Black Liberation and Socialism (7)
Speaker: George Novak. Title: 1776-1976 - Reform and Revolution in American History (8)
Speaker: Mary Pike. Title: The Socialist Suit Against the FBI (9)
Speaker: Andrew Pulley. Titles: Black Political Power; FBI Plot Against the Black Movement (10)
Speaker: Evelyn Reed. Titles: Is Biology Women's Destiny?; Woman's Evolution and Human Nature (11)
Speaker: Olga Rodriguez. Title: Chicano Liberation and Socialism (12)
Speaker: George Saunders. Title: Opposition Currents in the Soviet Union and Eastern Europe Today (13)
Speaker: Ralph Schoenman. Title: Blood on Their Hands (14)
Speaker: Syd Stapleton. Title: The Socialist Suit Against the FBI (15)
Speaker: Lea Tsemel. Title: Political Repression in Israel (16)
Speaker: Margaret Winter. Title: The Socialist Suit Against the FBI (17)
Speaker: Pat Wright. Titles: Black Women's Liberation; Women and the Cutbacks; Working Women and the ERA (18)

★ 214 ★
VILLANOVA UNIVERSITY
Public Relations Office
Villanova, Pennsylvania 19085 (215) 527-2100

Faculty and staff members are available to lecture on a wide variety of topics.

Accounting

Speaker: George J. Chorba. Titles: Cost Controls in Small Business; Financial Planning; Money Management; Motivation (1)
Speaker: Alvin A. Clay. Titles: Accounting Education; Careers in Accounting; International Accounting (2)

American Government and Politics

Speaker: Jeffrey W. Hahn. Titles: American Political Behavior; Candidate and Office-holder; Watergate and College Students (3)
Speaker: William Ray Heitzmann. Titles: American Jewish Voting Patterns; America's Political Cartoon Heritage (4)
Speaker: Robert W. Langran. Titles: Congress; The Constitution; The Legal Process; The Supreme Court (5)
Speaker: Thomas A. Losoncy. Title: New Frontiers Facing America (6)
Speaker: Jerome J. Niosi. Title: The Electoral College (7)

Art and Art History

Speaker: Rosalind Bloom. Titles: Realism in American Art; Women Artists (8)
Speaker: Henry B. Syvinski. Titles: Art; Religion (9)

Astronomy

Speaker: Edward M. Sion. Titles: Black Holes; Pulsars (10)

Athletics

Speaker: William Ray Heitzmann. Titles: Athletics and Academics; Basketball Coaching (11)

Black Studies

Speaker: Christopher S. Nwodo. Titles: Black Studies (12)

Business

Speaker: George J. Chorba. Title: Business Ethics (13)
Speaker: Thomas A. Losoncy. Title: Letters of Recommendation (14)

Career Opportunities

Speaker: Alvin A. Clay. Title: Accounting (15)
Speaker: June W. Lytel. Title: Journalism (16)

Civil Liberties

Speaker: Joseph Betz. Title: Civil Disobedience (17)

Communications

Speaker: June W. Lytel. Titles: Journalism; Management of School Publications (18)
Speaker: Jerome J. Niosi. Title: Teachers, Publications and Public Relations (19)

Computer Technology

Speaker: Stephen W. Ching. Title: Computer Technology (20)
Speaker: Joseph J. Hicks. Title: Computers (21)
Speaker: Thomas Scott. Title: Computers in Engineering and/or Science (22)

Consumerism

Speaker: Adolph S. Butkys. Title: Marketing and the Consumer Movement (23)
Speaker: Myrtle Feigenberg. Title: Nutrition and Consumerism (24)

Ecology

Speaker: John M. Hyson. Titles: Environmental Law; Land Use Planning (25)
Speaker: C. Michael Kelly. Title: Air Pollution Control (26)
Speaker: John J. Logue. Titles: The Fate of the Oceans; Peace, Ecology and Ocean Wealth (27)
Speaker: Lewis J. Mathers. Title: The Engineer and the Environment (28)
Speaker: Edward V. McAssey. Title: Energy Crisis and Engineering Control (29)
Speaker: Robert F. Sweeny. Title: Water Pollution Control (30)

Economics

Speaker: James J. Clarke. Title: Inflation (31)
Speaker: Joseph L. Lucia. Titles: Inflation and the Role of Government; The International Role of the Dollar (32)
Speaker: Saul Mason. Titles: Economics and Statistics; Monetary Theory; Money and Banking (33)
Speaker: Edward Mathis. Title: General Economic Conditions (34)
Speaker: Kishor Thanawala. Title: Economics (35)

Education

Speaker: William Ray Heitzmann. Title: Learning Games and Educational Simulations (36)
Speaker: Jerome J. Niosi. Titles: Declining Enrollment on Job Security; Developing Good Staff-Principal Relations; Learning Without Schools; Teachers, Publications and Public Relations (37)
Speaker: Christopher S. Nwodo. Title: Good Grades and Bad Education (38)
Speaker: John H. Schwarz. Titles: Faculty Job Exchanges; Higher Education (39)

Engineering

Speaker: Lucio Calabrese. Title: Energy Conversion (40)
Speaker: Ralph Koliner. Title: Engineering (41)
Speaker: John A. Myers. Title: Design of an Instant Coffee Plant (42)
Speaker: William J. Rice. Titles: Fluid Flow; Solar Energy (43)
Speaker: David J. Schorr. Title: The Engineer in Urban and Regional Planning (44)
Speaker: Edward M. Wallo. Title: Concrete (45)

English and Literature

Speaker: Margaret P. Esmonde. Titles: Literature for Children; Science Fiction/Fantasy Literature (46)
Speaker: John H. Schwarz. Titles: College Composition; 19th Century English Literature (47)

Ethnic Studies

Speaker: William Ray Heitzmann. Title: American Jewish Voting Patterns (48)
Speaker: Maria Plater-Zyberk. Title: Polish Civilization (49)

Foreign Countries

Speaker: Silvio E. Fittipaldi. Title: India (50)
Speaker: John H. Schwarz. Title: England (51)
Speaker: Kishor Thanawala. Title: South Asia (52)

Foreign Policy

Speaker: Jeffrey W. Hahn. Title: United States Foreign Policy (53)
Speaker: John J. Logue. Titles: The Challenge of the Expanding United Nations; Foreign Policy Alternatives (54)
Speaker: Jerome J. Niosi. Titles: American Foreign Policy; The Geopolitics of the Middle East; Peace in the Middle East? (55)
Speaker: Harry R. Strack. Title: Rhodesia and South Africa (56)

History

Speaker: William Ray Heitzmann. Title: America's Maritime Heritage (57)
Speaker: Jerome J. Niosi. Titles: American Revolution; Declaration of Independence (58)
Speaker: Maria Plater-Zyberk. Title: Polish History and Politics (59)

Hobbies

Speaker: Maria Plater-Zyberk. Title: Gardening (60)

Holidays

Speaker: George J. Chorba. Titles: Father's Day; Mother's Day (61)
Speaker: Jerome J. Niosi. Title: Memorial Day (62)

Law

Speaker: John M. Hyson. Titles: Environmental Law; Land Use Planning (63)

Mathematics

Speaker: Robert E. Beck. Titles: Decision-Making; Mathematical Sciences (64)

Mental Illness

Speaker: Bernard J. Gallagher. Title: Social and Cultural Influences on Mental Illness (65)

Modern Languages

Speaker: Charles H. Helmetag. Titles: German Drama; Walter Hasenclever: The Dramatist as Filmwriter (66)

Music

Speaker: Jerome J. Niosi. Title: Music is no Ugly Duckling (67)

Naval Science

Speaker: Thomas J. Culkin. Title: Marine and Naval Science (68)
Speaker: William Ray Heitzmann. Title: America's Maritime Heritage (69)
Speaker: James R. Johnson. Title: Naval Science (70)

Nursing and Health

Speaker: Myrtle Feigenberg. Title: Nutrition and Consumerism (71)
Speaker: Julia B. Paparella. Title: Continuing Education in Nursing (72)

Philosophy

Speaker: Joseph Betz. Titles: America and American Philosophy; American Philosophers and Natural Rights; A Philosophical Definition of Violence (73)
Speaker: Thomas A. Losoncy. Titles: Christian Humanism; Moral Character (74)
Speaker: Daniel T. Regan. Titles: American Social and Political Philosophy; New Morality (75)
Speaker: Frederick E. Van Fleteren. Title: Moral Philosophy (76)

Psychology

Speaker: David F. Bush. Titles: Family Goals and Communication; Human Needs, Goals and Financial Planning; Interpersonal Communication; Moral Judgment in Children, Youth and Adulthood; Psychological Aspects of Death and Dying (77)
Speaker: William Ray Heitzmann. Title: Behavior Modification (78)
Speaker: Paul Sheldon. Titles: Experimental Perception; Extra Sensory Perception; Human Factors Engineering (79)

Religion

Speaker: Silvio E. Fittipaldi. Titles: Christian-Catholic Theology; Christian-Jewish Relations; Oriental Religion; Religion and Psychology (80)
Speaker: Maria Plater-Zyberk. Title: Religion in Poland (81)
Speaker: Frederick E. Van Fleteren. Title: Saint Augustine (82)

Social Concerns

Speaker: Joseph Betz. Titles: Abortion; Drugs; The Just War Theory; The Justification of Revolutions; Morality and Law; Nuclear Disarmament; Theories of Punishment; Women's Liberation (83)
Speaker: Thomas A. Losoncy. Title: Abortion (84)
Speaker: Jerome J. Niosi. Title: All Men and Women are Created Equal (85)

Sociology

Speaker: Bernard J. Gallagher. Title: Social and Cultural Influences on Mental Illness (86)
Speaker: Jeffrey W. Hahn. Title: Soviet Socialization (87)

Transportation

Speaker: David J. Schorr. Title: Highway Safety (88)
Speaker: James J. Schuster. Title: Transportation (89)
Speaker: Theodore H. White. Title: The Engineer in Automobile Design and Production (90)

Villanova University

Speaker: Alvin A. Clay. Title: Villanova University (91)

Women

Speaker: Joseph Betz. Title: Women's Liberation (92)
Speaker: Rosalind Bloom. Title: Women Artists (93)
Speaker: Jerome J. Niosi. Title: Lib or Leadership (94)
Speaker: Beverly Schorr. Titles: Women and Higher Education; Women and Psychology (95)

★ 215 ★
VIRGINIA ELECTRIC AND POWER COMPANY
Post Office Box 2666
Richmond, Virginia 23261 (804) 771-4561

Offers speakers on electric energy to lecture before all types of groups and organizations. No fees.

Subjects: Conservation; Environment; Finance and Rates; Nuclear Reactors; Research and Development; Safety

★ 216 ★
VIRGINIA POLYTECHNIC INSTITUTE AND STATE UNIVERSITY
Virginia Tech Speakers Bureau
Blacksburg, Virginia 24061 (703) 951-6668

Speakers are provided to lecture on many topics throughout the state of Virginia. No fees other than reimbursement of travel expenses.

Speaker: Joseph B. Aceves. Titles: Modern Spain; Social Anthropology (1)
Speaker: Loyd D. Andrew. Titles: Education in Chile; Educational Values; Management by Objectives (2)
Speaker: Richard Arndt. Titles: Power From Space; Space Colonization (3)
Speaker: Robert C. Bates. Title: Human Cancer Viruses (4)
Speaker: Mary Ruth Bedford. Title: Dietetic Education (5)
Speaker: Albert S. Beecher. Titles: Landscaping; Plant Materials; Virginia Gardens (6)
Speaker: Wilson B. Bell. Titles: Intercollegiate Athletics and Higher Education; Private Support of Public Higher Education; Veterinary Medicine (7)
Speaker: Gilbert A. Bollinger. Titles: Earthquakes in the Southeastern United States; Earthquakes in Virginia (8)
Speaker: Kenley P. Bovard. Titles: Beef Cattle Breeding and Performance Testing; A Parent's Experiences with Mental Retardation (9)
Speaker: Roberts A. Braden. Titles: Higher Education; The Systematic Development of Instruction; Visualized Instruction (10)

Speaker: Halbert F. Brinson. Titles: Mechanical Behavior of Composites; Mechanical Behavior of Polymers; Photomechanics (11)
Speaker: J. Gordon Brown. Title: Student Affairs (12)
Speaker: Joseph J. Bryant. Titles: Careers in Journalism; Getting Your Club in the News; You and Your Land-Grant University (13)
Speaker: William C. Burleson. Titles: Public Relations and News; Serving Tech Territory; So You Want to Write News (14)
Speaker: Albin T. Butt. Titles: Effective Employment; Employee Benefit Programs; Employee Safety Programs (15)
Speaker: Dean Carter. Titles: Sculpture; Sculpture in the Landscape (16)
Speaker: Stuart K. Cassell. Title: The Development of Virginia Tech (17)
Speaker: Jerry A. Cherry. Titles: The Chicken; Poultry Science (18)
Speaker: Anne Cheney. Titles: Southern Writers; The Student/Athlete; Women Writers (19)
Speaker: George W. Claus. Titles: Helpful Bacteria; Photographing Wildflowers; Structure of Bacteria (20)
Speaker: Alan F. Clifford. Titles: Chemistry; Fluorine Compounds (21)
Speaker: James P. Clouse. Titles: Agricultural Education; Agriculture - A Vertical Frontier; Leadership (22)
Speaker: William F. Collins. Titles: Ice Cream; The Role of the Food Scientist; What Industry Expects of College Graduates (23)
Speaker: Germille Colmano. Titles: Health as Related to Light Intensity and Color; Sensation and Perception; Stress in Health and Disease (24)
Speaker: Roger E. Comely. Titles: The Elements of Menu Planning; Enjoying French and American Wines; How to Plan a Banquet (25)
Speaker: Gerald H. Cross. Titles: Pond Management; Urban Wildlife; Wildlife Management (26)
Speaker: Michael W. Crump. Titles: Effectiveness Training; Time Management; Why People Do Things (27)
Speaker: John R. Crunkilton. Titles: Conducting a Meeting; Teaching Techniques You Can Use; Teaching the Disadvantaged (28)
Speaker: James W. Dean. Titles: Career Planning; Leadership; Success in College (29)
Speaker: W.G. Devens. Titles: Careers in Engineering; Engineering Education; General Engineering (30)
Speaker: John W. Dickey. Titles: Land Use; Planning; Transportation (31)
Speaker: P.A. Distler. Titles: Dramatic Hero in the 20th Century; Racial Comedy in Vaudeville; State of Theater in America (32)
Speaker: Glen I. Earthman. Titles: Career Alternatives in Education; Trends in Educational Planning (33)
Speaker: John L. Espley. Title: Science Fiction (34)
Speaker: E.O. Essary. Titles: Cholesterol in Eggs; Eggs, Nutritional Value and Items of Interest; New Meat Product Development (35)
Speaker: George J. Flick. Titles: Marine Food Resources; Seafood Processing in Virginia; World Food Situation (36)
Speaker: William L. Flowers, Jr. Titles: Cultural Biases; National Legislative Policy; The Resident Continuing Education Center (37)
Speaker: Chester L. Foy. Titles: Pesticides, Pollution and People; Poison Ivy; Undergraduate Plant Protection Curriculum (38)
Speaker: Daniel Frederick. Title: Composites (39)
Speaker: Vicotria R. Fu. Titles: Adult-Child Interaction; Self-Concept of Children, Parents and Teachers; Sex-Role Development (40)
Speaker: A. Keith Furr. Title: Safety and Health Programs in Schools (41)
Speaker: J.C. Garrett. Titles: Community Improvement; Landscape Design; Village Redevelopment (42)
Speaker: David R. Goldfield. Titles: Can Our Cities Be Saved?; The Future of Suburbia; Virginia's Urban Past (43)
Speaker: George W. Gorsline. Titles: Computer Science at Virginia Tech; Management of ADP; What a Computer Is (44)
Speaker: Jack D. Graybeal. Title: Black Light (45)
Speaker: Paul H. Gunsten. Titles: Extramural Sport Clubs; Intramurals; Recreational Facilities at Virginia Tech (46)
Speaker: Kenneth H. Haines. Titles: The Feminist Movement; The Future of Cable Television; Tomorrow's Television Program (47)
Speaker: Laura J. Harper. Titles: Environmental Science; Is the American Family an Obsolete Institution?; Women's Roles in Modern Society (48)
Speaker: Ruth D. Harris. Titles: Career Education; Competency Based Education; Home Economics Education (49)
Speaker: William C. Havard. Titles: Liberal Arts; Nature of Southern Politics (50)
Speaker: Edmund G. Henneke. Title: Materials and Man (51)
Speaker: David E. Hill. Titles: College Youth; Leadership Development; Vocational Development (52)
Speaker: Edward G. Hoffman. Titles: Career Opportunities in the United States Air Force; History of Airpower; United States Air Force Academy (53)
Speaker: Lillian Holdeman. Titles: Botulism; Your Bacteria Keep You Company (54)

Speaker: Robert N. Holt. Title: Continuing Education (55)

Speaker: Hazel Hubbard. Titles: How to Read a Book; How to Use the Library; What the Carol Newman Library Can Do for You (56)

Speaker: Arden N. Huff. Titles: Equine Psychology; Horse Conformation; Virginia Horse Industry (57)

Speaker: Stanley A. Huffman, Jr. Titles: Flowers and Photography; Innovations in Teaching; Media and Learning (58)

Speaker: Harry H. Hull. Title: Jobs that Electrical Engineers Do (59)

Speaker: Overton R. Johnson. Titles: Togo, Northwest Africa; United States Army Reserve; Vocational Education (60)

Speaker: Thomas W. Johnson. Titles: RECON Literature Search Service; Water and Weather Data on the Computer (61)

Speaker: Wesley P. Judkins. Titles: Architecture of Flowers; Organic Gardening (62)

Speaker: Ronald E. Keister. Titles: Accounting and Accountability; Career Possibilities in the Field of Accounting; What Internal Auditing Can Do for Any Organization (63)

Speaker: Harold A. Kurstedt, Jr. Titles: Energy Alternatives; The Nuclear Power Question; Utilization of Atomic Energy (64)

Speaker: Fred M. Lamb. Titles: Furniture and Furniture Manufacturing; Job Safety and Health; Wood Use and Care in Housing (65)

Speaker: Joseph G. Lamoureux. Titles: The Highty-Tighties; Music at Virginia Tech; Music Education at Virginia Tech (66)

Speaker: Richard V. Lechowich. Title: Our Foods (67)

Speaker: John A.N. Lee. Titles: Computer Applications; Computer Appreciation; White Water Kayaking (68)

Speaker: Stephen D. Lequire. Title: Contemporary Ceramics (69)

Speaker: C. Ned Lester. Titles: Being Part of Your Community; Resources of the Extension Division (70)

Speaker: C. Hardy Long. Titles: Energy Conservation; Future of Energy; Heat Pumps and Solar Energy (71)

Speaker: Anthony Lopez. Titles: Effect of Food Processing on Nutrients in Foods; Recent Advances in Commercial Canning and Freezing of Foods; Why Additives in Foods? (72)

Speaker: Rebecca P. Lovingood. Titles: Household Appliances; Household Responsibility; Kitchen or Work Space Planning (73)

Speaker: James T. Lucas, Jr. Titles: Economy of the Peoples Republic of China; Economy of the Soviet Union (74)

Speaker: Richard L. Lynch. Titles: Cooperative Education; School-Community Relationships; Vocational Education (75)

Speaker: Robert H. McCollum. Titles: The Epidemic of Suicides; How to Live on 24 Hours a Day; Leisure Time in the 21st Century (76)

Speaker: Robert L. McConnell. Titles: Availability of Natural Resources; Economics of Recycling; Energy Prospects (77)

Speaker: Martin B. McMillion. Titles: Agricultural Education in Brazil; Getting My Article Published (78)

Speaker: James F. Marchman, III. Titles: Aircraft Noise; The Space Shuttle (79)

Speaker: Thomas J. Marlowe. Titles: Careers in Animal Science; Developing Efficient Breeding Program; Maximizing Beef Production (80)

Speaker: Harold P. Marshall. Titles: Automotive Pollution; Automotive Power Plants (81)

Speaker: Frank F. Marvin. Titles: Cartography; General Engineering (82)

Speaker: J.P.H. Mason, Jr. Titles: Agricultural Engineering as a Profession; Agricultural Engineering at Virginia Tech; Engineering in Agriculture (83)

Speaker: James R. Montgomery. Title: Post-Secondary Education in Next Ten Years (84)

Speaker: Laurence D. Moore. Titles: Effects of Air Pollution on Plants; The New Undergraduate Plant Protection Option (85)

Speaker: Robert W. Morrill. Title: Evolution of Alternative Schools (86)

Speaker: Joel A. Nachlas. Titles: IEOR in Nuclear Engineering; Industrial Engineering and Operations Research; Virginia Tech Lacrosse (87)

Speaker: Ronald J. Onega. Titles: Fusion Reactors; Nuclear Reactors (88)

Speaker: James J. Owen. Title: English Study Abroad (89)

Speaker: J.M. Oyler. Titles: Meeting the Needs for Veterinary Medical Education; Veterinary Medicine as a Career; Veterinary Medicine's Role in the Protection of Human Health (90)

Speaker: T.F. Parkinson. Titles: Nuclear Power; Nuclear Reactor (91)

Speaker: Steve R. Parson. Titles: Community Education; Community Involvement (92)

Speaker: Robert A. Paterson. Title: Biological Research in Antarctica (93)

Speaker: Alfred C. Payne. Titles: Is There a Religious Revival in Modern Russia?; Why is Everybody Suddenly Interested in Death?; Your Mental Health (94)

Speaker: Joseph C. Pitt. Titles: The Dynamics of Value Change; Philosophy and Technology; The Role of Philosophy (95)

Speaker: Robert F. Porter. Title: Art Criticism of History (96)

Speaker: Lawrence M. Potter. Titles: Poultry Nutrition; World Food Production (97)

Speaker: William Prince. Titles: Canoeing in

Virginia; Korea (98)
Speaker: Bruce R. Prouty. Titles: Estate Planning; Fire Safety in Health Facilities; Services to Small Businesses (99)
Speaker: Robert H. Pusey. Titles: Cooperative Education; State Technical Services; Technology Transfer (100)
Speaker: Ralph Ressler. Title: Career Development/Choice (101)
Speaker: James E. Roberts. Titles: Entomology; Home Garden Insects (102)
Speaker: Andrew Robeson. Titles: Public Concern About Nuclear Power; Role of Nuclear Power in Meeting the Energy Crisis; The Safety of Nuclear Power Plants (103)
Speaker: James W. Robinson. Titles: Arbitration of Labor-Management Disputes; Labor-Management Relations; Public Employee Bargaining (104)
Speaker: Jerald F. Robinson. Titles: Personnel Management; Public Employee Labor Relations (105)
Speaker: Cosby S. Rogers. Titles: Child-Rearing; Helping Children Deal with Death; Parent-Child Communications (106)
Speaker: G.E. Russell. Titles: Private Support for Higher Education; Virginia Tech Alumni Affairs; Virginia Tech Today (107)
Speaker: Joseph A. Schetz. Titles: The Love of Flight; The Space Program; What is Ocean Engineering? (108)
Speaker: Wilson E. Schmidt. Title: International Finance (109)
Speaker: Don R. Sebolt. Title: Current Trends in Physical Education (110)
Speaker: Arnold A. Sherman. Titles: American Character; American Revolution; Puritanism (111)
Speaker: Martin A. Siemoneit. Titles: The German Operetta; The Symbolist Movement in Literature and Art; The Use of Literature During Germany's Third Reich (112)
Speaker: John M. Skelly. Titles: Air Pollution in the Blue Ridge Mountains; Air Pollution - Plant Effects (113)
Speaker: Lyle H. Slack. Title: Ceramics-Fantastic New Material (114)
Speaker: Paul L. Smeal. Titles: Growing and Care of House Plants; Hobby Greenhouse Growing; Starting a Plant Growing Business (115)
Speaker: Donald W. Smith. Titles: General Surveying; Surveying Education and Opportunities; Surveying Property Lines (116)
Speaker: Wilson Snipes. Titles: Composition; Literary Criticism; Rhetoric (117)
Speaker: William E. Snizek. Title: The Cryonics Movement (118)
Speaker: Robert M. Spann. Titles: Energy; Regulation and Utilities; Tax Policies (119)
Speaker: Fred L. Spengler. Titles: The Air Force Academy; How to Establish an Organizational Training Program; Industrial Engineering as a Dynamic Profession (120)
Speaker: Richard A. Spray. Titles: Bicycle Safety; Energy-Environment-Conservation; Small Engines and You (121)
Speaker: Kenneth F. Strickland. Title: Aerobics (122)
Speaker: Robert F. Steffen. Titles: Cable Television; Instruction Development; Television in Education (123)
Speaker: Albert L. Sturm. Titles: Virginia Tech; Virginia's Constitutions (124)
Speaker: W. Robert Sullins. Titles: Developing Enthusiasm; Developing Professional Managers; Educating for the Future (125)
Speaker: George W. Swift. Title: Whitewater Paddling (126)
Speaker: Richard B. Talbot. Titles: Comparative Medicine; Veterinary Medicine; Veterinary Medicine as a Career (127)
Speaker: Larry T. Taylor. Title: Metal Ions (128)
Speaker: Thomas G. Teates. Titles: New Directions for Secondary Education?; Science Teacher Preparation; Science Teaching as a Career (129)
Speaker: D.P. Telionis. Titles: Aerodynamics of Sailing; Supersonic Flight (130)
Speaker: Vigdor L. Teplitz. Titles: Elementary Particles; Nuclear War (131)
Speaker: Marshall D. Tessnear. Titles: Emotional Difficulties and Mental Health of College Students (132)
Speaker: Ann E. Thompson. Titles: Extension and Continuing Education; Families and Communities; Professional Development (133)
Speaker: Forrest W. Thye. Titles: Athletic Performance and Nutrition; Dietary Fiber - Essential Nutrient?; Weight Control and Behavior Modification (134)
Speaker: Justo C. Ulloa. Titles: Cuban Literature; Foreign Languages and Careers; Spanish American Literature (135)
Speaker: Frans N. Van Damme. Title: Scientific Glassblowing (136)
Speaker: David H. Vaughan. Titles: Agricultural Engineering Profession; Energy in Agriculture; Solar Energy Applications in Agriculture (137)
Speaker: Jane H. Walter. Titles: Foreign Students at Virginia Tech; Intercultural Communications; Virginia Tech and Its International Programs (138)
Speaker: Anita H. Webb. Titles: Career Education; Careers in Home Economics; Metrics (139)
Speaker: Ryland E. Webb. Title: Applied Nutrition Program in Haiti (140)
Speaker: Helen L. Wells. Title: Housing is for People (141)
Speaker: Roy L. Wesley. Titles: Food Additives; Food Processing; Food Quality (142)

Speaker: Robert L. Whitelaw. Titles: Energy Conservation; The Free Market System; Transportation (143)
Speaker: Keith A. Wilkins. Titles: Communications; Journalism and the Mass Media; Meteorology (144)
Speaker: Joseph L. Wysocki. Titles: Housing Education; Housing for the Elderly; How to Buy a House (145)

W

★ 217 ★
WAR RESISTERS LEAGUE
339 Lafayette Street
New York, New York 10012 (212) 228-0450

Speakers offer lectures on war resistance and the nonviolent removal of all causes of war. Speakers' fees vary.

Speaker: William Douthard. Titles: Integration vs. Separation; Social Justice (1)
Speaker: David McReynolds. Title: Foreign Policy and Its Relationship to Pacifism, Socialism and Nonviolence (2)
Speaker: Jim Peck. Title: Nonviolent Action and Prisons (3)
Speaker: Igal Roodenko. Titles: Middle East Crisis; Nonviolence vs. Violence (4)

★ 218 ★
UNIVERSITY OF WASHINGTON
Speakers Bureau
4014 University Way, N.E.
Seattle, Washington 98105 (206) 543-9198

Arranges for lecturers to speak to community organizations, professional societies, high schools and community colleges on a great many fields. Most speakers are available without charge or for a modest fee. Often their fees go into a scholarship or research fund.

Adult Education

Title: Life-Long Learning

Affirmative Action

Titles: Assertiveness Training; Helpful Improvement Tools for Women

Africa

Titles: East African Wildlife; Social Change in Africa

Aging

Titles: Aging in Cross Cultural Perspective; Gerontology

American Ethnic Groups

Titles: Chicano History; The Legal Status and Economic Development of American Indian Tribes

Animals

Title: Pet Population Control

Anthropology

Title: Fossil Man

Archeology

Titles: Archeology of Washington State; Paleontological Field Work in Ethiopia

Architecture

Titles: Adaptation of Old Buildings to New Uses; Architectural History; Color in Interior Architecture

Art

Titles: History of Northwest Arts and Crafts; Macrame; Video Art

Asia, Far East

Titles: Japanese Theatre; Micronesia; Position of Women in China

Asia, Near East

Titles: Arabic Calligraphy; Egypt

Astronomy

Titles: How Hot is the Center of the Sun?; The Universe

Business Administration

Titles: How to Build a Work Team; The Multinational Company and Its Impact on International Relations; Real Estate Financing; Small Business Tax Problems

Career and Academic Counseling

Titles: The Job Market; Mid-Life Career Change

Cellular Sciences/Microbiology

Titles: Cell Division Research and Cancer; Human Genetic Engineering

Chemistry

Title: Border Area of Chemistry-Physics-Biology

Children/Adolescents

Titles: The Acting Bug; Adolescence; Child Abuse

Community and Public Services

Titles: Citizen Participation in Government Policy Making; School-Community Relations

Computers

Titles: Computer Simulation of Health Care Systems; Computers and the Privacy Issue

Dance

Title: Dance Therapy

Dentistry

Title: Dental Health Education

Drama

Title: Play Reviews

Drugs/Alcohol

Titles: Alcoholism and Social Drinking; Psychotropic Drugs

Economics

Titles: Environmental Economics; How to Stop Inflation

Education

Titles: Alternative Education; Compulsory Education; The Use of Instructional Television in School

Energy

Titles: Siting of Nuclear Power Plants; Solar Energy

Engineering

Titles: The Development of Lasers and Their Application; Metals Have Personalities

Environment

Titles: Interactions Between Man and Natural Ecosystems; Oil Tankers on Puget Sound

Europe

Titles: European Travel of the Type That is Close to the Earth; Spain; Yugoslavia

Fisheries

Titles: Aquaculture of Salmon; Effects of Shock Waves Upon Marine Fish

Forestry/Soils

Titles: The Forest Ecosystem; Land Use Allocation; Soils of Antarctica

Gardening/Plants

Titles: Houseplants; Mineral Nutrition of Plants

Geography/Maps

Titles: The Challenge of Maps for the Visually Handicapped; Growth Poles Theory

Geology

Titles: Glacial Ages, Glaciers; Mount Baker - Increased Thermal Activity

Handicapped

Titles: Integrating Handicapped and Normal Children in the Schools; Mental Retardation

Health Care

Titles: Emergency Medicine; Family Practice

History

Titles: Aspects of History and Philosophy of Science; European Intellectual History

Hobbies

Titles: Genealogy; Home Wine-Making; Underwater Photography

India

Title: Caste and Social Change in India

Law

Titles: Civil Liberties; Crime and Punishment; Specialities in Real Estate Law: Landlord-Tenant; The Supreme Court

Libraries

Titles: Information Explosion Faced by the Health Care Practitioner; Innovative Instructional Use of Media

Literature

Titles: The Bible as Literature; Relationship Between Literature and Liturgy

Marine Biology

Title: Coral Reefs

Mass Media

Titles: The Influence of Communication Media on Attitudes; When Do We Believe Our Mass Media?

Mathematics

Title: The Mathematics of the Mayans

Medicine: Technology

Titles: Current Techniques in Nuclear Medicine; Radiation Physics in Cancer Therapy

Medicine: Theory and Research

Titles: Environmental Causes of Birth Defects; How Nerves Transmit Biological Messages in Our Body

Medicine: Treatment

Titles: Megavitamin Therapy; The Phenomenon of Pain

Military

Title: Military History

Music

Titles: The History and Application of the Wind Quintet; Music-Drama

Myths and Mythology

Title: Greek and Roman Mythology

National Parks

Title: National Parks as Islands of Wilderness

North and South America

Titles: Cuba and Castro; Galapagos and its Organisms; Travel in the Caribbean and West Indies

Northwest Animals and Plants

Titles: Fauna of Pacific Northwest National Parks; Origins and History of Washington Flora

Nuclear Topics

Titles: Radioactivity in the Marine Environment; Risks of Nuclear Power

Nursing

Titles: Critical Care Nursing; Hospital Discharge

Nutrition

Titles: Nutrition and Mental Development; Vegetarian Nutrition and Cooking

Oceanography

Titles: National Policy for the Oceans; Tectonics of Ocean Ridges

Philosophy

Titles: Indian Philosophy; Involuntary Euthanasia; Socrates

Physics

Titles: Light and Color; Subnuclear Physics

Political Science

Titles: Political and Social History in Communist East Europe; What's Happening to the Political Parties?

Pollution

Titles: Air Quality Impact Studies; Noise Pollution; Residence Time of Aerosol in the Atmosphere

Printing and Publishing

Titles: History of American Magazines; New Technologies in Graphic Arts

Psychology: Family

Titles: Family Decision Making Process; Wilderness Family in British Columbia

Psychology: General

Titles: Achievement Motivation; ESP

Psychology: Therapy

Titles: Behavior Modification in Weight Reduction; Breaking Stereotypes

Religion

Titles: Comparative Religions; The Nature of Religion and Its Study

Russia

Titles: Anti-Semitism in the Soviet Union; Life in the Soviet Union

Safety

Titles: Electrical Safety at Home and in the Hospital; Industrial Safety

Sexuality

Titles: Human Sexuality; The Nature of Romantic Love

Sociology

Titles: Basic Institutional Change; Black Socio-Political Theory

Speech

Titles: Argumentation; Obscenity and Freedom of Expression

Sports

Titles: Athletics at the University of Washington; The Bicycle and the Airplane; How to Go About Developing Your Own Exercise Program; Skin Diving

Statistics

Title: Current Statistics on Violent Deaths Among Americans

Students

Titles: Student Attrition, Stopping Out, Transferring; Student Life: Issues and Programs

Technology

Titles: Science and Public Policy; Small Victories Over Doomsday: Making Technology Work

Terminal Illness

Title: Aging at Home

Transportation

Titles: Automobile Impact on Communities; Urban Transportation Systems

University of Washington

Titles: Health Sciences at the University; The Henry Suzzallo Years at the University of Washington; The University of Washington

Urban Planning

Titles: English Villages and Human Scale in Living Environments; Urban Land Use

Women's Issues

Titles: Prenatal Education for Parents; The Professions and the Socialization of Women; Sexism in Education

★ 219 ★
WASHINGTON CORRESPONDENTS BUREAU
4101 Glenrose Street
Kensington, Maryland 20795 (301) 942-4121

A group of journalists active in major national news organizations will speak on their first-hand experiences gained by covering the politicians in congress, the White House, and the bureaucracies. Fees are negotiable.

Speaker: Ed Bradley. Title: Politics (1)
Speaker: Marian Burros. Title: Consumer Issues (2)
Speaker: Barbara Cohen. Title: National Affairs (3)
Speaker: Richard Cohen. Title: Politics (4)
Speaker: Paul Duke. Title: Politics (5)
Speaker: Carl Leubsdorf. Title: Politics (6)
Speaker: Marianne Means. Title: Politics (7)
Speaker: Bob Pierpoint. Title: Politics (8)
Speaker: Eleanor Randolph. Titles: Politics; The White House (9)
Speaker: Mark Shields. Title: Politics (10)
Speaker: Warren Weaver. Title: The Supreme Court (11)

★ 220 ★
THE WASHINGTON REPORTERS GROUP
4101 Glenrose Street
Kensington, Maryland 20795 (301) 942-4121

A group of eight senior national correspondents headquartered in Washington who are available to discuss all aspects of the United States scene - the Presidency, congress, national security, foreign affairs, economics, politics or any related topics. Speakers are available for lectures or round-table discussions involving more than one of the group. Fees are variable.

Speaker: Peter Behr. Titles: Congress; The Oil Industry (1)
Speaker: James R. Dickenson. Titles: Congress; Politics (2)
Speaker: Jack W. Germond. Titles: Domestic Issues; Politics (3)
Speaker: Oswald L. Johnston. Titles: Foreign Policy; National Security (4)

Speaker: Harry Kelly. Titles: Congress; Law Enforcement; Politics (5)
Speaker: Tom Ottenand. Title: Politics (6)
Speaker: Frank Swoboda. Title: Economic Policy (7)
Speaker: Jules Witcover. Title: Politics (8)

★ 221 ★
IRV WEINER PROGRAMS, INC.
1236 Great Plain Avenue
Needham, Massachusetts 02192 (617) 449-1220

Presents lectures on magic, ESP, and psychological persuasion. Fees range from $700 to $850 based upon the details of the engagement.

Speaker: Irv Weiner. Titles: An Evening With Irv Weiner; Mr. Fingers, Artist in Residence; Mr. Fingers Goes to College; The Mr. Fingers Show (1)

★ 222 ★
WESTERN ELECTRIC COMPANY
Speakers Bureau
222 Broadway, Room 1407
New York, New York 10038 (212) 571-2637

Offers services of six hundred speakers on topics related to energy. There are no fees.

Titles: Calling on Science; Great Inventions; Human Factors Engineering; Laser; Metric System; Our American Heritage; Saving Energy; Solar Energy; Western Electric

★ 223 ★
WESTERN WASHINGTON UNIVERSITY
Bellingham, Washington 98225 (206) 676-3350

Faculty and administrators of the University provide lectures on almost any topic to clubs, civic groups, schools and other organizations.

Affirmative Action

Speaker: Mary Robinson. Title: Affirmative Action-Equal Opportunity (1)

Americana

Speaker: Laurence W. Brewster. Title: Abraham Lincoln the Speaker (2)
Speaker: Roscoe L. Buckland. Titles: The American and the Australian Outlaw; America's Three Most Popular Novelists; The Anglo-Saxon Myth in America; Three Romantic Heroines of the Wild West (3)

Astronomy

Speaker: Robert J. Quigley. Titles: Black Holes; Intelligent Life in the Universe; Modern Cosmology; Quasars and Pulsars; Relativity and the Non-scientists (4)

Climate

Speaker: Howard J. Critchfield. Title: Is the Climate Changing? (5)

Collective Bargaining

Speaker: Jon Monat. Titles: Collective Bargaining in Higher Education; Collective Bargaining in the Public Sector; Compensation Practices; Fair Employment Practices; Methods of Dispute Settlement in Employment; Personnel Administration (6)

Education

Speaker: Sharon Barnett. Titles: The Child Development Association; Competency-Based On-Site Learning in Early Childhood Education (7)
Speaker: Roscoe L. Buckland. Title: What Is a Bachelor's Degree? (8)
Speaker: Francis Hildebrand. Title: The Most Pressing Shortcoming of the Public Schools (9)
Speaker: James W. Scott. Title: Oxford, Cambridge and British Higher Education (10)
Speaker: Mary W. Watrous. Title: New Happenings in the High School (11)

Environment

Speaker: Steve Craig. Title: Whatcom County at the Crossroads (12)
Speaker: Robert S. Helgoe. Title: The Psychological Effects of Freeway Noises (13)
Speaker: Robert L. Monahan. Title: Suburban Development and Utopia (14)
Speaker: Ronald J. Taylor. Titles: Pollution Problems in Whatcom County; Wild Flowers and Plant Communities (15)
Speaker: Manfred C. Vernon. Title: Legal Problems of the Sea Around Us (16)

Foreign Affairs

Speaker: Harley E. Hiller. Titles: Canada, Past and Present; Development of Latin America (17)
Speaker: Ingeborg Paulus. Title: South African Apartheid (18)
Speaker: Mary Robinson. Title: Women in the Middle East (19)
Speaker: R.E. Stannard. Title: Foreign Correspondent (20)

Speaker: Manfred C. Vernon. Titles: Problems of the Middle East Today; United States Foreign Policy Today (21)

Government and Politics

Speaker: Michael W. Barnhart. Titles: One Man's View of the Washington State Legislature; The Politics of Social Change (22)
Speaker: James Davis. Titles: The Democratic National Committee; The President and Congress; Road to the White House; Watergate and Impeachment (23)

Health

Speaker: Salvatore F. Russo. Title: Chemistry of Hemoglobin (24)

Journalism

Speaker: R.E. Stannard. Title: Journalism Studies and Careers (25)

People

Speaker: Roscoe L. Buckland. Titles: Calendar and Culture; Living on the Frontier; They Never Really Owned the Land (26)

Poetry

Speaker: Knute R. Skinner. Title: Poetry Readings (27)

Population

Speaker: James W. Scott. Titles: Demographic and Socio-Economic Aspects of the Third World; World Population Growth (28)

Sports and Recreation

Speaker: Margaret Aitken. Title: Creative Playgrounds for Children (29)
Speaker: Francis Hildebrand. Title: Kayaking as a Sport for Those Over 35 (30)

Technology

Speaker: Clyde Hackler. Title: Technology at WWSC (31)

Travel and Exploration

Speaker: Howard J. Critchfield. Title: South African Landscapes (32)
Speaker: K. Peter Harder. Title: A Tourist's View of Soviet Economic Life (33)
Speaker: Francis Hildebrand. Titles: The Alaska Highway and McKinley National Park; Kayaking and Rafting Rivers; Under the Ocean Near Guam (34)
Speaker: Robert L. Monahan. Title: Leprechauns and Forests (35)
Speaker: Ingeborg Paulus. Titles: An East African Safari; East and South Africa; New Zealand (36)
Speaker: Maurice Schwartz. Titles: A Bellingham Geologist in Greece; Research Submarine Dive on Cobb Seamount (37)

Women

Speaker: Mary Robinson. Title: Concerns of Women (38)

★ 224 ★
WHITTIER COLLEGE
Whittier, California 90608 (213) 693-0771

Offers speakers in many fields to lecture to service organizations, women's clubs, and other such type groups in local areas. Fees vary.

Speaker: Maurine Behrens. Titles: Child Development; Fear of Success; Psychological Treatment (1)
Speaker: Phil Beukema. Titles: Dynamics of Management; System-Level Values (2)
Speaker: Donald Breese. Title: Popular Music of the 1920's (3)
Speaker: John F. Dean. Titles: Make Way for the Walking Wounded; Now Have Enough Things Black (4)
Speaker: Malcolm F. Farmer. Titles: Anthropology; Technology in Education (5)
Speaker: Stephen Gothold. Title: Music (6)
Speaker: Howard Harrison. Titles: American Foreign Policy; Chinese Foreign Policy; People's Republic of China (7)
Speaker: Richard B. Harvey. Titles: California Politics; General College Affairs; National Politics (8)
Speaker: Hilmi Ibrahim. Titles: Arab-Israeli Conflict; Islam; Leisure Problems (9)
Speaker: Lois James. Title: Macadamia Nuts in California (10)
Speaker: Jonathan Moody. Titles: Contemporary Religious Movements; Hare Krishna; Religious Ethics (11)
Speaker: Emelie Olson-Prather. Titles: Career vs. Motherhood; A Cross-Cultural Look at Human Sexuality; Home-care vs. Child Care; Minority Environment (12)
Speaker: Dallas Rhodes. Title: Environmental Geology (13)
Speaker: Ronald Roston. Titles: Compulsive Gambling; Ethics of Psychologists; Psychological Testing; Psychology of Dreams and Dreaming (14)
Speaker: Larry Thomas. Titles: Advertising; Political Campaigning; Public Relations for Small

Businesses; Urban Administration (15)
Speaker: Richard Thomson. Titles: The Importance of an Alumnus; The Plight of the Independent College (16)
Speaker: Richard H. Winters. Titles: The Bible; Estate Planning; Philosophy; Religion (17)

★ 225 ★
LOLA WILSON CELEBRITIES
139 South Beverly Drive
Beverly Hills, California 90212 (213) 278-8808

Makes available an annual roster of speakers who are prepared to lecture on various topics. Fees range from $400 to $2500 plus travel expenses.

Speaker: Richard Armour. Titles: A Light Look at Life; A Satirist at Work (1)
Speaker: James Bacon. Title: Hollywood and the International Jet Set (2)
Speaker: Murray Banks. Title: Anyone Who Goes to a Psychiatrist Should Have His Head Examined (3)
Speaker: Joyce Brothers. Title: Family Relations (4)
Speaker: Corinne Calvet. Titles: The Abuse of Women in Movies; How Visualization Made Me a Star; Sex, Spirit, and the Fountain of Youth; The Use of Color for the Control of Emotions (5)
Speaker: Canary. Title: Insights into the Male vs. Female Psyche (6)
Speaker: Scott Carpenter. Titles: The Future of Ocean Exploration; The Future of Space Activity (7)
Speaker: David Chagall. Titles: Luring the Robots; Why a Liberated Woman Makes for a Liberated Man (8)
Speaker: Criswell. Titles: Nostradamus' Forbidden Predictions; Your Incredible Future (9)
Speaker: Gisele Dallan. Titles: A Key to Self-Change; Man, Know Thyself! (10)
Speaker: Bruce Davis. Title: Alex Haley (11)
Speaker: Daryl D. Dayton. Titles: Asian Influences on American Music; Black Music in America; Twentieth Century American Music (12)
Speaker: William Fagan. Titles: Fertile Fields for Jobs; Techniques for Pushing Goods and Services (13)
Speaker: Stephen Fiske. Title: Songwriting (14)
Speaker: Anthony Forsythe. Titles: Current Trends in Decor; Economy in Decorating (15)
Speaker: Sydney Garfield. Title: Teeth (16)
Speaker: Joen Gladich. Titles: A Key to Self-Change; Man, Know Thyself! (17)
Speaker: Paul Gregory. Title: Perception Dynamics (18)
Speaker: Leo Guild. Title: A Book in Everyone's Life (19)
Speaker: Joyce Jillson. Titles: Getting What You Want With Astrology; How Astrology Can Help You Find Your Ideal Mate (20)
Speaker: David N. Kaye. Titles: The Cashless Society; The Computer and Electronics; The Home of the Future (21)
Speaker: Mary Lester. Titles: The Care and Consumption of Wines; How to Get the Best Wine Buy Moneywise (22)
Speaker: William Lester. Title: Capitalism and Socialism; The Face of Love (23)
Speaker: Halla Gudmundsdottir Linker. Titles: I Married Adventure; Vikings of My Iceland; Women of the World (24)
Speaker: H. Leith Loder. Titles: Body Language; The Trick of Selling Anything (25)
Speaker: Beatrice Lydecker. Titles: Communicate With Each Other; Emotional Problems of Animals (26)
Speaker: Patricia Manning. Title: Women of All Ages (27)
Speaker: Pamela Mason. Title: A Celebrity Speaks (28)
Speaker: Maxine Ordesky. Title: Reasons for Disorganization (29)
Speaker: Peter Mark Richman. Title: The Relationship and Difference Between Acting for Stage, Television and Films (30)
Speaker: Roberta Ritter. Title: Medical Malpractice (31)
Speaker: Cavett Robert. Title: Are You the Cause or the Result? (32)
Speaker: David St. Clair. Titles: Healing; How to Develop Your Psychic Abilities (33)
Speaker: Froma Sand. Titles: How to Overcome Loneliness; How to Recognize and Deal With Guilt (34)
Speaker: Wyn Sargent. Title: The Headhunters in Central Borneo and the Cannibals in West Irian (35)
Speaker: David J. Stevens-Allen. Titles: Our Foreign Policy of Ruin; Why We Can't Reform Government (36)
Speaker: Anne Strick. Titles: How to Win in a No-win System; The Myth of the Impartial Judge and Jury (37)
Speaker: Champion K. Teutsch. Titles: Reach Your Goals; Solve Your Problems (38)
Speaker: Paul Wallace. Titles: Dance in the American Musical Theater; The Dancer Preparing for a Career in Musical Comedy (39)
Speaker: Larry Wilde. Titles: The Art of Wit and Humor; What's Funny and Why? (40)
Speaker: William Winter. Title: Interpreting Today's World Headlines (41)
Speaker: Donna Workman. Titles: Carl Sandburg: Citizen, Writer; Carl Sandburg's Place in American Literature; Literary Influences (42)

Speaker: Sean Wright. Title: An Evening With Sherlock Holmes (43)
Speaker: Betty Wuliger. Title: Everything You Want to Know About Money (44)

★ 226 ★

WISCONSIN ELECTRIC POWER COMPANY
231 West Michigan Street
Milwaukee, Wisconsin 53201 (414) 277-2876

Provides lecturers on issues concerning nuclear power, alternate energy sources, the energy situation, and all other issues related to electric utility operation and the free enterprise system. All lectures provided free of charge.

Speaker: Jon C. Lundgren (1)

★ 227 ★

THE WOMEN'S CLASSICAL CAUCUS
c/o Professor Sarah B. Pomeroy
Department of Classics
Hunter College, CUNY
695 Park Avenue
New York, New York 10021 (212) 570-5566

The Women's Classical Caucus has recently organized a speakers bureau comprised of women who are experts in the fields of classical literature, history, religion, and archaeology. The bureau makes available to interested departments, groups, and institutions, the names, qualifications, and areas of expertise of women who are willing to lecture in the United States and Canada. Fees are variable.

Speaker: Helen H. Bacon. Titles: Aeneid; Greek Tragedy; Petronius; Robert Frost and the Classics (1)
Speaker: Sylvia Barnard. Title: Hellenistic Women Poets (2)
Speaker: Jean Rhys Bram. Titles: Greek and Roman History; Greek and Roman Mythology; Greek and Roman Religion (3)
Speaker: Valerie Broege. Titles: Catullus; Classical Mythology; Classical Themes in Science Fiction; The Classics and Images of America; The Classics and Popular Culture; Heroes and Hero Worship; History and Practice of Astrology; Women in Antiquity (4)
Speaker: Linda Clader. Titles: Helen of Troy; Poetic Immortality (5)
Speaker: Jenny Strauss Clay. Titles: Homer; Vergil (6)
Speaker: Dee Lesser Clayman. Titles: Hellenistic Poetry and Literary Criticism; Staging of Greek Tragedy; Uses of the Computer in Classical Scholarship (7)
Speaker: Phyllis Culham-Ertman. Titles: Greek and Latin Epigraphy; Greek History; Roman History (8)
Speaker: Ann Deagon. Titles: Panels on Creative Process; Poetry Readings; Poetry Workshops; The Poet as Woman (9)
Speaker: Sheila K. Dickison. Titles: Social History of Women in Antiquity; Tacitus (10)
Speaker: Gertrude Drake. Titles: Boethius; The Golden Ass; Mythology; Structured/Integrated Liberal Arts Programs; Vida's Christiad (11)
Speaker: Elizabeth A. Fisher. Titles: The Greeks and Latin Literature; Roman Literature in the Thirteenth-Century; Women in Sixth-Century Byzantium (12)
Speaker: Ruth Gais. Title: Classical Archaeology (13)
Speaker: Elizabeth R. Gebhard. Titles: Actors and Acting in the Ancient Theatre; Classical Archaeology; Greek and Roman Theatre; Mixed Theatres of the Empire; Stobi (14)
Speaker: Barbara K. Gold. Titles: Euripides; Mythology; Roman Lyric and Elegy; Roman Satire (15)
Speaker: Diane R. Gordon. Titles: Classical Mythology; Religion in the Ancient World; Women in History and Literature (16)
Speaker: Carola Greengard. Titles: Greek Tragedy; Hesiod; Homer and/or Early Babylonian Epic; Pindar (17)
Speaker: Judith P. Hallett. Titles: Ancient Attitudes Towards Sexuality and Bodily Functions; Ancient Greek Athletics; Etymology; The Family in Antiquity; Latin Literature; Teaching of Latin; Women in Antiquity (18)
Speaker: Karelisa Hartigan. Titles: Greek Drama; Myth in Modern Greek Poetry; Women in the Homeric World (19)
Speaker: Dorothy K. Hill. Title: Classical Archaeology (20)
Speaker: Phyllis B. Katz. Titles: Ancient Art and Myth; Ancient Women; Comparative Mythology; Lyric Poetry; Structuralism and the Classics (21)
Speaker: Eva C. Keuls. Title: Matrons and Misogynists (22)
Speaker: Barbara E. Killian. Titles: Latin; The Modern Student and Roman Satire; Ovid, The Wit of the Augustan Age; Roman Festivals; What Would Juvenal Say Today (23)
Speaker: Joy K. King. Titles: Propertius' Literary Programme; Tradition and Originality in Propertius' Monobiblos; The Unity of the Monobiblos; Women in Greek and Roman Literature; Women in Roman Elegy (24)
Speaker: Frances Coulborn Kohler. Titles: History of Classics in America; History of Greek and Roman Theater; Realism in Euripides; Structuralist

Approaches to Drama; Women in Ancient Greece (25)
Speaker: Ann Olga Koloski-Ostrow. Titles: Influence of Classics on English Literature; Pompeii and Herculaneum; Topography and Archaeology of Rome (26)
Speaker: Carol D. Lanham. Titles: Latin Letter-Writing; Medieval Latin (27)
Speaker: Mary R. Lefkowitz. Titles: Attitudes Toward Women in Antiquity; Greek Lyric Poetry; Women in Mythology (28)
Speaker: Julia W. Loomis. Titles: Classical Mythology; Conservatism; Cyprus in Modern Greek Poetry; Greek - An Ongoing Language From Ancient to Modern Times; Homer, the First Psychologist; The Image of Woman in 17th Century Metaphysical Poets; The Power of Women in First C. B. C. Roman Life (29)
Speaker: Sherry Marker. Titles: Byzantine Art; Greek and Roman History and Historiography (30)
Speaker: Mary Ella Milham. Titles: Apicius' Roman Cookbook; Platina; The Roman Geographers (31)
Speaker: Judith deLuce More. Titles: Ancient Forms of Sculpture; Ancient Law; Aspects of Ancient Town Planning; Aspects of Classical Influences on American Culture; Ovid's Metamorphoses (32)
Speaker: Kathleen Morgan. Titles: Latin Poetry; Mythology; Women in Antiquity (33)
Speaker: Martha C. Nussbaum. Titles: Ancient Philosophy; Greek Ethics; Nietzsche and Tragedy (34)
Speaker: Mary Kay Gamel Orlandi. Titles: Augustan Literature; Frivolous Narrative; Ovid; Pompeiian Mythological Painting (35)
Speaker: Jane E. Phillips. Title: Roman Mothers and the Lives of Their Adult Children (36)
Speaker: Sarah B. Pomeroy. Titles: Ancient History and Demography; Education of Women; Greek and Roman Women; Hellenistic Women (37)
Speaker: Jennifer Robert. Titles: Ancient History; Ancient Impeachment Proceedings; Ancient Views on the Value of Democracy; Athenian Democracy; Homer; Teaching Classics (38)
Speaker: Mary Ann Rossi. Titles: Euripidean Drama; Greek Art and Architecture; Greek Religion; Hellenistic Poetry; Reassessment of Status of Women in the Ancient World; Stoicism in Ancient Literature (39)
Speaker: Catharine P. Roth. Titles: History of Greek; History of Latin; Homer (40)
Speaker: Nancy F. Rubin. Titles: Semiotics in Literary Criticism; Structural Analysis of Myth; Typology of Myths (41)
Speaker: Jo-Ann Shelton. Titles: Chariot Racing in Imperial Rome; Seneca's Tragedies (42)
Speaker: Jane M. Snyder. Titles: Aspects of Greek Music; Epicureanism; Lucretius (43)
Speaker: Cora Angier Sowa. Titles: Ancient Myths in Modern Movies; Computer Applications in the Study of Literature; Holy Places; Science as a Mythology (44)
Speaker: Kay E. Stein. Titles: Alexander the Great; Archaeology of Classical and Hellenistic Greece; Archaeology of Crete and Mycenae; Holy Land Archaeology (45)
Speaker: Kathryn A. Thomas. Titles: Classical Numismatics; Classical Sites; Early Greek Lyric Poetry and Philosophy (46)
Speaker: Ruth S. Thomas. Titles: Polyphemus in Folktale, Homer, Literature and Art; Roman Engraved Gems (47)
Speaker: Carol Law Trachy. Titles: Artemis and the Women's Religion; The Goddesses of Greece; The Gorgon and the Gorgoneion; The Virgin in Greek Society; Women in Greek Drama; Women in Mythology (48)
Speaker: S.M. Treggiari. Title: Social History (49)
Speaker: Vera F. Vanderlip. Title: The Egyptian Hellenistic Cults (50)
Speaker: Winnie Frohn Villeneuve. Titles: Alexander Aphrodisiensis; The Greek Commentators on Aristotle and Their Method; The Presocratics; The Use of the Computer and Statistics in Literature and Linguistics (51)
Speaker: Cherryl A. Wagner. Title: Propaganda of the Augustan Age (52)
Speaker: Valerie M. Warrior. Title: Topography of Rome (53)
Speaker: Nancy Wiggers. Titles: Hellenistic Women Writers; Propertius (54)
Speaker: Nancy C. Wilkie. Titles: Archaeological Methodology; The Tholos Tomb at Nichoria (55)

★ 228 ★
WOMEN'S MARTIAL ARTS UNION
Post Office Box 879
New York, New York 10025 (212) 868-3380

Provides lectures and demonstrations on self-defense and the martial arts to women's groups. Fees are variable.

Titles: Judo; Karate; The Martial Arts; Rape and Self-Defense; Self-Defense; Tai Chi Ch'uan

★ 229 ★
WORLD MODELING ASSOCIATION
Post Office Box 100
Croton-on-Hudson, New York 10520 (914) 737-8512

Speakers offer lectures on beauty, nutrition, exercise, body language, oral communications, modeling,

photography, dancing, physical fitness, hairstyling, makeup, and public relations. Fees range from $150 to $500, plus expenses.

Speaker: Raymond Acton. Title: How to Dress Better for Less Money (1)
Speaker: Rachael Ewell. Title: Your Image and Self Motivation (2)
Speaker: Lisa Hoener. Title: Your Attitude Can Make You Young (3)
Speaker: Lisa Ferris Rubin. Title: In the Flow of Beauty (4)
Speaker: Ruth Tolman. Title: The Corner Stones of Success for Women in Business (5)

★ 230 ★
WORLD VISION INTERNATIONAL
919 West Huntington Drive
Monrovia, California 91016 (213) 357-1111

Speakers are available to lecture on areas such as world hunger, poverty, preaching and missions to churches and civic groups.

Speakers: F. Carlton Both (1); Patricia Chavez (2); Edward R. Dayton (3); Ted W. Engstrom (4); Edward L. Gruman (5); George E. Hahn (6); Samuel Kamaleson (7); Robert W. Latta (8); William E. Lundberg (9); Donald D. Maddox (10); W. Herbert Scott (11)

Y

★ 231 ★
YOUTH LIBERATION PRESS, INC.
2007 Washtenaw Avenue
Ann Arbor, Michigan 48104 (313) 995-4575

Lecturers are provided to speak on various issues relating to the rights of young people. Travel expenses and small honorariums ($25-$250).

Speaker: Al Autin. Title: A Young Person's Perspective on the Rights of Young People (1)
Speaker: Diana Autin. Title: The Legal Rights of Students and Young People (2)
Speaker: Keith Hefner. Titles: The Children's Rights Movement; The High School Underground Press; Student Rights; What is Young People's Liberation? (3)

SECTION II

SPEAKER INDEX

This index is an alphabetical listing of all the lecturers whose services may be arranged for, followed by the entry numbers for the speakers bureaus, and then the speaker code numbers in parentheses. These numbers refer users to descriptive entries in Section I, Speakers and Lecturers: How to Find Them.

For detailed instructions on the use and organization of this volume, see "Organization of the Volume," page vi, and "How to Use this Book," page vii.

SPEAKER INDEX

A

Aaron-Taylor, Susan 79 (1)
Abdullah, Yahya Sharif 1 (1)
Abel, Rudy E. 49 (1)
Abeles, Tom 163 (1)
Abend, Martin 71 (176)
Abernathy, Ralph 71 (117)
Abler, Ronald 151 (183)
Abraham, Lynn 176 (1)
Abrahams, Allen C. 138 (1)
Abrahams, Vivian 160 (1)
Abrams, Arnold G. 180 (1)
Abroms, Edward 49 (2)
Aceves, Joseph B. 216 (1)
Ackerman, Robert K. 52 (1)
Acton, Raymond 229 (1)
Adair, Doug 83 (1)
Adam, Heribert 171 (1)
Adams, Bill 180 (2)
Adams, Ernestyne James 181 (201), (256), (308)
Adams, Gerard 176 (2)
Adams, James D. 151 (231)
Adams, Murray C. 16 (1)
Adamsky, Richard A. 181 (89)
Adato, Perry Miller 49 (3)
Adelman, Richard C. 181 (13)
Adrosko, Rita J. 79 (2)
Affleck, William 49 (4)
Agabashian, Fred 33 (1)
Agate, Paul B. 151 (275)
Agronsky, Martin 71 (11), 112 (1), 135 (1),
Ahmad, Imam Masud 1 (2)
Ahmad, Mubashir 1 (3)
Ahmad, Rashid 1 (4)
Aitken, Margaret 223 (29)
Aker, F. David 181 (14)
Akers, Jack 173 (1)
Akers, Jean Palmer 42 (123)
Albert, Carl 71 (118)
Albert, Mary 71 (12)
Albert, Roslyn B. 136 (16)
Albertson, Jack 130 (1)
Albertson, Robert G. 159 (1)
Albi, Dominick 49 (5)
Albin, Bob 177 (1)
Albin, Marvin 117 (14)
Albinski, Henry S. 151 (189)
Alcorn, Gordon 159 (2)
Alcorn, Pat B. 136 (7)
Alexander, Bruce 171 (44)
Alexander, Marlene M. 65 (1)
Alexander, Marthann 79 (3)
Alexander, Shana 156 (1)
Allen, Craig G. 105 (65)
Allen, E.D. 171 (22)
Allen, Lewis 49 (6)
Allen, Mel 71 (203)
Allen, Ruthann 4 (1)
Allerup, N.P. 145 (1)
Alley, John 4 (2)
Allison, Priscilla H. 151 (61)
Alpers, Kenneth E. 67 (1)
Altmann, Anneliese 171 (45)
Ambruster, David L. 151 (35)
Ameringer, Charles D. 151 (213)
Ames, Kenneth A. 168 (1)
Ammond, Alene 176 (3)
Amory, Cleveland 97 (1)
Anderson, Arlynn L. 168 (2)
Anderson, Eulalee L. 57 (1)
Anderson, Garry G. 168 (3)
Anderson, Howard M. 180 (3)
Anderson, Jack 112 (2), 135 (2), 156 (2), 176 (4)
Anderson, Jeorgia 79 (4)
Anderson, Marian 154 (1)
Anderson, Martin 85 (1)
Anderson, Tom 6 (1)
Andrew, George 160 (2)
Andrew, Loyd D. 216 (2)
Andrzejewski, Julie 168 (4)
Anoff, Philip 130 (2)
Anthony, Frank 151 (62)
Anton, Paul 159 (3)
Antonio, Louis 49 (7)
Apke, Thomas M. 29 (191)
Aptheker, Herbert 71 (119)
Arble, William C. 151 (260)
Arceneaux, Clayton J. 174 (1)
Arch, James 135 (3), 180 (4)
Ardrey, Robert 112 (3)
Arledge, Roone 71 (204)
Armour, Richard 225 (1)
Armstrong, Ken 59 (1)
Armstrong, Neil 177 (2)
Arndt, Richard 216 (3)
Arnold, Jack 49 (8)
Arnold, James W. 105 (66)
Aronson, Nicole 56 (60), (90), (111)
Arthur, Guy B., Jr. 180 (5)
Asbury, William W. 151 (1)
Ashburn, Richie 176 (5)
Asija, Satya Pal 180 (6)
Askew, Raymond S. 16 (2)
Aslup, Robert F. 117 (36)
Asp, Carolyn 105 (16), (123)
Aten, Dennis 57 (2)
Atkin, Kenward L. 29 (33)
Atkins, Ferrel 57 (3)
Atwood, Walter F. 7 (1)
Auerbach, Gerald 49 (9)
Auerbach, Larry 49 (10)
Auld, Dennis 44 (1)
Aurand, Harold W. 151 (36)
Austin, Joan F. 79 (5)
Autin, Al 231 (1)
Autin, Diana 231 (2)
Autrey, Kenneth M. 16 (3)
Averbach, Bonnie 181 (1), (148)
Ayaga, Odeyo O. 181 (25), (90), (257), (331)

B

Baars, Theo D., Jr. 65 (2)
Baarsma, William 159 (4)
Babcock, Russell 143 (1)
Bachner, Annette 49 (11)
Bacon, Helen H. 227 (1)
Bacon, James 225 (2)
Badham, John 49 (12)
Baenninger, Ronald 181 (281)
Bagley, Worth H. 97 (2)
Bagrash, Frank M. 29 (85), (169), (229), (264)
Bailey, C. Ian 29 (86), (130), (299)
Bailey, Charles W. 131 (1)
Bailey, Ed 49 (13)
Bailey, F. Lee 156 (3), 177 (3)
Bailey, Harry A., Jr. 181 (26), (32), (202), (258)
Bailey, Paul M. 123 (1)
Bailey, Wilford S. 16 (4)
Baker, Dan 177 (4)
Baker, E.G. Stanley 52 (2)
Baker, Ira 56 (61)
Baker, James F. 49 (14)
Baker, Jerry 97 (3)
Baker, Mary 79 (6)
Baker, Norman 69 (1)
Baker, Russell 102 (1)
Baker, Sam 173 (2)
Bakr, Mamdouh 105 (116)
Balash, Muriel 49 (15)
Bale, Bob 180 (7)
Ball, F. Carlton 159 (5)
Ball, John K. 49 (16)
Ball, Lawrence C. 173 (3)
Ball, Maurcy 130 (3)
Balla, John C. 143 (2)
Bandera, Vladimir N. 181 (33), (203), (332)
Banerji, Ranan B. 181 (204)
Banister, Eric 171 (23)
Bank, Rose S. 79 (7)
Bank, Ted P., II 4 (3)
Banks, Clyde M. 65 (3)

Banks, Murray 112 (4), 177 (5), 225 (3)
Banow, Joel N. 49 (17)
Banzhaf, Parker C. 65 (4)
Baraka, Imamu Amiri 42 (11), (52)
Baran, Ernest 181 (155)
Barbee, Charles L. 49 (18)
Barber, Charles M. 142 (1)
Barish, Natalie 29 (113), (131), (170), (265)
Barkatullah, Qazi M. 1 (5)
Barnard, Daniel P. 173 (4)
Barnard, Sylvia 227 (2)
Barnes, Ben B. 16 (5)
Barnes, Clive 71 (1), 156 (4)
Barnes, Gordon 135 (4)
Barnett, Dick 71 (205)
Barnett, Sharon 223 (7)
Barnett, Suzanne W. 159 (6)
Barnhart, Michael W. 223 (22)
Baron, Allen 49 (19)
Baron, Carole M. 94 (1)
Barone, Marian T. 181 (2), (91)
Barone, Thomas F. 151 (123)
Barret, Clotilde 79 (8)
Barrett, Rona 71 (13)
Barrow, Willie 42 (12), (124)
Barry J. Robert 174 (2)
Barry, Mary E. 16 (6)
Barry, Paul 52 (3)
Bartel, Paul 49 (20)
Barth, John 71 (80)
Bartlett, Charles 97 (4)
Bartlett, Gary E. 168 (5)
Barto, Gordon 49 (21)
Barton, Michael 151 (214)
Barton, R.B. 117 (15), (107)
Bass, Saul 49 (22)
Bass, William T. 174 (3)
Bassman, Michael F. 56 (112)
Bastianutti, Diego 160 (3)
Bateman, Py 62 (1)
Bates, Robert C. 216 (4)
Bates, Ronald 180 (8)
Batra, Gopal K. 181 (156), (205), (333)
Batten, Hal J. 180 (9)
Batten, J.W. 56 (98)
Batten, Joe 112 (5), 135 (5), 177 (6), 180 (10)
Bauby, Cathrina 112 (6), 177 (7), 180 (11)
Bauer, Joe 180 (12)
Baum, Eric C. 67 (2)
Bauman, Dwight M. 31 (17), (40)
Baumann, Rich 67 (3)
Bauska, Barry 159 (7)
Bayh, Birch 112 (7), 176 (6)
Bayh, Marvella 97 (5)
Beach, James W. 151 (26)
Beale, Betty 112 (8)
Beall, John 57 (4)
Beaman, Frank 42 (36)
Beard, Timothy 154 (2)
Beasley, Edward 112 (9)
Beasley, Wayne T. 117 (64), (99)
Beattie, James M. 151 (19)
Beatty, Durwood 117 (1)
Beatty, John W. 151 (88)
Beavan, Gerald F. 127 (1)
Beaver, James E. 159 (8)
Beaver, Joseph C. 142 (2)
Beck, Edward S. 151 (161)
Beck, Ivan 160 (4)
Beck, Robert E. 214 (64)
Becker, Louis 142 (3)
Becker, Lucille F. 52 (4)
Beckman, William C. 174 (4)
Bedell, John W. 29 (280), (340)
Bedford, Mary Ruth 216 (5)
Beecher, Albert S. 216 (6)
Beecroft, Jay 177 (8)
Behlmer, Rudolph 49 (23)
Behr, Peter 220 (1)
Behrens, Maurine 224 (1)
Behrens, Peter J. 115 (203)
Belfer, Nancy 79 (9)
Bell, Mary A. 142 (4)
Bell, Steve 176 (7)
Bell, Tony 29 (281)
Bell, Wilson B. 216 (7)
Belli, Melvin 156 (5)
Bellis, Vincent J. 56 (66)
Bellizzi, John J. 88 (1)
Bellus, Dan 112 (10), 177 (9), 180 (13)
Bench, Johnny 42 (97)
Bender, Glenn F. 174 (5)
Bender, Harvey A. 211 (1)
Bender, May 147 (1)
Benedict, Richard 49 (24)
Benjamin, Lloyd 56 (9)
Bennett, Douglas 181 (34), (259), (334)
Bennett, Lerone 71 (120)
Bennett, Lerone, Jr. 42 (37), (53)
Bennett, Millard 180 (14)
Bennett, Richard 49 (25)
Bennett, Tom 171 (31)
Bentley, Doris B. 174 (6)
Benton, Suzanne 42 (1)
Bentsen, Lloyd 71 (121)
Berenbroick, Lester 52 (5)
Berens, John F. 105 (60)
Berg, Stuart 49 (26)
Bergen, Polly 97 (6), 156 (6)
Berger, Ruth 42 (114)
Bergman, Jules 176 (8)
Bergsten, Fred 135 (6)
Berk, Ginger 176 (9)
Berke, Jacqueline 52 (6)
Berkowitz, Freida Pastor 176 (10)
Berlin, Rosalind K. 79 (10)
Berlitz, Charles 156 (7)
Berman, Harry J. 151 (17)
Bermingham, Thomas J. 65 (5)
Bernard, Clara 176 (11)
Bernstein, Carl 176 (12)
Bernstein, Jeffry A. 159 (9)
Bernstein, Paul 27 (1)
Bernstein, Ralph 176 (13)
Berry, J. Raymond 159 (10)
Berry, Keith O. 159 (11)
Berry, Thomas 11 (1)
Bess, Dolores C. 174 (7)
Best, Eleanor 79 (11)
Bettelheim, Bruno 71 (81), 156 (8)
Betz, Joseph 214 (17), (73), (83), (92)
Betzendahl, Diane 176 (14)
Beukema, Phil 224 (2)
Beverly, Sherman, Jr. 142 (5)
Bevington, Gary 142 (6)
Bhakthan, N.M.G. 171 (24)
Bhatti, Bashir Ahmad 1 (6)
Bianco, Frank 49 (27)
Bicknell, John W. 52 (7)
Biddle, Ralph T. 8 (1)
Biederman, Edwin, Jr. 151 (124)
Bierbauer, Charles 176 (15)
Bierly, George W. 151 (2)
Bierly, Woodrow 151 (63)
Bigelow, Tom 33 (2)
Biggs, James W. 117 (65), (112)
Bihl, John M. 183 (1)
Billeaud, Frances P. 174 (8)
Bilson, Bruce 49 (28)
Binder, Arnold 27 (37)
Binns, E. Mallary 12 (1)
Binns, William H., Jr. 181 (157)
Birchard, Ralph E. 26 (15), (24), (113)
Bird, Charles 160 (5)
Bird, Christopher 134 (1)
Birdy, Earl J. 31 (9), (39)
Birnbaum, Robert 49 (29)
Bishop, Paula 112 (11)
Bistis, George N. 52 (8)
Bjerre, Jens 59 (2), 69 (2)
Bjorklund, L.R. 168 (6)
Black, Harry G. 42 (54)
Black, John W. 151 (3)
Black, Sophie K. 142 (7)
Blackburn, Edna 79 (12)
Blackwell, Duey 182 (1)

SPEAKER INDEX

Blair, Charles W. 174 (9)
Blair, Frank 156 (9)
Blair, Frank H., Jr. 143 (3)
Blakely, Henry 42 (55)
Blakely, James 112 (12)
Blanc, Mel 156 (10)
Bland, Jeffrey 159 (12)
Blanda, George 135 (7)
Blascovich, James J. 105 (99)
Blatchford, Joe 112 (13)
Blazer, Chuck 130 (4)
Bleich, Eli 49 (30)
Bleiler, Mae D. 151 (20)
Bleyer, Robert 49 (31)
Bliss, Edwin C. 180 (15)
Bloom, Arthur 49 (32)
Bloom, Mitchell 159 (13)
Bloom, Rosalind 214 (8), (193)
Blower, Kenneth E. 173 (5)
Blumberg, Dwayne D. 174 (10)
Blyth, Jack 147 (2)
Boardman, Blanche 65 (6)
Bobker, Lee 49 (33)
Bobrow, Edwin E. 180 (16)
Bohlin, Jill K. 142 (8)
Bollinger, Gilbert A. 216 (8)
Boltuck, Charles J. 168 (7)
Bond, Betty Jane 10 (1)
Bond, Margaret S. 56 (1)
Bonerz, Peter 49 (34)
Bonnell, Howard 177 (10)
Bonnette, Delta T. 174 (11)
Bonnette, Richard M. 174 (12)
Bonville, Robert E. 123 (2)
Book, Kenneth M. 132 (1)
Boone, Betty Jane 65 (7)
Boonin, Tobyann 176 (16)
Booth, F. Carlton 230 (1)
Booth, Heather 42 (148)
Booth, John 91 (1)
Booth, John N. 110 (1)
Borden, Chris 15 (1)
Borgen, Chris 71 (14)
Bork, Alfred 27 (19)
Bosner, Paul 49 (35)
Bossen, Robert H. 65 (8)
Bossing, Lewis 117 (37)
Bostick, Warren 27 (25)
Botdorf, Ruth 151 (264)
Boudin, Leonard 213 (1)
Bourke, J. David 67 (5)
Bouscaren, Anthony 14 (1)
Bovard, Kenley P. 216 (9)
Bowers, James 130 (5)
Bowers, Mary W. 142 (9)
Bowjer, Gordon 151 (253)
Bowman, Dawn 159 (14)
Boyajian, Aram 49 (36)
Boyan, Lee 180 (17)
Boyd, Ty 177 (11)
Brabant, Sarah C. 174 (13)
Brack, Harold A. 52 (9)
Braden, Roberts A. 216 (10)
Bradlee, Ben 71 (15)
Bradley, Bob 176 (17)
Bradley, David 49 (37)
Bradley, Ed 219 (1)
Bram, Jean Rhys 227 (3)
Bramlett, Gene A. 16 (7)
Branden, Nathaniel 71 (122)
Branson, Douglas M. 159 (15)
Brasseaux, Carl A. 174 (14)
Brattstrom, Bayard H. 29 (47), (69), (132), (266)
Braude, Michael 112 (14)
Braun, Vern 142 (10)
Braverman, Charles 49 (38)
Braverman, Robert 49 (39)
Breckenridge, Jay 151 (162)
Breese, Donald 224 (3)
Bregman, Buddy 49 (40)
Brehm, Anita 56 (62)
Breighner, Sandy 177 (12)
Brekke, Arnold 180 (18)
Brenk, Frederick E. 105 (17)
Brennan, Anne 11 (2)
Brennan, Peter 71 (68)
Brenner, Glenn 176 (18)
Bresler, Robert J. 151 (190)
Bresnan, Don 132 (2)
Brewer, Robert N. 16 (8)
Brewster, Laurence W. 223 (2)
Briggs, B. Bruce 71 (94)
Brigham, Edward, Jr. 91 (2)
Bringle, Edwina 79 (13)
Brinkley, David 135 (8), 156 (11), 176 (19)
Brinson, Halbert F. 216 (11)
Broadd, Harry A. 142 (11)
Broder, David S. 112 (15)
Brodey, Jean L. 181 (49), (67), (320)
Brodie, Earl D. 180 (19)
Brodsky, Ida 176 (20)
Broege, Valerie 227 (4)
Brokaw, Tom 176 (21)
Brommel, Bernard J. 142 (12)
Brooks, Benjamin 57 (5)
Brooks, Gwendolyn 42 (56)
Brooks, Lois Ziff 79 (14)
Brothers, Joyce 42 (88), 112 (16), 135 (9), 156 (12), 176 (22), 177 (13), 225 (4)
Broun, Charles W., Jr. 49 (41)
Browder, Anne 184 (1)
Brower, Jonathan J. 29 (282), (300)
Brown, Barbara 97 (7)
Brown, Claude 42 (57), (89), (125), 71 (181)
Brown, David B. 16 (9)
Brown, Edmund G., Sr. 8 (2)
Brown, Giles T. 29 (1), (14), (48), (70), (215), (224)
Brown, Himan 49 (42)
Brown, J. Gordon 216 (12)
Brown, Janice C. 79 (15)
Brown, Lester R. 112 (17)
Brown, Mark L. 151 (223)
Brown, Michael 49 (43)
Brown, Richard A. 46 (1)
Brown, Richard M. 105 (54)
Brown, Robert 154 (3)
Brown, Robert E. 151 (163)
Brown, Robert J. 151 (37)
Brown, Ron 177 (14)
Brownfeld, Allan C. 175 (1)
Brownlee, Ralph E. 105 (4)
Brozen, Yale 85 (2)
Brubaker, David 159 (16)
Brugel, John F. 151 (89)
Brun, Michael A. 117 (10), (29)
Bruteau, Beatrice 11 (3)
Bryan, W.R. 76 (1)
Bryant, Joseph J. 216 (13)
Bryant, Reginald 176 (23)
Buchanan, David 57 (6)
Buchanan, Patrick 71 (16), 156 (13)
Buchwald, Art 102 (2)
Buckland, Roscoe L. 223 (3), (8), (26)
Buckley, Chester 168 (8)
Buckley, James 49 (44), 71 (123)
Buckley, William F. 135 (10)
Bull, Robert J. 52 (10)
Bull, Vivian A. 52 (11)
Bullins, Ed 42 (27), (58), 154 (4)
Bumiller, Ted 110 (2)
Bunger, Robert Louis, Jr. 56 (2), (114)
Burch, Monte 112 (18)
Burge, Ethel 112 (19)
Burger, Mary Louise 142 (13)
Burhen, Jan 79 (16)
Burke, Robert L. 117 (66), (113)
Burke, Yvonne 71 (124)
Burkhart, Mary Quinn 16 (10)
Burleson, William C. 216 (14)
Burnett, Tobias W.T. 31 (23), (30)
Burnham, Kenneth E. 181 (206)
Burns, Stan 71 (17)
Burrell, Walter 42 (28)
Burros, Marian 219 (2)
Burrows, Thomas 49 (45)

Busalacchi, Louis J. 67 (6)
Bush, David F. 214 (77)
Bush, Louise F. 52 (12)
Busse, Jane 79 (17)
Butcher, Kathy 136 (1), (17)
Butkys, Adolph S. 214 (23)
Butler, Peter K. 67 (7)
Butler, Robert 49 (46)
Butler, William A. 57 (7)
Butler, Willis 59 (3)
Butrick, Frank M. 180 (20)
Butt, Albin T. 216 (15)
Butterworth, Joseph E. 29 (23), (107)
Buttram, Pat 112 (20)
Butts, Bob 57 (8)
Butz, Earl 112 (21), 156 (14)
Byrd, Lew H. 180 (21)
Byrd, Robert 71 (125)
Byrne, Kevin 105 (112)

C

Cahill, George F. 155 (1)
Cahlander, Adele 79 (18)
Cain, Joan A. 174 (15)
Cairney, John 97 (8)
Calabrese, Lucio 214 (40)
Calabro, Pat 46 (2)
Calamidas, Alec 151 (38)
Calderone, Mary 71 (82)
Caldwell, Betty A. 173 (6)
Callahan, Sidney 211 (2)
Callaway, Joe 97 (9)
Calvet, Corinne 225 (5)
Cameron, David A., Jr. 174 (16)
Cameron, Jo Anna 49 (47)
Camiel, Eric 49 (48)
Campbell, William E., Jr. 151 (64)
Canary 225 (6)
Canby, Vincent 71 (3), (107)
Cantrall, Otto L. 65 (9)
Caporali, John M. 151 (204)
Cappiello, Frank 97 (10)
Cappo, Joe 135 (11)
Capps, John T. 17 (1)
Capune, W. Garrett 29 (49), (133)
Caputo, Richard 151 (205)
Caradine, E. Everett, Jr. 174 (17)
Carlisle, Kitty 97 (11)
Carlisle, Robert 49 (49)
Carlson, Kenneth A. 75 (1)
Carnahan, Robert E. 151 (52)
Carney, Robert W. 180 (22)
Caron, Josiane 142 (14)
Carpenter, Liz 156 (15), 176 (24)
Carpenter, Lynn A. 151 (261)
Carpenter, Scott 225 (7)
Carr, Marion M. Odell 151 (65)
Carr, Martin 49 (50)
Carrier, David 31 (4)
Carroll, Chester C. 16 (11)
Carroll, Diane 56 (95)
Carroll, J.E. 65 (10)
Carroll, Paul 42 (59)
Carroll, Timothy 130 (6)
Carson, Ted 79 (19)
Carstens, Jane Ellen 174 (18)
Carter, Arnold 180 (23)
Carter, C.L. 180 (24)
Carter, Dean 216 (16)
Carter, Duane, Jr. 33 (3)
Carter, Glenn G. 151 (90)
Carter, Grace 79 (20)
Carter, J. Alan 123 (3)
Carter, Joe Douglas 151 (66)
Carter, Nick 177 (15)
Carter, Robert N. 180 (25)
Cartwright, Carol 151 (91)
Cartz, Louis 105 (18), (33)
Casey, Bernie 42 (2), (60)
Cassell, Stuart K. 216 (17)
Catell, Newton O. 151 (191)
Cates, Gilbert 49 (51)
Cathie, Walter C. 31 (15)
Cavender, A. Ray 16 (12)
Cawood, Robert 79 (21)
Cecilia-Mendez, Zeida 49 (52)
Chadwick, Russell 143 (4)
Chagall, David 225 (8)
Chambers, Everett 49 (53)
Chambliss, Thomas A. 56 (42)
Champion, John 49 (54)
Chan, Y. 151 (290)
Chancellor, John 135 (12)
Chang, Teh-Kuang 14 (2)
Chantrill, James 56 (99)
Chapin, Doloria 79 (22)
Chapin, Jack 151 (265)
Chapler, Chris 160 (6)
Chapman, Robert L. 52 (13)
Chapman, Sara A. 181 (77), (92)
Charlier, Roger H. 142 (15)
Charnin, Martin 49 (55)
Chase, Eleanor 79 (23)
Chasko, William E. 151 (125)
Chavez, Patricia 230 (2)
Chen, Robert P. 57 (9)
Chenault, Robert 49 (56)
Cheney, Anne 216 (19)
Cherne, Leo 71 (164)
Chernus, Jack 116 (1)
Cherry, Jerry A. 216 (18)
Cherry, William N. 117 (2)
Chetwynd, Hilary 79 (24)
Childress, Richard R. 117 (38)
Chillak, Edward W. 52 (14)
Ching, Stephen W. 214 (20)
Chiong, Miguel 160 (7)
Chodorov, Stephan 49 (57)
Choi-Duk-Shin 14 (3)
Chorba, George J. 214 (1), (13)
Chow, Ching-Wen 14 (4)
Christ, Donald G. 57 (10)
Christenberry, Chris 49 (58)
Christians, W.C. 180 (26)
Christianson, John N. 122 (22), 180 (27)
Christofferson, Thomas R. 52 (15)
Chudnow, Byron 49 (59)
Churchill, Winston 97 (12)
Ciccolella, Richard G. 14 (5)
Ciervo, Arthur 151 (67)
Cimbala, Stephen J. 151 (192)
Cimberg, Alan 122 (23), 177 (16), 180 (28)
Clabaugh, Maurice 117 (16)
Clader, Linda 227 (5)
Claflen, George L, Jr. 181 (78), (207), (260), (335)
Clampett, Bob 49 (60)
Clark, J. Rodney 65 (11)
Clark, Kenneth B. 71 (126)
Clark, Lindley 102 (3)
Clark, Ray K. 180 (29)
Clarke, Gary K. 112 (24)
Clarke, James J. 214 (31)
Clarke, R.B. 67 (8)
Clarke, Shirley 71 (108)
Claus, George W. 216 (20)
Clay, Alvin A. 214 (2), (15)
Clay, Jenny Strauss 227 (6)
Clay, Max 136 (2), (8)
Clayman, Dee Lesser 227 (7)
Clayson, Shelby J. 159 (17)
Clegg, Lee M. 67 (9)
Clement, Doris 79 (25)
Clement, Ted 79 (25)
Clennan, William A. 180 (30)
Cleveland, Peggy 180 (31)
Clifford, Alan F. 216 (21)
Close, Del 42 (29)
Clouse, James P. 216 (22)
Clouser, Richard A. 151 (92)
Clubb, O. Edmund 71 (127)
Coane, James 49 (61)
Coats, Jeff 177 (17), 180 (32)
Cobb, Calvin 130 (7)
Cobb, Gloria 42 (149)
Cobb, LaVarne 180 (33)
Cochran, John 171 (32)
Cochran, Lillian T. 52 (16)
Cockroft, Don 83 (2)
Coffer, William E. 29 (50), (87), (158), (192), (230), (254), (283), (331)

Cohen, Barbara 219 (3)
Cohen, Michael 46 (3)
Cohen, Richard 219 (4)
Cohen, Sara Kay 176 (25)
Coker, Samuel Terry 16 (13)
Colby, Bill 159 (18)
Colcord, Marshall 56 (16)
Cole, Charles C. 176 (26)
Coleman, Bernard D. 31 (8), (21)
Coleman, John 49 (62)
Coleman, Wayne 57 (11)
Colla, Richard 49 (63)
Colletto, James M. 29 (24), (301)
Collins, Gunther 49 (64)
Collins, William F. 216 (23)
Colmano, Germille 216 (24)
Combs, Ronald 142 (16)
Comely, Roger E. 216 (25)
Comer, James 42 (90)
Comfort, Alex 156 (16)
Cominos, Nicholas 49 (65)
Compton, Rod 56 (76)
Concannon, F.P. 65 (12)
Conklin, Bob 177 (18)
Conlbear, Kenneth 171 (14)
Conley, Harry L. 117 (3)
Connellan, Thomas K. 180 (34)
Conrad, Glenn R. 174 (19)
Conrad, James 40 (1)
Conroy, G. Dennis 99 (1)
Constandse, Martha E. 79 (26)
Cook, Ron 112 (25)
Cook, William J., Jr. 180 (35)
Coombs, Ilona C. 52 (17)
Coon, Lewis H. 57 (12)
Cooper, Dolores 176 (27)
Cooper, Don 91 (3)
Cooper, Hal 49 (66)
Cooper, Jane E. 151 (164)
Cooper, Lloyd G. 180 (36)
Cope, Louise Todd 79 (27)
Copeland, John W. 52 (18)
Cordes, Carroll 174 (20)
Corey, Gerald F. 29 (88), (231)
Corkrum, Ralph E. 159 (19)
Cormier, Raymond J. 181 (79), (138), (208)
Cornwall, Don 174 (21)
Correll, Leslie 79 (28)
Corrigan, John D. 180 (37)
Corwin, Norman 49 (67)
Costa, Joseph J. 151 (93)
Cote, Mary Louise 181 (158), (321)
Cotrone, Daniel 105 (92)
Coughlin, Robert W. 67 (10)
Courtney, Charles 52 (19)
Courtright, James B. 105 (2)
Cousins, Evert 11 (4)
Cousins, Morison 147 (3)
Cousins, Norman 97 (13)
Cousteau, Jean-Michel 112 (26), 156 (17)
Coutts, Lucille 79 (29)
Cowell, David A. 52 (20)
Cox, Miriam S. 29 (2), (15), (134), (185), (200), (332)
Crabb, Richard 112 (27)
Craig, Steve 223 (12)
Craik, Mary B. 168 (9)
Crane, Barry 49 (68)
Crane, Philip M. 85 (3)
Crane, William J. 57 (13)
Cranmer, H. Jerome 52 (21)
Cranston, Alan 71 (128)
Craven, Thomas 49 (69)
Crawford, Libby 79 (30)
Crawford, Margo 142 (17)
Creager, Clara H. 79 (31)
Crecine, John P. 31 (25), (34)
Creely, Daniel 142 (18)
Crepeau, Margaret T. 105 (89), (93)
Cribbin, James J. 135 (13)
Crim, Mort 71 (18), 176 (28)
Crist, Judith 71 (2), (109), 156 (18)
Criswell 225 (9)
Critchfield, Howard J. 223 (5), (32)
Crockett, Candace 79 (32)
Croskery, Robert W. 180 (38)
Cross, Gerald H. 216 (26)
Cross, Neill 49 (70)
Crump, Michael W. 216 (27)
Crunkilton, John R. 216 (28)
Cuff, David J. 181 (131), (209), (336)
Cukor, George 49 (71)
Culbertson, Ruth Pearson 79 (33)
Culham-Ertman, Phyllis 227 (8)
Culkin, Thomas J. 214 (68)
Cullen, Lloyd 177 (19), 180 (39)
Culligan, Joe 102 (4)
Culver, John C. 71 (129)
Cundiff, Merlyn 177 (20)
Cunningham, Dennis 176 (29)
Cunningham, Richard G. 151 (266)
Cunningham, Robert L. 151 (21)
Curiel, Ramon 27 (2)
Curran, Darryl J. 29 (9)
Curtis, Anthony R. 151 (68)
Curtis, Jon 173 (7)
Curzon, Albert 171 (33)
Cuscaden, Rob 42 (3)
Cusimano, Richard C. 174 (22)
Cussier, Edward L. 31 (11)
Cutler, William W., III 181 (93), (261)

D

Dahir, Sabir H. 151 (291)
Dallan, Gisele 225 (10)
Dallenbach, Wally 33 (4)
Dalton, Peter O. 65 (13)
Daly, John 130 (8)
Daly, John Charles 97 (14)
Dandois, Joseph E. 151 (53)
Danes, Zdenko F. 159 (20)
Danforth, Horace C. 65 (14)
Dang, Joseph N.P. 14 (6)
Danielewski, Tad 49 (72)
Daniels, Marc 49 (73)
Danska, Herbert 49 (74)
Danziger, Marvin 173 (8)
Dash, Sam 112 (28)
Daugherty, Duffy 71 (206)
Davenport, Beverly W. 29 (171)
Davenport, Calvin A. 29 (172), (267)
Davenport, Rita 177 (21)
David, Clive 97 (15)
David, Edmund 130 (9)
David, William J. 151 (4)
Davidson, Abraham A. 181 (80), (210), (301)
Davidson, James E. 150 (1)
Davidson, Martin 49 (75)
Davidson, Mary Frances 79 (34)
Davies, W. Lorne 171 (25)
Davis, A. Douglas 57 (14)
Davis, Alonzo 42 (4)
Davis, Bruce 225 (11)
Davis, Donald E. 16 (14)
Davis, Earle A., Jr. 27 (26)
Davis, Gunter 176 (30)
Davis, James 223 (23)
Davis, La Deva 176 (31)
Davis, Neil O. 16 (15)
Davis, Norman D. 16 (16)
Davis, Robert D. 16 (17)
Davis, Trenton 56 (25), (67)
Davis, William 154 (5)
Davison, Allan J. 171 (26)
Dayton, Daryl D. 225 (12)
Dayton, Edward R. 230 (3)
de Havilland, Olivia 97 (16)
de Jaegher, Raymond 14 (7)
De Jong, Peter 52 (23)
De Marco, Nicholas 49 (76)
De Mott, John 181 (68), (211)
de Pencier, Robert 160 (8)
De Santo, R. John 168 (10)
De Toth, Andre 49 (77)
De Veer, Robert 52 (24)

De Wolf, Rose 176 (32)
Deagon, Ann 277 (9)
Deal, Borden 154 (6)
Dean, James W. 216 (29)
Dean, John F. 224 (4)
Dean, Ken S. 117 (39)
Dean, William 130 (10)
DeArmond, Richard 171 (46)
Debnath, Lokenath 56 (68), (106), (125)
Dee, Merri 42 (38)
DeFlores, Robert 112 (29)
Dehoney, Martyvonne 52 (22)
Dehoney, Wayne 180 (40)
DeJersey, Katherine 42 (115)
Delaney, R.E. 112 (30), 135 (14)
Dellums, Ronald V. 71 (130)
DeLouise, Joseph 42 (116)
Demarest, David 31 (31)
Dempster, John M. 173 (9)
Demsetz, Harold 85 (4)
Denbow, Carl J. 117 (83)
Denbow, Terry 151 (69)
Dendel, Esther Warner 79 (35)
Dengler, Patricia L. 181 (50)
Dennard, James J. 123 (4)
Denny, Ronald J. 105 (70)
Derl-Davis, William 42 (30)
Derens, W.G. 216 (30)
DeRoche, Robert J. 105 (34), (113)
Desenberg, Irma E. 29 (10)
Deshotels, Warren J. 105 (117)
Devenyl, Denes 171 (7), (97)
DeVine, John W. 117 (17), (40)
DeVise, Pierre 42 (126)
DeWald, Samuel C. 151 (39)
Dewalt, Robert 130 (11)
Dewey, Hallie 177 (22), 180 (41)
Dey, Lala Kalyan 52 (25)
Deyell, Peter 49 (78)
Dhuru, Virendra B. 105 (28)
Diamonstein, Barbaralee 71 (4)
Dick, David 154 (7)
Dickenson, James R. 220 (2)
Dickerson, Nancy 102 (5)
Dickey, John W. 216 (31)
Dickison, Sheila K. 227 (10)
Dickinson, Winifred 151 (296)
Diebold, John 102 (6)
Dietze, Gottfried 85 (5)
Diles, Dave 112 (31)
Dillon, Mark 49 (79)
DiMento, Joseph 27 (3), (38)
Dimond, E. Grey 112 (32)
Dimond, Mary Clark 112 (33)
Distler, P.A. 216 (32)
Dittman, Roger 29 (51), (120), (177), (232), (255), (268)
Dixon, Jeane 112 (34), 135 (15), 156 (19)
Dixon, Maceo 213 (2)
Dmytryk, Edward 49 (80)
Dobbs, Frank W. 142 (19)
Dobkin, Lawrence 49 (81)
Dobmeyer, Edward R. 99 (2)
Dobriansky, Lev E. 85 (6)
Dodson, Fitzhugh J. 97 (17)
Dodson, Sid 110 (3)
Doerr, Edd 12 (2)
Doherty, Dennis J. 105 (35), (76), (104)
Dole, Robert 71 (131), 112 (35)
Dollar, Bobby G. 180 (42)
Domber, Edward A. 52 (26)
Dominguez, Carlos, Jr. 65 (15)
Dominick, Wayne D. 174 (23)
Doney, James 83 (3)
Doniger, Walter 49 (82)
Donnelly, John P. 105 (61)
Donner, Clive 49 (83)
Doris, Peter 160 (9)
Dornan, James E., Jr. 85 (7)
Dornoff, James 135 (16), 177 (23), 180 (43)
Dorrance, Rose 180 (44)
Dotson, Virginia 105 (77)
Doughty, Darrell J. 52 (27)
Douglas, John 116 (2)
Douglas, Mack 177 (24), 180 (45)
Douglas, Neil 51 (1)
Douglass, Merrill E. 180 (46)
Doukas, Peter H. 181 (159), (212)
Douthard, William 217 (1)
Dow, Ruth 57 (15)
Downes, Alan J. 168 (11)
Downes, Sheldon C. 56 (77)
Downing, Billie 117 (131)
Downs, Hugh 135 (17), 156 (20)
Drachkovitch, Milorad M. 85 (8)
Drake, Gertrude 227 (11)
Drake, James 49 (84)
Drath, Connie M. 184 (2)
Dreussi, Gina M. 98 (1)
Dreyer, Elizabeth 105 (105)
Driscoll, Philip 130 (12)
Druding, Susan C. 79 (36)
Drufenbrock, Diane 172 (1)
Drummond, Caroline 181 (81), (94), (139)
Dubeck, Leroy W. 181 (3), (95), (213), (276)
Dubin, Samuel S. 151 (40), 180 (47)
Dubois, Jean Louis 69 (3)
Ducharme, Mary H. 174 (29)
Ducharme, Robert J. 174 (25)
Duchin, Peter 102 (7)
Duckworth, L., Jr. 92 (1)
Duda, J.L. 151 (138)
Dugas, Edmond A. 174 (26)
Duke, Angier Biddle 97 (18)
Duke, (Mrs.) Angier Biddle 97 (19)
Duke, Paul 71 (19), 112 (36), 176 (33), 219 (5)
Duncan, J.W. 16 (18)
Duncan, Marion Claude 180 (48)
Dungan, James R. 151 (5)
Dunn, Cal 49 (85)
Dunn, J. Michael 105 (71), (114)
Dunn, Patricia 56 (43), (133)
Dupuis, Adrian 105 (36)
DuPuis, Mary M. 151 (94)
Durham, Joan 176 (34)
Durham, Leonard 57 (16)
Duro, Tom 177 (25)
Dutler, David C. 57 (17)
Dwyer, William F. 184 (3)
Dymally, Mervyn 71 (132)

E

Earick, Arthur D. 29 (52), (89), (135), (159), (314), (341)
Earthman, Glen I. 216 (33)
Eason, Byrdie E. 176 (27)
Ebaugh, Paul 151 (139)
Ebert, John 91 (4)
Ebert, Lawrence E. 159 (21)
Ebon, Martin 139 (2)
Eckroat, Larry R. 151 (165)
Eddleman, Cindy 27 (27)
Eder, Richard 97 (20)
Edge, Cecil 177 (26)
Edmonds, Charles P., III 16 (19)
Edwards, Douglas 71 (20), 135 (18), 154 (8), 156 (21), 176 (35), 177 (27)
Egan, Keith J. 105 (106)
Eggert, William R. 180 (49)
Egloff, William F. 57 (18)
Ehrhardt, David A. 67 (11)
Ehrhart, Dennis 174 (28)
Ehrlich, George E. 181 (160)
Eichelberger, Brenda 42 (150)
Eicher, Joan B. 79 (37)
Eisenberg, Nat 49 (86)
Eisenhower, John 156 (22)
Eisenmann, Gustave 49 (87)
Eisenstein, Mayer 122 (1)
Eiter, Richard H. 52 (28)
Elder, Harvey L. 117 (67), (92)
Elder, James T. 151 (41)
Elias, Edward M. 151 (140)

Elias, Paul 130 (13)
Ellenburg, Grace 56 (115)
Eller, Frank W. 56 (26), (100), (116)
Elliott, Barry 49 (88)
Elliott, Verda 79 (38)
Elliott, William F. 31 (16)
Ellison, Ralph 42 (61)
Ellsworth, Robert 102 (8)
Enders, Howard 49 (89)
Engle, A. William, Jr. 151 (185)
Englander, Roger 49 (90)
Engle, Hualing Nieh 42 (62)
Engle, Paul 42 (63)
Engstrom, Ted W. 230 (4)
Ensley, Harold 112 (37)
Ephron, Nora 102 (9)
Epstein, Janet 122 (2)
Erdman, Richard 49 (91)
Ericson, Lois 79 (39)
Erman, John 49 (92)
Ershkowitz, Herbert 181 (262)
Ervin, Sam 156 (23), 176 (36)
Erwin, Stuart 151 (297)
Esmonde, Margaret P. 214 (46)
Espley, John L. 216 (34)
Essary, E.O. 216 (35)
Essex, Harry 49 (93)
Etten, Marion 142 (20)
Evans, Bergen 71 (21)
Evans, David H. 29 (201), (220)
Evans, Donald E. 151 (95)
Evans, Jerry 49 (94)
Evans, M. Stanton 85 (9)
Evans, Mari 42 (64), (151)
Evans, Robert 180 (50)
Evans, Rowland 102 (10)
Everett, Grover W. 56 (69)
Everett, Nell C. 56 (63)
Everix, Pamela 108 (1)
Evers, Charles 71 (133)
Eversmeyer, Harold E. 177 (4), (13), (30)
Eveslage, Tom 168 (12)
Ewell, Rachel 229 (2)
Ezell, Wayland L. 168 (13)

F

Fackler, Herbert V. 174 (29)
Fadiman, Clifton 102 (11)
Fagan, William 225 (13)
Fahey, Joseph J. 103 (1)
Faichney, James 49 (95)
Fair, Don 176 (37)
Falbey, J. Wayne 65 (16)
Falis, Melvin 138 (2)
Falkenberg, Paul 49 (96)
Fantle, Karl S. 65 (17)
Farber, Barry 71 (22)
Fareed, Ahmed A. 142 (21)
Farenthold, Frances 176 (38)
Farmer, James 71 (134)
Farmer, Malcolm M. 224 (5)
Farnham, Emily 56 (10)
Farr, Robert 97 (21)
Farrah, George A. 168 (14)
Farrell, James T. 71 (182)
Farrell, Reid D. 65 (18)
Farrington, Diane G. 173 (10)
Fasheh, Issa I. 29 (25), (196), (216), (225), (315)
Fast, Julius 135 (19)
Faulk, John Henry 71 (23)
Faulkner, Janice Hardison 56 (131)
Faust, John R. 57 (19)
Fay, Edward E. 45 (1)
Fearnley, Joe 65 (19)
Fehrer, Linda 105 (37)
Feigenberg, Myrtle 214 (24), (71)
Feils, Stuart W. 173 (11)
Felack, Michael 151 (70)
Feldman, Reynold 142 (22)
Fenstermacher, Robert L. 52 (29)
Ferdun, Edrie 181 (82)
Ferguson, Frederick G. 151 (206)
Ferguson, Karen 57 (20)
Ferrar, Terry A. 151 (150)
Fettig, Art 180 (51)
Fiedler, E. Robert 49 (97)
Fiedler, Leslie 71 (183)
Field, Frank 71 (95)
Field, Tom 83 (4)
Fielding, Allen Fred 181 (161)
Fields, Dennis C. 168 (15)
Fields, Larry 176 (39)
Fields, Ronald J. 112 (38)
Fierman, Morton C. 29 (90), (114), (233)
Fierst, Dorothy K. 180 (52)
Figi, Mig 112 (39), 177 (28)
Finkel, Arnold 176 (40)
Fiore, Albert 49 (98)
Firoozi, Ferydoon 142 (23)
First, Jonathan 181 (96), (302)
Fischmann, Ruel 168 (16)
Fishbein, Morris 71 (96)
Fisher, Ed 83 (5)
Fisher, Elizabeth A. 227 (12)
Fiske, Stephen 225 (14)
Fitch, Dean 130 (14)
Fitch, Franklin G. 117 (41)
Fitch, James L. 117 (132)
Fittipaldi, Silvio E. 214 (50), (80)
Fitts, Robert H. 105 (115)
Fitzgerald, Geraldine 156 (24)
Flagge, John A. 123 (5)
Flarsheim, Henry 180 (53)
Fleischer, Richard 49 (99)
Fleishman, Joe 151 (18)
Fleming, E.J., III 132 (3)
Fleming, Ruth G. 56 (44)
Flener, Frederick O. 142 (24)
Fletcher, Peter W. 151 (304)
Flick, George J. 216 (36)
Flint, Cort R. 180 (54)
Florea, John 49 (100)
Flory, Joyce Ann 142 (25)
Flowers, William L., Jr. 216 (37)
Flynn, Dennis G. 67 (12)
Flynn, John 57 (21)
Flynn, Leo B. 105 (38)
Folwell, William H., III 151 (71)
Foner, Philip S. 213 (3)
Fontaine, Joan 71 (24), 112 (40)
Foos, Charles H. 123 (6)
Foran, David J. 105 (67)
Ford, Eileen 97 (22)
Ford, Frank 176 (41)
Ford, John P. 57 (22)
Ford, Louis 49 (101)
Ford, Nicholas S. 151 (247)
Ford, Sarah Ann 105 (39)
Fork, Donald J. 181 (69), (97)
Forrester, Kent 117 (88)
Forsythe, Anthony 225 (15)
Fort, Joel 71 (135)
Fortenberry, Charles N. 16 (20)
Foster, Ray 177 (29), 180 (55)
Foster, Richard 49 (102)
Foth, Dennis 171 (15)
Fouts, Ken 49 (103)
Fowler, Mary Ann 142 (26)
Fox, Thomas G. 151 (42)
Foy, Chester L. 216 (38)
Foy, James E. 16 (21)
France, Erwin 42 (127)
Francis, Arlene 156 (25)
Francisco, Clay 15 (2)
Francoeur, Robert T. 211 (3)
Francoeus, Robert 11 (5)
Frank, D. Michael 177 (30), 180 (56)
Frank, Gerold 71 (184)
Frank, Harry 16 (22)
Frank, Richard 27 (10)
Frank, Tom 151 (96)
Frankel, Sheldon S. 159 (22)
Frankenheimer, John 49 (104)
Frankforter, A. Daniel 151 (215)
Frankhouser, Willis M., Jr. 151 (207)
Franklin, Jerrold 181 (277)
Franklin, Joe 71 (25)
Franklin, Perry L. 171 (16)

Franklin, Ralph 110 (4)
Franklin, Wendall 49 (105)
Franz, George W. 151 (216)
Fraser, Alistair B. 151 (303)
Frazee, Charles A. 29 (178), (234)
Frazier, Joe 180 (57)
Frazier, Walt 71 (207)
Frederick, Daniel 216 (39)
Frederick, Duke 142 (27)
Frederick, Pauline 135 (20), 156 (26)
Fredericks, Kay 132 (4)
Freed, John E. 151 (232)
Freeman, Roger A. 85 (10)
Freeman, William E. 117 (114), (121)
French, Victor 49 (106)
Freudenberger, Daniel 49 (107)
Frey, John C. 151 (254)
Friedman, Frank L. 181 (51), (214)
Friedman, George A. 71 (83)
Friedman, Kim 49 (108)
Friedman, Si 147 (4)
Friel, Jonda 79 (40)
Friend, Robert 49 (109)
Frisbie, Alexander 49 (110)
Frost, Gordon W. 79 (41)
Frost, Ralph W. 180 (58)
Frost, Robert J., III 65 (20)
Frye, David 156 (27)
Fu, Vicotria R. 216 (40)
Fuentes, Carlos 52 (30)
Fugaro, Anthony 181 (162)
Fuhrmann, Brigita 79 (42)
Fuldheim, Dorothy 83 (6)
Fulghum, Robert S. 56 (78)
Fullager, R.K. 92 (2)
Fuller, R. Buckminster 134 (3)
Fulmer, Richard H. 151 (227)
Fung, Daniel Y.C. 151 (173)
Funt, B.L. 171 (34)
Furbay, John H. 100 (1), 177 (31), 180 (59)
Furino, Frank 49 (111)
Furr, A. Keith 216 (41)
Furrow, Stanley D. 151 (267)
Furst, John F. 150 (2)
Fyock, David H. 150 (3)

G

Gabbard, Lucina P. 57 (23)
Gable, John A. 167 (1)
Gabler, Howard 138 (3)
Gabryshak, Betty J. 105 (124)
Gaddis, Louise Tiranoff 49 (112)
Gage, Nick 71 (26)
Gais, Ruth 227 (13)
Gala, Basil E. 29 (76), (136), (173)
Gale, G. Fritz 65 (21)
Galey, Minaruth 181 (70), (98), (215)
Galfas, Timothy 49 (113)
Gallagher, Bernard J. 214 (65), (86)
Gallup, George 42 (13), 71 (136), 135 (21), 156 (28)
Galper, Jeffry 181 (263), (309)
Gamble, Hays B. 151 (225)
Gandolfo, Joe 177 (32)
Gange, Stary 25 (1)
Ganim, Gary 130 (15)
Gantt, Wilson 117 (42), (115), (127)
Garbo, Norman 97 (23)
Garcia, Ana M. 151 (233)
Garcia, Emilio 174 (30)
Gard, Grant 42 (65), 112 (41), 177 (33)
Gardiner, Jeanette 174 (31)
Gardner, Dick 177 (34), 180 (60)
Garfield, Gene J. 177 (68), (116)
Garfield, Sydney 225 (16)
Gargiulo, Michael 49 (114)
Gariepy, Dick 177 (35), 180 (61)
Garman, Robert E. 173 (12)
Garment, Leonard 71 (137)
Garmes, Lee 49 (115)
Garner, Ray 49 (116)
Garnett, Tay 49 (117)
Garrett, J.C. 216 (42)
Garrett, Lila 49 (118)
Garrett, Philip R. 142 (28)
Garth, Sheridan H. 103 (2)
Gary, Steve 176 (42)
Gass, Tyler E. 136 (12), (25)
Gates, James E. 180 (62)
Gaudet, Irby J., Jr. 174 (32)
Gautieri, Ronald F. 181 (163), (216)
Gavin, Mike 49 (119)
Gavrin, Irving 116 (3)
Gayle, Willie 177 (36)
Geary, Phillip 100 (2)
Gebhard, Elizabeth R. 227 (14)
Geddes, Bruce 49 (120)
Geer, Glenn B. 181 (83), (132), (217)
Gehlbach, Roger 171 (17)
Geiwitz, Allen R. 181 (164)
Geller, Uri 42 (117), 134 (4), 156 (29)
Gentry, Clyde 112 (42)
Gentry, Robert J. 174 (33)
George, Melvin R. 142 (29)
Georgiou, Peri P. 142 (30)
Gerber, Fred 79 (43)
Gerber, Nita 79 (43)
Gerber, Sanford 169 (1)
Gerhard, Glenn 151 (174)
Gerity, Patrick L. 83 (7)
German, Jack 65 (22)
Germond, Jack W. 220 (3)
Gerstle, Ralph 59 (4), 110 (5)
Gervasi, Frank 71 (177)
Geyer, Georgie Ann 135 (22)
Gholson, Ronald E. 57 (24)
Giacumakis, George J. Jr. 29 (3), (53), (91), (179), (217), (226), (235), (269)
Gianninoto, Frank 147 (5)
Giblin, Les 180 (63)
Gibson, Bill 49 (121)
Gibson, Jon L. 174 (34)
Gibson, Kenneth A. 71 (138)
Gichner, Lawrence E. 97 (24)
Giddens, E. Don 12 (3)
Gifford, Frank 154 (9)
Gil, David 172 (2)
Gilbert, Norma 52 (31)
Gilbert, R.L. 142 (31)
Gilde, L. 67 (13)
Giles, Howard C. 117 (18)
Gill, Donald A. 174 (35)
Gillespie, Joanna Bowen 52 (32)
Gillies, Jean 142 (32)
Gilman, Richard 29 (26), (34), (77), (92), (137)
Gilman, Stanley E. 151 (126)
Gilmore, Harold L. 151 (43)
Gilmour, Ernest H. 143 (5)
Gilmour, Joseph E., Jr. 151 (97)
Gilpatric, C. Edward 142 (33)
Gilpin, Nancy E. 181 (52), (71), (99), (322)
Ginn, Cheryl 176 (43)
Ginott, Alice 71 (84)
Ginsberg, Allen 71 (185)
Ginsberg-Place, Ruth 79 (44)
Ginzburg, Ralph 71 (27)
Girard, Joe 177 (37)
Girdler, R.J., Jr. 132 (5)
Gitomer, Nancy 77 (1)
Gladich, Joen 225 (17)
Glaser, Anton 151 (248)
Glaser, Mitch 93 (1)
Glass, Bill 112 (43), 177 (38)
Glass, Dorothea D. 181 (165)
Glasscock, Kip 177 (39)
Glazer, Edward 48 (1)
Glazer, Nathan 71 (85)

Glickman, Marty 71 (208)
Godbey, Gordon C. 151 (98)
Goddard, K. 92 (3)
Godfrey, Arthur 154 (10)
Goehl, Henry 181 (218), (314)
Goellner, Edward B. 174 (36)
Goetz, Theodore 49 (122)
Gold, Barbara K. 227 (15)
Gold, Herb 71 (186)
Goldberg, Arthur 102 (12)
Golden, Murray 49 (123)
Golden, R.A. 92 (4)
Golder, Richard 181 (166)
Goldfarb, Peter 49 (124)
Goldfield, David R. 216 (43)
Goldman, Carole 129 (1)
Goldman, Robert 31 (6)
Goldman, Stuart D. 151 (193)
Goldschmidt, Arthur E., Jr. 151 (194)
Goldshmidt, Wilfred 147 (6)
Goldspiel, Steven 50 (1)
Goldstein, Arthur J. 27 (28)
Goman, LaVerne 159 (23)
Gomez, Allen 49 (125)
Gonzalez, Rodrigo C. 142 (34)
Gonzalez-Cruz, Luis F. 151 (195)
Good, Cynthia D. 150 (4)
Good, Roland H., Jr. 151 (268)
Goodard, Dick 83 (8)
Goode, Mark 49 (126)
Goodel, Charles 71 (137)
Goodman, Ronald 79 (45)
Goodner, David M. 181 (167)
Goodnoff, Sol 49 (127)
Goodspeed, Charles 31 (22)
Goodwin, Frank 180 (64)
Gordon, Beverly 79 (46)
Gordon, Diane R. 227 (16)
Gordon, Lida G. 79 (47)
Gordon, Ruth 97 (25)
Gorsline, George W. 216 (44)
Gotbaum, Victor 71 (69)
Gothold, Stephen 224 (6)
Gotthoffer, Esther 79 (48)
Gottlieb, Michael 49 (128)
Gottlieb, Sanford 42 (14)
Gove, Bill 177 (40)
Gowdy, Curt 42 (98), 71 (209), 122 (44), 113 (11), 156 (30)
Gowen, Robert J. 56 (91), (117)
Goyert, Philip R., Jr. 174 (37)
Grachek, Arthur F. 168 (17)
Grady, William F. 181 (72), (100)
Graham, Charles J. 168 (18)
Graham, Jim 65 (23)
Graham, Kenneth R. 151 (54)
Graham, Maury 112 (45)
Graham, Robert J. 151 (234)
Graham, Virginia 135 (23), 176 (44)
Gramm, W. Phillip 135 (24)
Grandin-Nettles, Margareta 79 (49)
Grant, Jerry 33 (5)
Grant, Shirley M. 29 (27)
Grant, Susan 79 (50)
Grant, W. Harold 16 (23)
Grasselli, Jeanette 173 (13)
Graubart, Burton L. 29 (30)
Grauman, Walter 49 (129)
Gravel, Mike 71 (140), 112 (46)
Gray, Donald 11 (6)
Gray, Warren 49 (130)
Graybeal, David 52 (33)
Graybeal, Jack D. 216 (45)
Grayson, Persis 79 (51)
Graziano, Rocky 71 (210)
Greaves, Percy 6 (2)
Greaves, William 49 (131)
Green, Joe L. 174 (38)
Green, Robert L. 97 (26)
Greenblatt, Sidney 52 (34)
Greene, Errol L. 65 (24)
Greene, Jack B. 105 (40)
Greenfield, Concetta 31 (12), (26)
Greengard, Carola 227 (17)
Greenhill, Leslie P. 151 (99)
Greenlee, Sam 42 (66), 71 (110)
Greenspan, Bernard 52 (35)
Greenwald, Earl 181 (168)
Gregory, Paul 225 (18)
Grella, Michael A. 151 (100)
Gren, Jack 180 (65)
Griesbach, Marc F. 105 (41), (90)
Griessman, B. Eugene 16 (24)
Griffin, Robert J. 180 (66)
Griffith, Cyril E. 151 (217)
Griffith, James N. 180 (67)
Griffith, Joe 112 (47)
Griffith, John R. 57 (25)
Griffiths, Martha W. 112 (48)
Grimsal, Edward G., Jr. 174 (39)
Grimsby, Roger 154 (11)
Groah, William J., Jr. 80 (1)
Grode, John N. 151 (228)
Grogan, John 177 (41)
Gross, Charles A. 16 (25)
Gross, Dawyer D. 56 (137)
Gross, Jack L. 181 (35), (219)
Gross, Tennala A. 56 (126)
Grossman, Herbert 151 (151)
Grossman, Jack 42 (128)
Grossnickle, William F. 56 (134)
Grosswald, Emil 181 (149)
Grove, Ellis 151 (289)
Grubel, Herbert G. 171 (8)
Gruman, Edward L. 230 (5)
Grunerud, James J. 168 (19)
Guerra-Cunningham, Lucia 27 (11)
Guertner, Gary L. 29 (256), (292)
Guest, Bud 83 (9)
Guild, Leo 225 (19)
Guimaraes, Nestor 168 (20)
Gulati, Umesh C. 56 (17), (92), (118)
Gulati, Usha T. 56 (119)
Gulick, Evelyn M. 79 (52)
Gulje, Ulrich W., Sr. 169 (2)
Gunn, Andrew Leigh 12 (4)
Gunn, James 112 (49)
Gunsten, Paul H. 216 (46)
Gunter, Eldon 177 (42)
Gussow, Mel 71 (5)
Guthrie, Arthur 171 (9)
Gutman, William C. 181 (53)
Guy, Sallie T. 79 (53)
Guyer, Tennyson 112 (50), 177 (43)

H

Hackes, Peter 112 (51), 135 (25), 176 (45), 180 (68)
Hackler, Clyde 223 (31)
Hackler, George 57 (26)
Hadwiger, Kenneth E. 57 (27)
Haerr, Alvin R. 180 (69)
Hagar, Jonathon 110 (6)
Hagen, Owen 168 (21)
Hagenbuch, Keith M. 151 (258)
Haggai, Tom 112 (52), 177 (44)
Hahn, George E. 230 (6)
Hahn, Jeffrey W. 214 (3), (53), (87)
Hailey, Walter B., Jr. 180 (70)
Hailparn, Lydia 52 (36)
Haines, Kenneth H. 216 (47)
Hakeem, Hasan 1 (7)
Haldeman, James F. 151 (22)
Hale, William H., Jr. 180 (71)
Haley, Alex 102 (13)
Hall, David M. 16 (26)
Hall, Joanne A. 79 (54)
Hall, Laurence 112 (53)
Hall, Norman 49 (132)
Hall, R. Duane 3 (1)
Hall, Wesley W., Sr. 8 (3)
Hall, Woodie 180 (72)
Hallberg, Clarice L. 142 (35)
Haller, Mark H. 181 (264)

Hallett, Judith P. 227 (18)
Hallman, Ted 79 (55)
Halper, Lewis 130 (16)
Halsberg, Delaine 168 (22)
Halsman, Philippe 97 (27)
Halsted, George 180 (73)
Halton, Patrice Hoffman 168 (23)
Hamand, Lavern M. 57 (28)
Hamilton, Charles 42 (15), (129), 71 (141)
Hamilton, George 56 (79)
Hamilton, Neill Q. 52 (37)
Hamlin, Roy L. 46 (4)
Hammock, James W., Jr. 117 (69)
Hampshire, William B. 183 (2)
Hampton, Barbara L. 181 (27), (84)
Hamsa, Charles F. 174 (40)
Hanauer, Eric S. 29 (138), (270), (302), (316)
Hand, Irving 151 (226)
Haney, Art 56 (11)
Hankins, William W. 56 (27), (101)
Hanley, Frank L. 174 (41)
Hanna, Sherman D. 16 (27)
Hannan, Douglas 103 (3)
Hannan, Robert 65 (25)
Hanneman, Richard L. 133 (1)
Hans, Reid 168 (24)
Hansen, Arthur A. 29 (160), (333)
Hansen, Mark Victor 177 (45), 180 (74)
Hansen, Tim 159 (24)
Harder, K. Peter 223 (33)
Hardin, Burton E. 57 (29)
Hardin, Ian R. 16 (28)
Hardin, Paul 52 (38)
Harding, Vincent 42 (130)
Hare, Andrew 131 (2)
Hare, Nathan 71 (86)
Harkey, Bob 33 (6)
Harkness, William L. 151 (262)
Harmon, William R. 58 (1)
Harper, Betsy 56 (45)
Harper, David E. 52 (39)
Harper, Laura J. 216 (48)
Harrington, Bob 81 (1)
Harrington, William Franklin 180 (75)
Harris, Amy 112 (54)
Harris, Dorothy Lipp 180 (76)
Harris, Dorothy V. 151 (276)
Harris, Fred 71 (142)
Harris, L.H. 130 (17)
Harris, Leonard 71 (6)
Harris, Louis 49 (133)
Harris, Patricia A. 174 (42)
Harris, Philip R. 180 (77)
Harris, Ruth D. 216 (49)
Harris, Sidney J. 71 (28), 135 (26)
Harris, Sydney 112 (55)
Harris, Thomas Anthony 112 (56)
Harrison, A. Cleveland 16 (29)
Harrison, Howard 224 (7)
Harrison, Lillian K. 180 (78)
Harrop, Ronald 171 (35)
Hart, Arthur A. 79 (56)
Hart, Gary 112 (57)
Hart, William 172 (3)
Hartigan, Karelisa 227 (19)
Hartsook, John H. 181 (101)
Hartz, David 105 (78)
Harvey, Anthony 49 (134)
Harvey, Paul 112 (58), 135 (27), 156 (31), 177 (46)
Harvey, Richard B. 224 (8)
Harwood, Richard 49 (135)
Hasegawa, Saiji 14 (8)
Haskell, Floyd 112 (59)
Haskin, Lynn Martin 151 (72)
Hastings, (Mrs.) Donald 72 (1)
Hatalla, Josephine F. 151 (55)
Hatfield, Mark 71 (143)
Hatten, Roy 177 (47)
Haughton, Rosemary 211 (4)
Hauptli, Ellen 79 (57)
Hauptmann, Jerzy 85 (11)
Hauser, Rex 174 (43)
Hauser, Robert E. 151 (218)
Havard, William C. 216 (50)
Hawkens, Betty Jo 97 (28)
Hawley, Jane S. 142 (36)
Hayden, Bill 42 (131)
Hayden, Jeffrey 49 (136)
Hayes, Ira M. 118 (1), 177 (48), 180 (79)
Hayes, John P. 181 (73), (140)
Hayes, Kirby L. 16 (30)
Hayes, Peter Lind 97 (29)
Hayes, Timothy 49 (137)
Haynes, Trudy 176 (46)
Hays, Robert 180 (80)
Hays, Timothy 112 (60)
Hazo, Samuel 42 (67)
Head, Robert 117 (11)
Heard, J. Norman 174 (44)
Heavener, Mac D., Jr. 65 (26)
Hechinger, Fred 71 (87)
Hedges, Edith R. 57 (30)
Hefferan, Colien 151 (166)
Hefner, Keith 231 (3)
Hegarty, Christopher J. 42 (132), 177 (49), 180 (81)
Height, Dorothy J. 71 (144)
Heimgartner, Norman L. 159 (25)
Heimlich, Henry 135 (28)
Heinrichs, Waldo 181 (265), (337)
Heinsohn, Robert Jennings 151 (269)
Heisler, Ed 213 (4)
Heiss, Harold W., Jr. 136 (3), (26)
Heitzmann, William Ray 214 (4), (11), (36), (48), (57), (69), (78)
Helgoe, Robert S. 223 (13)
Hellwig, David J. 168 (25)
Helmetag, Charles H. 214 (66)
Helsel, Jack 176 (47)
Henderson, Don 176 (48)
Henderson, Edith 72 (2)
Henderson, Mary Lou 159 (26)
Henderson, Michael 182 (2)
Henderson, Skitch 71 (29)
Hendrick, James 16 (31)
Hendy, Martin 171 (27)
Henisch, Heinz K. 151 (73)
Henneke, Edmund G. 216 (51)
Hennessy, Jefferson T. 174 (45)
Henry, Bob 49 (138)
Henry, Janet 83 (10)
Henry, Kathleen M. 79 (58)
Henry, Paul 57 (31)
Henry, Porter 177 (50)
Henry, Richard L. 151 (277)
Herberg, Will 85 (12)
Herbison, Priscilla J. 168 (26)
Herlinger, Ilona 159 (27)
Herman, Fred 71 (165), 112 (61), 135 (29), 177 (51), 180 (82
Hermann, Beatrice 172 (4)
Herpel, George 177 (52)
Herring, Henry I. 151 (249)
Hersey, Ross 112 (62), 180 (83)
Hersh, Stuart 49 (139)
Hersh, Sy 71 (30)
Hershberger, Kenneth E. 151 (6)
Hesler, Richard 142 (37)
Hetznecker, William 181 (282)
Heumann, Joseph 57 (32)
Heyduck, Billy J. 57 (33)
Heyman, Lisa N. 181 (54), (220)
Hickey, William 83 (11)
Hicks, C. Norman 79 (59)
Hicks, Joseph J. 214 (21)
Hielscher, Newt 112 (63)
Hiers, Charles J. 16 (32)
Hifler, Joyce 97 (30)
Higginbotham, Peg 177 (53)
Higgins, Earl B. 16 (33)
Higgins, Joe 112 (64)
Higgins, Mary Lou 79 (60)
Higgs, Larry 49 (140)
Highsmith, James M. 168 (27)
Hildebrand, Francis 223 (9), (30), (34)

Hill, David E. 216 (52)
Hill, Dorothy K. 227 (20)
Hill, Jack 49 (141)
Hill, Mason L. 27 (4)
Hill, Michael 133 (2)
Hill, Morton A. 116 (4)
Hill, Shirley L. 29 (93), (342)
Hill, Walter E. 174 (46)
Hiller, Harley E. 223 (17)
Hillner, William M. 57 (34)
Hillson, C.J. 151 (152)
Hilton, Bruce 52 (40)
Hinman, Mary Bausch 79 (61)
Hinograd, A.J. 145 (3)
Hinton, Jerrold R. 65 (27)
Hintzman, D.E. 143 (6)
Hipple, G. Worthington 177 (54)
Hirschenson, Bernard 49 (142)
Hirshfeld, Marvin 181 (55)
Hitchcock, Walter B., Jr. 16 (34)
Hite, John B. 143 (7)
Hoade, Martin 49 (143)
Hobbs, Brenda Castille 174 (47)
Hobley, Marge Munn 142 (38)
Hobson, William G. 159 (28)
Hoch, Stewart 174 (48)
Hochberg, Victoria 49 (144)
Hoche, Henry 65 (28)
Hochschild, Richard 27 (29)
Hockman, Dan 57 (35)
Hodges, Richard E. 159 (29)
Hodgkinson, Brian 83 (12)
Hodson, Norma G. 16 (35)
Hoener, Lisa 229 (3)
Hoenig, Eugene M. 181 (169)
Hoffman, Barbara 159 (30)
Hoffman, Diane 84 (1)
Hoffman, Edward G. 216 (53)
Hoffman, Gary 49 (145)
Hoffman, Joshua 42 (5)
Hoffman, Lantz A. 151 (74)
Hoffman, Patricia 168 (28)
Hofstrom, Juanita 79 (62)
Hogan, Craig 67 (14)
Hogan, John 65 (29)
Holcomb, Thomas F. 117 (19), (43), (108)
Holdeman, Lillian 216 (54)
Holderby, Robert 42 (133)
Hollinder, Al 27 (39)
Hollingsworth, W.C. 67 (15)
Hollister, Charles A. 57 (36)
Holloman, Adelle 12 (5)
Holm, Margo 159 (31)
Holmes, Bruce B., Jr. 174 (49)
Holmes, Marjorie 97 (31)
Holroyd, Ruth 79 (63)
Holst, Art 112 (65), 177 (55)
Holt, Robert N. 216 (55)
Holtzman, Robert H. 181 (102), (303)
Holzer, Hans 154 (12)
Holzman, Red 71 (211)
Hommel, Flora 36 (1)
Hooks, Edgar 56 (28), (80)
Hopkins, Tom 177 (56)
Hopper, Paul T. 151 (235)
Horak, Stephan M. 57 (37)
Horgan, James D. 105 (118)
Horn, Kahn-Tineta 71 (97)
Horn, Michael H. 29 (71), (140), (271)
Horn, Walter V. 65 (30)
Hornung, Paul 71 (212)
Horrocks, Mike 157 (1)
Hortis, Theophanis 168 (29)
Horton, George R. 16 (36)
Horwitz, Murray 176 (49)
Hosman, Jean 129 (2)
Hostetler, Frank C. 142 (39)
Hotard, Stephen R. 174 (50)
Hottelet, Richard C. 102 (14)
Houlihan, John F. 151 (127)
Houmes, D.L. 67 (16)
House, Donald R. 16 (37)
Houston, Franklin S. 181 (36)
Hovanec, Evelyn 151 (236)
Howar, Barbara 156 (32)
Howard, Margaret F. 79 (64)
Howard, Milford Kenneth 16 (38)
Howard, Robert 117 (84)
Hower, Barbara 176 (50)
Hoy, David 112 (66), 180 (84)
Hoy, John C. 27 (20), (40)
Hoyt, George C. 171 (10), (57)
Hoyt, Milton 159 (32)
Hubbard, Hazel 216 (56)
Hubschman, Lynn 176 (51)
Hudiburgh, Kayren 178 (1)
Hudson, Leonard C. 180 (85)
Hudson, Max 65 (31)
Hudson, Randolph H. 142 (40)
Huff, Arden N. 216 (57)
Huffman, Dale L. 16 (39)
Huffman, Stanley A., Jr. 216 (58)
Hufnagle, Jon 177 (133)
Hughes, Irene 94 (2)
Hull, Harry H. 216 (59)
Hulse, Christopher R. 29 (54), (141), (161), (257), (284), (334)
Hultman, John 130 (18)
Hume, Bri 71 (31)
Humes, Ja es 176 (52)
Humphreys, Ben 177 (44)
Humphreys, Donald 181 (103), (133)
Humphries, Russell J. 180 (86)
Hunt, Edward E., Jr. 151 (208)
Hunt, Eugene B. 29 (108)
Hunt, Finley C., Jr. 49 (146)
Hunt, Joel 136 (13), (18)
Hunt, Jon H. 181 (104)
Hunter, Cecil 112 (67)
Hunter, Kenneth 129 (3)
Hunter, Richard S. 67 (17)
Hunter, Sam 71 (166)
Huntley, Dave 171 (36)
Hurley, Pat 56 (96)
Hurst, Allan 112 (68)
Hurst, Michael Eliot 171 (2), (48)
Husain, Asad 142 (41)
Hutchinson, John 171 (49)
Hutson, Don 112 (69), 177 (57), 180 (87)
Hyams, Peter 49 (147)
Hynek, J. Allen 135 (30)
Hynes, Teresa M. 29 (35), (142), (285), (308), (335)
Hyson, John M. 214 (25), (63)

I

Ibrahim, Hilmi 224 (9)
Ibsen, Charles A. 159 (33)
Iglewicz, Boris 181 (283)
Ikenberry, Stanley O. 151 (101)
Imus, Don 71 (32)
Iregbulem, Hilary I. 142 (42)
Irwin, J. David 16 (40)
Isard, Eleanore S. 181 (221), (284), (323)
Ishii, Thomas K. 105 (119)
Itkin, William 142 (43)
Ivory, James 49 (148)

J

Jacks, Lloyd B. 117 (20), (128), (137)
Jackson, Charles J. 142 (44)
Jackson, Henry 176 (53)
Jackson, Jesse 71 (145)
Jackson, Richard G. 117 (12)
Jacobs, Claire M. 142 (45)
Jacobson, Alan W. 65 (32)
Jaenike, Vaughn 57 (38)
Jaffa, Harry V. 85 (13)
Jaffe, Eugene 176 (54)
Jaglom, Henry 49 (149)
Jaipaul, Inderjit 181 (56)

Jakubek, Gene 180 (88)
Jala, Michael 14 (9)
James, Furney K. 56 (46)
James, Lois 224 (10)
Janeiro, Jan 79 (65)
Janeway, Eliot 42 (134), 71 (70), 112 (70), 135 (31)
Janeway, Elizabeth 42 (68), (152), 112 (71)
Janis, Phyllis M. 79 (66)
Jansen, Robert H. 180 (89)
Janssen, Peter 71 (88)
Jaroff, Leon 71 (98)
Jarriel, Tom 71 (33)
Jarvis, Charles 177 (58), 112 (72)
Jaquith, Cindy 213 (5)
Jaskoski, Helen M. 29 (162), (202), (336)
Javits, Marion 97 (32)
Jay, John 15 (3)
Jemian, Wartan A. 16 (41)
Jencks, Christopher 71 (89)
Jenkins, Stephen R. 16 (42)
Jenner, Bruce 156 (33)
Jenness, Linda 213 (6)
Jennings, Donald 160 (10)
Jennings, Peter R. 52 (41)
Jensen, Jim 154 (13)
Jensen, Linda R. 181 (105), (150)
Jewett, Joan 180 (90)
Jillson, Joyce 225 (20)
Johannes, John R. 105 (55)
Johanson, Donald C. 112 (73)
Johnson, Barent 52 (42)
Johnson, Bill 180 (91)
Johnson, Charles A. 133 (3)
Johnson, David C. 168 (30)
Johnson, David C. 174 (51)
Johnson, Dennis 135 (32)
Johnson, Earl 135 (33)
Johnson, F. Milam 56 (127)
Johnson, Fred M. 29 (72), (109), (186), (236), (272)
Johnson, Gerald W. 16 (43)
Johnson, Irving M. 59 (5)
Johnson, Jack B. 117 (100), (117)
Johnson, James C. 168 (31)
Johnson, James R. 214 (70)
Johnson, John C. 151 (141)
Johnson, Lamont 49 (150)
Johnson, Lane J. 181 (134), (222), (266)
Johnson, Marjorie Seddon 181 (106)
Johnson, Mildred 112 (74), 177 (59), 180 (92)
Johnson, Milford 168 (32)
Johnson, Nicholas 102 (15)
Johnson, Overton R. 216 (60)
Johnson, Raynolds 29 (36), (55), (78), (94), (115), (258)
Johnson, Thomas H. 56 (3), (47), (81)
Johnson, Thomas W. 216 (61)
Johnson, Violet 142 (46)
Johnston, Oswald L. 220 (4)
Johnston, Richard G. 151 (128)
Jones, A.L. 83 (13)
Jones, Arnold P., Jr. 142 (47)
Jones, Arthur 52 (43)
Jones, C. Eugene, Jr. 29 (28), (143), (273)
Jones, Charles 135 (34), 177 (60)
Jones, DeWitt 59 (6), 69 (4)
Jones, Donald 52 (44)
Jones, Doug 59 (7)
Jones, Douglas R. 56 (48)
Jones, Ernest A. 65 (33)
Jones, Eugene 49 (151)
Jones, George Hilton 57 (39)
Jones, Harry 83 (14)
Jones, Jack 176 (55)
Jones, Jeanetta L. 79 (67)
Jones, L. Bevel 180 (93)
Jones, Leo M. 105 (19)
Jones, Lowell 42 (16), (135)
Jones, Raymond P. 67 (18)
Jordan, Adiel Moncrief 180 (94)
Jordan, Barbara 177 (61)
Jordan, DuPree, Jr. 180 (95)
Jordan, June 42 (69), 71 (187)
Jorgensen, N.M. 56 (82), (138)
Josephson, Nors S. 29 (221), (227), (317)
Josey, Anita Norris 180 (96)
Joubert, Paul E. 174 (52)
Joy, Ron 49 (152)
Judd, Walter H. 14 (10)
Judkins, Wesley P. 216 (62)
Jupena, Urban 79 (68)
Juran, Nathan 49 (153)
Jutza, Michael 42 (31)

K

Kacin, Jay 49 (154)
Kagan, Jeremy 49 (155)
Kahrs, Karl H. 29 (56), (121), (259)
Kaimann, Richard A. 105 (5)
Kaiser, Jeffrey S. 105 (42)
Kalb, Marvin 71 (34)
Kaleem, Imam Ata Ullah 1 (8)
Kalser, Konstantin 49 (156)
Kalupa, Frank B. 29 (4), (37), (122), (318)
Kamaleson, Samuel 230 (7)
Kamau, Lucy J. 142 (48)
Kampen, Irene 97 (33)
Karayama, Masahide 14 (11)
Kane, Michael 49 (157)
Kane, R.W. 92 (5)
Kaneen, Brian D. 171 (50)
Kanin, Garson 97 (34)
Kaplan, Jonathan 49 (158)
Kaplan, Robert S. 31 (1), (38)
Kaplan, Sheldon 49 (159)
Kaplow, Herb 112 (75), 135 (35)
Kardatzke, Nyle 105 (32)
Karlin, Edith 79 (69)
Karlstrom, Ernest L. 159 (34)
Karpeles, Harry D. 181 (15), (57), (170), (223)
Karr, Norman 111 (1)
Karras, Alex 71 (213)
Karstedt, Bruce 180 (97)
Kasman, Mort 49 (160)
Kasper, Raymond 142 (49)
Katen, Tom 176 (56)
Kates, Nate 10 (2)
Katz, Max 49 (161)
Katz, Phyllis B. 227 (21)
Kauffman, Ron 180 (98)
Kaufman, Bel 112 (76)
Kaufman, Glen 79 (70)
Kaufman, Jerome 49 (162)
Kaufman, M.A. 143 (8)
Kaufman, Zenn 177 (62), 180 (99)
Kaye, Alan S. 29 (5), (16), (38), (57), (128), (163), (203), (218), (228), (237), (319), (328)
Kaye, David N. 225 (21)
Kazan, Elia 71 (111)
Kazin, Alfred 71 (188)
Kean, Glenn R. 151 (175)
Keeble, Troy 72 (4)
Keepin, C. Robert 95 (1)
Keeslar, Donald 49 (163)
Keeslar, Suzanne M. 117 (138)
Kefford, Michael 69 (5)
Kehoe, Alice B. 105 (1)
Keiper, Ronald R. 151 (305)
Keisch, Bernard 31 (5)
Keiser, Edmund D., Jr. 174 (53)
Keister, Ronald E. 216 (63)
Keith, Judith 112 (77)
Keleher, R.A. 92 (6)
Kellar, Kenneth C. 180 (100)
Keller, Harry 49 (164)
Keller, Howard H. 117 (87), (101), (139)
Kelly, B. Wayne 151 (44)
Kelly, C. Michael 214 (26)

Kelly, Harry 220 (5)
Kelly, Heather C. 174 (54)
Kelly, John M. 168 (33)
Kemp, Arthur 71 (71), (167), 85 (14)
Kemper, Joan Corrier 112 (78)
Kendall, A. Richard 181 (171)
Kendall, Robert D. 168 (34)
Kendrick, Lionel 56 (83)
Kenepp, Nancy 181 (172)
Kennedy, Donald E. 151 (224)
Kennedy, Keith A. 168 (35)
Kennedy, Ken 49 (165)
Kent, Deryck R. 27 (30)
Kent, George 42 (70)
Keogh, Eugene J. 8 (4)
Keovimol, Watana 14 (12)
Kern, Richard 69 (6)
Kerr, Stephen T. 159 (35)
Kerr, Thomas M. 31 (14)
Keto, Clement T. 181 (28), (267), (338)
Keuls, Eva C. 227 (22)
Key, Rhoderick E. 57 (40)
Kiang, Harry 142 (50)
Kidd, Billy 42 (99)
Kidder, Louise 181 (285), (324)
Kiem, Irv 130 (19)
Kierce, Harold F. 187 (1)
Kiker, Douglas 71 (35), 135 (36)
Kilgore, James 42 (71)
Killens, John 42 (72), 71 (189)
Killian, Albert F. 16 (44)
Killian, Barbara E. 227 (23)
Kilpatrick, James J. 102 (16)
Kim, Hyung I. 14 (13)
Kim, Jai-Kyup 159 (36)
Kim, Myong Whai 14 (14)
Kim, Y.H. 56 (4), (49)
Kimmick, Anthony J. 187 (2)
Kinder, Garry 112 (79)
Kinder, Jack 112 (80)
King, Alfred 56 (84)
King, Bucky 79 (71)
King, Durnford 49 (166)
King, Joy K. 227 (24)
King, Nelson B. 16 (45)
King, Thomas B. 151 (23)
Kinishi, Diane Reiko 99 (3)
Kintner, William R. 85 (15)
Kipp, Raymond J. 105 (120)
Kiraithe, Jacqueline M. 29 (95), (204), (297)
Kirchner, Grace L. 159 (37)
Kirk, Leo J. 123 (7)
Kirk, Robert W. 65 (34)
Kirk, Roy V. 117 (21)
Kirk, Russell 85 (16)
Kirk, William G. 57 (41)
Kirkpatrick, Robert T. 174 (55)
Kissell, Rick 172 (5)
Kistenmacher, Mildred L. 181 (16), (173)
Kitchen, Herman 4 (4)
Kitei, Michael 49 (167)
Kiteley, Gary W. 16 (46)
Kitman, Marvin 71 (7)
Klassen, Vuryl J. 29 (214)
Klavin, Gene 71 (36)
Kleiber, Douglas A. 168 (36)
Kleiman, Carol 135 (37)
Klein, M. Rosalie 105 (43)
Klein, Raymond H. 173 (14)
Klein, Sheila 79 (72)
Klein, Stewart 71 (8)
Kleinmann, Walter M., Jr. 123 (8)
Kleisar, Randal 49 (168)
Klement, John J. 173 (15)
Klevans, Edward H. 151 (129)
Kline, Herbert 49 (169)
Kline, James M. 117 (70)
Kling, George 130 (20)
Klitzke, Ramon A. 105 (56)
Klitzner, Alan 130 (21)
Klock, Joe 177 (63)
Kloke, Eloise E. 27 (5), (41)
Klomp, Robert C. 151 (102)
Knautz, Francis C. 123 (9)
Kneebone, Leon R. 151 (176)
Kneller, George R. 174 (56)
Knife, Dennis 49 (170)
Knight, Alice 11 (7)
Knight, Clifford B. 56 (29), (70)
Knowles, Ruth Sheldon 97 (35)
Knox, David 56 (5)
Knox, John, Jr. 52 (45)
Knubel, J. 92 (7)
Knudsen, Herbert D. 173 (16)
Knutson, Keith M. 168 (37)
Koch, Kenneth 71 (190)
Kochenbach, John 130 (22)
Koenecke, Alice 177 (78), (140)
Kogen, Ronald 57 (42)
Kohler, Frances Coulborn 227 (25)
Kohut, Robert I. 27 (31)
Kokoris, James A. 142 (51)
Koliner, Ralph 214 (41)
Koloski-Ostrow, Ann Olga 227 (26)
Koltun, Frances Lang 97 (36)
Konigsburg, Sidney 65 (35)
Kooyumjian, Mary L. 142 (52)
Korda, Michael 154 (14)
Korty, John 49 (171)
Koschel, Ed S. 180 (101)
Kotz, Samuel 181 (4), (151)
Kowalek, Jon W. 79 (73)
Kozak, Wlodzimierz M. 31 (24)
Kozik, Eugene 151 (45)
Kozlowski, Ed 147 (7)
Kraft, (Mrs.) Harold 167 (2)
Kraft, R. Wayne 11 (8)
Kraicer, Jacob 160 (11)
Krainin, Julian 49 (172)
Kramer, Hilton 71 (9)
Kramer, Jack 42 (100)
Kramer, Jerry 176 (57), 177 (64)
Kramer, Stanley 49 (173)
Krasnoff, Julienne Hallen 79 (74)
Kratochvil, Frank 49 (174)
Krause, Hal 177 (65)
Krause, Paul 57 (43)
Kraybill, Edward K. 151 (103)
Kraybill, Herbert K. 151 (186)
Kraybill, Wilbur K. 151 (104)
Kreamer, Jeanne T. 174 (57)
Kress, Roy A. 181 (107)
Kroger, Manfred 151 (177)
Krondahl, Hans 79 (75)
Krutz, Ronald L. 31 (18)
Krutza, June 57 (44)
Kubek, Anthony 14 (15), 85 (17)
Kuehn, John 49 (175)
Kuehnelt-Leddihn, Erik Von 85 (18)
Kuhn, Gerald D. 151 (178)
Kujundzic, Zeljko 151 (27)
Kulik, Buzz 49 (176)
Kumar, Frederick L. 117 (97)
Kumayama, Akihisa 3 (2)
Kumin, Maxine 71 (191)
Kummer, Mary J. 151 (142)
Kunkle, John F. 174 (58)
Kuntsler, William 42 (17), (136)
Kup, A.P. 171 (3)
Kuralt, Charles 135 (38), 154 (15)
Kurstedt, Harold A., Jr. 216 (64)
Kurtz, Donn M., II 174 (59)
Kuster, Bill 176 (58)
Kutney, Andrew J. 181 (58), (224), (325)
Kuykendall, John W. 16 (47)

L

La Lena, Connie 79 (76)
Labbauf, Abbas 151 (153)
Lacaze, Marie Louise 174 (60)
Lachman, Morton 49 (177)
Laczniak, Gene R. 105 (6)
Ladd, Clay 57 (45)
Ladd, Eleanor 181 (108)
Ladousa, Dickie 174 (61)
LaGoy, Stephen P. 151 (229)
Lahart, Joe 177 (66)

Laidman, Harvey 49 (178)
Lamb, Fred M. 216 (65)
Lambert, B. Geraldine 174 (62)
Lamont, Jay 176 (59), 181 (37), (225)
Lamoureux, Joseph G. 216 (66)
Lancaster, William W. 180 (102)
Landers, Ann 177 (67)
Landres, Paul 49 (179)
Lane, Benjamin A. 151 (105)
Langdale, Noah 177 (68)
Lange, George 69 (7)
Langran, Robert W. 214 (5)
Lanham, Ben T. 16 (48)
Lanham, Carol D. 227 (27)
Lanier, Gene D. 56 (50)
Lanier, Worth 16 (49)
Lantz, Harold 181 (174)
Lao, Rosina C. 56 (51), (135)
Lao, Y.J. 56 (71)
Lapoint, James J. 174 (63)
LaPorte, Robert, Jr. 151 (196)
Lapp, Charles 71 (168), 177 (69), 180 (103)
Lapsansky, Emma 181 (29), (268)
Lark, Ed 15 (4)
Larson, Reed 131 (3)
Larson, Roland E. 151 (250)
Larson, Thomas D. 151 (292)
Larson, Walter G. 168 (38)
Lassetter, Maggie S. 65 (36)
Laszlo, Andrew 49 (180)
Lathan, Stan 49 (181)
Latta, Robert W. 230 (8)
Lauda, Donald P. 57 (46)
Lauffer, Herbert 151 (278)
LaVallee-Williams, Marthe 181 (59), (74), (109), (315), (326)
Laven, Arnold 49 (182)
Lavenson, James 102 (17)
Lawler, Donald 56 (52), (64)
Lawler, Edwina G. 52 (46)
Lawless, Louie 49 (183)
Lawrason, Robin E. 181 (75), (110), (316)
Lawrence, Donald 180 (104)
Lawrence, J. 164 (1)
Lawrence, Robert S. 27 (21)
Lawson, Deborah 176 (60)
Lawson, Dorothy M. 57 (47)
Lawson, Hughie G. 117 (71)
Lawson, Jonathan 168 (39)
Leader, Anton 49 (184)
Leahy, Edward P. 56 (120)
Leahy, Robert 181 (5), (111)
Leahy, William 42 (137)
Lear, Len 176 (61)
Lease, A.A. 168 (40)
Leathers, Ronald 57 (48)
Leavell, J. Perry 52 (47)
Lebas, Sherry 174 (64)
Lebofsky, Dennis S. 181 (85), (112), (226), (304), (317)
LeBorg, Reginald 49 (185)
Lechowich, Richard V. 216 (67)
Leder, Hans H. 29 (96), (123), (164), (238)
Lederer, Francis 49 (186)
Ledridge, Paul Walton 65 (37)
Lee, Alan 49 (187)
Lee, Alfred McClung 52 (48)
Lee, Don L. 71 (192)
Lee, Fran 101 (1)
Lee, John A.N. 216 (68)
Lee, John W. 180 (105), 182 (3)
Lee, Juel 27 (22)
Leeds, Fredric 151 (28)
Leetch, Thomas 49 (188)
Lefkowitz, Mary R. 227 (28)
Legos, Patricia M. 181 (113), (227), (286)
Lehew, Harry D. 151 (75)
Lehman, John H. 173 (17)
Lehman, Ross B. 151 (76)
Lehr, Jay H. 136 (14), (19), (27)
Lehrer, Sam 176 (62)
Leifer, Calvin 181 (60), (114), (175)
Leigh, Peter R., II 57 (49)
Leitner, Ted 176 (63)
Leland, Robert 49 (189)
Lenaerts, Sue 178 (2)
Lenderman, Max L. 79 (77)
Lenhoff, Howard M. 27 (42)
Lenhoff, Sylvia G. 27 (23), (32), (43)
Lennon, Donald R. 56 (30)
Lens, Sidney 42 (18), (138)
Leonard, Lee 71 (37), (214), 130 (23)
Leonard, Sheldon 49 (190)
Leppert, Alfred M. 16 (50)
Lequire, Stephen D. 216 (69)
Lerner, Irving 49 (191)
Lerner, Joseph 49 (192)
Lerner, Jules 142 (53)
Lerner, Max 71 (38)
LeRoy, Mervyn 49 (193)
Lester, C. Ned 216 (70)
Lester, Mary 225 (22)
Lester, Michelle 79 (78)
Lester, William 225 (23)
Letterese, Peter D. 180 (106)
Leubsdorf, Carl 219 (6)
Lev, Benjamin 181 (339)
Leventhal, Jerome I. 181 (38), (61), (115)
Levertow, Denise 71 (193)
Levey, William 49 (194)
Levilain, Guy 168 (41)
Levin, Leonard 49 (195)
Levin, Meyer 71 (178)
Levin, Peter 49 (196)
Levine, Irving A. 71 (72)
Levine, Irving R. 71 (39), 112 (81), 135 (39)
Levine, Richard 138 (4)
Levine, Ruth Ellen 181 (176), (228)
Levinson, Mimi 79 (79)
Levinson, Sam 156 (34)
Levy, Maury 176 (64)
Levy, Steve 176 (65)
Lewis, Blake D., Jr. 151 (46)
Lewis, Claude 176 (66)
Lewis, Frederick C. 56 (53)
Lewis, Gary 67 (19)
Lewis, Joseph 49 (197)
Lewis, Ken 177 (70)
Lewis, Max L. 8 (5)
Lewis, Theodore G. 174 (65)
Lewis, W. David 16 (51)
Leyden, Michael B. 57 (50)
Licata, Kenneth 49 (198)
Liddle, Howard 181 (229), (287), (310)
Lieb, John A. 151 (154)
Lieberman, E. James 58 (2)
Lieberman, Harold 168 (42)
Liebler, Joan G. 181 (177)
Liebow, Ely 142 (54)
Lienhard, Joseph T. 105 (107)
Ligett, M.T. 67 (20)
Lignante, Bill 97 (37)
Lih-Wu, Han 14 (16)
Lilly, George T. 117 (80)
Lindauer, John 117 (22)
Lindberg, Phillip 57 (51)
Lindbergh, Jon Morrow 97 (38)
Linder, John E. 180 (107)
Lindman, Margaret L. 142 (55)
Lindquist, Carol U. 29 (239), (343)
Lindsey, Jason 49 (199)
Lindsey, Ouida 42 (39), (139)
Lindzey, James S. 151 (306)
Ling, Mona 177 (71)
Linker, Halla Gudmundsdottir 225 (24)
Linkletter, Art 112 (82), 135 (40), 156 (35), 177 (72)
Linkletter, Jack 102 (18), 112 (83)
Linn, John 57 (52)
Linn, Theodore Chace 52 (49)
Linville, George M. 65 (38)
Lipset, Seymour M. 71 (99)

Lipsio, Peter 4 (5)
Lisager, Peter 71 (40)
Liston, Albert M. 29 (73), (80), (260)
Littlefield, Nancy 49 (200)
Littleton, Taylor D. 16 (52)
Littman, Lynne 49 (201)
Litton, Martin 59 (8), 69 (8)
Livingston, Doc 49 (202)
Livingston, Savetta L. 79 (80)
Loberger, Gordon J. 117 (61)
Lobue, J.D. 49 (203)
Lockhart, Barbara D. 181 (6), (327)
Loder, H. Leith 225 (25)
Lodge, Elizabeth 176 (67)
Lodge, Henry Cabot 37 (39)
Loeb, Marshall 71 (73)
Loessin, Edgar 56 (12)
Lofgreen, Harold A. 168 (43)
Logan, Bob 42 (40)
Logue, John J. 214 (27), (54)
Lokey, Clarence W. 180 (108)
London, Jerry 49 (204)
Long, C. Hardy 216 (71)
Long, James W. 132 (6)
Long, Joseph B. 183 (3)
Long, Nate 49 (205)
Lonie, Don 177 (73)
Lono, J. Mark 52 (50)
Loomis, Horace B. 173 (18)
Loomis, Julia W. 227 (29)
Lopata, Helena 42 (140)
Lopata, Richard 42 (141)
Lopez, Anthony 216 (72)
Lopez, Jess A. 29 (58), (144), (193), (344)
Lopez, Jose E. 142 (56)
Lorayne, Harry 180 (109)
Lord, E.F. 92 (8)
Lord, Joseph 176 (68)
Lord, Walton J. 151 (29)
Lorde, Audre 42 (73)
Lorrah, Jean 117 (89), (96)
Losak, Stanley 49 (206)
Losoncy, Thomas A. 214 (6), (14), (74), (84)
Losso, Ernest 49 (207)
Lotlikar, Prabhakar D. 181 (178), (230)
Lotman, Arline 176 (69)
Lovell, R.T. 16 (53)
Lovett, Robert E. 27 (6)
Lovingood, Rebecca P. 216 (73)
Lovrinic, Jean 181 (318)
Lowell, Ross 49 (208)
Lowell, W.S. 57 (53)
Lowenthal, Lynn 176 (70)
Lower, Elmer W. 135 (41)
Lowry, Ted 49 (209)
Lowther, J. Stewart 159 (38)
Lubachko, Ivan S. 117 (62), (72), (141)
Lubell, Samuel 71 (146)
Lubin, Arthur 49 (210)
Lucas, James A. 142 (57)
Lucas, James T., Jr. 216 (74)
Lucas, Jerry 177 (74)
Luchs, Fred E. 180 (110)
Lucia, Joseph L. 214 (32)
Lumbleau, John 177 (75)
Lundberg, William E. 230 (9)
Lundgren, Jon C. 226 (1)
Lunger, Brett 33 (7)
Lupton, Charles 151 (187)
Lydecker, Beatrice 225 (26)
Lyle, Marguerite R. 174 (66)
Lyman, Bernard 171 (51)
Lynch, Catherine M. 151 (298)
Lynch, Margaret 11 (9)
Lynch, Richard L. 216 (75)
Lynn, Frank 65 (39)
Lynn, Joanne L. 29 (29), (97), (124), (145), (197), (205), (320)
Lynn, Paul K. 117 (81)
Lyons, C.P. 91 (5)
Lyras, Dean 49 (211)
Lyster, Patricia M. 79 (81)
Lytel, June W. 214 (16), (18)
Lywood, Denis 160 (12)

M

McAlindon, Harold R. 180 (11)
McAree, James 151 (197)
McAssey, Edward V. 214 (29)
McBride, Lois 79 (82)
McBride, Mary 42 (74)
McBride, Walter 79 (82)
McCahon, Robert 49 (212)
McCain, John S., Jr. 14 (17)
McCain, Roger A. 181 (39), (141), (231), (288)
McCall, Raymond J. 105 (100)
McCann, James K. 27 (7)
McCarren, Dale 42 (41)
McCarthy, Eugene 8 (6), 42 (19), 71 (147), 156 (36)
McCarthy, Gregory J. 151 (130)
McCarthy, J.F. 210 (1)
McCarthy, Miles D. 29 (98), (174), (274)
McCarty, John J. 180 (112)
McCauley, Bert J. 151 (293)
McClaren, Milton 171 (18), (37)
McClerren, B.F. 57 (57)
McClinton, Curtis R., Jr. 112 (84)
McClory, Sean 49 (213)
McCollum, Robert E. 181 (116)
McCollum, Robert H. 216 (76)
McConnell, Robert L. 216 (77)
McCord, R. Warren 16 (54)
McCormick, Barnes W. 151 (33)
McCormick, Robert H. 151 (47)
McCoy, Albert A. 65 (40)
McCredie, John W. 31 (19)
McCulloh, Byron 31 (29)
McCullough, George E. 65 (41)
McCulstion, John 159 (39)
McDonald, Clark E. 80 (2)
Macdonald, James 142 (58)
McDonald, Rita T. 105 (94), (101)
McDonald, W. Scott, Jr. 52 (51)
McDonough, Joseph 49 (214)
McElligott, James G. 181 (179)
McEnally, Terence E., Jr. 56 (128)
McFarland, G. Richmond 140 (1)
McFarland, Gene 57 (58)
McFarland, Kenneth 71 (169), 112 (85), 135 (42), 177 (76)
McFarland, Richard A. 29 (240)
McFarland, Richard F. 12 (6)
McGaughey, Robert H., III 117 (85)
McGhee, Clint 177 (77)
McGlachlin, Kay 178 (3)
McGrane, William J. 180 (113)
McGregor, Wallace 143 (9)
McGuire, Martin E. 56 (6), (31)
Macha, Roger L. 117 (5), (122)
McHugh, William P. 117 (9), (31)
McIntosh, Claudette E. 65 (42)
Mackal, Roy 42 (118)
McKay, Jim 42 (101), 71 (215), 112 (86), 156 (37)
Mackin, Catherine 112 (87), 135 (43), 176 (71)
McKinstry, Donald 151 (307)
McKinstry, Richard H. 151 (270)
McKirdy, Gail 129 (4)
McKnight, Conrad 174 (67)
McLaglen, Andrew 49 (215)
MacLaren, Fred 57 (54)
McLaren, Robert B. 29 (59), (99), (116), (241), (275), (321), (345)
McLaughlin, Wayne 136 (4), (20)
MacLeish, Rod 71 (41)
McMahon, Robert 3 (3)
McMillan, Malcolm C. 16 (55)
McMillan, Margaret 174 (68)
McMillion, Martin B. 216 (78)
McMullen, Jay 49 (216)

McMurry, Robert N. 180 (114)
MacNair, Wilmer 174 (69)
MacNeil, Robert 71 (42)
McNelly, Willis E. 29 (206)
McNicholas, Jean 98 (2)
McPherson, Michael L. 29 (146), (309)
McPhillips, Hugh 49 (217)
McQuaing, John H. 180 (115)
McReynolds, David 172 (6), 178 (4), 217 (2)
McReynolds, James 130 (24)
MacRury, King 180 (116)
McVittie, James L. 123 (10)
Maddox, Donald D. 230 (10)
Maddox, Lester 71 (148)
Madhubuti, Haki 42 (75)
Madsen, Bill 59 (9)
Madsen, Russell D. 168 (44)
Magidoff, Nila 97 (40)
Magner, Martin 49 (218)
Maley, Larry E. 67 (21)
Malik, Daud Abdul 1 (10)
Malik, Saeed Ahmad 1 (10)
Mallow, Mike 176 (72)
Malnati, Richard J. 181 (289)
Malone, Bobby G. 117 (45)
Mamoulian, Rouben 49 (219)
Mandell, Hans 49 (220)
Mandino, Og 177 (78)
Mandle, Joan D. 151 (167)
Mandlin, Harvey 49 (221)
Mangravite, Thomas 49 (222)
Mankiewicz, Joseph 49 (223)
Mann, Carol 42 (102)
Mann, Daniel 49 (224)
Mann, Donald H. 29 (80)
Manne, Henry G. 85 (19)
Manning, Patricia 225 (27)
Manoli, Sadanand G. 105 (20), (29)
Mansfield, Mike 71 (149)
Mansuy, Frank 151 (77)
Manuel, David P. 174 (70)
Manwaring, Robert T. 67 (22)
March, Alex 49 (225)
Marchman, James F. III. 216 (79)
Marciarose 176 (73)
Marcus, Edward 172 (7)
Marcus, Stanley 102 (19)
Mardell, Corol D. 142 (59)
Maresco, Richard E. 105 (72)
Margolis, Marjorie 71 (43)
Marine, Jules A. 180 (117)
Mark, Norman 42 (42)
Marker, Sherry 227 (30)
Markowski, Mel 56 (7)
Marks, Copeland H. 79 (83)
Marks, Gerald 160 (13)
Marlow, H. LeRoy 151 (287)
Marlowe, Thomas J. 216 (80)
Marmas, James G. 168 (45)
Marrero, Frank 49 (226)
Marshall, Harold P. 216 (81)
Marshall, Garry 49 (227)
Marshall, Leo 176 (74)
Marsicano, Arthur J. 151 (131)
Martel, Leon C. 102 (20)
Martel, Wallace N. 173 (19)
Martens, Frank H. 65 (43)
Martin, Jacquie 159 (40)
Martin, John Stokes 16 (56)
Martin, Leila 97 (41)
Martin, Ross 49 (228)
Martin, Sobey 49 (229)
Martin, W. Lee 180 (118)
Martin, William Oliver 85 (20)
Marton, Andrew 49 (230)
Martucci, Carmen 176 (75)
Marvin, Frank F. 216 (82)
Marvin, Grace 79 (84)
Marx, Maxine 154 (16)
Marx, Robert 42 (142)
Mascio, Afework A. 52 (52)
Masimini, Leslie 175 (2)
Maslansky, Paul 49 (231)
Mason, Eleanor C. 52 (53)
Mason, J.P.H., Jr. 216 (83)
Mason, Pamela 225 (28)
Mason, Saul 214 (33)
Masquelier, Roger 180 (119)
Massari, Mark 49 (232)
Massey, Morris 177 (79)
Masteller, Edward 151 (308)
Mastro, Julius 52 (54)
Matarazzo, S.M. 117 (46)
Mathers, Lewis J. 214 (28)
Mathews, H. Lee 151 (48)
Mathis, Edward 214 (34)
Mathis, Gilbert L. 117 (6), (23), (47)
Mattera, Joanne 79 (85)
Matthai, James P. 117 (32), (63)
Matzner, Gerhard C. 57 (55)
Maurer, David J. 57 (56)
Maxwell, Keith A. 159 (41)
Maxwell, Ronald 49 (233)
May, Judy 136 (21), (28)
May, Sandra A. 117 (48)
Mayberry, Arthur 105 (44)
Mayberry, Nancy 56 (121)
Mayer, Gerald 49 (234)
Mayer, H.K. 92 (9)
Mayer, Harold 49 (235)
Mayer, Jacquelyn 112 (88)
Mayer, Jean 176 (76)
Mayer, Nathaniel 181 (180)
Mayes, Jerry W. 117 (135)
Mazer, Ira 49 (236)
Meadows, Mark E. 16 (57)
Means, Marianne 219 (7)
Medler, Meredith A. 168 (46)
Mehl, Lewis 122 (3)
Meiklejohn, John 49 (237)
Meilach, Dona Z. 79 (86)
Mekas, Jonas 71 (112)
Melady, Thomas Patrick 97 (42)
Melhem, D.H. 42 (76)
Melo, Niels 49 (238)
Melton, Dave 112 (89)
Meltzer, Al 176 (77)
Meltzer, Bernard 176 (78)
Meltzer, Marilyn 79 (87)
Meltzer, Newton 49 (239)
Menard, Glenn 174 (71)
Menendez, Albert J. 12 (7)
Mentes, Matthew 59 (10)
Mentes, Sherilyn 59 (10)
Merchant, Larry 71 (216)
Merryman, Walker 184 (4)
Mertens, Gerald C. 168 (47)
Meserole, Harrison T. 151 (237)
Messick, Dale 42 (6)
Messuri, Anthony 49 (240)
Mester, Cathy S. 151 (78)
Metallinos, Nikos 181 (76), (86), (142), (232)
Metcalf, James 91 (6)
Metz, Donald L. 105 (21), (108)
Metzgar, G.F. 92 (10)
Metzler, James A. 52 (55)
Mewett, Jack H. 29 (310)
Mews, Marvin 49 (241)
Meyer, Betty 142 (60)
Meyer, Frank S. 85 (21)
Meyer, Harold 181 (17), (181)
Meyer, Peter B. 151 (49)
Meyers, Bruce F. 159 (42)
Meyers, Doris J. 151 (56)
Meyers, Gertrude 142 (61)
Meyers, Howard 110 (7)
Miah, Malik 213 (7)
Micali, Paul 135 (44), 180 (120)
Michaels, Jay 49 (242)
Michaels, Richard 49 (243)
Michaels-Paque, Joan 79 (98)
Michalec, John M. 67 (23)
Michelon, L.C. 180 (121)
Michl, H.E. 85 (22)
Middleton, John B. 150 (5)
Midgley, Stan 91 (7)
Milakofsky, Louis F. 151 (106)
Miles, Leland 97 (43)
Milham, Mary Ella 227 (31)
Milius, John 49 (244)

Millar, A. Craig 151 (107)
Miller, Arthur S. 181 (182)
Miller, Eugene W., Jr. 151 (198)
Miller, J. Philip 49 (245)
Miller, James 52 (56)
Miller, Joan D. 168 (48)
Miller, Len 27 (8)
Miller, Martin 168 (49)
Miller, Michael G. 117 (33), (90)
Miller, Richard L. 181 (18), (62), (340)
Miller, Robert 181 (233), (269)
Miller, Sayers, J., Jr. 151 (279)
Miller, William E. 71 (150)
Millet, Jeremy 174 (72)
Milligan, Edward A. 112 (90)
Milligan, John 160 (14)
Millison, Martin B. 181 (290)
Mills, James W. 52 (57)
Milson, Linda 105 (45)
Milton, Richard 49 (246)
Mindlin, Stan 130 (25)
Miner, W. Peter 49 (247)
Minnix, Bruce 49 (248)
Minow, Newton 42 (20), (43)
Miranda, A.J. Pete 49 (249)
Mitchell, Andrea 176 (79)
Mitchell, H.L. 172 (8)
Mitchell, Robert J. 49 (250)
Mitchell, Robin C. 105 (22), (46)
Mitford, Jessica 71 (194)
Mitten, Suzanne 62 (2)
Mizusawa, Kiyoe 151 (271)
Mlynaryk, Peter M. 29 (81)
Moellenbrock, George, Jr. 151 (188)
Moeller, H.G. 56 (142)
Moeller, Wayne E. 174 (73)
Moffat, Joseph F. 174 (74)
Mofield, William Ray 177 (86), (129)
Mohnac, Alex M. 181 (183)
Moll, Edward O. 57 (59)
Mollenhoff, Clark 112 (91)
Molnar, Thomas 85 (23)
Monahan, David 49 (251)
Monahan, Robert E. 151 (50)
Monahan, Robert L. 223 (14), (35)
Monat, Jon 223 (6)
Monsalvatge, Ray 177 (80), 180 (122)
Montagu, Ashley 71 (100), 156 (38), 176 (80)
Montagu, (Lord) 97 (44)
Montgomery, James R. 216 (84)
Montgomery, Robert L. 180 (123)
Montgomery, Terry 168 (50)
Montjar, Monty J. 151 (179)
Moody, Jonathan 224 (11)
Moore, Archie 71 (217)
Moore, Charles 56 (107)
Moore, L. David 34 (1)
Moore, Laurence D. 216 (85)
Moore, Oscar 56 (18)
Moore, Robin 97 (45)
Moore, Steven A. 65 (44)
Moore, William 110 (8)
Moorhead, Hugh S. 142 (62)
Moorman, Theo 79 (88)
Moran, Robert T. 3 (4)
Morda 42 (119)
More, Judith de Luce 227 (32)
Morehouse, Chauncey A. 151 (280)
Moreland, Muriel K. 174 (75)
Moreland, Steve J. 159 (43)
Morella, John R. 174 (76)
Morgan, Kathleen 227 (33)
Morgan, Marabel 156 (39)
Morgan, William W. 16 (58)
Morgenthau, Hans 71 (151)
Morley, John 130 (26)
Morman, Jean Mary 42 (7)
Morrill, Robert W. 216 (86)
Morris, Calvin 42 (21)
Morris, Jeannie 42 (103)
Morris, John 151 (281)
Morris, Johnny 42 (104)
Morris, Robert 14 (18)
Morrisey, George I. 180 (124)
Morrow, Bruce 71 (44)
Morrow, Mable 79 (89)
Morse, Hollingsworth 49 (252)
Morse, J. Mitchell 181 (143), (234), (305)
Morse, Jeffrey W. 159 (44)
Morse, Otis B., IV 151 (7)
Morse, Richard L.D. 112 (92)
Mortimer, Kenneth P. 151 (8)
Morton, Bruce G. 181 (184)
Morton, Joseph C. 142 (63)
Moses, Robert 71 (152)
Moskal, Lilyb 65 (45)
Motley, Red 177 (81)
Mouton, Jean 174 (77)
Moutz, Madora 65 (46)
Moutz, W.B. 65 (47)
Moyer, Ivan W., Jr. 151 (168)
Moyer, Kenneth E. 31 (2), (7)
Muehleman, Tom 117 (109)
Mueller-Roemer, Peter 56 (54), (129)
Muhammad, Askia 42 (44)
Muldawer, Leonard 181 (278)
Mulder, John 52 (58)
Mullally, Mike 57 (60)
Mullen, Sharman Stanic 151 (79)
Muller, Alfred 49 (253)
Muller, Kal 69 (9)
Mulligan, John P. 187 (3)
Mundt, Richard M. 180 (125)
Mundus, Frank 69 (10)
Murad, Ahmad 57 (61)
Muravin, Victor 180 (126)
Murdock, Charles K. 177 (82), 180 (127)
Murphy, George 135 (45)
Murphy, John J. 142 (64)
Murphy, John R. 180 (128)
Murphy, Paul 116 (5)
Murphy, Raymond 151 (108)
Murray, Louise 57 (62)
Murray, Warren 49 (254)
Murty, Vedula N. 151 (251)
Muschalek, George 105 (109)
Muskie, Edmund 176 (81)
Muzzarelli, Robert A. 56 (55)
Myers, John A. 214 (42)
Myers, Robert J. 181 (40)
Myers, Rowland M. 103 (4)
Myerson, Bess 71 (153), 135 (46), 156 (40)
Myhers, John 49 (255)
Myhrum, Robert 49 (256)

N

Nachlas, Joel A. 216 (87)
Nagel, Curtis 91 (8)
Nager, Norman R. 29 (39)
Nagle, James J. 52 (59)
Nahm, Andrew C. 14 (19)
Nail, Kenneth M. 45 (2)
Nakatsu, Kanju 160 (15)
Namasaka, Boaz N. 29 (6), (60), (82), (147), (194), (219), (242), (261), (329), (337)
Namath, Joe 156 (41)
Nance, Jack D. 171 (38)
Nanjundappa, G. 29 (287)
Narducci, Leo 97 (46)
Nash, Von 112 (93)
Nasir, Khalil Ahmad 1 (11)
Neff, Earl 83 (15)
Neff, William 49 (257)
Nelson, Alma 176 (82)
Nelson, Daniel J. 16 (59)
Nelson, David 49 (258)
Nelson, David 117 (95)
Nelson, Gaylord 71 (154), 112 (94)
Nelson, Gregory 52 (60)
Nelson, Murry R. 151 (109)

Nelson, P.E. 67 (24)
Nelson, Ralph 49 (259)
Nelson, Richard C. 151 (209)
Nettleton, Herbert 180 (129)
Neuhaus, Cable 151 (80)
Newby, Jeffrey 49 (260)
Newell, Howard F. 117 (24), (34)
Newfield, Jack 71 (45)
Newman, Edwin 71 (46)
Newman, Jim 177 (83)
Newnham, Robert 151 (255)
Newstreet, Richard A. 65 (48)
Newton, David S. 61 (60)
Newton, William 49 (261)
Nicely, James E. 57 (63)
Nichols, Frank 59 (11)
Nichols, Frank 110 (9)
Nicol, Alexander 49 (262)
Niemeyer, Gerhart 85 (24)
Nigh, George 112 (95)
Nightingale, Earl 135 (47), 177 (84)
Nin, Anais 71 (195)
Niosi, Jerome J. 214 (7), (19), (37), (55), (58), (62), (67), (85), (94)
Nisbet, Jacquetta 79 (90)
Nischan, Bodo 56 (32), (140)
Nissim-Sabat, Charles 142 (65)
Nist, Joan Stidham 16 (61)
Niu, M.C. 181 (19), (341)
Nizetich, Anthony V. 187 (4)
Noble, Gil 71 (47)
Noble, Judith G. 79 (91)
Nock, George R. 159 (45)
Noffsinger, Hugh A. 117 (49)
Noland, Andrew J. 180 (130)
Noland, Carol 57 (64)
Noran, R.L. 112 (96), 180 (131)
Nordberg, Robert B. 105 (47)
Norlem, J. Brent 168 (51)
Norman, Thom 177 (85), 180 (132)
Norris, Awbrey G. 16 (62)
Norris, Beverly 97 (47)
Norris, Clarence 97 (48)
Norris, Rufus 97 (49)
North, John 130 (27)
North, John T. 57 (65)
Nottingham, Walter G. 79 (92)
Novaco, R.W. 27 (44)
Novak, George 213 (8)
Novak, Karen Laub 211 (5)
Novak, Michael 211 (6)
Novak, Robert 102 (21)
Novey, Harold S. 27 (33)
Nowers, Phil 133 (4)
Nugent, John Peer 97 (50)
Nunn, William H. 168 (52)
Nussbaum, Jim 177 (86)
Nussbaum, Martha C. 277 (34)
Nwodo, Christopher S. 214 (12), (38)
Nyaggah, Mougo 29 (7), (180)
Nyquist, Janet 79 (93)

O

O'Brien, Harold J. 151 (81)
Occhiogrosso, Frank V. 52 (61)
O'Connell, Sheila 171 (19), (52)
O'Conner, Michael P. 56 (33), (72)
O'Connor, Len 135 (48)
O'Connor, Ulick 97 (51)
O'Dell, Peter 9 (1)
Oden, Thomas Clark 52 (62)
Odle, D. Richard 29 (11), (17), (148), (293), (311), (322)
O'Farrell, Leo 49 (263)
Offenbacher, Elmer L. 181 (7), (279)
Ofield, Jack 49 (264)
O'Gorman, Ned 42 (77), (91)
Oh, John K.C. 105 (57)
Oh, Tai K. 29 (149)
Ohaver, Allan R. 174 (78)
Okamoto, Shumpei 181 (270), (342)
O'Kane, James M. 52 (63)
Okuda, Kenji 171 (11)
Okun, Arthur M. 71 (74)
Oliver, James R. 174 (79)
Oliver, Robert T. 151 (110)
Ollman, Nadine 52 (64)
Ollom, John F. 52 (65)
Oloffs, Peter 171 (39)
Olsen, Roger A. 105 (58), (62), (79)
Olsman, Phil 49 (265)
Olson, Harry 135 (49)
Olson, Harry E., Jr. 112 (97)
Olson-Prather, Emelie 224 (12)
Oltman, William 159 (46)
Oltmans, William L. 97 (52)
Ondik, Michael 151 (309)
O'Neal, John 70 (1)
Onega, Ronald J. 216 (88)
O'Neil, Charles 117 (102)
Ongiri, David O. 151 (111)
Onli, Turtel 42 (8)
Onorato, Ed 151 (282)
Opitz, Edmund A. 85 (25)
Ordesky, Maxine 225 (29)
Ordung, Wyott 49 (266)
Ordway, Frederick 154 (17)
Orlandi, Mary Kay Gamel 227 (35)
Orr, Henry P. 16 (63)
Orris, Richard E. 150 (6)
Osgood, Charles 97 (53)
O'Shaughnessy, Marjorie 79 (94)
O'Sullivan, Sallie 79 (95)
Ott, Jack S. 173 (20)
Ott, John 134 (5)
Ott, Robert W. 151 (30)
Ottenand, Tom 220 (6)
Ottman, Sidney 169 (3)
Otto, Don H. 168 (53)
Overlock, Richard 147 (8)
Overton, D. William 65 (49)
Owen, Gordon 180 (133)
Owen, James J. 216 (89)
Owen, Lewis 103 (5)
Owens, Jesse 42 (105), 156 (42), 177 (87)
Oyler, J.M. 216 (90)

P

Paalborg, Jane E. 181 (117), (152)
Pabst, Alfred A. 168 (54)
Pace, Don M. 177 (73), (118)
Pace, John 132 (7)
Packard, George 176 (83)
Packard, Vance 102 (22)
Packenham, Michael 176 (84)
Padgett, Richard 56 (73)
Pain, James H. 52 (66)
Painter, Hal 79 (96)
Palazzolo, Tom 42 (32)
Paling, John 69 (11)
Palladino, Nunzlo J. 151 (132)
Palmer, Gail Branscome 136 (15), (22)
Palmer, H. Bruce 123 (11)
Palmer, Leigh Hunt 171 (40)
Palpant, Edgar H. 151 (310)
Paltrow, Bruce 49 (267)
Pambookian, Hagop S. 105 (23), (48), (80)
Pan, Stephan C.Y. 14 (20)
Pancheri, Lillian Unger 16 (64)
Panichello, Joe 180 (134)
Panofsky, H. 151 (155)
Papalas, Anthony J. 56 (93), (122)
Paparella, Julia B. 214 (72)
Papish, Norma 79 (97)

Pappas, Ike 112 (98)
Pardue, William P. 65 (50)
Paris, Jerry 49 (268)
Park, Chung Soo 14 (21)
Park, Richard S. 105 (73)
Park, Thomas C. 168 (55)
Parker, Bettye J. 142 (66)
Parker, Francine 49 (269)
Parkin, Blaine R. 151 (143)
Parkinson, T.F. 216 (91)
Parrott, Alton 110 (10)
Parseghian, Ara 42 (106), 177 (88)
Parson, Steve R. 216 (92)
Parsons, Benny 33 (8)
Parsons, Johnny 33 (9)
Partch, Max 168 (56)
Paschal, Herbert 56 (34)
Pastore, John 71 (155)
Pastors, Charles R. 142 (67)
Paterson, Robert A. 216 (93)
Patrikas, Elaine O. 181 (185), (235)
Pattee, Eldon 143 (10)
Patterson, Henry O. 151 (169)
Patterson, Richard 49 (270)
Patterson, Robert A. 151 (9)
Pauli, Karen 79 (99)
Paull, James F. 168 (57)
Pauls, Robert 163 (2)
Paulus, Ingeborg 233 (18), (36)
Pavan, Barbara 181 (118)
Payne, Alfred C. 216 (94)
Payne, Ethel 42 (45), (153)
Payne, Gregory 44 (2)
Payne, Reed 181 (119)
Payne, Roger 69 (12)
Payne, William J. 132 (8)
Peacock, Charles 130 (28)
Peale, Norman Vincent 176 (85), 177 (90)
Peale, Ruth Stafford 112 (99)
Pearson, Sharon 57 (66)
Peck, Jim 217 (3)
Peck, John 168 (58)
Pederson, Harry 59 (12)
Pedroso, Angelina 142 (68)
Peek, Philip M. 52 (67)
Peerce, Jan 154 (18)
Pehler, Jim 168 (59)
Pehowski, Marian 105 (68)
Pekarek, Mike 177 (91)
Pellegrini, Mario 49 (271)
Pelt, Therese 105 (81)
Pendergast, Patrick F. 16 (65)
Pendleton, Mary 79 (100)
Pendleton, Winston K. 180 (135)
Pennington, Beth 79 (101)
Penza, Ralph 176 (86)
Perine, James L. 151 (170)
Perkins, Donald Y. 16 (66)
Perkins, Eugene 42 (78), (92)
Perkins, Harold W. 151 (112)
Perkins, Jack 71 (48)
Perrigo, Lucia 110 (11)
Perry, Bonnie 176 (87)
Perry, Frank 123 (12)
Perry, William L. 151 (299)
Peter, Karl 171 (4)
Peter, Laurence J. 71 (75), 135 (50), 156 (43)
Peters, Issa 3 (5)
Peters, William 49 (272)
Peterson, Charles F. 181 (186), (236)
Peterson, Esther 102 (23)
Peterson, Harold 174 (80)
Peterson, Margi 105 (82)
Peterson, Richard 42 (143)
Peterson, William H. 85 (26)
Petrakis, Harry Mark 42 (79)
Petranto, Russell 49 (273)
Petrie, Garth F. 117 (50)
Petro, Sylvester 85 (27)
Petty, O.L., Jr. 132 (9)
Peyser, John 49 (274)
Peyton, Joe 159 (47)
Pfaltzgraff, Robert L., Jr. 85 (28)
Philips, Lee 49 (275)
Phillips, David Atlee 97 (54)
Phillips, Jane E. 227 (36)
Phillips, John N. 168 (60)
Phillips, John W. 159 (48)
Phillips, Joy 52 (68)
Phillips, Mary H. 168 (61)
Phillips, Kevin 71 (156)
Phillips, Phyllis P. 16 (67)
Phillips, Ronald 49 (276)
Phillips, Ted 94 (3)
Piacsek, Bela E. 105 (3)
Piasecki, Michael J. 105 (7)
Pick, Franz 71 (76)
Pickens, Phillip 65 (51)
Pickus, Morris I. 180 (136)
Piel, Gerard 102 (24)
Pierce, John E. 65 (52)
Pierpoint, Bob 219 (8)
Piers, Maria 42 (93)
Piersall, Jimmy 113 (2)
Pierson, Beverly 159 (49)
Pierucci, Francis 151 (300)
Pike, Mary 213 (9)
Pillay, K.K.S. 151 (156)
Pintoff, Ernest 49 (277), 71 (113)
Piper, Roswell M. 56 (19), (74)
Piranian, Louise 79 (102)
Pitt, Joseph C. 216 (95)
Pittman, Audrey S. 181 (30), (311)
Pittman, Everett 56 (108)
Pizzi, William J. 142 (69)
Plater-Zyberk, Maria 214 (49), (59), (60), (81)
Platt, Dorothy B. 181 (20)
Platus, Libby 79 (103)
Plimpton, George 71 (218), 97 (55)
Plumb, Charles 112 (100)
Pocock, Sylvia 79 (104)
Podolak, Ed 112 (101)
Pohlmann, Marjorie F. 79 (105)
Poindexter, Malcolm 176 (88)
Polakof, James 49 (278)
Pollack, Allan 71 (179)
Pollack, Robert L. 181 (187)
Pollak, June Salz 29 (61), (207), (243)
Pollard, Al 180 (137)
Polley, Roy J. 159 (50)
Pollock, Leland Wells 52 (69)
Pomeroy, Justin 13 (1)
Pomeroy, Sarah B. 227 (37)
Pool, Jonathan R. 58 (3)
Poor, Peter 49 (279)
Popovtzer, Mordecai M. 181 (188)
Porcella, Yvonne 79 (106)
Porter, Robert F. 216 (96)
Posner, Sally 79 (107)
Poss, Howard L. 181 (280)
Possony, Stefan T. 14 (22), 85 (29)
Post, Ted 49 (280)
Potter, Franklin 27 (12)
Potter, Lawrence M. 216 (97)
Potter, Rick 49 (281)
Powell, J. Lewis 135 (51), 180 (138)
Powell, Joe 177 (92)
Powell, John W. 151 (283)
Powell, Miles 180 (139)
Powell, Walter H. 181 (41)
Powers, Shorty 71 (101)
Powlison, Fraser 29 (150), (244)
Prado, Marcial 29 (125), (151), (208), (323)
Prakash, Ravi 27 (34)
Pray, Alfred R. 151 (210)
Preminger, Otto 49 (282), 71 (114)
Prendergast, Thomas L. 105 (91)
Pressman, Gabe 71 (49)
Presson, Alta V. 117 (79), (94)
Presson, William O. 117 (123)
Prewett, Clinton R. 56 (136)
Price, Bill 117 (51)
Price, Charles L. 56 (35)

Price, Glenda D. 181 (189)
Price, J. Lorell 151 (219)
Price, Michael J. 27 (45)
Price, Michael J. 105 (24)
Price, R. Alan 151 (238)
Price, Sterling 180 (140)
Price, Vincent 102 (25)
Prichard, Ernie 177 (93)
Prince, Dawn Stegenga 151 (57), (82)
Prince, William 216 (98)
Prinsky, Lorraine E. 29 (62), (288), (346)
Probst, Leonard 71 (10)
Prochnow, Joan E. 68 (1)
Prock, Leone 171 (20)
Proctor, Richard M. 79 (108)
Properzio, Paul G. 52 (70)
Prosser, Duane R. 151 (144)
Prouty, R. Bruce 216 (99)
Proxmire, William 112 (102)
Pruhs, Ronald 105 (30)
Pruitt, William J. 173 (21)
Pryor, Fred H. 112 (103)
Prystowsky, Harry 151 (10)
Przekop, Lawrence R. 29 (18), (100)
Puckett, Billy J. 117 (130)
Pullen, Rick D. 29 (40), (117)
Pulley, Andrew 213 (10)
Purcell, Charles W. 174 (81)
Pusey, Robert H. 216 (100)
Puthenpurayil, Joseph 151 (199)
Pyle, Richard 49 (283)
Pyms, Jack 65 (53)

Q

Qubein, Nido 42 (46), 112 (104), 176 (89), 177 (94), 180 (141)
Queeney, Donna S. 151 (288)
Quereshi, M.Y. 105 (102)
Quick, Marian A. 151 (113)
Quinn, Matt 176 (90)
Quinn, Sally 71 (50)
Quigley, Robert J. 223 (4)
Qureshi, Naimuddin 29 (19), (41), (63), (181), (198), (303), (330)

R

Rabi, I.I. 71 (102)
Rabinovitz, Amy 93 (2)
Rabinowe, Victoria 79 (109)
Radke, William 42 (144)
Rafferty, Max 71 (90)
Rafkin, Alan 49 (284)
Ragan, Fred 56 (94)
Rainbolt, William 49 (285)
Ralston, John 177 (95), 180 (142)
Ramirez, Judith 90 (1)
Ranck, James G. 52 (71)
Randall, Dudley 42 (80)
Randol, Monroe G. 65 (54)
Randolf, Linda 172 (9)
Randolph, Eleanor 219 (9)
Randolph, Jennings 112 (105)
Raneri, Marietta R. 151 (114)
Rang, Jack C. 57 (67)
Ransom, Jay Ellis 4 (6)
Rapf, Maurice 49 (286)
Rappaport, Herbert 181 (291)
Rappaport, Margaret M. 181 (237), (292)
Rapper, Irving 49 (287)
Rasky, Harry 49 (288)
Ratcheson, R.J. 145 (2)
Rather, Dan 156 (44), 176 (91)
Rausch, Erwin 180 (143)
Ray, Gale 79 (110)
Ray, Nicholas 154 (19)
Reagan, Ronald 112 (106), 156 (45)
Reasoner, Harry 71 (51)
Rechlicz, Gloria 105 (49)
Rechtsteiner, S. 67 (25)
Rechy, John 71 (196)
Reckinger, Nancy R. 29 (64), (101), (347)
Reddy, Dick 59 (13)
Reeck, Darrell 159 (51)
Reed, (Mrs.) Curtis 79 (111)
Reed, Evelyn 213 (11)
Reed, Jane 57 (68)
Reed, Rex 97 (56)
Reed, Russell A. 151 (294)
Reep, Edward 56 (13)
Rees, Jim 56 (20), (56)
Reethof, Gerhard 151 (145)
Reeves, John A. 52 (72)
Reeves, Roger A. 173 (22)
Reeves, William J. 29 (30), (348)
Regan, Daniel T. 214 (75)
Regensteiner, Else 79 (112)
Reha, Rose K. 168 (62)
Reichhardt, Richard 142 (70)
Reichle, F.A. 181 (190)
Reid, Charlotte 164 (2)
Reid, Kathy 62 (3)
Reid, Orien 176 (92)
Reilly, Paul 180 (144)
Reimann, Paul A. 52 (73)
Reinhart, Carl 27 (13)
Reisch, Walter 49 (289)
Reiss, Zenaide 79 (113)
Remick, Forrest J. 151 (133)
Remmers, Kurt W. 52 (74)
Renas, Stanley R. 142 (71)
Rense, William C. 174 (82)
Respess, James W. 12 (8)
Ressler, Ralph 216 (101)
Reyburn, Gerald 151 (220)
Reyhons, Ken 177 (96)
Reynolds, Barbara 42 (47), (81)
Reynolds, Frank 135 (52)
Reynolds, Gene 49 (290)
Reynolds, Jack 97 (57)
Rheinstein, Frederic 49 (291)
Rhodes, Dallas 224 (13)
Rhone, Richard S. 52 (75)
Riccardi, Mary Elinor 79 (114)
Rice, Bruce 112 (107)
Rice, Charles L. 52 (76)
Rice, Lawrence 174 (83)
Rice, William J. 214 (43)
Rich, Buddy 154 (20)
Rich, Lawrence M. 105 (110)
Richards, Bob 42 (107), 112 (108), 135 (53), 177 (97)
Richards, John Thomas 56 (57)
Richards, Maria A. 105 (83), (125)
Richards, Ron 49 (292)
Richardson, Bobby 177 (98)
Richardson, Gilbert P. 180 (145)
Richardson, Jack J. 57 (69)
Richardson, Jane 112 (109)
Richette, Lisa A. 176 (93)
Richey, Russell E. 52 (77)
Richman, Irwin 151 (257)
Richman, Peter Mark 225 (30)
Richter, Ken 91 (9)
Rickels, Patricia V. 174 (84)
Rickenbacker, William F. 135 (54)
Rickey, Charles 49 (293)
Ridgley, Louis E., Jr. 151 (58)
Rieck, Mary 151 (171)
Riedel, Richard L. 173 (23)
Riemer, Neal 52 (78)
Riess, Steven A. 142 (72)
Rietveld, Ronald D. 29 (338)
Riforgiato, Leonard R. 151 (221)
Riggs, Bobby 71 (219)
Rigsby, Gordon 49 (294)
Riis, Jon Eric 79 (115)
Rimmer, Robert 71 (91)
Rinfret, Pierre A. 135 (55)
Ring, John F. 65 (55)
Riola, Peter W. 46 (5)
Risberg, Douglas F. 168 (63)
Ritter, Roberta 225 (31)

Rivell, Amos C. 181 (63), (120)
Rivera, Geraldo 71 (52), 156 (46)
Roach, Richard R. 105 (111)
Robbins, Charles 71 (103)
Robbins, David A. 143 (11)
Robbins, Roland W. 103 (6)
Robbins, Willard 49 (295)
Robersen, William N. 105 (63)
Roberson, Don C. 173 (24)
Robert, Cavett 71 (170), 177 (99), 180 (146), 225 (32)
Robert, Jennifer 227 (38)
Roberts, Charles B. 16 (68)
Roberts, James E. 216 (102)
Roberts, John 59 (14), 110 (12)
Roberts, Robin 176 (94)
Roberts, Stanley 171 (5), (58)
Robertson, B.T. 16 (69)
Robertson, Oscar 71 (220)
Robertson, Richard J. 142 (73)
Robertson, Roderick 160 (16)
Robeson, Andrew 216 (103)
Robinette, Gladys H. 174 (85)
Robinette, Walter R. 174 (86)
Robins, John 49 (296)
Robinson, Byron M. 151 (115)
Robinson, Chris 49 (297)
Robinson, Edward A. 142 (74)
Robinson, Hamlin 159 (52)
Robinson, Irma F. 79 (116)
Robinson, James W. 216 (104)
Robinson, Jerald F. 216 (105)
Robinson, John W. 159 (53)
Robinson, Mary 223 (1), (19), (38)
Robinson, Richard K. 105 (8)
Robison, Mack 65 (56)
Rocco, Emma S. 151 (31)
Rocco, Frank 176 (95)
Rockerble, R.A. 171 (41), (53)
Rodabaugh, Karl 56 (8)
Rodes, Robert Michael, Jr. 52 (79)
Rodgers, Carolyn 42 (82)
Rodriguez, Eloy 27 (14)
Rodriguez, Olga 213 (12)
Rodwell, Marianne S. 79 (117)
Roesler, Ned 166 (1)
Roessler, Helmut R. 3 (6)
Rogell, Albert 49 (298)
Rogers, Cosby S. 216 (106)
Rogers, Donald L. 57 (70)
Rogers, Doug 49 (299)
Rogers, Will, Jr. 112 (110), 154 (21)
Rogge, Benjamin A. 85 (30)
Rohrlich, George F. 181 (42)
Rohrs, Harold Clark 52 (80)
Rolland, Herbert H. 173 (25)
Romano, John J. 151 (116)
Roney, Bob 59 (15)
Roodenko, Igal 217 (4)
Rook, Marcella Ruble 13 (2)
Rook, Thomas 49 (300)
Rooney, Andrew A. 112 (111)
Roos, Anne D. 181 (144)
Root, Bruce 67 (26)
Root, David A. 24 (1)
Rose, Joseph L. 117 (103), (119), (124)
Rosen, Moishe 93 (3)
Rosenberg, Bonita S. 181 (64), (191)
Rosenberg, Milton 42 (145)
Rosenfeld, Alvin 71 (180)
Rosenfield, Sheryl 130 (29)
Rosenhaft, Ann 172 (10)
Rosenman, Jill C. 181 (121)
Rosenthal, Eugene 168 (64)
Rosner, Charlotte 42 (154)
Ross, Herbert 49 (301)
Ross, William 171 (28)
Rossi, Mary Ann 227 (39)
Rossman, W. Richard 150 (7)
Rosten, Leo 71 (197)
Rosten, Norman 71 (198)
Roston, Ronald 224 (14)
Roth, Catharine P. 227 (40)
Roth, Wolfgang 154 (22)
Rothenberg, Marvin 49 (302)
Rouse, R. Dennis 16 (70)
Roussin, Ramon 159 (54)
Rousslang, Kenneth 159 (55)
Rowan, Robert W. 117 (52)
Rowe, David N. 14 (23)
Rowe, Kenneth E. 52 (81)
Rowe, Neil 130 (30)
Rowen, Carl 71 (53)
Rowland, Howard Ray 168 (65)
Rowland, Thomas V. 159 (56)
Roy, Rustum 151 (272)
Rubin, Lisa Ferris 229 (4)
Rubin, Nancy F. 227 (41)
Rubini, Dennis A. 181 (238)
Rudd, Hughes 156 (47)
Rudivoravan, (Princess) 97 (58)
Rugg, Fred E. 174 (87)
Ruiz, Jose Luis 49 (303)
Rukeyser, Merryle 71 (171)
Rumsfield, Donald 102 (26)
Rush, Richard D. 97 (59)
Rushfelt, Joy M. 79 (118)
Rusk, Dean 71 (157)
Ruskin, Phil 49 (304)
Russell, Anna 154 (23)
Russell, Bill 42 (108)
Russell, G.E. 216 (107)
Russell, Harold 112 (112)
Russell, J. Michael 29 (118), (245)
Russell, Joan 79 (119)
Russell, Mark 156 (48)
Russo, Salvatore F. 223 (24)
Rutan, Al 163 (3)
Rutherford, Johnny 42 (109)
Ryan, John A. 29 (152), (276)
Ryan, Michael Daniel 52 (82)
Rye, Donald 117 (53)
Ryl, Eden 177 (100)
Rymal, Kenneth S. 16 (71)

S

Sadler, William 42 (146)
Sadovszky, Otto J. 29 (12), (20), (31), (65), (102), (165), (209), (246), (289), (294), (298), (339), (349)
Saeed, Munawar 1 (12)
Safer, Morley 156 (49)
Sager, Cindy 79 (120)
Sagrera, Walter D. 117 (74)
Sahl, Mort 156 (50)
Saiet, Ronald A. 142 (75)
St. Clair, David 225 (33)
St. John, Adela Roger 71 (199)
Saint-Laurent, Henri 180 (147)
St. Martin, Allen H. 174 (88)
Salathe, Karl M. 52 (83)
Salerno, Ralph 97 (60)
Saline, Carol 176 (96)
Salisbury, Harrison 102 (27)
Salk, Jonas 156 (51)
Salkow, Sidney 49 (305)
Saltmarsh, Robert E. 57 (71)
Saltzman, Joan Reid 79 (121)
Saltzstein, Alan L. 29 (66), (262)
Salvia, Anthony A. 151 (252)
Samachson, Dorothy 42 (33)
Samp, Robert J. 180 (148)
Samuelson, Norbert M. 181 (87), (239), (293), (306), (343)
Sanchez, Sonia 42 (83), (155)
Sand, Froma 225 (34)
Sanders, Carol 57 (72)
Sanders, Claud D. 57 (73)
Sanders, Denis 49 (306)
Sanders, F. David 56 (36)
Sanders, J.W. 57 (74)
Sandrich, Jay 49 (307)
Sanford, Robert 130 (31)
Sankovitz, James L. 105 (50), (64)
Santucci, James A. 29 (13), (21), (129), (247)

Santulli, Michael A. 151 (157)
Saperstein, David 49 (308)
Sarama, Penny 176 (97)
Sargent, Joseph 49 (309)
Sargent, Wyn 225 (35)
Sarris, Andrew 71 (115)
Satlof, Ronald 49 (310)
Saunders, George 213 (13)
Saunders, Robert D., Jr. 67 (27)
Savage, John W., Jr. 8 (7)
Savage, Margaret 171 (29)
Savitch, Jessica 176 (98)
Sayetta, Tom C. 56 (130)
Scali, John 102 (28)
Scarza, Vincent 49 (311)
Schaap, Dick 71 (221)
Schabacker, John M. 52 (84)
Schaefer, George 49 (312)
Schafrath, Dick 83 (16)
Schanbacker, Eugene M. 117 (82), (142)
Schanker, Robert 151 (117)
Schatz, Madeline F. 29 (182), (222)
Schatzman, Dennis 31 (27), (35)
Schecterson, Jack 147 (9)
Scheier, Michael F. 31 (37)
Schenck, George 151 (134)
Schenk, William A. 98 (3)
Schenkel, Chris 71 (222)
Scherer, Ray 71 (54)
Schetz, Joseph A. 216 (108)
Scheuer, John 176 (99)
Scheuer, Thomas 49 (313)
Schick, Henry 8 (8)
Schiebel, Joseph 85 (31)
Schieber, Frank W. 65 (57)
Schieman, Richard D. 173 (26)
Schiff, Jack 177 (101)
Schild, Albert 181 (43), (153)
Schindler, Max 49 (316)
Schirra, Walter 135 (56)
Schlafly, Phyllis 14 (24), 112 (113)
Schlauch, Wolfgang 57 (75)
Schlesinger, Arthur 176 (100)
Schlesinger, James R. 71 (158)
Schlesinger, Lawrence E. 180 (149)
Schlick, John 56 (85)
Schlientz, Margaret Anne 105 (95)
Schlow, Marthamae C. 151 (200)
Schmelzel, E.W. 132 (10)
Schmidt, Arthur 181 (240), (344)
Schmidt, David L. 112 (114)
Schmidt, Eberhard A. 143 (12)
Schmidt, Robert L. 124 (1)
Schmidt, Wilson E. 216 (109)
Schnall, Maxine 176 (101)
Schneider, Alan 49 (314)
Schneider, Clarence E. 29 (210)
Schneider, Richard 49 (315)
Schoenman, Ralph 213 (14)
Scholes, Gene W. 57 (76)
Schonfeld, Moses 71 (55)
Schorr, Beverly 214 (95)
Schorr, Daniel 102 (29)
Schorr, David J. 214 (44), (88)
Schrag, Adele F. 181 (122)
Schrager, Joyce 42 (156)
Schram, Gene W. 57 (77)
Schreffler, Ken 176 (102)
Schreier, James W. 105 (9), (84)
Schroeder, Charles G. 16 (72)
Schroeder, Philis Alvic 79 (122)
Schulberg, Budd 71 (116)
Schultz, C.B. 67 (28)
Schultz, Whitt 135 (57), 180 (150)
Schulz, Richard 31 (20)
Schuster, James J. 214 (89)
Schustik, Bill 97 (61)
Schwartz, Alice M. 151 (32)
Schwartz, Allen 49 (317)
Schwartz, David 177 (102), 180 (151)
Schwartz, Jack 177 (103)
Schwartz, Loretta 176 (103)
Schwartz, Maurice 223 (37)
Schwartz, William F. 108 (2)
Schwarz, Abby 171 (42), (54)
Schwarz, John H. 214 (39), (47), (51)
Schwerdtfeger, Dale 168 (66)
Scott, Donald A. 52 (85)
Scott, Edwin H. 173 (27)
Scott, James W. 223 (28)
Scott, Ray 71 (223)
Scott, Thomas 214 (22)
Scott, W. Herbert 230 (11)
Scott, Walter 71 (56)
Scovill, Warner E. 173 (28)
Seale, William B. 177 (25)
Sebolt, Don R. 216 (110)
Secher, Bjorn 180 (152)
Secord, Arthur 71 (172), 177 (104)
Sedwick, John 49 (318)
Segall, M. Harvey 159 (57)
Segedin, Leopold B. 142 (76)
Seghal, Prem P. 56 (75)
Seiden, Don 42 (9), (94)
Seidman, Jules 49 (319)
Seinwerth, Herman W. 123 (13)
Sekely, Steve 49 (320)
Selame, Joseph 149 (10)
Self, William Lee 180 (153)
Selman, Joan 24 (2)
Seltzer, Leo 49 (321)
Semaan, Dick 177 (105), 180 (154)
Semenchuk, K. Anatole 49 (322)
Semple, Robert 160 (17)
Semrad, Alice 105 (96)
Senecal, Roland R. 10 (3)
Senungetuk, Joseph E. 79 (123)
Service, Kenneth 31 (10), (36)
Settembrini, Gioele 12 (9)
Settle, Phillip M. 57 (78)
Seward, D.M. 151 (11)
Shabica, Charles W. 142 (77)
Shachter, Jaqueline 181 (145)
Shackelford, Rufus 6 (3)
Shaffer, Dorothy 180 (155)
Shain, Herbert F. 123 (14)
Shank, Kathlene 57 (79)
Shanker, Albert 71 (77)
Shankman, Florence V. 181 (8) (123)
Shapiro, Stephen E. 116 (6)
Sharaway, H.S. 57 (80)
Sharf, Ray 56 (86)
Sharpe, William E. 151 (158)
Shatzman, Marci 176 (104)
Shavelson, Mel 49 (323)
Shawley, Stephen D. 79 (124)
Shay, Arnold 176 (105)
Shea, Jack 49 (324)
Shea, James M. 181 (9)
Shear, Barry 49 (325)
Shearin, P.L. 92 (11)
Sheehan, Don 180 (156)
Sheehan, T. Frank 18 (1)
Sheeks, Wayne 117 (98)
Sheen, Fulton J. 176 (106)
Sheeran, Dick 176 (107)
Sheikh, Anees E. 105 (103)
Sheldon, Harry J. 181 (319)
Sheldon, James 49 (326)
Sheldon, Paul 214 (79)
Shelley, Joshua 49 (327)
Shelton, Jo-Ann 227 (42)
Shemick, John M. 151 (118)
Shepherd, Robert E. 112 (115)
Sherman, Arnold A. 216 (111)
Sherman, Carl W. 151 (135)
Sherman, Vincent 49 (328)
Shi, J.E.B. 180 (157)
Shields, Alan John 16 (73)
Shields, Mark 219 (10)
Shields, Pat 49 (329)
Shiely, Catherine 105 (126)
Shiff, Robert A. 119 (1)
Shiflett, James 42 (34)
Shimkunas, Susan L. 79 (125)
Shin, Seon 160 (18)
Shires, William A. 56 (102)
Shoalts, Alvin B. 123 (15)

Shockley, William 71 (159)
Shoemaker, Charles C. 30 (1)
Sholar, Thomas P. 117 (54), (125)
Sholem, Lee 49 (330)
Shown, Vernon E. 117 (55), (120)
Shuff, Robert V. 57 (81)
Shull, Carl 57 (82)
Shuman, Robert L. 151 (12)
Sias, John D. 151 (83)
Sidey, Hugh 102 (30)
Sidney, George 49 (331)
Siebert, Donald R. 52 (86)
Siegchrist, Mark 105 (25)
Siemoneit, Martin A. 216 (112)
Siettmann, James P. 105 (26), (85)
Silberman, Charles 71 (92)
Silbersher, Marvin 49 (332)
Silk, Leonard 102 (31)
Silverstein, Elliot 49 (333)
Simboli, David R. 151 (239)
Simcock, Barbara 72 (3)
Simmons, Edward 49 (334)
Simmons, Michael K. 151 (240)
Simms, Jack 16 (74)
Simon, Douglas W. 52 (87)
Simon, Jack 49 (335)
Simonsen, August H. 151 (13)
Sims, E. Ralph 180 (158)
Sims, Melvin D. 29 (153), (211), (223), (304), (350)
Sinclair, Duncan 160 (19)
Sinclitico, Joseph A. 159 (58)
Singer, Alexander 49 (336)
Singer, Isaac B. 71 (200)
Singh, Avtar 56 (123)
Singh, Jane M. 151 (241)
Singleton, Gregory H. 142 (78)
Sink, Claire H. 151 (84)
Sion, Edward M. 214 (10)
Skaggs, Calvin L. 52 (88)
Skelly, John M. 216 (113)
Skimbo, Nicholas 151 (51
Skinner, Knute R. 223 (27)
Skvarla, Mervyn A. 142 (79)
Slack, Lyle H. 216 (114)
Slack, Ted C. 65 (58)
Slater, James R. 159 (59)
Slater, L.B. 65 (59)
Slatzer, Robert 49 (337)
Slavet, Arnold 8 (9)
Slickpoo, Allen P., Sr. 79 (126)
Sloman, Carol L. 159 (60)
Slook, Thomas H. 181 (10), (154)
Slough, Robert E., Jr. 123 (16)
Sloviter, Dolores Korman 181 (192), (241), (271), (312)
Slowik, Alfred A. 150 (8)
Small, Marvin B. 19 (1)
Small, Sally S. 151 (59)
Smeal, Paul L. 216 (115)
Smith, Andrew E. 123 (17)
Smith, Bradley H. 181 (88), (124)
Smith, Clifford 130 (32)
Smith, David 159 (61)
Smith, Donald W. 216 (116)
Smith, Frank E. 132 (11)
Smith, Hedrick 102 (32)
Smith, Hubert C. 151 (34)
Smith, James P., Jr. 181 (65)
Smith, June Warden 117 (56)
Smith, Lendon H. 113 (3)
Smith, Leonard J. 180 (159)
Smith, M. John 151 (119)
Smith, Mary 151 (242)
Smith, Max L. 132 (12)
Smith, Ralph B. 52 (89)
Smith, Rita 181 (21), (31), (135), (242), (294), (328)
Smith, Robert L. 151 (14)
Smith, Vernon 56 (124)
Smythe, Ted C. 29 (42), (67), (119), (312)
Snavely, Marcia K. 173 (29)
Snellenberg, Estelle Colwin 176 (108)
Sneva, Tom 33 (10)
Snider, H. Wayne 181 (44), (193), (243)
Snipes, Wilson 216 (117)
Snizek, William E. 216 (118)
Snodgrass, W.D. 71 (201)
Snow, Lee Erlin 79 (127)
Snyder, Jane M. 227 (43)
Snyder, Jimmy "The Greek" 42 (110), 156 (52)
Snyder, Judith P. 151 (15)
Snyder, Leroy 176 (109)
Snyder, Reginald 180 (160)
Snyder, Robert W. 173 (30)
Snyder, Shirley A. 151 (85)
Sochen, June 42 (157), 142 (80)
Sokolnicki, Alfred J. 105 (12), (27)
Solley, Bill 151 (230)
Sollo, Eugene D. 180 (161)
Someroski, Mel 79 (128)
Somerville, Thomas F. 159 (62)
Sonnenberg, Ray 180 (162)
Sood, Mohan K. 142 (81)
Sorensen, Ted 71 (104), 156 (53)
Soskis, David A. 181 (244), (295), (345)
South, James 151 (120)
Sowa, Cora Angier 227 (44)
Sowell, Edward F. 29 (110)
Sowell, Thomas 175 (3)
Spagrra, Paschal M. 181 (194)
Spann, Robert M. 216 (119)
Sparks, Sue C. 57 (83)
Spaulding, Robert R. 150 (9)
Spear, Joe 112 (116)
Spencer, Nancy A. 142 (82)
Spengler, Fred L. 216 (120)
Spetgang, Tillie 176 (110)
Spillman, Sanford 49 (338)
Spiro, Tom 172 (11)
Spitzer, Robert W. 112 (117)
Spock, Benjamin 178 (5)
Sprague, Ver Lynn 65 (60)
Spray, Richard A. 216 (121)
Sprott, J. Michael 16 (75)
Sreenivasam, Elsa M. 79 (129)
Stack, Lotus 79 (130)
Staight, Robert 177 (106), 180 (163)
Staley, Oren Lee 126 (1)
Stanaland, Eugene E. 16 (76)
Standish, Norman W. 173 (31)
Stanley, Anita Bacco 136 (5), (23)
Stanlis, Peter J. 85 (32)
Stannard, R.E. 223 (20), (25)
Stapleton, Syd 213 (15)
Starr, Bart 42 (111), 71 (224)
Stasavich, Clarence 56 (87)
Staub, Susan 131 (4)
Staubach, Roger 42 (112)
Staudacher, Joseph M. 105 (13)
Stearns, Michael 49 (339)
Stedman, Preston 29 (154)
Steel, Robert 49 (340)
Steele, Ralph 56 (37), (58), (88)
Stefanko, Robert 151 (136)
Steffen, Robert F. 216 (123)
Steffy, Denton A. 151 (146)
Steiger, Brad 134 (6)
Stein, Jack 151 (147)
Stein, Judith 79 (131)
Stein, Kay E. 227 (45)
Steiner, Joan Elizabeth 52 (90)
Steisel, Ira M. 181 (245), (296)
Stelle, Robert 130 (33)
Stemper, William H., Sr. 65 (61)
Stensland, Allen 168 (67)
Stephens, Jackie E. 143 (13)
Stephens, Jerome S., Jr. 150 (10)
Stephenson, Richard A. 56 (38)
Stephenson, William 56 (14), (109)

Sterling, Theodor D. 171 (12)
Sterling, Tom 69 (13)
Stern, Carl 71 (57), 176 (111)
Stern, Donald 49 (341)
Stern, Joel 102 (33)
Stern, Steven 49 (342)
Stevens, Carl 177 (107)
Stevens, Charles E. 56 (39), (110)
Stevens, Humphrey 142 (83)
Stevens, Melissa 179 (1)
Stevens, Patricia 179 (2)
Stevens-Allen, David J. 225 (36)
Stevenson, Adlai 71 (160)
Stevenson, Samantha 176 (112)
Stewart, Clete 42 (48)
Stewart, David 122 (4)
Stewart, Donald 180 (164)
Stewart, M. Edward 173 (32)
Stewart, Suzanne 180 (165)
Stiles, Bill 112 (118)
Stivers, Eugene H. 181 (125), (146), (246), (272), (297)
Stockdale, Bill 59 (16)
Stoessinger, John 71 (161)
Stokes, Carl 71 (58)
Stokes, Judy Ford 180 (166)
Stokes, Louis 180 (167)
Stokes, McNeill 180 (168)
Stoloff, Victor 49 (343)
Stominski, E.J. 92 (12)
Stone, Andrew 49 (344)
Stone, Chuck 42 (22), (49)
Stone, Dave 177 (108)
Stone, Ezra 49 (345)
Stone, I.F. 42 (23), (50), (147)
Stone, John W. 180 (169)
Stone, Jon 49 (346)
Stoner, Clarence H. 151 (284)
Storey, Rolland 180 (170)
Stowe, Wilmer C. 151 (159)
Strack, Harry R. 214 (56)
Strader, Gayle Gilbert 57 (84)
Strait, John A. 159 (63)
Stranahan, Joan 117 (57), (110)
Strazzella, James A. 181 (273)
Strick, Anne 225 (37)
Strickland, A.G. 180 (171)
Strickland, Kenneth F. 216 (122)
Strickler, Fay B. 151 (180)
Strock, Herbert 49 (347)
Strohecker, Edwin C. 117 (75)
Stroker, William 52 (91)
Strong, Harlan 130 (34)
Struever, Stuart 112 (119)
Stuart, Joseph 49 (348)
Stuart, Mary 156 (24)
Sturgeon, Paul 180 (172)
Sturm, Albert L. 216 (124)
Sturtz, Laurence E. 136 (9)
Styer, Sandra 142 (84)
Suart, George 171 (59)
Sugarman, Shirley 52 (92)
Sugg, Howard 56 (103)
Suhre, Lawrence R. 151 (243)
Sullins, W. Robert 216 (125)
Sullivan, Walter 97 (62)
Suloff, Charles E. 151 (263)
Summa, Bruce 177 (109)
Summers, Luis Henry 151 (148)
Surrency, Erwin C. 181 (136), (274), (346)
Susa, Jo 44 (3)
Sutton, Imre 29 (74), (166), (195)
Sutton, Kenneth 57 (85)
Sutton, Suzy 177 (110), 180 (173)
Swab, James L. 180 (174)
Swails, Richard G. 151 (60)
Swan, Jane D. 105 (86), (127)
Swanson, Gloria 97 (63)
Swayze, John Cameron 71 (59)
Sweeny, Robert F. 214 (30)
Sweet, Cody 112 (120), 176 (113), 177 (111), 180 (175)
Sweet, Guy V. 132 (13)
Sweeting, Roger 151 (285)
Swenson, Alf A. 168 (68)
Swerdloff, Arthur 49 (349)
Swett, Leonard W. 173 (33)
Swetz, Frank 151 (121)
Swift, George W. 216 (126)
Swoboda, Frank 220 (7)
Swope, Mary Ruth 57 (86)
Sykora, Merle H. 79 (132), 168 (69)
Syvinski, Henry B. 214 (9)
Szews, Alfred P. 105 (87)
Szymczak, Patricia A. 142 (85)
Szyszko, Barbara 105 (53)

T

Tacker, Harold 79 (133)
Tacker, Sylvia 79 (133)
Tackett, Amos 117 (7), (126)
Taft, Robert, Jr. 156 (54)
Taft, Thomas B. 105 (14)
Tait, Elaine 176 (114)
Tait, G. Thomas 151 (286)
Tait, Miriam A. 29 (43), (103), (175), (187), (313)
Taitt, Henry A. 57 (87)
Talbot, Richard B. 216 (127)
Tamplin, John C. 151 (244)
Tanja, Jon J. 16 (77)
Tannebring, William 49 (350)
Tapper, David 49 (351)
Tarkenton, Fran 42 (113)
Tarr, Joel A. 31 (13), (32)
Taylor, Charles 59 (17), 91 (10)
Taylor, Harold 71 (93)
Taylor, Janet Rousch 79 (134)
Taylor, John 117 (58)
Taylor, Jud 49 (352)
Taylor, Larry T. 216 (128)
Taylor, Maxine 180 (176)
Taylor, Ronald J. 223 (15)
Teague, Bob 71 (60), (225)
Teates, Thomas G. 216 (129)
Techter, David 42 (120)
Telionis, D.P. 216 (130)
Temple, Mary 79 (135)
Templeton, Mary Susan 56 (89)
Teplitz, Vigdor L. 216 (131)
TerHorst, J.F. 102 (34)
Terkel, Studs 42 (51), (84), 71 (105)
Terrell, Tracy D. 27 (15)
Terzian, Carl 112 (121), 180 (177)
Tessnear, Marshall D. 216 (132)
Teutsch, Champion K. 225 (38)
Thanawala, Kishor 214 (35), (52)
Thayer, Nelson S.T. 52 (93)
Theoharis, Athan 105 (59)
Thies, Anita H. 151 (86)
Thimmesch, Nick 112 (122), 175 (4)
Tho, Pauline N. Van 14 (25)
Thomas, Barry 29 (75), (277), (324)
Thomas, Kathryn A. 227 (46)
Thomas, Larry 224 (15)
Thomas, Lowell 71 (61), 97 (64)
Thomas, M. Donald 180 (178)
Thomas, Phillip A. 65 (62)
Thomas, Piri 42 (35), (85), 154 (25)
Thomas, Roy 130 (35)
Thomas, Ruth S. 227 (46)
Thomas, Walter I. 151 (24), (181)
Thomason, Roger K. 79 (136)
Thompson, Ann E. 216 (133)
Thompson, Bard 52 (94)
Thompson, J. Lee 49 (353)
Thompson, James T. 117 (8), (26), (35)
Thompson, Margaret 79 (137)
Thomson, Richard 224 (16)
Thoren, Donald Arthur 177 (112), 180 (179)
Thornburgh, Dan 57 (88)
Thorne, Fred 49 (354)

Thorne, Jim 97 (65)
Thornton, Jack 56 (21)
Thornton, Philip 49 (355)
Thorsen, Larry 57 (89)
Thurman, Ken 181 (126)
Thurman, Wayne L. 57 (90)
Thurmond, Strom 71 (162), 112 (123)
Thurston, Stephen 79 (138)
Thye, Forrest W. 216 (134)
Tice, James H. 150 (11)
Tiedge, James T. 105 (69)
Tiffany, Elizabeth G. 181 (22), (127)
Tiger, Lionel 102 (35)
Tighe, Kevin 49 (356)
Timberlake, Lewis 177 (113)
Tincher, Wilbur A. 16 (78)
Titus, Charles 57 (91)
Toback, Norman 49 (357)
Tobias, Marice 49 (358)
Tobin, Terry 105 (97)
Todd, Paul 151 (211)
Todd, Thomas 42 (24)
Toffel, Bill 176 (115)
Toffler, Alvin 102 (36)
Toker, Franklin 31 (3), (28)
Tolbert, Chip 111 (2)
Tole, Thomas M. 16 (79)
Tolley, Charles H. 117 (59)
Tolliver, Melba 71 (62)
Tolman, Ruth 229 (5)
Tomezsko, Edward, S.J. 151 (273)
Tonken, Winifred M. 79 (139)
Tonkin, Humphrey 58 (4)
Tonsor, Stephen J. 85 (33)
Topetzes, Nick J. 105 (98)
Torbert, Marianne 181 (11)
Tornabene, Phil 177 (114)
Tosi, Donald 136 (6), (10), (24)
Tower, Gail 181 (23), (195), (247)
Towner, Naomi Whiting 79 (140)
Townsend, Robert 71 (78)
Traas, Adrian G. 105 (74)
Trachtenberg, Leo 49 (359)
Trachy, Carol Law 227 (48)
Tracy, William T. 105 (15), (51)
Transier, Lee 181 (66), (128), (248)
Traube, Shepard 49 (360)
Trautmann, Frederick 181 (147) (298)
Trebby, James P. 105 (10)
Treggiari, S.M. 227 (49)
Tremble, Neal 142 (86)
Tremel, Charles L. 150 (12)
Trent, John 49 (361)
Trimble, Virginia 27 (16)
Triplett, George E. 29 (68), (104), (188), (263)
Tripp, Dave C. 180 (180)
Tritt, Francis 112 (124), 180 (181)
Trivett, John V. 171 (21)
Trotta, Liz 71 (63)
Trubkin, Loene 44 (4)
True, Herb 71 (173), 86 (1), 112 (125), 177 (125)
Truesdell, William D. 29 (126), (183), (199), (212), (248)
Trumble, Merta Sue 79 (141)
Tsemel, Lea 213 (16)
Tubbs, Carl 49 (362)
Tucker, Howard G. 27 (17)
Tuckerman, Murray M. 181 (196), (249)
Tulchin, Harold 49 (363)
Tullock, Gordon 85 (34)
Tumas, Elena V. 29 (127), (189), (213), (290), (295)
Turco, Salvatore 181 (197)
Turner, Alta R. 79 (142)
Turner, William 112 (126)
Tuuri, Walter R. 173 (34)
Tygart, Clarence E. 29 (105), (155), (176), (249), (291), (351)

U

Udall, Stewart 71 (106)
Uliassi, Edward C. 142 (87)
Ullman, Al 71 (79)
Ulloa, Justo C. 216 (135)
Ulmer, Gene C. 181 (137), (250), (347)
Ulmer, Ilona 181 (251), (329)
Umar, Farouk F. 117 (104)
Uni, Miriam 42 (95), 180 (182)
Upadhyay, Hansa D. 142 (88)
Ussery, Robert 56 (104)
Utley, Garrick 71 (64

V

Vachon, Reginald I. 16 (80)
Vairo, John D. 151 (16)
Valdivieso, Jorge H. 3 (7)
Valenta, Lubomir J. 27 (35)
Valentine, Robert 117 (76), (91), (136)
Valeriani, Richard 112 (127)
Vallarino, Lidia M. 16 (81)
Van Brackle, Henry L. 65 (63)
Van Damme, Frans N. 216 (136)
Van Den Haag, Ernest 85 (35)
Van Derbur, Marilyn 112 (128), 176 (116), 177 (116)
Van Dommelen, David B. 79 (143)
Van Fleteren, Frederick E. 214 (76), (82)
Van Gelder, Lydia 79 (144)
Van Horn, James E. 151 (172)
Van Horne, Harriet 71 (65)
Vance, Chuck 71 (174)
Vance, Mike 177 (117), 135 (58)
Vandegrift, Frank 16 (82)
Vanderbilt, Gloria 97 (66)
Vanderlip, Vera F. 227 (50)
Vandivier, Frances 181 (252), (313)
Var, Turgot 171 (6), (13)
Varnadore, E. Lee 65 (64)
Varner, James 52 (95)
Varney, Carleton 97 (67)
Varophas, Kusol 142 (89)
Vaughan, B.L. 212 (1)
Vaughan, David H. 216 (137)
Veatch, Frank 173 (35)
Venza, J. Riley 117 (77), (105)
Vernon, Manfred C. 223 (16), (21)
Verona, Stephen 49 (364)
Veseth, Michael 159 (64)
Vieweg, E. 92 (13)
Vigorito, John V. 174 (89)
Vilaro, Rudolfo E. 142 (90)
Villafana, Theodore 181 (198)
Villeneuve, Winnie Frohn 227 (51)
Vivas, Eliseo 85 (36)
Vodraska, Walter C. 174 (90)
Voegelin, Eric 85 (37)
Vogel, Francis X. 142 (91)
Voiers, Leslie C. 79 (145)
Volatis, Constantine 116 (7)
Volner, Jill 42 (25)
Volpicelli, Louis 49 (365)
Von Der Heide, John T., Jr. 52 (96)
Vonk, Paul Kenneth 180 (183)
Vukovich, Bill 33 (11)

W

Waas, Les 180 (184)
Waddell, Leyla Peck 57 (92)
Wadman, William W. 27 (9)
Waeker, Duhhaine 49 (366)

Wagenius, Terry 168 (70)
Wagner, Cherryl A. 227 (52)
Wagner, Esther 159 (65)
Wagner, Lou 176 (117)
Wagner, Robert F. 71 (163)
Waitley, Dennis 177 (118)
Walden, Daniel 151 (245)
Walden, John C. 16 (83)
Waldman, R. D. 92 (14)
Waldo, Robert 159 (66)
Walker, E. Jerry 180 (185)
Walker, Harold G. 123 (18)
Walker, Robert 142 (92)
Walker, Theodore 59 (18), 69 (14)
Walkington, David L. 29 (32), (106), (111), (278), (352)
Wall, Ruth 176 (118)
Wallace, Mike 156 (55)
Wallace, Paul 225 (39)
Wallace, Warren 49 (367)
Wallach, David L. 151 (274)
Waller, Irene 79 (146)
Walling, Marie 79 (147)
Wallo, Edward M. 214 (45)
Wallrof, Paul 159 (67)
Walsh, J.E. 92 (15)
Walsh, William M. 142 (93)
Walter, Jane H. 216 (138)
Walter, Robert L. 181 (129)
Walters, Bryan 42 (86)
Walters, Charles 49 (368)
Walters, Donald L. 181 (45), (130)
Walters, Dorothy M. 117 (119), 180 (186)
Walters, Frederick J. 180 (187)
Wanderman, Henry 56 (141)
Ward, Barbara 97 (68)
Ward, David L. 180 (188)
Ward, Machree A. 117 (111)
Ward, Marjorie E. 151 (301)
Ward, Robert L. 65 (65)
Ward, R.V. 210 (2)
Ward, William 130 (36)
Wardrep, Bruce 56 (22), (97)
Ware, Gussie M. 142 (94)
Warner, Richard W., Jr. 16 (84)
Warren, Ed 161 (1)
Warren, Lorraine 161 (2)
Warrior, Valerie M. 227 (53)
Washburne, Stephen S. 181 (199), (253)
Washbush, Diane M. 105 (52)
Wasserman, Albert 49 (369)
Wassmann, Felix S. 45 (3)
Waterman, Stanton 69 (15)
Waters, Paul W. 65 (66)
Watkins, Yancy 117 (134)
Watrous, Mary W. 223 (11)
Watson, Everett D. 112 (129)
Watson, Ulestine 142 (95)
Wattles, George M. 3 (8)
Watts, J. Robert 123 (19)
Waun, Roger J. 151 (87)
Waxlax, Robert 168 (71)
Waxman, Mark 49 (370)
Weaver, Ken 79 (148)
Weaver, Warren 219 (11)
Webb, Anita H. 216 (139)
Webb, Robert M. 174 (91)
Webb, Ryland E. 216 (140)
Webb, Yvonne 174 (92)
Webber, Arthur W. 29 (250)
Webber, Bill 176 (119)
Webber, Edith 56 (40), (132)
Weber, H.E. 151 (295)
Weber, Robert D. 180 (189)
Weber, Steven M. 159 (68)
Webre, Alfred 42 (121)
Webster, Nicholas 49 (371)
Weed, Merwin L. 151 (149)
Weete, John D. 16 (85)
Wegener, Ed 16 (86)
Wegman, W.J. 65 (67)
Weightman, Barbara A. 29 (8), (22), (167), (190), (325)
Weigle, Palmy 79 (149)
Weil, Helen H. 27 (18), (46)
Weiler, Conrad 181 (254), (275)
Weimer, Joan S. 52 (97)
Weiner, Barry Ross 8 (10)
Weiner, Irv 221 (1)
Weinstein, Allen 97 (69)
Weinstein, Alvin S. 31 (33)
Weintraub, Stanley 151 (246)
Weinzweig, Marjorie S. 29 (251), (326)
Weir, June 97 (70)
Weir, Raymond J. Jr. 7 (2)
Weis, Don 49 (372)
Weisman, Brice 49 (373)
Weissenborn, Albert E. 143 (14)
Welden, M.B. 92 (16)
Wellborn, Charles T. 180 (190)
Wells, Barron 174 (93)
Wells, Faye C. 117 (27)
Wells, Helen L. 216 (141)
Wells, Jane Freeman 117 (28)
Weltge, Sigrid 79 (150)
Wendkos, Stanley L. 181 (200)
Werbin, Irv 149 (11)
Werner, Hal 171 (30)
Werner, Jan 174 (94)
Werrenrath, Reinald 49 (374)
Wescott, Roger W. 52 (98)
Wesley, Roy L. 216 (142)
West, Steven L. 117 (106)
West, Virginia 79 (151)
Westfall, Carol D. 79 (152)
Westmoreland, William 156 (56)
Weston, Av 154 (26)
Wetterlind, Peter 57 (93)
Wetzel, Charles J. 52 (99)
Wetzel, Herbert A. 151 (25)
Weyman, Leo Hap 49 (375)
Whatley, Harold E. 34 (2)
Wheatley, Jon 171 (55), (60)
Wheeler, Thomas E. 124 (2)
Whinnen, W.J. 143 (15)
Whitaker, Jack 71 (226)
White, Dennis K. 105 (88)
White, Elliott 184 (24)
White, Geoffry D. 29 (44), (252)
White, J. Herbert 16 (87)
White, Louis Edward 16 (88)
White, Robert W. 27 (36)
White, Ronald 174 (95)
White, Sam 49 (376)
White, Somers H. 112 (130), 177 (120), 180 (191)
White, Theodore H. 214 (90)
Whitelaw, Robert L. 216 (143)
Whiting, Keith 143 (16)
Whitley, Steve 57 (94)
Whitten, Les 71 (66), 112 (131), 156 (57)
Wiancke, Gene 91 (11)
Wienberg, Harold 171 (43)
Wiercinski, Floyd J. 142 (96)
Wiggers, Nancy 227 (54)
Wiggins, James W. 85 (38)
Wiginton, John 160 (20)
Wilcher, Marshall E. 151 (201)
Wilcox, Olin R. 65 (68)
Wild, Rebecca Smith 57 (95)
Wilde, Larry 225 (40)
Wilden, Anthony 171 (56)
Wildman, Helen D. 27 (47)
Wiles, Gordon 49 (377)
Wiley, Charles 125 (1)
Wilkie, Nancy C. 227 (55)
Wilkins, Keith A. 216 (144)
Wilkinson, Charles 112 (132)
Willard, Valerie 176 (120)
Willerman, Marvin 142 (97)
Willett, Terry 160 (21)
Willey, Charles 112 (133), 177 (121)
Williams, Alfred B. 174 (96)
Williams, Delores T. 181 (12)
Williams, Don L. 105 (31)
Williams, Glenn D. 57 (96)
Williams, Harvey 27 (24)
Williams, Oscar 49 (378)
Williams, Paul 49 (379)
Williams, Richard 4 (7)

Williams, Thomas A. 56 (41), (59), (105)
Williams, Walter 175 (5)
Williams, Walter E. 181 (46), (255)
Williams, Wayne M. 117 (60)
Williamson, Homer E. 168 (72)
Williamson, Janet A. 151 (256)
Williamson, William O. 151 (259)
Willing, Sy 177 (122)
Wilsman, Leo G. 180 (192)
Wilson, Anne 97 (71)
Wilson, Earl 156 (58)
Wilson, Francis G. 85 (39)
Wilson, Heartsill 71 (175), 135 (59), 177 (123)
Wilson, Jack D. 117 (93)
Wilson, James T. 65 (69)
Wilson, Jean 79 (153)
Wilson, Justin 112 (134)
Wilson, Larry 177 (124)
Wilson, Roberta A. 159 (69)
Wilson, Samuel M. 181 (47)
Wilson, Stanley P. 16 (89)
Wilson, William 154 (27)
Wingard, Richard M. 16 (90)
Wingerter, Eugene J. 133 (5)
Winkless, Nelson Brock 49 (380)
Winslow, Louise 83 (17)
Winter, James O. 180 (193)
Winter, Margaret 213 (17)
Winter, William 225 (41)
Winterfelt, Rolf 29 (83)
Winters, Carl 112 (135), 177 (125), 180 (194)
Winters, Richard H. 224 (17)
Winther, Jorn 49 (381)
Wintner, Lori 49 (382)
Wirag, J. Robert 151 (212)
Wise, Jeffrey 168 (73)
Wise, Robert 49 (383)
Wiseman, Robert C. 57 (97)
Witalis, Edmond 49 (384)
Witchey, Ronald L. 29 (305)
Witcover, Jules 220 (8)
Withrow, Genna 122 (5)
Wittenberg, Barbara 79 (154)
Witzig, Warren F. 151 (137)
Woerpel, Dwayne R. 180 (195)
Wolf, Frank 52 (100)
Wolf, George D. 151 (222)
Wolfbein, Seymour L. 181 (48)
Wolfe, John 42 (87), 112 (136), 177 (126), 180 (196)
Wolfe, Tom 71 (202)
Wolff, Art 49 (385)
Wolfgang, Ken 15 (5)
Wolfram, Lynn E. 173 (36)
Wollenberg, Jackie 79 (155)
Wollin, Dorothy 168 (74)
Wood, Corinne S. 29 (168)
Wood, Noel T. 105 (11), (75)
Wooden, John 112 (137), 156 (59), 177 (127)
Woodeshick, Tom 176 (121)
Woodland, DeVon 126 (2)
Woodruff, Bill 176 (122), 180 (197)
Woodward, Bob 176 (123)
Woodward, James F. 29 (156), (184), (279)
Workman, Donna 225 (42)
Worth, Guthrie 29 (45), (84), (112), (157), (253)
Wray, John 49 (386)
Wright, Bob 97 (72)
Wright, James R. 56 (65)
Wright, Pat 213 (18)
Wright, Sean 225 (43)
Wuliger, Betty 225 (44)
Wunderle, Dale L. 173 (37)
Wydra, John 176 (124)
Wynn, Robert 49 (387)
Wysocki, Joseph L. 216 (145)

Y

Yadav, Bibhuti S. 181 (300), (307), (330)
Yacopino, Phyllis 79 (156)
Yates, Dorothy M. 65 (70)
Yates, Harold 49 (388)
Yates, Martha 180 (198)
Yatron, Georgine 151 (202)
Yawkey, Thomas Daniels 180 (199)
Yeager, Joseph H. 16 (91)
Yeager, Robert C. 150 (13)
Yessis, Michael 29 (296), (306)
Yoho, Dave 177 (128), 180 (200)
Yoo, Chai Hong 105 (121)
York, Alexandra 97 (73)
Yorks, Pamela 159 (70)
Young, Frank 42 (122)
Young, Joseph 42 (10)
Young, Robert L. 174 (97)

Z

Zabrowsky, Marian 176 (125)
Zafr, A. Muzaffar Ahmad 1 (13)
Zag, Karen 136 (11)
Zaretsky, Tuvya 93 (4)
Zavodni, John J. 151 (160)
Zegger, Robert Elie 142 (98)
Zeidler, Frank P. 172 (12)
Zelinsky, Wilbur 151 (184)
Zeltzer, Allen M. 29 (46), (327)
Zervanos, Stam M. 151 (302)
Ziegler, John H. 151 (182)
Zien, Kathleen L. 79 (157)
Zierten, Scott 172 (13)
Ziglar, Judge 177 (129), 180 (201)
Ziglar, Zig 112 (138), 177 (130), 180 (202)
Zimmerman, W.J. 151 (122)
Zinberg, Michael 49 (389)
Zincone, Louis H., Jr. 56 (23)
Zion, Sidney 71 (67)
Ziporyn, Marvin 42(26), (96)
Znamierowski, Nell 79 (158)
Zoll, Donald A. 85 (40
Zotto-Beltz, Mary Ann 79 (159)
Zuck, Florence M. 52 (101)
Zuck, Robert K. 52 (102)
Zugsmith, Albert 49 (390)
Zumwalt, Elmo 97 (74)
Zumwalt, Mouza Coutelais-du-Roche' 97 (75)
Zuniga, Frank 49 (391)
Zupko, Ronald E. 105 (122)

SECTION III

LECTURE TITLES AND KEYWORD INDEX

This index arranges lecture titles alphabetically and by keyword and provides entry numbers and, in parentheses, speaker code numbers which refer users to descriptive entries in Section I, Speakers and Lecturers: How to Find Them.

For detailed instructions on the use and organization of this volume, see "Organization of the Volume," page vi, and "How to Use this Book," page vii.

A

ABC's of Decision-Making 135 (5)
ABC's of Personally Controlling Stress at Home and at Work 136 (24)
ACT. Research Into the 117 (52)
ADP. Management of 216 (44)
ARC (Associations for Retarded). Organizations and Functions of 169 (2)
A. Solzhenitzyn and the Russian Writers' Tradition 29 (127), (213), (295)
Aalto. Architecture of Alvar 181 (78)
Aaron Burr, Rascal Patriot 103 (5)
Abandoned Wells on Ground Water. Impact of 136 (25)
Abet His Assassin? Did Lincoln Aides 29 (338)
Abnormal Psychology 105 (101)
Aboard for Siberia! All 59 (16)
Abortion 54, 105 (76), 214 (83), (84)
Abortion Legislation. Critique on Both Sides of 54
Abortion. Politics of 142 (78)
Abraham Lincoln 142 (27)
Abraham Lincoln a Christian? Was 29 (338)
Abraham Lincoln and the Emancipation of American Blacks 29 (338)
Abraham Lincoln the Speaker 223 (2)
Abroad. American Image 97 (18)
Abroad. Education 151 (111)
Abroad. English Study 216 (89)
Abroad in the Theatre 97 (20)
Abstractions in Fiber Forms. Nature - 79 (154)
Abstracts of Chemistry, Index Chemicus, and the Chemical Substructure Index. How to Use Current 84 (1)
Abundance in a Hungry World. United States Food 16 (3)
Abuse 181 (323)
Abuse - A Course for Parents and Teachers. Drug 56 (83)
Abuse. Alcohol and Drugs of 171 (53)
Abuse and Alcoholism. Patient Records in Drug 181 (177)
Abuse and Disaster. Drug 112 (82)
Abuse and Neglect. Child 159 (43)
Abuse and Their Action. Drugs 181 (159), (212)
Abuse. Authority, Its Use and 117 (28)
Abuse. Child 176 (93), 218
Abuse: Child and Woman 181 (221)
Abuse. Drug 16 (13), 54, 56 (83), 88 (1), 142 (69)
Abuse. Drug and Alcohol 151 (161)
Abuse. Drug Use 168 (29)
Abuse. Drug Use and 57 (69)
Abuse. Medical Professionals in Drug 88 (1)
Abuse, More and More Leisure. Drug Misuse and 56 (81)
Abuse of Women in Movies 225 (5)
Abuse Prevention. Drug 16 (84)
Abuse. Preventive Approaches to Alcohol and Drug 105 (88)
Abuse. Psychology of Drug 105 (106)
Abused. How Trademarks are Protected and 209
Abuser? Are You a Drug 181 (186), (236)
Abuses. Drugs and Athletics Uses and 56 (76)
Abuses. Nursing Home 176 (103)
Academic Administration 151 (8)
Academic Advising in Colleges and Universities 151 (116)
Academic Credit for Work Experience 16 (78)
Academic Decision. On Making a Good 151 (104)
Academic Freedom and Academic License 85 (16)
Academic Freedom. Model Code of Procedures for 105 (49)
Academic Governance 151 (8)
Academic License. Academic Freedom and 85 (16)
Academic Offerings. USL 174 (88)
Academic Programs and Aspirations 142 (40)
Academic Scholarships. No Need Athletic and 31 (15)
Academic World. Religion and the 29 (91), (235)
Academically. Black Community Competing 54
Academics. Athletics and 171 (22), 214 (11)
Academy. Air Force 216 (120)
Academy. United States Air Force 216 (53)
Academy. United States Naval 57 (53)
Acadian Education 174 (14)
Acadian Village 174 (40)
Acadiana. Mentally Retarded Citizens of 174 (44)
Acadians 174 (19)
Acceptable Quality Control 57 (11)
Access in Science and Business. Information 44 (1 - 4)
Access to Medical Records. Patients' 181 (185), (235)
Accident. Highway Safety is No 33 (1 - 11)
Accident Problem. Automobile 181 (44), (243)
Accidents. Alcohol and Traffic 168 (29)
Accidents Can Kill Businesses as Well as People 136 (4)
Account. Building for Your Own 65 (12)
Accountability 105 (42)
Accountability. Accounting and 216 (63)
Accountability. Educational 181 (104)
Accountability in America. Corporate 181 (32), (258)
Accounting 56 (16), 105 (10), 214 (15)
Accounting and Accountability 216 (63)
Accounting and Finance. Careers in 23
Accounting. Career Possibilities in the Field of 216 (63)
Accounting. Careers in 214 (2)
Accounting Education 214 (2)
Accounting Education. Changing Trends in 159 (50)
Accounting. Financial 159 (50)
Accounting for Inflation 31 (1)
Accounting in Economic Development 171 (13)

Accounting. International 214 (2)
Accounting. Managerial 159 (57)
Accounting Profession. Impact of Computers on the 171 (9)
Accounting Uniformity 171 (13)
Accounts Receivable. Efficient Handling of 136 (7)
Accounts. Tax-deferred Individual Retirement 18 (1)
Accounts. Tax-deferred Keogh Retirement 18 (1)
Accreditation of Engineering Education Degree Programs 151 (266)
Ace - Live Like a King. Sell Like an 112 (136)
Achieve Peace in the Middle East. How to 57 (61)
Achieve Productivity in Business. Overcoming Obstacles to 27 (8)
Achievement Motivation 56 (51), 218
Achievement Motivation. Introduction to 56 (135)
Achievement of Nationality in American Literature 16 (34)
Achieving More and Enjoying it Less? Are You 112 (54)
Achieving Success in the Free Enterprise System 180 (79)
Achieving Texture in Tapestry Weaving 79 (108)
Acid Dyes for Wool 79 (102), (141)
Acid Mine Drainage 151 (154)
Acquisition and Bilingual Children. Language 29 (95), (204)
Act Now. Think - 81 (1)
Acting 142 (74), 174 (48), 176 (49)
Acting Bug 218
Acting for Stage, Television and Films. Relationship and Difference Between 225 (30)
Acting in the Ancient Theatre. Actors and 227 (14)
Action. Affirmative 142 (47), 162
Action and Prisons. Nonviolent 217 (3)
Action and the Chicano. Affirmative 27 (2)
Action at the Pennsylvania State University. Affirmative 151 (1)
Action Complaints. How to Recognize Affirmative 151 (1)
Action. Drugs of Abuse and Their 181 (159), (212)
Action - Equal Opportunity. Affirmative 223 (1)
Action for the Disabled. Understanding Affirmative 151 (1)
Action. Search for Utopia Through Government 85 (11)
Action - The Manager's Role. Management by 135 (29)
Action. Volunteerism in 181 (66), (248)
Activation Analysis. Neutron 151 (156)
Activities and Suggestions for Invidivualizing and Informalizing Education. Opening Up the Classroom - 117 (48)
Activities. Creative 142 (13)
Activities for Everyone. Intramural Recreational 57 (17)
Activities for Public Places. Fiber 79 (128)
Activities for Teachers - Nursery - Fourth Grade. Language Arts and Math 117 (48)
Activities for the Classroom Teacher. Art, Music, and Cooking 117 (48)
Activities in Eastern North Carolina. History of Recreation, Physical Education, and Leisure 56 (28)
Activities. Language Arts and Related 117 (56)
Activities. Management of Commodity Futures Trading 138 (3), (4)
Activities. Occupational Therapeutic 159 (31)
Activities. Outdoor Recreational 105 (114)
Activities. Physical Education 151 (278)
Activities. Secondary School Student 57 (24)
Activities. Students and 105 (81)
Activities to Liven up Reading. Games and 181 (8)
Activity. Contemporary 79 (70)
Activity for the Overweight. Nutrition and 117 (79)
Activity. Future of Space 225 (7)
Activity. Mount Baker - Increased Thermal 218
Activity Professionals Response to Non-Traditional Students. Student 105 (38)
Activity. Programming a Successful Event or 105 (79)
Activity. Real Estate Market 29 (81)
Activity. Role of Open Markets in Coordinating and Directing Economic 85 (2)
Actor. Theater - Space - and the 29 (43), (313)
Actors and Acting in the Ancient Theatre 227 (14)
Acute Myocardial Infarction 27 (34)
Adam. Eve 'n 159 (1)
Adam's Slip. Kingdom of God and Secret of 1 (10)
Adaptation of Old Buildings to New Uses 218
Adaptations. Bolivian Fabrics and Contemporary 79 (18)
Adaptations in Saharan Africa. Prehistoric Cultural 117 (9)
Addiction and the Family. Heroin 171 (44)
Addiction - The Physiological and Pharmacological Aspects. Drug 54
Additives. Food 151 (177 - 179), 168 (29), 181 (178), (230), 216 (142)
Additives in Foods? Why 216 (72)
Adjustment 174 (50)
Adjustment Problems 174 (62)
Adjustment. Stress and Personal 174 (94)
Adjustment to Leisure 168 (36)
Administering and Evaluating Reading Programs. Planning, 142 (21)
Administering Intramurals. Programming, Organizing, and 57 (17)
Administering Through People 105 (51)
Administration. Academic 151 (8)
Administration and Colleges Today 16 (48)
Administration and Research. Informative Systems for Instruction, 57 (80)
Administration as a Career. Public 29 (262)
Administration at the High School or Elementary School Levels 56 (48)

Administration. Carter 154 (7)
Administration. Educational 105 (42)
Administration. Health Records 181 (185)
Administration. Implications of a New 102 (30)
Administration in the Public Schools. Personnel 16 (18)
Administration. Interpersonal Relationships in School 117 (41)
Administration. Judicial 181 (274)
Administration of an Intercollegiate Football Program 29 (24), (301)
Administration of Research on Campus 151 (139)
Administration. Office 174 (96)
Administration. Personnel 223 (6)
Administration. Personnel Management and 105 (11)
Administration. Programs in Office 174 (6)
Administration. Public 142 (33), (42), 168 (72)
Administration. Safety Programs and 23
Administration. School 168 (14)
Administration. School of Business and Public 159 (66)
Administration. School Organization and 117 (49)
Administration. Small Business 29 (83)
Administration. Trends in Educational 16 (56)
Administration. United States Foreign Assistance 151 (196)
Administration - What Washington Plans for United States Business. New 102 (10), (21)
Administrations. Business 180 (169)
Administrative Law 105 (56)
Administrative Management and Office Support Systems 119 (1)
Administrative Mindedness 105 (42)
Administrator and the School Board 105 (51)
Administrator. Liability and the 117 (46)
Admissions and Financial Aid. College 31 (16)
Admissions Game 151 (15)
Admissions. General College 54
Admissions. Graduate School 142 (95)
Admissions. Law School/Business School 142 (95)
Adolescence 151 (162), 181 (17), (181), 218
Adolescence Revisited 151 (170)
Adolescent Pregnancy. Medical and Psychological Aspects of 27 (30)
Adolescent With Special Problems. Educating the 142 (61)
Adolescents. Problems of 29 (88), (231)
Adolescents. Psychosocial Problems of Children and 181 (282)
Adopting Foreign Children 168 (48)
Adoption. Transracial 151 (111), 159 (41)
Adoptive Experience. Single Parent 181 (247)
Adornment. Body 79 (28)
Adornment From Non-Western Perspective. Jewelry and Body 79 (28)
Adult and Non-traditional Education 142 (33)
Adult-Child Interaction 216 (40)
Adult Children. Roman Mothers and the Lives of Their 227 (36)
Adult. Communications in the Brain Damaged 117 (133)
Adult Competency Ecucation versus Traditional Courses 16 (22)
Adult Contemporary Education versus Traditional Courses 16 (78)
Adult - Continuing Education 57 (26)
Adult Education 105 (34), 142 (95), 151 (98), 171 (15), 181 (111)
Adult Education by 1984? Compulsory 151 (98)
Adult Education. Continuing and 171 (18)
Adult Education in the United States 151 (122)
Adult Education. Some Major Issues in 151 (98)
Adult Exercise 168 (33)
Adult Farm Classes 117 (8)
Adult Physical Fitness 142 (86)
Adult. Teenage Problem - The 54
Adult Vocational Education. Liberalizing 151 (98)
Adulthood. Moral Judgment in Children, Youth and 214 (77)
Adults. Career Education for 16 (22)
Adults. Communication Problems of Children and 174 (8)
Adults. Physical Fitness for 151 (285)
Adults. Self-Esteem Exercises for 181 (292)
Adults. Sex Counseling for Single 29 (252)
Adults Should Know to Better Their Chances of Success. What Young 151 (38)
Adults. Speech and Language Difficulties in 56 (53)
Adults With and/or Hearing Problems. Rehabilitative Services for Children and 57 (63)
Advanced Batik 79 (108)
Advanced Loom-controlled Weaves 79 (114)
Advanced Spinning 79 (51)
Advances in Biology. Ethical Implications of 151 (164)
Advances in Commercial Canning and Freezing of Foods. Recent 216 (72)
Advances in Open Heart Surgery. New 181 (194)
Advent of Christ and Its Fulfillment. Second 1 (8)
Adventure. Afghanistan 29 (22), (167), (325)
Adventure. Antarctic 151 (301)
Adventure. Hawaiian 59 (7)
Adventure. I Married 225 (24)
Adventure. Peace Corps: The Modern 151 (118)
Adventure Road 83 (3)
Adventures. Alaskan 4 (6)
Adventures and Errands on the Original Horseless Carriage 56 (40)
Adventures. Great Sailing 59 (5)
Adventures in Attics 97 (24)
Adventures of a Man of Science 29 (186), (272)
Adventures of the Modern Day Prospector. Costs and 143 (13)
Adventures With Birds 168 (56)
Adversaries. News Media and Public Relations - Friendly 105 (67)
Advertise Your Company. How to 136 (5)

Advertising 29 (80), 65 (6), (17), (22), (26), (38), (39), (44), (45), (46), (52), (54), (68), (70), 117 (25), 142 (25), 180 (184), 224 (15)
Advertising and Marketing on Domestic and Foreign Levels. Role of Trademarks in 209
Advertising and Promotion 23
Advertising and Vulnerability of Man 117 (28)
Advertising Education. Obligation of Industry and the Role of Interships, in 151 (75)
Advertising. Images of Women in 168 (9)
Advertising Management 29 (33)
Advertising Program for the Media. Building an 168 (59)
Advertising/Promotion Around the World 3 (1)
Advertising. Sins of 135 (11)
Advertising. Story of Pabst History, Marketing and Advertising 145 (1 - 3)
Advertising Techniques. Television 151 (87)
Advertising. Truth in 105 (4)
Advertising - Why We Buy What We Do 117 (85)
Advising in Colleges and Universities. Academic 151 (116)
Advocacy. Child 181 (119)
Aeneid 227 (1)
Aerial Photos in Resource Management 151 (304)
Aerial Views of Washington Geology 159 (38)
Aerobic Dancing 174 (64)
Aerobics 216 (122)
Aerobics, the Art of Keeping Physically Fit 16 (18)
Aerodynamics of Sailing 216 (130)
Aerosol in the Atmosphere. Residence Time of 218
Aerospace Engineering as a Profession 151 (34)
Aerospace Engineering at Penn State 151 (34)
Aesthetic Education 142 (30)
Aesthetic Education of the Child 151 (30)
Aesthetics. Television 181 (76), (232)
Aesthetics. Weaving 79 (44)
Affair. Sex as a Family 159 (48)
Affairs. African 142 (48)
Affairs. Alumni 151 (3)
Affairs. American Indian 172 (4)
Affairs. Business 180 (75)
Affairs. Community 180 (100), (127)
Affairs. Consumer 135 (23), (46), 157 (1), 176 (44)
Affairs. Educational 180 (42)
Affairs. Faculty 151 (8)
Affairs. General College 224 (8)
Affairs in Africa. Current 171 (3)
Affairs in People's Republic of China. Current 181 (341)
Affairs. Indian 172 (3)
Affairs. International 29 (53), (217), (226), 172 (5), (11)
Affairs. Legal 176 (68)
Affairs Legislation. Consumer 16 (27)
Affairs. Military 151 (192)
Affairs. National 176 (19), 219 (3)
Affairs. North African 29 (3), (179), (217), (226)
Affairs. Origins of the American Tradition in Foreign 85 (7)
Affairs. Public 176 (84)
Affairs. Role of the United Nations in World 29 (63), (330)
Affairs. Soviet 85 (29)
Affairs. Student 216 (12)
Affairs. Urban 172 (12)
Affairs. Virginia Tech Alumni 216 (107)
Affairs: What Happened to Our Investment in Korea? Foreign 151 (110)
Affairs: What the Diplomats Are Doing and Why 151 (110)
Affairs. World 176 (7), (19), (35)
Affirmation in Contemporary Poetry 151 (105)
Affirmative Action 142 (47), 162
Affirmative Action and the Chicano 27 (2)
Affirmative Action at the Pennsylvania State University 151 (1)
Affirmative Action Complaints. How to Recognize 151 (1)
Affirmative Action - Equal Opportunity 223 (1)
Affirmative Action for the Disabled. Understanding 151 (1)
Affluence. Choral Music in a Time of 56 (107)
Affluence, Technology). Pollution is Great (Growth, Resources, Economics, 151 (225)
Affluent Society. Marcuse and the Hell of the 85 (36)
Affordable Trip to Europe. How to Plan an 117 (138)
Afghanistan 15 (1)
Afghanistan Adventure 29 (22), (167), (325)
Africa - An Emerging Giant 29 (1), (48)
Africa - An Overview 56 (2), (114)
Africa and the United States 181 (25), (257), (331)
Africa. Biologist in East 181 (18), (340)
Africa. Christianity in 29 (219), (242), (286)
Africa Culture. Contemporary 181 (25), (331)
Africa. Current Affairs in 171 (3)
Africa. East 174 (36), (82), (91)
Africa. East and South 223 (36)
Africa - In Myth and Folktale 29 (2), (200)
Africa. Islam in 1 (9)
Africa - Liberated or Oppressed. Women in 29 (7)
Africa. Modern 151 (111)
Africa. On Safari in 29 (319)
Africa: Politics. Contemporary 181 (25), (331)
Africa. Politics of 174 (59)
Africa. Prehistoric Cultural Adaptations in Saharan 117 (9)
Africa. Race Conflict in 29 (7)
Africa. Safari in 29 (5)
Africa. Social Change in 218
Africa. Southern 171 (1)
Africa. Squatter Settlements in 142 (48)
Africa - Tawny Lion of Tomorrow 57 (62)
Africa Today 85 (18)

LECTURE TITLES AND KEYWORD INDEX

Africa. Togo, Northwest 216 (60)
Africa. Travel in 29 (5), (319)
Africa. United States and Human Rights in Southern 181 (267)
Africa - United States Relations 97 (42)
Africa. Wildlife and Game Preserves of East 117 (142)
Africa - Women and Their Societies. Christianity in 29 (6)
Africa. Youth in 29 (7)
African Affairs 142 (48)
African Affairs. North 29 (3), (179), (217), (226)
African Animal Behavior 181 (281)
African Crisis - Blacks versus Whites 97 (50)
African Culture. Afro-Americans and 56 (2), (114)
African Culture and Its Transplantation to the New World 151 (218)
African Cultures and Societies 29 (7)
African Dress. Nigerian and 79 (37)
African Fabric Crafts 79 (35)
African History 29 (180), 151 (217), 171 (3), 181 (28)
African History to Americans 181 (267)
African. Jew-Afro-American and 29 (6), (60), (219), (329), (337)
African Literature in French 168 (41)
African Medicine Man and Western Psychotherapy 181 (291)
African Music and Culture 181 (27), (84)
African Safari. East 223 (36)
African Societies. Importance of Family in 29 (7)
African Territories. Portugal and Her 29 (7)
African Textiles 79 (14)
African Wildlife. East 218
Africanism. Pan- 151 (217), 181 (25), (331)
Afrikan Literature. Modern 142 (66)
Afro-American and African. Jew - 29 (6), (60), (219), (329), (337)
Afro-American History 151 (217)
Afro-American History and Culture 142 (7)
Afro-American in the United States Constitution 29 (82), (194), (337)
Afro-American Literary Criticism 142 (66)
Afro-American Literature 142 (66), (74)
Afro-American Music 181 (27), (84)
Afro-American Oral History 142 (66)
Afro-American Thought 181 (29)
Afro American Woman in American History. Black Psychology - The 29 (337)
Afro-American Women Writers 142 (66)
Afro-Americans and African Culture 56 (2), (114)
After Lebanon, What Next? 3 (5)
Age and Other Perils. Marriage, Middle 112 (60)
Age. Business in the Jet 100 (1)
Age for Learning to Read 171 (19)
Age of Confusion. Church in an 85 (18)
Age of Ideology. Relevance of Conservatism in an 85 (40)
Age of Radio. Golden 57 (67)
Age. Ovid, The Wit of the Augustan 227 (23)
Age. Propaganda of the Augustan 227 (52)
Age. Travel in the Jet 100 (2)
Aged. Architectural Barriers to the Handicapped and 151 (228)
Aged. Consumerism and the 168 (67)
Aged. Counseling and Working With the 181 (289)
Aged. Problems of the 168 (67)
Agencies. Banking Relations With Regulatory 117 (14)
Agencies. Intelligence 142 (64)
Agencies. Marketing for Non-profit Institutions and Public 181 (36)
Agencies. Supervisors in Health and Social Welfare 181 (56)
Agency. Environmental Protection 57 (94)
Agenda Setting 29 (42), (67)
Agenda Setting - Why We Think About What We Think About 29 (312)
Agent. How to Make Big Money as an Independent Sales 180 (16)
Agents. Anesthetic 181 (162)
Agents. Antimicrobial 54
Agents on Women. Impact of Environmental Hazardous 151 (153)
Ages. How Dark Were the Dark 54
Aggression 27 (44)
Aggression Control. Techniques of 31 (2)
Aggression, Violence and Human Nature 102 (35)
Aggressive Behavior 181 (28i)
Aging 151 (18)
Aging and Agism in the United States 172 (7)
Aging and Dying. On 142 (62)
Aging and Hormones 105 (3)
Aging at Home 218
Aging. Biology of 181 (13)
Aging. Exercise for the 174 (27)
Aging in Cross Cultural Perspective 218
Aging in Our Society 181 (15), (170), (223)
Aging: Realities and Myths 151 (17)
Aging. Vitamin Formula to Counter 27 (29)
Aging and Agism in the United States 172 (7)
Agony of Modern China 56 (117)
Agribusiness on the Economy. Significance of Agriculture and 16 (91)
Agricultural Economics 117 (6)
Agricultural Education 216 (22)
Agricultural Engineering As a Profession 216 (83)
Agricultural Engineering at Virginia Tech 216 (83)
Agricultural Experiment Station. Research in the 151 (181)
Agricultural Organizations. Food and 174 (4)
Agricultural Price Support Program 85 (22)
Agricultural Research 89 (16), 151 (24)
Agricultural Research. One Hundred Years of 16 (70)
Agriculture 180 (18)
Agriculture - A Vertical Frontier 216 (22)
Agriculture. Alabama 16 (75)

Agriculture and Agribusiness on the Economy. Significance of 16 (91)
Agriculture As It Relates to Industry 117 (2)
Agriculture Education in Brazil 216 (78)
Agriculture. Energy in 216 (137)
Agriculture. Engineering in 216 (83)
Agriculture Engineering Profession 216 (137)
Agriculture. Extension's Role in Today's 151 (23)
Agriculture. Food and Food-Related Research in 151 (181)
Agriculture in Berks County. Future of 151 (22)
Agriculture is More Than Agriculture 117 (2)
Agriculture. Land Use for 151 (21)
Agriculture. New Commitment to 151 (19)
Agriculture Organization of the United Nations. Food and 16 (45)
Agriculture Outlook 16 (91)
Agriculture. Pennsylvania 151 (22), (263)
Agriculture Production. Saving Energy While Increasing 16 (31)
Agriculture. Solar Energy Applications in 216 (137)
Agriculture. Vocational Education in 117 (4)
Ahmadiyyat the True Islam 1 (2), (7), (11)
Ahmadiyyat. Why I Believe in 1 (10)
Aid and Foreign Policy. Military 159 (36)
Aid. Canadian Foreign 171 (11)
Aid. College Admissions and Financial 31 (16)
Aid. First 142 (39), 174 (24)
Aid for Students in Post Secondary Education. Financial 54
Aid. Foreign Economic 56 (17)
Aid - How, When, Where. Financial 31 (15)
Aid. Student Financial 27 (22), 168 (32)
Aid? Who Needs a Hearing 151 (96)
Aides Abet His Assassin? Did Lincoln 29 (338)
Aids. Financial 57 (21)
Air and Water Pollution Control 204
Air Conservation 117 (32)
Air. Fight for Clean 54
Air Force Academy 216 (120)
Air Force Academy. United States 216 (53)
Air Force. Career Opportunities in the 216 (53)
Air Force Flying Career 174 (81)
Air Force. General 174 (81)
Air Force ROTC Program 174 (81)
Air Force School Systems 174 (81)
Air Force Teaching Methods 174 (81)
Air Isn't Good for the Economy. Smoke in the 54
Air Navigation 105 (70)
Air Pollution 54, 56 (69), 168 (29)
Air Pollution Control 214 (26)
Air Pollution Control. Air Quality Monitoring: 150 (8)
Air Pollution in the Blue Ridge Mountains 216 (113)
Air Pollution Metrorology 151 (155)
Air Pollution on Plants. Effects of 216 (85)
Air Pollution - Plant Effects 216 (113)
Air Quality Impact Studies 218
Air Quality Monitoring: Air Pollution Control 150 (8)
Air Turbulence. Clear 151 (155)
Aircraft. Building Plastic Model 151 (5)
Aircraft Noise 216 (79)
Airline Industry. United States Domestic 151 (290)
Airplane. Bicycle and the 218
Airplanes. Design and Construction of 151 (33)
Airport. Expansion of the Auburn 16 (46)
Airport. General Aviation and the Community 16 (46)
Airports. Bituminous Pavements for Highways and 151 (291)
Airpower. History of 216 (53)
Alabama Agriculture 16 (75)
Alabama Cooperative Extension Service 16 (75)
Alabama Counties. History of 16 (26)
Alabama Government 16 (55)
Alabama. Governors of 16 (55)
Alabama. Mushrooms of 16 (16)
Alabama National Guard 16 (44)
Alabama's Student Financial Assistance Program 16 (68)
Alaska 59 (3)
Alaska Highway and McKinley National Park 223 (34)
Alaska - It's Schools and People 57 (81)
Alaska. Long Distance Backpacking in 166 (1)
Alaska. Magnificent Fury of 51 (1)
Alaska, or New Mexico. Observations on Russia, 56 (116)
Alaska Wilderness Lake 59 (18), 69 (14)
Alaska. Wolf Research in 151 (302)
Alaska. Wood Block Printing in 79 (123)
Alaskan Adventures 4 (6)
Alaskan Exploration. Twenty Years of Change in 143 (9)
Alberta. Oil Sands of 181 (131), (336)
Alchemists in Our Public Schools 85 (10)
Alcohol Abuse. Drug and 151 (161)
Alcohol and Drug Abuse. Preventive Approaches to 105 (88)
Alcohol and Drugs of Abuse 171 (53)
Alcohol and the Driving Task 174 (12)
Alcohol and the Human Body 174 (12)
Alcohol and Traffic Accidents 168 (29)
Alcohol, Drinking Behavior, and College Students 151 (212)
Alcohol Education 56 (82)
Alcohol Intoxication. Facts People Should Know About 54
Alcoholism - A Business Problem 117 (15), (107)
Alcoholism and Social Drinking 218
Alcoholism in America 29 (280)
Alcoholism in Business 180 (66)
Alcoholism. Patient Records in Drug Abuse and 181 (177)
Alcoholism. Psychology of 105 (100)
Aleut - Eskimos 4 (6)
Aleutians. Exploring the 4 (1)
Alex Haley 225 (11)

Alexander Aphrodisiensis 227 (51)
Alexander the Great 227 (45)
Alexandrian Library 57 (92)
Algae and Cattle Kills. Toxic 168 (37)
Alice in Wonderland Fantasy. Is Our Representative Democratic Government a Reality or an 136 (19)
Alice in Wonderland Revisited 29 (200)
Alien Look at America's Faith 85 (18)
Alienation, Dissent, and the Intellectual 85 (12)
Alienation. Marxism and Human 159 (28)
Alienation of Today's World. How Collective Living Breaks Down the Isolation and 178 (1)
Alive Inside and Out. Be 112 (42)
Alkaloids. Medicinal Plant 54
All Aboard for Siberia! 59 (16)
All Aspects of Practice Management 8 (1)
All Men and Women Are Created Equal 214 (85)
Allergies 27 (33)
Allied Health 181 (189)
Allocation. Energy 57 (25)
Allocation. Land Use 218
Allowed to Read. Children's Books Only Grownups Should Be 29 (197), (205)
Almanac. Nature's Pollution 151 (156)
Alphabet. Development and Use of Chinese 3 (2)
Altered States of Consciousness 174 (55)
Alternate Energy 35
Alternate Sources of Energy 158
Alternative Education 57 (85), 218
Alternative Education and Freirian Model 142 (56)
Alternative Energy Sources 151 (123)
Alternative Funding Sources. Developing 57 (10)
Alternative Futures 159 (3)
Alternative. Independent Private Education as an 105 (38)
Alternative Life Styles 57 (8)
Alternative Methods of Entering Police Departments 29 (144), (344)
Alternative. Nuclear - The Viable 66 (3)
Alternative Schools. Evolution of 216 (86)
Alternative Social Institutions 172 (2)
Alternative Theatre in Chicago 142 (37)
Alternative to Monologue Preaching. Drama as a Sermonic 168 (34)
Alternatives Do You Have in Secondary Public Schools. What 29 (64), (101), (347)
Alternatives. Energy 16 (80), 66 (1), 152, 216 (64)
Alternatives for the Future. Energy 150 (3)
Alternatives in Education. Career 216 (33)
Alternatives in Public Schools 117 (57)
Alternatives in Social Studies. Viable 57 (24)
Alternatives. Moral Relativism and Its 85 (36)
Alternatives. Scientific Studies on Homebirth and Other 122 (3)
Alternatives to Both. Home Birth, Hospital Birth and 36 (1)
Alternatives to Government Programs. Private 85 (2)
Altoona Campus - Facilities and Services 151 (14)
Altoona Campus - History and Growth 151 (14)
Alumni Affairs 151 (3)
Alumni Affairs. Virginia Tech 216 (107)
Alumni and Eastern Illinois University 57 (91)
Alumni - No Raccoon-Coat Set. Today's 151 (76)
Alumni on the Pittsburgh Area. Impact of Duquesne University and 54
Alumni Ownership. USL Conference Center - 174 (3)
Alumni Program. Why an 57 (91)
Alumnus. Importance of an 224 (16)
Alvar Aalto. Architecture of 181 (78)
Amateur Among the Pros 97 (55)
Amateur C.B. Radio 151 (68)
Amateur Wine and Beer Making 174 (40)
Amazing Dutch. Holland and the 59 (14)
Amazing Korea 59 (1)
Amazon 69 (3)
Amazon. Colombia-Andes to the 59 (4)
Amazon. Colombia - From the Spanish Main to the 69 (7)
Amazon. Visit to the 29 (167), (190), (325)
Ambrose Bierce and Mark Twain. Diabolical Duo: 151 (243)
Ambulatory Pharmaceutical Services 54
Amendment: An Unqualified Right to be Unfair. First 117 (83)
Amendment. Equal Rights 56 (132), 174 (54)
Amendment - Is It Working. First 105 (54)
Amendment of 1972. Education 181 (6)
Amendment. Press and First 57 (88)
America 155 (1)
America: A Racial Paradise? Minority Studies: Beyond Takenism. Latin 168 (25)
America. Alcoholism in 29 (280)
America and American Philosophy 214 (73)
America and the Vietnam War 56 (91)
America and the World: Cross-Cultural Communication 151 (110)
America and the World: Whatever Happened to the Ivory Tower? 151 (110)
America. Anglo-Saxon Myth in 223 (3)
America. Archaeology (Prehistory) - Early Man of North 105 (1)
America as a Secularized Religious Faith 151 (221)
America Behind the Headlines 154 (15)
America - Biblical Themes. Defining 159 (1)
America. Black Music in 225 (12)
America. Black Playwright in 154 (4)
America. Black Women in 142 (17)
America. Botonical Gardens Arboretums in North 117 (5)
America. Building a New 211 (6)
America, Central America, Mexico and Greece. Trips to South 79 (117)
America. Changing Nature of 176 (15)
America. Changing Race Relations in 56 (4)
America. Changing Trends and Directions in 117 (100)
America. Classics and Images of 227 (4)

America. Colonial 142 (63)
America. Contemporary Crafts in 79 (73)
America. Corporate Accountability in 181 (32), (258)
America. Criminal Justice in 176 (62)
America. Critical Treatment of Women Dramatists in 29 (146), (309)
America. Deregulating 102 (14)
America. Development of Latin 223 (17)
America. Do You Want to Know About Latin 117 (103)
America? Does the New Left Represent The Greening of 85 (8)
America. Ecology of North 117 (30)
America - Europe - The Great Misunderstanding 85 (18)
America. Excitement of 189
America. Free Masonry in 19th Century 181 (262)
America. Future of Conservatism in Post-Liberal 85 (21)
America. General View of Textiles in 79 (2)
America. Hidden 103 (6)
America. History of Classics in 227 (25)
America: How Do We View One Another. United States and Latin 151 (213)
America? How Soon Will the Arabs Own 97 (45)
America Laugh. What Makes 105 (19)
America. Leadership and the Outlook for 102 (25)
America Means to Me. What 75 (1)
America. Medicinal Flowering Plants of South 27 (14)
America, Mexico and Greece. Trips to South America, Central 79 (117)
America. Miracle Called 112 (50)
America. Modern Latin 181 (344)
America. Music of the 18th Century 56 (39), (110)
America. My Discovery of 97 (40)
America. Need for Fundamental Political Changes in 178 (5)
America. New England - Cradle of 59 (14)
America. New Ethnicity in 168 (30)
America. New Frontiers Facing 214 (6)
America. Political Power in 181 (202), (258)
America. Portuguese Peasant in Europe and 29 (123), (164)
America - Prospects for Development. South 56 (6)
America. Religion and Culture in Present-day 85 (12)
America. Sexual Minorities in 181 (238)
America. Shakespeare in 151 (237)
America. Socialism and 181 (263)
America. Soviet Espionage in North 16 (18)
America. Stand Up 135 (59)
America. State of Theater in 216 (32)
America. Status of Religion in 16 (47)
America the Beautiful 59 (17)
America - The Greatness That is Ours 51 (1)
America: The Latin Review. United States and Latin 117 (102)
America to Americans. Selling 135 (42)
America Today. Latin 97 (54)
America. Transition in the Arts in 151 (157)
America. United States and Latin 151 (196)
America? What is Ahead 135 (31)
America. What's Ahead for 102 (27)
America. What's Right About 154 (8)
America. What's Right - What's Wrong With 85 (18)
America. What's Right With 125 (1), 135 (14)
America? Will the Sheiks Buy 181 (33), (203), (332)
America. Women in 142 (80)
American and African. Jew - Afro- 29 (6), (60), (219), (329), (337)
American and European Cinema 31 (12)
American and European Conservatism - Vital Link 85 (39)
American and German Government 85 (5)
American and the Australian Outlaw 223 (3)
American and World Culture. Polish Contributions to 105 (27)
American Antiques 103 (3)
American Art 181 (80)
American Art. Realism in 214 (8)
American Association of University Professors 181 (95)
American Ballet. Modern 97 (71)
American Black Homeland? West Africa - The 29 (7)
American Blacks. Abraham Lincoln and the Emancipation of 29 (338)
American Business - The Next Fifty Years 56 (19)
American Cancer Society 151 (83)
American Capitalism 142 (51)
American Catholicism. Berrigans and 105 (110)
American Ceramics. Contemporary 159 (39)
American Character 151 (214), 216 (111)
American Child 29 (280), (340)
American Children's Books. Early 174 (18)
American Cities. Historical Development of 181 (264)
American City. Quality of Life in the 31 (13)
American Colonial History 57 (35)
American Conscience 151 (214)
American Conservatives in the Middle of the Journey 85 (16)
American Constitutional Foundations 85 (9)
American Corporations With the Securities and Exchange Commission. Value and Uses of Financial Reports Filed by 50 (1)
American Crafts. Early 103 (5)
American Culture. Aspects of Classical Influences on 227 (32)
American Culture. Professional Baseball and 142 (72)
American Culture. Talks on 105 (27)
American Deserts. Great 69 (14)

American Dream...In Politics, Poetry and Humor 97 (9)
American Dyeing. Early 79 (111)
American Eccentrics. Great 102 (25)
American Economy. Long Run Outlook for the 85 (30)
American Economy Today 117 (24)
American Education. Anthropological Look at 29 (96), (164)
American Education. Concept of Public in 181 (261)
American Education. Crisis in 85 (10, (21)
American Education. Proposal for Improvement in 54
American Education Systems. Comparison of the German and 56 (54)
American Enterprise System 105 (6)
American Evacuation During World War II. Japanese 29 (139), (333)
American Family an Obsolete Institution? Is the 216 (48)
American Family. Changes in the 181 (237), (292)
American Family. Changing 151 (167)
American Family. Psychological Perspectives on the 181 (291)
American Fiction. Earliest 151 (237)
American Film 57 (32)
American Folk Heroes 29 (185), (200)
American Folk Music 29 (220)
American Folklore 29 (201)
American Foreign Policy 151 (192), 181 (265), (337), 214 (55), 224 (7)
American Foreign Policy. Contemporary Issues in 57 (19)
American Foreign Policy. Contemporary Problems of 159 (36)
American Foreign Policy. Current Issues in 117 (66), (113)
American Foreign Policy. Liberalism and the Tragedy of 85 (7)
American Foreign Policy. Quest for Purpose in Contemporary 85 (7)
American Foreign Policy. Realities of 85 (17)
American Future. Population Change and the 168 (42)
American Government and Politics 105 (55)
American Government's Issues and Problems: Democracy 117 (104)
American Heritage. Moravian Music - A Valuable 56 (110)
American Heritage. Our 222
American Higher Education. Distinguishing Features of 151 (103)
American Higher Education in the 1970's 168 (18)
American History 159 (16)
American History. Afro- 151 (217)
American History and Culture. Afro- 142 (17)
American History. Black and Compromises in 29 (261), (337)
American History I.Q. Your 151 (219)
American History. Lady Radicals In 151 (257)
American History. 1776-1976 - Reform and Revolution in 213 (8)
American History. World and 54
American History. Youth in 151 (221)
American Home 181 (268)
American Ideals of a Christian Capitalist Democracy 180 (183)
American Image Abroad 97 (18)
American Image. Making of an 97 (19)
American In the United States Constitution. Afro- 29 (82), (194), (337)
American Indian Affairs 172 (4)
American Indian and Black Genealogy 154 (2)
American Indian and the United States Government 29 (158), (254)
American Indian Contemporary Issues 29 (50), (158), (192), (283)
American Indian Education 29 (87)
American Indian History 29 (158), (331)
American Indian History, Legends and Culture 79 (126)
American Indian Poetry 29 (162)
American Indian. Rights of the 154 (21)
American Indian Textiles 79 (71)
American Indian Tribalism 29 (158), (230), (283)
American Indian Tribes. Legal Status and Economic Development of 218
American Indian Weaving Techniques and Contemporary Uses. Ancient 79 (90)
American Indians and Weaving. Meso 79 (110)
American Indians. Life and Culture of North 79 (124)
American Indians. Modern 105 (1)
American Indians of Southwest. Survey of Art of the 151 (27)
American Jazz 57 (42)
American Jewish Voting Patterns 214 (4), (48)
American Juvenile Periodicals. History of 117 (75)
American Law and Institutions 181 (274)
American Leaders. 2000 Young 135 (6)
American Life. Magazines and 105 (68)
American Literary Criticism. Afro- 142 (66)
American Literature 151 (232), (240)
American Literature. Achievement of Nationality in 16 (34)
American Literature. Afro- 142 (66), (74)
American Literature and Culture 142 (22)
American Literature Between the Great Wars 151 (231)
American Literature. Carl Sandburg's Place in 225 (42)
American Literature. Recent 117 (90)
American Literature. Spanish 216 (135)
American Literature. Women in 151 (234)
American Magazines. History of 218
American Medicine. Early 151 (257)
American Melting Pot 181 (256)
American Mercenary. Twentieth Century 154 (3)
American Mind, 1607-1900. Jewish Image in 181 (262)

American Music. Afro- 181 (27), (84)
American Music. Asian Influences on 225 (12)
American Music. Twentieth Century 225 (12)
American Musical Theater. Dance in the 225 (39)
American National Policy 174 (72)
American National Politics 151 (222)
American Oral History. Afro- 142 (66)
American People. Right to Work - Supported by Facts, Figures and the 131 (1)
American Philosophers and Natural Rights 214 (73)
American Philosophy. America and 214 (73)
American Pick-up Weaves. South 79 (107)
American Political Behavior 214 (3)
American Political Ideas 174 (72)
American Political Right. Varieties of the 85 (40)
American Political Tradition 85 (13)
American Political Tradition. Rediscovering the 85 (39)
American Politicians. Cautious Communicator: 151 (87)
American Politics 112 (15), 142 (64), 181 (262)
American Politics and Craziness 114 (3)
American Politics and Political Philosophy 85 (11)
American Politics. Equality and Liberty in 85 (13)
American Politics. Neighborhood Movement in 181 (275)
American Presidency 112 (13), 142 (27)
American Presidents. Early 142 (63)
American Psychiatry. History of 151 (214)
American Race Track Culture 142 (48)
American Relations. Future of Soviet - 85 (31)
American Relations. Japanese- 181 (270), (342)
American Relations With China and Japan 181 (265), (337)
American Religion? Disneyland: Entertainment or a New 159 (51)
American Religious Institutions 151 (215)
American Renaissance. Latin 151 (27)
American Revolution 117 (77), 142 (63), 174 (72), (83), 214 (58), 216 (11)
American Revolution Caused by a Conspiracy. Was the 105 (60)
American Revolution Considered as a Religious Revival 105 (60)
American Revolution. Latin 135 (22)
American Revolution. Second 174 (72)
American Role in Asia. Future of the 105 (57)
American Social and Political Philosophy 214 (75)
American Society 142 (78)
American Society. Psychotherapy in 181 (291)
American Space. Metropolitan Organization of 181 (134)
American Strategy in Foreign Policy 85 (29)
American Symphony Orchestra 57 (42)
American Thought. Afro- 181 (29)
American Tradition in Foreign Affairs. Origins of the 85 (7)
American Transportation Problems 16 (36)
American Voices. Three 102 (25)
American Way 112 (121)
American Way of Life. Environmental Quality and the 57 (94)
American West. Urban History and History of the 159 (16)
American Wines. Enjoying French and 216 (25)
American Woman 151 (72)
American Woman in American History. Black Psychology - 29 (337)
American Woman Novelist. Edith Wharton: 151 (238)
American Women in Autobiography. Her Own Words - Lives of 29 (336)
American Women in Autobiography. Lives of 29 (202)
American Women Writers. Afro- 142 (66)
American Word. Profit - An All- 112 (14)
Americana. Folklore 29 (185), (200), (332)
Americana in Asia. End of Pax 105 (57)
Americans. African History to 181 (267)
Americans Are Losing Faith in Free Enterprise. Why 102 (33)
Americans Are Not Born Stupid 168 (11)
Americans Are People 97 (43)
Americans. Current Statistics on Violent Deaths Among 218
Americans. Gertrude Stein's The Making of 181 (272)
Americans - Lincoln, the Master Politician. Great 151 (222)
Americans. Making of 181 (146)
Americans. Meaning of Japan for 168 (66)
Americans. Selling America to 135 (42)
Americans - Washington. Great
America's Bloodiest Day. Antietam - 57 (28)
America's Contribution to Theatre. Musical: 105 (26)
America's Faith. Alien Look at 85 (18)
America's First Olympic Team and Athletes 151 (275)
America's First Women Editor. Elizabeth Timothy - 56 (61)
America's Founding Fathers. Lincoln - Rutledge Romance - Hoax or Reality? Lincoln's Use and Abuse of 29 (338)
America's Goal - Justice Through Law 112 (28)
America's Maritime Heritage 214 (57), (69)
America's Negro Problem in Historical Perspective 85 (12)
Americas Oil Famine 97 (35)
America's Opportunity 112 (85)
America's Overseas Information 105 (54)
America's Pacific Paradise. Micronesia, 15 (1)
America's Political Cartoon Heritage 214 (4)
America's Population. Distribution Trends of 151 (84)
America's Role in World Affairs 102 (14)
America's Stake in Asia 102 (27)
America's Status in the World Today 102 (26)
America's Three Most Popular Novelists 223 (3)

LECTURE TITLES AND KEYWORD INDEX

Americas. Winter Holidays in the 15 (3)
Amnesty 105 (76)
Among Wild Whales 69 (12)
Amphibians and Reptiles of Louisiana 174 (53)
Amusement Only. For 97 (29)
Anaerobic Bacteria in Disease 56 (78)
Anaerobic Bacteriology in the Clinical Laboratory 56 (78)
Analog Computer. Designing An 181 (154)
Analysis and Design of Weaves. Drafting - 79 (78)
Analysis as a Science. Handwriting 94 (1)
Analysis. Cloth 79 (63)
Analysis in Curriculum Development. Systems 168 (15)
Analysis in Dental Research. Stress 105 (28)
Analysis. International Relations: Observations, Comments and 117 (104)
Analysis. Neutron Activation 151 (156)
Analysis of Energy Systems. Management and 163 (1)
Analysis of Large Corporations. Economic 85 (19)
Analysis of Mexico. Cultural and Political 117 (105)
Analysis of Myth. Structural 227 (41)
Analysis of Present Situation. Arab-Israeli Conflict - Its Origin and 117 (104)
Analysis of Sports Skills 151 (209)
Analysis. Organizational Transactional 27 (7)
Analysis. Transactional 151 (46), (77), 180 (32)
Analysis. Transportation Systems 151 (290)
Analyst. Reminiscences of a News 83 (6)
Analyzing Business Training Needs 151 (122)
Anarchism 181 (298)
Anarchism, Nihilism, and the New Left 85 (21)
Anatomy of the Brain or of the Visual System 27 (26)
Ancestors. Popular 154 (2)
Ancient American Indian Weaving Techniques and Contemporary Uses 79 (90)
Ancient and Medieval European History 151 (215)
Ancient and Modern Olympic Games. Differences in 151 (275)
Ancient and Modern Southwest Indian Spinning, Dyeing 79 (76)
Ancient Art and Myth 227 (21)
Ancient Astronauts. Lost Worlds and 174 (22)
Ancient Attitudes Towards Sexuality and Bodily Functions 227 (18)
Ancient. China: New, Old, 112 (32)
Ancient Egypt 57 (77)
Ancient Forms of Sculpture 227 (32)
Ancient Greece and Rome 54
Ancient Greece. Women in 227 (25)
Ancient Greek Athletics 227 (18)
Ancient History 151 (215), 227 (38)
Ancient History and Demography 227 (37)
Ancient Impeachment Proceedings 227 (38)
Ancient Indian Sacrifice 29 (21), (129), (247)
Ancient Law 227 (32)
Ancient Literature. Stoicism in 227 (39)
Ancient Mesoamerica 56 (1)
Ancient Myths in Modern Movies 227 (44)
Ancient New East 29 (217), (226)
Ancient Olympic Games. History of the 151 (275)
Ancient Peruvian Textiles 79 (63)
Ancient Philosophy 227 (34)
Ancient Religion and Philosophies 117 (64)
Ancient Textile Techniques for Today 79 (35)
Ancient Theatre. Actors and Acting in the 227 (14)
Ancient to Modern Times. Greek - An Ongoing Language From 227 (29)
Ancient Town Planning. Aspects of 227 (32)
Ancient Views on the Value of Democracy 227 (38)
Ancient Women 227 (21)
Ancient World. Occultism in the 151 (259)
Ancient World. Reassessment of Status of Women in the 227 (39)
Ancient World. Religion in the 227 (16)
And Who Shall Censor the Censors? 151 (74)
Andes to the Amazon. Colombia- 59 (4)
Anesthesia 181 (162), (172)
Anesthesia. Mystery of 181 (162)
Anesthetic Agents 181 (162)
Anglo-Saxon Myth in America 223 (3)
Angola Crisis 54
Animal and Plant Genetic Improvement 105 (2)
Animal Behavior. African 181 (281)
Animal Diseases and Resultant Food Loss 16 (45)
Animal Pests. Biological Control of Plant and 31 (8)
Animal Science. Careers in 216 (80)
Animal Today. On Being a Rational 168 (60)
Animal Training 142 (28)
Animals. Emotional Problems of 225 (26)
Animals for Biomedical Research. Use of 151 (206)
Animals. Humans and Other 181 (281)
Anne Wilson Speaks Contempo 97 (71)
Announcing and Script Writing. Radio and Television 142 (74)
Annual Giving 151 (188)
Antarctic Adventure 151 (301)
Antarctica. Biological Research in 216 (93)
Antarctica. Soils of 218
Anthem. Our National 57 (91)
Anthracite Mining. Labor and Industry in 151 (36)
Anthropological Look at American Education 29 (96), (164)
Anthropology 176 (80), 224 (5)
Anthropology and Dentistry 151 (208)
Anthropology. Contemporary Trends in 151 (214)
Anthropology in General 105 (1)
Anthropology. Medical 142 (48)
Anthropology of Haiti 142 (14)
Anthropology. Social 216 (1)
Anticonvulsants and Epilepsy 181 (164)
Antidote for Television. Storytelling - 29 (200)
Antietam - America's Bloodiest Day 57 (28)
Antimicrobial Agents 54
Antique Automobiles 16 (44)

Antique Clocks 168 (70)
Antique Firearms. Evolution of 117 (130)
Antique Spinning Wheels. Repair, Care, and Maintenance of 79 (99)
Antiques 142 (10), 174 (73)
Antiques. American 103 (3)
Antiques Around the World. Hunting 97 (24)
Antiques for Investment 103 (3)
Antiquity. Attitudes Toward Women in 227 (28)
Antiquity. Family in 227 (18)
Antiquity. Social History of Women in 227 (10)
Antiquity. Women in 227 (4), (18), (33)
Anti-rape Organizing 178 (2)
Anti-Semitism in the Soviet Union 218
Anti-submarine Warfare 105 (70)
Antitrust Law 105 (56)
Antitrust Section of the Attorney General's Office 168 (27)
Anxiety and Tension. How to Handle 174 (9)
Anxiety Control 105 (31)
Anxiety Reduction. Tension and 174 (94)
Anyone Who Goes to a Psychiatrist Should Have His Head Examined 225 (3)
Apartheid 181 (28), (338)
Apartheid. South African 223 (18)
Apathetic Bystander 56 (134)
Aphrodisiensis. Alexander 227 (51)
Apicius' Roman Cookbook 227 (31)
Aplenty. Poise 112 (19)
Appalachian People and Literature 168 (26)
Apparel and the Consumer 174 (54)
Appearance of the Promised Messiah and the Promised Mahdi 1 (8)
Appetite Regulatory Mechanisms in Obesity 171 (26)
Appliance Weaving. Small 79 (80)
Appliances. Household 216 (73)
Application. Development of Lasers and Their 218
Application. Meditation and Its Practical 108 (1), (2)
Application of Computers 174 (79)
Application of Historical Motifs in Weaving 79 (81)
Application of the Wind Quintet. History and 218
Applications. Computer 216 (68)
Applications in the Study of Literature. Computer 227 (44)
Applications. Lasers and Their 105 (119)
Applications. Lasers--Medical 29 (186)
Applications. Microwaves and Their 105 (119)
Applications of Computers. Civic 31 (17)
Applications of Radioisotopes. Industrial 54
Applications of Science and Technology. Future and 154 (17)
Applications. Real Estate Law 65 (5)
Applications to Real Estate Marketing. Computer 69 (65)
Applied General Systems Theory 159 (66)
Applied Nutrition Program in Haiti 216 (140)
Applique 79 (75)
Applique and Quilting 79 (84)
Applique. Design in Stitch and 79 (9)
Applique. Ethnic 79 (120)
Appointments. Federal Judicial 168 (57)
Appraisal. Performance 151 (46)
Appraising 65 (1), (10), (17), (22), (26), (33), (34), (37), (40), (43), (49), (50), (51), (58), (59), (61)
Appreciation. Art 142 (11)
Appreciation. Computer 216 (68)
Appreciation. Mathematics 181 (152)
Appreciation of Great Art 102 (25)
Appreciation of Music. Enjoyment and 54
Approach. Country Boy 65 (56)
Approach for Teaching and Learning 181 (122)
Approach to Classroom Discipline. Realistic and Humanistic 117 (51)
Approach to Discipline Problems - Effective Ways Parents Can Deal With and Understand Young Children. Positive 117 (48)
Approach to Foreign Language Teaching. Natural 27 (15)
Approach to Form and Fiber Fashion. Multiple 79 (106)
Approach to Music Teaching. Kodaly 54
Approach to Out-Patient Pharmacy Services. Clincial 54
Approach to Technology. Integrative 181 (47)
Approach to the Teaching of Reading. Using the Diagnostic 117 (36)
Approach to Treatment and Evaluation. Multi-disciplinary 159 (26)
Approach to Updating. Motivational 151 (40)
Approaches to Alcohol and Drug Abuse. Preventive 105 (88)
Approaches to Drama. Structuralist 227 (25)
Approaches to Drawing. Technical and Conceptual 117 (11)
Approaches to Learning. Multi-media Concepts and New 56 (50)
Approaches to Mental Handicap. Educational 117 (131)
Approaches to Tapestry. Design 79 (35)
Aptitude in the Arts. Attitudes and 181 (88)
Aquaculture of Salmon 218
Aqueous Solution Chemistry 159 (56)
Aquifers and Other Interesting Landforms. Glacial Deposition of 136 (13)
Arab-Israeli Conflict 57 (61), 181 (293), (306), 224 (9)
Arab-Israeli Conflict: Its Origin and Analysis of Present Situation 117 (104)
Arab Libraries in Jordan 29 (196), (225)
Arab World. Politics and Economics of the 57 (61)
Arabic Calligraphy 218
Arabic Language Today 29 (203), (218)
Arabs and Jews Were Friends. When 181 (306), (343)
Arabs. Jews and 29 (163), (218)

Arabs Own America? How Soon Will the 97 (45)
Ararat: Armenians and Their Contributions. People of 105 (23)
Arbitration 159 (58)
Arbitration of Labor-Management Disputes 216 (104)
Arboretum. Fullerton 29 (28), (143)
Arboretums in North America. Botanical Gardens - 117 (5)
Archaeological Methodology 227 (55)
Archaeological Research. Environmental Impact Studies and 117 (31)
Archaeology 142 (82)
Archaeology. Classical 227 (13), (14), (20)
Archaeology. Holy Land 227 (45)
Archaeology. Indians and 174 (34)
Archaeology. Medieval 31 (28)
Archaeology. Near Eastern 29 (226), (269)
Archaeology of Classical and Hellenistic Greece 227 (45)
Archaeology of Crete and Mycenae 227 (45)
Archaeology of Rome. Topography and 227 (26)
Archaeology of Washington State 218
Archaeology (Prehistory) - Early Man of North America 105 (1)
Archaeology. Romance of Undersea 4 (5)
Archaeology. What Science Can Do for 171 (36)
Archie Bunker to Fred Sanford. From 112 (9)
Architect. Choosing an 181 (78), (207)
Architects and Movements of the Nineteenth Century. Various 31 (3)
Architects Role in the Built Environment 174 (37)
Architectural Barriers 56 (77)
Architectural Barriers to the Handicapped and Aged 151 (228)
Architectural Commissions 79 (103)
Architectural Fiber Sculpture 79 (103)
Architectural History 218
Architecture 164 (1)
Architecture: An Edifice of Sound 151 (31)
Architecture and Preservation. History of Chicago 142 (79)
Architecture Aspects of Louisiana 174 (19)
Architecture. Color in Interior 218
Architecture. Cubism - Major Route of Modern Painting, Sculpture and 56 (10)
Architecture. External Influences on Synagogue 181 (306)
Architecture. Gothic 31 (3)
Architecture. Greek Art and 227 (39)
Architecture in South India. Art and 29 (13), (129)
Architecture. Isfahan is Half the World - Its Art and 151 (29)
Architecture of Alvar Aalto 181 (78)
Architecture of Colonial Philadelphia 151 (29)
Architecture of Flowers 216 (62)
Architecture of Frank Lloyd Wright 181 (78)
Architecture. Pennsylvania 151 (257)
Architecture. Synagogue 181 (87)
Archival Holdings 174 (19)
Are Students Today Better Prepared for a College Education? 16 (23), (78)
Are the Arts Interrelated in Your School? 181 (92)
Are United States Manufacturing Industries Monopolized? 85 (2)
Are You a Drug Abuser? 181 (186), (236)
Are You a Mystic? 54
Are You a Processionary Caterpillar 76 (1)
Are You Achieving More and Enjoying It Less? 112 (54)
Are You Losing Money in Inventory 136 (7)
Are You the Cause or the Result? 225 (32)
Areas of Risk, Management and Insurance 168 (68)
Arena of World Problems. Olympic Games: 151 (275)
Argentina 15 (2)
Argument. New Morality 105 (90)
Argumentation 218
Aristocracy. Authority and 85 (40)
Aristocracy Decadent? Is British 97 (44)
Aristotle and Their Method. Greek Commentators on 227 (51)
Arizona. Desert Pigs of 151 (302)
Armed Force. Draft versus An All-Volunteer 85 (1)
Armed Forces - Will it Work? Voluntary 159 (53)
Armenians and Their Contributions. People of Ararat: 105 (23)
Arms Control and Disarmament 85 (28)
Arms Control. Prospects for 151 (190)
Arms, Disarmament, and Security 56 (103)
Arms Limitation. Strategic 97 (74)
Arms Race? Is the United States Falling Behind? Where Are We Headed in the 102 (8)
Arms Race. Soviet-American 29 (256), (292)
Army Reserve. United States 216 (60)
Army. Voluntary 105 (74)
Around the World in Slides 151 (264)
Around-the-World Tropical Gardens 174 (44)
Arranging. Flower 16 (63)
Arrive at Selling Prices. How to 79 (96)
Arsenic and the Tacoma Smelter 159 (12)
Art 164 (1), 214 (9)
Art. American 181 (80)
Art and Architecture. Greek 227 (39)
Art and Architecture in South India 29 (13), (129)
Art and Architecture. Isfahan is Half the World - Its 151 (29)
Art and Craft of Threads 83 (17)
Art and Law 159 (30)
Art and Music. Similarities Between 20th Century 159 (21)
Art and Myth. Ancient 227 (21)
Art and Techniques of Bolivian Highland Weaving 79 (18)
Art and the Atom 31 (5)
Art and the Struggle Against Oppression. Theater 70 (1)
Art Appreciation 142 (11)

Art. Appreciation of Great 102 (25)
Art. Byzantine 227 (30)
Art. Children's 117 (12)
Art Concepts 142 (76)
Art. Contemporary 142 (76), 159 (18)
Art. Contemporary Trends in 151 (27)
Art Criticism of History 216 (96)
Art. Duquesne Tamburitzan Institute of Folk 54
Art. Early French Gothic 151 (28)
Art. Early Irish Christian 181 (79)
Art. Early Pagan Celtic 181 (79)
Art Exhibit. Jurying an 159 (18)
Art. Folklore and Legend of Birds in 57 (82)
Art Forgeries. Scientific Detection of 151 (73)
Art Form. Evolution of the 56 (13)
Art Form. Opera as a Contemporary 142 (16)
Art Form. Physics as an 151 (268)
Art Form. Textile Printing and Dyeing as an 79 (129)
Art Form. Weaving as an 79 (60)
Art Forms. Comparative 117 (11)
Art. French Impressionist 117 (138)
Art History 57 (52), 142 (11), (76)
Art History. Japanese 16 (32)
Art in Interior Design. Weaving as 79 (148)
Art in Mechanized Intelligence. State of the 181 (204)
Art in Nature 159 (5)
Art in Orange County 29 (10)
Art. Indian Culture and 57 (82)
Art. Integration of Science and 151 (27)
Art. Interdisciplinary Method of Teaching 142 (35)
Art. Japanese 151 (271)
Art. Jewish 181 (80), (301)
Art. Mexican Retablo and Related Folk 174 (41)
Art. Modern 181 (80), (210)
Art, Music and Children's Literature. Early Childhood Education in 142 (30)
Art, Music, and Cooking Activities for the Classroom Teacher 117 (48)
Art of Assemblage 176 (108)
Art of Asserting Yourself 57 (41)
Art of Being Average. Noble 112 (126)
Art of Communicating With Lasers and Lightwaves 144
Art of Driving Defensively 174 (12)
Art of Keeping Physically Fit. Aerobics, the 16 (18)
Art of Motivating People 151 (38)
Art of Parenting 117 (43)
Art of Peter Bruegel. Peasant in the 105 (61)
Art of Self Disclosure 57 (41)
Art of the American Indians of Southwest 151 (27)
Art of the Netherlands From the 15th to the 17th Century 56 (9)
Art of Various Parts of the World 117 (11)
Art of Wit and Humor 225 (40)
Art or Morality. Critical Judgments on 105 (66)
Art. Oriental 57 (44), 159 (18)
Art. Polyphemus in Folktale, Homer, Literature and 227 (47)
Art: Portrayed and Portrayers. Women in 151 (31)
Art. Public 79 (103)
Art: Reading Aloud. Lost 105 (26)
Art. Reading - the Magic 57 (62)
Art. Realism in American 214 (8)
Art. Reality of 56 (13)
Art. Shaker Textiles, Dyeing, Soft 79 (46)
Art Spirit 97 (66)
Art. Sports and 57 (82)
Art. State of the 67 (20)
Art Stitchery. Folk 79 (117)
Art. Survey of Medieval 56 (9)
Art. Symbolist Movement in Literature and 216 (112)
Art. Technique for Enjoying 105 (19)
Art Today 31 (4)
Art Treasures in Western Europe 56 (9)
Art. Video 218
Art Weaves 79 (48)
Art Weaves - the Weaver Controlled Weaves 79 (17)
Art Work. Discussion of Personal 117 (10)
Art World 176 (40)
Artemis and the Women's Religion 227 (48)
Artery By-Pass Surgery. Coronary 181 (194)
Arthur Godfrey. Life and Times of 154 (10)
Article Published. Getting My 216 (78)
Articulatory Phonetics 56 (65)
Artist. How to Train a Professional 16 (32)
Artist in Residence. Mr. Fingers, 221 (1)
Artist. Life of a Courtroom 97 (37)
Artist. Trials of a Woman 79 (79)
Artist. Zen and the 211 (5)
Artistry. Techniques of Portrait 168 (8)
Artist's Eye of Russia 29 (11), (17), (148), (293), (311), (322)
Artists of San Blas. Cuna Women - Mola 27 (47)
Artist's Way of Life 211 (5)
Artists. Women 214 (8), (93)
Arts 181 (77)
Arts and Crafts. Design in the 159 (18)
Arts and Crafts. History of Northwest 218
Arts and Crafts. Indian 79 (56)
Arts and Crafts of Ceylon 79 (128)
Arts and Culture. Eskimo 79 (123)
Arts and Math Activities for Teachers - Nursery - 4th Grade. Language 117 (48)
Arts and Quality of Life 57 (38)
Arts and Related Activities. Language 117 (56)
Arts and the Study Skills. Language 181 (319)
Arts as Preparation for an Uncertain Future. Liberal 151 (116)
Arts. Attitudes and Aptitude in the 181 (88)
Arts. Back to the Basics With the 151 (30)
Arts. Business and the 105 (6)
Arts. Careers in Teaching Industrial 117 (80)
Arts. Current State of the 29 (10)
Arts. Design and the Textile 79 (95)
Arts Education. Black Studies and Liberal 181 (25), (90)
Arts Education in Today's Society 151 (30)

Arts Education Today. Liberal 105 (35)
Arts. Educational Television in the 151 (32)
Arts. Fiber 79 (66)
Arts. Folk 57 (78)
Arts. Guatemala It's Textile 79 (41)
Arts in America. Transition in the 151 (157)
Arts in Elementary Schools 151 (32)
Arts in Schools Today 151 (30)
Arts in Society 16 (1)
Arts in the Modern School. Industrial 151 (118)
Arts in the Open School. Reading and Language 117 (36)
Arts in Vocational Education. Liberal 174 (91)
Arts. Inspiration for Weaving From Nature and the 79 (112)
Arts Interrelated in Your School? Are the 181 (92)
Arts. Liberal 216 (50)
Arts. Martial 228
Arts. New Technologies in Graphic 218
Arts. Performing 142 (92)
Arts Programs. Structured/Integrated Liberal 227 (11)
Arts, Reading, Mathematics and Science to Bilingual Classes in the Elementary Grades. Teaching Language 142 (90)
Arts Setting. Asian Studies in the Liberal 159 (6)
Arts. Teaching More Creatively in Reading and Language 57 (79)
Arts to the People and of the People 57 (38)
Arts? Who Needs Them? 57 (67)
Aseptic Bulk Storage and Transportation 67 (24), (25)
Aseptic Processing 67 (18)
Asia. America's Stake in 102 (27)
Asia and the United States. Family Life in 56 (123)
Asia. Emphasis of the United States in 117 (68)
Asia. End of Pax Americana in 105 (57)
Asia. Future of the American Role in 105 (57)
Asia. Future Role of United States Government in 159 (36)
Asia. Growth and Development in Southern 56 (123)
Asia. Middle East and South 142 (41)
Asia. Political, Cultural, Social and Economic Aspects of Southeast 142 (89)
Asia. Political Problems of 85 (18)
Asia. Politics of 174 (59)
Asia. South 214 (52)
Asia. Southeast 151 (189), 174 (91)
Asia. Today and Tomorrow 97 (57)
Asia Today. South East 85 (29)
Asia. Travel in 29 (16). (163), (319)
Asia. United States and 151 (196)
Asian Influences on American Music 225 (12)
Asian Politics. New Patterns of 105 (57)
Asian Studies in the Liberal Arts Setting 159 (6)
Ask Yourself 112 (74)
Aspect of Man's Life. Islamic Viewpoint on Any 1 (11)
Aspects. Drug Addiction - The Physiological and Pharmacological 54
Aspects. Negritude: Black and White 159 (40)
Aspects of Adolescent Pregnancy. Medical and Psychological 27 (30)
Aspects of Ancient Town Planning 227 (32)
Aspects of Bilingualism in Canada 56 (121)
Aspects of Business. Legal 105 (6)
Aspects of Childbearing. Various 105 (97)
Aspects of Classical Influences on American Culture 227 (32)
Aspects of Education. Legal 16 (83)
Aspects of Environmental Biology 57 (94)
Aspects of Greek Music 227 (43)
Aspects of Hardwood, Plywood, and Veneer. Technical 80 (1)
Aspects of History and Philosophy of Science 218
Aspects of Human Communication. Non-verbal 142 (37)
Aspects of India. Economic and Political 142 (81)
Aspects of Louisiana Architecture 174 (19)
Aspects of Mathematics. Philosophical 56 (129)
Aspects of NATO. Nonmilitary 151 (201)
Aspects of Organ Transplants. Legal and Medical 54
Aspects of Pollution. Economic 117 (35)
Aspects of Practice Management. All 8 (1)
Aspects of Real Estate. Motivational 65 (31)
Aspects of Southeast Asia. Political, Cultural, Social and Economic 142 (89)
Aspects of Sports Participation. Motivational 57 (74)
Aspects of the Energy Crisis. Economic 117 (35)
Aspects of the 19th Century Russian Literature 29 (127), (213)
Aspects of the Third World. Demographic and Socio-Economic 223 (28)
Aspects of This Overlooked Part of Communication. Non-Verbal Communication: A Program Dealing With the Many 117 (58)
Aspirations. Academic Programs and 142 (40)
Aspirations. Past Problems and Future 171 (59)
Ass. Golden 227 (11)
Assassin? Did Lincoln Aides Abet His 29 (338)
Assassination of John F. Kennedy 176 (56)
Assassination, Riot, Public Violence 29 (153)
Assassinations - The Kennedys and King. Political 54
Assateague Island. Wild Ponies of 151 (305)
Assemblage. Art of 176 (108)
Asserting Yourself. Art of 57 (41)
Assertion Training 29 (44), (252)
Assertive - Between Mouse and Monster. Becoming 29 (239), (343)
Assertive Training 105 (82), (88)
Assertiveness and Manipulation 168 (11)
Assertiveness Training 57 (71), 105 (77), (83), (86), 168 (23), 174 (94), 218
Assessment. Educational Quality 181 (116)
Assessment for Schools. Needs 181 (116)
Assessment. Psycho-Educational 142 (93)

Asset Not Listed on Your Balance Sheet. Trade Associations - A Business 136 (4)
Assignments. Inspirational and After Dinner 65 (60)
Assistance Administration. United States Foreign 151 (196)
Assistance in Statistics. United Nations Technical 151 (251)
Assistance is Available for Higher Education. Financial 105 (38)
Assistance Program. Alabama's Student Financial 16 (68)
Assistance Program Can Help You. How the Pennsylvania Technical 151 (47)
Associate Degree - A Historical Perspective 151 (2)
Associate Program. Child Development 174 (31)
Associate Relations. Realtor 65 (10), (36)
Associated Press 176 (13)
Association and You. United Nations 151 (65)
Association. Child Development 223 (7)
Association of University Professors. American 181 (95)
Association Today. National Water Works 136 (20)
Association Work. Trials and Tribulations of 136 (20)
Associations - A Business Asset Not Listed on Your Balance Sheet. Trade 136 (4)
Assumptions of Psychotherapy. Some Philosophical 29 (245)
Assurance. Quality 151 (43)
Asthma Sufferers. New Hope For 27 (33)
Astrology 180 (176)
Astrology. Astronomy and 181 (280)
Astrology Can Help You Find Your Ideal Mate. How 225 (20)
Astrology. Getting What You Want With 225 (20)
Astrology. History and Practice of 227 (4)
Astronautics. History of 154 (17)
Astronauts. Lost Worlds and Ancient 174 (22)
Astronomy 142 (31), (65)
Astronomy and Astrology 181 (280)
Astronomy. Universe According to Modern 181 (280)
Asymmetry of the Screen 181 (76)
Atchafalaya Basin. Research in the 174 (53)
Atheism and Its Tactics. New 85 (20)
Athenian Democracy 227 (38)
Athlete. Athletics and the Student 57 (60)
Athlete. Care of the 16 (38)
Athlete. Injury Prevention for the 151 (283)
Athlete. Recruiting the Student 57 (60)
Athlete. Student/ 216 (19)
Athletes. America's First Olympic Team and 151 (275)
Athletes. Growth and Development in Young 171 (28)
Athletes. How Science Produces Good 171 (23)
Athletes in Running. Expectations for College 168 (71)
Athletes. Sports and Christian 83 (2)
Athletic and Academic Scholarships. No Need 31 (15)
Athletic Injuries. Care and Prevention of 151 (279)
Athletic Injury 151 (283)
Athletic Injury/Illness Reporting System. National 151 (279)
Athletic Performance and Nutrition 216 (134)
Athletic Programs at Penn State 151 (281)
Athletic Skills. Improving Your 151 (209)
Athletic Training. Career in 151 (279)
Athletics 56 (82), (87), 159 (67), 180 (93)
Athletics. Ancient Greek 227 (18)
Athletics and Academics 171 (22), 214 (11)
Athletics and Education 57 (60)
Athletics and Higher Education. Intercollegiate 216 (7)
Athletics and Physical Education. Hypnosis In 151 (296)
Athletics and the Student Athlete 57 (60)
Athletics at Behrend College 151 (285)
Athletics at Carnegie-Mellon. Intramural 31 (9)
Athletics at the University of Washington 218
Athletics. Basketball and 151 (277), (284)
Athletics. Competitive 151 (285)
Athletics. Cryokinetic Therapy in 56 (76)
Athletics. Humorous Side of 151 (187)
Athletics in Education 56 (87)
Athletics. Intercollegiate 151 (285)
Athletics. Intramural 31 (39)
Athletics. Marquette 105 (112)
Athletics. Money in College 105 (112)
Athletics. Physical Education and 159 (47)
Athletics. Role of Women in 159 (69)
Athletics, Uses and Abuses. Drugs and 56 (76)
Athletics. Women's 105 (126)
Atlas. Man as 168 (60)
Atmosphere. Residence Time of Aerosol in the 218
Atom. Art and the 31 (5)
Atomic Energy 176 (45)
Atomic Energy. Utilization of 216 (64)
Attacks on the Auto Industry. Consumer 117 (16)
Attacks on Women's Rights 213 (5)
Attainment. Object of Man's Creation and the Means of Its 1 (11)
Attics. Adventures in 97 (24)
Attitude Can Make You Young. Your 229 (3)
Attitude Change. Three Processes of 56 (135)
Attitude. Management and 180 (130)
Attitude. Sinning 112 (132)
Attitudes About Business 23
Attitudes and Aptitude in the Arts 181 (88)
Attitudes and Values. Counseling for 151 (161)
Attitudes. Consumer 176 (87)
Attitudes. German 174 (33)
Attitudes. Influence of Communication Media on 218
Attitudes of University Students. Changing 27 (21)
Attitudes Toward Death and Dying. Changing 29 (281)
Attitudes Toward Women in Antiquity 227 (28)
Attitudes Towards Sexuality and Bodily Functions. Ancient 227 (18)

Attorney General's Office. Antitrust Section of the 168 (27)
Attorney Liaison. Realtor 65 (16)
Attorney Relationships. Realtor 65 (33)
Attorney. Working With Your CPA, Banker and 136 (7)
Attributes. Management 174 (43)
Attrition, Stopping Out, Transfering. Student 218
Auburn Airport. Expansion of the 16 (46)
Auctions. Real Estate 65 (23)
Audience With Laughter. How to Pulverize an 112 (67)
Audio-Visual Education 52 (74), 117 (41)
Audiovisual Instruction 174 (36)
Audiovisual Production 181 (69)
Audiovisual Production Techniques 181 (97)
Auditing Can Do for Any Organization. What Internal 216 (63)
Auditing 2000 A.D. 159 (50)
Audits 151 (9)
Augustan Age. Ovid, the Wit of the 227 (23)
Augustan Age. Propaganda of the 227 (52)
Augustan Literature 227 (35)
Augustine. Saint 214 (82)
Austen. In Search of Jane 151 (298)
Australia. Brawny 59 (1)
Australia by Camper 59 (16)
Australia. Impressions of 29 (326)
Australia. Outback 59 (1)
Australian Outlaw. American and the 223 (3)
Australian Politics and Foreign Policy 151 (189)
Australian Wildlife 29 (75), (277), (324)
Austria 15 (5), 59 (13)
Austria for All Seasons 51 (1)
Austria. Magnificent 59 (14)
Austria. Seven Days Around 29 (11), (148), (322)
Authenticity. Identity and 29 (251)
Authority and Aristocracy 85 (40)
Authority. Ecclesiastical 105 (104)
Authority, Its Use and Abuse 117 (28)
Authors. Children's 181 (145)
Auto Industry. Consumer Attacks on the 117 (16)
Autobiography. Her Own Words - Lives of American Women in 29 (336)
Autobiography. Lives of American Women in 29 (202)
Autocracy to Totalitariansim. From 57 (37)
Automated Flow Control Systems 67 (18)
Automation in Microbiology 151 (173)
Automobile Accident Problem 181 (44), (243)
Automobile Design and Production. Engineer in 214 (90)
Automobile Impact on Communities 218
Automobiles. Antique 16 (44)
Automotive Pollution 216 (81)
Automotive Power Plants 216 (81)
Autonomy? Community Economic Development - Dependence or 151 (49)
Availability of Natural Resources 216 (77)
Avant-Garde. Music of the 56 (108)
Avant-Garde Theater 159 (40)
Avenue Mannequins. Madison 142 (32)
Average. Noble Art of Being 112 (126)
Aviation 151 (33), 176 (74)
Aviation and the Community Airport. General 16 (46)
Aviation Benefits the Nation. General 19 (1)
Aviation Commission. Federal 176 (45)
Aviation. General 142 (69)
Aviation in Our Society 151 (34)
Aviation. Opportunities in 151 (34)
Avocation. Marriage - Vocation or 57 (41)
Avoid in Everyday Life. Legal Problems to 16 (80)
Avoid. Shocking Experience to 151 (261)
Awaken Your Sleeping Giant 112 (104)
Awakening as a Turning Point in Kentucky Religious History, 1780-1805. Second 117 (69)
Awareness 176 (71), (81)
Awareness - An Approach to Learning and Self. Environmental 29 (132)
Awareness. Environmental 29 (69)
Awareness. Human 180 (71)
Awareness. Improving Self- 171 (51)
Awareness of Environmental Problems. Public 151 (153)
Awareness of God 211 (6)
Awareness of Oneself. Goal Setting: Exercises to Increase 105 (78)
Awareness. Self 168 (73)
Awareness Through Face Language. Human 212 (1)
Awareness. Women's 174 (94)
Azusa to Marrakech. Footloose Family - 29 (4), (122), (318)

B

Babbitt - the Humanist as Critic of Contemporary Society. Irving 85 (32)
Babies. Test Tube 181 (20)
Babylonian Epic. Homer and/or Early 227 (17)
Bachelor's Degree? What Is a 223 (8)
Back to the Basics With the Arts 151 (30)
Backdoor to Siberia. Exploring 4 (3)
Background for the Crafts. Design - 79 (82)
Background Fruit Production 117 (5)
Background of Freedom of Press. Philosophical 117 (85)
Background of the Ethiopian Situation 56 (113)
Backpacking and Hiking. Camping, 174 (82)
Backpacking for the Beginner. Camping and 57 (68)
Backpacking in Alaska. Long Distance 166 (1)
Backpacking in Jasper National Park. Long Distance 166 (1)
Backpacking on the Pacific Crest Trail. Long Distance 166 (1)

Backroads, U.S.A. 59 (16)
Back-strap Loom 79 (80)
Backstrap Looms 79 (113)
Backstrap Weaving 79 (110)
Backyard Fruit Production 117 (122)
Backyard. University in Your 151 (7)
Bacteria. Helpful 216 (20)
Bacteria in Disease. Anaerobic 56 (78)
Bacteria in Hot Springs 159 (49)
Bacteria Keep You Company. Your 216 (54)
Bacteria. Photosynthetic 159 (49)
Bacteria. Structure of 216 (20)
Bacteriology in the Clinical Laboratory. Anaerobic 56 (78)
Bag Workshops 79 (150)
Bags and Handsome Ethnic Clothing 79 (39)
Bags. Summer and Winter 79 (30)
Baha'i Faith 142 (23)
Bahamas - Top to Bottom 59 (12)
Baikal and Irkutsk. Leningrad and the Environs of Lake 151 (296)
Bait in the Water. Keep Your 112 (37)
Bait - The Gambling Odds. Sucker 151 (249)
Baja California Dive Trip 29 (302), (316)
Baja. Sea and Shore of 59 (18), 69 (14)
Baker - Increased Thermal Activity. Mount 218
Baker's Witty World. Russell 102 (1)
Balance. Foriegn Policy and the Power 97 (2)
Balance of Research and Teaching in Nursing Education 105 (49)
Balancing the Parameters of a Reading Program 181 (108)
Balancing the Scales 20
Bald Eagle - National Symbol 4 (4)
Bali 15 (1)
Balkans 142 (6)
Ballet 142 (38)
Ballet. Modern American 97 (71)
Ballet Story 97 (71)
Band and Card Weaving. Inkle 79 (159)
Band Era. Big 112 (29)
Band Weaving 79 (133)
Bands. Techniques for Inkle 79 (133)
Bangkok 174 (82)
Bangladesh and India 69 (2)
Bangladesh. History of 56 (92)
Bangladesh, Pakistan, India. Indian Subcontinent - 16 (81)
Bank Marketing Storing and Selling Dollar 3 (3)
Bank or Real Estate, the Profession of Happy People. Lazy Man's Trip to the 65 (20)
Banker and Attorney. Working With Your CPA, 136 (7)
Banking 151 (9)
Banking. Money and 142 (23), 214 (33)
Banking Relations With Regulatory Agencies 117 (14)
Bankruptcies 23
Banks and Man. Outer 56 (33), (72)
Banquet. How to Plan a 216 (25)
Bar Weaves. Navajo and Hopi 79 (90)
Barbed Wire. Beef Buffalo 57 (28)
Bare Facts 17 (1)
Barefoot Sailing Charters 57 (27)
Bargaining: A Barter System of Justice. Plea 151 (229)
Bargaining. Collective 142 (42), 151 (8), 174 (17)
Bargaining in Education. Collective 117 (49)
Bargaining in Higher Education. Collective 29 (61), 223 (6)
Bargaining in the Public Sector. Collective 223 (6)
Bargaining. Public Employee 216 (104)
Bargaining. Teachers and Collective 181 (129)
Bargaining - the Good and the Bad. Collective 57 (65)
Barriers. Architectural 56 (77)
Barriers. Breaking the Time Trap 151 (35)
Barriers to Communication 57 (57)
Barriers to the Handicapped and Aged. Architectural 151 (228)
Barriers to the Handicapped and Aged. Transportation 151 (228)
Barriers to Women in Management 168 (62)
Base for Counseling. Philosophy as a 168 (1)
Baseball 113 (1), 142 (49)
Baseball and American Culture. Professional 142 (72)
Baseball and/or Athletics 151 (284)
Baseball Coaching 142 (49)
Baseball Hall of Fame 176 (94)
Baseball is a Funny Game...But This is Ridiculous 83 (14)
Basic Basketry, Wrapping. Children's Workshop in Knotless Netting, 79 (158)
Basic Economic Concepts 23
Basic Education? What is Fundamental 29 (64), (347)
Basic Industrial Resources of Blair County 151 (14)
Basic Institutional Change 218
Basic Insurance Needs of the Small and Medium Size Drilling Contractor 136 (8)
Basic Principles of Islam 1 (6)
Basic Principles of Wildlife Management and Conservation 151 (309)
Basic Research in the United States 181 (18)
Basic Skills 181 (116)
Basic Techniques 79 (63), (110)
Basic Theory 79 (53)
Basic Weaves. Three 79 (93)
Basic Weaving 79 (76)
Basic Weaving Techniques 79 (118)
Basketball 29 (153), (304), 113 (1)
Basketball and Athletics 151 (277)
Basketball Coaching 214 (11)
Basketball. Coaching of 151 (204)
Basketball. Warrior 105 (112)
Basketmaking 79 (125)
Basketry 79 (36), (39), (77), (86), (98), (103), (115), (138), (154), (159)

Basketry as Functional or Sculptural Forms. Contemporary 79 (135)
Basketry, Historical Introduction, Contemporary Investigations, Process, Structure and Motivation 79 (5)
Basketry Techniques 79 (4), (47)
Basketry - Techniques and Purposes. Salish Indian 151 (109)
Basketry. Techniques of 79 (151)
Basketry, Traditional and Contemporary 79 (1)
Basketry Workshops Making Christmas Ornaments, Using Thrums 79 (29)
Basketry, Wrapping. Children's Workshop in Knotless Netting, Basic 79 (158)
Baskets. Ethnic 79 (36)
Baskets. Knotted 79 (30)
Baskets of the World 79 (92)
Batch Weigh Systems 67 (18)
Batik 79 (129), (152)
Batik. Advanced 79 (108)
Batik and Tie-dye Techniques 79 (9)
Batik, Dye Painting 79 (79)
Batik, Tie-dye, Commercial Dyes for the Handcraft Person 79 (14)
Bauhaus on Contemporary Crafts. Influence of the 79 (150)
Be Alive Inside and Out 112 (42)
Be Curious: Practice Learning 151 (115)
Beaming. Warping and 79 (113)
Bear of Pennsylvania. Black 151 (306)
Beautiful. America the 59 (17)
Beauty Among Stars. Muhlenberg County, Kentucky, Its Strip Mining Industry, Its 117 (29)
Beauty. In the Flow of 229 (4)
Beauty is Not in the Eye of the Beholder 105 (90)
Beauty. Natural 97 (73)
Beauty. On the Nature of Truth, Goodness, and 117 (98)
Beauty Tips 179 (1)
Becoming Assertive - Between Mouse and Monster 29 (239), (343)
Beef Buffalo Barbed Wire 57 (28)
Beef Cattle Breeding and Performance Testing 216 (9)
Beef Production. Maximizing 216 (80)
Beef Project. Penn State Rockview 151 (182)
Beer Making. Amateur Wine and 174 (40)
Beginner. Camping and Backpacking for the 57 (68)
Beginners. 48 Techniques for 79 (74)
Beginning 4-H Weaving 79 (107)
Beginning 4-Harness Loom Weaving 79 (158)
Beginning Gymnastics and Tumbling 142 (60)
Beginning. Sound Comedy: In the 151 (289)
Beginning Weaving 79 (122), (145)
Beginnings of Photography 151 (73)
Beginnings of Religious Life 105 (107)
Behavior 180 (159)
Behavior. African Animal 181 (281)
Behavior. Aggressive 181 (281)
Behavior. American Political 214 (3)
Behavior, and College Students. Alcohol, Drinking 151 (212)
Behavior and Diet 113 (3)
Behavior and Learning Problems. Child With 117 (131)
Behavior and Motivation. Organizational 151 (43)
Behavior at Shopping Centers. Social 181 (290)
Behavior. Communications and Human 180 (76)
Behavior. Consumer 29 (33), (84), (157), (253)
Behavior Control. Ethics of 168 (47)
Behavior. Cross-cultural Studies of Drinking 168 (30)
Behavior. Deviant 174 (42)
Behavior. Effect of Environmental Pollutants on 168 (64)
Behavior. Effects of Human Biology on 102 (35)
Behavior. Electrical Potentials of the Brain and Their Relation to 171 (43)
Behavior. Environment and 105 (99)
Behavior. Fish 171 (42)
Behavior. Gambling 105 (99)
Behavior. Human 180 (113), (182)
Behavior in Sport 151 (276)
Behavior in the Physical, Intellectual and Emotional Domains. Teacher Modeling 117 (39)
Behavior Management. Childhood 174 (32)
Behavior Modification 117 (109), 142 (28), 168 (47), 181 (126), (296), 214 (78)
Behavior Modification and You 56 (5)
Behavior Modification in Business and Industry 168 (64)
Behavior Modification in Normal School Settings 117 (37)
Behavior Modification in Weight Reduction 218
Behavior Modification of the Retarded 168 (64)
Behavior Modification. Recreational 168 (64)
Behavior Modification. Weight Control and 216 (134)
Behavior Modifications 168 (7)
Behavior. Motivating Human 112 (68)
Behavior of Composites. Mechanical 216 (11)
Behavior of Pesticides in the Environment. Fate and 171 (39)
Behavior, Our Conceptions, Our View of Self and Others, How It Functions. Nature of Language - How it Influences Our 117 (61)
Behavior. Positive Health 181 (184)
Behavior. Risk Taking 105 (99)
Behavior. Teacher 181 (286)
Behavior. Voting 142 (64)
Behavioral Management of Children 174 (50)
Behavioral Pharmacology 142 (69)
Behavioral Sciences in Dentistry 105 (31)
Behavioral Teratology 168 (64)
Behaviorism in Education. Humanism versus 105 (36)
Behind the Headlines 29 (52)
Behind the Scenes in Television News 135 (41)
Beholder. Beauty is Not in the Eye of the 105 (90)
Beholder. Eye of the 189

Behrend College. Athletics at 151 (285)
Being a Human Teacher 29 (132)
Being an Eternal Quarterback 135 (7)
Being Part of Your Community 216 (70)
Believe is to Pray. To 105 (106)
Bell System: A Viewpoint 144
Bell System - It Works. One 144
Belle. Love and War: the Courtship of a Civil War 117 (69)
Bellingham Geologist in Greece 223 (37)
Bellow, Novelist. Saul 151 (245)
Ben. Martin Ritt, Latter-Day Son of 57 (95)
Benefactor of Humanity. Holy Prophet Muhammad as 1 (13)
Beneficiation. Energy Needs, Economic Choices, and Coal 151 (134)
Benefit Programs. Employee 23, 216 (15)
Benefits and Costs in Developing Rural Areas. Social 117 (100), (117)
Benefits. Business Practices and Employee 151 (1)
Benjamin Franklin 142 (63)
Bereavement, Grief, and Mourning 29 (281)
Berks Campus Has a New Library Building 151 (59)
Berks County 4-H Youth Programs 151 (20)
Berks County. Future of Agriculture in 151 (22)
Berlin - the Eternal Crisis 57 (75)
Bernhardt. Sarah 97 (28)
Berrigans and American Catholicism 105 (110)
Better Business Communications 174 (93)
Better Employer - Employee Relationship 117 (120)
Better Management of Time 56 (95)
Beverages. Bottling and Packaging Foods and 67 (10)
Bewitching Thailand 59 (1)
Beyond Management by Objectives 135 (33)
Bias in Television News 117 (84)
Bible 224 (17)
Bible as Literature 218
Bible. Bibliophile View of the 57 (92)
Bible. Evolution and the 168 (13)
Bible. Linguistic Study of the 29 (237)
Bible. Muhammad in the 1 (8)
Biblelands 59 (17)
Biblical Lebanon. Journey Through 105 (23)
Biblical Scenes of the Holy Land 159 (48)
Biblical Themes. Defining America - 159 (1)
Bibliophile View of the Bible 57 (92)
Bicentennial. Commentaries and Observations on the 54
Bicentennial. Newspaper and the 16 (15)
Bicentennial of Children 16 (61)
Bicentennial Orators 117 (76)
Bicycle and the Airplane 218
Bicycle Safety 216 (121)
Bicycling in Europe 29 (327)
Bierce and Mark Twain. Diabolical Duo: Ambrose 151 (243)
Bierce. Bitter 151 (243)
Big Band Era 112 (29)
Big Business 20
Big Government - When It Began 57 (56)
Big Power Confrontation in the Middle East 85 (31)
Bile. Rate Processes in 31
Bilingual Children. Language Acquisition and 29 (95), (204), (297)
Bilingual Classes in the Elementary Grades. Teaching Language Arts, Reading, Mathematics and Science to 142 (90)
Bilingual Education 142 (68), (90), 174 (58)
Bilingual Education. ESL - An Essential Component in 29 (297)
Bilingual Education. Essential Component in 29 (204)
Bilingual Education in California 29 (95), (204)
Bilingualism in Canada. Aspects of 56 (121)
Bill. 1976 Tax Reform 105 (7)
Bill of Rights. United States 31 (14)
Biochemical Genetics 142 (53)
Biochemistry 105 (2)
Biochemistry of a Cell 54
Biofeedback 4 (7), 171 (43)
Biofeedback and Self-Control 29 (240)
Biography and Truth 151 (246)
Biological Control of Plant and Animal Pests 31 (8)
Biological Messages in Our Body. How Nerves Transmit 218
Biological Research in Antarctica 216 (93)
Biological View. Northwest Trek, a Closer 159 (34)
Biologist in East Africa 181 (18), (340)
Biologist Looks at Evolution 100 Years After the Publication of the Origin of the Species 54
Biology 54, 142 (96)
Biology and Politics 181 (24)
Biology. Aspects of Environmental 57 (94)
Biology. Border Area of Chemistry - Physics 218
Biology. Deep-sea 29 (71), (140), (271)
Biology. Ethical Implications of Advances in 151 (164)
Biology. Marine 171 (42), 181 (18), (62)
Biology of Aging 181 (13)
Biology of South Puget Sound. Marine 159 (34)
Biology of Venereal Disease 29 (172), (267)
Biology on Behavior. Effects of Human 102 (35)
Biology. Plant 168 (13)
Biology. Teilhard and New 11 (5)
Biology Women's Destiny? Is 213 (11)
Biomass Conversion 163 (1)
Biomechanics of Human Movement 151 (209)
Biomechanics of Sport 29 (305)
Biomechanics of Tennis 29 (305)
Biomedical Engineering 181 (155)
Biomedical Research 16 (4)
Biomedical Research. Use of Animals for 151 (206)
Biomedical Revolution 171 (43)
Biomedical Technology. Wilkes-Barre Campus, Service From Mining to 151 (2)
Birches. Swinger of 151 (243)

Bird Songs 142 (2)
Birds 159 (2)
Birds. Adventures With 168 (56)
Birds in Art. Folklore and Legend of 57 (82)
Birds of Prey (Hawks and Owls) 151 (309)
Birmingham. Yesterday's 16 (55)
Birth and Alternatives to Both. Home Birth, Hospital 36 (1)
Birth and Death of a Lake 181 (133)
Birth Control 168 (23)
Birth Dearth 56 (21)
Birth Defects 181 (163)
Birth Defects. Drug-Induced 181 (216)
Birth Defects. Environmental Causes of 218
Birth Defects. Prenatal Detection of 27 (28)
Birth, Hospital Birth and Alternatives to Both. Home 36 (1)
Bitter Bierce 151 (243)
Bituminous Mining. Literature/Lore of 151 (236)
Bituminous Pavements for Highways and Airports 151 (291)
Black and Compromises in American History 29 (261), (337)
Black and White Aspects. Negritude: 159 (40)
Black Bear of Pennsylvania 151 (306)
Black Child. Special Learning Problems of the 142 (47)
Black Community Competing Academically 54
Black Community. Mental Health and the 181 (294)
Black Community. Philadelphia 181 (29)
Black Experience 151 (58)
Black Experience. Black Family 181 (30)
Black Family and Black Youth 151 (11)
Black Family, Black Experience 181 (30)
Black Family, Black Psychology 181 (31)
Black Folk Music in the South 29 (220)
Black Genealogy. American Indian and 154 (2)
Black History. Roots, a Saga of 102 (13)
Black Holes 214 (10), 223 (4)
Black Homeland? West Africa - the American 29 (7)
Black Humor: Humor of the Bruised Sensitivites 151 (243)
Black Liberation and Socialism 213 (7)
Black Liberation Movements 142 (17)
Black Light 216 (45)
Black Movement. FBI Plot Against the 213 (10)
Black Music in America 225 (12)
Black. Now Have Enough Things 224 (4)
Black Playwright in America 154 (4)
Black Political Power 213 (10)
Black Politics. Centrifugalism in 181 (26), (258)
Black Psychology 29 (242), 181 (294)
Black Psychology. Black Family 181 (31)
Black Psychology - the Afro American Woman in American History 29 (337)
Black Slang 29 (153), (211)
Black Socio-Political Theory 218
Black Students at Predominantly White Institutions. Student Development Programs for 105 (39)
Black Students. Teaching 174 (1)
Black Studies 214 (12)
Black Studies and Liberal Arts Education 181 (25), (90)
Black Woman 181 (328)
Black Women 181 (31)
Black Women in America 142 (17)
Black Women's Liberation 213 (18)
Black Youth. Black Family and 151 (111)
Blacks. Abraham Lincoln and the Emancipation of Americas 29 (338)
Blacks as Immigrants 168 (25)
Blacks in Sports 29 (153), (304)
Blacks versus Whites. African Crisis - 97 (50)
Blair County. Basic Industrial Resources of 151 (14)
Blanket. Navajo 79 (65)
Blending 67 (18)
Blessings of Liberty 85 (3)
Blind or Handicapped Student 181 (2), (91)
Blood Levels. Drug 54
Blood on Their Hands 213 (14)
Bloom Where You Are Planted 112 (99)
Blouse - Origin, Symbolism and Development. Mola 79 (25)
Blue Collar Worker 151 (52)
Blue. Red, White, and 189
Blue Ridge Mountains. Air Pollution in the 216 (113)
Blueprint on Fabric 79 (4)
Bobbin Lace, Needle Lace, Embroidery 79 (42)
Bobbin Lace, Traditional and Contemporary 79 (144)
Bodies and People in Process. Dance, 181 (82)
Body Adornment 79 (28)
Body Adornment From Non-Western Perspective. Jewelry and 79 (28)
Body. Alcohol and the Human 174 (12)
Body, and the Senses. Fiber, the 79 (27)
Body Covers 79 (79)
Body. How Nerves Transmit Biological Messages in Our 218
Body is Shouting at Me. Your 151 (41)
Body Language 112 (120), 135 (19), 176 (113), 225 (25)
Body Language and Other Nonverbal Languages 151 (61)
Body Language. Greater Understanding of People Through Face and 212 (1)
Body. Mind Over 151 (207)
Body to Science. Willing One's 181 (14)
Body. Wonders of the Human 54
Boethius 227 (11)
Bogs. Searching for Prairies, Forest and 168 (56)
Bold New Germany 51 (1)
Bolivian Fabrics and Contemporary Adaptations 79 (18)
Bolivian Highland Weaving. Art and Techniques of 79 (18)
Bonjour, France 59 (10)

Bonnie Scotland 59 (9)
Book. How to Get Your Child to Read a 151 (94)
Book. How to Read a 216 (56)
Book in Everyone's Life 225 (19)
Book Reviews 159 (23), (65)
Bookkeeping System. Introduction of the Basic 136 (7), (11)
Books 142 (7)
Books and Libraries in Society. Role of 29 (198)
Books. Children's 174 (77)
Books. Collecting Children's 117 (75)
Books. Comic 159 (23)
Books. Early American Children's 174 (18)
Books for Home Reading Programs. Good 168 (53)
Books Only Grownups Should be Allowed to Read. Children's 29 (197), (205)
Books. Valuing Children's 171 (19)
Books. Ways of Studying Children's 171 (19)
Bookshelf: Editor's Perspective. Concept to 151 (79)
Bootstrap. Myth of the 168 (25)
Border Area of Chemistry - Physics Biology 218
Born Again 154 (7)
Borneo and the Cannibals in West Irian. Head-hunters in Central 225 (35)
Bornese Festival for the Dead 57 (95)
Bosses. Women as 168 (62)
Botanical Gardens 117 (122)
Botanical Gardens - Arboretums in North America 117 (5)
Botswana Safari 29 (8), (167), (325)
Bottling and Packaging Foods and Beverages 67 (10)
Botulism 216 (54)
Bound Weave 79 (104), (113), (139)
Bound Weaves 79 (30)
Boy Scouts. Why 174 (79)
Braid. Osage 79 (80)
Braiding 79 (98)
Braiding. Ornamental 79 (122)
Braiding - Plaiting 79 (47)
Braids, Fringes and Joining Stitches 79 (53)
Braids, Tassels and Fringes 79 (80)
Brain Damaged Adult. Communications in the 117 (133)
Brain in Diseased States. Structure of 181 (169)
Brain or of the Visual System. Anatomy of the 27 (26)
Brain. Oscillations in the Eye and 31 (24)
Brain Research 142 (69), 181 (179)
Brain. Sleep and Dream Mechanisms of the 159 (68)
Brawny Australia 59 (1)
Brazil 2 (15), 56 (120), 57 (1)
Brazil. Agriculture Education in 216 (78)
Brazil. Fabulous Rio - Portrait of 110 (8)
Brazilian History. General 142 (56)
Brazilian Regime. Present 117 (102)
Bread Machine. Incredible 181 (33), (203), (332)
Breaking Stereotypes 218
Breaking the Time Trap Barriers 151 (35)
Breast Cancer 105 (127)
Breast Feeding 181 (251)
Brecht and His Theatre 154 (22)
Breeding and Performance Testing. Beef Cattle 216 (9)
Breeding Program. Developing Efficient 216 (80)
Bridge 142 (47)
Bridge. Longest 144
Bridge Structures. Highway 105 (121)
Bridges of Konigsberg. Graph Theory and the 151 (247)
Bridges. Silver 100 (2)
Brief Introduction to the History of the Earth 136 (15)
Bringing About Change in a Bureaucracy 16 (88)
British Aristocracy Decadent? Is 97 (44)
British Columbia. Indians of 151 (27)
British Columbia Milk-Marketing Board Rip-off 171 (8)
British Columbia. University Programs in Interior 171 (58)
British Columbia. Wilderness Family in 218
British Columbia's Economy. Tourism in 171 (13)
British Drama. New Stars of 57 (23)
British Higher Education. Oxford, Cambridge and 223 (10)
Broadcasting 113 (1), 180 (54)
Broadcasting and Broadcast Journalism 151 (68)
Broadcasting and Ma Bell. Cable 124 (2)
Broadcasting. Ethical Problems in 117 (84)
Broadcasting in Great Britain 29 (310)
Broadcasting's Fairness Doctrine 117 (86), (129)
Broadway, U.S.A. 59 (7)
Brocades. Weft 79 (90)
Brotherhood in Islam. Equality and 1 (13)
Brotherhood. World 83 (4)
Bruegel. Peasant in the Art of Peter 105 (61)
Bryophytes. Effect of Ionizing Radiation on 151 (151)
Buber. Education in the Thought of Martin 29 (233)
Buchwald at Large! 102 (2)
Buckeye Q 144
Bucks. Last of the 97 (51)
Buddhism 29 (247), 181 (307)
Buddhism in South and Southeast Asia 29 (129)
Buddhism. Zen 174 (55)
Buddhist Conception of Man 174 (89)
Buddhist Notion of Liberation 117 (97)
Buddhists, Confucianists, Taoists, Maoists, Jews, Christians and Muslims. World Religions - 54
Budget Development 151 (9)
Budget. European Travel on a 168 (61)
Budget in Today's Economy. Managing a Personal 16 (19)
Budget. Military 16 (62)
Budget. Teaching Weaving on a Zero 79 (107)
Budgetary Policy Processes. Federal Fiscal and 31 (25)

Budgeting for the City of Tacoma. Governmental 159 (4)
Budgeting. Personal 174 (63)
Budgets. Understanding School District 181 (45), (130)
Buffalo Barbed Wire. Beef 57 (28)
Bug. Acting 218
Build Your Own Information System 57 (93)
Building a Corporate Image 102 (19)
Building a New America 211 (6)
Building an Advertising Program for the Media 168 (59)
Building for Your Own Account 65 (12)
Building Plastic Model Aircraft 151 (5)
Buildings. Library 142 (29)
Buildings. Preservation of Historic 57 (92)
Buildings. Solar Energy to Heat Farm 16 (8)
Buildings. Solar Energy Utilization for Heating and Cooling 151 (126)
Buildings to New Uses. Adaptation of Old 218
Bulk Storage and Transportation. Aseptic 67 (24), (25)
Bunker to Fred Sanford. From Archie 112 (9)
Bureaucracy. Bringing About Change in a 16 (88)
Burke and Revolution. Edmund 85 (32)
Burke and Rousseau 85 (32)
Burke's Conception of History. Edmund 85 (32)
Burke's Theories of Metaphor. I.A. Richards' and Kenneth 151 (65)
Burns Story. Robert 97 (8)
Burr, Rascal Patriot. Aaron 103 (5)
Bushmen of Kalahari 69 (2)
Business 180 (83), (187)
Business Administration. Small 29 (83)
Business Administrations 180 (169)
Business Affairs 180 (75)
Business. Alcoholism in 180 (66)
Business and Computing in Education. Management Planning, Computing in 105 (5)
Business and Ecology 105 (6)
Business and Education. Women's Role in 117 (17)
Business and Government. Writing Reports in 168 (53)
Business and Industry. Behavior Modification in 168 (64)
Business and Its Environment 105 (6)
Business and Professional Speaking 142 (25)
Business and Public Administration. School of 159 (66)
Business and the Arts 105 (6)
Business Asset. Humor - A 112 (53)
Business Asset Not Listed on Your Balance Sheet. Trade Associations - A 136 (4)
Business. Attitudes About 23
Business. Big 20
Business Boom of the Seventies 112 (69)
Business Can Bring Personal Fulfillment in Life. How a Career in 23
Business. Changing Cultural Values Impact on 151 (48)
Business. Choosing the Form of 105 (7)
Business. College of 168 (45)
Business Communication 174 (96)
Business Communications. Better 174 (93)
Business Community. Cooperation Between the University and the 16 (36)
Business. Consumer End of 135 (11)
Business. Corner Stones of Success for Women in 229 (5)
Business. Cost Controlls in Small 214 (1)
Business. Economics and Politics of Government Regulation of 85 (19)
Business Education 174 (96)
Business. Education for 56 (19)
Business Education for the Future. Planning 117 (14)
Business Education. Programs in 174 (6)
Business Enterprise in the United States. Future of Small 159 (3)
Business. Environment and 56 (19), (74)
Business Ethics 105 (6), 214 (13)
Business. Experimenting With Democratic Management in 27 (1)
Business. Government and 174 (17)
Business. Government Regulations Economics and 54
Business/Government Relations 23
Business. How to Start a 23
Business. Human Relations in 56 (136)
Business in Greenville, North Carolina. Economic Impact of Students of East Carolina University on 56 (24)
Business in Saudi Arabia. Doing 3 (4), 210 (2)
Business in the Jet Age 100 (1)
Business, Industry, Stores, and Schools. Going Metric, In 57 (12)
Business. Information Access in Science and 44 (1 - 4)
Business. Legal Aspects of 105 (6)
Business. Living It in 180 (17)
Business Management. Small 181 (35), (219)
Business. Mathematics in the World of 181 (43), (153)
Business Meetings. Conducting 117 (128)
Business. Methods of Financial Management for a 151 (37)
Business. Minorities in 112 (84)
Business. Multinational Corporations in the Food 181 (34), (334)
Business. New Administration - What Washington Plans for United States 102 (10), (21)
Business? Now That You Can Run a Drilling Rig, Can You Run a Drilling 136 (7)
Business. Overcoming Obstacles to Achieve Productivity in 27 (8)
Business. People 180 (13)
Business. People Are My 105 (12)
Business Practices and Employee Benefits 151 (1)
Business Problem. Alcoholism - A 117 (15), (107)
Business Review. Current 29 (81)
Business. Role of Confidence in 102 (3)

Business. Roles of Unions in 54
Business School Admissions. Law School 142 (95)
Business. Services to Small 216 (99)
Business. Social Responsibility of 23, 168 (45)
Business - Society's Scapegoat 117 (15)
Business. Sports versus 112 (101)
Business. Starting a Plant Growing 216 (115)
Business. Status of Education as Viewed by 132 (11)
Business Subjects. Small 29 (83)
Business. Success in 180 (162)
Business Supports All Levels of Education. Why 132 (9)
Business Tax Problems. Small 218
Business - The Next Fifty Years. American 56 (19)
Business to Other Areas of the Social Structure. Changing Relationship of 56 (23)
Business. Tough Minded 180 (10)
Business Training Needs. Analyzing 151 (122)
Business. Trials, Tribulations and Joys of Family Owned 136 (7)
Business? What Counts in 102 (33)
Business? Why Do People Misunderstand 23
Business With an Empty Wagon. You Can't Do 112 (133)
Business World. Woman's Place in the 97 (32)
Business. Woman's Role in 117 (28)
Business. Women in 162
Businesses Are Financed. How 23
Businesses as Well as People. Accidents Can Kill 136 (4)
Businesses Fail: Why People Fail. Why 135 (58)
Businesses. Public Relations for Small 224 (15)
Businesses. Self-sufficient Energy Systems for Rural and Urban Dwellings and Small 163 (2)
Businessman: A Lawyer's View. Problems of the 136 (9)
Businessman. Tax Planning for the Individual and Small 29
Businessman's Glory Road 112 (135)
Businessmen Can Help Themselves. How 180 (19)
Busing. Integration - 117 (46)
Buy a Home Today 181 (225)
Buy a House. How to 216 (145)
Buy America? Will the Sheiks 181 (33), (203), (332)
Buyer. Dealing With a Newcomer 65 (29)
Buying and Selling for the Layperson. Home 56 (97)
Buying Motivations 65 (44)
Byrd. Word Painting in the Music of 151 (26)
Byron and Greece. Lord 142 (98)
Bystander. Apathetic 56 (134)
Byzantine Art 227 (30)
Byzantine Emperors 29 (178), (234)
Byzantium. Women in Sixth-Century 227 (12)

C

CIA - A Peculiar Service 97 (54)
CRTC Running Your Life? Is the 171 (5)
C.B. Radio. Amateur 151 (68)
C.B.C. Roman Life. Power of Women in First 227 (29)
Cabbages and Kings and Things. Of 97 (33)
Cable Broadcasting and Ma Bell 124 (2)
Cable Specifications. Power 150 (1)
Cable Television 105 (65), 181 (98), 216 (123)
Cable Television. Community Role of 181 (70), (215)
Cable Television for Education 181 (70)
Cable Television. Future of 216 (47)
Cable Television: 30 Years of Innovation and Service 124 (1)
Cabling, Fancy Designer Yarns. Plying, Doubling, 79 (22)
Cache in the Cornfield 112 (119)
Cactus. Huichol - Tribe of the Sacred 69 (9)
Cal State Fullerton 29 (27)
Cal State Fullerton Engineering Program 29 (108)
Cal State Fullerton Library. Microforms at the 29 (196)
Cal State Fullerton Library. Use of Microforms at the 29 (25)
Cal State Fullerton School of Business. Information Systems Degree Program in the 29 (92), (137)
Cal State Fullerton School of Business. New Information Systems Degree Program in the 29 (26)
Cal State Fullerton. Science and Engineering at 29 (32), (111)
Cal State Fullerton. Theater at 29 (311)
Calculus? What is 117 (92)
Calendar and Culture 223 (26)
California. Bilingual Education in 29 (95), (204)
California Dive Trip. Baja 29 (302), (316)
California Economic Forecast 29 (81)
California. Educational Opportunities in the University of 27 (23)
California Indian. Daily Life of the 29 (165), (339)
California Indians. Origin of the 29 (19), (165), (339)
California. Juvenile Justice in 29 (62), (288), (346)
California. Macademia Nuts in 224 (10)
California Politics 224 (8)
California State University Police Department 29 (144), (193)
California. Undersea Life in Southern 29 (270), (302)
California Weather. Southern 29 (152), (276)
California's Mission Trail 59 (10)
Caliphat. Islamic Conception of 1 (3)

Call Me Ms 27 (41)
Calligraphy. Arabic 218
Calling on Science 222
Cambridge and British Higher Education. Oxford, 223 (10)
Camel Girths. Western Indian 79 (131)
Camera. Creating With a Movie 168 (53)
Campaigning. Political 224 (15)
Campaigns and Candidates 159 (4)
Campaigns. Developing More Effective 151 (75)
Camper. Australia By 59 (16)
Camping 142 (39)
Camping and Backpacking for the Beginner 57 (68)
Camping, Backpacking and Hiking 174 (82)
Camps. Concentration 176 (105)
Campus Afloat. World 174 (91)
Campus. Computer's Role on the University 16 (5)
Campus Facilities 57 (51)
Campus Facilities and the Successful Program 57 (51)
Campus Planning - Luxury or Necessity 56 (101)
Campus. ROTC on the College 54
Campus. Radiation Safety at a University 27 (9)
Campus Security. Careers in 181 (58)
Can Capitalism Survive 154 (5)
Can Chimps Learn Human Language? 181 (314)
Can Computers Do Everything? 181 (204)
Can Exercise Help Your Heart? 171 (23)
Can Free Enterprise Survive Success? 102 (19)
Can Government Stabilize the Economy? 85 (22)
Can Legislation Improve Consumer Welfare? 54
Can Nuclear Weapons Be Controlled? 29 (256), (292)
Can Our Cities Be Saved? 216 (43)
Can There Be Anything New in Mathematics? 56 (129)
Can We Afford Liberty? 102 (12)
Can We Control the Future of Man? 29 (141), (161), (334)
Canada and Its Changing World 57 (62)
Canada. Aspects of Bilingualism in 56 (121)
Canada, Past and Present 223 (17)
Canada Today. United States and 151 (197)
Canadian Foreign Aid 171 (11)
Canadian Politics and Foreign Policy 151 (189)
Canadian Realistic Fiction for Children 171 (52)
Cancer. Breast 105 (127)
Cancer. Cell Division Research and 218
Cancer Cells. Differences in Normal and 31 (6)
Cancer Detection. Early Oral 181 (183)
Cancer. Eliminating 105 (127)
Cancer. Environment and 181 (178), (230)
Cancer of the Larynx. Speech After 117 (133)
Cancer. Oral 181 (182)
Cancer. Pelvic 181 (168)
Cancer Research 151 (211)
Cancer Society. American 151 (83)
Cancer Therapy. Radiation Physics in 218
Cancer Viruses. Human 216 (4)
Candidate and Office-holder 214 (3)
Candidates. Campaigns and 159 (4)
Candle Dipping 79 (101)
Cannibals in West Irian. Headhunters in Central Borneo and the 225 (35)
Cannibals. Last 69 (2)
Canning and Freezing. Home 16 (71)
Canning and Freezing of Foods. Recent Advances in Commercial 216 (72)
Canoeing 151 (304)
Canoeing in Virginia 216 (98)
Canvas Work. Creative 79 (127)
Canyon 110 (4)
Capital Outlay for Schools. Financing 117 (46)
Capital Punishment 159 (45)
Capital "You" 151 (112)
Capitalism 29 (80)
Capitalism. American 142 (51)
Capitalism and Socialism 225 (23)
Capitalism and the Ghetto 85 (2)
Capitalism and the Public Interest 85 (4)
Capitalism. Cars, Chaos and 171 (48)
Capitalism. Marx's Critique of 174 (89)
Capitalism, Racism and Poverty 85 (30)
Capitalism. Religion and 85 (25)
Capitalism Survive. Can 154 (5)
Capitalism. Swedish Road to 171 (2)
Capitalism? What is 85 (4)
Capitalist Democracy. American Ideals of a Christian 180 (183)
Capitol Campus 151 (222)
Capitol Hill Perspective. Right to Work 131 (2)
Carcass and Its Cuts. Lamb 151 (182)
Carcass and Its Cuts. Pork 151 (182)
Carcinoma Testicle. Prostate 181 (171)
Card Weaving 79 (32), (66), (113), (138)
Card Weaving. Inkle Band and 79 (159)
Card Weaving - Techniques and Design 79 (155)
Cardiac Pacemakers 181 (194)
Cardiac Rehabilitation 174 (27)
Cardiopulmonary Resuscitation 174 (24), 181 (162)
Cardiovascular Fitness 159 (14)
Care and Consumption of Wines 225 (22)
Care and Cultivation of Collectors 102 (19)
Care, and Maintenance of Antique Spinning Wheels. Repair, 79 (99)
Care and Prevention of Athletic Injuries 151 (279)
Care. Child 178 (5), 181 (313)
Care. Home Lawn 151 (25)
Care of House Plants. Growing and 216 (115)
Care of the Athlete 16 (38)
Care of the Hand Injured Patient 56 (79)
Career. Air Force Flying 174 (81)
Career Alternatives in Education 216 (33)
Career Centers 142 (44)
Career Change and Development 181 (49)
Career Change. Mid-life 181 (65), 218
Career Choices. Careers and 168 (38)
Career Decision Making. Parents' Role in 151 (88)

Career Development 142 (44), 174 (62)
Career Development and Placement Service 151 (60)
Career Development and Subject Matter Concepts 57 (72)
Career Development/Choice 216 (101)
Career Development for Women 16 (10)
Career Education 142 (44), (87), 181 (61), (115), 216 (49), (139)
Career Education and the Elementary School 57 (47)
Career Education and the Junior High School 57 (47)
Career Education Components 151 (58)
Career Education for Adults 16 (22)
Career Education for Career Planning 181 (61), (115)
Career Education Movement 57 (47)
Career Education Program Development 57 (72)
Career Education Programs. Involving the Community in 57 (72)
Career in Athletic Training 151 (279)
Career in Business Can Bring Personal Fulfillment in Life 23
Career in Engineering. Selecting a 151 (132)
Career in Musical Comedy. Dancer Preparing for a 225 (39)
Career More Exciting and Meaningful. How to Make Your 23
Career Opportunities by College or Major Career Planning 181 (50), (53)
Career Opportunities for College Graduates 181 (50), (53)
Career Opportunities in Linguistics 56 (65)
Career Opportunities in the Media 151 (72)
Career Opportunities in the Military 16 (62)
Career Opportunities in the United States Air Froce 216 (53)
Career Options. Maximizing Your 151 (90)
Career or Vocation. Choosing a 117 (80)
Career. Physics as a 105 (40)
Career Planning 105 (34), 181 (50, (52), 216 (29)
Career Planning and Job Hunting 57 (73)
Career Planning for the 1980's 27 (24)
Career Planning for Women 181 (52), (322)
Career Planning for Young People 16 (82)
Career Planning/Job Search for College Students 151 (54)
Career Possibilities in the Field of Accounting 216 (63)
Career. Public Administration as a 29 (262)
Career. Science Teaching as a 216 (129)
Career Versus Motherhood 224 (12)
Career. Veterinary Medicine as a 216 (90), (127)
Career Woman 180 (44)
Careers 142 (44)
Careers and Career Choices 168 (38)
Careers. Engineering 29 (23), (107), 151 (125)
Careers for Women 181 (49), (320)
Careers for Women. Geology and Hydrology 136 (22)
Careers for Women. Serial 29 (145)
Careers. Foreign Languages and 216 (135)
Careers in Accounting 214 (2)
Careers in Accounting and Finance 23
Careers in Animal Science 216 (80)
Careers in Campus Security 181 (58)
Careers in Communications 181 (49), (67)
Careers in Dental Research 181 (60)
Careers in Education 181 (52), (99)
Careers in Engineering 40 (16), 216 (30)
Careers in Engineering Technology 151 (53)
Careers in Home Economics 216 (139)
Careers in Journalism 181 (52), (71), 216 (13)
Careers in Library Service 151 (59)
Careers in Mathematics 151 (252)
Careers in Medical Technology 181 (64)
Careers in Physics 151 (274)
Careers in Science and Engineering 29 (111), (278)
Careers in Teaching Industrial Arts 117 (80)
Careers in the Health Care Field 181 (57), (170)
Careers. Journalism Studies and 223 (25)
Careers, Opportunities and Offerings. Industrial Education: 117 (81)
Caribbean and West Indies. Travel in the 218
Caribbean Literature. French 168 (41)
Caribbean Paradise 59 (14)
Carkhuff Learning and Counseling Models for Teachers 117 (39)
Carl Sandburg: Citizen, Writer 225 (42)
Carl Sandburg, Here and Now 97 (47), (49)
Carl Sandburg's Place in American Literature 225 (42)
Carnegie-Mellon University 31 (10)
Carriage. Adventures and Errands on the Original Horseless 56 (40)
Cars, Chaos and Capitalism 171 (48)
Carter Administration 154 (7)
Carter. Jimmy 175 (4)
Cartography 216 (82)
Cartoon Heritage. America's Political 214 (4)
Case for Conservatism 85 (39)
Cash Flow Planning 136 (7)
Cashless Society 225 (21)
Caste and Social Change in India 218
Caste System in India 56 (119)
Casting. Centrifugal 174 (61)
Castro. Cuba and 218
Casualty and Quantum Physics 56 (129)
Catholic Education 105 (47)
Catholic Education. Role of the Board in 105 (51)
Catholic Moral Theology. Roman 105 (111)
Catholic School in the United States. Role of 54
Catholic Theology. Christian- 214 (80)
Catholic Universities? Why 105 (41)
Catholic University. Idea of a 85 (33)
Catholicism. Berrigans and American 105 (110)
Catholicism. Relations of Protestantism and 174 (69)
Catholics are Excluded From Campus. Why Moderates, Conservatives, and 85 (33)

LECTURE TITLES AND KEYWORD INDEX

Cathy. Many Faces of 112 (6)
Cattle Breeding and Performance Testing. Beef 216 (9)
Cattle Kills. Toxic Algae and 168 (37)
Catullus 227 (4)
Cause and Effect of Education's Nervous Future 132 (1)
Causes and Effects of Inflation 117 (26)
Causes for Communication Gaps 171 (45)
Cautious Communicator: American Politicians 151 (87)
Cave Man to Space Man 135 (51), 144
Caves and Caving in Pennsylvania 151 (128)
Celebrity Speaks 225 (28)
Cell. Biochemistry of a 54
Cell Division Research and Cancer 218
Cell Membranes and Heroin 57 (20)
Celtic Art. Early Pagan 181 (79)
Cement Concrete as a Major Construction Material. Portland 151 (291)
Censors? And Who Shall Censor the 151 (74)
Censorship and Pornography 54
Censorship and the Press 168 (10)
Censorship in the Schools - A Threat to Freedom 151 (100)
Censorship Matters 142 (29)
Censorship: Past, Present, Future. No! No! No! 151 (85)
Censorship. Pornography and 85 (35)
Censorship: What Should Children Read? 151 (94)
Center. College 168 (5)
Center. Materials 174 (77)
Center. Milton S. Hershey Medical 151 (186)
Center. Resident Continuing Education 216 (37)
Centers. Learning Resource 181 (97)
Central America, Mexico and Greece. Trips to South America, 79 (117)
Central Borneo and the Cannibals in West Irian. Headhunters in 225 (35)
Central Cleaning 67 (18)
Central Economic Planning 105 (32)
Central Minnesota. Natural History of 168 (56)
Centrifugal Casting 174 (61)
Certrifugalism in Black Politics 181 (26), (258)
Ceramics 57 (33)
Ceramics. Contemporary 57 (44), 216 (69)
Ceramics. Contemporary American 159 (39)
Ceramics - Fantastic New Material 216 (114)
Ceramics. History of 57 (33)
Ceramics in the Public School System 56 (11)
Cerebral Palsy 181 (195)
Certification. Illinois Teacher 57 (48)
Certified Professional Secretary 174 (60)
Certified Professional Secretary Examination 117 (27)
Ceylon 15 (4)
Ceylon. Arts and Crafts of 79 (128)
Ceylon. Weaving of 79 (128)
Chain Warping 79 (147)
Challenge. Energy 47
Challenge in Education 29 (90)
Challenge of Building Peace 103 (1)
Challenge of Choice 27 (6)
Challenge of Leadership 189
Challenge of Maps for the Visually Handicapped 218
Challenge of the Expanding United Nations 214 (54)
Challenge to Change. Crisis: 180 (165)
Challenges of the Life Cycle 181 (246), (297)
Challenges to the Logical-Empirical School of Philosophy 29 (232), (268)
Chamber Music 16 (41)
Chambers of the Sea 69 (15)
Change and Development. Career 181 (49)
Change and the American Future. Population 168 (42)
Change. Basic Institutional 218
Change. Dynamics of Value 216 (95)
Change. Education for Social 54
Change in a Bureaucracy. Bringing About 16 (88)
Change in Africa. Social 218
Change in Alaskan Exploration. Twenty Years of 143 (9)
Change in India. Caste and Social 218
Change in Japan. Social and Techological 168 (66)
Change in South Africa 181 (28), (338)
Change in the Modern World. Theology of 54
Change. Management of 3 (4)
Change. Mid-life Career 181 (65), 218
Change. Politics of Social 223 (22)
Change. Process of Curriculum 168 (21)
Change Skills. Social 168 (4)
Change: The Individual and the Community. Social 168 (66)
Change. Women and Social 151 (167)
Changes in America. Need for Fundamental Political 178 (5)
Changes in Eastern North Carolina. Social 56 (31)
Changes in Nuclear Weapon Strategy 29 (255), (268)
Changes in Southern Politics. Trends and 16 (20)
Changes in the American Family 181 (237), (292)
Changing American Family 151 (167)
Changing Attitudes of University Students 27 (21)
Changing Attitudes Toward Death and Dying 29 (281)
Changing Cultural Values Impact on Business 151 (48)
Changing Family Life 168 (26)
Changing Higher Education 151 (120)
Changing Life Styles 102 (22), 176 (98)
Changing Nature of America 176 (15)
Changing Race Relations in America 56 (4)
Changing Relationship of Business to Other Areas of the Social Structure 56 (23)
Changing Religious-cultural Ideas 11 (1)
Changing Role of Women 56 (126)
Changing Societal Roles - Today and Tomorrow 57 (15)
Changing Trends and Directions in Americe 117 (100)

Changing Trends in Accounting Education 159 (50)
Changing Trends in Intramurals 57 (17)
Changing World 180 (59)
Changing World. Canada and Its 57 (62)
Changing World. Our 135 (47)
Changing World. Our Wildlife in a 151 (306)
Character. Moral 214 (74)
Character of Don Juan in Western Literature 151 (233)
Characteristics of a Helping Relationship 117 (44)
Chariot Racing in Imperial Rome 227 (42)
Charisma - Everybody Has It 112 (19)
Charismatic Renewal 105 (95)
Charles Dickens 181 (147)
Charles Ives. Music of 29 (221)
Charters. Barefoot Sailing 57 (27)
Chasing and Repousse Techniques 174 (61)
Chaucer's England 117 (89)
Cheap Energy. Clean and 54
Checkless Society 3 (3)
Chemical Dyeing. Handspinning and 79 (19)
Chemical Environment 56 (71)
Chemical Fertilizers. Population, the Food Chain, and 151 (134)
Chemical Industry to Midwestern United States Economics. Contributions of the 34 (1)
Chemical Substructure Index. How to Use Current Abstracts of Chemistry, Index Chemicus, and the 84 (1)
Chemical Technology: Opportunity for Women 151 (265)
Chemical Tests in Toxicology. Quick 54
Chemicals 73
Chemicals and Toxic Substances 204
Chemistry 216 (21)
Chemistry and Food 151 (264)
Chemistry, Index Chemicus, and the Chemical Substructure Index. How to Use Current Abstracts of 84 (1)
Chemistry of Hemoglobin 223 (24)
Chemistry of Smell 57 (6)
Chemistry of the Universe 142 (19)
Chemistry. Organic 181 (199)
Chemistry - Physics Biology. Border Area of 218
Chemist's View of the Energy Crisis 57 (6)
Cherokee Finger Weaving 79 (50)
Cherry, Bright Stack and Filling Equipment. Sweet Corn, Green Beans, 67 (6), (12)
Chess 181 (3)
Chess By Mail 174 (79)
Chicago. Alternative Theatre in 142 (37)
Chicago Architecture and Preservation. History of 142 (79)
Chicago Politics 142 (67)
Chicano. Affirmative Action and the 27 (2)
Chicano History 218
Chicano Liberation and Socialism 213 (12)
Chicken 216 (18)
Child About Drugs. How to Talk to Your 181 (186)
Child About Drugs. Talk to Your 181 (236)
Child Abuse 176 (93), 218
Child Abuse and Neglect 159 (43)
Child Advocacy 181 (119)
Child. Aesthetic Education of the 151 (30)
Child. American 29 (280), (340)
Child and Family. Emotionally Disturbed 16 (35)
Child and Multiple Handicaps 117 (132)
Child and Woman. Abuse: 181 (221)
Child Become High on Life. Helping Your 16 (84)
Child Care 142 (14), 178 (5), 181 (313)
Child Care. Home-care Versus 224 (12)
Child Communications. Parent- 216 (106)
Child Counseling 142 (93)
Child Development 105 (94), 142 (13), (45), (84), 224 (1)
Child Development Associate Program 174 (31)
Child Development Association 223 (7)
Child Development. Role of the Father in 105 (103)
Child Discipline, Cohabitation, Patterns of Family Interaction 56 (7)
Child. Discovering the 181 (292)
Child. Exceptional 174 (76)
Child For Success. How to Prepare Your 56 (59)
Child Growth and Development 174 (27)
Child. Handicapped 117 (132)
Child Has a Reading Problem. Your 174 (78)
Child in Today's Society. Exceptional 117 (133)
Child Interaction. Adult- 216 (40)
Child Language Disorders 181 (314)
Child Management 142 (28), 168 (7), (47)
Child Management in Dental Office 105 (30)
Child. Math for the Pre-school 181 (105), (150)
Child. Parents' Role in the Education of a Young 117 (45)
Child-Rearing Practices. Effects of Different Kinds of 105 (103)
Child. Special Learning Problems of the Black 142 (47)
Child Succeed in School. Parents - How to Help Your 29 (93)
Child to Read a Book. How to Get Your 151 (94)
Child. Understanding Your 105 (98)
Child. Urinary Infections in the 181 (171)
Child Welfare 168 (26), 181 (311)
Child With Behavior and Learning Problems 117 (131)
Child. Working Mothers - Are You Helping or Hurting Your 29 (239)
Childbearing. Various Aspects of 105 (97)
Childbirth 54
Childbirth and Methods for Combating Them. Major Causes of Pain in 36 (1)
Childbirth. Education for 181 (247)
Childbirth. Natural 181 (251), (329)
Childbirth to the Era of Feminism. Contribution of Psychoprophylactic 36 (1)
Childhood Behavior Management 174 (32)

Childhood. Curriculum for Early 142 (13)
Childhood Education 180 (199)
Childhood Education. Competency - Based - On - Site Learning in Early 223 (7)
Childhood Education. Directions in Early 151 (91)
Childhood Education. Early 56 (57), 142 (84), 171 (17), 174 (31)
Childhood Education in Art, Music and Children's Literature. Early 142 (30)
Childhood. What's Happening in Early 29 (93), (342)
Children. Adopting Foreign 168 (48)
Children and Adolescents. Psychosocial Problems of 181 (282)
Children and Adults. Communication Problems of 174 (8)
Children and Adults With and/or Hearing Problems. Rehabilitative Services for 57 (63)
Children and Professionals. Developing Moral Reasoning for 168 (63)
Children and Solutions. Parents of Handicapped 142 (61)
Children. Behavioral Management of 174 (50)
Children. Bicentennial of 16 (61)
Children. Canadian Realistic Fiction for 171 (52)
Children. Creative Playgrounds for 223 (29)
Children Deal With Death. Helping 216 (106)
Children. Delight - Keynote in Literature for 29 (200)
Children. Development of Minority and Under-Privileged 16 (33)
Children. Developmental Levels of 159 (25)
Children. Diagnosis and Evaluation of Gifted 181 (105)
Children. Dialectical Differences in 56 (53)
Children, Discipline, and Parents 151 (172)
Children. Education for Socio-economic Middleclass 174 (76)
Children. Effect of the Family Upon 57 (34)
Children. Effects of Television on 105 (103)
Children. Gifted and Talented 142 (52)
Children. Handicapped 57 (2)
Children in China 112 (33)
Children in the Schools. Integrating Handicapped and Normal 218
Children. Kidney Disease in 181 (158)
Children. Kidney Transplants in 181 (158)
Children. Language Acquisition and Bilingual 29 (95), (204), (297)
Children. Language and Speech Disorders in 56 (53)
Children. Language Development in Young 181 (319)
Children Learn. How 171 (21)
Children Learn Language. How 159 (29)
Children Literature 159 (23)
Children. Literature for 181 (144), 214 (46)
Children. Literature for Young 142 (84)
Children. Management of 174 (76)
Children. Mathematics for Young 142 (13)
Children. Mathematics. Teaching 151 (121)
Children, Parents, and Teachers. Self-concept of 216 (40)
Children. Parents - First Teachers of 151 (172)
Children. Positive Approach to Discipline Problems - Effective Ways Parents Can Deal With and Understand Young 177 (48)
Children. Problems of 181 (289)
Children. Raising 176 (20)
Children Reach Their Potential. Helping 105 (98)
Children Read? Censorship: What Should 151 (94)
Children. Reading Difficulties in 181 (107)
Children. Roman Mothers and the Lives of Their Adult 227 (36)
Children. Science for Young 142 (30)
Children. Selecting Good Literature for 56 (63)
Children. Services for Families and 181 (252), (313)
Children. Serving Handicapped 181 (119)
Children. Talking With 181 (282)
Children. Teaching Reading to Young 142 (30)
Children to Be More Creative - Ways Parents and Teachers Can Encourage Creativity. Helping 117 (48)
Children to Write Poetry. Stimulating 57 (79)
Children. Unwanted 176 (103)
Children. Vision in 29 (85), (169), (229)
Children With Special Needs. Preschool 142 (59)
Children. Working With Young Handicapped 151 (91)
Children, Youth and Adulthood. Moral Judgment In 214 (77)
Children's Art 117 (12)
Children's Authors 181 (145)
Children's Books 174 (77)
Children's Books. Collecting 117 (75)
Children's Books. Early American 174 (18)
Children's Books Only Grownups Should Be Allowed to Read 29 (197), (205)
Children's Books. Valuing 171 (19)
Children's Books. Ways of Studying 171 (19)
Children's Dentistry 181 (157)
Children's Literature 117 (56), 142 (13), 174 (18), (57), 181 (145)
Children's Literature and Film 151 (234)
Children's Literature. Early Childhood Education in Art, Music and 142 (30)
Children's Literature. History of 117 (75), 174 (18)
Children's Literature. Modern Trends in 57 (62)
Children's Literature. Racism in 151 (241)
Children's Literature. Sexism in 151 (241)
Children's Needs. Meeting 181 (11)
Children's Rights Movement 231 (3)
Children's School Success. Encouraging 117 (48)
Children's Weaving 79 (107)
Children's Workshop in Knotless Netting, Basic Basketry, Wrapping 79 (158)

Chile 56 (120)
Chile. Education in 216 (2)
Chile - Its History and Its Culture 27 (11)
Chimpanzees. Fertility and Longevity of Wild 151 (208)
Chimps Learn Human Language? Can 181 (314)
China 142 (50)
China After Mao 59 (2), 69 (2)
China. Agony of Modern 56 (117)
China and Japan. American Relations With 181 (265), (337)
China and the Modern World. Communist 85 (17)
China and the New Regime 97 (57)
China. Children in 112 (33)
China. Current Affairs in People's Republic of 181 (341)
China. Economic Development of Japan and 142 (51)
China. Economy of the People's Republic of 216 (74)
China. Education and the Social Revolution in 151 (121)
China. International Trade With 16 (6)
China. Life in 176 (109)
China. New 171 (2)
China: New, Old, Ancient 112 (32)
China. People's Republic of 224 (7)
China. Position of Women in 218
China. Taiwan and Communist 85 (17)
China Today 59 (2)
China. Women in Modern 112 (33)
China. Women in the People's Republic of 151 (11)
Chinas. News to and From the Two 105 (68)
Chinese Alphabet. Development and Use of 3 (2)
Chinese Export Porcelain 174 (41)
Chinese Family. Japanese and/or 168 (66)
Chinese Foreign Policy 224 (7)
Chinese History 159 (6)
Chinese Painting. Understanding 57 (52)
Choice is Yours 168 (38)
Cholesterol 57 (20)
Cholesterol in Eggs 216 (35)
Choosing an Architect 181 (78), (207)
Choosing the Form of Business 105 (7)
Choosing the Proper Contraceptive 57 (64)
Choral Music 142 (57)
Choral Music in a Time of Affluence 56 (107)
Choreography 142 (38)
Christ and Its Fulfillment. Second Advent of 1 (8)
Christ as Man and God 105 (109)
Christ. Images of 105 (106)
Christ in the Passover 93 (3)
Christiad. Vida's 227 (11)
Christian and Modern Science 151 (258)
Christian Art. Early Irish 181 (79)
Christian Athletes. Sports and 83 (2)
Christian Capitalist Democracy. American Ideals of a 180 (183)
Christian-Catholic Theology 214 (80)
Christian Church in the Fifth Century 29 (178), (234)
Christian Dialogue. Jewish- 181 (306)
Christian Ethics 105 (111)
Christian Faith. Experience of God Within 105 (109)
Christian Humanism 214 (74)
Christian-Jewish Relations 214 (80)
Christian Meaning of Being Man 105 (109)
Christian Monasticism. Origins of 29 (178), (234)
Christian Options in a Disintegrating Culture 211 (4)
Christian Tradition. Meditation - The 54
Christian? Was Abraham Lincoln a 29 (338)
Christian. Why I Am a 151 (258)
Christian Youth 180 (141)
Christianity in Africa 29 (219), (242), (286)
Christianity in Africa - Women and Their Societies 29 (6)
Christianity. Islam Versus 1 (2), (7)
Christians and Muslims. World Religions - Buddhists, Confucianists, Taoists, Maoists, Jews, 54
Christians. Educating 211 (4)
Christmas Ornaments, Using Thrums. Basketry Workshops Making 79 (29)
Christmas Where it Counts. Putting 75 (1)
Christmas. X More Weaving Months 'til 79 (30)
Ch'uan. Tai Chi 228
Church Colleges? Should Government Support 12
Church. Fathers of the 105 (107)
Church Groups. Episcopal 11 (7)
Church History 56 (139)
Church. History of the Early 105 (107)
Church in an Age of Confusion 85 (18)
Church in the Fifth Century. Christian 29 (178), (234)
Church. Monasticism in the Early 105 (107)
Church Must Be. What the 75 (1)
Church. Sacrament of Penance in the Early 105 (107)
Church-State Issue in Public Education 181 (102), (303)
Church Tax Exemptions. Future of 12
Churches in Change. Music of the 56 (107)
Cigarette Controversy 184 (1 - 4)
Cinema 181 (74)
Cinema. American and European 31 (12)
Cinema Today 31 (12)
Circle Is a Square. Heart of the 83 (5)
Cities Be Saved? Can Our 216 (43)
Cities Exist? Why Do 174 (51)
Cities. Historical Development of American 181 (264)
Cities. Land Use Within 174 (51)
Cities. Medieval 31 (28)
Cities. New 171 (48)
Cities of the World. Large 29 (319)
Cities, Seas, Sahara. Morocco 15 (2)
Cities - Understanding Their Locations. Pattern of 174 (51)

Citizen Involvement in Pollution Control 151 (160)
Citizen Participation in Government Policy Making 218
Citizen. What is the State Legislature Doing Which Affects the Ordinary 57 (49)
Citizen, Writer. Carl Sandburg: 225 (42)
Citizens of Acadiana. Mentally Retarded 174 (44)
Citizenship in a Democratic Society 168 (42)
Citizenship in an Ideological Environment - Thrust or Trick 85 (11)
City Government. Review of Various Types of 57 (49)
City. 19th Century 181 (262)
City of Stars to the City of Light. From the 97 (16)
City of Tacoma. Governmental Budgeting for the 159 (4)
City Planning 172 (12)
City. Quality of Life in the American 31 (13)
City Recycling. Neighborhoods and 181 (254), (275)
City Room to Corporate Office 151 (86)
Civic Applications of Computers 31 (17)
Civic Club. Join a 174 (40)
Civic Participation 65 (4), (46)
Civil Disobedience 151 (235), 214 (17)
Civil Engineering Land Marks. Historic 174 (90)
Civil Liberties 31 (14), 218
Civil Liberties During the Cold War Years 105 (59)
Civil Liberties. They Are Your 117 (103)
Civil Liberty. Economic Freedom and 174 (72)
Civil Rights 31 (14)
Civil Rights Laws 29 (60), (147), (194), (337)
Civil Rights Movement. John F. Kennedy and the 117 (66)
Civil Rights. Problems of 85 (5)
Civil Rights. Your 117 (103), (119)
Civil War 142 (27)
Civil War Belle. Love and War: The Courtship of a 117 (69)
Civil War Soldiers. Morals of 151 (214)
Civilization. Mexico-Culture and 142 (34)
Civilization of India. Culture and 181 (333)
Civilization. Polish 214 (49)
Civilization. Teeth and 151 (208)
Civilization. Western 142 (1)
Clasped Warp and Weft 79 (147)
Classic? What is a 97 (43)
Classical and Hellenistic Greece. Archaeology of 227 (45)
Classical Archaeology 227 (13), (14), (20)
Classical Greece 29 (317)
Classical Greek Drama 181 (81), (139)
Classical Influences on American Culture. Aspects of 227 (32)
Classical Mythology 227 (4), (16), (29)
Classical Numismatics 227 (46)
Classical Problems 181 (149)
Classical Scholarship. Uses of the Computer in 227 (7)
Classical Sites 227 (46)
Classical Themes in Science Fiction 227 (4)
Classics and Images of America 227 (4)
Classics and Popular Culture 227 (4)
Classics in America. History of 227 (25)
Classics on English Literature. Influence of 227 (26)
Classics. Robert Frost and the 227 (1)
Classics. Structuralism and the 227 (21)
Classics. Teaching 227 (38)
Classroom. Community and the 57 (47)
Classroom. Creative Writing in the 57 (79)
Classroom. Culture Conflict in the Classroom 174 (13)
Classroom Discipline. Realistic and Humanistic Approach to 117 (51)
Classroom. Humanism in the 16 (81)
Classroom Management 57 (34), 117 (37)
Classroom. Motivation in the 57 (70)
Classroom Teacher. Art, Music and Cooking Activities for the 117 (48)
Classroom to Community. From 105 (50)
Clay and Fiber 79 (71)
Clean Air. Fight for 54
Clean and Cheap Energy 54
Cleaning. Central 67 (18)
Cleaning Systems. Coal 150 (11)
Clear Air Turbulence 151 (155)
Clerical-Collar Mind 180 (94)
Cleveland 144
Clients 119 (1)
Climate Changing? Is the 223 (5)
Clinical Approach to Out-patient Pharmacy Services 54
Clinical Laboratory 105 (96)
Clinical Specialization 105 (95)
Clinical Supervision 174 (85)
Clinical Toxicology 54
Cloak and Dagger. Dixie Darlings of the 57 (96)
Clock Collecting and Repair 168 (70)
Clocks and Watches 151 (210)
Clocks. Antique 168 (70)
Closing 65 (5), (6), (7), (8), (9), (11), (14), (15), (16), (18), (20), (22), (24), (26), (30), (32), (33), (38), (39), (40), (42), (44), (48), (60), (63), (64), (70)
Closing and Negotiating the Sale 65 (61)
Cloth Analysis 79 (63)
Cloth and Costume as Design. Ethnic 79 (33)
Cloth Structure, Double Cloth 79 (6)
Clothes Assembled by Crochet or Knots. Woven 79 (60)
Clothing. Bags and Handsome Ethnic 79 (39)
Clothing Construction. Contemporary 79 (72)
Clothing. Designing Circular Weave 79 (10)
Clothing. Recycling 57 (84)
Club in the News. Getting Your 216 (13)

Club. Join a Civic 174 (40)
Club Sports 168 (5)
Clubs. Extramural Sport 216 (46)
Clubs. Welfare Roles of Country 117 (53)
Coaching 142 (46), 180 (5)
Coaching. Baseball 142 (49)
Coaching. Basketball 214 (11)
Coaching of Basketball 151 (204)
Coaching of Diving 181 (2)
Coaching Philosophy 168 (24)
Coal Benefication. Energy Needs, Economic Choices, and 151 (134)
Coal Cleaning Systems 150 (11)
Coal Mining. Modern 151 (136)
Coal Project. Western 47
Coast. Native Wildflowers of the West 159 (70)
Coastal and Marine Resources in Eastern North Carolina 56 (36), (38)
Coastal Wetlands 151 (159)
Cobb Seamount. Research Submarine Dive on 223 (37)
Cocurricular Education - Beyond the Classroom 151 (105)
Coffee Plant. Design of an Instant 214 (42)
Co-generation. Research and Development in 150 (9)
Cognition 142 (13)
Coiling 79 (145)
Cointelpro. From Pentagon Papers to 213 (1)
Cold War 57 (56)
Collecting and Repair. Clock 168 (70)
Collecting Children's Books 117 (75)
Collecting. Reptile 151 (307)
Collecting. Seashells and Shell 174 (30)
Collecting - the Pleasant Way to Become Wealthy 97 (36)
Collection Development 142 (29)
Collection of Tree Seeds in the Rocky Mountains 151 (310)
Collections in Following With the Squeaky Wheel Principle 136 (7)
Collective Bargaining 142 (42), 151 (8), 174 (17)
Collective Bargaining in Education 117 (49)
Collective Bargaining in Higher Education 29 (61), 223 (6)
Collective Bargaining in Private Industry 23
Collective Bargaining in the Public Sector 223 (6)
Collective Bargaining. Teachers and 181 (129)
Collective Bargaining - the Good and the Bad 57 (65)
Collective Living Breaks Down the Isolation and Alienation of Today's World. How 178 (1)
Collective Unconscious. Creative Process and the 154 (6)
Collectors. Care and Cultivation of 102 (19)
College Admissions and Financial Aid 31 (16)
College Admissions. General 54
College Affairs. General 224 (8)
College and Penn State. International in State 151 (173)
College Athletes in Running. Expectations for 168 (71)
College. Athletics at Behrend 151 (285)
College Athletics. Money in 105 (112)
College Campus. ROTC on the 54
College Center 168 (5)
College Composition 214 (47)
College Education. Cost of a 16 (68)
College Electoral 214 (7)
College Football Officiating 31 (39)
College Football. When the Muckrackers Took on 151 (69)
College Freshman. English and the 105 (46)
College Freshmen. Problems Faced by First Time 174 (88)
College. Future of the Independent 176 (26)
College Going. Trends in 151 (90)
College Graduate. Employment Trends for the 151 (60)
College Graduates. Career Opportunities for 181 (50), (53)
College Graduates. What Industry Expects of 216 (23)
College. How to Prepare for 29 (31), (102), (349)
College - Is There Life After College? 112 (64)
College Life: The Student and the Void 151 (105)
College. Making Plans for 151 (15)
College. Mr. Fingers Goes to 221 (1)
College of Business 168 (45)
College. Opportunity in the Two-year 56 (44)
College or Major. Career Opportunities by 181 (50)
College or Major Career Planning. Career Opportunities by 181 (53)
College. Plight of the Independent 224 (16)
College Program. Community 117 (59)
College Programs for Underachievers 105 (34)
College Sports. Economics of Pro and 54
College Student Growth 16 (72), 33 (16)
College Student. Older, Disadvantaged 181 (201), (308)
College Student. Religion and the 54
College Student. Sex and the 54
College Student. Today's 117 (127)
College Student. Values of Today's 16 (21)
College Student - Who Is He? Today's 117 (42)
College Students 151 (120)
College Students. Alcohol, Drinking Behavior, and 151 (212)
College Students. Career Planning/Job Search for 151 (54)
College Students. Counseling With 168 (28)
College Students. Four Decades of 151 (11)
College Students: How Have They Changed? 16 (57), 23 (16)
College Students. Watergate and 214 (3)
College Students - Where Their Heads Are At 29 (30), (348)
College. Success in 216 (29)
College. Transition From High School to 105 (34)
College Versus the Vocational Technical School. Community Junior 174 (1)

College. Vocational Students Can Go To 181 (55)
College? Why 151 (90)
College Youth 216 (52)
Colleges and Universities. Academic Advising in 151 (116)
Colleges and Universities. Government Support for Independent 105 (50)
Colleges and Universities. What Should the Public Expect From Our 151 (101)
Colleges Educate? Do 168)18)
Colleges. History and Development of the Land Grant 191 (122)
Colleges? Should Government Support Church 12
Colleges Today. Administration and 16 (48)
Collegiate Experience 151 (55)
Colombia 110 (5)
Colombia-Andes to the Amazon 59 (4)
Colombia - From the Spanish Main to the Amazon 69 (7)
Colonial America 142 (63)
Colonial History. American 57 (35)
Colonial Louisiana 174 (19)
Colonial North Carolina. Sound Society of 56 (34)
Colonial Pennsylvania 151 (216)
Colonial Philadelphia. Architecture of 151 (29)
Colonial Town Life in Eastern North Carolina 56 (30)
Colonialism - Myth and Reality 85 (18)
Colonization. Effects of 181 (21)
Colonization. Physiological Effects of 181 (31), (135)
Colonization. Social and Psychological Effects of 181 (31), (294)
Colonization. Space 216 (3)
Color 79 (29), (53), (139)
Color and Design 79 (75), (76), (106), (134)
Color and Design for Weavers 79 (108)
Color and Structure. Loom Controlled 79 (95)
Color and Texture in Weaving. Design, 79 (159)
Color and Weave Effect Method of Designing 79 (94)
Color and Weaving 79 (95)
Color Cubes 181 (1), (148)
Color. Design and 79 (48), (96)
Color, Design, and the Contemporary Scene 79 (158)
Color for the Control of Emotions. Use of 225 (5)
Color. Health as Related to Light Intensity and 216 (24)
Color in Interior Architecture 218
Color in Weaving 79 (81), (84), (116)
Color in Weaving, Design, and Pattern Weaving. Use of 79 (24)
Color. Light and 218
Color. Nature as a Source for Design and 79 (140)
Color - Physical and Psychological Investigation 79 (25)
Color Sensations. Subjective 31 (24)
Color Theory and Yarn Dyeing 79 (78)
Color - What It Can Do for You 79 (113)
Colorado 59 (11)
Colorado - Where the West Comes Alive 110 (9)
Coloring 181 (148)
Coloring Applied to Solitaire Games **181 (1)**
Column. How One Writes a Town-Gown 151 (76)
Combined Resist Dyeing Techniques 79 (108)
Comedy. Dancer Preparing for a Career in Musical 225 (39)
Comedy. Farm and Physical 151 (289)
Comedy: In the Beginning. Sound 151 (289)
Comedy in Vaudeville. Racial 216 (32)
Comedy of Love 86 (1)
Comic Books 159 (23)
Coming Political Upheaval 102 (36)
Commencement Speeches 168 (40)
Commentaries and Observations on the Bicentennial 54
Commentator. Historian as Social 174 (83)
Commentators on Aristotle and Their Method. Greek 227 (51)
(Commerical and Residential). Exchanging 65 (25)
Commercial Dye 79 (36)
Commercial Mushroom Industry 151 (176)
Commercial Property 65 (3), (17), (22), (25), (34), (50), (53), (54), (55), (56), (58), (62), (65), (66), (67)
Commercial Property and Investment 65 (61)
Commission. Federal Aviation 176 (45)
Commission. Value and Uses of Financial Reports Filed by American Corporation With the Securities and Exchange 50 (1)
Commission Weaving 79 (148)
Commission Weaving for Corporate Building 79 (118)
Commission. Working on 79 (105), (146)
Committee. Democratic National 223 (23)
Commodities in Economics 180 (29)
Commodity Futures Regulation 138 (2)
Commodity Futures Trading Activities. Management of 138 (3), (4)
Commodity Trading 38
Common Plant Diseases and Man 117 (13)
Communicate. How We 174 (66)
Communicate? What Do You Mean I Can't 29 (34), (137)
Communicate With Each Other 225 (26)
Communicate. You Can't Not 117 (136)
Communicating. Creative 102 (3)
Communicating, Too. Reading is Caring and 159 (54)
Communication 57 (27), 65 (6), 142 (71), (92), 159 (48)
Communication: A Program Dealing With the Many Aspects of This Overlooked Part of Communications. Non-verbal 117 (58)
Communication Among People 174 (1)
Communication and Better Relationships 159 (60)
Communication and Environment 135 (17)
Communication and Good Management 159 (60)
Communication and Human Relations 159 (60)
Communication and the Deaf 151 (92)

Communication and the Learning Process. Interpersonal 181 (110)
Communication and Word Power 151 (70)
Communication as a Management Tool 105 (15)
Communication. Barriers to 57 (57)
Communication Between the Sexes 142 (25)
Communication. Business 174 (96)
Communication. Development of Mass 117 (84)
Communication. Education for Improved 181 (94)
Communication. Essentials of Effective Personal 105 (12)
Communication. Family Goals and 214 (77)
Communication. Four Dimensions of 56 (56)
Communication Gaps. Causes for 171 (45)
Communication in Marriage 57 (8)
Communication in Small Groups 151 (78)
Communication. Interpersonal 105 (13), 117 (39), 142 (25), 214 (77)
Communication is Impossible 57 (57)
Communication. Leadership in Small Group 168 (17)
Communication. Marital 168 (73)
Communication Media on Attitudes. Influence of 218
Communication. Motivation and 180 (9)
Communication. Multisensory 181 (97)
Communication. Non-verbal 142 (25), 180 (155), (175)
Communication. Non-verbal Aspects of Human 142 (37)
Communication Now---More Than Ever 117 (135)
Communication of Feeling 105 (100)
Communication. Person-to-Person 174 (56)
Communication Problems of Children and Adults 174 (8)
Communication. Responsible 57 (57)
Communication. Salesmanship and 65 (32)
Communication Skills 180 (173)
Communication Strategies. Effective 105 (14)
Communication. Synergetic Models of 151 (65)
Communication Technology 29 (35), (142), (285)
Communication Technology - Past, Present and Future 29 (308), (335)
Communication: The Silent Messages. Nonverbal 151 (87)
Communication - The Subconscious Language. Nonverbal 117 (50)
Communication, Transportation, and Settlement Pattern 151 (183)
Communication. Women in 29 (35), (142), (285), (308), (335)
Communication. Written 168 (39)
Communications 56 (134), 142 (12), 180 (65), (73), (98), (104), (118), (144), (153), 216 (144)
Communications and Effective Speaking. Successful 180 (14)
Communications and Human Behavior 180 (76)
Communications and the Learning Process. Interpersonal 181 (316)
Communications. Better Business 174 (93)
Communications. Careers in 181 (49), (67)
Communications. Community 168 (12)
Communications. Corporate 162
Communications. Hollywood Story - Experience in 135 (45)
Communications. Human Relations and 168 (52)
Communications in a Multidisciplinary Setting 151 (79)
Communications in Modern Society. Mass 29 (55)
Communications in the Brain Damaged Adult 117 (133)
Communications. Industrial and Management 151 (81)
Communications is Understanding 189
Communications Law. Mass 168 (10)
Communications. Management 180 (123)
Communications. Mass- 102 (11), 168 (10)
Communications Media. Educational 181 (72), (100)
Communications. Parent-Child 216 (106)
Communications Problems. Homo Sapiens Characteristics Causing 151 (81)
Communications Vehicles. How to Buy 151 (75)
Communications With Internationals 151 (173)
Communicator: American Politicians. Cautious 151 (87)
Communism 159 (20), 175 (1), 180 (126)
Communism and Facism 151 (198)
Communism, Its Ideology and Morphology 85 (24)
Communist China and the Modern World 85 (17)
Communist China. Taiwan and 85 (17)
Communist Countries. Politics of Trading With 85 (6)
Communist East Europe. Political and Social History in 218
Communist Ideologies 54
Communist Ideology and Strategy 85 (15)
Communist Movement. Present Situation of the International 85 (8)
Communist Organization and Tactics 85 (15)
Communities. Automobile Impact on 218
Communities Can Improve the Quality of Education. How 151 (38)
Communities. Families and 216 (133)
Communities. Human Problems in Northern 171 (10)
Communities in the Pittsburgh Area. Ethnic 54
Communities. Intentional 151 (148)
Communities. Wild Flowers and Plant 223 (15)
Community Affairs 180 (100), (127)
Community and Individual Response to Crime 181 (285)
Community and Regional Planning and Development 16 (54)
Community and the Classroom 57 (47)
Community. Being Part of Your 216 (70)
Community - Challenge or Check. Life in the 85 (11)
Community College Program 117 (59)
Community Communications 168 (12)

Community Competing Academically. Black 54
Community Corrections Center. Jail as a 56 (142)
Community. Corrections in the 56 (142)
Community Development 16 (33)
Community Development. Economic or 16 (7)
Community Development. Neighborhoods, Housing and 181 (275)
Community Development. Projects and Programs for 117 (129)
Community Economic Development - Dependence or Autonomy? 151 (49)
Community Education 216 (92)
Community Education and Life-long Learning 57 (81)
Community for Our Time 211 (4)
Community. From Classroom to 105 (50)
Community Health 142 (39)
Community Improvement 216 (42)
Community in Career Education Programs. Involving the 57 (72)
Community in the Corporate State 151 (49)
Community Inland Resource Planning. Role of the 56 (22)
Community Involvement 216 (92)
Community Junior College Versus the Vocational Technical School 174 (1)
Community Mental Health 16 (81)
Community. Mental Health and the Black 181 (294)
Community. Music in the 54
Community Needs. Innovative Method of Forecasting 168 (57)
Community. Noise in Your 151 (141)
Community. Occupational Therapy in the 159 (31)
Community Organizing 172 (1)
Community. Penn State Services to the 151 (117)
Community. Philadelphia Black 181 (29)
Community Planning. State, Regional, and 151 (226)
Community Power 16 (1)
Community Property 159 (46)
Community Psychology 56 (136), 142 (73)
Community Public Relations 31 (35)
Community Public Relations. School/ 168 (10)
Community Recreation Facilities 16 (2)
Community Rehabilitation 56 (77)
Community Relations. School- 218
Community Relationships. School- 216 (75)
Community Resource Development 16 (12)
Community Resources for Better Living 57 (38)
Community Resources. Using 57 (47)
Community. Role and Place of Theatre in the Public 159 (62)
Community Role of Cable Television 181 (70), (215)
Community. Role of the Intelligence 102 (29)
Community. Role of the Student Press in Its School and 168 (51)
Community School Relationship 174 (85)
Community. Social Change: The Individual and the 168 (66)
Community Stores Can Be Used for Political Organizing. How Food Co-ops and 178 (1)
Community Support Reading? How Can Your 151 (94)
Community. Theatre in the 16
Community. University Relations With the 174 (89)
Community. Women in Education and the 174 (54)
Community's Newspaper? Your 181 (68), (211)
Company and Its Impact on International Relations. Multinational 218
Company - For Next to Nothing. How to Buy a 180 (20)
Company. How to Advertise Your 136 (5)
Comparative Art Forms 117 (11)
Comparative Economic Systems 117 (23), 142 (51)
Comparative Education 57 (1), 168 (55)
Comparative Linguistics 117 (87)
Comparative Medicine 216 (127)
Comparative Mythology 227 (21)
Comparative Religions 218
Comparative Revolutions 142 (1)
Comparison of the German and American Education Systems 56 (54)
Comparison of United States - U.S.S.R. Training for the Olympics 29 (296), (306)
Compensation. Louisiana Workmen's 174 (17)
Compensation Plans for Doctors. Deferred 8 (8)
Compensation Practices 223 (6)
Competence in Spite of Theory 135 (50)
Competence Skills. Interpersonal 151 (58)
Competency-based Degree Programs 142 (95)
Competency Based Education 216 (49)
Competency - Based-On-Site Learning in Early Childhood Education 223 (7)
Competition and Cooperation 171 (56)
Competition Versus Cooperation 117 (110)
Competitive Athletics 151 (285)
Competitive Swimming 56 (86)
Complaints. How to Recognize Affirmative Action 151 (1)
Complete Dentures 181 (174)
Composer. Meet the 31 (29)
Composers and Their Works. Individual Musical 54
Composers. Musical 54
Composites 216 (39)
Composition. College 214 (47)
Composition, Literary Criticism 216 (117)
Compounds. Fluorine 216 (21)
Comprehensive Exhibits 79 (89)
Comprehensive Musicianship 56 (108)
Compromises in American History. Black and 29 (261)
Compulsive Gambling 224 (14)
Compulsory Adult Education by 1984? 151 (98)
Compulsory Parenthood Education 151 (169)
Computability? What is 171 (35)
Computation. Limitations on Complexity of 181 (204)
Computer and Electronics 225 (21)
Computer and Statistics in Literature and Linguistics. Use of the 227 (51)
Computer Applications 216 (68)

Computer Applications in the Study of Literature 227 (44)
Computer Applications to Real Estate Marketing 69 (65)
Computer Appreciation 216 (68)
Computer-Assisted Instruction 16 (62)
Computer. Designing an Analog 181 (154)
Computer - Friend or Enemy 56 (126)
Computer. Household 174 (65)
Computer if Any? Which 29 (77)
Computer in Classical Scholarship. Uses of the 227 (7)
Computer in Its Language. Talking to the 57 (93)
Computer Interaction. Manager- 171 (9)
Computer Is. What a 216 (44)
Computer. Mathematics Versus the Modern 181 (154)
Computer Ombudsman Service of Vancouver 171 (12)
Computer on a Chip 31 (18)
Computer Programming 181 (214)
Computer Programming. New Techniques of 181 (51)
Computer Programs. Portability of 181 (214)
Computer Science 142 (3)
Computer Science at Virginia Tech 216 (44)
Computer Simulation of Health Care Systems 218
Computer Technology 214 (20)
Computer. Water and Weather Data on the 216 (61)
Computer. World's Biggest 144
Computerized Data Management 174 (23)
Computerized Information System Environment 174 (23)
Computers 214 (21)
Computers Affect You. How 56 (127)
Computers and Management 174 (43)
Computers and Our Lives 174 (11)
Computers and Society 142 (78)
Computers and the Privacy Issue 218
Computers. Application of 174 (79)
Computers. Civic Applications of 31 (17)
Computers Do Everything? Can 181 (204)
Computers - Future Trends. Mathematics and 142 (70)
Computers in Engineering and/or Science 214 (22)
Computers in Medicine 29 (173)
Computers in State Government. Use of 174 (79)
Computers on the Accounting Profession. Impact of 171 (9)
Computers. Playing Games With 181 (204)
Computer's Role on the University Campus 16 (5)
Computers. Teaching With 142 (70)
Concentration Camps 176 (105)
Concept of Public in American Education 181 (261)
Concept to Bookshelf: Editor's Perspective 151 (79)
Concepts of Public Choice 117 (18)
Conceptual Problems in Economics 181 (42)
Concerns of Women 223 (38)
Concrete 214 (45)
Concrete As a Major Construction Material. Portland Cement 151 (291)
Conditioning. Enjoying Fitness and 151 (204)
Conditioning for a Lifetime 159 (69)
Conditioning Young People. Training and 168 (33)
Condominiums 65 (1), (3), (16), (48), (49), (50), (55), (62)
Conducting a Meeting 216 (28)
Conducting Business Meetings 117 (128)
Conference Center - Alumi Ownership. USL 174 (3)
Conference. How to Plan a 57 (51)
Conference Participation and Leadership. Effective 56 (20)
Confessions of a Psychologist Father 97 (17)
Confidence in Business. Role of 102 (3)
Conflict 105 (93)
Conflict and Confrontation in Our Schools 54
Conflict and Resolution. Youth and Families: 151 (67)
Conflict. Arab-Israeli 57 (61), 181 (293), (306) 224 (9)
Conflict. Handling 57 (18)
Conflict in Interpersonal Relationships 159 (60)
Conflict in Schools 142 (97)
Conflict in the Classroom. Culture 174 (13)
Conflict. Sino-Soviet 85 (29)
Conflict. Youth in 54
Conflicts and Resolutions. Family- 29 (59), (99), (345)
Conflicts. Middle Eastern 29 (179), (226)
Conformation. Horse 216 (57)
Confrontation In Our Schools. Conflict and 54
Confucianists, Taoists, Maoists, Jews, Christians and Muslims. World Religions - Buddhists, 54
Congress 105 (55), 142 (64), 214 (5), 220 (1), (2), (5)
Congress. Penn State and the United States 151 (191)
Congress. President and 223 (23)
Congress. Programs of the Present 16 (20)
Conscience. American 151 (214)
Conscientious and Selective Objection 105 (76)
Consciousness. Altered States of 174 (55)
Conservation 159 (2)
Conservation. Air 117 (32)
Conservation and Regulation - State and Federal. Oil and Gas 151 (135)
Conservation. Basic Principles of Wildlife Management and 151 (309)
Conservation. Diamonds, Ecology and 143 (15)
Conservation. Energy 23, 25 (16), 57 (25), 80 (16), 151 (123), 216 (71), (143)
Conservation. Environment and 35
Conservation. Future of 85 (9)
Conservation. Human Erosion and Human 57 (69)
Conservation in the Home. Water 136 (22)
Conservation in Traffic Operations and Highway Design. Energy 174 (90)
Conservation in Transportation. Energy 174 (90)
Conservation of Human Resources 56 (80)
Conservation of Raw Materials 151 (253)
Conservation or Exploitation. Oceans - 97 (38)
Conservation. Outdoor Recreation and 171 (37)
Conservation. Soil 151 (21)

Conservation. Water 151 (158)
Conservation. Wildlife Filming and 4 (4)
Conservation With Water-saving Devices. Water 151 (304)
Conservatism 227 (29)
Conservatism and Intelligence 85 (23)
Conservatism. Case for 85 (39)
Conservatism in an Age of Ideology. Relevance of 85 (40)
Conservatism in Historical Perspective. Liberalism and 85 (12)
Conservatism in Post-Liberal America. Future of 85 (21)
Conservatism. New Winds - the Decline of Liberalism and the Rise of 85 (12)
Conservatism - Vital Link. American and European 85 (39)
Conservatism? What is 85 (21)
Conservative Tradition and Foreign Policy 85 (7)
Conservatives, and Catholics are Excluded From Campus. Why Moderates, 85 (33)
Conservatives in the Middle of the Journey. American 85 (16)
Constitution 176 (6), (36), 214 (5)
Constitution. Afro-American in the United States 214 (5), 29 (337)
Constitution. Decisions of the Supreme Court in Constructing the 54
Constitutional Foundations. American 85 (9)
Constitutional Government and Modern Democracy. Problems of 85 (5)
Constitutional Law 142 (67)
Constitutional/Moral Foreign Policy 102 (12)
Constitutions. Virginia's 216 (124)
Construction 65 (15), (33), (37), (56)
Construction Material. Portland Cement Concrete as a Major 151 (291)
Construction of Airplanes. Design and 151 (33)
Construction Technology Education 168 (6)
Constructions. Textile 79 (55)
Consumer Affairs 135 (23), (46), 157 (1), 176 (44)
Consumer Affairs Legislation 16 (27)
Consumer. Apparel and the 174 (54)
Consumer Attacks on the Auto Industry 117 (16)
Consumer Attitudes 176 (87)
Consumer Behavior 29 (33), (84), (157), (253)
Consumer Dilemma 176 (104)
Consumer Economics 142 (51)
Consumer Education. What I Learned as a Widow About 57 (64)
Consumer End of Business 135 (11)
Consumer Finance 174 (63)
Consumer Fraud 176 (61)
Consumer Interest. Meeting the Educational 27 (20)
Consumer Issues 219 (2)
Consumer Movement. Marketing and the 214 (23)
Consumer Problems. Energy 57 (84)
Consumer Product Safety 16 (6)
Consumer Product Safety Commission 105 (87)
Consumer Protection 29 (191), 176 (92)
Consumer Rights and Responsibilities 112 (92)
Consumer Safety 105 (87)
Consumer Tips 152
Consumer Welfare? Can Legislation Improve 54
Consumerism 168 (67)
Consumerism and the Aged 168 (67)
Consumerism as a Marketing Plan 102 (23)
Consumerism Boomerang 85 (19)
Consumerism: Choosing Health Care Professionals 181 (196)
Consumerism - Cognitive Dissonance Restated 117 (16)
Consumerism in Health 181 (170)
Consumerism. Nutrition and 214 (24), (71)
Consumerism - Threat to the Consumer 85 (30)
Consumerism Today 57 (84)
Consumerism: What's in Our Food 181 (249)
Consumerism. Who Killed the Ice Man - Or, An Answer to Ralph Nader and 85 (26)
Consumerism: You and Your Medicine Chest 181 (196), (249)
Consumers. Fifty Million 159 (35)
Consumers in Our Economy. Function of 168 (45)
Consumers. Metrics for 57 (84)
Consumers Talk 151 (175)
Contemplative Prayer in a Busy World 54
Contemporary Activity 79 (70)
Contemporary Africa Culture 181 (25), (331)
Contemporary Africa Politics 181 (25), (331)
Contemporary American Ceramics 159 (39)
Contemporary and Traditional Tapestry 79 (78)
Contemporary Art 142 (76), 159 (18)
Contemporary Basketry as Functional or Sculptural Forms 79 (135)
Contemporary Ceramics 57 (44), 216 (69)
Contemporary Clothing Construction 79 (72)
Contemporary Corruption of Language 85 (20)
Contemporary Crafts in America 79 (73)
Contemporary Dance 174 (75)
Contemporary Fiction and Non-fiction 159 (65)
Contemporary Fiction. Works of 159 (19)
Contemporary Film 57 (32)
Contemporary France 56 (115)
Contemporary French Government and Politics 57 (89)
Contemporary German 174 (33)
Contemporary International Relations 151 (193)
Contemporary Ireland. Problems and Hopes in 159 (65)
Contemporary Issues. American Indian 29 (192)
Contemporary Issues in American Foreign Policy 57 (19)
Contemporary Japan 151 (193)
Contemporary Literature 151 (232), 159 (24)
Contemporary Loom-Woven Hangings 79 (32)
Contemporary Music in Poland 54
Contemporary National Dress of Mayan Indians of Guatemala - Historical Interpretation and Future of the Tradition 79 (83)

Contemporary Novelists You Should Know 151 (234)
Contemporary Philosophy and Education 57 (85)
Contemporary Poetry 174 (29)
Contemporary Poetry. Affirmation in 151 (105)
Contemporary Printing 159 (18)
Contemporary Problems in International Relations 85 (15)
Contemporary Problems of American Foreign Policy 159 (36)
Contemporary Religious Movements 224 (11)
Contemporary Social Issues 85 (3)
Contemporary Social Problems 178 (5)
Contemporary Sprang 79 (38)
Contemporary Standards for Grammatical Correctness 117 (61)
Contemporary. Stitchery - Crewel or 79 (84)
Contemporary Tapestry Techniques 79 (39)
Contemporary Textiles 79 (136)
Contemporary Theatre 174 (48)
Contemporary Themes in Drama 54
Contemporary Themes in Fiction 54
Contemporary Themes in Poetry 54
Contemporary Theology. Issues in 54
Contemporary Trends in Anthropology 151 (214)
Contemporary Trends in Art 151 (27)
Contemporary Trends in Music 57 (4)
Contemporary Trends in Weaving 79 (112)
Contemporary Use of Primitive Knotless Netting 79 (52)
Contemporary Weaving 79 (71)
Continent. Darkening 97 (50)
Continent. Dawn in the Dark 100 (1)
Continents in Motion 97 (62)
Continuing Adult Education 171 (18)
Continuing Education 57 (35), 181 (111), (128), 216 (55)
Continuing Education and You 57 (26)
Continuing Education Center. Resident 216 (37)
Continuing Education. Higher Education and 181 (111)
Continuing Education in Nursing 214 (72)
Continuing Education Program 16 (10)
Continuing Professional Education: Its Importance 151 (40)
Continuous Progress Schools 174 (49)
Contraception Controversy 174 (69)
Contraceptive. Choosing the Proper 57 (64)
Contraceptives for Population Control 16 (30)
Contraction. Schools in an Era of 57 (81)
Contractions. Muscle 142 (96)
Contractor Status. Independent 65 (10)
Contractors. Safety Program for Drilling 136 (2)
Contracts in Gold, Silver, and Copper. Metals Futures 38
Contradictions in Mathematics 171 (35)
Contribution of Psychoprophylactic Childbirth to the Era of Feminism 36 (1)
Contributions of the Chemical Industry to Mid-western United States Economies 34 (1)
Control. Birth 168 (23)
Control. Cost 120
Control. Exercise and Weight 168 (33)
Control for Women. Figure 174 (64)
Control. Investment 151 (9)
Control. Population 105 (3), 174 (69)
Control. Pet Population 218
Control. Self 168 (47)
Control. Weight 151 (282), 176 (81)
Control Your Time at All Times 151 (38)
Controlled Fusion 151 (129)
Controlling Microbiological Food Hazards at Home 151 (178)
Controversies in Pulp Therapy 105 (30)
Convention Curcuit. Covering the 135 (36)
Conversational Quality. Speaking With a 168 (17)
Conversationalist. How to Become a More Interesting 105 (13)
Conversion. Biomass 163 (1)
Conversion. Energy 214 (40)
Conversion to the Metric System 174 (79)
Cookbook. Apicius' Roman 227 (31)
Cooking Activities for the Classroom Teacher. Art, Music, and 117 (48)
Cooking. Vegetarian Nutrition and 218
Cooperation Between the University and the Business Community 16 (36)
Cooperation. Competition and 171 (56)
Cooperation. Competition Versus 117 (110)
Cooperative Education 56 (45), 181 (115), 216 (74), (100)
Cooperative Education. Partners in Progress - 151 (95)
Cooperative Education. Total Education Through 16 (82)
Cooperative Enterprises 172 (9)
Cooperative Extension Programs 16 (12)
Cooperative Living 171 (1)
Cooperative Study and Interships in Higher Education 181 (51)
Cooperative? What Is a 151 (263)
Co-ops and Community Stores Can Be Used for Political Organizing. How Food 178 (1)
Copernican Revolution 29 (177), (232), (268)
Coping 180 (198)
Coping. Rehabilitation Psychology - 151 (18)
Copper. Metals Futures Contracts in Gold, Silver and 38
Copper. World of 143 (2)
Copyright Law as It Applies to Instructional Television 151 (66)
Coral Reefs 218
Corn, Green Beans, Cherry, Bright Stack and Filling Equipment. Sweet 67 (6), (12)
Corner Stones of Success for Women in Business 229 (5)
Cornfield. Cache in the 112 (119)
Coronary Artery By-pass Surgery 181 (194)
Corporate Accountability in America 181 (32), (258)

Corporate Building. Commission Weaving for 79 (118)
Corporate Communications 162
Corporate Image. Building a 102 (19)
Corporate Office. City Room to 151 (86)
Corporate Planning 151 (48)
Corporate Social Responsibility 159 (3)
Corporate State. Community in the 151 (49)
Corporation of the Future 102 (36)
Corporation of 2001 102 (6)
Corporations and Modern Society 159 (15)
Corporations and the Doctor. Professional 8 (9)
Corporations in the Food Business. Multinational 181 (34), (334)
Corporations. Social Responsibilities of the 85 (1)
Corporations With the Securities and Exchange Commission. Value and Uses of Financial Reports Filed by American 50 (1)
Corps of Engineers, History and Current Roles 105 (74)
Correction of Facial Deformities 181 (161)
Corrections Center. Jail as a Community 56 (142)
Corrections in the Community 56 (142)
Correspondent. Foreign 223 (20)
Corrosion Resistant Plating for Processing Equipment 67 (11)
Corrupt Society 97 (45)
Corruption of Language. Contemporary 85 (20)
Cosmology 142 (65)
Cosmology - Man's Place in the Universe 27 (16)
Cosmology. Modern 223 (4)
Cosmology. New 29 (186), (272)
Cost and Decision Making 174 (43)
Cost Containment 180 (34)
Cost Control 120
Cost Controls in Small Business 214 (1)
Cost of a College Education 16 (68)
Cost of Health Care. Rising 8 (6)
Cost of Imported Oil 31 (23)
Cost of Medical Care. Rising 27 (25)
Cost of Money. High 168 (67)
Cost of Transfers 85 (34)
Costa Rica - Tropical Plants 159 (70)
Costs and Adventures of the Modern Day Prospector 143 (13)
Costs. Meeting College 57 (83)
Costs of Regulatory Delays. Human 31 (30)
Costs. Rising Health Care 54
Costume as Design. Ethnic Cloth and 79 (33)
Costume Design 79 (109)
Costume. Ethnic 79 (57)
Could the West Fall Without a Shot Being Fired? 97 (12)
Council on Physical Fitness. President's 105 (114)
Counseling and Genetic Engineering. Genetic 105 (104)
Counseling and Guidance. General 142 (93)
Counseling and Psychotherapy 29 (231)
Counseling and Working With the Aged 181 (289)
Counseling. Child 142 (93)
Counseling Executives 180 (38)
Counseling. Family 180 (88)
Counseling/Family Therapy. Family 181 (287), (310)
Counseling for Attitudes and Values 151 (161)
Counseling for Couples. Sex 29 (252)
Counseling for Single Adults. Sex 29 (252)
Counseling. Genetic 29 (113), (131), (170), 151 (164), 181 (173)
Counseling. Group 142 (93)
Counseling Groups and Techniques. Uses of 151 (161)
Counseling. Guidance and 105 (47), 142 (4), (44)
Counseling. Individual 142 (93)
Counseling/Marital Therapy. Marital 181 (287), (310)
Counseling. Marriage 29 (231), 16 (35)
Counseling Models for Teachers. Carkhuff Learning and 117 (39)
Counseling. Personal 180 (108)
Counseling. Philosophy as a Base for 168 (1)
Counseling. Prenatal Diagnosis of Genetic 151 (165)
Counseling the Nontraditional Student 151 (161)
Counseling With College Students 168 (28)
Counselor. High School 174 (76)
Counselor. Liability and the Guidance 117 (46)
Counselors. Training of 181 (287), (310)
Counter-Revolution 85 (23)
Countries. Love Charms of 29 174 (92)
Countries. Post Disaster Housing in Developing 31 (22)
Countries. Problems of Development in the Less Developed 159 (52)
Country Boy Approach 65 (56)
Country Clubs. Welfare Roles of 117 (53)
Country? What is an Underdeveloped 29 (328)
Country. Yankee 103 (6)
Country's History. Some Other 168 (25)
County Government in Illinois Could be Improved. How 57 (49)
Couples. Sex Counseling for 29 (252)
Courage. How to Live With 75 (1)
Court. Supreme 214 (5), 218, 219 (1)
Courthouses. Louisiana 174 (19)
Courtroom Artist. Life of a 97 (37)
Courts 176 (1)
Courtship of a Civil War Belle. Love and War: The 117 (69)
Craft of Threads. Art and 83 (17)
Craft Pottery. Japanese Folk 57 (44)
Crafts. African Fabric 79 (35)
Crafts. Design - Background for the 79 (82)
Crafts. Design in the Arts and 159 (18)
Crafts. Early American 103 (5)
Crafts. History of Northwest Arts and 218

Crafts in a Museum. Place of 79 (73)
Crafts in America. Contemporary 79 (73)
Crafts. Indian Arts and 79 (56)
Crafts of Ceylon. Arts and 79 (128)
Crafts of the Southern Highlands 79 (51)
Crafts. Pattern in Design and the 79 (108)
Creating the Contemporary From the Traditional 79 (53)
Creating With a Movie Camera 168 (53)
Creating With Media 57 (97)
Creating Your Own Image and Lifestyle 97 (26)
Creative Activities 142 (13)
Creative Canvas Work 79 (127)
Creative Communicating 102 (3)
Creative Crochet and Double Weave 79 (60)
Creative Designing With Concepts or Ideas 79 (98)
Creative Drama: A Basic Skill for Living 159 (54)
Creative Education 180 (150)
Creative Engineering 171 (7)
Creative Fabric Designing 79 (53)
Creative Management 171 (7)
Creative Persuasion 112 (61)
Creative Photography 171 (47)
Creative Playgrounds for Children 223 (29)
Creative Potential in Technical Editing 151 (79)
Creative Process and the Collective Unconscious 154 (6)
Creative Process. Panels on 227 (9)
Creative Selling 65 (46), (47)
Creative Stitchery 79 (82), (127)
Creative Weaving and Wall Hangings 79 (95)
Creative Writing 142 (66), 174 (29)
Creative Writing: A Basic Skill for Living 159 (54)
Creative Writing in the Classroom 57 (79)
Creativity 142 (43)
Creativity. Helping Children to Be More Creative - Ways Parents and Teachers Can Encourage 117 (48)
Creativity in Elementary School Math 181 (105), (150)
Creativity in Music 57 (4)
Credit for Work Experience. Academic 16 (78)
Credit. Speak Up For 48 (1)
Credit. Using 16 (19)
Crete and Mycenae. Archaeology of 227 (45)
Crewel or Contemporary. Stitchery 79 (84)
Cricket and Field Hockey. Introduction to 29 (303)
Crime 176 (37), (61), 180 (194)
Crime and Economic Conditions 174 (70)
Crime and Police. Urban 181 (264)
Crime and Punishment 174 (52), 218
Crime and Science 159 (11)
Crime. Community and Individual Response to 181 (285)
Crime in Society 29 (153), (350)
Crime. Organized 97 (60), 168 (49), 181 (264)
Crime. White Collar 168 (49)
Crimes. How to Protect Yourself Against White Collar 97 (21)
Criminal Information 180 (6)
Criminal Investigations. Nuclear Methods in 151 (156)
Criminal Justice 65 (16), 181 (273)
Criminal Justice Education Through Berks Campus 151 (230)
Criminal Justice Field 181 (220)
Criminal Justice in America 176 (62)
Criminal Justice System 151 (229), (230), 181 (54)
Criminal Justice System. Major Problems in Our 57 (49)
Criminal Law 159 (45), 181 (273)
Criminal Law and Justice 159 (63)
Criminal Procedure 159 (45), 181 (273)
Criminal. Professional 168 (49)
Criminal Related Areas 159 (63)
Crisis and Engineering Control. Energy 214 (29)
Crisis. Angola 54
Crisis. Berlin - the Eternal 57 (75)
Crisis - Blacks Versus Whites. African 97 (50)
Crisis: Challenge to Change 180 (165)
Crisis. Cyprus 171 (6)
Crisis. Educational 54
Crisis. Energy 151 (131), 181 (137), (253)
Crisis. Environmental 52 (59), 54
Crisis - Fact or Fiction. Food 112 (21)
Crisis. Impending Mineral 143 (9)
Crisis in American Education 85 (10), (21)
Crisis? Is There an Energy 54
Crisis. Middle East 217 (4)
Crisis of Faith. Today's 105 (104)
Crisis of Our Time? What is the Moral 85 (12)
Crisis of Our Times. Talent Waste - the Moral 54
Crisis. Panama 151 (83)
Crisis. Product Liability 181 (44)
Crisis. Public Relations in 29 (39)
Crisis: Real and Unreal. Energy 181 (250)
Crisis. United States Energy 143 (8)
Crisis. Writing 16 (34)
Critical Care Nursing 218
Critical Judgments on Art or Morality 105 (66)
Critical Skills for Effective Life Making 57 (71)
Critical Treatment of Women Dramatists in America 29 (146), (309)
Critique on Both Sides of Abortion Legislation 54
Critiques 79 (140)
Crochet 79 (39), (47), (77), (103)
Crochet and Double Weave. Creative 79 (60)
Crochet. Sculptural 79 (127)
Crochet. Structural Design in Free 79 (145)
Crocheted Tapestries and Sculpture 79 (92)
Cross-Cultural Look at Human Sexuality 224 (12)
Cross-Cultural Studies of Drinking Behavior 168 (30)
Cross-Cultural Studies of Stereotypes 105 (102)

Cross-tension Knotting 79 (103)
Crown and the Shadow 112 (88)
Cryogenics 159 (55)
Cryokinetic Therapy in Athletics 56 (76)
Cryonics Movement 216 (118)
Cuba 151 (233)
Cuba and Castro 218
Cuban History 142 (68)
Cuban Literature 216 (135)
Cuban Revolution 151 (195)
Cubes. Color 181 (1), (148)
Cubism - Major Route of Modern Painting, Sculpture and Architecture 56 (10)
Culinary Creativity 136 (17)
Cultivation of Collectors. Care and 102 (19)
Cults. Egyptian Hellenistic 227 (50)
Cultural Adaptations in Saharan Africa. Prehistoric 117 (9)
Cultural and Political Analysis of Mexico 117 (105)
Cultural Biases 216 (37)
Cultural Facts About Pakistan. Social and 29 (19), (181)
Cultural Geography of the U.S.A. Cultural Region and General 151 (184)
Cultural History. United States 142 (80)
Cultural Ideas. Changing Religious - 11 (1)
Cultural Influences on Mental Illness. Social and 214 (65), (86)
Cultural Look at Human Sexuality. Cross- 224 (12)
Cultural Perspective. Aging in Cross 218
Cultural Region and General Cultural Geography of the U.S.A. 151 (184)
Cultural, Social and Economic Aspects of Southeast Asia. Political, 142 (89)
Cultural Studies of Drinking Behavior. Cross- 168 (30)
Cultural Values. Impact of Social Science on 105 (21)
Cultural Values Impact on Business. Changing 151 (48)
Culture 176 (46)
Culture. African Music and 181 (27), (84)
Culture. Afro-American History and 142 (17)
Culture. Afro-Americans and African 56 (2)
Culture. American Indian History, Legends and 79 (126)
Culture. American Literature and 142 (22)
Culture. American Race Track 142 (48)
Culture and Art. Indian 57 (82)
Culture and Civilization. Mexico - 142 (34)
Culture and Civilization of India 181 (333)
Culture and Its Transplantation to the New World. African 151 (218)
Culture and Politics. German 56 (139)
Culture and Society. Japanese 151 (271)
Culture. Aspects of Classical Influences on 227 (32)
Culture. Calendar and 223 (26)
Culture Changes of Modern Hawaiians. Ethnicity and 29 (141), (161), (257), (284)
Culture. Chile - Its History and Its 27 (11)
Culture. Christian Options in a Disintegrating 211 (4)
Culture. Classics and Popular 227 (4)
Culture Conflict in the Classroom 174 (13)
Culture. Contemporary Africa 181 (25), (331)
Culture, Drugs, and Revolution. Youth 54
Culture. East European 29 (127), (213), (290)
Culture. Eskimo Arts and 79 (123)
Culture. Ethnicity and 181 (176), (228)
Culture. European Travel and 151 (297)
Culture. European Travel Relative to Spanish and Italian 151 (300)
Culture. Garden Flowers - Varieties and 117 (5)
Culture in Present-day America. Religion and 85 (12)
Culture. India, Its Religions, Political Systems, and 151 (199)
Culture. Korean 168 (55)
Culture. Language as Living Symbols of a 27 (18)
Culture - Marriage Customs, Holidays and Festivals. Indian 117 (97)
Culture of North American Indians. Life and 79 (124)
Culture of Poverty and Political Culture in Hawaii 29 (141), (161), (257), (284)
Culture. Polish 105 (27)
Culture. Polish Contributions to American and World 105 (27)
Culture. Professional Baseball and American 142 (72)
Culture Shock 117 (138)
Culture. Talks on American 105 (27)
Cultures and Societies. African 29 (7)
Cultures. Women in Other 57 (1)
Cumpolsory Education 218
Cuna Indians of the San Blas Islands and the Mayans of Yucatan. Hammocks as Made By the 79 (25)
Cuna Women - Mola Artists of San Blas 27 (47)
Curmudgeon at Large 97 (1)
Current Affairs in Africa 171 (3)
Current Affairs in People's Republic of China 181 (341)
Current Business Review 29 (81)
Current Economic Situation 151 (37)
Current Events 181 (233), (269)
Current Issues in American Foreign Policy 117 (66), (113)
Current Issues in Education 168 (55)
Current Issues in Mass Media 29 (36), (55), (115)
Current Mathematics Trends and Programs 181 (117)
Current Policy, Future Implications 117 (24)
Current Political Issues 168 (26)
Current Problems in Medical Politics 30 (1)
Current Public Policies and Problems 117 (68), (116)

Current Scene. Orbital View of the 97 (14)
Current State of the Arts 29 (10)
Current State of the Economy. Perspectives on the 168 (43)
Current Statistics on Violent Deaths Among Americans 218
Current Techniques in Nuclear Medicine 218
Current Trends in Decor 225 (15)
Current Trends in Physical Education 216 (110)
Current Trends in Portal Hypertension 181 (190)
Current Trends in Special Education 181 (126)
Curriculum 142 (83)
Curriculum Change. Process of 168 (21)
Curriculum Design 168 (15)
Curriculum Development 142 (21)
Curriculum Development. Systems Analysis in 168 (15)
Curriculum. English 168 (53)
Curriculum for Early Childhood 142 (13)
Curriculum. Organizing the English 57 (48)
Curriculum. Penn State 151 (55)
Curriculum Planning 142 (4)
Curriculum. School 168 (14)
Customs, Holidays and Festivals. Indian Culture - Marriage 117 (97)
Customs in India. Fashions and 56 (119)
Cutaneous Reactions to Cosmetics and Topical Pharmaceutics 54
Cutbacks. Women and the 213 (18)
Cypress Sanctuary - Fisheating Creek. Florida 69 (6)
Cypress Swamp. Hidden Worlds of Florida's Big 69 (6)
Cyprus Crisis 171 (6)
Cyprus Dilemma 56 (124)
Cyprus in Modern Greek Poetry 227 (29)
Czechoslovakia 159 (20)
Czechoslovakia and Ukraine 15 (2)

D

DNA Molecule Research. Recombinant 174 (46)
D.H. Lawrence 29 (207), (243)
Dagger. Dixie Darlings of the Cloak and 57 (96)
Daily Life of the California Indian 29 (165), (339)
Dakar to Timbuctu 59 (9)
Dance 181 (77)
Dance, Bodies and People in Process 181 (82)
Dance. Contemporary 174 (75)
Dance. Disco and Soul 29 (153), (223)
Dance. Education 181 (77)
Dance Education in the Schools 181 (92)
Dance in the American Musical Theater 225 (39)
Dance. Modern 142 (38)
Dancer Preparing for a Career in Musical Comedy 225 (39)
Dance Therapy 218
Dancing. Aerobic 174 (64)
Dancing. Greek Folk 181 (86)
Dangers and Opportunities. Middle East - 85 (29)
Dark Ages. How Dark Were the 54
Dark Continent. Dawn in the 100 (1)
Dark. Farming in the 151 (25)
Darkening Continent 97 (50)
Darlings of the Cloak and Dagger. Dixie 57 (96)
Darwin's Islands 181 (20)
Data Interpretation. Sports Injury Research: 151 (283)
Data Management. Computerized 174 (23)
Data Management Systems 151 (45)
Data on Stock and Bond Markets. Effects of Financial 31 (1)
Data Processing Feasibility 105 (5)
Data Processing in Pre-costing Meals 16 (90)
Data Processing. M.I.S. and 168 (20)
Data Processing. Management of 105 (5)
Data. Quality of Statistical 151 (251)
Data Systems for Higher Education 57 (93)
Dawn in the Dark Continent 100 (1)
Day Care 142 (13)
Day. How to Live on 24 Hours a 216 (76)
Daytime Dramas. What It's Like to be Queen of the 154 (24)
Dead. Bornese Festival aor the 57 (95)
Dead? Is the Sales-person 16 (6)
Deaf Children. Developmental Levels of 159 (25)
Deaf. Communication and the 151 (92)
Dealing With a Newcomer Buyer 65 (29)
Dealing With the F.B.I. On 97 (69)
Dearth. Birth 56 (21)
Death and Dying 57 (8), 105 (92)
Death and Dying. Changing Attitudes Toward 29 (281)
Death and Dying. Psychological Aspects of 214 (77)
Death and Grief 168 (67)
Death. Dignified 29 (281)
Death. Helping Children Deal With 216 (106)
Death in Literature. Love and 105 (16)
Death in Modern and Premodern Societies 29 (281)
Death Investigations. Role of Toxicology in 54
Death. Life After 1 (4), (8)
Death of a Lake. Birth and 181 (133)
Death of English? Will the Public Schools Be the 168 (51)
Death of Liberalism 85 (20), (40)
Death of the Lecture: Using the Personalized System of Instruction in Higher Education 151 (169)
Death of the White Liberal 151 (170)
Death on the Cross. Proofs Concerning Jesus' Survival From 1 (9)
Death - Some Philosophical Considerations. Life After 105 (91)
Death? Why is Everybody Suddenly Interested in 216 (94)

Deaths Among Americans. Current Statistics on Violent 218
Deaths. Narcotic 54
Debate. "Johnny Can't Write" 105 (46)
Debussy and Ravel. Piano Sonority and the Poetic Impulse of 174 (41)
Decade Ahead. National Priorities in the 85 (10)
Decades of College Students. Four 151 (11)
Decanal Roel 151 (256)
Decathlon. What Research Tells Us About the 29 (305)
Decentralized Energy Production 163 (2)
Decision-Making 214 (64)
Decision-Making. ABC's of 135 (5)
Decision Making. Cost and 174 (43)
Decision Making. Parents' Role in Career 151 (88)
Decision-Making. Political 159 (4)
Decision-Making. Practical 168 (11)
Decision-Making. Problem-solving and 168 (17)
Decision Making Process. Family 218
Decision. On Making a Good Academic 151 (104)
Decision. Political 117 (106)
Decisions of the Supreme Court in Constructing the Constitution 54
Declaration of Independence 214 (58)
Declaration of Independence. Meaning of the 85 (13)
Decline of Liberalism and the Rise of Conservatism. New Winds - the 85 (12)
Decline of the Law 159 (8)
Declining Enrollment on Job Security 214 (37)
Decor. Current Trends in 225 (15)
Decorating. Economy in 225 (15)
Decoration. Fabric 79 (45)
Decorative Wall Hangings 79 (143)
Dedicated Dollars 18 (1)
Deep. Man Dives 97 (38)
Deep. Master Hunters of the 69 (10)
Deep Sea Biology 29 (71), (140), (271)
Deep Throat, the Mystery of Watergate 105 (54)
Deer. White Tail 151 (309)
Defects. Birth 181 (163)
Defects. Drug-induced Birth 181 (216)
Defects. Environmental Causes of Birth 218
Defects. Prenatal Detection of Birth 27 (28)
Defects. Prenatal Diagnosis of Genetic 211 (1)
Defense Establishment 54
Defense for Women. Personal 151 (205)
Defense for Women. Self- 174 (64)
Defense Mechanisms. Role Playing and 57 (13)
Defense of the Holy Quran. In 1 (6)
Defense Policies. United States 29 (256), (292)
Defense Spending 54
Defense. Women's Self 62 (1), (2), (3)
Defensively. Art of Driving 174 (12)
Deferred Compensation Plans for Doctors 8 (8)
Deferred. · Dream 97 (5)
Deferred Gift for the University. Planning a 151 (187)
Deficiencies: Need for Remediation. Writing 151 (114)
Defining America - Biblical Themes 159 (1)
Deformities. Correction of Facial 181 (161)
Deformities. Facial 181 (183)
Degree - A Historical Perspective. Associate 151 (2)
Degree. Facing Employment With a College 16 (36)
Degree. Planning Your Own 168 (22)
Degree Programs. Accreditation of Engineering Education 151 (266)
Degree Programs. Competency-based 142 (95)
Degree? What Is a Bachelor's 223 (8)
Dehydrated Food Products, Grain and Other Moisture Measurements in Food Processing. Measurement of Moisture in 67 (21)
Delaware County Campus - Its Mission and History 151 (16)
Delays. Human Costs of Regulatory 31 (30)
Delegation 182 (1 - 3)
Delight - Keynote in Literature for Children 29 (200)
Delightfull Denmark 59 (14)
Delinquency as a Persistent Social Problem. Juvenile 27 (37)
Delivery of Educational Services. Regional 57 (10)
Delivery of Health Care. Issues in the 27 (36)
Delivery System of Government Projects. Incursions Into the Private 30 (1)
Demand. Oil and Gas Industry, Supply and 151 (135)
Demand. Person These Times 75 (1)
Democracy. American Government's Issues and Problems: 117 (104)
Democracy. American Ideas of a Christian Capitalist 180 (183)
Democracy. Ancient Views on the Value of 227 (38)
Democracy. Athenian 227 (38)
Democracy. Future of 85 (18)
Democracy. Leadership in a 117 (65), (112)
Democracy. Mrs. Gandhi and Indian 117 (97)
Democracy. Problems of Constitutional Government and Modern 85 (5)
Democracy. Role of Persuasion in a 117 (65), (112)
Democracy. Struggle for Union 213 (4)
Democracy. Values of Free Speech in a 117 (65), (112)
Democrat. Robert Frost - Individualistic 85 (32)
Democratic Government a Reality or an Alice in Wonderland Fantasy. Is Our Representative 136 (19)
Democratic Management in Business. Experimenting With 27 (1)
Democratic National Committee 223 (23)
Democratic Party 176 (53)
Democratic Revolution. Venezuela: The 151 (213)
Democratic Socialist Ideas. Libertarian Socialist and 181 (288)

Democratic Society. Citizenship in a 168 (42)
Democratic Society. Violence in a 85 (35)
Demographic and Socio-economic Aspects of the Third World 223 (28)
Demography. Ancient History and 227 (37)
Demonstration. Remembering Names - A 105 (13)
Demonstrations and Programs. String Quartet - for School 117 (95)
Demonstrations in Physics and Young and Old. Dramatic 27 (12)
Demystification of Education Technology 181 (110)
Denmark. Delightful 59 (14)
Denmark. Modern 168 (65)
Denmark Study Program. SCS 168 (54)
Density Level and Belt Scale Process Gauges. Nuclear 67 (19)
Dental Education. Research in 181 (114)
Dental Education. Role of Research in 181 (175)
Dental Health Education 218
Dental Materials 105 (28)
Dental Office. Child Management in 105 (30)
Dental Research 181 (175)
Dental Research. Careers in 181 (60)
Dental Research. Stress Analysis in 105 (28)
Dentistry and Health 105 (29)
Dentistry. Anthropology and 151 (208)
Dentistry. Behavioral Sciences in 105 (31)
Dentistry. Children's 181 (157)
Dentistry. Geriatric 181 (174)
Dentistry. Modern Pediatric 105 (30)
Dentistry. Modern Trends in 105 (28)
Dentures. Complete 181 (174)
Dentures. Fractional 181 (174)
Dentures. Implant 181 (174)
Dependence or Automony? Community Economic Development - 151 (49)
Deposit of Social Security Checks. Direct 18 (1)
Deposition of Aquifers and Other Interesting Land-forms. Glacial 136 (13)
Depreciation and Shelter. Tax 61 (65)
Deprogramming. Religious Kidnapping and 12
Deregulating America 102 (14)
Desegregation. Fight for School 213 (2)
Desert Pigs of Arizona 151 (302)
Deserts. Great American 69 (14)
Design 79 (49), (61), (88)
Design and Color 79 (48), (96)
Design and Color. Nature as a Source for 79 (140)
Design and Construction of Airplanes 151 (33)
Design and Corporate Graphics. Packaging 147 (1 - 11)
Design, and Pattern Weaving. Use of Color in Weaving, 79 (24)
Design and Production. Engineer in Automobile 214 (90)
Design and Rug Weaving. Rug 79 (78)
Design, and the Contemporary Scene. Color, 79 (158)
Design and the Crafts. Pattern in 79 (108)
Design and the Textile Arts 79 (95)
Design Approaches to Tapestry 79 (35)
Design - Background for the Crafts 79 (82)
Design. Card Weaving - Techniques and 79 (155)
Design. Color and 79 (75), (76), (106), (134)
Design, Color, and Texture in Weaving 79 (159)
Design Conceptualizing. Liturgical 79 (132)
Design. Costume 79 (109)
Design. Curriculum 168 (15)
Design. Dress 79 (106)
Design. Ecclesiastical 79 (75)
Design. Energy Conservation in Traffic Operations and Highway Design 174 (90)
Design. Ethnic Cloth and Costume as 79 (33)
Design. Floral 117 (7), (126)
Design for Hand Spinners. Yarn 79 (91)
Design for Weavers. Color and 79 (108)
Design for Weaving 79 (118)
Design. Housing 181 (78)
Design. Imagination and Textile 79 (156)
Design in Free Crochet. Structural 79 (145)
Design in Nature and Weaving 79 (132)
Design in San Francisco. Urban 181 (260)
Design in Stitch and Applique 79 (9)
Design in the Arts and Crafts 159 (18)
Design - Inspiration From Nature 79 (82)
Design Inspiration - Nature and Pottery 159 (5)
Design. Interior 168 (69)
Design. Landscape 216 (42)
Design. Library 142 (79)
Design. Multiple Harness Fabric 79 (8)
Design. Neighborhood 181 (78)
Design of an Instant Coffee Plant 214 (42)
Design of Highways. Earthquake Resistant 105 (121)
Design of Weaves. Drafting - Analysis and 79 (78)
Design. Sanitary 67 (18)
Design. Tapestry Weaving, History and 79 (44)
Design, Textiles 79 (89)
Design. Urban 181 (78)
Design Vertically in Weaving. Gaining 79 (94)
Design. Weave 79 (76)
Design, Weave, and Construct a Variety of Chairs, Swings, Hammocks. How to 79 (87)
Design. Weaving as Art in Interior 79 (148)
Design. Work 105 (116)
Design. Yarn 79 (72)
Designer. Interior 164 (1)
Designer. Weaver as 79 (55)
Designer Yarns. Plying, Doubling Cabling Fancy 79 (22)
Designing 79 (39), (117)
Designing an Analog Computer 181 (154)
Designing and Lighting for Theatre. Directing, 159 (62)
Designing and Weaving With Supplementary Warps 79 (38)
Designing Circular Weave Clothing 79 (10)

Designing. Color and Weave Effect Method of 79 (94)
Designing. Creative Fabric 79 (53)
Designing Effective Instruction 57 (76)
Designing Fabrics. Fundamentals of Drafting and 79 (93)
Designing. Fashion 97 (46)
Designing for Textiles 79 (32)
Designing for Theatre and Opera 154 (22)
Designing in Fiber, Yarn, Fabric 79 (146)
Designing Piping Systems 67 (18)
Designing. Theory and 79 (104)
Designing With Concepts or Ideas. Creative 79 (98)
Designing Within a Rectangle 79 (94)
Designs in Guatemalan Weaving 79 (26)
Designs in Weaving. Inca 79 (26)
Destiny? Is Biology Women's 213 (11)
Destiny. Man - His Origin, Purpose, 56 (138)
Detection. Early Oral Cancer 181 (183)
Detection of Art Forgeries. Scientific 151 (73)
Detection of Birth Defects. Prenatal 27 (28)
Detective Fiction 142 (54)
Detente 54
Detentes. European Security and 29 (56), (121), (259)
Developing a Positive Sense of Self Worth 77 (1)
Developing Alternative Funding Sources 57 (10)
Developing Countries. Human Nutrition in 16 (53)
Developing Countries. Post Disaster Housing in 31 (22)
Developing Efficient Breeding Program 216 (80)
Developing Enthusiasm 216 (125)
Developing Good Staff-principal Relations 214 (37)
Developing Moral Reasoning for Children and Professionals 168 (63)
Developing More Effective Campaigns 151 (75)
Developing Nations. Management in 151 (43)
Developing Professional Managers 216 (125)
Developing Reading Centers 142 (30)
Developing Rural Areas. Social Benefits and Costs in 117 (100), (117)
Developing Skill Areas. Instructional Materials for 142 (30)
Developing Your Own Exercise Program. How to Go About 218
Development: A Participative Strategy. Student Leadership 151 (107)
Development. Accounting in Economic 171 (13)
Development: Alleviating World Poverty. Dynamics of International 151 (196)
Development, and Literature. Violin - History, 57 (42)
Development and Placement Service. Career 151 (60)
Development and Renewal. Sacrament of Penance, Its 105 (104)
Development and Subject Matter Concepts. Career 57 (72)
Development and Use of Chinese Alphabet 3 (2)
Development and Utopia. Suburban 223 (14)
Development as a Tapestry Weaver. Woven Image - My 79 (44)
Development Associate Program. Child 174 (31)
Development Association. Child 223 (7)
Development. Budget 151 (9)
Development. Career 142 (44), 174 (62)
Development. Career Change and 181 (49)
Development. Career Education Program 57 (72)
Development. Child 105 (94), 142 (13), (45), (84), 224 (1)
Development. Child Growth and 174 (27)
Development/Choice. Career 216 (101)
Development. Collection 142 (29)
Development. Community 16 (33)
Development. Community and Regional Planning and 16 (54)
Development. Community Resource 16 (12)
Development. Curriculum 142 (21)
Development - Dependence or Autonomy? Community Economic 151 (49)
Development. Drafting and Loom Controlled Pattern 79 (95)
Development. Economic 171 (11), 181 (42)
Development. Economic or Community 16 (7)
Development. Educational Materials 142 (36)
Development. Energy 57 (25)
Development. Exceptional 181 (126)
Development for Women. Career 16 (10)
Development. Human 181 (22)
Development. Human Resources 180 (36)
Development in Co-generation. Research and 150 (9)
Development in Nepal. Educational 29 (18), (100)
Developments in Religion. Recent 56 (137)
Development in Southern Asia. Growth and 56 (123)
Development in the First Year of Life 181 (23)
Development in the Less Developed Countries. Problems of 159 (52)
Development in Young Athletes. Growth and 171 (28)
Development in Young Children. Language 181 (319)
Development. Instructional 168 (15)
Development. Leadership 105 (82), 216 (52)
Development. Management Training and 180 (24)
Development. Mola Blouse - Origin Symbolism and 79 (25)
Development. Moral Judgment 142 (84)
Development. Motor 181 (11)
Development. Neighborhoods, Housing and Community 181 (275)
Development. Normal Gross and Fine Motor 159 (26)
Development. Normal Language 56 (53)

Development. Northern 171 (10)
Development. Nutrition and Mental 218
Development of American Cities. Historical 181 (264)
Development of American Indian Tribes. Legal Status and Economic 218
Development of Instruction. Systematic 216 (10)
Development of Japan and China. Economic 142 (51)
Development of Lasers and Their Application 218
Development of Latin America 223 (17)
Development of Mass Communication 117 (84)
Development of Minority and Underprivileged Children 16 (33)
Development of Post-secondary Education Programs 151 (97)
Development of Speech and Language Skills. Normal 174 (8)
Development of the East Carolina University Campus 56 (27)
Development of the Land Grant Colleges. History and 191 (122)
Development of the University Student 16 (21)
Development of Virginia Tech 216 (17)
Development. Perceptual Motor 159 (26)
Development. Personal 180 (152)
Development. Personality 65 (36)
Development. Problems of Political 151 (189)
Development, Production and Processing of Vegetable Seeds Used in the Food Processing Industry 67 (26), (27)
Development Programs for Black Students at Pre-cominantly White Institutions. Student 105 (39)
Development. Projects and Programs for Community 117 (129)
Development. Psychology of Normal Human Growth and 117 (111)
Development. Reflexive 159 (26)
Development. Role of the Father in Child 105 (103)
Development Services. Penn State's Management 151 (287)
Development. Sex-role 142 (84)
Development. South America - Prospects for 56 (6)
Development. Systems Analysis in Curriculum 168 (15)
Development. Union Growth and 174 (17)
Development. Vocational 216 (52)
Developmental Disabilities 181 (131)
Developmental Levels of Children 159 (25)
Developmental Levels of Deaf Children 159 (25)
Developmental Process in Humans 174 (1)
Developmentally Disabled Infants Learn. Helping 169 (1)
Developmentally Disabled. Planning for the 27 (32)
Developments in Religion. Recent 56 (137)
Developments. Latest Energy 151 (125)
Developments of Point Defiance Park - The People Speak. Future 159 (34)
Developments. Residential 65 (27)
Developments. Tennis-oriented 65 (27)
Deviance - Society's Whipping Boy 29 (282)
Deviant Behavior 174 (42)
Deviation. Psychology of Sexual 105 (100)
Devices. New Radiological Imaging 181 (198)
Devices. Water Conservation With Water-saving 151 (304)
Devices. Weaving on Small 79 (3)
Devonshire. Extant Wood Screens in 151 (26)
Diabetic Ischemic 181 (190)
Diabetic Retinopathy. Electric Signs of 31 (24)
Diabolical Duo: Ambrose Bierce and Mark Twain 151 (243)
Diagnosis and Evaluation of Gifted Children 181 (105)
Diagnosis and Treatment of Reading Disabilities 142 (21)
Diagnosis of Genetic Counseling. Prenatal 151 (165)
Diagnosis of Genetic Defects. Prenatal 211 (1)
Diagnosis of Renal Masses 181 (171)
Diagnosis. Prenatal 181 (173)
Diagnosis. Prenatal Genetic 181 (167)
Diagnostic Approach to the Teaching of Reading. Using the 117 (36)
Diagnostics. Drug Induced Modification of 54
Dial (A Screening Test) 142 (59)
Dialectical Differences in Children 56 (53)
Dialects 142 (2)
Dialects in the World. Spanish 29 (208)
Dialects. Social 181 (218), (314)
Dialogue. Jewish-Christian 181 (306)
Dialogue. Science Religion 29 (241), (275)
Diamonds, Ecology and Conservation 143 (15)
Diamonds Fund. Four 151 (186)
Diary. Nepal Photo 4 (2)
Dickens. Charles 181 (147)
Dickerson's Washington. Nancy 102 (5)
Did Lincoln Aides Abet His Assassin? 29 (338)
Did You Know That...? 117 (124)
Diet. Behavior and 113 (3)
Diet Therapy for Sick People 117 (94)
Diet. Nutrition and 181 (166)
Dietary Fiber - Essential Nutrient? 216 (134)
Dietetic Education 216 (5)
Difference. Effective Guidance Does Make a 54
Differences in Ancient and Modern Olympic Games 151 (275)
Differences in Children. Dialectical 56 (53)
Differences in Normal and Cancer Cells 31 (6)
Different. Equal But 102 (23)
Different. Teaching the Culturally 57 (85)
Different Worlds: United States and Soviet Education Compared. Two 159 (35)
Difficult Job. Parenting, A 57 (34)
Difficulties in Adults. Speech and Language 56 (53)
Difficulties in Children. Reading 181 (107)
Difficulties. Preventing Reading 171 (19)

Dignified Death 29 (281)
Dimensional Fiber Forms 79 (33)
Dimensional Macrame. Three- 79 (86)
Dimensional Tapestries. Stuffed/Quilted 3- 79 (137)
Dimensional Tapestry Using Double Weave 79 (119)
Dimensional Weaving. Three- 79 (17)
Dimensions of Communication. Four 56 (56)
Dinner Assignments. Inspirational and After 65 (60)
Diplomats Are Doing and Why. Foreign Affairs: What the 151 (110)
Dipping. Candle 79 (101)
Direct Deposit of Social Security Checks 18 (1)
Direct Response Marketing of Insurance 127 (1)
Directing 174 (48)
Directing, Designing and Lighting for Theatre 159 (62)
Directing Economic Activity. Role of Open Markets in Coordinating and 85 (2)
Directing Theatre Groups 142 (74)
Direction of Higher Education 168 (50)
Direction. Scriptural 105 (105)
Directions. Energy Trends and 29 (81)
Directions in America. Changing Trends and 117 (100)
Directions in Continuing Education. New 171 (18)
Directions in Early Childhood Education 151 (91)
Directions in Language Study. New 181 (315)
Disabilities. Developmental 181 (313)
Disabilities. Diagnosis and Treatment of Reading 142 (21)
Disabilities - Fact or Fancy? Learning 151 (100)
Disabilities. Learning 117 (131), 142 (59), 171 (20)
Disability. Helping the Family Adapt To a 159 (31)
Disability. Reading 181 (121)
Disabled Infants Learn. Helping Developmentally 169 (1)
Disabled. Planning for the Developmentally 27 (32)
Disabled Populations 181 (126)
Disabled. Sexuality of the 181 (165)
Disabled. Understanding Affirmative Action for the 151 (1)
Disadvantaged College Student. Older, 181 (201), (308)
Disadvantaged. Education of the 56 (42)
Disadvantaged. Mainstreaming the 181 (104)
Disadvantaged Pupil. Teaching the 174 (1)
Disadvantaged. Teaching the 216 (28)
Disarmament, and Security. Arms, 56 (103)
Disarmament. Arms Control and 85 (28)
Disarmament. Nuclear 214 (83)
Disarmament. Peace and 172 (6)
Disaster. Drug Abuse and 112 (82)
Disaster Housing in Developing Countries. Post 31 (22)
Disaster or Opportunity? Divorce: 29 (150), (244)
Disaster Public Relations 29 (39)
Discharge. Hospital 218
Discipline, and Parents. Children, 151 (172)
Discipline, Cohabitation, Patterns of Family Interaction. Child 56 (7)
Discipline in the School Setting 117 (58)
Discipline Problems - Effective Ways Parents Can Deal With and Understand Young Children. Positive Approach to 117 (48)
Discipline. Realistic and Humanistic Approach to Classroom 117 (51)
Disclosure. Art of 57 (41)
Disclosure Myth. Full 85 (19)
Disco and Soul Dance 29 (153), (223)
Discovering Single Blessedness 151 (11)
Discovering the Child 181 (292)
Discovery of America. My 97 (40)
Discovery of Soloman Gold Mines 1 (9)
Discovery. Search and 181 (124)
Discovery. Thrill of 143 (1)
Discrimination, A Universal Imperative 85 (38)
Discrimination Against the Older Worker 142 (71)
Discrimination. Economics of 181 (46)
Discretion in Our System of Justice 151 (229)
Discrimination. Subtleties of Sex 159 (60)
Discussion of Personal Art Work 117 (10)
Discussion Techniques 142 (25)
Disease. Anaerobic Bacteria in 56 (78)
Disease. Biology of Veneral 29 (172), (267)
Disease in Children. Kidney 181 (158)
Disease. Mental Retardation as a Social 159 (43)
Disease. Occupational Lung 181 (156)
Disease. Stress in Health and 216 (24)
Diseased States. Structure of Brain in 181 (169)
Diseases and Man. Common Plant 117 (13)
Diseases and the Resultant Food Loss. Animal 16 (45)
Diseases. Respiratory 181 (156)
Diseases. Rheumatic 181 (160)
Disenfranchized. Sexually 168 (4)
Disinfection. Hospital 168 (29)
Disintegrating Culture. Christian Options in a 211 (4)
Disneyland: Entertainment or a New American Religion? 159 (51)
Disobedience. Civil 151 (235), 214 (17)
Disorders. Child Language 181 (314)
Disorders. Hearing 56 (55), 151 (96)
Disorders in Children. Language and Speech 56 (53)
Disorders in Public Schools. Management of Speech 56 (55)
Disorders of the Aged. Hearing 151 (96)
Disorders. Psychosomatic 105 (100)
Disorders. Speech and Hearing 56 (55)
Disorders. Speech and Language 16 (67)
Disorganization. Reasons for 225 (29)
Disposal. Nuclear Waste 31 (30)
Disposal of Nuclear Power Plant Waste 151 (128)
Dispute Settlement in Employment. Methods of 223 (6)

Dissemination of Information 29 (41)
Dissent and the Intellectual 85 (20)
Dissent, and the Intellectual. Alienation, 85 (12)
Dissidents. Visit With Soviet 27 (42)
Dissonance Restated. Consumeriam - Cognitive 117 (16)
Distaffs 79 (22)
Distaffs From Greece, Turkey, and Yugoslavia. Primitive Spinners - Spindles and/or 79 (20)
Distinguishing Features of American Higher Education 151 (103)
Distributing of Income. Income Tax and the 151 (166)
Distribution - A Vital Link for Education 132 (7)
Distribution System. Planning the 150 (12)
Distribution Trends of America's Population 151 (184)
Distributive Education 181 (38), (55), (61), (115)
Distributor Does It All. Your School 132 (6)
Disturbed Child and Family. Emotionally 16 (35)
Disturbed Child. How to Create a 57 (41)
Dive on Cobb Seamount. Research Submarine 223 (37)
Dive Trip. Baja California 29 (302), (316)
Divergent Thinging 142 (43)
Diversity and Political Life. Genetic 181 (24)
Dives Deep. Man 97 (38)
Diving. Coaching of 181 (2)
Diving. Scuba 142 (31), 181 (5)
Diving. Skin 218
Diving. Wreck 29 (138), (302)
Division Research and Cancer. Cell 218
Division. Resources of the Extension 216 (70)
Divorce and Remarriage 105 (76)
Divorce: Disaster or Opportunity? 29 (150), (244)
Dixie Darlings of the Cloak and Dagger 57 (96)
Dizziness 27 (31)
Do Colleges Educate? 168 (18)
Do Engineers Make Good Managers? 151 (45)
Do Students Still Need Private Philanthropy? 151 (89)
Do You Have What It Takes to be a Teacher? 168 (38)
Do You Hear Me? 151 (57), (82)
Do You Mean to Tell Me You Are Still Smoking? 151 (83)
Do You Really Want Cheap Meat? 151 (175)
Do You Want to Know About Latin America 117 (103)
Doctor. Professional Corporations and the 8 (9)
Doctors and Their Spouses. Estate Planning for 8 (5)
Doctors. Deferred Compensation Plans for 8 (8)
Doctors. Early and Current Economic Education of Young 8 (3)
Doctors. Estate Planning for 8 (10)
Doctors to Get Involved in Politics. Need for 8 (7)
Doctrine and Equal Time. Fairness 117 (84)
Doctrine. Broadcasting's Fairness 117 (86), (129)
Doctrine of the Mormon Church. History and 56 (138)
Documentaries. Presidential 135 (12)
Does Nature Obey Mathematical Laws? 56 (129)
Does the New Left Represent "The Greening of America"? 85 (8)
Dog Obedience 142 (26)
Dog Story. King of the Shaggy 112 (62)
Doing Business in Saudi Arabia 3 (4), 210 (2)
Doing Theology in the Parish 105 (106)
Dollar. Bank Marketing Storing and Selling 3 (3)
Dollar Continues to Buy Less - With or Without Wage - Price Controls. Why Your 85 (26)
Dollar. International Role of the 214 (32)
Dollar. Stretching Your Food 57 (15)
Dollars. Dedicated 18 (1)
Dollars for Scholars 151 (89)
Dollars. From Lettuce Seed to Fifty Million 151 (185)
Domestic Airline Industry. United States 151 (290)
Domestic and Foreign Levels. Role of Trademarks in Advertising and Marketing on 209
Domestic Issues 220 (3)
Dominican Crisis 105 (54)
Don Juan in Western Literature. Character of 151 (233)
Don't Blame the Mass Media 29 (42), (67), (312)
Don't Eat Your Neighbor's Salad 151 (61)
Don't Flunk the Teacher 112 (76)
Don't Just Stand There - Worry 112 (115)
Don't Let the Bugs Get the Best of You 136 (25)
Don't Take Yourself Too Seriously 57 (96)
Doomsdayers. Making Sense of the 54
Doors. Opening the 144
Dory. Grand Canyon by 69 (8)
Dosage Forms. Prolonged Release 54
Dostoevsky's Grand Inquisitor, Slavery and Freedom 85 (36)
Double and Quadruple Weaves 79 (138)
Double Cloth. Cloth Structure, 79 (6)
Double Cloths 79 (21)
Double Gang Weaving on Eight Harnesses 79 (132)
Double, Multilayered Weaves 79 (118)
Double Weave 79 (30), (48), (62), (63), (65), (77), (84), (104), (113), (139), (140), (145)
Double Weave and Hand Manipulated Double Weave Tapestry 79 (69)
Double Weave. Creative Crochet and 79 (60)
Double Weave. Dimensional Tapestry Using 79 (119)
Double Weave - Four Harness Tapestry 79 (74)
Double Weave Tapestry. Double Weave and Hand Manipulated 79 (69)
Double Weave With Weighted Warps 79 (13)
Double Weaves, Samplers, and Tapestry 79 (7)
Doubles and Singles Strategy in Tennis 29 (305)
Doubling, Cabling, Fancy Designer Yarns. Plying, 79 (22)
Doubt. Management by 171 (7)
Doups. Leno Weaves Using 79 (24)
Down to Earth 143 (4)

Downs of Weight Control. Ups and Downs 57 (30)
Dracula Meets the New Woman 117 (89)
Draft. Profile 79 (23)
Draft Versus An All Volunteer Armed Force 85 (1)
Drafting 79 (63), (81)
Drafting - Analysis and Design of Weaves 79 (78)
Drafting and Designing Fabrics. Fundamentals of 79 (93)
Drafting and Loom Controlled Pattern Development 79 (95)
Drafting for Creative Insight 79 (55)
Drafting for Four-Harness Looms. Pattern 79 (122)
Drafting for Multi-harness Looms. Pattern 79 (122)
Drafting). Have You Tried This? (Name 79 (23)
Drafting. Introduction to Weaving and 79 (64)
Drafting Methods 79 (64)
Drafting. 3-D 79 (104)
Drainage. Acid Mine 151 (154)
Drama 142 (74)
Drama: A Basic Skill for Living. Creative 159 (54)
Drama as a Sermonic Atlernative to Monologue Preaching 168 (34)
Drama. Classical Greek 181 (81), (139)
Drama. Contemporary Themes in 54
Drama. Euripidean 227 (39)
Drama. German 214 (66)
Drama. Greek 227 (19)
Drama. Music 218
Drama. New Stars of British 57 (23)
Drama of Nuptse 69 (5)
Drama. Structuralist Approaches to 227 (25)
Drama. Women in Greek 227 (48)
Dramas. What It's Like to be Queen of the Daytime 154 (24)
Dramatic Demonstrations in Physics for Young and Old 27 (12)
Dramatic Hero in the 20th Century 216 (32)
Dramatic Readings 159 (27)
Dramatist as Filmwriter. Walter Hasenclever: The 214 (66)
Dramatists in America. Critical Treatment of Women 29 (146), (309)
Drawdowns 79 (63)
Drawing. Technical and Conceptual Approaches to 117 (11)
Drawing: Universal Graphic Language. Technical 117 (82)
Dream Deferred 97 (5)
Dream...In Politics, Poetry and Humor. American 97 (9)
Dream. In Pursuit of a 144
Dream. Mechanisms of the Brain. Sleep and 159 (68)
Dream of a Utopia in Government Structure 85 (11)
Dreaming. Psychology of 151 (169)
Dreaming. Psychology of Dreams and 224 (14)
Dreams and Dreaming. Psychology of 224 (14)
Dreams. Impossible 112 (27)
Dress Better for Less Money. How to 229 (1)
Dress Design 79 (106)
Dress - Historical, Folk, and Traditional. Psychology of Clothing and 79 (28)
Dress. Nigerian and African 79 (37)
Dress of Mayan Indians of Guatemala - Historical Interpretation and Future of the Tradition. Contemporary National 79 (83)
Drilling and Production. Oil and Gas Industry - 151 (135)
Drilling Business? Now That You Can Run a Drilling Rig, Can You Run a 136 (7)
Drilling Contractors. Safety Program For 136 (2)
Drilling Industry. Mathematics of the Well 136 (3)
Drilling. Offshore 74
Drilling Regulations in Plain Talk. Your State's 136 (26)
Drilling Rig, Can You Run a Drilling Business? Now That You Can Run a 136 (7)
Drinking 113 (2)
Drinking. Alcoholism and Social 218
Drinking Behavior, and College Students. Alcohol, 151 (212)
Drinking Behavior. Cross-Cultural Studies of 168 (30)
Drinking From Old Wells 75 (1)
Drinking Water. Earthy Odors in 16 (85)
Drive Systems. Fluid 67 (23)
Driving Defensively. Art of 174 (12)
Driving. Smith System of 189
Driving Task. Alcohol and the 174 (12)
Drop Spindle. Wool Spinning on 79 (59)
Drug Abuse 16 (13), 54, 56 (83), 88 (1), 142 (69)
Drug Abuse - A Course for Parents and Teachers 56 (83)
Drug Abuse and Alcoholism. Patient Records in 181 (177)
Drug Abuse and Disaster 112 (82)
Drug Abuse. Medical Professionals in 88 (1)
Drug Abuse Prevention 16 (84)
Drug Abuse. Preventive Approaches to Alcohol and 105 (88)
Drug Abuse. Psychology of 105 (100)
Drug Abuser? Are You a 181 (186), (236)
Drug Addiction - The Physiological and Pharmacological Aspects 54
Drug and Alcohol Abuse 151 (161)
Drug Blood Levels 54
Drug Induced Birth Defects 181 (216)
Drug Induced Modification of Diagnostics 54
Drug Interactions. Prescription 54
Drug Misuse and Abuse, More and More Leisure 56 (81)
Drug Problems in Organizations 105 (84)
Drug Reactions. Patient Susceptibility to Adverse 54
Drug Scene 57 (69)
Drug Security. Hospital 88 (1)

Drug Treatment of the Mentally Retarded 181 (164)
Drug Use, Abuse 168 (29)
Drug Use and Abuse 57 (69)
Drugs 113 (2), 142 (44), 214 (83)
Drugs and Athletics, Uses and Abuses 56 (76)
Drugs and Food. Interactions Between 54
Drugs, and Revolution. Youth Culture, 54
Drugs. How to Talk to Your Child About 181 (186)
Drugs in Society 29 (171)
Drugs in Sports 151 (283)
Drugs. Misuse of 181 (216)
Drugs of Abuse. Alcohol and 171 (53)
Drugs of Abuse and Their Action 181 (159), (212)
Drugs. Psychotropic 218
Drugs. Talk to Your Child About 181 (236)
Duchin. Musical World of Peter 102 (7)
Duckling. Music is No Ugly 214 (67)
Duo: Ambrose Bierce and Mark Twain. Diabolical 151 (243)
Duquesne Tamburitzan Institute of Folk Art 54
Duquesne University and Alumni on the Pittsburgh Area. Impact of 54
Duquesne University Tamburitzans 54
Dutch. Holland and the Amazing 59 (14)
Dutch: Land of the Hex Sign. Pennsylvania 117 (75)
Duties and Responsibilities of Boards of Education. Legal 57 (55)
Dwellings and Small Businesses. Self-Sufficient Energy Systems for Rural and Urban 163 (2)
Dwellings. Integrated Energy 163 (2)
Dye. Commercial 79 (36)
Dye Experimentation With Mordants. Innovative Natural 79 (156)
Dye Painting. Batik, 79 (79)
Dye Plants. Navajo Carding and Spinning Along With Rugs and Navajo 79 (61)
Dye Techniques 79 (33)
Dye Theory 79 (36)
Dye. Tie- 79 (129)
Dyeing 79 (13), (36)
Dyeing. Ancient and Modern Southwest Indian Spinning, 79 (76)
Dyeing and Spinning Techniques. Innovative 79 (109)
Dyeing as an Art Form. Textile Printing and 79 (129)
Dyeing. Color Theory and Yarn 79 (78)
Dyeing. Early American 79 (111)
Dyeing for Weavers 79 (130)
Dyeing. Handspinning and Chemical 79 (19)
Dyeing. Indigo 79 (14)
Dyeing. Indigo Natural 79 (36)
Dyeing. Natural 79 (85), (101), (107)
Dyeing. Natural Lichen 79 (156)
Dyeing of Wool. Spinning and Natural 79 (54)
Dyeing, Soft Art. Shaker Textiles, 79 (46)
Dyeing. Soft Skins 79 (152)
Dyeing. Spinning and Natural 79 (144)
Dyeing. Spinning and Vegetable 79 (15)
Dyeing Techniques. Combined Resist 79 (108)
Dyeing. Vegetable 79 (20), (34)
Dyeing, Weaving, Sheep Raising. Spinning, 79 (12)
Dyeing. Weaving, Spinning and 79 (43)
Dyeing With Natural Dyes 79 (89)
Dyeing Wool With Natural Materials 79 (149)
Dyes and Pigments 79 (129)
Dyes. Dyeing With Natural 79 (89)
Dyes for the Handcraft Person. Batik, Tie-Dye, Commercial 79 (14)
Dyes for Wool. Acid 79 (102), (141)
Dyes, Fragrances, Culinary. Herbs for 79 (111)
Dyes. Ikat, Shibori, and Tritik, Using Commercial 79 (144)
Dyes. Man Made 79 (108)
Dyes. Natural 79 (50)
Dyes, Quilting, Spinning. Natural 79 (58)
Dying. Changing Attitudes Toward Death and 29 (281)
Dying. Death and 57 (8), 105 (92)
Dying. On Aging and 142 (62)
Dying. Process of 31 (20)
Dying. Psychological Aspects of Death and 214 (77)
Dynamics. Group 142 (73), 174 (32), 189
Dynamics of International Development: Alleviating World Poverty 151 (196)
Dynamics of Management 224 (2)
Dynamics of Value Change 216 (95)
Dynamics of Weight Control 105 (81)
Dynamics. Perception 225 (18)
Dysfunction. Understanding Sexual 29 (250)

E

ERA. Working Women and the 213 (18)
ESL - An Essential Component in Bilingual Education 29 (297)
ESP 112 (66), 168 (47), 180 (84), (131), 218
ESP and You 154 (12)
ESP Through the Tarot 117 (96)
Eagle - National Symbol. Bald 4 (4)
Earl Long and Louisiana Education 174 (38)
Earliest American Fiction 151 (237)
Early American Children's Books 174 (18)
Early American Crafts 103 (5)
Early American Dyeing 79 (111)
Early American Medicine 151 (257)
Early American Presidents 142 (63)
Early and Current Economic Education of Young Doctors 8 (3)
Early Childhood Education 56 (57), 171 (17), (31)
Early Childhood Education in Art, Music and Children's Literature 142 (30)

LECTURE TITLES AND KEYWORD INDEX

Early Education and Intervention 142 (45)
Early French Gothic Art 151 (28)
Early Greek Lyric Poetry and Philosophy 227 (46)
Early Irish Christian Art 181 (79)
Early Oral Cancer Detection 181 (183)
Early Pagan Celtic Art 181 (79)
Early Photography in Eastern Europe 151 (73)
Earner Families - How They Spend and Save. Two 151 (166)
Ears. Goldmine Between Your 135 (57)
Earth. Brief Introduction to the History of the 136 (15)
Earth. Down to 143 (4)
Earth. European Travel of the Type That is Close to the 218
Earth Fibers 79 (152)
Earth. Handful of 56 (62)
Earth. Mission to 57 (22)
Earth. Plate Tectonics and Our Restless 142 (88)
Earth Resources 154 (17)
Earth Resources. Remote Sensing of 151 (139)
Earthquake Resistant Design of Highways 105 (121)
Earthquakes 29 (152), (276)
Earthquakes and the Prediction 142 (88)
Earthquakes in the Southeastern United States 216 (8)
Earthquakes in Virginia 216 (8)
Earthquakes - Prediction, Control, and Nuclear Power Plants. Energy and Petroleum Resources, 27 (4)
Earth's Interior 159 (20)
Earthy Odors in Drinking Water 16 (85)
Easel. Pull Up An 97 (23)
East Africa 174 (36), (82), (91)
East Africa. Biologist in 181 (18), (340)
East Africa. Wildlife and Game Preserves of 117 (142)
East African Safari 223 (36)
East African Wildlife 218
East. Ancient New 29 (217), (226)
East and South Africa 223 (36)
East and South Asia. Middle 142 (41)
East and West 105 (20)
East and West Can Meet 97 (58)
East Asia Today. South 85 (29)
East. Big Power Confrontation in the Middle 85 (31)
East Carolina University Campus. Development of the 56 (27)
East Carolina University on Business in Greenville, North Carolina. Economic Impact of Students of 56 (24)
East Central Illinois. What the Music Department Has to Offer 57 (40)
East Checkerboard. Middle 29 (215), (224)
East Conflicts. Middle 29 (217)
East Conflict. Terrorism in the Middle 181 (345)
East Crisis. Middle 217 (4)
East. Current Situation in the Middle 151 (194)
East - Dangers and Opportunities. Middle 85 (29)
East Europe. Political and Social History in Communist 218
East European Culture 29 (127), (213), (290)
East. Geography of the Middle 117 (63)
East. Geopolitics of the Middle 214 (55)
East. Government and Politics of the Middle 117 (104)
East. How to Achieve Peace in the Middle 57 (61)
East in the United States Energy Picture. Middle 56 (15)
East in War and Peace. Middle 181 (339)
East. Issues in the Middle 54
East. Middle 142 (23), 175 (1), (4)
East? Peace in the Middle 214 (55)
East. Politics of the Middle 174 (59)
East Problems and the U.S.A. Middle 151 (291)
East Revisited. Far 97 (52)
East. Role of the United Nations in the Middle 102 (28)
East. Social Change in the Middle 56 (6)
East. Soviet Strategy in the Middle 85 (31)
East Studies at Penn State. Middle 151 (194)
East to West. Quilting, 79 (120)
East Today. Problems of the Middle 223 (21)
East. Travel in the Middle 29 (163), (218), (228), (319)
East Unveiled. Middle 100 (1)
East-West Relations 57 (75)
East. Women in the Middle 223 (19)
Eastern Archaeology. Near 29 (226), (269)
Eastern Conflicts. Middle 29 (179), (226)
Eastern Europe. Early Photography in 151 (73)
Eastern Europe. Politics in 54
Eastern Europe Today 56 (112)
Eastern Europe Today. Opposition Currents in the Soviet Union and 213 (13)
Eastern Illinois University. Alumni and 57 (91)
Eastern North Carolina. Environmental Services in 56 (25)
Eastern North Carolina. History of Recreation, Physical Education, and Leisure Activities in 56 (28)
Eastern North Carolina. Railroad Travel in 56 (35)
Eastern North Carolina - The Year 2000 56 (36), (38)
Eastern North Carolina Waterways. Future of 56 (29)
Eastern North Carolina's Relative Location 56 (36), (38)
Eastern North Carolinians. Religious Roots of 56 (32)
Eating Low on the Food Chain 181 (184)
Eccentrics. Great American 102 (25)
Ecclesiastical Authority 105 (104)
Ecclesiastical Design 79 (75)
Ecclesiastical Vestments 79 (125)
Ecclesiastical Weaving 79 (81)

Echocardiography 27 (34)
Ecletic Enrollment Projection Model 57 (93)
Ecological Problems in North Carolina 56 (66)
Ecological Problems. Ways Mathematics Can Help With 31 (21)
Ecological Questions. Modern 54
Ecology 181 (31)
Ecology and Conservation. Diamonds, 143 (15)
Ecology, and Ocean Wealth. Peace, 214 (27)
Ecology. Business and 105 (6)
Ecology. Human 54
Ecology. Microbial 159 (49)
Ecology of North America 117 (30)
Ecology. Politics 29 (47), (69), (132), (266)
Ecology. Property and 29 (74), (195)
Economic Activity. Role of Open Markets in Coordinating and Directing 85 (2)
Economic Aid. Foreign 56 (17)
Economic Analysis of Large Corporations 85 (19)
Economic and Political Aspects of India 142 (81)
Economic Aspects of Pollution 117 (35)
Economic Aspects of Southeast Asia. Political, Cultural, Social and 142 (89)
Economic Aspects of the Energy Crisis 117 (35)
Economic Aspects of the Third World. Demographic and Socio- 223 (28)
Economic Choices, and Coal Beneficiation. Energy Needs, 151 (134)
Economic Concepts. Basic 23
Economic Conditions 16 (76)
Economic Conditions. Crime and 174 (70)
Economic Conditions. General 214 (34)
Economic Crises 151 (49)
Economic Development 171 (11), 181 (42)
Economic Development. Accounting in 171 (13)
Economic Development - Dependence or Autonomy? 151 (49)
Economic Development of American Indian Tribes. Legal Status and 218
Economic Development of Japan and China 142 (51)
Economic Education 168 (45)
Economic Education of Young Doctors. Early and Current 8 (3)
Economic Forecast 29 (81)
Economic Forecast. California 29 (81)
Economic Forecasting 181 (48)
Economic Freedom 175 (5)
Economic Freedom and Civil Liberty 174 (72)
Economic Growth 174 (70)
Economic Growth. Environmental Quality and the Problem of 29 (73), (79), (260)
Economic Impact of Students of East Carolina University on Business in Greenville, North Carolina 56 (24)
Economic Issues. National 151 (42)
Economic Life. Tourists's View of Soviet 223 (33)
Economic Literacy 117 (17), (40)
Economic Motivations 181 (42)
Economic or Community Development 16 (7)
Economic Order. New International 57 (61)
Economic Outlook 65 (1), 102 (31), 117 (23)
Economic Planning. Central 105 (32)
Economic Policy 159 (64), 220 (7)
Economic Policy. Government 117 (26)
Economic Policy. National 174 (70)
Economic Problems of India and Pakistan. Social and 56 (118)
Economic Relationships 159 (52)
Economic Security and Public Policy 181 (42)
Economic Shortages 54
Economic Situation. Current 151 (37)
Economic Situation. International 57 (61)
Economic Status of Women in the Home 90 (1)
Economic Systems. Comparative 117 (23, 142 (51)
Economic Systems. Prices and Production in Variant 85 (14)
Economics 142 (71), 174 (63), 176 (2), (54), 180 (62), (121), 214 (35)
Economics, Affluence, Technology). Pollution is Great (Growth, Resources, 151 (225)
Economics. Agricultural 117 (6)
Economics and Business. Government Regulations in 54
Economics and Environmental Quality Control 168 (43)
Economics and Had the Sense Not to Ask. More Than You Ever Wanted to Know About 105 (32)
Economics and Politics of Government Regulation of Business 85 (19)
Economics and Politics of Local Government 54
Economics and Statistics 214 (33)
Economics, and the Welfare State. Paternalism, 85 (14)
Economics and Trade. International 138 (1)
Economics and Urban Policy. Social Problems in 85 (1)
Economics. Careers in Home 216 (139)
Economics. Commodities in 180 (29)
Economics. Conceptual Problems in 181 (42)
Economics. Consumer 142 (51)
Economics Education. Home 216 (49)
Economics. Energy 174 (70)
Economics. Environmental 218
Economics. Home 176 (31)
Economics in One Easy Lesson 151 (50)
Economics. International 54, 117 (23), 142 (51)
Economics. Kelsonian 181 (39)
Economics of Discrimination 181 (46)
Economics of Education 117 (47)
Economics of Environmental Quality 117 (34)
Economics of Minimal Government 105 (32)
Economics of Pro and College Sports 54
Economics of Racism and Poverty 168 (41)
Economics of Real Estate 65 (4), (14), (15), (18), (19), (34), (50), (51), (54), (56), (58), (59), (62), (65), (66), (67), (69)
Economics of Recycling 216 (77)

Economics of Regional Planning 168 (43)
Economics of Revolution 85 (34)
Economics of Rights - Property and Personal 85 (14)
Economics of Scale and Choice of Technology 151 (134)
Economics of ---. Simple 105 (32)
Economics of Taxes 54
Economics of the Arab World. Politics 57 (61)
Economics of Union Electric's Operations 189
Economics. Race and 175 (3)
Economics. Trends in Home 117 (78)
Economies. Contributions of the Chemical Industry to Midwestern United States 34 (1)
Economy 97 (68), 135 (24), (55)
Economy Affects Your Future. How Today's 97 (68), 135 (39)
Economy? Can Government Stabilize the 85 (22)
Economy. Function of Consumers in Our 168 (45)
Economy. Government Expenditures and the 54
Economy. Government Policy and the 16 (37)
Economy. How Industries Affect Hawaii's 23
Economy in Decorating 225 (15)
Economy. Investments and Today's 16 (79)
Economy. Long Run Outlook for the American 85 (30)
Economy. Managing a Personal Budget in Today's 16 (19)
Economy. National 117 (22)
Economy. National United States 65 (35)
Economy. North Carolina's Changing Position in the Tobacco 56 (18)
Economy of the Medical Profession. Political 85 (14)
Economy of the People's Republic of China 216 (74)
Economy of the Soviet Union 216 (74)
Economy on Work and Play. Effects of the 142 (78)
Economy Over the Next Five Years 102 (3)
Economy. Perspectives on the Current State of the 168 (43)
Economy. Post-Election 97 (10)
Economy. Profits and Their Importance to the 34 (1)
Economy. Science in the 171 (34)
Economy. Significance of Agriculture and Agri-business on the 16 (91)
Economy. Smoke in the Air Isn't Good for the 54
Economy. State of the 174 (17), (63)
Economy Today. American 117 (24)
Economy. Tourism in British Columbia's 171 (13)
Ecosystem. Forest 218
Ecosystems. Interactions Between Man and Natural 218
Edgar Allan Poe. Mystery of 151 (237)
Edibility of Wild Plants. Folklore and 57 (82)
Edible Fungi 151 (176)
Edith Wharton: American Woman Novelist 151 (238)
Editing. Creative Potential in Technical 151 (79)
Editing, Ethics. Newspapers, Reporting, 151 (68)
Editing Scholarly Works 174 (19)
Editor. Elizabeth Timothy - America's First 56 (61)
Editor's Perspective. Concept to Bookshelf: 151 (79)
Edmund Burke and Revolution 85 (32)
Edmund Burke's Conception of History 85 (32)
Educate? Do Colleges 168 (18)
Educating Christians 211 (4)
Educating for the Future 216 (125)
Educating Hearing Impaired 151 (113)
Educating the Adolescent With Special Problems 142 (61)
Education 29 (91), 117 (54), 176 (16)
Education Abroad 151 (111)
Education. Acadian 174 (14)
Education. Accounting 214 (2)
Education Activities. Physical 151 (278)
Education. Adult 105 (34), 142 (95), 151 (98), 171 (15), 181 (111)
Education. Adult and Non-traditional 142 (33)
Education. Adult-Continuing 57 (26)
Education. Aesthetic 142 (30)
Education. Agricultural 216 (22)
Education. Alcohol 56 (82)
Education. Alternative 57 (85), 218
Education Amendment of 1972 181 (6)
Education. American Indian 29 (87)
Education and Athletics. Physical 159 (47)
Education and Board Education Programs 65 (43)
Education and Continuing Education. Higher 181 (111)
Education and Freirian Model. Alternative 142 (56)
Education and Industry. Psychological Testing in 105 (102)
Education and Intervention. Early 142 (45)
Education and Its Moral Implications. Jewish 29 (90), (114), (233)
Education and Leisure Activities in Eastern North Carolina. History of Recreation, Physical 56 (28)
Education and Life-long Learning. Community 57 (81)
Education and Opportunities. Surveying 216 (116)
Education, and Self-Development Concepts. Transportation, 46 (1 - 5)
Education and Technology 142 (75)
Education and the Community. Women in 174 (54)
Education and the Elementary School. Career 57 (47)
Education and the Future 57 (46), 168 (21)
Education and the Junior High School. Career 57 (47)
Education and the Social Revolution in China 151 (121)
Education and the World of Work. Higher 27 (20)
Education and You. Continuing 57 (26)
Education. Anthropological Look at American 29 (96), (164)
Education? Are Students Today Better Prepared for a College 16 (23), (78)

Education as an Alternative. Independent Private 105 (38)
Education as Viewed by Business. Status of 132 (11)
Education at Virginia Tech. Music 216 (66)
Education. Athletics and 57 (60)
Education. Athletics in 56 (87)
Education. Audio-visual 52 (74), 117 (41)
Education. Balance of Research and Teaching in Nursing 105 (49)
Education Become Meaningful and a Lifetime Reward? How Can 151 (38)
Education - Beyond the Classroom. Cocurricular 151 (105)
Education. Bilingual 142 (68), (90), 174 (58)
Education. Black Studies and Liberal Arts 181 (25), (90)
Education. Business 174 (96)
Education by 1984? Compulsory Adult 151 (98)
Education. Cable Television for 181 (70)
Education. Career 142 (44), (87), 181 (61), (115), 216 (49)
Education. Career Alternatives in 216 (33)
Education. Careers in 181 (52), (99)
Education: Careers, Opportunities and Offerings. Industrial 117 (81)
Education. Catholic 105 (47)
Education Center. Resident Continuing 216 (37)
Education. Challenge in 29 (90)
Education. Changing Higher 151 (120)
Education. Changing Trends in Accounting 159 (50)
Education. Childhood 180 (199)
Education. Church-State Issue in Public 181 (102), (303)
Education. Collective Bargaining in 117 (49)
Education. Collective Bargaining in Higher 29 (61), 223 (6)
Education. Community 216 (92)
Education. Comparative 57 (1), 168 (55)
Education Compared. Two Different Worlds: United States and Soviet 159 (35)
Education. Competency Based 216 (49)
Education. Competency-Based-On-Site Learning in Early Childhood 223 (7)
Education Components. Career 151 (58)
Education. Compulsory 218
Education. Compulsory Parenthood 151 (169)
Education. Concept of Public in American 181 (261)
Education. Construction Technology 168 (6)
Education. Contemporary Philosophy and 57 (85)
Education. Continuing 57 (35), 181 (111), (128), 216 (55)
Education. Continuing and Adult 171 (18)
Education. Cooperative 56 (45), 181 (115), 216 (74), (100)
Education. Cooperative Study and Internships in Higher 181 (51)
Education. Cost of a College 16 (68)
Education. Creative 180 (150)
Education. Crisis in American 85 (10), (21)
Education. Current Issues in 168 (55)
Education. Current Trends in Physical 216 (110)
Education. Current Trends in Special 181 (126)
Education. Dance 181 (77)
Education in the Schools. Dance 181 (92)
Education. Data Systems for Higher 57 (93)
Education. Death of the Lecture: Using the Personalized System of Instruction in Higher 151 (169)
Education Degree Programs. Accreditation of Engineering 151 (266)
Education. Dental Health 218
Education. Dietetic 216 (5)
Education. Direction of Higher 168 (50)
Education. Directions in Early Childhood 151 (91)
Education. Distinguishing Features of American Higher 151 (103)
Education. Distribution - A Vital Link for 132 (7)
Education. Distributive 181 (38), (55), (61), (115)
Education. ESL - An Essential Component in Bilingual 29 (297)
Education. Earl Long and Louisiana 174 (38)
Education. Early Childhood 56 (57), 142 (84), 171 (17), 174 (31)
Education. Economic 168 (45)
Education. Economics of 117 (47)
Education. Elementary 56 (48), 174 (25), (49)
Education. Elementary Health 174 (24)
Education. Elementary Physical 181 (11)
Education. Engineering 216 (30)
Education. English 142 (36), (74)
Education. Environmental 56 (75), 171 (37)
Education. Essential Component in Bilingual 29 (204)
Education. Evaluation and 171 (20)
Education. Existentialism and 105 (36)
Education. Extension and Continuing 216 (133)
Education Factory. Life in an 151 (7)
Education. Faculty Union and Higher 181 (109)
Education. Federal Government and Indian 159 (32)
Education. Financial Aid for Students in Post Secondary 54
Education. Financial Assistance is Available for Higher 105 (38)
Education. Financing Postsecondary 105 (50)
Education for Adults. Career 16 (22)
Education for All 174 (79)
Education for Business 56 (19)
Education for Career Planning. Career 181 (61), (115)
Education for Childbirth 181 (247)
Education for Elementary Teachers. Health 181 (113)
Education for Human Sexuality 56 (3), (47)
Education for Improved Communication 181 (94)
Education for Leisure. Physical Recreation and 171 (27)

Education for Present and Future Technology 105 (117)
Education for Parents. Prenatal 218
Education for Parents. Sex 57 (64)
Education for Social Change 54
Education for Socio-Economic Middleclass Children 174 (76)
Education for the Future. Planning Business 117 (14), 174 (83)
Education for the 70s 54
Education for What? 85 (3)
Education. Future and 57 (24)
Education. Future of 29 (19)
Education. Future of Elementary 57 (79)
Education. Future of Higher 142 (33)
Education: Future Trends. Engineering 151 (266)
Education. Goal and Objectives of 117 (49)
Education. Good Grades and Bad 214 (38)
Education. Graduate 57 (27), 151 (256)
Education. Health 142 (39)
Education. Higher 151 (140), 214 (39), 216 (10)
Education. Higher Education and Continuing 181 (111)
Education. Home Economics 216 (49)
Education. Housing 216 (145)
Education. How Communities Can Improve the Quality of 151 (38)
Education. Huey Long and Louisiana 174 (38)
Education. Human Relations 77 (1)
Education. Humanism Versus Behaviorism in 105 (36)
Education. Humanistic 29 (88)
Education. Humanistic Physical 181 (11)
Education. Humorous Look at 29 (68), (104), (188)
Education. Hypnosis in Athletics and Physical 151 (286)
Education Implications for Pennsylvania. Foreign Student 151 (107)
Education in Agriculture. Vocational 117 (4)
Education in Art, Music and Children's Literature. Early 142 (30)
Education in Brazil. Agriculture 216 (78)
Education in California. Bilingual 29 (95), (204)
Education in Chile 216 (2)
Education in Louisiana. Future of Higher 174 (79)
Education in Next Ten Years. Post-secondary 216 (84)
Education in Nursing. Continuing 214 (72)
Education in Pennsylvania. Role of Private Higher 54
Education in the Ground Water Industry: What You Didn't Learn at Daddy's Knee 136 (1)
Education in the 1970's. American Higher 85 (33), 168 (18)
Education in Real Estate 65 (36)
Education in the 70's and Beyond. Humanizing 168 (21)
Education in the Seventies. Plans and Problems of 16 (48)
Education in the Social Sciences 142 (87)
Education in the Thought of A.J. Heschel. Ideas on 29 (90), (233)
Education in the Thought of Martin Buber 29 (233)
Education in the U.S.S.R. 117 (72)
Education in the United States. Adult 151 (122)
Education in Today's Society. Arts 151 (30)
Education in Washington. Financing Public 159 (53)
Education. Individualized - Personalized 117 (50)
Education. Industrial 168 (40)
Education. Industrial Technology 168 (6)
Education. Intercollegiate Athletics and Higher 216 (7)
Education. Issues in Nursing 151 (256)
Education: Its Importance. Continuing Professional 151 (40)
Education. Journalism 142 (36)
Education. Legal 159 (58)
Education. Legal Aspects of 16 (83)
Education. Legal Duties and Responsibilities of Boards of 57 (55)
Education. Liberal Arts in Vocational 174 (91)
Education. Liberalizing Adult Vocational 151 (98)
Education. Life-long 16 (88)
Education. Longs and Louisiana 174 (38)
Education. Mainstreaming in Special 159 (25)
Education. Major Areas of Health 181 (227)
Education. Management Planning, Computing in Business and Computing in 105 (5)
Education. Manufacturing Technology 168 (6)
Education. Matching Models in 57 (70)
Education. Media in 57 (97)
Education. Meeting the Needs for Veterinary Medical 216 (90)
Education. Methods of Instructing in Secondary 117 (41)
Education. Metric 142 (24)
Education. Mime in Elementary and Secondary 29 (43), (103), (187)
Education. Minorities and Public 181 (93)
Education. Motivation in 112 (128)
Education? Movement 181 (77), (92)
Education Movement. Career 57 (47)
Education. Multi-cultural 142 (74)
Education. Nature of Undergraduate 16 (52)
Education. Need for Continuing 151 (117)
Education. Need for Sex 151 (160)
Education. New Directions for Secondary 216 (129)
Education. New Directions in Continuing 171 (18)
Education. New Life Through Higher 151 (103)
Education. New Physical 29 (86), (130), (299)
Education. Non-traditional 142 (66), (95)
Education. Non-traditional Higher 142 (22)
Education. Nursing 105 (43)
Education. Obligation of Industry and the Role of Internships, in Advertising 151 (75)
Education of a Young Child. Parents' Role in the 117 (45)

Education of Handicapped Individuals 151 (228)
Education of the Child. Aesthetic 151 (30)
Education of the Disadvantaged 56 (42)
Education of the Gifted 174 (84), (95)
Education of Women 227 (37)
Education of Young Doctors. Early and Current Economic 8 (3)
Education. Ombudsman in Public 57 (10)
Education. Open 151 (111), 181 (118)
Education. Opening Up the Classroom - Activities and Suggestions for Individualizing and Informalizing 117 (48)
Education. Oxford, Cambridge and British Higher 223 (10)
Education. Partners in Progress - Cooperative 151 (95)
Education. Philosophical Considerations in 168 (1)
Education. Philosophy of 105 (47)
Education. Photography in 171 (47)
Education. Physical 117 (123), 174 (16), (26)
Education. Politics and 102 (29)
Education. Politics and Higher 168 (50)
Education. Politics of 16 (83), 142 (33)
Education. Preparing for Higher 105 (38)
Education. Private Support for Higher 216 (107)
Education. Private Support of Public Higher 216 (7)
Education. Problems of Higher 85 (5)
Education. Professional 174 (86)
Education Program. Continuing 16 (10)
Education Program Development. Career 57 (72)
Education Program in Pennsylvania. Expanded Nutrition 151 (171)
Education Programs. Development of Post-secondary 151 (97)
Education Programs. Education and Board 65 (43)
Education. Programs in Business 174 (6)
Education Programs. Involving the Community in Career 57 (72)
Education - Promise or Ruin? Public 151 (100)
Education. Proposal for Improvement in American 54
Education. Recurrent 171 (15)
Education. Religion and Public 12
Education. Research in 181 (89), (130)
Education. Research in Dental 181 (114)
Education. Role of Instructional Materials in 132 (4)
Education. Role of Music in 54
Education. Role of Research in Dental 181 (175)
Education. Role of the Board in Catholic 105 (51)
Education. Role of Vocational 117 (40)
Education. Safety 142 (39)
Education. Secondary 142 (36)
Education. Secondary Teacher 142 (74)
Education. Serious Look at 29 (68), (104)
Education. Sex 54, 105 (3), 142 (39)
Education. Sexism in 218
Education. Some Major Issues in Adult 151 (98)
Education. Soviet 57 (10)
Education. Speak Out for Higher 16 (87)
Education. Speak Up for 132 (3)
Education. Special 56 (57), 174 (47)
Education. State Office and Public 57 (10)
Education. Student Teaching in Teacher 117 (60)
Education. Survival of Public 57 (65)
Education Systems. Comparison of the German and American 56 (54)
Education. Teacher 174 (86), 181 (89), (122)
Education Technology. Demystification of 181 (110)
Education. Technology in 224 (5)
Education. Television in 216 (123)
Education Through Berks Campus. Criminal Justice 151 (230)
Education Through Cooperative Education. Total 16 (82)
Education Today. Liberal Arts 105 (35)
Education. Today's Need for Continuing 151 (102)
Education. Total Education Through Cooperative 16 (82)
Education. Trends in Elementary 159 (29), 181 (118)
Education. Trends in Engineering 151 (132)
Education. Trends in Higher 29 (59), (99)
Education to 2000 A.D. Tuning 151 (112)
Education. Unionism in Higher 142 (65)
Education: United States and U.S.S.R. Engineering 151 (2)
Education. Utilization of Local History in 142 (5)
Education Versus Traditional Courses. Adult Contemporary 16 (22), (78)
Education. Veterinary Medical 16 (4)
Education. Vocational 181 (60), (63), (75), (104),)115), (120)
Education. What I Learned As a Widow About Consumer 57 (64)
Education? What is Fundamental Basic 29 (64), (101), (347)
Education: Whatever Happened to the Ivory Tower? 151 (110)
Education. Who Controls 29 (94)
Education. Why Business Supports All Levels of 132 (9)
Education? Why Life-long 168 (22)
Education. Why Your Elementary School Needs Physical 174 (16)
Education. Women and Higher 105 (86), 181 (109), (326), 214 (95)
Education. Women's Role in Business and 117 (17)
Educational Accountability 181 (104)
Educational Administration 105 (42)
Educational Administration. Trends in 16 (56)
Educational Affairs 180 (42)
Educational and Political Organizations. Future of Free Enterprise for Local Civic, Social, 74

LECTURE TITLES AND KEYWORD INDEX

Educational Approaches to Mental Handicap 117 (131)
Educational Assessment. Psycho- 142 (93)
Educational Communications Media 181 (72), (100)
Educational Consumer Interest. Meeting the 27 (20)
Educational Crisis 54
Educational Development in Nepal 29 (18), (100)
Educational Innovations 171 (17)
Educational Leadership 56 (136)
Educational Lobbying 54
Educational Materials 180 (143)
Educational Materials Development 142 (36)
Educational Measurement 142 (21)
Educational Media 174 (57), 181 (70), (98)
Educational. Moral 181 (102)
Educational Opportunities in the University of California 27 (23)
Educational Opportunities. Jewish Faith and Jewish 181 (96), (302)
Educational Opportunity Program 105 (44)
Educational or Instructional Television 168 (15)
Educational Philosopher's Role Today 181 (102)
Educational Planning. Long Range 57 (10)
Educational Planning. Trends in 216 (33)
Educational Process. Peopling: Humanizing the 117 (43)
Educational Programs in Public Policy 31 (34)
Educational Quality Assessment 181 (116)
Educational Services. Regional Delivery of 57 (10)
Educational Setting. Value Clarification in the 117 (58)
Educational Simulations. Learning Games and 214 (36)
Educational System for Mentally Retarded 169 (3)
Educational System. German (and Scandinavian) 151 (235)
Educational Technology. Science Teacher and 29 (100)
Educational Television 181 (70), (98), (215)
Educational Television and Commercial Television 142 (83)
Educational Television in the Arts 151 (32)
Educational Television. Twenty Years of 16 (86)
Educational Theatre. Multi-media Presentation of 105 (24)
Educational Values 216 (2)
Education's Nervous Future. Cause and Effect of 132 (1)
Educator and the Media 105 (65)
Educator. Museum as 151 (30)
Educator: The Resident Hall Dilemma. Landlord or 151 (105)
Effect. Law of 31 (7)
Effect of Education's Nervous Future. Cause and 132 (1)
Effect of Environmental Pollutants on Behavior 168 (64)
Effect of Food Processing on Nutrients in Foods 216 (72)
Effect of Ionizing Radiation on Bryophytes 151 (151)
Effect of the Family Upon Children 57 (34)
Effective Are Our Public Schools? How 159 (53)
Effective Conference Participation and Leadership 56 (20)
Effective Communication Strategies 105 (14)
Effective Employment 216 (15)
Effective Guidance Does Make a Difference 54
Effective Instruction. Designing 57 (76)
Effective Leadership 151 (46)
Effective Life Making. Critical Skills for 57 (71)
Effective Management. Management Science, 105 (5)
Effective Manager 151 (39)
Effective Media 57 (76)
Effective Newspaper Publicity 151 (84)
Effective Newspaper. Your Organization Can Have an 168 (51)
Effective Public Relations 168 (65)
Effective Sales Management 180 (81)
Effective Speaking. Successful Communications and 180 (14)
Effective Time Management 180 (3)
Effectively. Manage Your Time 151 (35)
Effectiveness. Organizational 56 (136)
Effectiveness. Managerial Values and Organizational 117 (21)
Effectiveness. Prayer and Its 1 (8)
Effectiveness. Psychological 105 (100)
Effectiveness Through Facilitative Communication. Improving Personal 16 (57)
Effectiveness Training 216 (27)
Effects. Inflation and Its 174 (40)
Effects of Air Pollution on Plants 216 (85)
Effects of Colonization 181 (21)
Effects of Colonization. Physiological 181 (31), (135)
Effects of Colonization. Social and Psychological 181 (31), 294
Effects of Different Kinds of Child-rearing Practices 105 (103)
Effects of Environmental Pollutants. Health 204
Effects of Financial Data on Stock and Bond Markets 31 (1)
Effects of Freeway Noises. Psychological 223 (13)
Effects of Human Biology on Behavior 102 (35)
Effects of Inflation. Causes and 117 (26)
Effects of Loneliness to Organizations 151 (38)
Effects of Nuclear Radiation 31 (30)
Effects of Pesticides. Health 171 (39)
Effects of Shock Waves Upon Marine Fish 218
Effects of Television on Children 105 (103)
Effects of Television on Society 159 (62)
Effects of the Economy on Work and Play 142 (78)
Effects of Thermal Pollution on Rivers 57 (16)
Effects of Work on Health 29 (155), (176), (291)
Efficiency 120
Efficiency. Electric Motors - Energy 67 (8)
Efficiency. Energy 189
Efficiency in Technological Societies. Physiological 56 (80)
Efficient Handling of Accounts Receivable 136 (7)

Efficient Learning. Piaget - Some Ideas on 57 (50)
Eggs. Cholesterol in 216 (35)
Eggs, Nutritional Value and Items of Interest 216 (35)
Egypt 57 (92), 218
Egypt. Ancient 57 (77)
Egypt - Gift of the Nile 59 (7)
Egypt - Old and New 29 (227), (317)
Egyptian Hellenistic Cults 227 (50)
Eight Harness Looms. Theory and Use of Multilayer Weaving on 79 (52)
8 Harnesses. Double Gang Weaving on 79 (132)
18th Century America. Music of the 56 (39), (110)
18th Century English Painting 56 (10)
18th Century Italian Creche Figure. 17th and 174 (41)
18th Century Literature 117 (88)
1877. Great Labor Uprising of 213 (3)
1812. Forgotten Hero of the War of 57 (91)
1812. Governor Isaac Shelby and the War of 117 (69)
84 Students a Day. Europe on 168 (21)
Einstein's Theory of Relativity 56 (130)
Elderly. Housing for the 216 (145)
Elderly. Law and the 181 (192), (241), (271), (312)
Elected Officials. Packaging Our 117 (106)
Election Economy. Post- 97 (10)
Election of the President 105 (58)
Elections 105 (55)
Elections. West German Politics After the 1976 29 (259)
Elective Studies 168 (22)
Electoral College 214 (7)
Electoral Politics. How to Spread Feminist and Socialist Ideas Through 178 (1)
Electric Generation at a Fossil-fuel Steam Electric Plant 150 (11)
Electric Industry. OSHA Requirements and Safety Measures in the 150 (6)
Electric Motors - Energy Efficiency 67 (8)
Electric Plant. Electric Generation at a Fossil-fuel Steam 150 (11)
Electric Power and Common Sense 189
Electric Signs of Diabetic Retinopathy 31 (24)
Electric Systems. Interconnected 189
Electric Thermal Storage 150 (2)
Electrical Engineers Do. Jobs That 216 (59)
Electrical Potentials of the Brain and Their Relation to Behavior 171 (43)
Electrical Safety 105 (87)
Electrical Safety at Home and in the Hospital 218
Electrical Safety - Safety House 152
Electricity. Miracle of 152
Electrodiagnosis 181 (155)
Electromyography. Single Fiber 181 (155)
Electron Microscope 171 (33)
Electron Microscopy of Nervous System 181 (169)
Electronic Journalism. Impact of 154 (13)
Electronic Journalism Phenomenon. Human Intrigue and 176 (43)
Electronic Music 57 (4)
Electronics. Computer and 225 (21)
Electrospinograms 181 (155)
Elegy. Roman Lyric and 227 (15)
Elegy. Women in Roman 227 (24)
Elementary and Secondary Schools. Innovation Practices for Improving the Instructional Staff in the 117 (58)
Elementary Education 56 (48), 174 (25), (49)
Elementary Education. Future of 57 (79)
Elementary Health Education 174 (24)
Elementary Math and Science 174 (49)
Elementary Math. Modern 56 (48)
Elementary Particles 181 (277), 216 (131)
Elementary Physical Education 181 (11)
Elementary Principal 181 (118)
Elementary School. Career Education and the 57 (47)
Elementary School Levels. Administration at the High School or 56 (48)
Elementary School Mathematics 142 (26)
Elementary School - Mathematics Can Be Fun 151 (250)
Elementary School Science. Look at 57 (50)
Elementary Teachers. Health Education for 181 (113)
Elements in Properly Preparing a Real Estate Sales Contract 65 (41)
Elements of Menu Planning 216 (25)
Elements Which Contribute to Stress on the Job. Occupational Stress: The 117 (19)
Eliminating Cancer 105 (127)
Eliot and the Religious Search. T.S. 105 (106)
Elizabeth Timothy - America's First Woman Editor 56 (61)
Elsewhere in the Universe. Life 57 (87)
Emancipation of American Blacks. Abraham Lincoln and the 29 (338)
Embroidery 79 (146)
Embroidery. Bobbin Lace, Needle Lace, 79 (42)
Embroidery. Excitement of 79 (97)
Embroidery. Pueblo 79 (89)
Embroidery Weaves 79 (67), (84)
Emergency Medicine 218
Emergency Psychiatric Measures 105 (95)
Emerging Clinical Role of the Pharmacist 16 (77)
Emerging Giant. Africa - An 29 (48)
Emerging United States 85 (28)
Emotional Difficulties and Mental Health of College Students 216 (132)
Emotional Domains. Teacher Modeling Behavior in the Physical, Intellectual and 117 (39)
Emotional Problems of Animals 225 (26)
Emotionally Disturbed Child and Family 16 (35)
Emotions. Use of Color for the Control of 225 (5)
Emperors. Byzantine 29 (178), (234)
Emphasis of the United States in Asia 117 (68)
Empire. Ferment in the Soviet 85 (6)
Empire. Mixed Theatres of the 227 (14)
Empirical School of Philosophy. Challenges to the Logical 29 (232)

Employee Bargaining. Public 216 (104)
Employee Benefit Programs 23, 216 (15)
Employee Benefits. Business Practices and 151 (1)
Employee Labor Relations. Public 216 (105)
Employee Motivation. Increasing Productivity Through 67 (2)
Employee Relations 162, 180 (179)
Employee Relationship. Better Employer- 117 (120)
Employee Safety Programs 216 (15)
Employee Selection 180 (114)
Employees Into Unwanted Labor Unions. Right to Work - Forcing Public 131 (4)
Employer-Employee Relationship. Better 117 (120)
Employment and Unemployment Manpower 181 (48)
Employment Compliance in Municipal Governments. Equal 29 (66), (262)
Employment. Effective 216 (15)
Employment in Today's World. Preparing for 117 (80)
Employment Interview. Historical Overview of Equal Employment Opportunity and Affirmative Action Laws and Regulations, the 27 (2)
Employment Interviewing 151 (57)
Employment. Methods of Dispute Settlement in 223 (6)
Employment Practices. Fair 223 (6)
Employment Rights and Opportunities. Women's 27 (2)
Employment Trends for the College Graduate 151 (60)
Employment With a College Degree. Facing 16 (36)
Enameling Technique. Weaving and 79 (128)
Encounter Groups. Therapeutic and 29 (231)
Encouraging Children's School Success 117 (48)
Encouraging Creativity. Helping Children to Be More Creative - Ways Parents and Teachers Can 117 (48)
End of Pax Americana in Asia 105 (57)
Endocrinologist. When Should You Consult an 27 (35)
Enduring Values. Love, Spontaneity and 85 (35)
Enemy. Computer - Friend or 56 (126)
Energy 29 (72), (109), (236), 216 (119)
Energy Allocation 57 (25)
Energy. Alternate 35
Energy. Alternate Sources of 158
Energy Alternatives 16 (80), 66 (1), 152, 216 (64)
Energy Alternatives for the Future 150 (3)
Energy and Mineral Resources 142 (81)
Energy and Morality 83 (13)
Energy and Petroleum Resources, Earthquakes - Prediction, Control, and Nuclear Power Plants 27 (4)
Energy and Pollution 56 (71)
Energy and the Environment 204
Energy and the Future 174 (39)
Energy Applications in Agriculture. Solar 216 (137)
Energy. Atomic 176 (45)
Energy Challenge 47
Energy. Clean and Cheap 54
Energy Conservation 16 (25), (80), 23, 57 (25), 151 (123), 214 (40), 216 (71), (143)
Energy Conservation in Traffic Operations and Highway Design 174 (90)
Energy Conservation in Transportation 174 (90)
Energy Consumer Problems 57 (84)
Energy Crisis 151 (131), 181 (137), (253)
Energy Crisis and Engineering Control 214 (29)
Energy Crisis. Chemist's View of the 57 (6)
Energy Crisis. Economic Aspects of the 117 (35)
Energy Crisis? Is There an 54
Energy Crisis: Real and Unreal 181 (250)
Energy Crisis. Role of Nuclear Power in Meeting the 216 (103)
Energy Crisis. United States 143 (8)
Energy Crisis? What 102 (24)
Energy Development 57 (25)
Energy Developments. Latest 151 (125)
Energy Dilemma. Solving the United States 151 (136)
Energy Dwellings. Integrated 163 (2)
Energy Economics 174 (20)
Energy Efficiency 189
Energy Efficiency. Electric Motors - 67 (8)
Energy - Environment 142 (81)
Energy - Environment - Conservation 216 (121)
Energy Facility Siting 151 (150)
Energy for the Future 151 (132)
Energy From Garbage 16 (50)
Energy. Future of 216 (71)
Energy. Geothermal 181 (137)
Energy-Going...Going...Gone 152
Energy. Heat Pumps and Solar 216 (71)
Energy in Agriculture 216 (137)
Energy in the Future 150 (2)
Energy in the Home. How You Can Save 16 (80)
Energy. Kaleidoscope of 152
Energy Needs, Economic Choices, and Coal Beneficiation 151 (134)
Energy Options for Food Production 47
Energy Outlook. General 35
Energy Parks 151 (150)
Energy Picture. Middle East in the United States 56 (15)
Energy Policy. Environmental and 151 (150)
Energy Policy. United States 57 (89)
Energy. Politics of Nuclear 117 (106)
Energy Production. Decentralized 163 (2)
Energy Prospects 216 (77)
Energy. Prospects for Solar 29 (110)
Energy Question 210 (1)
Energy Regulation. Nuclear 151 (133)
Energy Research. Look at 16 (2)
Energy. Saving 222
Energy - Saving Homes for Profit and Comfort 18 (1)
Energy Savings by Preventive Maintenance 151 (47)
Energy Situation. Our 31 (23)

Energy. Solar 105 (117), 214 (43), 218, 222
Energy Sources. Alternative 151 (123)
Energy Sources. Non-polluting 142 (15)
Energy Systems for Rural and Urban Dwellings and Small Businesses. Self-sufficient 163 (2)
Energy Systems. Integrated 163 (1)
Energy Systems. Integrated Farmstead 163 (3)
Energy Systems. Management and Analysis of 163 (1)
Energy - The Tip of the Iceberg 56 (29)
Energy to Heat Farm Buildings. Solar 16 (8)
Energy Trends and Directions 29 (81)
Energy - Use it Wisely. It's Your 47
Energy Utilization for Heating and Cooling Buildings. Solar 151 (126)
Energy. Utilization of Atomic 216 (64)
Energy, Where Art Thou? 29 (109)
Energy - Where Will It Come From? 151 (127)
Energy While Increasing Agriculture Production. Saving 16 (31)
Energy. Why Nuclear 151 (129)
Energy Wise Are You. How 66 (2)
Enforcement. Law 220 (5)
Enforcement of Pollution Control Laws 204
Engineer and the Environment 214 (28)
Engineer in Automobile Design and Production 214 (90)
Engineer in Urban and Regional Planning 214 (44)
Engineering 16 (40), 174 (97), 214 (41)
Engineering and Engineering Technology at Penn State 151 (149)
Engineering and Motivation. Human 180 (146)
Engineering and Operations Research. Industrial 216 (87)
Engineering and the Future of Man. Genetic 151 (164)
Engineering and/or Science. Computers in 214 (22)
Engineering as a Dynamic Profession. Industrial 216 (120)
Engineering as a Profession. Aerospace 151 (34)
Engineering as a Profession. Agricultural 216 (83)
Engineering at Cal State Fullerton. Science and 29 (32), (111)
Engineering at Penn State. Aerospace 151 (34)
Engineering at Virginia Tech. Agricultural 216 (83)
Engineering. Biomedical 181 (155)
Engineering Careers 29 (23), (107), 151 (125)
Engineering. Careers in 16 (40), 216 (30)
Engineering. Careers in Science and 29 (111), (278)
Engineering. Creative 171 (7)
Engineering Control. Energy Crisis and 214 (29)
Engineering Education 216 (30)
Engineering Education Degree Programs. Accreditation of 151 (266)
Engineering Education: Future Trends 151 (266)
Engineering Education. Trends in 151 (132)
Engineering Education: United States and U.S.S.R. 151 (2)
Engineering Fair. International Science 29 (111), (278), (352)
Engineering. General 216 (30), (82)
Engineering. Genetic 105 (2), 151 (151), 181 (19)
Engineering. Genetic Counseling and Genetic 105 (104)
Engineering. Human Factors 214 (79), 222
Engineering. Human Genetic 218
Engineering. IEOR in Nuclear 216 (87)
Engineering in Agriculture 216 (83)
Engineering. Industrial 105 (116)
Engineering Land Marks. Historic Civil 174 (90)
Engineering: Life in Our Hands. Genetic 102 (24)
Engineering. Minorities and Women in Science and 29 (111), (278)
Engineering. Naval Ships 105 (73)
Engineering on the Last Frontier 151 (138)
Engineering. Opportunities for Women in 151 (142)
Engineering Profession. Agriculture 216 (137)
Engineering Program. Cal State Fullerton 29 (108)
Engineering. Rehabilitation 181 (180)
Engineering Research at Penn State 151 (139)
Engineering. Science and 29 (278)
Engineering. Selecting a Career in 151 (132)
Engineering. Systems 151 (45)
Engineering Team 151 (131)
Engineering Technology 151 (140), 174 (97)
Engineering Technology at Penn State. Engineering and 151 (149)
Engineering Technology. Careers in 151 (53)
Engineering Technology. Mechanical 151 (146)
Engineering - The Challenge of the Future 151 (144)
Engineering: The Full Scope. Genetic 159 (44)
Engineering? What is Ocean 216 (108)
Engineers and Research Scientists. Social Responsibility of 16 (11)
Engineers Do. Jobs That Electrical 216 (59)
Engineers, History and Current Roles. Corps of 105 (74)
Engineers Make Good Managers? Do 151 (45)
Engines and You. Small 216 (121)
Engines for Power or Vehicular Transportation 151 (295)
Engines. Turbine Type 151 (295)
Engines. Wave Engines - A Different Concept in 151 (295)
England 57 (44), (92), 214 (51)
England and France. Popular Recreation and Reform in the 19th Century 142 (98)
England. Chaucer's 117 (89)
England. French Writers and Opinions on 142 (98)
England is Closing 151 (197)
England. Pathways Through 59 (16)
England. There'll Always Be An 59 (17)
England. University in France and 105 (33)
English and the College Freshman 105 (46)
English as a Third Language 151 (239)
English Curriculum 168 (53)
English Curriculum. Organizing the 57 (48)

English Education 142 (36), (74)
English Infant Schools. Visit to 168 (61)
English Language. Origin of the 29 (209), (298)
English Literature. Influence of Classics on 227 (26)
English Literature. 19th Century 214 (47)
English or the Mayor's? King's 181 (317)
English Painting. 18th Century 56 (10)
English Prisons. 19th Century 159 (61)
English Sentence. Grammar of the 57 (48)
English Study Abroad 216 (89)
English Syntax. Phonology, Morphology of 56 (65)
English Teaching Methods 168 (53)
English Villages and Human Scale in Living Environments 218
English? What Good is a Major in 29 (29), (97)
English? Will the Public Schools Be the Death of 168 (51)
Engraved Gems. Roman 227 (47)
Enhanced in the Food Processing Industry. How Productivity Can Be 67 (1)
Enhanced Oil Recovery in Pennsylyania 151 (138)
Enhancing Marital Happiness 29 (252)
Enhancing Sexual Pleasure 29 (252)
Enhancing Your Features 176 (9)
Enjoying Art. Technique for 105 (19)
Enjoying Fitness and Conditioning 151 (204)
Enjoying French and American Wines 216 (25)
Enjoying Your Work 180 (51)
Enjoyment and Appreciation of Music 54
Enrichment of Marriage Relationships 57 (71)
Enrollment on Job Security. Declining 214 (37)
Enrollment Projection Model. Eclectic 57 (93)
Entering Police Departments. Alternative Methods of 29 (144), (344)
Entering Police Departments. Methods of 29 (58)
Enterprise for Local Civic, Social, Educational and Political Organizations. Future of Free 74
Enterprise. Free 23
Enterprise. Future of Private 102 (6)
Enterprise in the United States. Future of Small Business 159 (3)
Enterprise Survive Success? Can Free 102 (19)
Enterprise System. Achieving Success in the Free 180 (79)
Enterprise System. American 105 (6)
Enterprise System. Free 151 (51), 180 (107)
Enterprise. Why Americans Are Losing Faith in Free 102 (33)
Enterprises. Cooperative 172 (9)
Entertainment or a New American Religion? Disneyland: 159 (51)
Enthusiasm. Power of 135 (16)
Entomology 216 (102)
Entrepreneurs: Male and Female 105 (84)
Environment 117 (33), 171 (37), 176 (46), (81)
Environment and Behavior 105 (99)
Environment and Business 56 (19), (74)
Environment and Cancer 181 (178), (230)
Environment and Conservation 35
Environment. Architects Role in the Built 174 (37)
Environment. Business and Its 105 (6)
Environment. Chemical 56 (71)
Environment. Communication and 135 (17)
Environment. Computerized Information System 174 (23)
Environment - Conservation. Energy - 216 (121)
Environment. Energy - 142 (81)
Environment. Energy and the 204
Environment. Engineer and the 214 (28)
Environment. Fate and Behavior of Pesticides in the 171 (39)
Environment for Survival 97 (13)
Environment. Garments - Our Immediate 79 (32)
Environment. Harmful Plants in the 117 (1)
Environment. Health in the Occupational 151 (153)
Environment in Eastern North Carolina. Population on the Physical 56 (36), (38)
Environment. Labor and the 172 (13)
Environment. Law and 29 (74), (195)
Environment. Long-range Planning for Our 171 (37)
Environment. Man and His 56 (73)
Environment. Man's 174 (91)
Environment. Minority 224 (12)
Environment on an International Scale. Preserve the 181 (346)
Environment. Preserve the 181 (136)
Environment. Radioactivity in the Marine 218
Environment Relations. Man 16 (28)
Environment. Save the 142 (15)
Environment. Surveys in a Group 181 (283)
Environment - Thrust or Trick. Citizenship in an Ideological 85 (11)
Environment. Today's Man and the 152
Environment. Today's Woman and the 152
Environmental and Energy Policy 151 (150)
Environmental Awareness 29 (69)
Environmental Awareness - An Approach to Learning and Self 29 (132)
Environmental Biology. Aspects of 57 (94)
Environmental Causes of Birth Defects 218
Environmental Concerns 158
Environmental Crisis 52 (59), 54
Environmental Economics 218
Environmental Education 56 (75), 171 (37)
Environmental Geology 224 (13)
Environmental Hazardous Agents on Women. Impact of 151 (153)
Environmental Health Hazards 181 (184)
Environmental Impact Studies and Archaeological Research 117 (31)
Environmental Issues 187 (4)
Environmental Law 159 (41), 214 (25), (63)
Environmental Law and Management 27 (3)
Environmental Microbiology 168 (29)
Environmental Pollutants. Health Effects of 204

Environmental Pollutants on Behavior. Effect of 168 (64)
Environmental Polluters. Vanadium - Tattletale of 27 (9)
Environmental Pollution 56 (67)
Environmental Pollution and Food 151 (177)
Environmental Preservation 57 (25)
Environmental Problems 56 (103), 73, 176 (45)
Environmental Problems. Public Awareness of 151 (153)
Environmental Programs. International 204
Environmental Protection Agency 57 (94)
Environmental Protection Systems 150 (11)
Environmental Psychology 168 (74)
Environmental Quality and the American Way of Life 57 (94)
Environmental Quality and the Problem of Economic Growth 29 (73), (79), (260)
Environmental Quality Control. Economics and 168 (43)
Environmental Quality. Economics of 117 (34)
Environmental Radiation 204
Environmental Science 216 (48)
Environmental Services in Eastern North Carolina 56 (25)
Environmental Services in North Carolina 56 (67)
Environmental Standards for Generating Station Operations 150 (4)
Environmental Systems 150 (3)
Environments. English Villages and Human Scale in Living 218
Environs of Lake Baikal and Irkutsk. Leningrad and the 151 (296)
Enzymes - Life's Key Chemicals 54
Epic. Homer and/or Early Babylonian 227 (17)
Epic Voyages of Ra 69 (1)
Epicureanism 227 (43)
Epidemic of Suicides 216 (76)
Epigraphy. Greek and Latin 227 (8)
Epilepsy. Anticonvulsants and 181 (164)
Episcopal Church Groups 11 (7)
Equal. All Men and Women Are Created 214 (85)
Equal at Last. Women in Real Estate 65 (20)
Equal But Different 102 (23)
Equal Employment Compliance in Municipal Governments 29 (66), (262)
Equal Employment Opportunity and Affirmative Action Laws and Regulations, the Employment Interview. Historical Overview of 27 (2)
Equal Opportunity. Affirmative Action - 223 (1)
Equal Rights Amendment 56 (132), 174 (54)
Equal Rights for Women? What's Wrong With 112 (113)
Equal Time. Fairness Doctrine and 117 (84)
Equality 172 (2)
Equality and Brotherhood in Islam 1 (13)
Equality and Liberty in American Politics 85 (13)
Equality of Women 54
Equality. Two Ideas of 85 (25)
Equation. Safety - Maintenance - Common Sense 132 (13)
Equine Psychology 216 (57)
Equipment and Facilities. Standards for Sports 151 (280)
Equipment. Corrosion Ressistant Plating for Processing 67 (11)
Equipment. Evaluation of Sports 151 (280)
Equipment. Refuse Collection, Solid Wastes' Handling 133 (4)
Equipment Safety. Playground 132 (8)
Equipment. Sweet Corn, Green Beans, Cherry, Bright Stack and Filling 67 (6), (12)
Erect. When Man First Walked 112 (73)
Erie County. Natural Areas of 151 (308)
Erie County. Streams of 151 (308)
Eros, Sex and Marriage 85 (18)
Erosion and Human Conservation. Human 57 (69)
Errands on the Original Horseless Carriage. Adventures and 56 (40)
Error Correcting Codes 151 (147)
Escape From Poor Postal Service 3 (8)
Eskimo Arts and Culture 79 (123)
Eskimos. Aleut- 4 (6)
Eskimos. Living With the 4 (3)
Esperanto After Ninety Years 58 (2)
Esperanto and the Right to Communicate 58 (3)
Esperanto in the Orient. Status of 58 (1)
Esperanto in the World Today 58 (4)
Espionage in North America. Soviet 16 (18)
Essential Component in Bilingual Education 29 (204)
Essentials of Effective Personal Communication 105 (12)
Establishment. Defense 54
Estate Planning 54, 159 (46), 216 (99), 224 (17)
Estate Planning for Doctors 8 (10)
Estate Planning for Doctors and Their Spouses 8 (5)
Estate Planning for Women 136 (21)
Eternal Crisis. Berlin the 57 (75)
Eternal Crisis. International Monetary Structure - An 85 (14)
Eternal Quarterback. Being an 135 (7)
Eternal Spring. Guatemala - Land of 117 (140)
Ethic. Social Sex and the Work 211 (3)
Ethical and Social Problems in Medicine 16 (64)
Ethical Dilemma. Management's 181 (47)
Ethical Impact. Science and It's 142 (19)
Ethical Implications of Advances in Biology 151 (164)
Ethical Problems in Broadcasting 117 (84)
Ethical/Theological Topics. Lectures on Social/ Political/ 168 (34)
Ethics 65 (2), (4), (5), (6), (7), (9), (10), (14), (15), (17), (18), (22), (24), (30), (31), (33), (36), (37), (38), (39), (42), (43), (46), (47), (51), (53), (54), (55), (56), (59), (65), (66), (68), (70)
Ethics and Genetic Research 29 (113), (131), (265)

Ethics and Profits 102 (31)
Ethics and the News Media 181 (68)
Ethics and the Press 29 (40), (117)
Ethics. Business 105 (6), 214 (13)
Ethics. Christian 105 (111)
Ethics. Greek 227 (34)
Ethics in a Technological Era 159 (12)
Ethics in Nursing. Medico-moral Legal 105 (49)
Ethics. Medical 105 (104)
Ethics. Newspapers, Reporting, Editing, 151 (68)
Ethics of Behavior Control 168 (47)
Ethics of News Media 56 (102)
Ethics of Psychologists 224 (14)
Ethics. Religious 224 (11)
Ethics: Scoops to Scandals. Journalism 151 (86)
Ethics. Sexual 105 (104)
Ethics. Social Responsibility and Management 151 (43)
Ethiopia. Paleontological Field Work in 218
Ethiopia, the Country and Her People 117 (142)
Ethiopian Situation. Background of the 56 (113)
Ethnic Applique 79 (120)
Ethnic Baskets 79 (36)
Ethnic Cloth and Costume as Design 79 (33)
Ethnic Clothing. Bags and Handsome 79 (39)
Ethnic Communities in the Pittsburgh Area 54
Ethnic Costume 79 (57)
Ethnic Groups and Contemporary Adaptions. Textile Techniques of 79 (8)
Ethnic Politics 54
Ethnicity and Culture 181 (176), (228)
Ethnicity and Culture Changes of Modern Hawaiians 29 (141), (161), (257), (284)
Ethnicity in America. New 168 (30)
Ethnicity. New 211 (6)
Etymology 227 (18)
Euripidean Drama 227 (39)
Euripides 227 (15)
Euripides. Realism in 227 (25)
Europe After Helsinki 97 (52)
Europe and America. Portuguese Peasant in 29 (123), (164)
Europe. Art Treasures in Western 56 (9)
Europe. Bicycling in 29 (327)
Europe. Early Photography in Eastern 151 (73)
Europe. Four Seasons in 29 (321)
Europe. How to Plan an Affordable Trip to 117 (138)
Europe. John Scali's 102 (28)
Europe. Most Exciting Road Through 51 (1)
Europe. New Immigrants in 168 (30)
Europe 1975 117 (137)
Europe on 84 Students a Day 168 (21)
Europe. Opera in the United States and 154 (22)
Europe. Political and Social History in Communist East 218
Europe. Politics in Eastern 54
Europe - The Great Misunderstanding. America - 85 (18)
Europe Today. Eastern 56 (112)
Europe Today. Opposition Currents in the Soviet Union and Eastern 213 (13)
Europe Today. Western 168 (65)
Europe. Traveling Through 142 (34)
Europe. Travelogue of Western 117 (138)
Europe. Urban Spaces of 181 (335)
Europe. Youth Hosteling in 151 (298)
European Cinema. American and 31 (12)
European Conservatism - Vital Link. American and 85 (39)
European Culture. East 29 (127), (213)
European History. Ancient and Medieval 151 (215)
European Intellectual History 218
European Security and Detentes 29 (56), (121), (259)
European Security. United States and 85 (28)
European Travel and Culture 151 (297)
European Travel of the Type That is Close to the Earth 218
European Travel on a Budget 168 (61)
European Travel Relative to Spanish and Italian Culture 151 (300)
European Unity 57 (75)
Euthanasia 54
Euthanasia. Involuntary 218
Evacuation During World War II. Japanese American 29 (139), (333)
Evaluating Reading Programs. Planning, Administering and 142 (21)
Evaluation and Education 171 (20)
Evaluation and Improvement of Instruction. Teacher 105 (48)
Evaluation and Research 168 (14)
Evaluation. Interdisciplinary Research Management and 151 (254)
Evaluation Methods. Program 159 (13)
Evaluation. Multidisciplinary Approach to Treatment and 159 (26)
Evaluation of Gifted Children. Diagnosis and 181 (105)
Evaluation of Instruction. Student 174 (57)
Evaluation of Sports Equipment 151 (280)
Evaluation. Performance 181 (47), (299)
Eve 'n Adam 159 (1)
Evening With Irv Weiner 221 (1)
Evening With Sherlock Holmes 225 (43)
Event or Activity. Programming a Successful 105 (79)
Events. Current 181 (233), (269)
Everest. Soldiers on 69 (5)
Everybody is Somebody: The Self-concept 117 (43)
Everyday Life in France 56 (111)
Everyday Life in the Soviet Union 97 (40)
Everyday Problems in Writing 168 (53)
Everyone Can Take a Pleasing Photograph 136 (16)

Everyone. Intramural Recreational Activities for 57 (17)
Everyone Plays a Part 97 (11)
Everything You Ever Wanted to Know About Plastic Well Casing---But Were Afraid to Ask 136 (25)
Everything You Want to Know About Money 225 (44)
Everything You Wanted to Know About Washington But Didn't Know Who to Ask 135 (25)
Evidence and the Law 159 (8)
Evidence for Ghosts and Psychic Photography. Scientific 154 (12)
Evidence. Utilization of Physical 159 (11)
Evoked Electrospinograms 181 (155)
Evolution and Human Nature. Women's 213 (11)
Evolution and the Bible 168 (13)
Evolution. Human 57 (77), 142 (58)
Evolution of a Clinical Pharmacy Services 54
Evolution of Alternative Schools 216 (86)
Evolution of Antique Firearms 117 (130)
Evolution of Pittsburgh 31 (32)
Evolution of the Art Form 56 (13)
Evolution of the Radio 171 (32)
Evolution of the Universe 142 (31)
Evolution 100 Years After the Publication of the Origin of the Species. Biologist Looks at 54
Evolution. Prehistoric Man and 174 (22)
Evolution. Studies in Plant 168 (13)
Examination. Certified Professional Secretary 117 (27)
Examplar. Holy Prophet Muhammad as an 1 (12)
Excellence. In Pursuit of 176 (98)
Excellence. Party Planning Par 97 (15)
Excellence. Professional 57 (96)
Exceptional Child 174 (76)
Exceptional Child in Today's Society 117 (133)
Exceptional Development 181 (126)
Excesses. Federal Regulation and Its 34 (1)
Exchange Commission. Value and Uses of Financial Reports Filed by American Corporations With the Securities and 50 (1)
Exchange. Learning- 99 (1), (2), (3)
Exchanges. Faculty Job 214 (39)
Exchanging 65 (12), (41), (43), (53), (54), (61), (65), (69)
Exchanging (Commercial and Residential) 65 (25)
Excitement of America 189
Excitement of Embroidery 79 (97)
Exciting and Meaningful. How to Make Your Career More 23
Excluded From Campus. Why Moderates, Conservatives, and Catholics are 85 (33)
Executive Orders. Federal Laws, Regulations, and 151 (1)
Executive Speaking 180 (138)
Executive State. Ideology of the 151 (190)
Executives. Counseling 180 (38)
Executives. Fitness for Busy 176 (75)
Exemptions. Future of Church Tax 12
Exercise 159 (17), 105 (115)
Exercise. Adult 168 (33)
Exercise and Weight Control 168 (33)
Exercise for the Aging 174 (27)
Exercise Help Your Heart? Can 171 (23)
Exercise in Our Society. Role of 168 (33)
Exercise Physiology 174 (27)
Exercise Program. How to Go About Developing Your Own 218
Exercise. Therapeutic 57 (2)
Exercises for Adults. Self-esteem 181 (292)
Exercises for the Office 174 (64)
Exercises to Increase Awareness of Oneself. Goal Setting: 105 (78)
Exhibit. Jurying an Art 159 (18)
Exhibits. Comprehensive 79 (89)
Existence of God 1 (3)
Existence of God. Proofs of the 1 (6)
Existential Psycho-analysis 181 (291)
Existentialism 54, 174 (55)
Existentialism and Education 105 (36)
Existentialism and the Modern Youth 29 (102), (246), (349)
Existentialism. Literature of 159 (40)
Existentialism. Notion of Person in 117 (97)
Exorcism: Fact or Fiction 134 (2)
Exorcism. Possession and 154 (12)
Exotic Places. Photographing 29 (38), (319)
Expanded Honeycomb 79 (147)
Expanded Nutrition Education Program in Pennsylvania 151 (171)
Expansion of the Auburn Airport 16 (46)
Expectations for College Athletes in Running 168 (71)
Expedition. New Guinea 59 (2)
Expenditures and the Economy. Government 54
Experience. Academic Credit for Work 16 (78)
Experience. Black 151 (58)
Experience. Black Family, Black 181 (30)
Experience. Collegiate 151 (55)
Experience in Communications. Hollywood Story - 135 (45)
Experience. Non-violence and the Gandhi 54
Experience of God Within Christian Faith 105 (109)
Experience. Russian 15 (2)
Experience. Single Parent Adoptive 181 (247)
Experience. Southern 16 (24)
Experience to Avoid. Shocking 151 (261)
Experience. Using Language 57 (79)
Experience. Wildnerness 16 (72)
Experiences. Palatable Writing 151 (231)
Experiences With Mental Retardation. Parent's 216 (9)
Experiences With Mind Control 4 (7)
Experiment Station. Research in the Agricultural 151 (181)
Experimental and Sculptural Techniques. Fiber-fabric 79 (98)
Experimental Perception 214 (79)
Experimental Weaving 79 (140)

Experimentation With Mordants. Innovative Natural Dye 79 (156)
Experimenting With Democratic Management in Business 27 (1)
Expert. Metrications: Too Important to Leave to the 151 (248)
Expert Witness. Scientist as an 159 (11)
Explained. Racism 29 (49)
Exploded. Talent Myth 56 (13)
Exploding Technology - A New Way of Life 102 (22)
Exploitation. Oceans - Conservation or 97 (38)
Exploration and Production. Offshore 35
Exploration. Future of Ocean 225 (7)
Exploration. Humor in 4 (3)
Exploration of the Solar System 154 (17)
Exploration. Twenty Years of Change in Alaskan 143 (9)
Exploration (United States). Oil and Gas 151 (124)
Explorations in Tubular Weave 79 (109)
Explorations of the Role Fiber Has in Our Lives 79 (27), (46)
Exploring Backdoor to Siberia 4 (3)
Exploring the Aleutians 4 (1)
Exploring the Unconscious 4 (7)
Exploring Warmth 168 (64)
Exploring Weaving on Primitive Looms 79 (85)
Explosion and Implosion. Population- 85 (38)
Explosion Faced by the Health Care Practitioner. Information 218
Explosion. Population 29 (47), (69), (132), (266)
Explosion. Sports 16 (74)
Export Procelain. Chinese 174 (41)
Expository Writing - A Necessary Skill 57 (66)
Expression. Obscenity and Freedom of 218
Extant Wood Screens in Devonshire 151 (26)
Extension and Continuing Education 216 (133)
Extension Division. Resources of the 216 (70)
Extension or Public Service. University 16 (7)
Extension Programs. Cooperative 16 (12)
Extension Service. Alabama Cooperative 16 (75)
Extension's Role in Today's Agriculture 151 (23)
Extensions and Continuing 142 (10)
External Influences on Synagogue Architecture 181 (306)
Extra Mile 18 (1)
Extra Sensory Perception 214 (79)
Extramural Sport Clubs 216 (46)
Extremities. Strains of the Lower 57 (2)
Eye and Brain. Oscillations in the 31 (24)
Eye-Ball to Eye-Ball 83 (16)
Eye Cannot See. World That the 69 (11)
Eye, Light, and Illusions 56 (130)
Eye of a Needle. Nature Through the 79 (82)
Eye of Russia. Artist's 29 (11), (17), (148), (293), (311), (322)
Eye of the Beholder 189
Eye of the Beholder. Beauty is Not in the 105 (90)
Eyewitness to the Modern Time 154 (11)

F

F.B.I. 105 (59)
FBI Files. Hiss Case and the 97 (69)
F.B.I. On Dealing With the 97 (69)
FBI Plot Against the Black Movement 213 (10)
FBI. Socialist Suit Against the 213 (9), (15), (17)
Fabric. Blueprint on 79 (4)
Fabric Crafts. African 79 (35)
Fabric Decoration 79 (45)
Fabric Design. Multiple Harness 79 (8)
Fabric Designing. Creative 79 (53)
Fabric. Designing in Fiber, Yarn 79 (146)
Fabric Experimental and Sculptural Techniques. Fiber- 79 (98)
Fabric. Manipulation of 79 (92)
Fabric. Photographic Images on 79 (129)
Fabric Processes in Rural India 79 (45)
Fabric With Photo Silkscreen. Photo Imagery on 79 (4)
Fabrics and Contemporary Adaptations. Bolivian 79 (18)
Fabrics. Fashion 79 (84), (136), (151)
Fabrics. Finishing Touches for Handwoven 79 (151)
Fabrics for Workshops 79 (105)
Fabrics. Fundamentals of Drafting and Designing 79 (93)
Fabrics. Historic 79 (70)
Fabrics. Printing on Photosensitized 79 (4)
Fabulous Rio- Portrait of Brazil 110 (8)
Face and Body Language. Greater Understanding of People Through 212 (1)
Face Language. How to Increase Your Psychic Abilities Through 212 (1)
Face Language. Human Awareness Through 212 (1)
Face of Love 225 (23)
Faced Loom Controlled Patterning. Weft 79 (132)
Faces of Cathy. Many 112 (6)
Faces of France 15 (1)
Faces of France. Many 110 (2)
Facial Deformities 181 (183)
Facial Deformities. Correction of 181 (161)
Facilitative Communication. Improving Personal Effectiveness Through 16 (58)
Facilities and Services. Altoona Campus - 51 (14)
Facilities and the Successful Program. Campus 57 (51)
Facilities at Virginia Tech. Recreational 216 (46)
Facilities. Campus 57 (51)
Facilities. Community Recreation 16 (2)
Facilities. Fire Safety in Health 216 (99)
Facilities Planning 105 (116)
Facilities. Standards for Sports Equipment and 151 (280)

Facility. Function and Operation of a Major Futures Trading 38
Facility Siting. Energy 151 (150)
Facility. Today's University 29 (105), (155), (291)
Facing Employment With a College Degree 16 (36)
Facism. Communism and 151 (198)
Fact or Fancy? Learning Disabilities - 151 (100)
Fact or Fancy? Spiritualism - 151 (259)
Fact or Fiction. Exorcism: 134 (2)
Fact or Fiction. Flying Saucers - 83 (15)
Fact or Inference: For Those Who Jump to Conclusions 151 (168)
Factors Engineering. Human 214 (79), 222
Factory. Life in an Education 151 (7)
Facts About Pakistan. Social and Cultural 29 (19), (181)
Facts About the Nature of Knowledge. Truth, Objectivity and Some Interesting 85 (20)
Facts and Prevention. Food Poisoning - 151 (173)
Facts. Bare 17 (1)
Facts, Figures and the American People. Right to Work - Supported by 131 (1)
Facts People Should Know About Alcohol Intoxication 54
Faculty Affairs 151 (8)
Faculty Job Exchanges 214 (39)
Faculty Participation in University Governance 105 (49)
Faculty. Teaching Staff or 181 (110)
Faculty Union and Higher Education 181 (109)
Fair Employment Practices 223 (6)
Fair. International Science and Engineering 29 (111), (278), (352)
Fair Trial. Free Press and 181 (68), (211)
Fairness Doctrine and Equal Time 117 (84)
Fairness Doctrine. Broadcasting's 117 (86), (129)
Fairy Tales 159 (23)
Faith. Alien Look at America's 85 (18)
Faith. America as a Secularized Religious 151 (221)
Faith and Jewish Educational Opportunities. Jewish 181 (96), (302)
Faith. Baha'i 142 (23)
Faith. Experience of God Within Christian 105 (109)
Faith in Free Enterprise. Why Americans are Losing 102 (33)
Faith. Today's Crisis of 105 (104)
Faith Versus Science 151 (149)
Fall of Rome. Morality and the 56 (93)
Fall of the Model-T Ford, 1909-1927. Rise and 151 (294)
Fall Without a Shot Being Fired? Could the West 97 (12)
Fallacy of Libertarianism 85 (40)
Families and Children. Services for 181 (252), (313)
Families and Communities 216 (133)
Families: Conflict and Resolution. Youth and 151 (167)
Families - How They Spend and Save. Two Earner 151 (166)
Families, Individuals and Groups. Psychotherapy With 159 (37)
Family Adapt to a Disability. Helping the 159 (31)
Family Affair. Sex as a 159 (48)
Family an Obsolete Institution? Is the American 216 (48)
Family and Black Youth. Black 151 (111)
Family - Azusa to Marrakech. Footloose 29 (4), (122), (318)
Family, Black Experience. Black 181 (30)
Family, Black Psychology. Black 181 (31)
Family. Changes in the American 181 (237), (292)
Family. Changing American 151 (167)
Family - Conflicts and Resolutions 29 (59), (99), (345)
Family Counseling 180 (88)
Family Counseling/Family Therapy 181 (287), (310)
Family Decision Making Process 218
Family. Emotionally Disturbed Child and 16 (35)
Family Farm System 126 (1), (2)
Family Goals and Communication 214 (77)
Family. Heroin Addiction and the 171 (44)
Family History. Tracing Your 176 (67)
Family. Homosexuality, Marriage and the 181 (238)
Family in African Societies. Importance of 29 (7)
Family in Antiquity 227 (18)
Family in British Columbia. Wilderness 218
Family in Historical Perspective 142 (78)
Family Interaction. Child Discipline, Cohabitation, Patterns of 56 (7)
Family Interaction. Patterns of 56 (7)
Family. Japanese and/or Chinese 168 (66)
Family Life. Changing 168 (26)
Family Life in Asia and the United States 56 (123)
Family Living 176 (51)
Family Mime 29 (43), (103), (187), (313)
Family. Nutrition for the 117 (79)
Family. Once and Future 211 (2)
Family Owned Business. Trials, Tribulations and Joys of 136 (7)
Family Practice 218
Family Problems. Solving 168 (7)
Family. Psychological Perspectives on the American 181 (291)
Family Relations 225 (4)
Family Relations. Marriage and 16 (35)
Family Relationships. Marital/ 181 (229), (287), (310)
Family Roots. How to Find Your 154 (2)
Family. Sociology of the 159 (33)
Family Still Basic? Is the 151 (93)
Family Therapy 142 (93)

Family Therapy. Family Counseling/ 181 (287), (310)
Family Therapy. Marriage and 176 (25)
Family Upon Children. Effect of the 57 (34)
Fanatic Ideologies in Our Midst 85 (16)
Fantasy. Function and 79 (33)
Fantasy. Is Our Representative Democratic Government a Reality or an Alice in Wonderland 136 (19)
Fantasy Literature. Science Fiction/ 214 (46)
Fantasy. Los Angeles Contemporary Photography Premeditated 29 (9)
Far East Revisited 97 (52)
Far East. Travel in the 29 (128), (319)
Farm and Physical Comedy 151 (289)
Farm Buildings. Solar Energy to Heat 16 (8)
Farm Classes. Adult 117 (8)
Farm Real Estate Value Trends 16 (91)
Farm System. Family 126 (1), (2)
Farm. Tractor Safety on the 151 (263)
Farmers in a Changing World 117 (2)
Farmers Union. Southern Tenant 172 (8)
Farming in the Dark 151 (25)
Farmlands 151 (225)
Farms. Groves, Ranches, 65 (34)
Fascination of Literature - Why We Enjoy Stories, Poems, and Plays 54
Fascism. Free Institutions Versus 142 (1)
Fashion 176 (114)
Fashion Designing 97 (46)
Fashion Fabrics 79 (84), (136), (151)
Fashion. Four Ws of 97 (70)
Fashion Merchandising 142 (8)
Fashion. Multiple Approach to Form and Fiber 79 (106)
Fashion Scene. Male 111 (1), (2)
Fashions and Customs in India 56 (119)
Fate and Behavior of Pesticides in the Environment 171 (39)
Fate of the Oceans 214 (27)
Father. Confessions of a Psychologist 97 (17)
Father in Child Development. Role of the 105 (103)
Father. Life and Times of My 112 (110)
Fathers are Parents Too 159 (48)
Fathers Day 214 (61)
Fathers. Founding 181 (259)
Fathers. Lincoln-Rutledge Romance - Hoax or Reality? Lincoln's Use and Abuse of America's Founding 29 (338)
Fathers of the Church 105 (107)
Fathers. Spirituality of the 105 (107)
Fathom World. Four 59 (12)
Fatigue 105 (115)
Faulkner: Prose Poet. William 159 (19)
Fauna of Pacific Northwest National Parks 218
Fear of Success 224 (1)
Feasibility. Data Processing 105 (5)
Feasibility. Market 65 (1)
Feathers of Selling. Nuts, Guts, and 180 (2)
Features. Enhancing Your 176 (9)
Features. Local Geologic 151 (13)
Features of American Higher Education. Distinguishing 151 (103)
Federal and Pennsylvania Income Tax 151 (44)
Federal Aviation Commission 176 (45)
Federal Fiscal and Budgetary Policy Processes 31 (25)
Federal Government and Indian Education 159 (32)
Federal Income Tax Topics. Other 105 (7)
Federal Income Taxation 159 (9)
Federal Judicial Appointments 168 (57)
Federal Labor Relations 174 (17)
Federal Laws, Regulations, and Executive Orders 151 (1)
Federal. Oil and Gas Conservation and Regulation - State and 151 (135)
Federal Regulation 34 (1)
Federal Regulation and Its Excesses 34 (1)
Federal Taxation 54
Federalism. Problems of 85 (5)
Feed? How Many People Can We 151 (160)
Feed Them? How Shall We 151 (19)
Feeding. Breast 181 (251)
Feeling. Communication of 105 (100)
Feelings and Imagery in the Selection of Food 171 (51)
Female. Entrepreneurs: Male and 105 (84)
Female Psyche. Insights Into the Male Versus 225 (6)
Female Sexuality 168 (23)
Feminine. Teilhard and the 11 (2)
Femininity and Liberated Women 179 (2)
Femininity and Sport Participation. Masculinity- 151 (276)
Feminism 168 (4), 171 (54)
Feminism and Socialism 213 (5)
Feminism. Contribution of Psychoprophylactic Childbirth to the Era of 36 (1)
Feminism. Medieval 151 (215)
Feminism. Socialist- 172 (4)
Feminist and Socialist Ideas Through Electoral Politics. How to Spread 178 (1)
Feminist Movement 216 (47)
Fencing 142 (49)
Ferment in the Soviet Empire 85 (6)
Ferns, and Wildflowers of Washington. Trees, 159 (59)
Fertile Fields for Jobs 225 (13)
Fertility and Longevity of Wild Chimpanzees 151 (208)
Fertility. Food, Fuel and 56 (17)
Fertility. How Wagelessness in the Home Effects Women's Options for 90 (1)
Fertilization 181 (18)
Fertilizers. Population, the Food Chain, and Chemical 151 (134)
Festival for the Dead. Bornese 57 (95)

Festival. Latern 168 (52)
Festivals. Folk 54
Festivals. Indian Culture - Marriage Customs, Holidays and 117 (97)
Festivals. Romen 227 (23)
Fiber 79 (154)
Fiber Activities for Public Places 79 (128)
Fiber and Yarn Manipulation 79 (146)
Fiber Arts 79 (66)
Fiber. Clay and 79 (71)
Fiber Electromyography. Single 181 (155)
Fiber - Essential Nutrient? Dietary 216 (134)
Fiber-fabric Experimental and Sculptural Techniques 79 (98)
Fiber Fashion. Multiple Approach to Form and 79 (106)
Fiber Forms and Small Loom Techniques 79 (129)
Fiber Forms. Dimensional 79 (33)
Fiber. Forms in 79 (151)
Fiber Forms. Nature - Abstractions in 79 (154)
Fiber. Functional Sculpture 79 (138)
Fiber Happenings 79 (86)
Fiber Has in Our Lives. Explorations of the Role 79 (27), (46)
Fiber. International Scene in 79 (151)
Fiber Magic 79 (138)
Fiber Paintings 79 (75)
Fiber, People, Places 79 (5)
Fiber. Ritual Objects in 79 (92)
Fiber Sculpture. Architectural 79 (103)
Fiber Techniques in Weaving 79 (29)
Fiber, The Body, and the Senses 79 (27)
Fiber, Yarn, Fabric. Designing in 79 (146)
Fibers 79 (36)
Fibers and Textiles 151 (32)
Fibers. Earth 79 (152)
Fibers. Hand Spinning - All Kinds of 79 (51)
Fibers - History, Function, Identification 79 (19)
Fibers. Nature 168 (69)
Fiction and Non-fiction. Contemporary 159 (65)
Fiction and the Future. Science 56 (64)
Fiction and Utopias. Science 181 (141), (231)
Fiction. Classical Themes in Science 227 (4)
Fiction. Contemporary Themes in 54
Fiction. Detective 142 (54)
Fiction. Earliest American 151 (237)
Fiction. Exorcism: Fact or 134 (2)
Fiction/Fantasy Literature. Science 214 (46)
Fiction. Flying Saucers - Fact or 83 (15)
Fiction For Children. Canadian Realistic 171 (52)
Fiction. Future and Science 29 (206)
Fiction. Ideas in Science 151 (235)
Fiction of Technical Writing 151 (79)
Fiction. Science 16 (51), 112 (49), 216 (34)
Fiction - The New Methodology. Science 56 (64)
Fiction: What It's All About. Science 117 (88)
Fiction. Works of Contemporary 159 (19)
Fields. Life and Times of W.C. 112 (38)
Fifteen Years of Change. Washington Whirl - 97 (5)
15th to the 17th Century. Art of the Netherlands From the 56 (9)
5th Century. Christian Church in the 29 (178), (234)
Fifty Million Consumers 159 (35)
Fifty Million Dollars. From Lettuce Seed to 151 (185)
Fifty Years. American Business - the Next 56 (19)
Fight for Clean Air 54
Fight for School Desegregation 213 (2)
Fight for Them. Our Freedoms and How to 97 (48)
Fighting for Freedom in South Africa 175 (2)
Figure Control for Women 174 (64)
Files. Hiss Case and the FBI 97 (69)
Film 176 (29)
Film. American 57 (32)
Film and Television as an Industrial Process 57 (32)
Film. Children's Literature and 151 (234)
Film. Contemporary 57 (32)
Film-making 154 (19)
Film Stars are Made and Promoted. How Television and 176 (102)
Film. Underground 168 (16)
Film. Women in 142 (80)
Filming and Conservation. Wildlife 4 (4)
Films. Producing 180 (50)
Filmwriter. Walter Hasenclever: The Dramatist as 214 (66)
Final Hunter. Man: The 112 (3)
Final Religion for Mankind. Islam the 1 (4)
Finance 65 (9), (14), (18), (22), (26), (31), (34), (35), (49), (54), (61), (64), (65), (66), 105 (10)
Finance. Careers in Accounting and 23
Finance. Consumer 174 (63)
Finance. International 216 (109)
Finance. Personal 168 (45)
Finance. Public 174 (17)
Financed. How Businesses are 23
Finances. High International 54
Finances. Public 174 (70)
Financial Accounting 159 (50)
Financial Aid. College Admissions and 31 (16)
Financial Aid for Students in Post Secondary Education 54
Financial Aid - How, When, Where 31 (15)
Financial Aid. Student 27 (22), 168 (32)
Financial Aids 57 (21)
Financial Assistance is Available for Higher Education 105 (38)
Financial Assistance Program. Alabama's Student 16 (68)
Financial Data on Stock and Bond Markets. Effects of 31 (1)
Financial Management for a Business. Methods of 151 (37)
Financial Planning 214 (1)
Financial Planning and Management 23
Financial Planning. Human Needs, Goals and 214 (77)

Financial Reports Filed by American Corporations With the Securities and Exchange Commission. Value and Uses of 50 (1)
Financial Statement. How to Read a 151 (50)
Financing 65 (32)
Financing Capital Outlay for Schools 117 (46)
Financing Postsecondary Education 105 (50)
Financing Public Education in Washington 159 (53)
Financing. Real Estate 218
Findings Which May Lead to Human Cures. Veterinary 16 (69)
Fine Turf 117 (7), (126)
Finger Weaving 79 (40), (98), (113), (142)
Finger Weaving. Cherokee 79 (50)
Fingers, Artist in Residence. Mr. 221 (1)
Fingers Goes to College. Mr. 221 (1)
Fingers Show. Mr. 221 (1)
Finishing Touches for Handwoven Fabrics 79 (151)
Finland. Focus on 110 (3)
Fire Next Time. South Africa - 29 (7)
Fire Prevention 151 (260)
Fire Safety 151 (260)
Fire Safety in Health Facilities 216 (99)
Firearms. Evolution of Antique 117 (130)
First Aid 142 (39), 174 (24)
First Amendment: An Unqualified Right to Be Unfair 117 (83)
First Amendment - Is It Working 105 (54)
First Amendment. Press and 57 (88)
First Ladies. Tattle Tales About 112 (11)
First Olympic Team and Athletes. America's 151 (275)
First Person Monologues 168 (34)
First Person Singular 97 (11)
First Time College Freshmen. Problems Faced by 174 (88)
First Un-Americans 105 (60)
First Woman Editor. Elizabeth Timothy - America's 56 (61)
First Year of Life. Development in the 181 (23)
Fiscal and Budgetary Policy Processes. Federal 31 (25)
Fiscal and Monetary Policies 56 (23)
Fiscal Planning 151 (9)
Fiscal Policy. Government 174 (21)
Fish Behavior 171 (42)
Fish. Effects of Shock Waves Upon Marine 218
Fish to Increase World Protein Supply. Growing 16 (53)
Fisheating Creek. Florida - Cypress Sanctuary 69 (6)
Fisheries 174 (4)
Fishes. Management of 57 (16)
Fishing 113 (1), 142 (10), (18), 176 (117)
Fishing Rights. Indian 159 (24)
Fitness. Adult Physical 142 (86)
Fitness and Conditioning. Enjoying 151 (204)
Fitness. Cardiovascular 159 (14)
Fitness for Adults. Physical 151 (285)
Fitness for Busy Executives 176 (75)
Fitness for Your Future 171 (30)
Fitness. Physical 142 (18), (20), 151 (205), 159 (67), 174 (27)
Fitness. President's Council on Physical 105 (114)
Fitness. Yoga, Health, and 57 (80)
Five Basic Methods of Salesmanship 135 (44)
500 Years. Michelangelo Inspires After 151 (264)
Five Years. Economy Over the Next 102 (3)
Flame Retardent Textiles 16 (28)
Flamespread Testing and Structural Testing 80 (2)
Flannel Board Usage 142 (94)
Flashback! 1976 Student is a 171 (58)
Fleece. Potentials of 79 (27)
Fleeces for Hand Spinning. Selection and Preparation of 79 (59)
Flight. Love of 216 (108)
Flight. Supersonic 216 (130)
Flooring. Laminated Hardwood Block 80 (2)
Flora. Origins and History of Washington 218
Floral Design 117 (7), (126)
Florida - Cypress Sanctuary-Fisheating Creek 69 (6)
Florida's Big Cypress Swamp. Hidden Worlds of 69 (6)
Flow Characteristics of Solids - Liquid Mixtures in Pumps and Piping 67 (5)
Flow Control Systems. Automated 67 (18)
Flow. Fluid 214 (43)
Flow in Living Color. Ground Water 136 (14)
Flow Planning. Cash 136 (7)
Flower Arranging 16 (63)
Flowering Plants of South America. Medicinal 27 (14)
Flowers and Photography 216 (58)
Flowers and Plant Communities. Wild 223 (15)
Flowers and Their Habitats. Wild 168 (56)
Flowers. Architecture of 216 (62)
Flowers. Garden 117 (122)
Flowers. Pollination of 159 (70)
Flowers - Varieties and Culture. Garden 117 (5)
Flowers. Wild 151 (308)
Fluid Drive Systems 67 (23)
Fluid Flow 214 (43)
Fluids. Use of Intravenous 16 (77)
Fluorine Compounds 216 (21)
Flushing Horizontal Form, Fill and Seal Packaging. Gas 67 (15)
Flying 151 (33)
Flying Career. Air Force 174 (81)
Flying Free 4 (1)
Flying Saucers - Fact or Fiction 83 (15)
Focus on Finland 110 (3)
Folk, and Traditional. Psychology of Clothing and Dress - Historical, 79 (28)
Folk Art. Duquesne Tamburitzan Institute of 54
Folk Art. Mexican Retablo and Related 174 (41)
Folk Art Stitchery 79 (117)
Folk Arts 57 (78)

Folk Craft Pottery. Japanese 57 (44)
Folk Dancing. Greek 181 (86)
Folk Festivals 54
Folk Hero of Turkey. Hodja - 29 (200)
Folk Heroes. American 29 (185), (200)
Folk Literature 159 (23)
Folk Music 142 (57)
Folk Music. American 29 (220)
Folk Music in the South. Black 29 (220)
Folklore. American 29 (201)
Folklore Americana 29 (185), (200), (332)
Folklore and Edibility of Wild Plants 57 (82)
Folklore and Legend of Birds in Art 57 (82)
Folklore and Processes of Spinning. History, 79 (99)
Folklore and Reality. Shark - 69 (10)
Folklore. Greece - In Myth and 29 (200)
Folklore in History 54
Folklore. Oriental - Myth and 29 (15), (200)
Folklore. Research in Greek 181 (142)
Folktale. Africa - In Myth and 29 (2), (200)
Folktale, Homer, Literature and Art. Polyphemus in 227 (47)
Food Abundance in a Hungry World. United States 16 (3)
Food Additives 151 (177), (178), (179), 168 (29), 181 (178), (230), 216 (142)
Food and Agricultural Organizations 174 (4)
Food and Agriculture Organization of the United Nations 16 (45)
Food and Food Production Research 151 (24)
Food and Food-related Research in Agriculture 151 (181)
Food and Health 176 (76)
Food and Nutrition 187 (1)
Food and Nutrition Beliefs 57 (30)
Food Business. Multinational Corporations in the 181 (34), (334)
Food Chain, and Chemical Fertilizers. Population, the 151 (134)
Food Chain. Eating Low on the 181 (184)
Food. Chemistry and 151 (264)
Food Composition, Food Safety and Food Fermentations 16 (71)
Food Consciousness. Raising 151 (177)
Food. Consumerism: What's in Our 181 (249)
Food Co-ops and Community Stores Can Be Used for Political Organizing. How 178 (1)
Food Crisis - Fact or Fiction 112 (21)
Food Dollar. Stretching Your 57 (15)
Food. Environmental Pollution and 151 (177)
Food. Feelings and Imagery in the Selection of 171 (51)
Food From the Sea 29 (71), (140), (271)
Food, Fuel and Fertility 56 (17)
Food Hazards at Home. Controlling Microbiological 151 (178)
Food? How Safe is Your 151 (177)
Food in Your Home. Preserving 151 (180)
Food. Interactions Between Drugs and 54
Food Laws. Food Regulations 151 (177)
Food Loss. Animal Diseases and the Resultant 16 (45)
Food Management 180 (166)
Food. Naturally Occuring Toxic Substances 151 (177)
Food Pharmacology 171 (26)
Food Plant Noise Control 67 (4)
Food Plant Waste Water. Land Treatment of 67 (13)
Food Poisoning - Facts and Prevention 151 (173)
Food Problems. World 112 (17 (117)
Food Processing 216 (142)
Food Processing Industry. Development, Production and Processing of Vegetable Seeds Used in the 67 (26), (27)
Food Processing Industry. How Productivity Can be Enhanced in the 67 (1)
Food Processing. Measurement of Moisture in Dehydrated Food Products, Grain and Other Moisture Measurements in 67 (21)
Food Processing on Nutrients in Foods. Effect of 216 (72)
Food Processing. Pumps for 67 (18)
Food Production and World Population 16 (89)
Food Production. Energy Options for 47
Food Production. Organophosphate Pesticides and 117 (3)
Food Production Research. Food and 151 (24)
Food Production. World 216 (97)
Food Products, Grain and Other Moisture Measurements in Food Processing. Measurement of Moisture in Dehydrated 67 (21)
Food Quality 216 (142)
Food Regulations and Food Laws 151 (177)
Food-related Research in Agriculture. Food and 151 (181)
Food Resources. Marine 216 (36)
Food Scientist. Role of the 216 (23)
Food Services. Institutional 16 (90)
Food Situation. World 16 (30), 117 (8), 216 (36)
Food We Eat. Technology and the 151 (177)
Foods and Beverages. Bottling and Packaging 67 (10)
Foods. Effect of Food Processing on Nutrients in 216 (72)
Foods. Nutrition and Health 151 (174)
Foods of the Future 151 (177)
Foods. Optical Causes of Color in 67 (17)
Foods. Our 216 (67)
Foods. Preserving Your Home-Produced 151 (178)
Foods. Recent Advances in Commercial Canning and Freezing of 216 (72)
Foods? Why Additives in 216 (72)
Foot Forward. How to Put Your Best 168 (38)
Football 29 (301), 113 (1), 151 (282)
Football Officiating. College 31 (39)
Football. Officiating High School 16 (42)

Football Program. Administration of an Inter-collegiate 29 (24), (301)
Football. When the Muckrackers Took on College 151 (69)
Footloose Family - Azusa to Marrakech 29 (4), (122), (318)
For Amusement Only 97 (29)
For Better or Worse 75 (1)
For God's Sake, Laugh 105 (26)
For Humans Only 144
For Your Information 151 (63)
Forceps, and Seawater. Scalpel, 56 (88)
Forcing Public Employees into Unwanted Labor Unions. Right to Work - 131 (4)
Ford, 1909-1927. Rise and Fall of the Model-T 151 (294)
Forecast. Economic 29 (81)
Forecasting and Research 65 (1)
Forecasting Community Needs. Innovative Method of 168 (57)
Forecasting. Economic 181 (48)
Forecasting. Land Use 151 (290)
Foreign Affairs. Origins of the American Tradition in 85 (7)
Foreign Affairs: What Happened to Our Investment in Korea? 151 (110)
Foreign Affairs: What the Diplomats Are Doing and Why 151 (110)
Foreign Aid. Canadian 171 (11)
Foreign Assistance Administration. United States 151 (196)
Foreign Children. Adopting 168 (48)
Foreign Correspondent 223 (20)
Foreign Economic Aid 56 (17)
Foreign Language Pedagogy 142 (6)
Foreign Language Skills 174 (58)
Foreign Language Teaching. Natural Approach to 27 (15)
Foreign Languages 174 (15)
Foreign Languages and Careers 216 (135)
Foreign Levels. Role of Trademarks in Advertising and Marketing on Domestic and 209
Foreign Policy 220 (4)
Foreign Policy Alternatives 214 (54)
Foreign Policy. American 151 (192), 181 (265), (337), 214 (55), 224 (7)
Foreign Policy. American Strategy in 85 (29)
Foreign Policy and Its Relationship to Pacifism, Socialism and Nonviolence 217 (2)
Foreign Policy and the Power Balance 97 (2)
Foreign Policy and United States Governmental Machinery for Carrying it Out. United States 85 (15)
Foreign Policy. Australian Politics and 151 (189)
Foreign Policy. Canadian Politics and 151 (189)
Foreign Policy. Chinese 224 (7)
Foreign Policy. Conservative Tradition and 85 (7)
Foreign Policy. Constitutional/Moral 102 (12)
Foreign Policy. Contemporary Issues in American 57 (19)
Foreign Policy. Contemporary Problems of American 159 (36)
Foreign Policy. Current Issues in American 117 (66), (113)
Foreign Policy. Liberalism and the Tragedy of American 85 (7)
Foreign Policy. Military Aid and 159 (36)
Foreign Policy of Ruin. Our 225 (36)
Foreign Policy. Organizing and Managing United States 151 (196)
Foreign Policy. Quest for Purpose in Contemporary American 85 (7)
Foreign Policy. Realities of American 85 (17)
Foreign Policy. Religious Subversion of 180 (145)
Foreign Policy. Sources and Goals of Soviet 85 (31)
Foreign Policy. Soviet 54, 57 (37)
Foreign Policy Today. United States 223 (21)
Foreign Policy. Toward a Wiser 85 (16)
Foreign Policy. Trends in United States 85 (21)
Foreign Policy. United States 85 (28), 117 (68), 214 (53)
Foreign Student Education Implications for Pennsylvania 151 (107)
Foreign Students at Virginia Tech 216 (138)
Foreign Students in the U.S.A. 31 (26)
Foreign Students. Strangers in Paradise - 151 (200)
Foreign Trade 174 (70)
Forensic Science 159 (11)
Forest and Bogs. Searching for Prairies, 168 (56)
Forest Ecosystem 218
Forest Recreation 151 (304)
Forestry as Adapted to a Power Company 150 (5)
Forestry Techniques 159 (13)
Forests. Leprechauns and 223 (35)
Forever. Why Not Live 45 (2)
Forgeries. Scientific Detection of Art 151 (73)
Forgotten Hero of the War of 1812 57 (91)
Form and Fiber Fashion. Multiple Approach to 79 (106)
Form and Meaning in Our Times. Mythology - 54
Form. Evolution of the Art 56 (13)
Form, Fill and Seal Packaging. Gas Flushing Horizontal 67 (15)
Form of Business. Choosing the 105 (7)
Form. Opera as a Contemporary Art 142 (16)
Form. Physics as an Art 151 (268)
Form. Textile Printing and Dyeing as an Art 79 (129)
Form. Weaving as an Art 79 (60)
Form With Respect to Time and Space. Reappraisal of Organic 54
Formation. Television and Public Opinion 168 (50)
Formation. Weave 79 (140)
Former Governor Looks at Health Programs 8 (2)
Forming a Rifle, Pistol, or Shotgun Class 57 (58)
Forms and Small Loom Techniques. Fiber 79 (129)
Forms. Comparative Art 117 (11)
Forms. Contemporary Basketry as Functional or Sculptural 79 (135)

Forms. Dimensional Fiber 79 (33)
Forms in Fiber 79 (151)
Forms. Light 79 (90)
Forms. Nature - Abstractions in Fiber 79 (154)
Forms of Sculpture. Ancient 227 (32)
Forms. Office Management, Operation, and 65 (32)
Forms. Prolonged Release Dosage 54
Forms. Weaving Stuffed 79 (10)
Formula to Counter Aging. Vitamin 27 (29)
Fortune. Mysterious Laws of Chance and 29 (136)
48 Techniques for Beginners 79 (74)
49'ers. Nutrition for Modern 57 (30)
Fossil-fuel Steam Electric Plant. Electric Generation at a 150 (11)
Fossil Man 218
Fossils 159 (38)
Fossils. Hunting for Gems and 4 (6)
Fossils of Mazon Creek 57 (77)
Foundation Grants. How to Research 105 (53)
Foundations. American Constitutional 85 (9)
Foundations in Wisconsin. Philanthropic 105 (53)
Founding Fathers 181 (259)
Founding Fathers. Lincoln - Rutledge Romance - Hoax or Reality? Lincoln's Use and Abuse of America's 29 (338)
Fountain of Youth. Sex, Spirit, and the 225 (5)
Fountains in the Landscape 181 (132)
Four Continents. Student Unrest in 85 (18)
Four Decades of College Students 151 (11)
Four Diamonds Fund 151 (186)
Four Dimensions of Communication 56 (56)
Four Fathom World 59 (12)
4-H Weaving. Beginning 79 (107)
4-H Youth Programs. Berks County 151 (20)
4-Harness Loom Weaving. Beginning 79 (158)
Four-harness Looms. Pattern Drafting for 79 (122)
Four Harness Tapestry. Double Weave - 79 (74)
Four Harness Weaving 79 (50)
Four Seasons in Europe 29 (321)
Four Things We Must Learn 75 (1)
Four Ws of Fashion 97 (70)
Fourth Branch of Government 117 (106)
4th Grade. Language Arts and Math Activities for Teachers - Nursery - 117 (48)
Foxes That Nibble Your Vines. Little 75 (1)
Fractional Dentures 181 (174)
Fracture Traces to Locate Water Wells. Using 136 (12)
Fragrances, Culinary. Herbs for Dyes, 79 (111)
Frame Loom. Rigid Heddle 79 (135)
Frame Loom Tapestry 79 (107)
Frame Loom Tapestry Weaving 79 (9)
Frame Loom Workshop 79 (68)
Frame Looms 79 (50)
Frame Set Ups. Weaving Off-loom-Board or 79 (127)
Frame Weaving. Nail 79 (106)
Frames of Reference 181 (88)
France 57 (92)
France and England. University in 105 (33)
France. Bonjour, 59 (10)
France. Contemporary 56 (115)
France. Everyday Life in 56 (111)
France. Faces of 15 (1)
France. Many Faces of 110 (2)
France. Popular Recreation and Reform in the 19th Century England and 142 (98)
France. Renaissance in 57 (92)
Franchising 65 (11), (31), (54)
Franco. Spain After 29 (125), (151), (323)
Frank Lloyd Wright 142 (79)
Frank Lloyd Wright. Architecture of 181 (78)
Frank Lloyd Wright's Own Homes - The Two Taliesins 151 (29)
Franklin. Benjamin 142 (63)
Franklin to Fusion 152
Fraser's MBA Program. Simon 171 (57)
Fraud. Consumer 176 (61)
Fred Sanford. From Archie Bunker to 112 (9)
Free Crochet. Structural Design in 79 (145)
Free Enterprise 23
Free Enterprise for Local Civic, Social, Educational and Political Organizations. Future of 74
Free Enterprise System 151 (51), 180 (107)
Free Enterprise System. Achieving Success in the 180 (79)
Free Enterprise. Why Americans Are Losing Faith in 102 (33)
Free-form Wall Hangings 79 (140)
Free Institutions Versus Fascism 142 (1)
Free Market System 216 (43)
Free Masonry in 19th Century America 181 (262)
Free Press and Fair Trial 181 (68)
Free Press Versus Fair Trial 181 (211)
Free Society. Labor Policy of the 85 (27)
Free Society. Teaching and Learning in a 174 (1)
Free Speech. How Free is 117 (135)
Free Speech in a Democracy. Values of 117 (65)
Freedom 155 (1)
Freedom and Academic License. Academic 85 (16)
Freedom and Civil Liberty. Economic 174 (72)
Freedom and Responsibilities of the Press 102 (27)
Freedom and the Common Law Tradition 85 (27)
Freedom. Censorship in the Schools - A Threat to 151 (100)
Freedom. Dostoevsky's Grand Inquisitor, Slavery and 85 (36)
Freedom. Economic 175 (5)
Freedom. God and Political 85 (25)
Freedom in South Africa. Fighting for 175 (2)
Freedom. Intellectual 56 (50)
Freedom, Law and Political Institutions. Order, 85 (40)
Freedom. Model Code of Procedures for Academic 105 (49)
Freedom Nobody Wants 85 (25)

Freedom of Choice. Sex, Monogamy and the 211 (3)
Freedom of Expression. Obscenity and 218
Freedom of or From Religion 151 (200)
Freedom of Press. Philosophical Background of 117 (85)
Freedom of Speech and Press 56 (94)
Freedom of the Scholastic Press 168 (12)
Freedom - The Remarkable Identity. Property and 85 (27)
Freedom Versus Security 3 (8)
Freedoms and How to Fight for Them. Our 97 (48)
Freedom's Unfinished Tasks 12
Freeway Noises. Psychological Effects of 223 (13)
Freezing of Foods. Recent Advances in Commercial Canning and 216 (72)
Freirian Model. Alternative Education and 142 (56)
French. African Literature in 168 (41)
French and American Wines. Enjoying 216 (25)
French Caribbean Literature 168 (41)
French Fries Made From Riced Potatoes 67 (14)
French Gastronomy 151 (28)
French Gothic Art. Early 151 (28)
French Government and Politics. Contemporary 57 (89)
French Hero. Medieval 181 (138)
French History. Great Names in 56 (90)
French Horn Performance 57 (29)
French: How We Differ 117 (138)
French Impressionist Art 117 (138)
French Literature. Great Names in 56 (60)
French Revolution 117 (74)
French Revolution and Napoleon 117 (64)
French: What We Have in Common 117 (138)
French Writers and Opinions on England 142 (98)
Freshman. English and the College 105 (46)
Freshmen. Problems Faced by First Time College 174 (88)
Friend or Enemy. Computer - 56 (126)
Friends Are Racists. Some of My Best 168 (11)
Friends. When Arabs and Jews Were 181 (306), (343)
Friendship. Melville and Hawthorne, A Timely 105 (22)
Fringes and Joining Stitches. Braids, 79 (53)
Fringes. Braids, Tassels and 79 (80)
Frivolous Narrative 227 (35)
From Archie Bunker to Fred Sanford 112 (9)
From Autocracy to Totalitarianism 57 (37)
From Classroom to Community 105 (50)
From Judaism to Islam 1 (1)
From Lettuce Seed to Fifty Million Dollars 151 (185)
From Pentagon Papers to Cointelpro 213 (1)
From the City of Stars to the City of Light 97 (16)
From the Land of the Phamlysoun 56 (26)
Front Line and the Bottom Line 135 (32)
Frontier. Agriculture - A Vertical 216 (22)
Frontier. Engineering on the Last 151 (138)
Frontier. Living on the 223 (26)
Frontier. Mind - The Last 151 (203)
Frontiers of Wildlife Photography 69 (11)
Frost and the Classics. Robert 227 (1)
Frost - Individualistic Democrat. Robert 85 (32)
Frost. New England of Robert 69 (4)
Frost's New England. Robert 59 (6)
Frozen Tombs of Siberia. Scythian 29 (20)
Fruit Production. Background 117 (5), (122)
Frustrations to Enhance Productivity. Identify 151 (38)
Fuel and Fertility. Food, 56 (17)
Fuel for the Future 20
Fuel Shortages 158
Fuel Tomorrow. Yesterday's 66 (5)
Full Disclosure Myth 85 (19)
Fullerton Arboretum 29 (28), (143), (273)
Fullerton Library. Microforms at the Cal State 29 (196)
Fullerton. Theater at Cal Stste 29 (311)
Fun Being Successful. It's 81 (1)
Fun. Elementary School - Mathematics Can Be 151 (250)
Fun. How to Have 97 (25)
Fun Making Money. It's 81 (1)
Fun. No Seats - No 112 (8)
Fun. Selling Can be 180 (139)
Function and Fantasy 79 (33)
Function and Operation of a Major Futures Trading Facility 38
Function, Identification. Fibers - History, 79 (19)
Function. Muscle 105 (115)
Function of Consumers in Our Economy 168 (45)
Functional or Sculptural Forms. Contemporary Basketry as 79 (135)
Functional Sculpture in Fiber 79 (138)
Functions of ARC (Associations for Retarded) Organizations and 169 (2)
Functions of USL. Service 174 (88)
Fund. Four Diamonds 151 (186)
Fund of Philadelphia. People's 181 (309)
Fund Raising. Creative Direct Mail for 151 (188)
Fundamental Basic Education? What is 347 (29)
Fundamental Political Changes in America. Need for 178 (5)
Fundamental Principles of Islam 1 (1)
Fundamentals of Drafting and Designing Fabrics 79 (93)
Funding of Research 29 (255), (268)
Funding Sources. Developing Alternative 57 (10)
Funds. Kinds of No-Load Mutual 140 (1)
Funds. Services Offered by No-Load Mutual 140 (1)
Funds. Trust 54
Fungi. Edible 151 (176)
Funny Game...But This is Ridiculous. Baseball is a 83 (14)
Funny Thing Happened on the Way... 83 (10)

Funny? What's So 151 (243)
Furnace. Out of This 31 (31)
Furnishings. Home 56 (96)
Furnishings. Structuring Woven 79 (87)
Furniture and Furniture Manufacturing 216 (65)
Furniture Refinishing Techniques 151 (97)
Furniture Styles. Historical 56 (96)
Fusion. Controlled 151 (129)
Fusion. Franklin to 152
Fusion Reactors 216 (88)
Future 168 (47)
Future and Applications of Science and Technology 154 (17)
Future and Education 57 (24)
Future and Science Fiction 29 (206)
Future Comes From. Where the 168 (11)
Future. Communication Technology - Past, Present and 29 (308), (335)
Future Control of the Oceans 57 (19)
Future. Corporation of the 102 (36)
Future Developments of Point Defiance Park - The People Speak 159 (34)
Future. Educating for the 216 (125)
Future. Education and the 57 (46), 168 (21)
Future. Education for the 174 (83)
Future. Energy Alternatives for the 150 (3)
Future. Energy and the 174 (39)
Future. Energy for the 151 (132)
Future. Energy in the 150 (2)
Future. Engineering - The Challenge of the 151 (144)
Future Family. Once and 221 (2)
Future. Fitness for Your 171 (30)
Future. Foods of the 151 (177)
Future. Fuel for the 20
Future. Home of the 225 (21)
Future. How Today's Economy Affects Your 135 (39)
Future Implications. Current Policy, 117 (24)
Future Implications for the 174 (31)
Future. Invent Your Own 151 (35)
Future is Here 176 (69)
Future. Liberal Arts as Preparation for an Uncertain 151 (116)
Future Life Style. Shaping a 102 (15)
Future. Management of the 135 (13)
Future. Metric System in Your 168 (35)
Future. No! No! No! Censorship: Past, Present, 151 (85)
Future. Nutrition for the 159 (12)
Future of Agriculture in Berks County 151 (22)
Future of Cable Television 216 (47)
Future of Church Tax Exemptions 12
Future of Conservation 85 (9)
Future of Conservatism in Post-Liberal America 85 (21)
Future of Democracy 85 (18)
Future of Eastern North Carolina Waterways 56 (29)
Future of Education 27 (19), (104)
Future of Elementary Education 57 (79)
Future of Energy 216 (71)
Future of Free Enterprise for Local Civic, Social, Educational and Political Organizations 74
Future of Higher Education 142 (33)
Future of Higher Education in Louisiana 174 (79)
Future of Man 29 (54)
Future of Man? Can We Control the 29 (141), (161), (334)
Future of Man. Genetic Engineering and the 151 (164)
Future of Man. Genetics and 29 (113), (131), (170)
Future of Ocean Exploration 225 (7)
Future of Private Enterprise 102 (6)
Future of Small Business Enterprise in the United States 159 (3)
Future of Soviet - American Relations 85 (31)
Future of Space Activity 225 (7)
Future of Suburbia 216 (43)
Future of the American Role in Asia 105 (57)
Future of the Independent College 176 (26)
Future of the South 16 (24)
Future of the South. Technology and the 16 (32), (51)
Future of the Tradition. Contemporary National Dress of Mayan Indians of Guatemala - Historical Interpretation and 79 (83)
Future of Tory Radicalism. Nature and 85 (40)
Future of Universities 171 (60)
Future of Work and Leisure 181 (12)
Future of Working 57 (85)
Future. Penn State and the 151 (101)
Future. Planning Business Education for the 117 (14)
Future. Planning for the 102 (33)
Future. Population Change and the American 168 (42)
Future Promises and Perils 151 (236)
Future. Religion and the 11 (4)
Future Role of United States Government in Asia 159 (36)
Future. Science Fiction and the 56 (64)
Future. Sex Past and 142 (62)
Future. Technology and the 57 (46)
Future Trends. Engineering Education: 151 (266)
Future Trends in Meat 151 (182)
Future Trends in Psychology 105 (102)
Future Trends. Mathematics and Computers - 142 (70)
Future. Urban Society and the 181 (240)
Future. Your Incredible 225 (9)
Futures. Alternative 159 (3)
Futures Trading Facility. Function and Operation of a Major 38
Futurology 181 (231)

G

Gaining Design Vertically in Weaving 79 (94)
Galapagos and Its Organisms 218
Galilee. Two From 97 (31)
Gambling Behavior 105 (99)
Gambling. Compulsive 224 (14)
Gambling. Mathematics in 29 (214)
Gambling Odds. Sucker Bait - The 151 (249)
Gambling. Probability and 56 (130)
Gambling. Question of Legalized 97 (60)
Game. Admissions 151 (15)
Game...But This is Ridiculous. Baseball is a Funny 83 (14)
Game. Get in the 112 (43)
Game. How to Improve Your 29 (306)
Game of Go. Japanese 151 (210)
Game Preserves of East Africa. Wildlife and 117 (142)
Game. Ratings 105 (69)
Games and Activities to Liven Up Reading 181 (8)
Games and Educational Simulations. Learning 214 (36)
Games and Puzzles in Elementary Topography 151 (247)
Games: Arena of World Problems. Olympic 151 (275)
Games. Coloring Applied to Solitaire 181 (1)
Games. Differences in Ancient and Modern Olympic 151 (275)
Games. History of the Ancient Olympic 151 (275)
Games. Mathematical 181 (1), (148)
Games of Chance. Mathematics in 181 (4), (151)
Games 30 Years Ago. Olympic 181 (2)
Games With Computers. Playing 181 (204)
Gaming. Operational 151 (148)
Gandhi and Indian Democracy. Mrs. 117 (97)
Gandhi Experience. Non-violence and the 54
Gang Weaving 79 (140)
Gang Weaving on 8 Harnesses. Double 79 (132)
Gap. Head 'Em Off at the 76 (1)
Gaps. Causes for Communication 171 (45)
Garbage. Energy From 16 (50)
Garbage or Gold. Solid Wastes and Their Management 16 (2)
Garden Flowers 117 (122)
Garden Flowers - Varieties and Culture 117 (5)
Garden. Home Vegetable 151 (25)
Garden Insects. Home 216 (102)
Gardening 214 (60)
Gardening. Landscape 16 (63)
Gardening. Organic 216 (62)
Gardening Problems 189
Gardening. Vegetable 174 (2)
Gardening With Vegetables. Home 117 (5), (122)
Gardens 117 (7), (126)
Gardens - Arboretums in North America. Botanical 117 (5)
Gardens. Around-the-World Tropical 174 (44)
Gardens. Botanical 117 (122)
Gardens. Japanese 57 (44)
Gardens. Notes on Home 56 (100)
Gardens. Virginia 216 (6)
Garfield Thomas Water Tunnel. Research at the 151 (143)
Garments 79 (159)
Garments. Loom-Designed 79 (136)
Garments. Loom Shaped 79 (16)
Garments Made on Loom 79 (147)
Garments - Our Immediate Environment 79 (32)
Garments. Shaped 79 (138)
Gas Conservation and Regulation - State and Federal. Oil and 151 (135)
Gas Exploration (United States). Oil and 151 (124)
Gas Flushing Horizontal Form, Fill and Seal Packaging 67 (15)
Gas Industry - Drilling and Production. Oil and 151 (135)
Gas Industry - Supply and Demand. Oil and 151 (135)
Gas Storage. Underground 151 (135)
Gas Shortages. Natural 74
Gas Supply. Realities of Oil and 181 (131), (209)
Gastronomy. French 151 (28)
Gauges. Nuclear Density, Level and Belt Scale Process 67 (19)
Gauze Weaves 79 (113)
Gems and Fossils. Hunting for 4 (6)
Gems. Roman Engraved 227 (47)
Gemstones 105 (18), 151 (255)
Genealogy 218
Genealogy. American Indian and Black 154 (2)
General Air Force 174 (81)
General. Anthropology in 105 (1)
General Aviation 142 (69)
General Aviation and the Community Airport 16 (46)
General Aviation Benefits the Nation 19 (1)
General Brazilian History 142 (56)
General College Admissions 54
General College Affairs 224 (8)
General Counseling and Guidance 142 (93)
General Economic Conditions 214 (34)
General Energy Outlook 35
General Engineering 216 (30), (82)
General History 174 (80)
General Lafayette's Visit to Louisiana 174 (14)
General Management 105 (9)
General Picture. Minority Groups - A 27 (42)
General Psychology 174 (32), (62)
General Public Policy Issues 133 (2)
General R.E. Lee. Our Greatest 57 (28)
General Relativity 142 (65)

General Sales and Marketing 23
General Surveying 216 (116)
General Systems Theory. Applied 159 (66)
General View of Textiles in America 79 (2)
Generating Station Operations. Environmental Standards for 150 (4)
Generation at a Fossil-fuel Steam Electric Plant. Electric 150 (11)
Generics. Selection and Purchase of 54
Genes and Society 211 (1)
Genesis of Landscape Painting 56 (13)
Genetic Counseling 29 (113), (131), (170), 151 (164), 181 (173)
Genetic Counseling and Genetic Engineering 105 (104)
Genetic Counseling. Prenatal Diagnosis of 151 (165)
Genetic Defects. Prenatal Diagnosis of 211 (1)
Genetic Diagnosis. Prenatal 181 (167)
Genetic Diversity and Political Life 181 (24)
Genetic Engineering 105 (2), 151 (151), 181 (19)
Genetic Engineering and the Future of Man 151 (164)
Genetic Engineering. Genetic Counseling and 105 (104)
Genetic Engineering. Human 218
Genetic Engineering: Life in Our Hands 102 (24)
Genetic Engineering: The Full Scope 159 (44)
Genetic Improvement. Animal and Plant 105 (2)
Genetic Manipulation 151 (211)
Genetic Research. Ethics and 29 (113), (131), (265)
Genetically Superior Trees. Mass Production of 151 (310)
Genetics 181 (16), (173)
Genetics and Future of Man 29 (113), (131), (170)
Genetics and Mental Retardation 29 (131)
Genetics. Biochemical 142 (53)
Genetics. Human 105 (2), 142 (53), 181 (20)
Genetics of Mental Retardation 29 (170), (265)
Genetics. Society and 29 (113), (131), (170)
Genius in the Average Man. There is 112 (108), 135 (53)
Geographers. Roman 227 (31)
Geography as a Profession 29 (89), (159), (341)
Geography Behind the Headlines 29 (135), (159)
Geography of the Middle East 117 (63)
Geography of the Soviet Union 117 (63)
Geography of the U.S.A. Cultural Region and General Cultural 151 (184)
Geography - Past Connotations Versus Current Trends 174 (51)
Geologic Features. Local 151 (13)
Geologic History. Pollen Grains and 159 (38)
Geologist in Greece. Bellingham 223 (37)
Geology. Aerial Views of Washington 159 (38)
Geology and Hydrology Careers for Women 136 (22)
Geology. Environmental 224 (13)
Geology of Coles County, Illinois. Glacial 57 (22)
Geology of Lower Puget Sound 159 (38)
Geology of Minnesota 168 (3)
Geology of Minnesota. Glacial 168 (3)
Geology of Northeastern Washington and the Spokane Area 143 (14)
Geology of Philadelphia 181 (137)
Geology of Pittsburgh Area 151 (13)
Geology of Various Western United States National Parks 168 (3)
Geopolitics of the Middle East 214 (55)
Geostrategic Problems 85 (29)
Geothermal Energy 181 (137)
Geriatric Dentistry 181 (174)
Geriatric. Physical Rehabilitation Needs of the 56 (89)
German and American Education Systems. Comparison of the 56 (54)
German (and Scandinavian) Educational System 151 (235)
German Attitudes 174 (33)
German. Contemporary 174 (33)
German Culture and Politics 56 (139)
German Drama 214 (66)
German Government. American and 85 (5)
German Kabarett and Its Influence. Pre-Hitler 154 (22)
German Manager 3 (6)
German Operetta 216 (112)
German Politics After the 1976 Elections. West 29 (259)
Germany 15 (4), 59 (13)
Germany. Bold New 51 (1)
Germany - History and Prospects. Soviet Union and 85 (31)
Germany. Modern 57 (75)
Germany. Social Insurance in 3 (6)
Germany. 20th Century 142 (1)
Germany. West 142 (22)
Germany's Third Reich. Use of Literature 216 (112)
Gerontology 218
Gertrude Stein's the Making of Americans 181 (272)
Gestalt Therapy 27 (45), 57 (71)
Gestalt Therapy and Sartrian Theory 29 (245)
Get in the Game 112 (43)
Getting a Greater Return on Your Money 97 (59)
Getting Back to Nature 16 (72)
Getting Into the Health Professions 29 (98), (174), (274)
Getting More for Your Money 54
Getting My Article Published 216 (78)
Getting the Most From the Best 75 (1)
Getting the Most From Transportation Technology 151 (293)
Getting Things Done 180 (15)
Getting What You Want With Astrology 225 (20)
Getting Your Club in the News 216 (13)
Gettysburg, the Valley Campaign 57 (96)
Ghana 174 (91)

Ghandi and Martin Luther King. Mahatma 103 (1)
Ghetto. Capitalism and the 85 (2)
Ghetto. Growing Up in the 154 (25)
Ghosts and Psychic Photography. Scientific Evidence for 154 (12)
Ghosts, Witches 161 (1), (2)
Giant. Africa - An Emerging Giant 29 (1), (48)
Giant. Awaken Your Sleeping 112 (104)
Gift for the University. Planning a Deferred 151 (187)
Gift of Prophecy 112 (34), 135 (15)
Gift of the Nile. Egypt - 59 (7)
Gifted and Talented Children 142 (52)
Gifted. Education of the 174 (84), (95)
Girls. Just for Us 97 (6)
Girls, Ladies, Women, or Persons? 151 (61)
Girths. Western Indian Camel 79 (131)
Give a Speech in One Easy Lesson 174 (66)
Give Up or Get Involved 112 (30)
Giving. Annual 151 (188)
Giving is Old But New to P. S.U. 151 (185)
Giving to Penn State. Private 151 (187)
Glacial Ages, Glaciers 218
Glacial Deposition of Aquifers and Other Interesting Landforms 136 (13)
Glacial Geology of Coles County, Illinois 57 (22)
Glacial Geology of Minnesota 168 (3)
Glaciers. Glacial Ages, 218
Glands. Tumors of Salivary 181 (175)
Glands. Ultrastructure of Salivary 181 (175)
Glass Blowing 151 (267)
Glassblowing. Scientific 216 (136)
Glimpse Into the Life and Teachings of Muhammad 1 (8)
Global Minds for a Global World 100 (1)
Global World. Global Minds for a 100 (1)
Glorious Koran 29 (218), (228), (237)
Glory Road. Businessman's 112 (135)
Glycosides. Medicinal Plant 54
Gnostic Tradition and Its Varieties 85 (23)
Gnosticism and Politics 85 (37)
Go. Japanese Game of 151 (210)
Goal and Objectives of Education 117 (49)
Goal - Justice Through Law. America's 112 (28)
Goal Setting - A Means to Self Improvement 112 (78)
Goal Setting: Exercises to Increase Awareness of Oneself 105 (78)
Goal Setting. Time Planning and 65 (32)
Goals and Communication. Family 214 (77)
Goals and Financial Planning. Human Needs, 214 (77)
Goals of Soviet Foreign Policy. Sources 85 (31)
Goals. Reach Your 225 (38)
God and Political Freedom 85 (25)
God and Secret of Adam's Slip. Kingdom of 1 (10)
God. Awareness of 211 (6)
God. Christ as Man and 105 (109)
God. Existence of 1 (3)
God. Islamic Conception of 1 (2), (8)
God. Man Relationship With 1 (4)
God. Phenomenology and 117 (97)
God. Proofs of the Existence of 1 (6)
God. Sartre and Man's Search for a Missing 29 (118), (245)
God Within Christian Faith. Experience of 105 (109)
Goddesses of Greece 227 (48)
Godfrey. Life and Times of Arthur 154 (10)
God's Sake, Laugh. For 105 (26)
Going Metric, In Business, Industry, Stores, and Schools 57 (12)
Gold Mines. Discovery of Soloman 1 (9)
Gold, Silver, and Copper. Metals Futures Contracts in 38
Gold. Solid Wastes and Their Management Garbage or 16 (2)
Golden Age of Radio 57 (67)
Golden Ass 227 (11)
Golden Triangle. Red China, Laos, Thailand, and the 54
Golden Twenties 57 (56)
Golden Years of Hollywood 112 (40)
Goldmine Between Your Ears 135 (57)
Good Books for Home Reading Programs 168 (53)
Good Grades and Bad Education 214 (38)
Good Laugh and Something to Think About 112 (63)
Good Life Possible Today? Is the 85 (36)
Goodness, and Beauty. On the Nature of Truth, 117 (98)
Goods and Services. Techniques for Pushing 225 (13)
Goose Rhymes. Historical Origin of Mother 56 (63)
Gorgon and the Gorgoneion 227 (48)
Gothic Architecture 31 (3)
Gothic Art. Early French 151 (28)
Governance. Academic 151 (8)
Governance. Faculty Participation in University 105 (49)
Government 176 (79), (81)
Government a Reality or an Alice in Wonderland Fantasy. Is Our Representative Democratic 136 (19)
Government Action. Search for Utopia Through 85 (11)
Government. Alabama 16 (55)
Government. American and German 85 (5)
Government. American Indian and the United States 29 (158), (254)
Government and Business 174 (17)
Government and Indian Education. Federal 159 (32)
Government and Modern Democracy. Problems of Constitutional 85 (5)
Government and Organization. Neighborhood 181 (275)
Government and Politics. American 105 (55)

Government and Politics. Contemporary French 57 (89)
Government and Politics of the Middle East 117 (104)
Government Economic Policy 117 (26)
Government. Economics and Politics of Local 54
Government. Economics of Minimal 105 (32)
Government Expenditures and the Economy 54
Government Fiscal Policy 174 (21)
Government. Fourth Branch of 117 (106)
Government in Asia. Future Role of United States 159 (36)
Government in Illinois Could be Improved. How County 57 (49)
Government. Inflation and the Role of 214 (32)
Government into a Corner. Painting 85 (25)
Government. Lobbying in State and Local 31 (27)
Government. Local 105 (56)
Government. Morality in 97 (74)
Government. Opening Up Systems of 174 (79)
Government Policy and the Economy 16 (37)
Government Policy Making. Citizen Participation in 218
Government Printing Office and You 56 (99)
Government. Problems and Issues in Local 54
Government Programs. Private Alternatives to 85 (2)
Government. Proper Relationship Between Broadcast Journalists and the 117 (84)
Government. Public Involvement in 176 (3)
Government Regulation of Business. Economics and Politics of 85 (19)
Government Regulations in Economics and Business 54
Government Relations. Business/ 23
Government. Review of Various Types of City 57 (49)
Government Stabilize the Economy? Can 85 (22)
Government. State and Local 16 (43)
Government Structure. Dream of a Utopia in 85 (11)
Government Support Church Colleges? Should 12
Government Support for Independent Colleges and Universities 105 (50)
Government the Source of Monopoly. Is 85 (2)
Government. Use of Computers in State 174 (79)
Government - When It Began. Big 57 (56)
Government. Why We Can't Reform 225 (36)
Government. Writing Reports in Business and 168 (53)
Governmental Budgeting for the City of Tacoma 159 (4)
Governmental Machinery for Carrying It Out. United States Foreign Policy and United States 85 (15)
Governments. Equal Employment Compliance in Municipal 29 (66), (262)
Government's Issues and Problems: Democracy. American 117 (104)
Governor Isaac Shelby and the War of 1812 117 (69)
Governor Looks at Health Programs. Former 8 (2)
(Governor William W. Scranton). Pennsylvania Politics 151 (222)
Governors of Alabama 16 (55)
Grade. Language Arts and Math Activities for Teachers - Nursery - 4th 117 (48)
Grades and Bad Education. Good 214 (38)
Grades. Teaching Language Arts, Reading, Mathematics and Science to Bilingual Classes in the Elementary 142 (90)
Graduate Education 57 (27), 151 (256)
Graduate. Employment Trends for the College 151 (60)
Graduate School Admissions 142 (95)
Graduates. Career Opportunities for College 181 (50), (53)
Graduates. What Industry Expects of College 216 (23)
Grain and Other Moisture Measurements in Food Processing. Measurement of Moisture in Dehydrated Food Products, 67 (21)
Grains and Geologic History. Pollen 159 (38)
Grammar and Literature. Transformational 29 (210)
Grammar of the English Sentence 57 (48)
Grammar. Transformational 56 (65)
Grammatical Correctness. Contemporary Standards for 117 (61)
Grand Canyon 59 (8)
Grand Canyon by Dory 69 (8)
Grand Inquisitor, Slavery and Freedom. Dostoevsky's 85 (36)
Grandeur. Roman 16
Grant Colleges. History and Development of the Land 191 (122)
Grants. How to Research Foundation 105 (53)
Graph Theory and the Bridges of Konigsberg 151 (247)
Graphic Arts. New Technologies in 218
Graphic Language. Technical Drawing: Universal 117 (82)
Graphic Methods. Graphics and 168 (15)
Graphics and Graphic Methods 168 (15)
Graphics. Landscape 181 (83), (132)
Graphics. Packaging Design and Corporate 147 (1 - 11)
Grasp. Reach Beyond Your 135 (49)
Gratuitous Sex and Violence on Television 116 (1), (2), (6)
Great. Alexander the 227 (45)
Great American Deserts 69 (14)
Great American Eccentrics 102 (25)
Great Americans - Lincoln, the Master Politician 151 (222)
Great Americans - Washington 151 (222)

Great Art. Appreciation of 102 (25)
Great Britain. Brodcasting in 29 (310)
Great Britain. U.S.A. and 181 (118)
Great Day. Tomorrow be a 25 (1)
Great Ice Storm 47
Great Inventions 222
Great Labor Uprising of 1877 213 (3)
Great Letter-writers 159 (65)
Great Misunderstanding. America - Europe - The 85 (18)
Great Names in French History 56 (90)
Great Names in French Literature 56 (60)
Great Sailing Adventures 59 (5)
Great Smokey Mountains 69 (6)
Great Stories I Have Heard 75 (1)
Great Trans-Canada Train Ride 59 (17)
Great Western Movie Scene 112 (20)
Great World of Sports 112 (107)
Greater Understanding of People Through Face and Body Language 212 (1)
Greatest General R.E. Lee. Our 57 (28)
Greatness That is Ours. America - The 51 (1)
Greece 15 (2), 105 (17), 142 (55), 174 (82)
Greece and Rome. Ancient 54
Greece. Archaeology of Classical and Hellenistic 227 (45)
Greece. Bellingham Geologist in 223 (37)
Greece. Classical 29 (317)
Greece. Goddesses of 227 (48)
Greece - In Myth and Folklore 29 (200)
Greece - Islands to the Mountains 59 (10)
Greece. Lord Byron and 142 (98)
Greece Today 56 (122)
Greece. Trips to South America, Central America, Mexico and 79 (117)
Greece, Turkey, and Yugoslavia. Primitive Spinners-Spindles and/or Distaffs From 79 (20)
Greece. Women in Ancient 227 (25)
Greek - An Ongoing Language From Ancient to Modern Times 227 (29)
Greek and Latin Epigraphy 227 (8)
Greek and Roman History 227 (3)
Greek and Roman History and Historiography 227 (30)
Greek and Roman Literature. Women in 227 (24)
Greek and Roman Mythology 218, 227 (3)
Greek and Roman Religion 227 (3)
Greek and Roman Theatre 227 (14)
Greek and Roman Theater. History of 227 (25)
Greek and Roman Women 227 (37)
Greek Art and Architecture 227 (39)
Greek Athletics. Ancient 227 (18)
Greek Commentators on Aristotle and Their Method 227 (51)
Greek Drama 227 (19)
Greek Drama. Classical 181 (81), (139)
Greek Drama. Women in 227 (48)
Greek Ethics 227 (34)
Greek Folk Dancing 181 (86)
Greek Folklore. Research in 181 (142)
Greek History 227 (8)
Greek. History of 227 (40)
Greek Lyric Poetry 227 (28)
Greek Lyric Poetry and Philosophy. Early 227 (46)
Greek Music. Aspects of 227 (43)
Greek Mythology. Landscape of 29 (124), (197), (205), (320)
Greek or Roman Literature 105 (16)
Greek or Roman Religion 105 (16)
Greek Poetry. Cyprus in Modern 227 (29)
Greek Poetry. Myth in Modern 227 (19)
Greek Religion 227 (39)
Greek Society. Virgin in 227 (48)
Greek Traditions of Textiles 79 (156)
Greek Tragedy 227 (1), (17)
Greek Tragedy. Staging of 227 (7)
Greeks and Latin Literature 227 (12)
Green Scum on Lakes 168 (37)
Greenbeans, Cherry, Bright Stack and Filling Equipment. Sweet Corn, 67 (6), (12)
Greenhouse Growing. Hobby 216 (115)
Greening of America? Does the New Left Represent 85 (8)
Greenland, Newfoundland. Vikings - Iceland, 151 (220)
Greenville and the Medical Rehabilitation Community 56 (77)
Greenville, North Carolina. Economic Impact of Students of East Carolina University on Business in 56 (24)
Grey Owl. Three Months With 171 (14)
Grid. Managerial 189
Grief, and Mourning. Bereavement, 29 (281)
Grief. Death and 168 (67)
Grief. Normal Gratifications of 56 (133)
Gross and Fine Motor Development. Normal 159 (26)
Ground Water Flow in Living Color 136 (14)
Ground Water. Impact of Abandoned Wells on 136 (25)
Ground Water Industry: What You Didn't Learn at Daddy's Knee. Education in the 136 (1)
Ground Water Pollution Control 136 (14)
Ground Water Source Heat Pump 136 (25)
Group Communication. Leadership in Small 168 (17)
Group Counseling 142 (93)
Group Dynamics 142 (73), 174 (32), 189
Group Environment. Surveys in a 181 (283)
Group Processes 168 (74)
Group Psychotherapy. Individual or 181 (289)
Group Relations. Minority 168 (66)
Group. Specific Art Interest of a 29 (10)
Group Therapy 142 (73)
Group Therapy. Individual and 181 (289)
Grouping Within the Schools 56 (48)
Groups - A General Picture. Minority 27 (42)

Groups - A General Picture. Minority 27 (42)
Groups and Techniques. Uses of Counseling 151 (161)
Groups. Communication in Small 151 (78)
Groups. Directing Theatre 142 (74)
Groups. Episcopal Church 11 (7)
Groups. New Religious 181 (206)
Groups. Parent's 142 (4)
Groups. Psychotherapy With Families, Individuals and 159 (37)
Groups. Therapeutic and Encounter 29 (231)
Groves, Ranches, Farms 65 (34)
Grow in Contemporary Society. Helping the Physically Handicapped Child to 56 (89)
Growing and Care of House Plants 216 (115)
Growing Fish to Increase World Protein Supply 16 (53)
Growing Up in the Ghetto 154 (25)
Grownups Should be Allowed to Read. Children's Books Only 29 (197), (205)
Growth. Altoona Campus - History and 151 (14)
Growth and Development, Child 174 (27)
Growth and Development in Southern Asia 56 (123)
Growth and Development in Young Athletes 171 (28)
Growth and Development. Psychology of Normal Human 117 (111)
Growth and Development. Union 174 (17)
Growth. College Student 16 (33), (72)
Growth. Economic 174 (70)
Growth. Environmental Quality and the Problem of Economic 29 (73), (260)
Growth. Guru and Spiritual 54
Growth of Technocratic Society 171 (2)
Growth Poles Theory 218
Growth. Population 181 (131), (336)
(Growth, Resources, Economics, Affluence, Technology). Pollution is Great 151 (225)
Growth Still Possible - and Desirable? Is 151 (49)
Growth. Why We Need Zero Population 168 (58)
Growth. World Population 223 (28)
Guam. Under the Ocean Near 223 (34)
Guaranteed Sales 65 (54)
Guaranteed Trade Sales Plan 65 (18)
Guard. Alabama National 16 (44)
Guatemala and Yucatan 59 (4)
Guatemala - Historical Interpretation and Future of the Tradition. Contemporary National Dress of Mayan Indians of 79 (83)
Guatemala It's Textile Arts 79 (41)
Guatemala - Land of Eternal Spring 117 (140)
Guatemala. Textiles of 79 (48)
Guatemalan Weaving. Designs in 79 (26)
Guerilla Warfare 142 (27), (89)
Guest. Ovid Pierce's The Wedding 56 (36)
Guidance 174 (1)
Guidance and Counseling 105 (47), 142 (4), (44)
Guidance Counselor. Liability and the 117 (46)
Guidance Does Make a Difference. Effective 54
Guidance. General Counseling and 142 (93)
Guidance on Personality. Impact of 54
Guidance. Vocational 180 (180)
Guide to Working With Homespun. Practical 79 (130)
Guilt. How to Recognize and Deal With 225 (34)
Guinea Expedition. New 59 (2)
Guru and Spiritual Growth 54
Guts, and Feathers of Selling. Nuts, 180 (2)
Gymnastics 142 (46)
Gymnastics and Tumbling. Beginning 142 (60)
Gymnastics: From High School to the Olympics. Men's 168 (2)

H

H.E.L.P. (Health Education Learning Program). Project 16 (49)
Habitats. Wild Flowers and Their 168 (56)
Haiti. Anthropology of 142 (14)
Haiti. Applied Nutrition Program in 216 (140)
Haley. Alex 225 (11)
Halfway Houses 16 (73)
Hall Dilemma. Landlord or Educator: The Resident 151 (105)
Hall of Fame. Baseball 176 (94)
Ham Radio? What is 174 (79)
Hamilton and Jefferson: Comparison and Contrast of Philosophies 117 (77)
Hammock Twining 79 (50)
Hammocks as Made by the Cuna Indians of the San Blas Islands and the Mayans of Yucatan 79 (25)
Hammocks. How to Design, Weave, and Construct a Variety of Chairs, Swings, 79 (87)
Hand Injured Patient. Care of the 56 (79)
Hand Spinning 79 (3), (101)
Hand Spinning - All Kinds of Fibers 79 (51)
Handball. Team 105 (114)
Handful of Earth 56 (62)
Handicap. Educational Approaches to Mental 117 (131)
Handicapped 112 (112)
Handicapped and Aged. Architectural Barriers to the 151 (228)
Handicapped and Aged. Transportation Barriers to the 151 (228)
Handicapped and Normal Children in the Schools. Integrating 218
Handicapped. Challenge of Maps for the Visually 218
Handicapped Child 117 (132)
Handicapped Child to Grow in Contemporary Society. Helping the Physically 56 (89)
Handicapped Children 57 (2)
Handicapped Children and Solutions. Parents of 142 (61)

Handicapped Children. Serving 181 (119)
Handicapped Children. Working With Young 151 (91)
Handicapped. Housing - A Problem for the 151 (225)
Handicapped Individuals. Education of 151 (228)
Handicapped Individuals. Legal Rights of Mentally/ Physically 151 (228)
Handicapped. Law and the 57 (5)
Handicapped. Services for the 144
Handicapped Student. Blind or 181 (2), (91)
Handicaps. Child and Multiple 117 (132)
Handicrafted Textiles. Nigerian 79 (37)
Handling Conflict 57 (18)
Handling the Stress of Life 151 (39)
Hands. Blood on Their 213 (14)
Handspinning and Chemical Dyeing 79 (19)
Handwriting Analysis as a Science 94 (1)
Hangings 79 (21)
Hanoi. Tower of 117 (93)
Happiness in Your Marriage. Keeping 56 (5)
Happiness. Science and 85 (36)
Happiness, Success and Prosperity. Ways to Attain Health, Wealth, 180 (33)
Hardwood Block Flooring. Laminated 80 (2)
Hardwood, Plywood and Veneer. Technical Aspects of 80 (1)
Hardwood, Plywood, and Veneer. Use, Manufacturing, and Marketing of 80 (2)
Hardwood Plywood. Prefinished 80 (2)
Hare Krishna 224 (11)
Harmful Plants in the Environment 117 (1)
Harness Weaving 79 (11)
Harriet Beecher Stowe 181 (147)
Hasenclever: The Dramatist as Filmwriter. Walter 214 (66)
Hattie Larlham Story 98 (1 - 3)
Have We Come a Long Way? 151 (94)
Have You Had Your Annual Shake-up? 102 (18)
Have You Listened Lately? 151 (172)
Have You Tried This? Name Drafting 79 (23)
Having Fun Fund-raising 29 (154)
Hawaii 4 (15), 142 (22), (85)
Hawaii. Culture of Poverty and Political Culture in 29 (141), (284)
Hawaii. Culture of Poverty and Political Cultures in 29 (257)
Hawaiian Adventure 59 (7)
Hawaiians. Ethnicity and Culture Changes of Modern 29 (141), (161), (257), (284)
Hawaii's Economy. How Industries Affect 23
(Hawks and Owls). Birds of Prey 151 (309)
Hawthorne, A Timely Friendship. Melville and 105 (22)
Hazards At Home. Controlling Microbiological Food 151 (178)
Hazards. Environmental Health 181 (184)
Hazleton Campus of Penn State 151 (4)
Head 'Em Off at the Gap 76 (1)
Headhunters in Central Borneo and the Cannibals in West Irian 225 (35)
Headlines. America Behind the 154 (15)
Headlines. Behind the 29 (52)
Headlines. Geography Behind the 29 (135)
Headlines. Interpreting Today's World 225 (41)
Healing 105 (95), 225 (33)
Health 176 (70)
Health. Allied 181 (189)
Health and Disease. Stress in 216 (24)
Health, and Fitness. Yoga 57 (80)
Health and Light 134 (5)
Health and Social Welfare Agencies. Supervisors in 181 (56)
Health and Social Welfare. History of Public 171 (49)
Health and the Black Community. Mental 181 (294)
Health as Related to Light Intensity and Color 216 (24)
Health Behavior. Positive 181 (184)
Health Care 180 (111), 181 (176)
Health Care Costs. Rising 54
Health Care Field. Careers in the 181 (57), (170)
Health Care. Issues in the Delivery of 27 (36)
Health Care Practitioner. Information Explosion Faced by the 218
Health Care Professionals. Consumerism: Choosing 181 (196)
Health Care Revolution 181 (170)
Health Care. Rising Cost of 8 (6)
Health Care Services 16 (60)
Health Care Systems. Computer Simulation of 218
Health. Community 142 (39)
Health. Community Mental 16 (81)
Health Consultation. Mental 181 (282)
Health. Consumerism in 181 (170)
Health. Dentistry and 105 (29)
Health Education 142 (39)
Health Education. Dental 218
Health Education. Elementary 174 (24)
Health Education for Elementary Teachers 181 (113)
Health Education. Major Areas of 181 (227)
Health Effects of Environmental Pollutants 204
Health Effects of Pesticides 171 (39)
Health. Effects of Work on 29 (155), (176), (291)
Health Facilities. Fire Safety in 216 (99)
Health. Food and 176 (76)
Health Foods. Nutrition and 151 (174)
Health for Daily Living. Mental 117 (108)
Health Hazards. Environmental 181 (184)
Health in the Occupational Environment 151 (153)
Health Information System 181 (185)
Health Insurance. National 27 (25), 54

Health. Job Safety and 216 (65)
Health. Mental 57 (34), 105 (94), 113 (2), 142 (44), 181 (31)
Health. Obesity and 151 (208)
Health of College Students. Emotional Difficulties and Mental 216 (132)
Health. Personality and Mental 105 (98)
Health. Preventative Mental 142 (45)
Health Professions. Getting into the 29 (98), (174), (274)
Health Programs. Former Governor Looks at 8 (2)
Health Programs in Schools. Safety and 216 (41)
Health Quackery 168 (29)
Health. Radiation, Radioactivity and the Public 27 (9)
Health Records Administration 181 (185)
Health Sciences at the University 218
Health Sciences Careers 27 (27)
Health Subjects 142 (20)
Health. Urban Living Problems Related to 56 (80)
Health. Veterinary Medicine's Role in the Protection of Human 216 (90)
Health, Wealth, Happiness, Success and Prosperity. Ways to Attain 180 (33)
Health. Your Mental 216 (94)
Hearing 181 (318)
Hearing Aid? Who Needs a 151 (96)
Hearing Disorders 56 (55), 151 (96)
Hearing Disorders of the Aged 151 (96)
Hearing Disorders. Speech and 56 (55)
Hearing Impaired 151 (113)
Hearing Impaired. Educating 151 (113)
Hearing Impaired. How Penn State Serves 151 (113)
Hearing Loss 181 (318)
Hearing Loss. What it Means to Have a 117 (132)
Hearing. Noise on 181 (318)
Hearing Problems. Rehabilitative Services for Children and Adults With and/or 57 (63)
Hearing Therapy Services. Speech and 174 (47)
Heart? Can Exercise Help Your 171 (23)
Heart of the Circle Is a Square 83 (5)
Heart Surgery. New Advances in Open 181 (194)
Heat Farm Buildings. Solar Energy to 16 (8)
Heat Pumps and Solar Energy 216 (71)
Heating and Cooling Buildings. Solar Energy Utilization for 151 (126)
Heddle Frame Loom. Rigid 79 (135)
Heimlich Maneuver 135 (28)
Helen of Troy 227 (5)
Helicopters 151 (33)
Hell of the Affluent Society. Marcuse and the 85 (36)
Hellenistic Cults. Egyptian 227 (50)
Hellenistic Greece. Archaeology of Classical and 227 (45)
Hellenistic Poetry 227 (39)
Hellenistic Poetry and Literary Criticism 227 (7)
Hellenistic Women 227 (37)
Hellenistic Women Poets 227 (2)
Hellenistic Women Writers 227 (54)
Hello Ohio! 144
Helpful Bacteria 216 (20)
Helpful Hints for Hopeful Heroes 3 (1)
Helpful Improvement Tools for Women 218
Helping Children Deal With a Death 216 (106)
Helping Children Reach Their Potential 105 (98)
Helping Children to Be More Creative - Ways Parents and Teachers Can Encourage Creativity 117 (48)
Helping Developmentally Disabled Infants Learn 169 (1)
Helping Relationship. Characteristics of a 117 (44)
Helping the Family Adapt to a Disability 159 (31)
Helping the Physically Handicapped Child to Grow in Contemporary Society 56 (89)
Helping Your Child Become High on Life 16 (84)
Helplessness 181 (242)
Helsinki. Europe After 97 (52)
Hemoglobin. Chemistry of 223 (24)
Henry Suzzallo Years at the University of Washington 218
Her Own Words - Lives of American Women in Autobiography 29 (336)
Herbs for Dyes, Fragrances, Culinary 79 (111)
Herculaneum. Pompeii and 227 (26)
Heredity, and I.Q. Race, 181 (242), (294)
Heritage. America's Maritime 214 (57), (69)
Heritage. America's Political Cartoon 214 (4)
Heritage House 29 (143)
Heritage. Moravian Music - A Valuable American 56 (110)
Heritage. Our American 222
Hero in the 20th Century. Dramatic 216 (32)
Hero. Medieval French Hero 181 (138)
Hero of the War of 1812. Forgotten 57 (91)
Hero of Turkey. Hodja - Folk 29 (200)
Hero Worship. Heroes and 227 (4)
Heroes. American Folk 29 (185), (200)
Heroes and Hero Worship 227 (4)
Heroes. Helpful Hints for Hopeful 3 (1)
Heroes in History 142 (98)
Heroin Addiction and the Family 171 (44)
Heroin. Cell Membranes and 57 (20)
Heroines of the Wild West. Three Romantic 223 (3)
Hershey Medical Center. Milton S. 151 (10), (186)
Heschel. Education in the Thought of A.J. 29 (233)
Heschel. Ideas on Education in the Thought of A.J. 29 (90)
Hesiod 227 (17)
Hex Sign. Pennsylvania Dutch: Land of the 117 (75)
Hidden America 103 (6)
Hidden Sea 69 (15)

Hidden Worlds of Florida's Big Cypress Swamp 69 (6)
High Cost of Money 168 (67)
High International Finances 54
High School. Career Education and the Junior 57 (47)
High School Counselor 174 (76)
High School Football. Officiating 16 (42)
High School Journalism 168 (10)
High School. New Happenings in the 223 (11)
High School or Elementary School Levels. Administration at the 56 (48)
High School Student Recruitment 105 (37)
High School to College. Transition From 105 (34)
High School to the Olympics. Men's Gymnastics: From 168 (2)
High School Underground Press 231 (3)
High Sierra. John Muir's 59 (6)
High Sierra. Yosemite and the 59 (15)
Higher Education 151 (140), 214 (39), 216 (10)
Higher Education and Continuing Education 181 (111)
Higher Education and the World of Work 27 (20)
Higher Education. Changing 151 (120)
Higher Education. Collective Bargaining in 223 (6)
Higher Education. Cooperative Study and Internships in 181 (51)
Higher Education. Data Systems for 57 (93)
Higher Education. Death of the Lecture: Using the Personalized System of Instruction in 151 (169)
Higher Education. Direction of 168 (50)
Higher Education. Distinguishing Features of American 151 (103)
Higher Education. Faculty Union and 181 (109)
Higher Education. Financial Assistance is Available for 105 (38)
Higher Education. Future of 142 (33)
Higher Education in Louisiana. Future of 174 (79)
Higher Education in Pennsylvania. Role of Private 54
Higher Education in the 1970's. American 168 (18)
Higher Education. Intercollegiate Athletics and 216 (7)
Higher Education. New Life Through 151 (103)
Higher Education. Non-traditional 142 (22)
Higher Education. Oxford, Cambridge and British 223 (10)
Higher Education. Politics and 168 (50)
Higher Education. Preparing for 105 (38)
Higher Education. Private Support for 216 (107)
Higher Education. Private Support of Public 216 (7)
Higher Education. Problems of 85 (5)
Higher Education. Speak Out for 16 (87)
Higher Education. Trends in 29 (59)
Higher Education. Unionism in 142 (65)
Higher Education. Women and 105 (86), 181 (109), (326), 214 (95)
Highland Weaving. Art and Techniques of Bolivian 79 (18)
Highlands. Crafts of the Southern 79 (51)
Highlights of the Louvre 117 (138)
Highty-Tighties 216 (66)
Highway and McKinley National Park. Alaska 223 (34)
Highway and Traffic Safety 16 (9)
Highway Bridge Structures 105 (121)
Highway Design. Energy Conservation in Traffic Operations and 174 (90)
Highway Safety 214 (88)
Highway Safety is no Accident 33 (1 - 11)
Highways and Airports. Bituminous Pavements for 151 (291)
Highways. Earthquake Resistant Design of 105 (121)
Hiking. Camping, Backpacking and 174 (82)
Hill. Sagamore 167 (2)
Hinduism 181 (307)
Hiss Case and the FBI Files 97 (69)
Historian as Social Commentator 174 (83)
Historic Buildings. Preservation of 57 (92)
Historic Civil Engineering Land Marks 174 (90)
Historic Fabrics 79 (70)
Historic Places. National Register for 174 (19)
Historic Preservation 174 (37)
Historic Spinning Wheels 79 (101)
Historical Development of American Cities 181 (264)
Historical, Folk, and Traditional. Psychology of Clothing and Dress - 79 (28)
Historical Furniture Styles 56 (96)
Historical Interpretation and Future of the Tradition. Contemporary National Dress of Mayan Indians of Guatemala - 79 (83)
Historical Introduction, Contemporary Investigations, Process, Structure and Motivation. Basketry, 79 (5)
Historical Look at Jesus Christ 57 (91)
Historical Motifs in Weaving. Application of 79 (81)
Historical Origin of Mother Goose Rhymes 56 (63)
Historical Overview of Equal Employment Opportunity and Affirmative Action Laws and Regulations, the Employment Interview 27 (2)
Historical Periods in Music 54
Historical Perspective. America's Negro Problem in 85 (12)
Historical Perspective. Associate Degree - A 151 (2)
Historical Perspective. Family in 142 (78)
Historical Perspective. Liberalism and Conservatism in 85 (12)
Historical View. Plight of the Woman Writer: 151 (114)
Histories. Shakespeare's 159 (19)
Historiography. Greek and Roman History and 227 (30)
History 142 (12)
History. African 29 (180), 151 (217), 171 (3), 181 (28)

History. Afro-American 151 (217)
History. Afro-American Oral 142 (66)
History. American 159 (16)
History. American Colonial 57 (35)
History. American Indian 29 (158), (331)
History. Ancient 151 (215), 227 (38)
History. Ancient and Medieval European 151 (215)
History and Application of the Wind Quintet 218
History and Culture. Afro-American 142 (17)
History and Current Roles. Corps of Engineers, 105 (74)
History and Current Status of Instructional Television at Penn State 151 (66)
History and Demography. Ancient 227 (37)
History and Design. Tapestry Weaving, 79 (44)
History and Development of the Land Grant Colleges 191 (122)
History and Doctrine of the Mormon Church 56 (138)
History and Growth. Altoona Campus - 151 (14)
History and Historiography. Greek and Roman 227 (30)
History and Its Culture. Chile - Its 27 (11)
History and Literature. Women in 227 (16)
History and Methods of Kindergarten 117 (56)
History and Philosophy of Science 142 (31)
History and Philosophy of Science. Aspects of 218
History and Politics. Polish 214 (59)
History and Prophecy. Israel in 45 (3)
History and Prospects. Soviet Union and Germany - 85 (31)
History and Teaching. Oral 181 (93)
History. Architectural 218
History. Art 57 (52), 142 (11), (76)
History. Art Criticism of 216 (96)
History. Black and Compromises in American 29 (261), (337)
History. Black Psychology - The Afro American Woman in American 29 (337)
History. Chicano 218
History. Chinese 159 (6)
History. Church 56 (139)
History. Cuban 142 (68)
History. Delaware County Campus - Its Mission and 151 (16)
History, Development, and Literature. Violin - 57 (42)
History. Edmund Burke's Conception of 85 (32)
History. European Intellectual 218
History, Folklore and Processes of Spinning 79 (99)
History. Folklore in 54
History, Function, Identification. Fibers - 79 (19)
History. General 174 (80)
History. General Brazilian 142 (56)
History. Great Names in French 56 (90)
History. Greek 227 (8)
History. Greek and Roman 227 (3)
History. Heroes in 142 (98)
History I.Q. Your American 151 (219)
History, Importance and Fundamentals. Plastics Technology: 117 (81)
History in Communist East Europe. Political and Social 218
History in Education. Utilization of Local 142 (5)
History. Japanese Art 16 (32)
History. Jewish 142 (3)
History. Labor 151 (224)
History. Lady Radicals in American 151 (257)
History, Legends and Culture. American Indian 79 (126)
History, Marketing and Advertising. Story of Pabst 145 (1 - 3)
History. Medieval Rome - The New Social 27 (10)
History. Military 218
History of Airpower 216 (53)
History of Alabama Counties 16 (26)
History of American Juvenile Periodicals 117 (75)
History of American Magazines 218
History of American Psychiatry 151 (214)
History of Astronautics 154 (17)
History of Bangladesh 56 (92)
History of Central Minnesota. Natural 168 (56)
History of Ceramics 57 (33)
History of Chicago Architecture and Preservation 142 (79)
History of Children's Literature 117 (75), 174 (18)
History of Classics in America 227 (25)
History of Greek 227 (40)
History of Greek and Roman Theater 227 (25)
History of India and Pakistan 56 (92)
History of Latin 227 (40)
History of Livingston County 117 (73)
History of New Iberia 174 (19)
History of Northwest Arts and Crafts 218
History of Printed Textiles 79 (120)
History of Public Health and Social Welfare 171 (49)
History of Recreation, Physical Education, and Leisure Activities in Eastern North Carolina 56 (28)
History of Social Studies in Schools 151 (109)
History of the American West. Urban History and 159 (16)
History of the Ancient Olympic Games 151 (275)
History of the Early Church 105 (107)
History of the Earth. Brief Introduction to the 136 (15)
History of the Lamaze Method in the United States 36 (1)
History of Washington Flora. Origins and 218
History of Watercolor Painting 56 (13)
History of Women in Antiquity. Social 227 (10)
History. Opera 142 (16)
History. Orange County 29 (139), (160), (333)
History. Party 172 (5)
History. Pollen Grains and Geologic 159 (38)
History. Role of Women in 54
History. Roman 227 (8)

History. Roots, a Saga of Black History 102 (13)
History, 1780-1805. Second Awakening as a Turning Point in Kentucky Religious 117 (69)
History. 1776-1976 - Reform and Revolution in American 213 (8)
History. Social 142 (78), 227 (49)
History. Some Other Country's 168 (25)
History Techniques. Oral 142 (5)
History. Textile 79 (36), (150)
History to Americans. African 181 (267)
History. Tracing Your Family 176 (67)
History. Trojan War: Myth or 56 (93)
History. United States Cultural 142 (80)
History. United States 181 (269)
History. Women in 168 (46)
History. World and American 54
History. Youth in American 151 (221)
History. Youth Movements in 85 (33)
Hobbies in the Teaching of Phyics. Use of 57 (87)
Hobby Greenhouse Growing 216 (115)
Hobby Printing. Professional and 151 (68)
Hockey. Ice 105 (113)
Hockey. Introduction to Cricket and Field 29 (303)
Hodja - Folk Hero of Turkey 29 (200)
Holdings. Archival 174 (19)
Holes. Black 214 (10), 223 (4)
Holidays and Festivals. Indian Culture - Marriage Customs, 117 (97)
Holidays in the Americas. Winter 15 (3)
Holland and the Amazing Dutch 59 (14)
Hollywood and the International Jet Set 225 (2)
Hollywood. Golden Years of 112 (40)
Hollywood Story - Experience in Communications 135 (45)
Holmes. Evening With Sherlock 225 (43)
Holmes. Sherlock 142 (54)
Holy Land Archaeology 227 (45)
Holy Land. Biblical Scenes of the 159 (48)
Holy Land. Israel - the 59 (16)
Holy Land. Tour Through the 29 (216), (225), (315)
Holy Lands 59 (16)
Holy Places 227 (44)
Holy Prophet Muhammad as an Examplar 1 (12)
Holy Prophet Muhammad as Benefactor of Humanity 1 (13)
Holy Prophet Muhammad. Jesus as Precursor of the 1 (5)
Holy Quran. In Defense of the 1 (6)
Holy Quran. Jesus in the 1 (8)
Home. Aging at 218
Home. American 181 (268)
Home and at Work. ABC's of Personally Controlling Stress at 136 (24)
Home and in the Hospital. Electrical Safety at 218
Home and Make Money. How to Live in a Stately 97 (44)
Home and Office. Security Systems for 29 (136)
Home Birth, Hospital Birth and Alternatives to Both 36 (1)
Home Buying and Selling for the Layperson 56 (97)
Home Canning and Freezing 16 (71)
Home - Care Versus Child Care 224 (12)
Home. Controlling Microbiological Food Hazards at 151 (178)
Home. Economic Status of Women in the 90 (1)
Home Economics 176 (31)
Home Economics. Careers in 216 (139)
Home Economics Education 216 (49)
Home Economics. Trends in 117 (78)
Home Furnishings 56 (96)
Home Garden Insects 216 (102)
Home Gardening With Vegetables 117 (5), (122)
Home Gardens. Notes on 56 (100)
Home. How and Where to Buy a 181 (37)
Home. How to Improve Safety in the 16 (58)
Home. How You Can Save Energy in the 16 (80)
Home (Interiors). Put a Little Weaving in Your 79 (30)
Home Landscape 181 (132), (217)
Home Lawn Care 151 (25)
Home. Lighting in the 56 (95)
Home of the Future 225 (21)
Home. Ornamentals Around the 151 (25)
Home. Preserving Food in Your 151 (180)
Home-Produced Foods. Preserving Your 151 (178)
Home Reading Programs. Good Books for 168 (53)
Home. Selecting a 56 (96)
Home Today. Buy a 181 (225)
Home Trade-in Program 65 (25)
Home Vegetable Garden 151 (25)
Home. Water Conservation in the 136 (22)
Home. Weaving for My 79 (10)
Home. Weed Control Around the 117 (1)
Home Wine-making 218
Homebirth and Other Alternatives. Scientific Studies on 122 (3)
Homebirth. Practicing Physician in 122 (1)
Homebirth: The Way of the Future 122 (4)
Homebirths and the Nurse Midwife 122 (2)
Homer 227 (6), (38), (40)
Homer and/or Early Babylonian Epic 227 (17)
Homer, Literature and Art. Polyphemus in Folktale, 227 (47)
Homer, the First Psychologist 227 (29)
Homeric World. Women in the 227 (19)
Homes and Parks. Mobile 65 (53)
Homes for Profit and Comfort. Energy-saving 18 (1)
Homes. Mobile 65 (1)
Homes - the Two Taliesins. Frank Lloyd Wright's Own 151 (29)
Homestake Mine 143 (7)
Homo Sapiens Characteristics Causing Communications Problems 151 (81)
Homosexuality 171 (48)

Homosexuality, Marriage and the Family 181 (238)
Honeycomb. Expanded 79 (147)
Hong Kong 59 (3), 174 (82)
Hong Kong and Macao 59 (1)
Hong Kong. Transportation in 151 (290)
Hope. World's Only 45 (1)
Hopibar Weaves. Navajo and 79 (90)
Hopi Weaving Techniques. Navajo and 79 (100)
Hormones. Aging and 105 (3)
Hormones and Human Reproduction 171 (24)
Horn Performance. French 57 (29)
Horse Conformation 216 (57)
Horse Industry. Virginia 216 (57)
Horseless Carriage. Adventures and Errands on the 56 (40)
Horticulture Research and Teaching. Scope of 16 (66)
Hospital Birth and Alternatives to Both. Home Birth, 36 (1)
Hospital Discharge 218
Hospital Disinfection 168 (29)
Hospital Drug Security 88 (1)
Hospital. Electrical Safety at Home and in the 218
Hospital Operations 151 (9)
Hospital Pharmacy 181 (197)
Hostages and Victims. Terrorists, 181 (244), (295)
Hosteling in Europe. Youth 151 (298)
Hot Springs. Bacteria in 159 (49)
Hour Power 182 (1 - 3)
House. Electrical Safety - Safety 152
House. Heritage 29 (143)
House. How to Buy a 216 (145)
House. Poisons Around the 181 (216)
Household Appliances 216 (73)
Household Computer 174 (65)
Household Responsibility 216 (73)
Houseplant I Did't Like. I Never Met a 97 (3)
Houseplants 218
Houses. Halfway 16 (73)
Housewife's Dilemma 135 (37)
Housing - A Problem for the Handicapped 151 (228)
Housing and Community Development. Neighborhoods, 181 (275)
Housing Design 181 (78)
Housing Education 216 (145)
Housing for the Elderly 216 (145)
Housing in Developing Countries. Post Disaster 31 (22)
Housing is for People 216 (141)
Housing. Wood Use and Care in 216 (65)
How a Career In Business Can Bring Personal Fulfillment in Life 23
How a Water Witch Drowns in a Dry Hole 136 (14)
How and Where to Buy a Home 181 (37)
How and Why of Conducting a Meeting 105 (85)
How Astrology Can Help You Find Your Ideal Mate 225 (20)
How Businesses are Financed 23
How Businessmen Can Help Themselves 180 (19)
How Can Education Become Meaningful and a Lifetime Reward? 151 (38)
How Can Your Community Support Reading 151 (94)
How Children Learn 171 (21)
How Children Learn Language 159 (29)
How Collective Living Breaks Down the Isolation and Alienation of Today's World 178 (1)
How Come Less Poverty and More Welfare 85 (35)
How Communities Can Improve the Quality of Education 151 (38)
How Computers Affect You 56 (127)
How County Government in Illinois Could Be Improved 57 (49)
How Dark Were the Dark Ages 54
How Do We Go From Here? 56 (70)
How Effective Are Our Public Schools? 159 (53)
How Energy Wise Are You? 66 (2)
How Food Co-ops and Community Stores Can Be Used for Political Organizing 178 (1)
How Free is Free Speech 117 (135)
How Have They Changed? College Students: 16 (23)
How Hot is the Center of the Sun? 218
How Industries Affect Hawaii's Economy 23
How Industries Market Their Products/Services 23
How Long Has This Been Going On 112 (47)
How Man Came to the New World 4 (3)
How Many People Can We Feed? 151 (160)
How Much is Too Much 56 (29)
How Nerves Transmit Biological Messages in Our Body 218
How One Writes a Town-Gown Column 151 (76)
How Parents Can Change Our Schools 112 (89)
How Penn State Serves Hearing Impaired 151 (113)
How Productivity Can Be Enhanced in the Food Processing Industry 67 (1)
How Public Relations Can Benefit You 136 (16)
How Safe is Your Food? 151 (177)
How Science Produces Good Athletes 171 (23)
How Scientists Communicate - If and When They Do! 151 (73)
How Shall We Feed Them? 151 (19)
How Soon Will the Arabs Own America? 97 (45)
How Sport Involvement Socializes Individuals 151 (276)
How Television and Film Stars are Made and Promoted 176 (102)
How the News is Collected 16 (74)
How to Achieve Peace in the Middle East 57 (61)
How to Advertise Your Company 136 (5)
How to Arrive at Selling Prices 79 (96)
How to Be a Jew for Jesus 93 (4)
How to Be a Star Salesman 112 (79)
How to Become a More Interesting Conversationalist 105 (13)
How to Build a Work Team 218
How to Buy a Company - For Next to Nothing 180 (20)

How to Buy a House 216 (145)
How to Buy Communications Vehicles 151 (75)
How to Choose a Vocation 151 (103)
How to Choose Your Pharmacist 181 (186)
How to Control the Time of Your Life 180 (46)
How to Cope With Stress 151 (38)
How to Create a Distrubed Child 57 (41)
How to Deal Successfully With People 180 (4)
How to Design Machines to Be Reliable and Safe 151 (145)
How to Design, Weave, and Construct a Variety of Chairs, Swings, Hammocks 79 (87)
How to Develop Your Psychic Abilities 225 (33)
How to Do a Better Job 180 (41)
How to Dress Better for Less Money 229 (1)
How to Enrich Your Marriage 168 (73)
How to Establish an Organizational Training Program 216 (120)
How to Find Your Family Roots 154 (2)
How to Get the Best Wine Buy Moneywise 225 (22)
How to Get the Most for Your Invested Money 140 (1)
How to Get Your Child to Read a Book 151 (94)
How to Go About Developing Your Own Exercise Program 218
How to Handle Anxiety and Tension 174 (9)
How to Have Fun 97 (25)
How to Improve Safety in the Home 16 (58)
How to Improve Your Game 29 (306)
How to Increase Your Motivation Level 23
How to Increase Your Psychic Abilities Through Face Language 212 (1)
How to Kill Stress Before it Kills You 102 (4)
How to Know When You Are Doing a Good Job 29 (84)
How to Lie With Statistics 151 (17)
How to Live in a Stately Home and Make Money 97 (44)
How to Live on 24 Hours a Day 216 (76)
How to Live With Courage 75 (1)
How to Make a Habit of Succeeding 180 (45)
How to Make Big Money as an Independent Sales Agent 180 (16)
How to Make Your Career More Exciting and Meaningful 23
How to Manage by Objectives 151 (39)
How to Manage Your Time 151 (67)
How to Overcome Loneliness 225 (34)
How to Parent 97 (17)
How to Plan a Banquet 216 (25)
How to Plan a Conference 57 (51)
How to Plan an Affordable Trip to Europe 117 (138)
How to Prepare for College 29 (31), (102), (349)
How to Prepare Your Child for Success 56 (59)
How to Protect Yourself Against White Collar Crimes 97 (21)
How to Pulverize an Audience With Laughter 112 (67)
How to Put Your Best Foot Forward 168 (38)
How to Read a Book 216 (56)
How to Read a Financial Statement 151 (50)
How to Read More Effectively 136 (23)
How to Recognize Affirmative Action Complaints 151 (1)
How to Recognize and Deal With Guilt 225 (34)
How to Reduce the Chances of Obsolescence 151 (38)
How to Relax and Live Longer 29 (250)
How to Remember What You Read 171 (16)
How to Research Foundation Grants 105 (53)
How to Run a Meeting Effectively 105 (77)
How to Sell Almost Anything to Almost Anyone 102 (18)
How to Sell Successfully 112 (80)
How to Sell Twice as Much in Half the Time 112 (130)
How to Spread Feminist and Socialist Ideas Through Electoral Politics 178 (1)
How to Square the Ideological Circle 85 (14)
How to Start a Business 23
How to Stop Inflation 218
How to Talk Like a Philadelphian 181 (226), (317)
How to Talk to Your Child About Drugs 181 (186)
How to Teach Weaving 79 (145)
How to Train a Professional Artist 16 (32)
How to Travel 151 (11)
How to Understand and be Understood 102 (18)
How to Use Current Abstracts of Chemistry, Index Chemicus, and the Chemical Substructure Index 84 (1)
How to Use the Library 216 (56)
How to Use the Manual of Water Well Construction Standards 136 (27)
How to Use the Science Citation Index 84 (1)
How to Use the Social Sciences Citation Index 84 (1)
How to Visualize Ideas Before Weaving 79 (105)
How to Win in a No-win System 225 (37)
How to Win Without Cheating 113 (3)
How to Work Harder and Get Less 85 (26)
How Today's Economy Affects Your Future 135 (39)
How Trademarks are Protected and Abused 209
How Trademarks are Selected 209
How Visualization Made Me a Star 225 (5)
How Wagelessness in the Home Effects Women's Options for Fertility 90 (1)
How We Communicate 174 (66)
How You Can Save Energy in the Home 16 (80)
Huey Long and Louisiana Education 174 (38)
Huichol-Tribe of the Sacred Cactus 69 (9)
Human Alienation. Marxism and 159 (28)
Human Awareness 180 (71)
Human Awareness Through Face Language 212 (1)
Human. Becoming 171 (38)
Human Behavior 180 (113), (182)
Human Behavior. Communications and 180 (76)
Human Biology on Behavior. Effects of 102 (35)
Human Body. Alcohol and the 174 (12)

Human Body. Wonders of the 54
Human Cancer Viruses 216 (4)
Human Communication. Non-verbal Aspects of 142 (37)
Human Costs of Regulatory Delays 31 (30)
Human Cures. Veterinary Findings Which May Lead to 16 (69)
Human Development 181 (22)
Human Ecology 54
Human Engineering and Motivation 180 (146)
Human Erosion and Human Conservation 57 (69)
Human Evolution 57 (77), 142 (58)
Human Factors Engineering 214 (79), 222
Human Genetic Engineering 218
Human Genetics 105 (2), 142 (53), 181 (20)
Human Growth and Development. Psychology of Normal 117 (111)
Human Interactions 135 (9)
Human Intrigue and Electronic Journalism Phenomenon 176 (43)
Human Language? Can Chimps Learn 181 (314)
Human Mind. Journey to the Depths of the 112 (96)
Human Movement. Biomechanics of 151 (209)
Human Myotatic Reflex 181 (155)
Human Nature. Aggression, Violence and 102 (35)
Human Nature. Women's Evolution and 213 (11)
Human Needs, Goals and Financial Planning 214 (77)
Human Nutrition in Developing Countries 16 (53)
Human Past. Reconstructing the 171 (38)
Human Potential 105 (77)
Human Potential Movement 57 (71)
Human Potential: You Can Achieve! Your 105 (34)
Human Problems in Northern Communities 171 (10)
Human Race. Let's Join the 100 (1)
Human Relations 65 (36), 105 (13), 180 (22), (25), (133)
Human Relations and Communications 168 (52)
Human Relations. Communication and 159 (60)
Human Relations Education 77 (1)
Human Relations in Business 56 (136)
Human Relations Motivation 16 (43)
Human Relations Problems Still Facing Us 174 (79)
Human Relationships 174 (62)
Human Relationships - Component of Teacher Preparation 117 (45)
Human Relationships. Improving 181 (289)
Human Reproduction 181 (20)
Human Reproduction. Hormones and 171 (24)
Human Resources. Conservation of 56 (80)
Human Resources Development 180 (36)
Human Rights in Southern Africa. United States and 181 (267)
Human Rights in the Soviet Union. Nationalism and 57 (37)
Human Rights. Language and 171 (50)
Human Rights. Russia, the Refusedniks and 27 (43)
Human Rights. United States and 181 (28)
Human Rights Violations 154 (27)
Human Scale in Living Environments. English Villages and 218
Human Service Workers. Volunteers and 181 (56)
Human Sexuality 29 (174), (274), 181 (221), (227), (284), (286), 218
Human Sexuality. Cross-cultural Look at 224 (12)
Human Sexuality. Education for 56 (3), (47)
Human Systems 142 (73)
Human Teacher. Being a 29 (132)
Human Value. Science and 151 (273)
Human Values. Technology and 105 (118), 151 (157), (272)
Humanism. Christian 214 (74)
Humanism in the Classroom 16 (81)
Humanism in the Public Schools. Myth of 12
Humanism Versus Behaviorism in Education 105 (36)
Humanism - What is It? 117 (110)
Humanist as Critic of Contemporary Society. Irving Babbit - the 85 (32)
Humanistic Approach to Classroom Discipline. Realistic and 117 (51)
Humanistic Education 29 (88)
Humanistic Physical Education 181 (11)
Humanities Research 171 (55)
Humanity. Holy Prophet Muhammad as Benefactor of 1 (13)
Humanity. Islam as Religion of 1 (2)
Humanizing Education in the 70's and Beyond 168 (21)
Humanizing Instruction 181 (115)
Humanizing the Educational Process. Peopling: 117 (43)
Humans and Other Animals 181 (281)
Humans. Developmental Process in 174 (1)
Humans Only. For 144
Humor 180 (67)
Human - A Business Asset 112 (53)
Humor. American Dream...In Politics, Poetry and 97 (9)
Humor. Art of Wit and 225 (40)
Humor: Humor of the Bruised Sensitivites: Black 151 (243)
Humor in Exploration 4 (3)
Humor of Mark Twain. Life and 117 (91)
Humor of the Bruised Sensitivites. Black Humor: 151 (243)
Humor Power 86 (1)
Humor. Soviet 105 (68)
Humor. Soviet Underground 27 (46)
Humor. Your Greatest Sense - Your Sense of 112 (39)
Humorous 56 (98)
Humorous Look at Education 29 (68), (104), (188)
Humorous Look at Politics 29 (68), (188), (263)
Humorous Side of Athletics 151 (187)
Hungarian Weaving 79 (40)

Hungary 59 (10)
Hunger 176 (103)
Hunger in the United States 168 (4)
Hunger. World 57 (19)
Hungry World. Meat in a 16 (39)
Hungry World. United States Food Abundance in a 16 (3)
Hunter. Man: The Final 112 (3)
Hunters of the Deep. Master 69 (10)
Hunting Antiques Around the World 97 (24)
Hunting. Career Planning and Job 57 (73)
Hunting for Gems and Fossils 4 (6)
Hunting With Justin Wilson 112 (134)
Hutterites of the Western Plain 171 (4)
Hydraulic Ram 136 (26)
Hydrogen From the Sun 151 (127)
Hydrology Careers for Women. Geology and 136 (22)
Hypertension. Current Trends in Portal 181 (190)
Hypertension. Silent Killer - 16 (13)
Hypnosis 176 (95)
Hypnosis in Athletics and Physical Education 151 (286)
Hypnotism. Phenomena of the Mind - Mentalism and 114 (2)

I

IEOR In Nuclear Engineering 216 (87)
I.A. Richards' and Kenneth Burke's Theories of Metaphor 151 (65)
I.Q. and You 151 (207)
I.Q. Meaning of the 181 (245), (296)
I.Q. Race, Heredity, and 181 (242), (294)
I.Q. Your American History 151 (219)
I Hate Music 29 (222)
I Haven't a Thing to Wear 112 (77)
I Like Me 81 (1)
I Married Adventure 225 (24)
I Never Met a Houseplant I Didn't Like 97 (3)
I'm Okay - You're Okay 112 (56)
Ice Cream 216 (23)
Ice Hockey 105 (113)
Ice Man - Or, An Answer to Ralph Nader and Consumerism. Who Killed the 85 (26)
Ice. Physics of 181 (279)
Ice Skating. Physics of 181 (7), (279)
Ice Storm. Great 47
Iceberg. Energy - the Tip of the 56 (29)
Iceland, Greenland, Newfoundland. Vikings - 151 (220)
Iceland. Vikings of My 225 (24)
Idea of a Catholic University 85 (33)
Idea of Progress Today 85 (32)
Ideal Mate. How Astrology Can Help You Find Your 225 (20)
Ideals of a Christian Capitalist Democracy. American 180 (183)
Ideas. American Political 174 (72)
Ideas Before Weaving. How to Visualize 79 (105)
Ideas. Changing Religious-Cultural 11 (1)
Ideas. Creative Designing With Concepts or 79 (98)
Ideas for Profitable Selling. Proven 180 (89)
Ideas. Impacts of the Prophets of Israel Upon Religious 29 (114)
Ideas in Science Fiction 151 (235)
Ideas. Libertarian Socialist and Democratic Socialist 181 (288)
Ideas of Equality. Two 85 (25)
Ideas on Education in the Thought of A.J. Heschel 29 (90)
Ideas on Efficient Learning. Piaget - Some 57 (50)
Ideas. Teilhard's Religious 11 (6)
Ideas Through Electoral Politics. How to Spread Feminist and Socialist 178 (1)
Ideas. Title 57 (79)
Identification. Fibers - History, Function, 79 (19)
Identify Frustrations to Enhance Productivity 151 (38)
Identity and Authenticity 29 (251)
Identity. Property and Freedom - the Remarkable 85 (27)
Identity. Soul and the Search for 29 (164), (238)
Ideological Circle. How to Square the 85 (14)
Ideological Environment - Thrust or Trick. Citizenship in an 85 (11)
Ideologies. Communist 54
Ideologies in Our Midst. Fanatic 85 (16)
Ideology and Morphology. Communism, Its 85 (24)
Ideology and Strategy. Communist 85 (15)
Ideology in the 1970's. Operational Significance of Marxist-Leninist 85 (31)
Ideology of the Executive State 151 (190)
Ideology. Philosophical Truth and the Meaning of 85 (20)
Ideology. Relevance of Conservatism in an Age of 85 (40)
Ikat 79 (36), (65), (115)
Ikat, Shibori, and Tritik, Using Commercial Dyes 79 (144)
Ikat. Warp and Weft 79 (68)
Ikat Warps 79 (62)
Illinois Could be Improved. How County Government in 57 (49)
Illinois. Glacial Geology of Coles County, 57 (22)
Illinois: How We Pay for Them. Schools in 57 (55)
Illinois Legislature 142 (67)
Illinois Teacher Certification 57 (48)
Illinois University. Alumni and Eastern 57 (91)
Illinois. What the Music Department Has to Offer East Central 57 (40)

Illness Reporting System. National Athletic Injury/ 151 (279)
Illness. Social and Cultural Influences on Mental 214 (65), (86)
Illumination and Zen 117 (97)
Illusions. Eye, Light, and 56 (130)
Illustrative Slides. Poetry Readings With 117 (10)
Image Abroad. American 97 (18)
Image and Lifestyle. Creating Your Own 97 (26)
Image and Self Motivation. Your 229 (2)
Image. Building a Corporate 102 (19)
Image in the American Mind, 1607-1900. Jewish 181 (262)
Image. Making of an American 97 (19)
Image - My Development as a Tapestry Weaver. Woven 79 (44)
Image. Non-objective 151 (73)
Image of Woman in 17th Century Meta-physical Poets 227 (29)
Image. Your 176 (98)
Imagery in the Selection of Food. Feelings and 171 (51)
Imagery on Fabric With Photo Silkscreen. Photo 79 (4)
Images of America. Classics and 227 (4)
Images of Christ 105 (106)
Images of Women in Advertising 168 (9)
Images on Fabric. Photographic 79 (129)
Imagination and Textile Design 79 (156)
Imagination. Reviving the Moral 85 (16)
Imaging Devices. New Radiological 181 (198)
Immediate Environment. Garments - Our 79 (32)
Immigrant Women in the Hierarchy of Wages. Place of 90 (1)
Immigrants. Blacks as 168 (25)
Immigrants in Europe. New 168 (30)
Immortal Poland 110 (6)
Immorality. Poetic 227 (5)
Impact of Abandoned Wells on Ground Water 136 (25)
Impact of Computers on the Accounting Profession 171 (9)
Impact of Duquesne University and Alumni on the Pittsburgh Area 54
Impact of Electronic Journalism 154 (13)
Impact of Environmental Hazardous Agents on Women 151 (153)
Impact of Guidance on Personality 54
Impact of Mass Media on Values 168 (50)
Impact of Social Sciences on Cultural Values 105 (21)
Impact of Technology on International Relations 85 (15)
Impact of Technology on Society 142 (65)
Impact of the Prophets of Israel Upon Religious Ideas 29 (114)
Impacted Teeth 181 (161)
Impaired. Educating Hearing 151 (113)
Impaired. Hearing 151 (113)
Impaired. How Penn State Serves Hearing 151 (113)
Impartial Judge and Jury. Myth of the 225 (37)
Impeachment Proceedings. Ancient 227 (38)
Impeachment. Watergate and 223 (23)
Impending Mineral Crisis 143 (9)
Imperative. Discrimination, a Universal 85 (38)
Imperative. Territory - The 112 (3)
Imperial Presidency 151 (221)
Imperial Rome. Chariot Racing in 227 (42)
Imperialism. Theories of 142 (56)
Implant Dentures 181 (174)
Implications for the Future 174 (31)
Implications of a New Administration 102 (30)
Implosion. Population - Explosion and 85 (38)
Importance of an Alumnus 224 (16)
Importance of Family in African Societies 29 (7)
Importance of Scholarship to Society 85 (25)
Important? What Is 168 (65)
Imported Oil. Cost of 31 (23)
Imports. Steel 20
Impossible. Communication is 57 (57)
Impossible Dreams 112 (27)
Impressionist Art. French 117 (138)
Impressionist Museum. Visit to the Jeu de Paume- 117 (138)
Impressions of Australia 29 (326)
Improve Your Quality of Living 151 (180)
Improvement. Animal and Plant Genetic 105 (2)
Improvement. Community 216 (42)
Improvement. Goal Setting - A Means to Self 112 (78)
Improvement in American Education. Proposal for 54
Improvement of Instruction at Penn State 151 (99)
Improvement of Instruction. Teacher Evaluation and 105 (48)
Improvement. Self- 180 (90)
Improvement Tools for Women. Helpful 218
Improving Human Relationships 181 (289)
Improving Personal Effectiveness Through Facilitative Communication 16 (57)
Improving Productivity in Marketing Operations 29 (84), (112)
Improving Schools 54
Improving Self-awareness 171 (51)
Improving Teacher-Student Relationship 117 (55), (120)
Improving the Instructional Staff in the Elementary and Secondary Schools. Innovation Practices for 117 (58)
Improving Your Athletic Skills 151 (209)
Improvisation 174 (48)
In Defense of the Holy Quran 1 (6)
In Pursuit of a Dream 144
In Pursuit of Excellence 176 (98)
In Search of Singapore 15 (5)
In Search of the Santa Maria 4 (4)
In the Flow of Beauty 229 (4)
In the Public Interest 102 (23)
Inalienable Rights. What Happened to Our 117 (118)

Inca Designs in Weaving 79 (26)
Incentive Marketing Field. Techniques of the 130 (1 - 36)
Income Tax and the Distributing of Income 151 (166)
Income Tax. Federal and Pennsylvania 151 (44)
Income. Tax Inferred and Exempt 151 (44)
Income Tax Topics. Other Federal 105 (7)
Income Taxation. Federal 159 (9)
Income Taxes and How They Affect You 151 (50)
Increasing Agriculture Production. Saving Energy While 16 (31)
Increasing Productivity Through Employee Motivation 67 (2)
Incredible Bread Machine 181 (33), (203), (332)
Incursions Into the Private Delivery System of Government Projects 30 (1)
Independence. Declaration of 214 (58)
Independence. Meaning of the Declaration of 85 (13)
Independent College. Future of the 176 (26)
Independent College. Plight of the 224 (16)
Independent Colleges and Universities. Government Support for 105 (50)
Independent Contractor Status 65 (10)
Independent Private Education as an Alternative 105 (38)
Independent Sales Agent. How to Make Big Money an an 180 (16)
Index Chemicus, and the Chemical Substructure Index. How to Use Current Abstracts of Chemistry, 84 (1)
Index. How to Use Current Abstracts of Chemistry, Index Chemicus, and the Chemical Substructure 84 (1)
Index. How to Use the Science Citation 84 (1)
Index. How to Use the Social Sciences Citation 84 (1)
India 15 (5), 174 (82), 214 (50)
India and Pakistan. History of 56 (92)
India and Pakistan. Social and Economic Problems of 56 (118)
India and the Orient 105 (20)
India and the United States 151 (197)
India. Bangladesh and 69 (2)
India. Caste and Social Change in 218
India. Caste System in 56 (119)
India. Culture and Civilization of 181 (333)
India. Economic and Political Aspects of 142 (81)
India. Fabric Processes in Rural 79 (45)
India. Fashions and Customs in 56 (119)
India. Indian Subcontinent - Bangladesh, Pakistan, 16 (81)
India, Its Religions, Political Systems, and Culture 151 (199)
India. Philosophy of 142 (81)
India. Regal 112 (109)
India. Religion Traditions in 56 (123)
India. Religious Traditions of 56 (140)
India. Role of Women in 56 (119)
India. Soul of 59 (2)
India. Viewpoint 79 (45)
India. Weaving of Tribal 79 (115)
Indian Affairs 172 (3)
Indian Affairs. American 172 (4)
Indian Affairs. New Insights Into 112 (90)
Indian and Black Genealogy. American 154 (2)
Indian and the United States Government. American 29 (158), (254)
Indian Arts and Crafts 79 (56)
Indian Basketry - Techniques and Purposes. Salish 151 (109)
Indian Camel Girths. Western 79 (131)
Indian Contemporary Issues. American 29 (50), (158), (192), (283)
Indian Culture and Art 57 (82)
Indian Culture - Marriage Customs, Holidays and Festivals 117 (97)
Indian. Daily Life of the California 29 (165), (339)
Indian Democracy. Mrs. Gandhi and 117 (97)
Indian Education. American 29 (87)
Indian Education. Federal Government and 159 (32)
Indian Fishing Rights 159 (24)
Indian History. American 29 (158), (331)
Indian History, Legends and Culture. American 79 (126)
Indian Land Rights 29 (166), (195)
Indian Philosophy 218
Indian Poetry. American 29 (162)
Indian Reservations and the States 29 (166), (195)
Indian. Rights of the American 154 (21)
Indian Sacrifice. Ancient 29 (21), (129), (247)
Indian Scene 142 (81)
Indian Spinning, Dyeing. Ancient and Modern Southwest 79 (76)
Indian Subcontinent - Bangladesh, Pakistan, India 16 (81)
Indian Textiles 79 (131)
Indian Textiles. American 79 (71)
Indian Tribalism. American 29 (158), (230), (283)
Indian Tribes. Legal Status and Economic Development of 218
Indian Way of Life 142 (81)
Indian Weaving Techniques and Contemporary Uses. Ancient American 79 (90)
Indians and Archaeology 174 (34)
Indians and Weaving. Meso American 79 (110)
Indians in North Carolina. Tuscarora 56 (34)
Indians. Life and Culture of North American 79 (124)
Indians. Modern American 105 (1)
Indians of British Columbia 151 (27)
Indians of Guatemala - Historical Interpretation and Future of the Tradition. Contemporary National Dress of Mayan 79 (83)

Indians of Southwest. Survey of Art of the American 151 (27)
Indians of the San Blas Islands and the Mayans of Yucatan. Hammocks as Made by the Cuna 79 (25)
Indians. Origin of the California 29 (19), (165), (339)
Indigo Dyeing 79 (14)
Indigo Natural Dyeing 79 (36)
Individual and Group Therapy 181 (289)
Individual and Small Businessman. Tax Planning for the 29 (307)
Individual and the Community. Social Change: The 168 (66)
Individual Counseling 142 (93)
Individual Musical Composers and Their Works 54
Individual or Group Psychotherapy 181 (289)
Individual Response to Crime. Community and 181 (285)
Individual Retirement Accounts. Tax-deferred 18 (1)
Individual Sports. Lifetime 105 (114)
Individualistic Democrat. Robert Frost - 85 (32)
Individualized Learning 181 (103)
Individualized Learning Strategies of Materials 181 (75), (110)
Individualized - Personalized Education 117 (50)
Individualizing and Informalizing Education. Opening Up the Classroom - Activities and Suggestions for 117 (48)
Individualizing Instruction 181 (98)
Individuals and Groups. Psychotherapy With Families, 159 (37)
Individuals. Education of Handicapped 151 (228)
Individuals. How Sport Involvement Socializes 151 (276)
Individuals in the Corporate Society 102 (35)
Individuals. Legal Rights of Mentally/Physically Handicapped 151 (228)
Individuals of Local Prominence 174 (19)
Indonesia 142 (22)
Induced Modification of Diagnostics. Drug 54
Industrial and Management Communications 151 (81)
Industrial and Municipal Wastewater Treatment 204
Industrial Applications of Radioisotopes 54
Industrial Arts. Careers in Teaching 117 (80)
Industrial Arts in the Modern School 151 (118)
Industrial Education 168 (40)
Industrial Education: Careers, Opportunities and Offerings 117 (81)
Industrial Engineering 105 (116)
Industrial Engineering and Operations Research 216 (87)
Industrial Engineering as a Dynamic Profession 216 (120)
Industrial Process. Film and Television as an 57 (32)
Industrial Psychology and Relations 180 (8)
Industrial Real Estate 65 (62)
Industrial Resources of Blair County. Basic 151 (14)
Industrial Revolution. Korea: The Land of 151 (118)
Industrial Safety 218
Industrial Technology 57 (11)
Industrial Technology Education 168 (6)
Industrial Technology. Man and Modern 168 (6)
Industrial Wastewater Control 105 (120)
Industrial Waste-water. Removal of Suspended Solids From 67 (22)
Industries Affect Hawaii's Economy. How 23
Industries. Job Opportunities in 23
Industries Market Their Products/Services. How 23
Industries Monololized? Are United States Manufacturing 85 (2)
Industry 180 (26), 187 (4)
Industry. OSHA Requirements and Safety Measures in the Electric 150 (6)
Industry. Agriculture as it Relates to 117 (2)
Industry and Telecommunication Policy. Telephone 151 (183)
Industry and the Role of Interships in Advertising Education. Obligation of 151 (75)
Industry. Behavior Modification in Business and 168 (64)
Industry. Collective Bargaining in Private 23
Industry. Commercial Mushroom 151 (176)
Industry. Consumer Attacks on the Auto 117 (16)
Industry - Drilling and Production. Oil and Gas 151 (135)
Industry Expects of College Graduates. What 216 (23)
Industry. How Productivity Can Be Enhanced in the Food Processing 67 (1)
Industry in Anthracite Mining. Labor and 151 (36)
Industry, Its Beauty Among Stars. Muhlenberg County, Kentucky, Its Strip Mining 117 (29)
Industry. Mathematics of the Well Drilling 136 (3)
Industry. Metric Conversion and the Water Well 136 (28)
Industry. New Technology in the Meat 16 (39)
Industry. Northern 171 (10)
Industry. Oil 220 (1)
Industry. Psychological Testing in Education and 105 (102)
Industry. Steel 20
Industry, Stores, and Schools. Going Metric - In Business 57 (12)
Industry - Supply and Demand. Oil and Gas 151 (135)
Industry to Midwestern United States Economies. Contributions of the Chemical 34 (1)
Industry. United States Domestic Airline 151 (290)
Industry. Virginia Horse 216 (57)
Industry: What You Didn't Learn at Daddy's Knee. Education in the Ground Water 136 (1)

Infant Mortality. Nuclear Radiation and 151 (262)
Infant Mortality. Statistics and 151 (262)
Infant Schools. A Visit to English 168 (61)
Infants Learn. Helping Developmentally Disabled 169 (1)
Infarction. Acute Myocardial 27 (34)
Infections in the Child. Urinary 181 (171)
Infectious Process 168 (29)
Inference: For Those Who Jump to Conclusions. Factor 151 (168)
Inflation 159 (64), 174 (21), (70), 214 (31)
Inflation. Accounting for 31 (1)
Inflation and Its Effects 174 (40)
Inflation and the Role of Government 214 (32)
Inflation and Unemployment 56 (17)
Inflation - Can It be Controlled? 85 (14)
Inflation: Causes and Cures 16 (37)
Inflation. Causes and Effects of 117 (26)
Inflation. How to Stop 218
Inflation. Problems in 54
Inflation/Recession 174 (63)
Inflation. Why Don't They Stop 85 (10)
Inflationary Times. Management in 171 (9)
Influence of Classics on English Literature 227 (26)
Influence of Communication Media on Attitudes 218
Influence of the Bauhaus on Contemporary Crafts 79 (150)
Informalizing Education. Opening Up the Classroom - Activities and Suggestions for Individualizing and 117 (48)
Information Access in Science and Business 44 (1), (2), (3), (4),
Information. America's Overseas 105 (54)
Information. Criminal 180 (6)
Information. Dissemination of 29 (41)
Information Explosion Faced by the Health Care Practitioner 218
Information. For Your 151 (63)
Information. Medical Technology--Professional 105 (45)
Information Processing Systems. Trends in 31 (19)
Information Retrieval 119 (1)
Information Services. News and 112 (51)
Information System. Build Your Own 57 (93)
Information System Environment. Computerized 174 (23)
Information System. Health 181 (185)
Information System Implementation. Problems in Management 171 (9)
Information Systems 174 (43)
Information Systems Degree Program in the Cal State Fullerton School of Business 29 (92), (137)
Information Systems. Management 159 (13), (57)
Information Systems. Marketing Research and 105 (8)
Informative Systems for Instruction, Administration and Research 57 (80)
Injured Patient. Care of the Hand 56 (79)
Injuries. Care and Prevention of Athletic 151 (279)
Injury. Athletic 151 (283)
Injury/Illness Reporting System. National Athletic 151 (279)
Injury Law. Personal 159 (22)
Injury Prevention for the Athlete 151 (283)
Injury Research: Data Interpretation. Sports 151 (283)
Inkle Band and Card Weaving 79 (159)
Inkle Bands. Techniques for 79 (133)
Inkle Looms 79 (50)
Inkle Weaves. Unusual 79 (90)
Inkle Weaving 79 (66), (107)
Inland. Yankee Sails 59 (5)
Inlay 79 (117)
Inner Space. Mysteries of 97 (65)
Inner Way 211 (5)
Innovation and Change. Management of 105 (116)
Innovation and Service. Cable Television: 30 Years of 124 (1)
Innovation Practices for Improving the Instructional Staff in the Elementary and Secondary Schools 117 (58)
Innovation. Tapestry - Tradition and 79 (112)
Innovations. Educational 171 (17)
Innovations in Teaching 216 (58)
Innovations. Transportation 117 (17)
Innovative Dyeing and Spinning Techniques 79 (109)
Innovative Instructional Use of Media 218
Innovative Method of Forecasting Community Needs 168 (57)
Innovative Natural Dye Experimentation With Mordants 79 (156)
Inquisitor, Slavery and Freedom. Dostoevsky's Grand 85 (36)
Insects 151 (308)
Insects. Home Garden 216 (102)
In-Service Training of Teachers 142 (36)
Insight. Drafting for Creative 79 (55)
Insights Into the Male Versus Female Psyche 225 (6)
Insights. Photographic 97 (27)
Inspection Systems. Taptone Quality 67 (7)
Inspiration for Weaving From Nature and the Arts 79 (112)
Inspiration From Nature. Design - 79 (82)
Inspiration - Nature and Pottery. Design 159 (5)
Inspirational and After Dinner Assignments 65 (60)
Inspirations 11 (9)
Instant Coffee Plant. Design of an 214 (42)
Instant Turmoil 76 (1)
Institute of Folk Art. Duquesne Tamburitzan 54
Institute of Transportation. Research Program of the UCI 27 (39)
Institutional Change. Basic 218
Institutional Food Services 16 (90)
Institutional Public Relations 29 (39)
Institutions. Alternative Social 172 (2)
Institutions. American Law and 181 (274)

Institutions. American Religious 151 (215)
Institutions and Public Agencies. Marketing for Non-profit 181 (36)
Institutions. Order, Freedom, Law and Political 85 (40)
Institutions. Student Development Programs for Black Students at Predominantly White 105 (39)
Institutions to the Taxpaying Public. Responsibilities of Public 16 (87)
Institutions Versus Fascism. Free 142 (1)
Instructing in Secondary Education. Methods of 117 (41)
Instruction, Administration and Research. Informative Systems for 57 (80)
Instruction at Penn State. Improvement of 151 (99)
Instruction. Audiovisual 174 (36)
Instruction. Computer-assisted 16 (62)
Instruction. Designing Effective 57 (76)
Instruction Development 216 (123)
Instruction. Humanizing 181 (115)
Instruction in Higher Education. Death of the Lecture: Using the Personalized System of 151 (169)
Instruction in Spanish 181 (101)
Instruction. Individualizing 181 (98)
Instruction. Student Evaluation of 174 (57)
Instruction. Systematic Development of 216 (10)
Instruction. Teacher Evaluation and Improvement of 105 (48)
Instruction. Visualized 216 (10)
Instructional Development 168 (15)
Instructional Materials for Developing Skill Areas 142 (30)
Instructional Materials in Education. Role of 132 (4)
Instructional Problems 57 (76)
Instructional Services 151 (99)
Instructional Staff in the Elementary and Secondary Schools. Innovation Practices for Improving the 117 (58)
Instructional Technology 181 (97)
Instructional Television as a Teaching Tool 151 (66)
Instructional Television at Penn State. History and Current Status of 151 (66)
Instructional Television. Copyright Law as It Applies to 151 (66)
Instructional Television. Educational or 168 (15)
Instructional Television in School. Use of 218
Instructional Use of Media. Innovative 218
Insurance and the Rate of Unemployment. Unemployment 171 (8)
Insurance. Areas of Risk, Management and 168 (68)
Insurance. Direct Response Marketing of 127 (1)
Insurance in Germany. Social 3 (6)
Insurance. Medical Malpractice 181 (44), (193)
Insurance. National Health 27 (25), 54
Insurance Needs of the Small and Medium Size Drilling Contractor. Basic 136 (8)
Integrated Energy Dwellings 163 (2)
Integrated Energy Systems 163 (1)
Integrated Farmstead Energy Systems 163 (3)
Integrated Liberal Arts Programs. Structured/ 227 (11)
Integrating Handicapped and Normal Children in the Schools 218
Integration - Busing 117 (46)
Integration of Science and Art 151 (27)
Integration. Problems in School 56 (49)
Integration Versus Separation 217 (1)
Integrative Approach to Technology 181 (47)
Intellectual. Alienation, Dissent, and the 85 (12)
Intellectual and Emotional Domains. Teacher Modeling Behavior in the Physical, 117 (39)
Intellectual. Dissent and the 85 (20)
Intellectual Freedom 56 (50)
Intellectual History. European 218
Intelligence Agencies 142 (64)
Intelligence, and Personality Tests. Interest, 168 (28)
Intelligence Community. Presidency and the 105 (59)
Intelligence Community. Role of the 102 (29)
Intelligence. Conservatism and 85 (23)
Intelligence in the Universe 154 (17)
Intelligence. State of the Art in Mechanized 181 (204)
Intelligence Testing 142 (21)
Intelligent Life in the Universe 223 (4)
Intentional Communities 151 (148)
Interaction. Adult-Child 216 (40)
Interaction. Child Discipline, Cohabitation, Patterns of Family 56 (7)
Interaction. Manager-Computer 171 (9)
Interaction. Patterns of Family 56 (7)
Interactions Between Drugs and Food 54
Interactions Between Man and Natural Ecosystems 218
Interactions. Human 135 (9)
Interactions. Prescription Drug 54
Intercollegiate Athletics 151 (285)
Intercollegiate Athletics and Higher Education 216 (7)
Intercollegiate Football Program. Administration of an 29 (24), (301)
Interconnected Electric Systems 189
Intercultural Communications 216 (138)
Interdisciplinary Method of Teaching Art 142 (35)
Interdisciplinary Research in Universities. Role of 151 (73)
Interdisciplinary Research Management and Evaluation 151 (254)
Interest. Capitalism and the Public 85 (4)
Interest. In the Public 102 (23)
Interest, Intelligence, and Personality Tests 168 (28)
Interest. Meeting the Educational Consumer 27 (20)

Interest of a Group. Specific Art 29 (10)
Interesting Facts About the Nature of Knowledge. Truth, Objectivity and Some 85 (20)
Interference to Your Television 9 (1)
Intergroup Relations 168 (63)
Interior Architecture. Color in 218
Interior British Columbia. University Programs 171 (58)
Interior Design 168 (69)
Interior Design. Weaving as Art in 79 (148)
Interior Designer 164 (1)
Interior. Earth's 159 (20)
(Interiors). Put a Little Weaving in Your Home 79 (30)
Internal Auditing Can Do for Any Organization. What 216 (63)
International Accounting 214 (2)
International Affairs 29 (53), (217), (226), 172 (5), (11)
International Communist Movement. Present Situation of the 85 (8)
International Development: Alleviating World Poverty. Dynamics of 151 (196)
International Economic Order. New 57 (61)
International Economic Situation 57 (61)
International Economics 54, 117 (23), 142 (51)
International Economics and Trade 138 (1)
International Environmental Programs 204
International Finance 216 (109)
International Finances. High 54
International Jet Set. Hollywood and the 225 (2)
International Law 154 (27)
International Monetary Structure - An Eternal Crisis 85 (14)
International Programs. Virginia Tech and Its 216 (138)
International Relations 56 (103), 142 (41), 151 (192)
International Relations. Contemporary 151 (193)
International Relations. Contemporary Problems in 85 (15)
International Relations. Impact of Technology on 85 (15)
International Relations. Multinational Company and Its Impact on 218
International Relations: Observations, Comments and Analysis 117 (104)
International Role of the Dollar 214 (32)
International Scale. Preserve the Environment on an 181 (346)
International Scene in Fiber 79 (151)
International Scene - Sovereighnty and Suppression. Politics on the 85 (11)
International Science and Engineering Fair 29 (111), (278), (352)
International System in the 1970's 85 (28)
International Terrorism 181 (244), (345)
International Trade in the Seventies 85 (22)
International Trade With China 16 (6)
Internationals. Communications With 151 (173)
Internationals in State College and Penn State 151 (173)
Internships 168 (10)
Internships in Advertising Education. Obligation of Industry and the Role of 151 (75)
Internships in Higher Education. Cooperative Study and 181 (51)
Interpersonal Communication 105 (13), 117 (39), 142 (25), 214 (77)
Interpersonal Communication and the Learning Process 181 (110), (316)
Interpersonal Competence Skills 151 (58)
Interpersonal Relations 57 (18), 117 (115)
Interpersonal Relationships. Conflict in 159 (60)
Interpersonal Relationships in School Administration 117 (41)
Interpersonal Relationships. Power in 16 (1)
Interpretation and Future of the Tradition. Contemporary National Dress of Mayan Indians of Guatemala - Historical 79 (83)
Interpretation and the Liturgy. Oral 105 (110)
Interpretation. Sports Injury Research: Data 151 (283)
Interpreting Today's World Headlines 225 (41)
Interrelationships of Non-loom Techniques 79 (8)
Inter-Relationships with Law and Society 54
Intervention. Early Education and 142 (45)
Intervention. Rape 62 (1), (2), (3)
Interview. Historical Overview of Equal Employment Opportunity and Affirmative Action Laws and Regulations, the Employment 27 (2)
Interviewing 142 (25)
Interviewing. Employment 151 (57)
Interviewing. Oral 29 (153), (211)
Intramural Athletics 31 (39)
Intramural Athletics at Carnegie-Mellon 31 (9)
Intramural Programming 105 (114)
Intramural Recreational Activities for Everyone 57 (17)
Intramurals 216 (46)
Intramurals. Changing Trends in 57 (17)
Intramurals. Programming, Organizing, and Administering 57 (17)
Intravenous Fluids. Use of 16 (77)
Intrigue and Electronic Journalism Phenomenon. Human 176 (43)
Introduction, Contemporary Investigations, Process, Structure and Motivation. Basketry, Historical 79 (5)
Intoxication. Facts People Should Know About Alcohol 54
Introduction of the Basic Bookkeeping System 136 (7), (11)
Introduction to Achievement Motivation 56 (135)
Introduction to Convexity 117 (93)
Introduction to Cricket and Field Hockey 29 (303)
Introduction to the History of the Earth. Brief 136 (15)

Introduction to Urban and Regional Planning 56 (101)
Introduction to Weaving and Drafting 79 (64)
Intuitive Topology 117 (93)
Invent Your Own Future 151 (35)
Inventions. Great 222
Inventive Wearables 79 (33)
Inventory. Are You Losing Money in 136 (7)
Invest. To Invest or Not To 29 (76)
Invested Money. How to Get the Most for Your 140 (1)
Investigating Reporting. New Spirit in 135 (2)
Investigation. Color-physical and Psychological 79 (25)
Investigations. Nuclear Methods in Criminal 151 (156)
Investigations, Process, Structure and Motivation. Basketry, Historical Introduction, Contemporary 79 (5)
Investigations. Role of Toxicology in Death 54
Investigative Security-Consulting. Licensed Private 180 (86)
Investigators. Scientific 105 (117)
Investment. Antiques for 103 (3)
Investment. Commercial Property and 65 (61)
Investment Control 151 (9)
Investment in Korea? Foreign Affairs: What Happened to Our 151 (110)
Investment Real Estate 65 (3), (7), (12), (16), (17), (19), (23), (25), (29), (34), (43), (49), (50), (55), (56), (58), (61), (62), (65), (66), (67), (69)
Investments 23, 117 (114), (121)
Investments and Today's Economy 16 (79)
Investments. Real Estate 181 (37)
Invisible. Seeing the 181 (278)
Invisible Taxes for Religion. Public Utility 12
Involuntary Euthanasia 218
Involvement. Community 216 (92)
Involvement in Government. Public 176 (3)
Involvement in Pollution Control. Citizen 151 (160)
Involvement Socializes Individuals. How Sport 151 (276)
Involving the Community in Career Education Programs 57 (72)
Ionizing Radiation on Bryophytes. Effect of 151 (151)
Ions. Metal 216 (128)
Iran 15 (1), 174 (82)
Ireland 15 (1), 59 (9)
Ireland. Problems and Hopes in Contemporary 159 (65)
Irian. Headhunters in Central Borneo and the Cannibals in West 225 (35)
Iris. Journey to the 105 (19)
Irish Christian Art. Early 181 (79)
Irish Literacy Renaissance 97 (51)
Irish Literature 174 (29)
Irish Republic. Quality of Life in the 159 (65)
Irish Women. Trends Among Irish Youth and 159 (65)
Irish Youth and Irish Women. Trends Among 159 (65)
Irkutsk. Leningrad and the Environs of Lake Baikal and 151 (296)
Iron Curtain and in the Soviet Union. Life Behind the 29 (65), (289)
Irrefragable Man 85 (38)
Irresponsible, What Can We Do? When the Mass Media Are 29 (119), (312)
Irresponsible. When the Mass Media Are 29 (42)
Irv Weiner. Evening With 221 (1)
Irving Babbitt - the Humanist as Critic of Contemporary Society 85 (32)
Is a High Level of Unemployment Really Necessary? 151 (42)
Is All Truth and Morality Relative 85 (20)
Is Biology Women's Destiny? 213 (11)
Is British Aristocracy Decadent? 97 (44)
Is Government the Source of Monopoly 85 (2)
Is Growth Still Possible - and Desirable? 151 (49)
Is Literacy Obsolete 29 (205)
Is Mining Important to You 143 (3)
Is My Land Your Land? 151 (225)
Is Our Representative Democratic Government a Reality or an Alice in Wonderland Fantasy 136 (19)
Is the CRTC Running Your Life? 171 (5)
Is the American Family an Obsolete Institution? 216 (48)
Is the Climate Changing? 223 (5)
Is the Family Still Basic? 151 (93)
Is the Good Life Possible Today? 85 (36)
Is the Party Over? 151 (219)
Is the Sales Person Dead? 16 (6)
Is There a Religious Revival in Modern Russia? 216 (94)
Is There an Energy Crisis? 54
Is Your Leadership Showing? 112 (124)
Isaac Shelby and the War of 1812. Governor 117 (69)
Ischemic. Diabetic 181 (190)
Isfahan is Half the World - Its Art and Architecture 151 (29)
Islam 224 (9)
Islam. Ahmadiyyat or the True 1 (2), (7), (11)
Islam and the World Peace 1 (2)
Islam and the World Problems 1 (11)
Islam as Religion of Humanity 1 (2)
Islam. Basic Principles of 1 (6)
Islam. Equality and Brotherhood in 1 (13)
Islam. From Judaism to 1 (1)
Islam. Fundamental Principles of 1 (1)
Islam in Africa 1 (9)
Islam in the World Today 29 (57), (218), (228), (237)
Islam My Best Choice 1 (13)
Islam. New World Order of 1 (1)

Islam. Peculiarities of 1 (10)
Islam. Principles of 1 (12)
Islam. Religion of 142 (41)
Islam. Short Sketch of 1 (8)
Islam the Final Religion for Mankind 1 (4)
Islam the Only Solution for the World Problems 1 (7)
Islam Versus Christianity 1 (2), (7)
Islamic Conception of Caliphat 1 (3)
Islamic Conception of God 1 (2), (8)
Islamic Conception of Purpose of Life 1 (3)
Islamic Morals 1 (2)
Islamic Prayer 1 (12)
Islamic Viewpoint on Any Aspect of Man's Life 1 (11)
Islamic Worship 1 (8)
Island. Trinidad, Tropical 151 (299)
Island. Wild Ponies of Assateague 151 (305)
Islands and the Mayans of Yucatan. Hammocks as Made by the Cuna Indians of the San Blas 79 (25)
Islands. Darwin's 181 (20)
Islands of Wilderness. National Parks as 218
Islands to the Mountains. Greece - 59 (10)
Islands. Yankee Sails the Trade Wind 59 (5)
Isms. Today's 117 (64), (99)
Isolation and Alienation of Today's World. How Collective Living Breaks Down the 178 (1)
Isolationism 181 (265)
Israel in History and Prophecy 45 (3)
Israel. Modern 27 (42)
Israel. Political Repression in 213 (16)
Israel. Rise of the Modern State of 181 (143), (293), (306)
Israel - the Holy Land 59 (16)-
Israel: Then and Now 15 (2)
Israel Upon Religious Ideas. Impact of the Prophets of 29 (114)
Israeli Conflict. Arab- 57 (61), 181 (293), (306), 224 (9)
Israeli Conflict: Its Origin and Analysis of Present Situation. Arab- 117 (104)
Issues in Contemporary Theology 54
Issues in Nursing Education 151 (256)
Issues in Testing 117 (52)
Issues in the Delivery of Health Care 27 (36)
Issues in the Middle East 54
Issues Nobody Likes to Talk About 112 (48)
It Takes a Long Time to Become Young 97 (34)
Italian Creche Figure. 17th and 18th Century 174 (41)
Italian Culture. European Travel Relative to Spanish and 151 (300)
Italy. Mark Twain in 59 (13)
It's a Man's World, Too 151 (242)
It's Fun Being Successful 81 (1)
It's Fun Making Money 81 (1)
It's No Sin to be Rich 154 (5)
It's Your Energy - Use It Wisely 47
Ives. Music of Charles 29 (221)
Ivory Tower? America and the World: Whatever Happened to the 151 (110)
Ivory Tower? Education: Whatever Happened to the 151 (110)

J

Jail as a Community Corrections Center 56 (142)
James Joyce 181 (143)
James A. Michener 181 (140)
Janacek. Music of Leos 29 (221)
Jane Austen. In Search of 151 (298)
Japan 57 (44), 168 (52), 174 (82), 181 (342)
Japan. American Relations With China and 181 (265), (337)
Japan and China. Economic Development of 142 (51)
Japan and Korea. National Security Problems Involving 159 (36)
Japan. Contemporary 151 (193)
Japan for Americans. Meaning of 168 (66)
Japan. Social and Techological Change in 168 (66)
Japan. Soul of 15 (5)
Japan. Who Reads What In 105 (68)
Japanese American Evacuation During World War II 29 (139), (333)
Japanese-American Relations 181 (270), (342)
Japanese and/or Chinese Family 168 (66)
Japanese Art 151 (271)
Japanese Art History 16 (32)
Japanese Culture and Society 151 (271)
Japanese Folk Craft Pottery 57 (44)
Japanese Game of Go 151 (210)
Japanese Gardens 57 (44)
Japanese Lifestyles. Modern 168 (66)
Japanese Management 29 (149)
Japanese Rage for Order 57 (95)
Japanese Studies 168 (52)
Japanese Theatre 218
Japanese Village 168 (52)
Japanese Women's Lib 57 (95)
Jasper National Park. Long Distance Backpacking in 166 (1)
Jazz 142 (38)
Jazz. American 57 (42)
Jazz. West Coast 181 (79)
Jefferson: Comparison and Contrast of Philosophies. Hamilton and 117 (77)
Jesus as Precursor of the Holy Prophet Muhammad 1 (5)
Jesus Christ. Historical Look at 57 (91)
Jesus. How to be a Jew for 93 (4)
Jesus in the Holy Quran 1 (8)

Jesus in the Quran 1 (1)
Jesus. Why I a Jew Believe in Jesus 93 (2)
Jesus' Survival From Death on the Cross. Proofs Concerning 1 (9)
Jet Age. Business in the 100 (1)
Jet Age. Travel in the 100 (2)
Jet Set. Hollywood and the International 225 (2)
Jeu de Paume-Impressionist Museum. Visit to the 117 (138)
Jew-Afro-American and African 29 (6), (60), (219), (329), (337)
Jew, Believe in Jesus. Why I a 93 (2)
Jew for Jesus. How to Be a 93 (4)
Jewelry and Body Adornment From Non-western Perspective 79 (28)
Jewels of the Mediterranean. Rare 59 (9)
Jewish Art 181 (80), (301)
Jewish-Christian Dialogue 181 (306)
Jewish Education and Its Moral Implications 29 (90), (114), (233)
Jewish Educational Opportunities. Jewish Faith and 181 (96), (302)
Jewish Faith and Jewish Educational Opportunities 181 (96), (302)
Jewish History 142 (3)
Jewish Image in the American Mind, 1607-1900 181 (262)
Jewish Literature 142 (3)
Jewish Relations. Christian- 214 (80)
Jewish School. Running a Secular 181 (112), (304)
Jewish Scientists. Outstanding 181 (279)
Jewish Thought. Modern Trends in 181 (306)
Jewish Thought. Trends in 181 (239)
Jewish Voting Patterns. American 214 (4), (48)
Jews and Arabs 29 (163), (218)
Jews, Christians and Muslims. World Religions - Buddhists, Confucianists, Taoists, Maoists, 54
Jews Were Friends. When Arabs and 181 (306), (343)
Jimmy Carter 175 (4)
Job Exchanges. Faculty 214 (39)
Job. How to Do a Better 180 (41)
Job. How to Know When You are Doing a Good 29 (84), (112)
Job Hunting. Career Planning and 57 (73)
Job Market 218
Job. Occupational Stress: The Elements Which Contribute to Stress on the 117 (19)
Job Opportunities in Industries 23
Job. Parenting, a Difficult 57 (34)
Job Performance. Verbal, Vocal and Visual Cues to Better 180 (1)
Job Safety and Health 216 (65)
Job Satisfaction. Vocational and 181 (65)
Job Satisfying. Make Your 181 (65)
Job Search for College Students. Career Planning/ 151 (54)
Job Security. Declining Enrollment on 214 (37)
Job Success. Social Competencies and 117 (20)
Job Success: What It Takes to Make It 117 (19)
Jobs. Fertile Fields for 225 (13)
Jobs. Placement of Students in 56 (46)
Jobs That Electrical Engineers Do 216 (59)
Jogging 142 (18), 151 (205), 181 (9)
John F. Kennedy and the Civil Rights Movement 117 (66)
John F. Kennedy. Assassination of 176 (56)
John Muir's High Sierra 59 (6), 69 (4)
John Scali's Europe 102 (28)
John Witherspoon. Visit With Reverend 151 (41)
Johnny Can't Write Debate 105 (46)
Johnny Still Can't Read. Why 151 (100)
Johnny Through. Seeing Through Johnny So as to See 105 (98)
Johnny's Writing. What We Can Do About 57 (66)
Join a Civic Club 174 (40)
Joining Stitches. Braids, Fringes and 79 (53)
Jordan. Arab Libraries in 29 (196), (225)
Journalism 57 (88), 176 (64), 180 (128), 214 (16), (18)
Journalists and the Government. Proper Relationship Between Broadcast 117 (84)
Journalism and the Mass Media 216 (144)
Journalism. Broadcasting and Broadcast 151 (68)
Journalism. Careers in 181 (52), (71), 216 (13)
Journalism Education 142 (36)
Journalism Ethics: Scoops to Scandals 151 (86)
Journalism. High School 168 (10)
Journalism. Impact of Electronic 154 (13)
Journalism. Magazine 151 (68)
Journalism Phenomenon. Human Intrigue and Electronic 176 (43)
Journalism. Professional 135 (20)
Journalism Studies and Careers 223 (25)
Journalism. Television 154 (26)
Journey. American Conservatives in the Middle of the 85 (16)
Journey Through Biblical Lebanon 105 (23)
Journey to Inner Peace. Yoga - A 151 (88)
Journey to the Depths of the Human Mind 112 (96)
Journey to the Iris 105 (19)
Journeys to the Unconscious 211 (5)
Joy of Creating 79 (106)
Joyce. James 181 (143)
Joys of Family Owned Business. Trials, Tribulations and 136 (7)
Judaism 56 (141)
Judaism to Islam. From 1 (1)
Judge and Jury. Myth of the Impartial 225 (37)
Judging 142 (46)
Judgment Development. Moral 142 (84)
Judgment in Children, Youth and Adulthood. Moral 214 (77)
Judgments on Art or Morality. Critical 105 (66)
Judicial Administration 181 (274)
Judicial Appointments. Federal 168 (57)
Judicial Boards at Marquette. Student 105 (62)

Judo 228
Jugoslavija. Self-management of Science in 29 (120), (255), (268)
Jungle Law. Underwater 112 (26)
Junior College Versus the Vocational Technical School. Community 174 (1)
Junior High School. Career Education and the 57 (47)
Jury. Myth of the Impartial Judge and 225 (37)
Jurying an Art Exhibit 159 (18)
Just for Us Girls 97 (6)
Just War 105 (76)
Just War Theory 214 (83)
Justice. Criminal 16 (65), 181 (273)
Justice. Criminal Law and 159 (63)
Justice. Discretion in Our System of 151 (229)
Justice Education Through Berks Campus. Criminal 151 (230)
Justice Field. Criminal 181 (220)
Justice in America. Criminal 176 (62)
Justice in California. Juvenile 29 (62), (288), (346)
Justice. Law, Order, and 85 (35)
Justice. Plea Bargaining: A Barter System of 151 (229)
Justice System. Criminal 151 (229), (230), 181 (54)
Justice System. Major Problems in Our Criminal 57 (49)
Justice Through Law. America's Goal - 112 (28)
Justification of Revolutions 214 (83)
Justin Wilson. Hunting With 112 (134)
Juvenal Say Today. What Would 227 (23)
Juvenile Delinquency as a Persistent Social Problem 27 (37)
Juvenile Justice in California 29 (62), (288), (346)
Juvenile Periodicals. History of American 117 (75)

K

Kabarett and Its Influence. Pre-Hitler German 154 (22)
Kalahari. Bushmen of 69 (2)
Kaleidoscope of Energy 152
Karate 228
Karate. Women's Sport 62 (1)
Kayaking and Rafting Rivers 223 (34)
Kayaking as a Sport for Those Over 35 223 (30)
Kayaking. White Water 216 (68)
Keep Your Bait in the Water 112 (37)
Keeping Happiness in Your Marriage 56 (5)
Keeping Pace With Tomorrow 118 (1)
Keeping Up-to-Date 151 (40)
Keeping Your Marriage Alive and Growing 159 (48)
Kelsonian Economics 181 (39)
Kennedy and the Civil Rights Movement. John F. 117 (66)
Kennedy. Assassination of John F. 176 (56)
Kennedys and King. Political Assassinations - The 54
Kenneth Burke's Theories of Metaphor. I.A. Richards' and 151 (65)
Kentucky 117 (119)
Kentucky in the War Between the States. West 117 (67)
Kentucky - Its Strip Mining Industry, Its Beauty Among Stars. Muhlenberg County, 117 (29)
Kentucky - Present Status and Future Prospects. Tourism in West 117 (121)
Kentucky Religious History, 1780-1805. Second Awakening as a Turning Point in 117 (69)
Kentucky. Tourism in West 117 (114)
Kentuckyhenge: Stonehenge Revisited 117 (70)
Kenya. River People - the Pokomo of 56 (2), (114)
Keogh Retirement Accounts. Tax-deferred 18 (1)
Key Chemicals. Enzymes - Life's 54
Key to Learning. Motivation - A 117 (134)
Key to Self-change 225 (10), (17)
Keynote in Literature for Children. Delight - 29 (200)
Kidnapping and Deprogramming. Religious 12
Kidney Disease in Children 181 (158)
Kidney Transplants in Children 181 (158)
Kill Each Other? Why Do We 112 (3)
Killer - Hypertension. Silent 16 (13)
Kills. Toxic Algae and Cattle 168 (37)
Kindergarten. History and Methods of 117 (56)
Kinds of No-Load Mutual Funds 140 (1)
King. Mahatma Ghandi and Martin Luther 103 (1)
King of the Shaggy Dog Story 112 (62)
King. Political Assassinations - the Kennedys and 54
King. Sell Like an Ace - Live Like a 112 (136)
Kingdom of God and Secret of Adam's Slip 1 (10)
Kings and Things. Of Cabbages and 97 (33)
King's English or the Mayor's? 181 (317)
King-size Clean-up 20
Kitchen or Work Space Planning 216 (73)
Knitting. Peruvian Needle 79 (65)
Knotless Netting 79 (40), (103)
Knotless Netting, Basic Basketry, Wrapping. Children's Workshop in 79 (158)
Knotless Netting. Contemporary Use of Primitive 79 (52)
Knots. Woven Clothes Assembled by Crochet or 79 (60)
Knotted Baskets 79 (30)
Knotting 79 (39), (98), (146)
Knotting. Cross-tension 79 (103)
Knowledge Most Worth Having 168 (42)
Knowledge or Certainty. Scientific Truth - 57 (6)
Knowledge. Truth, Objectivity and Some Interesting Facts About the Nature of 85 (20)

Kodaly Approach to Music Teaching 54
Konigsberg. Graph Theory and the Bridges of 151 (247)
Koran. Glorious 29 (218), (228), (237)
Korea 216 (98)
Korea. Amazing 59 (1)
Korea? Foreign Affairs: What Happened to Our Investment in 151 (110)
Korea. National Security Problems Involving Japan and 159 (36)
Korea: The Land of Industrial Revolution 151 (118)
Korean Culture 168 (55)
Krishna. Hare 224 (11)
Kubler-Ross Revisited 29 (281)

L

Labor and Industry in Anthracite Mining 151 (36)
Labor and the Environment 172 (13)
Labor History 151 (224)
Labor Law 180 (168)
Labor-Management Disputes. Arbitration of 216 (104)
Labor-Management Relations 216 (104)
Labor Negotiations 151 (9)
Labor Policy of the Free Society 85 (27)
Labor Relations 172 (12)
Labor Relations. Federal 174 (17)
Labor Relations. Public Employee 216 (105)
Labor Relations. Public Sector 181 (41)
Labor Relations Today 151 (223)
Labor Studies 151 (224)
Labor Unions. Right to Work - Forcing Public Employees into Unwanted 131 (4)
Labor Uprising of 1877. Great 213 (3)
Laboratory. Anaerobic Bacteriology in the Clinical 56 (78)
Laboratory. Clinical 105 (96)
Laboratory Medicine 171 (41)
Lace 79 (71), (139)
Lace. Layering, Transparency, and 79 (27)
Lace, Needle Lace, Embroidery. Bobbin 79 (42)
Lace, Traditional and Contemporary. Bobbin 79 (144)
Lace Weaves. Weaver Controlled and Loom Controlled 79 (69)
Lace Weaving the Easy Way 79 (147)
Laces. Needle 79 (98)
Lacrosse. Virginia Tech 216 (87)
Ladies. Tattle Tales About First 112 (11)
Ladies, Women, or Persons? Girls, 151 (61)
Lady in Tennis Shoes Syndrome. Old 168 (22)
Lady Radicals in American History 151 (257)
Lafayette's Visit to Louisiana. General 174 (14)
Lake. Alaska Wilderness 59 (18), 69 (14)
Lake Baikal and Irkutsk. Leningrad and the Environs of 151 (296)
Lake. Birth and Death of a 181 (133)
Lake Michigan 142 (77)
Lakes. Green Scum on 168 (37)
Lamaze Method in the United States. History of the 36 (1)
Lamb Carcass and Its Cuts 151 (182)
Laminated Hardwood Block Flooring 80 (2)
Land and People. U.S.S.R. - 117 (62), (72)
Land Archaeology. Holy 227 (45)
Land. Biblical Scenes of the Holy 159 (48)
Land Grant Colleges. History and Development of the 191 (122)
Land Grant University. You and Your 216 (13)
Land? Is My Land Your 151 (225)
Land. Israel - the Holy 59 (16)
Land Marks. Historic Civil Engineering 174 (90)
Land of Eternal Spring. Guatemala - 117 (140)
Land of Industrial Revolution. Korea: the 151 (118)
Land of Natural Wonders. Venezuela - 69 (7)
Land of the Hex Sign. Pennsylvania Dutch: 117 (75)
Land of the Phamlysoun. From the 56 (26)
Land of the Setting Sun. Megrab - 69 (3)
Land. Paradox of a Forgotten 168 (26)
Land Rights. Indian 29 (166), (195)
Land Subsidence 136 (12)
Land. They Never Really Owned the 223 (26)
Land. Tour Through the Holy 29 (216), (225), (315)
Land Treatment of Food Plant Waste Water 67 (13)
Land Use 54, 216 (31)
Land Use Allocation 218
Land Use for Agriculture 151 (21)
Land Use Forecasting 151 (290)
Land Use Issues and Concerns 151 (23)
Land Use Legislation. National 174 (28)
Land Use Planning 16 (54), 214 (25), (63)
Land Use Planning and Mineral Potential 143 (6)
Land Use Planning. Urban 142 (50)
Land Use. Transportation and 151 (290)
Land Use. Urban 218
Land Use Within Cities 174 (51)
Landfills, Resource Recovery, and Handling of Hazardous Waste. Sanitary 133 (3)
Landforms. Glacial Deposition of Aquifers and Other Interesting 136 (13)
Landing Sites. UFOs and Their 94 (3)
Landlord or Educator: The Resident Hall Dilemma 151 (105)
Landlord - Tenant Law 29 (121)
Landlord - Tenant. Specialties in Real Estate Law: 218
Lands. Holy 59 (16)
Landscape Design 216 (42)
Landscape. Fountains in the 181 (132)
Landscape Gardening 16 (63)
Landscape Graphics 181 (83), (132)
Landscape. Home 181 (132), (217)

Landscape of Greek Mythology 29 (124), (197), (205), (320)
Landscape Painting. Genesis of 56 (13)
Landscape. Philadelphia 181 (132)
Landscape Plant Materials 16 (63)
Landscape. Sculpture in the 216 (16)
Landscapes. South African 223 (32)
Landscaping 117 (7), (126), 216 (6)
Language Acquisition and Bilingual Children 29 (95), (204), (297)
Language and Human Rights 171 (50)
Language and Mind 181 (314)
Language and Other Nonverbal Languages. Body 151 (61)
Language and Reading 159 (29)
Language and Speech Disorders in Children 56 (53)
Language and Spelling 159 (29)
Language and Thinking 181 (314)
Language Arts and Math Activities for Teachers - Nursery - 4th Grade 117 (48)
Language Arts and Related Activities 117 (56)
Language Arts and the Study Skills 181 (319)
Language Arts in the Open School. Reading and 117 (36)
Language Arts, Reading, Mathematics and Science to Bilingual Classes in the Elementary Grades. Teaching 142 (90)
Language Arts. Teaching More Creatively in Reading and 57 (79)
Language as Living Symbols of a Culture 27 (18)
Language. Body 112 (120), 135 (19), 176 (113), 225 (25)
Language? Can Chimps Learn Human 181 (314)
Language. Contemporary Corruption of 85 (20)
Language Development in Young Children 181 (319)
Language Development. Normal 56 (53)
Language Difficulties in Adults. Speech and 56 (53)
Language Disorders. Child 181 (314)
Language Disorders. Speech and 16 (67)
Language. English as a Third 151 (239)
Language Experience. Using 57 (79)
Language From Ancient to Modern Times. Greek - An Ongoing 227 (29)
Language. Greater Understanding of People Through Face and Body 212 (1)
Language. How Children Learn 159 (29)
Language - How it Influences Our Behavior, Our Conceptions, Our View of Self and Others, How it Functions. Nature of 117 (61)
Language. How to Increase Your Psychic Abilities Through Face 212 (1)
Language. Human Awareness Through Face 212 (1)
Language Learning. Phonetics and 29 (203)
Language. Non-Verbal Communication - the Sub-conscious 117 (50)
Language. Origin of the English 29 (209), (298)
Language Pedagogy. Foreign 142 (6)
Language Problems. Prevention of Speech and 57 (63)
Language. Proper 142 (2)
Language. Sexism in 168 (9)
Language Skills. Foreing 174 (58)
Language Skills. Normal Development of Speech and 174 (8)
Language. Social Levels of 142 (2)
Language Study. New Directions in 181 (315)
Language Study. Unity of 181 (59)
Language. Talking to the Computer in Its 57 (93)
Language Teaching. Linguistics and 117 (87)
Language Teaching. Natural Approach to Foreign 27 (15)
Language. Technical Drawing Universal Graphic 117 (82)
Language Today. Arabic 29 (203), (218)
Languages and Careers. Foreign 216 (135)
Languages and Mind. Relationship of 171 (46)
Languages. Body Language and Other Nonverbal 151 (61)
Languages. Foreign 174 (15)
Languages. Oriental 168 (55)
Languages. Slavic 171 (46)
Laos, Thailand, and the Golden Triangle. Red China, 54
Large Cities of the World 29 (319)
Larlham Story. Hattie 98 (1), (2), (3)
Larynx. Speech After Cancer of the 117 (133)
Laser 56 (130), 222
Laser. Physics of the 171 (40)
Lasers 29 (272), 151 (147)
Lasers and Lightwaves. Art of Communicating With 144
Lasers and Their Application. Development of 218
Lasers and Their Applications 105 (119)
Lasers--Medical Applications 29 (186)
Last Cannibals 69 (2)
Last of the Bucks 97 (51)
Latern Festical 168 (52)
Latest Energy Developments 151 (125)
Latest Reading Controversy 57 (54)
Latin 227 (23)
Latin America: A Racial Paradise? Minority Studies: Beyond Takenism 168 (25)
Latin America. Development of 223 (17)
Latin America. Do You Want to Know About 117 (103)
Latin America: How Do We View One Another. United States and 151 (213)
Latin America. Modern 181 (344)
Latin America: The Latin Review. United States and 117 (102)
Latin America Today 97 (54)
Latin America. United States and 151 (196)
Latin American Renaissance 151 (27)
Latin American Revolution 135 (22)
Latin Epigraphy. Greek and 227 (8)
Latin. History of 227 (40)
Latin Letter-writing 227 (27)
Latin Literature 227 (18)

Latin Literature. Greeks and 227 (12)
Latin. Medieval 227 (27)
Latin Poetry 227 (33)
Latin Review. United States and Latin America: The 117 (102)
Latin. Teaching of 227 (18)
Latino Women in the United States. Role of the 142 (68)
Laugh and Something to Think About. Good 112 (63)
Laugh. For God's Sake, 105 (26)
Laugh. Open Wide and 112 (72)
Laugh. What Makes America 105 (19)
Laughing Matters 20
Laughter and Tears as Communication 105 (93)
Laughter. How to Pulverize an Audience With 112 (67)
Laughter. Line of 151 (289)
Laughter. Livin' on Love and 112 (12)
Laughter. Look Back in 97 (63)
Laughter. Psychology of 151 (270)
Law 54, 176 (111)
Law. Administrative 105 (56)
Law. America's Goal - Justice Through 112 (28)
Law. Ancient 227 (32)
Law and Environment 29 (74), (195)
Law and Institutions. American 181 (274)
Law and Justice. Criminal 159 (63)
Law and Management. Environmental 27 (3)
Law and Political Institutions. Order, Freedom, 85 (40)
Law and Race 181 (46), (255)
Law and Society 159 (41)
Law and Society. Inter-Relationships With 54
Law and the Elderly 181 (192), (241), (271), (312)
Law and the Handicapped 57 (5)
Law and the Poor. Minimum Wage 85 (22)
Law and the Rule of Lawyers. Rule of the 85 (40)
Law. Antitrust 105 (56)
Law Applications. Real Estate 65 (5)
Law. Art and 159 (30)
Law as It Applies to Instructional Television. Copyright 151 (66)
Law. Constitutional 142 (67)
Law. Criminal 159 (45), 181 (273)
Law. Decline of the 159 (8)
Law Enforcement 220 (5)
Law. Environmental 159 (41), 214 (25), (63)
Law. Evidence and the 159 (8)
Law. International 154 (27)
Law: Is It Enforceable? Ohm's 151 (73)
Law. Labor 180 (168)
Law. Landlord-Tenant 29 (121)
Law: Landlord-Tenant. Specialties in Real Estate 218
Law. Mass Communications 168 (10)
Law Matters. Public 57 (36)
Law. Morality and 54, 214 (83)
Law. Obscenity Problem and Obscenity 116 (1 - 7)
Law of Effect 31 (7)
Law of the Sea 3 (7), 187 (2)
Law, Order, and Justice 85 (35)
Law. Patent, Trademark and Copyright 105 (56)
Law. Personal Injury 159 (22)
Law. Real Estate 65 (22)
Law. Real Estate License 65 (36), (51)
Law School/Business School Admissions 142 (95)
Law School Study 105 (56)
Law Schools 159 (42)
Law. Social Welfare 105 (56)
Law. Student and the 168 (19)
Law. Teacher and the 168 (19)
Law. Teacher, the Pupil and the 57 (55)
Law Tradition. Freedom and the Common 85 (27)
Law. Underwater Jungle 112 (26)
Law With University Students 16 (81)
Lawn Care 117 (7), (126), 189
Lawn Care. Home 151 (25)
Lawn Management. Zoysia 189
Lawrence. D.H. 29 (207), (243)
Laws and Regulations, the Employment Interview. Historical Overview of Equal Employment Opportunity and Affirmative Action 27 (2)
Laws. Civil Rights 29 (60), (147), (194), (337)
Laws - Cure for or a Cause of Poverty? Minimum Wage 85 (2)
Laws? Does Nature Obey Mathematical 56 (129)
Laws. Enforcement of Pollution Control 204
Laws. Food Regulations and Food 151 (177)
Laws of Chance and Fortune. Mysterious 29 (136)
Laws, Regulations, and Executive Orders. Federal 151 (1)
Lawyer's View. Problems of the Businessman: A 136 (9)
Lawyers. Rule of the Law and the Rule of 85 (40)
Lay Midwife in Today's Society 122 (5)
Layer. Threats to the Ozone 151 (155)
Layered Weaving 79 (29), (40)
Layering, Transparency, and Lace 79 (27)
Layman. Metrics for the 57 (70)
Layperson. Home Buying and Selling for the 56 (97)
Lazy Man's Trip to the Bank or Real Estate, the Profession of Happy People 65 (20)
Leader. Profile of a 29 (136)
Leader? What Makes a 112 (125)
Leaders. 2000 Young American 135 (6)
Leadership 105 (81), 117 (46), 216 (22), (29)
Leadership and Productivity 56 (134)
Leadership and the Outlook for America 102 (25)
Leadership. Challenge of 189
Leadership Development 105 (82), 216 (52)
Leadership Development: A Participative Strategy. Student 151 (107)
Leadership. Educational 56 (136)
Leadership. Effective 151 (46)
Leadership. Effective Conference Participation and 56 (20)

Leadership in a Democracy 117 (65), (112)
Leadership in Small Group Communication 168 (17)
Leadership. Lib or 214 (94)
Leadership. Management/ 23
Leadership. Nature of 102 (30)
Leadership of Man 112 (68)
Leadership. Personality/ 105 (77)
Leadership Showing? Is Your 112 (124)
Leadership Training 180 (195)
Leaf Printing 79 (36)
Learn to Live a Fuller and More Rewarding Life 151 (38)
Learning and Counseling Models for Teachers. Carkhuff 117 (39)
Learning and Self. Environmental Awareness - An Approach to 29 (132)
Learning. Approach for Teaching and 181 (122)
Learning. Be Curious: Practice 151 (115)
Learning Centers 142 (13)
Learning. Community Education and Life-long 57 (81)
Learning Disabilities 142 (59), 117 (131), 171 (20)
Learning Disabilities - Fact or Fancy? 151 (100)
Learning-exchange 99 (1), (2), (3)
Learning for Tomorrow 102 (36)
Learning Games and Educational Simulations 214 (36)
Learning in a Free Society. Teaching and 174 (1)
Learning in Early Childhood Education. Competency - Based-on-Site 223 (7)
Learning. Individualized 181 (103)
Learning. Life-long 57 (26), 151 (119), 168 (21), 218
Learning. Mastery 181 (89)
Learning. Meanings of Lifelong 57 (85)
Learning. Media and 216 (58)
Learning. Media in Teaching and 181 (75), (110)
Learning. Motivation - A Key to 117 (134)
Learning. Multi-media Concept and New Approaches to 56 (50)
Learning. Phonetics and Language 29 (203)
Learning. Piaget - Some Ideas on Efficient 57 (50)
Learning Problems. Child With Behavior and 117 (131)
Learning Problems of the Black Child. Special 142 (47)
Learning Process 117 (60)
Learning Process. Interpersonal Communications and the 181 (110), (316)
Learning Resource Centers 181 (97)
Learning Strategies of Materials. Individualized 181 (75), (110)
Learning. Subordination of Teaching to 171 (21)
Learning. Theories of 105 (47)
Learning to Read 171 (16)
Learning to Read. Age for 171 (19)
Learning to See in Nature and Relate to Your Weaving 79 (77)
Learning Without Schools 214 (37)
Leasing 120
Lebanon 57 (92)
Lebanon. Journey Through Biblical 105 (23)
Lebanon, What Next? After 3 (5)
Lecture: Using the Personalized System of Instruction in Higher Education. Death of the 151 (169)
Lectures on Social/Political/Ethical/Theological Topics 168 (34)
Lee. Our Greatest General R.E. 57 (28)
Left. Anarchism, Nihilism, and the New 85 (21)
Left and the New Right. New 85 (9)
Left. New 85 (23), (24)
Left - Old and New 172 (6)
Left Represent The Greening of America? Does the 85 (8)
Leftover Warp 79 (53)
Legal Affairs 176 (68)
Legal and Medical Aspects of Organ Transplants 54
Legal Aspects of Business 105 (6)
Legal Aspects of Education 16 (83)
Legal Duties and Responsibilities of Boards of Education 57 (55)
Legal Education 159 (58)
Legal Ethics in Nursing. Medico-Moral 105 (49)
Legal Problems of the Sea Around Us 223 (16)
Legal Problems to Avoid in Everyday Life 16 (80)
Legal Process 214 (5)
Legal Rights of Mentally/Physically Handicapped Individuals 151 (228)
Legal Rights of Students and Young People 231 (2)
Legal Status and Economic Development of American Indian Tribes 218
Legalized Gambling. Question of 97 (60)
Legend of Birds in Art. Folklore and 57 (82)
Legendary Siam 15 (5)
Legends and Culture. American Indian History, 79 (126)
Legislation. Consumer Affairs 16 (27)
Legislation. Critique on Both Sides of Abortion 54
Legislation Improve Consumer Welfare? Can 54
Legislation. National Land Use 174 (28)
Legislative Policy. National 216 (37)
Legislature Doing Which Affects the Ordinary Citizen. What is the State 57 (49)
Legislature. Illinois 142 (67)
Legislature. One Man's View of the Washington State 223 (22)
Leisure Activities in Eastern North Carolina. History of Recreation Physical Education and 56 (28)
Leisure. Adjustment to 168 (36)
Leisure. Drug Misuse and Abuse, More and More 56 (81)
Leisure. Future of Work and 181 (12)
Leisure. Physical Recreation and Education for 171 (27)
Leisure Problems 224 (9)
Leisure Time in the 21st Century 216 (76)

Len O'Connor Reports 135 (48)
Leningrad and the Environs of Lake Baikal and Irkutsk 151 (296)
Leninist Ideology in the 1970's. Operational Significance of Marxist - 85 (31)
Leno 79 (139)
Leno Weaves Using Doups 79 (24)
Lenos 79 (63)
Leos Janacek. Music of 29 (221)
Leprechauns and Forests 223 (35)
Lesotho 171 (11)
Lesson. Economics in One Easy 151 (50)
Lesson. Give a Speech in One Easy 174 (66)
Let's Join the Human Race 100 (1)
Let's Not Save the World 85 (25)
Letters of Recommendation 214 (14)
Letter-writers. Great 159 (65)
Letter-writing. Latin 227 (27)
Lettuce Seed to Fifty Million Dollars. From 151 (185)
Level Values. System- 224 (2)
Liability and the Administrator 117 (46)
Liability and the Guidance Counselor 117 (46)
Liability and the School Nurse 117 (46)
Liability and the Teacher 117 (46)
Liability and the Vocational Teacher 117 (46)
Liability Crisis. Product 181 (44)
Liability. Perspectives in Product 31 (33)
Liability. School Board 117 (46)
Liaison. Realtor Attorney 65 (16)
Lib. Japanese Women's 57 (95)
Lib or Leadership 214 (94)
Liberal America. Future of Conservatism in Post- 85 (21)
Liberal Arts 216 (50)
Liberal Arts as Preparation for an Uncertain Future 151 (116)
Liberal Arts Education. Black Studies and 181 (25), (90)
Liberal Arts Education Today 105 (35)
Liberal Arts in Vocational Education 174 (91)
Liberal Arts Programs. Structured/Integrated 227 (11)
Liberal Arts Setting. Asian Studies in the 159 (6)
Liberal. Death of the White 151 (170)
Liberalism and Conservatism in Historical Perspective 85 (12)
Liberalism and the Rise of Conservatism. New Winds - the Decline of 85 (12)
Liberalism and the Tragedy of American Foreign Policy 85 (7)
Liberalism. Death of 85 (20), (40)
Liberalism. Neo-conservatism and Neo- 85 (18)
Liberalizing Adult Vocational Education 151 (98)
Liberated Man. Why a Liberated Woman Makes for a 225 (8)
Liberated or Oppressed. Women in Africa - 29 (7)
Liberated Woman Makes for a Liberated Man. Why a 225 (8)
Liberated Women. Femininity and 179 (2)
Liberation 142 (25)
Liberation and Sexual Roles. Women's 85 (35)
Liberation and Socialism. Black 213 (7)
Liberation and Socialism. Chicano 213 (12)
Liberation. Black Women's 213 (18)
Liberation. Buddhist Notion of 117 (97)
Liberation in Spain. Women's 213 (6)
Liberation Movement. Women's 151 (167)
Liberation Movements. Black 142 (17)
Liberation of the White Male Professional 159 (24)
Liberation. Philosophy and Women's 29 (251)
Liberation. Psychological 181 (146)
Liberation? What is Young People's 231 (3)
Liberation. Women's 214 (83), (92)
Liberator of Woman. Muhammad the 1 (2)
Libertarian Socialist and Democratic Socialist Ideas 181 (288)
Libertarianism. Fallacy of 85 (40)
Liberties. Civil 31 (14), 218
Liberties During the Cold War Years. Civil 105 (59)
Liberties. They Are Your Civil 117 (103)
Liberty 155 (1), 174 (72)
Liberty and Our Third Century. Religious 12
Liberty. Blessings of 85 (3)
Liberty? Can We Afford 102 (12)
Liberty. Economic Freedom and Civil 174 (72)
Liberty in American Politics. Equality and 85 (13)
Liberty. Religious Roots of 85 (9)
Liberty. Security Versus 159 (32)
Libraries 142 (7), 159 (23)
Libraries in Jordan. Arab 29 (196), (225)
Libraries in Society. Role of Books and 29 (198)
Libraries. School 159 (23)
Library. Alexandrian 57 (92)
Library Building. Berks Campus Has a New 151 (59)
Library Buildings 142 (29)
Library Can Do for You. What the Carol Newman 216 (56)
Library Design 142 (79)
Library. How to Use the 216 (56)
Library Management 142 (29)
Library. Microforms at the Cal State Fullerton 29 (196)
Library Service. Careers in 151 (59)
License. Academic Freedom and Academic 85 (16)
License Law. Real Estate 65 (36), (51)
Licensed Private Investigative Security-Consulting 180 (86)
Lichen Dyeing. Natural 79 (156)
Lie With Statistics. How to 151 (17)
Lie With Statistics. Statistics/Probability - How to 151 (252)
Life After Death 1 (4), (8)
Life After Death - Some Philosophical Considerations 105 (91)

Life After College? College - Is There 112 (64)
Life and Culture of North American Indians 79 (124)
Life and Hard Times as a Weaving Woman. My 79 (50)
Life and Humor of Mark Twain 117 (91)
Life and Music. My 154 (1)
Life and Teachings of Muhammad. Glimpse Into the 1 (8)
Life and Times of Arthur Godfrey 154 (10)
Life and Times of My Father 112 (110)
Life and Times of W.C. Fields 112 (38)
Life. Artist's Way of 211 (5)
Life. Arts and Quality of 57 (38)
Life. Beginnings of Religious 105 (107)
Life Behind the Iron Curtain and in the Soviet Union 29 (65), (289), (294)
Life. Book in Everyone's 225 (19)
Life Career Change. Mid- 218
Life. Changing Family 168 (26)
Life Cycle. Challenges of the 181 (246), (297)
Life. Development in the First Year of 181 (23)
Life Elsewhere in the Universe 57 (87)
Life. Environmental Quality and the American Way of 57 (94)
Life. Exploding Technology - A New Way of 102 (22)
Life. Genetic Diversity and Political 181 (24)
Life. Handling the Stress of 151 (39)
Life. Helping Your Child Become High on 16 (84)
Life. How a Career in Business Can Bring Personal Fulfillment in 23
Life. How to Control the Time of Your 180 (46)
Life in an Education Factory 151 (7)
Life in Asia and the United States. Family 56 (123)
Life in China 176 (109)
Life in Eastern North Carolina. Colonial Town 56 (30)
Life in France. Everyday 56 (111)
Life in Our Hands. Genetic Engineering: 102 (24)
Life in Southern California. Undersea 29 (270), (302)
Life in the American City. Quality of 31 (13)
Life in the Community - Challenge or Check 85 (11)
Life in the Irish Republic. Quality of 159 (65)
Life in the Philippines. Village 151 (162)
Life in the Soviet Union 218
Life in the Soviet Union. Everyday 97 (40)
Life in the Universe. Intelligent 223 (4)
Life. Indian Way of 142 (81)
Life Is in Your Hands. Palmistry: Your 117 (96)
Life? Is the CRTC Running Your 171 (5)
Life is Tremendous 135 (34)
Life. Islamic Conception of Purpose 1 (3)
Life. Islamic Viewpoint on Any Aspect of Man's 1 (11)
Life: Issues and Programs. Student 218
Life. Learn to Live a Fuller and More Rewarding 151 (38)
Life. Legal Problems to Avoid in Everyday 16 (80)
Life. Light Look at 225 (1)
Life. Magazines and American 105 (68)
Life Making. Critical Skills for Effective 57 (71)
Life Management Skills 117 (110)
Life. Meaningfulness in the Process of 174 (9)
Life. Metrics for Everyday 151 (248)
Life. Motivation in One's 105 (80)
Life. Music and My 154 (20)
Life of a Courtroom Artist 97 (37)
Life of a Public Wife in Washington 97 (75)
Life of Plants. Secret 134 (1)
Life of the California Indian. Daily 29 (165), (339)
Life on the University Campus. Student 16 (21)
Life - Options and Opportunities. Quality of 57 (15)
Life. Origin of 151 (211)
Life. Philosophy and Ordinary 171 (55)
Life Possible Today? Is the Good 85 (36)
Life. Power of Women in First C.B.C. Roman 227 (29)
Life. Quality of 16 (7), 97 (19)
Life. Relaxation Response: How to Use Mental Relaxation Techniques to Enrich Your 136 (23)
Life. Run for Your 151 (67)
Life. Survival and Length of 180 (148)
Life: The Student and the Void. College 151 (105)
Life. Three Ways to Manage Your 75 (1)
Life Through Higher Education. New 151 (103)
Life. Tourist's View of Soviet Economic 223 (33)
Life. Toy Department of 112 (31)
Life. Transference in Everyday 181 (125)
Life. Women in Political 56 (131)
Life-long Education 16 (88)
Life-long Learning 57 (26), 151 (119), 168 (21), 218
Life-long Learning. Community Education and 57 (81)
Life's Key Chemicals. Enzymes - 54
Lifesaving. Scuba 181 (5)
Lifestyle. Creating Your Own Image and 97 (26)
Life-Style. Shaping a Future 102 (15)
Life-Style. Weaving as a 79 (31)
Lifestyles. Alternative 57 (8)
Lifestyles. Changing 102 (22), 176 (98)
Lifestyles. Modern Japanese 168 (66)
Lifetime. Conditioning for a 159 (69)
Lifetime Individual Sports 105 (114)
Light and Color 218
Light, and Illusions. Eye, 56 (130)
Light. Black 216 (45)
Light. From the City of Stars to the City of 97 (16)
Light Forms 79 (90)

Light. Health and 134 (5)
Light Intensity and Color. Health as Related to 216 (24)
Light Look at Life 225 (1)
Light. Polarized 56 (128)
Lighter Side of the News 97 (53)
Lighting for Theatre. Directing, Designing and 159 (62)
Lighting in the Home 56 (95)
Lightwaves. Art of Communicating With Lasers and 144
Limitation. Strategic Arms 97 (74)
Limitations on Complexity of Computation 181 (204)
Limits for Children. Setting 117 (50)
Limits of Majority Rule 85 (25)
Limits. Relativism and Its 85 (38)
Lincoln a Christian? Was Abraham 29 (338)
Lincoln. Abraham 142 (27)
Lincoln Aides Abet His Assassin? Did 29 (338)
Lincoln and the Emancipation of American Blacks. Abraham 29 (338)
Lincoln. Mary Todd 57 (28)
Lincoln the Man Not Myth 57 (28)
Lincoln, the Master Politician. Great Americans - 151 (222)
Lincoln the Speaker. Abraham 223 (2)
Lincoln's Use and Abuse of America's Founding Fathers. Lincoln - Rutledge Romance - Hoax or Reality? 29 (338)
Line. Front Line and the Bottom 135 (32)
Line of Laughter 151 (289)
Linguist Does. What a 29 (203)
Linguistic Study of the Bible 29 (237)
Linguistics 142 (6)
Linguistics and Language Teaching 117 (87)
Linguistics and Literature 151 (235)
Linguistics. Career Opportunities in 56 (65)
Linguistics. Comparative 117 (87)
Linguistics. Study of 171 (46)
Linguistics. Use of the Computer and Statistics in Literature and 227 (51)
Lion of Tomorrow. Africa - Tawny 57 (62)
Liquid Mixtures in Pumps and Piping. Flow Characteristics of Solids - 67 (5)
Listen? Why Don't They 151 (81)
Listening 181 (319)
Listening: Do We 174 (66)
Listening is Money--Both Ways 105 (13)
Listening, Then Speaking 168 (17)
Listing 65 (7), (8), (9), (11), (12), (13), (14), (15), (17), (20), (21), (22), (24), (26), (29), (30), (31), (32), (37), (38), (39), (40), (41), (42), (45), (47), (48), (52), (55), (59), (61), (63), (64), (67), (68)
Listing. Multiple 65 (10)
Literacy. Economic 117 (17), (40)
Literacy Obsolete. Is 29 (205)
Literacy Renaissance. Irish 97 (51)
Literacy. Visual 168 (15), 181 (97)
Literacy? What is 159 (54)
Literary Criticism. Afro-American 142 (66)
Literary Criticism. Composition, 216 (117)
Literary Criticism. Hellinstic Poetry and 227 (7)
Literary Criticism. Semiotics in 227 (41)
Literary Influences 225 (42)
Literary Programme. Propertius' 227 (24)
Literature. Achievement of Nationality in American 16 (34)
Literature. Afro-American 142 (66), (74)
Literature. American 151 (232), (240)
Literature and Art. Polyphemus in Folktale, Homer, 227 (47)
Literature and Art. Symbolist Movement in 216 (112)
Literature and Culture. American 142 (22)
Literature and Film. Children's 151 (234)
Literature and Linguistics. Use of the Computer and Statistics in 227 (51)
Literature and Liturgy. Relationship Between 218
Literature and Society 29 (213), (290)
Literature. Appalachian People and 168 (26)
Literature. Aspect of the 19th Century Russian 29 (127), (213)
Literature. Augustan 227 (35)
Literature Between the Great Wars. American 151 (231)
Literature. Bible as 218
Literature. Carl Sandburg's Place in American 225 (42)
Literature. Character of Don Juan in Western 151 (233)
Literature. Children's 117 (56), 142 (13), 159 (23), 174 (18), (57), 181 (45)
Literature. Computer Applications in the Study of 227 (44)
Literature. Contemporary 151 (232), 159 (24)
Literature. Cuban 216 (135)
Literature During Germany's Third Reich. Use of 216 (112)
Literature. Early Childhood Education in Art, Music and Children's 142 (30)
Literature. 18th Century 117 (88)
Literature. Folk 159 (23)
Literature for Children 181 (144), 214 (46)
Literature for Children. Delight - Keynote in 29 (200)
Literature for Children. Selecting Good 56 (63)
Literature for Young Children 142 (84)
Literature. French Caribbean 168 (41)
Literature. Great Names in French 56 (60)
Literature. Greek or Roman 105 (16)
Literature. Greeks and Latin 227 (12)
Literature. History of Children's 117 (75), 174 (18)
Literature in French. African 168 (41)
Literature in the Thirteenth-Century. Roman 227 (12)

Literature. Influence of Classics on English 227 (26)
Literature. Irish 174 (29)
Literature. Jewish 142 (3)
Literature. Latin 227 (18)
Literature. Linguistics and 151 (235)
Literature/Lore of Bituminous Mining 151 (236)
Literature. Love and Death in 105 (16)
Literature. Male-Female Roles in Russian Culture as Relected in Nineteenth and Twentieth Century 27 (18)
Literature. Modern Afrikan 142 (66)
Literature. Modern Trends in Children's 57 (62)
Literature. 19th Century English 214 (47)
Literature of Existentialism 159 (40)
Literature. Popular 142 (27)
Literature. Profiles in 181 (145)
Literature. Racism in Children's 151 (241)
Literature. Rebel in 159 (40)
Literature. Recent American 117 (90)
Literature. Romantic and Victorian 105 (25)
Literature. Science Fiction/Fantasy 214 (46)
Literature Search Service. RECON 216 (61)
Literature: Selected Topics. Myth and 151 (236)
Literature. Sexism in Children's 151 (241)
Literature. Spanish American 216 (135)
Literature. Stoicism in Ancient 227 (39)
Literature. Technology in 151 (245)
Literature. Transformational Grammar and 29 (210)
Literature. Violin - History, Development and 57 (42)
Literature - Why We Enjoy Stories, Poems, and Plays. Fascination of 54
Literature. Women in 105 (123)
Literature. Women in American 151 (234)
Literature. Women in Greek and Roman 227 (24)
Literature. Women in History and 227 (16)
Literature. Yiddish 142 (54)
Little Foxes That Nibble Your Vines 75 (1)
Liturgical Design Conceptualizing 79 (132)
Liturgy. Oral Interpretation and the 105 (110)
Liturgy. Relationship Between Literature and 218
Live Forever. Why Not 45 (2)
Live on 24 Hours a Day. How to 216 (76)
Liven Up Reading 181 (123)
Lives of American Women in Autobiography 29 (202)
Livin' on Love and Laughter 112 (12)
Living. Community Resources for Better 57 (38)
Living. Cooperative 171 (1)
Living. Creative Drama: A Basic Skill for 159 (54)
Living. Creative Writing: A Basic Skill for 159 (54)
Living Environments. English Villages and Human Scale in 218
Living. Family 176 (51)
Living. Improve Your Quality of 151 (180)
Living It in Business 180 (17)
Living. Mental Health for Daily 117 (108)
Living. Modern Nutrition for Everyday 181 (187)
Living on the Frontier 223 (26)
Living Patterns. Medieval 31 (28)
Living Problems Related to Health. Urban 56 (80)
Living. University Residential 57 (31)
Living. Urban Renewal for Better 29 (135), (159)
Living. Values for 112 (52)
Living With Crisis 112 (71)
Living With the Eskimos 4 (3)
Livingston County. History 117 (73)
Load Management Opportunities 150 (9)
Lobbying. Educational 54
Lobbying in State and Local Government 31 (27)
Local Geologic Features 151 (13)
Local Government 105 (56)
Local Government. Economics and Politics of 54
Local Government. Lobbying in State and 31 (27)
Local Government. Problems and Issues in 54
Local Government. State and 16 (43)
Local History in Education. Utilization of 142 (5)
Local Politics 174 (59)
Local Prominence. Individuals of 174 (19)
Locating Self in Society 168 (66)
Location and Therapy. School Site 142 (79)
Location. Eastern North Carolina's Relative 56 (36), (38)
Locations. Pattern of Cities - Understanding Their 174 (51)
Logic and Truth Tables 171 (35)
Logical-Empirical School of Philosophy. Challenges to the 29 (232), (268)
London. Royal 59 (7)
London Through the Centuries 142 (98)
Loneliness to Organizations. Effects of 151 (38)
Loneliness. How to Overcome 225 (34)
Long and Louisiana Education. Earl 174 (38)
Long and Louisiana Education. Huey 174 (38)
Long Distance Backpacking in Alaska 166 (1)
Long Distance Backpacking in Jasper National Park 166 (1)
Long Distance Backpacking on the Pacific Crest Trail 166 (1)
Long Distance Running 168 (71)
Long Range Educational Planning 57 (10)
Long Range Planning for Our Environment 171 (37)
Long Run Outlook for the American Economy 85 (30)
Longest Bridge 144
Longevity of Wild Chimpanzees. Fertility and 151 (208)
Longs and Louisiana Education 174 (38)
Look at Elementary School Science 57 (50)
Look at Energy Research 16 (2)
Look Back in Laughter 97 (63)
Look From Washington 97 (4)
Look. You 97 (67)
Looking at Sports From the Broadcasting Booth 112 (44)
Loom. Back-strap 79 (80)
Loom Controlled Color and Structure 79 (95)

Loom Controlled Lace Weaves. Weaver Controlled and 79 (69)
Loom Controlled Pattern Development. Drafting and 79 (95)
Loom Controlled Patterning. Weft Faced 79 (132)
Loom Controlled Weaves. Advanced 79 (114)
Loom for Navajo. Vertical 79 (8)
Loom. Garments Made on 79 (147)
Loom. Making a Warp and Setting Up a 79 (24)
Loom. Pattern Drfating for Multi-harness 79 (122)
Loom. Rigid Heddle Frame 79 (135)
Loom Shaped Garments 79 (16)
Loom. Stitchery on the 79 (71)
Loom Tapestry. Frame 79 (107)
Loom Tapestry Weaving. Frame 79 (9)
Loom Techniques. Fiber Forms and Small 79 (129)
Loom. Unconventional Ways of Using Your 79 (31)
Loom. Warp Weighted 79 (155)
Loom Weaving. Beginning 4-harness 79 (158)
Loom Weaving. Off- 79 (150)
Loom. Weaving With a Simple 79 (62)
Loom Workshop. Frame 79 (68)
Loom-designed Garments 79 (136)
Looms 79 (89)
Looms. Backstrap 79 (113)
Looms. Exploring Weaving on Primitive 79 (85)
Looms. Frame 79 (50)
Looms. Inkle 79 (50)
Looms. Pattern Drafting for Four-harness 79 (122)
Looms. Special Projects for 2 Harness 79 (130)
Looms. Tapestry and Tapestry 79 (113)
Looms. Theory and Use of Multilayer Weaving on Eight Harness 79 (52)
Loom-woven Hangings. Contemporary 79 (32)
Loose Warp Weaving 79 (89)
Lord Byron and Greece 142 (98)
Lore of Bituminous Mining. Literature/ 151 (236)
Los Angeles Contemporary Photography Premeditated Fantasy 29 (9)
Loss. Animal Diseases and the Resultant Food 16 (45)
Loss. Hearing 181 (318)
Loss. What it Means to Have a Hearing 117 (132)
Lost Art: Reading Aloud 105 (26)
Lost Worlds and Ancient Astronauts 174 (22)
Louisiana. Amphibians and Reptiles of 174 (53)
Louisiana Architecture. Aspects of 174 (19)
Louisiana. Colonial 174 (19)
Louisiana Courthouses 174 (19)
Louisiana Education. Earl Long and 174 (38)
Louisiana Education. Huey Long and 174 (38)
Louisiana Education. Longs and 174 (38)
Louisiana. Future of Higher Education in 174 (79)
Louisiana. General Lafayette's Visit to 174 (14)
Louisiana Place Names 174 (35)
Louisiana. Poisonous Snakes of 174 (53)
Louisiana. Poverty in 174 (70)
Louisiana Secondary Schools. Science in 174 (53)
Louisiana Transportation Systems 174 (74)
Louisiana. Urban Poverty in 174 (70)
Louisiana Workmen's Compensation 174 (17)
Louisiana. Washington, 174 (37)
Louisiana's Wildlife Resource 174 (20)
Louvre. Highlights of the 117 (138)
Love and Death in Literature 105 (16)
Love and Laughter. Livin' on 112 (12)
Love and War: The Courtship of a Civil War Belle 117 (69)
Love Charms of 29 Countries 174 (92)
Love. Comedy of 86 (1)
Love. Face of 225 (23)
Love. Meaning of 56 (5)
Love. Nature of Romantic 218
Love of Flight 216 (108)
Love. Psychology of 97 (23)
Love, Sex, and Marriage. Your Questions Answered on 56 (5)
Love, Spontaneity and Enduring Values 85 (35)
Love. To Russia With 151 (296)
Low Bid of Syndrome 132 (5)
Lowell Thomas Remembers 97 (64)
Lower Puget Sound. Geology of 159 (38)
Lucretius 227 (43)
Luddites. New 85 (38)
Lumber 73
Luminescence Phenomena 159 (55)
Lung Disease. Occupational 181 (156)
Lung. Smoking and the 181 (156), (205)
Lure to Young and Old. University Park: Its 151 (6)
Luring the Robots 225 (8)
Luther King. Mahatma Ghandi and Martin 103 (1)
Luxury or Necessity. Campus Planning - 56 (101)
Lyric and Elegy. Roman 227 (15)
Lyric Poetry 227 (21)
Lyric Poetry and Philosophy. Early Greek 227 (46)
Lyric Poetry. Greek 227 (28)

M

M's and O's 79 (23)
MBA Program. Simon Fraser's 171 (57)
MSU. Management at 117 (21)
MSU. Reading and 117 (134)
MSU's Right to Read Program 117 (134)
M.I.S. and Data Processing 168 (20)
Ma Bell. Cable Broadcasting and 124 (2)
Macademia Nuts in California 224 (10)
Macao. Hong Kong and 59 (1)
Machine. Incredible Bread 181 (33), (203), (332)
Machine Operators. Training 67 (16)
Machinery for Carrying it Out. United States Foreign Policy and United States Governmental 85 (15)

Machinery. Noise Control in 151 (145)
Machines to Be Reliable and Safe. How to Design 151 (145)
McKeesport Campus. Penn State 51 (13)
McKinley National Park. Alaska Highway and 223 (34)
Macrame 79 (48), (66), (136), 218
Macrame. Three-Dimensional 79 (86)
Madison Avenue Mannequins 142 (32)
Magazine Journalism 151 (68)
Magazines and American Life 105 (68)
Magazines. History of American 218
Magazines. Men's 181 (73)
Magic 114 (1)
Magic and Reality. Myth, 57 (62)
Magic Around the World. Winter 15 (3)
Magic Art. Reading - the 57 (62)
Magic. Fiber 79 (138)
Magic of Thinking Big 180 (151)
Magic of Venice 59 (7)
Magic Shows 168 (47)
Magical Movie Music 56 (109)
Magnetic Resonance Techniques. Nuclear 159 (56)
Magnificent Austria 59 (14)
Magnificent Fury of Alaska 51 (1)
Mahatma Ghandi and Martin Luther King 103 (1)
Mahdi. Appearance of the Promised Messiah and the Promised 1 (8)
Mail. Chess by 174 (79)
Mail for Fund Raising. Creative Direct 151 (188)
Main to the Amazon. Colombia - From the Spanish 69 (7)
Mainstreaming 142 (4), 181 (119)
Mainstreaming in Special Education 159 (25)
Mainstreaming: Pros and Cons 117 (131)
Mainstreaming the Disadvantaged 181 (104)
Maintenance and Rehabilitation. Well 136 (25)
Maintenance. Energy Savings by Preventive 151 (47)
Maintenance Management 171 (7)
Maintenance of Antique Spinning Wheels. Repair, Care, and 79 (99)
Maintenance. Tree 189
Majestic Rhine 59 (14)
Major Areas of Health Education 181 (227)
Major. Career Opportunities by College or 181 (50)
Major Causes of Pain in Childbirth and Methods for Combating Them 36 (1)
Major in English? What Good is a 29 (29), (97)
Major Problems in Our Criminal Justice System 57 (49)
Majority in the Minority 151 (56)
Majority Rule. Limits of 85 (25)
Make Today Count 182 (1), (2), (3)
Make Way for the Walking Wounded 224 (4)
Make Your Job Satisfying 181 (65)
Making a Good Academic Decision. On 151 (104)
Making a Warp and Setting Up a Loom 79 (24)
Making Money. It's Fun 81 (1)
Making of Americans 181 (46)
Making of an American Image 97 (19)
Making Out a Will 54
Making Plans for College 151 (15)
Making Radioactive Wastes Safe 151 (272)
Making Sea Movies 69 (15)
Making Sense of the Doomsdayers 54
Making Soap 56 (104)
Making the Wheels Turn 27 (5)
Making Wearables 79 (29)
Malaysian Turtles 57 (59)
Malaysian Wildlife 57 (59)
Male and Female. Entrepreneurs: 105 (84)
Male Fashion Scene 111 (1), (2)
Male-Female Roles in Russian Culture as Reflected in Nineteenth and Twentieth Century Literature 27 (18)
Male Professional. Liberation of the White 159 (24)
Male Versus Female Psyche. Insights Into the 225 (6)
Malpractice Insurance. Medical 181 (44), (193)
Malpractice. Medical 54, 225 (31)
Mammals. Marine 187 (3)
Man. Advertising and Vulnerability of 117 (28)
Man and Evolution. Prehistoric 174 (22)
Man and God. Christ as 105 (109)
Man and His Environment 56 (73)
Man and Modern Industrial Technology 168 (6)
Man and Natural Ecosystems. Interactions Between 218
Man and the Environment. Today's 152
Man and Western Psychotherapy. African Medicine 181 (291)
Man as Atlas 168 (60)
Man. Buddhist Conception of 174 (89)
Man Came to the New World. How 4 (3)
Man? Can We Control the Future of 29 (141), (161), (334)
Man. Cave Man to Space 135 (51)
Man. Christian Meaning of Being 105 (109)
Man. Common Plant Diseases and 117 (13)
Man Dives Deep 97 (38)
Man Environment Relations 16 (28)
Man First Walked Erect. When 112 (73)
Man. Fossil 218
Man. Future of 29 (54)
Man. Genetic Engineering and the Future of 151 (164)
Man. Genetics and Future of 29 (113), (131), (170)
Man - His Origin, Purpose, Destiny 56 (138)
Man. Irrefragable 85 (38)
Man, Know Thyself! 225 (10)
Man. Leadership of 112 (68)
Man Made Dyes 79 (108)
Man. Materials and 216 (51)
Man Not Myth. Lincoln the 57 (28)
Man of North America. Archaeology (Prehistory) - Early 105 (1)

Man of Science. Adventures of a 29 (186), (272)
Man on the Moon Means for You. What a 112 (25)
Man - Or, an Answer to Ralph Nader and Consumerism. Who Killed the Ice 85 (26)
Man. Outer Banks and 56 (33), (72)
Man Relationship With God 1 (4)
Man: The Final Hunter 112 (3)
Man. Theories of 29 (141), (284)
Man. There is Genius in the Average 112 (108)
Man. There's Genius in the Average 135 (53)
Man Today. USSR and Soviet 85 (18)
Man. Uncommon 135 (27)
Man. Why a Liberated Woman Makes for a Liberated 225 (8)
Man/Woman Relationships 211 (2)
Manage by Objectives. How to 151 (39)
Manage Your Life. Three Ways to 75 (1)
Manage Your Time Effectively 151 (35)
Manage Your Time. How to 151 (67)
Management 112 (23), (114), 120, 142 (71), 151 (140), 180 (37), (52), (61), (69), (74), (87), (95), (102), (105), (112), (116), (119), (124), (136), (158), (171), (174), (181), (188), (189), (190), (191), (197), 181 (41)
Management. Advertising 29 (33)
Management. Aerial Photos in Resource 151 (304)
Management. All Aspects of Practice 8 (1)
Management and Administration. Personnel 105 (11)
Management and Analysis of Energy Systems 163 (1)
Management and Attitude 180 (130)
Management and Conservation. Basic Principles of Wildlife 151 (309)
Management and Evaluation. Interdisciplinary Research 151 (254)
Management and Insurance. Areas of Risk, 168 (68)
Management and Motivation 180 (85)
Management and Motivation. Personnel 181 (41)
Management and Office Support Systems. Administrative 119 (1)
Management and Organization 180 (77)
Management at MSU 117 (21)
Management Attributes 174 (43)
Management. Barriers to Women in 168 (62)
Management by Action - The Manager's Role 135 (29)
Management by Doubt 171 (7)
Management by Motivation 112 (22)
Management by Objectives 29 (45), (84), (112), 136 (10), 151 (46), 159 (66), 216 (2)
Management by Objectives. Beyond 135 (33)
Management by Walking Around 102 (17)
Management. Child 142 (28), 168 (7), (47)
Management. Childhood Behavior 174 (32)
Management. Classroom 57 (34), 117 (37)
Management. Communication and Good 159 (60)
Management Communications 180 (123)
Management Communications. Industrial and 151 (81)
Management. Computerized Data 174 (23)
Management. Computers and 174 (43)
Management. Creative 171 (7)
Management Development Services. Penn State's 151 (287)
Management Disputes. Arbitration of Labor - 216 (104)
Management. Dynamics of 224 (2)
Management. Effective Sales 180 (81)
Management. Effective Time 180 (3)
Management. Environmental Law and 27 (3)
Management Ethics. Social Responsibility and 151 (43)
Management. Financial Planning and 23
Management. Food 180 (166)
Management for a Business. Methods of Financial 151 (37)
Management. General 105 (9)
Management in Business. Experimenting With Democratic 27 (1)
Management in Dental Office. Child 105 (30)
Management in Developing Nations 151 (43)
Management in Inflationary Times 171 (9)
Management in Selling. Personal 112 (124)
Management Information System Implementation. Problems in 171 (9)
Management Information Systems 159 (13), (57)
Management. Japanese 29 (149)
Management/Leadership 23
Management. Library 142 (29)
Management. Maintenance 171 (7)
Management. Marketing Management - Product 105 (8)
Management. Meeting 151 (71)
Management. Money 176 (99), 214 (1)
Management. Motivational 180 (49)
Management. Natural Resource 151 (254)
Management of ADP 216 (44)
Management of Change 3 (4)
Management of Children 174 (76)
Management of Children. Behavioral 174 (50)
Management of Commodity Futures Trading Activities 138 (3), (4)
Management of Data Processing 105 (5)
Management of Fishes 57 (16)
Management of Innovation and Change 105 (116)
Management of Patient Care 105 (95)
Management of School Publications 214 (18)
Management of Speech Disorders in Public Schools 56 (55)
Management of the Future 135 (13)
Management of Time. Better 56 (95)
Management. Office 65 (8), (9), (11), (12), (15), (19), 28), (38), (48), (52), (53), (63), (64), (68), (70)
Management, Operation, and Forms. Office 65 (32)

Management Opportunities. Load 150 (9)
Management. Personal Time 151 (48)
Management. Personnel 142 (42), 216 (105)
Management. Personnel. Sales and 180 (106)
Management Planning, Computing in Business and Computing in Education 105 (5)
Management. Pond 216 (26)
Management. Problems and Solutions in Radioactive Waste 151 (130)
Management. Property 65 (5), (17), (28), (35), (43), (55)
Management. Records 119 (1), 168 (44)
Management Relations. Labor- 216 (104)
Management. Risk 181 (44)
Management. Sales 23, 180 (55), (92), (103), (178)
Management. Sales and 180 (132)
Management Science, Effective Management 105 (5)
Management Skills. Life 117 (110)
Management. Small Business 181 (35), (219)
Management. Solid Wastes and Their 16 (2)
Management Systems. Data 151 (45)
Management. Timber 73
Management. Time 216 (27)
Management Tool. Communication as a 105 (15)
Management. Tough-minded 135 (5)
Management Training and Development 180 (24)
Management. Transit 105 (116)
Management. Tree Trimming and Right-of-way 150 (7)
Management. Waste 133 (1), (5)
Management. Wildlife 216 (26)
Management. Worker Self- 181 (39)
Management. Zoysia Lawn 189
Management's Ethical Dilemma 181 (47)
Manager/Computer Interaction 171 (9)
Manager. Effective 151 (39)
Manager. German 3 (6)
Managerial Accounting 159 (57)
Managerial Grid 189
Managerial Values and Organizational Effectiveness 117 (21)
Manager's Role. Management by Action - the 135 (29)
Managers. Developing Professional 216 (125)
Managers? Do Engineers Make Good 151 (45)
Managing a Personal Budget in Today's Economy 16 (19)
Managing in Changing Times 112 (103)
Managing Other People Time 182 (1), (2), (3)
Managing United States Foreign Policy. Organizing and 151 (196)
Managing Your Time 57 (15), 151 (39)
Mandalas 79 (40)
Mandalay. Road to 110 (10)
Maneuver. Heimlich 135 (28)
Manipulated Tensions 79 (140)
Manipulation. Assertiveness and 168 (11)
Manipulation. Fiber and Yarn 79 (146)
Manipulation. Genetic 151 (211)
Manipulation of Fabric 79 (92)
Mankind. Islam the Final Religion for 1 (4)
Mankind. Prospects for 97 (39), 102 (20)
Mannequins. Madison Avenue 142 (32)
Manpower. Employment and Unemployment 181 (48)
Man's Creation and the Means of Its Attainment. Object of 1 (11)
Man's Environment 174 (91)
Man's Life. Islamic Viewpoint on Any Aspect of 1 (11)
Man's Place in the Universe. Cosmology - 27 (16)
Man's Search for a Missing God. Sartre and 29 (245)
Man's Trip to the Bank or Real Estate, the Profession of Happy People. Lazy 65 (20)
Manual of Water Well Construction Standards. How to Use the 136 (27)
Manufacturing, and Marketing of Hardwood, Plywood, and Venerr. Use, 80 (2)
Manufacturing. Furniture and Furniture 216 (65)
Manufacturing Industries Monopolized? Are United States 85 (2)
Manufacturing. Shoe 170
Manufacturing Technology Education 168 (6)
Many Faces of Cathy 112 (6)
Many Faces of France 110 (2)
Many Possibilities of Men 54
Mao. China After 59 (2), 69 (2)
Maoists, Jews, Christians and Muslims. World Religions - Buddhists, Confucianists, Taoists, 54
Map Coloring Problems 151 (247)
Maps for the Visually Handicapped. Challenge of 218
Marathon 105 (115)
Marcuse and the Hell of the Affluent Society 85 (36)
Margery the Medium 57 (39)
Marine and Naval Science 214 (68)
Marine Biology 171 (42), 181 (18), (62)
Marine Biology of South Puget Sound 159 (34)
Marine Environment. Radioactivity in the 218
Marine Fish. Effects of Shock Waves Upon 218
Marine Food Resources 216 (36)
Marine Mammals 187 (3)
Marine Resources in Eastern North Carolina. Coastal and 56 (36), (38)
Marital Communication 168 (73)
Marital Counseling/Marital Therapy 181 (287), (310)
Marital/Family Relationships 181 (229), (287), (310)
Marital Happiness. Enhancing 29 (252)
Marital Relationship 159 (33)
Marital Therapy. Marital Counseling/ 181 (287), (310)
Maritime Heritage. America's 214 (57), (69)
Mark Twain. Diabolical Duo: Ambrose Bierce and 151 (243)

Mark Twain in Italy 59 (13)
Mark Twain in Switzerland 59 (13)
Mark Twain. Life and Humor of 117 (91)
Market Feasibility 65 (1)
Market. Job 218
Market. Solving Social Problems Through the 85 (4)
Market Speculation. Stock 16 (17)
Market System. Free 216 (43)
Market Targets 57 (18)
Market Their Products/Services. How Industries 23
Marketing 117 (25), 142 (71), 176 (92), 180 (21), (91), (156), (157), (161), (170)
Marketing and Advertising. Story of Pabst History, 145 (1), (2), (3)
Marketing and the Consumer Movement 214 (23)
Marketing Board Rip-off. British Columbia Milk- 171 (8)
Marketing. Computer Applications to Real Estate 69 (65)
Marketing Field. Techniques of the Incentive 130 (1 - 36)
Marketing for Non-Profit Institutions and Public Agencies 181 (36)
Marketing. General Sales and 23
Marketing Management - Product Management 105 (8)
Marketing. Modern 105 (4)
Marketing Objectives 29 (84)
Marketing of Hardwood, Plywood, and Veneer. Use, Manufacturing, and 80 (2)
Marketing of Insurance. Direct Response 127 (1)
Marketing on Domestic and Foreign Levels. Role of Trademarks in Advertising and 209
Marketing Operations. Improving Productivity in 29 (112)
Marketing Plan. Consumerism as a 102 (23)
Marketing Research and Information Systems 105 (8)
Marketing. Sales and 180 (53), (101)
Marketing, Storing and Selling Dollar. Bank 3 (3)
Marketing. Transit 105 (8)
Marketing Your Work 79 (159)
Markets. Effects of Financial Data on Stock and Bond 31 (1)
Markets in Coordinating and Directing Economic Activity. Role of Open 85 (2)
Markets. Regulation of Securities 85 (19)
Marquette Athletics 105 (112)
Marquette. Student Judicial Boards at 105 (62)
Marquette University Impact on Milwaukee 105 (64)
Marquette University Today 105 (63)
Marrakech. Footloose Family - Azusa to 29 (4), (122), (318)
Marriage Alive and Growing. Keeping Your 159 (48)
Marriage and Family Relations 16 (35)
Marriage and Family Therapy 176 (25)
Marriage and the Family. Homosexuality, 181 (238)
Marriage. Communication in 57 (8)
Marriage Counseling 16 (35), 29 (231)
Marriage Customs, Holidays and Festivals. Indian Culture - 117 (97)
Marriage. Eros, Sex and 85 (18)
Marriage. How to Enrich Your 168 (73)
Marriage. Keeping Happiness in Your 56 (5)
Marriage, Middle Age and Other Perils 112 (60)
Marriage. Non-Sexist 159 (60)
Marriage. Preparing for 168 (73)
Marriage Relationships. Enrichment of 57 (71)
Marriage - Vocation or Avocation 57 (41)
Marriage. Your Questions Answered on Love, Sex, and 56 (5)
Mars. Viking on 29 (152), (276)
Marsh - A Quiet Mystery 69 (13)
Martial Arts 228
Martin Luther King. Mahatma Ghandi and 103 (1)
Martin Ritt, Latter-Day Son of Ben 57 (95)
Martin Van Buren 151 (216)
Marxes Are the Craziest People 154 (16)
Marxism 85 (8)
Marxism and Human Alienation 159 (28)
Marxism and Its Revolutionists 85 (23)
Marxist - Lenninist Ideology in the 1970's. Operational Significance of 85 (31)
Marx's Critique of Capitalism 174 (89)
Mary Todd Lincoln 57 (28)
Masculinity-Femininity and Sport Participation 151 (276)
Maskmaking 79 (125)
Masonry in 19th Century America. Free 181 (262)
Mass Communication. Development of 117 (84)
Mass Communications 102 (11), 168 (10)
Mass Communications in Modern Society 29 (36), (55)
Mass Communications Law 168 (10)
Mass Media 180 (12)
Mass Media Are Irresponsible, What Can We Do? When the 29 (119), (312)
Mass Media Are Irresponsible. When the 29 (42)
Mass Media. Current Issues in 29 (36), (55), (115)
Mass Media. Don't Blame the 29 (42), (67), (312)
Mass Media. Journalism and the 216 (144)
Mass Media Myth. Modern 105 (69)
Mass Media on Values. Impact of 168 (50)
Mass Media. Television and the 142 (25)
Mass Media? When Do We Believe Our 218
Mass Production of Genetically Superior Trees 151 (310)
Mass Society 181 (248)
Mass Transit 54
Massachusetts. Witchcraft at Salem: An Overview of the Witchcraft Trials at Salem, 117 (71)
Masses. Diagnosis of Renal 181 (171)
Master Hunters of the Deep 69 (10)
Mastery Learning 181 (89)

Matching Models in Education 57 (70)
Mate. How Astrology Can Help You Find Your Ideal 225 (20)
Material. Portland Cement Concrete As a Major Construction 151 (291)
Material Wall Hangings. Plant 79 (96)
Materials and Man 216 (51)
Materials and Processes. New 151 (125)
Materials Center 174 (77)
Materials. Dental 105 (28)
Materials Development. Educational 142 (36)
Materials. Dyeing Wool With Natural 79 (149)
Materials. Educational 180 (143)
Materials for Developing Skill Areas. Instructional 142 (30)
Materials in Education. Role of Instructional 132 (4)
Materials. Individualized Learning Strategies of 181 (75), (110)
Materials. Landscape Plant 16 (63)
Materials. Mystique of 151 (259)
Materials. Plant 216 (6)
Materials Science. Modern 16 (41)
Materials. Sexism in Reading 57 (54)
Materials. Weaving With Natural 79 (107)
Math Activities for Teachers - Nursery - 4th Grade. Language Arts and 117 (48)
Math and Science. Elementary 174 (49)
Math. Creativity in Elementary School Math 181 (105), (150)
Math for the Pre-school Child 181 (105), (150)
Math. Modern Elementary 56 (48)
Math: What Went Wrong? Modern 151 (121)
Mathematical Games 181 (1), (148)
Mathematical Laws? Does Nature Obey 56 (129)
Mathematical Models 142 (70)
Mathematical Recreations 181 (1), (148)
Mathematical Sciences 214 (64)
Mathematical Statistics and/or Probability 27 (17)
Mathematics and Computers - Future Trends 142 (70)
Mathematics and Music 56 (106)
Mathematics and Science to Bilingual Classes in the Elementary Grades. Teaching Language Arts, Reading, 142 (90)
Mathematics Appreciation 181 (152)
Mathematics as a Tool 56 (126)
Mathematics at Murray State University. Programs in 117 (92)
Mathematics Can Be Fun. Elementary School - 151 (250)
Mathematics Can Help With Ecological Problems. Ways 31 (21)
Mathematics? Can There be Anything New in 56 (129)
Mathematics. Careers in 151 (252)
Mathematics. Contradictions in 171 (35)
Mathematics. Elementary School 142 (26)
Mathematics for Young Children 142 (13)
Mathematics in Gambling 29 (214)
Mathematics in Games of Chance 181 (4), (151)
Mathematics in the Modern World 181 (153)
Mathematics in the World of Business 181 (43), (153)
Mathematics. Motivation in the Teaching of 117 (92)
Mathematics. New 181 (153)
Mathematics of the Mayans 218
Mathematics of the Well Drilling Industry 136 (3)
Mathematics. Philosophical Aspects of 56 (129)
Mathematics. Professional Opportunities in 27 (17)
Mathematics. Reading 174 (67)
Mathematics. Teaching Children 151 (121)
Mathematics. Teaching of 171 (21)
Mathematics - the Queen and Servant 56 (125)
Mathematics Trends and Programs 181 (152)
Mathematics Trends and Programs. Current 181 (117)
Mathematics Versus the Modern Computer 181 (154)
Matrimony. Sacrament of 105 (104)
Matrons and Misogynists 227 (22)
Maturation. Sexual 105 (3)
Maximizing Beef Production 216 (80)
Maximizing Your Career Options 151 (90)
Mayan Indians of Guatemala - Historical Interpretation and Future of the Tradition. Contemporary National Dress of 79 (83)
Mayans. Mathematics of the 218
Mayans of Yucatan. Hammocks as Made by the Cuna Indians of the San Blas Islands and the 79 (25)
Mayor's? King's English or the 181 (317)
Maze. Solving the 144
Mazon Creek. Fossils of 57 (77)
Meals. Data Processing in Pre-costing 16 (90)
Meaning in Our Times. Mythology - Form and 54
Meaning of Being Man. Christian 105 (109)
Meaning of Ideology. Philosophical Truth and the 85 (20)
Meaning of Japan for Americans 168 (66)
Meaning of Love 56 (5)
Meaning of the Declaration of Independence 85 (13)
Meaning of the I.Q. 181 (245), (296)
Meaningful. How to Make Your Career More Exciting and 23
Meaningfulness in the Process of Life 174 (9)
Meaningless. Words Are 117 (115)
Meanings of Lifelong Learning 57 (85)
Measurement and Control. Moisture 67 (3)
Measurement and Work Simplification. Work 119 (1)
Measurement. Educational 142 (21)
Measurement in the Office. Production Standards and Work 117 (14)
Measurement of Moisture in Dehydrated Food Products, Grain and Other Moisture Measurements in Food Processing 67 (21)
Measurement. Police Traffic Radar Speed 105 (119)
Measurement. Population 174 (51)

Measurement. Reading 142 (21)
Measurements in Food Processing. Measurement of Moisture in Dehydrated Food Products, Grain and Other Moisture 67 (21)
Measures. Emergency Psychiatric 105 (95)
Measures in the Electric Industry. OSHA Requirements and Safety 150 (6)
Measures. Prosthetic 181 (174)
Meat? Do You Really Want Cheap 151 (175)
Meat. Future Trends in 151 (182)
Meat in a Hungry World 16 (39)
Meat Industry. New Technology in the 16 (39)
Meat Product Development. New 216 (35)
Meat We Eat 151 (182)
Mechanical Behavior of Composites 216 (11)
Mechanical Behavior of Polymers 216 (11)
Mechanical Engineering Technology 151 (146)
Mechanics of Technical Reports Proposals 151 (79)
Mechanisms in Obesity. Appetite Regulatory 171 (26)
Mechanisms of the Brain. Sleep and Dream 159 (68)
Mechanisms. Role Playing and Defense 57 (13)
Mechanized Intelligence. State of the Art in 181 (204)
Media 176 (4), (5), (14), (17), (28), (30), (32), (39), (41), (47), (55), (72), (78), (83), (86), (88), (90), (91), (96), (98), (100), (101), (107), (110), (119), (124)
Media and Learning 216 (58)
Media and Public Relations - Friendly Adversaries. News 105 (67)
Media Are Irresponsible, What Can We Do? When the Mass 29 (119), (312)
Media Behind the News 151 (77)
Media. Building an Advertising Program for the 168 (59)
Media. Career Opportunities in the 151 (72)
Media. Creating With 57 (97)
Media Criticism. Television, 57 (32)
Media. Current Issues in Mass 29 (36), (55), (115)
Media. Don't Blame Mass 29 (42), (67), (312)
Media. Educational 174 (57), 181 (70), (98)
Media. Educational Communications 181 (72), (100)
Media. Educator and the 105 (65)
Media. Effective 57 (76)
Media. Ethics and the News 181 (68)
Media. Ethics of News 56 (102)
Media in Education 57 (97)
Media in Teaching and Learning 181 (75), (110)
Media. Innovative Instructional Use of 218
Media. Journalism and the Mass 216 (144)
Media. Mass 180 (12)
Media. Multi- 180 (129)
Media Myth. Modern Mass 105 (69)
Media. News 176 (66)
Media on Attitudes. Influence of Communication 218
Media on Values. Impact of Mass 168 (50)
Media. Politics and the 154 (26)
Media. Presidency and the 27 (40)
Media. Public Relations: Getting to the 151 (86)
Media Strategy 29 (33)
Media. Television and the Mass 142 (25)
Media Weaving. Mixed 79 (79)
Media - What's It All About 29 (46)
Media? When Do We Believe Our Mass 218
Media. Women in the 151 (72)
Medical and Psychological Aspects of Adolescent Pregnancy 27 (30)
Medical Anthropology 142 (48)
Medical Applications. Lasers-- 29 (186)
Medical Aspects of Organ Transplants. Legal and 54
Medical Care. Rising Cost of 27 (25)
Medical Center. UCI 27 (36)
Medical Center. Milton S. Hershey 151 (10), (186)
Medical Education. Meeting the Needs for Veterinary 216 (90)
Medical Education. Veterinary 16 (4)
Medical Ethics 105 (104)
Medical Malpractice 54, 225 (31)
Medical Malpractice Insurance 181 (44), (193)
Medical Microbiology 54
Medical Politics. Current Problems in 30 (1)
Medical Procedures. Radiation Safety in 181 (198)
Medical Profession. Political Economy of the 85 (14)
Medical Professionals in Drug Abuse 88 (1)
Medical Records. Patients' Access to 181 (185), (235)
Medical Rehabilitation Community. Greenville and the 56 (77)
Medical School. So You Want to Get Into 27 (25)
Medical Technology 181 (189), (191)
Medical Technology. Careers in 181 (64)
Medical Technology--Professional Information 105 (45)
Medical Technology--Recruitment 105 (45), (52)
Medicinal Flowering Plants of South America 27 (14)
Medicinal Plant Alkaloids 54
Medicinal Plant Glycosides 54
Medicine, a Young and Growing Profession. Sports 56 (76)
Medicine as a Career. Veterinary 216 (90), (127)
Medicine Chest. Consumerism: You and Your 181 (196), (249)
Medicine. Comparative 216 (127)
Medicine. Computers in 29 (173)
Medicine. Current Techniques in Nuclear 218
Medicine. Early American 151 (257)
Medicine. Emergency 218
Medicine. Ethical and Social Problems in 16 (64)
Medicine. Laboratory 171 (41)

Medicine Man and Western Psychotherapy. African 181 (291)
Medicine. Rehabilitation 181 (155)
Medicine. Religion and 75 (1)
Medicine. Veterinary 216 (7), (127)
Medicine. Women in 181 (158), (321)
Medicine's Role in the Protection of Human Health. Veterinary 216 (90)
Medico-Moral Legal Ethics in Nursing 105 (49)
Medieval 54
Medieval and Renaissance Music 142 (57)
Medieval Archaeology 31 (28)
Medieval Art. Survey of 56 (9)
Medieval Cities 31 (28)
Medieval European History. Ancient and 151 (215)
Medieval Feminism 151 (215)
Medieval French Hero 181 (138)
Medieval Latin 227 (27)
Medieval Living Patterns 31 (28)
Medieval Rome - the New Social History 27 (10)
Meditation 176 (81)
Meditation and Its Practical Application 108 (1), (2)
Meditation - the Christian Tradition 54
Meditation in Public Schools. Transcendental 12
Meditation? What's the Fuss About 54
Mediterranean. Rare Jewels of the 59 (9)
Mediterranean. Yankee Sails the 59 (5)
Medium. Margery the 57 (39)
Meet the Composer 31 (29)
Meeting Children's Needs 181 (11)
Meeting College Costs 57 (83)
Meeting. Conducting a 216 (28)
Meeting Effectively. How to Run a 105 (77)
Meeting. How and Why of Conducting a 105 (85)
Meeting Management 151 (71)
Meeting the Educational Consumer Interest 27 (20)
Meeting the Needs for Veterinary Medical Education 216 (90)
Meetings. Conducting Business 117 (128)
Meetings. Sales 65 (46)
Meetings. Saving Time in Running 105 (13)
Megalopolis 181 (134), (222)
Megavitamin Therapy 218
Megrab - Land of the Setting Sun 69 (3)
Mellon University. Carnegie- 31 (10)
Melting Pot. American 181 (256)
Melville 105 (22)
Melville and Hawthorne, a Timely Friendship 105 (22)
Membrane Separations 31 (11)
Membranes and Heroin. Cell 57 (20)
Memorial Day 214 (62)
Memory Techniques 180 (164)
Memory Training 180 (109)
Men and Women are Created Equal. All 214 (85)
Men in the Women's Movement. Role of 142 (57)
Men. Many Possibilities of 54
Men's Gymnastics: From High School to the Olympics 168 (2)
Men's Magazines 181 (73)
Mental Development. Nutrition and 218
Mental Handicap. Educational Approaches to 117 (131)
Mental Health 57 (34), 113 (2), 105 (94), 142 (44), 181 (31)
Mental Health and the Black Community 181 (294)
Mental Health. Community 16 (81)
Mental Health Consultation 181 (282)
Mental Health for Daily Living 117 (108)
Mental Health of College Students. Emotional Difficulties and 216 (132)
Mental Health. Personality and 105 (98)
Mental Health. Preventative 142 (45)
Mental Health. Your 216 (94)
Mental Illness. Social and Cultural Influences on 214 (65), (86)
Mental Relaxation Techniques to Enrich Your Life. Relaxation Response: How to Use 136 (23)
Mental Retardation 56 (57), 117 (131), 159 (43), 218
Mental Retardation as a Social Disease 159 (43)
Mental Retardation. Genetics and 29 (131)
Mental Retardation. Genetics of 29 (170), (265)
Mental Retardation. Parent's Experiences With 216 (9)
Mentalism and Hypnotism. Phenomena of the Mind - 114 (2)
Mentally/Physically Handicapped Individuals. Legal Rights of 151 (228)
Mentally Retarded Citizens of Acadiana 174 (44)
Mentally Retarded. Drug Treatment of the 131 (164)
Mentally Retarded. Educational System for 169 (3)
Menu Planning. Elements of 216 (25)
Mercenary. Twentieth Century American 154 (3)
Merchandising 65 (47)
Merchandising. Fashion 142 (8)
Merchandising. Residential 65 (46)
Mercury Pollution 151 (156)
Merry-Go-Round. Washington 135 (2)
Mesoamerica. Ancient 56 (1)
Meso-American Indians and Weaving 79 (110)
Messages in Our Body. How Nerves Transmit Biological 218
Messages. Nonverbal Communication: The Silent 151 (87)
Messiah and the Promised Mahdi. Appearance of the Promised 1 (8)
Messiah and the Signs of the Time. Promised 1 (5)
Metal Ions 216 (128)
Metal Thread Work 79 (71)
Metals Futures Contracts in Gold, Silver, and Copper 38
Metals Have Personalities 218
Metamorphoses. Ovids 227 (32)
Metaphor. I.A. Richard's and Kenneth Burke's Theories of 151 (65)

Metaphysical Poets. Image of Woman in 17th Century 227 (29)
Metaphysics 174 (55)
Meteorology 216 (144)
Meteorology. Air Pollution 151 (155)
Meters. Poetic 142 (2)
Methadone 88 (1)
Methane Production. Small Scale 163 (3)
Method in the United States. History of the Lamaze 36 (1)
Method of Designing. Color and Weave Effect 79 (94)
Method of Forecasting Community Needs. Innovative 168 (57)
Method of Teaching Art. Interidsciplinary 142 (35)
Methodologies. User Oriented Planning 151 (148)
Methodology. Archaeological 227 (55)
Methodology. Science Fiction - the New 56 (64)
Methodology. Trends in 56 (42)
Methods. Air Force Teaching 174 (81)
Methods. Drafting 79 (64)
Methods. English Teaching 168 (53)
Methods for Combating Them. Major Causes of Pain in Childbirth and 36 (1)
Methods. Graphics and Graphic 168 (15)
Methods in Criminal Investigations. Nuclear 151 (156)
Methods in the Social Sciences. Quantitative 142 (78)
Methods of Dispute Settlement in Employment 223 (6)
Methods of Entering Police Departments 29 (58)
Methods of Entering Police Departments. Alternative 29 (144), (344)
Methods of Financial Management for a Business 151 (37)
Methods of Instructing in Secondary Education 117 (41)
Methods of Kindergarten. History and 117 (56)
Methods of Salesmanship. Five Basic 135 (44)
Methods of Treadling. Special 79 (94)
Methods. Program Evaluation 159 (13)
Methods to Elementary School Children. Teaching Research 142 (5)
Metric Conversion 57 (11)
Metric Conversion and the Water Well Industry 136 (28)
Metric Education 142 (24)
Metric, In Business, Industry, Stores, and Schools. Going 57 (12)
Metric System 105 (122), 117 (92), 142 (26), 222
Metric System and Conversion 105 (116)
Metric System. Conversion to the 174 (79)
Metric System in Your Future 168 (35)
Metric System, Its Impact and Its Implementation 117 (82)
Metric System Now or Later 151 (149)
Metrication: Too Important to Leave to the Expert 151 (248)
Metrics 216 (139)
Metrics for Consumers 57 (84)
Metrics for Everyday Life 151 (248)
Metrics for the Layman 57 (70)
Metrics. S.I. Metrics Versus Old 151 (248)
Metrics. Sensible Ways to Teach 151 (248)
Metrification 171 (9)
Metropolitan Organization of American Space 181 (134)
Mexican Retablo and Related Folk Art 174 (41)
Mexican Tapestry Weaving 79 (54)
Mexico and Greece. Trips to South America, Central America, 79 (117)
Mexico. Cultural and Political Analysis of 117 (105)
Mexico - Culture and Civilization 142 (34)
Mexico. Mormons in 29 (139), (160)
Mexico. Wonderful 59 (9)
Michelangelo Inspires After 500 Years 151 (264)
Michener. James A. 181 (140)
Michigan. Lake 142 (77)
Microbial Ecology 159 (49)
Microbiological Food Hazards at Home. Controlling 151 (178)
Microbiology 54
Microbiology. Automation in 151 (173)
Microbiology. Environmental 168 (29)
Microbiology. Medical 54
Microforms at the Cal State Fullerton Library 29 (25), (196)
Micronesia 218
Micronesia, America's Pacific Paradise 15 (1)
Microprocessors 151 (147)
Microscope. Electron 171 (33)
Microscopy of Nervous System. Electron 181 (169)
Microscopic World 151 (159)
Microwave Oven Safety 105 (119)
Microwaves and Their Applications 105 (119)
Middle Age and Other Perils. Marriage, 112 (60)
Middle East 142 (23), 175 (1), (4)
Middle East and South Asia 142 (41)
Middle East. Big Power Confrontation in the 85 (31)
Middle East Checkerboard 29 (48), (215), (224)
Middle East Conflict. Terrorism in the 181 (345)
Middle East Conflicts 29 (217)
Middle East Crisis 217 (4)
Middle East. Current Situation in the 151 (194)
Middle East - Dangers and Opportunities 85 (29)
Middle East. Geography of the 117 (63)
Middle East. Geopolitics of the 214 (55)
Middle East. Government and Politics of the 117 (104)
Middle East. How to Achieve Peace in the 57 (61)
Middle East in the United States Energy Picture 56 (15)
Middle East in War and Peace 181 (339)
Middle East. Issues in the 54

Middle East Oil in a Revolutionary Age 3 (5)
Middle East? Peace in the 214 (55)
Middle East. Politics of the 174 (59)
Middle East Problems and the U.S.A. 151 (291)
Middle East. Role of the U.N. in the 102 (28)
Middle East. Social Change in the 56 (6)
Middle East. Soviet Strategy in the 85 (31)
Middle East Studies at Penn State 151 (194)
Middle East Today. Problems of the 223 (21)
Middle East. Travel in the 29 (163), (218), (228), (319)
Middle East Unveiled 100 (1)
Middle East. Women in the 223 (19)
Middle Eastern Conflicts 29 (179), (226)
Middle of the Journey. American Conservatives in the 85 (16)
Middle Years of Womanhood 181 (221), (284), (323)
Middleclass Children. Education for Socio-Economic 174 (76)
Mid-Life Career Change 181 (65), 218
Midst. Fanatic Ideologies in Our 85 (16)
Midwestern United States Economies. Contributions of the Chemical Industry to 34 (1)
Midwife. Homebirths and the Nurse 122 (2)
Midwife in Today's Society. Lay 122 (5)
Migration. Puerto Rican 142 (56)
Mile. Extra 18 (1)
Miles van der Rohe 142 (79)
Military Affairs 151 (192)
Military Aid and Foreign Policy 159 (36)
Military Budget 16 (62)
Military. Career Opportunities in the 16 (62)
Military History 218
Military. New 16 (62)
Milk-Marketing Board Rip-off. British Columbia 171 (8)
Milton S. Hershey Medical Center 151 (10), (186)
Milwaukee. Marquette University Impact on 105 (64)
Mime. Family 29 (43), (103), (187), (313)
Mime in Elementary and Secondary Education 29 (43), (103), (187)
Mind-bodies. Unlocking the 97 (7)
Mind. Clerical-Collar 180 (94)
Mind Control. Experiences With 4 (7)
Mind. Journey to the Depths of the Human 112 (96)
Mind. Language and 181 (314)
Mind-Mentalism and Hypnotism. Phenomena of the 114 (2)
Mind Over Body 151 (207)
Mind. Mysterious World of the 56 (105)
Mind. Relationship of Languages and 171 (46)
Mind. Success is a State of 135 (3)
Mind - the Last Frontier 151 (203)
Mindedness. Administrative 105 (42)
Minding the Store 102 (19)
Minds for a Global World. Global 100 (1)
Mine Drainage. Acid 151 (154)
Mine. Homestake 143 (7)
Mine. What Does it Take to Find a 143 (12)
Mineral Crisis. Impending 143 (9)
Mineral Nutrition of Plants 218
Mineral Potential. Land Use Planning and 143 (6)
Mineral Resources. Energy and 142 (81)
Mineral Wealth of South Africa 181 (137), (347)
Minerals and Mountains 143 (11)
Minerals. Rocks and 142 (81)
Mines. Discovery of Soloman Gold 1 (9)
Mines in the Western States. Wilderness Studies of the Bureau of 143 (10)
Minimal Government. Economics of 105 (32)
Minimum Wage Law and the Poor 85 (22)
Minimum Wage Laws - Cure for Or a Cause of Poverty? 85 (2)
Mining Important to You. Is 143 (3)
Mining Industry, Its Beauty Among Stars. Muhlenberg County, Kentucky, Its Strip 117 (29)
Mining. Labor and Industry in Anthracite 151 (36)
Mining. Literature/Lore of Bituminous 151 (236)
Mining. Modern Coal 151 (136)
Mining to Biomedical Technology. Wilkes-Barre Campus, Service From 151 (2)
Ministerial Rhetoric 151 (78)
Ministry to the University 105 (105)
Minnesota. Geology of 168 (3)
Minnesota. Glacial Geology of 168 (3)
Minnesota. Natural History of Central 168 (56)
Minnesota Politics 168 (72)
Minorities 176 (23), (66)
Minorities and Public Education 181 (93)
Minorities and Women in Science and Engineering 29 (111), (278)
Minorities in America. Sexual 181 (238)
Minorities in Business 112 (84)
Minority and Underpriviledged Children. Development of 16 (33)
Minority Environment 224 (12)
Minority Group Relations 168 (66)
Minority Groups A General Picture 27 (42)
Minority. Majority in the 151 (56)
Minority Studies: Beyond Takenism. Latin America: A Racial Paradise? 168 (25)
Minority Women 142 (14)
Miracle Called America 112 (50)
Miracle of Being You 75 (1)
Miracle of Electricity 152
Miracles in Monologue 97 (28)
Mirages 151 (303)
Misogynists. Matrons and 227 (22)
Mission and History. Delaware County Campus - Its 151 (16)
Missing God. Sartre and Man's Search for a 29 (245)
Mission to Earth 57 (22)
Mission Trail. California's 59 (10)
Mistakes We Make About the Aged 57 (85)

Mr. Fingers, Artist in Residence 221 (1)
Mr. Fingers Goes to College 221 (1)
Mr. Fingers Show 221 (1)
Mr. Rooney Goes to Washington 112 (111)
Mrs. Gandhi and Indian Democracy 117 (97)
Misunderstand Business? Why Do People 23
Misunderstanding. America - Europe - the Great 85 (18)
Misuse and Abuse, More and More Leisure. Drug 56 (81)
Misuse of Drugs 181 (216)
Mixed Media Weaving 79 (79)
Mixed Stitchery 79 (71)
Mixed Textile Techniques 79 (71)
Mixed Theatres of the Empire 227 (14)
Mixtures in Pumps and Piping. Flow Characteristics of Solids - Liquid 67 (5)
Mobile Homes 65 (1)
Mobile Homes and Parks 65 (53)
Mock Tapestry 79 (132)
Model Aircraft. Building Plastic 151 (5)
Model. Alternative Education and Freirian 142 (56)
Model Code of Procedures for Academic Freedom 105 (49)
Model. Eclectic Enrollment Projection 57 (93)
Model. Sinclair's 181 (134)
Model-T Ford, 1909-1927. Rise and Fall of the 151 (294)
Modeling Behavior in the Physical, Intellectual and Emotional Domains. Teacher 117 (39)
Models for Teachers. Carkhuff Learning and Counseling 117 (39)
Models in Education. Matching 57 (70)
Models. Mathematical 142 (70)
Models of Communication. Synergetic 151 (65)
Moderates, Conservatives, and Catholics are Excluded From Campus. Why 85 (33)
Modern Adventure. Peace Corps: The 151 (118)
Modern Africa 151 (111)
Modern Afrikan Literature 142 (66)
Modern American Ballet 97 (71)
Modern American Indians 105 (1)
Modern and Contemporary Philosophies 117 (98)
Modern and Premodern Societies. Death in 29 (281)
Modern Art 181 (80), (210)
Modern Astronomy. Universe According to 181 (280)
Modern China. Agony of 56 (117)
Modern China. Women in 112 (33)
Modern Coal Mining 151 (136)
Modern Computer. Mathematics Versus the 181 (154)
Modern Corporate Critics. Response to 85 (19)
Modern Cosmology 223 (4)
Modern Dance 142 (38)
Modern Democracy. Problems of Constitutional Government and 85 (5)
Modern Denmark 168 (65)
Modern Ecological Questions 54
Modern Elementary Math 56 (48)
Modern 49'ers. Nutrition for 57 (30)
Modern Germany 57 (75)
Modern Greek Poetry. Cyprus in 227 (29)
Modern Greek Poetry. Myth in 227 (19)
Modern Hawaiians. Ethnicity and Culture Changes of 29 (141), (257), (284)
Modern Industrial Technology. Man and 168 (6)
Modern Israel 27 (42)
Modern Japanese Lifestyles 168 (66)
Modern Latin America 181 (344)
Modern Marketing 105 (4)
Modern Mass Media Myth 105 (69)
Modern Materials Science 16 (41)
Modern Math: What Went Wrong? 151 (121)
Modern Movies. Ancient Myths in 227 (44)
Modern Nutrition for Everyday Living 181 (187)
Modern Obstetrical Care 181 (167)
Modern Painting, Sculpture and Architecture. Cubism - Major Route of 56 (10)
Modern Pediatric Dentistry 105 (30)
Modern School. Industrial Arts in the 151 (118)
Modern Society. Corporations and 159 (15)
Modern Society. Mass Communication in 29 (36)
Modern Society. Recreation in a 181 (12)
Modern Southwest Indian Spinning, Dyeing. Ancient and 79 (76)
Modern Spain 216 (1)
Modern State of Israel. Rise of the 181 (293), (306), (343)
Modern Student and Roman Satire 227 (23)
Modern Swedish Tapestries 79 (75)
Modern Time. Eyewitness to the 154 (11)
Modern Times. Greek - An Ongoing Language From Ancient to 227 (29)
Modern Trends in Children's Literature 57 (62)
Modern Trends in Dentistry 105 (28)
Modern Trends in Jewish Thought 181 (306)
Modern World. Communist China and the 85 (17)
Modern World. Mathematics in the 181 (153)
Modern World. Religion in the 54
Modern World. Theology of Change in the 54
Modern Youth. Existentialism and the 29 (102), (349)
Modification and You. Behavior 56 (5)
Modification. Behavior 117 (109), 142 (28), 168 (7), (47), 181 (126), (296), 214 (78)
Modification in Business and Industry. Behavior 168 (64)
Modification in Normal School Settings. Behavior 117 (37)
Modification in Weight Reduction. Behavior 218
Modification of Diagnostics. Drug Induced 54
Modification of the Retarded. Behavior 168 (64)
Modification. Recreational Behavior 168 (64)
Modification. Weight Control and Behavior 216 (34)
Moisture in Dehydrated Food Products, Grain and

Other Moisture Measurements in Food Processing. Measurement of 67 (21)
Moisture Measurement and Control 67 (3)
Moisture Measurements in Food Processing. Measurement of Moisture in Dehydrated Food Products, Grain and Other 67 (21)
(Moksha). Vedanta Concept of Salvation 117 (97)
Mola Artists of San Blas. Cuna Women - 27 (47)
Mola Blouse - Origin, Symbolism and Development 79 (25)
Molecule Research. Recombinant DNA 174 (46)
Moment. World at the 83 (6)
Monarchy 154 (5)
Monasticism 29 (126), (183), (199), (212), (248)
Monasticism and... 29 (126), (183), (199), (212), (248)
Monasticism in the Early Church 105 (107)
Monastricism. Origins of Christian 29 (178), (234)
Monetary Policies. Fiscal and 56 (23)
Monetary Structure - An Eternal Crisis. International 85 (14)
Monetary Theory 214 (33)
Money and Banking 142 (23), 214 (33)
Money and Retirement 151 (166)
Money as an Independent Sales Agent. How to Make Big 180 (16)
Money--Both Ways. Listening Is 105 (13)
Money. Everything You Want to Know About 225 (44)
Money. Getting a Greater Return on Your 97 (59)
Money. Getting More for Your 54
Money. High Cost of 168 (67)
Money. How to Dress Better for Less 229 (1)
Money. How to Get the Most for Your Invested 140 (1)
Money. How to Live in a Stately Home and Make 97 (44)
Money in College Athletics 105 (112)
Money in Inventory. Are You Losing 136 (7)
Money. It's Fun Making 81 (1)
Money Management 176 (99), 214 (1)
Money Wisely. Spending 174 (63)
Moneywise. How to Get the Best Wine Buy 225 (22)
Mongolian Puzzle 29 (14), (48)
Monitoring: Air Pollution Control. Air Quality 150 (8)
Monobiblos. Tradition and Originality in Propertius' 227 (24)
Monobiblos. Unity of the 227 (24)
Monogamy and the Freedom of Choice. Sex, 211 (3)
Monologue. Miracles in 97 (28)
Monologue Preaching. Drama as a Sermonic Alternative to 168 (34)
Monologues. First Person 168 (34)
Monopolized? Are United States Manufacturing Industries 85 (2)
Monopoly. Is Government the Source of 85 (2)
Monopoly. Myth of 85 (30)
Monster. Becoming Assertive - Between Mouse and 29 (239), (343)
Monster. Paris, That Beloved 117 (138)
Moon Means for You. What a Man on the 112 (25)
Moon. Theories of the Origin of the 151 (274)
Moorman Technique 79 (88)
Moral Character 214 (74)
Moral Crisis of Our Time? What is the 85 (12)
Moral Crisis of Our Times. Talent Waste - the 54
Moral Educational 181 (102)
Moral Foreign Policy. Constitutional/ 102 (12)
Moral Imagination. Reviving the 85 (16)
Moral Implications. Jewish Education and Its 29 (90), (114), (233)
Moral Judgment Development 142 (84)
Moral Judgment in Children, Youth and Adulthood 214 (77)
Moral Legal Ethics in Nursing. Medico - 105 (49)
Moral Philosophy 214 (76)
Moral Question of Nuclear Power 151 (133)
Moral Reasoning for Children and Professionals. Developing 168 (63)
Moral Relativism and Its Alternative 85 (36)
Moral Values in the Public Schools. Teaching 159 (32)
Morality and Law 54, 214 (83)
Morality and the Fall of Rome 56 (93)
Morality Argument. New 105 (90)
Morality. Critical Judgments on Art or 105 (66)
Morality. Energy and 83 (13)
Morality in Government 97 (74)
Morality. New 105 (104), 214 (75)
Morality Relative. Is All Truth and 85 (20)
Morality? What is the New 85 (12)
Morals. Islamic 1 (2)
Morals of Civil War Soldiers 151 (214)
Moravian Music - A Valuable American Heritage 56 (110)
Mordants. Innovative Natural Dye Experimentation With 79 (156)
More About Everything 97 (33)
More Beautiful You 97 (22)
More Power to You 152
More Than You Ever Wanted to Know About Economics and Had the Sense Not to Ask 105 (32)
Mormon Church. History and Doctrine of the 56 (138)
Mormons in Mexico 29 (139), (160)
Morocco: Cities, Seas, Sahara 15 (2)
Morphology. Communism, Its Ideology and 85 (24)
Morphology, Syntax of English. Phonology, 56 (65)
Mortality. Nuclear Radiation and Infant 151 (262)

Mortality. Statistics and Infant 151 (262)
Most Exciting Road Through Europe 51 (1)
Most Pressing Shortcoming of the Public Schools 223 (9)
Mother Goose Rhymes. Historical Origin of 56 (63)
Motherhood. Career Versus 224 (12)
Motherhood. Unmarried 142 (14)
Mother's Day 214 (61)
Mothers and the Lives of Their Adult Children. Roman 227 (36)
Mothers - Are You Helping or Hurting Your Child? Working 29 (239), (343)
Motifs in Weaving. Application of Historical 79 (81)
Motion. Continents in 97 (62)
Motion. Rehabilitation - Putting People in 56 (79)
Motivating for Profit 54
Motivating Human Behavior 112 (68)
Motivating People. Art of 151 (38)
Motivation 57 (73), 65 (2), (66), 112 (93), (137), 142 (47), (71), 176 (28), (57), (89), (116), (122), 180 (35), (56), (115), (125), (134), (193), 214 (1)
Motivation - A Key to Learning 117 (134)
Motivation. Achievement 56 (51), 218
Motivation and Communication 180 (9)
Motivation. Basketry, Historical Introduction, Contemporary Investigations Process, Structure and 79 (5)
Motivation for the Older Professional 151 (40)
Motivation. Human Engineering and 180 (146)
Motivation. Human Relations 16 (43)
Motivation in Education 112 (128)
Motivation in One's Life 105 (80)
Motivation in the Classroom 57 (70)
Motivation in the Teaching of Mathematics 117 (92)
Motivation. Increasing Productivity Through Employee 67 (2)
Motivation. Introduction to Achievement 56 (135)
Motivation Level. How to Increase Your 23
Motivation. Management and 180 (85)
Motivation. Management by 112 (22)
Motivation of People for Profits 65 (20)
Motivation of Self and Others 151 (46)
Motivation. Organizational Behavior and 151 (43)
Motivation. Personal 180 (40)
Motivation. Personnel Management and 181 (41)
Motivation. Persuasion and 65 (28)
Motivation. Sales and 180 (117)
Motivation. Self- 65 (45)
Motivation - Success and You 112 (129)
Motivation. Your Image and Self 229 (2)
Motivation - Youth in Real Estate 65 (42)
Motivational Approach to Updating 151 (40)
Motivational Aspects of Real Estate 65 (31)
Motivational Aspects of Sports Participation 57 (74)
Motivational Management 180 (49)
Motivations. Buying 65 (44)
Motivations. Economic 181 (42)
Motor Development 181 (11)
Motor Development. Normal Gross and Fine 159 (26)
Motor Development. Perceptual 159 (26)
Motors - Energy Efficiency. Electric 67 (8)
Mount Baker - Increased Thermal Activity 218
Mountain Yesterdays. Rocky 57 (3)
Mountains. Air Pollution in the Blue Ridge 216 (113)
Mountains. Collection of Tree Seeds in the Rocky 151 (310)
Mountains. Great Smokey 69 (6)
Mountains. Greece - Islands to the 59 (10)
Mountains. Minerals and 143 (11)
Mountains. Origin of 142 (88)
Mourning. Bereavement, Grief, and 29 (281)
Mouse and Monster. Becoming Assertive - Between 29 (239), (343)
Movement. Biomechanics of Human 151 (209)
Movement. Career Education 57 (47)
Movement. Children's Rights 231 (3)
Movement Education? 181 (77), (92)
Movement. FBI Plot Against the Black 213 (10)
Movement. Feminist 216 (47)
Movement From 1930 to Today. Negritude 168 (41)
Movement. Human Potential 57 (71)
Movement in American Politics. Neighborhood 181 (275)
Movement. John F. Kennedy and the Civil Rights 117 (66)
Movement. Marketing and the Consumer 214 (23)
Movement. Present Situation of the International Communist 85 (8)
Movement. Role of Men in the Women's 142 (57)
Movement Therapy 29 (103), (175)
Movement. Womens 168 (46)
Movement. Women's Liberation 151 (167)
Movements. Black Liberation 142 (17)
Movements. Contemporary Religious 224 (11)
Movements in History. Youth 85 (33)
Movements of the Nineteenth Century. Various Architects and 31 (3)
Movements. Radical 85 (8)
Movie Camera. Creating With a 168 (53)
Movie Music. Magical 56 (109)
Movie Scene. Great Western 112 (20)
Movies. Abuse of Women in 225 (5)
Movies and Television. Social Significance of 105 (66)
Movies. Ancient Myths in Modern 227 (44)
Movies. Making Sea 69 (15)
Movies. Religion and the 105 (110)
Movies. Rex Reed at the 97 (56)
Moving and Transportation 180 (192)
Much. How Much is Too 56 (29)
Muckrackers Took on College Football. When the 151 (69)

Muhammad as an Examplar. Holy Prophet 1 (12)
Muhammad as Benefactor of Humanity. Holy Prophet 1 (13)
Muhammad. Glimpse Into the Life and Teachings of 1 (8)
Muhammad in the Bible 1 (8)
Muhammad. Jesus as Precursor of the Holy Prophet 1 (5)
Muhammad the Liberator of Woman 1 (2)
Muhlenberg County, Kentucky - Its Strip Mining Industry, Its Beauty Among Stars 117 (29)
Muir's High Sierra. John 59 (6), 69 (4)
Multi-Cultural Education 142 (74)
Multidisciplinary Approach to Treatment and Evaluation 159 (26)
Multidisciplinary Setting. Communications in a 151 (79)
Multi-harness Looms. Pattern Drafting for 79 (122)
Multi-harness Weaving 79 (140)
Multi-Image Production Techniques 142 (75)
Multilayer Weaving on Eight Harness Looms. Theory and Use of 79 (52)
Multilayered Weaves. Double, 79 (118)
Multi-Media 180 (129)
Multi-Media Concepts and New Approaches to Learning 56 (50)
Multi-Media Presentation of Educational Theatre 105 (24)
Multinational Company and Its Impact on International Relations 218
Multinational Corporations in the Food Business 181 (34), (334)
Multiple Approach to Form and Fiber Fashion 79 (106)
Multiple Handicaps. Child and 117 (132)
Multiple Harness Fabric Design 79 (8)
Multiple Harness Weaving 79 (93)
Multiple Listing 65 (10)
Multisensory Communication 181 (97)
Multitrack Recording Techniques 57 (29)
Municipal Governments. Equal Employment Compliance in 29 (66)
Municipal Wastewater Treatment. Industrial and 204
Murray State University. Programs in Mathematics at 117 (92)
Muscle Contractions 142 (96)
Muscle Function 105 (115)
Museum and Youth Science Center 29 (106), (278)
Museum and Youth Science Center of North Orange County 29 (352)
Museum as Educator 151 (30)
Museum. Organizing the Small 57 (56)
Museum. Place of Crafts in a 79 (73)
Museum. Visit to the Jeu de Paume-Impressionist 117 (138)
Mushroom Industry. Commercial 151 (176)
Mushrooms of Alabama 16 (16)
Music 151 (29), 224 (6)
Music - A Valuable American Heritage. Moravian 56 (110)
Music. Afro-American 181 (27), (84)
Music. American Folk 29 (220)
Music and Children's Literature. Early Childhood Education in Art, 192 (30)
Music, and Cooking Activities for the Classroom Teacher. Art, 117 (48)
Music and Culture. African 181 (27), (84)
Music and My Life 154 (20)
Music. Asian Influences on American 225 (12)
Music. Aspects of Greek 227 (43)
Music at Virginia Tech 216 (66)
Music. Chamber 16 (41)
Music. Choral 142 (57)
Music. Contemporary Trends In 57 (4)
Music. Creativity in 57 (4)
Music Department Has to Offer East Central Illinois. What the 57 (40)
Music - Drama 218
Music Education at Virginia Tech 216 (66)
Music. Electronic 57 (4)
Music. Enjoyment and Appreciation of 54
Music. Folk 142 (57)
Music. Historical Periods in 54
Music. I Hate 29 (222)
Music in a Time of Affluence. Choral 56 (107)
Music in America. Black 225 (12)
Music in Education. Role of 54
Music in Poland. Contemporary 54
Music in the Community 54
Music in the South. Black Folk 29 (220)
Music is No Ugly Duckling 214 (67)
Music. Magical Movie 56 (109)
Music. Mathematics and 56 (106)
Music. Medieval and Renaissance 142 (57)
Music. My Life and 154 (1)
Music of Byrd. Word Painting in the 151 (26)
Music of Charles Ives 29 (221)
Music of Leos Janacek 29 (221)
Music of the Avant-Garde 56 (108)
Music of the Churches in Change 56 (107)
Music of the 18th Century America 56 (39), (110)
Music of the 1920's. Popular 224 (3)
Music of the Spheres. Poetry: 151 (244)
Music. Orchestral 142 (57)
Music. Physics of 171 (40)
Music. Similarities Between 20th Century Art and 159 (21)
Music. Styles of 54
Music: Sung and Unsung. Women in 151 (31)
Music Teaching. Kodaly Approach to 54
Music. Twentieth Century American 225 (12)
Music. What It Means to Understand 54
Music. Women in 29 (182), (222)
Music World 154 (23)
Music. World of 154 (18)
Musical: America's Contribution to Theatre 105 (26)
Musical Comedy. Dancer Preparing for a Career in 225 (39)

Musical Composers 54
Musical Composers and Their Works. Individual 54
Musical Nicknames 176 (10)
Musical Theater. Dance in the American 225 (39)
Musical Theatre Cavalcade 97 (72)
Musical World of Peter Duchin 102 (7)
Musicianship. Comprehensive 56 (108)
Muslims. World Religions - Buddhists, Confucianists, Taoists, Maoists, Jews, Christians and 54
Mussolini 117 (74)
Mutual Funds. Kinds of No-Load 140 (1)
Mutual Funds. Services Offered by No-Load 140 (1)
My Discovery of America 97 (40)
My Life and Hard Times as a Weaving Woman 79 (50)
My Life and Music 154 (1)
Mycenae. Archaeology of Crete and 227 (45)
Myocardial Infarction. Acute 27 (34)
Myotatic Reflex. Human 181 (155)
Myself as Seen in My Voice 57 (90)
Mysteries of Inner Space 97 (65)
Mysterious Laws of Chance and Fortune 29 (136)
Mysterious World of the Mind 56 (105)
Mystery. Marsh - A Quiet 69 (13)
Mystery of Anesthesia 181 (162)
Mystery of Watergate. Deep Throat, the 105 (54)
Mystery of Edgar Allan Poe 151 (237)
Mystic? Are You a 54
Mysticism 105 (106), 174 (55)
Mysticism/Non-Western Philosophy 142 (22)
Mystique of Materials 151 (259)
Myth. Ancient Art and 227 (21)
Myth and Folklore. Greece - In 29 (200)
Myth and Folklore. Oriental: 29 (15), (200)
Myth and Folktale. Africa: In 29 (2), (200)
Myth and Literature: Selected Topics 151 (236)
Myth and Reality. Colonialism - 85 (18)
Myth Exploded. Talent 56 (13)
Myth. Full Disclosure 85 (19)
Myth in America. Anglo-Saxon 223 (3)
Myth in Modern Greek Poetry 227 (19)
Myth. Lincoln the Man No 57 (28)
Myth, Magic and Reality 57 (62)
Myth. Modern Mass Media 105 (69)
Myth of Humanism in the Public Schools 12
Myth of Monopoly 85 (30)
Myth of the Bootstrap 168 (25)
Myth of the Impartial Judge and Jury 225 (37)
Myths of Today 85 (36)
Myth or History. Trojan War: 56 (93)
Myth. Structural Analysis of 227 (41)
Mythological Painting. Poempeiian 227 (35)
Mythology 227 (11), (15), (33)
Mythology. Classical 227 (4), (16), (29)
Mythology. Comparative 227 (21)
Mythology - Form and Meaning in Our Times 54
Mythology. Greek and Roman 218, 227 (3)
Mythology. Landscape of Greek 29 (124), (197), (205), (320)
Mythology. Science as a 227 (44)
Mythology. Women in 227 (28), (48)
Myths. Aging: Realities and 151 (17)
Myths in Modern Movies. Ancient 227 (44)
Myths in the World of Sport 29 (282), (300)
Myths. Typology of 227 (41)

N

NATO and Southern Africa 168 (41)
NATO. Nonmilitary Aspects of 151 (201)
Nader and Consumerism. Who Killed the Ice Man - Or, an Answer to Ralph 85 (26)
Nail Frame Weaving 79 (106)
(Name Drafting). Have You Tried This? 79 (23)
Names - A Demonstration. Remembering 105 (13)
Names in French History. Great 56 (90)
Names in French Literature. Great 56 (60)
Names. Louisiana Place 174 (35)
Nancy Dickerson's Washington 102 (5)
Napoleon 117 (74)
Napoleon. French Revolution and 117 (64)
Narcotic Deaths 54
Narrative. Frivolous 227 (35)
Nation. General Aviation Benefits the 19 (1)
Nation of Strangers 102 (22)
Nation. State of Our 135 (1)
National Affairs 176 (19), 219 (3)
National Anthem. Our 57 (91)
National Athletic Injury/Illness Reporting System 151 (279)
National Committee. Democratic 223 (23)
National Concern. Right to Work - A 131 (3)
National Dress of Mayan Indians of Guatemala - Historical Interpretation and Future of the Tradition. Contemporary 79 (83)
National Economic Issues 151 (42)
National Economic Policy 174 (70)
National Economy 117 (22)
National Guard. Alabama 16 (44)
National Health Insurance 27 (25), 54
National Land Use Legislation 174 (28)
National Legislative Policy 216 (37)
National Outlook 97 (39)
National Park. Alaska Highway and McKinley 223 (34)
National Park. Long Distance Backpacking in Jasper 166 (1)
National Parks as Islands of Wilderness 218
National Parks. Fauna of Pacific Northwest 218
National Parks. Geology of Various Western United States 168 (3)
National Parks of the Southwest 57 (43)
National Policy. American 174 (72)

National Policy for the Oceans 218
National Politics 224 (8)
National Politics. American 151 (222)
National Priorities in the Decade Ahead 85 (10)
National Register for Historic Places 174 (19)
National Security 220 (4)
National Security Policy. United States 85 (15)
National Security Problems Involving Japan and Korea 159 (36)
National Symbol. Bald Eagle - 4 (4)
National United States Economy 65 (35)
National Water Work Association Today 136 (20)
Nationalism and Human Rights in the Soviet Union 57 (37)
Nationalism. Puerto Rican 142 (56)
Nationality in American Literature. Achievement of 16 (34)
Nations Association and You. United 151 (65)
Nations in World Affairs. Role of the United 29 (330)
Nations. Management in Developing 151 (43)
Nations. United States Relations With the 57 (19)
Native Wildflowers of the West Coast 159 (20)
Natural Approach to Foreign Language Teaching 27 (15)
Natural Areas of Erie County 151 (308)
Natural Beauty 97 (73)
Natural Childbirth 181 (251), (329)
Natural Dye Experimentation With Mordants. Innovative 79 (156)
Natural Dyeing 79 (85), (101), (107)
Natural Dyeing. Indigo 79 (36)
Natural Dyeing of Wool. Spinning and 79 (54)
Natural Dyeing. Spinning and 79 (144)
Natural Dyes 79 (50)
Natural Dyes. Dyeing With 79 (89)
Natural Dyes, Quilting, Spinning 79 (58)
Natural Ecosystems. Interactions Between Man and 218
Natural Gas Shortages 74
Natural History of Central Minnesota 168 (56)
Natural Lichen Dyeing 79 (156)
Natural Materials. Dyeing Wool With 79 (149)
Natural Materials. Weaving With 79 (107)
Natural Resource Management 151 (254)
Natural Resources. Availability of 216 (77)
Natural Rights. American Philosophers and 214 (73)
Natural Wonders. Venezuela - Land of 69 (7)
Naturally Occuring Toxic Substances in Food 151 (177)
Nature - Abstractions in Fiber Forms 79 (154)
Nature. Aggression, Violence and Human 102 (35)
Nature and Future of Tory Radicalism 85 (40)
Nature and Pottery. Design Inspiration - 159 (5)
Nature and Relate to Your Weaving. Learning to See In 79 (77)
Nature and the Arts. Inspiration for Weaving From 79 (112)
Nature and Weaving. Design in 79 (132)
Nature. Art in 159 (5)
Nature as a Source for Design and Color 79 (140)
Nature as Source 79 (35)
Nature. Design - Inspiration From 79 (82)
Nature Fibers 168 (69)
Nature. Getting Back to 16 (72)
Nature Obey Mathematical Laws? Does 56 (129)
Nature of America. Changing 176 (15)
Nature of Knowledge. Truth, Objectivity and Some Interesting Facts About the 85 (20)
Nature of Language - How it Influences Our Behavior, Our Conceptions, Our View of Self and Others, How it Functions 117 (61)
Nature of Leadership 102 (30)
Nature of Religion and Its Study 218
Nature of Romantic Love 218
Nature of Southern Politics 216 (50)
Nature of Truth, Goodness, and Beauty. On the 117 (98)
Nature of Undergraduate Education 16 (52)
Nature. Photographing 4 (2)
Nature Through the Eye of a Needle 79 (82)
Nature. Woman's Evolution and Human 213 (11)
Nature's Pollution Almanac 151 (156)
Nature's Way - Nuclear Power 152
Nautical Navigation 105 (70)
Navajo and Hopibar Weaves 79 (90)
Navajo and Hopi Weaving Techniques 79 (100)
Navajo Blanket 79 (65)
Navajo Carding and Spinning Along With Rugs and Navajo Dye Plants 79 (61)
Navajo Spindle, Large Orifice Spinners. Saxony Wheel, Walking Wheel, 79 (59)
Navajo. Vertical Loom for 79 (8)
Navajo Weaving 79 (61), (85), (89), (91), (92), (134)
Naval Academy. United States 57 (53)
Naval ROTC 105 (70)
Naval Science 214 (70)
Naval Science. Marine and 214 (68)
Naval Ships Engineering 105 (73)
Naval Supremacy. Russia's Challenge to Our 97 (74)
Naval Weapons 105 (71)
Navigation. Air 105 (70)
Navigation. Nautical 105 (70)
Navy 105 (75)
Navy ROTC 105 (75)
Navy. Women in the 105 (124)
Near Eastern Archaeology 29 (226), (269)
Necessity. Campus Planning - Luxury or 56 (101)
Need Athletic and Academic Scholarships. No 31 (15)
Need for Continuing Education 151 (117)
Need for Continuing Education. Today's 151 (102)
Need for Doctors to Get Involved in Politics 8 (7)
Need for Fundamental Political Changes in America 178 (5)

Need for Remediation. Writing Deficiencies: 151 (114)
Need for Retirement Planning 8 (4)
Need for Sex Education 151 (160)
Need for Speech Training 117 (135)
Need to Know About Yourself. What You 75 (1)
Needle Knitting. Peruvian 79 (65)
Needle Lace, Embroidery. Bobbin Lace, 79 (42)
Needle Laces 79 (98)
Needle. Nature Through the Eye of a 79 (82)
Needlelace 79 (29)
Needs. Analyzing Business Training 151 (122)
Needs Assessment for Schools 181 (116)
Needs, Economic Choices, and Coal Beneficiation. Energy 151 (134)
Needs, Goals and Financial Planning. Human 214 (77)
Needs. Innovative Method of Forecasting Community 168 (57)
Needs. Meeting Children's 181 (11)
Needs of the Geriatric. Physical Rehabilitation 56 (89)
Needs of the Small and Medium Size Drilling Contractor. Basic Insurance 136 (8)
Needs. Preschool Children With Special 142 (59)
Needs Them? Arts? Who 57 (67)
Needs You. Your Newspaper 57 (88)
Neglect. Child Abuse and 159 (43)
Neglect. Social Change, Revolution, and the Politics of Benign 85 (12)
Neglected Textile Techniques. Selected, 79 (33)
Negotiating the Sale 65 (21)
Negotiating the Sale. Closing and 65 (61)
Negotiations in the Public Sector. Professional 117 (38)
Negotiations. Labor 151 (9)
Negritude: Black and White Aspects 159 (40)
Negritude Movement From 1930 to Today 168 (41)
Negro Problem in Historical Perspective. America's 85 (12)
Neighborhood Design 181 (78)
Neighborhood Government and Organization 181 (275)
Neighborhood Movement in American Politics 181 (275)
Neighborhoods and City Recycling 181 (254), (275)
Neighborhoods, Housing and Community Development 181 (275)
Neighbors to the North. Our 56 (121)
Neo-Colonialism and the Third World 142 (56)
Neo-Conservatism and Neo-Liberalism 85 (18)
Neo-Liberalism. Neo-Conservatism and 85 (18)
Nepal 15 (1), 69 (5), 174 (82)
Nepal. Educational Development in 29 (18), (100)
Nepal Photo Diary 4 (2)
Nerves Transmit Biological Messages in Our Body. How 218
Nervous System 181 (195)
Nervous System. Electron Microscopy of 181 (169)
Netherlands from the 15th to the 17th Century. Art of the 56 (9)
Netting 79 (39)
Netting, Basic Basketry, Wrapping. Children's Workshop in Knotless 79 (158)
Netting. Contemporary Use of Primitive Knotless 79 (52)
Netting. Knotless 79 (40), (103)
Neutron Activation Analysis 151 (156)
New Administration - What Washington Plans for United States Business 102 (10), (21)
New Advances in Open Heart Surgery 181 (194)
New Atheism and Its Tactics 85 (20)
New China 171 (2)
New Cities 171 (48)
New Commitment to Agriculture 151 (19)
New Cosmology 29 (186), (272)
New Day - A New Way 112 (83)
New Deal. Socialism and the 172 (8)
New Directions for Secondary Education 216 (129)
New Directions in Continuing Education 171 (18)
New Directions in Language Study 181 (315)
New East. Ancient 29 (217), (226)
New England and the Sea 97 (61)
New England - Cradle of America 59 (14)
New England of Robert Frost 69 (4)
New England. Robert Frost's 59 (6)
New Ethnicity 211 (6)
New Ethnicity in America 168 (30)
New Frontiers Facing America 214 (6)
New Guinea Expedition 59 (2)
New Happenings in the High School 223 (11)
New Hebrides. People of 69 (9)
New Hope for Asthma Sufferers 27 (33)
New Iberia. History of 174 (19)
New Immigrants in Europe 168 (30)
New Information Systems Degree Program in the Cal State Fullerton School of Business 29 (26)
New Insights Into Indian Affairs 112 (90)
New International Economic Order 57 (61)
New Kind of Power 189
New Left 85 (23), (29)
New Left and the New Right 85 (9)
New Life Through Higher Education 151 (103)
New Look at the Old Jerusalem 57 (62)
New Luddites 85 (38)
New Materials and Processes 151 (125)
New Mathematics 181 (153)
New Meat Product Development 216 (35)
New Mexico. Observations on Russia, Alaska, or 56 (116)
New Military 16 (62)
New Morality 105 (104), 214 (75)
New Morality Argument 105 (90)
New Norway 59 (14)
New Patterns of Asian Politics 105 (57)
New Physical Education 29 (86), (130), (299)
New Radiological Imaging Devices 181 (198)
New Religious Groups 181 (206)
New South 154 (7)
New South, Today and Tomorrow 154 (6)
New Spirit in Investigating Reporting 135 (2)

New Spirituality 181 (208)
New Stars of British Drama 57 (23)
New Techniques of Computer Programming 181 (51)
New Technologies in Graphic Arts 218
New Technology in the Meat Industry 16 (39)
New Undergraduate Plant Protection Option 216 (85)
New Vikings 97 (62)
New Winds - the Decline of Liberalism and the Rise of Conservatism 85 (12)
New Woman in a New World 151 (11)
New Women 211 (2)
New World. How Man Came to the 4 (3)
New World. New Woman in a 151 (11)
New World Order of Islam 1 (1)
New Zealand 52 (76), 223 (36)
Newcomer Buyer. Dealing With a 65 (29)
Newfoundland 69 (13)
Newfoundland. Vikings - Iceland, Greenland, 151 (220)
Newman Library Can Do for You. What the Carol 216 (56)
News Analyst. Reminiscences of a 83 (6)
News and Information Services 112 (51)
News and the World Today 135 (10)
News. Behind the Scenes in Television 135 (41)
News. Bias in Television 117 (84)
News. Getting Your Club in the 216 (13)
News in the Soviet Union 105 (68)
News in Washington 112 (2)
News is Collected. How th 16 (74)
News. Lighter Side of the 97 (53)
News Media 176 (66)
News Media and Public Relations - Friendly Adversaries 105 (67)
News. Media Behind the 151 (77)
News Media. Ethics and the 181 (68)
News Media. Ethics of 56 (102)
News of Penn State 151 (64)
News. People in the 176 (73)
News. Public Relations and 216 (14)
News. Radio/Television 168 (10)
News. Six O'Clock 151 (80)
News. So You Want to Write 216 (14)
News to and From the Two Chinas 105 (68)
Newscasting 112 (1), (36), (58), (75), (81), (87), (91), (98), (116), (122), (127), (131), 135 (8), (18), (26), (35), (38), (43), (52)
Newsletters. Producing Attractive 151 (84)
Newsman's Sermon 181 (68)
Newspaper and the Bicentennial 15 (16)
Newspaper Needs You. Your 57 (88)
Newspaper Publicity. Effective 151 (84)
Newspaper. Putting Together the Campus 117 (85)
Newspaper? Your Community's 181 (68), (211)
Newspaper. Your Organization Can Have an Effective 168 (51)
Newspapering, Today and Yesterday 56 (102)
Newspapers, Reporting, Editing, Ethics 151 (68)
Next 200 Years 102 (20)
Nibble Your Vines. Little Foxes That 75 (1)
Nicknames. Musical 176 (10)
Nietzsche and Tragedy 227 (34)
Nigerian and African Dress 79 (37)
Nigerian Handicrafted Textiles 79 (37)
Nihilism, and the New Left. Anarchism, 85 (21)
Nile. Egypt - Gift of the 59 (7)
Nile. Yankee Sails the 59 (5)
1909-1927. Rise and Fall of the Model-T Ford, 151 (294)
1980's. Career Planning for the 27 (24)
1980's. Real Estate Professional of the 181 (37)
1984? Compulsory Adult Education by 151 (98)
1990. USSR in 97 (52)
1970's. American Higher Education in the 168 (18)
1970's. Education in the 85 (33)
1970's. International System in the 85 (28)
1970's. Operational Significance of Marxist-Leninist Ideology in the 85 (31)
1970's Style. Sport - 171 (25)
1975. Europe 117 (137)
1976 Elections. West German Politics After the 29 (259)
1976 Student is a Flashback! 171 (58)
1976 Tax Reform Bill 105 (7)
1972. Education Amendment of 181 (6)
1930 to Today. Negritude Movement From 168 (41)
1920's. Popular Music of the 224 (3)
Nineteenth and Twentieth Century Literature. Male - Female Roles in Russian Culture as Reflected in 27 (18)
19th Century America. Free Masonry in 181 (262)
19th Century City 181 (262)
19th Century England and France. Popular Recreation and Reform in the 142 (98)
19th Century English Literature 214 (47)
19th Century English Prisons 159 (61)
19th Century Russian Literature. Aspect of the 29 (127), (213)
Nineteenth Century. Various Architects and Movements of the 31 (3)
Ninety Years. Esperanto After 58 (2)
Nixon's Early Years. Richard M. 29 (139), (333)
No Need Athletic and Academic Scholarships 31 (15)
No! No! No! Censorship: Past, Present, Future 151 (85)
No Seats - No Fun 112 (8)
Noble Art of Being Average 112 (126)
Noise. Aircraft 216 (79)
Noise Control. Food Plant 67 (4)
Noise Control in Machinery 151 (145)
Noise in Your Community 151 (141)
Noise is Pollution 151 (26)
Noise on Hearing 181 (138)
Noise Pollution 204, 218
Noises. Psychological Effects of Freeway 223 (13)
No-Load Mutual Funds. Kinds of 140 (1)

No-Load Mutual Funds. Services Offered by 140 (1)
Non-Crystalline Solids 151 (73)
Non-Fiction. Contemporary Fiction and 159 (65)
Nongradedness 181 (118)
Non-Loom Techniques 79 (118), (140)
Non-Loom Techniques. Interrelationships of 79 (8)
Nonmilitary Aspects of NATO 151 (201)
Non-Objective Image 151 (73)
Non-Parenthood 129 (1 - 4)
Non-Polluting Energy Sources 142 (15)
Non-Profit Institutions and Public Agencies. Marketing for 181 (36)
Nonscientists. Relativity and the 223 (4)
Nonsense About Race. Sense and 4 (3)
Nonsense Poetry 56 (63)
Nonsense. Sense and 112 (20)
Non-Sexist Marriage 159 (60)
Non-Traditional Education 142 (66), (95)
Non-Traditional Education. Adult and 142 (33)
Non-Traditional Higher Education 142 (22)
Nontraditional Student. Counseling the 151 (161)
Non-Verbal Aspects of Human Communication 142 (37)
Nonverbal Communication 142 (25), 180 (155), (175)
Non-Verbal Communication: A Program Dealing With the Many Aspects of This Overlooked Part of Communications 117 (58)
Nonverbal Communication: The Silent Messages 151 (87)
Non-Verbal Communication - The Subconscious Language 117 (50)
Nonverbal Side of Sales 151 (41)
Non-Violence 178 (4)
Non-Violence and the Gandhi Experience 54
Nonviolence. Foreign Policy and Its Relationship to Pacifism, Socialism and 217 (2)
Nonviolence Versus Violence 217 (4)
Nonviolent Action and Prisons 217 (3)
Non-Western Philosophy. Mysticism 142 (22)
Non-Woven Structures. Woven and/or 79 (70)
Normal Children in the Schools. Integrating Handicapped and 218
Normal Development of Speech and Language Skills 174 (8)
Normal Gratifications of Grief 56 (133)
Normal Gross and Fine Motor Development 159 (26)
Normal Human Growth and Development. Psychology of 117 (111)
Normal Language Development 56 (53)
Norway 15 (4)
Norway. New 59 (14)
Norway - The Bold Vikings 51 (1)
North African Affairs 29 (3), (179), (217), (226)
North America. Archaeology (Prehistory) - Early Man of 105 (1)
North America. Botanical Gardens - Arboretums in 117 (5)
North America. Ecology of 117 (30)
North America. Soviet Espionage in 16 (18)
North American Indians. Life and Culture of 79 (124)
North Carolina and the United States. Political Parties in 56 (131)
North Carolina. Coastal and Marine Resources in Eastern 56 (36), (38)
North Carolina. Colonial Townlife in Eastern 56 (30)
North Carolina. Ecological Problems in 56 (66)
North Carolina. Economic Impact of Students of East Carolina University on Business in Greenville, 56 (24)
North Carolina. Environmental Services in 56 (67)
North Carolina. Environmental Services in Eastern 56 (25)
North Carolina. History of Recreation, Physical Education, and Leisure Activities in Eastern 56 (28)
North Carolina. Ovid Pierce's View of Eastern 56 (36)
North Carolina. Population on the Physical Environment in Eastern 56 (36), (38),
North Carolina. Railroad Travel in Eastern 56 (35)
North Carolina. Social Changes in Eastern 56 (31)
North Carolina. Sound Society of Colonial 56 (34)
North Carolina - the Year 2000. Eastern 56 (36), (38)
North Carolina. Tuscarora Indians in 56 (34)
North Carolina Waterways. Future of Eastern 56 (29)
North Carolinians. Religious Roots of Eastern 56 (32)
North Carolina's Changing Position in the Tobacco Economy 56 (18)
North Carolina's Relative Location. Eastern 56 (36), (38)
North Orange County. Museum and Youth Science Center of 29 (352)
North. Our Neighbors to the 56 (121)
Northern Communities. Human Problems in 171 (10)
Northern Development 171 (10)
Northern Industry 171 (10)
Northwest Africa. Togo, 216 (60)
Northwest Arts and Crafts. History of 218
Northwest National Parks. Fauna of Pacific 218
Northwest Trek, a Closer Biological View 159 (34)
Nostradamus' Forbidden Predictions 225 (9)
Notes on Home Gardens 56 (100)
Notion of Liberation. Buddhist 117 (97)
Notion of Person in Existentialism 117 (97)
Novelist. Edith Wharton: American Woman 151 (238)
Novelist. Saul Bellow, 151 (245)

Novelists. America's Three Most Popular 223 (3)
Novelists You Should Know. Contemporary 151 (234)
Novelty Yarns, Their Creation and Use 79 (130)
Now Have Enough Things Black 224 (4)
Now That You Can Run a Drilling Rig, Can You Run a Drilling Business? 136 (7)
NROTC 105 (71), (72), (73)
Nuclear Density Level and Belt Scale Process Gauges 67 (19)
Nuclear Disarmament 214 (83)
Nuclear Energy. Politics of 117 (106)
Nuclear Energy Regulation 151 (133)
Nuclear Energy. Why 151 (129)
Nuclear Engineering. IEOR in 216 (87)
Nuclear Magnetic Resonance Techniques 159 (56)
Nuclear Medicine. Current Techniques in 218
Nuclear Methods in Criminal Investigations 151 (156)
Nuclear Physics 142 (65)
Nuclear Power 29 (51), 181 (18), 189, 216 (91)
Nuclear Power - Boom or Bust? 29 (255), (268)
Nuclear Power in Meeting the Energy Crisis. Role of 216 (103)
Nuclear Power. Moral Question of 151 (133)
Nuclear Power. Nature's Way 152
Nuclear Power Option in Perspective 27 (9)
Nuclear Power Plant Waste. Disposal of 151 (128)
Nuclear Power Plants. Energy and Petroleum Resources, Earthquakes - Prediction, Control, and 27 (4)
Nuclear Power Plants. Safety of 151 (132), 216 (103)
Nuclear Power Plants. Siting of 218
Nuclear Power: Problems and Promise 151 (137)
Nuclear Power. Public Concern About 216 (103)
Nuclear Power Question 216 (64)
Nuclear Power. Risks of 218
Nuclear Radiation and Infant Mortality 151 (262)
Nuclear Radiation. Effects of 31 (30)
Nuclear Reactors 216 (88), (91)
Nuclear Safety and Risks in Perspective 31 (30)
Nuclear - the Viable Alternative 66 (3)
Nuclear War 216 (131)
Nuclear Waste Disposal 31 (30)
Nuclear Weapon Strategy 29 (51)
Nuclear Weapon Strategy. Changes in 29 (255), (268)
Nuclear Weapons be Controlled? Can 29 (256), (292)
Number System. Our 117 (92)
Number Theory? 181 (149)
Numismatics. Classical 227 (46)
Nuptse. Drama of 69 (5)
Nurse. Liability and the School 117 (46)
Nurse Midwife. Homebirths and the 122 (2)
Nursery - 4th Grade. Language Arts and Math Activities for Teachers - 117 (48)
Nursing 174 (7)
Nursing. Continuing Education in 214 (72)
Nursing. Critical Care 218
Nursing Education 105 (43)
Nursing Education. Balance of Research and Teaching in 105 (49)
Nursing Education. Issues in 151 (256)
Nursing Home Abuses 176 (103)
Nursing. Medico - Moral Legal Ethics in 105 (49)
Nursing. Psychiatric 105 (95)
Nutrient? Dietary Fiber - Essential 216 (134)
Nutrients in Foods. Effect of Food Processing on 216 (72)
Nutrition 142 (20), 176 (31), (70), (82)
Nutrition and Activity for the Overweight 117 (79)
Nutrition and Consumerism 214 (24), (71)
Nutrition and Cooking. Vegetarian 218
Nutrition and Diet 181 (166)
Nutrition and Health Foods 151 (174)
Nutrition and Mental Development 218
Nutrition and You 57 (86)
Nutrition. Athletic Performance and 216 (134)
Nutrition Beliefs. Food and 57 (30)
Nutrition Education Program in Pennsylvania. Expanded 151 (171)
Nutrition. Food and 187 (1)
Nutrition for Everyday Living. Modern 181 (187)
Nutrition for Modern 49'ers 57 (30)
Nutrition for the Family 117 (79)
Nutrition for the Future 159 (12)
Nutrition for the Two of You 57 (30)
Nutrition in Developing Countries. Human 16 (53)
Nutrition - It's Your Choice 57 (15)
Nutrition of Plants. Mineral 218
Nutrition. Poultry 216 (97)
Nutrition Program in Haiti. Applied 216 (40)
Nutritional Value and Items of Interest. Eggs, 216 (35)
Nuts and Bolts of Photography 151 (71)
Nuts and Bolts of Success 112 (5)
Nuts, Guts, and Feathers of Selling 180 (2)
Nuts in California. Macademia 224 (10)

O

OSHA Requirements and Safety Measures in the Electric Industry 150 (6)
OTC Prescription Drug Interactions 54
O.K. Let's Talk About It 180 (11)
Obedience. Dog 142 (26)
Obesity and Health 151 (208)
Obesity. Appetite Regulatory Mechanisms in 171 (26)
Obesity. Psychology of 105 (100), (102)
Object of Man's Creation and the Means of Its Attainment 1 (11)
Obligation of Industry and the Role of Interships in Advertising Education 151 (75)

Obscenity and Freedom of Expression 218
Obscenity Law. Obscenity Problem and 116 (1 - 7)
Obscenity Problem and Obscenity Law 116 (1 - 7)
Observations on Russia, Alaska, or New Mexico 56 (116)
Observing the World Around Us 171 (51)
Obstetrical Care. Modern 181 (167)
Occult Scene of the 70's 154 (12)
Occultism in the Ancient World 151 (259)
Occupational Lung Disease 181 (156)
Occupational Outlook 151 (55)
Occupational Stress: The Elements Which Contribute to Stress on the Job 117 (19)
Occupational Therapeutic Activities 159 (31)
Occupational Therapy 181 (127)
Occupational Therapy in the Community 159 (31)
Occupational Therapy Yesterday, Today, and Tomorrow 159 (31)
Ocean Engineering? What is 216 (108)
Ocean Exploration. Future of 225 (7)
Ocean Near Guam. Under the 223 (34)
Ocean Ridges. Tectonics of 218
Ocean Wealth. Peace, Ecology, and 214 (27)
Oceans 56 (68)
Oceans - Conservation or Exploitation 97 (38)
Oceans. Fate of the 214 (27)
Oceans. Future Control of the 57 (19)
Oceans. National Policy for the 218
O'Connor Reports. Len 135 (48)
Odd Thing Happened on the Way to the Office 113 (3)
Odors in Drinking Water. Earthy 16 (85)
Odyssey. 2001: A Space 154 (17)
Of Cabbages and Kings and Things 97 (33)
Off-Loom-Board or Frame Set Ups. Weaving 79 (127)
Off-Loom Techniques 79 (53)
Off-Loom Weaving 79 (85), (150)
Off-Loom Weaving Techniques 79 (149)
Offenses. Sex 29 (49)
Office Administration 174 (96)
Office and Public Education. State 57 (10)
Office and You. Government Printing 56 (99)
Office. Antitrust Section of the Attorney General's 168 (27)
Office. Exercises for the 174 (64)
Office Management 65 (8), (9), (11), (12), (15), (19), (28), (38), (48), (52), (53), (63), (64), (68), (70)
Office Management, Operation, and Forms 65 (32)
Office Operations 65 (47)
Officers Training Corps. Reserve 105 (74)
Officials. Packaging Our Elected 117 (106)
Officiating and Professionalism 105 (114)
Officiating High School Football 16 (42)
Officiating. Sport 57 (74)
Officiating Sports 151 (93)
Offshore Drilling 74
Offshore Exploration and Production 35
Ohio! Hello 144
Ohio River Valley Sanitary Water Commission 151 (154)
Ohm's Law: Is It Enforceable? 151 (73)
Oil and Gas Conservation and Regulation - State and Federal 151 (135)
Oil and Gas Exploration (United States) 151 (124)
Oil and Gas Industry - Drilling and Production 151 (135)
Oil and Gas Industry - Supply and Demand 151 (135)
Oil and Gas Supply. Realities of 181 (131), (209)
Oil and You 174 (87)
Oil. Cost of Imported 31 (23)
Oil Famine. Americas 97 (35)
Oil in a Revolutionary Age. Middle East 3 (5)
Oil Industry 220 (1)
Oil Recovery in Pennsylvania. Enhanced 151 (138)
Oil Sands of Alberta 181 (131), (336)
Oil Tankers on Puget Sound 218
Old Lady in Tennis Shoes Syndrome 168 (22)
Old Testament 52 (73)
Old. You're Never Too 105 (34)
Older, Disadvantaged College Student 181 (201), (308)
Olympic Games: Arena of World Problems 151 (275)
Olympic Games. Differences in Ancient and Modern 151 (275)
Olympic Games. History of the Ancient 151 (275)
Olympic Games 30 Years Ago 181 (2)
Olympic Team and Athletes. America's First 151 (275)
Olympics 182 (6)
Olympics. Comparison of United States - U.S.S.R. Training for the 29 (296), (306)
Olympics. Men's Gymnastics: From High School to the 168 (2)
Ombudsman 29 (260)
Ombudsman in Public Education 57 (10)
Ombudsman Service of Vancouver. Computer 171 (12)
On Aging and Dying 142 (62)
On Being a Rational Animal Today 168 (60)
On Being a Translator 151 (235)
On Dealing With the F.B.I. 97 (69)
On Making a Good Academic Decision 151 (104)
On Safari in Africa 29 (319)
On the Nature of Truth, Goodness, and Beauty 117 (98)
On the Sunny Side of the Street 83 (9)
Once and Future Family 211 (2)
One Bell System - It Works 144
One Hundred Percent Commission Concept 65 (15)
One Hundred Years of Agricultural Research 16 (70)
One Man's View of the Washington State Legislature 223 (22)

Only a Day to Anywhere 100 (1)
Ontology of Values 29 (116), (241)
Open Concept Schools - What Are They? 159 (53)
Open Education 151 (111), 181 (118)
Open Road 112 (45)
Open Wide and Laugh 112 (72)
Opening the Doors 144
Opening Up Systems of Government 174 (79)
Opening Up the Classroom - Activities and Suggestions for Individualizing and Informalizing Education 117 (48)
Opera 181 (85)
Opera as a Contemporary Art Form 142 (16)
Opera. Designing for Theatre and 154 (22)
Opera History 142 (16)
Opera in the United States and Europe 154 (22)
Operas. Soap 176 (125)
Operation of Radio and Television Stations 117 (86)
Operation Tigris 69 (1)
Operational Gaming 151 (148)
Operational Significance of Marxist - Leninist Ideology in the 1970's 85 (31)
Operations Research 142 (70)
Operetta. German 216 (112)
Opportunities for Women in Engineering 151 (142)
Opportunities in Aviation 151 (34)
Opportunity in the Two-Year College 56 (44)
Opposition Currents in the Soviet Union and Eastern Europe Today 213 (13)
Optical Causes of Color in Foods 67 (17)
Oral Cancer 181 (182)
Oral Cancer Detection. Early 181 (183)
Oral History and Teaching 181 (93)
Oral History Techniques 142 (5)
Oral Interpretation and the Liturgy 105 (110)
Oral Interviewing 29 (153), (211)
Oral Surgery 181 (161)
Orange County. Art in 29 (10)
Orange County History 29 (139), (160), (333)
Orbital View of the Current Scene 97 (14)
Orchestra. American Symphony 57 (42)
Orchestral Music 142 (57)
Orchids as Windowsill Plants 151 (237)
Order, Freedom, Law and Political Institutions 85 (40)
Organ Transplants. Legal and Medical Aspects of 54
Organic Chemistry 181 (199)
Organic Form With Respect to Time and Space. Reappraisal of 54
Organic Gardening 216 (62)
Organization and Functions of ARC (Associations for Retarded) 169 (2)
Organization Can Have an Effective Newspaper. Your 168 (51)
Organization. Management and 180 (77)
Organization Versus Order 105 (32)
Organizational Behavior and Motivation 151 (43)
Organizational Effectiveness 56 (136)
Organizational Transactional Analysis 27 (7)
Organizations. Professional Teacher 174 (49)
Organized Crime 97 (60), 168 (49), 181 (264)
Organizing and Managing United States Foreign Policy 151 (196)
Organizing the English Curriculum 57 (48)
Organizing the Small Museum 57 (56)
Organizing Women 142 (14)
Organophosphate Pesticides and Food Production 117 (3)
Orient 142 (55)
Orient. India and the 105 (20)
Orient. Pearls of the 151 (264)
Orient. Status of Esperanto in the 58 (1)
Oriental Art 57 (44), 159 (18)
Oriental Languages 168 (55)
Oriental: Myth and Folklore 29 (15), (200)
Oriental Philosophy 117 (97)
Oriental Religion 214 (80)
Orientation 65 (46)
Origin of Life 151 (211)
Origin of Mountains 142 (88)
Origin of the California Indians 29 (19), (165), (339)
Origin of the English Language 29 (209), (298)
Origins and History of Washington Flora 218
Origins of Christian Monasticism 29 (178), (234)
Origins of the American Tradition in Foreign Affairs 85 (7)
Ornamental Braiding 79 (122)
Ornamentals Around the Home 151 (25)
Ornaments in the Scandinavian Manner. Weaving Straw 79 (38)
Osage Braid 79 (80)
Oscillations in the Eye and Brain 31 (24)
Osteoporosis 181 (188)
Other Federal Income Tax Topics 105 (7)
Our American Heritage 222
Our Changing World 135 (47)
Our Energy Situation 31 (23)
Our Foods 216 (67)
Our Foreign Policy of Ruin 225 (36)
Our Freedoms and How to Fight for Them 97 (48)
Our Greatest General R.E. Lee 57 (28)
Our National Anthem 57 (91)
Our Neighbors to the North 56 (121)
Our Number System 117 (92)
Our Plundered Planet 29 (48), (70)
Our Police Problems 29 (49)
Our Police Problems - Whose Fault 29 (133)
Our Wildlife in a Changing World 151 (306)
Out of This Furnace 31 (31)
Out-Patient Pharmacy Services. Clinical Approach to 54
Outback Australia 59 (1)
Outdoor Recreation and Conservation 171 (37)
Outdoor Recreational Activities 105 (114)
Outer Banks and Man 56 (33), (72)
Outlaw. American and the Australian 223 (3)

Outstanding Jewish Scientists 181 (279)
Oven Safety. Microwave 105 (119)
Overcoming Objections 65 (11), (44)
Overcoming Obstacles to Achieve Productivity in Business 27 (8)
Overcoming Problems in Slack Fill 67 (9)
Overseas Information. America's 105 (54)
Overshot and What You Can Do With It 79 (145)
Overweight. Nutrition and Activity for the 117 (79)
Ovid 227 (35)
Ovid Pierce on What the Present Can Learn From the Past 56 (36)
Ovid Pierce's The Wedding Guest 56 (36)
Ovid Pierce's View of Eastern North Carolina 56 (36)
Ovid, the Wit of the Augustan Age 227 (23)
Ovids Metamorphoses 227 (32)
Owl. Three Months With Grey 171 (14)
Owls). Birds of Prey (Hawks and 151 (309)
Oxford, Cambridge and British Higher Education 223 (10)

P

PVC Rollers and Pulleys. V-trough Carriers and 67 (28)
P.S.U. Giving is Old But New to 151 (185)
Pabst History, Marketing and Advertising. Story of 145 (1), (2), (3)
Pace With Tomorrow. Keeping 118 (1)
Pacemakers. Cardiac 181 (194)
Pacific Crest Trail. Long Distance Backpacking on the 166 (1)
Pacific Northwest National Parks. Fauna of 218
Pacific Paradise. Micronesia, America's 15 (1)
Pacifism, Socialism and Nonviolence. Foreign Policy and Its Relationship to 217 (2)
Packaging Design and Corporate Graphics 147 (1 - 11)
Packaging. Gas Flushing Horizontal Form, Fill and Seal 67 (15)
Packaging Foods and Beverages. Bottling and 67 (10)
Packaging Our Elected Officials 117 (106)
Paddling. Whitewater 216 (126)
Pagan Celtic Art. Early 181 (79)
Pain in Childbirth and Methods for Combating Them. Major Causes of 36 (1)
Pain. Phenomenon of 218
Painted Warp 79 (147)
Painterly Photography and Photographic Painting 151 (73)
Painting. Batik, Dye 79 (79)
Painting. 18th Century English 56 (10)
Painting. Genesis of Landscape 56 (13)
Painting Government Into a Corner 85 (25)
Painting. History of Watercolor 56 (13)
Painting in the Music of Byrd. Word 151 (26)
Painting. Painterly Photography and Photographic 151 (73)
Painting. Poempeiian Mythological 227 (35)
Painting, Sculpture and Architecture. Cubism - Major Route of Modern 56 (10)
Painting. Understanding Chinese 57 (52)
Paintings. Fiber 79 (75)
Pakistan. History of India and 56 (92)
Pakistan, India. Indian Subcontinent - Bangladesh, 16 (81)
Pakistan. Social and Cultural Facts About 29 (19), (181)
Pakistan. Social and Economic Problems of India and 56 (118)
Palatable Writing Experiences 151 (231)
Paleontological Field Work in Ethiopia 218
Palestine Problem - Prospects for Peace 151 (291)
Palmistry: Your Life Is in Your Hands 117 (96)
Palsy. Cerebral 181 (195)
Pan-Africanism 151 (217), 181 (25), (331)
Panama Canal Treaty Talks 151 (213)
Panama Crisis 151 (83)
Panels on Creative Process 227 (9)
Paper. Pulp and 73
Paper. Weaving on 79 (105)
Paper. Working on 79 (6)
Papers. Rickenbacker 135 (54)
Paradise. Caribbean 59 (14)
Paradise - Foreign Students. Strangers in 151 (200)
Paradise. Micronesia, America's Pacific 15 (1)
Paradise? Minority Studies: Beyond Takenism. Latin America: A Racial 168 (25)
Paradox of a Forgotten Land 168 (26)
Parameters of a Reading Program. Balancing the 181 (108)
Paraplegia. Thriving in Spite of 151 (136)
Paraprofessionals in Psychology. Training 168 (7)
Parapsychology 105 (77), 134 (4)
Parasitology. Veterinary 16 (4)
Paratransit 31 (40)
Parent Adoptive Experience. Single 181 (247)
Parent-Child Communications 216 (106)
Parent-Child Relationship 142 (45)
Parent. How to 97 (17)
Parenteral Therapy 181 (197)
Parenthood Education. Compulsory 151 (169)
Parenthood. Non- 129 (1 - 4)
Parenthood. Single 142 (14)
Parenting 142 (45)
Parenting, a Difficult Job 57 (34)
Parenting. Art of 117 (43)
Parenting With Versality 181 (292)
Parents and Reading 151 (93)
Parents and Teachers Can Encourage Creativity. Helping Children to Be More Creative - Ways 117 (48)

Parents and Teachers. Drug Abuse - A Course for 56 (83)
Parents, and Teachers. Self-concept of Children, 216 (40)
Parents and the Reading Program 181 (107), (123)
Parents Can Change Our Schools. How 112 (89)
Parents Can Deal With and Understand Young Children. Positive Approach to Discipline Problems - Effective Ways 117 (48)
Parents. Children, Discipline, and 151 (172)
Parent's Experiences With Mental Retardation 216 (9)
Parents - First Teachers of Children 151 (172)
Parent's Groups 142 (4)
Parents - How to Help Your Child Succeed in School 29 (93), (342)
Parents of Handicapped Children and Solution 142 (61)
Parents. Prenatal Education for 57 (64)
Parents' Rights 57 (5)
Parents' Role in Career Decision Making 151 (88)
Parents' Role in the Education of a Young Child 117 (45)
Parents. Sex Education for 57 (64)
Parents Too. Fathers are 159 (48)
Paris 142 (98)
Paris of the Parisians 59 (7)
Paris, That Beloved Monster 117 (138)
Parish. Doing Theology in the 105 (106)
Parisians. Paris of the 59 (7)
Park: Its Lure to Young and Old. University 151 (6)
Park Ranger in South Dakota 57 (43)
Parks. Energy 151 (150)
Parks. Mobile Homes and 65 (53)
Parks of the Southwest. National 57 (43)
Parliamentary Procedure. Use of 117 (128)
Part-time Student 171 (15)
Participation and Leadership. Effective Conference 56 (20)
Participation. Civic 65 (4), (46)
Participation in Government Policy Making. Citizen 218
Participation in University Governance. Faculty 105 (49)
Participation in University Policy Making. Student 16 (21)
Participation. Masculinity-Femininity and Sport 151 (276)
Participation. Motivational Aspects of Sports 57 (74)
Participative Strategy. Student Leadership Development: A 151 (107)
Particles. Elementary 181 (277), 216 (131)
Parties in North Carolina and the United States. Political 56 (131)
Parties. Political 105 (55)
Parties? What's Happening to the Political 218
Partly Cloudy. Six Inches of 83 (8)
Partners in Progress 151 (12)
Partners in Progress - Berks County and the Berks Campus of Penn State 151 (112)
Partners in Progress - Cooperative Education 151 (95)
Party. Democratic 176 (53)
Party History 172 (5)
Party Over? Is the 151 (219)
Party Planning Par Excellence 97 (15)
Passover. Christ in the 93 (3)
Past Preserved for the Present 174 (41)
Past Problems and Future Aspirations 171 (59)
Patchwork. Seminole 79 (125)
Patent, Trademark and Copyright Law 105 (56)
Paternalism, Economics, and the Welfare State 85 (14)
Pathology. Teaching 181 (182)
Pathways Through England 59 (16)
Patient Care. Management of 105 (95)
Patient. Care of the Hand Injured 56 (79)
Patient Records in Drug Abuse and Alcoholism 181 (177)
Patient Susceptibility to Adverse Drug Reactions 54
Patients' Access to Medical Records 181 (185), (235)
Patolas 79 (131)
Patriot. Aaron Burr, Rascal 103 (5)
Patriotism 189
Pattern 79 (139)
Pattern Development. Drafting and Loom Controlled 79 (95)
Pattern Drafting for Four-harness Looms 79 (122)
Pattern Drafting for Multi-harness Looms 79 (122)
Pattern in Design and the Crafts 79 (108)
Pattern Making and Clothing Construction and Theory 79 (28)
Pattern of Cities - Understanding Their Locations 174 (51)
Pattern Weaving. Use of Color in Weaving, Design, and 79 (24)
Patterning. Weft Faced Loom Controlled 79 (132)
Patterns, A Contemporary View 79 (119)
Patterns. American Jewish Voting 214 (14), (48)
Patterns. Communication Transportation, and Settlement 151 (183)
Patterns. Medieval Living 31 (28)
Patterns of Asian Politics. New 105 (57)
Patterns of Family Interaction 56 (7)
Patterns. Presidential Voting 181 (266)
Pavement Skid Resistance for Safe Travel 151 (291)
Pavements for Highways and Airports. Bituminous 151 (291)
Pax Americana in Asia. End of 105 (57)
Pay for Them. Schools in Illinois: How We 57 (55)
Pay What You Pay. Why You 66 (4)
Payroll Taxes 105 (7)
Peace and Disarmament 172 (6)
Peace. Challenge of 103 (1)
Peace Corps: The Modern Adventure 151 (118)
Peace, Ecology, and Ocean Wealth 214 (27)

Peace in the Middle East? 214 (55)
Peace in the Middle East. How to Achieve 57 (61)
Peace. Islam and the World 1 (2)
Peace. Middle East in War and 181 (339)
Peace. Palestine Problem - Prospects for 151 (291)
Peace. United Nations and World 102 (14)
Peace. Yoga - A Journey to Inner 151 (88)
Pearl Harbor 181 (265)
Pearls of the Orient 151 (264)
Peasant in Europe and America. Portuguese 29 (123), (164)
Peasant in the Art of Peter Bruegel 105 (61)
Pebble Weave. Peruvian 79 (90)
Peculiar Service. CIA - A 97 (54)
Peculiarities of Islam 1 (10)
Pedagogy. Foreign Language 142 (6)
Pedestrian Pittsburgh 31 (31)
Pediatric Dentistry. Modern 105 (30)
Pediatrician Straightens Out the World 113 (3)
Pelvic Cancer 181 (168)
Penalty or Permissiveness 83 (12)
Penance in the Early Church. Sacrament of 105 (107)
Penance, Its Development and Renewal. Sacrament of 105 (104)
Penn State. Aerospace Engineering at 151 (34)
Penn State and the Future 151 (101)
Penn State and the United States Congress 151 (191)
Penn State. Athletic Programs at 151 (281)
Penn State Curriculum 151 (55)
Penn State Does for You. What 151 (67)
Penn State. Engineering and Engineering Technology at 151 (149)
Penn State. Engineering Research at 151 (139)
Penn State. Hazleton Campus of 151 (4)
Penn State. History and Current Status of Instructional Television at 151 (66)
Penn State. Improvement of Instruction at 151 (99)
Penn State. Internationals in State College and 151 (173)
Penn State McKeesport Campus 51 (13)
Penn State. Middle East Studies at 151 (194)
Penn State. News of 151 (64)
Penn State. Partners in Progress - Berks County and the Berks Campus of 151 (112)
Penn State. Private Giving to 151 (187)
Penn State Rockview Beef Project 151 (182)
Penn State Serves Hearing Impaired. How 151 (113)
Penn State Services to the Community 151 (117)
Penn State - Something for Everyone 151 (203)
Penn State. Sports Research at 151 (209)
Penn State Students 151 (108)
Penn State Way. Power Volleyball the 151 (286)
Penn State? Why Private Support for 151 (185)
Penn State's Commonwealth Campus System 151 (64)
Penn State's Management Development Services 151 (287)
Penn State's Many Faces 151 (6)
Pennsylvania Agriculture 151 (22), (263)
Pennsylvania Architecture 151 (257)
Pennsylvania. Black Bear of 151 (306)
Pennsylvania. Caves and Caving in 151 (128)
Pennsylvania. Colonial 151 (216)
Pennsylvania Dutch: Land of the Hex Sign 117 (75)
Pennsylvania. Enhanced Oil Recovery in 151 (138)
Pennsylvania. Expanded Nutrition Education Program in 151 (171)
Pennsylvania. Foreign Student Education Implications for 151 (107)
Pennsylvania Income Tax. Federal and 151 (44)
Pennsylvania. Poisonous Plants of 54
Pennsylvania Politics (Governor William W. Scranton) 151 (222)
Pennsylvania. Revolutionary 151 (216)
Pennsylvania. Role of Private Higher Education in 54
Pennsylvania 1776 151 (257)
Pennsylvania State University. Affirmative Action at the 151 (1)
Pennsylvania State University - Is It for You? 151 (90)
Pennsylvania Technical Assistance Program Can Help You. How the 151 (47)
Pennsylvania. Transportation in 151 (292)
PENNTAP Can Help 151 (123)
PENNTAP Style. Technology Transfer 151 (124)
PENNTAP Style. Transferring Technology 151 (288)
Pentagon Papers to Cointelpro. From 213 (1)
People. Accidents Can Kill Businesses as Well as 136 (4)
People. Administering Through 105 (51)
People. Alaska - It's Schools and 57 (81)
People. Americans Are 97 (43)
People and Literature. Appalachian 168 (26)
People and Of the People. Arts to the 57 (38)
People and Their Problems 112 (16)
People Are My Business 105 (12)
People are People 100 (2)
People. Art of Motivating 151 (38)
People. Arts to the People and of the 57 (38)
People Business 180 (13)
People Can We Feed? How Many 151 (160)
People. Communication Among 174 (1)
People. Diet Therapy for Sick 117 (94)
People. Ethiopia, the County and Her 117 (142)
People Fail. Why Businesses Fail: Why 135 (58)
People for Profits. Motivation of 65 (20)
People. Housing is for 216 (141)
People. How to Deal Successfully With 180 (4)
People in Motion. Rehabilitation - Putting 56 (79)
People in Process. Dance, Bodies and 181 (82)
People in the News 176 (73)
People. Lazy Man's Trip to the Bank or Real Estate, the Profession of Happy 65 (20)
People. Legal Rights of Students and Young 231 (2)
People. Marxes Are the Craziest 154 (16)
People Misunderstand Business? Why do 23

People of Ararat: Armeniams and Their Contributions 105 (23)
People of New Hebrides 69 (9)
People. Pesticides, Pollution and 216 (38)
People, Places. Fiber, 79 (5)
People. Plants are Like 97 (3)
People Play. Why 151 (276)
People. Press and the 102 (34)
People, Quality, and Priorities 151 (101)
People. Relating to 169 (74)
People. Right to Work - Supported by Facts, Figures and the American 131 (1)
People Should Know About Alcohol Intoxication. Facts 54
People - the Pokomo of Kenya. River 56 (2), (114)
People Through Face and Body Language. Greater Understanding of 212 (1)
People Time. Managing Other 182 (1), (2), (3)
People. Too Many 54
People. Training and Conditioning Young 168 (33)
People. U.S.S.R. Land and 117 (62), (72)
People. Working With Young 159 (67)
People. Young Person's Perspective on the Rights of Young 231 (1)
People's Fund of Philadelphia 181 (309)
People's Liberation? What is Young 231 (3)
People's Republic of China 224 (7)
People's Republic of China. Current Affairs in 181 (341)
People's Republic of China. Economy of the 216 (74)
People's Republic of China. Women in the 151 (11)
People's Right to Know 181 (68)
Peopling: Humanizing the Educational Process 117 (43)
Percent Commission Concept. One Hundred 65 (15)
Perception 151 (62)
Perception and the Real World. Visual 29 (229), (264)
Perception Dynamics 225 (18)
Perception. Experimental 214 (79)
Perception. Extra Sensory 214 (79)
Perception. Sensation and 216 (24)
Perception. Speech 151 (96)
Perceptual Motor Development 159 (26)
Performance Appraisal 151 (46)
Performance Evaluation 181 (47), (299)
Performance. French Horn 57 (29)
Performance Testing. Beef Cattle Breeding and 216 (9)
Performance. Verbal, Vocal and Visual Cues to Better Job 180 (1)
Performing Arts 142 (92)
Perils. Future Promises and 151 (236)
Periodicals. History of American Juvenile 117 (75)
Periods in Music. Historical 54
Permanent Things. Protest, Revolution, and the 85 (16)
Permissiveness. Penalty or 83 (12)
Persistent Social Problem. Juvenile Delinquency as a 27 (37)
Person Dead? Is the Sales 16 (6)
Person in Existentialism. Notion of 117 (97)
Person Monologues. First 168 (34)
Person Singular. First 97 (11)
Person These Times Demand 75 (1)
Person Tick. What Makes a 105 (98)
Person-to-Person Communication 174 (56)
Personal Adjustment. Stress and 174 (94)
Personal Art Work. Discussion of 117 (10)
Personal Budgeting 174 (63)
Personal Communication. Essentials of Effective 105 (12)
Personal Counseling 180 (108)
Personal Defense for Women 151 (205)
Personal Development 180 (152)
Personal. Economics of Rights - Property and 85 (14)
Personal Finance 168 (45)
Personal Injury Law 159 (22)
Personal Management in Selling 112 (124)
Personal Motivation 180 (40)
Personal Revolution 181 (292)
Personal. Strictly 112 (55)
Personal Time Management 151 (48)
Personalities. Metals Have 218
Personality 151 (163)
Personality and Mental Health 105 (98)
Personality Development 65 (36)
Personality. Impact of Guidance on 54
Personality/Leadership 105 (77)
Personality Tests. Interest, Intelligence, and 168 (28)
Personalized Education. Individualized - 117 (50)
Personally Useful Psychology. Teaching 57 (45)
Personnel Administration 223 (6)
Personnel Administration in the Public Schools 16 (18)
Personnel Management 142 (42), 216 (105)
Personnel Management and Administration 105 (11)
Personnel Management and Motivation 181 (41)
Personnel. Sales and Management 180 (106)
Personnel - 1776-2076 105 (9)
Persons? Girls, Ladies, Women, or 151 (61)
Perspectives in Product Liability 31 (33)
Perspectives in Product Safety 31 (33)
Perspectives on Pollution 31 (13)
Perspectives on the Current State of the Economy 168 (43)
Persuasion 142 (25)
Persuasion and Motivation 65 (28)
Persuasion. Creative 112 (61)
Persuasion in a Democracy. Role of 117 (65), (112)
Persuasive Speaker 168 (17)
Persuasive Writing 168 (39)
Peruvian Needle Knitting 79 (65)
Peruvian Pebble Weave 79 (90)
Peruvian Pick-up 79 (145)
Peruvian Textiles 79 (65)

Peruvian Textiles. Ancient 79 (63)
Pesticides 171 (39)
Pesticides and Food Production. Organophosphate 117 (3)
Pesticides. Health Effects of 171 (39)
Pesticides in the Environment. Fate nand Behavior of 171 (39)
Pesticides. Pollution and People 216 (38)
Pesticides, Pollution and Politics 16 (14)
Pesticides Regulation 204
Pesticides. Safe Use of 189
Pests. Biological Control of Plant and Animal 31 (8)
Pet Population Control 218
Peter Bruegel. Peasant in the Art of 105 (61)
Peter Duchin. Musical World of 102 (7)
Petroleum Resources, Earthquakes - Prediction, Control, and Nuclear Power Plants. Energy and 27 (4)
Petronius 227 (1)
Pets 176 (60)
Phamlysoun. From the Land of the 56 (26)
Phantom. Unisex 171 (28)
Pharmaceutical Services. Ambulatory 54
Pharmaceutical Services. Why and How of Ambulatory 54
Pharmaceutics. Cutaneous Reactions to Cosmetics and Topical 54
Pharmacist. Emerging Clinical Role of the 16 (77)
Pharmacist. How to Choose Your 181 (186)
Pharmacological Aspects. Drug Addiction - the Physiological and 54
Pharmacology. Behavioral 142 (69)
Pharmacology. Food 171 (26)
Pharmacy Clinic - Outgrow of the Clinical Pharmacy 54
Pharmacy. Hospital 181 (197)
Pharmacy. Practice of a Clinical 54
Pharmacy Services 16 (60)
Pharmacy Services. Clinical Approach to Out-patient 54
Pharmacy Services. Evolution of A Clinical 54
Phenomena of the Mind - Mentalism and Hypnotism 114 (2)
Phenomenology and God 117 (97)
Phenomenon of Pain 218
Philadelphia 181 (184)
Philadelphia. Architecture of Colonial 151 (29)
Philadelphia Black Community 181 (29)
Philadelphia. Geology of 181 (137)
Philadelphia Landscape 181 (132)
Philadelphia. People's Fund of 181 (309)
Philadelphian. How to Talk Like a 181 (226), (317)
Philanthropic Foundations in Wisconsin 105 (53)
Philanthropy? Do Students Still Need Private 151 (89)
Philippines. Village Life in the 151 (162)
Philippines. Visit to the 151 (299)
Philosopher's Role Today. Educational 181 (102)
Philosophers and Natural Rights. American 214 (73)
Philosophical Aspects of Mathematics 56 (129)
Philosophical Assumptions of Psychotherapy. Some 29 (245)
Philosophical Background of Freedom of Press 117 (85)
Philosophical Considerations in Education 168 (1)
Philosophical Considerations. Life After Death - Some 105 (91)
Philosophical Definition of Violence 214 (73)
Philosophical Truth and the Meaning of Ideology 85 (20)
Philosophies. Ancient Religion and 117 (64)
Philosophies. Hamilton and Jefferson: Comparison and Controls of 117 (77)
Philosophies. Modern and Contemporary 117 (98)
Philosophy 224 (17)
Philosophy. America and American 214 (73)
Philosophy. American Politics and Political 85 (11)
Philosophy. American Social and Political 214 (75)
Philosophy. Ancient 227 (34)
Philosophy and Education. Contemporary 57 (85)
Philosophy and Ordinary Life 171 (55)
Philosophy and Psychology of Yoga 181 (300)
Philosophy and Technology 216 (95)
Philosophy and Women's Liberation 29 (251)
Philosophy as a Base for Counseling 168 (1)
Philosophy. Challenges to the Logical-Empirical School of 29 (232), (268)
Philosophy. Coaching 168 (24)
Philosophy. Early Greek Lyric Poetry and 227 (46)
Philosophy. Indian 218
Philosophy. Moral 214 (76)
Philosophy. Mysticism/Non-Western 142 (22)
Philosophy of Education 105 (47)
Philosophy of India 142 (81)
Philosophy of Religion 56 (137)
Philosophy of Science. Aspects of History and 218
Philosophy of Science. History and 142 (31)
Philosophy of Suffering 105 (89)
Philosophy. Oriental 117 (97)
Philosophy. Restoration of 85 (23)
Philosophy. Role of 216 (95)
Philosophy. Social Policy and 172 (2)
Philosophy. Socrates and the Unwritten 174 (5)
Philosophy. Teilhard and 11 (3)
Philosophy? What is 174 (89)
Philosophy. Worth of 105 (90)
Phone for All It's Worth. Use Your 144
Phonetics and Language Learning 29 (203)
Phonetics. Articulatory 56 (65)
Phonology, Morphology, Syntax of English 56 (65)
Photo Diary. Nepal 4 (2)
Photo Imagery on Fabric With Photo Silkscreen (4)
Photo Silkscreen. Photo Imagery on Fabric With 79 (4)
Photograph. Everyone Can Take a Pleasing 136 (16)
Photographic Images on Fabric 79 (129)
Photographic Insights 97 (27)

Photographic Painting. Painterly Photography and 151 (73)
Photographing Exotic Places 29 (38), (319)
Photographing Nature 4 (2)
Photographing Wildflowers 216 (20)
Photographs. Unusual 174 (79)
Photography 168 (16)
Photography and Photographic Painting. Painterly 151 (73)
Photography as Self-Expression 171 (47)
Photography. Beginnings of 151 (73)
Photography. Creative 171 (47)
Photography. Flowers and 216 (58)
Photography. Frontiers of Wildlife 69 (11)
Photography in Eastern Europe. Early 151 (73)
Photography in Education 171 (47)
Photography. Nuts and Bolts of 151 (71)
Photography Premeditated Fantasy. Los Angeles Contemporary 29 (9)
Photography. Scientific Evidence for Ghosts and Psychic 154 (12)
Photography. Underwater 218
Photomechanics 216 (11)
Photomicrography 181 (169)
Photos in Resource Management. Aerial 151 (304)
Photosensitized Fabrics. Printing on 79 (4)
Photosynthetic Bacteria 159 (49)
Physical and Psychological Investigation. Color - 79 (25)
Physical Comedy. Farm and 151 (289)
Physical Education 117 (123), 174 (16), (26)
Physical Education Activities 151 (278)
Physical Education and Athletics 159 (47)
Physical Education, and Leisure Activities in Eastern North Carolina. History of Recreation, 56 (28)
Physical Education. Current Trends in 216 (110)
Physical Education. Elementary 181 (11)
Physical Education. Humanistic 181 (11)
Physical Education. Hypnosis in Athletics and 151 (286)
Physical Education. New 29 (86), (130), (299)
Physical Education. Why Your Elementary School Needs 174 (16)
Physical Environment in Eastern North Carolina. Population on the 56 (36), (38)
Physical Evidence. Utilization of 159 (11)
Physical Fitness 142 (18), (20), 151 (205), 159 (67), 174 (27)
Physical Fitness. Adult 142 (86)
Physical Fitness for Adults 151 (285)
Physical Fitness. President's Council on 105 (114)
Physical, Intellectual and Emotional Domains. Teacher Modeling Behavior in the 117 (39)
Physical Recreation and Education for Leisure 171 (27)
Physical Rehabilitation Needs of the Geriatric 56 (89)
Physical Therapy 159 (17), 181 (200)
Physical Therapy as a Career 56 (79)
Physically Fit. Aerobics, the Art of Keeping 16 (18)
Physically Handicapped Individuals. Legal Rights of Mentally/ 151 (228)
Physician in Homebirth. Practicing 122 (1)
Physics 57 (7), (14), 142 (3)
Physics as a Career 105 (40)
Physics as an Art Form 151 (268)
Physics Biology. Border Area of Chemistry 218
Physics. Careers in 151 (274)
Physics. Casualty and Quantum 56 (129)
Physics for Young and Old. Dramatic Demonstrations in 27 (12)
Physics in Cancer Therapy. Radiation 218
Physics. Nuclear 142 (65)
Physics of Ice 181 (279)
Physics of Ice Skating 181 (7), (279)
Physics of Low Temperature 171 (40)
Physics of Music 171 (40)
Physics of the Laser 171 (40)
Physics. Subnuclear 218
Physics. Use of Hobbies in the Teaching of 57 (87)
Physiological and Pharmacological Aspects. Drug Addiction - the 54
Physiological Effects of Colonization 181 (31), (135)
Physiological Efficiency in Technological Societies 56 (80)
Physiological Psychology 151 (18)
Physiology 54
Physiology. Exercise 174 (27)
Piaget - Some Ideas on Efficient Learning 57 (50)
Piano Sonority and the Poetic Impulse of Debussy and Ravel 174 (41)
Pick-up 79 (139)
Pick-up. Peruvian 79 (145)
Pick-up Weaves. South American 79 (107)
Picture. Minority Groups - A General 27 (42)
Pictorial Stitchery 79 (75)
Pierce on What the Present Can Learn From the Past. Ovid 56 (36)
Pierce's The Wedding Guest. Ovid 56 (36)
Pierce's View of Eastern North Carolina. Ovid 56 (36)
Piety of Celluloid Sin. Popcorn and the 56 (14)
Piget 142 (13)
Pigments. Dyes and 79 (129)
Pigs of Arizona. Desert 151 (302)
Pile Weaves 79 (153)
Pillow Workshops 79 (150)
Pilot Training. Undergraduate 174 (81)
Pin Warp 79 (106)
Pindar 227 (17)
Piping. Flow Characteristics of Solids - Liquid Mixtures in Pumps and 67 (5)
Piping Systems. Designing 67 (18)
Pistol, or Shotgun Class. Forming a Rifle, 57 (58)
Pittsburgh Area. Geology of 151 (13)

Pittsburgh Area. Impact of Duquesne University and Alumni on the 54
Pittsburgh Area. Ethnic Communities in the 54
Pittsburgh. Evolution of 31 (32)
Pittsburgh. Pedestrian 31 (31)
Place in the Business World. Woman's 97 (32)
Place in the Universe. Cosmology - Man's 27 (16)
Place Names. Louisiana 174 (35)
Place of Crafts in a Museum 79 (73)
Place of Immigrant Women in the Hierarchy of Wages 90 (1)
Place of Theatre in the Public Community. Role and 159 (62)
Placement Service. Career Development and 151 (60)
Placement of Students in Jobs 56 (46)
Places. Fiber Activities for Public Places 79 (128)
Places. Fiber, People, 79 (5)
Places. National Register for Historic 174 (19)
Places. Photographing Exotic 29 (38), (319)
Plain Weave Tapestry Techniques 79 (153)
Plaiting 79 (152)
Plaiting. Braiding- 79 (47)
Plan a Conference. How to 57 (51)
Plan. Consumerism as a Marketing 102 (23)
Plan. Guaranteed Trade Sales 65 (18)
Planet. Our Plundered 29 (48), (70)
Planned Selling 112 (61)
Planner and the Public. Planning Process - 56 (101)
Planning 142 (39), 174 (28), 216 (31)
Planning a Deferred Gift for the University 151 (187)
Planning a Three-D Project 79 (40)
Planning, Administering and Evaluating Reading Programs 142 (21)
Planning and Control 54
Planning and Development. Community and Regional 16 (54)
Planning and Goal Setting. Time 65 (32)
Planning and Job Hunting. Career 57 (73)
Planning and Management. Financial 23
Planning and Mineral Potential. Land Use 143 (6)
Planning. Aspects of Ancient Town 227 (32)
Planning Business Education for the Future 117 (14)
Planning. Career 105 (34), 181 (50), (52), 216 (29)
Planning. Career Education for Career 181 (61), (115)
Planning. Career Opportunities by College or Major Career 181 (53)
Planning. Cash Flow 136 (7)
Planning. Central Economic 105 (32)
Planning. City 172 (12)
Planning, Computing in Business and Computing in Education. Management 105 (5)
Planning. Corporate 151 (48)
Planning. Curriculum 142 (4)
Planning. Economics of Regional 168 (43)
Planning. Elements of Menu 216 (25)
Planning. Engineer in Urban and Regional 214 (44)
Planning. Estate 54, 159 (46), 224 (17)
Planning. Facilities 105 (116)
Planning. Financial 214 (1)
Planning. Fiscal 151 (9)
Planning for Doctors and Their Spouses. Estate 8 (5)
Planning for Doctors. Estate 8 (10)
Planning for our Environment. Long-range 171 (37)
Planning for the Developmentally Disabled 27 (32)
Planning for the Future 102 (33)
Planning for the Individual and Small Businessman. Tax 29 (307)
Planning for the 1980's. Career 27 (24)
Planning for Travel 29 (135)
Planning for Travel Pleasure 29 (159)
Planning for Wholesalers. Time-phased Order 29 (77)
Planning for Women. Career 181 (52), (322)
Planning for Women. Estate 136 (21)
Planning for Young People. Career 16 (82)
Planning. Human Needs, Goals and Financial 214 (77)
Planning. Introduction to Urban and Regional 56 (101)
Planning/Job Search for College Students. Career 151 (54)
Planning. Kitchen or Work Space 216 (73)
Planning. Land Use 16 (54), 214 (25)
Planning. Long Range Educational 57 (10)
Planning - Luxury or Necessity. Campus 56 (101)
Planning Methodologies. User Oriented 151 (148)
Planning. Need for Retirement 8 (4)
Planning Par Excellence. Party 97 (15)
Planning. Problems of Social 85 (4)
Planning Process - the Planner and the Public 56 (101)
Planning. Program 105 (81)
Planning. Regional Power 189
Planning. Role of the Community in Land Resource 56 (22)
Planning. State, Regional, and Community 151 (226)
Planning. Techniques of Urban 54
Planning the Distribution System 150 (12)
Planning. Transportation 151 (290)
Planning Travel Pleasure 29 (314)
Planning. Trends in Educational 216 (33)
Planning. University 151 (5)
Planning. Urban Land Use 142 (50)
Planning. Weave 79 (64)
Planning Your Own Degree 168 (22)
Plans and Problems of Education in the Seventies 16 (48)
Plans for College. Making 151 (15)
Plans for Doctors. Deferred Compensation 8 (8)
Plant Alkaloids. Medicinal 54

Plant and Animal Pests. Biological Control of 31 (8)
Plant Biology 168 (13)
Plant Communities. Wild Flowers and 223 (15)
Plant. Design of an Instant Coffee 214 (42)
Plant Diseases and Man. Common 117 (13)
Plant Effects. Air Pollution - 216 (113)
Plant. Electric Generation at a Fossil-fuel Steam Electric 150 (11)
Plant Evolution. Studies in 168 (13)
Plant Genetic Improvement. Animal and 105 (2)
Plant Glycosides. Medicinal 54
Plant Growing Business. Starting a 216 (115)
Plant Material Wall Hangings 79 (96)
Plant Materials 216 (6)
Plant Materials. Landscape 16 (63)
Plant Noise Control. Food 67 (4)
Plant Protection Curriculum. Undergraduate 216 (38)
Plant Protection Option. New Undergraduate 216 (85)
Plant Sex 29 (273)
Plant Taxanomist. Role of 168 (13)
Plant Waste. Disposal of Nuclear Power 151 (128)
Plant Waste Water. Land Treatment of Food 67 (13)
Planting. Tree 189
Plants are Like People 97 (3)
Plants. Automotive Power 216 (81)
Plants. Costa Rica - Tropical 159 (70)
Plants. Effects of Air Pollution on 216 (85)
Plants. Energy and Petroleum Resources, Earthquakes - Prediction, Control, and Nuclear Power 27 (4)
Plants. Folklore and Edibility of Wild 57 (82)
Plants. Growing and Care of House 216 (115)
Plants in the Environment. Harmful 117 (1)
Plants. Mineral Nutrition of 218
Plants. Navajo Carding and Spinning Along With Rugs and Navajo Dye 79 (61)
Plants of Pennsylvania. Poisonous 54
Plants of South America. Medicinal Flowering 27 (14)
Plants of the Past 159 (38)
Plants. Orchids as Windowsill 151 (237)
Plants. Poisonous 16 (13)
Plants. Safety of Nuclear Power 151 (132), 216 (103)
Plants. Secret Life of 134 (1)
Plants. Siting of Nuclear Power 218
Plants. Wild 159 (2)
Plastic Model Aircraft. Building 151 (5)
Plastics Technology: History, Importance and Fundamentals 117 (81)
Plastic Well Casing---But Were Afraid to Ask. Everything You Ever Wanted to Know About 136 (25)
Plate Tectonics and Our Restless Earth 142 (88)
Platina 227 (31)
Plating for Processing Equipment. Corrosion Resistant 67 (11)
Play. Effects of the Economy on Work and 142 (78)
Play Reviews 218
Play. Why People 151 (276)
Playground Equipment Safety 132 (8)
Playgrounds for Children. Creative 223 (29)
Playing and Defense Mechanisms. Role 57 (13)
Playing Games With Computers 181 (204)
Plays a Part. Everyone 97 (11)
Plays. Fascination of Literature Why We Enjoy Stories, Poems, and 54
Playwright in America. Black 154 (4)
Plea Bargaining: A Barter System of Justice 151 (229)
Pleasant Way to Become Wealthy. Collecting - The 97 (36)
Pleasure. Enhancing Sexual 29 (252)
Pleasure. Planning for Travel 29 (159), (314)
Plight of the Independent College 224 (16)
Plight of the Woman Writer: Historical View 151 (114)
Plot Against the Black Movement. FBI 213 (10)
Plundered Planet. Our 29 (48), (70)
Plying, Doubling, Cabling, Fancy Designer Yarns 79 (22)
Plywood 73
Plywood and Veneer. Technical Aspects of Hardwood, 80 (1)
Plywood, and Veneer. Use, Manufacturing, and Marketing of 80 (2)
Plywood. Prefinished Hardwood 80 (2)
Poe. Mystery of Edgar Allan 151 (237)
Poem is Born 29 (134), (200)
Poems, and Plays. Fascination of Literature - Why We Enjoy Stories, 54
Poet as Woman 227 (9)
Poet. William Faulkner: Prose 159 (19)
Poetic Immorality 227 (5)
Poetic Impulse of Debussy and Ravel. Piano Sonority and the 174 (41)
Poetic Meters 142 (2)
Poetry 181 (144)
Poetry. Affirmation in Contemporary 151 (105)
Poetry. American Indian 29 (162)
Poetry and Humor. American Dream...In 97 (9)
Poetry and Literary Criticism. Hellinistic 227 (7)
Poetry and Philosophy. Early Greek Lyric 227 (46)
Poetry. Contemporary 174 (29)
Poetry. Contemporary Themes in 54
Poetry. Cyprus in Modern Greek 227 (29)
Poetry. Greek Lyric 227 (28)
Poetry. Hellenistic 227 (39)
Poetry. Latin 227 (33)
Poetry. Lyric 227 (21)
Poetry: Music of the Spheres 151 (244)
Poetry. Myth in Modern Greek 227 (19)
Poetry. Nonsense 56 (63)
Poetry. Power of 57 (62)
Poetry. Prayer and 105 (106)
Poetry Readings 159 (7), 223 (27), 227 (9)
Poetry Readings With Illustrative Slides 117 (10)
Poetry. Rural 168 (39)

Poetry. Stimulating Children to Write 57 (79)
Poetry. Vietnamese 168 (41)
Poetry Workshops 227 (9)
Poets. Hellenistic Women 227 (2)
Poets. Image of Woman in 17th Century Metaphysical 227 (29)
Point Defiance Park - The People Speak. Future Developments of 159 (34)
Poise A Plenty 112 (19)
Poison Ivy 216 (38)
Poison Prevention 16 (13)
Poisoning - Facts and Prevention. Food 151 (173)
Poisonous Plants 16 (13)
Poisonous Plants of Pennsylvania 54
Poisonous Snakes of Louisiana 174 (53)
Poisons 181 (163)
Poisons Around the House 181 (216)
Pokomo of Kenya. River People - The 56 (2), (114)
Poland 59 (10)
Poland. Contemporary Music in 54
Poland. Immortal 110 (6)
Poland. Religion in 214 (81)
Polarized Light 56 (128)
Poles Theory. Growth 218
Police and Politics 83 (7)
Police Car. View From a 75 (1)
Police Department. California State University 29 (144), (193)
Police Departments. Alternative Methods of Entering 29 (144), (344)
Police Departments. Methods of Entering 29 (58)
Police Problems. Our 29 (49)
Police Problems - Whose Fault. Our 29 (133)
Police Traffic Radar Speed Measurement 105 (119)
Police. Urban Crime and 181 (264)
Policies and Problems. Current Public 117 (68), (116)
Policies. Fiscal and Monetary 56 (23)
Policies, Property Tax, Tax Reform. Tax 159 (64)
Policies. Soviet Foreign 54
Policies. United States Defense 29 (256), (292)
Policy Alternatives. Foreign 214 (54)
Policy. American Foreign 151 (192), 181 (265), (337), 214 (55), 224 (7)
Policy. American National 174 (72)
Policy. American Strategy in Foreign 85 (29)
Policy and Its Relationship to Pacifism, Socialism and Nonviolence. Foreign 217 (2)
Policy and Philosophy. Social 172 (2)
Policy and the Economy. Government 16 (37)
Policy and the Power Balance. Foreign 97 (2)
Policy and United States Governmental Machinery for Carrying It Out. United States Foreign 85 (15)
Policy. Australian Politics and Foreign 151 (189)
Policy. Canadian Politics and Foreign 151 (189)
Policy. Chinese Foreign 224 (7)
Policy. Conservative Tradition and Foreign 85 (7)
Policy. Constitutional/Moral Foreign 102 (12)
Policy. Contemporary Issues in American Foreign 57 (19)
Policy. Contemporary Problems of American Foreign 159 (36)
Policy. Current Issues in American Foreign 117 (66), (113)
Policy. Economic 159 (64), 220 (7)
Policy. Economic Security and Public 181 (42)
Policy. Educational Programs in Public 31 (34)
Policy. Environmental and Energy 151 (150)
Policy for the Oceans. National 218
Policy. Foreign 220 (4)
Policy, Future Implications. Current 117 (24)
Policy. Government Economic 117 (26)
Policy. Government Fiscal 174 (21)
Policy Issues. General Public 133 (2)
Policy. Liberalism and the Tragedy of American Foreign 85 (7)
Policy Making. Citizen Participation in Government 218
Policy Making. Student Participation in University 16 (21)
Policy. Military Aid and Foreign 159 (36)
Policy. National Economic 174 (70)
Policy of Ruin. Our Foreign 225 (36)
Policy of the Free Society. Labor 85 (27)
Policy. Organizing and Managing United States 151 (196)
Policy Processes. Federal Fiscal and Budgetary 31 (25)
Policy. Public 117 (103), (119)
Policy. Quest for Purpose in Contemporary American Foreign 85 (7)
Policy. Realities of American Foreign 85 (17)
Policy. Religious Subversion of Foreign 180 (145)
Policy. Science and Public 218
Policy. Social Problems in Economics and Urban 85 (1)
Policy. Sources and Goals of Soviet Foreign 85 (31)
Policy. Soviet Foreign 57 (37)
Policy. Statistics, Society, and Public 151 (262)
Policy. Telephone Industry and Telecommunication 151 (183)
Policy Today. United States Foreign 223 (21)
Policy. Toward a Wiser Foreign 85 (16)
Policy. Trends in United States Foreign 85 (21)
Policy. United States Energy 57 (89)
Policy. United States Foreign 85 (28), 117 (68)
Policy. United States National Security 85 (15)
Polish Civilization 214 (49)
Polish Contributions to American and World Culture 105 (27)
Polish Culture 105 (27)
Polish History and Politics 214 (59)
Political Analysis of Mexico. Cultural and 117 (105)
Political and Social History in Communist East Europe 218

Political Aspects of India. Economic and 142 (81)
Political Assassinations - The Kennedys and King 54
Political Behavior. American 214 (3)
Political Campaigning 224 (15)
Political Cartoon Heritage. America's 214 (4)
Political Changes in America. Need for Fundamental 178 (5)
Political, Cultural, Social and Economic Aspects of Southeast Asia 142 (89)
Political Culture in Hawaii. Culture of Poverty and 29 (141), (161), (257), (284)
Political Decision 117 (106)
Political Decision-Making 159 (4)
Political Development. Problems of 151 (189)
Political Economy of the Medical Profession 85 (14)
Political/Ethical/Theological Topics. Lectures on Social/ 168 (34)
Political Freedom. God and 85 (25)
Political Ideas. American 174 (72)
Political Implications of Social Services 181 (309)
Political Institutions. Order, Freedom, Law and 85 (40)
Political Issues. Current 168 (26)
Political Life. Genetic Diversity and 181 (24)
Political Life. Women in 56 (131)
Political Organizations. Future of Free Enterprise for Local Civic, Social, Educational and 74
Political Organizing 172 (11)
Political Organizing. How Food Co-ops and Community Stores Can Be Used for 178 (1)
Political Parties 105 (55)
Political Parties in North Carolina and the United States 56 (131)
Political Parties? What's Happening to the 218
Political Philosophy. American Politics and 85 (11)
Political Philosophy. American Social and 214 (75)
Political Power. Black 213 (10)
Political Power in America 181 (202), (258)
Political Problems of Asia 85 (18)
Political Pressures. ROTC - The 54
Political Repression in Israel 213 (16)
Political Right. Varieties of the American 85 (40)
Political Scene 176 (21)
Political Systems, and Culture. India, Its Religions, 151 (199)
Political Theory. Reconstruction of 85 (24)
Political Tradition. American 85 (13)
Political Tradition. Rediscovering the American 85 (39)
Political Upheaval. Coming 102 (36)
Politician. Great Americans - Lincoln, the Master 151 (222)
Politicians. Cautious Communicator: American 151 (87)
Politics 112 (7), (35), (46), (57), (59), (94), (102), (105), (106), (123), 176 (38), (71), (79), 180 (57), (167), 219 (1), (4), (5), (6), (7), (8), (10), 220 (2), (3), (5), (6), (8)
Politics After the 1976 Elections. West German 29 (259)
Politics After Watergate 151 (190)
Politics. American 112 (15), 142 (64), 181 (262)
Politics. American Government and 105 (55)
Politics. American National 151 (222)
Politics and Craziness. American 114 (3)
Politics and Economics of the Arab World 57 (61)
Politics and Education 102 (29)
Politics and Foreign Policy. Australian 151 (189)
Politics and Foreign Policy. Canadian 151 (189)
Politics and Higher Education 168 (50)
Politics and Political Philosophy. American 85 (11)
Politics and the Media 154 (26)
Politics. Biology and 181 (24)
Politics. California 224 (8)
Politics. Centrifugalism in Black 181 (26), (258)
Politics. Chicago 142 (67)
Politics. Contemporary Africa: 181 (25), (331)
Politics. Contemporary French Government 57 (89)
Politics. Current Problems in Medical 30 (1)
Politics. Equality and Liberty in American 85 (13)
Politics. Ethnic 54
Politics. German Culture and 56 (139)
Politics. Gnosticism and 85 (37)
Politics (Governor William W. Scranton). Pennsylvania 151 (222)
Politics. How to Spread Feminist and Socialist Ideas Through Electoral 178 (1)
Politics. Humorous Look at 29 (68), (188), (263)
Politics in Eastern Europe 54
Politics in the USSR 54
Politics. International 52 (75)
Politics. Local 174 (59)
Politics. Minnesota 168 (72)
Politics. National 224 (8)
Politics. Nature of Southern 216 (50)
Politics. Need for Doctors to Get Involved in 8 (7)
Politics. Neighborhood Movement in American 181 (275)
Politics. New Patterns of Asian 105 (57)
Politics of Abortion 142 (78)
Politics of Africa 174 (59)
Politics of Asia 174 (59)
Politics of Benign Neglect. Social Change, Revolution, and the 85 (12)
Politics of Ecology 29 (47), (69), (132), (266)
Politics of Education 16 (83), 142 (33)
Politics of Government Regulation of Business. Economics and 85 (19)
Politics of Local Government. Economics and 54
Politics of Nuclear Energy 117 (106)
Politics of Punishment 151 (227)
Politics of Social Change 223 (22)
Politics of Surrender 85 (9)
Politics of the Middle East 174 (59)
Politics of the Middle East. Government and 117 (104)
Politics on the International Scene - Sovereignty and Suppression 85 (11)

Politics of Trading With Communist Countries 85 (6)
Politics. Pesticides, Pollution and 16 (14)
Politics, Poetry and Humor. American Dream... In 97 (9)
Politics. Police and 83 (7)
Politics. Polish History and 214 (59)
Politics. Practical 189
Politics. Presidential 151 (190)
Politics. Religion and 85 (24)
Politics. Serious Look at 29 (68), (188), (263)
Politics. Sex and 178 (3)
Politics. State 172 (3), (5), 174 (59)
Politics. Trends and Changes in Southern 16 (20)
Politics. Urban 54, 142 (33), 168 (72)
Politics. West German 29 (56)
Pollen Grains and Geologic History 159 (38)
Pollination of Flowers 159 (70)
Pollutants. Health Effects of Environmental 204
Pollutants on Behavior. Effect of Environmental 168 (64)
Polluters. Vanadium - Tattletale of Environmental 27 (9)
Polluting Energy Sources. Non- 142 (15)
Pollution. Air 54, 56 (69), 168 (29)
Pollution Almanac. Nature's 151 (156)
Pollution and Food. Environmental 151 (177)
Pollution and People. Pesticides, 216 (38)
Pollution and Politics. Pesticides, 16 (14)
Pollution and You 57 (94)
Pollution: Are We Through Yet? 151 (151)
Pollution. Automotive 216 (81)
Pollution Control. Air 214 (26)
Pollution Control. Air and Water 204
Pollution Control. Air Quality Monitoring: Air 150 (8)
Pollution Control. Citizen Involvement in 151 (160)
Pollution Control. Ground Water 136 (14)
Pollution Control Laws. Enforcement of 204
Pollution Control. Water 214 (30)
Pollution. Economic Aspects of 117 (35)
Pollution. Energy and 56 (71)
Pollution. Environmental 56 (67)
Pollution in the Blue Ridge Mountains. Air 216 (113)
Pollution is Great (Growth, Resources, Economics, Affluence, Technology) 151 (225)
Pollution. Mercury 151 (156)
Pollution Meteorology. Air 151 (155)
Pollution. Noise 204, 218
Pollution. Noise is 151 (26)
Pollution on Plants. Effects of Air 216 (85)
Pollution on Rivers. Effects of Thermal 57 (16)
Pollution. Perspectives on 31 (13)
Pollution - Plant Effects. Air 216 (113)
Pollution Problems 168 (37)
Pollution Problems in Whatcom County 223 (15)
Pollution. Water 54, 56 (69), 105 (120), 168 (29)
Pollution. Web of 57 (59)
Polymers. Mechanical Behavior of 216 (11)
Polyphemus in Folktale, Homer, Literature and Art 227 (47)
Pompeii and Herculaneum 227 (26)
Pompeiian Mythological Painting 227 (35)
Pond Management 216 (26)
Ponies of Assateague Island. Wild 151 (305)
Poor. Minimum Wage Law and the 85 (22)
Popcorn and the• Piety of Celluloid Sin 56 (14)
Popular Ancestors 154 (2)
Popular Culture. Classics and 227 (4)
Popular Literature 142 (27)
Popular Music of the 1920's 224 (3)
Popular Novelists. America's Three Most 223 (3)
Popular Recreation and Reform in the 19th Century Century England and France 142 (98)
Population Change and the American Future 168 (42)
Population Control 105 (3), 174 (69)
Population Control. Contraceptives for 16 (30)
Population Control. Pet 218
Population. Distribution Trends of America's 151 (184)
Population Explosion 29 (47), (69), (132), (266)
Population - Explosion and Implosion 85 (38)
Population. Food Production and World 16 (89)
Population Growth 181 (131), (336)
Population Growth. Why We Need Zero 168 (58)
Population Growth. World 223 (28)
Population Measurement 174 (51)
Population on the Physical Environment in Eastern North Carolina 56 (36), (38)
Population Problem 29 (287), 174 (51), (69)
Population, the Food Chain, and Chemical Fertilizers 151 (134)
Population Trends 174 (51)
Populations and Their Trends. World 16 (30)
Populations. Disabled 181 (126)
Porcelain. Chinese Export 174 (41)
Pork Carcass and Its Cuts 151 (182)
Pornography 181 (238)
Pornography and Censorship 85 (35)
Pornography and Propaganda 171 (56)
Pornography. Censorship and 54
Portability of Computer Programs 181 (214)
Portal Hypertension. Current Trends in 181 (190)
Portland Cement Concrete as a Major Construction Material 151 (291)
Portrait Artistry. Techniques of 168 (8)
Portrait of Brazil. Fabulous Rio - 110 (8)
Portraits. Woven 79 (75)
Portugal 15 (1), 59 (11)
Portugal and Her African Territories 29 (7)
Portuguese Peasant in Europe and America 29 (123), (164)
Position of Women in China 218
Positive Approach to Discipline Problems - Effective Ways Parents Can Deal With and Understand Young Children 117 (48)
Positive Health Behavior 181 (184)
Positive Sense of Self Worth. Developing a 77 (1)

Positive Thinking 180 (70), (140)
Positively. Think 180 (142)
Possession and Exorcism 154 (12)
Possibilities of Men. Many 54
Postal Service and Its Problems 151 (183)
Postal Service. Escape From Poor 3 (8)
Post-Disaster Housing in Developing Countries 31 (22)
Post-Election Economy 97 (10)
Post-Liberal America. Future of Conservatism in 85 (21)
Postsecondary Education. Financing 105 (50)
Post-Secondary Education in Next Ten Years 216 (84)
Post-Watergate Presidency 181 (258)
Pot. American Melting 181 (256)
Potatoes. French Fries Made From Riced 67 (14)
Potential. Helping Children Reach Their 105 (98)
Potential. Human 105 (77)
Potential in Technical Editing. Creative 151 (79)
Potential. Land Use Planning and Mineral 143 (6)
Potential Movement. Human 57 (71)
Potential of Women 176 (26)
Potential: You Can Achieve! Your Human 105 (34)
Potentials of Fleece 79 (27)
Potentials of the Brain and Their Relation to Behavior. Electrical 171 (43)
Pottery. Design Inspiration - Nature and 159 (5)
Pottery. Japanese Folk Craft 57 (44)
Poultry Nutrition 216 (97)
Poultry Science 216 (18)
Poverty - A Critical View. War on 85 (25)
Poverty and More Welfare. How Come Less 85 (35)
Poverty and Political Culture in Hawaii. Culture of 29 (141), (161), (257), (284)
Poverty and Unemployment 181 (333)
Poverty. Capitalism, Racism and 85 (30)
Poverty. Dynamics of International Development: Alleviating World 151 (196)
Poverty. Economics of Racism and 168 (41)
Poverty in Louisiana 174 (70)
Poverty in Louisiana. Urban 174 (70)
Poverty in the United States Increasing or Decreasing? Is 117 (24)
Poverty. Minimum Wage Laws - Cure for or a Cause of 85 (2)
Power and Common Sense. Electric 189
Power Balance. Foreign Policy and the 97 (2)
Power. Black Political 213 (10)
Power - Boom or Bust? Nuclear 29 (255), (268)
Power Cable Specifications 150 (1)
Power. Communication and Word 151 (70)
Power. Community 16 (1)
Power Company. Forestry as Adapted to a 150 (5)
Power Confrontation in the Middle East. Big 85 (31)
Power From Space 216 (3)
Power. Hour 182 (1), (2), (3)
Power. Humor 86 (1)
Power in America. Political 181 (202), (258)
Power in Interpersonal Relationships 16 (1)
Power in Meeting the Energy Crisis. Role of Nuclear 216 (103)
Power in Our Society 154 (14)
Power. Moral Question of Nuclear 151 (133)
Power. Nature's Way - Nuclear 152
Power. New Kind of 189
Power. Nuclear 29 (51), 181 (18), 189, 216 (91)
Power of a Woman. Selling 180 (186)
Power of Enthusiasm 135 (16)
Power of One 151 (41)
Power of Poetry 57 (62)
Power of Radio 151 (70)
Power of Women in First C.B.C. Roman Life 227 (29)
Power Option in Perspective. Nuclear 27 (9)
Power or Vehicular Transportation. Engines for 151 (295)
Power Planning. Regional 189
Power Plant Waste. Disposal of Nuclear 151 (128)
Power Plants. Automotive 216 (81)
Power Plants. Energy and Petroleum Resources, Earthquakes - Prediction, Control, and Nuclear 27 (4)
Power Plants. Safety of Nuclear 151 (132), 216 (103)
Power Plants. Siting of Nuclear 218
Power: Problems and Promise. Nuclear 151 (137)
Power. Public Concern About Nuclear 216 (103)
Power Question. Nuclear 216 (64)
Power. Risks of Nuclear 218
Power. Sea 105 (75)
Power to You. More 152
Power Volleyball the Penn State Way 151 (286)
Power. Women and 154 (14)
Practical Application. Meditation and Its 108 (1), (2)
Practical Decision-Making 168 (11)
Practical Guide to Working With Homespun 79 (130)
Practical Politics 189
Practice. Family 218
Practice Learning. Be Curious: 151 (115)
Practice Management. All Aspects of 8 (1)
Practice of a Clinical Pharmacy 54
Practice of Public Relations 31 (36)
Practices and Employee Benefits. Business 151 (1)
Practices. Compensation 223 (6)
Practices. Effects of Different Kinds of Child-Rearing 105 (103)
Practices. Fair Employment 223 (6)
Practices for Improving the Instructional Staff in the Elementary and Secondary Schools. Innovation 117 (58)
Practicing Physician in Homebirth 122 (1)
Practitioner. Information Explosion Faced by the Health Care 218
Prairies, Forest and Bogs. Searching for 168 (56)
Praise of Science. In 171 (33)
Pray. To Believe is to 105 (106)

Prayer and Its Effectiveness 1 (8)
Prayer and Poetry 105 (106)
Prayer and Spirituality 105 (105)
Prayer in a Busy World. Contemplative 54
Prayer. Islamic 1 (12)
Prayer. Scriptural 105 (105)
Prayer. What is 105 (106)
Preaching. Drama as a Sermonic Alternative to Monologue 168 (34)
Pre-Costing Meals. Data Processing in 16 (90)
Precursor of the Holy Prophet Muhammad. Jesus as 1 (5)
Predicting Texture 31 (11)
Prediction, Control, and Nuclear Power Plants. Energy and Petroleum Resources, Earthquakes - 27 (4)
Prediction. Earthquakes and the 142 (88)
Predictions. Nostradamus' Forbidden 225 (9)
Prefinished Hardwood Plywood 80 (2)
Pregnancy 54
Pregnancy. Medical and Psychological Aspects of Adolescent 27 (30)
Prehistoric Cultural Adaptations in Saharan Africa 117 (9)
Prehistoric Man and Evolution 174 (22)
Prehistoric View of Women 29 (168)
(Prehistory) - Early Man of North America. Archaeology 105 (1)
Pre-Hitler German Kabarett and Its Influence 154 (22)
Prejudice. Psychology of 105 (103)
Prejudice. Racial, Religious and Sexual 181 (234), (305)
Premodern Societies. Death in Modern and 29 (281)
Prenatal Detection of Birth Defects 27 (28)
Prenatal Diagnosis 181 (173)
Prenatal Diagnosis of Genetic Counseling 151 (165)
Prenatal Diagnosis of Genetic Defects 211 (1)
Prenatal Education for Parents 218
Prenatal Genetic Diagnosis 181 (167)
Preparation for an Uncertain Future. Liberal Arts as 151 (116)
Preparation. Human Relationships - Component of Teacher 117 (45)
Preparation of Fleeces for Hand Spinning. Selection and 79 (59)
Prepare for College. How to 29 (31), (102), (349)
Prepare Your Child for Success. How to 56 (59)
Prepared for a College Education? Are Students Today Better 16 (23), (78)
Preparing for a Career in Musical Comedy. Dancer 225 (39)
Preparing for Employment in Today's World 117 (80)
Preparing for Higher Education 105 (38)
Preparing for Marriage 168 (73)
Pre-School Child. Math for the 181 (105), (150)
Preschool Children With Special Needs 142 (59)
Prescription Drug Interactions 54
Present Brazilian Regime 117 (102)
Present Situation of the International Communist Movement 85 (8)
Presentation of Educational Theatre. Multi-Media 105 (2
Presentations. Sales 180 (23)
Presenting Offer and Counter-offer 65 (8)
Preservation. Environmental 57 (25)
Preservation. Historic 174 (37)
Preservation. History of Chicago Architecture and 142 (79)
Preservation of Historic Buildings 57 (92)
Preserve the Environment 181 (136)
Preserve the Environment on an International Scale 181 (346)
Preserving Food in Your Home 151 (180)
Preserving Your Home-Produced Foods 151 (178)
Presidency 105 (55)
Presidency. American 112 (13), 142 (27)
Presidency and the Intelligence Community 105 (59)
Presidency and the Media 27 (40)
Presidency. Imperial 151 (221)
Presidency. Post-Watergate 181 (258)
President and Congress 223 (23)
President. Election of the 105 (58)
Presidential Documentaries 135 (12)
Presidential Politics 151 (190)
Presidential Voting Patterns 181 (266)
Presidents 142 (64)
Presidents and the Press 168 (10)
President's Council on Physical Fitness 105 (114)
Presidents. Early American 142 (63)
Presocratics 227 (51)
Press and Fair Trial. Free 181 (68)
Press and First Amendment 57 (88)
Press and the People 102 (34)
Press. Associated 176 (13)
Press. Censorship and the 168 (10)
Press. Ethics and the 29 (40), (117)
Press. Freedom and Responsibilities of the 102 (27)
Press. Freedom of Speech and 56 (94)
Press. Freedom of the Scholastic 168 (12)
Press. High School Underground 231 (3)
Press in Its School and Community. Role of the Student 168 (51)
Press. Philosophical Background of Freedom of 117 (85)
Press. Presidents and the 168 (10)
Press Versus Fair Trial. Free 181 (211)
Press. What's Wrong With the 151 (67)
Pressures. ROTC - The Political 54
Preventing Reading Difficulties 171 (19)
Prevention. Drug Abuse 16 (84)
Prevention. Fire 151 (260)
Prevention. Food Poisoning - Facts and 151 (173)
Prevention for the Athlete. Injury 151 (283)
Prevention of Athletic Injuries. Care and 151 (279)
Prevention of Speech and Language Problems 57 (63)

Prevention. Poison 16 (13)
Prevention. Rape 62 (1), (2), (3), 181 (224), (325)
Preventive Approaches to Alcohol and Drug Abuse 105 (88)
Preventive Maintenance. Energy Savings by 151 (47)
Preventive Mental Health 142 (45)
Price Controls - Do They Work. Wage and 85 (22)
Price Controls. Why Your Dollar Continues to Buy Less - With or Without Wage 85 (26)
Price Support Program. Agricultural 85 (22)
Prices and Production in Variant Economic Systems 85 (14)
Prices. How to Arrive at Selling 79 (96)
Primitive Knotless Netting. Contemporary Use of 79 (52)
Primitive Looms. Exploring Weaving on 79 (85)
Primitive Spinners - Spindles and/or Distaffs From Greece, Turkey, and Yugoslavia 79 (20)
Principal. Elementary 181 (118)
Principal of Profit 132 (12)
Principle. Collections in Following With the Squeaky Wheel 136 (7)
Principles of Islam 1 (12)
Principles of Islam. Basic 1 (6)
Principles of Islam. Fundamental 1 (1)
Principles of Wildlife Management and Conservation. Basic 151 (309)
Printed Textiles. History of 79 (120)
Printing and Dyeing as an Art Form. Textile 79 (129)
Printing. Contemporary 159 (18)
Printing in Alaska. Wood Block 79 (123)
Printing. Leaf 79 (36)
Printing Office and You. Government 56 (99)
Printing on Photosensitized Fabrics 79 (4)
Printing. Professional and Hobby 151 (68)
Printmaking 16 (32)
Priorities in the Decade Ahead. National 85 (10)
Priorities. People, Quality, and 151 (101)
Prison, Its Problems and Prospects 56 (142)
Prison. Reform of the 168 (49)
Prisoners? Why Rehabilitate 29 (49), (133)
Prisons. 19th Century English 159 (61)
Prisons. Nonviolent Action and 217 (3)
Prisons: Rehabilitation or Punishment? 159 (28)
Privacy Issue. Computers and the 218
Privacy. Right of 181 (211)
Private Alternatives to Government Programs 85 (2)
Private and Public. Self-consciousness - 31 (37)
Private Delivery System of Government Projects. Incursions into the 30 (1)
Private Education as an Alternative. Independent 105 (38)
Private Enterprise. Future of 102 (6)
Private Giving for the Public Good 151 (185)
Private Giving to Penn State 151 (187)
Private Higher Education in Pennsylvania. Role of 54
Private Industry. Collective Bargaining in 23
Private Investigative Security-Consulting. Licensed 180 (86)
Private Philanthropy? Do Students Still Need 151 (89)
Private Property Rights. Protection of 65 (24)
Private Support for Higher Education 216 (107)
Private Support for Penn State? Why 151 (185)
Private Support of Public Higher Education 216 (7)
Pro and College Sports. Economics of 54
Pro on the Go 112 (65)
Probability and Gambling 56 (130)
Probability - How to Lie With Statistics. Statistics/ 151 (252)
Probability. Mathematical Statistics and/or 27 (17)
Probable Causes of Success 112 (10)
Problems and Hopes in Contemporary Ireland 159 (65)
Problems and Issues in Local Government 54
Problems and Solutions in Radioactive Waste Management 151 (130)
Problems Faced by First Time College Freshmen 174 (88)
Problems in Inflation 54
Problems in Management Information System Implementation 171 (9)
Problems in School Integration 56 (49)
Problems of Adolescents 29 (88), (231)
Problems of Children 181 (289)
Problems of Civil Rights 85 (5)
Problems of Constitutional Government and Modern Democracy 85 (5)
Problems of Development in the Less Developed Countries 159 (52)
Problems of Federalism 85 (5)
Problems of Higher Education 85 (5)
Problems of Political Development 151 (189)
Problems of Social Planning 85 (4)
Problems of the Aged 168 (67)
Problems of the Businessman: A Lawyer's View 136 (9)
Problems of the Middle East Today 223 (21)
Problems of University Students 174 (9)
Problems. People and Their 112 (16)
Problems. Solve Your 225 (38)
Problems. Today's 176 (11)
Problems. We Create Our Own 112 (41)
Problems. Youth-Oriented 135 (40)
Problem-Solving 105 (82)
Problem-Solving and Decision-Making 168 (17)
Problem-Solving Techniques 151 (103)
Procedure. Criminal 159 (45), 181 (273)
Procedure. Use of Parliamentary 117 (128)
Procedures for Academic Freedom. Model Code of 105 (49)
Procedures. Radiation Safety in Medical 181 (198)
Proceedings. Ancient Impeachment 227 (38)

Process. Infectious 168 (29)
Process. Legal 214 (5)
Process of Curriculum Change 168 (21)
Process of Dying 31 (20)
Process. Students' Rights and Due 117 (46)
Processes. Group 168 (74)
Processes in Bile. Rate 31 (11)
Processes. New Materials and 151 (125)
Processing. Aseptic 67 (18)
Processing Equipment. Corrosion Resistant Plating for 67 (11)
Processing. Food 216 (142)
Processing. Word 119 (1)
Processionary Caterpillar. Are You a 76 (1)
Producing Attractive Newsletters 151 (84)
Producing Films 180 (50)
Product Development. New Meat 216 (35)
Product Liability Crisis 181 (44)
Product Liability. Perspectives in 31 (33)
Product Management. Marketing Management - 105 (8)
Product Safety 105 (87)
Product Safety Commission. Consumer 105 (87)
Product Safety. Consumer 16 (6)
Product Safety. Perspectives in 31 (33)
Production and Processing of Vegetable Seeds Used in the Food Processing Industry. Development, 67 (26), (27)
Production and World Population. Food 16 (89)
Production. Audiovisual 181 (69)
Production. Background Fruit 117 (5)
Production. Backyard Fruit 117 (122)
Production. Decentralized Energy 163 (2)
Production. Energy Options for Food 47
Production. Engineer in Automobile Design and 214 (90)
Production in Variant Economic Systems. Prices and 85 (14)
Production. Maximizing Beef 216 (80)
Production of Genetically Superior Trees. Mass 151 (310)
Production. Offshore Exploration and 35
Production. Oil and Gas Industry - Drilling and 151 (135)
Production. Organophosphate Pesticides and Food 117 (3)
Production Research. Food and Food 151 (24)
Production. Saving Energy While Increasing Agriculture 16 (31)
Production. Shoe 170
Production. Small Scale Methane 163 (3)
Production Standards and Work Measurement in the Office 117 (14)
Production Techniques. Audiovisual 181 (97)
Production Techniques. Multi-Image 142 (75)
Production Techniques. Television 151 (66)
Production. World Food 216 (97)
Productivity Can Be Enhanced in the Food Processing Industry. How 67 (1)
Productivity. Identify Frustrations to Enhance 151 (38)
Productivity in Business. Overcoming Obstacles to Achieve 27 (8)
Productivity in Marketing Operations. Improving 29 (84), (112)
Productivity. Leadership and 56 (134)
Productivity Through Employee Motivation. Increasing 67 (2)
Products/Services. How Industries Market Their 23
Profession. Aerospace Engineering as a 151 (34)
Profession. Agricultural Engineering as a 216 (83)
Profession. Geography as a 29 (89), (159), (341)
Profession. Impact of Computers on the Accounting 171 (9)
Profession of Happy People. Lazy Man's Trip to the Bank or Real Estate, the 65 (20)
Profession. Political Economy of the Medical 85 (14)
Profession. Sports Medicine a Young and Growing 56 (76)
Profession. Teaching as a 56 (42)
Professional and Hobby Printing 151 (68)
Professional Artist. How to Train a 16 (32)
Professional Baseball and American Culture 142 (72)
Professional Corporations and the Doctor 8 (9)
Professional Criminal 168 (49)
Professional Development 216 (133)
Professional Education 174 (86)
Professional Education: Its Importance. Continuing 151 (40)
Professional Excellence 57 (96)
Professional Information. Medical Technology-- 105 (45)
Professional Journalism 135 (20)
Professional. Liberation of the White Male 159 (24)
Professional. Motivation for the Older 151 (40)
Professional Negotiations in the Public Sector 117 (38)
Professional Obsolescence 151 (40), 180 (47)
Professional of the 1980's. Real Estate 181 (37)
Professional Opportunities in Mathematics 27 (17)
Professional. Real Estate 181 (225)
Professional Secretary. Certified 174 (60)
Professional Secretary Examination. Certified 117 (27)
Professional Speaking. Business and 142 (25)
Professional Teacher Organizations 174 (49)
Professionalism. Officiating and 105 (114)
Professionalization of Teaching 181 (102)
Professionals. Consumerism: Choosing Health Care 181 (196)
Professionals. Developing Moral Reasoning for Children and 168 (63)
Professionals in Drug Abuse. Medical 88 (1)
Professionals Response to Non-traditional Students. Student Activity 105 (38)
Professions and the Socialization of Women 218
Professions. Getting Into the Health 29 (98), (174), (274)

Professors. American Association of University 181 (95)
Professors and Their Impact on Students 16 (23)
Profile Draft 79 (23)
Profile of a Leader 29 (136)
Profile. Student 168 (38)
Profiles in Literature 181 (145)
Profit - An All-American Word 112 (14)
Profit and Comfort. Energy-saving Homes for 18 (1)
Profit is a Six Letter Word 76 (1)
Profit. Motivating for 54
Profit. Principal of 132 (12)
Profit. Prophets 56 (37)
Profit? What is 23
Profitability 144
Profitable Selling. Proven Ideas for 180 (89)
Profits and Their Importance to the Economy 34 (1)
Profits - Business/Government Relationship 34 (2)
Profits. Ethics and 102 (31)
Profits. Motivation of People for 65 (20)
Profits - Spoils or Just Rewards 117 (15)
Profits. Understanding 20
Program. Administration of an Intercollegiate Football 29 (24), (301)
Program. Agricultural Price Support 85 (22)
Program. Air Force ROTC 174 (81)
Program. Alabama's Student Financial Assistance 16 (68)
Program. Balancing the Parameters of a Reading 181 (108)
Program. Cal State Fullerton Engineering 29 (108)
Program. Campus Facilities and the Successful 57 (51)
Program Can Help You. How the Pennsylvania Technical Assistance 151 (47)
Program. Child Development Associate 174 (31)
Program. Community College 117 (59)
Program. Continuing Education 16 (10)
Program Dealing With the Many Aspects of This Overlooked Part of Communications. Non-Verbal Communication: A 117 (58)
Program. Developing Efficient Breeding 216 (80)
Program Development. Career Education 57 (72)
Program. Educational Opportunity 105 (44)
Program Evaluation Methods 159 (13)
Program for Drilling Contractors. Safety 136 (2)
Program for the Media. Building an Advertising 168 (59)
Program. Home Trade-in 65 (25)
Program. How to Go About Developing Your Own Exercise 218
Program in Pennsylvania. Expanded Nutrition Education 151 (171)
Program in the Cal State Fullerton School of Business. Information Systems Degree 29 (26), (92), (137)
Program. MSU's Right to Read 117 (134)
Program of the UCI Institute of Transportation. Research 27 (39)
Program. Parents and the Reading 181 (107), (123)
Program Planning 105 (81)
Program. Realtor Associate 65 (10)
Program. SCS Denmark Study 168 (54)
Program. Simon Fraser's MBA 171 (57)
Program. Successful Weight Reduction 181 (245), (296)
Program. Why an Alumni 57 (91)
Programming a Successful Event or Activity 105 (79)
Programming. Computer 181 (214)
Programming. Intramural 105 (114)
Programming. New Techniques of Computer 181 (51)
Programming, Organizing, and Administering Intramurals 57 (17)
Programming. Student 174 (71)
Programs. Accreditation of Engineering Education Degree 151 (266)
Programs and Administration. Safety 23
Programs and Aspirations. Academic 142 (40)
Programs at Penn State. Athletic 151 (281)
Programs. Berks County 4-H Youth 151 (20)
Programs. Competency-based Degree 142 (95)
Programs. Cooperative Extension 16 (12)
Programs. Current Mathematics Trends and 181 (117)
Programs. Development of Post-Secondary Education 151 (97)
Programs. Education and Board Education 65 (43)
Programs. Employee Benefit 23
Programs for Black Students at Predominantly White Institutions. Student Development 105 (39)
Programs for Community Development. Projects and 117 (129)
Programs for Underachievers. College 105 (34)
Programs. Former Governor Looks at Health 8 (2)
Programs. Good Books for Home Reading 168 (53)
Programs in Business Education 174 (6)
Programs in Interior British Columbia. University 171 (58)
Programs in Mathematics at Murray State University 117 (92)
Programs in Office Administration 174 (6)
Programs in Public Policy. Educational 31 (34)
Programs. International Environmental 204
Programs. Involving the Community in Career Education 57 (72)
Programs. Mathematics Trends and 181 (152)
Programs of Readings for Special Occasions 105 (85)
Programs of the Present Congress 16 (20)
Programs. Planning, Administering and Evaluating Reading 142 (21)
Programs. Portability of Computer 181 (214)
Programs. Private Alternatives to Government 85 (2)
Programs. Public School String 117 (95)
Programs. Reading 29 (95)
Programs. String Quartet - for School Demonstrations and 117 (95)
Programs. Student Life: Issues and 218

Programs. Traffic Safety 56 (84), (85)
Programs. Training 180 (80)
Programs. USL Scholarship 174 (88)
Programs. USL Service 174 (58)
Progress - Berks County and the Berks Campus of Penn State. Partners in 151 (112)
Progress - Cooperative Education. Partners in 151 (95)
Progress. Partners in 151 (12)
Progress Schools. Continuous 174 (49)
Progress Today. Idea of 85 (32)
Project H.E.L.P. (Health Education Learning Program) 16 (49)
Project. Penn State Rockview Beef 151 (182)
Project. Planning a Three-D 79 (40)
Project. Western Coal 47
Projection Model. Eclectic Enrollment 57 (93)
Projects and Programs for Community Development 117 (129)
Projects for 2 Harness Looms. Special 79 (130)
Projects. Incursions Into the Private Delivery System of Government 30 (1)
Prolonged Release Dosage Forms 54
Prominence. Individuals of Local 174 (19)
Promise. Nuclear Power: Problems and 151 (137)
Promise or Ruin? Public Education - 151 (100)
Promised Mahdi. Appearance of the Promised Messiah and the 1 (8)
Promised Messiah and the Promised Mahdi. Appearance of the 1 (8)
Promised Messiah and the Signs of the Time 1 (5)
Promises and Perils. Future 151 (236)
Promotion. Advertising and 23
Promotion Around the World. Advertising/ 3 (1)
Pronouns. Spanish 29 (208)
Proofs Concerning Jesus' Survival From Death on the Cross 1 (9)
Proofs of the Existence of God 1 (6)
Propaganda of the Augustan Age 227 (52)
Propaganda. Pornography and 171 (56)
Proper Contraceptive. Choosing the 57 (64)
Proper Language 142 (2)
Proper Relationship Between Broadcast Journalists and the Government 117 (84)
Propertius 227 (54)
Propertius' Literary Programme 227 (24)
Propertius' Monobiblos. Tradition and Originality in 227 (24)
Property and Ecology 29 (74), (195)
Property and Freedom - the Remarkable Identity 85 (27)
Property and Investment. Commercial 65 (61)
Property and Personal. Economics of Rights - 85 (14)
Property. Commercial 65 (3), (17), (22), (25), (34), (50), (53), (54), (55), (56), (58), (62), (65), (66), (67)
Property. Community 159 (46)
Property Lines. Surveying 216 (116)
Property Management 65 (5), (17), (28), (35), (43), (55)
Property. Qualifying the Seller and His 65 (41)
Property Rights. Protection of Private 65 (24)
Property Tax, Tax Reform. Tax Policies, 159 (64)
Prophecy. Gift of 112 (34), 135 (15)
Prophecy. Israel in History and 45 (3)
Prophet Muhammad as an Examplar. Holy 1 (12)
Prophet Muhammad as Benefactor of Humanity. Holy 1 (13)
Prophet Muhammad. Jesus as Prescusor of the Holy 1 (5)
Prophets of Israel Upon Religious Ideas. Impact of the 29 (114)
Prophets of Profit 56 (37)
Proposal for Improvement in American Education 54
Proposals. Mechanics of Technical Reports 151 (79)
Pros. Amateur Among the 97 (55)
Pros and Cons. Mainstreaming: 117 (131)
Prose Poet. William Faulner: 159 (19)
Prospect Before Us 102 (11)
Prospecting 65 (8), (44)
Prospector. Costs and Adventures of the Modern Day 143 (13)
Prospects for Mankind 97 (39), 102 (20)
Prospects for Solar Energy 29 (110)
Prosperity. Ways to Attain Health, Wealth, Happiness, Success and 180 (33)
Prostate Carcinoma Testicle 181 (171)
Prosthetic Measures 181 (174)
Protect Yourself Against White Collar Crimes. How to 97 (21)
Protected and Abused. How Trademarks are 209
Protecting Title to Realty 65 (16)
Protection Agency. Environmental 57 (94)
Protection. Consumer 29 (191), 176 (92)
Protection Curriculum. Undergraduate Plant 216 (38)
Protection for Senior Citizens. Self 62 (1)
Protection of Human Health. Veterinary Medicine's Role in the 216 (90)
Protection of Private Property Rights 65 (24)
Protection of Workers 151 (153)
Protection Option. New Undergraduate Plant 216 (85)
Protection Systems. Environmental 150 (11)
Protective Relaying 150 (13)
Protein. Structure of a 54
Protein Supply. Growing Fish to Increase World 16 (53)
Protest, Revolution, and the Permanent Things 85 (16)
Protestantism and Catholicism. Relations of 174 (69)
Proton. Structure of the 181 (277)
Proven Ideas for Profitable Selling 180 (89)
Provence 142 (98)
Providing Structure in the Unstructured Classroom 117 (51)
Provocative Contractual Questions for School Purchasers 132 (2)
Psyche. Insights Into the Male Versus Female 225 (6)

Psychiatric Concepts 105 (95)
Psychiatric Measures. Emergency 105 (95)
Psychiatric Nursing 105 (95)
Psychiatrist Comes. What to Do Until the 112 (4)
Psychiatrist Should Have His Head Examined. Anyone Who Goes to a 225 (3)
Psychiatry. History of American 151 (214)
Psychic Abilities. How to Develop Your 225 (33)
Psychic Abilities Through Face Language. How to Increase Your 212 (1)
Psychic Phenomena 176 (34), (97), (120), 180 (96)
Psychic Photography. Scientific Evidence for Ghosts and 154 (12)
Psychic World 94 (2)
Psychoanalysis. Existential 181 (291)
Psycho-Educational Assessment 142 (93)
Psychological Aspects of Adolescent Pregnancy. Medical and 27 (30)
Psychological Aspects of Death and Dying 214 (77)
Psychological Effectiveness 105 (100)
Psychological Effects of Colonization. Social and 181 (31), (294)
Psychological Effects of Freeway Noises 223 (13)
Psychological Investigation. Color - Physical and 79 (25)
Psychological Liberation 181 (146)
Psychological Perspectives on the American Family 181 (291)
Psychological Self-help 57 (45)
Psychological Testing 224 (14)
Psychological Testing in Education and Industry 105 (102)
Psychological Tests 174 (76)
Psychological Treatment 224 (1)
Psychologists. Ethics of 224 (14)
Psychologist Father. Confessions of a 97 (17)
Psychologist. Homer, the First 227 (29)
Psychology 151 (271), 176 (22), 180 (122), (149),
Psychology. Adnormal 105 (101)
Psychology and Relations. Industrial 180 (8)
Psychology. Black 29 (242), 181 (294)
Psychology. Black Family, Black 181 (31)
Psychology. Community 56 (136), 142 (73)
Psychology - Coping. Rehabilitation 151 (18)
Psychology. Environmental 168 (74)
Psychology. Equine 216 (57)
Psychology. Future Trends in 105 (102)
Psychology. General 174 (32), (62)
Psychology of Alcoholism 105 (100)
Psychology of Clothing and Dress - Historical, Folk, and Traditional 79 (28)
Psychology of Dreaming 151 (169)
Psychology of Dreams and Dreaming 224 (14)
Psychology of Drug Abuse 105 (100)
Psychology of Laughter 151 (270)
Psychology of Love 97 (23)
Psychology of Normal Human Growth and Development 117 (111)
Psychology of Obesity 105 (100), (102)
Psychology of Prejudice 105 (103)
Psychology of Selling 136 (6)
Psychology of Sex 174 (76)
Psychology of Sexual Deviation 105 (100)
Psychology of Sleep 151 (169)
Psychology of Sport 168 (36), (71)
Psychology of Stress 151 (203)
Psychology of Women 16 (81), 181 (324)
Psychology of Yoga. Philosophy and 181 (300)
Psychology. Physiological 151 (18)
Psychology. Religion and 168 (47), 214 (80)
Psychology. Sport 171 (29)
Psychology. Teaching Personally Useful 57 (45)
Psychology Testing 57 (13)
Psychology - the Afro American Woman in American History. Black 29 (337)
Psychology. Training Paraprofessionals in 168 (7)
Psychology. Women and 214 (95)
Psychology. Yoga 151 (88)
Psychoprophylactic Childbirth to the Era of Feminism. Contribution of 36 (1)
Psychosocial Problems of Children and Adolescents 181 (282)
Psychosomatic Disorders 105 (100)
Psychotherapeutics 181 (164)
Psychotherapy 142 (73)
Psychotherapy. African Medicine Man and Western 181 (291)
Psychotherapy. Counseling and 29 (231)
Psychotherapy in American Society 181 (291)
Psychotherapy. Individual or Group 181 (289)
Psychotherapy. Some Philisophical Assumptions of 29 (245)
Psychotherapy With Families, Individuals and Groups 159 (37)
Psychotropic Drugs 218
Public Administration 142 (33), (42), 168 (72)
Public Administration as a Career 29 (262)
Public Administration. School of Business and 159 (66)
Public Affairs 176 (84)
Public Agencies. Marketing for Non-profit Institutions and 181 (36)
Public Art 79 (103)
Public Awareness of Environmental Problems 151 (153)
Public Choice. Concepts of 117 (18)
Public Community. Role and Place of Theatre in the 159 (62)
Public Concern About Nuclear Power 216 (103)
Public Education. Church-State Issue in 181 (102), (303)
Public Education in Washington. Financing 159 (53)
Public Education. Minorities and 181 (93)
Public Education. Ombudsman in 57 (10)
Public Education - Promise or Ruin? 151 (100)
Public Education. Religion and 12
Public Education. State Office and 57 (10)
Public Education. Survival of 57 (65)

Public Employee Bargaining 216 (104)
Public Employee Labor Relations 216 (105)
Public Employees Into Unwanted Labor Unions. Right to Work - Forcing 131 (4)
Public Expect From Our Colleges and Universities. What Should the 151 (101)
Public Finance 174 (17), (70)
Public Good. Private Giving for the 151 (185)
Public Health and Social Welfare. History of 171 (49)
Public Health. Radiation, Radioactivity and the 27 (9)
Public Higher Education. Private Support of 216 (7)
Public in American Education. Concept of 181 (261)
Public Interest. Capitalism and the 85 (4)
Public Interest. In the 102 (23)
Public Involvement in Government 176 (3)
Public Law Matters 57 (36)
Public Opinion Formation. Television and 168 (50)
Public Places. Fiber Activities for 79 (128)
Public. Planning Process - the Planner and the 56 (101)
Public Policies and Problems. Current 117 (68), (116)
Public Policy 117 (103), (119)
Public Policy. Economic Security and 181 (42)
Public Policy. Educational Programs in 31 (34)
Public Policy Issues. General 133 (2)
Public Policy. Science and 218
Public Policy. Statistics, Society, and 151 (262)
Public Relations 29 (36), (37), (55), (78), (94), (258), 56 (102), 65 (6), (22), (30), (33), (38), (39), (41), (42), (45), (46), (55), (59), (60), (63), (66), (68), 180 (135), (137), (177)
Public Relations and News 216 (14)
Public Relations by Objective 29 (39)
Public Relations Can Benefit You. How 136 (16)
Public Relations Can Do for You. What 151 (67)
Public Relations. Community 31 (35)
Public Relations. Disaster 29 (39)
Public Relations. Effective 168 (65)
Public Relations for Small Businesses 224 (15)
Public Relations for Your Organization 151 (84)
Public Relations - Friendly Adversaries. News Media and 105 (67)
Public Relations: Getting to the Media 151 (86)
Public Relations in Crisis 29 (39)
Public Relations. Institutional 29 (39)
Public Relations. Practice of 31 (36)
Public Relations. School/Community 168 (10)
Public Relations. Teachers, Publications and 214 (19), (37)
Public Relations. Techniques of 168 (50)
Public. Responsibilities of Public Institutions to the Taxpaying 16 (87)
Public School Curriculum 16 (56)
Public School String Programs 117 (95)
Public Schools. Alchemists in Our 85 (10)
Public Schools. Alternatives in 117 (57)
Public Schools Be the Death of English? Will the 168 (51)
Public Schools? How Effective Are Our 159 (53)
Public Schools. Management of Speech Disorders in 56 (55)
Public Schools. Most Pressing Shortcoming of the 223 (9)
Public Schools. Myth of Humanism in the 12
Public Schools. Personnel Administration in the 16 (18)
Public School System. Ceramics in the 56 (11)
Public Schools. Teaching Moral Values in the 159 (32)
Public Schools. Transcendental Meditation 12
Public Schools. What Alternatives Do You Have in Secondary 29 (347)
Public Sector. Collective Bargaining in the 223 (6)
Public Sector Labor Relations 181 (41)
Public Sector. Professional Negotiations in the 117 (38)
Public. Self-consciousness - Private and 31 (37)
Public Service. University Extension or 16 (7)
Public Speaking 142 (25)
Public Speaking is Easy 105 (13)
Public Television. Role and Responsibility of 16 (86)
Public Utility Invisible Taxes for Religion 12
Public Violence. Assassination, Riot, 29 (153)
Public Wife in Washington. Life of a 97 (75)
Publication of the Origin of the Species. Biologist Looks at Evolution 100 Years After the 54
Publications and Public Relations. Teachers, 214 (19), (37)
Publications. Management of School 214 (18)
Public's Right to Know 102 (29)
Publicity. Effective Newspaper 151 (84)
Published. Getting My Article 216 (78)
Pueblo Embroidery 79 (89)
Puerto Rican Migration 142 (56)
Puerto Rican Nationalism 142 (56)
Puerto Rico 59 (14), 110 (12)
Puerto Rico and the United States. Relationship Between 151 (202)
Puget Sound. Geology of Lower 159 (38)
Puget Sound. Marine Biology of South 159 (34)
Puget Sound. Oil Tankers on 218
Pull Up an Easel 97 (23)
Pulleys. V-trough Carriers and PVC Rollers and 67 (28)
Pulp and Paper 73
Pulp Therapy. Controversies in 105 (30)
Pulsars 214 (10)
Pulsars. Quasars and 223 (4)
Pump. Ground Water Source Heat 136 (25)
Pumps and Piping. Flow Characteristics of Solids - Liquid Mixtures in 67 (5)
Pumps and Solar Energy. Heat 216 (71)

Pumps for Food Processing 67 (18)
Punishment. Capital 159 (45)
Punishment. Crime and 174 (52), 218
Punishment. Politics of 151 (227)
Punishment? Prisons: Rehabilitation or 159 (28)
Punishment. Right to 168 (16)
Punishment. Theories of 214 (83)
Pupil and the Law. Teacher, the 57 (55)
Pupil. Teaching the Disadvantaged 174 (1)
Purchase of Generics. Selection and 54
Purchasers. Provocative Contractual Questions for School 132 (2)
Purchasing Questions. Ten Most Asked 132 (10)
Puritanism 216 (111)
Purpose, Destiny. Man - His Origin, 56 (138)
Purpose in Contemporary American Foreign Policy. Quest for 85 (7)
Purpose of a University 174 (10)
Purpose of Life. Islamic Conception of 1 (3)
Purposes. Salish Indian Basketry - Techniques and 151 (109)
Pursuit of a Dream. In 144
Pushing Goods and Services. Techniques for 225 (13)
Put a Little Weaving in Your Home (Interiors) 79 (30)
Put Some Wind in Your Sails 105 (13)
Putting Christmas Where It Counts 75 (1)
Putting People in Motion. Rehabilitation - 56 (79)
Putting Together the Campus Newspaper 117 (85)
Puzzle. Mongolian 29 (14), (48)
Puzzles in Elementary Topography. Games and 151 (247)

Q

Q. Buckeye 144
Quackery. Health 168 (29)
Quadruple Weaves. Double and 79 (138)
Qualifying 65 (6), (7), (8), (9), (11), (13), (14), (22), (24), (26), (30), (31), (32), (38), (40), (42), (44), (48), (52), (59), (60), (63), (64), (68)
Qualifying the Seller and His Property 65 (41)
Quality, and Priorities. People, 151 (101)
Quality and the American Way of Life. Environmental 57 (94)
Quality and the Problem of Economic Growth. Environmental 29 (73), (260)
Quality Assessment. Educational 181 (116)
Quality Assurance 151 (43)
Quality Control. Acceptable 57 (11)
Quality Control. Economics and Environmental 168 (43)
Quality Control. Water 150 (4)
Quality. Economics of Environmental 117 (34)
Quality. Food 216 (142)
Quality Impact Studies. Air 218
Quality Inspection Systems. Taptone 67 (7)
Quality Monitoring: Air Pollution Control. Air 150 (8)
Quality of Education. How Communities Can Improve the 151 (38)
Quality of Life 7 (16), 97 (19)
Quality of Life. Arts and 57 (38)
Quality of Life in the American City 31 (13)
Quality of Life in the Irish Republic 159 (65)
Quality of Life - Options and Opportunities 57 (15)
Quality of Living. Improve Your 151 (180)
Quality of Statistical Data 151 (251)
Quality. Speaking With a Conversational 168 (17)
Quality. Water 57 (94)
Quantitative Methods in the Social Sciences 142 (78)
Quantum Physics. Casualty and 56 (129)
Quarterback. Being an Eternal 135 (7)
Quartet - for School Demonstrations and Programs. String 117 (95)
Quasars and Pulsars 223 (4)
Queen and Servant. Mathematics - the 56 (125)
Queen of the Daytime Dramas. What It's Like to be 154 (24)
Quest for Purpose in Contemporary American Foreign Policy 85 (7)
Question of Legalized Gambling 97 (60)
Question of Nuclear Power. Moral 151 (133)
Questioning Schools of Teachers 117 (45)
Questions 181 (149)
Questions Answered on Love, Sex, and Marriage. Your 56 (5)
Questions. Modern Ecological 54
Questions. Ten Most Asked Purchasing 132 (10)
Quick Chemical Tests in Toxicology 54
Quiet Mystery. Marsh - A 69 (13)
Quilted 3-Dimensional Tapestries. Stuffed/ 79 (137)
Quilting 79 (98)
Quilting. Applique and 79 (84)
Quilting, East to West 79 (120)
Quilting. Quilts and 16 (64)
Quilting, Spinning. Natural Dyes, 79 (58)
Quilting, Traditional and Contemporary 79 (1)
Quilts and Quilting 16 (64)
Quintet. History and Application of the Wind 218
Quran. In Defense of the Holy 1 (6)
Quran. Jesus in the 1 (1)
Quran. Jesus in the Holy 1 (8)

R

RA. Epic Voyages of 69 (1)
RECON Literature Search Service 216 (61)
ROTC. Naval 105 (70)
ROTC. Navy 105 (75)

ROTC on the College Campus 54
ROTC Program. Air Force 174 (81)
ROTC - the Political Pressures 54
Raccoon-Coat Set. Today's Alumni - No 151 (76)
Race and Economics 175 (3)
Race Conflict in Africa 29 (7)
Race, Heredity, and I.Q. 181 (242), (294)
Race? Is the United States Falling Behind? Where Are We Headed in the Arms 102 (8)
Race. Law and 181 (46), (255)
Race. Let's Join the Human 100 (1)
Race Relations 16 (24)
Race Relations in America. Changing 56 (4)
Race Relations in the South 56 (8)
Race. Sense and Nonsense About 4 (3)
Race. Soviet-American Arms 29 (256), (292)
Race Track Culture. American 142 (48)
Races. Sailing to Win 181 (10)
Racial Adoption. Trans- 159 (41)
Racial Comedy in Vaudeville 216 (32)
Racial Paradise? Minority Studies: Beyond Takenism. Latin America: A 168 (25)
Racial, Religious and Sexual Prejudice 181 (234), (305)
Racing in Imperial Rome. Chariot 227 (42)
Racism 181 (242)
Racism and Poverty. Capitalism, 85 (30)
Racism and Poverty. Economics of 168 (41)
Racism and Sexism 142 (14)
Racism Explained 29 (49), (133)
Racism in Children's Literature 151 (241)
Racists. Some of My Best Friends Are 168 (11)
Radar Speed Measurement. Police Traffic 105 (119)
Radiation and Infant Mortality. Nuclear 151 (262)
Radiation. Effects of Nuclear 31 (30)
Radiation. Environmental 204
Radiation on Bryophytes. Effect of Ionizing 151 (151)
Radiation Physics in Cancer Therapy 218
Radiation, Radioactivity and the Public Health 27 (9)
Radiation Safety at a University Campus 27 (9)
Radiation Safety in Medical Procedures 181 (198)
Radical Movements 85 (8)
Radicalism. Nature and Future of Tory 85 (40)
Radicals in American History. Lady 151 (257)
Radio 168 (59)
Radio. Amateur C.B. 151 (68)
Radio and Television Announcing and Script Writing 142 (74)
Radio and Television Stations. Operation of 117 (86)
Radio. Evolution of the 171 (32)
Radio. Golden Age of 57 (67)
Radio - My Time is Your Time 29 (46)
Radio. Power of 151 (70)
Radio. Television and 176 (115)
Radio/Television News 168 (10)
Radio? What is Ham 174 (79)
Radioactive Waste Management. Problems and Solutions in 151 (130)
Radioactive Wastes Safe. Making 151 (272)
Radioactivity and the Public Health. Radiation, 27 (9)
Radioactivity in the Marine Environment 218
Radioisotopes. Industrial Applications of 54
Radiological Imaging Devices. New 181 (198)
Rafting Rivers. Kayaking and 223 (34)
Railroad Travel in Eastern North Carolina 56 (35)
Raising Children 176 (20)
Raising. Creative Direct Mail for Fund 151 (188)
Raising Food Consciousness 151 (177)
Raising. Spinning, Dyeing, Weaving Sheep 79 (12)
Raising. Women's Consciousness 105 (125)
Ralph Nader and Consumerism. Who Killed the Ice Man - Or, an Answer to 85 (26)
Ram. Hydraulic 136 (26)
Ranches, Farms. Groves, 65 (34)
Ranger in South Dakota. Park 57 (43)
Rape 105 (125), 168 (23)
Rape and Self-Defense 228
Rape Intervention 62 (1), (2), (3)
Rape Organizing. Anti- 178 (2)
Rape Prevention 62 (1), (2), (3), 181 (224), (325)
Rape: Victims of Crises 151 (88)
Rare Jewels of the Mediterranean 59 (9)
Rascal Patriot. Aaron Burr, 103 (5)
Rate Processes in Bile 31 (11)
Rating Your School 117 (50)
Ratings Game 105 (69)
Ravel. Piano Sonority and the Poetic Impulse of Debussy and 174 (41)
Raw Materials. Conservation of 151 (253)
Rawhide 79 (89)
Reach Beyond Your Grasp 135 (49)
Reach Your Goals 225 (38)
Reactor. Nuclear 216 (91)
Reactors. Fusion 216 (88)
Reactors. Nuclear 216 (88)
Read a Book. How to 216 (56)
Read a Book. How to Get Your Child to 151 (94)
Read. Age for Learning to 171 (19)
Read? Censorship: What Should Children 151 (94)
Read. Children's Book Only Grownups Should be Allowed to 29 (197), (205)
Read. How to Remember What You 171 (16)
Read. Learning to 171 (16)
Read More Effectively. How to 136 (23)
Read. Why Johnny Still Can't 151 (100)

Readers Theatre 159 (10)
Reading 174 (78), 181 (106)
Reading Aloud. Lost Art: 105 (26)
Reading and Does it Work? What is Speed 171 (16)
Reading and Language Arts in the Open School 117 (36)
Reading and Language Arts. Teaching More Creatively in 57 (79)
Reading and MSU 117 (134)
Reading and Writing 142 (41)
Reading Centers. Developing 142 (30)
Reading Controversy. Latest 57 (54)
Reading Difficulties in Children 181 (107)
Reading Difficulties. Preventing 171 (19)
Reading Disabilities. Diagnosis and Treatment 142 (21)
Reading Disability 181 (121)
Reading. Games and Activities to Liven Up 181 (8)
Reading? How Can Your Community Support 151 (94)
Reading is Caring and Communicating, Too 159 (54)
Reading. Language and 159 (29)
Reading. Liven Up 181 (123)
Reading Materials. Sexism in 57 (54)
Reading Mathematics 174 (67)
Reading, Mathematics and Science to Bilingual Classes in the Elementary Grades. Teaching Language Arts, 142 (90)
Reading Measurement 142 (21)
Reading. Parents and 151 (93)
Reading Problem. Your Child Has a 174 (78)
Reading Problems at the Elementary and Secondary Schools 142 (21)
Reading Program. Balancing the Parameters of a 181 (108)
Reading Program. Parents and the 181 (107), (123)
Reading Programs 29 (95)
Reading Programs. Good Books for Home 168 (53)
Reading Programs. Planning, Administering and Evaluating 142 (21)
Reading. Remedial 142 (9)
Reading Skills 142 (21)
Reading Skills in the Elementary Schools. Teaching 117 (36)
Reading. Speed 57 (54), 174 (78)
Reading Success 181 (123)
Reading. Teaching 181 (123)
Reading. Teaching of 171 (21)
Reading - the Magic Art 57 (62)
Reading to Young Children. Teaching 142 (30)
Reading. Using the Diagnostic Approach to the Teaching of 117 (36)
Readings. Dramatic 159 (27)
Readings for Special Occasions. Programs of 105 (85)
Readings. Poetry 159 (7), 223 (27), 227 (9)
Readings With Illustrative Slides. Poetry 117 (10)
Real Estate 176 (59), (78), 180 (7), (39)
Real Estate Actions 65 (23)
Real Estate. Economics of 65 (4), (14), (15), (18), (19), (34), (50), (51), (54), (56), (58), (59), (62), (65), (66), (67), (69)
Real Estate. Education in 65 (36)
Real Estate - Equal at Last. Women in 65 (20)
Real Estate Financing 218
Real Estate. Industrial 65 (62)
Real Estate. Investment 65 (3), (7), (12), (16), (17), (19), (23), (25), (29), (34), (43), (49), (50), (55), (56), (58), (61), (62), (65), (66), (67), (69)
Real Estate Investments 181 (37)
Real Estate Law 65 (22)
Real Estate Law Applications 65 (5)
Real Estate Law: Landlord-Tenant. Specialties in 218
Real Estate License Law 65 (36), (51)
Real Estate Market Activity 29 (81)
Real Estate Marketing. Computer Applications to 69 (65)
Real Estate. Motivation - Youth in 65 (42)
Real Estate. Motivational Aspects of 65 (31)
Real Estate Professional 181 (225)
Real Estate Professional of the 1980's 181 (37)
Real Estate Sales Contract. Elements in Properly Preparing a 65 (41)
Real Estate the Profession of Happy People. Lazy Man's Trip to the Bank or 65 (20)
Real Estate Today 181 (37)
Real Estate Value Trends. Farm 16 (91)
Realism in American Art 214 (8)
Realism in Euripides 227 (25)
Realistic and Humanistic Approach to Classroom Discipline 117 (51)
Realistic Fiction for Children. Canadian 171 (52)
Realities and Myths. Aging: 151 (17)
Realities and American Foreign Policy 85 (17)
Realities of Oil and Gas Supply 181 (131), (209)
Reality of Art 56 (13)
Realtor Associate Program 65 (10)
Realtor Associate Relations 65 (10), (36)
Realtor Attorney Liaison 65 (16)
Realtor Attorney Relationships 65 (33)
Realty. Protecting Title to 65 (16)
Reappraisal of Organic Form With Respect to Time and Space 54
Reason and Rebellion 85 (40)
Reasoning for Children and Professionals. Developing Moral 168 (63)
Reasons for Disorganization 225 (29)

Reassessment of Status of Women in the Ancient World 227 (39)
Rebel in Literature 159 (40)
Rebellion. Reason and 85 (40)
Rebels Gone. Where Have All the 27 (20)
Recent Advances in Commercial Canning and Freezing of Foods 216 (72)
Recent American Literature 117 (90)
Recent Developments in Religion 56 (137)
Recession. Inflation/ 174 (63)
Reclaiming the Past With Tape Recorders 117 (69)
Recombinant DNA Molecule Research 174 (46)
Recommendation. Letters of 214 (14)
Reconstructing the Human Past 171 (38)
Reconstruction 142 (27)
Reconstruction of Political Theory 85 (24)
Recorders. Reclaiming the Past With Tape 117 (69)
Recording Techniques. Multitrack 57 (29)
Recordkeeping 105 (7)
Records Administration. Health 181 (185)
Records in Drug Abuse and Alcoholism. Patient 181 (177)
Records Management 119 (1), 168 (44)
Records. Patients' Access to Medical 181 (185), (235)
Recovery in Pennsylvania. Enhanced Oil 151 (138)
Recreation 117 (54), (125)
Recreation and Conservation. Outdoor 171 (37)
Recreation and Education for Leisure. Physical 171 (27)
Recreation and Reform in the 19th Century England and France. Popular 142 (98)
Recreation Facilities. Community 16 (2)
Recreation. Forest 151 (304)
Recreation in a Modern Society 181 (12)
Recreation of Sex 211 (3)
Recreation, Physical Education, and Leisure Activities in Eastern North Carolina. History of 56 (28)
Recreation. Singing as 56 (107)
Recreational Activities for Everyone. Intramural 57 (17)
Recreational Activities. Outdoor 105 (114)
Recreational Behavior Modification 168 (64)
Recreational Facilities at Virginia Tech 216 (46)
Recreations. Mathematical 181 (1), (148)
Recruiting the Student Athlete 57 (60)
Recruitment. High School Student 105 (37)
Recruitment. Medical Technology-- 105 (45), (52)
Rectangle. Designing Within a 79 (94)
Recurrent Education 171 (15)
Recycling Clothing 57 (84)
Recycling. Economics of 216 (77)
Recycling. Neighborhoods and City 181 (254), (275)
Recycling. Textile 79 (27)
Red China, Laos, Thailand, and the Golden Triangle 54
Red, White, and Blue 189
Redevelopment. Village 216 (42)
Rediscovering the American Political Tradition 85 (39)
Reduction. Behavior Modification in Weight 218
Reduction Program. Successful Weight 181 (245), (296)
Reduction. Tension and Anxiety 174 (94)
Reed at the Movies. Rex 97 (56)
Reefs. Coral 218
Reference. Frames of 181 (88)
Refinishing Techniques. Furniture 151 (97)
Reflex. Human Myotatic 181 (155)
Reflexive Development 159 (26)
Reform and Revolution in American History. 1776-1976 213 (8)
Reform Bill. 1976 Tax 105 (7)
Reform Government. Why We Can't 225 (36)
Reform in the 19th Century England and France. Popular Recreation and 142 (98)
Reform of the Prison 168 (49)
Reform. Social Security - Current Problems and Prospects for 31 (38)
Reform. Tax 54
Reform. Tax Policies Property Tax, Tax 159 (64)
Reform. Welfare 54, 172 (10)
Reformation of Sixteenth Century 168 (46)
Reforming? What Needs 29 (64), (101)
Reforming? Why? How Do You Get Involved? Rise - What Needs 29 (347)
Refuse Collection, Solid Wastes Handling Equipment 133 (4)
Refusedniks and Human Rights. Russia, the 27 (43)
Regal India 112 (109)
Regime. China and the New 97 (57)
Regime. Present Brazilian 117 (102)
Region and General Cultural Geography of the U.S.A. Cultural 151 (184)
Regional, and Community Planning. State, 151 (226)
Regional Delivery of Educational Services 57 (10)
Regional Planning and Development. Community and 16 (54)
Regional Planning. Economics of 168 (43)
Regional Planning. Engineer in Urban and 214 (44)
Regional Planning. Introduction to Urban and 56 (101)
Regional Power Planning 189
Register for Historic Places. National 174 (19)
Regulation and Its Excesses. Federal 34 (1)
Regulation and Utilities 216 (119)
Regulation. Commodity Futures 138 (2)
Regulation. Federal 34 (1)
Regulation. Nuclear Energy 151 (133)
Regulation of Business. Economics and Politics of Government 85 (19)
Regulation of Securities Markets 85 (19)
Regulation of Transportation 31 (40)
Regulation. Pesticides 204
Regulation - State and Federal. Oil and Gas Conservation and 151 (135)

Regulation. Utility 23
Regulations, and Executive Orders. Federal Laws, 151 (1)
Regulations and Food Laws. Food 151 (177)
Regulations in Economics and Business. Government 54
Regulations in Plain Talk. Your State's Drilling 136 (26)
Regulations, the Employment Interview. Historical Overview of Equal Employment Opportunity and Affirmative Action Laws and 27 (2)
Regulatory Agencies. Banking Relations With 117 (14)
Regulatory Delays. Human Costs of 31 (30)
Regulatory Mechanisms in Obesity. Appetite 171 (26)
Rehabilitate Prisoners? Why 29 (49), (133)
Rehabilitation 181 (165), (200)
Rehabilitation. Cardiac 174 (27)
Rehabilitation. Community 56 (77)
Rehabilitation Community. Greenville and the Medical 56 (77)
Rehabilitation Engineering 181 (180)
Rehabilitation Medicine 181 (155)
Rehabilitation Needs of the Geriatric. Physical 56 (89)
Rehabilitation or Punishment? Prisons: 159 (28)
Rehabilitation Psychology - Coping 151 (18)
Rehabilitation - Putting People in Motion 56 (79)
Rehabilitation Services 181 (176)
Rehabilitation Therapy 142 (73)
Rehabilitation. Well Maintenance and 136 (25)
Rehabilitative Services for Children and Adults With an/or Hearing Problems 57 (63)
Reich. Use of Literature During Germany's Third 216 (112)
Relating to People 169 (74)
Relation to Behavior. Electrical Potentials of the Brain and Their 171 (43)
Relations. Africa - United States 97 (42)
Relations and Communications. Human 168 (52)
Relations and News. Public 216 (14)
Relations. Business/Government 23
Relations by Objective. Public 29 (39)
Relations Can Benefit You. How Public 136 (16)
Relations Can Do for You. What Public 151 (67)
Relations. Christian-Jewish 214 (80)
Relations. Communication and Human 159 (60)
Relations. Community Public 31 (35)
Relations. Contemporary International 151 (193)
Relations. Contemporary Problems in International 85 (15)
Relations. Developing Good Staff-Principal 214 (37)
Relations. Disaster Public 29 (39)
Relations. East-West 57 (75)
Relations Education. Human 77 (1)
Relations. Effective Public 168 (65)
Relations. Employee 162, 180 (179)
Relations. Family 225 (4)
Relations. Federal Labor 174 (17)
Relations for Small Businesses. Public 224 (15)
Relations for Your Organization. Public 151 (84)
Relations - Friendly Adversaries. News Media and Public 105 (67)
Relations. Future of Soviet-American 85 (31)
Relations: Getting to the Media. Public 151 (86)
Relations. Human 65 (36), 105 (13), 180 (22), (25), (133)
Relations. Impact of Technology on International 85 (15)
Relations in America. Changing Race 56 (4)
Relations in Business. Human 56 (136)
Relations in Crisis. Public 29 (39)
Relations in the South. Race 56 (8)
Relations. Industrial Psychology and 180 (8)
Relations. Institutional Public 29 (39)
Relations. Intergroup 168 (63)
Relations. International 56 (103), 151 (192), 142 (41)
Relations. Interpersonal 57 (18), 117 (115)
Relations. Japanese-American 181 (270), (342)
Relations. Labor 172 (12)
Relations. Man Environment 16 (28)
Relations. Marriage and Family 16 (35)
Relations. Minority Group 168 (66)
Relations Motivation. Human 16 (43)
Relations. Multinational Company and Its Impact on International 218
Relations: Observations, Comments and Analysis. International 117 (104)
Relations of Protestantism and Catholicism 174 (69)
Relations. Practice of Public 31 (36)
Relations Problems Still Facing Us. Human 174 (79)
Relations. Public 29 (36), (37), (55), (78), (94), (258), 56 (102), 65 (6), (22), (30), (33), (38), (39), (41), (42), (45), (46), (55), (59), (60), (63), (66), (68), 180 (135), (137), (177)
Relations. Public Sector Labor 181 (41)
Relations. Race 16 (24)
Relations. Realtor Associate 65 (10), (36)
Relations. School-Community 218
Relations. School/Community Public 168 (10)
Relations. Teachers, Publications and Public 214 (19), (37)
Relations Today. Labor 151 (223)
Relations With China and Japan. American 181 (265), (337)
Relations With Regulatory Agencies. Banking 117 (14)
Relations With the Community. University 174 (89)
Relations With the Third World. United States 57 (19)
Relations With the United Nations. United States 57 (19)
Relationship and Difference Between Acting for Stage, Television and Films 225 (30)
Relationship. Better Employer-Employee 117 (120)

Relationship Between Broadcast Journalists and the Government. Proper 117 (84)
Relationship Between Literature and Liturgy 218
Relationship Between Puerto Rico and the United States 151 (202)
Relationship. Characteristics of a Helping 117 (44)
Relationship. Improving Teacher-Student 117 (55), (120)
Relationship. Marital 159 (33)
Relationship of Languages and Mind 171 (46)
Relationship of the United States to the United Nations 16 (59)
Relationship. Parent-Child 142 (45)
Relationship. Profits - Business/Government 34 (2)
Relationship to Pacifism, Socialism and Nonviolence. Foreign Policy and Its 217 (2)
Relationship With God. Man 1 (4)
Relationships. Communication and Better 159 (60)
Relationships. Community School 174 (85)
Relationships - Component of Teacher Preparation. Human 117 (45)
Relationships. Conflict in Interpersonal 159 (60)
Relationships. Economic 159 (52)
Relationships. Enrichment of Marriage 57 (71)
Relationships. Human 174 (62)
Relationships. Improving Human 181 (289)
Relationships in School Administration. Interpersonal 117 (41)
Relationships. Man/Woman 211 (2)
Relationships. Marital/Family 181 (229), (287), (310)
Relationships. Power in Interpersonal 16 (1)
Relationships. Realtor Attorney 65 (33)
Relativism and Its Limits 85 (38)
Relativity and the Nonscientists 223 (4)
Relativity. Einstein's Theory of 56 (130)
Relativity. General 142 (65)
Relax and Live Longer. How to 29 (250)
Relaxation 176 (81)
Relaxation Response: How to Use Mental Relaxation Techniques to Enrich Your Life 136 (23)
Relaxation Techniques to Enrich Your Life. Relaxation Response: How to Use Mental 136 (23)
Relaying. Protective 150 (13)
Release Dosage Forms. Prolonged 54
Relevance of Conservatism in an Age of Ideology 85 (40)
Reliability 151 (147)
Relief Surfaces 79 (47)
Religion 52 (76), 142 (78), 176 (28), (85), (106), 180 (185), 214 (9), 224 (17)
Religion and Capitalism 85 (25)
Religion and Culture in Present-Day America 85 (12)
Religion and Its Study. Nature of 218
Religion and Medicine 75 (1)
Religion and Philosophies. Ancient 117 (64)
Religion and Politics 85 (24)
Religion and Psychology 168 (47), 214 (80)
Religion and Public Education 12
Religion and the Academic World 29 (91), (235)
Religion and the College Student 54
Religion and the Future 11 (4)
Religion and the Movies 105 (110)
Religion. Artemis and the Women's 227 (48)
Religion Dialogue. Science 29 (241), (275)
Religion? Disneyland: Entertainment or a New American 159 (51)
Religion for Mankind. Islam the Final 1 (4)
Religion. Freedom of or From 151 (200)
Religion. Greek 227 (39)
Religion. Greek and Roman 227 (3)
Religion. Greek or Roman 105 (16)
Religion in America. Status of 16 (47)
Religion in Poland 214 (81)
Religion in the Ancient World 227 (16)
Religion in the Modern World 54
Religion of Humanity. Islam as 1 (2)
Religion of Islam 142 (41)
Religion. Oriental 214 (80)
Religion. Philosophy of 56 (137)
Religion. Public Utility Invisible Taxes for 12
Religion. Recent Developments in 56 (137)
Religion. Science and 174 (53)
Religion. Science Versus 29 (156), (184), (279)
Religion. Sociology of 105 (108)
Religion. Sports as a 211 (6)
Religion Survive? Will 29 (155), (249), (291)
Religion. Technology and 16 (51)
Religion Traditions in India 56 (123)
Religions - Buddhists, Confucianists, Taoists, Maoists, Jews, Christians and Muslims. World 54
Religions. Comparative 218
Religions, Political Systems, and Culture. India, Its 151 (199)
Religions. World's 56 (137)
Religious and Sexual Prejudice. Racial, 181 (234), (305)
Religious-Cultural Ideas. Changing 11 (1)
Religious Ethics 224 (11)
Religious Faith. America as a Secularized 151 (221)
Religious Groups. New 181 (206)
Religious History, 1780-1805. Second Awakening as a Turning Point in Kentucky 117 (69)
Religious Ideas. Impact of the Prophets of Israel Upon 29 (114)
Religious Ideas. Teilhard's 11 (6)
Religious Institutions. American 151 (215)
Religious Kidnapping and Deprogramming 12
Religious Liberty and Our Third Century 12
Religious Life. Beginnings of 105 (107)
Religious Movements. Contemporary 224 (11)
Religious Revival. American Revolution Considered as a 105 (60)
Religious Revival in Modern Russia? Is There a 216 (94)

Religious Roots of Eastern North Carolinians 56 (32)
Religious Roots of Liberty 85 (9)
Religious Search. T.S. Eliot and the 105 (106)
Religious Subversion of Foreign Policy 180 (145)
Religious Traditions of India 56 (140)
Remarriage. Divorce and 105 (76)
Remedial Reading 142 (9)
Remediation. Writing Deficiencies: Need for 151 (114)
Remember What You Read. How to 171 (16)
Remembering Names--A Demonstration 105 (13)
Reminiscences of a News Analyst 83 (6)
Remote Sensing of Earth Resources 151 (139)
Removal of Suspended Solids From Industrial Waste Water 67 (22)
Renaissance 117 (74)
Renaissance in France 57 (92)
Renaissance. Irish Literacy 97 (51)
Renaissance. Latin American 151 (27)
Renaissance Music. Medieval and 142 (57)
Renaissance 2000 - You Are What You Value 180 (78)
Renal Masses. Diagnosis of 181 (171)
Renewal. Charismatic 105 (95)
Renewal for Better Living. Urban 29 (135), (159)
Renewal. Sacrament of Penance, Its Development and 105 (104)
Renewal. Separation-Loss-Grief: 181 (284)
Renewal. Urban 29 (52), 85 (1)
Rep Weaving. Workshops on 79 (148)
Repair, Care, and Maintenance of Antique Spinning Wheels 79 (99)
Repair. Clock Collecting and 168 (70)
Report. World 97 (13)
Reporting, Editing, Ethics. Newspapers, 151 (68)
Reporting. New Spirit in Investigating 135 (2)
Reporting System. National Athletic Injury/Illness 151 (279)
Reports Filed by American Corporations With the Securities and Exchange Commission. Value and Uses of Financial 50 (1)
Reports in Business and Government. Writing 168 (53)
Reports. Len O'Connor 135 (48)
Reports Proposals. Mechanics of Technical 151 (79)
Repousse Techniques. Chasing and 174 (61)
Representative Democratic Government a Reality or an Alice in Wonderland Fantasy. Is Our 136 (19)
Repression in Israel. Political 213 (16)
Reproduction. Hormones and Human 171 (24)
Reproduction. Human 181 (20)
Reptile Collecting 151 (307)
Reptiles of Louisiana. Amphibians and 174 (53)
Republic of China. Women in the Peoples' 151 (11)
Republic. Quality of Life in the Irish 159 (65)
Requirements and Safety Measures in the Electric Industry. OSHA 150 (6)
Research 142 (9), (96)
Research. Agricultural 16 (89), 151 (24)
Research and Cancer. Cell Division 218
Research and Development in Co-generation 150 (9)
Research and Information Systems. Marketing 105 (8)
Research and Teaching in Nursing Education. Balance of 105 (49)
Research and Teaching. Scope of Horticulture 16 (66)
Research at Penn State. Engineering 151 (139)
Research at Penn State. Sports 151 (209)
Research at the Garfield Thomas Water Tunnel 151 (143)
Research. Biomedical 16 (4)
Research. Brain 142 (40), 181 (179)
Research. Cancer 151 (211)
Research. Careers in Dental 181 (60)
Research: Data Interpretation. Sports Injury 151 (283)
Research. Dental 181 (175)
Research. Environmental Impact Studies and Archaeological 117 (31)
Research. Ethics and Genetic 29 (113), (131), (265)
Research. Evaluation and 168 (14)
Research. Food and Food Production 151 (24)
Research. Forecasting and 65 (1)
Research Foundation Grants. How to 105 (53)
Research. Funding of 29 (255), (268)
Research. Humanities 171 (55)
Research in Agriculture. Food and Food-Related 151 (181)
Research in Alaska. Wolf 151 (302)
Research in Antarctica. Biological 216 (93)
Research in Dental Education 181 (114)
Research in Dental Education. Role of 181 (175)
Research in Education 181 (89), (130)
Research in Greek Folklore 181 (142)
Research in the Agricultural Experiment Station 151 (181)
Research in the Atchafalaya Basin 174 (53)
Research in the United States. Basic 181 (18)
Research in the University. Role of 151 (266)
Research in Universities. Role of Interdisciplinary 151 (73)
Research. Industrial Engineering and Operations 216 (87)
Research. Informative Systems for Instruction, Administration and 57 (80)
Research into the ACT 117 (52)
Research. Look at Energy 16 (2)
Research Management and Evaluation. Interdisciplinary 151 (254)
Research Means to the University. What 16 (11)
Research Methods to Elementary School Children. Teaching 142 (5)
Research on Campus. Administration of 151 (139)
Research. One Hundred Years of Agricultural 16 (70)
Research. Operations 142 (70)

Research Organization 151 (266)
Research Program of the UCI Institute of Transportation 27 (39)
Research. Recombinant DNA Molecule 174 (46)
Research Scientists. Social Responsibility of Engineers and 16 (11)
Research. Space 171 (31)
Research. Stress Analysis in Dental 105 (28)
Research Submarine Dive on Cobb Seamount 223 (37)
Research Tell Us? What Does the 181 (122)
Research Tells Us About the Decathlon. What 29 (305)
Research. Use of Animals for Biomedical 151 (206)
Reservations and the States. Indian 29 (166), (195)
Reserve Officers Training Corps 105 (74)
Reserve. United States Army 216 (60)
Residence Time of Aerosol in the Atmosphere 218
Resident Continuing Education Center 216 (37)
Resident Hall Dilemma. Landlord or Educator: The 151 (105)
Residential Developments 65 (27)
Residential). Exchanging (Commercial and 65 (25)
Residential Living. University 57 (31)
Residential Merchandising 65 (46)
Resolution. Youth and Families: Conflict and 151 (167)
Resource Centers. Learning 181 (97)
Resource Development. Community 16 (12)
Resource. Louisiana's Wildlife 174 (20)
Resource Management. Aerial Photos in 151 (304)
Resource Management. Natural 151 (254)
Resource Planning. Role of the Community in Land 56 (22)
Resource Rooms 142 (4)
Resources. Availability of Natural 216 (77)
Resources. Conservation of Human 56 (80)
Resources Development. Human 180 (36)
Resources. Earth 154 (17)
Resources, Earthquakes - Prediction, Control, and Nuclear Power Plants. Energy and Petroleum 27 (4)
Resources, Economics, Affluence, Technology). Pollution is Great (Growth, 151 (225)
Resources. Energy and Mineral 142 (81)
Resources for Better Living. Community 57 (38)
Resources in Eastern North Carolina. Coastal and Marine 56 (36), (38)
Resources of Blair County. Basic Industrial 151 (14)
Resources of the Extension Division 216 (70)
Resources. Remote Sensing of Earth 151 (139)
Resources Unlimited 112 (100)
Resources. Using Community 57 (47)
Respiratory Diseases 181 (156)
Response to Modern Corporate Critics 85 (19)
Responsibilities of Public Institutions to the Taxpaying Public 16 (87)
Responsible Communication 57 (57)
Restoration of Philosophy 85 (23)
Restorations. Road to Ruins and 103 (6)
Resuscitation. Cardiopulmonary 174 (24), 181 (162)
Retablo and Related Folk Art. Mexican 174 (41)
Retardation as a Social Disease. Mental 159 (43)
Retardation. Genetics and Mental 29 (131)
Retardation. Genetics of Mental 29 (170), (265)
Retardation. Mental 56 (57), 117 (131), 159 (43), 218
Retardation. Parent's Experiences With Mental 216 (9)
Retarded. Behavior Modification of the 168 (64)
Retarded Citizens of Acadiana. Mentally 174 (44)
Retarded. Drug Treatment of the Mentally 181 (164)
Retarded. Educational System for Mentally 169 (3)
Retarded). Organization and Functions of ARC (Associations for 169 (2)
Retardent Textiles. Flame 16 (28)
Retinopathy. Electric Signs of Diabetic 31 (24)
Retirement Accounts. Tax-deferred Keogh 18 (1)
Retirement. Money and 151 (166)
Retirement Planning. Need for 8 (4)
Retrospective of Own and Students' Work 79 (1)
Return. Tax 168 (44)
Revenue Sharing 159 (64)
Reverend John Witherspoon. Visit With 151 (41)
Review. Current Business 29 (81)
Review of Various Types of City Government 57 (49)
Review. United States and Latin America: Latin 117 (102)
Reviews. Book 159 (23), (65)
Reviews. Play 218
Revival in Modern Russia? Is There a Religious 216 (94)
Reviving the Moral Imagination 85 (16)
Revolution. American 117 (64), 142 (63), 174 (72), (83), 214 (58), 216 (11)
Revolution and Napoleon. French 117 (64)
Revolution, and the Permanent Things. Protest, 85 (16)
Revolution, and the Politics of Benign Neglect. Social Change, 85 (12)
Revolution. Biomedical 171 (43)
Revolution Caused by a Conspiracy. Was the American 105 (60)
Revolution Considered as a Religious Revival. American 105 (60)
Revolution. Copernican 29 (177), (232), (268)
Revolution. Counter- 85 (23)
Revolution. Cuban 151 (195)
Revolution. Economics of 85 (34)
Revolution. Edmund Burke and 85 (32)
Revolution. French 117 (74)
Revolution. Health Care 181 (170)
Revolution in American History. 1776-1976 - Reform and 213 (8)
Revolution in China. Education and the Social 151 (121)
Revolution. Korea: The Land of Industrial 151 (118)

Revolution. Latin American 135 (22)
Revolution. Personal 181 (292)
Revolution. Road to 103 (5)
Revolution. Science, Technology, and the Cultural 85 (33)
Revolution. Second American 174 (72)
Revolution. Sexual 211 (2)
Revolution. Venezuela: The Democratic 151 (213)
Revolution. Vietnamese 168 (41)
Revolution. Youth Culture, Drugs and 54
Revolutionary Age. Middle East Oil in a 3 (5)
Revolutionary Pennsylvania 151 (216)
Revolutionists. Marxism and Its 85 (23)
Revolutions. Comparative 142 (1)
Revolutions. Justification of 214 (83)
Reward. How Can Education Become Meaningful and a Lifetime 151 (38)
Rewards. Profits - Spoils or Just 117 (15)
Rex Reed at the Movies 97 (56)
Rhetoric 216 (117)
Rhetoric. Ministerial 151 (78)
Rheumatic Diseases 181 (160)
Rhine. Majestic 59 (14)
Rhodesia and South Africa 214 (56)
Rhymes. Historical Origin of Mother Goose 56 (63)
Rich. It's No Sin to be 154 (5)
Richard M. Nixon's Early Years 29 (139), (333)
Richards' and Kenneth Burke's Theories of Metaphor. I.A. 151 (65)
Rickenbacker Papers 135 (54)
Ridges. Tectonics of Ocean 218
Rifle, Pistol, or Shotgun Class. Forming a 57 (58)
Right About America. What's 154 (8)
Right. New Left and the New 85 (9)
Right of Privacy 181 (211)
Right-of-Way Management. Tree Trimming and 150 (7)
Right to be Unfair. First Amendment: An Unqualified 117 (83)
Right to Communicate. Esperanto and the 58 (3)
Right to Know. People's 181 (68)
Right to Know. Public's 102 (29)
Right to Punishment 168 (16)
Right to Read Program. MSU's 117 (134)
Right to Work - A National Concern 131 (3)
Right to Work - Capitol Hill Perspective 131 (2)
Right to Work - Forcing Public Employees Into Unwanted Labor Unions 131 (4)
Right to Work - Supported by Facts, Figures and the American People 131 (1)
Right. Varieties of the American Political 85 (40)
Right - What's Wrong With America. What's 85 (18)
Right With America. What's 125 (1), 135 (14)
Right. Women's 142 (25)
Rights Amendment. Equal 56 (132), 174 (54)
Rights. American Philosophers and Natural 214 (73)
Rights and Due Process. Students' 117 (46)
Rights and Opportunities. Women's Employment 27 (2)
Rights and Responsibilities. Consumer 112 (92)
Rights. Attacks on Women's 213 (5)
Rights. Civil 31 (14)
Rights for Women? What's Wrong With Equal 112 (113)
Rights in Southern Africa. United States and Human 181 (267)
Rights in the Soviet Union. Nationalism and Human 57 (37)
Rights. Indian Fishing 159 (24)
Rights. Indian Land 29 (166), (195)
Rights. Language and Human 171 (50)
Rights Laws. Civil 29 (60), (147), (337)
Rights Movement. Children's 231 (3)
Rights Movement. John F. Kennedy and the Civil 117 (66)
Rights of Mentally/Physically Handicapped Individuals. Legal 151 (228)
Rights of Students and Young People. Legal 231 (2)
Rights of the American Indian 154 (21)
Rights of Young People. Young Person's Perspective on the 231 (1)
Rights. Parents' 57 (5)
Rights. Problems of Civil 85 (5)
Rights - Property and Personal. Economics of 85 (14)
Rights. Protection of Private Property 65 (24)
Rights. Russia, the Refusedniks and Human 27 (43)
Rights. Student 168 (12), 231 (3)
Rights. United States and Human 181 (28)
Rights. United States Bill of 31 (14)
Rights Violations. Human 154 (27)
Rights? What Happened to Our Inalienable 117 (73), (118)
Rights. Your Civil 117 (103), (119)
Rigid Heddle Frame Loom 79 (135)
Rio - Portrait of Brazil. Fabulous 110 (8)
Riot, Public Violence. Assassination, 29 (153)
Riots - Causes and Remedies 85 (35)
Rise and Fall of the Model-T Ford, 1909-1927 151 (294)
Rise of the Modern State of Isreal 181 (293), (306), (343)
Rise - What Needs Reforming? Why? How Do You Get Involved? 29 (347)
Rising Cost of Health Care 8 (6)
Rising Cost of Medical Care 27 (25)
Rising Health Care Costs 54
Risk Management 181 (44)
Risk, Management and Insurance. Areas of 168 (68)
Risk Taking Behavior 105 (99)
Risks of Nuclear Power 218
Ritt, Latter-Day Son of Ben. Martin 57 (95)
Ritual Objects in Fiber 79 (92)
River People - the Pokomo of Kenya 56 (2), (114)
River Valley Sanitary Water Commission. Ohio 151 (154)
Rivers. Effects of Thermal Pollution on 57 (16)
Rivers. Kayaking and Rafting 223 (34)

Rivers of the West. Wild 69 (8)
Rivers. Scenic 151 (304)
Road. Adventure 83 (3)
Road. Businessman's Glory 112 (135)
Road Not Taken 56 (52)
Road. Open 112 (45)
Road Through Europe. Most Exciting 51 (1)
Road to Mandalay 110 (10)
Road to Revolution 103 (5)
Road to Ruins and Restorations 103 (6)
Road to the White House 223 (23)
Robert Burns Story 97 (8)
Robert Frost and the Classics 227 (1)
Robert Frost - Individualistic Democrat 85 (32)
Robert Frost. New England of 69 (4)
Robert Frost's New England 59 (6)
Robots. Luring the 225 (8)
Rocks and Minerals 142 (81)
Rockview Beef Project. Penn State 151 (182)
Rocky Mountain Yesterdays 57 (3)
Rocky Mountains. Collection of Tree Seeds in the 151 (310)
Roel. Decanal 151 (256)
Rogers. World of Will 154 (21)
Role and Place of Theatre in the Public Community 159 (62)
Role and Responsibility of Public Television 16 (86)
Role of Books and Libraries in Society 29 (198)
Role of Confidence in Business 102 (3)
Role of Exercise in Our Society 168 (33)
Role of Instructional Materials in Education 132 (4)
Role of Men in the Women's Movement 142 (57)
Role of Music in Education 54
Role of Nuclear Power in Meeting the Energy Crisis 216 (103)
Role of Open Markets in Coordinating and Directing Economic Activity 85 (2)
Role of Persuasion in a Democracy 117 (65), (112)
Role of Philosophy 216 (95)
Role of Plant Taxanomist 168 (13)
Role of Private Higher Education in Pennsylvania 54
Role of Research in Dental Education 181 (175)
Role of Research in the University 151 (266)
Role of the Board in Catholic Education 105 (51)
Role of the Catholic School in the United States 54
Role of the Community in Land Resource Planning 56 (22)
Role of the Father in Child Development 105 (103)
Role of the Food Scientist 216 (23)
Role of the Intelligence Community 102 (29)
Role of the Latino Women in the United States 142 (68)
Role of the Student Press in Its School and Community 168 (51)
Role of the United Nations in the Middle East 102 (28)
Role of the United Nations in World Affairs 29 (63), (330)
Role of the University Theatre 16 (29)
Role of Toxicology in Death Investigations 54
Role of Trademarks in Advertising and Marketing on Domestic and Foreign Levels 209
Role of United States Government in Asia. Future 159 (36)
Role of Vocational Education 117 (40)
Role of Women in Athletics 159 (69)
Role of Women in History 54
Role of Women in India 56 (119)
Role of Women in Today's World 174 (15)
Role Playing and Defense Mechanisms 57 (13)
Roles of Unions in Business 54
Roman Catholic Moral Theology 105 (111)
Roman Cookbook. Apicius' 227 (31)
Roman Elegy. Women in 227 (24)
Roman Engraved Gems 227 (47)
Roman Festivals 227 (23)
Roman Geographers 227 (31)
Roman Grandeur 16 (61)
Roman History 227 (8)
Roman History and Historiography. Greek and 227 (30)
Roman History. Greek and 227 (3)
Roman Life. Power of Women in First C.B.C. 227 (29)
Roman Literature. Greek or 105 (16)
Roman Literature in the Thirteenth-Century 227 (12)
Roman Literature. Women in Greek and 227 (24)
Roman Lyric and Elegy 227 (15)
Roman Mothers and Lives of Their Adult Children 227 (36)
Roman Mythology. Greek and 218, 227 (3)
Roman Religion. Greek and 227 (3)
Roman Religion. Greek or 105 (16)
Roman Satire 227 (15)
Roman Satire. Modern Student and 227 (23)
Roman Theater. History of Greek and 227 (25)
Roman Theatre. Greek and 227 (14)
Roman Women. Greek and 227 (37)
Romance - Hoax or Reality? Lincoln's Use and Abuse of America's Founding Fathers. Lincoln-Rutledge 29 (338)
Romance of Undersea Archaeology 4 (5)
Romance of Words 103 (4)
Romantic and Victorian Literature 105 (25)
Romantic Heroines of the Wild West. Three 223 (3)
Romantic Love. Nature of 218
Rome 105 (17)
Rome. Ancient Greece and 54
Rome. Chariot Racing in Imperial 227 (42)
Rome. Morality and the Fall of 56 (93)
Rome - The New Social History. Medieval 27 (10)
Rome. Topography and Archaeology of 227 (26)
Rome. Topography of 227 (53)
Room to Corporate Office. City 151 (86)
Rooms. Resource 142 (4)
Rooney Goes to Washington. Mr. 112 (111)

Roosevelt. Theodore 167 (1)
Roots, a Saga of Black History 102 (13)
Roses 189
Rotary 168 (32)
Round Trip to 2000 A.D. 102 (24)
Rousseau. Burke and 85 (32)
Royal London 59 (7)
Rug Design and Rug Weaving 79 (78)
Rug Techniques 79 (69), (118)
Rug Techniques - Creatively Used 79 (38)
Rug Weaves 79 (107)
Rug Weaving 79 (8), (17), (85)
Rug Weaving. Rug Design and 79 (78)
Rugs 79 (48), (49), (61)
Rugs and Navajo Dye Plants. Navajo Carding and Spinning Along With 79 (61)
Rugs and Rya 79 (75)
Rugs. Sculptural Shaped 79 (68)
Rugs. Weft Face 79 (159)
Rugs. Wool Rag 79 (137)
Ruins and Restorations. Road to 103 (6)
Rule. Limits of Majority 85 (25)
Rule of Lawyers. Rule of the Law and the 85 (40)
Rule of the Law and the Rule of Lawyers 85 (40)
Run for Your Life 151 (67)
Running a Secular Jewish School 181 (112), (304)
Running. Expectations for College Athletes in 168 (71)
Running. Long-Distance 168 (71)
Rural and Urban Dwellings and Small Businesses. Self-sufficient Energy Systems for 163 (2)
Rural Areas. Social Benefits and Costs in Developing 117 (100), (117)
Rural Poetry 168 (39)
Russell Baker's Witty World 102 (1)
Russia, Alaska, or New Mexico. Observations on 56 (116)
Russia. Artist's Eye of 29 (11), (17), (148), (293), (311), (322)
Russia Few Ever Get to See 51 (1)
Russia? Is There a Religious Revival in Modern 216 (94)
Russia - Past and Present 57 (37)
Russia, the Refusedniks and Human Rights 27 (43)
Russia With Love. To 151 (296)
Russian Culture as Reflected in Nineteenth and Twentiety Century Literature. Male-Female Roles in 27 (18)
Russian Experience 15 (2)
Russian Literature. Aspect of the 19th Century 29 (127), (213)
Russian Writers' Tradition. A. Solzhenitzyn and the 29 (127), (213), (295)
Russians 102 (32)
Russians. Vulnerable 85 (6)
Russia's Challenge to Our Naval Supremancy 97 (74)
Rutledge Romance - Hoax or Reality? Lincoln's Use and Abuse of America's Founding Fathers. Lincoln - 29 (338)
Rya. Rugs and 79 (75)

S

SCS Denmark Study Program 168 (54)
S.I. Metrics Versus Old Metrics 151 (248)
Sacrament of Matrimony 105 (104)
Sacrament of Penance in the Early Church 105 (107)
Sacrament of Penance, Its Development and Renewal 105 (104)
Sacred Cactus. Huichol - Tribe of the 69 (9)
Sacrifice. Ancient Indian 29 (129), (247)
Safari. An East African 223 (36)
Safari. Botswana 29 (8), (167), (325)
Safari in Africa 29 (5)
Safari in Africa. On 29 (319)
Save Energy in the Home. How You Can 16 (80)
Safe. Making Radioactive Wastes 151 (272)
Safe Travel. Pavement Skid Resistance for 151 (291)
Safe Use of Pesticides 189
Safety 120
Safety and Food Fermentations. Food Composition, Food 16 (71)
Safety and Health. Job 216 (65)
Safety and Health Programs in Schools 216 (41)
Safety and Risks in Perspective. Nuclear 31 (30)
Safety at a University Campus. Radiation 27 (9)
Safety at Home and in the Hosptial. Electrical 218
Safety. Bicycle 216 (121)
Safety Commission. Consumer Product 105 (87)
Safety. Consumer 105 (87)
Safety. Consumer Product 16 (6)
Safety Education 142 (39)
Safety. Electrical 105 (87)
Safety. Fire 151 (260)
Safety. Highway 214 (88)
Safety. Highway and Traffic 16 (9)
Safety House. Electrical Safety - 152
Safety in Health Facilities. Fire 216 (99)
Safety in Medical Procedures. Radiation 181 (198)
Safety in the Home. How to Improve 16 (58)
Safety. Industrial 218
Safety is No Accident. Highway 33 (1 - 11)
Safety - Maintenance - Common Sense Equation 132 (13)
Safety Measures in the Electric Industry. OSHA Requirements and 150 (6)
Safety. Microwave Oven 105 (119)
Safety of Nuclear Power Plants 151 (132), 216 (103)
Safety on the Farm. Tractor 151 (263)
Safety. Perspectives in Product 31 (33)
Safety. Playground Equipment 132 (8)
Safety. Product 105 (87)
Safety Program for Drilling Contractors 136 (2)
Safety Programs and Administration 23

Safety Programs. Employee 216 (15)
Safety Programs. Traffic 56 (84), (85)
Safety. Water 56 (86), 174 (68)
Saga of Black History. Roots, A 102 (13)
Sagamore Hill 167 (2)
Sahara. Morocco: Cities, Seas, 15 (2)
Saharan Africa. Prehistoric Cultural Adaptations in 117 (9)
Sailing 27 (13)
Sailing Adventures. Great 59 (5)
Sailing. Aerodynamics of 216 (130)
Sailing Charters. Barefoot 57 (27)
Sailing. Science of 181 (10)
Sailing to Win Races 181 (10)
Sails Inland. Yankee 59 (5)
Sails. Put Some Wind in Your 105 (13)
Sails Scandinavia. Yankee 59 (5)
Sails the Mediterranean. Yankee 59 (5)
Sails the Nile. Yankee 59 (5)
Sails the Trade Wind Islands. Yankee 59 (5)
Saint Augustine 214 (82)
Saint Cloud State University 168 (65)
Saint Cloud State University Today and Tomorrow 168 (18)
Salad. Don't Eat Your Neighbor's 151 (61)
Sale. Closing and Negotiating the 65 (61)
Sale. Negotiating the 65 (21)
Salem: An Overview of the Witchcraft Trials at Salem, Massachusetts 117 (71)
Sales 180 (27), (163)
Sales Agent. How to Make Big Money as an Independent 180 (16)
Sales and Management 180 (132)
Sales and Management Personnel 180 (106)
Sales and Marketing 180 (53), (101)
Sales and Marketing. General 23
Sales and Motivation 180 (117)
Sales Contract. Elements in Properly Preparing a Real Estate 65 (41)
Sales. Guaranteed 65 (54)
Sales Management 23, 180 (55), (92), (103), (178)
Sales Management. Effective 180 (81)
Sales Meetings 65 (46)
Sales. Nonverbal Side of 151 (41)
Sales Person Dead? Is the 16 (6)
Sales Plan. Guaranteed Trade 65 (18)
Sales Presentations 180 (23)
Sales Training 180 (120), (147), (196)
Salesman. How to be a Star 112 (79)
Salesmanship 65 (6), (7), (8), (9), (11), (12), (13), (14), (19), (20), (24), (26), (28), (30), (31), (37), (38), (39), (42), (43), (44), (45), (48), (52), (53), (60), (61), (63), (64), (68), 180 (28), (60), (63), (64), (72), (82), (172), (200), (201), (202)
Salesmanship and Communication 65 (32)
Salesmanship. Five Basic Methods of 135 (44)
Salesmen Training 65 (6), (9), (11), (12), (13), (17), (18), (19), (20), (23), (28), (30), (31), (32), (39), (42), (43), (44), (45), (47), (48), (52), (53), (55), (60), (63), (64), (68), (70)
Salish Indian Basketry - Techniques and Purposes 151 (109)
Salivary Glands. Tumors of 181 (175)
Salivary Glands. Ultrastructure of 181 (175)
Salmon. Aquaculture of 218
Salvation 1 (8)
Salvation (Moksha). Vedanta Concept of 117 (97)
Salvation? Sea Our 151 (159)
Samplers, and Tapestry. Double Weaves, 79 (7)
Sampling Techniques 79 (84)
San Blas. Cuna Women - Mola Artists of 27 (47)
San Blas Island and the Mayans of Yucatan. Hammocks as Made by the Cuna Indians of the 79 (25)
San Francisco 15 (4)
San Francisco. Urban Design in 181 (260)
Sanctuary - Fisheating Creek. Florida - Cypress 69 (6)
Sanctuary. Tucker Wildlife 29 (75), (277), (324)
Sandburg: Citizen, Writer. Carl 225 (42)
Sandburg, Here and Now. Carl 97 (47), (49)
Sandburg's Place in American Literature. Carl 225 (42)
Sands of Alberta. Oil 181 (131), (336)
Sanford. From Archie Bunker to Fred 112 (9)
Sanitary Design 67 (18)
Sanitary Landfills, Resource Recovery, and Handling of Hazardous Waste 133 (3)
Sanitary Water Commission. Ohio River Valley 151 (154)
Santa Maria. In Search of the 4 (4)
Sarah Bernhardt 97 (28)
Sartre and Man's Search for a Missing God 29 (118), (245)
Sartre's Theory of Sexuality 29 (118), (245)
Sartrian Theory. Gestalt Therapy and 29 (245)
Satire. Modern Student and Roman 227 (23)
Satire. Roman 227 (15)
Satirist at Work 225 (1)
Satisfaction. Vocational and Job 181 (65)
Saucers - Fact or Fiction. Flying 83 (15)
Saudi Arabia. Doing Business in 3 (4), 210 (2)
Saul Bellow, Novelist 151 (245)
Save the Environment 142 (15)
Save the World. Let's Not 85 (25)
Save. Two Earner Families - How They Spend and 151 (166)
Saved? Can Our Cities Be 216 (43)
Saved? Should the University be 85 (3)
Saving Devices. Water Conservation With Water- 151 (304)
Saving Energy 222
Saving Energy While Increasing Agriculture Production 16 (31)
Saving Homes for Profit and Comfort. Energy- 18 (1)
Saving Time in Running Meetings 105 (13)

Savings by Preventive Maintenance. Energy 151 (47)
Saxony Wheel, Walking Wheel, Navajo Spindle, Large Orifice Spinners 79 (59)
Say is What You Get. What You 117 (136)
Scale and Choice of Technology. Economics of 151 (134)
Scale Process Gauges. Nuclear Density, Level and Belt 67 (19)
Scales. Balancing the 20
Scali's Europe. John 102 (28)
Scalpel, Forceps, and Seawater 56 (88)
Scandals. Journalism Ethics: Scoops to 151 (86)
Scandinavia 57 (92)
Scandinavia. Yankee Sails 59 (5)
Scandinavian) Educational System. German (and 151 (235)
Scandinavian Manner. Weaving Straw Ornaments in the 79 (38)
Scapegoat. Business - Society's 117 (15)
Scene. Color, Design, and the Contemporary 79 (158)
Scenes of the Holy Land. Biblical 159 (48)
Scenic Rivers 151 (304)
Schistik's Variety of Songs 97 (61)
Scholarly Works. Editing 174 (19)
Scholars. Dollars for 151 (89)
Scholarship Programs. USL 174 (88)
Scholarship to Society. Importance of 85 (25)
Scholarship. Uses of the Computer in Classical 227 (7)
Scholarships 57 (21)
Scholarships. No Need Athletic and Academic 31 (15)
Scholastic Press. Freedom of the 168 (12)
School Administration 168 (14)
School Administration. Interpersonal Relationships in 117 (41)
School Admissions. Graduate 142 (95)
School Admissions. Law School/Business 142 (95)
School and Community. Role of the Student Press in Its 168 (51)
School? Are the Arts Interrelated in Your 181 (92)
School Board. Administrator and the 105 (51)
School Board Liability 117 (46)
School Board? Should You Trust Your 151 (106)
School/Business School Admissions. Law 142 (95)
School. Career Education and the Elementary 57 (47)
School. Career Education and the Junior High 57 (47)
School Children. Teaching Research Methods to Elementary 142 (5)
School. Community Junior College Versus the Vocational Technical 174 (1)
School/Community Public Relations 168 (10)
School-Community Relationships 216 (75), 218
School Counselor. High 174 (76)
School Curriculum 168 (14)
School Curriculum. Public 16 (56)
School Demonstrations and Programs. String Quartet - for 117 (95)
School Desegregation. Fight for 213 (2)
School Distributor Does It All. Your 132 (6)
School District Budgets. Understanding 181 (45), (130)
School Football. Officiating High 16 (42)
School in the United States. Role of the Catholic 54
School. Industrial Arts in the Modern 151 (118)
School Integration. Problems in 56 (49)
School Journalism. High 168 (10)
School Levels. Administration at the High 56 (48)
School Libraries 159 (23)
School Math. Creativity in Elementary 181 (105), (150)
School - Mathematics Can Be Fun. Elementary 151 (250)
School Mathematics. Elementary 142 (26)
School Needs Physical Education. Why Your Elementary 174 (16)
School. New Happenings in the High 223 (11)
School Nurse. Liability and the 117 (46)
School of Business and Public Administration 159 (66)
School of Business. Information Systems Degree Program in the Cal State Fullerton 29 (92)
School of Philosophy. Challenges to the Logical Empirical 29 (232), (268)
School or Elementary School Levels. Administration at the High 56 (48)
School Organization 142 (91)
School Organization and Administration 117 (49)
School. Parents - How to Help Your Child Succeed in 29 (93), (342)
School Publications. Management of 214 (18)
School Purchasers. Provocative Contractual Questions for 132 (2)
School. Rating Your 117 (50)
School. Reading and Language Arts in the Open 117 (36)
School Relationship. Community 174 (85)
School. Running a Secular Jewish 181 (112), (304)
School Science. Look at Elementary 57 (50)
School Setting. Discipline in the 117 (58)
School Settings. Behavior Modification in Normal 117 (37)
School Site Location and Therapy 142 (79)
School. So You Want to Get Into Medical 27 (25)
School String Programs. Public 117 (95)
School Student Activities. Secondary 57 (24)
School Student Recruitment. High 105 (37)
School Study. Law 105 (56)
School Success. Encouraging Children's 117 (48)
School System. Ceramics in the Public 56 (11)
School Systems. Air Force 174 (81)
School. Teaching and Reading Skills in the Elementary 117 (36)
School to College. Transition From High 105 (34)

School to the Olympics. Men's Gymnastics: From High 168 (2)
School. Trends in the Elementary 174 (85)
School Underground Press. High 231 (3)
School. Use of Instructional Television in 218
School. What Does Your Child Get Out of 57 (13)
Schools - A Threat to Freedom. Censorship in the 151 (100)
Schools. Alchemists in Our Public 85 (10)
Schools. Alternatives in Public 117 (57)
Schools and People. Alaska - It's 57 (81)
Schools. Arts in Elementary 151 (32)
Schools Be the Death of English? Will the Public 168 (51)
Schools. Conflict and Confrontation In Our 54
Schools. Conflict in 142 (97)
Schools. Continuous Progress 174 (49)
Schools. Dance Education in the 181 (92)
Schools. Evolution of Alternative 216 (86)
Schools. Financing Capital Outlay for 117 (46)
Schools. Going Metric - In Business, Industry, Stores, and 57 (12)
Schools. Grouping Within the 56 (48)
Schools. History of Social Studies in 151 (109)
Schools? How Effective Are Our Public 159 (53)
Schools. How Parents Can Change Our 112 (89)
Schools. Improving 54
Schools in an Era of Contraction 57 (81)
Schools in Illinois: How We Pay for Them 57 (55)
Schools. Innovation Practices for Improving the Instructional Staff in the Elementary and Secondary 117 (58)
Schools. Integrating Handicapped and Normal Children in the 218
Schools. Law 159 (42)
Schools. Learning Without 214 (37)
Schools. Management of Speech Disorders in Public 56 (55)
Schools. Most Pressing Shortcoming of the Public 223 (9)
Schools. Myth of Humanism in the Public 12
Schools. Needs Assessment for 181 (116)
Schools of Teachers. Questioning 117 (45)
Schools. Personnel Administration in the Public 16 (18)
Schools. Reading Problems at the Elementary and Secondary 142 (21)
Schools. Safety and Health Programs in 216 (41)
Schools. Science in Louisiana Secondary 174 (53)
Schools. Tax Support for Sectarian 12
Schools Teach? What Should the 151 (100)
Schools. Teaching Moral Values in the Public 159 (32)
Schools Today. Arts in 151 (30)
Schools. Transcendental Meditation in Public 12
Schools. Visit to English Infant 168 (61)
Schools? What Alternatives Do You Have in Secondary Public 29 (64), (101), (347)
Schools - What Are They? Open Concept 159 (53)
Science 176 (8)
Science. Adventures of a Man of 29 (186), (272)
Science and Art. Integration of 151 (27)
Science and Business. Information Access in 44 (1 - 4)
Science and Engineering 29 (278)
Science and Engineering at Cal State Fullerton 29 (32), (111)
Science and Engineering. Careers in 29 (111), (278)
Science and Engineering Fair. International 29 (111), (278), (352)
Science and Engineering. Minorities and Women in 29 (111), (278)
Science and Happiness 85 (36)
Science and Human Value 151 (273)
Science and It's Ethical Impact 142 (19)
Science and Public Policy 218
Science and Religion 174 (53)
Science and Technology. Future and Applications of 154 (17)
Science and Technology. U.S.A. - 151 (131)
Science as a Mythology 227 (44)
Science. Aspects of History and Philosophy of 218
Science at Virginia Tech. Computer 216 (44)
Science. Calling on 222
Science Can Do for Archaeology. What 171 (36)
Science. Careers in Animal 216 (80)
Science Center. Museum and Youth 29 (106), (278)
Science Center of North Orange County. Museum and Youth 29 (352)
Science. Christian and Modern 151 (258)
Science Citation Index. How to Use the 84 (1)
Science. Computer 142 (3)
Science. Computers in Engineering and/or 214 (22)
Science. Crime and 159 (11)
Science, Effective Management. Management 105 (5)
Science. Elementary Math and 174 (49)
Science. Environmental 216 (48)
Science. Faith Versus 151 (149)
Science Fiction 16 (51), 112 (49), 216 (34)
Science Fiction and Utopias 181 (141), (231)
Science Fiction and the Future 56 (64)
Science Fiction. Classical Themes in 227 (4)
Science Fiction/Fantasy Literature 214 (46)
Science Fiction. Future and 29 (206)
Science Fiction. Ideas in 151 (235)
Science Fiction - the New Methodology 56 (64)
Science Fiction: What It's All About 117 (88)
Science for Young Children 142 (30)
Science. Forensic 159 (11)
Science. Handwriting Analysis as a 94 (1)
Science. History and Philosophy of 142 (31)
Science in Jugoslavija. Self-Management of 29 (120), (255), (268)
Science in Louisiana Secondary Schools 174 (53)
Science. In Praise of 171 (33)
Science in the Economy 171 (34)
Science. Look at Elementary School 57 (50)

Science. Marine and Naval 214 (68)
Science. Modern Materials 16 (41)
Science. Naval 214 (70)
Science Never Tasted Like This 57 (50)
Science of Sailing 181 (10)
Science on the Stage 159 (40)
Science. Poultry 216 (18)
Science Produces Good Athletes. How 171 (23)
Science Religion Dialogue 29 (241), (275)
Science. Space 56 (98)
Science Teacher and Educational Technology 29 (100)
Science Teacher Preparation 216 (129)
Science Teaching as a Career 216 (129)
Science, Technology, and Society 151 (269), (272)
Science, Technology, and the Cultural Revolution 85 (33)
Science. Teilhard and 11 (8)
Science to Bilingual Classes in the Elementary Grades. Teaching Language Arts, Reading, Mathematics and 142 (90)
Science Versus Religion 29 (156), (184), (279)
Science. Willing One's Body to 181 (14)
Science. Women in 57 (20), 171 (54)
Sciences at the University. Health 218
Sciences Careers. Health 27 (27)
Sciences Citation Index. How to Use the Social 84 (1)
Sciences. Education in the Social 142 (87)
Sciences in Dentistry. Behavioral 105 (31)
Sciences. Mathematical 214 (64)
Sciences on Cultural Values. Impact of Social 105 (21)
Sciences. Quantitative Methods in the Social 142 (78)
Scientific Detection of Art Forgeries 151 (73)
Scientific Evidence for Ghosts and Psychic Photography 154 (12)
Scientific Glassblowing 216 (136)
Scientific Investigators 105 (117)
Scientific Studies on Homebirth and Other Alternatives 122 (3)
Scientific Truth - Knowledge or Certainty 57 (6)
Scientist as an Expert Witness 159 (11)
Scientist. Role of the Food 216 (23)
Scientists Communicate - If and When They Do! How 151 (73)
Scientists. Outstanding Jewish 181 (279)
Scientists. Social Responsibility of Engineers and Research 16 (11)
Scoops to Scandals. Journalism Ethics: 151 (86)
Scope of Horticulture Research and Teaching 16 (66)
Scotland 57 (44)
Scotland and Wales 15 (4)
Scotland. Bonnie 59 (9)
Scouting 168 (32)
Scouts. Why Boy 174 (79)
Scranton). Pennsylvania Politics (Governor William W. 151 (222)
Screen. Asymmetry of the 181 (76)
Screening Test). Dial (A 142 (59)
Screens in Devonshire. Extant Wood 151 (26)
Script Writing. Radio and Television Announcing and 142 (74)
Scriptural Direction 105 (105)
Scriptural Prayer 105 (105)
Scuba Diving 142 (31), 181 (5)
Scuba Lifesaving 181 (5)
Sculptural Crochet 79 (127)
Sculptural Forms. Contemporary Basketry as Functional or 79 (135)
Sculptural Shaped Rugs 79 (68)
Sculptural Techniques. Fiber-Fabric Experimental and 79 (98)
Sculptural Twining 79 (35)
Sculpture 216 (16)
Sculpture. Ancient Forms of 227 (32)
Sculpture and Architecture. Cubism - Major Route of Modern Painting, 56 (10)
Sculpture. Architectural Fiber 79 (103)
Sculpture. Crocheted Tapestries and 79 (92)
Sculpture in Fiber. Functional 79 (138)
Sculpture in the Landscape 216 (16)
Sculpture. Soft 79 (47), (129)
Scum on Lakes. Green 168 (37)
Scythian Frozen Tombs of Siberia 29 (12), (20), (165)
Sea and Shore of Baja 69 (14), (18)
Sea and Us 142 (15)
Sea Around Us. Legal Problems of the 223 (16)
Sea Biology. Deep 29 (271)
Sea. Chambers of the 69 (15)
Sea. Food From the 29 (71), (140), (271)
Sea. Hidden 69 (15)
Sea. Law of the 3 (7), 187 (2)
Sea Movies. Making 69 (15)
Sea. New England and the 97 (61)
Sea Our Salvation? 151 (159)
Sea Power 105 (75)
Sea. Village Beneath the 59 (12)
Seafood Processing in Virginia 216 (36)
Seal Packaging. Gas Flushing Horizontal Form, Fill and 67 (15)
Seamount. Research Submarine Dive on Cobb 223 (37)
Search and Discovery 181 (124)
Search for a Missing God. Sartre and Man's 29 (118), (245)
Search for College Students. Career Planning/Job 151 (54)
Search for Identity. Soul and the 29 (164), (238)
Search for Utopia Through Government Action 85 (11)
Search of Jane Austen. In 151 (298)
Search of Singapore. In 15 (5)
Search of the Santa Maria. In 4 (4)
Search Service. RECON Literature 216 (61)
Search. T.S. Eliot and the Religious 105 (106)
Searching for Prairies, Forest and Bogs 168 (56)
Seas, Sahara. Morocco: Cities, 15 (2)

Seashells and Shell Collecting 174 (30)
Seasons. Austria for All 51 (1)
Seasons in Europe. Four 29 (321)
Seats - No Fun. No 112 (8)
Seawater. Scalpel, Forceps, and 56 (88)
Seaweed Utilization 151 (152)
Second Advent of Christ and Its Fulfillment 1 (8)
Second American Revolution 174 (72)
Second Awakening as a Turning Point in Kentucky Religious History, 1780-1805 117 (69)
Secondary Education 142 (36)
Secondary Education. Financial Aid for Students in Post 54
Secondary Education. Mime in Elementary and 29 (43), (103), (187)
Secondary Education. New Directions for 216 (129)
Secondary Public Schools. What Alternatives Do You Have in 29 (347)
Secondary School Student Activities 57 (24)
Secondary Schools. Innovation Practices for Improving the Instructional Staff in the Elementary and 117 (58)
Secret Life of Plants 134 (1)
Secret of Adam's Slip. Kingdom of God and 1 (10)
Secretarial Support. Text-Editing, and 119 (1)
Secretary. Certified Professional 174 (60)
Secretary Examination. Certified Professional 117 (27)
Secrets of the Wildlife World 69 (11)
Sectarian Schools. Tax Support for 12
Sectional Warping 79 (147)
Secular Jewish School. Running a 181 (112), (304)
Secularized Religious Faith. America as a 151 (221)
Securities and Exchange Commission. Value and Uses of Financial Reports Filed by American Corporations With the 50 (1)
Securities Markets. Regulation of 85 (19)
Security and Detentes. European 29 (56), (121), (259)
Security and Public Policy. Economic 181 (42)
Security. Arms, Disarmament, and 56 (103)
Security. Careers in Campus 181 (58)
Security-Consulting. Licensed Private Investigative 180 (86)
Security. Declining Enrollment on Job 214 (37)
Security. Freedom Versus 3 (8)
Security. Hospital Drug 88 (1)
Security. National 220 (4)
Security Policy. United States National 85 (15)
Security Problems Involving Japan and Korea. National 159 (36)
Security Systems for Home and Office 29 (136)
Security. United States and European 85 (28)
Security Versus Liberty 159 (32)
See in Nature and Relate to Your Weaving. Learning to 79 (77)
See. World That the Eye Cannot 69 (11)
See You at the Top 112 (138)
Seed to Fifty Million Dollars. From Lettuce 151 (185)
Seeds in the Rocky Mountains. Collection of Tree 151 (310)
Seeds Used in the Food Processing Industry. Development, Production and Processing of Vegetable 67 (26), (27)
Seeing the Invisible 181 (278)
Seeing Through Johnny So as to See Johnny Through 105 (98)
Selected. How Trademarks are 209
Selected, Neglected Textile Techniques 79 (33)
Selecting a Career in Engineering 151 (132)
Selecting a Home 56 (96)
Selecting Good Literature for Children 56 (63)
Selection and Preparation of Fleeces for Hand Spinning 79 (59)
Selection and Purchase of Generics 54
Selection. Employee 180 (114)
Selection of Food. Feelings and Imagery in the 171 (51)
Selection. Vehicle 120
Self and Others, How it Functions. Nature of Language - How it Influences Our Behavior, Our Conceptions, Our View of 117 (61)
Self. Environmental Awareness - An Approach to Learning and 29 (132)
Self Worth. Developing a Positive Sense of 77 (1)
Self-Awareness 168 (73)
Self-Awareness. Improving 171 (51)
Self-Change. Key to 225 (10), (17)
Self-Concept. Everybody is Somebody: The 117 (43)
Self-Concept of Children, Parents, and Teachers 216 (40)
Self-Consciousness - Private and Public 31 (37)
Self-Control 168 (47)
Self-Control. Biofeedback and 29 (240)
Self-Defense for Women 174 (64)
Self-Defense. Rape and 228
Self-Defense. Women's 62 (1), (2), (3)
Self-Development Concepts. Transportation, Education, and 46 (1 - 5)
Self-Disclosure - A View of Self 105 (89)
Self-Disclosure. Art of 57 (41)
Self-Esteem Exercises for Adults 181 (292)
Self-Expression. Photography as 171 (47)
Self-Help. Psychological 57 (45)
Self-Improvement 180 (90)
Self-Management of Science in Jugoslavija 29 (120), (255), (268)
Self-Management. Worker 181 (39)
Self-Motivation 65 (45)
Self-Motivation. Your Image and 229 (2)
Self-Protection for Senior Citizens 62 (1)
Self-Sufficient Energy Systems for Rural and Urban Dwellings and Small Businesses 163 (2)
Sell Almost Anything to Almost Anyone. How to 102 (18)

Sell Like an Ace - Live Like a King 112 (136)
Sell Successfully. How to 112 (80)
Sell Twice as Much in Half the Time. How to 112 (130)
Seller and His Property. Qualifying the 65 (41)
Selling 117 (25)
Selling America to Americans 135 (42)
Selling Can be Fun 180 (139)
Selling. Creative 65 (46), (47)
Selling Dollar. Bank Marketing, Storing and 3 (3)
Selling for the Layperson. Home Buying and 56 (97)
Selling. Nuts, Guts, and Feathers of 180 (2)
Selling. Planned 112 (61)
Selling Prices. How to Arrive at 79 (96)
Selling Power of a Woman 180 (186)
Selling. Proven Ideas for Profitable 180 (89)
Selling. Psychology of 136 (6)
Selling. Successful 180 (43)
Seminole Patchwork 79 (125)
Semiotics in Literary Criticism 227 (41)
Seneca's Tragedies 227 (42)
Senior Citizens. Self Protection for 62 (1)
Sensation and Perception 216 (24)
Sensations. Subjective Color 31 (24)
Sense and Nonsense 112 (20)
Sense and Nonsense About Race 4 (3)
Sense Not to Ask. More Than You Ever Wanted to Know About Economics and Had the 105 (32)
Sense of Self Worth. Developing a Positive 77 (1)
Sense of the Doomsdayers. Making 54
Senses. Fiber, the Body, and the 79 (27)
Sensible Ways to Teach Metrics 151 (248)
Sensing of Earth Resources. Remote 151 (139)
Sensitivities. Black Humor Humor of the Bruised 151 (243)
Sensitivity 176 (81)
Sensory Perception. Extra 214 (79)
Sentence. Grammar of the English 57 (48)
Separation 181 (221)
Separation. Integration Versus 217 (1)
Separation-Loss-Grief: Renewal 181 (284)
Separations. Membrane 31 (11)
Serial Careers for Women 29 (145)
Serious Look at Education 29 (68), (104)
Serious Look at Politics 29 (68), (263)
Seriously. Don't Take Yourself Too 57 (96)
Sermon. Newsman's 181 (68)
Sermonic Atlernative to Monologue Preaching. Drama as a 168 (34)
Servant. Mathematics - the Queen and 56 (125)
Services for Families and Children 181 (252), (313)
Services for the Handicapped 144
Services Offered by No-Load Mutual Funds 140 (1)
Services to Small Business 216 (99)
Serving Handicapped Children 181 (119)
Serving Tech Territory 216 (14)
Setting Limits for Children 117 (50)
Settlement in Employment. Methods of Dispute 223 (6)
Settlement Pattern. Communication, Transportation, and 151 (183)
Settlements in Africa. Squatter 142 (48)
Seven Days Around Austria 29 (11), (148), (322)
1780-1805. Second Awakening as a Turning Point in Kentucky Religious History, 117 (69)
1776-1976 - Reform and Revolution in American History 213 (8)
1776. Pennsylvania 151 (257)
1776-2076. Personnel 105 (9)
17th and 18th Century Italian Creche Figure 174 (41)
17th Century. Art of the Netherlands From the 15th to the 56 (9)
17th Century Metaphysical Poets. Image of Woman in 227 (29)
70's and Beyond. Humanizing Education in the 168 (21)
Seventies. Business Boom of the 112 (69)
70s. Education for the 54
Seventies. International Trade in the 85 (22)
70's. Occult Scene of the 154 (12)
Seventies. Plans and Problems of Education in the 16 (48)
Seventies. Survival in the 112 (70)
'76. Spirit of 57 (91)
Sewage Treatment 150 (4)
Sex and Marriage. Eros, 85 (18)
Sex, and Marriage. Your Questions Answered on Love, 56 (5)
Sex and Politics 178 (3)
Sex and Reality. Utopianism, 85 (35)
Sex and Society 168 (66)
Sex and the College Student 54
Sex and the Work Ethic. Social 211 (3)
Sex and Violence on Television. Gratuitous 116 (1), (2), (6)
Sex as a Family Affair 159 (48)
Sex Counseling for Couples 29 (252)
Sex Counseling for Single Adults 29 (252)
Sex Discrimination. Subtleties of 159 (60)
Sex Education 54, 105 (3), 142 (39)
Sex Education for Parents 57 (64)
Sex Education. Need for 151 (160)
Sex, Monogamy and the Freedom of Choice 211 (3)
Sex Offenses 29 (49), (133)
Sex Past and Future 142 (62)
Sex. Plant 29 (273)
Sex. Psychology of 174 (76)
Sex. Recreation of 211 (3)
Sex, Spirit, and the Fountain of Youth 225 (5)
Sexes. Communication Between the 142 (25)
Sexism 168 (4)
Sexism in Children's Literature 151 (241)
Sexism in Education 218
Sexism in Language 168 (9)

Sexism in Reading Materials 57 (54)
Sexism. Racism and 142 (14)
Sex-Role Development 142 (84), 216 (40)
Sexual Deviation. Psychology of 105 (100)
Sexual Dysfunction. Understanding 29 (250)
Sexual Ethics 105 (104)
Sexual Maturation 105 (3)
Sexual Minorities in America 181 (238)
Sexual Pleasure. Enhancing 29 (252)
Sexual Prejudice. Racial, Religious and 181 (234), (305)
Sexual Revolution 211 (2)
Sexual Roles. Women's Liberation and 85 (35)
Sexuality 168 (73)
Sexuality and Bodily Functions. Ancient Attitudes Towards 227 (18)
Sexuality. Cross-Cultural Look at Human 224 (12)
Sexuality. Education for Human 56 (3), (47)
Sexuality. Female 168 (23)
Sexuality. Human 29 (174), (274), 181 (221), (227), (284), (286), 218
Sexuality of the Disabled 181 (165)
Sexuality. Sartre's Theory of 29 (118), (245)
Sexually Disenfranchized 168 (4)
Shadow and Splendor 110 (7), (11)
Shadow. Crown and the 112 (88)
Shaggy Dog Story. King of the 112 (62)
Shake-up? Have You Had Your Annual 102 (18)
Shaker Textiles, Dyeing, Soft Art 79 (46)
Shakespeare 105 (16)
Shakespeare in America 151 (237)
Shakespeare's Histories 159 (19)
Shape of Things to Come 100 (1)
Shaped Garments 79 (138)
Shaped Garments. Loom 79 (16)
Shaping a Future of Life Style 102 (15)
Sharing. Revenue 159 (64)
Shark - Folklore and Reality 69 (10)
Sharks - Past and Present 112 (26)
Sheep Raising. Spinning, Dyeing, Weaving 79 (12)
Sheepraising Business and the Wool-raising Game. Spin-offs From the 79 (20)
Sheiks Buy America? Will the 181 (33), (203), (332)
Shelby and the War of 1812. Governor Isaac 117 (69)
Shell Collecting. Seashells and 174 (30)
Shelter. Tax Depreciation and 61 (65)
Shelters. Super Tax 181 (37)
Sherlock Holmes 142 (54)
Sherlock Holmes. Evening With 225 (43)
Shibori, and Tritik, Using Commercial Dyes. Ikat, 79 (144)
Ships Engineering. Naval 105 (73)
Shock. Culture 117 (138)
Shock Waves Upon Marine Fish. Effects of 218
Shocking Experience to Avoid 151 (261)
Shoe Manufacturing 170
Shoe Production 170
Shoes Syndrome. Old Lady in Tennis 168 (22)
Shooting. Successful Shotgun 57 (58)
Shopping Centers. Social Behavior at 181 (290)
Shore of Baja. Sea and 59 (18), 64 (14)
Short Sketch of Islam 1 (8)
Shortages. Economic 54
Shortages. Fuel 158
Shortages. Natural Gas 74
Shortcoming of the Public Schools. Most Pressing 223 (9)
Shot Being Fired? Could the West Fall Without a 97 (12)
Shotgun Class. Forming a Rifle, Pistol, or 57 (58)
Shotgun Shooting. Successful 57 (58)
Should Government Support Church Colleges? 12
Should the University be Saved? 85 (3)
Should You Trust Your School Board? 151 (106)
Show. Mr. Fingers 221 (1)
Showing 65 (7), (8), (9), (14), (20), (24), (26), (29), (30), (32), (37), (39), (48), (52), (63), (64), (70)
Showmanship 180 (99)
Shows. Magic 168 (47)
Shuttle. Space 216 (79)
Siam. Legendary 15 (5)
Siberia! All Aboard for 59 (16)
Siberia. Exploring Backdoor to 4 (3)
Siberia. Scythian Frozen Tombs of 29 (12), (20), (165)
Sick People. Diet Therapy for 117 (94)
Side of Sales. Nonverbal 151 (41)
Side of the News. Lighter 97 (53)
Side of the Street. On the Sunny 83 (9)
Siege of Vicksburg 117 (67)
Sierra. John Muir's High 59 (6), 69 (4)
Sierra. Yosemite and the High 59 (15)
Sign. Pennsylvania Dutch: Land of the Hex 117 (75)
Significance of Agriculture and Agribusiness on the Economy 16 (91)
Significance of Marxist-Leninist Ideology in the 1970's. Operational 85 (31)
Significance of Movies and Television. Social 105 (66)
Signs of Diabetic Retinopathy. Electric 31 (24)
Signs of the Time. Promised Messiah and the 1 (5)
Sikkim. Weaving of 79 (128)
Silent Killer - Hypertension 16 (13)
Silent Messages. Nonverbal Communication: The 151 (87)
Silkscreen. Photo Imagery on Fabric With Photo 79 (4)
Silver and Copper. Metals Futures Contracts in Gold, 38
Silver Bridges 100 (2)
Simple Loom. Weaving With a 79 (62)
Similarities Between 20th Century Art and Music 159 (21)

Simon Fraser. Teacher Training at 171 (21)
Simon Fraser's MBA Program 171 (57)
Simple Economics of---- 105 (32)
Simplification. Work Measurement and Work **119** (1)
Simulation of Health Care Systems. Computer 218
Simulations. Learning Games and Educational 214 (36)
Sin. Popcorn and the Piety of Celluloid 56 (14)
Sin. Theology of 105 (104)
Sin to be Rich. It's No 154 (5)
Sinclair's Model 181 (134)
Singapore. In Search of 15 (5)
Singing as Recreation 56 (107)
Single Adults. Sex Counseling for 29 (252)
Single Fiber Electromyography 181 (155)
Single Parent Adoptive Experience 181 (247)
Single Parenthood 142 (14)
Singles Strategy in Tennis. Doubles and 29 (305)
Singular. First Person 97 (11)
Sino-Soviet Conflict 85 (29)
Sino-Soviet Conflict and the United States 151 (193)
Sins of Advertising 135 (11)
Site Location and Therapy. School 142 (79)
Sites. Classical 227 (46)
Sites. UFOs and Their Landing 94 (3)
Siting. Energy Facility 151 (150)
Siting of Nuclear Power Plants 218
Situation. Arab-Israeli Conflict: Its Origin and Analysis of Present 117 (104)
Situation. Background of the Ethiopian 56 (113)
Situation. Current Economic 151 (37)
Situation in the Middle East. Current 151 (194)
Situation. International Economic 57 (61)
Situation of the International Communist Movement. Present 85 (8)
Situation. Our Energy 31 (23)
Situation. World Food 16 (30), 117 (8)
Six Inches of Partly Cloudy 83 (8)
Six Letter Word. Profit is a 76 (1)
Six O'Clock News 151 (80)
1607-1900. Jewish Image in the American Mind, 181 (262)
Sixteenth Century. Reformation of 168 (46)
Sixth-Century Byzantium. Women in 227 (12)
Skating. Physics of Ice 181 (7), (279)
Sketch of Islam. Short 1 (8)
Ski Down the Years 15 (3)
Skid Resistance for Safe Travel. Pavement 151 (291)
Skill Areas. Instructional Materials for Developing 142 (30)
Skill. Expository Writing - A Necessary 57 (66)
Skills. Analysis of Sports 151 (209)
Skills. Basic 181 (116)
Skills. Communication 180 (173)
Skills for Effective Life Making. Critical 57 (71)
Skills. Foreign Language 174 (58)
Skills. Improving Your Athletic 151 (209)
Skills in the Elementary Schools. Teaching and Reading 117 (36)
Skills. Interpersonal Competence 151 (58)
Skills. Language Arts and the Study 181 (319)
Skills. Life Management 117 (110)
Skills. Normal Development of Speech and Language 174 (8)
Skills. Reading 142 (21)
Skills. Social Change 168 (4)
Skills. Study 181 (123)
Skin Diving 218
Skins Dyeing. Soft 79 (152)
Slack Fill. Overcoming Problems in 67 (9)
Slang. Black 29 (153), (211)
Slang. Spanish 29 (208)
Slavery and Freedom. Dostoevsky's Grand Inquisitor, 85 (36)
Slavic Languages 171 (46)
Sleep and Dream Mechanisms of the Brain 159 (68)
Sleep. Phsychology of 151 (169)
Slides. Around the World in 151 (264)
Slides. Poetry Reading With Illustrative 117 (10)
Slippery Wire and Other Telephone Stuff 144
Slip is Showing. Your 151 (242)
Slip. Kingdom of God and Secret of Adam's 1 (10)
Small Appliance Weaving 79 (80)
Small Business Administration 29 (83)
Small Business Management 181 (35), (219)
Small Business. Services to 216 (99)
Small Business Subjects 29 (83)
Small Business Tax Problems 218
Small Businessman. Tax Planning for the Individual and 29 (307)
Small Devices. Weaving on 79 (3)
Small Engines and You 216 (121)
Small is Beautiful 151 (49)
Small Loom Techniques. Fiber Forms and 79 (129)
Small Museum. Organizing the 57 (56)
Small Scale Methane Production 163 (3)
Small Victories Over Doomsday: Making Technology Work 218
Smell. Chemistry of 57 (6)
Smelter. Arsenic and the Tacoma 159 (12)
Smith System of Driving 189
Smoke in the Air Isn't Good for the Economy 54
Smokey Mountains. Great 69 (6)
Smoking 113 (2)
Smoking and the Lung 181 (156), (205)
Smoking - Can I Quit 117 (109)
Smoking? Do You Mean to Tell Me You are Still 151 (83)
Snakes of Louisiana. Poisonous 174 (53)
Snakes. Venom in Harmless 151 (307)
So You Want to Be a Writer 105 (68)
So You Want to Get Into Medical School 27 (25)
So You Want to Write News 216 (14)
Soap Making 79 (101)
Soap. Making 56 (104)
Soap Operas 176 (125)
Soccer 151 (278)
Social and Cultural Facts About Pakistan 29 (19), (181)

Social and Cultural Influences on Mental Illness 214 (65), (86)
Social and Economic Aspects of Southeast Asia. Political, Cultural, 142 (89)
Social and Economic Problems of India and Pakistan 56 (118)
Social and Political Philosophy. American 214 (75)
Social and Psychological Effects of Colonization 181 (31), (294)
Social and Technological Change in Japan 168 (66)
Social Anthropology 216 (1)
Social Behavior at Shopping Centers 181 (290)
Social Benefits and Costs in Developing Rural Areas 117 (100), (117)
Social Change. Education for 54
Social Change in Africa 218
Social Change in India. Caste and 218
Social Change in the Middle East 56 (6)
Social Change. Politics of 223 (22)
Social Change, Revolution, and the Politics of Benign Neglect 85 (12)
Social Change Skills 168 (4)
Social Change. Teaching About 27 (38)
Social Change: The Individual and the Community 168 (66)
Social Change. Tradition and 85 (23)
Social Change. Women and 151 (167)
Social Changes in Eastern North Carolina 56 (31)
Social Commentator. Historian as 174 (83)
Social Competencies and Job Success 117 (20)
Social Consequences of Television 57 (32)
Social Dialects 181 (218), (314)
Social Disease. Mental Retardation as a 159 (43)
Social Drinking. Alcoholism and 218
Social, Educational and Political Organizations. Future of Free Enterprise for Local Civic, 74
Social History 142 (78), 227)49)
Social History in Communist East Europe. Political and 218
Social History. Medieval Rome - The New 27 (10)
Social History of Women in Antiquity 227 (10)
Social Impact of Technology 168 (42)
Social Institutions. Alternative 172 (2)
Social Insurance in Germany 3 (6)
Social Issues 174 (42)
Social Issues. Contemporary 85 (3)
Social Levels of Language 142 (2)
Social Planning. Problems of 85 (4)
Social Policy and Philosophy 172 (2)
Social/Political/Ethical/Theological Topics. Lectures on 168 (34)
Social Problem. Juvenile Delinquency as a Persistent 27 (37)
Social Problems. Contemporary 178 (5)
Social Problems in Economics and Urban Policy 85 (1)
Social Problems in Medicine. Ethical and 16 (64)
Social Problems Through the Market. Solving 85 (4)
Social Responsibilities of Business 23
Social Responsibilities of the Corporations 85 (1)
Social Responsibility and Mangement Ethics 151 (43)
Social Responsibility. Corporate 159 (3)
Social Responsibility of Business 168 (45)
Social Responsibility of Engineers and Research Scientists 16 (11)
Social Revolution in China. Education and the 151 (121)
Social Sciences Citation Index. How to Use the 84 (1)
Social Sciences. Education in the 142 (87)
Social Sciences on Cultural Values. Impact of 105 (21)
Social Sciences. Quantitative Methods in the 142 (78)
Social Security 181 (40)
Social Security Checks. Direct Deposit of 18 (1)
Social Security - Current Problems and Prospects for Reform 31 (38)
Social Services. Political Implications of 181 (309)
Social Sex and the Work Ethic 211 (3)
Social Significance of Movies and Television 105 (66)
Social Stresses and Strains. Sport- 29 (282), (300)
Social Structure. Changing Relationship of Business to Other Areas of the 56 (23)
Social Studies in Schools. History of 151 (109)
Social Studies. Viable Alternatives in 57 (24)
Social Welfare 117 (100), (117), 181 (308)
Social Welfare Agencies. Supervisors in Health and 181 (56)
Social Welfare. History of Public Health and 171 (49)
Social Welfare Law 105 (56)
Social Workers. Supervision of 181 (56)
Socialism and America 181 (263)
Socialism and Nonviolence. Foreign Policy and Its Relationship to Pacifism, 217 (2)
Socialism and the New Deal 172 (8)
Socialism. Black Liberation and 213 (7)
Socialism. Capitalism and 225 (23)
Socialism. Chicano Liberation and 213 (12)
Socialist-Feminism 172 (4)
Socialism. Feminism and 213 (5)
Socialist and Democratic Socialist Ideas. Libertarian 181 (288)
Socialist Ideas Through Electoral Politics. How to Spread Feminist and 178 (1)
Socialist Ideas. Libertarian Socialist and Democratic 181 (288)
Socialist Suit Against the FBI 213 (9), (15), (17)
Socialization of Women 168 (9)
Socialization of Women. Professions and the 218
Socialization. Soviet 214 (87)
Societal Roles - Today and Tomorrow. Changing 57 (15)
Societies. African Cultures and 29 (7)

Societies. Christianity in Africa - Women and Their 29 (6)
Societies. Death in Modern and Premodern 29 (281)
Societies. Importance of Family in African 29 (7)
Societies. Physiological Efficiency in Technological 56 (80)
Society. Aging in Our 181 (15), (170), (223)
Society. American 142 (78)
Society. American Cancer 151 (83)
Society and Genetics 29 (113), (131), (170)
Society, and Public Policy. Statistics, 151 (262)
Society and the Future. Urban 181 (240)
Society. Arts Education in Today's 151 (30)
Society. Arts in 16 (1)
Society. Aviation in Our 151 (34)
Society. Cashless 225 (21)
Society. Checkless 3 (3)
Society. Citizenship in a Democratic 168 (42)
Society. Computers and 142 (78)
Society. Corporations and Modern 159 (15)
Society. Corrupt 97 (45)
Society. Crime in 29 (153), (350)
Society. Drugs in 29 (171)
Society. Effects of Television on 159 (62)
Society. Exceptional Child in Today's 117 (133)
Society. Genes and 211 (1)
Society. Growth of Technocratic 171 (2)
Society. Helping the Physically Handicapped Child to Grow in Contemporary 56 (89)
Society. Impact of Technology on 142 (65)
Society. Importance of Scholarship to 85 (25)
Society in M. Zoshchenko's Writings. Soviet 29 (127), (189), (295)
Society. Individuals in the Corporate 102 (35)
Society. Inter-relationships With Law and 54
Society. Irving Babbitt - The Humanist as Critic of Contemporary 85 (32)
Society. Japanese Culture and 151 (271)
Society. Labor Policy of the Free 85 (27)
Society. Law and 159 (41)
Society. Lay Midwife in Today's 122 (5)
Society. Literature and 29 (213), (290)
Society. Locating Self in 168 (66)
Society. Marcuse and the Hell of the Affluent 85 (36)
Society. Mass 181 (248)
Society. Mass Communication in Modern 29 (36), (55)
Society of Colonial North Carolina. Sound 56 (34)
Society. Power in Our 154 (14)
Society. Psychotherapy in American 181 (291)
Society. Recreation in a Modern 181 (12)
Society. Role of Books and Libraries in 29 (198)
Society. Role of Exercise in Our 168 (33)
Society. Science, Technology, and 151 (269), (272)
Society. Sex and 168 (66)
Society. Sport and 168 (71)
Society. Sport in 29 (130), (299)
Society. Teaching and Learning in a Free 174 (1)
Society? Techno 102 (11)
Society. Technology Transfer From Universities to 151 (141)
Society. University and the Order of 85 (37)
Society. Violence in a Democratic 85 (35)
Society. Virgin in Greek 227 (48)
Society. Women in 57 (8)
Society's Scapegoat. Business - 117 (15)
Society's Whipping Boy. Deviance - 29 (282)
Socio-Economic Aspects of the Third World. Demographic and 223 (28)
Socio-Economic Middleclass Children. Education for 174 (76)
Socio-Political Theory. Black 218
Sociology 174 (69)
Sociology of Religion 105 (108)
Sociology of Sport 57 (74)
Sociology of the Family 159 (33)
Socrates 218
Socrates and the Unwritten Philosophy 174 (5)
Sodom and Tomorrow 85 (38)
Soft Sculpture 79 (47), (129)
Soft Skins Dyeing 79 (152)
Soil 117 (32), 151 (21)
Soil Conservation 151 (21)
Soils of Antarctica 218
Solar Energy 105 (117), 214 (43), 218, 222
Solar Energy Applications in Agriculture 216 (137)
Solar Energy. Heat Pumps and 216 (71)
Solar Energy. Prospects for 29 (110)
Solar Energy to Heat Farm Buildings 16 (8)
Solar Energy Utilization for Heating and Cooling Buildings 151 (126)
Solar System. Exploration of the 154 (17)
Soldiers. Morals of Civil War 151 (214)
Soldiers on Everest 69 (5)
Solid Wastes and Their Management 16 (2)
Solids From Industrial Waste Water. Removal of Suspended 67 (22)
Solids - Liquid Mixtures in Pumps and Piping. Flow Characteristics of 67 (5)
Solids. Non-crystalline 151 (73)
Solitaire Games. Coloring Applied to **181 (1)**
Soloman Gold Mines. Discovery of 1 (9)
Solution for the World Problems. Islam the Only 1 (7)
Solution Chemistry. Aqueous 159 (56)
Solutions. Parents of Handicapped Children and 142 (61)
Solutions in Radioactive Waste Management. Problems and 151 (130)
Solve Your Problems 225 (38)
Solving Family Problems 168 (7)
Solving. Problem- 105 (82)
Solving Social Problems Through the Market 85 (4)
Solving the Maze 144
Solving the United States Energy Dilemma 151 (136)

Solzhenitzyn and the Russian Writers' Tradition. A. 29 (127), (213), (295)
Some Funny Things About Women 102 (9)
Some Major Issues in Adult Education 151 (98)
Some of My Best Friends Are Racists 168 (11)
Some Other Country's History 168 (25)
Some Philosophical Assumptions of Psychotherapy 29 (245)
Something Must Be Wrong 151 (93)
Son of Ben. Martin Ritt, Latter-Day 57 (95)
Songs. Bird 142 (2)
Songs. Schistik's Variety of 97 (61)
Songwriting 225 (14)
Sonority and the Poetic Impulse of Debussy and Ravel. Piano 174 (41)
Soon Will the Arabs Own America? How 97 (45)
Soul and the Search for Identity 29 (164), (238)
Soul Dance. Disco and 29 (153), (223)
Soul of India 59 (2)
Soul of Japan 15 (5)
Sound. Architecture: An Edifice of 151 (31)
Sound Comedy: In the Beginning 151 (289)
Sound Society of Colonial North Carolina 56 (34)
Source Heat Pump. Ground Water 136 (25)
Source for Design and Color. Nature as a 79 (140)
Source. Nature as 79 (35)
Source of Monopoly. Is Government the 85 (2)
Sources. Alternative Energy 151 (123)
Sources and Goals of Soviet Foreign Policy 85 (31)
Sources. Developing Alternative Funding 57 (10)
Sources. Non-polluting Energy 142 (15)
Sources of Energy. Alternate 158
South Africa 52 (76), 175 (1)
South Africa. Change in 181 (28), (338)
South Africa. East and 223 (36)
South Africa. Fighting for Freedom in 175 (2)
South Africa - Fire Next Time 29 (7)
South Africa. Mineral Wealth of 181 (137), (347)
South Africa. Rhodesia and 214 (56)
South African Apartheid 223 (18)
South African Landscapes 223 (32)
South America, Central America, Mexico and Greece. Trips to 79 (117)
South America. Medicinal Flowering Plants of 27 (14)
South America - Prospects for Development 56 (6)
South American Pick-up Weaves 79 (107)
South and Southeast Asia. Buddhism in 29 (129)
South Asia 214 (52)
South Asia. Middle East and 142 (41)
South. Black Folk Music in the 29 (220)
South Dakota. Park Ranger in 57 (43)
South East Asia Today 85 (29)
South. Future of the 16 (24)
South India. Art and Architecture in 29 (13), (129)
South. New 154 (7)
South Puget Sound. Marine Biology of 159 (34)
South. Race Relations in the 56 (8)
South. Technology and the Future of the 16 (32), (51)
South, Today and Tomorrow. New 154 (6)
Southeast Asia 151 (189), 174 (91)
Southeast Asia. Buddhism in South and 29 (129)
Southeast Asia. Political, Cultural, Social and Economic Aspects of 142 (89)
Southeastern United States. Earthquakes in the 216 (8)
Southern Africa 171 (1)
Southern Africa. NATO and 168 (41)
Southern Africa. United States and Human Rights in 181 (267)
Southern Asia. Growth and Development in 56 (123)
Southern California. Undersea Life in 29 (270), (302)
Southern California Weather 29 (152), (276)
Southern Experience 16 (24)
Southern Highlands. Crafts of the 79 (51)
Southern Politics. Nature of 216 (50)
Southern Politics. Trends and Changes in 16 (20)
Southern Tenant Farmers Union 172 (8)
Southern Writers 216 (19)
Southwest Indian Spinning, Dyeing. Ancient and Modern 79 (76)
Southwest. National Parks of the 57 (43)
Southwest. Survey of Art of the American Indians of 151 (27)
Sovereignty and Suppression. Politics on the International Scene - 85 (11)
Soviet Affairs 85 (29)
Soviet-American Arms Race 29 (256), (292)
Soviet-American Relations. Future of 85 (31)
Soviet Conflict. Sino- 85 (29)
Soviet Conflict and the United States. Sino- 151 (193)
Soviet Dissidents. Visit With 27 (42)
Soviet Economic Life. Tourist's View of 223 (33)
Soviet Education 57 (10)
Soviet Education Compared. Two Different Worlds: United States and 159 (35)
Soviet Empire. Ferment in the 85 (6)
Soviet Espionage in North America 16 (18)
Soviet Foreign Policy 54, 57 (37)
Soviet Foreign Policy. Sources and Goals of 85 (31)
Soviet Humor 105 (68)
Soviet Man Today. USSR and 85 (18)
Soviet Socialization 214 (87)
Soviet Society in M. Zoshchenko's Writings 29 (127), (189), (213), (295)
Soviet Strategy in the Middle East 85 (31)
Soviet Underground Humor 27 (46)
Soviet Union 143 (5), 171 (2)
Soviet Union and Eastern Europe Today. Opposition Currents in the 213 (13)
Soviet Union and Germany - History and Prospects 85 (31)
Soviet Union and the Third World 85 (31)
Soviet Union. Anti-Semitism in the 218
Soviet Union. Economy of the 216 (74)

Soviet Union. Everyday Life in the 97 (40)
Soviet Union. Geography of the 117 (63)
Soviet Union. Life Behind the Iron Curtain and in the 29 (65), (289), (294)
Soviet Union. Life in the 218
Soviet Union. Nationalism and Human Rights in the 57 (37)
Soviet Union. News in the 105 (68)
Soviet Union. Sport in the 29 (306)
Soviet Union Today 117 (101), (139)
Space Activity. Future of 225 (7)
Space-and the Actor. Theater- 29 (43), (313)
Space Colonization 216 (3)
Space Man. Cave Man to 135 (51)
Space. Metropolitan Organization of American 181 (134)
Space. Mysteries of Inner 97 (65)
Space Odyssey. 2001: A 154 (17)
Space Planning. Kitchen or Work 216 (73)
Space. Power From 216 (3)
Space Program 216 (108)
Space. Reappraisal of Organic Form With Respect to Time and 54
Space Research 171 (31)
Space Science 56 (98)
Space Shuttle 216 (79)
Space. Technology From 135 (56)
Space Travel 142 (31)
Space. Voyage Into 29 (186), (272)
Spaceman. Caveman to 144
Spaces of Europe. Urban 181 (335)
Spain 218
Spain After Franco 29 (125), (151), (323)
Spain. Modern 216 (1)
Spain. Spotlight on 110 (1)
Spain. Women's Liberation in 213 (6)
Spanish American Literature 216 (135)
Spanish and Italian Culture. European Travel Relative to 151 (300)
Spanish Dialects in the World 29 (208)
Spanish. Instruction in 181 (101)
Spanish Main to the Amazon. Colombia - From the 69 (7)
Spanish Pronouns 29 (208)
Spanish Slang 29 (208)
Speak Out for Higher Education 16 (87)
Speak Up for Credit 48 (1)
Speak Up for Education 132 (3)
Speaker. Abraham Lincoln the 223 (2)
Speaker. Persuasive 168 (17)
Speaking About Speaking 151 (83)
Speaking. Business and Professional 142 (25)
Speaking. Executive 180 (138)
Speaking is Easy. Public 105 (13)
Speaking. Listening, Then 168 (17)
Speaking. Public 142 (25)
Speaking. Successful Communications and Effective 180 (14)
Speaking With a Conversational Quality 168 (17)
Speaks. Celebrity 225 (28)
Speaks Contempo. Anne Wilson 97 (71)
Special Education 56 (57), 174 (47)
Special Education. Current Trends in 181 (126)
Special Education. Mainstreaming in 159 (25)
Special Learning Problems of the Black Child 142 (47)
Special Methods of Treadling 79 (94)
Special Projects for 2 Harness Looms 79 (130)
Specialization. Clinical 105 (95)
Specialties in Real Estate Law: Landlord-Tenant 218
Species. Biologist Looks at Evolution 100 Years After the Publication of the Origin of the 54
Specific Art Interest of a Group 29 (10)
Specifications. Power Cable 150 (1)
Speculation. Stock Market 16 (17)
Speech After Cancer of the Larynx 117 (133)
Speech and Hearing Disorders 56 (55)
Speech and Hearing Therapy Services 174 (47)
Speech and Language Difficulties in Adults 56 (53)
Speech and Language Disorders 16 (67)
Speech and Language Problems. Prevention of 57 (63)
Speech and Language Skills. Normal Development of 174 (8)
Speech and Press. Freedom of 56 (94)
Speech Disorders in Children. Language and 56 (53)
Speech Disorders in Public Schools. Management of 56 (55)
Speech. How Free is Free 117 (135)
Speech in a Democracy. Values of Free 117 (65), (112)
Speech in One Easy Lesson. Give a 174 (66)
Speech Perception 151 (96)
Speech Problems 57 (90)
Speech Training. Need for 117 (135)
Speeches. Commencement 168 (40)
Speed Measurement. Police Traffic Radar 105 (119)
Speed Reading 57 (54), 174 (78)
Speed Reading and Does it Work? What is 171 (16)
Speed Warping 79 (93)
Spelling. Language and 159 (29)
Spend and Save. Two Earner Families - How They 151 (166)
Spending. Defense 54
Spending Money Wisely 174 (63)
Spheres. Poetry: Music of the 151 (244)
Spin-offs From the Sheepraising Business and the Wool-raising Game 79 (20)
Spindle and Wheel. Spinning With 79 (62)
Spindle, Large Orifice Spinners. Saxony Wheel, Walking Wheel, Navajo 79 (59)
Spindle. Wool Spinning on Drop 79 (59)
Spindles and/or Distaffs From Greece, Turkey, and Yugoslavia. Primitive Spinners - 79 (20)
Spinners. Saxony Wheel, Walking Wheel, Navajo Spindle, Large Orifice 79 (59)

Spinners - Spindles and/or Distaffs From Greece, Turkey, and Yugoslavia. Primitive 79 (20)
Spinners. Yarn Design for Hand 79 (91)
Spinning 79 (13), (36), (50), (76), (89), (91), (110), (146)
Spinning. Advanced 79 (51)
Spinning - All Kinds of Fibers. Hand 79 (51)
Spinning Along With Rugs and Navajo Dye Plants. Navajo Carding and 79 (61)
Spinning and Dyeing. Weaving, 79 (43)
Spinning and Natural Dyeing 79 (144)
Spinning and Natural Dyeing of Wool 79 (54)
Spinning and Vegetable Dyeing 79 (15)
Spinning, Dyeing. Ancient and Modern Southwest Indian 79 (76)
Spinning, Dyeing, Weaving, Sheep Raising 79 (12)
Spinning. Hand 79 (3), (101)
Spinning. History, Folklore and Processes of 79 (99)
Spinning. Natural Dyes, Quilting, 79 (58)
Spinning on Drop Spindle. Wool 79 (59)
Spinning. Selection and Preparation of Fleeces for Hand 79 (59)
Spinning Techniques. Innovative Dyeing and 79 (109)
Spinning - Techniques, Trends 79 (22)
Spinning Wheels. Historic 79 (101)
Spinning Wheels. Repair, Care, and Maintenance of Antique 79 (99)
Spinning With Spindle and Wheel 79 (62)
Spirit, and the Fountain of Youth. Sex, 225 (5)
Spirit. Art 97 (66)
Spirit in Investigating Reporting. New 135 (2)
Spirit of '76 57 (91)
Spiritual Growth. Guru and 54
Spiritual Revival on the University Campus 16 (21)
Spirituality. New 181 (208)
Spirituality of the Fathers 105 (107)
Spirituality. Prayer and 105 (105)
Spiritualism - Fact or Fancy? 151 (259)
Splendor. Shadow and 110 (7), (11)
Splendored Thing. Wisdom - A Many 57 (96)
Split-ply Twining 79 (131)
Spokane Area. Geology of Northeastern Washington and the 143 (14)
Spontaneity and Enduring Values. Love, 85 (35)
Sport and Society 168 (71)
Sport. Behavior in 151 (276)
Sport. Biomechanics of 29 (305)
Sport Clubs. Extramural 216 (46)
Sport for Those Over 35. Kayaking as a 223 (30)
Sport in Society 29 (130), 111 (299)
Sport in the Soviet Union 29 (306)
Sport Involvement Socializes Individuals. How 151 (276)
Sport Karate. Women's 62 (1)
Sport Participation. Masculinity-Femininity and 151 (276)
Sport. Myths in the World of 29 (282), (300)
Sport - 1970s Style 171 (25)
Sport Officiating 57 (74)
Sport Psychology 171 (29)
Sport. Psychology of 168 (36), (71)
Sport - Social Stresses and Strains 29 (282), (300)
Sport. Sociology of 57 (74)
Sport. Women in 151 (276), 159 (14), 181 (6), (327)
Sports 113 (2), 176 (42), (77), (112), (121)
Sports and Art 57 (82)
Sports and Christian Athletes 83 (2)
Sports as a Religion 211 (6)
Sports. Blacks in 29 (153), (304)
Sports. Club 168 (5)
Sports Clubs 105 (114)
Sports. Drugs in 151 (283)
Sports. Economics of Pro and College 54
Sports Equipment and Facilities. Standards for 151 (280)
Sports Equipment. Evaluation of 151 (280)
Sports Explosion 16 (74)
Sports From the Broadcasting Booth. Looking at 112 (44)
Sports. Great World of 112 (107)
Sports Injury Research: Data Interpretation 151 (283)
Sports. Lifetime Individual 105 (114)
Sports Medicine, a Young and Growing Profession 56 (76)
Sports. Officiating 151 (93)
Sports Participation. Motivational Aspects of 57 (74)
Sports Research at Penn State 151 (209)
Sports Skills. Analysis of 151 (209)
Sports Versus Business 112 (101)
Sports. Wide World of 112 (86)
Sports. Women in 171 (29)
Sportscasting 176 (18), (48), (63), (65)
Spotlight on Spain 110 (1)
Spouses. Estate Planning for Doctors and Their 8 (5)
Sprang. Contemporary 79 (38)
Spring. Guatemala - Land of Eternal 117 (140)
Springs. Bacteria in Hot 159 (49)
Square. Heart of the Circle Is a 83 (5)
Square the Ideological Circle. How to 85 (14)
Squatter Settlements in Africa 142 (48)
Sri Lanka 59 (4)
Stabilize the Economy? Can Government 85 (22)
Stack and Filling Equipment. Sweet Corn, Green Beans, Cherry, Bright 67 (6), (12)
Staff in the Elementary and Secondary Schools. Innovation Practices for Improving the Instructional 117 (58)
Staff or Faculty. Teaching 181 (110)
Staff-Principal Relations. Developing Good 214 (37)
Stage. Science on the 159 (40)
Stage, Television and Films. Relationship and Difference Between Acting for 225 (30)
Staging of Greek Tragedy 227 (7)
Stake in Asia. America's 102 (27)
Stand Up America 135 (59)

Standards and Work Measurement in the Office. Production 117 (14)
Standards for Generating Station Operations. Environmental 150 (4)
Standards for Grammatical Correctness. Contemporary 117 (61)
Standards for Sports Equipment and Facilities 151 (280)
Standards. How to Use the Manual of Water Well Construction 136 (27)
Star. How Visualization Made Me a 225 (5)
Star Salesman. How to be a 112 (79)
Starmaidens and Numerous Others 134 (6)
Stars 142 (31)
Stars are Made and Promoted. How Television and Film 176 (102)
Stars. Muhlenberg County, Kentucky, Its Strip Mining Industry, Its Beauty Among 117 (29)
Stars of British Drama. New 57 (23)
Stars to the City of Light. From the City of 97 (16)
Start a Business. How to 23
Starting a Plant Growing Business 216 (115)
State and Federal. Oil and Gas Conservation and Regulation - 151 (135)
State and Local Government 16 (43)
State and Local Government. Lobbying in 31 (27)
State. Archeology of Washington 218
State College and Penn State. Internationals in 151 (173)
State. Community in the Corporate 151 (49)
State Government. Use of Computers in 174 (79)
State. Ideology of the Executive 151 (190)
State Issue in Public Education. Church- 181 (102), (303)
State Legislature Doing Which Affects the Ordinary Citizen. What is the 57 (49)
State Legislature. One Man's View of the Washington 223 (22)
State of Israel. Rise of the Modern 181 (293), (306), (343)
State of Mind. Success is a 135 (3)
State of Our Nation 135 (1)
State of the Art 67 (20)
State of the Art in Mechanized Intelligence 181 (204)
State of the Arts. Current 29 (10)
State of the Economy 174 (17), (63)
State of the Economy. Perspectives on the Current 168 (43)
State of Theater in America 216 (32)
State Office and Public Education 57 (10)
State. Paternalism, Economics, and the Welfare 85 (14)
State Politics 172 (3), (5), 174 (59)
State, Regional, and Community Planning 151 (226)
State Technical Services 216 (100)
State University. Affirmative Action at the Pennsylvania 151 (1)
State University - Is It for You? Pennsylvania 151 (90)
State University Police Department. California 29 (193)
State University. Programs in Mathematics at Murray 117 (92)
State University. Saint Cloud 168 (65)
State University Today and Tomorrow. Saint Cloud 168 (18)
State. Wayward Welfare 85 (10)
Stately Home and Make Money. How to Live in a 97 (44)
Statement. How to Read a Financial 151 (50)
State's Drilling Regulations in Plain Talk. Your 136 (26)
States. Indian Reservations and the 29 (166), (195)
States. West Kentucky in the War Between the 117 (67)
States. Wilderness Studies of the Bureau of Mines in the Western 143 (10)
Station Operations. Environmental Standards for Generating 150 (4)
Station. Research in the Agricultural Experiment 151 (181)
Stations. Operation of Radio and Television 117 (86)
Statistical Data. Quality of 151 (251)
Statistics and Infant Mortality 151 (262)
Statistics and/or Probability. Mathematical 27 (17)
Statistics. Economics and 214 (33)
Statistics. How to Lie With 151 (17)
Statistics in Literature and Linguistics. Use of the Computer and 227 (51)
Statistics on Violent Deaths Among Americans. Current 218
Statistics/Probability - How to Lie With Statistics 151 (252)
Statistics, Society, and Public Policy 151 (262)
Statistics. United Nations Technical Assistance in 151 (251)
Status and Economic Development of American Indian Tribes. Legal 218
Status and Future Prospects. Tourism in West Kentucky - Present 117 (121)
Status in the World Today. America's 102 (26)
Status. Independent Contractor 65 (10)
Status of Education as Viewed by Business 132 (11)
Status of Esperanto in the Orient 58 (1)
Status of Instructional Television at Penn State. History and Current 151 (66)
Status of Religion in America 16 (47)
Status of Women in the Ancient World. Reassessment of 227 (39)
Status of Women in the Home. Economic 90 (1)
Steam Electric Plant. Electric Generation at a Fossil-fuel 150 (11)
Steamboats on the Teche 174 (14)
Steel Imports 20

Steel Industry 20
Stein's: The Making of Americans. Gertrude 181 (272)
Stereotypes. Breaking 218
Stereotypes. Cross-cultural Studies of 105 (102)
Still the Last, Best Hope 76 (1)
Stimulating Children to Write Poetry 57 (79)
Stitch and Applique. Design in 79 (9)
Stitchery 79 (98)
Stitchery. Creative 79 (82), (127)
Stitchery - Crewel or Contemporary 79 (84)
Stitchery. Folk Art 79 (117)
Stitchery. Mixed 79 (71)
Stitchery on the Loom 79 (71)
Stitchery. Pictorial 79 (75)
Stitches. Braids, Fringes and Joining 79 (53)
Stobi 227 (14)
Stock and Bond Markets. Effects of Financial Data on 31 (1)
Stock Market Speculation 16 (17)
Stoicism in Ancient Literature 227 (39)
Stonehenge Revisited. Kentuckyhenge: 117 (70)
Stop Inflation. Why Don't They 85 (10)
Storage and Transportation. Aseptic Bulk 67 (24), (25)
Storage. Electric Thermal 150 (2)
Storage. Underground Gas 151 (135)
Store. Minding the 102 (19)
Stores, and Schools. Going Metric - In Business, Industry, 57 (12)
Stores Can be Used for Political Organizing. How Food Co-ops and Community 178 (1)
Stories I Have Heard. Great 75 (1)
Stories, Poems, and Plays. Fascination of Literature - Why We Enjoy 54
Storing and Selling Dollar. Bank Marketing, 3 (3)
Storm and Stress 151 (170)
Storm. Great Ice 47
Story of Pabst History, Marketing and Advertising 145 (1), (2), (3)
Story. Tell and Show Your 151 (71)
Storytelling - Antidote for Television 29 (200)
Stowe. Harriet Beecher 181 (147)
Strains of the Lower Extremities 57 (2)
Strains. Sport - Social Stresses and 29 (282), (300)
Strangers in Paradise - Foreign Students 151 (200)
Strangers. Nation of 102 (22)
Strategic Arms Limitation 97 (74)
Strategies. Effective Communication 105 (14)
Strategies for Changing That Work 117 (100)
Strategies of Materials. Individualized Learning 181 (75), (110)
Strategies. Value Clarifying 56 (43)
Strategy. Changes in Nuclear Weapon 29 (255), (268)
Strategy. Communist Ideology and 85 (15)
Strategy in Foreign Policy. American 85 (29)
Strategy in Tennis. Doubles and Singles 29 (305)
Strategy in the Middle East. Soviet 85 (31)
Strategy. Media 29 (33)
Strategy. Nuclear Weapon 29 (51)
Strategy. Student Leadership Development: A Participative 151 (107)
Straw Ornaments in the Scandinavian Manner. Weaving 79 (38)
Strawberries. Think 102 (17)
Streams of Erie County 151 (308)
Street. On the Sunny Side of the 83 (9)
Stress 27 (44)
Stress Analysis in Dental Research 105 (28)
Stress and Personal Adjustment 174 (94)
Stress at Home and at Work. ABC's of Personally Controlling 136 (24)
Stress Before it Kills You. How to Kill 102 (4)
Stress. How to Cope With 151 (38)
Stress in Health and Disease 216 (24)
Stress of Life. Handling the 151 (39)
Stress on the Job. Occupational Stress: The Elements Which Contribute to 117 (19)
Stress. Psychology of 151 (203)
Stress. Storm and 151 (170)
Stresses and Strains. Sport-Social 29 (282), (300)
Stretching Your Food Dollar 57 (15)
Strictly Personal 112 (55)
String Programs. Public School 117 (95)
String Quartet - For School Demonstrations and Programs 117 (95)
Strip Mining Industry, Its Beauty Among Stars. Muhlenberg County, Kentucky - Its 117 (29)
Structural Analysis of Myth 227 (41)
Structural Design in Free Crochet 79 (145)
Structural Testing. Flamespread Testing and 80 (2)
Structuralism and the Classics 227 (21)
Structuralist Approaches to Drama 227 (25)
Structure and Motivation. Basketry, Historical Introduction, Contemporary Investigations, Process, 79 (5)
Structure. Changing Relationship of Business to Other Areas of the Social 56 (23)
Structure, Double Cloth. Cloth 79 (6)
Structure in the Unstructured Classroom. Providing 117 (51)
Structure. Loom Controlled Color and 79 (95)
Structure of a Protein 54
Structure of Bacteria 216 (20)
Structure of Brain in Diseased States 181 (169)
Structure of the Proton 181 (277)
Structured/Integrated Liberal Arts Programs 227 (11)
Structures. Highway Bridge 105 (121)
Structures. 3-D 79 (6)
Structures. Woven and/or Non-woven 79 (70)
Structuring Woven Furnishings 79 (87)
Struggle Against Oppression. Theater Art and the 70 (1)
Struggle for Union Democracy 213 (4)
Student Activities. Secondary School 57 (24)
Student Activity Professionals Response to Non-Traditional Students 105 (38)

Student Affairs 216 (12)
Student and Roman Satire. Modern 227 (23)
Student and the Law 168 (19)
Student and the Void. College Life: The 151 (105)
Student/Athlete 216 (19)
Student Athlete. Athletics and the 57 (60)
Student Athlete. Recruiting the 57 (60)
Student Attrition, Stopping Out, Transferring 218
Student. Blind or Handicapped 181 (2), (91)
Student. Counseling the Nontraditional 151 (161)
Student. Development of the University 16 (21)
Student Development Programs for Black Students at Predominantly White Institutions 105 (39)
Student Education Implications for Pennsylvania. Foreign 151 (107)
Student Evaluation of Instruction 174 (57)
Student Financial Aid 27 (22), 168 (32)
Student Financial Assistance Program. Alabama's 16 (68)
Student Growth. College 16 (33), (72)
Student is a Flashback! 1976 171 (58)
Student Judicial Boards at Marquette 105 (62)
Student Leadership Development: A Participative Strategy 151 (107)
Student Life: Issues and Programs 218
Student Life on the University Campus 16 (21)
Student. Older, Disadvantaged College 181 (201), (308)
Student Organizations. Vocational 181 (55)
Student Participation in University Policy Making 16 (21)
Student. Part-time 171 (15)
Student Press in Its School and Community. Role of the 168 (51)
Student Profile 168 (38)
Student Programming 174 (71)
Student Recruitment. High School 105 (37)
Student Relationship. Improving Teacher 117 (55), (120)
Student. Religion and the College 54
Student Rights 168 (12), 231 (3)
Student. Sex and the College 54
Student Teaching 174 (86)
Student Teaching in Teacher Education 117 (60)
Student. Today's College 117 (127)
Student Union 174 (71)
Student. University Comes to the 151 (103)
Student Unrest in Four Continents 85 (18)
Student. Values of Today's College 16 (21)
Student. Well Travelled 159 (7)
Student - Who Is He? Today's College 117 (42)
Student-Centered Teaching 117 (44)
Students 174 (1)
Students a Day. Europe on 84 168 (21)
Students. Alcohol, Drinking Behavior and College 151 (212)
Students and Activities 105 (81)
Students and Young People. Legal Rights of 231 (2)
Students at Predominantly White Institutions. Student Development Programs for Black 105 (39)
Students at Virginia Tech. Foreign 216 (138)
Students Can Go to College. Vocational 181 (55)
Students. Career Planning/Job Search for College 151 (54)
Students. Changing Attitudes of University 27 (21)
Students. College 151 (120)
Students. Counseling With College 168 (28)
Students. Emotional Difficulties and Mental Health of College 216 (132)
Students. Four Decades of College 151 (11)
Students Go. Where Do the 57 (13)
Students: How Have They Changed? College 16 (23), (57)
Students in Jobs. Placement of 56 (46)
Students in Post Secondary Education. Financial Aid for 54
Students in the U.S.A. Foreign 31 (26)
Students. Law With University 16 (81)
Students Learn? Where Do 151 (120)
Students of East Carolina University on Business in Greenville, North Carolina. Economic Impact of 56 (24)
Students. Penn State 151 (108)
Students. Problems of University 174 (9)
Students. Professors and Their Impact on 16 (23)
Students Still Need Private Philanthropy? Do 151 (89)
Students. Strangers in Paradise - Foreign 151 (200)
Students. Teaching Black 174 (1)
Students Today Better Prepared for a College Education? Are 16 (23), (78)
Students. Today's University 29 (291), (351)
Students Versus Universities 85 (35)
Students. Watergate and College 214 (3)
Students - Where Their Heads are at. College 29 (30), (348)
Students' Rights and Due Process 117 (46)
Students' Work. Retrospective of Own and 79 (1)
Studies in Plant Evolution 168 (13)
Study of Linguistics 171 (46)
Study Skills 181 (123)
Studying Children's Books. Ways of 171 (19)
Stuffed Forms. Weaving 79 (10)
Stuffed/Quilted 3-Dimensional Tapestries 79 (137)
Stupid. Americans Are Not Born 168 (11)
Style. Shaping a Future Life 102 (15)
Style. Transferring Technology PENNTAP 151 (288)
Style. Weaving as a Life 79 (31)
Styles. Alternative Life 57 (8)
Styles. Changing Life 102 (22)
Styles. Historical Furniture 56 (96)
Styles of Music 54
Subconscious Language. Non-Verbal Communication - The 117 (50)
Subcontinent - Bangladesh, Pakistan, India. Indian 16 (81)
Subject Matter Concepts. Career Development and 57 (72)

Subjective Color Sensations 31 (24)
Subjects. Health 142 (20)
Subjects. Small Business 29 (83)
Submarine Dive on Cobb Seamount. Research 223 (37)
Submarine Warfare. Anti- 105 (70)
Submarines 105 (75)
Subnuclear Physics 218
Subordination of Teaching to Learning 171 (21)
Subsidence. Land 136 (12)
Substances. Chemicals and Toxie 204
Substructure Index. How to Use Current Abstracts of Chemistry, Index Chemicus, and the Chemical 84 (1)
Subtleties of Sex Discrimination 159 (60)
Suburban Development and Utopia 223 (14)
Suburbia. Future of 216 (43)
Subversion of Foreign Policy. Religious 180 (145)
Succeed in School. Parents - How to Help Your Child 29 (93), (342)
Succeeding. How to Make a Habit of 180 (45)
Success 180 (154), (160)
Success and Motivation 180 (97)
Success and Prosperity. Ways to Attain Health, Wealth, Happiness, 180 (33)
Success and You. Motivation - 112 (129)
Success? Can Free Enterprise Survive 102 (19)
Success. Encouraging Children's School 117 (48)
Success. Fear of 224 (1)
Success for Women in Business. Corner Stones of 229 (5)
Success. How to Prepare Your Child for 56 (59)
Success in Business 180 (162)
Success in College 216 (29)
Success in the Free Enterprise System 180 (79)
Success is a State of Mind 135 (3)
Success. Nuts and Bolts of 112 (5)
Success. Probable Causes of 112 (10)
Success. Reading 181 (123)
Success. Social Competencies and Job 117 (20)
Success: What it Takes to Make It. Job 117 (19)
Success. What Young Adults Should Know to Better Their Chances of 151 (38)
Successful Communications and Effective Speaking 180 (14)
Successful. It's Fun Being 81 (1)
Successful Program. Campus Facilities and the 57 (51)
Successful Selling 180 (43)
Successful Shotgun Shooting 57 (58)
Successful Weight Reduction Program 181 (245), (296)
Sucker Bait - the Gambling Odds 151 (249)
Sufferers. New Hope for Asthma 27 (33)
Suffering. Philosophy of 105 (89)
Sufficient Energy Systems for Rural and Urban Dwellings and Small Businesses. Self- 163 (2)
Suggestions for Individualizing and Informalizing Education. Opening Up the Classroom - Activities and 117 (48)
Suicides. Epidemic of 216 (76)
Suit Against the FBI. Socialist 213 (9), (15), (17)
Summer and Winter Bags 79 (30)
Summer. Swedish 59 (13)
Sun? How Hot is the Center of the 218
Sun. Hydrogen From the 151 (127)
Sun. Megrab - Land of the Setting 69 (3)
Sundials 181 (132)
Sunny Side of the Street. On the 83 (9)
Super Tax Shelters 181 (37)
Supersonic Flight 216 (130)
Superstitious Influences. Voodoo and 174 (92)
Supervision. Clinical 174 (85)
Supervision of Social Workers 181 (56)
Supervision Techniques 181 (176)
Supervisors in Health and Social Welfare Agencies 181 (56)
Supplementary Warps 79 (139), (140)
Supplementary Warps. Designing and Weaving With 79 (38)
Supply and Demand. Oil and Gas Industry - 151 (135)
Supply. Growing Fish to Increase World Protein 16 (53)
Supply. Realities of Oil and Gas 181 (131), (209)
Support for Higher Education. Private 216 (107)
Support for Independent Colleges and Universities. Government 105 (50)
Support for Sectarian Schools. Tax 12
Support Program. Agricultural Price 85 (22)
Support Systems. Administrative Management and Office 119 (1)
Support Televised Violence or I'll Kill You 105 (69)
Support. Text-Editing, and Secretarial 119 (1)
Suppression. Politics on the International Scene - Sovereignty and 85 (11)
Supremacy. Russia's Challenge to Our Naval 97 (74)
Supreme Court 214 (5), 218, 219 (11)
Supreme Court in Constructing the Constitution. Decisions of the 54
Surfaces. Relief 79 (47)
Surgery. Coronary Artery By-Pass 181 (194)
Surgery. New Advances in Open Heart 181 (194)
Surgery. Oral 181 (161)
Surprising Switzerland 59 (11)
Surrender. Politics of 85 (9)
Survey of Art of the American Indians of Southwest 151 (27)
Survey of Medieval Art 56 (9)
Surveying 65 (27)
Surveying Education and Opportunities 216 (116)
Surveying. General 216 (116)
Surveying Property Lines 216 (116)
Surveys in a Group Environment 181 (283)
Survival. Environment for 97 (13)
Survival From Death on the Cross. Proofs Concerning Jesus' 1 (9)

Survival in the Seventies 112 (70)
Survival of Public Education 57 (65)
Survival. Threat to Our 125 (1)
Survival Within By Doing Without 151 (220)
Survival and Length of Life 180 (148)
Survive. Can Capitalism 154 (5)
Survive. Will Religion 29 (155), (249), (291)
Susceptibility to Adverse Drug Reactions. Patient 54
Suspended Solids From Industrial Waste Water. Removal of 67 (22)
Suzzallo Years at the University of Washington. Henry 218
Swamp. Hidden Worlds of Florida's By Cypress 69 (6)
Swedish Road to Capitalism 171 (2)
Swedish Summer 59 (13)
Swedish Tapestries. Modern 79 (75)
Sweet Corn, Green Beans, Cherry, Bright Stack and Filling Equipment 67 (6), (12)
Swimming. Competitive 56 (86)
Swing Over Today's World Headlines 103 (2)
Swinger of Birches 151 (243)
Swings, Hammocks. How to Design, Weave, and Construct a Variety of Chairs, 79 (87)
Switzerland 15 (1), 59 (14)
Switzerland in Winter 15 (3)
Switzerland. Mark Twain in 59 (13)
Switzerland. Surprising 59 (11)
Switzerland Today 59 (3)
Symbol. Bald Eagle - National 4 (4)
Symbolism and Development. Mola Blouse - Origin, 79 (25)
Symbolist Movement in Literature and Art 216 (112)
Symbols of a Culture. Language as Living 27 (18)
Symphony Orchestra. American 57 (42)
Synagogue Architecture 181 (87)
Synagogue Architecture. External Influences on 181 (306)
Syndication 65 (12), (16), (19), (24), (53), (57), (61), (65)
Syndrome. Low Bid of 132 (5)
Syndrome. Old Lady in Tennis Shoes 168 (22)
Synergetic Models of Communication 151 (65)
Syntax of English. Phonology, Morphology, 56 (65)
System-Level Values 224 (2)
Systematic Development of Instruction 216 (10)
Systems Analysis in Curriculum Development 168 (15)
Systems Engineering 151 (45)

T

T.S. Eliot and the Religious Search 105 (106)
Tacitus 227 (10)
Tacoma. Governmental Budgeting for the City of 159 (4)
Tacoma Smelter. Arsenic and the 159 (12)
Tai Chi Ch'uan 228
Tail Deer. White 151 (309)
Taiwan 4 (15), 57 (9)
Taiwan and Communist China 85 (17)
Take Charge of Yourself 112 (97)
Takenism. Latin America: A Racial Paradise? Minority Studies: Beyond 168 (25)
Talent Myth Exploded 56 (13)
Talent Waste - The Moral Crisis of Our Times 54
Talented Children. Gifted and 142 (52)
Tales. Fairy 159 (23)
Tales of the Tobacco Country 56 (41)
Taliesins. Frank Lloyd Wright's Own Homes - The Two 151 (29)
Talk. Consumers 151 (175)
Talk, I'll Listen, for a Change. You 83 (5)
Talk to Your Child About Drugs 181 (236)
Talking to the Computer in Its Language 57 (93)
Talking With Children 181 (282)
Talks on American Culture 105 (27)
Tamburitzan Institute of Folk Art. Duquesne 54
Tamburitzans. Duquesne University 54
Tankers on Puget Sound. Oil 218
Taoists, Maoists, Jews, Christians and Muslims. World Religions - Buddhists, Confucianists, 54
Tape Recorders. Reclaiming the Past With 117 (69)
Tapestries and Sculpture. Crocheted 79 (92)
Tapestries. Modern Swedish 79 (75)
Tapestries. Stuffed/Quilted 3-Dimensional 79 (137)
Tapestry 79 (48), (117), (138), (140), (159)
Tapestry and Tapestry Looms 79 (113)
Tapestry. Contemporary and Traditional 79 (78)
Tapestry. Design Approaches to 79 (35)
Tapestry. Double Weave and Hand Manipulated Double Weave 79 (69)
Tapestry. Double Weave - Four Harness 79 (74)
Tapestry. Double Weaves, Samplers, and 79 (7)
Tapestry. Frame Loom 79 (107)
Tapestry. Mock 79 (132)
Tapestry Techniques 79 (68), (76), (96)
Tapestry Techniques. Contemporary 79 (39)
Tapestry Techniques. Plain Weave 79 (153)
Tapestry - Tradition and Innovation 79 (112)
Tapestry, Traditional and Contemporary 79 (49)
Tapestry Using Double Weave. Dimensional 79 (119)
Tapestry Weaver. Woven Image - My Development as a 79 (44)
Tapestry Weaving 79 (75), (85), (110)
Tapestry Weaving. Achieving Texture in 79 (108)
Tapestry Weaving. Frame Loom 79 (9)
Tapestry Weaving, History and Design 79 (44)
Tapestry Weaving. Mexican 79 (54)
Taptone Quality Inspection Systems 67 (7)
Tarot. ESP Through the 117 (96)
Task. Alcohol and the Driving 174 (12)
Tasks for Teachers 29 (90)
Tasks. Freedom's Unfinished 12

Tassels and Fringes. Braids, 79 (80)
Tatting 79 (146)
Tattle Tales About First Ladies 112 (11)
Tax and the Distributing of Income. Income 151 (166)
Tax-Deferred Individual Retirement Accounts 18 (1)
Tax-Deferred Keogh Retirement Accounts 18 (1)
Tax Depreciation and Shelter 61 (65)
Tax Exemptions. Future of Church 12
Tax. Federal and Pennsylvania Income 151 (44)
Tax Inferred and Exempt Income 151 (44)
Tax Planning for the Individual and Small Businessman 29 (307)
Tax Policies 216 (119)
Tax Policies, Property Tax, Tax Reform 159 (64)
Tax Problems. Small Business 218
Tax Reform 54
Tax Reform Bill. 1976 105 (7)
Tax Reform. Tax Policies, Property Tax, 159 (64)
Tax Return 168 (44)
Tax Shelters. Super 181 (37)
Tax Support for Sectarian Schools 12
Tax Topics. Other Federal Income 105 (7)
Taxanomist. Role of Plant 168 (13)
Taxation 23, 159 (22)
Taxation. Federal 54
Taxation. Federal Income 159 (9)
Taxes and How They Affect You. Income 151 (50)
Taxes. Economics of 54
Taxes for Religion. Public Utility Invisible 12
Taxes. Payroll 105 (7)
Taxies 31 (40)
Taxpaying Public. Responsibilities of Public Institutions to the 16 (87)
Teacher and Educational Technology. Science 29 (100)
Teacher and the Law 168 (19)
Teacher. Art, Music, and Cooking Activities for the Classroom 117 (48)
Teacher Behavior 181 (286)
Teacher. Being a Human 29 (132)
Teacher Certification. Illinois 57 (48)
Teacher? Do You Have What It Takes to Be a 168 (38)
Teacher. Don't Flunk the 112 (76)
Teacher Education 174 (86), 181 (89), (122)
Teacher Education. Secondary 142 (74)
Teacher Education. Student Teaching in 117 (60)
Teacher Evaluation and Improvement of Instruction 105 (48)
Teacher. Liability and the 117 (46)
Teacher. Liability and the Vocational 117 (46)
Teacher Modeling Behavior in the Physical, Intellectual and Emotional Domains 117 (39)
Teacher Organizations. Professional 174 (49)
Teacher Preparation. Human Relationships - Component of 117 (45)
Teacher Preparation. Science 216 (129)
Teacher - Student Relationship. Improving 117 (55), (120)
Teacher, the Pupil and the Law 57 (55)
Teacher Training 142 (36)
Teacher Training at Simon Fraser 171 (21)
Teachers and Collective Bargaining 181 (129)
Teachers Can Encourage Creativity. Helping Children to Be More Creative - Ways Parents and 117 (48)
Teachers. Carkhuff Learning and Counseling Models for 117 (39)
Teachers. Drug Abuse - A Course for Parents and 56 (83)
Teachers. Health Education for Elementary 181 (113)
Teachers. In-Service Training of 142 (36)
Teachers-Nursery-4th Grade. Language Arts and Math Activities for 117 (48)
Teachers of Children. Parents - First 151 (172)
Teachers, Publications and Public Relations 214 (19), (37)
Teachers. Questioning Schools of 117 (45)
Teachers. Self-Concept of Children, Parents, and 216 (40)
Teachers. Tasks for 29 (90)
Teaching About Social Change 27 (38)
Teaching and Learning. Approach for 181 (122)
Teaching and Learning in a Free Society 174 (1)
Teaching and Learning. Media in 181 (75), (110)
Teaching and Reading Skills in the Elementary Schools 117 (36)
Teaching Art. Interdisciplinary Method of 142 (35)
Teaching as a Career. Science 216 (129)
Teaching as a Profession 56 (42)
Teaching Black Students 174 (1)
Teaching Children Mathematics 151 (121)
Teaching Classics 227 (38)
Teaching in Nursing Education. Balance of Research and 105 (49)
Teaching in Teacher Education. Student 117 (60)
Teaching Industrial Arts. Careers in 117 (80)
Teaching. Innovations in 216 (58)
Teaching. Kodaly Approach to Music 54
Teaching Language Arts, Reading, Mathematics and Science to Bilingual Classes in the Elementary Grades 142 (90)
Teaching. Linguistics and Language 117 (87)
Teaching Methods. Air Force 174 (81)
Teaching Methods. English 168 (53)
Teaching Moral Values in the Public Schools 159 (32)
Teaching More Creatively in Reading and Language Arts 57 (79)
Teaching. Natural Approach to Foreign Language 27 (15)
Teaching of Latin 227 (18)
Teaching of Mathematics 171 (21)
Teaching of Mathematics. Motivation in the 117 (92)
Teaching of Physics. Use of Hobbies in the 57 (87)

Teaching of Reading 171 (21)
Teaching of Reading. Using the Diagnostic Approach to the 117 (36)
Teaching. Oral History and 181 (93)
Teaching Pathology 181 (182)
Teaching Personally Useful Psychology 57 (45)
Teaching. Professionalization of 181 (102)
Teaching Reading 181 (123)
Teaching Reading to Young Children 142 (30)
Teaching Research Methods to Elementary School Children 142 (5)
Teaching. Scope of Horticulture Research, and 16 (66)
Teaching Staff or Faculty 181 (110)
Teaching. Student 174 (86)
Teaching. Student-Centered 117 (44)
Teaching. Team 181 (118)
Teaching Techniques 142 (39)
Teaching Techniques You Can Use 216 (28)
Teaching the Culturally Different 57 (85)
Teaching the Disadvantaged 216 (28)
Teaching the Disadvantaged Pupil 174 (1)
Teaching to Learning. Subordination of 171 (21)
Teaching Tool. Instructional Television as a 151 (66)
Teaching Weaving on a Zero Budget 79 (107)
Teaching With Computers 142 (70)
Teachings of Muhammad. Glimpse Into the Life and 1 (8)
Team and Athletes. America's First Olympic 151 (275)
Team. Engineering 151 (131)
Team Handball 105 (114)
Team Teaching 181 (118)
Teche Country 174 (19)
Teche. Steamboats on the 174 (14)
Technical and Conceptual Approaches to Drawing 117 (11)
Technical Aspects of Hardwood, Plywood, and Veneer 80 (1)
Technical Assistance in Statistics. United Nations 151 (251)
Technical Assistance Program Can Help You. How the Pennsylvania 151 (47)
Technical Drawing: Universal Graphic Language 117 (82)
Technical Editing. Creative Potential in 151 (79)
Technical Reports Proposals. Mechanics of 151 (79)
Technical School. Community Junior College Versus the Vocational 174 (1)
Technical Services. State 216 (100)
Technical Training 174 (97)
Technical Writing. Fiction of 151 (79)
Technique for Enjoying Art 105 (19)
Technique. Moorman 79 (88)
Technique. Weaving and Enameling 79 (128)
Techniques and Contemporary Uses. Ancient American Indian Weaving 79 (90)
Techniques and Design. Card Weaving - 79 (155)
Techniques and Purposes. Salish Indian Basketry - 151 (109)
Techniques. Audiovisual Production 181 (97)
Techniques. Basic 79 (63), (110), (118)
Techniques. Basketry 79 (4), (47)
Techniques. Batik and Tie-dye 79 (9)
Techniques. Chasing and Repousse 174 (61)
Techniques. Combined Resist Dyeing 79 (108)
Techniques. Contemporary Tapestry 79 (39)
Techniques - Creatively Used. Rug 79 (38)
Techniques. Discussion 142 (25)
Techniques. Dye 79 (33)
Techniques. Fiber-fabric Experimental and Sculptural 79 (98)
Techniques. Fiber Forms and Small Loom 79 (129)
Techniques for Beginners. 48 79 (74)
Techniques for Inkle Bands 79 (133)
Techniques for Pushing Goods and Services 225 (13)
Techniques for Today. Ancient Textile 79 (35)
Techniques. Forestry 159 (13)
Techniques. Furniture Refinishing 151 (97)
Techniques in Nuclear Medicine. Current 218
Techniques in Weaving. Fiber 79 (29)
Techniques. Innovative Dyeing and Spinning 79 (109)
Techniques. Interrelationships of Non-loom 79 (8)
Techniques. Memory 180 (164)
Techniques. Mixed Textile 79 (71)
Techniques. Multi-Image Production 142 (75)
Techniques. Multitrack Recording 57 (29)
Techniques. Navajo and Hopi Weaving 79 (100)
Techniques. Non-Loom 79 (118), (140)
Techniques. Nuclear Magnetic Resonance 159 (56)
Techniques of Aggression Control 31 (2)
Techniques of Basketry 79 (151)
Techniques of Bolivian Highland Weaving. Art and 79 (18)
Techniques of Computer Programming. New 181 (51)
Techniques of Ethnic Groups and Contemporary Adaptions. Textile 79 (8)
Techniques of Portrait Artistry 168 (8)
Techniques of Public Relations 168 (50)
Techniques of the Incentive Marketing Field 130 (1 - 36)
Techniques of Urban Planning 54
Techniques. Off-Loom 79 (53)
Techniques. Off-Loom Weaving 79 (149)
Techniques. Oral History 142 (5)
Techniques. Plain Weave Tapestry 79 (153)
Techniques. Problem-Solving 151 (103)
Techniques. Rug 79 (69), (118)
Techniques. Sampling 79 (84)
Techniques. Selected, Neglected Textile 79 (33)
Techniques. Supervision 181 (176)
Techniques. Tapestry 79 (68), (76), (96)
Techniques. Teaching 142 (39)
Techniques. Telephone 65 (32), 180 (31)
Techniques. Television Advertising 151 (87)
Techniques. Television Production 151 (66)

Techniques to Enrich Your Life. Relaxation Response: How to Use Mental Relaxation 136 (23)
Techniques. Track and Field 171 (30)
Techniques, Trends. Spinning - 79 (22)
Techniques. Two Harness 79 (3)
Techniques. Uses of Counseling Groups and 151 (161)
Techniques You Can Use. Teaching 216 (28)
Techno Society? 102 (11)
Technological Change in Japan. Social and 168 (66)
Technological Era. Ethics in a 159 (12)
Technological Societies. Physiological Efficiency in 56 (80)
Technologies in Graphic Arts. New 218
Technology 168 (40)
Technology - A New Way of Life. Exploding 102 (22)
Technology and Human Values 105 (118), 151 (157), (272)
Technology and Religion 16 (51)
Technology, and Society. Science 151 (269), (272)
Technology, and the Cultural Revolution. Science, 85 (33)
Technology and the Food We Eat 151 (177)
Technology and the Future 57 (46)
Technology and the Future of the South 16 (32), (51)
Technology and Values 57 (46)
Technology at Penn State. Engineering and Engineering 151 (49)
Technology at WWSC 223 (31)
Technology. Careers in Engineering 151 (53)
Technology. Careers in Medical 181 (64)
Technology. Communication 29 (35), (142), (285)
Technology. Computer 214 (20)
Technology. Demystification of Education 181 (110)
Technology. Economics of Scale and Choice of 151 (134)
Technology. Education and 142 (75)
Technology Education. Construction 168 (6)
Technology. Education for Present and Future 105 (117)
Technology Education. Industrial 168 (6)
Technology Education. Manufacturing 168 (6)
Technology. Engineering 151 (140), 174 (97)
Technology From Space 135 (56)
Technology. Future and Applications of Science and 154 (17)
Technology. Getting the Most From Transportation 151 (293)
Technology: History, Improtance and Fundamentals. Plastics 117 (81)
Technology in Education 224 (5)
Technology in Literature 151 (245)
Technology in the Meat Industry. New 16 (39)
Technology. Industrial 57 (11)
Technology. Instructional 181 (97)
Technology. Integrative Approach to 181 (47)
Technology. Man and Modern Industrial 168 (6)
Technology. Mechanical Engineering 151 (146)
Technology. Medical 181 (189), (191)
Technology on International Relations. Impact of 85 (15)
Technology on Society. Impact of 142 (65)
Technology: Opportunity for Women. Chemical 151 (265)
Technology - Past, Present and Future. Communication 29 (308), (335)
Technology PENNTAP Style. Transferring 151 (288)
Technology. Philosophy and 216 (95)
Technology). Pollution is Great (Growth, Resources, Economics, Affluence, 151 (225)
Technology--Professional Information. Medical 105 (45)
Technology--Recruitment. Medical 105 (45), (52)
Technology. Science Teacher and Educational 29 (100)
Technology. Social Impact of 168 (42)
Technology Transfer 216 (100)
Technology Transfer From Universities to Society 151 (141)
Technology Transfer - PENNTAP 151 (124)
Technology. Transferring 151 (47)
Technology. Transportation 151 (290)
Technology. U.S.A. - Science and 151 (131)
Technology. Understanding 151 (269)
Technology. Wilkes-Barre Campus, Service From Mining to Biomedical 151 (2)
Technology Work. Small Victories Over Doomsday: Making 218
Tectonics and Our Restless Earth. Plate 142 (88)
Tectonics of Ocean Ridges 218
Teenage Problem - The Adult 54
Teeth 225 (16)
Teeth and Civilization 151 (208)
Teeth. Impacted 181 (161)
Teilhard and New Biology 11 (5)
Teilhard and Philosophy 11 (3)
Teilhard and Science 11 (8)
Teilhard and the Feminine 11 (2)
Teilhard's Religious Ideas 11 (6)
Telecommunication Policy. Telephone Industry and 151 (183)
Telephone Industry and Telecommunication Policy 151 (183)
Telephone Stuff. Slippery Wire and Other 144
Telephone Techniques 65 (32), 180 (31)
Telephone. Terror by 144
Television 168 (59)
Television Advertising Techniques 151 (87)
Television Aesthetics 181 (76), (232)
Television and Film Stars are Made and Promoted. How 176 (102)
Television and Films. Relationship and Difference Between Acting for Stage, 225 (30)
Television and Public Opinion Formation 168 (50)
Television and Radio 176 (115)

Television and the Mass Media 142 (25)
Television and You 83 (1)
Television Announcing and Script Writing. Radio and 142 (74)
Television as a Teaching Tool. Instructional 151 (66)
Television as an Industrial Process. Film and 57 (32)
Television at Penn State. History and Current Status of Instructional 151 (66)
Television. Cable 105 (65), 181 (98), 216 (123)
Television. Community Role of Cable 181 (70), (215)
Television. Copyright Law as It Applies to Instructional 151 (66)
Television. Educational 181 (70), (98), (215)
Television. Educational or Instructional 168 (15)
Television. Educational Television and Commercial 142 (83)
Television for Education. Cable 181 (70)
Television. Future of Cable 216 (47)
Television. Gratuitous Sex and Violence on 116 (1), (2), (6)
Television in Education 216 (123)
Television in School. Use of Instructional 218
Television in the Arts. Educational 151 (32)
Television. Interference to Your 9 (1)
Television - Is It Really That Bad? 83 (11)
Television Journalism 154 (26)
Television, Media Criticism 57 (32)
Television News. Behind the Scenes in 135 (41)
Television News. Bias in 117 (84)
Television News. Radio/ 168 (10)
Television on Children. Effects of 105 (103)
Television on Society. Effects of 159 (62)
Television or Not Television and Your Family 105 (85)
Television Production Techniques 151 (66)
Television Program. Tomorrow's 216 (47)
Television. Role and Responsibility of Public 16 (86)
Television. Social Consequences of 57 (32)
Television. Social Significance of Movies and 105 (66)
Television Stations. Operation of Radio and 117 (86)
Television. Storytelling - Antidote for 29 (200)
Television: 30 Years of Innovation and Service. Cable 124 (1)
Television. Twenty Years of Educational 16 (86)
Tell and Show Your Story 151 (71)
Telling It Like It Is - and Isn't 105 (68)
Temperature. Physics of Low 171 (40)
Ten Most Asked Purchasing Questions 132 (10)
Ten Years From Now 54
Tenant Farmers Union. Southern 172 (8)
Tenant Law. Landlord- 29 (121)
Tennis 151 (278)
Tennis. Biomechanics of 29 (305)
Tennis. Doubles and Singles Strategy in 29 (305)
Tennis-oriented Developments 65 (27)
Tennis Shoes Syndrome. Old Lady in 168 (22)
Tension and Anxiety Reduction 174 (94)
Tension. How to Handle Anxiety and 174 (9)
Teratology. Behavioral 168 (64)
Territories. Portugal and Her African 29 (7)
Territory - The Imperative 112 (3)
Terror by Telephone 144
Terrorism in the Middle East Conflict 181 (345)
Terrorism. International 181 (244), (345)
Terrorists, Hostages and Victims 181 (244), (295)
Test Tube Babies 181 (20)
Testicle. Prostate Carcinoma 181 (171)
Testing 142 (9)
Testing and Structural Testing. Flamespread 80 (2)
Testing. Flamespread Testing and Structural 80 (2)
Testing in Education and Industry. Psychological 105 (102)
Testing. Intelligence 142 (21)
Testing. Issues in 117 (52)
Testing. Psychological 224 (14)
Testing. Psychology 57 (13)
Tests in Toxicology. Quick Chemical 54
Tests. Interest, Intelligence, and Personality 168 (28)
Tests. Psychological 174 (76)
Tests. Use of 56 (134)
Text-Editing, and Secretarial Support 119 (1)
Textile Arts. Design and the 79 (95)
Textile Arts. Guatemala It's 79 (41)
Textile Constructions 79 (55)
Textile Design. Imagination and 79 (156)
Textile History 79 (36), (150)
Textile Printing and Dyeing as an Art Form 79 (129)
Textile Recycling 79 (27)
Textile Techniques for Today. Ancient 79 (35)
Textile Techniques. Mixed 79 (71)
Textile Techniques of Ethnic Groups and Contemporary Adaptions 79 (8)
Textile Techniques. Selected, Neglected 79 (33)
Textiles 79 (45), 124 (54)
Textiles. African 79 (14)
Textiles. American Indian 79 (71)
Textiles. Ancient Peruvian 79 (63)
Textiles. Contemporary 79 (136)
Textiles. Design, 79 (89)
Textiles. Designing for 79 (32)
Textiles, Dyeing, Soft Art. Shaker 79 (46)
Textiles. Fibers and 151 (32)
Textiles. Flame Retardent 16 (28)
Textiles. Greek Traditions of 79 (156)
Textiles. History of Printed 79 (120)
Textiles in America. General View of 79 (2)
Textiles. Indian 79 (131)
Textiles. Nigerian Handicrafted 79 (37)
Textiles of Guatemala 79 (48)
Textiles. Peruvian 79 (65)

Texture 79 (139)
Thailand, and the Golden Triangle. Red China, Laos, 54
Thailand. Bewitching 59 (1)
Theater Art and the Struggle Against Oppression 70 (1)
Theater at Cal State Fullerton 29 (311)
Theater. Avant-Garde 159 (40)
Theater. Dance in the American Musical 225 (39)
Theater. History of Greek and Roman 227 (25)
Theater in America. State of 216 (32)
Theater-Space-and the Actor 29 (43), (313)
Theatre 56 (12), 176 (29), (46), (48)
Theatre. Abroad in the 97 (20)
Theatre. Actors and Acting in the Ancient 227 (14)
Theatre and Opera. Designing for 154 (22)
Theatre. Brecht and His 154 (22)
Theatre Cavalcade. Musical 97 (72)
Theatre. Contemporary 174 (48)
Theatre. Directing, Designing and Lighting for 159 (62)
Theatre. Greek and Roman 227 (14)
Theatre Groups. Directing 142 (74)
Theatre in Chicago. Alternative 142 (37)
Theatre in the Community 16 (29)
Theatre in the Public Community. Role and Place of 159 (62)
Theatre. Japanese 218
Theatre. Multi-Media Presentation of Educational 105 (24)
Theatre. Musical: America's Contribution to 105 (26)
Theatre. Readers 159 (10)
Theatre. Role of the University 16 (29)
Theatres of the Empire. Mixed 227 (14)
Theme. Variations on a 79 (74)
Themes. Defining America - Biblical 159 (1)
Themes in Drama. Contemporary 54
Themes in Fiction. Contemporary 54
Themes in Poetry. Contemporary 54
Theodore Roosevelt 167 (1)
Theological Topics. Lectures on Social/Political/ Ethical/ 168 (34)
Theology 174 (69)
Theology. Christian-Catholic 124 (80)
Theology in the Parish. Doing 105 (106)
Theology. Issues in Contemporary 54
Theology of Change in the Modern World 54
Theology of Sin 105 (104)
Theology. Roman Catholic Moral 105 (111)
Theories of Imperialism 142 (56)
Theories of Learning 105 (47)
Theories of Man 29 (141), (284)
Theories of Metaphor. I.A. Richard's and Kenneth Burke's 151 (65)
Theories of Punishment 214 (83)
Theories of the Origin of the Moon 151 (274)
Theory and Designing 79 (104)
Theory and the Bridges of Konigsberg. Graph 151 (247)
Theory and Use of Multilayer Weaving on Eight Harness Looms 79 (52)
Theory and Yarn Dyeing. Color 79 (78)
Theory. Applied General Systems 159 (66)
Theory. Basic 79 (53)
Theory. Black Socio-Political 218
Theory. Competence in Spite of 135 (50)
Theory. Dye 79 (36)
Theory. Gestalt Therapy and Sartrian 29 (245)
Theory. Growth Poles 218
Theory. Monetary 214 (33)
Theory? Number 181 (149)
Theory of Relativity. Einstein's 56 (130)
Theory of Sexuality. Sartre's 29 (118), (245)
Theory. Pattern Making and Clothing Construction and 79 (28)
Theory. Reconstruction of Political 85 (24)
Therapeutic Activities. Occupational 159 (31)
Therapeutic and Encounter Groups 29 (231)
Therapeutic Exercise 57 (2)
Therapy and Sartrian Theory. Gestalt 29 (245)
Therapy as a Career. Physical 56 (79)
Therapy. Controversies in Pulp 105 (30)
Therapy. Dance 218
Therapy. Family 142 (93)
Therapy. Family Counseling/Family 181 (287), (310)
Therapy for Sick People. Diet 117 (94)
Therapy. Gestalt 27 (45), 57 (71)
Therapy. Group 142 (73)
Therapy in Athletics. Cryokinetic 56 (76)
Therapy in the Community. Occupational 159 (31)
Therapy. Individual and Group 181 (289)
Therapy. Marital Counseling/Marital 181 (287), (310)
Therapy. Marriage and Family 176 (25)
Therapy. Megavitamin 218
Therapy. Movement 29 (103), (175)
Therpay. Occupational 181 (127)
Therapy. Parenteral 181 (197)
Therapy. Physical 159 (17), 181 (200)
Therapy. Radiation Physics in Cancer 218
Therapy. Rehabilitation 142 (73)
Therapy. School Site Location and 142 (79)
Therapy Services. Speech and Hearing 174 (47)
Therapy Yesterday, Today, and Tomorrow. Occupational 159 (31)
There is Genius in the Average Man 112 (108)
There Is No Easy Way 112 (37)
There'll Always Be an England 59 (17)
There's Genius in the Average Man 135 (53)
Thermal Activity. Mount Baker - Increased 218
Thermal Pollution on Rivers. Effects of 57 (16)
Thermal Storage. Electric 150 (2)
They Are Your Civil Liberties 117 (103)
They Never Really Owned the Land 223 (26)

Think-Act Now 81 (1)
Think About Not Thinking 56 (58)
Think and Remember 180 (30)
Think on These Things 97 (30)
Think Positively 180 (142)
Think Strawberries 102 (17)
Third Century. Religious Liberty and Our 12
Third Reich. Use of Literature During Germany's 216 (112)
Third World 168 (41)
Third World. Demographic and Socio-Economic Aspects of the 223 (28)
Third World. Neo-Colonialism and the 142 (56)
Third World. Soviet Union and the 85 (31)
Third World. United States Relations With the 57 (19)
Thirteenth-Century. Roman Literature in the 227 (12)
30 Years Ago. Olympic Games 181 (2)
30 Years of Innovation and Service. Cable Television: 124 (1)
35. Kayaking as a Sport for Those Over 223 (30)
Thomas Remembers. Lowell 97 (64)
Thomas Water Tunnel. Research at the Garfield 151 (143)
Thread Work. Metal 79 (71)
Threads. Art and Craft of 83 (17)
Threat to Our Survival 125 (1)
Threats to the Ozone Layer 151 (155)
Three American Voices 102 (25)
Three Basic Weaves 79 (93)
Three Bronson Weaves With Variations 79 (94)
3-D Drafting 79 (104)
Three-D Project. Planning a 79 (40)
3-D Structures 79 (6)
3-D Weaving 79 (71)
3-D Workshops 79 (150)
Three-Dimensional Macrame 79 (86)
Three-Dimensional Weaving 79 (17), (71)
Three Months With Grey Owl 171 (14)
Three Processes of Attitude Change 56 (135)
Three Romantic Heroines of the Wild West 223 (3)
Three Ways to Manage Your Life 75 (1)
Thrill of Discovery 143 (1)
Thriving in Spite of Paraplegia 151 (136)
Thrums. Basketry Workshops Making Christmas Ornaments, Using 79 (29)
Tie-dye 79 (129)
Tie-dye, Commercial Dyes for the Handcraft Person. Batik, 79 (14)
Tie-dye Techniques. Batik and 79 (9)
Tigris. Operation 69 (1)
Timber Management 73
Timbuctu. Dakar to 59 (9)
Time and Space. Reappraisal of Organic Form With Respect to 54
Time at All Times. Control Your 151 (38)
Time. Better Management of 56 (95)
Time. Community for Our 211 (4)
Time Control 65 (44)
Time Effectively. Manage Your 151 (35)
Time. Fairness Doctrine and Equal 117 (84)
Time. How to Manage Your 151 (67)
Time in Running Meetings. Saving 105 (13)
Time is Your Time. Radio - 29 (46)
Time Management 216 (27)
Time Management. Personal 151 (48)
Time. Managing Other People 182 (1), (2), (3)
Time. Managing Your 151 (15), (39)
Time of Affluence. Choral Music in a 56 (107)
Time of Your Life. How to Control the 180 (46)
Time Out 182 (1), (2), (3)
Time-Phased Order Planning for Wholesalers 29 (77)
Time Planning and Goal Setting 65 (32)
Time. Promised Messiah and the Signs of the 1 (5)
Time to Become Young. It Takes a Long 97 (34)
Time Trap Barriers. Breaking the 151 (35)
Time? What is the Moral Crisis of Our 85 (12)
Times as a Weaving Woman. My Life and Hard 79 (50)
Times Demand. Person These 75 (1)
Times. Managing in Changing 112 (103)
Times. Mythology - Form and Meaning in Our 54
Times of My Father. Life and 112 (110)
Times of W.C. Fields. Life and 112 (38)
Times. Talent Waste - The Moral Crisis of Our 54
Timothy - America's First Woman Editor. Elizabeth 56 (61)
Tips. Beauty 179 (1)
Tips. Consumer 152
Title Ideas 57 (79)
Title to Realty. Protecting 65 (16)
To Believe is to Pray 105 (106)
To Invest or Not to Invest 29 (76)
Tobacco Country. Tales of the 56 (41)
Tobacco Economy. North Carolina's Changing Position in the 56 (18)
Today's Alumni - No Raccoon-coat Set 151 (76)
Today's College Student 117 (127)
Today's College Student - Who Is He? 117 (42)
Today's Crisis of Faith 105 (104)
Today's Isms 117 (64), (99)
Today's Man and the Environment 152
Today's Need for Continuing Education 151 (102)
Today's Problems 176 (11)
Today's University Facility 29 (105), (155), (291)
Today's University Students 29 (291), (351)
Today's Woman 112 (99)
Today's Woman and the Environment 152
Togo, Northwest Africa 216 (60)
Tombs of Siberia. Scythian Frozen 29 (12), (20), (165)
Tomorrow be a Great Day 25 (1)
Tomorrow's Television Program 216 (47)
Too Many People 54
Too Much of a Good Thing 56 (70)
Topography and Archaeology of Rome 227 (26)
Topography. Games and Puzzles in Elementary 151 (247)

Topography of Rome 227 (53)
Topology. Intuitive 117 (93)
Tory Radicalism. Nature and Future of 85 (40)
Total Education Through Cooperative Education 16 (82)
Totalitarianism. From Autocracy to 57 (37)
Tough Minded Business 180 (10)
Tough-Minded Management 135 (5)
Tour Through the Holy Land 29 (216), (225), (315)
Tourism 171 (13)
Tourism in British Columbia's Economy 171 (13)
Tourism in West Kentucky 117 (114)
Tourism in West Kentucky - Present Status and Future Prospects 117 (121)
Tourist's View of Soviet Economic Life 223 (33)
Toward a Wiser Foreign Policy 85 (16)
Towards a New World 134 (3)
Tower? America and the World: Whatever Happened to the Ivory 151 (110)
Tower? Education: Whatever Happened to the Ivory 151 (110)
Tower of Hanoi 117 (93)
Town-Gown Column. How One Writes a 151 (76)
Town Life in Eastern North Carolina. Colonial 56 (30)
Town Planning. Aspects of Ancient 227 (32)
Toxic Algae and Cattle Kills 168 (37)
Toxic Substances. Chemicals and 204
Toxic Substances in Food. Naturally Occuring 151 (177)
Toxicology. Clinical 54
Toxicology in Death Investigations. Role of 54
Toxicology. Quick Chemical Tests in 54
Toy Department of Life 112 (31)
Tracing Your Family History 176 (67)
Track and Field 168 (71)
Track and Field Techniques 171 (30)
Tractor Safety on the Farm 151 (263)
Trade Associations - A Business Asset Not Listed on Your Balance Sheet 136 (4)
Trade. Foreign 174 (70)
Trade-in Program. Home 65 (25)
Trade in the Seventies. International 85 (22)
Trade. International Economics and 138 (1)
Trade Sales Plan. Guaranteed 65 (18)
Trade Wind Islands. Yankee Sails the 59 (5)
Trade With China. International 16 (6)
Trademarks Are Protected and Abused. How 209
Trademarks are Selected. How 209
Trademarks Are. What 209
Trademarks in Advertising and Marketing on Domestic and Foreign Levels. Role of 209
Trademarks Matter. Why 209
Trading Activities. Management of Commodity Futures 138 (3), (4)
Trading. Commodity 38
Trading Facility. Function and Operation of a Major Futures 38
Trading With Communist Countries. Politics of 85 (6)
Tradition and Originality in Propertius' Monobiblos 227 (24)
Tradition and Social Change 85 (23)
Traffic Accidents. Alcohol and 168 (29)
Traffic Forecasting 151 (290)
Traffic Operations and Highway Design. Energy Conservation in 174 (90)
Traffic Radar Speed Measurement. Police 105 (119)
Traffic Safety. Highway and 16 (9)
Traffic Safety Programs 56 (84), (85)
Tragedies. Seneca's 227 (42)
Tragedy. Greek 227 (1), (17)
Tragedy. Nietzsche and 227 (34)
Tragedy of American Foreign Policy. Liberalism and the 85 (7)
Tragedy. Staging of Greek 227 (7)
Training and Conditioning Young People 168 (33)
Training and Development. Management 180 (24)
Training. Animal 142 (28)
Training. Assertion 29 (44), (252)
Training. Assertive 105 (82), (88)
Training. Assertiveness 57 (71), 105 (77), (83), (86), 168 (23), 174 (94), 218
Training at Simon Fraser. Teacher 171 (21)
Training. Career in Athletic 151 (279)
Training Corps. Reserve Officers 105 (74)
Training. Effectiveness 216 (27)
Training for the Olympics. Comparison of United States - U.S.S.R. 29 (296), (306)
Training. Leadership 180 (195)
Training Machine Operators 67 (16)
Training. Memory 180 (109)
Training. Need for Speech 117 (135)
Training Needs. Analyzing Business 151 (122)
Training of Counselors 181 (287), (310)
Training of Teachers. In-Service 142 (36)
Training Paraprofessionals in Physchology 168 (7)
Training Program. How to Establish an Organizational 216 (120)
Training Programs 180 (80)
Training. Sales 180 (120), (147), (196)
Training. Salesmen 65 (6), (9), (11), (12), (13), (17), (18), (19), (20), (23), (28), (30), (31), (32), (39), (42), (43), (44), (45), (47), (48), (52), (53), (55), (60), (63), (64), (68), (70)
Training. Teacher 142 (36)
Training. Technical 174 (91)
Training. Undergraduate Pilot 174 (81)
Training. Volunteerism and 151 (161)
Training. Weight 142 (18)
Trampoline 174 (45)
Transactional Analysis 105 (77), 151 (46), 180 (32)
Transactional Analysis. Organizational 27 (7)
Transcendental Meditation in Public Schools 12
Transference in Everyday Life 181 (125)
Transferring Technology 151 (47)
Transferring Technology PENNTAP Style 151 (288)
Transformational Grammar 56 (65)
Transformational Grammar and Literature 29 (210)

Transit Management 105 (116)
Transit Marketing 105 (8)
Transit. Mass 54
Transition From High School to College 105 (34)
Transition in the Arts in America 151 (157)
Translator. On Being a 151 (235)
Transplantation to the New World. African Culture and Its 151 (218)
Transplants in Children. Kidney 181 (158)
Transplants. Legal and Medical Aspects of Organ 54
Transportation 168 (31), 214 (89), 216 (31), (43)
Transportation and Land Use 151 (290)
Transportation, and Settlement Pattern. Communication, 151 (183)
Transportation. Aseptic Bulk Storage and 67 (24), (25)
Transportation Barriers to the Handicapped and Aged 151 (228)
Transportation, Education, and Self-development Concepts 46 (1 - 5)
Transportation. Energy Conservation in 174 (90)
Transportation. Engines for Power or Vehicular 151 (295)
Transportation in Hong Kong 151 (290)
Transportation in Pennsylvania 151 (292)
Transportation Innovations 117 (17)
Transportation. Moving and 180 (192)
Transportation Planning 151 (290)
Transportation Problems. American 16 (36)
Transportation. Regulation of 31 (40)
Transportation. Research Program of the UCI Institute of 27 (39)
Transportation Systems Analysis 151 (290)
Transportation Systems. Louisiana 174 (74)
Transportation Systems. Urban 218
Transportation Technology 151 (290)
Transportation Technology. Getting the Most From 151 (293)
Transracial Adoption 151 (111), 159 (41)
Travel 176 (27), 180 (58)
Travel and Culture. European 151 (297)
Travel. How to 151 (11)
Travel in Africa 29 (5), (319)
Travel in Asia 29 (16), (163), (319)
Travel in Eastern North Carolina. Railroad 56 (35)
Travel in the Caribbean and West Indies 218
Travel in the Far East 29 (218), (319)
Travel in the Jet Age 100 (2)
Travel in the Middle East 29 (163), (218), (228), (319)
Travel of the Type That is Close to the Earth. European 218
Travel on a Budget. European 168 (61)
Travel. Pavement Skid Resistance for Safe 151 (291)
Travel. Planning for 29 (135)
Travel Pleasure. Planning 29 (159), (314)
Travel Relative to Spanish and Italian Culture. European 151 (300)
Travel. Space 142 (31)
Traveling Through Europe 142 (34)
Travelogue of Western Europe 117 (138)
Treasures in Western Europe 56 (9)
Tree Maintenance 189
Tree Planting 189
Tree Seeds in the Rocky Mountains. Collection of 151 (310)
Tree Trimming and Right-of-Way Management 150 (7)
Trees, Ferns, and Wildflowers of Washington 159 (59)
Trees. Mass Production of Genetically Superior 151 (310)
Trends Among Irish Youth and Irish Women 159 (65)
Trends and Changes in Southern Politics 16 (20)
Trends in Accounting Education. Changing 159 (50)
Trends in College Going 151 (90)
Trends in Educational Administration 16 (56)
Trends in Educational Planning 216 (33)
Trends in Elementary Education 159 (29), 181 (118)
Trends in Engineering Education 151 (132)
Trends in Higher Education 29 (59), (99)
Trends in Home Economics 117 (78)
Trends in Information Processing Systems 31 (19)
Trends in Jewish Thought 181 (239)
Trends in Methodology 56 (42)
Trends in the Elementary School 174 (85)
Trends in United States Foreign Policy 85 (21)
Trials and Tribulations of Association Work 136 (20)
Trials of a Woman Artist 79 (79)
Trials, Tribulations and Joys of Family Owned Business 136 (7)
Tribalism. American Indian 29 (230), (283)
Trinidad, Tropical Island 151 (299)
Trips to South America, Central America, Mexico and Greece 79 (117)
Tritik, Using Commercial Dyes. Ikat, Shibori, and 79 (144)
Trojan War: Myth or History 56 (93)
Troy. Helen of 227 (5)
Trust Funds 54
Trusts 159 (46)
Truth About Witchcraft 154 (12)
Truth in Advertising 105 (4)
Truth, Objectivity and Some Interesting Facts About the Nature of Knowledge 85 (20)
Tube Babies. Test 181 (20)
Tubular Weave. Explorations in 79 (109)
Tucker Wildlife Sanctuary 29 (75), (277), (324)
Tumbling. Beginning Gymnastics and 142 (60)
Tumors of Salivary Glands 181 (175)
Tuning Education to 2000 A.D. 151 (112)
Tunnel. Research at the Garfield Thomas Water 151 (143)
Turbine Type Engines 151 (295)
Turbulence. Clear Air 151 (155)
Turkey 59 (3), 174 (82)
Turkey, and Yugoslavia. Primitive Spinners - Spindles and/or Distaffs From Greece, 79 (20)

Turkey. Hodja - Folk Hero of 29 (200)
Turkey - Yesterday's Tomorrow 51 (1)
Turmoil to Tranquility 105 (67)
Turtles. Malaipian 57 (59)
Tuscarora Indians in North Carolina 56 (34)
Twain. Diabolical Duo: Ambrose Bierce and Mark 151 (243)
Twain in Italy. Mark 59 (13)
Twain in Switzerland. Mark 59 (13)
Twain. Life and Humor of Mark 117 (91)
Twenties. Golden 57 (56)
Twentieth Century American Mercenary 154 (3)
Twentieth Century American Music 225 (12)
20th Century Art and Music. Similarities Between 159 (21)
20th Century. Dramatic Hero in the 216 (32)
20th Century Germany 142 (1)
20th Century. World in the 142 (1)
Twenty Years of Change in Alaskan Exploration 143 (9)
Twenty Years of Educational Television 16 (86)
Twill 79 (81), (139)
Twining 79 (98), (113)
Twining. Hammock 79 (50)
Twining. Sculptural 79 (35)
Twining. Split-ply 79 (131)
Twining. Warp and Weft 79 (133)
Twining. Warp-weighted 79 (29)
Two Earner Families - How They Spend and Save 151 (166)
Two From Galilee 97 (31)
Two Harness Techniques 79 (3)
200 Years. Next 102 (20)
Two Ideas of Equality 85 (25)
2000 A.D. Auditing 159 (50)
2000 A.D. Round Trip to 102 (24)
2000 A.D. Tuning Education to 151 (112)
2001: A Space Odyssey 154 (17)
2001. Corporation of 102 (6)
2000. Eastern North Carolina the Year 56 (36), (38)
2000 - You Are What You Value. Renaissance 180 (78)
2000 Young American Leaders 135 (6)
Typology of Myths 227 (41)

U

UCI Institute of Transportation. Research Program of the 27 (39)
UCI Medical Center 27 (36)
UFO's 135 (30), 181 (213), (276)
UFOs and Their Landing Sites 94 (3)
U.S.A. and Great Britain 181 (118)
U.S.A. Backroads, 59 (16)
U.S.A. Broadway, 59 (7)
U.S.A. Cultural Region and General Cultural Geography of the 151 (184)
U.S.A. Foreign Students in the 31 (26)
U.S.A. Middle East Problems and the 151 (291)
U.S.A. - Science and Technology 151 (131)
USL Academic Offerings 174 (88)
USL Conference Center - Alumi Ownership 174 (3)
USL Scholarship Programs 174 (88)
USL. Service Functions of 174 (88)
USL Service Programs 174 (88)
U.S.S.R. 57 (92), 117 (141)
USSR and Soviet Man Today 85 (18)
U.S.S.R. Education in the 117 (72)
U.S.S.R. Engineering Education: United States and 151 (2)
USSR in 1990 97 (52)
U.S.S.R. - Land and People 117 (62), (72)
USSR. Politics in the 54
U.S.S.R. Training for the Olympics. Comparison of United States - 29 (296), (306)
Ukraine. Czechoslovakia and 15 (2)
Ultrasonics 142 (96)
Ultrastructure of Salivary Glands 181 (175)
Uncommon Man 135 (27)
Unconventional Ways of Using Your Loom 79 (31)
Under the Ocean Near Guam 223 (34)
Underachievers. College Programs for 105 (34)
Underdeveloped Country? What is an 29 (328)
Undergraduate Education. Nature of 16 (52)
Undergraduate Pilot Training 174 (81)
Undergraduate Plant Protection Curriculum 216 (38)
Undergraduate Plant Protection Option. New 216 (85)
Underground Film 168 (16)
Underground Gas Storage 151 (135)
Underground Humor. Soviet 27 (46)
Underground Press. High School 231 (3)
Underprivileged Children. Development of Minority and 16 (33)
Undersea Archaeology. Romance of 4 (5)
Undersea Life in Southern California 29 (270), (302)
Understanding Affirmative Action for the Disabled 151 (1)
Understanding Chinese Painting 57 (52)
Understanding Profits 20
Understanding School District Budgets 181 (45), (130)
Understanding Sexual Dysfunction 29 (250)
Understanding Technology 151 (269)
Understanding Your Child 105 (98)
Underwater Jungle Law 112 (26)
Underwater Photography 218
Unemployment 174 (70)
Unemployment. Inflation and 56 (17)
Unemployment Insurance and the Rate of Unemployment 171 (8)
Unemployment Manpower. Employment and 181 (48)
Unemployment. Poverty and 181 (333)
Unemployment Problems 54

Unemployment Really Necessary? Is a High Level of 151 (42)
Ungavà Venture 143 (16)
Union and Higher Education. Faculty 181 (109)
Union Democracy. Struggle for 213 (4)
Union Electric System 189
Union Electric's Operations. Economics of 189
Union Growth and Development 174 (17)
Union. Southern Tenant Farmers 172 (8)
Union. Student 174 (71)
Unionism in Higher Education 142 (65)
Unions in Business. Roles of 54
Unions. Right to Work - Forcing Public Employees Into Unwanted Labor 131 (4)
Unisex Phantom 171 (28)
United Nations 52 (75), 174 (4)
United Nations and World Peace 102 (14)
United Nations Association and You 151 (65)
United Nations. Challenge of the Expanding 214 (54)
United Nations. Food and Agriculture Organization of the 16 (45)
United Nations in the Middle East. Role of the 102 (28)
United Nations in World Affairs. Role of the 29 (63), (330)
United Nations Must Face Up to Its Responsibilities 97 (42)
United Nations. Relationship of the United States to the 16 (59)
United Nations Technical Assistance in Statistics 151 (251)
United Nations. United States Relations With the 57 (19)
United States. Adult Education in the 151 (122)
United States. Africa and the 181 (25), (257), (331)
United States. Aging and Agism in the 172 (7)
United States Air Force Academy 216 (53)
United States Air Force. Career Opportunities in the 216 (53)
United States and Asia 151 (196)
United States and Canada Today 151 (197)
United States and Europe. Opera in the 154 (22)
United States and European Security 85 (28)
United States and Human Rights 181 (28)
United States and Human Rights in Southern Africa 181 (267)
United States and Latin America 151 (196)
United States and Latin America: How Do We View One Another 151 (213)
United States and Latin America: The Latin Review 117 (102)
United States and U.S.S.R. Engineering Education: 151 (2)
United States and Soviet Education Compared. Two Different Worlds: 159 (35)
United States Army Reserve 216 (60)
United States. Basic Research in the 181 (18)
United States Bill of Rights 31 (14)
United States Business. New Administration - What Washington Plans for 102 (10), (21)
United States Congress. Penn State and the 151 (191)
United States Constitution. Afro-American in the 29 (82), (194), (337)
United States Cultural History 142 (80)
United States Defense Policies 29 (256), (292)
United States Domestic Airline Industry 151 (290)
United States. Earthquakes in the Southeastern 216 (8)
United States Economies. Contributions of the Chemical Industry to Midwestern 34 (1)
United States Economy. National 65 (35)
United States. Emerging 85 (28)
United States Energy Crisis 143 (8)
United States Energy Dilemma. Solving the 151 (136)
United States Energy Picture. Middle East in the 56 (15)
United States Energy Policy 57 (89)
United States Falling Behind? Where Are We Headed in the Arms Race? Is the 102 (8)
United States. Family Life in Asia and the 56 (123)
United Stated Food Abundance in a Hungry World 16 (3)
United States Foreign Assistance Administration 151 (196)
United States Foreign Policy 85 (28), 117 (68), 214 (53)
United States Foreign Policy and United States Governmental Machinery for Carrying it Out 85 (15)
United States Foreign Policy. Organizing and Managing 151 (196)
United States Foreign Policy Today 223 (21)
United States Foreign Policy. Trends in 85 (21)
United States. Future of Small Business Enterprise in the 159 (3)
United States Government. American Indian and the 29 (158), (254)
United States Government in Asia. Future Role of 159 (36)
United States Governmental Machinery for Carrying it Out. United States Foreign Policy and 85 (15)
United States History 181 (269)
United States. History of the Lamaze Method in the 36 (1)
United States. Hunger in the 168 (4)
United States in Asia. Emphasis of the 117 (68)
United States Increasing or Decreasing? Is Poverty in the 117 (24)
United States. India and the 151 (197)
United States Manufacturing Industries Monopolized? Are 85 (2)
United States National Parks. Geology of Various Western 168 (3)
United States National Security Policy 85 (15)

United States Naval Academy 57 (53)
(United States). Oil and Gas Exploration 151 (124)
United States. Political Parties in North Carolina and the 56 (131)
United States Relations. Africa - 97 (42)
United States Relations With the Third World 57 (19)
United States Relations With the United Nations 57 (19)
United States. Relationship Between Puerto Rico and the 151 (202)
United States Role in Vietnam 85 (17)
United States. Role of the Catholic School in the 54
United States. Role of the Latino Women in the 142 (68)
United States. Sino-Soviet Conflict and the 151 (193)
United States to the United Nations. Relationship of the 16 (59)
United States - USSR Training for the Olympics. Comparison of 29 (296), (306)
Unity of Language Study 181 (59)
Unity of the Monobiblos 227 (24)
Unity Versus Trinity 1 (5)
Universal Graphic Language. Technical Drawing: 117 (82)
Universe 218
Universe According to Modern Astronomy 181 (280)
Universe. Chemistry of the 142 (19)
Universe. Cosmology - Man's Place in the 27 (16)
Universe. Intelligence in the 154 (17)
Universe. Intelligent Life in the 223 (4)
Universe. Life Elsewhere in the 57 (87)
Universities. Academic Advising in Colleges and 151 (116)
Universities. Future of 171 (60)
Universities. Government Support for Independent Colleges and 105 (50)
Universities. Role of Interdisciplinary Research in 151 (73)
Universities. Students Versus 85 (35)
Universities to Society. Technology Transfer From 151 (141)
Universities. What Should the Public Expect From Our Colleges and 151 (101)
Universities? Why Catholic 105 (41)
University 171 (60)
University. Affirmative Action at the Pennsylvania State 151 (1)
University. Alumni and Eastern Illinois 57 (91)
University and Alumni on the Pittsburgh Area. Impact of Duquesne 54
University and the Business Community. Cooperation Between the 16 (36)
University and the Order of Society 85 (37)
University be Saved? Should the 85 (3)
University Campus. Computer's Role on the 16 (5)
University Campus. Radiation Safety at a 27 (9)
University Campus. Spiritual Revival on the 16 (21)
University Campus. Student Life on the 16 (21)
University. Carnegie-Mellon 31 (10)
University Comes to the Student 151 (103)
University Extension or Public Service 16 (7)
University Facility. Today's 29 (105), (155), (291)
University Governance. Faculty Participation in 105 (49)
University. Health Sciences at the 218
University. Idea of a Catholic 85 (33)
University Impact on Milwaukee. Marquette 105 (64)
University in France and England 105 (33)
University in Your Backyard 151 (7)
University - Is it For You? Pennsylvania State 151 (90)
University. Ministry to the 105 (105)
University of California. Educational Opportunities in the 27 (23)
University of Washington 218
University of Washington. Athletics at the 218
University of Washington. Henry Suzzallo Years at the 218
University on Business in Greenville, North Carolina. Economic Impact of Students of East Carolina 56 (24)
University Operations 151 (9)
University Park: Its Lure to Young and Old 151 (6)
University Planning 151 (5)
University. Planning a Deferred Gift for the 151 (187)
University Police Department. California 29 (193)
University Policy Making. Student Participation in 16 (21)
University Professors. American Association of 181 (95)
University Programs in Interior British Columbia 171 (58)
University. Programs in Mathematics at Murray State 117 (92)
University. Purpose of a 174 (10)
University Relations With the Community 174 (89)
University Residential Living 57 (31)
University. Role of Research in the 151 (266)
University. Saint Cloud State 168 (65)
University Student. Development of the 16 (21)
University Students. Changing Attitudes of 27 (21)
University Students. Law With 16 (81)
University Students. Problems of 174 (9)
University Students. Today's 29 (291), (351)
University Tamburitzans. Duquesne 54
University Theatre. Role of the 16 (29)
University Today and Tomorrow. Saint Cloud State 168 (18)
University Today. Marquette 105 (63)
University. Villanova 214 (91)
University. What Research Means to the 16 (11)

University. You and Your Land - Grant 216 (13)
Unlocking the Mind-bodies 97 (7)
Unmarried Motherhood 142 (14)
Unusual Inkle Weaves 79 (90)
Unusual Photographs 174 (79)
Unwanted Children 176 (103)
Ups and Downs of Weight Control 57 (30)
Urban Affairs 172 (12)
Urban and Regional Planning. Engineer in 214 (44)
Urban and Regional Planning. Introduction to 56 (101)
Urban Crime and Police 181 (264)
Urban Design 181 (78)
Urban Design in San Francisco 181 (260)
Urban Dwellings and Small Businesses. Self-sufficient Energy Systems for Rural and 163 (2)
Urban History and History of the American West 159 (16)
Urban Land Use 218
Urban Land Use Planning 142 (50)
Urban Living Problems Related to Health 56 (80)
Urban Past. Virginia's 216 (43)
Urban Planning. Techniques of 54
Urban Policy. Social Problems in Economics and 85 (1)
Urban Politics 54, 142 (33), 168 (72)
Urban Poverty in Louisiana 174 (70)
Urban Problems 135 (21)
Urban Renewal 29 (52), 85 (1)
Urban Renewal for Better Living 29 (135), (159)
Urban Society and the Future 181 (240)
Urban Spaces of Europe 181 (335)
Urban Transportation Systems 218
Urban Wildlife 216 (26)
Urinary Infections in the Child 181 (171)
Use, Manufacturing, and Marketing of Hardwood, Plywood, and Veneer 80 (2)
Use of Animals for Biomedical Research 151 (206)
Use of Color for the Control of Emotions 225 (5)
Use of Color in Weaving, Design, and Pattern Weaving 79 (24)
Use of Computers in State Government 174 (79)
Use of Hobbies in the Teaching of Physics 57 (87)
Use of Instructional Television in School 218
Use of Intravenous Fluids 16 (77)
Use of Literature During Germany's Third Reich 216 (112)
Use of Microforms at the Cal. State Fullerton Library 29 (25)
Use of Parliamentary Procedure 117 (128)
Use of Tests 56 (134)
Use of the Computer and Statistics in Literature and Linguistics 227 (51)
Use Your Phone for All It's Worth 144
User Oriented Planning Methodologies 151 (148)
Uses of Counseling Groups and Techniques 151 (161)
Uses of the Computer in Classical Scholarship 227 (7)
Using Community Resources 57 (47)
Using Credit 16 (19)
Using Fracture Traces to Locate Water Wells 136 (12)
Using Language Experience 57 (79)
Using the Diagnostic Approach to the Teaching of Reading 117 (36)
Utilities. Regulation and 216 (119)
Utility Invisible Taxes for Religion. Public 12
Utility Rate Cases 150 (10)
Utility Regulation 23
Utilization of Atomic Energy 216 (64)
Utilization of Local History in Education 142 (5)
Utilization of Physical Evidence 159 (11)
Utopia 85 (37)
Utopia in Government Structure. Dream of a 85 (11)
Utopia. Suburban Development and 223 (14)
Utopia Through Government Action. Search for 85 (11)
Utopianism, Sex and Reality 85 (35)
Utopias. Science Fiction and 181 (141), (231)

V

V-trough Carriers and PVC Rollers and Pulleys 67 (28)
Vacation. How to Choose a 151 (103)
Valley Sanitary Water Commission. Ohio River 151 (154)
Value and Uses of Financial Reports Filed by American Corporations With the Securities and Exchange Commission 50 (1)
Value Clarification in the Educational Setting 117 (58)
Value Clarifying Strategies 56 (43)
Values Clarification 142 (39), 174 (94)
Values for Living 112 (52)
Values of Free Speech in a Democracy 117 (65)
Values of Speech in a Democracy 117 (112)
Values of Today's College Student 16 (21)
Values That Use Us 159 (1)
Valuing Children's Books 171 (19)
Van Buren. Martin 151 (216)
Van der Rohe. Miles 142 (79)
Vanadium - Tattletale of Environmental Polluters 27 (9)
Vancouver. Computer Ombudsman Service of 171 (12)
Vanishing Old West 15 (4)
Variations on a Theme 79 (74)
Variations on a Weave 79 (31)
Varieties of the American Political Right 85 (40)
Various Architects and Movements of the Nineteenth Century 31 (3)
Various Aspects of Childbearing 105 (97)
Vaudeville. Racial Comedy in 216 (32)
Vedanta Concept of Salvation (Moksha) 117 (97)

Vegetable Dyeing 79 (20), (34)
Vegetable Dyeing. Spinning and 79 (15)
Vegetable Garden. Home 151 (25)
Vegetable Gardening 174 (2)
Vegetable Seeds Used in the Food Processing Industry. Development, Production and Processing of 67 (26), (27)
Vegetables. Home Gardening With 117 (5), (122)
Vegetarian Nutrition and Cooking 218
Vehicle Selection 120
Vehicles. How to Buy Communications 151 (75)
Veneer. Technical Aspects of Hardwood, Plywood and 80 (1)
Veneer. Use, Manufacturing, and Marketing of Hardwood, Plywood, and 80 (2)
Venereal Disease. Biology of 29 (172), (267)
Venezuela - Land of Natural Wonders 69 (7)
Venezuela: The Democratic Revolution 151 (213)
Venice. Magic of 59 (7)
Venom in Harmless Snakes 151 (307)
Verbal, Vocal and Visual Cues to Better Job Performance 180 (1)
Vergil 227 (6)
Vertical Loom for Navajo 79 (8)
Veterinary Findings Which May Lead to Human Cures 16 (69)
Veterinary Medical Education 16 (4)
Veterinary Medical Education. Meeting the Needs for 216 (90)
Veterinary Medicine 216 (7)
Veterinary Medicine As a Career 216 (90), (127)
Veterinary Medicine's Role in the Protection of Human Health 216 (90)
Veterinary Parasitology 16 (4)
Viable Alternatives in Social Studies 57 (24)
Vibrancy and Values 181 (292)
Vicksburg. Siege of 117 (67)
Victimology 168 (49)
Victims of Crises. Rape: 151 (88)
Victims. Terrorists, Hostages and 181 (244), (295)
Victorian Literature. Romantic and 105 (25)
Victories Over Doomsday: Making Technology Work. Small 218
Vida's Christiad 227 (11)
Video Art 218
Viet Nam and Its Consequences 85 (21)
Vietnam. United States Role in 85 (17)
Vietnam War. America and the 56 (91)
Vietnam? Why 117 (66)
Vietnamese Poetry 168 (41)
Vietnamese Revolution 168 (41)
View From a Police Car 75 (1)
Viewpoint India 79 (45)
Viking on Mars 29 (152), (276)
Vikings - Iceland, Greenland, Newfoundland 151 (220)
Vikings. New 97 (62)
Vikings. Norway - the Bold 51 (1)
Vikings of My Iceland 225 (24)
Village. Acadian 174 (40)
Village Beneath the Sea 59 (12)
Village. Japanese 168 (52)
Village Life in the Philippines 151 (162)
Village Redevelopment 216 (42)
Villages and Human Scale in Living Environments. English 218
Villains Still Pursue Me 102 (25)
Villanova University 214 (91)
Violence and Human Nature. Aggression, 102 (35)
Violence. Assassination, Riot, Public 29 (153)
Violence in a Democratic Society 85 (35)
Violence. Nonviolence Versus 217 (4)
Violence on Television. Gratuitous Sex and 116 (1) (2), (6)
Violence or I'll Kill You. Support Televised 105 (69)
Violence. Philosophical Definition of 214 (73)
Violin - History, Development, and Literature 57 (42)
Violin Making 57 (29)
Virgin in Greek Society 227 (48)
Virginia. Canoeing in 216 (98)
Virginia. Earthquakes in 216 (8)
Virginia Gardens 216 (6)
Virginia Horse Industry 216 (57)
Virginia. Seafood Processing in 216 (36)
Virginia Tech 216 (124)
Virginia Tech. Agricultural Engineering at 216 (83)
Virginia Tech Alumni Affairs 216 (107)
Virginia Tech and Its International Programs 216 (138)
Virginia Tech. Computer Science at 216 (44)
Virginia Tech. Development of 216 (17)
Virginia Tech. Foreign Students at 216 (138)
Virginia Tech Lacrosse 216 (87)
Virginia Tech. Music at 216 (66)
Virginia Tech. Recreational Facilities at 216 (46)
Virginia Tech Today 216 (107)
Virginia's Constitutions 216 (124)
Virginia's Urban Past 216 (43)
Viruses. Human Cancer 216 (4)
Vision in Children 29 (85), (169), (229)
Visit to English Infant Schools 168 (61)
Visit to the Amazon 29 (129), (167), (325)
Visit to the Jeu de Paume-Impressionist Museum 117 (138)
Visit to the Philippines 151 (299)
Visit With Reverend John Witherspoon 151 (41)
Visit With Soviet Dissidents 27 (42)
Visual Education. Audio- 117 (41)
Visual Literacy 168 (15), 181 (97)
Visual Perception and the Real World 29 (229), (264)
Visual System. Anatomy of the Brain or of the 27 (26)
Visualization Made Me a Star. How 225 (5)
Visualized Instruction 216 (10)
Vitamin Formula to Counter Aging 27 (29)

Vitamins 54
Vocation. Choosing a Career or 117 (80)
Vocation. How to Choose a 151 (103)
Vocation or Avocation. Marriage - 57 (41)
Vocational and Job Satisfaction 181 (65)
Vocational Development 216 (52)
Vocational Education 181 (63), (104), (115), (120), 216 (60), (75)
Vocational Education in Agriculture 117 (4)
Vocational Education. Liberal Arts in 174 (91)
Vocational Education. Liberalizing Adult 151 (98)
Vocational Education. Role of 117 (40)
Vocational Guidance 180 (180)
Vocational Student Organizations 181 (55)
Vocational Students Can Go to College 181 (55)
Vocational Teacher. Liability and the 117 (46)
Vocational Technical School. Community Junior College Versus the 174 (1)
Voice Is You. Your 144
Voice Reveals About You. What Your 105 (13)
Volcanoes 181 (137)
Volleyball the Penn State Way. Power 151 (286)
Voluntary Armed Forces - Will it Work? 159 (53)
Voluntary Army 105 (74)
Volunteer Armed Force. Draft Versus An All- 85 (1)
Volunteerism and Training 151 (161)
Volunteerism in Action 181 (66), (248)
Volunteers and Human Service Workers 181 (56)
Voodoo and Superstitious Influences 174 (92)
Voters and Voting 105 (55)
Voting Behavior 142 (64)
Voting Patterns. American Jewish 214 (4), (48)
Voting Patterns. Presidential 181 (266)
Voting. Voters and 105 (55)
Voyage Into Space 29 (186), (272)
Voyages of RA. Epic 69 (1)
Vulnerable Russians 85 (6)

W

Ws of Fashion. Four 97 (70)
WWSC. Technology at 223 (31)
W.C. Fields. Life and Times of 112 (38)
Wage and Price Controls - Do They Work 85 (22)
Wage Law and the Poor. Minimum 85 (22)
Wage Laws - Cure for or a Cause of Poverty? Minimum 85 (2)
Wage-price Controls 56 (17)
Wage-price Controls. Why Your Dollar Continues to Buy Less - With or Without 85 (26)
Wagelessness in the Home Effects Women's Options for Fertility. How 90 (1)
Wages. Place of Immigrant Women in the Hierarchy of 90 (1)
Wagon. You Can't do Business With an Empty 112 (133)
Wales. Scotland and 15 (4)
Wall Handings 79 (6), (48), (88), (112)
Wall Hangings. Creative Weaving 79 (95)
Wall Hangings. Decorative 79 (143)
Wall Hangings. Free-form 79 (140)
Wall Hangings. Plant Material 79 (96)
Wallhangings 79 (49)
Walter Hasenclever: The Dramatist as Filmwriter 214 (66)
War. America and the Vietnam 56 (91)
War and Peace. Middle East in 181 (339)
War Belle. Love and War: The Courtship of a Civil 117 (69)
War Between the States. West Kentucky in the 117 (67)
War. Civil 142 (27)
War. Cold 57 (56)
War. Just 105 (76)
War: Myth or History. Trojan 56 (93)
War. Nuclear 216 (131)
War of 1812. Forgotten Hero of the 57 (91)
War of 1812. Governor Isaac Shelby and the 117 (69)
War on Poverty - A Critical View 85 (25)
War Soldiers. Morals of Civil 151 (214)
War: The Courtship of a Civil War Belle. Love and 117 (69)
War Theory. Just 214 (83)
War Years. Civil Liberties During the Cold 105 (59)
Warfare. Anti-submarine 105 (70)
Warfare. Guerilla 142 (27), (89)
Warp and Setting Up a Loom. Making a 79 (24)
Warp and Weft. Clasped 79 (147)
Warp and Weft Ikat 79 (68)
Warp and Weft Twining 79 (133)
Warp. Leftover 79 (53)
Warp. Painted 79 (147)
Warp. Pin 79 (106)
Warp Weaving. Loose 79 (89)
Warp Weighted Loom 79 (155)
Warp Weighted Looms 79 (113)
Warp-Weighted Twining 79 (29)
Warp Weighting 79 (155)
Warping and Beaming 79 (133)
Warping. Chain 79 (147)
Warping. Sectional 79 (147)
Warping. Speed 79 (93)
Warping Without Cross 79 (21)
Warps. Designing and Weaving With Supplementary 79 (38)
Warps. Double Weave With Weighted 79 (13)
Warps. Ikat 79 (62)
Warps. Supplementary 79 (139), (140)
Warrior Basketball 105 (112)
Wars. American Literature Between the Great 151 (231)
Was Abraham Lincoln a Christian? 29 (338)
Was the American Revolution Caused by a Conspiracy 105 (60)

Washington and the Spokane Area. Geology of Northeastern 143 (14)
Washington. Athletics at the University of 218
Washington But Didn't Know Who to Ask. Everything You Wanted to Know About 135 (25)
Washington. Financing Public Education in 159 (53)
Washington Flora. Origins and History of 218
Washington Geology. Aerial Views of 159 (38)
Washington. Great Americans - 151 (222)
Washington. Henry Suzzallo Years at the University of 218
Washington. Life of a Public Wife in 97 (75)
Washington. Look From 97 (4)
Washington, Louisiana 174 (37)
Washington Merry-Go-Round 135 (2)
Washington. Mr. Rooney Goes to 112 (111)
Washington. Nancy Dickerson's 102 (5)
Washington. News in 112 (2)
Washington Outlook 102 (26)
Washington Plans for United States Business. New Administration - What 102 (10), (21)
Washington Scene 176 (24), (33), (50), (52), 180 (68)
Washington State. Archeology of 218
Washington State Legislature. One Man's View of the 223 (22)
Washington. Trees, Ferns, and Wildflowers of 159 (59)
Washington. University of 218
Washington Whirl - Fifteen Years of Change 97 (5)
Washington Wonderland 102 (16)
Waste Management 133 (1), (5)
Waste Management. Problems and Solutions in Radioactive 151 (130)
Waste. Sanitary Landfills, Resource Recovery, and Handling of Hazardous 133 (3)
Waste - the Moral Crisis of Our Times. Talent 54
Wastes' Handling Equipment. Refuse Collection, Solid 133 (4)
Wastes Safe. Making Radioactive 151 (272)
Wastewater Control. Industrial 105 (120)
Wastewater Treatment 105 (120)
Wastewater Treatment. Industrial and Municipal 204
Watches. Clocks and 151 (210)
Water 117 (32)
Water and Weather Data on the Computer 216 (61)
Water Commission. Ohio River Valley Sanitary 151 (154)
Water Conservation 151 (158)
Water Conservation in the Home 136 (22)
Water Conservation With Water-saving Devices 151 (304)
Water. Earthy Odors in Drinking 16 (85)
Water Flow in Living Color. Ground 136 (14)
Water. Impact of Abandoned Wells on Ground 136 (25)
Water Industry: What You Didn't Learn at Daddy's Knee. Education in the Ground 136 (1)
Water Kayaking. White 216 (68)
Water. Keep Your Bait in the 112 (37)
Water. Land Treatment of Food Plant Waste 67 (13)
Water Pollution 54, 56 (69), 105 (120), 168 (29)
Water Pollution Control 214 (30)
Water Pollution Control. Air and 204
Water Pollution Control. Ground 136 (14)
Water Quality 57 (94)
Water Quality Control 150 (4)
Water. Removal of Suspended Solids From Industrial Waste 67 (22)
Water Safety 56 (86), 174 (68)
Water-saving Devices. Water Conservation With 151 (304)
Water Source Heat Pump. Ground 136 (25)
Water Tunnel. Research at the Garfield Thomas 151 (143)
Water, Water Everywhere and Not a Drop to Drink 16 (42)
Water Well Construction Standards. How to Use the Manual of 136 (27)
Water Well Industry. Metric Conversion and the 136 (28)
Water Wells. Using Fracture Traces to Locate 136 (12)
Water Witch Drowns in a Dry Hole. How a 136 (14)
Water Works Association Today. National 136 (20)
Watercolor Painting. History of 56 (13)
Watergate 176 (12), (123)
Watergate and College Students 214 (3)
Watergate and Impeachment 223 (23)
Watergate. Deep Throat, the Mystery of 105 (54)
Watergate. Politics After 151 (190)
Watergate Presidency. Post- 181 (258)
Waterways. Future of Eastern North Carolina 56 (29)
Wave Engines - A Different Concept in Engines 151 (295)
Wave Phenomena 56 (125)
Waves Upon Marine Fish. Effects of Shock 218
Ways Mathematics Can Help With Ecological Problems 31 (21)
Ways of Studying Children's Books 171 (19)
Ways to Attain Health, Wealth, Happiness, Success and Prosperity 180 (33)
Wayward Welfare State 85 (10)
We Are What We Watch 151 (72)
We Create Our Own Problems 112 (41)
Wealth, Happiness, Success and Prosperity. Ways to Attain Health, 180 (33)
Wealth of South Africa. Mineral 181 (137), (347)
Wealth. Peace, Ecology, and Ocean 214 (27)
Wealthy. Collecting - the Pleasant Way to Become 97 (36)

Weapon Strategy. Changes in Nuclear 29 (255), (268)
Weapon Strategy. Nuclear 29 (51)
Weapons be Controlled? Can Nuclear 29 (256), (292)
Weapons. Naval 105 (71)
Wearables. Inventive 79 (33)
Wearables. Making 79 (29)
Weather 176 (58)
Weather Data on the Computer. Water and 216 (61)
Weather- or Whether 135 (4)
Weather. Southern California 29 (152), (276)
Weave, and Construct a Variety of Chairs, Swings, Hammocks. How to Design, 79 (87)
Weave and Hand Manipulated Double Weave Tapestry. Double 79 (69)
Weave. Bound 79 (104), (113), (139)
Weave Clothing. Designing Circular 79 (10)
Weave. Creative Crochet and Double 79 (60)
Weave Design 79 (76)
Weave. Dimensional Tapestry Using Double 79 (119)
Weave. Double 79 (30), (48), (62), (63), (77), (84), (104), (113), (139), (145)
Weave Effect Method of Designing. Color and 79 (94)
Weave. Explorations in Tubular 79 (109)
Weave Formation 79 (140)
Weave - Four Harness Tapestry. Double 79 (74)
Weave. Peruvian Pebble 79 (90)
Weave Planning 79 (64)
Weave Tapestry. Double Weave and Hand Manipulated Double 79 (69)
Weave Tapestry Techniques. Plain 79 (153)
Weave. Variations on a 79 (31)
Weave With Weighted Warps. Double 79 (13)
Weaver as Designer 79 (55)
Weaver Controlled and Loom Controlled Lace Weaves 79 (69)
Weavers. Color and Design for 79 (108)
Weavers. Dyeing for 79 (130)
Weaves. Advanced Loom Controlled 79 (114)
Weaves. Art 79 (48)
Weaves. Bound 79 (30)
Weaves. Double 79 (65)
Weaves. Double and Quadruple 79 (138)
Weaves. Double, Multilayered 79 (118)
Weaves. Drafting - Analysis and Design of 79 (78)
Weaves. Embroidery 79 (67), (84)
Weaves. Gauze 79 (113)
Weaves. Navajo and Hopi Bar 79 (90)
Weaves. Pile 79 (153)
Weaves. Rug 79 (107)
Weaves, Samplers, and Tapestry. Double 79 (7)
Weaves. South American Pick-up 79 (107)
Weaves - the Weaver Controlled Weaves. Art 79 (17)
Weaves. Three Basic 79 (93)
Weaves. Unusual Inkle 79 (90)
Weaves Using Doups. Leno 79 (24)
Weaves. Weaver Controlled and Loom Controlled Lace 79 (69)
Weaves With Variations. Three Bronson 79 (94)
Weaving 79 (146)
Weaving. Achieving Texture in Tapestry 79 (108)
Weaving Aesthetics 79 (44)
Weaving and Drafting. Introduction to 79 (64)
Weaving and Enameling Technique 79 (128)
Weaving and Wall Hangings. Creative 79 (95)
Weaving. Application of Historical Motifs in 79 (81)
Weaving. Art and Techniques of Bolivian Highland 79 (18)
Weaving as a Life Style 79 (31)
Weaving as an Art Form 79 (60)
Weaving as Art in Interior Design 79 (148)
Weaving. Backstrap 79 (110)
Weaving. Band 79 (133)
Weaving. Basic 79 (76)
Weaving. Beginning 79 (122), (145)
Weaving. Beginning 4-H 79 (107)
Weaving. Beginning 4-Harness Loom 79 (158)
Weaving. Card 79 (66), (113)
Weaving. Cherokee Finger 79 (50)
Weaving. Children's 79 (107)
Weaving. Color and 79 (95)
Weaving. Color in 79 (81), (84), (116)
Weaving. Commission 79 (148)
Weaving. Contemporary 79 (71)
Weaving. Contemporary Trends in 79 (112)
Weaving, Design, and Pattern Weaving. Use of Color in 79 (24)
Weaving. Design, Color and Texture in 79 (159)
Weaving. Design for 79 (118)
Weaving. Design in Nature and 79 (132)
Weaving. Designs in Guatemalan 79 (26)
Weaving. Double 79 (140)
Weaving. Ecclesiastical 79 (81)
Weaving. Experimental 79 (140)
Weaving. Fiber Techniques 79 (29)
Weaving. Finger 79 (40), (98), (113), (142)
Weaving for Corporate Building. Commission 79 (118)
Weaving for My Home 79 (10)
Weaving. Four Harness 79 (50)
Weaving. Frame Loom Tapestry 79 (9)
Weaving From Nature and the Arts. Inspiration for 79 (112)
Weaving. Gaining Design Vertically in 79 (94)
Weaving. Gang 79 (140)
Weaving. Harness 79 (11)
Weaving, History and Design. Tapestry 79 (44)
Weaving. How to Teach 79 (145)
Weaving. How to Visualize Ideas Before 79 (105)
Weaving. Hungarian 79 (40)
Weaving in Other Countries 79 (112)
Weaving in the Round 79 (60)
Weaving in Your Home (Interiors). Put a Little 79 (30)

Weaving. Inca Designs in 79 (26)
Weaving. Inkle 79 (66), (107)
Weaving. Inkle Band and Card 79 (159)
Weaving. Layered 79 (29), (40)
Weaving. Learning to See in Nature and Relate to Your 79 (77)
Weaving. Loose Warp 79 (89)
Weaving. Meso American Indians and 79 (110)
Weaving. Mexican Tapestry 79 (54)
Weaving. Mixed Media 79 (79)
Weaving Months 'til Christmas. X More 79 (30)
Weaving. Multi-Harness 79 (140)
Weaving. Multiple Harness 79 (93)
Weaving. Nail Frame 79 (106)
Weaving. Navajo 79 (61), (85), (89), (91), (92), (134)
Weaving of Ceylon 79 (128)
Weaving of Sikkim 79 (128)
Weaving of Tribal India 79 (115)
Weaving. Off-loom 79 (85), (86), (150)
Weaving Off-loom-board or Frame Set Ups 79 (127)
Weaving on a Zero Budget. Teaching 79 (107)
Weaving on Eight Harness Looms. Theory and Use of Multilayer 79 (52)
Weaving on 8 Harnesses. Double Gang 79 (132)
Weaving on Paper 79 (105)
Weaving on Primitive Looms. Exploring 79 (85)
Weaving on Small Device 79 (3)
Weaving. Rug 79 (8), (17), (85)
Weaving. Rug Design and Rug 79 (78)
Weaving, Sheep Raising. Spinning, Dyeing, 79 (12)
Weaving. Small Appliance 79 (80)
Weaving, Spinning and Dyeing 79 (43)
Weaving Straw Ornaments in the Scandinavian Manner 79 (38)
Weaving Stuffed Forms 79 (10)
Weaving. Tapestry 79 (75), (85), (110)
Weaving Techniques and Contemporary Uses. Ancient American Indian 79 (90)
Weaving - Techniques and Design. Card 79 (155)
Weaving Techniques. Basic 79 (118)
Weaving Techniques. Navajo and Hopi 79 (100)
Weaving Techniques. Off-loom 79 (149)
Weaving the Easy Way. Lace 79 (147)
Weaving. 3-D 79 (71)
Weaving. Three Dimensional 79 (17)
Weaving Today 79 (92)
Weaving With a Simple Loom 79 (62)
Weaving With Natural Materials 79 (107)
Weaving With Supplementary Warps. Designing and 79 (38)
Weaving With Yarn and Words 79 (153)
Weaving Woman. My Life and Hard Times as a 79 (50)
Weaving. Workshops on Rep 79 (148)
Web of Pollution 57 (59)
Wedding Guest. Ovid Pierce's the 56 (36)
Weed Control Around the Home 117 (1)
Weft Brocades 79 (90)
Weft. Clasped Warp and 79 (147)
Weft Face Rugs 79 (159)
Weft Faced Loom Controlled Patterning 79 (132)
Weft Ikat. Warp and 79 (68)
Weft Twining. Warp and 79 (133)
Weigh Systems. Batch 67 (18)
Weight Control 151 (282), 176 (81)
Weight Control and Behavior Modification 216 (134)
Weight Control. Dynamics of 105 (81)
Weight Control. Exercise and 168 (33)
Weight Control. Ups and Downs of 57 (30)
Weight Reduction. Behavior Modification in 218
Weight Reduction Program. Successful 181 (245), (296)
Weight Training 142 (18)
Weighted Looms. Warp 79 (113)
Weiner. Evening With Irv 221 (1)
Welfare Agencies. Supervisors in Health and Social 181 (56)
Welfare? Can Legislation Improve Consumer 54
Welfare. Child 168 (26), 181 (311)
Welfare. History of Public Health and Social 171 (49)
Welfare. How Come Less Poverty and More 85 (35)
Welfare Law. Social 105 (56)
Welfare Reform 54, 172 (10)
Welfare Roles of Country Clubs 117 (53)
Welfare. Social 117 (100), (117), 181 (308)
Welfare State. Paternalism, Economics, and the 85 (14)
Welfare State. Wayward 85 (10)
Well Casing---But Were Afraid to Ask. Everything You Ever Wanted to Know About Plastic 136 (25)
Well Construction Standards. How to Use the Manual of Water 136 (27)
Well Drilling Industry. Mathematics of the 136 (3)
Well Industry. Metric Conversion and the Water 136 (28)
Well Maintenance and Rehabilitation 136 (25)
Well Travelled Student 159 (7)
Wells on Ground Water. Impact of Abandoned 136 (25)
Wells. Using Fracture Traces to Locate Water 136 (12)
West Africa - the American Black Homeland? 29 (7)
West Can Meet. East and 97 (58)
West Coast Jazz 181 (79)
West Coast. Native Wildflowers of the 159 (70)
West Comes Alive. Colorado - Where the 110 (9)
West. East and 105 (20)
West Fall Without a Shot Being Fired? Could the 97 (12)
West German Politics 29 (56)
West German Politics After the 1976 Elections 29 (259)
West Germany 142 (22)
West Indies 56 (120)

West Indies. Travel in the Caribbean and 218
West Irian. Headhunters in Central Borneo and the Cannibals in 225 (35)
West Kentucky in the War Between the States 117 (67)
West Kentucky - Present Status and Future Prospects. Tourism in 117 (121)
West Kentucky. Tourism in 117 (114)
West. Quilting, East to 79 (120)
West. Three Romantic Heroines of the Wild 223 (3)
West. Urban History and History of the American 159 (16)
West. Vanishing Old 15 (4)
West Virginia 168 (26)
West Virginia. Whitewater Rafting in 136 (18)
West. Wild Rivers of the 69 (8)
Western Civilization 142 (1)
Western Coal Project 47
Western Electric 222
Western Europe. Art Treasures in 56 (9)
Western Europe Today 168 (65)
Western Europe. Travelogue of 117 (138)
Western Indian Camel Girths 79 (131)
Western Literature. Character of Don Juan in 151 (233)
Western Movie Scene. Great 112 (20)
Western Plain. Hutterites of the 171 (4)
Western Psychotherapy. African Medicine Man and 181 (291)
Western States. Wilderness Studies of the Bureau of Mines in the 143 (10)
Western United States National Parks. Geology of Various 168 (3)
Wetlands. Coastal 151 (159)
We've Come a Long Way Baby 97 (41)
Whales. Among Wild 69 (12)
Wharton: American Woman Novelist. Edith 151 (238)
What a Computer Is 216 (44)
What a Linguist Does 29 (203)
What a Man on the Moon Means for You 112 (25)
What Alternatives Do You Have in Secondary Public Schools 29 (64), (101), (347)
What America Means to Me 75 (1)
What Counts in Business? 102 (33)
What Do You Mean I Can't Communicate? 29 (34), (77), (137)
What Does it Take to Find a Mine 143 (12)
What Does the Research Tell Us? 181 (122)
What Does Your Child Get Out of School 57 (13)
What Energy Crisis? 102 (24)
What Funny and Why? 225 (40)
What Good is a Major in English? 29 (29), (97)
What Happened to Our Inalienable Rights? 117 (73), (118)
What I Learned as a Widow About Consumer Education 57 (64)
What Industry Expects of College Graduates 216 (23)
What Internal Auditing Can Do for Any Organization 216 (63)
What Is a Bachelor's Degree? 223 (8)
What is a Classic? 97 (43)
What Is a Cooperative? 151 (263)
What is Ahead America? 135 (31)
What is an Underdeveloped Country? 29 (328)
What is Calculus? 117 (92)
What is Capitalism? 85 (4)
What is Computability? 171 (35)
What is Conservatism? 85 (21)
What is Fundamental Basic Education? 29 (64), (101), (347)
What is Ham Radio? 174 (79)
What Is Important? 168 (65)
What is Literacy? 159 (54)
What is Ocean Engineering? 216 (108)
What is Philosophy? 174 (89)
What is Prayer 105 (106)
What is Profit? 23
What is Speed Reading and Does it Work? 171 (16)
What is the Moral Crisis of Our Time? 85 (12)
What is the New Morality? 85 (12)
What is the State Legislature Doing Which Affects the Ordinary Citizen 57 (49)
What is Young People's Liberation? 231 (3)
What It Means to Have a Hearing Loss 117 (132)
What It Means to Understand Music 54
What It's Like to be Queen of the Daytime Dramas 154 (24)
What Makes a Leader? 112 (125)
What Makes a Person Tick 105 (98)
What Makes America Laugh 105 (19)
What Needs Reforming? 29 (64), (101)
What Penn State Does for You 151 (67)
What Public Relations Can Do for You 151 (67)
What Research Means to the University 16 (11)
What Research Tells Us About the Decathlon 29 (305)
What Science Can Do for Archaeology 171 (36)
What Should the Public Expect From our Colleges and Universities 151 (101)
What Should the Schools Teach? 151 (100)
What the Carol Newman Library Can Do for You 216 (56)
What the Church Must Be 75 (1)
What the Music Department Has to Offer East Central Illinois 57 (40)
What to Do Until the Psychiatrist Comes 112 (4)
What Trademarks Are 209
What We Believe 93 (1)
What We Can do About Johnny's Writing 57 (66)
What We Can Do Together 112 (95)
What Work Should Mean 57 (85)
What Would Juvenal Say Today 227 (23)
What You Need to Know About Yourself 75 (1)
What You Say is What You Get 117 (136)
What You See is What You Get 180 (48)
What Young Adults Should Know to Better Their Chances of Success 151 (38)

What Your Voice Reveals About You 105 (13)
Whatcom County at the Crossroads 223 (12)
Whatcom County. Pollution Problems in 223 (15)
What's Ahead for America 102 (27)
What's Going on in There? 112 (118)
Whats Happening in Early Childhood 29 (93), (342)
What's Happening to the Political Parites? 218
What's Right About America 154 (8)
What's Right - What's Wrong With America 85 (18)
What's Right With America 125 (1), 135 (14)
What's So Funny? 151 (243)
What's the Fuss About Meditation? 54
What's Wrong With Equal Rights for Women? 112 (113)
What's Wrong With the Press 151 (67)
Wheel Principle. Collections in Following With the Squeaky 136 (7)
Wheels Turn. Making the 27 (5)
When Arabs and Jews Were Friends 181 (306)
When Do We Believe Our Mass Media? 218
When Man First Walked Erect 112 (73)
When Mass Media Are Irresponsible, What Can We Do? 29 (312)
When Should You Consult an Endocrinologist 27 (35)
When the Mass Media Are Irresponsible 29 (42)
When the Mass Media Are Irresponsible, What Can We Do? 29 (119)
When the Muckrackers Took on College Football 151 (69)
Where Are We Headed in the Arms Race? Is the United States Falling Behind? 102 (8)
Where Do Students Learn? 151 (120)
Where Do the Students Go 57 (13)
Where Do We Go From Here? 97 (4)
Where Have All the Rebels Gone 27 (20)
Where the Future Comes From 168 (11)
Which Computer If Any? 29 (77)
Which is the Real You 97 (31)
White, and Blue. Red, 189
White Aspects. Negritude: Black and 159 (40)
White Collar Crime 168 (49)
White Collar Crimes. How to Protect Yourself Against 97 (21)
White House 219 (9)
White House. Road to the 223 (23)
White Institutions. Student Development Programs for Black Students at Predominantly 105 (39)
White Liberal. Death of the 151 (170)
White Male Professional. Liberation of the 159 (24)
White Tail Deer 151 (309)
White Water Kayaking 216 (68)
Whites. African Crisis - Blacks Versus 97 (50)
Whitewater Paddling 216 (126)
Whitewater Rafting in West Virginia 136 (18)
Who Am I? 105 (80)
Who Controls Education 29 (94)
Who Controls You? 168 (11)
Who Killed the Ice Man - Or, an Answer to Ralph Nader and Consumerism 85 (26)
Who Needs a Hearing Aid? 151 (96)
Who Reads What in Japan 105 (68)
Wholesalers. Time-phased Order Planning for 29 (77)
Why a Liberated Woman Makes for a Liberated Man 225 (8)
Why Additives in Foods? 216 (72)
Why Americans Are Losing Faith in Free Enterprise 102 (33)
Why An Alumni Program 57 (91)
Why and How of Ambulatory Pharmaceutical Services 54
Why Boy Scouts 174 (79)
Why Business Supports All Levels of Education 132 (9)
Why Businesses Fail: Why People Fail 135 (58)
Why Catholic Universities? 105 (41)
Why College? 151 (90)
Why Do Cities Exist? 174 (51)
Why Do People Misunderstand Business? 23
Why Do We Kill Each Other? 112 (3)
Why Don't They Listen? 151 (81)
Why Don't They Stop Inflation 85 (10)
Why I a Jew, Believe in Jesus 93 (2)
Why I am a Christian 151 (258)
Why I Believe in Ahmadiyyat 1 (10)
Why is Everybody Suddenly Interested in Death? 216 (94)
Why Johnny Still Can't Read 151 (100)
Why Life-long Education? 168 (22)
Why Moderates, Conservatives, and Catholics are Excluded From Campus 85 (33)
Why Not Live Forever 45 (2)
Why Nuclear Energy 151 (129)
Why People Do Things 216 (27)
Why People Play 151 (276)
Why Private Support for Penn State? 151 (185)
Why Rehabilitate Prisoners? 29 (49), (133)
Why Trademarks Matter 209
Why Vietnam? 117 (66)
Why We Can't Reform Government 225 (36)
Why We Need Zero Population Growth 168 (58)
Why You Pay What You Pay 66 (4)
Why Your Dollar Continues to Buy Less - With or Without Wage-price Controls 85 (26)
Why Your Elementary School Needs Physical Education 174 (16)
Wide World of Sports 112 (86)
Widow About Consumer Education. What I Learned as a 57 (64)
Widowhood 29 (281)
Wife in Washington. Life of a 97 (75)
Wild Chimpanzees. Fertility and Longevity of 151 (208)
Wild Flowers 151 (308)
Wild Flowers and Plant Communities 223 (15)
Wild Flowers and Their Habitats 168 (56)

Wild Plants 159 (2)
Wild Ponies of Assateague Island 151 (305)
Wild Rivers of the West 69 (8)
Wild Whales. Among 69 (12)
Wilderness Experience 72 (16)
Wilderness Family in British Columbia 218
Wilderness Lake. Alaska 59 (18), 69 (14)
Wilderness. National Parks as Islands of 218
Wilderness Studies of the Bureau of Mines in the Western States 143 (10)
Wilderness. Windows to 57 (3)
Wildflowers of the West Coast. Native 159 (70)
Wildflowers of Washington. Trees, Ferns, and 159 (59)
Wildflowers. Photographing 216 (20)
Wildlife 112 (18)
Wildlife and Game Preserves of East Africa 117 (142)
Wildlife. Australian 29 (75), (277), (324)
Wildlife. East African 218
Wildlife Filming and Conservation 4 (4)
Wildlife in a Changing World. Our 151 (306)
Wildlife. Malaysian 57 (59)
Wildlife Management 216 (26)
Wildlife Management and Conservation. Basic Principles of 151 (309)
Wildlife Photography. Frontiers of 69 (11)
Wildlife Resource. Louisiana's 174 (20)
Wildlife Sanctuary. Tucker 29 (75), (277), (324)
Wildlife. Urban 216 (26)
Wildlife World. Secrets of the 69 (11)
Wilkes-Barre Campus, Service From Mining to Biomedical Technology 151 (2)
Will. Making Out a 54
Will Religion Survive? 29 (155), (249), (291)
Will Rogers. World of 154 (21)
Will the Public Schools Be the Death of English? 168 (51)
Will the Sheiks Buy America? 181 (33), (203), (332)
William Faulkner: Prose Poet 159 (19)
William W. Scranton). Pennsylvania Politics (Governor) 151 (222)
Willing One's Body to Science 181 (14)
Wills 159 (46)
Wilson. Hunting With Justin 112 (134)
Wilson Speaks Contempo. Anne 97 (71)
Win Without Cheating. How to 113 (3)
Wind Islands, Yankee Sails the Trade 59 (5)
Wind Quintet. History and Application of the 218
Windows to Wilderness 57 (3)
Windowsill Plants. Orchids as 151 (237)
Winds - the Decline of Liberalism and the Rise of Conservatism. New 85 (12)
Wine 176 (84)
Wine and Beer Making. Amateur 174 (40)
Wine Buy Moneywise. How to Get the Best 225 (22)
Winemaking 16 (17)
Winemaking. Home 218
Wines. Care and Consumption of 225 (22)
Wines. Enjoying French and American 216 (25)
Winning 56 (87)
Winning Attitude 112 (132)
Winter Bags. Summer and 79 (30)
Winter Holidays in the Americas 15 (3)
Winter Magic Around the World 15 (3)
Winter. Switzerland in 15 (3)
Wire and Other Telephone Stuff. Slippery 144
Wisconsin. Philanthropic Foundations in 105 (53)
Wisdom - A Many Splendored Thing 57 (96)
Wit and Humor. Art of 225 (40)
Witch Drowns in a Dry Hole. How a Water 136 (14)
Witchcraft at Salem: An Overview of the Witchcraft Trials at Salem, Massachusetts 117 (71)
Witchcraft Trials at Salem, Massachusetts. Witchcraft at Salem: An Overview of the 117 (71)
Witchcraft. Truth About 154 (12)
Witches. Ghosts, 161 (1), (2)
Witherspoon. Visit With Reverend John 151 (41)
Witness. Scientist as an Expert 159 (11)
Wolf Research in Alaska 151 (302)
Woman 181 (330)
Woman. Abuse: Child and 181 (221)
Woman. American 151 (72)
Woman and the Environment. Today's 152
Woman Artist. Trials of a 79 (79)
Woman. Black 181 (328)
Woman. Career 180 (44)
Woman. Dracula Meets the New 117 (89)
Woman Editor. Elizabeth Timothy - America's First 56 (61)
Woman in a New World. New 151 (11)
Woman in 17th Century Metaphysical Poets. Image of 227 (29)
Woman Makes for a Liberated Man. Why a Liberated 225 (8)
Woman. Muhammad the Liberator of 1 (2)
Woman. My Life and Hard Times as a Weaving 79 (50)
Woman Novelist. Edith Wharton: American 151 (238)
Woman. Poet as 227 (9)
Woman Relationships. Man/ 211 (2)
Woman. Selling Power of a 180 (186)
Woman. Today's 112 (99)
Woman Writer: Historical View. Plight of the 151 (114)
Womanhood. Middle Years of 181 (221), (284), (323)
Woman's Evolution and Human Nature 213 (11)
Woman's Place in the Business World 97 (32)
Woman's Role in Business 117 (28)
Women 171 (54)
Women. Ancient 227 (21)
Women and Higher Education 105 (86), (95), (109), (326)

Women and Power 154 (14)
Women and Psychology 214 (95)
Women and Social Change 151 (167)
Women and Sport 151 (276)
Women and the Cutbacks 213 (18)
Women and the ERA. Working 213 (18)
Women and Their Societies. Christianity in Africa - 29 (6)
Women are Created Equal. All Men and 214 (85)
Women Artists 214 (8), (93)
Women as Bosses 168 (62)
Women. Black 181 (31)
Women. Career Development for 16 (10)
Women. Career Planning for 181 (52), (322)
Women. Careers for 181 (49), (320)
Women. Changing Role of 56 (126)
Women. Chemical Technology: Opportunity for 151 (265)
Women. Concerns of 223 (38)
Women Dramatists in America. Critical Treatment of 29 (146), (309)
Women. Education of 227 (37)
Women. Equality of 54
Women. Estate Planning for 136 (21)
Women. Femininity and Liberated 179 (2)
Women. Figure Control for 174 (64)
Women. Geology and Hydrology Careers for 136 (22)
Women. Greek and Roman 227 (37)
Women. Hellenistic 227 (37)
Women. Helpful Improvement Tools for 218
Women. Impact of Environmental Hazardous Agents on 151 (153)
Women in Advertising. Images of 168 (9)
Women in Africa - Liberated or Oppressed 29 (7)
Women in America 142 (80)
Women in America. Black 142 (17)
Women in American Literature 151 (234)
Women in Ancient Greece 227 (25)
Women in Antiquity 227 (18), (33)
Women in Antiquity. Attitudes Toward 227 (28)
Women in Antiquity. Social History of 227 (10)
Women in Art: Portrayed and Portrayers 151 (31)
Women in Athletics. Role of 159 (69)
Women in Autobiography. Her Own Words - Lives of American 29 (202), (336)
Women in Business 162
Women in Business. Corner Stones of Success for 229 (5)
Women in China. Position of 218
Women in Communication 29 (35), (142), (285), (308), (335)
Women in Education and the Community 174 (54)
Women in Engineering. Opportunities for 151 (142)
Women in Film 142 (80)
Women in First C.B.C. Roman Life. Power of 227 (29)
Women in Greek and Roman Literature 227 (24)
Women in Greek Drama 227 (48)
Women in History 168 (46)
Women in History and Literature 227 (16)
Women in History. Role of 54
Women in India. Role of 56 (119)
Women in Literature 105 (123)
Women in Management. Barriers to 168 (62)
Women in Medicine 181 (158), (321)
Women in Modern China 112 (33)
Women in Movies. Abuse of 225 (5)
Women in Music 29 (182), (222)
Women in Music: Sung and Unsung 151 (31)
Women in Mythology 227 (28), (48)
Women in Other Cultures 57 (1)
Women in Political Life 56 (131)
Women in Real Estate - Equal at Last 65 (20)
Women in Roman Elegy 227 (24)
Women in Science 57 (20), 171 (54)
Women in Science and Engineering. Minorities and 29 (111), (278)
Women in Sixth-Century Byzantium 227 (12)
Women in Society 57 (8)
Women in Sport 159 (14), 181 (6), (327)
Women in Sports 171 (29)
Women in the Ancient World. Reassessment of Status of 227 (39)
Women in the Hierarchy of Wages. Place of Immigrant 90 (1)
Women in the Home. Economic Status of 90 (1)
Women in the Homeric World 227 (19)
Women in the Media 151 (72)
Women in the Middle East 223 (19)
Women in the Navy 105 (124)
Women in the Peoples' Republic of China 151 (11)
Women in the United States. Role of the Latino 142 (68)
Women in Today's World. Role of 174 (15)
Women. Minority 142 (14)
Women - Mola Artists of San Blas. Cuna 27 (47)
Women. New 211 (2)
Women of All Ages 225 (27)
Women of the World 225 (24)
Women, or Persons? Girls, Ladies, 151 (61)
Women. Organizing 142 (14)
Women. Personal Defense for 151 (205)
Women Poets. Hellenistic 227 (2)
Women. Potential of 176 (26)
Women. Prehistoric View of 29 (168)
Women. Professions and the Socialization of 218
Women. Psychology of 81 (16), 181 (324)
Women. Self-Defense for 174 (64)
Women. Serial Careers for 29 (145)
Women Services 142 (14)
Women. Socialization of 168 (9)
Women. Some Funny Things About 102 (9)
Women. Trends Among Irish Youth and Irish 159 (65)
Women? What's Wrong With Equal Rights for 112 (113)
Women Writers 216 (19)
Women Writers. Afro-American 142 (66)
Women Writers. Hellenistic 227 (54)

Women's Athletics 105 (126)
Women's Awareness 174 (94)
Women's Consciousness Raising 105 (125)
Women's Destiny? Is Biology 213 (11)
Women's Employment Rights and Opportunities 27 (2)
Women's Issue 174 (13)
Womens Issues 174 (42)
Women's Lib. Japanese 57 (95)
Women's Liberation 214 (83), (92)
Women's Liberation and Sexual Roles 85 (35)
Women's Liberation. Black 213 (18)
Women's Liberation in Spain 213 (6)
Women's Liberation Movement 151 (167)
Women's Liberation. Philosophy and 29 (251)
Womens Movement 168 (46)
Women's Movement. Role of Men in the 142 (57)
Women's Options for Fertility. How Wagelessness in the Home Effects 90 (1)
Women's Religion. Artemis and the 227 (48)
Women's Right 142 (25)
Women's Rights. Attacks on 213 (5)
Women's Role in Business and Education 117 (17)
Women's Roles in Modern Society 216 (48)
Women's Self Defense 62 (1), (2), (3)
Women's Sport Karate 62 (1)
Wonderful Mexico 59 (9)
Wonders of the Human Body 54
Wood Block Printing in Alaska 79 (123)
Wood Screens in Devonshire. Extant- 151 (26)
Wood Use and Care in Housing 216 (65)
Wool. Acid Dyes for 79 (102), (141)
Wool Rag Rugs 79 (137)
Wool-raising Game. Spin-offs From the Sheep-raising Business and the 79 (20)
Wool. Spinning and Natural Dyeing of 79 (54)
Wool Spinning on Drop Spindle 79 (59)
Wool With Natural Materials. Dyeing 79 (149)
Word Painting in the Music of Byrd 151 (26)
Word Power. Communication and 151 (70)
Word Processing 119 (1)
Words are Meaningless 117 (115)
Words. Romance of 103 (4)
Work - A National Concern. Right to 131 (3)
Work. ABC's of Personally Controlling Stress at Home and at 136 (24)
Work and Leisure. Future of 181 (12)
Work - Capitol Hill Perspective. Right to 131 (2)
Work Design 105 (116)
Work. Enjoying Your 180 (51)
Work Ethic. Social Sex and the 211 (3)
Work Experience. Academic Credit for 16 (78)
Work - Forcing Public Employees into Unwanted Labor Unions. Right to 131 (4)
Work. Higher Education and the World of 27 (20)
Work Measurement and Work Simplification **119 (1)**
Work Measurement in the Office. Production Standards and 117 (14)
Work on Health. Effects of 29 (155), (176)
Work. Satirist at 225 (1)
Work Should Mean. What 57 (85)
Work Simplification. Work Measurement and **119 (1)**
Work. Strategies for Changing That 117 (100)
Work -Supported by Facts, Figures and the American People. Right to 131 (1)
Work. Trials and Tribulations of Association 136 (20)
Work. Wage and Price Controls - Do They 85 (22)
Worker. Blue Collar 151 (52)
Worker Self-Management 181 (39)
Working. Future of 57 (85)
Working Mothers - Are You Helping or Hurting Your Child 29 (239), (343)
Working on Commission 79 (105), (146)
Working on Paper 79 (6)
Working With Young Handicapped Children 151 (91)
Working With Young People 159 (67)
Working With Your CPA, Banker and Attorney 136 (7)
Working Women and the ERA 213 (18)
Workmen's Compensation. Louisiana 174 (17)
Works of Contemporary Fiction 159 (19)
Workshop. Frame Loom 79 (68)
Workshop in Knotless Netting, Basic Basketry, Wrapping. Children's 79 (158)
Workshops. Bag 79 (150)
Workshops. Fabrics for 79 (105)
Workshops on Rep Weaving 79 (148)
Workshops. Pillow 79 (150)
Workshops. Poetry 227 (9)
Workshops. 3-D 79 (150)
World Affairs 176 (7), (19), (35)
World and American History 54
World at the Moment 83 (6)
World Brotherhood 83 (4)
World Campus Afloat 174 (91)
World Direct to You 144
World Food Problems 112 (17), (117)
World Food Production 216 (97)
World Food Situation 16 (30), 117 (8), 216 (36)
World Hunger 57 (19)
World in the 20th Century 142 (1)
World of Copper 143 (2)
World of Music 154 (18)
World of Will Rogers 154 (21)
World Population Growth 223 (28)
World Populations and Their Trends 16 (30)
World Religions - Buddhists, Confucianists, Taoists, Maoists, Jews, Christians and Muslims 54
World Report 97 (13)
World That the Eye Cannot See 69 (11)
World War II. Japanese American Evacuation During 29 (139), (333)
World's Biggest Computer 144
World's Only Hope 45 (1)

World's Religions 56 (137)
Worship. Heroes and Hero 227 (4)
Worship. Islamic 1 (8)
Worth of Philosophy 105 (90)
Woven and/or Non-woven Structures 79 (70)
Woven Clothes Assembled by Crochet or Knots 79 (60)
Woven Furnishings. Structuring 79 (87)
Woven Image - My Development as a Tapestry Weaver 79 (44)
Woven Portraits 79 (75)
Wrapping 79 (47)
Wreck Diving 29 (138), (302)
Wrestling 151 (282)
Wright. Architecture of Frank Lloyd 181 (78)
Wright. Frank Lloyd 142 (79)
Wright's Own Homes - the Two Taliesins. Frank Lloyd 151 (29)
Writer. Carl Sandburg: Citizen, 225 (42)
Writer: Historical View. Plight of the Woman 151 (114)
Writer. So You Want to Be a 105 (68)
Writers. Afro-American Women 142 (66)
Writers and Opinions on England. French 142 (98)
Writers. Hellenistic Women 227 (54)
Writers. Southern 216 (19)
Writer's Tradition. A. Solzhenitzn and the Russian 29 (127), (295)
Writers. Women 216 (19)
Writing: A Basic Skill for Living. Creative 159 (54)
Writing - A Necessary Skill. Expository 57 (66)
Writing. Creative 142 (66), 174 (29)
Writing Crisis 16 (34)
Writing Deficiencies: Need for Remediation 151 (114)
Writing. Everyday Problems in 168 (53)
Writing Experiences. Palatable 151 (231)
Writing. Fiction of Technical 151 (79)
Writing in the Classroom. Creative 57 (79)
Writing. Persuasive 168 (39)
Writing. Reading and 142 (41)
Writing Reports in Business and Government 168 (53)
Writing. What We Can Do About Johnny's 57 (66)
Writings. Soviet Society in the Zoshchenko's 29 (127), (189), (213), (295)
Written Communication 168 (39)

X

X More Weaving Months 'til Christmas 79 (30)

Y

Yankee Country 103 (6)
Yankee Sails Inland 59 (5)
Yankee Sails Scandinavia 59 (5)
Yankee Sails the Mediterranean 59 (5)
Yankee Sails the Nile 59 (5)
Yankee Sails the Trade Wind Islands 59 (5)
Yankees 97 (1)
Yarn and Words. Weaving With 79 (153)
Yarn Design 79 (72)
Yarn Design for Hand Spinners 79 (91)
Yarn Dyeing. Color Theory and 79 (78)
Yarn, Fabric. Designing in Fiber, 79 (146)
Yarn Manipulation. Fiber and 79 (146)
Yarns. Plying, Doubling, Cabling, Fancy Designer 79 (22)
Yarns, Their Creation and Use. Novelty 79 (130)
Yesterday's Birmingham 16 (55)
Yesterday's Fuel Tomorrow 66 (5)
Yiddish Literature 142 (54)
Yoga 176 (82), 181 (307)
Yoga - A Journey to Inner Peace 151 (88)
Yoga, Health, and Fitness 57 (80)
Yoga. Philosophy and Psychology of 181 (300)
Yoga Psychology 151 (88)
Yogurt 151 (177)
Yosemite and the High Sierra 59 (15)
You and Your Land - Grant University 216 (13)
You Can't Do Business With an Empty Wagon 112 (133)
You Can't Not Communicate 117 (136)
You Look 97 (67)
You Talk, I'll Listen, For a Change 83 (5)
Young Person's Perspective on the Rights of Young People 231 (1)
Your American History I.Q. 151 (219)
Your Attitude Can Make You Young 229 (3)
Your Bacteria Keep You Company 216 (54)
Your Body is Shouting at Me 151 (41)
Your Child Has a Reading Problem 174 (78)
Your Civil Rights 117 (103), (119)
Your Community's Newspaper? 181 (68), (211)
Your Greatest Sense - Your Sense of Humor 112 (39)
Your Human Potential: You Can Achieve! 105 (34)
Your Image 176 (98)
Your Image and Self Motivation 229 (2)
Your Incredible Future 225 (9)
Your Mental Health 216 (94)
Your Newspaper Needs You 57 (88)
Your Organization Can Have an Effective Newspaper 168 (51)
Your Questions Answered on Love, Sex, and Marriage 56 (5)
Your School Distributor Does It All 132 (6)

Your Slip is Showing 151 (242)
Your State's Drilling Regulations in Plain Talk 136 (26)
Your Voice Is You 144
You're Never Too Old 105 (34)
Youth 180 (110)
Youth and Adulthood. Moral Judgment in Children, 214 (77)
Youth and Families: Conflict and Resolution 151 (167)
Youth and Irish Women. Trends Among Irish 159 (65)
Youth. Black Family and Black 151 (111)
Youth. Christian 180 (141)
Youth. College 216 (52)
Youth Culture, Drugs, and Revolution 54
Youth. Existentialism and the Modern 29 (102), (246), (349)
Youth Hosteling in Europe 151 (298)
Youth in Africa 29 (7)
Youth in American History 151 (221)
Youth in Conflict 54
Youth in Real Estate. Motivation - 65 (42)
Youth Movements in History 85 (33)
Youth-Oriented Problems 135 (40)
Youth Programs. Berks County 4-H 151 (20)
Youth Science Center. Museum and 29 (106)
Youth Science Center of North Orange County. Museum and 29 (352)
Youth. Sex, Spirit, and the Fountain of 225 (5)
You've Come A Long Way Baby 151 (200)
You've Got a Lot Going for You 112 (100)
Yucatan. Guatemala and 59 (4)
Yucatan. Hammocks as Made by the Cuna Indians of the San Blas Islands and the Mayans of 79 (25)
Yugoslavia 171 (2), 218
Yugoslavia. Primitive Spinners - Spindles and/or Distaffs From Greece, Turkey, and 79 (20)

Z

Zen and the Artist 211 (5)
Zen Buddahism 174 (55)
Zen. Illumination and 117 (97)
Zero Budget. Teaching Weaving on a 79 (107)
Zero Population Growth. Why We Need 168 (58)
Zoology 112 (24)
Zoshchenko's Writings. Soviet Society in M. 29 (127), (189), (213), (295)
Zoysia Lawn Management 189

SECTION IV

GEOGRAPHIC INDEX

This index arranges speakers bureaus by state and city, followed by their entry numbers referring to their listings in Section I, Speakers and Lecturers: How to Find Them.

ALABAMA

Auburn

Auburn University 16

ARIZONA

Glendale

American Graduate School of International Management 3

CALIFORNIA

Angwin

Pacific Union College 146

Beverly Hills

Lola Wilson Celebrities 225

Fresno

Cal-Land Improvement Contractors 25

Fullerton

California State University, Fullerton 29

Glendale

Glendale Federal Savings and Loan Association 75

Hillsborough

Fame, Limited 59

Hollywood

Directors Guild of America 49

Irvine

University of California, Irvine 27

Los Angeles

Getty Oil Company 74

Monrovia

World Vision International 230

Oakland

Unique Programs, Inc. 190

San Francisco

Chevron U.S.A. Inc. 35

Federal Reserve Bank of San Francisco 61

Network Against Psychiatric Assault 137

San Jose

Associated Film Artists 15

San Luis Obispo

California Polytechnic State University 28

San Rafael

Jews for Jesus 93

Santa Barbara

C.A.L.M. - Child Abuse Listening Mediation, Inc. 24

Santa Barbara Council for the Retarded 169

Whittier

Whittier College 224

COLORADO

Lakewood

Concerns of People, Inc. 39

CONNECTICUT

Hamden

Quest Associates 161

CONNECTICUT (continued)

Newington

American Radio Relay League 9

West Hartford

Handweavers Guild of America 79

Mixter Artist Management 114

DISTRICT OF COLUMBIA

The Ahmadiyya Movement in Islam, Inc. 1

Esperanto League for North America 58

Food Processing Machinery and Supplies Association 67

The Heritage Foundation 82

National Association of Housing Cooperatives 121

National Cable Television Association 124

National Solid Waste Management Association 133

Public Citizen Visitors Center 157

Speakers Bureau of America, Inc. 175

Spokespeople 178

The Tobacco Institute 184

Tuna Research Foundation, Inc. 187

United States Consumer Product Safety Commission 191

United States Department of Agriculture 192

United States Department of Defense 193

Department of the Air Force 194

Department of the Army 195

Department of the Navy 196

United States Marine Corps 197

United States Department of Health, Education and Welfare
Social Security Administration 199

United States Department of State
Arms Control and Disarmament Agency 200

Foreign Service Institute 201

United States Department of the Interior
Bureau of Indian Affairs 202

United States Department of Transportation
United States Coard Guard 203

United States Environmental Protection Agency 204

United States International Communications Agency 205

United States Interstate Commerce Commission 206

United States National Transportation Safety Board 207

United States Postal Service 208

Washington Correspondents Bureau 219

The Washington Reporters Group 220

FLORIDA

Crawfordville

Time Life and Lee Inc. 182

Fort Lauderdale

First Federal of Broward 63

Miami

Florida Power and Light 66

Orlando

The American Sunbathing Associaton, Inc. 10

Florida Association of Realtors 65

FLORIDA (continued)

Tallahassee

Florida A&M University 64

GEORGIA

Atlanta

Georgia Federal Savings and Loan Association 72

National Speakers' and Psychics' Registry 134

Success Leaders Speakers Service 180

HAWAII

Honolulu

Business Communication Council 23

ILLINOIS

Charleston

Eastern Illinois University 57

Chicago

Burns Sports Celebrity Service, Inc. 22

Chemetron Corporation 34

James A. H. Conrad 40

The Contemporary Forum 42

Carl M. Johnson 94

National Association of Suggestion Systems 123

Northeastern Illinois University 142

Evanston

Ancient Arts of the Future 13

The Learning Exchange 99

Lake Forest

National Speakers Bureau, Inc. 135

Park Ridge

Tool and Die Institute 185

Skokie

The Gilbert Miller Agency 113

INDIANA

Highland

Calumet Area Foundation for Medical Care, Inc. 30

Indianapolis

Leo Crowder Productions, Inc. 43

International Entertainment Bureau 86

Richmond

Earlham College 55

IOWA

Cedar Rapids

Coe College 37

Corning

National Farmers Organization 126

Des Moines

Dial Corporation 48

Iowa City

Iowa Mountaineers, Inc. 91

KANSAS

Leawood

Mid West Program Service, Inc. 112

Manhattan

Kansas State University 95

Salina

Kansas Wesleyan University 96

Wichita

Beech Aircraft Corporation 19

KENTUCKY

Louisville

Data Courier, Inc. 44

Murray

Murray State University 117

LOUISIANA

Lafayette

University of Southwestern Louisiana 174

New Orleans

Free Southern Theater 70

Bob Harrington 81

MARYLAND

Baltimore

Baltimore Federal Savings and Loan Association 18

National Organization for Non-Parents 129

Bethesda

Disclosure Incorporated 50

College Park

University of Maryland 106

Hyattsville

American Polygraph Association 7

Kensington

Washington Correspondents Bureau 219

The Washington Reporters Group 220

Rockville

United States Department of Health, Education and Welfare
Public Health Service 198

Silver Spring

Americans United 12

National Micrographics Association 128

MASSACHUSETTS

Boston

Martin A. Forrest 69

Massachusetts Bar Association 107

East Sandwich

University Speakers Bureau 211

Lynn

Shoe Suppliers of America 170

Needham

Irv Weiner Programs, Inc. 221

GEOGRAPHIC INDEX

MICHIGAN

Ann Arbor

Youth Liberation Press, Inc. 231

Detroit

Childbirth Without Pain Education Association 36

Detroit Edison 47

Kalamazoo

American Institute for Exploration 4

MINNESOTA

Foreston

RAP and Associates 163

Minneapolis

American Collectors Association, Inc. 2

Medtronic, Inc. 109

Saint Cloud

Saint Cloud State University 168

Saint Peter

Gustavus Adolphus College 78

MISSOURI

Kansas City

Patricia Stevens Model and Merchandising Agency 179

United Telecommunications, Inc. 210

Marble Hill

National Association of Parents and Professionals for Safe Alternatives in Childbirth 122

Saint Louis

Monsanto Company 115

Union Electric Speakers Forum 189

NEW JERSEY

East Rutherford

Dawn Bible Students Association 45

Madison

Drew University 52

Morristown

Jersey Central Power and Light Company 92

New Providence

International Industrial Television Association 87

Newark

Public Service Electric and Gas Company 158

Union

National Premium Sales Executives, Inc. 130

NEW YORK

Albany

International Narcotic Enforcement Officers Association 88

Croton-on-Hudson

World Modeling Association 229

Delhi

Ned Roesler 166

Forest Hills

Lecture Services, Inc. 100

NEW YORK (continued)

Hartsdale

Program Corporation of America 156

New York

American Montessori Society 5

American Professional Practice Association 8

American Teilhard Association for the Future of Man 11

Asian Speakers Bureau 14

Blackman and Raber Limited 21

Commodity Exchange, Inc. 38

Consolidated Edison Company of New York, Inc. 41

Richard Fulton Inc. 71

Keedick Lecture Bureau, Inc. 97

Fran Lee Foundation Inc. 101

The Leigh Bureau 102

Mahgo Enterprises, Inc. 104

Men's Fashion Association of America 111

Morality in Media, Inc. 116

Naremco Services, Inc. 119

National Association of Fleet Administrators, Inc. 120

National Committee for Responsible Patriotism 125

New York Mercantile Exchange 138

Newsweek, Inc. 139

Package Designers Council 147

Pinkerton's Inc. 153

Podium Management Associates, Inc. 154

Trans World Airlines 186

The United States Trademark Association 209

Viewpoint Speakers Bureau 213

War Resisters League 217

Western Electric Company 222

The Women's Classical Caucus 227

Women's Martial Arts Union 228

Oyster Bay

Theodore Roosevelt Association 167

Roslyn

Ann Lewis Program Service 103

Schenectady

Union College 188

NORTH CAROLINA

Charlotte

North Carolina National Bank 141

Dunn

Bald Headed Men of America 17

Durham

Duke University 53

Greenville

East Carolina University 56

Winston-Salem

R. J. Reynolds Tobacco Company 165

OHIO

Akron

The Goodyear Tire and Rubber Company 76

OHIO (continued)

Bay Village

Charles Hutaff 83

Cleveland

Delta Nu Alpha Transportation Fraternity 46

Ohio Bell Telephone Company 144

Sohio Speakers Bureau 173

Cleveland Heights

International Platform Association 89

Columbus

Speakers Unlimited 177

Tin Research Institute, Inc. 183

Dayton

NCR Corporation 118

Mantua

The Hattie Larlham Foundation, Inc. 98

Rocky River

Reid Interiors 164

Toledo

Champion Spark Plug Company 33

Worthington

National Water Well Association 136

OKLAHOMA

Norman

Douglas Management 51

OREGON

Portland

Georgia-Pacific Corporation 73

Pearl Harbor Survivors Association, Inc. 149

PENNSYLVANIA

Bethlehem

Bethlehem Steel Corporation 20

Bryn Mawr

Intercollegiate Studies Institute, Inc. 85

Johnstown

Pennsylvania Electric Company 150

Philadelphia

The Green Circle Program, Inc. 77

Institute for Scientific Information 84

Philadelphia Electric Speakers Bureau 152

The Speaker's Bureau of Philadelphia 176

Temple University 181

Pittsburgh

Carnegie-Mellon University 31

Duquesne University 54

The "Pride In America" Company 155

University Park

The Pennsylvania State University 151

Valley Forge

National Liberty Corporation 127

No-Load Mutual Fund Association 140

PENNSYLVANIA (continued)

Villanova

Villanova University 124

TENNESSEE

Memphis

Center for Southern Folklore 32

Memphis State University 110

Nashville

George Peabody College for Teachers 148

Pigeon Forge

The American Party 6

TEXAS

Carrollton

B. L. Vaughan and Associates 212

VIRGINIA

Arlington

Hardwood Plywood Manufacturers Association 80

National School Supply and Equipment Association 132

Blacksburg

Virginia Tech Speakers Bureau 216

Fairfax

National Right to Work Committee 131

Richmond

Federal Reserve Bank of Richmond 60

Virginia Electric and Power Company 215

WASHINGTON

Bellingham

Western Washington University 223

Seattle

Feminist Karate Union 62

Rainier National Bank 162

University of Washington 218

Spokane

Northwest Mining Association 143

Tacoma

University of Puget Sound 159

WISCONSIN

Milwaukee

Food Shoppers Union 68

Marquette University 105

Pabst Brewing Company 145

Socialist Party, USA 172

Wisconsin Electric Power Company 226

Wauwatosa

Meditation Institute 108

CANADA

Alberta - Calgary

The University of Calgary 26

British Columbia - Burnaby

Simon Fraser University 171

CANADA (continued)

Ontario - Kingston

Queen's University 160

Ontario - Toronto

International Wages for Housework Campaign - Canada 90

SECTION V

LIST OF SUBJECT HEADINGS

SUBJECT INDEX

This index is a detailed and comprehensive list of subjects on which lecturers speak. The entry numbers and, in parentheses, speaker code numbers given here refer users to descriptive entries in the speakers bureau listings in Section I, Speakers and Lecturers: How to Find Them.

For detailed instructions on the use and organization of this volume, see "Organization of the Volume," page vi, and "How to Use this Book," page vii.

LIST OF SUBJECT HEADINGS

Abortion
Accounting
Acupuncture
Advertising
Africa
Aging
Agriculture
Alaska
Alcoholism
American Indians
Ancient World
Animals
Anthropology
Antiques
Archaeology
Architecture
Art
Astrology
Astronomy
Audiovisual
Australia and New Zealand
Automation--See Computers
Automobiles
Aviation

Banking
Biofeedback
Biology
Blacks
Body Language--See Nonverbal Communication
Business and Industry
Business/Government Relations

Canada
Careers
Cartography--See Geography
Ceramics
Chemical Industry
Chemistry
Chicanos
Child Abuse
Children
Children's Literature
China
Civil Liberties
Civil Rights
Clocks
Collecting and Collectors
College Students
Colleges and Universities
Communication
Communism
Communities
Computers
Concentration Camps
Conservation
Construction
Consumer Affairs
Continuing Education
Cooking
Counseling
Creativity
Crime
Criminal Justice

Dance
Data Processing--See Computers
Death
Dentistry
Developing Countries
Discrimination--See Racial Relations
Diseases and Body Disorders
Drama--See Theater
Drug Abuse
Drugs

Earthquakes--See Geology
Eastern United States
Ecology
Economics
Education
Electricity
Employment
Energy
Engineering
English Language--See Language
Entertainment
Environment
Equal Employment
Eskimos
Espionage--See Intelligence Activities
Estate Planning
Ethics and Morals
Europe
Exercise--See Physical Fitness

Family Relations
Far East
Fashion
Films
Financial Management
Folklore
Food and Beverages
Food Supply
Foreign Languages
Foreign Policy--See International Affairs
Fossils
France
Fund Raising
Future of Society

Gambling
Games
Gardening--See Horticulture
Gems
Genealogy
Genetics
Geography
Geology
Geriatrics--See Aging
Germany
Gestalt
Government
Graphoanalysis
Great Britain and Ireland

Handicapped
Handicrafts
Hawaii
Health
Health Professions
History
Home Management
Horticulture
Human Relations
Human Rights--See Civil Liberties
Humor
Hypnotism

India
Industry --See Business and Industry
Inflation--See Economics
Information Systems
Insurance
Intelligence Activities
Interior Decorating
International Affairs
International Business
Interviewing
Ireland--See Great Britain and Ireland
Islam
Israel

Japan
Journalism and The Press

Judaism
Judicial System

Labor Relations
Land Use
Landscaping
Language
Lasers
Latin America
Law
Leadership
Libraries
Linguistics
Literature
Local History

Magic
Management
Manufacturing--See Business and Industry
Marine Life
Maritime
Marketing
Marriage--See Family Relations
Mathematics
Media
Medical Science
Medieval World
Meditation
Meeting Management
Memory
Mental Health
Meteorology
Metric System
Mexican-American--See Chicanos
Middle East
Military
Minerals
Mining
Minorities
Morals-- See Ethics and Morals
Motivation
Museums
Music
Mythology

National Defense
New Zealand--See Australia and New Zealand
News Media--See Media
Newspapers--See Journalism and The Press
Nonverbal Communication

Nuclear Energy
Nursing--See Health Professions
Nutrition

Office Management
Oil and Gas

Pacific Regions
Palmistry
Parapsychology--See Psychic Phenomena
Peace
Perception
Personal Development
Personnel Administration
Pets--See Animals
Pharmaceuticals--See Drugs
Philosophy
Photography
Physical Education
Physical Fitness
Physicians--See Health Professions
Physics
Physiology
Plant Life
Poetry
Poison
Polar Regions
Police
Politics
Pollution--See Ecology
Population
Postal Service
Pregnancy and Childbirth
Prisons--See Criminal Justice
Propaganda
Psychic Phenomena
Psychology
Public Administration
Public Relations
Publishing

Racial Relations
Radio
Railroads
Rape--See Crime
Reading
Real Estate
Recreation
Religion
Research
Retirement

Russia

Safety
Sailing--See Water Sports
Sales
School Administration
Science
Science Fiction
Sculpture
Secretaries
Security
Self Improvement--See Personal Development
Sex and Sexuality
Social Problems
Social Responsibilities
Social Sciences
Social Welfare
Solar Energy
South America
Southeast Asia
Southern United States
Space
Spain
Spanish American--See Chicanos
Speech
Sports
State and Local Government
Statistics
Stock Market

Taxes
Technology
Television
Textiles
Theater
Time Management
Traffic Safety
Transactional Analysis
Transportation
Travel
Travel Films

United Nations
United States
United States History
Universities--See Colleges and Universities
Urban Affairs

Values
Veterinary Medicine
Vocations--See Careers

Wastes and Refuse
Water Sports
Weather--See Meteorology
Weight Reduction--See Physical Fitness
Western United States
Wilderness
Wildlife
Women
Writing

Yoga
Youth

Zoology

A

ABORTION
See also: PREGNANCY AND CHILDBIRTH

Duquesne University 54
Marquette University 105
Doherty, Dennis J. (76)
Northeastern Illinois University 142
Singleton, Gregory H. (78)
Villanova University 214
Betz, Joseph (83)
Losoncy, Thomas A. (84)

ACCOUNTING

Business Communication Council 23
Carnegie-Mellon University 31
Kaplan, Robert S. (1)
Duquesne University 54
East Carolina University 56
Colcord, Marshall (16)
Marquette University 105
Trebby, James P. (10)
National Water Well Association 136
Alcorn, Pat B. (7)
Zag, Karen (11)
Puget Sound, University of 159
Polley, Roy J. (50)
Segall, M. Harvey (57)
Simon Fraser University 171
Guthrie, Arthur (9)
Var, Turgut (13)
Villanova University 214
Clay, Alvin A. (2), (15)
Virginia Polytechnic Institute and State University 216
Keister, Ronald E. (63)

ACUPUNCTURE

Ancient Arts of the Future 13
Pomeroy, Justin (1)

ADVERTISING

American Graduate School of International Management 3
Hall, Duane R. (1)
Business Communication Council 23
California State University, Fullerton 29
Atkin, Kenward L. (33)
Mann, Donald H. (80)
First Federal of Broward 63
Florida Association of Realtors 65
Boardman, Blanche (6)
Fantle, Karl S. (17)
German, Jack (22)
Heavener, Mac D., Jr. (26)
Linville, George M. (38)
Lynn, Frank (39)
Moore, Steven A. (44)
Moskal, Lilyb (45)
Moutz, Madora (46)
Pierce, John E. (52)
Randol, Monroe (54)
Wilcox, Olin R. (68)
Yates, Dorothy M. (70)
Georgia Federal Savings and Loan Association 72
Marquette University 105
Brownlee, Ralph E. (4)
Murray State University 117
McGaughey, Robert H. III (85)
Seale, William B. (25)
Wells, Jane Freeman (28)
National Speakers Bureau, Inc. 135
Cappo, Joe (11)
National Water Well Association 136
Stanley, Anita Bacco (5)
Northeastern Illinois University 142
Flory, Joyce Ann (25)
Walker, Robert (92)
Pabst Brewing Company 145
Allerup, N.P. (1)
Ratcheson, R.J. (2)
Winograd, A.J. (3)
Pennsylvania State University 151
Lehew, Harry D. (75)
Waun, Roger J. (87)
Saint Cloud State University 168
Craik, Mary B. (9)
Pehler, Jim (59)
Success Leaders Speakers Service 180
Waas, Les (184)
United States Trademark Association 209
Whittier College 224
Thomas, Larry (15)

AFRICA

Ahmadiyya Movement in Islam, Inc. 1
Malik, Daud Abdul (9)
Associated Film Artists 15
Francisco, Clay (2)
California State University, Fullerton 29
Brown, Giles T. (1), (48)
Cox, Miriam S. (2), (200)
Giacumakis, George J. (3), (179), (217), (226)
Josephson, Nors S. (227), (317)
Kalupa, Frank B. (4), (318)
Kaye, Alan S. (5), (163), (319)
Namasaka, Boaz N. (6), (60), (219), (242), (329), (337)
Nanjundappa, Boaz N. (286)
Nyaggah, Mougo (7), (180)
Weightman, Barbara A. (8), (167), (325)
Drew University 52
Mascio, Afeword A. (52)
Peek, Philip M. (67)
Rice, Charles L. (76)
Weimer, Joan S. (97)
Wolf, Frank (100)
Duquesne University 54
East Carolina University 56
Birchard, Ralph (113)
Bunger, Robert Louis, Jr. (2), (114)
Eastern Illinois University 57
Murray, Louise (62)
Waddell, Leyla Peck (92)
Fame Limited 59
Johnson, Irving M. (5)
Jones, Doug (7)
Madsen, Bill (9)
Forrest, Martin A. 69
Bjerre, Jens (2)
Intercollegiate Studies Institute, Inc. 85
Kuehnelt-Leddikin, Erik Von (18)
Keedick Lecture Bureau, Inc. 97
Melady, Thomas Patrick (42)
Nugent, John Peer (50)
Lecture Services, Inc. 100
Furbay, John H. (1)
Murray State University 117
McHugh, William P. (9)
Schanbacker, Eugene M. (142)
Northeastern Illinois University 142
Kamau, Lucy J. (48)
Pennsylvania State University 151
Griffith, Cyril E. (217)
Hauser, Robert E. (218)
Ongiri, David O. (111)
Puget Sound, University of 159
Reeck, Darrell (51)

AFRICA (continued)

Saint Cloud State University 168
Levilain, Guy (41)
Simon Fraser University 171
Adam, Heribert (1)
Kup, A.P. (3)
Southwestern Louisiana, University of 174
Goellner, Edward B. (36)
Kurtz, Donn M. II (59)
Rense, William C. (82)
Webb, Robert M. (91)
Speakers Bureau of America, Inc. 175
Brownfeld, Allan C. (1)
Masimini, Leslie (2)
Temple University 181
Ayaga, Odeyo O. (25), (257), (331)
Baenninger, Ronald (281)
Hampton, Barbara L. (27), (84)
Keto, Clement T. (28), (267), (338)
Miller, Richard L. (18), (340)
Rappaport, Herbert (291)
Ulmer, Gene C. (137), (347)
Villanova University 214
Strack, Harry R. (56)
Virginia Polytechnic Institute and State University 216
Johnson, Overton R. (60)
Washington, University of 218
Western Washington University 223
Critchfield, Howard J. (32)
Paulus, Ingeborg (18), (36)

AGING

California, Irvine, University of 27
Hochschild, Richard (29)
East Carolina University 56
Templeton, Mary Susan (89)
Eastern Illinois University 57
Sutton, Kenneth (85)
Feminist Karate Union 62
Bateman, Py (1)
Marquette University 105
Piacsek, Bela E. (3)
Northeastern Illinois University 142
Moorhead, Hugh S. (62)
Renas, Stanley R. (71)
Pennsylvania State University 151
Berman, Harry J. (17)
Fleishman, Joe (18)
Frank, Tom (96)
Grode, John N. (228)
Queen's University 160
Andrew, George (2)
Saint Cloud State University 168
Stensland, Allen (67)
Socialist Party, USA 172
Marcus, Edward (7)
Southwestern Louisiana, University of 174
Eason, Byrdie E. (27)
Speakers Bureau of Philadelphia 176
Schwartz, Loretta (103)
Success Leaders Speakers Service 180
Samp, Robert J. (148)
Temple University 181
Adelman, Richard C. (13)
Karpeles, Harry D. (15), (170), (223)
Lantz, Harold (174)
Malnati, Richard J. (289)
Sloviter, Dolores Korman (192), (241), (271), (312)
Virginia Polytechnic Institute and State University 216
Wysocki, Joseph L. (145)
Washington, University of 218

AGRICULTURE
See also: FOOD AND BEVERAGES; FOOD SUPPLY

Auburn University 16
Brewer, Robert N. (8)
Hendrick, James (31)
King, Nelson B. (45)
Rouse, R. Dennis (70)
Sprott, J. Michael (75)
Wilson, Stanley P. (89)
Yeager, Joseph H. (91)
California Polytechnic State University 28
East Carolina University 56
Moore, Oscar (18)
Florida Association of Realtors 65
Kirk, Robert W. (34)
Georgia-Pacific Corporation 73
Handweavers Guild of America 79
Blackburn, Edna (12)
Carter, Grace (20)
Intercollegiate Studies Institute, Inc. 85
Michl, H.E. (22)
Kansas Wesleyan University 96
Maryland, University of 106
Monsanto Company 115
Murray State University 117
Cherry, William N. (2)
Conley, Harry L. (3)
Eversmeyer, Harold E. (4)
Mathis, Gilbert (6)
Thompson, James T. (8)
National Farmers Organization 126
Staley, Oren Lee (1)
Woodland, De Von (2)
Pennsylvania State University 151
Beattie, James M. (19)
Bleiler, Mae E. (20)
Cunningham, Robert L. (21)
Gamble, Hays B. (225)
Haldeman, James E. (22)
King, Thomas B. (23)
Suloff, Charles E. (263)
Thomas, Walter I. (24), (181)
Wetzel, Herbert A. (25)
Reynolds Tobacco Company, R.J. 165
Socialist Party, USA 172
Mitchell, H.L. (8)
Southwestern Louisiana, University of 174
Beckman, William C. (4)
Success Leaders Speakers Service 180
Brekke, Arnold (18)
United States Department of Agriculture 192
Virginia Polytechnic Institute and State University 216
Bovard, Kenley P. (9)
Cherry, Jerry A. (18)
Clouse, James P. (22)
McMillion, Martin B. (78)
Marlowe, Thomas J. (80)
Mason, J.P.H., Jr. (83)
Vaughan, David H. (137)

ALASKA

American Institute for Exploration 4
Allen, Ruthann (1)
Ransom, Jay Ellis (6)
Douglas Management 51
Douglas, Neil (1)
East Carolina University 56
Eller, Frank (116)
Eastern Illinois University 57
Shuff, Robert V. (81)
Fame Limited 59
Butler, Willis (3)
Walker, Theodore J. (18)
Forrest, Martin A. 69
Walker, Theodore (14)

ALASKA (continued)

Northwest Mining Association 143
McGregor, Wallace (9)
Pennsylvania State University 151
Zervanos, Stam M. (302)
Roesler, Ned 166
Roesler, Ned (1)
Western Washington University 223
Hildebrand, Francis (34)

ALCOHOLISM

California State University, Fullerton 29
Bedell, John W. (280)
Duquesne University 54
East Carolina University 56
Jorgensen, N.M. (82)
Marquette University 105
McCall, Raymond J. (100)
White, Dennis K. (88)
Miller Agency, Gilbert 113
Piersall, Jimmy (2)
Mixter Artist Management 114
Tracy, Heddie, Sr. (4)
Murray State University 117
Barton, R.B. (15), (107)
Pennsylvania State University 151
Beck, Edward S. (161)
Wirag, J. Robert (212)
Saint Cloud State University 168
Hortis, Theophanis (29)
Johnson, David C. (30)
Simon Fraser University 171
Rockerble, R.A. (53)
Southwestern Louisiana, University of 174
Bonnette, Richard M. (12)
Success Leaders Speakers Service 180
Griffin, Robert J. (66)
Temple University 181
Liebler, Joan G. (177)
Washington, University of 218

AMERICAN INDIANS
See also: ESKIMOS; MINORITIES

California State University, Fullerton 29
Coffer, William E. (50), (87), (158), (192), (230), (254), (283), (331)
Jaskowski, Helen M. (162)
Qureshi, Naimuddin (19)
Sadovszky, Otto J. (165), (339)
Sutton, Imre (166), (195)
East Carolina University 56
Paschal, Herbert (34)
Eastern Illinois University 57
Shull, Earl (82)
Handweavers Guild of America 79
Hart, Arthur A. (56)
King, Bucky (71)
Marks, Copeland H. (83)
Shawley, Stephen D. (124)
Slickpoo, Allen P. (126)
Turner, Alta R. (142)
Marquette University 105
Kehoe, Alice B. (1)
Mid West Program Service, Inc. 112
Milligan, Edward A. (90)
Pennsylvania State University 151
Kujundzic, Zeljko (27)
Podium Management Associates, Inc. 154
Beard, Timothy (2)
Rogers, Will, Jr. (21)
Puget Sound, University of 159
Hansen, Tim (24)
Hoyt, Milton (32)
Socialist Party, USA 172
Hart, William (3)
Hermann, Beatrice (4)
Southwestern Louisiana, University of 174
Gibson, Jon L. (34)
United States Department of the Interior 202
Washington, University of 218

ANCIENT WORLD

Auburn University 16
Nist, Joan Stidham (61)
California State University, Fullerton 29
Lynn, Joanne L. (124), (197), (205), (320)
Josephson, Nors S. (317)
Drew University 52
Properzio, Paul G. (70)
Duquesne University 54
East Carolina University 56
Bond, Margaret S. (1)
Papalas, Anthony J. (93)
Eastern Illinois University 57
Murray, Louise (62)
Schram, Frederick R. (77)
Marquette University 105
Asp, Carolyn (16)
Brenk, Frederick E. (17)
Murray State University 117
Beasley, Wayne T. (64)
Kline, James M. (70)
Pennsylvania State University 151
Frankforter, A. Daniel (215)
Williamson, William O. (259)
Southwestern Louisiana, University of 174
Cusimano, Richard C. (22)
Women's Classical Caucus 227
Bram, Jean Rhys (3)
Broege, Valerie (4)
Clader, Linda (5)
Clay, Jenny Strauss (6)
Clayman, Dee Lesser (7)
Culham-Ertman, Phyllis (8)
Dickison, Sheila K. (10)
Drake, Gertrude (11)
Fisher, Elizabeth A. (12)
Gebhard, Elizabeth R. (14)
Gold, Barbara K. (15)
Gordon, Diane R. (16)
Greengard, Carola (17)
Hallett, Judith P. (18)
Hartigan, Karelisa (19)
Katz, Phyllis B. (21)
Killian, Barbara E. (23)
King, Joy K. (24)
Kohler, Frances Coulborn (25)
Koloski-Ostrow, Ann Olga (26)
Lanham, Carol D. (27)
Loomis, Julia W. (29)
Marker, Sherry (30)
Milham, Mary Ella (31)
More, Judith de Luce (32)
Morgan, Kathleen (33)
Nussbaum, Martha C. (34)
Orlandi, Mary Kay Gamel (35)
Phillips, Jane E. (36)
Pomeroy, Sarah B. (37)
Robert, Jennifer (38)
Rossi, Mary Ann (39)
Shelton, Jo-Ann (42)
Snyder, Jane M. (43)
Stein, Kay E. (45)
Thomas, Kathryn A. (46)
Thomas, Ruth S. (47)
Trachy, Carol Law (48)
Vanderlip, Vera F. (50)
Villeneuve, Winnie Frohn (51)
Wagner, Cherryl A. (52)
Warrior, Valerie M. (53)
Wiggers, Nancy (54)
Wilkie, Nancy C. (55)

ANIMALS
See also: MARINE LIFE; WILDLIFE; ZOOLOGY

Northeastern Illinois University 142
Fowler, Mary Ann (26)
Garrett, Philip R. (28)
Pennsylvania State University 151
Ferguson, Frederick G. (206)
Hunt, Edward E., Jr. (208)
Saint Cloud State University 168
Partch, Max (56)
Speaker's Bureau of Philadelphia 176
Lawson, Deborah (60)
Temple University 181
Baenninger, Ronald (281)
Goehl, Henry (314)
Virginia Polytechnic Institute and State University 216
Cherry, Jerry A. (18)
Huff, Arden N. (57)
Marlowe, Thomas J. (80)
Potter, Lawrence M. (97)
Washington, University of 218
Wilson Celebrities, Lola 225
Lydecker, Beatrice (26)

ANTHROPOLOGY

American Institute for Exploration 4
Bank, Ted P. II (3)
California State University, Fullerton 29
Hulse, Christopher R. (141), (161), (284)
Leder, Hans H. (96), (164)
Wood, Corinne S. (168)
Drew University 52
Wescott, Roger W. (98)
Eastern Illinois University 57
Schram, Frederick R. (77)
Marquette University 105
Kehoe, Alice B. (1)
Mid West Program Service, Inc. 112
Johanson, Donald C. (73)
Murray State University 117
McHugh, William P. (9)
National Speakers Bureau, Inc. 135
Powell, J. Lewis (51)
Northeastern Illinois University 142
Caron, Josiane (14)
Kamaw, Lucy J. (48)
MacDonald, James (58)
Pennsylvania State University 151
Barton, Michael (214)
Hunt, Edward E., Jr. (208)
Simon Fraser University 171
Nance, Jack D. 38
Southwestern Louisiana, University of 174
Cusimano, Richard C. (22)
Speaker's Bureau of Philadelphia 176
Montagu, Ashley (80)
Virginia Polytechnic Institute and State University 216
Aceves, Joseph B. (1)
Washington, University of 218
Whittier College 224
Farmer, Malcolm F. (5)

ANTIQUES

Auburn University 16
Killian, Albert F. (44)
Conrad, James A.H. 40
Conrad, James (1)
Keedick Lecture Bureau, Inc. 97
Gichner, Lawrence E. (24)
Lewis Program Service, Ann 103
Hannan, Douglas (3)
Murray State University 117
Puckett, Billy J. (130)
Northeastern Illinois University 142
Braun, Vern (10)
Reid Interiors 164
Reid, Charlotte (2)
Saint Cloud State University 168
Wagenius, Terry (70)
Southwestern Louisiana, University of 174
Moeller, Wayne E. (73)

ARCHAEOLOGY

American Institute for Exploration 4
Lipsio, Peter (5)
California State University, Fullerton 29
Giacumakis, George J. (226), (269)
Carnegie-Mellon University 31
Toker, Franklin (28)
Drew University 52
Bull, Robert J. (10)
Marquette University 105
Kehoe, Alice B. (1)
Murray State University 117
McHugh, William P. (31)
Northeastern Illinois University 142
Spencer, Nancy A. (82)
Simon Fraser University 171
Huntley, Dave (36)
Southwestern Louisiana, University of 174
Gibson, Jon L. (34)
Washington, University of 218
Women's Classical Caucus 227
Gais, Ruth (13)
Gebhard, Elizabeth R. (14)
Hill, Dorothy K. (20)
Koloski-Ostrow, Ann Olga (26)
Stein, Kay E. (45)
Wilkie, Nancy C. (55)

ARCHITECTURE

California Polytechnic State University 28
California State University, Fullerton 29
Santucci, James A. (13), (129)
Carnegie-Mellon University 31
Toker, Franklin (3)
East Carolina University 56
Farnham, Emily (10)
Northeastern Illinois University 142
Skvarla, Melvyn A. (79)
Pennsylvania State University 151
Grode, John N. (228)
Lord, Walton J. (29)
Richman, Irwin (257)
Rocco, Emma S. (31)
Reid Interiors 164
Lawrence, J. (1)
Southwestern Louisiana, University of 174
Conrad, Glenn R. (19)
Goyert, Philip R., Jr. (37)
Temple University 181
Claflen, George L., Jr. (78), (207)
Samuelson, Norbert M. (87), (306)
Washington, University of 218
Women's Classical Caucus 227
Rossi, Mary Ann (39)

ART
See also: CERAMICS; SCULPTURE

ART

Auburn University 16
Adams, Murray C. (1)
Hiers, Charles J. (32)
California State University, Fullerton 29
Desenberg, Irma E. (10)
Odle, D. Richard (11), (148)
Sadovszky, Otto J. (12)
Santucci, James A. (13), (129)
Carnegie-Mellon University 31
Carrier, David (4)
Keisch, Bernard (5)
Contemporary Forum 42
Drew University 52
Dehoney, Martyvonne (22)
Peek, Philip M. (67)
East Carolina University 56
Benjamin, Lloyd (9)
Farnham, Emily (10)
Reep, Edward (13)
Eastern Illinois University 57
Jaenike, Vaughn (38)
Krutza, June (44)
Linn, John (52)
Rang, Jack C. (67)
Settle, Phillip M. (78)
Shull, Carl (82)
Fulton Inc., Richard 71
Keedick Lecture Bureau, Inc. 97
Lignante, Bill (37)
Vanderbilt, Gloria (66)
Learning Exchange 99
Leigh Bureau 102
Price, Vincent (25)
Marquette University 105
Donnelly, John P. (61)
Jones, Leo M. (19)
Laczniak, Gene R. (6)
Maryland, University of 106
Murray State University 117
Brun, Michael A. (10)
Head, Robert (11)
Jackson, Richard G. (12)
Keeslar, Suzanne M. (138)
Newsweek, Inc. 139
Northeastern Illinois University 142
Broadd, Harry A. (11)
Combs, Ronald (16)
Hallberg, Clarice L. (35)
Segedin, Leopold B. (76)
Walker, Robert (92)
Pennsylvania State University 151
Beach, James W. (26)
Botdorf, Ruth (264)
Henisch, Heinz K. (73)
Kujundzic, Zeljko (27)
Leeds, Fredric (28)
Lord, Walton J. (29)
Mizusawa, Kiyoe (271)
Ott, Robert W. (30)
Rocco, Emma S. (31)
Santulli, Michael A. (157)
Schwartz, Alice M. (32)
Puget Sound, University of 159
Ball, F. Carlton (5)
Colby, Bill (18)
Ebert, Laurence E. (21)
Hoffman, Barbara (30)
Reid Interiors 164
Lawrence, J. (1)
Saint Cloud State University 168
Buckley, Chester (8)
Simon Fraser University 171
Wheatley, Jon (55)
Southwestern Louisiana, University of 174
Hanley, Frank L. (41)
Ladousa, Dickie (61)
Speaker's Bureau of Philadelphia 176
Finkel, Arnold (40)
Haynes, Trudy (46)
Snellenburg, Estelle Colwin (108)
Temple University 181
Chapman, Sara A. (77), (92)
Cormier, Raymond J. (79)
Davidson, Abraham A. (80), (210), (301)
Geer, Glenn B. (83)
Lebofsky, Dennis S. (85)
Smith, Bradley H. (88)
University Speakers Bureau 211
Novak, Karen Laub (5)
Villanova University 214
Bloom, Rosalind (8), (93)
Syvinski, Henry B. (9)
Virginia Polytechnic Institute and State University 216
Porter, Robert F. (96)
Siemoneit, Martin A. (112)
Washington, University of 218
Women's Classical Caucus 227
Katz, Phyllis B. (21)
Marker, Sherry (30)
Rossi, Mary Ann (39)
Thomas, Ruth S. (47)

ASTROLOGY

Ancient Arts of the Future 13
Rook, Marcella Ruble (2)
Contemporary Forum 42
Success Leaders Speakers Service 180
Taylor, Maxine (176)
Temple University 181
Poss, Howard L. (280)
Wilson Celebrities, Lola 225
Jillson, Joyce (20)
Women's Classical Caucus 227
Broege, Valerie (4)

ASTRONOMY

See also: SPACE

California State University, Fullerton 29
Johnson, Fred M. (272)
Drew University 52
Fenstermacher, Robert L. (29)
Northeastern Illinois University 142
Gilbert, R.L. (31)
Nissim-Sabat, Charles (65)
Pennsylvania State University 151
Wallach, David L. (274)
Temple University 181
Poss, Howard L. (280)
Villanova University 214
Sion, Edward M. (10)
Washington, University of 218
Western Washington University 223
Quigley, Robert J. (4)

AUDIOVISUAL

Drew University 52
Remmers, Kurt W. (74)
East Carolina University 56
Lanier, Gene D. (50)
Eastern Illinois University 57
Scholes, Gene W. (76)
Wiseman, Robert C. (97)
Marquette University 105
Allen, Craig G. (65)
Price, Michael J. (24)
Taft, Thomas B. (14)
Murray State University 117
Fitch, Franklin G. (41)
National Micrographics Association 128
Northeastern Illinois University 142
Saiet, Ronald A. (75)
Saint Cloud State University 168
Fields, Dennis C. (15)
Southwestern Louisiana, University of 174
Goellner, Edward B. (36)
Kreamer, Jeanne T. (57)
Temple University 181
Fork, Donald J. (69), (97)

AUDIOVISUAL (continued)

Galey, Minaruth (70), (98)
Grady, William F. (72), (100)
Lawrason, Robin E. (75), (110)
Virginia Polytechnic Institute and State University 216
Huffman, Stanley A., Jr. (58)
Steffen, Robert F. (123)
Washington, University of 218

AUSTRALIA AND NEW ZEALAND

California State University, Fullerton 29
Thomas, Barry (75), (277), (324)
Weinzweig, Marjorie S. (326)
Drew University 52
Rice, Charles L. (76)
Fame Limited 59
Armstrong, Ken (1)
Stockdale, Bill (16)
Pennsylvania State University 151
Albinski, Henry S. (189)
Western Washington University 223
Buckland, Roscoe L. (3)
Paulus, Ingeborg (36)

AUTOMATION
See: COMPUTERS

AUTOMOBILES
See also: TRAFFIC SAFETY; TRANSPORTATION

Auburn University 16
Brown, David B. (9)
Killian, Albert F. (44)
Carnegie-Mellon University 31
Baumann, Dwight M. (40)
Champion Spark Plug Company 33
East Carolina University 56
Webber, Edith (40)
Murray State University 117
Clabaugh, Maurice (16)
National Association of Fleet Administrators, Inc. 120
Pennsylvania State University 151
Reed, Russell A. (294)
Weber, H.E. (295)
Simon Fraser University 171
Hurst, Michael Eliot (48)
Southwestern Louisiana, University of 174
Bonnette, Richard M. (12)
Temple University 181
Snider, H. Wayne (44), (243)
Union Electric Speakers Forum 189
Villanova University 214
Schorr, David J. (88)
White, Theodore H. (90)
Virginia Polytechnic Institute and State University 216
Marshall, Harold P. (81)
Washington, University of 218

AVIATION
See also: TRANSPORTATION

Auburn University 16
Kiteley, Gary W. (46)
Beech Aircraft Corporation 19
Small, Marvin B. (1)
Marquette University 105
Denny, Ronald J. (70)
National Speakers Bureau, Inc. 135
Rickenbacker, William F. (54)
Northeastern Illinois University 142
Pizzi, William J. (69)
Pennsylvania State University 151
Chan, Y. (290)
Dahir, Sabir H. (291)
McCormick, Barnes W. (33)
Smith, Hubert C. (34)
Southwestern Louisiana, University of 174
Purcell, Charles W. (81)
Speaker's Bureau of Philadelphia 176
Hackes, Peter (45)
Marshall, Leo (74)
Trans World Airlines 186
United States Department of Defense 194
Virginia Polytechnic Institute and State University 216
Hoffman, Edward G. (53)
Marchman, James F., III (79)
Schetz, Joseph A. (108)
Spengler, Fred L. (120)
Telionis, D.P. (130)
Washington, University of 218

B

BANKING

American Graduate School of International Management 3
McMahon, Robert (3)
Baltimore Federal Savings and Loan Association 18
Sheehan, T. Frank (1)
Duquesne University 54
Federal Reserve Bank of Richmond 60
Federal Reserve Bank of San Francisco 61
First Federal of Boward 63
Georgia Federal Savings and Loan Association 72
Murray State University 117
Albin, Marvin (14)
North Carolina National Bank 141
Northeastern Illinois University 142
Firoozi, Ferydoon (23)
Pennsylvania State University 151
Patterson, Robert A. (9)
Rainier National Bank 162
Villanova University 214
Mason, Saul (33)
Wilson Celebrities, Lola 225
Kaye, David N. (21)

BIOFEEDBACK

American Institute for Exploration 4
Williams, Richard (7)
California State University, Fullerton 29
McFarland, Richard A. (240)
Simon Fraser University 171
Wienberg, Harold (43)

BIOLOGY
See also: BIOFEEDBACK; GENETICS; PHYSIOLOGY

American Teilhard Association for the Future of Man 11
Francoeus, Robert (5)
California State University, Fullerton 29

BIOLOGY (continued)

Davenport, Calvin A. (172), (267)
Horn, Michael H. (71), (140), (271)
Carnegie-Mellon University 31
Coleman, Bernard D. (8)
Cussier, Edward L. (11)
Goldman, Robert (6)
Drew University 52
Baker, E.G. Stanley (2)
Bistis, George N. (8)
Bush, Louise F. (12)
Hilton, Bruce (40)
Phillips, Joy (68)
Pollock, Leland Wells (69)
Duquesne University 54
Eastern Illinois University 57
Whitley, Steve (94)
Leigh Bureau 102
Tiger, Lionel (35)
Marquette University 105
Courtright, James B. (2)
Piacsek, Bela E. (3)
Maryland, University of 106
Northeastern Illinois University 142
Mac Donald, James (58)
Wiercinski, Floyd J. (96)
Pennsylvania State University 151
Cooper, Jane E. (164)
Ferguson, Frederick G. (206)
Fung, Daniel Y.C. (173)
Todd, Paul (211)
Puget Sound, University of 159
Karlstrom, Ernest L. (34)
Pierson, Beverly (49)
Rousslang, Kenneth (55)
Saint Cloud State University 168
Ezell, Wayland L. (13)
Hortis, Theophanis (29)
Simon Fraser University 171
Schwarz, Abby (42)
Wienberg, Harold (43)
Temple University 181
Adelman, Richard C. (13)
Miller, Richard L. (18), (62), (340)
Tiffany, Elizabeth G. (22)
White, Elliott (24)
Virginia Polytechnic Institute and State University 216
Claus, George W. (20)
Holdeman, Lillian (54)
Paterson, Robert A. (93)
Washington, University of 218

BLACKS
See also: MINORITIES; RACIAL RELATIONS

California State University, Fullerton 29
Evans, David H. (220)
Namasaka, Boaz N. (82), (194), (242), (261), (337)
Nyaggah, Mougo (7)
Rietveld, Ronald D. (338)
Sims, Melvin D. (153), (211), (223), (304)
Drew University 52
Varner, James (95)
Duquesne University 54
Intercollegiate Studies Institute, Inc. 85
Herberg, Will (12)
Leigh Bureau 102
Haley, Alex (13)
Marquette University 105
Ford, Sarah Ann (39)
Northeastern Illinois University 142
Crawford, Margo (17)
Jones, Arnold P., Jr. (47)
Parker, Bettye J. (66)
Robinson, Edward A. (74)
Pennsylvania State University 151
Griffith, Cyril E. (217)
Hauser, Robert E. (218)
Ongiri, David O. (111)
Ridgley, Louis E., Jr. (58)
Podium Management Associates, Inc. 154
Beard, Timothy (2)
Bullins, Ed (4)
Thomas, Piri (25)
Puget Sound, University of 159
Martin, Jacquie (40)
Saint Cloud State University 168
Hellwig, David J. (25)
Levilain, Guy (41)
Southwestern Louisiana, University of 174
Arceneaux, Clayton J. (1)
Temple University 181
Ayaga, Odeyo O. (25), (90)
Bailey, Harry A., Jr. (26), (258)
Hampton, Barbara L. (84)
Keto, Clement T. (28), (338)
Lapsansky, Emma (29)
Pittman, Audrey S. (30)
Smith, Rita (31), (294), (328)
Viewpoint Speakers Bureau 213
Dixon, Maceo (2)
Miah, Malik (7)
Pulley, Andrew (10)
Wright, Pat (18)
Villanova University 214
Nwodo, Christopher S. (12)
Washington, University of 218
Western Washington University 223
Paulus, Ingeborg (18)
Wilson Celebrities, Lola 225
Davis, Bruce (11)
Dayton, Daryl D. (12)

BODY LANGUAGE
See: NONVERBAL COMMUNICATION

BUSINESS AND INDUSTRY
See also: BUSINESS/GOVERNMENT RELATIONS; CHEMICAL INDUSTRY; INTERNATIONAL BUSINESS

Auburn University 16
Horton, George B. (36)
Bethlehem Steel Corporation 20
Business Communication Council 23
California, Irvine, University of 27
Miller, Len (8)
California Polytechnic State University 28
California State University, Fullerton 29
Gilman, Richard (77)
Mann, Donald H. (80)
Mlynaryk, Peter M. (81)
Winterfelt, Rolf (83)
Chemetron Corporation 34
Whatley, Harold E. (2)
East Carolina University 56
Piper, Roswell M. (19), (74)
Zincone, Louis H., Jr. (23)
First Federal of Broward 63
Getty Oil Company 74
Hardwood Plywood Manufacturers Association 80
Grooh, William J., Jr. (1)
Mc Donald, Clark E. (2)
Intercollegiate Studies Institute, Inc. 85
Anderson, Martin (1)
Brozen, Yale (2)
Demsetz, Harold (4)
Manne, Henry G. (19)
Rogge, Benjamin A. (30)
Leigh Bureau 102
Clark, Lindley (3)
Diebold, John (6)

BUSINESS AND INDUSTRY (continued)

Evans, Rowland (10)
Marcus, Stanley (19)
Novak, Robert (21)
Silk, Leonard (31)
Stern, Joel (33)
Toffler, Alvin (36)
Marquette University 105
Kaimann, Richard A. (5)
Laczniak, Gene R. (6)
Piasecki, Michael J. (7)
Maryland, University of 106
Mid West Program Service, Inc. 112
Braude, Michael (14)
Hutson, Don (69)
McClinton, Curtis R., Jr. (84)
Winters, Carl (135)
Monsanto Company 115
Murray State University 117
Albin, Marvin (14)
Barton, R.B. (15)
Giles, Howard C. (18)
Wells, Jane Freeman (28)
NCR Corporation 118
Hayes, Ira M. (1)
National Committee for Responsible Patriotism 125
Wiley, Charles (1)
National School Supply and Equipment Association 132
Petty, O.L., Jr. (9)
Smith, Frank E. (11)
Smith, Max L. (12)
National Water Well Association 136
Alcorn, Pat B. (7)
Butcher, Kathy (1)
Heiss, Harold W., Jr. (3)
McLaughlin, Wayne (4)
Sturtz, Laurence E. (9)
Northeastern Illinois University 142
Watson, Ulestine (95)
Package Designers Council 147
Pennsylvania State University 151
Mathews, H. Lee (48)
Skimbo, Nicholas (51)
Zimmerman, W.J. (122)
Puget Sound, University of 159
Anton, Paul (3)
Branson, Douglas M. (15)
Waldo, Robert (66)
Rainier National Bank 162
Saint Cloud State University 168
Highsmith, James M. (27)
Marmas, James G. (45)
Shoe Suppliers of America 170
Simon Fraser University 171
Hoyt, George C. (57)
Socialist Party, USA 172
Randolph, Linda (9)
Southwestern Louisiana, University of 174
Bentley, Doris B. (6)
Wells, Barron (93)
Williams, Alfred (13), (96)
Success Leaders Speakers Service 180
Batten, Joe (10)
Boyan, Lee (17)
Brodie, Earl D. (19)
Butrick, Frank M. (20)
Christians, W.C. (26)
Harrington, William Franklin (75)
Hayes, Ira M. (79)
Hersey, Ross (83)
Linder, John E. (107)
Sonnenberg, Ray (162)
Walters, Frederick J. (187)
Temple University 181
Bailey, Harry A., Jr. (32), (258)
Bandera, Vladimir N. (33)
Gross, Jack L. (35)
Snider, H. Wayne (44)
Tool and Die Institute 185
Tuna Research Foundation, Inc. 187
Nizetich, Anthony V. (4)
United States Interstate Commerce Commission 206
United States Trademark Association 209
Villanova University 214
Chorba, George J. (13)
Virginia Polytechnic Institute and State University 216
Prouty, Bruce R. (99)
Spengler, Fred L. (120)

BUSINESS/GOVERNMENT RELATIONS

Business Communication Council 23
Chemetron Corporation 34
Moore, L. David (1)
Whatley, Harold E. (2)
Disclosure Inc. 50
Goldspiel, Steven (1)
Duquesne University 54
Intercollegiate Studies Institute Inc. 85
Brozen, Yale (2)
Manne, Henry G. (19)
Leigh Bureau 102
Evans, Rowland (10)
Johnson, Nicholas (15)
Novak, Robert (21)
Murray State University 117
Albin, Marvin (14)
National Water Well Association 136
Heiss, Harold W., Jr. (26)
Lehr, Jay H. (27)
Pennsylvania State University 151
Kroger, Manfred (177)
Remick, Forrest J. (133)
Sherman, Carl W. (135)
Southwestern Louisiana, University of 174
Caradine, E. Everett (17)
Virginia Polytechnic Institute and State University 216
Spann, Robert M. (119)

C

CANADA

East Carolina University 56
Mayberry, Nancy (121)
Eastern Illinois University 57
Murray, Louise (62)
Fame Limited 59
Taylor, Charles (17)
Forrest, Martin A. 69
Sterling, Tom (13)
Pennsylvania State University 151
Albinski, Henry S. (189)
McAree, James (197)
Simon Fraser University 171
Hoyt, George C. (10)
Okuda, Kenji (11)
Var, Turgut (13)
Washington, University of 218
Western Washington University 223
Hiller, Harley E. (17)

CAREERS

Auburn University 16
Frank, Harry (22)
Horton, George B. (36)
Vandegrift, Frank (82)
Business Communication Council 23
California, Irvine, University of 27
Hoy, John C. (20)

CAREERS (continued)

Williams, Harvey (24)
California State University, Fullerton 29
Lynn, Joanne M. (145)
East Carolina University 56
James, Furney K. (46)
Eastern Illinois University 57
Lawson, Dorothy M. (47)
Sanders, Carol (72)
Sanders, Claud D. (73)
Marquette University 105
DeRoche, Robert J. (34)
Maryland, University of 106
Murray State University 117
Lilly, George T. (80)
Northeastern Illinois University 142
Jackson, Charles J. (44)
Uliassi, Edward C. (87)
Pennsylvania State University 151
Beatty, John W. (88)
Carter, Glenn G. (90)
Graham, Kenneth R. (54)
Hatalla, Josephine F. (55)
Kraybill, Edward K. (103)
Ridgley, Louis E., Jr. (58)
Romano, John J. (116)
Swails, Richard G. (60)
Saint Cloud State University 168
Larson, Walter G. (38)
Southwestern Louisiana, University of 174
Lambert, B. Geraldine (62)
Success Leaders Speakers Service 180
Dubin, Samuel S. (47)
Tripp, Dave C. (180)
Temple University 181
Brodey, Jean L. (49), (320)
Dengler, Patricia L. (50)
Gilpin, Nancy E. (52), (322)
Gutman, William C. (53)
Hunt, Jon H. (104)
Leventhal, Jerome I. (61), (115)
Rivell, Amos C. (63), (120)
Smith, James P., Jr. (65)
Transier, Lee (66)
Virginia Polytechnic Institute and State University 216
Collins, William F. (23)
Dean, James W. (29)
Harris, Ruth D. (49)
Hill, David E. (52)
Johnson, Overton R. (60)
Lynch, Richard L. (75)
Ressler, Ralph (101)
Webb, Anita H. (139)
Washington, University of 218
Wilson Celebrities, Lola 225
Fagan, William (13)

CARTOGRAPHY
See: GEOGRAPHY

CERAMICS

East Carolina University 56
Haney, Art (11)
Eastern Illinois University 57
Heyduck, Billy J. (33)
Krutza, June (44)
Puget Sound, University of 159
Ball, F. Carlton (5)
McCulstion, John (39)
Southwestern Louisiana, University of 174
Hanley, Frank L. (41)
Virginia Polytechnic Institute and State University 216
Lequire, Stephen D. (69)
Slack, Lyle H. (114)

CHEMICAL INDUSTRY

Chemetron Corporation 34
Moore, L. David (1)
Georgia-Pacific Corporation 73
Monsanto Company 115
Pennsylvania State University 151
Schenck, George (134)

CHEMISTRY

Drew University 52
Miller, James (56)
Nelson, Gregory (60)
Scott, Donald A. (85)
Duquesne University 54
Eastern Illinois University 57
Buchanan, David (6)
Northeastern Illinois University 142
Dobbs, Frank W. (19)
Pennsylvania State University 151
Botdorf, Ruth (264)
Chapin, Jack (265)
Puget Sound, University of 159
Rowland, Thomas V. (56)
Temple University 181
Washburne, Stephen S. (199)
Virginia Polytechnic Institute and State University 216
Brinson, Halbert F. (11)
Clifford, Alan F. (21)
Frederick, Daniel (39)
Taylor, Larry T. (128)
Washington, University of 218
Western Washington University 223
Russo, Salvatore F. (24)

CHICANOS
See also: LATIN AMERICA; MINORITIES; RACIAL RELATIONS

California, Irvine, University of 27
Curiel, Ramon (2)
Northeastern Illinois University 142
Pedroso, Angelina (68)
Viewpoint Speakers Bureau 213
Rodriguez, Olga (12)
Washington, University of 218

CHILD ABUSE
See also: FAMILY RELATIONS

C.A.L.M. - Child Abuse Listening Mediation, Inc. 24
Root, David A. (1)
Selman, Joan (2)
Puget Sound, University of 159
Moreland, Steve J. (43)
Speaker's Bureau of Philadelphia 176
Richette, Lisa A. (93)
Temple University 181
Isard, Eleanore S. (221)
Washington, University of 218

CHILDREN
See also: FAMILY RELATIONS; YOUTH

American Montessori Society 5
Auburn University 16
Higgins, Earl B. (33)
Hodson, Norma G. (35)
California, Irvine, University of 27
Goldstein, Arthur I. (28)
California Polytechnic State University 28

CHILDREN (continued)

California State University, Fullerton 29
Bagrash, Frank M. (85), (169), (229)
Bedell, John W. (280), (340)
Hill, Shirley L. (93), (342)
Kiraithe, Jacqueline M. (95)
Lindquist, Carol U. (239), (343)
East Carolina University 56
Lewis, Frederick C. (53)
Markowski, Mel (7)
Richards, John Thomas (57)
Williams, Thomas A. (59)
Marquette University 105
McDonald, Rita T. (94)
Sheikh, Anees E. (103)
Topetzes, Nick J. (98)
Murray State University 117
Downing, Billie (131)
Fitch, James L. (132)
Hufnagle, Jon (133)
May, Sandra A. (48)
Petrie, Garth F. (50)
Northeastern Illinois University 142
Burger, Mary Louise (13)
Caron, Josiane (14)
Garrett, Philip R. (28)
Georgiou, Peri P. (30)
Jacobs, Claire M. (45)
Jones, Arnold P., Jr. (47)
Kooyumjian, Mary L. (52)
Mardell, Carol D. (59)
Styer, Sandra (84)
Pennsylvania State University 151
Cartwright, Carol (91)
Du Puis, Mary M. (94)
Harkness, William L. (262)
Ott, Robert W. (30)
Van Horn, James E. (172)
Puget Sound, University of 159
Heimgartner, Norman L. (25)
Henderson, Mary Lou (26)
Hodges, Richard E. (29)
Saint Cloud State University 168
Boltuck, Charles J. (7)
Herbison, Priscilla J. (26)
Mertens, Gerald C. (47)
Santa Barbara Council for the Retarded 169
Gerber, Sanford (1)
Southwestern Louisiana, University of 174
Eason, Byrdie E. (27)
Gardiner, Jeanette (31)
Gaudet, Irby J., Jr. (32)
Hotard, Stephen R. (50)
Morella, John R. (76)
Speaker's Bureau of Philadelphia 176
Brodsky, Ida (20)
Schwartz, Loretta (103)
Spokespeople 178
Spock, Benjamin (5)
Yawkey, Thomas Daniels (199)
Temple University 181
Hetznecker, William (282)
Malnati, Richard J. (289)
Payne, Reed (119)
Pittman, Audrey S. (311)
Sheldon, Harry J. (319)
Thurman, Ken (126)
Tiffany, Elizabeth G. (22)
Torbert, Marianne (11)
Tower, Gail (23)
Vandivier, Frances (252), (313)
Villanova University 214
Bush, David F. (77)
Virginia Polytechnic Institute and State University 216
Fu, Victoria R. (40)
Rogers, Cosby S. (106)
Washington, University of 218
Western Washington University 223
Aitken, Margaret (29)
Barnett, Sharon (7)
Whittier College 224
Behrens, Maurine (1)
Olson-Prather, Emelie (12)
Youth Liberation Press, Inc. 231
Hefner, Keith (3)

CHILDREN'S LITERATURE

California State University, Fullerton 29
Lynn, Joanne L. (205)
East Carolina University 56
Everett, Nell C. (63)
Eastern Illinois University 57
Murray, Louise (62)
Murray State University 117
Smith, June Warden (56)
Strohecker, Edwin C. (75)
Northeastern Illinois University 142
Burger, Mary Louise (13)
Styer, Sandra (84)
Pennsylvania State University 151
Graham, Robert J. (234)
Singh, Jane M. (241)
Puget Sound, University of 159
Goman, LaVerne (23)
Simon Fraser University 171
O'Connell, Sheila (19), (52)
Southwestern Louisiana, University of 174
Carstens, Jane Ellen (18)
Kreamer, Jeanne T. (57)
Mouton, Jean (77)
Villanova University 214
Esmonde, Margaret P. (46)

CHINA
See also: FAR EAST

American Graduate School of International Management 3
Kumayama, Akihisa (2)
Auburn University 16
Barry, Mary E. (6)
Drew University 52
Greenblatt, Sidney (34)
Duquesne University 54
East Carolina University 56
Gowne, Robert J. (117)
Fame Limited 59
Armstrong, Ken (1)
Bjerre, Jens (2)
Butler, Willis (3)
Forrest, Martin A. 69
Bjerre, Jens (2)
Intercollegiate Studies Institute Inc. 85
Kubek, Anthony (17)
Keedick Lecture Bureau, Inc. 97
Reynolds, Jack (57)
Mid West Program Service, Inc. 112
Dimond, E. Grey (32)
Dimond, Mary Clark (33)
Northeastern Illinois University 142
Kiang, Harry (50)
Kokoris, James A. (51)
Pennsylvania State University 151
Seward, D.M. (11)
Swetz, Frank (121)
Puget Sound, University of 159
Barnett, Suzanne W. (6)
Simon Fraser University 171
Hurst, Michael Eliot (2)
Speaker's Bureau of Philadelphia 176
Snyder, Leroy (109)
Temple University 181
Heinrichs, Waldo (265), (337)
Niu, M.C. (341)
Virginia Polytechnic Institute and State University 216
Lucas, James T., Jr. (74)
Washington, University of 218

CHINA (continued)

Whittier College 224
Harrison, Howard (7)

CIVIL LIBERTIES

Americans United 12
Carnegie-Mellon University 31
Kerr, Thomas M. (14)
Contemporary Forum 42
Drew University 52
Copeland, John W. (18)
Courtney, Charles (19)
East Carolina University 56
Lanier, Gene D. (50)
Ragan, Fred (94)
Eastern Illinois University 57
Thornburgh, Dan (88)
Heritage Foundation 82
Intercollegiate Studies Institute, Inc. 85
Crane, Philip M. (3)
Evans, M. Stanton (9)
Herberg, Will (12)
Jaffa, Harry V. (13)
Kemp, Arthur (14)
Kirk, Russell (16)
Martin, William Oliver (20)
Opitz, Edmund A. (25)
Petro, Sylvester (27)
Van Den Haag, Ernest (35)
Zoll, Donald A. (40)
Keedick Lecture Bureau, Inc. 97
Norris, Clarence (48)
Leigh Bureau 102
Goldberg, Arthur (12)
Salisbury, Harrison (27)
Schorr, Daniel (29)
Marquette University 105
Brown, Richard M. (54)
Theoharis, Athan (59)
Murray State University 117
Biggs, James W. (65), (112)
Denbow, Carl J. (83)
McGaughey, Robert H., III (85)
Mayes, Jerry W. (135)
Pace, Don M. (73), (118)
Rose, Joseph L. (103)
Northeastern Illinois University 142
George, Melvin R. (29)
Pennsylvania State University 151
Du Puis, Mary M. (94)
Grella, Michael A. (100)
Hoffman, Lantz A. (74)
Hopper, Paul T. (235)
Snyder, Shirley A. (85)
Podium Management Associates, Inc. 154
Wilson, William (27)
"Pride in America" Company 155
Cahill, George F. (1)
Puget Sound, University of 159
Hoyt, Milton (32)
Southwestern Louisiana, University of 174
Millet, Jeremy (72)
Temple University 181
DeMott, John (211)
Keto, Clement T. (28)
Villanova University 214
Betz, Joseph (17)
Washington, University of 218
Youth Liberation Press, Inc. 231
Autin, Al (1)
Autin, Diana (2)
Hefner, Keith (3)

CIVIL RIGHTS
See also: EQUAL EMPLOYMENT

California State University, Fullerton 29
Namasaka, Boaz N. (60), (147), (194), (337)
Carnegie-Mellon University 31
Kerr, Thomas M. (14)
Drew University 52
Cowell, David A. (20)
Intercollegiate Studies Institute, Inc. 85
Gietze, Gottfried (5)
Massachusetts Bar Association 107
Murray State University 117
Burke, Robert L. (66)
Pace, Don M. (118)
Rose, Joseph L. (103), (119)
Northeastern Illinois University 142
Jones, Arnold P., Jr. (47)
Renas, Stanley R. (71)
Pennsylvania State University 151
Asbury, William W. (1)
Socialist Party, USA 172
Gil, David (2)

CLOCKS

Pennsylvania State University 151
Pray, Alfred R. (210)
Saint Cloud State University 168
Wagenius, Terry (70)
Temple University 181
Geer, Glenn B. (132)

COLLECTING AND COLLECTORS

American Institute for Exploration 4
Ransom, Jay Ellis (6)
Conrad, James A.H. 40
Conrad, James (1)
Murray State University 117
Strohecker, Edwin C. (75)
Saint Cloud State University 168
Wagenius, Terry (70)
Southwestern Louisiana, University of 174
Garcia, Emilio (30)

COLLEGE STUDENTS

Auburn University 16
Foy, James F. (21)
Grant, W. Harold (23)
Higgins, Earl B. (33)
Meadows, Mark E. (57)
Schroeder, Charles G. (72)
Tincher, Wilbur A. (78)
California, Irvine, University of 27
Hoy, John C. (20)
Lawrence, Robert S. (21)
Lee, Juel (22)
California State University, Fullerton 29
Reeves, William J. (30), (348)
Sadovszky, Otto J. (31), (102), (349)
Tygart, Clarence E. (155), (291), (351)
Carnegie-Mellon University 31
Cathie, Walter C. (15)
Elliott, William F. (16)
Greenfield, Concetta (26)
Drew University 52
Bush, Louise F. (12)
Mills, James W. (57)
Duquesne University 54
East Carolina University 56
James, Furney K. (46)
Eastern Illinois University 57
Crane, William J. (13)
Flynn, John (21)
Henry, Paul (31)
Sparks, Sue C. (83)

COLLEGE STUDENTS (continued)

Intercollegiate Studies Institute, Inc. 85
Kuehnelt-Leddihin, Erik Von (18)
Van Den Haag, Ernest (35)
Marquette University 105
Fehrer, Linda (37)
Flynn, Leo B. (38)
Ford, Sarah Ann (39)
Pelt, Therese (81)
Murray State University 117
Gantt, Wilson (42), (127)
Matarazzo, S.M. (46)
Pennsylvania State University 151
Brugel, John E. (89)
Carter, Glenn G. (90)
Graham, Kenneth R. (54)
Hatalla, Josephine F. (55)
Kraybill, Edward K. (103)
Kraybill, Wilbur K. (104)
Lane, Benjamin A. (105)
Millar, Craig A. (107)
Murphy, Raymond (108)
Schlow, Marthamae C. (200)
Seward, D.M. (11)
Snyder, Judith P. (15)
South, James (120)
Swails, Richard G. (60)
Wirag, J. Robert (212)
Puget Sound, University of 159
Bauska, Barry (7)
Saint Cloud State University 168
Eveslage, Tom (12)
Hoffman, Patricia (28)
Johnson, Milford (32)
Larson, Walter G. (38)
Simon Fraser University 171
Roberts, Stanley (58)
Southwestern Louisiana, University of 174
Arceneaux, Clayton J. (1)
Blair, Charles W. (9)
Menard, Glenn (71)
St. Martin, Allen H. (88)
Temple University 181
Adams, Ernestyne James (201), (308)
Barone, Marian T. (2), (91)
Hirshfeld, Marvin (55)
Villanova University 214
Hahn, Jeffrey W. (3)
Virginia Polytechnic Institute and State University 216
Brown, J. Gordon (12)
Cheney, Anne (19)
Dean, James W. (29)
Hill, David E. (52)
Tessnear, Marshall D. (132)
Walter, Jane H. (138)
Washington, University of 218
Youth Liberation Press, Inc. 231
Autin, Diana (2)
Hefner, Keith (3)

COLLEGES AND UNIVERSITIES
See also: COLLEGE STUDENTS

Auburn University 16
Bramlett, Gene A. (7)
Carroll, Chester C. (11)
Cavender, A. Ray (12)
Foy, James F. (21)
Horton, George B. (36)
Lanham, Ben T. (48)
Roberts, Charles B. (68)
California, Irvine, University of 27
Lenhoff, Sylvia G. (23)
California State University, Fullerton 29
Grant, Shirley M. (27)
Jones, C. Eugene (28), (143)
Pollak, June Salz (61)
Tygart, Clarence E. (105), (155), (291)
Carnegie-Mellon University 31
Cathie, Walter C. (15)
Elliott, William F. (16)
Service, Kenneth (10)
Drew University 52
DeVeer, Robert (24)
Lono, J. Mark (48)
Duquesne University 54
East Carolina University 56
Birchard, Ralph (24)
Hankins, William W. (27), (101)
Eastern Illinois University 57
Henry, Paul (31)
Lindberg, Phillip (51)
Sparks, Sue C. (83)
Titus, Charles (91)
Wetterlind, Peter (93)
Marquette University 105
Cartz, Louis (33)
Flynn, Leo B. (38)
Griesbach, Marc F. (41)
Olsen, Roger A. (62)
Rechlicz, Gloria (49)
Robersen, William N. (63)
Sankovitz, James L. (50), (64)
Maryland, University of 106
Murray State University 117
Tolley, Charles H. (59)
Northeastern Illinois University 142
Nissim-Sabat, Charles (65)
Pennsylvania State University 151
Asbury, William W. (1)
Behrens, Peter J. (203)
Bierly, George W. (2)
Black, John W. (3)
Brugel, John E. (89)
Campbell, William E., Jr. (64)
Carter, Glenn G. (90)
Catell, Newton O. (191)
Ciervo, Arthur (67)
Cunningham, Richard G. (266)
David, William J. (4)
Dungan, James R. (5)
Ebaugh, Paul (139)
Engel, A. William, Jr. (185)
Fung, Daniel Y.C. (173)
Greenhill, Leslie P. (99)
Hatalla, Josephine F. (55)
Hershberger, Kenneth E. (6)
Ikenberry, Stanley O. (101)
Johnson, John C. (141)
Kraybill, Herbert K. (103), (186)
Lane, Benjamin A. (105)
Lehman, Ross B. (76)
Lupton, Charles (187)
Moellenbrock, George, Jr. (188)
Morse, Otis B., IV (7)
Mortimer, Kenneth P. (8)
Patterson, Robert A. (9)
Perkins, Harold W. (112)
Quick, Marian A. (113)
Romano, John J. (116)
Schanker, Robert (117)
Simonsen, August H. (13)
Smith, Robert L. (14)
Snyder, Judith P. (15)
Vairo, John D. (16)
Weed, Merwin L. (149)
Williamson, Janet A. (256)
Zimmerman, W.J. (122)
Queen's University 160
Sinclair, Duncan (19)
Saint Cloud State University 168
Bartlett, Gary E. (5)
Graham, Charles J. (18)
Johnson, Milford (32)
Rowland, Howard Ray (65)
Simon Fraser University 171
Hoyt, George C. (57)
Roberts, Stanley (58)
Suart, George (59)
Wheatley, Jon (60)
Southwestern Louisiana, University of 174
Arceneaux, Clayton J. (1)
Bass, William T. (3)

COLLEGES AND UNIVERSITIES (continued)

Blumberg, Dwayne D. (10)
St. Martin, Allen H. (88)
Vigorito, John V. (89)
Speaker's Bureau of Philadelphia 176
Cole, Charles C. (26)
Temple University 181
Dubeck, Leroy W. (95)
LaVallee-Williams, Marthe (109)
Villanova University 214
Clay, Alvin A. (91)
Schwarz, John H. (39)
Virginia Polytechnic Institute and State University 216
Bell, Wilson B. (7)
Bryant, Joseph J. (13)
Cassell, Stuart K. (17)
Lester, C. Ned (70)
Russell, G.E. (107)
Sturm, Albert L. (124)
Walter, Jane H. (138)
Washington, University of 218
Western Washington University 223
Buckland, Roscoe L. (8)
Scott, James W. (10)
Whittier College 224
Harvey, Richard B. (8)
Thomson, Richard (16)

COMMUNICATION
See also: HUMAN RELATIONS; INTERVIEWING; JOURNALISM AND THE PRESS; LANGUAGE; MEDIA; NONVERBAL COMMUNICATION; READING; SPEECH; WRITING

Auburn University 16
Meadows, Mark E. (57)
California Polytechnic State University 28
California State University, Fullerton 29
Gilman, Richard (34), (77), (137)
Hynes, Teresa M. (35), (142), (285), (308), (335),
Qureshi, Naimuddin (41)
Contemporary Forum 42
Drew University 52
Brack, Harold A. (9)
East Carolina University 56
Grossnickle, William F. (134)
Rees, Jim (56)
Eastern Illinois University 57
Hadwiger, Kenneth E. (27)
McClerren, B.F. (57)
Fulton Inc., Richard 71
Leigh Bureau 102
Culligan, Joe (4)
Linkletter, Jack (18)
Marquette University 105
Crepeau, Margaret T. (93)
Sokolnicki, Alfred J. (12)
Staudacher, Joseph M. (13)
Taft, Thomas B. (14)
Tracy, William T. (15)
Maryland, University of 106
Murray State University 117
Dean, Ken S. (39)
Gantt, Vernon W. (115)
Mayes, Jerry W. (135)
Valentine, Robert (136)
National Speakers Bureau, Inc. 135
Downs, Hugh (17)
Murphy, George (45)
Northeastern Illinois University 142
Brommel, Bernard J. (12)
Flory, Joyce Ann (25)
Renas, Stanley R. (71)
Walker, Robert (92)
Ohio Bell Telephone Company 144
Pennsylvania State University 151
Carr, Marion M. Odell (65)
Clouser, Richard A. (92)
Felack, Michael (70)
Folwell, William H., III (71)
Henisch, Heinz K. (73)
Mester, Cathy S. (78)
Mullen, Sharman Stanic (79)
O'Brien, Harold J. (81)
Prince, Dawn Stegenga (57), (82)
Ridgley, Louis E., Jr. (58)
Waun, Roger J. (87)
Puget Sound, University of 159
Phillips, John W. (48)
Solman, Carol L. (60)
Saint Cloud State University 168
Eveslage, Tom (12)
Grachek, Arthur F. (17)
Nunn, William H. (52)
Simon Fraser University 171
Altmann, Anneliese (45)
Southwestern Louisiana, University of 174
Arceneaux, Clayton J. (1)
Billeaud, Frances P. (8)
Kneller, George R. (56)
Lyle, Marguerite R. (66)
Wells, Barron (93)
Williams, Alfred B. (96)
Success Leaders Speakers Service 180
Batten, Hal (9)
Bauby, Cathrina (11)
Bennett, Millard (14)
Cleveland, Peggy (31)
Gren, Jack (65)
Halsted, George (73)
Harris, Dorothy Lipp (76)
Kauffman, Ron (98)
Lawrence, Donald (104)
Martin, W. Lee (118)
Montgomery, Robert L. (123)
Reilly, Paul (144)
Self, William Lee (153)
Sutton, Suzy (173)
Temple University 181
Brodey, Jean L. (49), (67)
Drummond, Caroline (94)
Fork, Donald J. (97)
Grady, William F. (72), (100)
Lawrason, Robin E. (110), (316)
Lebofsky, Dennis S. (226), (317)
Union Electric Speakers Forum 189
United States International Communications Agency 205
United Telecommunications, Inc. 210
Villanova University 214
Bush, David F. (77)
Virginia Polytechnic Institute and State University 216
Walter, Jane H. (138)
Wilkins, Keith A. (144)
Wilson Celebrities, Lola 225
Lydecker, Beatrice (26)
World Modeling Association 229

COMMUNISM

Duquesne University 54
Intercollegiate Studies Institute, Inc. 85
Dobriansky, Lev E. (6)
Drachkovitch, Milorad M. (8)
Kintner, William R. (15)
Kubek, Anthony (17)
Molnar, Thomas (23)
Niemeyer, Gerhart (24)
Schiebel, Joseph (31)
Pennsylvania State University 151
Miller, Eugene W., Jr. (198)
Puget Sound, University of 159
Danes, Zdenko F. (20)
Hobson, William G. (28)

COMMUNISM (continued)

Southwestern Louisiana, University of 174
Vigorito, John V. (89)
Speakers Bureau of America, Inc. 175
Brownfeld, Allan C. (1)
Success Leaders Speakers Service 180
Muravin, Victor (126)
Washington, University of 218

COMMUNITIES
See also: URBAN AFFAIRS

Auburn University 16
Adams, Murray C. (1)
Askew, Raymond S. (2)
Bramlett, Gene A. (7)
Cavender, A. Ray (11)
Higgins, Earl B. (33)
McCord, R. Warren (54)
Carnegie-Mellon University 31
Schatzman, Dennis (35)
Contemporary Forum 42
East Carolina University 56
Wardrep, Bruce (22)
Eastern Illinois University 57
Jaenike, Vaughn (38)
Lawson, Dorothy M. (47)
Sanders, Carol (72)
Intercollegiate Studies Institute, Inc. 85
Hauptmann, Jerzy (11)
Maryland, University of 106
Murray State University 117
Mofield, William Ray (129)
Pennsylvania State University 151
Calamidas, Alec (38)
Johnson, John C. (141)
Meyer, Peter B. (49)
Summers, Luis Henry (148)
Saint Cloud State University 168
Eveslage, Tom (12)
Johnson, Milford (32)
Paull, James F. (57)
Southwestern Louisiana, University of 174
Hamsa, Charles F. (40)
Success Leaders Speakers Service 180
Kellar, Kenneth C. (100)
Murdock, Charles K. (127)
Temple University 181
Weiler, Conrad (254), (275)
Virginia Polytechnic Institute and State University 216
Garrett, J.C. (42)
Lester, C. Ned (70)
Lynch, Richard L. (75)
Parson, Steve R. (92)
Thompson, Ann E. (133)
Washington, University of 218

COMPUTERS
See also: INFORMATION SYSTEMS

Auburn University 16
Barnes, Ben B. (5)
Wingard, Richard M. (90)
California State University, Fullerton 29
Gala, Basil E. (173)
Gilman, Richard (26), (77), (92), (137)
Carnegie-Mellon University 31
Bauman, Dwight M. (17)
Krutz, Ronald L. (18)
McCredie, John W. (19)
Data Courier, Inc. 44
Drew University 52
Metzler, James A. (55)
East Carolina University 56
Gross, Tennala A. (126)
Johnson, F. Milam (127)
Eastern Illinois University 57
Wetterlind, Peter (93)
Florida Association of Realtors 65
Wilson, James T. (69)
Marquette University 105
Kaimann, Richard A. (5)
Northeastern Illinois University 142
Becker, Louis (3)
Reichhardt, Richard (70)
Singleton, Gregory H. (78)
Ohio Bell Telephone Company 144
Pennsylvania State University 151
Fung, Daniel Y.C. (173)
Kozik, Eugene (45)
Stein, Jack (147)
Queen's University 160
Wiginton, John (20)
Saint Cloud State University 168
Guimaraes, Nestor (20)
Simon Fraser University 171
Guthrie, Arthur (9)
Sterling, Theodor D. (12)
Southwestern Louisiana, University of 174
Bonnette, Delta T. (11)
Dominick, Wayne D. (23)
Hauser, Rex (43)
Lewis, Theodore G. (65)
Oliver, James R. (79)
Temple University 181
Banerji, Ranan B. (204)
Friedman, Frank L. (51), (214)
Slook, Thomas H. (154)
Villanova University 214
Ching, Stephen W. (20)
Hicks, Joseph J. (21)
Scott, Thomas (22)
Virginia Polytechnic Institute and State University 216
Gorsline, George W. (44)
Johnson, Thomas W. (61)
Lee, John A.N. (68)
Washington, University of 218
Wilson Celebrities, Lola 225
Kaye, David N. (21)
Women's Classical Caucus 227
Clayman, Dee Lesser (7)
Sowa, Cora Angier (44)
Villeneuve, Winnie Frohn (51)

CONCENTRATION CAMPS

Speaker's Bureau of Philadelphia 176
Shay, Arnold (105)

CONSERVATION
See also: ECOLOGY

American Institute for Exploration 4
Kitchen, Herman (4)
Auburn University 16
Gross, Charles A. (25)
Vachon, Reginald I. (80)
Business Communication Council 23
Cal-Land Improvement Contractors 25
Chevron U.S.A. Inc. 35
Consolidated Edison Company of New York, Inc. 41
Detroit Edison 47
Eastern Illinois University 57
Griffith, John R. (25)
National Water Well Association 136
Palmer, Gail Branscome (22)
Northwest Mining Association 143
Whinnen, W.J. (15)
Pennsylvania State University 151
Barone, Thomas F. (123)
Bowjer, Gordon (253)
Cunningham, Robert L. (21)

CONSERVATION (continued)

Fletcher, Peter W. (304)
Frey, John C. (254)
McCormick, Robert H. (47)
Ondik, Michael (309)
Sharpe, William E. (158)
Sherman, Carl W. (135)
Philadelphia Electric Speakers Bureau 152
Puget Sound, University of 159
Alcorn, Gordon (2)
Reynolds Tobacco Company, R.J. 165
Simon Fraser University 171
McClaren, Milton (37)
United States Department of Agriculture 192
United States Environmental Protection Agency 204
Virginia Electric and Power Company 215
Virginia Polytechnic Institute and State University 216
Long, C. Hardy (71)
McConnell, Robert L. (77)
Spray, Richard A. (121)
Whitelaw, Robert L. (143)
Western Electric Company 222

CONSTRUCTION

Marquette University 105
Bakr, Mamdouh (116)
Yoo, Chai Hong (121)
Pennsylvania State University 151
Dahir, Sabir H. (291)
Saint Cloud State University 168
Bjorklund, L.R. (6)
Villanova University 214
Wallo, Edward M. (45)
Virginia Polytechnic Institute and State University 216
Lamb, Fred M. (65)

CONSUMER AFFAIRS

Auburn University 16
Barry, Mary E. (6)
Hanna, Sherman D. (27)
California State University, Fullerton 29
Apke, Thomas M. (191)
Atkin, Kenward L. (33)
Worth, Guthrie (84), (157), (253)
Carnegie-Mellon University 31
Weinstein, Alvin S. (33)
Consolidated Edison Company of New York, Inc. 41
Duquesne University 54
Eastern Illinois University 57
Noland, Carol (64)
Strader, Gayle Gilbert (84)
Food Shoppers Union 68
Prochnow, Joan E. (1)
Intercollegiate Studies Institute, Inc. 85
Manne, Henry G. (19)
Peterson, William H. (26)
Rogge, Benjamin A. (30)
Keedick Lecture Bureau, Inc. 97
Farr, Robert (21)
Lee Foundation Inc., Fran 101
Lee, Fran (1)
Leigh Bureau 102
Peterson, Esther (23)
Marquette University 105
Brownlee, Ralph E. (4)
Szews, Alfred P. (87)
Massachusetts Bar Association 107
Mid West Program Service, Inc. 112
Morse, Richard L.D. (92)
Murray State University 117
Clabaugh, Maurice (16)
National Speakers Bureau, Inc. 135
Cappo, Joe (11)
Graham, Virginia (23)
Myerson, Bess (46)
Northeastern Illinois University 142
Kokoris, James A. (51)
Pennsylvania State University 151
Kean, Glenn R. (175)
Philadelphia Electric Speakers Bureau 152
Public Citizen Visitors Center 157
Horrocks, Mike (1)
Puget Sound, University of 159
Kerr, Stephen T. (35)
Saint Cloud State University 168
Marmas, James G. (45)
Stensland, Allen (67)
Simon Fraser University 171
Grubel, Herbert G. (8)
Southwestern Louisiana, University of 174
Kelly, Heather C. (54)
Lapoint, James J. (63)
Speaker's Bureau of Philadelphia 176
Graham, Virginia (44)
Lear, Len (61)
Perry, Bonnie (87)
Reid, Orien (92)
Shatzman, Marci (104)
Temple University 181
Karpeles, Harry D. (170)
Tuckerman, Murray M. (196), (249)
United States Consumer Product Safety Commission 191
Villanova University 214
Butkys, Adolph S. (23)
Feigenberg, Myrtle (24), (71)
Washington Correspondents Bureau 219
Burros, Marian (2)

CONTINUING EDUCATION

Auburn University 16
Burkhart, Mary Quinn (10)
Frank, Harry (22)
Tincher, Wilbur A. (78)
White, Louis Edward (88)
Eastern Illinois University 57
Hackler, George (26)
Hockman, Dan (35)
Shuff, Robert V. (81)
Sutton, Kenneth (85)
Marquette University 105
DeRoche, Robert J. (34)
Murray State University 117
Thompson, James T. (8)
Northeastern Illinois University 142
Braun, Vern (10)
Gilpatric, C. Edward (33)
Watson, Ulestine (95)
Pennsylvania State University 151
Dubin, Samuel S. (40)
Godbey, Gordon C. (98)
Klamp, Robert C. (102)
Schanker, Robert (117)
Smith, M. John (119)
Zimmerman, W.J. (122)
Saint Cloud State University 168
Hagen, Owen (21)
Halberg, Delaine (22)
Simon Fraser University 171
Foth, Dennis (15)
McClaren, Milton (18)
Temple University 181
Leahy, Robert (111)
Transier, Lee (128)
Villanova University 214
Paparella, Julia B. (72)
Virginia Polytechnic Institute and State University 216
Flowers, William L., Jr. (37)
Holt, Robert N. (55)

CONTINUING EDUCATION (continued)

Parson, Steve R. (92)
Thompson, Ann E. (133)
Washington, University of 218

COOKING

Auburn University 16
Davis, Robert D. (17)
Rymal, Kenneth S. (71)
Eastern Illinois University 57
Dow, Ruth (15)
National Water Well Association 136
Butcher, Kathy (17)
Pennsylvania State University 151
Kuhn, Gerald D. (178)
Leeds, Fredric (28)
Strickler, Fay B. (180)
Southwestern Louisiana, University of 174
Hamsa, Charles F. (40)
Virginia Polytechnic Institute and State University 216
Comely, Roger E. (25)
Washington, University of 218

COUNSELING

California State University, Fullerton 29
Corey, Gerald F. (231)
Drew University 52
Mills, James W. (57)
Duquesne University 54
Marquette University 105
Norberg, Robert B. (47)
Murray State University 117
Matarazzo, S.M. (46)
Northeastern Illinois University 142
Bell, Mary A. (4)
Jackson, Charles J. (44)
Walsh, William M. (93)
Pennsylvania State University 151
Beck, Edward S. (161)
Romano, John J. (116)
Saint Cloud State University 168
Ames, Kenneth A. (1)
Hoffman, Patricia (28)
Southwestern Louisiana, University of 174
Arceneaux, Clayton J. (1)
Morella, John R. (76)
Success Leaders Speakers Service 180
Lokey, Clarence W. (108)
Temple University 181
Liddle, Howard (287), (310)

CREATIVITY

California State University, Fullerton 29
Cox, Miriam S. (134), (200)
Podium Management Associates, Inc. 154
Deal, Borden (6)
Women's Classical Caucus 227
Deagon, Ann (9)

CRIME
See also: CRIMINAL JUSTICE; POLICE

California State University, Fullerton 29
Capune, W. Garrett (49), (133)
Sims, Melvin D. (153), (350)
Feminist Karate Union 62
Bateman, Py (1)
Mitten, Suzanne (2)
Reid, Kathy (3)
Intercollegiate Studies Institute, Inc. 85
Van Den Haag, Ernest (35)
Keedick Lecture Bureau, Inc. 97
Farr, Robert (21)
Salerno, Ralph (60)
Weinstein, Allen (69)
Marquette University 105
Richards, Marva A. (125)
Maryland, University of 106
Pennsylvania State University 151
Beatty John W. (88)
Pinkerton's Inc. 153
Puget Sound, University of 159
Berry, Keith O. (11)
Nock, George R. (45)
Strait, John A. (63)
Saint Cloud State University 168
Halton, Patrice Hoffman (23)
Miller, Martin (49)
Southwestern Louisiana, University of 174
Joubert, Paul E. (52)
Manuel, David P. (70)
Speaker's Bureau of Philadelphia 176
Fair, Don (37)
Lear, Len (61)
Spokespeople 178
Lenaerts, Sue (2)
Success Leaders Speakers Service 180
Asija, Satya Pal (6)
Winters, Carl (194)
Temple University 181
Haller, Mark H. (264)
Kidder, Louise (285)
Kutney, Andrew J. (224), (325)
Soskis, David A. (244), (295), (345)
Villanova University 214
Betz, Joseph (73)
Women's Martial Arts Union 228

CRIMINAL JUSTICE
See also: CRIME; POLICE

American Polygraph Association 7
Atwood, Walter F. (1)
Weir, Raymond J., Jr. (2)
Auburn University 16
Pendergast, Patrick F. (65)
Shields, Alan John (73)
California State University, Fullerton 29
Capune, W. Garrett (49), (133)
Prinsky, Lorraine E. (62), (288), (346)
Contemporary Forum 42
East Carolina University 56
Moeller, H.G. (142)
Eastern Illinois University 57
Leigh, Peter R., II (49)
Intercollegiate Studies Institute, Inc. 85
Van Den Haag, Ernest (35)
Maryland, University of 106
Massachusetts Bar Association 107
Mid West Program Service, Inc. 112
Dash, Sam (28)
Newsweek, Inc. 139
Pennsylvania State University 151
Fulmer, Richard H. (227)
LaGoy, Stephen P. (229)
Pillay, K.K.S. (156)
Solley, Bill (230)
Puget Sound, University of 159
Berry, Keith O. (11)
Hobson, William G. (28)
Nock, George R. (45)
Smith, David (61)
Strait, John A. (63)

CRIMINAL JUSTICE (continued)

Saint Cloud State University 168
Fischmann, Ruel (16)
Miller, Martin (49)
Southwestern Louisiana, University of 174
Joubert, Paul E. (52)
Speaker's Bureau of Philadelphia 176
Lehrer, Sam (62)
Success Leaders Speakers Service 180
Asija, Satya Pal (6)
Temple University 181
DeMott, John (211)
Heyman, Lisa N. (54), (220)
Strazzella, James A. (273)
Villanova University 214
Betz, Joseph (83)
War Resisters League 217
Peck, Jim (3)
Washington, University of 218
Washington Reporters Group 220
Kelly, Harry (5)
Wilson Celebrities, Lola 225
Strick, Anne (37)

D

DANCE

California State University, Fullerton 29
Sims, Melvin D. (153), (223)
Keedick Lecture Bureau, Inc. 97
Wilson, Anne (71)
Northeastern Illinois University 142
Hobley, Marge Munn (38)
Walker, Robert (92)
Southwestern Louisiana, University of 174
Lebas, Sherry (64)
Moreland, Muriel K. (75)
Temple University 181
Chapman, Sara A. (77), (92)
Ferdun, Edrie (82)
Metallinois, Nilos (86)
Washington, University of 218
Wilson Celebrities, Lola 225
Wallace, Paul (39)
World Modeling Association 229

DATA PROCESSING
See: COMPUTERS

DEATH
See also: ESTATE PLANNING

California State University, Fullerton 29
Bell, Tony (281)
Carnegie-Mellon University 31
Schulz, Richard (20)
Duquesne University 54
East Carolina University 56
Dunn, Patricia (133)
Eastern Illinois University 57
Butts, Bob (8)
Marquette University 105
Cotrone, Daniel (92)
Prendergast, Thomas L. (91)
Northeastern Illinois University 142
Moorhead, Hugh S. (62)
Pennsylvania State University 151
Harkness, William L. (262)
Saint Cloud State University 168
Stensland, Allen (67)
Temple University 181
Aker, F. David (14)
Villanova University 214
Bush, David F. (77)
Virginia Polytechnic Institute and State University 216
McCollum, Robert H. (76)
Payne, Alfred C. (94)
Rogers, Cosby S. (106)
Washington, University of 218

DENTISTRY

Marquette University 105
Dhuru, Virendra B. (28)
Manoli, Sadanand G. (29)
Pruhs, Ronald (30)
Williams, Don L. (31)
Pennsylvania State University 151
Hunt, Edward E., Jr. (208)
Temple University 181
Binns, William H., Jr. (157)
Fielding, Allen Fred (161)
Lantz, Harold (174)
Leifer, Calvin (60), (114), (175)
Washington, University of 218

DEVELOPING COUNTRIES

Auburn University 16
Lovell, T.R. (53)
California State University, Fullerton 29
Kaye, Alan S. (328)
Carnegie-Mellon University 31
Goodspeed, Charles (22)
Drew University 52
Jennings, Peter R. (41)
Mascio, Afework A. (52)
Eastern Illinois University 57
Faust, John R. (19)
Intercollegiate Studies Institute, Inc. 85
Schiebel, Joseph (31)
Northeastern Illinois University 142
Lopez, Jose E. (56)
Pennsylvania State University 151
Gilmore, Harold L. (43)
LaPorte, Robert, Jr. (196)
Puget Sound, University of 159
Robinson, Hamlin (52)
Saint Cloud State University 168
Levilain, Guy (41)
Virginia Polytechnic Institute and State University 216
Webb, Ryland E. (140)
Western Washington University 223
Scott, James W. (28)

DISCRIMINATION
See: RACIAL RELATIONS

DISEASES AND BODY DISORDERS

Auburn University 16
Coker, Samuel Terry (13)
California, Irvine, University of 27
Kohut, Robert I. (31)
Novey, Harold S. (33)
Prakash, Ravi (34)
Valenta, Lubomir J. (35)
California State University, Fullerton 29
Davenport, Calvin A. (172), (267)
Carnegie-Mellon University 31
Kozak, Wlodzimierz M. (24)
East Carolina University 56
Fulghum, Robert S. (78)
Muzzarelli, Robert A. (55)
Eastern Illinois University 57
Aten, Dennis (2)
Marquette University 105
Swan, Jane D. (127)
Pennsylvania State University 151
Sias, John D. (83)
Todd, Paul (211)

DISEASES AND BODY DISORDERS (continued)

Saint Cloud State University 168
  Hortis, Theophanis (29)
Temple University 181
  Batra, Gopal K. (156)
  Cote, Mary Louise (158)
  Ehrlich, George E. (160)
  Geiwitz, Allen R. (164)
  Greenwald, Earl (168)
  Hoenig, Eugene M. (169)
  Kendall, A. Richard (171)
  Lotlikar, Prabhakar D. (178), (230)
  Miller, Arthur S. (182)
  Mohnac, Alex M. (183)
  Popovtzer, Mordecai M. (188)
  Reichle, F.A. (190)
  Tower, Gail (195)
Virginia Polytechnic Institute and State University 216
  Bates, Robert C. (4)
  Colmano, Germille (24)
  Holdeman, Lillian (54)
Washington, University of 218

DRAMA
  See: THEATER

DRUG ABUSE

Auburn University 16
  Coker, Samuel Terry (13)
  Warner, Richard W., Jr. (84)
California State University, Fullerton 29
  Davenport, Beverly Wills (171)
Duquesne University 54
East Carolina University 56
  Compton, Rod (76)
  Johnson, Thomas H. (81)
  Kendrick, Lionel (83)
Eastern Illinois University 57
  Richardson, Jack J. (69)
International Narcotic Enforcement Officers Association 88
  Bellizzi, John J. (1)
Marquette University 105
  McCall, Raymond J. (100)
  Schreier, James W. (84)
  White, Dennis K. (88)
Mid West Program Service, Inc. 112
  Linkletter, Art (82)
Miller Agency, Gilbert 113
  Piersall, Jimmy (2)
Northeastern Illinois University 142
  Pizzi, William J. (69)
Pennsylvania State University 151
  Beck, Edward S. (161)
  Powell, John W. (283)
Saint Cloud State University 168
  Hortis, Theophanis (29)
Simon Fraser University 171
  Alexander, Bruce (44)
  Rockerble, R.A. (53)
Temple University 181
  Doukas, Peter H. (159), (212)
  Gautieri, Ronald F. (216)
  Liebler, Joan G. (177)
  Peterson, Charles F. (186), (236)
Villanova University 214
  Betz, Joseph (83)
Washington, University of 218

DRUGS

Auburn University 16
  Newton, David S. (60)
California State University, Fullerton 29
  Davenport, Beverly Wills (171)
Contemporary Forum 42
Duquesne University 54
Eastern Illinois University 57
  Ferguson, Karen (20)
  Richardson, Jack J. (69)
Northeastern Illinois University 142
  Jackson, Charles J. (44)
  Pizzi, William J. (69)
Pennsylvania State University 151
  Powell, John W. (283)
Queen's University 160
  Beck, Ivan (4)
  Marks, Gerald (13)
  Nakatsu, Kanju (15)
Saint Cloud State University 168
  Hortis, Theophanis (29)
Simon Fraser University 171
  Alexander, Bruce (44)
  Rockerble, R.A. (53)
Temple University 181
  Gautieri, Ronald F. (216)
  Geiwitz, Allen R. (164)
  Peterson, Charles F. (186)
  Tuckerman, Murray M. (196), (249)
  Turco, Salvatore (197)
United States Department of Health, Education and Welfare 198

E

EARTHQUAKES
  See: GEOLOGY

EASTERN UNITED STATES

Fame Limited 59
  Jones, Dewitt (6)
  Roberts, John (14)
Forrest, Martin A. 69
  Jones, Dewitt (4)
Keedick Lecture Bureau, Inc. 97
  Schustik, Bill (61)
Murray State University 117
  Strohecker, Edwin C. (75)
Saint Cloud State University 168
  Herbison, Priscilla J. (26)

ECOLOGY
  See also: CONSERVATION; WASTES AND REFUSE

Auburn University 16
  Askew, Raymond S. (2)
  Davis, Donald E. (14)
  Hardin, Ian R. (28)
Bethlehem Steel Corporation 20
California, Irvine, University of 27
  Wadman, William W. (9)
California State University, Fullerton 29
  Brattstrom, Bayard H. (47), (69), (132), (266)
  Brown, Giles T. (48), (70)
  Liston, Albert M. (73), (260)
  Sutton, Imre (74), (195)
Carnegie-Mellon University 31
  Coleman, Bernard D. (21)
  Tarr, Joel A. (13)
Duquesne University 54
East Carolina University 56
  Bellis, Vincent J. (66)
  Davis, Trenton (67)
  Everett, Grover W. (69)
  Lao, Y.J. (71)
  Padgett, Richard (73)
Eastern Illinois University 57
  Durham, Leonard (16)
  Moll, Edward O. (59)
  Whitley, Steve (94)

ECOLOGY (continued)

Georgia-Pacific Corporation 73
Marquette University 105
Kipp, Raymond J. (120)
Laczniak, Gene R. (6)
Murray State University 117
Brun, Michael A. (29)
Eversmeyer, Harold E. (30)
McHugh, William P. (31)
Matthai, James P. (32)
Thompson, James T. (35)
National Solid Waste Management Association 133
Hill, Michael (2)
National Water Well Association 136
Lehr, Jay H. (14)
Northeastern Illinois University 142
Charlier, Roger H. (15)
Northwest Mining Association 143
Whinnen, W.J. (15)
Pennsylvania Electric Company 150
Good, Cynthia D. (4)
Slowik, Alfred A. (8)
Tice, James H. (11)
Pennsylvania State University 151
Beach, James W. (26)
Ferrar, Terry A. (150)
Fletcher, Peter W. (304)
Gamble, Hays B. (225)
Grossman, Herbert (151)
Hillson, C.J. (152)
Johnson, John C. (141)
Kroger, Manfred (177)
Labbauf, Abbas (153)
Lieb, John A. (154)
Panofsky, H. (155)
Pillay, K.K.S. (156)
Reethof, Gerhard (145)
Schenck, George (134)
Sharpe, William E. (158)
Stowe, Wilmer C. (159)
Zavodni, John J. (160)
Puget Sound, University of 159
Karlstrom, Ernest L. (34)
Maxwell, Keith A. (41)
Pierson, Beverly (49)
Saint Cloud State University 168
Hortis, Theophanis (29)
Knutson, Keith M. (37)
Lofgreen, Harold A. (43)
Simon Fraser University 171
Oloffs, Peter (39)
Temple University 181
Smith, Rita (31)
Tuna Research Foundation, Inc. 187
Nizetich, Anthony V. (4)
United States Environmental Protection Agency 204
Villanova University 214
Hyson, John M. (25), (63)
Kelly, C. Michael (26)
Logue, John J. (27)
Mathers, Lewis J. (28)
Sweeny, Robert F. (30)
Virginia Polytechnic Institute and State University 216
Cross, Gerald H. (26)
Foy, Chester L. (38)
Henneke, Edmund G. (51)
McConnell, Robert L. (77)
Marchman, James F. III (79)
Marshall, Harold P. (81)
Moore, Laurence D. (85)
Skelly, John M. (113)
Spray, Richard A. (121)
Washington, University of 218
Western Washington University 223
Helgoe, Robert S. (13)
Taylor, Ronald J. (15)

ECONOMICS

American Party 6
Anderson, Tom (1)
Greaves, Percy (2)
Shackelford, Rufus (3)
Auburn University 16
House, Donald R. (37)
Stanaland, Eugene E. (76)
Tole, Thomas M. (79)
Business Communication Council 23
California State University, Fullerton 29
Liston, Albert M. (73), (79), (260)
Mlynaryk, Peter M. (81)
Chemetron Corporation 34
Moore, L. David (1)
Contemporary Forum 42
Drew University 52
Bull, Vivian A. (11)
Cranmer, H. Jerome (21)
Duquesne University 54
East Carolina University 56
Gulati, Umesh C. (17)
Eastern Illinois University 57
Murad, Ahmad (61)
Federal Reserve Bank of Richmond 60
Federal Reserve Bank of San Francisco 61
First Federal of Broward 63
Florida Association of Realtors 65
Alexander, Marlene M. (1)
Banzhaf, Parker C. (4)
Danforth, Horace C. (14)
Dominquez, Carlos, Jr. (15)
Farrell, Reid D. (18)
Fearnley, Joe (19)
Kirk, Robert W. (34)
Konigsburg, Sidney (35)
Pardue, William P. (50)
Pickens, Phillip (51)
Randol, Monroe G. (54)
Robison, Mack (56)
Slack, Ted C. (58)
Slater, L.B. (59)
Thomas, Phillip A. (62)
Ward, Robert L. (65)
Waters, Paul W. (66)
Wegman, W.J. (67)
Wilson, James T. (69)
Fulton Inc., Richard 71
Georgia Federal Savings and Loan Association 72
Intercollegiate Studies Institute, Inc. 85
Anderson, Martin (1)
Brozen, Yale (2)
Demsetz, Harold (4)
Freeman, Roger A. (10)
Kemp, Arthur (14)
Manne, Henry G. (19)
Michl, H.E. (22)
Opitz, Edmund A. (25)
Peterson, William H. (26)
Rogge, Benjamin A. (30)
Tullock, Gordon (34)
Keedick Lecture Bureau, Inc. 97
Cappiello, Frank (10)
Ward, Barbara (68)
Leigh Bureau 102
Clark, Lindley (3)
Silk, Leonard (31)
Marquette University 105
Kardatzke, Nyle (32)
Murray State University 117
DeVine, John W. (17), (40)
Lindauer, John (22)
Mathis, Gilbert L. (6), (23), (47)
Newell, Howard F. (24)
Thompson, James T. (26)
National Speakers Bureau, Inc. 135
Gramm, W. Phillip (24)
Levine, Irving R. (39)
Rinfret, Pierre A. (55)
New York Mercantile Exchange 138
Abrahams, Allen C. (1)
North Carolina National Bank 141
Northeastern Illinois University 142
Kokoris, James A. (51)

ECONOMICS (continued)

Renas, Stanley R. (71)
Singleton, Gregory H. (78)
Pennsylvania State University 151
Brown, Robert J. (37)
Fox, Thomas G. (42)
Gamble, Hays B. (225)
LaPorte, Robert, Jr. (196)
Meyer, Peter B. (49)
Monahan, Robert E. (50)
Schenck, George (134)
Puget Sound, University of 159
Robinson, Hamlin (52)
Veseth, Michael (64)
Saint Cloud State University 168
Levilain, Guy (41)
Lofgreen, Harold A. (43)
Marmas, James G. (45)
Simon Fraser University 171
Okuda, Kenji (11)
Var, Turgut (13)
Southwestern Louisiana, University of 174
Caradine, E. Everett (17)
Cornwall, Don (21)
Hamsa, Charles F. (40)
Lapoint, James J. (63)
Manuel, David P. (70)
Millet, Jeremy (72)
Speakers Bureau of America, Inc. 175
Sowell, Thomas (3)
Williams, Walter (5)
Speaker's Bureau of Philadelphia 176
Adams, Gerard (2)
Jaffe, Eugene (54)
Success Leaders Speakers Service 180
Clark, Ray K. (29)
Gates, James E. (62)
Michelon, L.C. (121)
Temple University 181
McCain, Roger A. (39)
Rohrlich, George F. (42)
Williams, Walter E. (46)
Wolfbein, Seymour L. (48)
Villanova University 214
Clarke, James J. (31)
Jucia, Joseph L. (32)
Mason, Saul (33)
Mathis, Edward (34)
Thanawala, Kishor (35)
Virginia Polytechnic Institute and State University 216
Lucas, James T., Jr. (74)
Whitelaw, Robert L. (143)
Washington, University of 218
Washington Reporters Group 220
Swoboda, Frank (7)

EDUCATION
See also: COLLEGE STUDENTS; COLLEGES AND UNIVERSITIES; CONTINUING EDUCATION; SCHOOL ADMINISTRATION

American Montessori Society 5
Americans United 12
Auburn University 16
Duncan, J.W. (18)
Lanham, Ben T. (48)
Littleton, Taylor D. (52)
Martin, John Stokes (56)
Norris, Aubrey G. (62)
Roberts, Charles B. (68)
Tincher, Wilbur A. (78)
Vallarino, Lidia M. (81)
Vandegrift, Frank (82)
Walden, John C. (83)
White, J. Herbert (87)
California, Irvine, University of 27
Bork, Alfred (19)
Hoy, John C. (20)
California State University, Fullerton 29
Brattstrom, Bayard H. (132)
Corey, Gerald F. (88)
Fierman, Morton C. (90), (233)
Giacumakis, George J. (91), (235)
Johnson, Raynolds (94)
Kiraithe, Jacqueline M. (95), (204), (297)
Leder, Hans H. (96), (164)
McLaren, Robert B. (59), (99)
Przekop, Lawrence R. (100)
Reckinger, Nancy R. (64), (101), (347)
Sadovszky, Otto J. (102)
Tait, Miriam A. (103), (187)
Triplett, George E. (68), (104), (188)
Drew University 52
Baker, E.G. Stanley (2)
Chillak, Edward W. (14)
Domber, Edward A. (26)
Gillespie, Joanna Bowen (32)
Hardin, Paul (38)
Johnson, Barent (42)
Lono, J. Mark (48)
Salathe, Karl M. (83)
Thompson, Bard (94)
Duquesne University 54
East Carolina University 56
Chambliss, Thomas A. (42)
Fleming, Ruth G. (44)
Harper, Betsy (45)
Jones, Douglas R. (48)
Lanier, Gene D. (50)
Lao, Rosina C. (51)
Lawler, Donald (52)
Mueller-Roemer, Peter (54)
Muzzarelli, Robert A. (55)
Prewett, Clinton R. (136)
Richards, John Thomas (57)
Eastern Illinois University 57
Anderson, Eulalee L. (1)
Christ, Donald G. (10)
Crane, William J. (13)
Gholson, Ronald E. (24)
Hadwiger, Kenneth E. (27)
Hillner, William M. (34)
Lauda, Donald P. (46)
Lawson, Dorothy M. (47)
Leathers, Ronald (48)
Leyden, Michael B. (50)
Matzner, Gerhard C. (55)
North, John T. (65)
Rogers, Donald L. (70)
Scholes, Gene W. (76)
Shank, Kathlene (79)
Sharaway, H.S. (80)
Shuf, Robert V. (81)
Sutton, Kenneth (85)
Fulton Inc., Richard 71
Intercollegiate Studies Institute Inc. 85
Crane, Philip M. (3)
Dietze, Gottfried (5)
Freeman, Roger A. (10)
Kirk, Russell (16)
Meyer, Frank S. (21)
Tonsor, Stephen J. (33)
Voegelin, Eric (37)
Learning Exchange 99
Conroy, G. Dennis (1)
Dobmeyer, Edward R. (2)
Kinishi, Diane Reiko (3)
Leigh Bureau 102
Schorr, Daniel (29)
Toffler, Alvin (36)
Marquette University 105
DeRoche, Robert J. (34)
Doherty, Dennis J. (35)
Dupuis, Adrian (36)
Flynn, Leo B. (38)
Kaimann, Richard A. (5)
Mayberry, Arthur (44)
Mitchell, Robin C. (46)
Nordberg, Robert B. (47)
Pambookian, Hagop S. (48)

EDUCATION (continued)

Rechlicz, Gloria (49)
Sankovitz, James L. (50)
Swan, Jane D. (86)
Maryland, University of 106
Mid West Program Service, Inc. 112
Higgins, Joe (64)
Kaufman, Bel (76)
Melton, Dave (89)
Van Derbur, Marilyn (128)
Murray State University 117
Aslup, Robert F. (36)
Bossing, Lewis (37)
Dean, Ken S. (39)
DeVine, John W. (40)
Elder, Harvey L. (92)
Fitch, Franklin G. (41)
Holcomb, Thomas F. (43)
Humphreys, Ben (44)
Malone, Bobby G. (45)
Mathis, Gilbert L. (47)
May, Sandra A. (48)
Mayes, Jerry W. (135)
Noffsinger, Hugh A. (49)
Petrie, Garth F. (50)
Price, Bill (51)
Rowan, Robert W. (52)
Sholar, Thomas P. (54)
Shown, Vernon E. (55), (120)
Smith, June Warden (56)
Stranahan, Joan (57)
Taylor, John (58)
Tolley, Charles H. (59)
Watkins, Yancy (134)
Williams, Wayne M. (60)
National School Supply and Equipment Association 132
Book, Kenneth M. (1)
Fleming, E.J., III (3)
Fredericks, Kay (4)
Petty, O.L., Jr. (9)
Smith, Frank E. (11)
National Speakers Bureau, Inc. 135
Peter, Laurence J. (50)
Newsweek, Inc. 139
Northeastern Illinois University 142
Bell, Mary A. (4)
Beverly, Sherman, Jr. (5)
Bowers, Mary W. (9)
Burger, Mary Louise (13)
Fareed, Ahmed A. (21)
Feldman, Reynold (22)
Fowler, Mary Ann (26)
Georgiou, Peri P. (30)
Gilpatric, C. Edward (33)
Hawley, Jane S. (36)
Hostetler, Frank C. (39)
Hudson, Randolph H. (40)
Jones, Arnold P., Jr. (47)
Lopez, Jose E. (56)
Mardell, Carol D. (59)
Meyers, Gertrude (61)
Parker, Bettye J. (66)
Pedroso, Angelina (68)
Reichhardt, Richard (70)
Robinson, Edward A. (74)
Saiet, Ronald A. (75)
Stevens, Humphrey (83)
Uliassi, Edward C. (87)
Vilaro, Rudolfo E. (90)
Walsh, William M. (93)
Ware, Gussie M. (94)
Watson, Ulestine (95)
Willerman, Marvin (97)
Peabody College for Teachers, George 148
Pennsylvania State University 151
Bierly, George W. (2)
Calamidas, Alec (38)
Carter, Joe Douglas (66)
Cartwright, Carol (91)
Elias, Edward M. (140)
Evans, Donald E. (95)
Gilmour, Joseph E., Jr. (97)
Greenhill, Leslie P. (99)
Grella, Michael A. (100)
Hopper, Paul T. (235)
Ikenberry, Stanley O. (101)
Kraybill, Edward K. (103)
Kraybill, Wilbur K. (104)
Lane, Benjamin A. (105)
Larson, Roland E. (250)
Millar, Craig A. (107)
Morse, Otis B., IV (7)
Nelson, Murry R. (109)
Oliver, Robert T. (110)
Ongiri, David O. (111)
Ott, Robert W. (30)
Patterson, Henry O. (169)
Perkins, Harold W. (112)
Robinson, Byron M. (115)
Schwartz, Alice M. (32)
Shemick, John M. (118)
South, James (120)
Swetz, Frank (121)
Williamson, Janet A. (256)
Puget Sound, University of 159
Hodges, Richard E. (29)
Hoyt, Milton (32)
Kerr, Stephen T. (35)
Robinson, John W. (53)
Queen's University 160
Nakatsu, Kanju (15)
Sinclair, Duncan (19)
Saint Cloud State University 168
Ames, Kenneth A. (1)
Farrah, George A. (14)
Fields, Dennis C. (15)
Graham, Charles J. (18)
Grunerud, James J. (19)
Hagen, Owen (21)
Halberg, Delaine (22)
Larson, Walter G. (38)
Montgomery, Terry (50)
Pabst, Alfred A. (54)
Park, Thomas C. (55)
Simon Fraser University 171
Conlbear, Kenneth (14)
Foth, Dennis (15)
Gehlbach, Roger (17)
O'Connell, Sheila (19)
Prock, Leone (20)
Trivett, John V. (21)
Wheatley, Jon (60)
Southwestern Louisiana, University of 174
Arceneaux, Clayton J. (1)
Brabant, Sarah C. (13)
Ducharme, Robert J. (25)
Green, Joe L. (38)
Holmes, Bruce B., Jr. (49)
Kreamer, Jeanne T. (57)
Kunkle, John F. (58)
Morella, John R. (76)
Oliver, James R. (79)
Rice, Lawrence (83)
Rickels, Patricia V. (84)
Robinette, Gladys H. (85)
Robinette, Walter R. (86)
Webb, Robert M. (91)
White, Ronald (95)
Speaker's Bureau of Philadelphia 176
Boonin, Tobyann (16)
Success Leaders Speakers Service 180
Dollar, Bobby G. (42)
Rausch, Erwin (143)
Schieltz, Whitt (150)
Yawkey, Thomas Daniels (199)
Temple University 181
Adamsky, Richard A. (89)
Chapman, Sara A. (92)
Cutter, William W. III (93), (261)
Drummond, Caroline (94)
Fork, Donald J. (97)
Friedman, Frank L. (51)
Gilpin, Nancy E. (52), (99)
Hirshfield, Marvin (55)
Holtzman, Robert H. (102), (303)
Humphreys, Donald (103)
Hunt, Jon H. (104)
Jensen, Linda R. (105), (150)

EDUCATION (continued)

Kress, Roy A. (107)
La Vallee-Williams, Marthe (109), (326)
Lawrason, Robin E. (110), (316)
Leahy, Robert (111)
Legos, Patricia M. (113), (286)
Leventhal, Jerome I. (61), (115)
Lockhart, Barbara D. (6)
Pavan, Barbara (118)
Rivell, Amos C. (120)
Schrag, Adele F. (122)
Shankman, Florence V. (123)
Sheldon, Harry J. (319)
Thurman, Ken (126)
Walter, Robert L. (129)
Walters, Donald L. (130)
Viewpoint Speakers Bureau 213
Dixon, Maceo (2)
Villanova University 214
Heitzmann, William Ray (36)
Lytel, June W. (18)
Niosi, Jerome J. (19), (37)
Nivodo, Christopher S. (38)
Schorr, Beverly (95)
Schwarz, John H. (39)
Virginia Polytechnic Institute and State University 216
Andrew, Loyd D. (2)
Bell, Wilson B. (7)
Braden, Roberts A. (10)
Crunkilton, John R. (28)
Earthman, Glen I. (33)
Furr, A. Keith (41)
Harris, Ruth D. (49)
Havard, William C. (50)
Huffman, Stanley A., Jr. (58)
Lynch, Richard L. (75)
Montgomery, James R. (84)
Morrill, Robert W. (86)
Owen, James J. (89)
Pusey, Robert H. (100)
Russell, G.E. (107)
Sullins, W. Robert (125)
Teates, Thomas G. (129)
Walter, Jane H. (138)
Washington, University of 218
Western Washington University 223
Buckland, Roscoe L. (8)
Hildebrand, Francis (9)
Scott, James W. (10)
Watrous, Mary W. (11)
Whittier College 224
Farmer, Malcolm F. (5)

ELECTRICITY
See also: ENERGY

Consolidated Edison Company of New York, Inc. 41
Detroit Edison 47
Florida Power and Light 66
Jersey Central Power and Light Company 92
Pennsylvania Electric Company 150
Davidson, James E. (1)
Furst, John N. (2)
Good, Cynthia D. (4)
Middleton, John B. (5)
Orris, Richard E. (6)
Rossman, W. Richard (7)
Spaulding, Robert R. (9)
Stephens, Jerome S. Jr. (10)
Tice, James H. (11)
Tremel, Charles L. (12)
Yeager, Robert C. (13)
Pennsylvania State University 151
Carpenter, Lynn A. (261)
Henisch, Heinz K. (73)
Philadelphia Electric Speakers Bureau 152
Public Service Electric and Gas Company 158
Union Electric Speakers Forum 189
Virginia Electric and Power Company 215
Virginia Polytechnic Institute and State University 216
Hull, Harry H. (59)
Western Electric Company 222
Wisconsin Electric Power Company 226

EMPLOYMENT
See also: EQUAL EMPLOYMENT; INTERVIEWING

Duquesne University 54
East Carolina University 56
Gulati, Umesh C. (17)
James, Furney K. (46)
Eastern Illinois University 57
Sutton, Kenneth (85)
Intercollegiate Studies Institute, Inc. 85
Brozen, Yale (2)
Michl, H.E. (22)
Peterson, William H. (26)
Petro, Sylvester (27)
International Wages for Housework Campaign - Canada 90
Ramirez, Judith (1)
Murray State University 117
Holcomb, Thomas F. (19)
Jacks, Lloyd B. (20)
Lilly, George T. (80)
Pennsylvania State University 151
Carnahan, Robert E. (52)
Fox, Thomas G. (42)
Graham, Kenneth R. (54)
Hatalla, Josephine F. (55)
Labbauf, Abbas (153)
Prince, Dawn Stegenga (57)
Swails, Richard G. (60)
Simon Fraser University 171
Grubel, Herbert G. (8)
Southwestern Louisiana, University of 174
Manuel, David P. (70)
Temple University 181
Batra, Gopal K. (333)
Wolfbein, Seymour L. (48)
Virginia Polytechnic Institute and State University 216
Butt, Albin T. (15)

ENERGY
See also: ELECTRICITY; NUCLEAR ENERGY; OIL AND GAS; SOLAR ENERGY

Auburn University 16
Askew, Raymond S. (2)
Gross, Charles A. (25)
Hendrick, James (31)
Vachon, Reginald I. (80)
Bethlehem Steel Corporation 20
Business Communication Council 23
California, Irvine, University of 27
Hill, Mason L. (4)
California State University, Fullerton 29
Johnson, Fred M. (72), (109), (236), (272)
Mlynaryk, Peter M. (81)
Carnegie-Mellon University 31
Burnett, Tobias W.T. (23)
Chevron U.S.A. Inc. 35
Consolidated Edison Company of New York, Inc. 41
Detroit Edison 47
Duquesne University 54
East Carolina University 56
Birchard, Ralph E. (15)
Gulati, Umesh C. (17)
Knight, Clifford B. (29)
Lao, Y.J. (71)
Eastern Illinois University 57
Buchanan, David (6)

ENERGY (continued)
Griffith, John R. (25)
Strader, Gayle Gilbert (84)
Thorsen, Larry (89)
Florida Power and Light 66
Getty Oil Company 74
Jersey Central Power and Light Company 92
Keedick Lecture Bureau, Inc. 97
Knowles, Ruth Sheldon (35)
Leigh Bureau 102
Piel, Gerard (24)
Murray State University 117
Thompson, James T. (35)
Newsweek, Inc. 139
Northeastern Illinois University 142
Charlier, Roger H. (15)
Sood, Mohan K. (81)
Northwest Mining Association 143
Kaufman, M.A. (8)
McGregor, Wallace (9)
Pennsylvania Electric Company 150
Furst, John N. (2)
Fyock, David H. (3)
Tice, James H. (11)
Pennsylvania State University 151
Barone, Thomas F. (123)
Chasko, William E. (125)
Ferrar, Terry A. (150)
Houlihan, John F. (127)
McCormick, Robert H. (47)
Marsicano, Arthur J. (131)
Palladino, Nunzio J. (132)
Schenck, George (134)
Stefanko, Robert (136)
Philadelphia Electric Speakers Bureau 152
Public Service Electric and Gas Company 158
Rap and Associates 163
Abeles, Tom (1)
Pauls, Robert (2)
Rutan, Al (3)
Sohio Speakers Bureau 173
Southwestern Louisiana, University of 174
Grimsal, Edward G., Jr. (39)
Manuel, David P. (70)
Rugg, Fred E. (87)
Vodraska, Walter C. (90)
Temple University 181
Cuff, David J. (131), (209), (336)
Ulmer, Gene C. (137), (250)
Washburne, Stephen S. (253)
Union Electric Speakers Forum 189
United States Environmental Protection Agency 204
United Telecommunications, Inc. 210
McCarthy, J.F. (1)
Villanova University 214
Calabrese, Lucio (40)
McAssey, Edward V. (29)
Virginia Electric and Power Company 215
Virginia Polytechnic Institute and State University 216
Arndt, Richard (3)
Kurstedt, Harold A., Jr. (64)
Long, C. Hardy (71)
McConnell, Robert L. (77)
Marshall, Harold P. (81)
Robeson, Andrew (103)
Spann, Robert M. (119)
Spray, Richard A. (121)
Vaughan, David H. (137)
Whitelaw, Robert L. (143)
Washington, University of 218
Western Electric Company 222
Wisconsin Electric Power Company 226

ENGINEERING
See also: CONSTRUCTION

Auburn University 16
Irwin, J. David (40)
California Polytechnic State University 28
California State University, Fullerton 29
Butterworth, Joseph D. (23), (107)
Hunt, Eugene B. (108)
Walkington, David L. (32), (111), (278), (352)
Carnegie-Mellon University 31
Cussier, Edward L. (11)
Drew University 52
McDonald, W. Scott, Jr. (51)
Food Processing Machinery and Supplies Association 67
Bourke, J. David (5)
Hollingsworth, W.C. (15)
Jones, Raymond P. (18)
Michalec, John M. (23)
Marquette University 105
Bakr, Mamdough (116)
Traas, Adrian G. (74)
Maryland, University of 106
Pennsylvania State University 151
Bierly, George W. (2)
Chasko, William E. (125)
Cunningham, Richard G. (266)
Dandois, Joseph E. (53)
Duda, J.L. (138)
Ebaugh, Paul (139)
Elias, Edward M. (140)
Kozik, Eugene (45)
Kummer, Mary J. (142)
Marsicano, Arthur J. (131)
Palladino, Nunzio J. (132)
Parkin, Blaine R. (143)
Prosser, Duane R. (144)
Reethof, Gerhard (145)
Smith, Hubert C. (34)
Steffy, Denton A. (146)
Weed, Merwin L. (149)
Queen's University 160
Lywood, Denis (12)
Simon Fraser University 171
Devenyl, Denes (7)
Southwestern Louisiana, University of 174
Vodraska, Walter C. (90)
Young, Robert L. (97)
Temple University 181
Baran, Ernest (155)
Mayer, Nathaniel (180)
Villanova University 214
Koliner, Ralph (41)
McAssey, Edward V. (29)
Mathers, Lewis J. (28)
Myers, John A. (42)
Rice, William J. (43)
Schorr, David J. (44)
Scott, Thomas (22)
Wallo, Edward M. (45)
White, Theodore H. (90)
Virginia Polytechnic Institute and State University 216
Devens, W.G. (30)
Hull, Harry H. (59)
Marvin, Frank F. (82)
Mason, J.P.H., Jr. (83)
Nachlas, Joel A. (87)
Schetz, Joseph A. (108)
Smith, Donald W. (116)
Spengler, Fred L. (120)
Washington, University of 218
Western Electric Company 222

ENGLISH LANGUAGE
See: LANGUAGE

ENTERTAINMENT
See also: HUMOR; MAGIC

Crowder Productions, Inc., Leo 43

ENTERTAINMENT (continued)

Glendale Federal Savings and Loan Association 75
Carlson, Kenneth A. (1)
Goodyear Tire and Rubber Company 76
Bryan, W.R. (1)
Harrington, Bob 81
Harrington, Bob (1)
Hutaff, Charles 83
International Entertainment Bureau 86
True, Herb (1)
International Platform Association 89
Keedick Lecture Bureau, Inc. 97
Leigh Bureau 102
Baker, Russell (1)
Buchwald, Art (2)
Duchin, Peter (7)
Haley, Alex (13)
Price, Vincent (25)
Maryland, University of 106
Mid West Program Service, Inc. 112
Miller Agency, Gilbert 113
National Speakers Bureau, Inc. 135
Ohio Bell Telephone Company 144
Podium Management Associates, Inc. 154
Godfrey, Arthur (10)
Marx, Maxine (16)
Peerce, Jan (18)
Rich, Buddy (20)
Rogers, Will, Jr. (21)
Stuart, Mary (24)
Program Corporation of America 156
Puget Sound, University of 159
Reeck, Darrell (51)
Speaker's Bureau of Philadelphia 176
Haynes, Trudy (46)
Schreffler, Ken (102)
Zabrowsky, Marian (125)
Success Leaders Speakers Service 180
Kaufman, Zenn (99)
Weiner Programs, Inc., Irv 221
Weiner, Irv (1)
Wilson Celebrities, Lola 225
Bacon, James (2)
Calvet, Corinne (5)
Mason, Pamela (28)

ENVIRONMENT
See also: ECOLOGY

Auburn University 16
Hardin, Ian R. (28)
California, Irvine, University of 27
DiMento, Joseph F. (3)
California State University, Fullerton 29
Brattstrom, Bayard H. (69), (132)
Liston, Albert M. (73), (79), (260)
Sutton, Imre (74), (195)
Chevron U.S.A. Inc. 35
Consolidated Edison Company of New York, Inc. 41
Drew University 52
Nagle, James J. (59)
Pollock, Leland Wells (69)
Duquesne University 54
East Carolina University 56
Davis, Trenton (25), (67)
Knight, Clifford B. (29), (70)
Lao, Y.J. (71)
O'Conner, Michael P. (72)
Piper, Roswell M. (19), (74)
Seghal, Prem P. (75)
Sugg, Howard (103)
Eastern Illinois University 57
Whitley, Steve (94)
Fulton, Inc., Richard 71
Georgia-Pacific Corporation 73
Keedick Lecture Bureau, Inc. 97
Cousins, Norman (13)
Murray State University 117
Miller, Michael G. (33)
Newell, Howard F. (34)
National Speakers Bureau, Inc. 135
Downs, Hugh (17)
Pennsylvania Electric Company 150
Fyock, David H. (3)
Good, Cynthia D. (4)
Slowik, Alfred A. (8)
Pennsylvania State University 151
Ferrar, Terry A. (150)
Frey, John C. (254)
Labbauf, Abbas (153)
Philadelphia Electric Speakers Bureau 152
Public Service Electric and Gas Company 158
Puget Sound, University of 159
Maxwell, Keith A. (41)
Queen's University 160
Semple, Robert (17)
Saint Cloud State University 168
Rosenthal, Eugene (64)
Simon Fraser University 171
McClaren, Milton (37)
Oloffs, Peter (39)
Southwestern Louisiana, University of 174
Ehrhart, Dennis (28)
Webb, Robert M. (91)
Speaker's Bureau of Philadelphia 176
Hackes, Peter (45)
Muskie, Edmund (81)
Temple University 181
Lotlikar, Prabhakar D. (178), (230)
Morton, Bruce G. (184)
Surrency, Erwin C. (136), (346)
Tuna Research Foundation, Inc. 187
Nizetich, Anthony V. (4)
United States Environmental Protection Agency 204
Villanova University 214
Hyson, John M. (25), (63)
Mathers, Lewis J. (28)
Virginia Electric and Power Company 215
Virginia Polytechnic Institute and State University 216
Harper, Laura J. (48)
Spray, Richard A. (121)
Washington, University of 218
Western Washington University 223
Craig, Steve (12)
Helgoe, Robert S. (13)
Monahan, Robert L. (14)
Taylor, Ronald J. (15)

EQUAL EMPLOYMENT

California, Irvine, University of 27
Curiel, Ramon (2)
California State University, Fullerton 29
Saltzstein, Alan L. (66), (262)
East Carolina University 56
Webber, Edith (132)
Northeastern Illinois University 142
Jones, Arnold P., Jr. (47)
Renas, Stanley R. (71)
Pennsylvania State University 151
Asbury, William W. (1)
Western Washington University 223
Robinson, Mary (1)

ESKIMOS
See also: AMERICAN INDIANS

American Institute for Exploration 4
Bank, Ted P. II (3)

ESKIMOS (continued)

Ransom, Jay Ellis (6)
Handweavers Guild of America 79
Senungetuk, Joseph E. (123)

ESPIONAGE
See: INTELLIGENCE ACTIVITIES

ESTATE PLANNING
See also: RETIREMENT

American Professional Practice Association 8
Lewis, Max L. (5)
Weiner, Barry Ross (10)
Duquesne University 54
Massachusetts Bar Association 107
National Water Well Association 136
May, Judy (21)
Puget Sound, University of 159
Oltman, William (46)
Temple University 181
Aker, F. David (14)
Virginia Polytechnic Institute and State University 216
Prouty, Bruce R. (99)
Whittier College 224
Winters, Richard H. (17)

ETHICS AND MORALS
See also: SOCIAL RESPONSIBILITIES; VALUES

California State University, Fullerton 29
Barish, Natalie (113), (131), (265)
Pullen, Rick D. (40), (117)
Drew University 52
Copeland, John W. (18)
Hilton, Bruce (40)
Jones, Donald (44)
Oden, Thomas Clark (62)
Duquesne University 54
Florida Association of Realtors 65
Baars, Theo D., Jr. (2)
Banzhof, Parker C. (4)
Bermingham, Thomas J. (5)
Boardman, Blanche (6)
Boone, Betty Jane (7)
Cantrall, Otto L. (9)
Carroll, J.E. (10)
Danforth, Horace C. (14)
Dominguez, Carlos, Jr. (15)
Fantle, Karl S. (17)
Farrell, Reid D. (18)
German, Jack (22)
Greene, Errol L. (24)
Horn, Walter V. (30)
Hudson, Max (31)
Jones, Ernest A. (33)
Lassetter, Maggie S. (36)
Ledridge, Paul Walton (37)
Linville, George M. (38)
Lynn, Frank (39)
McIntosh, Claudette E. (42)
Martens, Frank H. (43)
Moutz, Madora (46)
Moutz, W.B. (47)
Pyms, Jack (53)
Randol, Monroe G. (54)
Ring, John F. (55)
Robison, Mack (56)
Slater, L.B. (59)
Ward, Robert L. (65)
Waters, Paul W. (66)
Wilcox, Olin R. (68)
Yates, Dorothy M. (70)
Hutaff, Charles 83
Jones, A.L. (13)
Intercollegiate Studies Institute, Inc. 85
Herberg, Will (12)
Kirk, Russell (16)
Martin, William Oliver (20)
Vivas, Eliseo (36)
Keedick Lecture Bureau, Inc. 97
Moore, Robin (45)
Zumwalt, Elmo (74)
Leigh Bureau 102
Silk, Leonard (31)
Marquette University 105
Doherty, Dennis J. (104)
Griesbach, Marc F. (90)
Laczniak, Gene R. (6)
Roach, Richard R. (111)
Murray State University 117
Howard, Robert (84)
Northeastern Illinois University 142
Dobbs, Frank W. (19)
Pennsylvania State University 151
Barton, Michael (214)
Cooper, Jane E. (164)
Gilmore, Harold L. (43)
Remick, Forrest J. (133)
Thies, Anita H. (86)
Puget Sound, University of 159
Bland, Jeffrey (12)
Hoyt, Milton (32)
Saint Cloud State University 168
Risberg, Douglas F. (63)
Temple University 181
DeMott, John (68), (211)
Holtzman, Robert H. (102)
Villanova University 214
Betz, Joseph (83)
Bush, David F. (77)
Chorba, George J. (13)
Losoncy, Thomas A. (74)
Regan, Daniel T. (75)
Van Fleteran, Frederick E. (76)
Whittier College 224
Moody, Jonathan (11)
Roston, Ronald (14)
Women's Classical Caucus 227
Nussbaum, Martha C. (34)

EUROPE
See also: FRANCE; GERMANY; GREAT BRITAIN AND IRELAND; SPAIN

Associated Film Artists 15
Borden, Chris (1)
Francisco, Clay (2)
Jay, John (3)
Lark, Ed (4)
Wolfgang, Ken (5)
California State University, Fullerton 29
Dittman, Roger R. (120), (255), (268)
Kahrs, Karl H. (56), (121), (259)
Leder, Hans H. (123), (164)
McLaren, Robert G. (321)
Nyaggah, Mougo (7)
Odle, D. Richard (11), (148), (322)
Tumas, Elena V. (127), (213), (290)
Zeltzer, Allen M. (327)
Douglas Management 51
Douglas, Neil (1)
Drew University 52
Salathe, Karl M. (83)
Von Der Heide, John T. (96)
Duquesne University 54
East Carolina University 56
Bassman, Michael F. (112)
Papalas, Anthony J. (122)
Eastern Illinois University 57
Schlauch, Wolfgang (75)
Waddell, Leyla Peck (92)
Fame Limited 59
Butler, Willis (3)

EUROPE (continued)

Johnson, Irving M. (5)
Jones, Doug (7)
Madsen, Bill (9)
Mentes, Matthew and Sherilyn (10)
Nichols, Frank (11)
Reddy, Dick (13)
Roberts, John (14)
Keedick Lecture Bureau, Inc. 97
Oltmans, Willem L. (52)
Leigh Bureau 102
Scali, John (28)
Marquette University 105
Sokolnicki, Alfred J. (27)
Memphis State University 110
Booth, John N. (1)
Bumiller, Ted (2)
Dodson, Sid (3)
Hagar, Jonathan (6)
Murray State University 117
Jacks, Lloyd P. (137)
Keeslar, Suzanne M. (138)
Northeastern Illinois University 142
Bevington, Gary (6)
Gonzalez, Rodrigo C. (34)
Lindman, Margaret R. (55)
Pennsylvania State University 151
Erwin, Stuart (297)
Frankforter, A. Daniel (215)
Lynch, Catherine M. (298)
Pierucci, Francis (300)
Reyburn, Gerald (220)
Puget Sound, University of 159
Danes, Zdenko F. (20)
Saint Cloud State University 168
Hagen, Owen (21)
Johnson, David C. (30)
Phillips, Mary H. (61)
Rowland, Howard Ray (65)
Simon Fraser University 171
Hurst, Michael Eliot (2)
Southwestern Louisiana, University of 174
Rense, William C. (82)
Temple University 181
Claflen, George L., Jr. (335)
Viewpoint Speakers Bureau 213
Saunders, George (13)
Villanova University 214
Plater-Zyberk, Maria (49), (59)
Washington, University of 218

EXERCISE
See: PHYSICAL FITNESS

F

FAMILY RELATIONS
See also: CHILDREN; PREGNANCY AND CHILDBIRTH; SEX AND SEXUALITY; WOMEN

Auburn University 16
Hodson, Norma G. (35)
Warner, Richard W., Jr. (84)
C.A.L.M. - Child Abuse Listening Mediation, Inc. 24
Root, David A. (1)
Selman, Joan (2)
California State University, Fullerton 29
Corey, Gerald F. (231)
Lindquist, Carol H. (239), (343)
McLaren, Robert B. (59), (99), (345)
Powlison, Fraser (150), (244)
White, Geoffrey D. (252)
Drew University 52
Gilbert, Norma (31)
Gillespie, Joanna Bowen (32)
Graybeal, David (33)
Lee, Alfred McClung (48)
Duquesne University 54
East Carolina University 56
Knox, David (5)
Markowski, Mel (7)
Singh, Avtar (123)
Eastern Illinois University 57
Butts, Bob (8)
Hillner, William M. (34)
Kirk, William G. (41)
Noland, Carol (64)
Saltmarsh, Robert E. (71)
Intercollegiate Studies Institute, Inc. 85
Kuehnelt-Leddikin, Erik Von (18)
International Wages for Housework Campaign - Canada 90
Ramirez, Judith (1)
Keedick Lecture Bureau, Inc. 97
Dodson, Fitzhugh J. (17)
Marquette University 105
Doherty, Dennis J. (76), (104)
Sheikh, Anees E. (103)
Topetzes, Nick J. (98)
Maryland, University of 106
Massachusetts Bar Association 107
Mid West Program Service, Inc. 112
Hays, Timothy (60)
Murray State University 117
Holcomb, Thomas F. (43)
Malone, Bobby G. (45)
May, Sandra A. (48)
Northeastern Illinois University 142
Caron, Josiane (14)
Jacobs, Claire M. (45)
Meyers, Gertrude (61)
Singleton, Gregory H. (78)
Walsh, William M. (93)
Pennsylvania State University 151
Beatty, John W. (88)
Costa, Joseph J. (93)
DuPuis, Mary M. (94)
Mandle, Joan D. (167)
Ongiri, David O. (111)
Paterson, Henry O. (169)
Seward, D.M. (11)
Van Horn, James E. (172)
Puget Sound, University of 159
Ibsen, Charles A. (33)
Maxwell, Keith A. (41)
Phillips, John W. (48)
Sloman, Carol L. (60)
Saint Cloud State University 168
Boltuck, Charles J. (7)
Herbison, Priscilla J. (26)
Miller, Joan D. (48)
Wise, Jeffrey (73)
Simon Fraser University 171
Alexander, Bruce (44)
Speaker's Bureau of Philadelphia 176
Cohen, Sara Kay (25)
Hubschman, Lynn (51)
Success Leaders Speakers Service 180
Jakubek, Gene (88)
Temple University 181
Isard, Eleanore S. (221), (284)
Liddle, Howard (229), (287), (310)
Rappaport, Herbert (291)
Rappaport, Margaret M. (237), (292)
Rubini, Dennis A. (238)
Tower, Gail (247)
Vandivier, Frances (252), (313)
University Speakers Bureau 211
Callahan, Sidney (2)
Francoeur, Robert B. (3)
Villanova University 214
Bush, David F. (77)
Chorba, George J. (61)
Virginia Polytechnic Institute and State University 216

FAMILY RELATIONS (continued)

Bovard, Kenley P. (9)
Fu, Victoria R. (40)
Harper, Laura J. (48)
Rogers, Cosby S. (106)
Thompson, Ann E. (133)
Washington, University of 218
Whittier College 224
Olson-Prather, Emelie (12)
Wilson Celebrities, Lola 225
Brothers, Joyce (4)
Women's Classical Caucus 227
Hallett, Judith P. (18)
Phillips, Jane E. (36)

FAR EAST
See also: CHINA; JAPAN

Asian Speakers Bureau 14
Associated Film Artists 15
Lark, Ed (4)
Wolfgang, Ken (5)
California State University, Fullerton 29
Brown, Giles T. (14), (48)
Cox, Miriam S. (15), (200)
Kaye, Alan S. (16), (128), (163), (319)
Santucci, James A. (129)
Drew University 52
Jennings, Peter R. (41)
Rodes, Robert Michael, Jr. (79)
Von Der Heide, John T., Jr. (96)
East Carolina University 56
Singh, Avtar (123)
Fame Limited 59
Armstrong, Ken (1)
Forrest, Martin A. 69
Baker, Norman (1)
Kefford, Michael (5)
Intercollegiate Studies Institute, Inc. 85
Kuehnelt-Leddikin, Erik Von (18)
Possony, Stefan T. (29)
Keddick Lecture Bureau, Inc. 97
Oltmans, Willem L. (52)
Reynolds, Jack (57)
Leigh Bureau 102
Salisbury, Harrison (27)
Marquette University 105
Manoli, Sadanand G. (20)
Oh, John K.C. (57)
Pehowski, Marian (68)
Murray State University 117
Garfield, Gene J. (68)
Northeastern Illinois University 142
Lindman, Margaret R. (55)
Pennsylvania State University 151
Botdorf, Ruth (264)
Goldman, Stuart D. (193)
LaPorte, Robert, Jr. (196)
Oliver, Robert T. (110)
Shemick, John M. (118)
Puget Sound, University of 159
Barnett, Suzanne W. (6)
Kim, Jai-Kyup (36)
Saint Cloud State University 168
Park, Thomas C. (55)
Southwestern Louisiana, University of 174
Kurtz, Donn M., II (59)
Rense, William C. (82)
Virginia Polytechnic Institute and State University 216
Prince, William (98)
Washington, University of 218

FASHION

Keedick Lecture Bureau, Inc. 97
Narducci, Leo (46)
Weir, June (70)
Men's Fashion Association of America 111
Karr, Norman (1)
Tolbert, Chip (2)
Mid West Program Service, Inc. 112
Keith, Judith (77)
Northeastern Illinois University 142
Bohlin, Jill K. (8)
Gillies, Jean (32)
Southwestern Louisiana, University of 174
Kelly, Heather C. (54)
Speaker's Bureau of Philadelphia 176
Berk, Ginger (9)
Tait, Elaine (114)
Stevens Model and Merchandising Agency, Patricia 179
Stevens, Melissa (1)
World Modeling Association 229
Acton, Raymond (1)

FILMS

American Institute for Exploration 4
Kitchen, Herman (4)
Carnegie-Mellon University 31
Greenfield, Concetta (12)
Contemporary Forum 42
Directors Guild of America 49
Drew University 52
Skaggs, Calvin L. (88)
East Carolina University 56
Stephenson, William (14), (109)
Eastern Illinois University 57
Heumann, Joseph (32)
Forrest, Martin A. 69
Waterman, Stanton (15)
Fulton Inc., Richard 71
Keedick Lecture Bureau, Inc. 97
DeHavilland, Olivia (16)
Reed, Rex (56)
Swanson, Gloria (63)
Leigh Bureau 102
Price, Vincent (25)
Marquette University 105
Arnold, James W. (66)
Rich, Lawrence M. (110)
Mid West Program Service, Inc. 112
Buttram, Pat (20)
Fields, Ronald J. (38)
Fontaine, Joan (40)
National Speakers Bureau, Inc. 135
Murphy, George (45)
Northeastern Illinois University 142
Sochen, June (80)
Pennsylvania State University 151
Graham, Robert J. (234)
Podium Management Associates, Inc. 154
Ray, Nicholas (19)
Saint Cloud State University 168
Fischmann, Ruel (16)
Otto, Don H. (53)
Speaker's Bureau of Philadelphia 176
Dunningham, Dennis (29)
Schreffler, Ken (102)
Success Leaders Speakers Service 180
Evans, Robert (50)
Temple University 181
LaVallee-Williams, Marthe (74)
Villanova University 214
Helmetag, Charles H. (66)
Wilson Celebrities, Lola 225
Bacon, James (2)
Calvet, Corinne (5)
Mason, Pamela (28)
Richman, Peter Mark (30)

FILMS (continued)

Women's Classical Caucus 227
Sowa, Cora Angier (44)

FINANCIAL MANAGEMENT
See also: ESTATE PLANNING

American Collectors Association, Inc. 2
American Graduate School of International Management 3
McMahon, Robert (3)
Auburn University 16
Edmonds, Charles P., III (19)
Tole, Thomas M. (79)
Baltimore Federal Savings and Loan Association 18
Sheehan, T. Frank (1)
Business Communication Council 23
California State University, Fullerton 29
Gala, Basil E. (76)
Chemetron Corporation 34
Moore, L. David (1)
Whatley, Harold E. (2)
Dial Corporation 48
Glazer, Edward (1)
Disclosure Inc. 50
Goldspiel, Steven (1)
Duquesne University 54
East Carolina University 56
Zincone, Louis H., Jr. (23)
Florida Association of Realtors 65
Banks, Clyde M. (3)
Boone, Betty Jane (7)
Concannon, F.P. (12)
Falbey, J. Wayne (16)
Fantle, Karl S. (17)
Fearnley, Joe (19)
Graham, Jim (23)
Hannan, Robert (25)
Hogan, John (29)
Kirk, Robert W. (34)
Martens, Frank H. (43)
Overton, D. William (49)
Pardue, William P. (50)
Ring, John F. (55)
Robison, Mack (56)
Schieber, Frank W. (57)
Slack, Ted C. (58)
Stemper, William H., Sr. (61)
Thomas, Phillip A. (62)
Ward, Robert L. (65)
Waters, Paul W. (66)
Wegman, W.J. (67)
Wilson, James T. (69)
Georgia Federal Savings and Loan Association 72
Keedick Lecture Bureau, Inc. 97
Rush, Richard D. (59)
Marquette University 105
Trebby, James P. (10)
Murray State University 117
Freeman, William E. (114), (121)
National Water Well Association 136
Alcorn, Pat B. (7)
No-Loan Mutual Fund Association 140
McFarland, G. Richmond (1)
Pennsylvania State University 151
Brown, Robert J. (37)
Hefferan, Colien (166)
Monahan, Robert E. (50)
Patterson, Robert A. (9)
Podium Management Associates, Inc. 154
Davis, William (5)
Queen's University 160
Wiginton, John (20)
Rainier National Bank 162
Saint Cloud State University 168
Marmas, James G. (45)
Stensland, Allen (67)
Southwestern Louisiana, University of 174
Lapoint, James J. (63)
Manuel, David P. (70)
Speaker's Bureau of Philadelphia 176
Scheuer, John (99)
Success Leaders Speakers Service 180
Connellan, Thomas K. (34)
Temple University 181
Lamont, Jay (37)
Villanova University 214
Bush, David F. (77)
Chorba, George J. (1)
Wilson Celebrities, Lola 225
Kaye, David N. (21)
Wuliger, Betty (44)

FOLKLORE

California State University, Fullerton 29
Cox, Miriam S. (185), (200), (332)
Evans, David H. (201)
Center for Southern Folklore 32
Drew University 52
Peek, Philip M. (67)
Duquesne University 54
Eastern Illinois University 57
Shull, Carl (82)
Puget Sound, University of 159
Goman, LaVerne (23)
Southwestern Louisiana, University of 174
Webb, Yvonne (92)
Temple University 181
Metallinois, Nikos (142)
Women's Classical Caucus 227
Thomas, Ruth S. (47)

FOOD AND BEVERAGES
See also: AGRICULTURE; FOOD SUPPLY; NUTRITION

Auburn University 16
Huffman, Dale L. (39)
Rymal, Kenneth S. (71)
Weete, John D. (85)
Wingard, Richard M. (90)
Chemetron Corporation 34
Detroit Edison 47
Duquesne University 54
Eastern Illinois University 57
Hedges, Edith R. (30)
Food Processing Machinery and Supplies Association 67
Alpers, Kenneth E. (1)
Baum, Eric C. (2)
Baumann, Rich (3)
Body Guard, Inc. (4)
Bourke, J. David (5)
Busalacchi, Louis J. (6)
Butler, Peter K. (7)
Clarke, R.B. (8)
Clegg, Lee M. (9)
Coughlin, Robert W. (10)
Ehrhardt, David A. (11)
Flynn, Dennis G. (12)
Gilde, L. (13)
Hogan, Craig (14)
Hollingsworth, W.C. (15)
Houmes, D.L. (16)
Hunter, Richard S. (17)
Jones, Raymond P. (18)
Lewis, Gary (19)
Ligett, M.T. (20)
Maley, Larry E. (21)
Manwaring, Robert T. (22)
Michalec, John M. (23)
Nelson, P.E. (24)
Rechtsteiner, S. (25)
Root, Bruce (26)
Saunders, Robert D. Jr. (27)

FOOD AND BEVERAGES
(continued)

Schultz, C.B. (28)
Maryland, University of 106
Monsanto Company 115
Pabst Brewing Company 145
Allerup, N.P. (1)
Ratcheson, R.J. (2)
Wingrad, A.J. (3)
Pennsylvania State University 151
Botdorf, Ruth (264)
Fung, Daniel Y.C. (173)
Gerhard, Glenn (174)
Kean, Glenn R. (175)
Kneebone, Leon R. (176)
Kroger, Manfred (177)
Kuhn, Gerald D. (178)
Montjar, Monty J. (179)
Strickler, Fay B. (180)
Thomas, Walter I. (181)
Ziegler, John H. (182)
Saint Cloud State University 168
Hortis, Theophanis (29)
Simon Fraser University 171
Davison, Allan J. (26)
Southwestern Louisiana, University of 174
Beckman, William C. (4)
Hamsa, Charles F. (40)
Speaker's Bureau of Philadelphia 176
Mayer, Jean (76)
Pakenham, Michael (84)
Success Leaders Speakers Service 180
Stokes, Judy Ford (166)
Temple University 181
Bennett, Douglas (34), (334)
Lotlikar, Prabhakar D. (178), (230)
Tuckerman, Murray M. (249)
Tuna Research Foundation, Inc. 187
Kierce, Harold F. (1)
United States Department of Health, Education and Welfare 198
Villanova University 214
Myers, John A. (42)
Virginia Polytechnic Institute and State University 216
Bovard, Kenley P. (9)
Cherry, Jerry A. (18)
Collins, William F. (23)
Essary, E.O. (35)
Flick, George J. (36)
Lechowich, Richard V. (67)
Lopez, Anthony (72)
Marlowe, Thomas J. (80)
Potter, Lawrence M. (97)
Wesley, Roy L. (142)
Whittier College 224
James, Lois (10)
Wilson Celebrities, Lola 225
Lester, Mary (22)

FOOD SUPPLY
See also: POPULATION

Auburn University 16
Autrey, Kenneth M. (3)
Hayes, Kirby L. (30)
Huffman, Dale L. (39)
King, Nelson B. (45)
Lovell, R.T. (53)
Wilson, Stanley P. (89)
California State University, Fullerton 29
Horn, Michael H. (71), (140), (271)
Drew University 52
Jennings, Peter R. (41)
East Carolina University 56
Gulati, Umesh C. (17)
Eastern Illinois University 57
Faust, John R. (19)
Food Shoppers Union 68
Mid West Program Service, Inc. 112
Brown, Lester R. (17)
Butz, Earl L. (21)
Spitzer, Robert W. (117)
Murray State University 117
Thompson, James T. (8)
Pennsylvania State University 151
Beattie, James M. (19)
Kroger, Manfred (177)
Schenck, George (134)
Thomas, Walter I. (24)
Zavodni, John J. (160)
Puget Sound, University of 159
Bland, Jeffrey (12)
Saint Cloud State University 168
Andrzejewski, Julie (4)
Speaker's Bureau of Philadelphia 176
Schwartz, Loretta (103)
Virginia Polytechnic Institute and State University 216
Flick, George J. (36)
Potter, Lawrence M. (97)
World Vision International 230

FOREIGN LANGUAGES
See also: LANGUAGE

American Graduate School of International Management 3
Kumayama, Akihisa (2)
California, Irvine, University of 27
Terrell, Tracy D. (15)
California State University, Fullerton 29
Kaye, Alan S. (203), (218)
Prado, Marcial (208)
Esperanto League for North America 58
Harmon, William R. (1)
Lieberman, E. James (2)
Pool, Jonathan R. (3)
Tonkin, Humphrey (4)
Learning Exchange 99
Northeastern Illinois University 142
Bevington, Gary (6)
Pedroso, Angelina (68)
Vilaro, Rudolfo E. (90)
Pennsylvania State University 151
Hopper, Paul T. (235)
Queen's University 160
Bastianutti, Diego (3)
Saint Cloud State University 168
Park, Thomas C. (55)
Simon Fraser University 171
DeArmond, Richard (46)
Southwestern Louisiana, University of 174
Cain, Joan A. (15)
Gentry, Robert J. (33)
Kunkle, John F. (58)
Temple University 181
Hartsook, John H. (101)
Virginia Polytechnic Institute and State University 216
Ulloa, Justo C. (135)
Women's Classical Caucus 227
Hallett, Judith P. (18)
Killian, Barbara E. (23)
Lanham, Carol D. (27)
Loomis, Julia W. (29)
Roth, Catharine P. (40)

FOREIGN POLICY
See: INTERNATIONAL AFFAIRS

FOSSILS

American Institute for Exploration 4
Ransom, Jay Ellis (6)

FOSSILS (continued)

Eastern Illinois University 57
Schram, Frederick R. (77)
Puget Sound, University of 159
Lowther, J. Stewart (38)
Washington, University of 218

FRANCE
See also: EUROPE

Associated Film Artists 15
Borden, Chris (1)
Drew University 52
Christofferson, Thomas R. (15)
East Carolina University 56
Aronson, Nicole (111)
Ellenburg, Grace (115)
Eastern Illinois University 57
Thorsen, Larry (89)
Waddell, Leyla Peck (92)
Fame Limited 59
Mentes, Matthew and Sherilyn (10)
Marquette University 105
Cartz, Louis (33)
Memphis State University 110
Bumiller, Ted (2)
Murray State University 117
Beasley, Wayne T. (64)
Keeslar, Suzanne M. (138)
Sagrera, Walter D. (74)
Northeastern Illinois University 142
Gonzalez, Rodrigo C. (34)
Zegger, Robert Elie (98)

FUND RAISING

California State University, Fullerton 29
Stedman, Preston (154)
Drew University 52
Salathe, Karl M. (83)
Marquette University 105
Szyszko, Barbara (53)
Pennsylvania State University 151
Engel, A. William, Jr. (185)
Kraybill, Herbert K. (186)
Lupton, Charles (187)
Moellenbrock, George, Jr. (188)

FUTURE OF SOCIETY

American Teilhard Association for the Future of Man 11
Cousins, Evert (4)
California State University, Fullerton 29
Hulse, Christopher R. (54), (141), (161), (334)
McNelly, Willis E. (206)
East Carolina University 56
Lawler, Donald (64)
Eastern Illinois University 57
Lauda, Donald P. (46)
Keedick Lecture Bureau, Inc. 97
Lodge, Henry Cabot (39)
Oltmans, Willem L. (52)
Lecture Services, Inc. 100
Furbay, John H. (1)
Leigh Bureau 102
Diebold, John (6)
Fadiman, Clifton (11)
Johnson, Nicholas (15)
Martel, Leon C. (20)
Piel, Gerard (24)
Salisbury, Harrison (27)
Stern, Joel (33)
Toffler, Alvin (36)
Marquette University 105
Schreier, James W. (9)
National Speakers' and Psychics' Registry 134
Fuller, R. Buckminster (3)
National Speakers Bureau, Inc. 135
Janeway, Eliot (31)
Pennsylvania State University 151
Perkins, Harold W. (112)
Podium Management Associates, Inc. 154
Ordway, Frederick (17)
Puget Sound, University of 159
Anton, Paul (3)
Polley, Roy J. (50)
Saint Cloud State University 168
Downes, Alan J. (11)
Hagen, Owen (21)
Lieberman, Harold (42)
Mertens, Gerald C. (47)
Speaker's Bureau of Philadelphia 176
Lotman, Arline (69)
Temple University 181
McCain, Roger A. (231)
Schmidt, Arthur (240)
Wilson Celebrities, Lola 225
Criswell (9)

G

GAMBLING

California State University, Fullerton 29
Gala, Basil E. (136)
Klassen, Vuryl J. (214)
East Carolina University 56
Sayetta, Tom C. (130)
Keedick Lecture Bureau, Inc. 97
Salerno, Ralph (60)
Marquette University 105
Blascovich, James J. (99)
Northeastern Illinois University 142
Kamau, Lucy J. (48)
Pennsylvania State University 151
Herring, Henry I. (249)
Temple University 181
Kotz, Samuel (4), (151)
Whittier College 224
Roston, Ronald (14)

GAMES
See also: RECREATION

Northeastern Illinois University 142
Jones, Arnold P., Jr. (47)
Pennsylvania State University 151
Ford, Nicholas S. (247)
Pray, Alfred R. (210)
Southwestern Louisiana, University of 174
Oliver, James R. (79)
Temple University 181
Averbach, Bonnie (1), (148)
Banerji, Ranan B. (204)
Dubeck, Leroy W. (3)
Shankman, Florence V. (8)
Villanova University 214
Heitzmann, William Ray (36)

GARDENING
See: HORTICULTURE

GEMS
See also: MINERALS

American Institute for Exploration 4
Ransom, Jay Ellis (6)
Northwest Mining Association 143
Whinnen, W.J. (15)
Pennsylvania State University 151
Newnham, Robert (255)
Women's Classical Caucus 227
Thomas, Ruth S. (47)

GENEALOGY

Leigh Bureau 102
Haley, Alex (13)
Podium Management Associates, Inc. 154
Beard, Timothy (2)
Speaker's Bureau of Philadelphia 176
Lodge, Elizabeth (67)
Washington, University of 218

GENETICS

California State University, Fullerton 29
Barish, Natalie (113), (131), (170), (265)
Drew University 52
Nagle, James J. (59)
Leigh Bureau 102
Piel, Gerard (24)
Marquette University 105
Courtright, James B. (2)
Doherty, Dennis J. (104)
Northeastern Illinois University 142
Lerner, Jules (53)
Pennsylvania State University 151
Cooper, Jane E. (164)
Eckroat, Larry R. (165)
Grossman, Herbert (151)
Todd, Paul (211)
Puget Sound, University of 159
Morse, Jeffrey W. (44)
Southwestern Louisiana, University of 174
Hill, Walter E. (46)
Temple University 181
Goodner, David M. (167)
Kistenmacher, Mildred L. (16), (173)
Niu, M.C. (19)
Platt, Dorothy B. (20)
White, Elliott (24)
University Speakers Bureau 211
Bender, Harvey A. (1)
Washington, University of 218

GEOGRAPHY

California State University, Fullerton 29
Earick, Arthur F. (89), (135), (159), (341)
Murray State University 117
Matthai, James P. (63)
Pennsylvania State University 151
Abler, Ronald (183)
Zelinsky, Wilbur (184)
Southwestern Louisiana, University of 174
Johnson, David C. (51)
Virginia Polytechnic Institute and State University 216
Marvin, Frank F. (82)
Washington, University of 218
Women's Classical Caucus 227
Milham, Mary Ella (31)
Warrior, Valerie M. (53)

GEOLOGY

California, Irvine, University of 27
Hill, Mason L. (4)
California State University, Fullerton 29
Ryan, John A. (152), (276)
Eastern Illinois University 57
Ford, John P. (22)
Marquette University 105
Yoo, Chai Hong (121)
National Water Well Association 136
Gass, Tyler E. (12)
Hunt, Joel (13)
Lehr, Jay H. (14)
Palmer, Gail Branscome (15), (22)
Northeastern Illinois University 142
Sood, Mohan K. (81)
Upadhyay, Hansa D. (89)
Northwest Mining Association 143
Weissenborn, Albert E. (14)
Pennsylvania State University 151
Ebaugh, Paul (139)
Johnston, Richard G. (128)
Simonsen, August H. (13)
Puget Sound, University of 159
Lowther, J. Stewart (38)
Saint Cloud State University 168
Anderson, Garry G. (3)
Temple University 181
Humphreys, Donald (133)
Ulmer, Gene C. (137)
Virginia Polytechnic Institute and State University 216
Bollinger, Gilbert A. (8)
Washington, University of 218
Western Washington University 223
Schwartz, Maurice (37)
Whittier College 224
Rhodes, Dallas (13)

GERIATRICS
See: AGING

GERMANY
See also: EUROPE

American Graduate School of International Management 3
Roessler, Helmut R. (6)
Associated Film Artists 15
Lark, Ed (4)
California State University, Fullerton 29
Kahrs, Karl H. (56), (259)
Douglas Management 51
Douglas, Neil (1)
Drew University 52
Schabacker, John M. (84)
East Carolina University 56
Nischan, Bodo (139)
Eastern Illinois University 57
Schlauch, Wolfgang (75)
Fame Limited 59
Reddy, Dick (13)
Intercollegiate Studies Institute, Inc. 85
Dietze, Gottfried (5)
Schiebel, Joseph (31)
Northeastern Illinois University 142
Barber, Charles M. (1)
Feldman, Reynold (22)
Pennsylvania State University 151
Hopper, Paul T. (235)
Southwestern Louisiana, University of 174
Gentry, Robert J. (33)
Virginia Polytechnic Institute and State University 216
Siemoneit, Martin A. (112)

GESTALT

California, Irvine, University of 27
Price, Michael J. (45)
California State University, Fullerton 29
Russell, J. Michael (245)
Contemporary Forum 42
Eastern Illinois University 57
Saltmarsh, Robert E. (71)

GOVERNMENT

See also: PUBLIC ADMINISTRATION; STATE AND LOCAL GOVERNMENT

California State University, Fullerton 29
Liston, Albert M. (260)
Carnegie-Mellon University 31
Crecine, John P. (25), (34)
Contemporary Forum 42
Eastern Illinois University 57
Maurer, David J. (56)
Fulton Inc., Richard 71
Heritage Foundation 82
Intercollegiate Studies Institute, Inc. 85
Brozen, Yale (2)
Dietze, Gottfried (5)
Freeman, Roger A. (10)
Hauptmann, Jerzy (11)
Kemp, Arthur (14)
Kuehnelt-Leddihin, Erick Von (18)
Opitz, Edmund A. (25)
Marquette University 105
Johannes, John R. (55)
Maryland, University of 106
Murray State University 117
Biggs, James W. (65), (112)
National Water Well Association 136
Lehr, Jay H. (19)
Socialist Party, USA 172
Drufenbrock, Diane (1)
Gil, David (2)
Kissell, Rick (5)
Southwestern Louisiana, University of 174
Oliver, James R. (79)
Speaker's Bureau of Philadelphia 176
Ammond, Alene (3)
Bayh, Birch (6)
Ervin, Sam (36)
Mitchell, Andrea (79)
Muskie, Edmund (81)

GRAPHOANALYSIS

Johnson, Carl M. 94
Baron, Carole M. (1)

GREAT BRITAIN AND IRELAND

See also: EUROPE

Associated Film Artists 15
Borden, Chris (1)
Lark, Ed (4)
California State University, Fullerton 29
Mewett, Jack H. (310)
Drew University 52
Lee, Alfred McClung (48)
Salathe, Karl M. (83)
Eastern Illinois University 57
Krutza, June (44)
Waddell, Leyla Peck (92)
Fame Limited 59
Jones, Doug (7)
Madsen, Bill (9)
Stockdale, Bill (16)
Taylor, Charles (17)
Keedick Lecture Bureau, Inc. 97
Montagu, Lord (44)
O'Connor, Ulick (51)
Marquette University 105
Cartz, Louis (33)
Northeastern Illinois University 142
Zegger, Robert Elie (98)
Pennsylvania State University 151
McAree, James (197)
Puget Sound, University of 159
Smith, David (61)
Wagner, Esther (65)
Saint Cloud State University 168
Phillips, Mary H. (61)
Temple University 181
Pavan, Barbara (118)
Villanova University 214
Schwarz, John H. (51)
Western Washington University 223
Scott, James W. (10)

H

HANDICAPPED

California, Irvine, University of 27
Lenhoff, Sylvia G. (32)
East Carolina University 56
Downes, Sheldon C. (77)
Hamilton, George (79)
Richards, John Thomas (57)
Templeton, Mary Susan (89)
Eastern Illinois University 57
Aten, Dennis (2)
Brooks, Benjamin L. (5)
Nicely, James E. (63)
Larlham Foundation, Inc., Hattie 98
Dreussi, Gina M. (1)
McNicholas, Jean (2)
Schenk, William A. (3)
Mid West Program Service, Inc. 112
Russell, Harold (112)
Murray State University 117
Downing, Billie (131)
Fitch, James L. (132)
Hufnagle, Jon (133)
Northeastern Illinois University 142
Mardell, Carol D. (59)
Meyers, Gertrude (61)
Ohio Bell Telephone Company 144
Pennsylvania State University 151
Asbury, William W. (1)
Cartwright, Carol (91)
Clouser, Richard A. (92)
Frank, Tom (96)
Grode, John N. (228)
Quick, Marian A. (113)
Stefanko, Robert (136)
Puget Sound, University of 159
Heimgartner, Norman L. (25)
Holm, Margo (31)
Moreland, Steve J. (43)
Saint Cloud State University 168
Rosenthal, Eugene (64)
Santa Barbara Council for the Retarded 169
Gerber, Sanford (1)
Gulje, Ulrich W., Sr. (2)
Ottman, Sidney (3)
Simon Fraser University 171
Prock, Leone (20)
Southwestern Louisiana, University of 174
Heard, J. Norman (44)

HANDICAPPED (continued)

Hobbs, Brenda Castille (47)
Morella, John R. (76)
Temple University 181
Barone, Marian T. (2), (91)
Geiwitz, Allen R. (164)
Glass, Dorothea D. (165)
Levine, Ruth Ellen (176)
Lovrinic, Jean (318)
Mayer, Nathaniel (180)
Payne, Reed (119)
Rosenman, Jill C. (121)
Smith, Rita (242)
Thurman, Ken (126)
Tiffany, Elizabeth G. (127)
Wendkos, Stanley L. (200)
Virginia Polytechnic Institute and State University 216
Bovard, Kenley P. (9)
Washington, University of 218

HANDICRAFTS
See also: CERAMICS

Auburn University 16
Pancheri, Lillian Unger (64)
East Carolina University 56
Ussery, Robert (104)
Eastern Illinois University 57
Settle, Phillip M. (78)
Handweavers Guild of America 79
Aaron-Taylor, Susan (1)
Adrosko, Rita J. (2)
Alexander, Marthann (3)
Anderson, Jeorgia (4)
Austin, Joan F. (5)
Baker, Mary (6)
Bank, Rose S. (7)
Barret, Clotilde (8)
Belfer, Nancy (9)
Berlin, Rosalind K. (10)
Best, Eleanor (11)
Blackburn, Edna (12)
Bringle, Edwina (13)
Brooks, Lois Ziff (14)
Brown, Janice C. (15)
Burhen, Jan (16)
Busse, Jane (17)
Cahlander, Adele (18)
Carson, Ted (19)
Carter, Grace (20)
Cawood, Robert (21)
Chapin, Doloria (22)
Chase, Eleanor (23)
Chetwynd, Hilary (24)
Clement, Doris and Ted (25)
Constandse, Martha E. (26)
Cope, Louise Todd (27)
Correll, Leslie (28)
Coutts, Lucille (29)
Crawford, Libby (30)
Creager, Clara H. (31)
Crockett, Candace (32)
Culbertson, Ruth Pearson (33)
Davidson, Mary Frances (34)
Dendel, Esther Warner (35)
Druding, Susan C. (36)
Eicher, Joan B. (37)
Elliott, Verda (38)
Ericson, Lois (39)
Friel, Jonda (40)
Frost, Gordon W. (41)
Fuhrmann, Brigita (42)
Gerber, Fred and Nita (43)
Ginsberg-Place, Ruth (44)
Goodman, Ronald (45)
Gordon, Beverly (46)
Gordon, Lida G. (47)
Gotthoffer, Esther (48)
Grandin-Nettles, Margareta (49)
Grant, Susan (50)
Grayson, Persis (51)
Gulick, Evelyn M. (52)
Guy, Sallie T. (53)
Hall, Joanne A. (54)
Hallman, Ted (55)
Hart, Arthur A. (56)
Hauptli, Ellen (57)
Henry, Kathleen M. (58)
Hicks, C. Norman (59)
Higgins, Mary Lou (60)
Hinman, Mary Bausch (61)
Hofstrom, Juanita (62)
Holroyd, Ruth (63)
Howard, Margaret F. (64)
Janeiro, Jan (65)
Janis, Phyllis M. (66)
Jones, Jeanetta L. (67)
Jupena, Urban (68)
Karlin, Edith (69)
Kaufman, Glen (70)
King, Bucky (71)
Klein, Sheila (72)
Kowalek, Jon W. (73)
Krasnoff, Julienne Hallen (74)
Krondahl, Hans (75)
La Lena, Connie (76)
Lenderman, Max L. (77)
Lester, Michelle (78)
Levinson, Mimi (79)
Livingston, Savetta L. (80)
Lyster, Patricia M. (81)
McBride, Lois and Walter (82)
Marks, Copeland H. (83)
Marvin, Grace (84)
Mattera, Joanne (85)
Meilach, Dona Z. (86)
Meltzer, Marilyn (87)
Moorman, Theo (88)
Morrow, Mable (89)
Nisbet, Jacquetta (90)
Noble, Judith G. (91)
Nottingham, Walter G. (92)
Nyquist, Janet (93)
O'Shaughnessy, Marjorie (94)
O'Sullivan, Sallie (95)
Painter, Hal (96)
Papish, Norma (97)
Paque, Joan Michaels (98)
Pauli, Karen (99)
Pendleton, Mary (100)
Pennington, Beth (101)
Piranian, Louise (102)
Platus, Libby (103)
Pocock, Sylvia (104)
Pohlmann, Marjorie F. (105)
Porcella, Yvonne (106)
Posner, Sally (107)
Proctor, Richard M. (108)
Rabinowe, Victoria (109)
Ray, Gale (110)
Reed, Mrs. Curtis (111)
Regensteiner, Else (112)
Reiss, Zenaide (113)
Riccardi, Mary Elinor (114)
Riis, Jon Eric (115)
Robinson, Irma F. (116)
Rodwell, Marianne S. (117)
Rushfelt, Joy M. (118)
Russell, Joan (119)
Sager, Cindy (120)
Saltzman, Joan Reid (121)
Schroeder, Philis Alvic (122)
Senungetuk, Joseph E. (123)
Shawley, Stephen D. (124)
Shimkunas, Susan L. (125)
Slickpoo, Allen P. (126)
Snow, Lee Erlin (127)
Someroski, Mel (128)
Sreenivasam, Elsa M. (129)
Stack, Lotus (130)
Stein, Judith (131)
Sykora, Merle H. (132)
Tacker, Sylvia and Harold (133)
Taylor, Janet Rush (134)
Temple, Mary (135)
Thomason, Roger K. (136)
Thompson, Margaret (137)
Thurston, Stephen (138)
Tonken, Winifred M. (139)
Towner, Naomi Whiting (140)
Trumble, Merta Sue (141)
Turner, Alta R. (142)

HANDICRAFTS (continued)

Handweavers Guild of America 79
Van Dommelen, David B. (143)
Van Gelder, Lydia (144)
Voiers, Leslie C. (145)
Waller, Irene (146)
Walling, Marie (147)
Weaver, Ken (148)
Weigle, Palmy (149)
Weltge, Sigrid (150)
West, Virginia (151)
Westfall, Carol D. (152)
Wilson, Jean (153)
Wittenberg, Barbara (154)
Wollenberg, Jackie (155)
Yacopino, Phyllis (156)
Zien, Kathleen L. (157)
Znamierowski, Nell (158)
Zotto-Beltz, Mary Ann (159)
Learning Exchange 99
Lewis Program Service, Ann 103
Owen, Lewis (5)
Maryland, University of 106
Pennsylvania State University 151
Curtis, Anthony R. (68)
Dungan, James R. (5)
Gilmour, Joseph E., Jr. (97)
Grella, Michael A. (100)
Nelson, Murry R. (109)
Puget Sound, University of 159
Colby, Bill (18)
Reid Interiors 164
Reid, Charlotte (2)
Southwestern Louisiana, University of 174
Ladousa, Dickie (61)
Speaker's Bureau of Philadelphia 176
Snellenburg, Estelle Colwin (108)
Washington, University of 218

HAWAII

Associated Film Artists 15
Lark, Ed (4)
Business Communication Council 23
California State University, Fullerton 29
Hulse, Christopher R. (141), (161), (257), (284)
Fame Limited 59
Jones, Doug (7)
Northeastern Illinois University 142
Feldman, Reynold (22)
Szymczak, Patricia A. (85)

HEALTH
See also: DISEASES AND BODY DISORDERS; HEALTH PROFESSIONS; MEDICAL SCIENCE; MENTAL HEALTH; NUTRITION; PHYSICAL FITNESS; PHYSIOLOGY

American Professional Practice Association 8
Brown, Edmund G., Sr. (2)
McCarthy, Eugene J. (6)
Auburn University 16
Lanier, Worth (49)
Newton, David S. (60)
California, Irvine, University of 27
Bostick, Warren (25)
Valenta, Lubomir J. (35)
Wadman, William W. (9)
California State University, Fullerton 29
Tygart, Clarence E. (155), (176), (291)
Calumet Area Foundation for Medical Care, Inc. 30
Shoemaker, Charles C. (1)
Drew University 52
Mascio, Afework A. (52)
Duquesne University 54
East Carolina University 56
Hooks, Edgar W. (80)
Marquette University 105
Manoli, Sadanand G. (29)
Taft, Thomas B. (14)
Maryland, University of 106
Northeastern Illinois University 142
Etten, Marion (20)
Hostetler, Frank C. (39)
Pennsylvania State University 151
Harkness, William L. (262)
Hunt, Edward E., Jr. (208)
Kraybill, Herbert K. (186)
Labbauf, Abbas (153)
Prystowsky, Harry (10)
Saint Cloud State University 168
Hortis, Theophanis (29)
Simon Fraser University 171
Hutchinson, John (49)
Southwestern Louisiana, University of 174
Ducharme, Mary H. (24)
Speaker's Bureau of Philadelphia 176
Lowenthal, Lynn (70)
Mayer, Jean (76)
Success Leaders Speakers Service 180
McAlindon, Harold R. (111)
Temple University 181
Batra, Gopal K. (205)
Karpeles, Harry D. (170)
Legos, Patricia M. (113), (227)
Levine, Ruth Ellen (176)
Morton, Bruce G. (184)
Tobacco Institute 184
Browder, Anne (1)
Drath, Connie M. (2)
Dwyer, William F. (3)
Merryman, Walker (4)
United States Environmental Protection Agency 204
Virginia Polytechnic Institute and State University 216
Bedford, Mary Ruth (5)
Colmano, Germille (24)
Furr, A. Keith (41)
Lamb, Fred M. (65)
Prouty, Bruce R. (99)
Washington, University of 218
Wilson Celebrities, Lola 225
Ritter, Roberta (31)
St. Clair, David (33)

HEALTH PROFESSIONS
See also: DENTISTRY

American Professional Practice Association 8
Biddle, Ralph T. (1)
Hall, Wesley W., Sr. (3)
Keogh, Eugene J. (4)
Lewis, Max L. (5)
Savage, John W., Jr. (7)
Schick, Henry (8)
Slavet, Arnold (9)
Weiner, Barry Ross (10)
Auburn University 16
Bailey, Wilford S. (4)
Pancheri, Lillian Unger (64)
Tanja, Jon J. (77)
California, Irvine, University of 27
Bostick, Warren (25)
Eddleman, Cindy (27)
White, Robert W. (36)
California State University, Fullerton 29
McCarthy, Miles D. (98), (174), (274)
Calumet Area Foundation for Medical Care, Inc. 30
Shoemaker, Charles C. (1)
Drew University 52
Baker, E.G. Stanley (2)
Duquesne University 54

HEALTH PROFESSIONS
(continued)

East Carolina University 56
Downes, Sheldon C. (77)
Hamilton, George (79)
Intercollegiate Studies Institute, Inc. 85
Kemp, Arthur (14)
International Narcotic Enforcement Officers Association 88
Bellizzi, John J. (1)
Marquette University 105
Doherty, Dennis J. (104)
Klein, M. Rosalie (43)
Milson, Linda (45)
Rechlicz, Gloria (49)
Schlientz, Margaret Anne (95)
Washburn, Diane M. (52)
Murray State University 117
Matarazzo, S.M. (46)
National Association of Parents and Professionals for Safe Alternatives in Childbirth (NAPSAC) 122
Eisenstein, Mayer (1)
Epstein, Janet (2)
Northeastern Illinois University 142
Etten, Marion (20)
Pennsylvania State University 151
Patterson, Robert A. (9)
Williamson, Janet A. (256)
Southwestern Louisiana, University of 174
Bess, Dolores C. (7)
Temple University 181
Cote, Mary Louise (321)
Jaipaul, Inderjit (56)
Karpeles, Harry D. (57), (170)
Levine, Ruth Ellen (176)
Patrikas, Elaine O. (185), (235)
Price, Glenda D. (189)
Rosenberg, Bonita S. (64), (191)
Snider, H. Wayne (193)
Tuckerman, Murray M. (196), (249)
Villanova University 214
Paparella, Julia B. (72)
Virginia Polytechnic Institute and State University 216
Oyler, J.M. (90)
Talbot, Richard B. (127)
Washington, University of 218
Wilson Celebrities, Lola 225
Ritter, Roberta (31)

HISTORY
See also: ANCIENT WORLD; LOCAL HISTORY; MEDIEVAL WORLD

California, Irvine, University of 27
Frank, Richard (10)
California State University Fullerton 29
Dittman, Roger R. (177)
Frazee, Charles A. (178)
Drew University 52
Leavell, J. Perry (47)
Von Der Heide, John T., Jr. (96)
Wetzel, Charles J. (99)
Duquesne University 54
East Carolina University 56
Aronson, Nicole (90)
Eastern Illinois University 57
Waddell, Leyla Peck (92)
Intercollegiate Studies Institute, Inc. 85
Stanlis, Peter J. (32)
Maryland, University of 106
Murray State University 117
Beasley, Wayne T. (64)
Burke, Robert L. (66)
Elder, Harvey L. (67)
Hammock, James W., Jr. (69)
Lawson, Hughie G. (71)
Sagrera, Walter D. (74)
Strohecker, Edwin C. (75)
Northeastern Illinois University 142
Barber, Charles M. (1)
Brommel, Bernard J. (12)
Singleton, Gregory H. (78)
Zegger, Robert Elie (98)
Pennsylvania State University 151
Frankforter, A. Daniel (215)
Reyburn, Gerald (220)
Saint Cloud State University 168
Medler, Meredith A. (46)
Simon Fraser University 171
Wheatley, Jon (55)
Southwestern Louisiana, University of 174
Peterson, Harold (80)
Rice, Lawrence (83)
Temple University 181
Cutler, William W., III (93)
Virginia Polytechnic Institute and State University 216
Porter, Robert F. (96)
Washington, University of 218
Women's Classical Caucus 227
Dickison, Sheila K. (10)
Marker, Sherry (30)
Pomeroy, Sarah B. (37)
Robert, Jennifer (38)
Treggiari, S.M. (49)

HOME MANAGEMENT
See also: COOKING; HORTICULTURE; INTERIOR DECORATING

Auburn University 16
Edmonds, Charles P., III (19)
Morgan, William W. (58)
Vachon, Reginald I. (80)
Baltimore Federal Savings and Loan Association 18
Sheehan, T. Frank (1)
California Polytechnic State University 28
California State University, Fullerton 29
Apke, Thomas M. (191)
Gala, Basil E. (136)
East Carolina University 56
Carroll, Diane (95)
Hurley, Pat (96)
Wardrep, Bruce (97)
Eastern Illinois University 57
Dow, Ruth (15)
Murray State University 117
Koenecke, Alice (78)
National Water Well Association 136
Palmer, Gail Branscome (22)
Pennsylvania State University 151
Hefferan, Colien (166)
Kuhn, Gerald D. (178)
Strickler, Fay B. (180)
Southwestern Louisiana, University of 174
Lewis, Theodore G. (65)
Speaker's Bureau of Philadelphia 176
Davis, LaDeva (31)
Virginia Polytechnic Institute and State University 216
Harris, Ruth D. (49)
Lamb, Fred M. (65)
Lovingood, Rebecca P. (73)
Webb, Anita H. (139)
Wysocki, Joseph L. (145)
Wilson Celebrities, Lola 225
Kaye, David N. (21)

HORTICULTURE

Auburn University 16
Orr, Henry P. (63)
Perkins, Donald Y. (66)
East Carolina University 56
Eller, Frank W. (100)
Eastern Illinois University 57
Krutza, June (44)
Murray State University 117
Beatty, Durwood (1)
Macha, Roger L. (5), (122)
Tackett, Amos (7), (126)
Pennsylvania State University 151
Meserole, Harrison T. (237)
Wetzel, Herbert A. (25)
Reid Interiors 164
Reid, Charlotte (2)
Southwestern Louisiana, University of 174
Barry, J. Robert (2)
Heard, J. Norman (44)
Union Electric Speakers Forum 189
Villanova University 214
Plater-Zyberk, Maria (60)
Virginia Polytechnic Institute and State University 216
Beecher, Albert S. (6)
Judkins, Wesley P. (62)
Roberts, James E. (102)
Smeal, Paul L. (115)
Washington, University of 218

HUMAN RELATIONS

Auburn University 16
Adams, Murray C. (1)
Johnson, Gerald W. (43)
Drew University 52
Bicknell, John W. (7)
East Carolina University 56
Dunn, Patricia (133)
Grossnickle, William F. (134)
Prewett, Clinton R. (136)
Eastern Illinois University 57
Egloff, William F. (18)
Florida Association of Realtors 65
Lassetter, Maggie S. (36)
Green Circle Program, Inc. 77
Gitomer, Nancy (1)
Hutaff, Charles 83
Field, Tom (4)
Fisher, Ed (5)
Keedick Lecture Bureau, Inc. 97
Garbo, Norman (23)
Lecture Services, Inc. 100
Furbay, John H. (1)
Geary, Phillip (2)
Leigh Bureau 102
Packard, Vance (22)
Tiger, Lionel (35)
Marquette University 105
Crepeau, Margaret T. (93)
Sokolnicki, Alfred J. (12)
Staudacher, Joseph M. (13)
Mid West Program Service, Inc. 112
Sweet, Cody (120)
Murray State University 117
Gantt, Vernon W. (115)
Humphreys, Ben (44)
Malone, Bobby G. (45)
Stranahan, Joan (110)
National Speakers Bureau, Inc. 135
Brothers, Joyce (9)
Puget Sound, University of 159
Sloman, Carol L. (60)
Saint Cloud State University 168
Downes, Alan J. (11)
Nunn, William H. (52)
Risberg, Douglas F. (63)
Schwerdtfeger, Dale (66)
Wollin, Dorothy (74)
Simon Fraser University 171
Wilden, Anthony (56)
Southwestern Louisiana, University of 174
Kneller, George R. (56)
Lambert, B. Geraldine (62)
Oliver, James R. (79)
Success Leaders Speakers Service 180
Arch, James (4)
Bellus, Dan (13)
Carney, Robert W. (22)
Carter, Robert N. (25)
Harris, Dorothy Lipp (76)
McGrane, William J. (113)
Owen, Gordon (133)
Robert, Cavett (146)
Uni, Miriam (182)
Temple University 181
Malnati, Richard J. (289)
Union Electric Speakers Forum 189
Vaughan and Associates, B.L. 212
Vaughan, B.L. (1)

HUMAN RIGHTS

See: CIVIL LIBERTIES

HUMOR

See also: ENTERTAINMENT

Bald Headed Men of America 17
Capps, John T. (1)
California, Irvine, University of 27
Weil, Helen H. (46)
California State University, Fullerton 29
Cox, Miriam S. (185)
Johnson, Fred M. (186)
Tait, Miriam A. (187)
Triplett, George E. (68), (104), (188)
Tumas, Elena V. (189), (213)
East Carolina University 56
Batten, J.W. (98)
Harrington, Bob 81
Harrington, Bob (1)
International Entertainment Bureau 86
True, Herb (1)
Keedick Lecture Bureau, Inc. 97
Callaway, Joe (9)
Leigh Bureau 102
Baker, Russell (1)
Buchwald, Art (2)
Ephron, Nora (9)
Marquette University 105
Jones, Leo M. (19)
Pehowski, Marian (68)
Siettman, James P. (26)
Mid West Program Service, Inc. 112
Blakely, James (12)
Buttram, Pat (20)
Fields, Ronald J. (38)
Figi, Mig (39)
Hall, Laurence (53)
Hersey, Ross (62)
Hielscher, Newt (63)
Hunter, Cecil (67)
Jarvis, Charles W. (72)
Rogers, Will, Jr. (110)
Murray State University 117
Valentine, Robert (91)
Pennsylvania State University 151
Grove, Ellis (289)
Lupton, Charles (187)
McKinstry, Richard H. (270)
Suhre, Lawrence R. (243)
Podium Management Associates, Inc. 154
Rogers, Will, Jr. (21)
Success Leaders Speakers Service 180
Griffith, James N. (67)

HUMOR (continued)

Virginia Polytechnic Institute and State University 216
Distler, P.A. (32)
Wilson Celebrities, Lola 225
Armour, Richard (1)
Wilde, Larry (40)

HYPNOTISM

Duquese University 54
Mixter Artist Management 114
Kolisch, John (2)
Pennsylvania State University 151
Tait, G. Thomas (286)
Speaker's Bureau of Philadelphia 176
Rocco, Frank (95)

I

INDIA

American Institute for Exploration 4
Alley, John (2)
Associated Film Artists 15
Borden, Chris (1)
Lark, Ed (4)
Wolfgang, Ken (5)
Auburn University 16
Vallarino, Lidia M. (81)
California State University, Fullerton 29
Przekop, Lawrence R. (18), (100)
Qureshi, Naimuddin (19), (181)
Santucci (13), (21), (129), (247)
East Carolina University 56
Gulati, Umesh C. (92), (118)
Gulati, Usha T. (119)
Singh, Avtar (123), (140)
Fame Limited 59
Bjerre, Jens (2)
Gerstle, Ralph (4)
Forrest, Martin A. 69
Bjerre, Jens (2)
Kefford, Michael (5)
Handweavers Guild of America 79
Someroski, Mel (128)
Marquette University 105
Manoli, Sadanand G. (20)
Mid West Program Service, Inc. 112
Richardson, Jane (109)
Murray State University 117
Kumar, Frederick L. (97)
Northeastern Illinois University 142
Sood, Mohan K. (81)
Pennsylvania State University 151
McAree, James (197)
Puthenpurayil, Joseph (199)
Southwestern Louisiana, University of 174
Rense, William C. (82)
Temple University 181
Batra, Gopal K. (333)
Villanova University 214
Fittipaldi, Silvio E. (50)
Washington, University of 218

INDUSTRY
See: BUSINESS AND INDUSTRY

INFLATION
See: ECONOMICS

INFORMATION SYSTEMS
See also: COMPUTERS; LIBRARIES

Eastern Illinois University 57
Wetterlind, Peter (93)
Marquette University 105
Robinson, Richard K. (8)
Naremco Services, Inc. 119
Schiff, Robert A. (1)
Puget Sound, University of 159
Segall, M. Harvey (57)
Saint Cloud State University 168
Guimaraes, Nestor (20)
Simon Fraser University 171
Guthrie, Arthur (9)
Southwestern Louisiana, University of 174
Dominick, Wayne D. (23)
Hauser, Rex (43)
Temple University 181
Patrikas, Elaine O. (185)

INSURANCE

California, Irvine, University of 27
Bostick, Warren (25)
Duquesne University 54
National Liberty Corporation 127
Beavan, Gerald F. (1)
National Water Well Association 136
Clay, Max (8)
Saint Cloud State University 168
Swenson, Alf A. (68)
Temple University 181
Snider, H. Wayne (44), (193)

INTELLIGENCE ACTIVITIES

Auburn University 16
Duncan, J.W. (18)
Keedick Lecture Bureau, Inc. 97
Phillips, David Atlee (54)
Weinstein, Allen (69)
Leigh Bureau 102
Schorr, Daniel (29)
Marquette University 105
Brown, Richard M. (54)
Theoharis, Athan (59)
Northeastern Illinois University 142
Murphy, John J. (64)
Viewpoint Speakers Bureau 213
Boudin, Leonard (1)
Pike, Mary (9)
Pulley, Andrew (10)
Stapleton, Syd (15)
Winter, Margaret (17)

INTERIOR DECORATING

East Carolina University 56
Carroll, Diane (95)
Hurley, Pat (96)
Reid Interiors 164
Lawrence, J. (1)
Reid, Charlotte (2)
Saint Cloud State University 168
Sykora, Merle H. (69)
Virginia Polytechnic Institute and State University 216
Lamb, Fred M. (65)
Lovingood, Rebecca P. (73)
Wilson Celebrities, Lola 225
Forsythe, Anthony (15)

INTERNATIONAL AFFAIRS
See also: DEVELOPING COUNTRIES; INTERNATIONAL BUSINESS; UNITED NATIONS

American Party 6
Anderson, Tom (1)
Shackelford, Rufus (3)
Auburn University 16
Autrey, Kenneth M. (3)
California State University, Fullerton 29
Giacumakis, George J. (53), (217), (226)
Kahrs, Karl H. (56), (121)
Carnegie-Mellon University 31
Goodspeed, Charles (22)
Contemporary Forum 42
Drew University 52
Rhone, Richard S. (75)
Simon, Douglas W. (87)
Duquesne University 54
East Carolina University 56
Gulati, Umesh C. (17)
Sugg, Howard (103)
Eastern Illinois University 57
Faust, John R. (19)
Horak, Stephan M. (37)
Maurer, David J. (56)
Murad, Ahmad (61)
Schlauch, Wolfgang (75)
Hutaff, Charles 83
Fuldheim, Dorothy (6)
Intercollegiate Studies Institute, Inc. 85
Dobriansky, Lev E. (6)
Dornan, James E., Jr. (7)
Hauptmann, Jerzy (11)
Kintner, William R. (15)
Kirk, Russell (16)
Kubek, Anthony (17)
Kuehnelt-Leddihin, Erik Von (18)
Meyer, Frank S. (21)
Opitz, Edmund (25)
Pfaltzgraff, Robert L., Jr. (28)
Possony, Stefan T. (29)
Schiebel, Joseph (31)
Keedick Lecture Bureau, Inc. 97
Bagley, Worth H. (2)
Churchill, Winston (12)
Cousins, Norman (13)
Duke, Angier Biddle (18)
Melady, Thomas Patrick (42)
Moore, Robin (45)
Phillips, David Atlee (54)
Rudivoravan, Princess (58)
Zumwalt, Elmo (74)
Leigh Bureau 102
Goldberg, Arthur (12)
Hottelet, Richard C. (14)
Rumsfeld, Donald (26)
Salisbury, Harrison (27)
Lewis Program Service, Ann 103
Garth, Sheridan (2)
Marquette University 105
Manoli, Sadanand G. (20)
Oh, John K.C. (57)
Murray State University 117
Burke, Robert L. (66), (113)
Garfield, Gene J. (68)
O'Neil, Charles (102)
Umar, Farouk F. (104)
Newsweek, Inc. 139
Northeastern Illinois University 142
Husain, Asad (41)
Lopez, Jose E. (56)
Pennsylvania State University 151
Albinski, Henry S. (189)
Ameringer, Charles D. (213)
Cimbala, Stephen J. (192)
Dahir, Sabir H. (291)
Fung, Daniel Y.C. (173)
Goldman, Stuart D. (193)
LaPorte, Robert, Jr. (196)
McAree, James (197)
Oliver, Robert T. (110)
Sias, John D. (83)
Wilcher, Marshall E. (201)
Yatron, Georgine (202)
Podium Management Associates, Inc. 154
Wilson, William (27)
Puget Sound, University of 159
Kim, Jai-Kyup (36)
Queen's University 160
Bastianutti, Diego (3)
Saint Cloud State University 168
Levilain, Guy (41)
Simon Fraser University 171
Okuda, Kenji (11)
Socialist Party, USA 172
Kissell, Rick (5)
Spiro, Tom (11)
Speaker's Bureau of Philadelphia 176
Bell, Steve (7)
Brinkley, David (19)
Edwards, Douglas (35)
Success Leaders Speakers Service 180
Richardson, Gilbert P. (145)
Temple University 181
Ayaga, Odeyo O. (25), (257), (331)
Heinrichs, Waldo (265), (337)
Keto, Clement T. (267)
Okamoto, Shumpei (270), (342)
Samuelson, Norbert M. (293), (343)
Soskis, David A. (244), (345)
United States Department of Defense 193
United States Department of State 200
United States Department of State 201
United States Environmental Protection Agency 204
United States International Communications Agency 205
Viewpoint Speakers Bureau 213
Saunders, George (13)
Villanova University 214
Hahn, Jeffrey W. (53)
Logue, John J. (54)
Niosi, Jerome J. (55)
War Resisters League 217
McReynolds, David (2)
Washington, University of 218
Washington Reporters Group 220
Johnston, Oswald L. (4)
Western Washington University 223
Stannard, R.E. (20)
Vernon, Manfred C. (21)
Whittier College 224
Harrison, Howard (7)
Wilson Celebrities, Lola 225
Stevens-Allen, David J. (36)
Winter, William (41)
World Vision International 230

INTERNATIONAL BUSINESS

American Graduate School of International Management 3
Moran, Robert T. (4)
Roessler, Helmut R. (6)
Auburn University 16
Barry, Mary E. (6)
Bethlehem Steel Corporation 20
Carnegie-Mellon University 31
Burnett, Tobias W.T. (23)
Duquesne University 54
Intercollegiate Studies Institute, Inc. 85
Michl, H.E. (22)
Lecture Services, Inc. 100
Furbay, John H. (2)
Murray State University 117
Mathis, Gilbert L. (23)
New York Mercantile Exchange 138

INTERNATIONAL BUSINESS (continued)

Abrahams, Allen C. (1)
Northeastern Illinois University 142
Kokoris, James A. (51)
Pennsylvania State University 151
Gilmore, Harold L. (43)
Temple University 181
Bandera, Vladimir N. (33), (203), (332)
Bennett, Douglas (34), (334)
United States Trademark Association 209
United Telecommunications, Inc. 210
Ward, R.V. (2)
Villanova University 214
Clay, Alvin A. (2)
Lucia, Joseph L. (32)
Virginia Polytechnic Institute and State University 216
Schmidt, Wilson E. (109)
Washington, University of 218
Washington Reporters Group 220
Behr, Peter (1)

INTERVIEWING

California, Irvine, University of 27
Curiel, Ramon (2)
California State University, Fullerton 29
Sims, Melvin D. (153), (211)
Northeastern Illinois University 142
Flory, Joyce Ann (25)
Pennsylvania State University 151
Prince, Dawn Stegenga (57)

IRELAND
See: GREAT BRITAIN AND IRELAND

ISLAM

Ahmadiyya Movement in Islam, Inc. 1
Abdullah, Yahya Sharif (1)
Ahmad, Imam Masud (2)
Ahmad, Mubashir (3)
Ahmad, Rashid (4)
Barkatullah, Qazi M. (5)
Bhatti, Bashir Ahmad (6)
Hakeem, Hasan (7)
Kaleem, Imam Ata Ullah (8)
Malid, Daud Abdul (9)
Malik, Saeed Ahmad (10)
Nasir, Khalil Ahmad (11)
Saeed, Munawar (12)
Zafr, A. Muzaffar Ahmad (13)
California State University, Fullerton 29
Kaye, Alan S. (57), (218), (228), (237)
Northeastern Illinois University 142
Husain, Asad (41)
Whittier College 224
Ibrahim, Hilmi (9)

ISRAEL
See also: JUDAISM; MIDDLE EAST

Associated Film Artists 15
Francisco, Clay (2)
California, Irvine, University of 27
Lenhoff, Howard M. (42)
Dawn Bible Students Association 45
Wassmann, Felix S. (3)
Fame Limited 59
Stockdale, Bill (16)
Temple University 181
Samuelson, Norbert M. (293), (306), (343)
Viewpoint Speakers Bureau 213
Tsemel, Lea (16)

J

JAPAN
See also: FAR EAST

Auburn University 16
Hiers, Charles J. (32)
California State University, Fullerton 29
Oh, Tai K. (149)
Drew University 52
Hamilton, Neill Q. (37)
Eastern Illinois University 57
Krutza, June (44)
Wild, Rebecca Smith (95)
Marquette University 105
Pehowski, Marian (68)
Northeastern Illinois University 142
Kokoris, James A. (51)
Pennsylvania State University 151
Goldman, Stuart D. (193)
Mizusawa, Kiyoe (271)
Puget Sound, University of 159
Kim, Jai-Kyup (36)
Saint Cloud State University 168
Nunn, William H. (52)
Schwerdtfeger, Dale (66)
Southwestern Louisiana, University of 174
Rense, William C. (82)
Temple University 181
Heinrichs, Waldo (265), (337)
Okamoto, Shumpei (270), (342)
Washington, University of 218

JOURNALISM AND THE PRESS
See also: PUBLISHING

Auburn University 16
Davis, Neil O. (15)
Simms, Jack (74)
California, Irvine, University of 27
Hoy, John C. (40)
California State University, Fullerton 29
Earick, Arthur D. (52)
Hynes, Teresa M. (35), (308)
Pullen, Rick D. (40), (117)
Contemporary Forum 42
East Carolina University 56
Shires, William A. (102)
Eastern Illinois University 57
Thornburgh, Dan (88)
Hutaff, Charles 83
Fuldheim, Dorothy (6)
Leigh Bureau 102
Salisbury, Harrison (27)
ter Horst, J.F. (34)
Marquette University 105
Foran, David J. (67)
Pehowski, Marian (68)
Mid West Program Service, Inc. 112
Hackes, Peter (51)
Murray State University 117
Howard, Robert (84)
McGaughey, Robert H., III (85)
National Speakers Bureau, Inc. 135
Anderson, Jack (2)
Buckley, William F. (10)
Frederick, Pauline (20)

JOURNALISM AND THE PRESS (continued)

Northeastern Illinois University 142
  Hawley, Jane S. (36)
Pennsylvania State University 151
  Ciervo, Arthur (67)
  Curtis, Anthony R. (68)
  Hoffman, Lantz A. (74)
  Lehman, Ross B. (76)
  Sink, Claire H. (84)
  Snyder, Shirley A. (85)
  Thies, Anita H. (86)
Podium Management Associates, Inc. 154
  Jensen, Jim (13)
  Kuralt, Charles (15)
  Weston, Av (26)
Saint Cloud State University 168
  DeSanto, R. John (10)
  Eveslage, Tom (12)
  Norlem, J. Brent (51)
Speaker's Bureau of Philadelphia 176
  Bernstein, Carl (12)
  Bernstein, Ralph (13)
  Ginn, Cheryl (43)
  Levy, Maury (64)
  Woodward, Bob (123)
Success Leaders Speakers Service 180
  Murphy, John R. (128)
Temple University 181
  DeMott, John (68), (211)
  Gilpin, Nancy E. (52), (71)
Villanova University 214
  Lytel, June W. (16), (18)
Virginia Polytechnic Institute and State University 216
  Bryant, Joseph J. (13)
  Burleson, William C. (14)
  Wilkins, Keith A. (144)
Washington, University of 218
Washington Correspondents Bureau 219
Washington Reporters Group 220
Western Washington University 223
  Stannard, R.E. (20), (25)

JUDAISM

Ahmadiyya Movement in Islam, Inc. 1
  Abdullah, Yahya Sharif (1)
California State University, Fullerton 29
  Fierman, Morton C. (90), (114), (233)
  Kaye, Alan S. (163), (218)
  Namasaka, Boaz N. (6), (60), (219), (329), (337)
East Carolina University 56
  Wanderman, Henry (141)
Jews for Jesus 93
  Glaser, Mitch (1)
  Rabinowitz, Amy (2)
  Rosen, Moishe (3)
  Zaretsky, Tuvya (4)
Northeastern Illinois University 142
  Becker, Louis (3)
  Liebow, Ely (54)
Temple University 181
  Davidson, Abraham A. (80), (301)
  Ershkowitz, Herbert (262)
  First, Jonathan (96), (302)
  Lebofsky, Dennis S. (112), (304)
  Offenbacher, Elmer L. (279)
  Samuelson, Norbert M. (87), (239), (306)
Villanova University 214
  Fittipaldi, Silvio E. (80)
  Heitzmann, William Ray (4), (48)
Washington, University of 218

JUDICIAL SYSTEM
  See also: CRIMINAL JUSTICE

California State University, Fullerton 29
  Prinsky, Lorraine E. (62), (288), (346)
Intercollegiate Studies Institute, Inc. 85
  Van Den Haag, Ernest (35)
Keedick Lecture Bureau, Inc. 97
  Lignante, Bill (37)
Massachusetts Bar Association 107
Mid West Program Service, Inc. 112
  Dash, Sam (28)
Newsweek, Inc. 139
Pennsylvania State University 151
  LaGoy, Stephen P. (229)
Puget Sound, University of 159
  Berry, Keith O. (11)
Saint Cloud State University 168
  Paull, James F. (57)
Speaker's Bureau of Philadelphia 176
  Abraham, Lynn (1)
Temple University 181
  DeMott, John (211)
  Surrency, Erwin C. (274)
Villanova University 214
  Langran, Robert W. (5)
War Resisters League 217
  Douthard, William (1)
  Peck, Jim (3)
  Roodenko, Igal (4)
Washington, University 218
Washington Correspondents Bureau 219
  Weaver, Warren (11)
Wilson Celebrities, Lola 225
  Strick, Anne (37)

L

LABOR RELATIONS

Business Communication Council 23
California State University, Fullerton 29
  Pollak, June Salz (61)
Contemporary Forum 42
Duquesne University 54
Eastern Illinois University 57
  North, John T. (65)
Massachusetts Bar Association 107
Murray State University 117
  Childress, Richard R. (38)
  Noffsinger, Hugh A. (49)
National Right to Work Committee 131
  Bailey, Charles W. (1)
  Hare, Andrew (2)
  Larson, Reed (3)
  Staub, Susan (4)
Northeastern Illinois University 142
  Iregbulem, Hilary I. (42)
  Nissim-Sabat, Charles (65)
Pennsylvania State University 151
  Aurand, Harold W. (36)
  Brown, Mark L. (223)
  Kennedy, Donald E. (224)
  Labbauf, Abbas (153)
  Mortimer, Kenneth P. (8)
  Patterson, Robert A. (9)
Puget Sound, University of 159
  Sinclitico, Joseph A. (58)
Socialist Party, USA 172
  Zeidler, Frank P. (12)
  Zierten, Scott (13)
Southwestern Louisiana, University of 174
  Caradine, E. Everett (17)
Success Leaders Speakers Service 180
  Bates, Ronald (8)

LABOR RELATIONS (continued)

Stokes, McNeill (168)
Thoren, Donald Arthur (179)
Temple University 181
McCain, Roger A. (39)
Powell, Walter H. (41)
Walter, Robert L. (129)
Viewpoint Speakers Bureau 213
Foner, Philip (3)
Heisler, Ed (4)
Virginia Polytechnic Institute and State University 216
Butt, Albin T. (15)
Robinson, James W. (104)
Robinson, Jerald F. (105)
Western Washington University 223
Monat, Jon (6)

LAND USE
See also: ECOLOGY; URBAN AFFAIRS

Auburn University 16
McCord, R. Warren (54)
Duquesne University 54
Murray State University 117
Johnson, Jack B. (100), (117)
Northeastern Illinois University 142
Kiang, Harry (50)
Pennsylvania State University 151
Chan, Y. (290)
Gamble, Hays B. (225)
Hand, Irving (226)
Southwestern Louisiana, University of 174
Ehrhart, Dennis (28)
Johnson, David C. (51)
Villanova University 214
Hyson, John M. (25), (63)
Virginia Polytechnic Institute and State University 216
Dickey, John W. (31)
Washington, University of 218

LANDSCAPING

Auburn University 16
Orr, Henry P. (63)
Murray State University 117
Tackett, Amos (7), (126)
Pennsylvania State University 151
Wetzel, Herbert A. (25)
Temple University 181
Geer, Glenn B. (132), (217)
Virginia Polytechnic Institute and State University 216
Beecher, Albert S. (6)
Carter, Dean (16)
Garrett, J.C. (42)

LANGUAGE
See also: FOREIGN LANGUAGES; LINGUISTICS

California, Irvine, University of 27
Weil, Helen H. (18)
California State University, Fullerton 29
Kaye, Alan S. (203)
Kiraithe, Jacqueline M. (95), (204), (297)
Lynn, Joanne L. (29), (97)
Sadovszky, Otto J. (209), (298)
Schneider, Clarence E. (210)
Sims, Melvin D. (153), (211)
Drew University 52
Chapman, Robert L. (13)
East Carolina University 56
Lewis, Frederick C. (53)
Wright, James R. (65)
Eastern Illinois University 57
Leathers, Ronald (48)
Intercollegiate Studies Institute, Inc. 85
Martin, William Oliver (20)
Lewis Program Service, Ann 103
Myers, Rowland M. (4)
Marquette University 105
Mitchell, Robin C. (46)
Maryland, University of 106
Murray State University 117
Gantt, Vernon W. (115)
Keller, Howard H. (87)
Loberger, Gordon J. (61)
Northeastern Illinois University 142
Beaver, Joseph C. (2)
Pennsylvania State University 151
Carr, Marion M. Odell (65)
Simboli, David R. (239)
Puget Sound, University of 159
Hodges, Richard E. (29)
Saint Cloud State University 168
Norlem, J. Brent (51)
Otto, Don H. (53)
Simon Fraser University 171
DeArmond, Richard (46)
Kaneen, Brian D. (50)
Temple University 181
Goehl, Henry (218), (314)
LaVallee-Williams, Marthe (59), (315)
Lebofsky, Dennis S. (317)
Sheldon, Harry J. (319)

LASERS

California State University, Fullerton 29
Johnson, Fred M. (186), (272)
Drew University 52
Siebert, Donald R. (86)
East Carolina University 56
Sayetta, Tom C. (130)
Marquette University 105
Ishii, Thomas K. (119)
Ohio Bell Telephone Company 144
Pennsylvania State University 151
Stein, Jack (147)
Simon Fraser University 171
Palmer, Leigh Hunt (40)
Washington, University of 218
Western Electric Company 222

LATIN AMERICA

California, Irvine, University of 27
Wildman, Helen D. (47)
Drew University 52
DeVeer, Robert (24)
Fuentes, Carlos (30)
Jennings, Peter R. (41)
East Carolina University 56
Leahy, Edward P. (120)
Fame Limited 59
Madsen, Bill (9)
Pederson, Harry (12)
Roberts, John (14)
Walker, Theodore J. (18)
Forrest, Martin A. 69
Walker, Theodore (14)
Keedick Lecture Bureau, Inc. 97
Phillips, David Atlee (54)
Marquette University 105
Brown, Richard M. (54)
Memphis State University 110
Roberts, John (12)
Murray State University 117
O'Neil, Charles (102)
Rose, Joseph L. (103)
Venza, J. Riley (105)
National Speakers Bureau, Inc. 135
Geyer, Georgie Ann (22)

LATIN AMERICA (continued)

Northeastern Illinois University 142
Gonzalez, Rodrigo C. (34)
Lopez, Jose E. (56)
Pedroso, Angelina (68)
Pennsylvania State University 151
Ameringer, Charles D. (213)
Garcia, Ana M. (233)
Gonzalez-Cruz, Luis F. (195)
Kujundzic, Zeljko (27)
LaPorte, Robert, Jr. (196)
Perry, William L. (299)
Sias, John D. (83)
Yatron, Georgine (202)
Saint Cloud State University 168
Hellwig, David J. (25)
Levilain, Guy (41)
Temple University 181
Schmidt, Arthur (344)
Virginia Polytechnic Institute and State University 216
Webb, Ryland E. (140)
Washington, University of 218
Western Washington University 223
Hiller, Harley E. (17)

LAW
See also: CRIMINAL JUSTICE; JUDICIAL SYSTEM

American Graduate School of International Management 3
Valdivieso, Jorge H. (7)
Auburn University 16
Fortenberry, Charles N. (20)
Vachon, Reginald I. (80)
Vallarino, Lidia M. (81)
California, Irvine, University of 27
DiMento, Joseph F. (3)
California State University, Fullerton 29
Apke, Thomas M. (191)
Namasaka, Boaz N. (147), (194), (337)
Sutton, Imre (74), (195)
Contemporary Forum 42
Drew University 52
Hardin, Paul (38)
Duquesne University 54
East Carolina University 56
Webber, Edith (132)
Eastern Illinois University 57
Brooks, Benjamin L. (5)
Hollister, Charles A. (36)
Matzner, Gerhard C. (55)
Florida Association of Realtors 65
Bermingham, Thomas J. (5)
Falbey, J. Wayne (16)
German, Jack (22)
Jones, Ernest A. (33)
Lassetter, Maggie S. (36)
Pickens, Phillip (51)
Intercollegiate Studies Institute, Inc. 85
Petro, Sylvester (27)
Van Den Haag, Ernest (35)
Zoll, Donald A. (40)
Marquette University 105
Klitzke, Ramon A. (56)
Laczniak, Gene R. (6)
Maryland, University of 106
Massachusetts Bar Association 107
Mid West Program Service, Inc. 112
Dash, Sam (28)
Morality in Media, Inc. 116
Chernus, Jack (1)
Douglas, John (2)
Gavrin, Irving (3)
Hill, Morton A. (4)
Murphy, Paul (5)
Shapiro, Stephen E. (6)
Volatis, Constantine (7)
Murray State University 117
Matarazzo, S.M. (46)
National Water Well Association 136
Sturtz, Laurence E. (9)
Northeastern Illinois University 142
Pastors, Charles R. (67)
Watson, Ulestine (95)
Pennsylvania State University 152
Grode, John N. (228)
LaGoy, Stephen P. (229)
Podium Management Associates, Inc. 154
Wilson, William (27)
Puget Sound, University of 159
Beaver, James E. (8)
Frankel, Sheldon S. (22)
Hoffman, Barbara (30)
Maxwell, Keith A. (41)
Meyers, Bruce F. (42)
Nock, George R. (45)
Oltman, William (46)
Sinclitico, Joseph A. (58)
Strait, John A. (63)
Saint Cloud State University 168
DeSanto, R. John (10)
Grunerud, James J. (19)
Highsmith, James M. (27)
Paull, James F. (57)
Southwestern Louisiana, University of 174
Ehrhart, Dennis (28)
Speaker's Bureau of Philadelphia 176
Lord, Joseph (68)
Stern, Carl (111)
Success Leaders Speakers Service 180
Stokes, McNeill (168)
Temple University 181
Sloviter, Dolores Korman (192), (241), (271), (312)
Strazzella, James A. (273)
Surrency, Erwin C. (274)
Williams, Walter E. (46), (255)
United States Environmental Protection Agency 204
Villanova University 214
Betz, Joseph (83)
Hyson, John M. (25), (63)
Langran, Robert W. (5)
Virginia Polytechnic Institute and State University 216
Flowers, William L., Jr. (37)
Washington, University of 218
Western Washington University 223
Vernon, Manfred C. (16)
Women's Classical Caucus 227
More, Judith de Luce (32)
Youth Liberation Press, Inc. 231
Autin, Diana (2)

LEADERSHIP

Business Communication Council 23
California State University, Fullerton 29
Gala, Basil E. (136)
East Carolina University 56
Grossnickle, William F. (134)
Prewett, Clinton R. (136)
Rees, Jim (20)
Leigh Bureau 102
Sidey, Hugh (30)
Marquette University 105
Dotson, Virginia (77)
Pelt, Therese (81)
Peterson, Margi (82)
Maryland, University of 106
Mid West Program Service, Inc. 112
Hurst, Allan (68)
Tritt, Francis (124)
True, Herb (125)
Murray State University 117
Biggs, James W. (65), (112)
Matarazzo, S.M. (46)

LEADERSHIP (continued)

National Speakers Bureau, Inc. 135
Bergsten, Fred (6)
Pennsylvania State University 151
Lewis, Blake D., Jr. (46)
Saint Cloud State University 168
Grachek, Arthur F. (17)
Success Leaders Speakers Service 180
Woerpel, Dwayne R. (195)
Union Electric Speakers Forum 189
Villanova University 214
Niosi, Jerome J. (94)
Virginia Polytechnic Institute and State University 216
Clouse, James P. (22)
Dean, James W. (29)
Hill, David E. (52)

LIBRARIES
See also: INFORMATION SYSTEMS

California State University, Fullerton 29
Fasheh, Issa I. (25), (196), (225)
Gilman, Richard (26), (92), (137)
Lynn, Joanne L. (197), (205)
Qureshi, Naimuddin (198)
Truesdell, William D. (199), (212)
Carnegie-Mellon University 31
McCredie, John W. (19)
Data Courier, Inc. 44
Auld, Dennis (1)
Payne, Gregory (2)
Susa, Jo (3)
Trubkin, Loene (4)
Drew University 52
Jones, Arthur (43)
Eastern Illinois University 57
Waddell, Leyla Peck (92)
Institute for Scientific Information 84
Hoffman, Diane (1)
National Micrographics Association 128
Northeastern Illinois University 142
Black, Sophie K. (7)
George, Melvin R. (29)
Skvarla, Melvyn A. (79)
Pennsylvania State University 151
Small, Sally S. (59)
Puget Sound, University of 159
Goman, LaVerne (23)
Southwestern Louisiana, University of 174
Conrad, Glenn R. (19)
Mouton, Jean (77)
Temple University 181
Fork, Donald J. (97)
Virginia Polytechnic Institute and State University 216
Hubbard, Hazel (56)
Washington, University of 218

LINGUISTICS
See also: LANGUAGE

California State University, Fullerton 29
Kaye, Alan S. (203), (237)
East Carolina University 56
Wright, James R. (65)
Murray State University 117
Keller, Howard H. (87)
Northeastern Illinois University 142
Bevington, Gary (6)
Pennsylvania State University 151
Hopper, Paul T. (235)
Simon Fraser University 171
DeArmond, Richard (46)
Women's Classical Caucus 227
Villeneuve, Winnie Frohn (51)

LITERATURE
See also: CHILDREN'S LITERATURE; FOLKLORE; POETRY; SCIENCE FICTION

Auburn University 16
Hitchcock, Walter B., Jr. (34)
California, Irvine, University of 27
Weil, Helen H. (18)
California State University, Fullerton 29
Cox, Miriam S. (200)
Jaskowski, Helen M. (202), (336)
Lynn, Joanne L. (205)
Pollak, June Salz (207), (243)
Schneider, Clarence E. (210)
Tumas, Elena V. (127), (213), (290)
Contemporary Forum 42
Drew University 52
Becker, Lucille F. (4)
Bicknell, John W. (7)
Coombs, Llona C. (17)
Jones, Arthur (43)
Lawler, Edwina G. (46)
Mulder, John (58)
Occhiogrosso, Frank V. (61)
Ollman, Nadine (64)
Rice, Charles L. (76)
Skaggs, Calvin L. (88)
Steiner, Joan Elizabeth (90)
Duquesne University 54
East Carolina University 56
Aronson, Nicole (60)
Sanders, F. David (36)
Fulton Inc., Richard 71
Intercollegiate Studies Institute, Inc. 85
Stanlis, Peter J. (32)
Vivas, Eliseo (36)
Keedick Lecture Bureau, Inc. 97
Cairney, John (8)
Marquette University 105
Asp, Carolyn (16), (123)
Mitchell, Robin C. (22)
Siegchrist, Mark (25)
Maryland, University of 106
Murray State University 117
Forrester, Kent (88)
Lorrah, Jean (89)
Miller, Michael G. (90)
Valentine, Robert (91)
Northeastern Illinois University 142
Feldman, Reynold (22)
Frederick, Duke (27)
Liebow, Ely (54)
Parker, Bettye J. (66)
Robinson, Edward A. (74)
Zegger, Robert Elie (98)
Pennsylvania State University 151
Adams, James D. (231)
Freed, John E. (232)
Garcia, Ana M. (233)
Graham, Robert J. (234)
Hopper, Paul T. (235)
Hovanec, Evelyn (236)
Lynch, Catherine M. (298)
Meserole, Harrison T. (237)
Price, R. Alan (238)
Simmons, Michael K. (240)
Suhre, Laurence R. (243)
Walden, Daniel (245)
Weintraub, Stanley (246)
Puget Sound, University of 159
Corkrum, Ralph E. (19)
Goman, LaVerne (23)
Hansen, Tim (24)
Martin, Jacquie (40)
Wagner, Esther (65)
Saint Cloud State University 168
Levilain, Guy (41)

LITERATURE (continued)

Simon Fraser University 171
Wheatley, Jon (55)
Southwestern Louisiana, University of 174
Fackler, Herbert V. (29)
Temple University 181
Cormier, Raymond J. (138)
Hayes, John P. (140)
Morse, J. Mitchell (143)
Roos, Anne D. (144)
Shachter, Jaqueline (145)
Stivers, Eugene H. (272)
Trautmann, Fredrick (147)
Villanova University 214
Schwarz, John H. (47)
Virginia Polytechnic Institute and State University 216
Cheney, Anne (19)
Distler, P.A. (32)
Owen, James J. (89)
Siemoneit, Martin A. (112)
Snipes, Wilson (117)
Ulloa, Justo C. (135)
Washington, University of 218
Western Washington University 223
Buckland, Roscoe L. (3)
Wilson Celebrities, Lola 225
Davis, Bruce (11)
Workman, Donna (42)
Wright, Sean (43)
Women's Classical Caucus 227
Bacon, Helen H. (1)
Broege, Valerie (4)
Clayman, Dee Lesser (7)
Culham-Ertman, Phyllis (8)
Drake, Gertrude (11)
Fisher, Elizabeth A. (12)
Gold, Barbara K. (15)
Gordon, Diane R. (16)
Greengard, Carola (17)
Hallett, Judith P. (18)
Katz, Phyllis B. (21)
Killian, Barbara E. (23)
King, Joy K. (24)
Kohler, Frances Coulborn (25)
Koloski-Ostrow, Ann Olga (26)
Loomis, Julia W. (29)
More, Judith de Luce (32)
Nussbaum, Martha C. (34)
Orlandi, Mary Kay Gamel (35)
Robert, Jennifer (38)
Rossi, Mary Ann (39)
Roth, Catharine P. (40)
Rubin, Nancy F. (41)
Shelton, Jo-Ann (42)
Snyder, Jane M. (43)
Sowa, Cora Angier (44)
Thomas, Ruth S. (47)
Villeneuve, Winnie Frohn (51)
Wiggers, Nancy (54)

LOCAL HISTORY

Auburn University 16
Hall, David M. (26)
McMillan, Malcolm C. (55)
California State University, Fullerton 29
Hansen, Arthur A. (139), (160), (333)
Jones, C. Eugene (28), (143)
Carnegie-Mellon University 31
Demarest, David (31)
Tarr, Joel A. (32)
East Carolina University 56
Eller, Frank W. (26)
Hooks, Edgar (28)
Lennon, Donald R. (30)
McGuire, Martin (31)
Nischan, Bodo (32)
O'Conner, Michael P. (33)
Paschal, Herbert (34)
Price, Charles L. (35)
Sanders, F. David (36)
Steele, Ralph (37)
Stephenson, Richard A. (38)
Stevens, Charles E. (39)
Webber, Edith (40)
Williams, Thomas A. (41)
Murray State University 117
Freeman, William E. (114)
Hammock, James W., Jr. (69)
Kline, James M. (70)
Pace, Don M. (73)
Strohecker, Edwin C. (75)
Northeastern Illinois University 142
Beverly, Sherman, Jr. (5)
Skvarla, Melvyn A. (79)
Pennsylvania State University 151
Smith, Robert L. (14)
Saint Cloud State University 168
Partch, Max (56)
Southwestern Louisiana, University of 174
Brasseaux, Carl A. (14)
Conrad, Glenn R. (19)
Gill, Donald A. (35)
Goyert, Philip R., Jr. (37)
Green, Joe L. (38)
Hamsa, Charles F. (40)
Heard, J. Norman (44)
Virginia Polytechnic Institute and State University 216
Goldfield, David R. (43)

M

MAGIC

Eastern Illinois University 57
Murray, Louise (62)
Mixter Artist Management 114
Dacri, Steve (1)
Saint Cloud State University 168
Mertens, Gerald C. (47)
Weiner Programs, Inc., Irv 221
Weiner, Irv (1)

MANAGEMENT

See also: LEADERSHIP; MEETING MANAGEMENT; MOTIVATION; OFFICE MANAGEMENT; PERSONNEL ADMINISTRATION; PUBLIC ADMINISTRATION; SCHOOL ADMINISTRATION

Auburn University 16
White, Louis Edward (88)
Business Communication Council 23
California, Irvine, University of 27
Bernstein, Paul (1)
Kloke, Eloise E. (5)
California State University, Fullerton 29
Oh, Tai K. (149)
Winterfelt, Rolf (83)
Worth, Guthrie (45), (84), (112)
Drew University 52
McDonald, W. Scott, Jr. (51)
Smith, Ralph B. (89)
Duquesne University 54
East Carolina University 56
Prewett, Clinton R. (136)
Eastern Illinois University 57
Coleman, Wayne (11)
Fulton Inc., Richard 71
Leigh Bureau 102
Lavenson, James (17)
Marquette University 105
Bakr, Mamdouh (116)
Kaimann, Richard A. (5)
Schreier, James W. (9)
Tracy, William T. (15)
Maryland, University of 106

MANAGEMENT (continued)

Mid West Program Service, Inc. 112
Christianson, J.N. (22)
Cimberg, Alan (23)
Schmidt, David L. (114)
Murray State University 117
Kirk, Roy V. (21)
Shown, Vernon E. (120)
Wells, Jane Freeman (28)
Naremco Services, Inc. 119
Schiff, Robert A. (1)
National Association of Suggestion Systems 123
National Speakers Bureau, Inc. 135
Batten, Joe (5)
Cribbin, James J. (13)
Herman, Fred (29)
Johnson, Earl (33)
Vance, Mike (58)
National Water Well Association 136
Alcorn, Pat B. (7)
Butcher, Kathy (1)
McLaughlin, Wayne (20)
Tosi, Donald (10)
Northeastern Illinois University 142
Renas, Stanley R. (71)
Pennsylvania State University 151
Calamidas, Alec (38)
DeWald, Samuel C. (39)
Elias, Edward M. (140)
Frey, John C. (254)
Gilmore, Harold L. (43)
Lewis, Blake D., Jr. (46)
Marlow, H. LeRoy (287)
Mathews, H. Lee (48)
O'Brien, Harold J. (81)
Puget Sound, University of 159
Bloom, Mitchell (13)
Segall, M. Harvey (57)
Waldo, Robert (66)
Rainier National Bank 162
Saint Cloud State University 168
Madsen, Russell D. (44)
Reha, Rose K. (62)
Swenson, Alf A. (68)
Simon Fraser University 171
Devenyl, Denes (7)
Guthrie, Arthur (9)
Southwestern Louisiana, University of 174
Hauser, Rex (43)
Speakers Unlimited 177
Success Leaders Speakers Service 180
Carter, C.L. (24)
Cooper, Lloyd G. (36)
Corrigan, John D. (37)
Croskery, Robert W. (38)
Fierst, Dorothy K. (52)
Gariepy, Dick (61)
Haerr, Alvin R. (69)
Hansen, Mark Victor (74)
Harris, Philip R. (77)
Hays, Robert (80)
Hudson, Leonard C. (85)
Hutson, Don (87)
Jordan, DuPree, Jr. (95)
Lancaster, William W. (102)
Lee, John W. (105)
Letterese, Peter D. (106)
McCarty, John J. (112)
McMurry, Robert N. (114)
MacRury, King (116)
Masquelier, Roger (119)
Montgomery, Robert L. (123)
Noland, Andrew J. (130)
Norman, Thom (132)
Pickus, Morris I. (136)
Sims, E. Ralph (158)
Stone, John W. (169)
Strickland, A.G. (171)
Swab, James L. (174)
Thoren, Donald Arthur (179)
Tritt, Frances (181)
Ward, David L. (188)
Weber, Robert D. (189)
Wellborn, Charles T. (190)
White, Sommers H. (191)
Woodruff, Bill (197)
Temple University 181
Gross, Jack L. (35), (219)
Powell, Walter H. (41)
Wilson, Samuel M. (47)
Union Electric Speakers Forum 189
Villanova University 214
Losoncy, Thomas A. (14)
Virginia Polytechnic Institute and State University 216
Andrew, Loyd D. (2)
Spengler, Fred L. (120)
Sullins, W. Robert (125)
Washington, University of 218
Whittier College 224
Beukema, Phil (2)

MANUFACTURING
See: BUSINESS AND INDUSTRY

MARINE LIFE

California State University, Fullerton 29
Hanover, Eric S. (270), (302)
Horn, Michael H. (71), (140), (271)
Drew University 52
Bush, Louise F. (12)
Pollock, Leland Wells (69)
Eastern Illinois University 57
Durham, Leonard (16)
Forrest, Martin A. 69
Mundus, Frank (10)
Payne, Roger (12)
Mid West Program Service, Inc. 112
Cousteau, Jean-Michel (26)
Pennsylvania State University 151
Hillson, C.J. (152)
Puget Sound, University of 159
Karlstrom, Ernest L. (34)
Simon Fraser University 171
Schwarz, Abby (42)
Southwestern Louisiana, University of 174
Beckman, William C. (4)
Garcia, Emilio (30)
Keiser, Edmund D., Jr. (53)
Temple University 181
Miller, Richard L. (18), (62)
Tuna Research Foundation, Inc. 187
Kimmick, Anthony J. (2)
Virginia Polytechnic Institute and State University 216
Cross, Gerald H. (26)
Flick, George J. (36)
Washington, University of 218

MARITIME

American Graduate School of International Management 3
Valdivieso, Jorge H. (7)
East Carolina University 56
Debnath, Lokenath (68)
Knight, Clifford B. (29)
Stephenson, Richard A. (38)
Eastern Illinois University 57
Faust, John R. (19)
Keedick Lecture Bureau, Inc. 97
Lindbergh, Jon Morrow (38)
Northeastern Illinois University 142
Charlier, Roger H. (15)
Shabica, Charles W. (77)
Pennsylvania State University 151
Stowe, Wilmer C. (159)

MARTIME (continued)

Temple University 181
Humphreys, Donald (133)
United States Department of Transportation 203
Villanova University 214
Heitzmann, William Ray (57), (69)
Logue, John J. (27)
Virginia Polytechnic Institute and State University 216
Schetz, Joseph A. (108)
Washington, University of 218
Western Washington University 223
Vernon, Manfred C. (16)
Wilson Celebrities, Lola 225
Carpenter, Scott (7)

MARKETING

Business Communication Council 23
California State University, Fullerton 29
Worth, Guthrie (84), (112)
Eastern Illinois University 57
Egloff, William F. (18)
First Federal of Broward 63
Georgia Federal Savings and Loan Association 72
Leigh Bureau 102
Peterson, Esther (23)
Marquette University 105
Brownlee, Ralph E. (4)
Robinson, Richard K. (8)
Murray State University 117
Seale, William B. (25)
National Liberty Corporation 127
Beavan, Gerald F. (1)
National Premium Sales Executives, Inc. 130
Northeastern Illinois University 142
Bohlin, Jill K. (8)
Renas, Stanley R. (71)
Pabst Brewing Company 145
Allerup, N.P. (1)
Ratcheson, R.J. (2)
Winograd, A.J. (3)
Package Designers Council 147
Reynolds Tobacco Company, R.J. 165
Speaker's Bureau of Philadelphia 176
Reid, Orien (92)
Success Leaders Speakers Service 180
Byrd, Lew H. (21)
Flarsheim, Henry (53)
Johnson, Bill (91)
Koschel, Ed S. (101)
Sheehan, Don (156)
Shi, J.E.B. (157)
Sollo, Eugene D. (161)
Storey, Rolland (170)
Temple University 181
Houston, Franklin S. (36)
United States Trademark Association 209
Villanova University 214
Butkep, Adolph S. (23)
Wilson Celebrities, Lola 225
Fagan, William (13)

MARRIAGE

See: FAMILY RELATIONS

MATHEMATICS

See also: STATISTICS

California, Irvine, University of 27
Tucker, Howard G. (17)
California State University, Fullerton 29
Klassen, Vuryl J. (214)
Carnegie-Mellon University 31
Coleman, Bernard D. (21)
Drew University 52
Chillak, Edward W. (14)
Greenspan, Bernard (35)
East Carolina University 56
Debnath, Lokenath (106), (125)
Gross, Tennala A. (126)
Mueller-Roemer, Peter (129)
Sayetta, Tom C. (130)
Maryland, University of 106
Murray State University 117
Elder, Harvey L. (92)
Wilson, Jack D. (93)
Northeastern Illinois University 142
Reichhardt, Richard (70)
Singleton, Gregory H. (78)
Pennsylvania State University 151
Berman, Harry J. (17)
Ford, Nicholas S. (247)
Harkness, William L. (262)
Larson, Roland E. (250)
Murty, Vedula N. (251)
Salvia, Anthony A. (252)
Swetz, Frank (121)
Simon Fraser University 171
Harrop, Ronald (35)
Southwestern Louisiana, University of 174
McKnight, Conrad (67)
Temple University 181
Averbach, Bonnie (1), (148)
Grosswald, Emil (149)
Jensen, Linda R. (105), (150)
Kotz, Samuel (4), (151)
Paalborg, Jane E. (117), (152)
Schild, Albert (43), (153)
Slook, Thomas H. (154)
Villanova University 214
Beck, Robert E. (64)
Washington, University of 218

MEDIA

See also: JOURNALISM AND THE PRESS; PROPAGANDA; RADIO; TELEVISION

California, Irvine, University of 27
Hoy, John C. (40)
California State University, Fullerton 29
Atkin, Kenward L. (33)
Hynes, Teresa M. (35), (308)
Johnson, Raynolds (36), (55), (115)
Mewett, Jack H. (310)
Pullen, Rick D. (40), (117)
Smythe, Ted C. (42), (67), (119), (312)
Zeltzer, Allen M. (46)
Contemporary Forum 42
East Carolina University 56
Shires, William A. (102)
Eastern Illinois University 57
Heumann, Joseph (32)
Leigh Bureau 102
Fadiman, Clifton (11)
Marquette University 105
Allen, Craig G. (65)
Arnold, James W. (66)
Foran, David J. (67)
Pehowski, Marian (68)
Tiedge, James T. (69)
Mid West Program Service, Inc. 112
Agronsky, Martin (1)
Anderson, Jack (2)
Duke, Paul (36)
Gowdy, Curt (44)
Hackes, Peter (51)
Harvey, Paul (58)
Kaplow, Herb (75)

MEDIA (continued)

Levine, Irving R. (81)
Mackin, Catherine (87)
Mollenhoff, Clark (91)
Pappas, Ike (98)
Spear, Joe (116)
Thimmesch, Nick (122)
Valeriani, Richard (127)
Whitten, Les (131)
Miller Agency, Gilbert 113
Gowdy, Curt (1)
Morality in Media, Inc. 116
Chernus, Jack (1)
Douglas, John (2)
Gavrin, Irving (3)
Hill, Morton A. (4)
Murphy, Paul (5)
Shapiro, Stephen E. (6)
Volatis, Constantine (7)
Murray State University 117
Denbow, Carl J. (83)
Howard, Robert (84)
McGaughey, Robert H., III (85)
Mofield, William Ray (86), (129)
National Speakers Bureau, Inc. 135
Barnes, Gordon (4)
Brinkley, David (8)
Buckley, William F. (10)
Chancellor, John (12)
Downs, Hugh (17)
Edwards, Douglas (18)
Frederick, Pauline (20)
Harris, Sidney J. (26)
Harvey, Paul (27)
Kaplow, Herb (35)
Kiker, Douglas (36)
Kuralt, Charles (38)
Lower, Elmer W. (41)
Mackin, Catherine (43)
Murphy, George (45)
Nightingale, Earl (47)
O'Connor, Len (48)
Reynolds, Frank (52)
Northeastern Illinois University 142
Flory, Joyce Ann (25)
Walker, Robert (92)
Pennsylvania State University 151
Abler, Ronald (183)
Curtis, Anthony R. (68)
Felack, Michael (70)
Haskin, Lynn Martin (72)
Lehew, Harry D. (75)
Mansuy, Frank (77)
Neuhaus, Cable (80)
Thies, Anita H. (86)
Podium Management Associates, Inc. 154
Jensen, Jim (13)
Kuralt, Charles (15)
Weston, Av (26)
Saint Cloud State University 168
DeSanto, R. John (10)
Montgomery, Terry (50)
Pehler, Jim (59)
Simon Fraser University 171
Wilden, Anthony (56)
Speaker's Bureau of Philadelphia 176
Anderson, Jack (4)
Ashburn, Richie (5)
Bernstein, Carl (12)
Bernstein, Ralph (13)
Betzendahl, Diane (14)
Bradley, Bob (17)
Brenner, Glenn (18)
Brinkley, David (19)
Crim, Mort (28)
David, Gunter (30)
DeWolf, Rose (32)
Fields, Larry (39)
Ford, Frank (41)
Ginn, Cheryl (43)
Helsel, Jack (47)
Henderson, Don (48)
Jones, Jack (55)
Leitner, Ted (63)
Levy, Steve (65)
Lewis, Claude (66)
Mallow, Mike (72)
Marciarose (73)
Meltzer, Bernard (78)
Packard, George (83)
Penza, Ralph (86)
Poindexter, Malcolm (88)
Quinn, Matt (90)
Rather, Dan (91)
Saline, Carol (96)
Savitch, Jessica (98)
Schlesinger, Arthur (100)
Schnall, Maxine (101)
Sheeran, Dick (107)
Spetgang, Tillie (110)
Webber, Bill (119)
Woodward, Bob (123)
Wydra, John (124)
Success Leaders Speakers Service 180
Bauer, Joe (12)
Flint, Cort R. (54)
Nettleton, Herbert (129)
Temple University 181
Brodey, Jean L. (49), (67)
DeMott, John (68), (211)
United States International Communications Agency 205
United Telecommunications, Inc. 210
Virginia Polytechnic Institute and State University 216
Wilkins, Keith A. (144)
Washington, University of 218
Washington Correspondents Bureau 219
Washington Reporters Group 220

MEDICAL SCIENCE
See also: DENTISTRY; DISEASES AND BODY DISORDERS; HEALTH PROFESSIONS; VETERINARY MEDICINE

Auburn University 16
Bailey, Wilford S. (4)
Tanja, Jon J. (77)
California, Irvine, University of 27
Goldstein, Arthur I. (28)
Kent, Deryck R. (30)
Prakash, Ravi (34)
California State University, Fullerton 29
Gala, Basil E. (173)
Johnson, Fred M. (186)
Chemetron Corporation 34
Duquesne University 54
East Carolina University 56
Fulghum, Robert S. (78)
Hamilton, George (79)
Lee Foundation Inc., Fran 101
Lee, Fran (1)
Marquette University 105
Dhuru, Virendra B. (28)
Pruhs, Ronald (30)
Semrad, Alice (96)
Medtronic, Inc. 109
Newsweek, Inc. 139
Northeastern Illinois University 142
Kamau, Lucy J. (48)
Pizzi, William J. (69)
Pennsylvania State University 151
Ferguson, Frederick G. (206)
Hunt, Edward E., Jr. (208)
Richman, Irwin (257)
Todd, Paul (211)
Queen's University 160
Doris, Peter (9)
Lywood, Denis (12)
Saint Cloud State University 168
Hortis, Theophanis (29)

MEDICAL SCIENCE (continued)

Simon Fraser University 171
Rockerble, R.A. (41)
Wienberg, Harold (43)
Temple University 181
Baran, Ernest (155)
Batra, Gopal K. (205)
Cote, Mary Louise (158)
Fielding, Allen Fred (161)
Fugaro, Anthony (162)
Hoenig, Eugene M. (169)
Kendall, A. Richard (171)
Kenepp, Nancy (172)
Leifer, Calvin (175)
McElligott, James G. (179)
Mayer, Nathaniel (180)
Miller, Arthur S. (182)
Mohnac, Alex M. (183)
Patrikas, Elaine O. (235)
Popovtzer, Mordecai M. (188)
Price, Glenda D. (189)
Reichle, F.A. (190)
Rosenberg, Bonita S. (191)
Spagna, Paschal M. (194)
Turco, Salvatore (197)
Villagana, Theodore (198)
Virginia Polytechnic Institute and State University 216
Talbot, Richard B. (127)
Washington, University of 218

MEDIEVAL WORLD

California, Irvine, University of 27
Frank, Richard (10)
Carnegie-Mellon University 31
Toker, Franklin (28)
Duquesne University 54
East Carolina University 56
Benjamin, Lloyd (9)
Pennsylvania State University 151
Frankforter, A. Daniel (215)
Women's Classical Caucus 227
Fisher, Elizabeth A. (12)
Lanham, Carol D. (27)

MEDITATION

Americans United 12
Duquesne University 54
Meditation Institute 108
Everix, Pamela (1)
Schwartz, William F. (2)
Speaker's Bureau of Philadelphia 176
Muskie, Edmund (81)

MEETING MANAGEMENT

East Carolina University 56
Rees, Jim (20)
Eastern Illinois University 57
Lindberg, Phillip (51)
Marquette University 105
Dotson, Virginia (77)
Olsen, Roger A. (79)
Siettmann, James P. (85)
Staudacher, Joseph M. (13)
Murray State University 117
Jacks, Lloyd P. (128)
National Water Well Association 136
Butcher, Kathy (1)
Pennsylvania State University 151
Folwell, William H., III (71)
Virginia Polytechnic Institute and State University 216
Crunkilton, John R. (28)

MEMORY

Marquette University 105
Staudacher, Joseph M. (13)
Simon Fraser University 171
Franklin, Perry L. (16)
Success Leaders Speakers Service 180
Clennan, William A. (30)
Lorayne, Harry (109)
Stewart, Donald (164)

MENTAL HEALTH
See also: PSYCHOLOGY

Auburn University 16
Vallarino, Lidia M. (81)
California, Irvine, University of 27
Novaco, R.W. (44)
Contemporary Forum 42
Eastern Illinois University 57
Hillner, William M. (34)
Ladd, Clay (45)
Marquette University 105
McCall, Raymond J. (100)
McDonald, Rita T. (94)
Schlientz, Margaret Anne (95)
Topetzes, Nick J. (98)
Miller Agency, Gilbert 113
Piersall, Jimmy (2)
Murray State University 117
Holcomb, Thomas F. (108)
Northeastern Illinois University 142
Jackson, Charles J. (44)
Jacobs, Claire M. (45)
Temple University 181
Smith, Rita (31), (294)
Villanova University 214
Gallagher, Bernard J. (65), (86)
Virginia Polytechnic Institute and State University 216
Payne, Alfred C. (94)
Tessnear, Marshall D. (132)

METEOROLOGY

California State University, Fullerton 29
Ryan, John A. (152), (276)
National Speakers Bureau, Inc. 135
Barnes, Gordon (4)
Pennsylvania State University 151
Fraser, Alistair B. (303)
Panofsky, H. (155)
Speaker's Bureau of Philadelphia 176
Kuster, Bill (58)
Virginia Polytechnic Institute and State University 216
Johnson, Thomas W. (61)
Wilkins, Keith A. (144)
Western Washington University 223
Critchfield, Howard J. (5)

METRIC SYSTEM

Eastern Illinois University 57
Coleman, Wayne (11)
Coon, Lewis H. (12)
Rogers, Donald L. (70)
Strader, Gayle Gilbert (84)
Marquette University 105
Bakr, Mamdouh (116)
Zupko, Ronald E. (122)
Murray State University 117
Elder, Harvey L. (92)
Schanbacker, Eugene M. (82)
National Water Well Association 136
May, Judy (28)

METRIC SYSTEM (continued)

Northeastern Illinois University 142
 Flener, Frederick O. (24)
 Fowler, Mary Ann (26)
Pennsylvania State University 151
 Glaser, Anton (248)
 Weed, Merwin L. (149)
Saint Cloud State University 168
 Kennedy, Keith A. (35)
Simon Fraser University 171
 Guthrie, Arthur (9)
Southwestern Louisiana, University of 174
 Oliver, James R. (79)
Virginia Polytechnic Institute and State University 216
 Webb, Anita H. (139)
Western Electric Company 222

MEXICAN-AMERICAN
 See: CHICANOS

MIDDLE EAST
 See also: ISRAEL

American Graduate School of International Management 3
 Moran, Robert T. (4)
 Peters, Issa (5)
Associated Film Artists 15
 Borden, Chris (1)
California State University, Fullerton 29
 Brown, Giles T. (48), (215), (228)
 Fasheh, Issa I. (196), (216), (225), (315)
 Giacumakis, George J. (179), (217), (226), (269)
 Kaye, Alan S. (163), (218), (228), (319)
 Weightman, Barbara A. (22), (167), (325)
Douglas Management 51
 Douglas, Neil (1)
Drew University 52
 Berke, Jacqueline (6)
 Bull, Vivian A. (11)
 Cowell, David A. (20)
Duquesne University 54
East Carolina University 56
 Birchard, Ralph E. (15)
 McGuire, Martin E. (6)
 Smith, Vernon (124)
Eastern Illinois University 57
 Murad, Ahmad (61)
 Waddell, Leyla Peck (92)
Fame Limited 59
 Butler, Willis (3)
 Stockdale, Bill (16)
 Taylor, Charles Forbes (17)
Fulton Inc., Richard 71
Intercollegiate Studies Institute, Inc. 85
 Possony, Stefan T. (29)
 Schiebel, Joseph (31)
Keedick Lecture Bureau, Inc. 97
 Moore, Robin (45)
Lecture Services, Inc. 100
 Furbay, John H. (1)
Leigh Bureau 102
 Scali, John (28)
Marquette University 105
 Pambookian, Hagop S. (23)
Murray State University 117
 Matthai, James P. (63)
 Umar, Farouk F. (104)
Northeastern Illinois University 142
 Firoozi, Ferydoon (23)
 Husain, Asad (41)
Pennsylvania State University 151
 Dahir, Sabir H. (291)
 Goldschmidt, Arthur E., Jr. (194)
 Lord, Walton J. (29)
Simon Fraser University 171
 Var, Turgut (6)
Southwestern Louisiana, University of 174
 Kurtz, Donn M., II (59)
 Rense, William C. (82)
Speakers Bureau of America, Inc. 175
 Brownfeld, Allan C. (1)
 Thimmesch, Nick (4)
Temple University 181
 Lev, Benjamin (339)
 Samuelson, Norbert M. (293), (306)
 Soskis, David A. (345)
United Telecommunications, Inc. 210
 Ward, R.V. (2)
Villanova University 214
 Niosi, Jerome J. (55)
War Resisters League 217
 Roodenko, Igal (4)
Washington, University of 218
Western Washington University 223
 Robinson, Mary (19)
 Vernon, Manfred C. (21)
Whittier College 224
 Ibrahim, Hilmi (9)

MILITARY

Auburn University 16
 Killian, Albert F. (44)
 Norris, Awbrey G. (62)
Duquesne University 54
Eastern Illinois University 57
 Lowell, W.S. (53)
Intercollegiate Studies Institute, Inc. 85
 Anderson, Martin (1)
Keedick Lecture Bureau, Inc. 97
 Zumwalt, Elmo (74)
Marquette University 105
 Denny, Ronald J. (70)
 Doherty, Dennis J. (76)
 Dunn, J. Michael (71)
 Gabryshak, Betty J. (124)
 Maresco, Richard E. (72)
 Park, Richard S. (73)
 Traas, Adrian G. (74)
 Wood, Noel T. (75)
National Speakers Bureau, Inc. 135
 Rickenbacker, William F. (54)
Pennsylvania State University 151
 Bresler, Robert J. (190)
 Cimbala, Stephen J. (192)
Puget Sound, University of 159
 Robinson, John W. (53)
Queen's University 160
 Willett, Terry (21)
Southwestern Louisiana, University of 174
 Purcell, Charles W. (81)
United States Department of Defense 193
United States Department of Defense 194
United States Department of Defense 195
United States Department of Defense 196
United States Department of Defense 197
United States Department of State 200
Villanova University 214
 Culkin, Thomas J. (68)
 Johnson, James R. (70)
Virginia Polytechnic Institute and State University 216
 Hoffman, Edward G. (53)
 Johnson, Overton R. (60)
 Spengler, Fred L. (120)
Washington, University of 218

MINERALS
See also: GEMS; MINING

Detroit Edison 47
Northwest Mining Association 143
Balla, John C. (2)
Hintzman, D.E. (6)
McGregor, Wallace (9)
Robbins, David A. (11)
Whinnen, W.J. (15)
Podium Management Associates, Inc. 154
Ordway, Frederick (17)
Temple University 181
Ulmer, Gene C. (137), (347)
Tin Research Institute, Inc. 183
Bihl, John M. (1)
Hampshire, William B. (2)
Long, Joseph B. (3)
Washington, University of 218

MINING
See also: MINERALS

Northwest Mining Association 143
Babcock, Russell (1)
Balla, John C. (2)
Blair, Frank H., Jr. (3)
Chadwick, Russell (4)
Hintzman, D.E. (6)
Hite, John B. (7)
McGregor, Wallace (9)
Pattee, Edon (10)
Robbins, David A. (11)
Schmidt, Eberhard A. (12)
Stephens, Jackie E. (13)
Whinnen, W.J. (15)
Whiting, Keith (16)
Pennsylvania State University 151
Aurand, Harold W. (33)
Hovanec, Evelyn (236)
Lieb, John A. (154)
Stefanko, Robert (136)
Puget Sound, University of 159
Bland, Jeffrey (12)

MINORITIES
See also: AMERICAN INDIANS; BLACKS; CHICANO; EQUAL EMPLOYMENT

Auburn University 16
Higgins, Earl B. (33)
California, Irvine, University of 27
Curiel, Ramon (2)
Lenhoff, Howard M. (42)
Drew University 52
Copeland, John W. (18)
DeJong, Peter (23)
Duquesne University 54
East Carolina University 56
Chambliss, Thomas A. (42)
Jones, Douglas R. (48)
Eastern Illinois University 57
Sutton, Kenneth (85)
Marquette University 105
Mayberry, Arthur (44)
Mid West Program Service, Inc. 112
McClinton, Curtis R., Jr. (84)
Murray State University 117
Matarazzo, S.M. (46)
Northeastern Illinois University 142
Caron, Josiane (14)
Rainier National Bank 162
Saint Cloud State University 168
Hellwig, David J. (25)
Johnson, David C. (30)
Schwerdtfeger, Dale (66)
Southwestern Louisiana, University of 174
Brabant, Sarah C. (13)
Speaker's Bureau of Philadelphia 176
Bryant, Reginald (23)
Lewis, Claude (66)
Temple University 181
Adams, Ernestyne James (201), (256), (308)
Cutler, William W., III (93)
Hunt, Jon H. (104)
Levine, Ruth Ellen (176), (228)
Morse, J. Mitchell (234), (305)
Rubini, Dennis A. (238)
University Speakers Bureau 211
Novak, Michael (6)
Virginia Polytechnic Institute and State University 216
Crunkilton, John R. (28)
Flowers, William L., Jr. (37)
Whittier College 224
Olson-Prather, Emelie (12)

MORALS
See: ETHICS AND MORALS

MOTIVATION

Auburn University 16
Johnson, Gerald W. (43)
Business Communication Council 23
Drew University 52
Domber, Edward A. (26)
East Carolina University 56
Lao, Rosina C. (51), (135)
Eastern Illinois University 57
Rogers, Donald L. (70)
Sanders, Claud D. (73)
Florida Association of Realtors 65
Baars, Theo D., Jr. (2)
Frost, Robert J., III (20)
Hoche, Henry (28)
Hudson, Max (31)
McIntosh, Claudette E. (42)
Moore, Steven A. (44)
Moskal, Lilyb (45)
Waters, Paul W. (66)
Food Processing Machinery and Supplies Association 67
Baum, Eric C. (2)
Fulton Inc., Richard 71
Marquette University 105
Pambookian, Hagop S. (80)
Mid West Program Service, Inc. 112
Christianson, J.N. (22)
Hurst, Allan (68)
Nash, Von (93)
Van Derbur, Marilyn (128)
Watson, Everett D. (129)
Wooden, John (137)
Murray State University 117
Watkins, Yancy (134)
Northeastern Illinois University 142
Jones, Arnold P., Jr. (47)
Renas, Stanley R. (71)
Pennsylvania State University 151
Calamidas, Alec (38)
Dubin, Samuel S. (40)
Gilmore, Harold L. (43)
Lewis, Blake D., Jr. (46)
Speaker's Bureau of Philadelphia 176
Crim, Mort (28)
Kramer, Jerry (57)
Qubein, Nido (89)
Van Derbur, Marilyn (116)
Woodruff, Bill (122)
Speakers Unlimited 177
Success Leaders Speakers Service 180
Batten, Hal J. (9)
Cook, William J., Jr. (35)
Dehoney, Wayne (40)
Eggert, William R. (49)
Frank, D. Michael (56)

MOTIVATION (continued)

Hudson, Leonard C. (85)
Karstedt, Bruce (97)
McQuaing, John H. (115)
Marine, Jules A. (117)
Mundt, Richard M. (125)
Panichello, Joe (134)
Robert, Cavett (146)
Winter, James O. (193)
Villanova University 214
Chorba, George J. (1)
Washington, University of 218
World Modeling Association 229
Ewell, Rachael (2)

MUSEUMS

California State University, Fullerton 29
Walkington, David L. (106), (278), (352)
Eastern Illinois University 57
Maurer, David J. (56)
Handweavers Guild of America 79
Kowalek, Jon W. (73)
Murray State University 117
Keeslar, Suzanne M. (138)
Pennsylvania State University 151
Ott, Robert W. (30)

MUSIC

Auburn University 16
Jemian, Wartan A. (41)
California State University, Fullerton 29
Evans, David H. (220)
Josephson, Nors S. (221)
Schatz, Madeline F. (182), (222)
Carnegie-Mellon University 31
McCulloh, Byron (29)
Drew University 52
Berenbroick, Lester (5)
Hailparn, Lydia (36)
Duquesne University 54
East Carolina University 56
Debnath, Lokenath (106)
Moore, Charles (107)
Pittman, Everett (108)
Stephenson, William E. (109)
Stevens, Charles (39), (110)
Eastern Illinois University 57
Beall, John (4)
Hardin, Burton E. (29)
Key, Rhoderick E. (40)
Kogen, Ronald (42)
Keedick Lecture Bureau, Inc. 97
Schustik, Bill (61)
Wright, Bob (72)
Learning Exchange 99
Leigh Bureau 102
Duchin, Peter (7)
Marquette University 105
Siettman, James P. (26)
Mid West Program Service, Inc. 112
DeFlores, Robert (29)
Murray State University 117
Nelson, David (95)
Northeastern Illinois University 142
Combs, Ronald (16)
Hobley, Marge Munn (38)
Lucas, James A. (57)
Walker, Robert (92)
Pennsylvania State University 151
Beach, James W. (26)
Lord, Walton J. (29)
Rocco, Emma S. (31)
Podium Management Associates, Inc. 154
Anderson, Marian (1)
Peerce, Jan (18)
Rich, Buddy (20)
Roth, Wolfgang (22)
Russell, Anna (23)
Puget Sound, University of 159
Ebert, Lawrence E. (21)
Simon Fraser University 171
Palmer, Leigh Hunt (40)
Southwestern Louisiana, University of 174
Hanley, Frank L. (41)
Speaker's Bureau of Philadelphia 176
Berkowitz, Freida Pastor (10)
Temple University 181
Cormier, Raymond J. (79)
Hampton, Barbara L. (27), (84)
Lebofsky, Dennis S. (85)
Villanova University 214
Niosi, Jerome J. (67)
Virginia Polytechnic Institute and State University 216
Lamoureux, Joseph G. (66)
Washington, University of 218
Whittier College 224
Breese, Donald (3)
Gothold, Stephen (6)
Wilson Celebrities, Lola 225
Dayton, Daryl D. (12)
Fiske, Stephen (14)
Wallace, Paul (39)
Women's Classical Caucus 227
Snyder, Jane M. (43)

MYTHOLOGY
See also: ANCIENT WORLD

Duquesne University 54
Eastern Illinois University 57
Murray, Louise (62)
Pennsylvania State University 151
Hovanec, Evelyn (236)
Washington, University of 218
Women's Classical Caucus 227
Bram, Jean Rhys (3)
Broege, Valerie (4)
Drake, Gertrude (11)
Gold, Barbara K. (15)
Gordon, Diane R. (16)
Hartigan, Karelisa (19)
Katz, Phyllis B. (21)
Lefkowitz, Mary R. (28)
Loomis, Julia W. (29)
Morgan, Kathleen (33)
Orlandi, Mary Kay Gamel (35)
Rubin, Nancy F. (41)
Sowa, Cora Angier (44)
Trachy, Carol Law (48)

N

NATIONAL DEFENSE
See also: INTERNATIONAL AFFAIRS; MILITARY

American Party 6
Anderson, Tom (1)
Shackelford, Rufus (3)
California State University, Fullerton 29
Dittman, Roger R. (51), (255), (268)
Guertner, Gary L. (256), (292)
Duquesne University 54
East Carolina University 56
Sugg, Howard (103)
Heritage Foundation 82
Intercollegiate Studies Institute, Inc. 85
Kintner, William R. (15)
Pfaltzgraff, Robert L., Jr. (28)
Keedick Lecture Bureau, Inc. 97
Zumwalt, Elmo (74)
Leigh Bureau 102
Ellsworth, Robert (8)

NATIONAL DEFENSE (continued)

Pennsylvania State University 151
Bresler, Robert J. (190)
Wilcher, Marshall E. (201)
Puget Sound, University of 159
Robinson, John W. (53)
United States Department of Defense 193
United States Department of Defense 194
United States Department of Defense 195
United States Department of Defense 196
United States Department of Defense 197
United States Department of State 200
Villanova University 214
Betz, Joseph (83)
Washington Reporters Group 220
Johnston, Oswald L. (4)

NEW ZEALAND
See: AUSTRALIA AND NEW ZEALAND

NEWS MEDIA
See: MEDIA

NEWSPAPERS
See: JOURNALISM AND THE PRESS

NONVERBAL COMMUNICATION

Mid West Program Service, Inc. 112
Sweet, Cody (120)
Murray State University 117
Petrie, Garth F. (50)
Taylor, John (58)
National Speakers Bureau, Inc. 135
Fast, Julius (19)
Northeastern Illinois University 142
Flory, Joyce Ann (25)
Hesler, Richard (37)
Pennsylvania State University 151
Allison, Priscilla H. (61)
Elder, James T. (41)
Waun, Roger J. (87)
Speaker's Bureau of Philadelphia 176
Sweet, Cody (113)
Success Leaders Speakers Service 180
Shaffer, Dorothy (155)
Sweet, Cody (175)
Vaughan and Associates, B.L. 212
Vaughan, B.L. (1)
Wilson Celebrities, Lola 225
Loder, H. Leith (25)

NUCLEAR ENERGY
See also: ENERGY

California, Irvine, University of 27
Hill, Mason L. (4)
Wadman, William W. (9)
Carnegie-Mellon University 31
Burnett, Tobias W. T. (30)
Florida Power and Light 66
Kansas State University 95
Keepin, G. Robert (1)
Murray State University 117
West, Steven L. (106)
Pennsylvania State University 151
Grossman, Herbert (151)
Harkness, William L. (262)
Johnston, Richard G. (128)
Klevans, Edward H. (129)
McCarthy, Gregory J. (130)
Palladino, Nunzio J. (132)
Pillay, K.K.S. (156)
Remick, Forrest J. (133)
Roy, Rustum (272)
Witzig, Warren F. (137)
Philadelphia Electric Speakers Bureau 152
Speaker's Bureau of Philadelphia 176
Hackes, Peter (45)
Temple University 181
Miller, Richard L. (18)
Union Electric Speakers Forum 189
United States Environmental Protection Agency 204
Virginia Electric and Power Company 215
Virginia Polytechnic Institute and State University 216
Kurstedt, Harold A., Jr. (64)
Nachlas, Joel A. (87)
Onega, Ronald J. (88)
Parkinson, T.F. (91)
Robeson, Andrew (103)
Teplitz, Vigdor L. (131)
Washington, University of 218
Wisconsin Electric Power Company 226

NURSING
See: HEALTH PROFESSIONS

NUTRITION
See also: FOOD AND BEVERAGES

American Montessori Society 5
Auburn University 16
Lovell, R.T. (53)
California, Irvine, University 27
Hochschild, Richard (29)
Duquesne University 54
Eastern Illinois University 57
Dow, Ruth (15)
Ferguson, Karen (20)
Hedges, Edith R. (30)
Swope, Mary Ruth (86)
Maryland, University of 106
Miller Agency, Gilbert 113
Smith, Lendon H. (3)
Murray State University 117
Presson, Alta V. (79), (94)
Northeastern Illinois University 142
Etten, Marion (20)
Pennsylvania State University 151
Gerhard, Glenn (174)
Kroger, Manfred (177)
Rieck, Mary (171)
Puget Sound, University of 159
Bland, Jeffrey (12)
Simon Fraser University 171
Lyman, Bernard (51)
Speaker's Bureau of Philadelphia 176
Davis, LaDeva (31)
Lowenthal, Lynn (70)
Mayer, Jean (76)
Nelson, Alma (82)
Temple University 181
Golder, Richard (166)
Morton, Bruce G. (184)
Pollack, Robert L. (187)
Tuna Research Foundation, Inc. 187
Kierce, Harold F. (1)
Villanova University 214
Feigenberg, Myrtle (24), (71)
Virginia Polytechnic Institute and State University 216

NUTRITION (continued)

Bedford, Mary Ruth (5)
Essary, E.O. (35)
Lopez, Anthony (72)
Thye, Forrest W. (134)
Webb, Ryland E. (140)
Washington, University of 218
World Modeling Association 229

O

OFFICE MANAGEMENT
See also: SECRETARIES

California State University, Fullerton 29
Gala, Basil E. (136)
Florida Association of Realtors 65
Bossen, Robert H. (8)
Cantrall, Otto L. (9)
Clark, J. Rodney (11)
Concannon, F.P. (12)
Dominguez, Carlos, Jr. (15)
Fearnley, Joe (19)
Hoche, Henry (28)
Jacobson, Alan W. (32)
Linville, George M. (38)
Moutz, W.B. (47)
Newstreet, Richard A. (48)
Pierce, John E. (52)
Pyms, Jack (53)
Van Brackle, Henry L. (63)
Varnadore, E. Lee (64)
Wilcox, Olin R. (68)
Yates, Dorothy M. (70)
Murray State University 117
Albin, Marvin (14)
Naremco Services, Inc. 119
Schiff, Robert A. (1)
Southwestern Louisiana, University of 174
Bentley, Doris B. (6)
Williams, Alfred B. (96)

OIL AND GAS
See also: ENERGY

American Graduate School of International Management 3
Peters, Issa (5)
California, Irvine, University of 27
Hill, Mason L. (4)
Carnegie-Mellon University 31
Burnett, Tobias W.T. (23)
Chevron U.S.A. Inc. 35
Consolidated Edison Company of New York, Inc. 41
Getty Oil Company 74
Keedick Lecture Bureau, Inc. 97
Knowles, Ruth Sheldon (35)
Pennsylvania State University 151
Bierderman, Edwin Jr. (124)
Duda, J.L. (138)
Sherman, Carl W. (135)
Public Service Electric and Gas Company 158
Southwestern Louisiana, University of 174
Rugg, Fred E. (87)
Temple University 181
Cuff, David J. (131), (209), (336)
Washington, University of 218
Washington Reporters Group 220
Behr, Peter (1)

P

PACIFIC REGIONS

Associated Film Artists 15
Borden, Chris (1)
Fame Limited 59
Bjerre, Jens (2)
Forrest, Martin A. 69
Muller, Kal (9)
Pennsylvania State University 151
Perry, William L. (299)
Western Washington University 223
Hildebrand, Francis (34)

PALMISTRY

Ancient Arts of the Future 13
Pomeroy, Justin (1)
Murray State University 117
Lorrah, Jean (96)

PARAPSYCHOLOGY
See: PSYCHIC PHENOMENA

PEACE

Ahmadiyya Movement in Islam, Inc. 1
Ahmad, Imam Masud (2)
Drew University 52
DeVeer, Robert (24)
Wetzel, Charles J. (99)
Duquesne University 54
Eastern Illinois University 57
Murad, Ahmad (61)
Gustavus Adolphus College 78
Hutaff, Charles 83
Field, Tom (4)
Leigh Bureau 102
Hottelet, Richard C. (14)
Lewis Program Service, Ann 103
Fahey, Joseph J. (1)
Marquette University 105
Doherty, Dennis J. (76)
Oh, John K.C. (57)
Pennsylvania State University 151
Bresler, Robert J. (190)
Shemick, John M. (118)
Socialist Party, USA 172
McReynolds, David (6)
Spokespeople 178
McReynolds, David (4)
Villanova University 214
Betz, Joseph (83)
Logue, John J. (27)
War Resisters League 217
McReynolds, David (2)
Peck, Jim (3)
Roodenko, Igal (4)

PERCEPTION

California State University, Fullerton 29
Bagrash, Frank M. (85), (169), (229), (264)
Carnegie-Mellon University 31
Kozak, Wlodzimierz M. (24)
East Carolina University 56
Sayetta, Tom C. (130)
Food Processing Machinery and Supplies Association 67
Hunter, Richard S. (17)
Pennsylvania State University 151
Anthony, Frank (62)
Henisch, Heinz K. (73)
Simon Fraser University 171
Lyman, Bernard (51)
Villanova University 214
Sheldon, Paul (79)

PERCEPTION (continued)

Virginia Polytechnic Institute and State University 216
Colmano, Germille (24)
Wilson Celebrities, Lola 225
Gregory, Paul (18)

PERSONAL DEVELOPMENT
See also: MEMORY; TIME MANAGEMENT

Auburn University 16
Meadows, Mark E. (57)
California State University, Fullerton 29
Lindquist, Carol U. (239)
Webber, Arthur W. (250)
White, Geoffry D. (44), (252)
Carnegie-Mellon University 31
Moyer, Kenneth E. (2)
Scheier, Michael F. (37)
East Carolina University 56
Knox, David (5)
Lao, Rosina C. (135)
Eastern Illinois University 57
Dow, Ruth (15)
Kirk, William G. (41)
Ladd, Clay (45)
Saltmarsh, Robert E. (71)
Williams, Glenn D. (96)
Florida Association of Realtors 65
Lassetter, Maggie S. (36)
Glendale Federal Savings and Loan Association 75
Carlson, Kenneth A. (1)
Green Circle Program, Inc. 77
Gitomer, Nancy (1)
Harrington, Bob 81
Harrington, Bob (1)
Keedick Lecture Bureau, Inc. 97
Ford, Eileen (22)
Gordon, Ruth (25)
Green, Robert L. (26)
Kanin, Garson (34)
York, Alexandra (73)
Leigh Bureau 102
Culligan, Joe (4)
Linkletter, Jack (18)
Marquette University 105
DeRoche, Robert J. (34)
Dotson, Virginia (77)
Hartz, David (78)
Pambookian, Hagop S. (80)
Peterson, Margi (82)
Richards, Marva A. (83)
Staudacher, Joseph M. (13)
Sean, Jane D. (86)
White, Dennis K. (88)
Mid West Program Service, Inc. 112
Banks, Murray (4)
Batten, Joe (5)
Bellus, Dan (10)
Burge, Ethel (19)
Gard, Grant C. (41)
Gentry, Clyde (42)
Harris, Amy (54)
Harris, Sydney (55)
Harris, Thomas Anthony (56)
Janeway, Elizabeth (71)
Johnson, Mildred (74)
Kemper, Joan Corrier (78)
Linkletter, Jack (83)
Olson, Harry E., Jr. (97)
Plumb, Charles (100)
Richards, Bob (108)
Turner, William (126)
Wilkinson, Charles (132)
Ziglar, Zig (138)
Murray State University 117
Holcomb, Thomas F. (43)
Stranahan, Joan (110)
National Speakers Bureau, Inc. 135
Arch, Jim (3)
Dornoff, James (16)
Jones, Charles (34)
Olson, Harry (49)
Richards, Bob (53)
Schultz, Whitt (57)
Vance, Mike (58)
National Water Well Association 136
Stanley, Anita Bacco (23)
Tosi, Donald (24)
Northeastern Illinois University 142
Itkin, William (43)
Pennsylvania State University 151
Ambruster, David L. (35)
Brown, Robert E. (163)
Calamidas, Alec (38)
DeWald, Samuel C. (39)
Elder, James T. (41)
Frankhouser, Willis M. Jr. (207)
Ridgley, Louis E., Jr. (58)
Robinson, Byron M. (115)
Strickler, Fay B. (180)
Saint Cloud State University 168
Downes, Alan J. (11)
Grachek, Arthur F. (17)
Larson, Walter G. (38)
Mertens, Gerald C. (47)
Wise, Jeffrey (73)
Wollin, Dorothy (74)
Simon Fraser University 171
Lyman, Bernard (51)
Southwestern Louisiana, University of 174
Blair, Charles W. (9)
Werner, Jan (94)
Speaker's Bureau of Philadelphia 176
Berk, Ginger (9)
Muskie, Edmund (81)
Savitch, Jessica (98)
Wall, Ruth (118)
Stevens Model and Merchandising Agency, Patricia 179
Success Leaders Speakers Service 180
Abrams, Arnold G. (1)
Bliss, Edwin C. (15)
Cobb, LaVarne (33)
Dewey, Hallie (41)
Douglas, Mack (45)
Dubin, Samuel S. (47)
Fettig, Art (51)
Hailey, Walter B., Jr. (70)
Hale, William H., Jr. (71)
Jewett, Joan (90)
Jordan, Adiel Moncrief (94)
Price, Sterling (140)
Ralston, John (142)
Schwartz, David (151)
Secher, Bjorn (152)
Semaan, Dick (154)
Snyder, Reginald (160)
Yates, Martha (198)
Temple University 181
Rappaport, Margaret M. (292)
Smith, James P., Jr. (65)
Stivers, Eugene H. (246), (297)
University Speakers Bureau 211
Novak, Karen Laub (5)
Vaughan and Associates, B.L. 212
Vaughan, B.L. (1)
Virginia Polytechnic Institute and State University 216
Crump, Michael W. (27)
Sullins, W. Robert (125)
Wilson Celebrities, Lola 225
Calvet, Corinne (5)
Dallan, Gisele (10)
Gladich, Joen (17)
Gregory, Paul (18)
Guild, Leo (19)
Robert, Cavett (32)
Sand, Froma (34)
Strick, Anne (37)
Teutsch, Champion K. (38)
World Modeling Association 229
Ewell, Rachael (2)
Hoener, Lisa (3)
Rubin, Lisa Ferris (4)
Tolman, Ruth (5)

PERSONNEL ADMINISTRATION

Auburn University 16
Duncan, J.W. (18)
Marquette University 105
Schreier, James W. (9)
Wood, Noel T. (11)
Northeastern Illinois University 142
Iregbulem, Hilary I. (42)
Pennsylvania State University 151
Lewis, Blake D., Jr. (46)
Rainier National Bank 162
Temple University 181
Powell, Walter H. (41)
Wilson, Samuel M. (47), (299)
Villanova University 214
Losoncy, Thomas A. (14)
Virginia Polytechnic Institute and State University 216
Butt, Albin T. (15)
Robinson, Jerald F. (105)
Western Washington University 223
Monat, Jon (6)

PETS
See: ANIMALS

PHARMACEUTICALS
See: DRUGS

PHILOSOPHY

American Teilhard Association for the Future of Man 11
Bruteau, Beatrice (3)
California, Irvine, University of 27
Trimble, Virginia (16)
California State University, Fullerton 29
Dittman, Roger R. (232), (268)
Johnson, Fred M. (272)
Leder, Hans H. (164), (238)
Russell, J. Michael (118), (245)
Sadovszky, Otto J. (246)
Weinzweig, Marjorie (251)
Drew University 52
Johnson, Barent (42)
Knox, John, Jr. (45)
Lawler, Edwina G. (46)
Riemer, Neal (78)
Duquesne University 54
East Carolina University 56
Jorgensen, N.M. (138)
Intercollegiate Studies Institute, Inc. 85
Martin, William Oliver (20)
Molnar, Thomas (23)
Stanlis, Peter J. (32)
Van Den Haag, Ernest (35)
Vivas, Eliseo (36)
Voegelin, Eric (37)
Wiggins, James W. (38)
Marquette University 105
Crepeau, Margaret T. (89)
Dupuis, Adrian (36)
Griesbach, Marc F. (90)
Prendergast, Thomas L. (91)
Maryland, University of 106
Murray State University 117
Beasley, Wayne T. (64)
Kumar, Frederick L. (97)
Sheeks, Wayne (98)
Northeastern Illinois University 142
Feldman, Reynold (22)
Nissim-Sabat, Charles (65)
Pennsylvania State University 151
Moyer, Ivan W., Jr. (168)
Saint Cloud State University 168
Ames, Kenneth A. (1)
Phillips, John N. (60)
Simon Fraser University 171
Wheatley, Jon (55)
Southwestern Louisiana, University of 174
Bender, Glenn F. (5)
Kirkpatrick, Robert T. (55)
Vigorito, John V. (89)
Villanova University 214
Betz, Joseph (73)
Regan, Daniel T. (75)
Van Fleteren, Frederick E. (76)
Virginia Polytechnic Institute and State University 216
Pitt, Joseph C. (95)
Washington, University of 218
Whittier College 224
Winters, Richard H. (17)
Women's Classical Caucus 227
Nussbaum, Martha C. (34)
Rossi, Mary Ann (39)
Rubin, Nancy F. (41)
Snyder, Jane M. (43)
Thomas, Kathryn A. (46)
Villeneuve, Winnie Frohn (51)

PHOTOGRAPHY

American Institute for Exploration 4
Alley, John (2)
California State University, Fullerton 29
Curran, Darryl J. (9)
Kaye, Alan S. (38), (319)
Forrest, Martin A. 69
Paling, John (11)
Keedick Lecture Bureau, Inc. 97
Halsman, Philippe (27)
National Water Well Association 136
Albert, Roslyn B. (16)
Pennsylvania State University 151
Fletcher, Peter W. (304)
Folwell, William H., III (71)
Henisch, Heinz K. (73)
Saint Cloud State University 168
Fischmann, Ruel (16)
Simon Fraser University 171
Devenyl, Denes (47)
Southwestern Louisiana, University of 174
Oliver, James R. (79)
Virginia Polytechnic Institute and State University 216
Claus, George W. (20)
Huffman, Stanley A., Jr. (58)
Washington, University of 218
World Modeling Association 229

PHYSICAL EDUCATION

Auburn University 16
Jenkins, Stephen R. (42)
California State University, Fullerton 29
Bailey, C. Ian (86), (130), (299)
Carnegie-Mellon University 31
Birdy, Earl J. (9), (39)
Drew University 52
Harper, David E. (39)
Mason, Eleanor C. (53)
Reeves, John A. (72)
East Carolina University 56
Hooks, Edgar (28)
Jorgensen, N.M. (82)
Stasavich, Clarence (87)
Eastern Illinois University 57
Dutler, David C. (17)
Mullally, Mike (60)
Marquette University 105
Byrne, Kevin (112)
Dunn, J. Michael (114)
Maryland, University of 106
Murray State University 117
Presson, William O. (123)
Northeastern Illinois University 142
Johnson, Violet (46)

PHYSICAL EDUCATION
(continued)

Pennsylvania State University 151
Caporali, John M. (204)
Lauffer, Herbert (278)
Miller, Sayers J., Jr. (279)
Morris, John (281)
Nelson, Richard C. (209)
Stoner, Clarence H. (284)
Sweeting, Roger (285)
Tait, G. Thomas (286)
Puget Sound, University of 159
Peyton, Joe (47)
Wallrof, Paul (67)
Wilson, Roberta A. (69)
Saint Cloud State University 168
Anderson, Arlynn L. (2)
Hans, Reid (24)
Waxlax, Robert (71)
Southwestern Louisiana, University of 174
Cameron, David A. (16)
Dugas, Edmond A. (26)
Temple University 181
Torbert, Marianne (11)
Villanova University 214
Heitzmann, William Ray (11)
Virginia Polytechnic Institute and State University 216
Bell, Wilson B. (7)
Cheney, Anne (19)
Gunsten, Paul H. (46)
Sebolt, Don R. (110)

PHYSICAL FITNESS

American Sunbathing Association, Inc. 10
Auburn University 16
Duncan, J.W. (18)
Eastern Illinois University 57
Aten, Dennis (2)
Hedges, Edith R. (30)
Sharaway, H.S. (80)
Feminist Karate Union 62
Bateman, Py (1)
Mitten, Suzanne (2)
Reid, Kathy (3)
Marquette University 105
Dunn, J. Michael (114)
Fitts, Robert H. (115)
McCall, Raymond J. (100)
Pelt, Therese (81)
Quereshi, M.Y. (102)
Murray State University 117
Muehleman, Tom (109)
Presson, Alta V. (79)
Northeastern Illinois University 142
Creely, Daniel (18)
Etten, Marion (20)
Tremble, Neal (86)
Pennsylvania State University 151
Caporali, John M. (204)
Caputo, Richard (205)
Ciervo, Arthur (67)
Hunt, Edward E., Jr. (208)
Miller, Sayers J., Jr. (279)
Nelson, Richard C. (209)
Onorato, Ed (282)
Sias, John D. (83)
Sweeting, Roger (285)
Puget Sound, University of 159
Bowman, Dawn (14)
Clayson, Shelby J. (17)
Wallrof, Paul (67)
Wilson, Roberta A. (69)
Queen's University 160
Andrew, George (2)
Saint Cloud State University 168
Kelly, John M. (33)
Simon Fraser University 171
Allen, E.D. (22)
Banister, Eric (23)
Hendy, Martin (27)
Werner, Hal (30)
Southwestern Louisiana, University of 174
Eason, Byrdie E. (27)
Lebas, Sherry (64)
Speaker's Bureau of Philadelphia 176
Martucci, Carmen (75)
Muskie, Edmund (81)
Temple University 181
Shea, James M. (9)
Steisel, Ira M. (245), (296)
Virginia Polytechnic Institute and State University 216
Strickland, Kenneth F. (122)
Thye, Forrest W. (134)
Washington, University of 218
Women's Martial Arts Union 228
World Modeling Association 229

PHYSICIANS

See: HEALTH PROFESSIONS

PHYSICS

See also: LASERS

California, Irvine, University of 27
Potter, Franklin (12)
East Carolina University 56
Debnath, Lokenath (125)
McEnally, Terence E., Jr. (128)
Mueller-Roemer, Peter (129)
Sayetta, Tom C. (130)
Eastern Illinois University 57
Butler, William A. (7)
Davis, A. Douglas (14)
Taitt, Henry A. (87)
Marquette University 105
Greene, Jack B. (40)
Maryland, University of 106
Northeastern Illinois University 142
Becker, Louis (3)
Nissim-Sabat, Charles (65)
Pennsylvania State University 151
Good, Roland H., Jr. (268)
Wallach, David L. (274)
Simon Fraser University 171
Palmer, Leigh Hunt (40)
Temple University 181
Franklin, Jerrold (277)
Muldawer, Leonard (278)
Offenbacher, Elmer L. (279)
Virginia Polytechnic Institute and State University 216
Brinson, Halbert F. (11)
Taylor, Larry T. (128)
Teplitz, Vigdor L. (131)
Washington, University of 218
Western Washington University 223
Quigley, Robert J. (4)

PHYSIOLOGY

California, Irvine, University of 27
Davis, Earle A., Jr. (26)
Carnegie-Mellon University 31
Kozak, Wlodzimierz M. (24)
Duquesne University 54
Northeastern Illinois University 142
Wiercinski, Floyd J. (96)
Queen's University 160
Abrahams, Vivian (1)
Andrew, George (2)
Bird, Charles (5)
Chapler, Chris (6)
Chiong, Miguel (7)
Doris, Peter (9)
Jennings, Donald (10)
Kraicer, Jacob (11)
Milligan, John (14)
Shin, Seon (18)

PHYSIOLOGY (continued)

Simon Fraser University 171
Bhakthan, N.M.G. (24)
Davison, Allan J. (26)
Wienberg, Harold (43)
Temple University 181
Batra, Gopal K. (156), (205)
Leifer, Calvin (175)
Lovrinic, Jean (318)
McElligott, James G. (179)
Smith, Rita (135)
Tower, Gail (195)
Washington, University of 218
Western Washington University 223
Russo, Salvatore F. (24)

PLANT LIFE
See also: HORTICULTURE

Auburn University 16
Coker, Samuel Terry (13)
Davis, Norman D. (16)
Orr, Henry P. (63)
Perkins, Donald Y. (66)
California, Irvine, University of 27
Rodriguez, Eloy (14)
California State University, Fullerton 29
Jones, C. Eugene (273)
Carnegie-Mellon University 31
Coleman, Bernard D. (8)
Drew University 52
Bistis, George N. (8)
Zuck, Florence M. (101)
Zuck, Robert K. (102)
Duquesne University 54
Eastern Illinois University 57
Shull, Carl (82)
Food Processing Machinery and Supplies Association 67
Root, Bruce (26)
Saunders, Robert D., Jr. (27)
Handweavers Guild of America 79
Reed, Mrs. Curtis (111)
Keedick Lecture Bureau, Inc. 97
Baker, Jerry (3)
Marquette University 105
Courtright, James B. (2)
Murray State University 117
Beatty, Durwood (1)
Eversmeyer, Harold E. (13)
Macha, Roger L. (5), (122)
Tackett, Amos (7), (126)
National Speakers' and Psychics' Registry 134
Bird, Christopher (1)
Pennsylvania State University 151
Grossman, Herbert (151)
Hillson, C.J. (152)
Meserole, Harrison T. (237)
Palpant, Edgar H. (310)
Wetzel, Herbert A. (25)
Puget Sound, University of 159
Alcorn, Gordon (2)
Bloom, Mitchell (13)
Lowther, J. Stewart (38)
Slater, James R. (59)
Yorks, Pamela (70)
Saint Cloud State University 168
Ezell, Wayland L. (13)
Southwestern Louisiana, University of 174
Heard, J. Norman (44)
Union Electric Speakers Forum 189
Virginia Polytechnic Institute and State University 216
Beecher, Albert S. (6)
Foy, Chester L. (38)
Huffman, Stanley A., Jr. (58)
Judkins, Wesley P. (62)
Moore, Laurence D. (85)
Skelly, John M. (113)
Smeal, Paul L. (115)
Washington, University of 218
Western Washington University 223
Taylor, Ronald J. (15)

POETRY

California State University, Fullerton 29
Cox, Miriam S. (134), (200)
Jaskowski, Helen M. (162)
Contemporary Forum 42
Duquesne University 54
East Carolina University 56
Everett, Nell C. (63)
Eastern Illinois University 57
Murray, Louise (62)
Fulton Inc., Richard 71
Keedick Lecture Bureau, Inc. 97
Cairney, John (8)
Callaway, Joe (9)
Norris, Beverly (47)
Norris, Rufus (49)
Marquette University 105
Egan, Keith J. (106)
Murray State University 117
Brun, Michael A. (10)
Northeastern Illinois University 142
Beaver, Joseph C. (2)
Pennsylvania State University 151
Lane, Benjamin A. (105)
Tamplin, John C. (244)
Puget Sound, University of 159
Bauska, Barry (7)
Saint Cloud State University 168
Lawson, Jonathan (39)
Southwestern Louisiana, University of 174
Fackler, Herbert V. (29)
Temple University 181
Roos, Anne D. (144)
Western Washington University 223
Skinner, Knute R. (27)
Wilson Celebrities, Lola 225
Workman, Donna (42)
Women's Classical Caucus 227
Bacon, Helen H. (1)
Barnard, Sylvia (2)
Clader, Linda (5)
Clay, Jenny Strauss (6)
Clayman, Dee Lesser (7)
Deagon, Ann (9)
Greengard, Carola (17)
Hartigan, Karelisa (19)
Katz, Phyllis B. (21)
Lefkowitz, Mary R. (28)
Loomis, Julia W. (29)
Morgan, Kathleen (33)
Rossi, Mary Ann (39)
Thomas, Kathryn A. (46)

POISON

Auburn University 16
Coker, Samuel Terry (13)
Duquesne University 54
Puget Sound, University of 159
Bland, Jeffrey (12)
Simon Fraser University 171
Oloffs, Peter (39)
Temple University 181
Gautierei, Ronald F. (163), (216)
Union Electric Speakers Forum 189
United States Environmental Protection Agency 204
Virginia Polytechnic Institute and State University 216
Foy, Chester L. (38)

POLAR REGIONS

Pennsylvania State University 151
Ward, Marjorie E. (301)
Virginia Polytechnic Institute and State University 216

POLAR REGIONS (continued)

Paterson, Robert A. (93)
Washington, University of 218

POLICE
See also: CRIME; CRIMINAL JUSTICE; SECURITY

California State University, Fullerton 29
Capune, W. Garrett (49), (133)
Lopez, Jess A. (58), (144), (193), (344)
Glendale Federal Savings and Loan Association 75
Carlson, Kenneth A. (1)
Hutaff, Charles 83
Gerity, Patrick L. (7)
Marquette University 105
Ishii, Thomas K. (119)
Pennsylvania State University 151
Pillay, K.K.S. (156)
Pinkerton's Inc. 153
Success Leaders Speakers Service 180
Humphries, Russell J. (86)
Temple University 181
Haller, Mark H. (264)
Kutney, Andrew J. (58)
Washington Reporters Group 220
Kelly, Harry (5)

POLITICS
See also: COMMUNISM; PROPAGANDA

Auburn University 16
Fortenberry, Charles N. (20)
California, Irvine, University of 27
Hoy, John C. (40)
California State University, Fullerton 29
Triplett, George E. (68), (188), (263)
Carnegie-Mellon University 31
Schatzman, Dennis (27)
Contemporary Forum 42
Drew University 52
Jones, Donald (44)
Mastro, Julius (54)
Riemer, Nela (78)
Rodes, Robert Michael, Jr. (79)
Simon, Douglas W. (87)
Wolf, Frank (100)
Duquesne University 54
East Carolina University 56
Faulkner, Janice Hardison (131)
Eastern Illinois University 57
Horak, Stephan M. (37)
Hutaff, Charles 83
Gerity, Patrick L. (7)
Intercollegiate Studies Institute, Inc. 85
Dornan, James E. Jr. (7)
Drachkovitch, Milorad M. (8)
Evans, M. Stanton (9)
Hauptmann, Jerzy (11)
Herberg, Will (12)
Jaffa, Harry V. (13)
Kirk, Russell (16)
Kuehnelt-Leddihin, Eric Von (18)
Martin, William Oliver (20)
Meyer, Frank S. (21)
Molnar, Thomas (23)
Niemeyer, Gerhart (24)
Opitz, Edmund A. (25)
Stanlis, Peter J. (32)
Tullock, Gordon (34)
Voegelin, Eric (37)
Wilson, Francis G. (39)
Zoll, Donald A. (40)
Kansas Wesleyan University 96
Keedick Lecture Bureau, Inc. 97
Bartlett, Charles (4)
Bayh, Marvella (5)
Callaway, Joe (9)
Cappiello, Frank (10)
Daly, John Charles (14)
Lodge, Henry Cabot (39)
Osgood, Charles (53)
Zumwalt, Elmo (74)
Zumwalt, Mouza Coutelais-du-Roche' (75)
Leigh Bureau 102
Dickerson, Nancy (5)
Kilpatrick, James J. (16)
Rumsfeld, Donald (26)
Schorr, Daniel (29)
Sidey, Hugh (30)
Toffler, Alvin (36)
Lewis Program Service, Ann 103
Garth, Sheridan (2)
Marquette University 105
Brown, Richard M. (54)
Johannes, John R. (55)
Olsen, Roger A. (58)
Theoharis, Athan (59)
Maryland, University of 106
Massachusetts Bar Association 107
Mid West Program Service, Inc. 112
Anderson, Jack (2)
Bayh, Birch (7)
Bishop, Paula (11)
Blatchford, Joe (13)
Broder, David S. (15)
Dole, Robert (35)
Gravel, Mike (46)
Hart, Gary (57)
Haskell, Floyd (59)
Nelson, Gaylord (94)
Proxmire, William (102)
Randolph, Jennings (105)
Reagan, Ronald (106)
Rooney, Andrew A. (111)
Thurmond, Strom (123)
Mixter Artist Management 114
Thompson, Hunter S. (3)
Murray State University 117
Beasley, T. Wayne (64), (99)
Garfield, Gene J. (68)
Johnson, Jack B. (100)
Rose, Joseph L. (103), (119)
Uman, Farouk F. (104)
West, Steven L, (106)
National Speakers Bureau, Inc. 135
Anderson, Jack (2)
Chancellor, John (12)
Hackes, Peter (25)
Nightingale, Earl (47)
O'Connor, Len (48)
Newsweek, Inc. 139
Northeastern Illinois University 142
Barber, Charles M. (1)
Frederick, Duke (27)
Gilpatric, C. Edward (33)
Lopez, Jose E. (56)
Murphy, John J. (64)
Pastors, Charles R. (67)
Pennsylvania State University 151
Albinski, Henry S. (189)
Bresler, Robert J. (190)
Catell, Newton O. (191)
Miller, Eugene W., Jr. (198)
Perine, James L. (170)
Riforgiato, Leonard R. (221)
Waun, Roger J. (87)
Wolf, George D. (222)
Podium Management Associates, Inc. 154
Davis, William (5)
Dick, David (7)
Grimsby, Roger (11)
Korda, Michael (14)
Weston, Av (26)
Puget Sound, University of 159
Baarsma, William (4)
Saint Cloud State University 168
De Santo, R. John (10)
Herbison, Priscilla J. (26)
Williamson, Homer E. (72)

POLITICS (continued)

Socialist Party, USA 172
Drufenbrock, Diane (1)
Gil, David (2)
Hart, William (3)
Kissell, Rick (5)
McReynolds, David (6)
Mitchell, H.L. (8)
Spiro, Tom (11)
Southwestern Louisiana, University of 174
Kurtz, Donn M., II (59)
Millet, Jeremy (72)
Vigorito, John V. (89)
Speakers Bureau of America, Inc. 175
Thimmesch, Nick (4)
Speaker's Bureau of Philadelphia 176
Bayh, Birch (6)
Bernstein, Carl (12)
Brinkley, David (19)
Brokaw, Tom (21)
Carpenter, Liz (24)
Duke, Paul (33)
Ervin, Sam (36)
Farenthold, Frances (38)
Howar, Barbara (50)
Humes, James (52)
Jackson, Henry (53)
Katen, Tom (56)
Mackin, Catherine (71)
Mitchell, Andrea (79)
Pakenham, Michael (84)
Woodward, Bob (123)
Spokespeople 178
Hudiburgh, Kayren (1)
McGlachlin, Kay (3)
McReynolds, David (4)
Spock, Benjamin (5)
Success Leaders Speakers Service 180
Frazier, Jo (57)
Hackes, Peter (68)
Stokes, Louis (167)
Vonk, Paul Kenneth (183)
Temple University 181
Bailey, Harry A., Jr. (202), (258)
Ershkowitz, Herbert (262)
Galper, Jeffry (263), (309)
Johnson, Lane J. (266)
McCain, Roger A. (288)
Miller, Robert (233), (269)
Trautmann, Fredrick (298)
Weiler, Conrad (275)
White, Elliott (24)
Union Electric Speakers Forum 189
United States International Communications Agency 205
Viewpoint Speakers Bureau 213
Boudin, Leonard (1)
Jaquith, Cindy (5)
Miah, Malik (7)
Pike, Mary (9)
Pulley, Andrew (10)
Rodriguez, Olga (12)
Stapleton, Syd (15)
Tsemel, Lea (16)
Winter, Margaret (17)
Villanova University 214
Betz, Joseph (83)
Hahn, Jeffrey W. (3)
Heitzmann, William Ray (4), (48)
Langran, Robert W. (5)
Losoncy, Thomas A. (6)
Niosi, Jerome W. (7)
Virginia Polytechnic Institute and State University 216
Flowers, William L., Jr. (37)
Havard, William C. (50)
War Resisters League 217
Douthard, William (1)
McReynolds, David (2)
Washington, University of 218
Washington Correspondents Bureau 219
Bradley, Ed (1)
Cohen, Barbara (3)
Cohen, Richard (4)
Duke, Paul (5)
Leubsdorf, Carl (6)
Means, Marianne (7)
Pierpoint, Bob (8)
Randolph, Eleanor (9)
Shields, Mark (10)
Washington Reporters Group 220
Behr, Peter (1)
Dickenson, James R. (2)
Germond, Jack W. (3)
Johnston, Oswald L. (4)
Kelly, Harry (5)
Ottenand, Tom (6)
Witcover, Jules (8)
Western Washington University 223
Barnhart, Michael W. (22)
Davis, James (23)
Whittier College 224
Harvey, Richard B. (8)
Thomas, Larry (15)
Wilson Celebrities, Lola 225
Lester, William (23)
Stevens-Allen, David J. (36)
Women's Classical Caucus 227
Robert, Jennifer (38)

POLLUTION
See: ECOLOGY

POPULATION
See also: FOOD SUPPLY

Auburn University 16
Hayes, Kirby L. (30)
Wilson, Stanley P. (89)
California State University, Fullerton 29
Brattstrom, Bayard H. (47), (69), (132), (266)
Nanjundappa, G. (287)
Drew University 52
Cochran, Lillian T. (16)
Nagle, James J. (59)
Duquesne University 54
East Carolina University 56
Thornton, Jack (21)
Intercollegiate Studies Institute, Inc. 85
Wiggins, James W. (38)
Marquette University 105
Piacsek, Bela E. (3)
National Organization for Non-Parents 129
Pennsylvania State University 151
Schenck, George (134)
Zavodni, John J. (160)
Zelinsky, Wilbur (184)
Saint Cloud State University 168
Lieberman, Harold (42)
Peck, John (58)
Southwestern Louisiana, University of 174
Johnson, David C. (51)
Mac Nair, Wilmer (69)
Temple University 181
Cuff, David J. (131), (336)
Western Washington University 223
Scott, James W. (28)

POSTAL SERVICE

American Graduate School of International Management 3
Wattles, George M. (8)
Pennsylvania State University 151
Abler, Ronald (183)
United States Postal Service 208

PREGNANCY AND CHILDBIRTH

California, Irvine, University of 27
Kent, Deryck R. (30)
Childbirth Without Pain Education Association 36
Hommel, Flora (1)
Duquesne University 54
Marquette University 105
Tobin, Terry (97)
National Association of Parents and Professionals for Safe Alternatives in Childbirth (NAPSAC) 122
Eisenstein, Mayer (1)
Epstein, Janet (2)
Mehl, Lewis (3)
Stewart, David (4)
Withrow, Genna (5)
Pennsylvania State University 151
Eckroat, Larry R. (165)
Temple University 181
Gautieri, Ronald F. (163)
Goodner, David M. (167)
Kistenmacher, Mildred L. (173)
Platt, Dorothy B. (20)
Tower, Gail (247)
Ulmer, Ilona (251), (329)
University Speakers Bureau 211
Bender, Harvey A. (1)
Washington, University of 218

PRISONS
See: CRIMINAL JUSTICE

PROPAGANDA

Drew University 52
Lee, Alfred McClung (48)
Simon Fraser University 171
Wilden, Anthony (56)
Women's Classical Caucus 227
Wagner, Cherryl A. (52)

PSYCHIC PHENOMENA

American Institute for Exploration 4
Williams, Richard (7)
Ancient Arts of the Future 13
Rook, Marcella Ruble (2)
Contemporary Forum 42
Duquesne University 54
East Carolina University 56
Williams, Thomas A. (105)
Hutaff, Charles 83
Neff, Earl (15)
Johnson, Carl M. 94
Hughes, Irene (2)
Phillips, Ted (3)
Marquette University 105
Dotson, Virginia (77)
Mid West Program Service, Inc. 112
Dixon, Jeane (34)
Hoy, David (66)
Noran, R.L. (96)
Mixter Artist Management 114
Kolisch, John (2)
Murray State University 117
Lorrah, Jean (96)
National Speakers' and Psychics' Registry 134
Bird, Christopher (1)
Ebon, Martin (2)
Geller, Uri (4)
Steiger, Brad (6)
National Speakers Bureau, Inc. 135
Dixon, Jeane (15)
Pennsylvania State University 151
Williamson, William O. (259)
Podium Management Associates, Inc. 154
Holzer, Hans (12)
Quest Associates 161
Warren, Ed (1)
Warren, Lorraine (2)
Saint Cloud State University 168
Mertens, Gerald C. (47)
Southwestern Louisiana, University of 174
Kirkpatrick, Robert T. (55)
Speaker's Bureau of Philadelphia 176
Durham, Joan (34)
Sarama, Penny (97)
Willard, Valerie (120)
Success Leaders Speakers Service 180
Hoy, David (84)
Josey, Abita Norris (96)
Noran, R.L. (131)
Temple University 181
Dubeck, Leroy W. (213), (276)
University Speakers Bureau 211
Novak, Karen Laub (5)
Vaughan and Associates, B.L. 212
Vaughan, B.L. (1)
Villanova University 214
Sheldon, Paul (79)
Washington, University of 218
Weiner Programs, Inc., Irv 221
Weiner, Irv (1)
Wilson Celebrities, Lola 225
Criswell (9)
St. Clair, David (33)

PSYCHOLOGY
See also: GESTALT

California State University, Fullerton 29
Corey, Gerald F. (231)
Namasaka, Boaz N. (242)
Russell, J. Michael (245)
Tait, Miriam A. (103), (175)
Contemporary Forum 42
Drew University 52
Ranck, James G. (71)
Sugarman, Shirley (92)
Thayer, Nelson S.T. (93)
East Carolina University 56
Grossnickle, William F. (134)
Lao, Rosina C. (135)
Prewett, Clinton R. (136)
Eastern Illinois University 57
Crane, William J. (13)
Ladd, Clay (45)
Marquette University 105
Blascovich, James J. (99)
Crepau, Margaret (89)
McCall, Raymond J. (100)
McDonald, Rita T. (101)
Quereshi, M.Y. (102)
Schlientz, Margaret Anne (95)
Shiekh, Anees E. (103)
Topetzes, Nick J. (98)
Mid West Program Service, Inc. 112
Ardrey, Robert (3)
Brothers, Joyce (16)
Noran, R.L. (96)
Murray State University 117
Muehleman, Tom (109)
Stranahan, Joan (110)
Ward, Machree A. (111)
National Speakers Bureau, Inc. 135
Brothers, Joyce (9)
Network Against Psychiatric Assault 137
Northeastern Illinois University 142
Garrett, Philip R. (28)
Itkin, William (43)
Robertson, Richard J. (73)
Walsh, William M. (93)
Pennsylvania State University 151
Barton, Michael (214)
Behrens, Peter J. (203)
Fleishman, Joe (18)
Frankhouser, Willis M., Jr. (207)

PSYCHOLOGY (continued)

McKinstry, Richard H. (270)
Mizusawa, Kiyoe (271)
Patterson, Henry O. (169)
Puget Sound, University of 159
Kirchner, Grace L. (37)
Weber, Steven M. (68)
Saint Cloud State University 168
Boltuck, Charles J. (7)
Hoffman, Patricia (28)
Mertens, Gerald C. (47)
Rosenthal, Eugene (64)
Wollin, Dorothy (74)
Southwestern Louisiana, University of 174
Gaudet, Irby J., Jr. (32)
Hotard, Stephen R. (50)
Lambert, B. Geraldine (62)
Morella, John R. (76)
Speaker's Bureau of Philadelphia 176
Brothers, Joyce (22)
Success Leaders Speakers Service 180
Bates, Ronald (8)
McGrane, William J. (113)
Monsalvatge, Ray (122)
Schlesinger, Lawrence E. (149)
Smith, Leonard J. (159)
Uni, Miriam (182)
Temple University 181
Baenninger, Ronald (281)
Hetznecker, William (282)
Iglewicz, Boris (283)
Kidder, Louise (324)
Legos, Patricia M. (286)
Malnati, Richard J. (289)
Millison, Martin B. (290)
Rappaport, Herbert (291)
Rappaport, Margaret M. (292)
Smith, Rita (294)
Steisel, Ira M. (245), (296)
Stivers, Eugene H. (297)
Thurman, Ken (126)
Villanova University 214
Gallagher, Bernard J. (65), (86)
Heitzmann, William Ray (78)
Schorr, Beverly (95)
Sheldon, Paul (79)
Bush, David F. (77)
Fittipaldi, Silvio E. (80)
Virginia Polytechnic Institute and State University 216
Crump, Michael W. (27)
Tessnear, Marshall D. (132)
Thye, Forrest W. (134)
Washington, University of 218
Whittier College 224
Behrens, Maurine (1)
Roston, Ronald (14)
Wilson Celebrities, Lola 225
Banks, Murray (3)

PUBLIC ADMINISTRATION

California State University, Fullerton 29
Saltzstein, Alan L. (262)
Northeastern Illinois University 142
Gilpatric, C. Edward (33)
Iregbulem, Hilary I. (42)
Puget Sound, University of 159
Waldo, Robert (66)
Saint Cloud State University 168
Williamson, Homer E. (72)
Southwestern Louisiana, University of 174
Caradine, E. Everett (17)
Virginia Polytechnic Institute and State University 216
Robinson, James W. (104)
Robinson, Jerald F. (105)
Western Washington University 223
Monat, Jon (6)

PUBLIC RELATIONS
See also: FUND RAISING

California State University, Fullerton 29
Johnson, Raynolds (36), (55), (78), (94), (258)
Kalupa, Frank B. (37)
Nager, Norman R. (39)
Carnegie-Mellon University 31
Schatzman, Dennis (35)
Service, Kenneth (36)
Drew University 52
Lono, J. Mark (48)
East Carolina University 56
Shires, William A. (102)
First Federal of Broward 63
Florida Association of Realtors 65
Banzhof, Parker C. (4)
Boardman, Blanche (6)
German, Jack (22)
Horn, Walter V. (30)
Jones, Ernest A. (33)
Linville, George M. (38)
Lynn, Frank (39)
McCullough, George E. (41)
McIntosh, Claudette E. (42)
Moskal, Lilyb (45)
Moutz, Madora (46)
Ring, John F. (55)
Robison, Mack (56)
Slater, L.B. (59)
Sprague, Ver Lynn (60)
Van Brackle, Henry L. (63)
Waters, Paul W. (66)
Wilcox, Olin R. (68)
Leigh Bureau 102
Marcus, Stanley (19)
Marquette University 105
Foran, David J. (67)
National Water Well Association 136
Albert, Roslyn B. (16)
Pennsylvania State University 151
Ciervo, Arthur (67)
Sink, Claire H. (84)
Thies, Anita H. (86)
Saint Cloud State University 168
DeSanto, R. John (10)
Montgomery, Terry (50)
Rowland, Howard Ray (65)
Success Leaders Speakers Service 180
Pendleton, Winston K. (135)
Pollard, Al (137)
Terzian, Carl (177)
Villanova University 214
Niosi, Jerome J. (19), (37)
Virginia Polytechnic Institute and State University 216
Bryant, Joseph J. (13)
Burleson, William C. (14)
Whittier College 224
Thomas, Larry (15)
World Modeling Association 229

PUBLISHING

Contemporary Forum 42
East Carolina University 56
Baker, Ira (61)
Chantrill, James (99)
Marquette University 105
Pehowski, Marian (68)
Murray State University 117
Strohecker, Edwin C. (75)
Northeastern Illinois University 142
Black, Sophie K. (7)
Pennsylvania State University 151
Curtis, Anthony R. (68)
Mullen, Sharman Stanic (79)
Sink, Claire H. (84)

PUBLISHING (continued)

Southwestern Louisiana, University of 174
Conrad, Glenn R. (19)
Temple University 181
Hayes, John P. (73)
Villanova University 214
Lytel, June W. (18)
Niosi, Jerome J. (19), (37)
Virginia Polytechnic Institute and State University 216
McMillion, Martin B. (78)
Washington, University of 218
Youth Liberation Press, Inc. 231
Hefner, Keith (3)

R

RACIAL RELATIONS
See also: EQUAL EMPLOYMENT; MINORITIES

Auburn University 16
Griessman, B. Eugene (24)
California State University, Fullerton 29
Capune, W. Garrett (49), (133)
Nyaggah, Mougo (7)
East Carolina University 56
Kim, Y.H. (4), (49)
Rodabaugh, Karl (8)
Intercollegiate Studies Institute, Inc. 85
Rogge, Benjamin A. (30)
Wiggins, James W. (38)
Keedick Lecture Bureau, Inc. 97
Nugent, John Peer (50)
Maryland, University of 106
Northeastern Illinois University 142
Caron, Josiane (14)
Pennsylvania State University 151
Ongiri, David O. (111)
Singh, Jane M. (241)
Podium Management Associates, Inc. 154
Thomas, Piri (25)
Puget Sound, University of 159
Maxwell, Keith A. (41)
Saint Cloud State University 168
Downes, Alan J. (11)
Levilain, Guy (41)
Miller, Joan D. (48)
Speakers Bureau of America, Inc. 175
Sowell, Thomas (3)
Temple University 181
Keto, Clement T. (28), (338)
Morse, J. Mitchell (234), (305)
Smith, Rita (242), (294)
Williams, Walter E. (46), (255)
Viewpoint Speakers Bureau 213
Dixon, Maceo (2)
Rodriguez, Olga (12)
Virginia Polytechnic Institute and State University 216
Distler, P.A. (32)
Western Washington University 223
Paulus, Ingeborg (18)

RADIO
See also: MEDIA

American Radio Relay League 9
California State University, Fullerton 29
Mewett, Jack H. (310)
Zeltzer, Allen M. (46)
Eastern Illinois University 57
Rang, Jack C. (67)
Murray State University 117
Mofield, William Ray (86)
Northeastern Illinois University 142
Robinson, Edward A. (74)
Pennsylvania State University 151
Curtis, Anthony R. (68)
Felack, Michael (70)
Podium Management Associates, Inc. 154
Godfrey, Arthur (10)
Saint Cloud State University 168
De Santo, R. John (10)
Pehler, Jim (59)
Simon Fraser University 171
Cochran, John (32)
Southwestern Louisiana, University of 174
Oliver, James R. (79)
Speaker's Bureau of Philadelphia 176
Toffel, Bill (115)
Zabrowsky, Marian (125)
United States International Communications Agency 205

RAILROADS

Chemetron Corporation 34
East Carolina University 56
Price, Charles L. (35)

RAPE
See: CRIME

READING

Eastern Illinois University 57
MacLaren, Fred (54)
Murray, Louise (62)
Shank, Kathlene (79)
Marquette University 105
Siettman, James P. (26)
Murray State University 117
Aslup, Robert F. (36)
Watkins, Yancy (134)
National Water Well Association 136
Stanley, Anita Bacco (23)
Northeastern Illinois University 142
Bowers, Mary W. (9)
Fareed, Ahmed A. (21)
Georgiou, Peri P. (30)
Husain, Asad (41)
Pennsylvania State University 151
Costa, Joseph J. (93)
Du Puis, Mary M. (94)
Grella, Michael A. (100)
Puget Sound, University of 159
Berry, J. Raymond (10)
Hodges, Richard E. (29)
Roussin, Ramon (54)
Saint Cloud State University 168
Otto, Don H. (53)
Simon Fraser University 171
Franklin, Perry L. (16)
O'Connell, Sheila (19)
Trivett, John V. (21)
Southwestern Louisiana, University of 174
Ohaver, Allan R. (78)
Temple University 181
Johnson, Marjorie, Seddon (106)
Kress, Roy A. (107)
Ladd, Eleanor (108)
Rosenman, Jill C. (121)
Shankman, Florence V. (8) (123)
Virginia Polytechnic Institute and State University 216
Hubbard, Hazel (56)
Wilson Celebrities, Lola 225
Guild, Leo (19)

REAL ESTATE

California State University, Fullerton 29
Apke, Thomas M. (191)
Mlynaryk, Peter M. (81)
East Carolina University 56
Hurley, Pat (96)
Wardrep, Bruce (97)
Federal Reserve Bank of San Francisco 61
Florida Association of Realtors 65
Alexander, Narlene (1)
Baars, Theo D., Jr. (2)
Banks, Clyde M. (3)
Banzhaf, Parker C. (4)
Bermingham, Thomas J. (5)
Boardman, Blanche (6)
Boone, Betty Jane (7)
Bossen, Robert H. (8)
Cantrall, Otto L. (9)
Carroll, J.E. (10)
Clark, J. Rodney (11)
Concannon, F.P. (12)
Dalton, Peter O. (13)
Danforth, Horace C. (14)
Dominguez, Carlos, Jr. (15)
Falbey, J. Wayne (16)
Fantle, Karl S. (17)
Farrell, Reid D. (18)
Fearnley, Joe (19)
Frost, Robert J., III (20)
Gale, G. Fritz (21)
German, Jack (22)
Graham, Jim (23)
Greene, Errol L. (24)
Hannan, Robert (25)
Heavener, Mac D., Jr. (26)
Hinton, Jerrold R. (27)
Hoche, Henry (28)
Hogan, John (29)
Horn, Walter V. (30)
Hudson, Max (31)
Jacobson, Alan W. (32)
Jones, Ernest A. (33)
Kirk, Robert W. (34)
Konigsburg, Sidney (35)
Lassetter, Maggie S. (36)
Ledridge, Paul Walton (37)
Linville, George M. (38)
Lynn, Frank (39)
McCoy, Albert A. (40)
McCullough, George E. (41)
McIntosh, Claudette E. (42)
Martens, Frank H. (43)
Moore, Steven A. (44)
Moskal, Lilyb (45)
Moutz, Madora (46)
Moutz, W.B. (47)
Newstreet, Richard A. (48)
Overton, D. William (49)
Pardue, William P. (50)
Pickens, Phillip (51)
Pierce, John E. (52)
Pyms, Jack (53)
Randol, Monroe G. (54)
Ring, John F. (55)
Robison, Mack (56)
Schieber, Frank W. (57)
Slack, Ted C. (58)
Slater, L.B. (59)
Sprague, Ver Lynn (60)
Stemper, William H., Sr. (61)
Thomas, Phillip A. (62)
Van Brackle, Henry L. (63)
Varnadore, E. Lee (64)
Ward, Robert L. (65)
Waters, Paul W. (66)
Wegman, W.J. (67)
Wilcox, Olin R. (68)
Wilson, James T. (69)
Yates, Dorothy M. (70)
Georgia Federal Savings and Loan Association 72
Massachusetts Bar Association 107
National Association of Housing Cooperatives 121
Speaker's Bureau of Philadelphia 176
Lamont, Jay (59)
Meltzer, Bernard (78)
Success Leaders Speakers Service 180
Bale, Bob (7)
Cullen, Lloyd (39)
Temple University 181
Lamont, Jay (37), (225)
Virginia Polytechnic Institute and State University 216
Lamb, Fred M. (65)
Wells, Helen L. (141)
Wysocki, Joseph L. (145)
Washington, University of 218

RECREATION
See also: GAMES; PHYSICAL FITNESS; SPORTS; WATER SPORTS

Auburn University 16
Askew, Raymond S. (2)
East Carolina University 56
Hooks, Edgar (28)
Johnson, Thomas H. (81)
Eastern Illinois University 57
Krause, Paul (43)
Reed, Jane (68)
Marquette University 105
Dunn, J. Michael (114)
Maryland, University of 106
Murray State University 117
Freeman, William E. (114), (121)
Sholar, Thomas P. (54), (125)
Northeastern Illinois University 142
Hostetler, Frank C. (39)
Pennsylvania State University 151
Fletcher, Peter W. (304)
Johnston, Richard G. (128)
Roesler, Ned (166)
Roesler, Ned (1)
Saint Cloud State University 168
Kleiber, Douglas A. (36)
Rosenthal, Eugene (64)
Simon Fraser University 171
Hendy, Martin (27)
McClaren, Milton (37)
Southwestern Louisiana, University of 174
Rense, William C. (82)
Temple University 181
Williams, Delores T. (12)
Virginia Polytechnic Institute and State University 216
Gunsten, Paul H. (46)
McCollum, Robert H. (76)
Western Washington University 223
Aitken, Margaret (29)
Whittier College 224
Ibrahim, Hilmi (9)

RELIGION
See also: ISLAM; JUDAISM

Ahmadiyya Movement in Islam, Inc. 1
Abdullah, Yahya Sharif (1)
Ahmad, Imam Masud (2)
Ahmad, Mubashir (3)
Ahmad, Rashid (4)
Barkatullah, Qazi M. (5)
Bhatti, Bashir Ahmad (6)
Hakeem, Hasan (7)
Kaleem, Imam Atah Ullah (8)
Malik, Daud Abdul (9)
Malik, Saeed Ahmad (10)
Nasir, Khalil Ahmad (11)
Saeed, Munawar (12)
Zafr, A. Muzaffar Ahmad (13)
American Party 6
Anderson, Tom (1)
Shackelford, Rufus (3)

RELIGION (continued)

American Teilhard Association for the Future of Man 11
Berry, Thomas (1)
Brennan, Anne (2)
Bruteau, Beatrice (3)
Cousins, Evert (4)
Francoeus, Robert (5)
Gray, Donald (6)
Knight, Alice (7)
Kraft, R. Wayne (8)
Lynch, Margaret (9)
Americans United 12
Auburn University 16
Foy, James F. (21)
Kuykendall, John W. (47)
Lewis, W. David (51)
California State University, Fullerton 29
Fasheh, Issa I. (216), (225), (315)
Fierman, Morton C. (114)
Frazee, Charles A. (178), (234)
Giacumakis, George J. (91), (235)
McLaren, Robert B. (241), (275)
Namasaka, Boaz N. (6), (219), (242)
Nanjundappa, Boaz N. (286)
Russell, J. Michael (118)
Santucci, James A. (247)
Truesdell, William D. (183), (212), (248)
Tygart, Clarence E. (155), (249), (291)
Woodward, James F. (156), (184), (279)
Contemporary Forum 42
Dawn Bible Students Association 45
Fay, Edward E. (1)
Nail, Kenneth M. (2)
Wassmann, Felix S. (3)
Drew University 52
Ackerman, Robert K. (1)
Berenbroick, Lester (5)
Brack, Harold A. (9)
Courtney, Charles (19)
DeJong, Peter (23)
Dey, Lala Kalyan (25)
Doughty, Darrell J. (27)
Graybeal, David (33)
Hamilton, Neill Q. (37)
Johnson, Barent (42)
Jones, Donald (44)
Knox, John, Jr. (45)
Linn, Theodore Chace (49)
Oden, Thomas Clark (62)
Ollom, John F. (65)
Pain, James H. (66)
Ranck, James G. (71)
Reimann, Paul A. (73)
Rice, Charles L. (76)
Richey, Russell E. (77)
Rowe, Kenneth E. (81)
Ryan, Michael Daniel (82)
Stroker, William (91)
Sugarman, Shirley (92)
Thayer, Nelson S.T. (93)
Thompson, Bard (94)
Duquesne University 54
East Carolina University 56
Gross, Dawyer D. (137)
Jorgensen, N.M. (138)
Moore, Charles (107)
Nischan, Bodo (139)
Singh, Avtar (123), (140)
Eastern Illinois University 57
Titus, Charles (91)
Waddell, Leyla Peck (92)
Glendale Federal Savings and Loan Association 75
Carlson, Kenneth A. (1)
Harrington, Bob 81
Harrington, Bob (1)
Hutaff, Charles 83
Cockroft, Don (2)
Intercollegiate Studies Institute, Inc. 85
Herberg, Will (12)
Kuehnelt-Leddihin, Erik Von (18)
Martin, William Oliver (20)
Niemeyer, Gerhart (24)
Opitz, Edmund A. (25)
Tonsor, Stephen J. (33)
Jews for Jesus 93
Glaser, Mitch (1)
Rabinowitz, Amy (2)
Rosen, Moishe (3)
Zaretsky, Tuvya (4)
Kansas Wesleyan University 96
Keedick Lecture Bureau, Inc. 97
Holmes, Marjorie (31)
Marquette University 105
Doherty, Dennis J. (104)
Dreyer, Elizabeth (105)
Egan, Keith J. (106)
Lienhard, Joseph T. (107)
Metz, Donald L. (108)
Muschalek, George (109)
Pambookian, Hagop S. (23)
Rich, Lawrence M. (110)
Roach, Richard R. (111)
Maryland, University of 106
Murray State University 117
Kumar, Frederick L. (97)
Mayes, Jerry W. (135)
Newsweek, Inc. 139
Northeastern Illinois University 142
Firoozi, Ferydoon (23)
Singleton, Gregory H. (78)
Pennsylvania State University 151
Frankforter, A. Daniel (215)
Hagenbuch, Keith M. (258)
Mester, Cathy S. (78)
Riforgiato, Leonard R. (221)
Schlow, Marthamae C. (200)
Puget Sound, University of 159
Albertson, Robert G. (1)
Phillips, John W. (48)
Saint Cloud State University 168
Ezell, Wayland L. (13)
Kendall, Robert D. (34)
Mertens, Gerald C. (47)
Southwestern Louisiana, University of 174
Keiser, Edmund D., Jr. (53)
Kirkpatrick, Robert T. (55)
MacNair, Wilmer (69)
Vigorito, John V. (89)
Speaker's Bureau of Philadelphia 176
Crim, Mort (28)
Peale, Norman Vincent (85)
Sheen, Fulton J. (106)
Success Leaders Speakers Service 180
Qubein, Nido (141)
Richardson, Gilbert P. (145)
Walker, E. Jerry (185)
Temple University 181
Burnham, Kenneth E. (206)
Cormier, Raymond J. (208)
Holtzman, Robert H. (102), (303)
Morse, J. Mitchell (305)
Samuelson, Norbert M. (306)
Yadav, Bibhuti S. (307)
University Speakers Bureau 211
Haughton, Rosemary (4)
Novak, Michael (6)
Villanova University 214
Fittipaldi, Silvio E. (80)
Losoncy, Thomas A. (74)
Plater-Zyberk, Maria (81)
Syvinski, Henry B. (9)
Van Fleteren, Frederick E. (82)
Virginia Polytechnic Institute and State University 216
Payne, Alfred C. (94)
Washington, University of 218
Whittier College 224
Moody, Jonathan (11)
Winters, Richard H. (17)
Women's Classical Caucus 227
Bram, Jean Rhys (3)

RELIGION (continued)

Gordon, Diane R. (16)
Rossi, Mary Ann (39)
Sowa, Cora Angier (44)
Trachy, Carol Law (48)
Vanderlip, Vera F. (50)
World Vision International 230

RESEARCH

Auburn University 16
Carroll, Chester C. (11)
California State University, Fullerton 29
Dittman, Roger R. (255), (268)
Northeastern Illinois University 142
Wiercinski, Floyd J. (96)
Pennsylvania State University 151
Cunningham, Richard G. (266)
Ebaugh, Paul (139)
Ferguson, Frederick G. (206)
Frey, John C. (254)
Henisch, Heinz K. (73)
Queen's University 160
Milligan, John (14)
Nakatsu, Kanju (15)
Southwestern Louisiana, University of 174
Keiser, Edmund D., Jr. (53)
Temple University 181
Miller, Richard L. (18)

RETIREMENT
See also: ESTATE PLANNING

American Professional Practice Association 8
Keogh, Eugene J. (4)
Baltimore Federal Savings and Loan Association 18
Sheehan, T. Frank (1)
Georgia Federal Savings and Loan Association 72
Pennsylvania State University 151
Hefferan, Colien (166)
United States Department of Health, Education and Welfare 199

RUSSIA

American Institute for Exploration 4
Bank, Ted P., II (3)
Associated Film Artists 15
Francisco, Elay (2)
California, Irvine, University of 27
Lenhoff, Howard M. (42)
Lenhoff, Sylvia G. (43)
Weil, Helen H. (18), (46)
California State University, Fullerton 29
Odle, D. Richard (11), (17), (148), (293), (311), (322)
Sadovszky, Otto J. (12), (20), (65), (165), (289), (294)
Tumas, Elena V. (127), (189), (213), (295)
Yessis, Michael (296), (306)
Douglas Management 51
Douglas, Neil (1)
Drew University 52
Eiter, Richard H. (28)
Duquesne University 54
East Carolina University 56
Eller, Frank W. (116)
Eastern Illinois University 57
Horak, Stephan M. (37)
Waddell, Leyla Peck (92)
Fame Limited 59
Reddy, Dick (13)
Stockdale, Bill (16)
Intercollegiate Studies Institute, Inc. 85
Dobriansky, Lev E. (6)
Kuehnelt-Leddihin, Erik Von (18)
Possony, Stefan T. (29)
Schiebel, Joseph (31)
Keedick Lecture Bureau, Inc. 97
Magidoff, Nila (40)
Oltmans, Willem L. (52)
Leigh Bureau 102
Smith, Hedrick (32)
Marquette University 105
Pehowski, Marian (68)
Murray State University 117
Keller, Howard H. (101), (139)
Lubachko, Ivan S. (62), (72), (141)
Matthai, James P. (63)
Northwest Mining Association 143
Gilmour, Ernest H. (5)
Pennsylvania State University 151
Dickinson, Winifred (296)
Goldman, Stuart D. (193)
Puget Sound, University of 159
Kerr, Stephen T. (35)
Simon Fraser University 171
Hurst, Michael Eliot (2)
Viewpoint Speakers Bureau 213
Saunders, George (13)
Villanova University 214
Hahn, Jeffrey W. (87)
Virginia Polytechnic Institute and State University 216
Lucas, James T., Jr. (74)
Payne, Alfred C. (94)
Washington, University of 218
Western Washington University 223
Harder, K. Peter (33)

S

SAFETY
See also: TRAFFIC SAFETY

Auburn University 16
Barry, Mary E. (6)
Hardin, Ian R. (28)
Morgan, William W. (58)
Business Communication Council 23
Cal-Land Improvement Contractors 25
Marquette University 105
Ishii, Thomas K. (119)
Szews, Alfred P. (87)
National School Supply and Equipment Association 132
Payne, William J. (8)
Sweet, Guy V. (13)
National Water Well Association 136
Clay, Max (2)
McLaughlin, Wayne (4)
Northeastern Illinois University 142
Hostetler, Frank C. (39)
Pennsylvania Electric Company 150
Orris, Richard E. (6)
Pennsylvania State University 151
Arble, William C. (260)
Carpenter, Lynn A. (261)
Labbauf, Abbas (153)
Reethof, Gerhard (145)
Suloff, Charles E. (263)
Philadelphia Electric Speakers Bureau 152
Southwestern Louisiana, University of 174
Ducharme, Mary H. (24)
McMillan, Margaret (68)
Union Electric Speakers Forum 189
United States Consumer Product Safety Commission 191
United States National Transportation Safety Board 207
Virginia Electric and Power Company 215

SAFETY (continued)

Virginia Polytechnic Institute and State University 216
Butt, Albin T. (15)
Furr, A. Keith (41)
Lamb, Fred M. (65)
Prouty, Bruce R. (99)
Washington, University of 218

SAILING
See: WATER SPORTS

SALES
See also: ADVERTISING; MARKETING; PUBLIC RELATIONS

Auburn University 16
Barry, Mary E. (6)
Business Communication Council 23
First Federal of Broward 63
Florida Association of Realtors 65
Boardman, Blanche (6)
Boone, Betty Jane (7)
Bossen, Robert H. (8)
Cantrall, Otto L. (9)
Clark, J. Rodney (11)
Concannon, F.P. (12)
Dalton, Peter O. (13)
Danforth, Horace C. (14)
Dominquez, Carlos (15)
Fantle, Karl S. (17)
Farrell, Reid D. (18)
Fearnley, Joe (19)
Frost, Robert J., III (20)
Graham, Jim (23)
Greene, Errol L. (24)
Heavener, Mac D., Jr. (26)
Hoche, Henry (28)
Horn, Walter V. (30)
Hudson, Max (31)
Jacobson, Alan W. (32)
Ledridge, Paul Walton (37)
Linville, George M. (38)
Lynn, Frank (39)
McIntosh, Claudette E. (42)
Martens, Frank H. (43)
Moore, Steven A. (44)
Moskal, Lilyb (45)
Moutz, Madora (46)
Moutz, W.B. (47)
Newstreet, Richard A. (48)
Pierce, John E. (52)
Pyms, Jack (53)
Ring, John F. (55)
Sprague, Ver Lynn (60)
Stemper, William H., Sr. (61)
Van Brackle, Henry L. (63)
Varnadore, E. Lee (64)
Wilcox, Olin R. (68)
Yates, Dorothy M. (70)
Leigh Bureau 102
Linkletter, Jack (18)
Mid West Program Service, Inc. 112
Herman, Fred (61)
Kinder, Garry (79)
Kinder, Jack (80)
Tritt, Francis (124)
White, Somers H. (130)
Wolfe, John (136)
Murray State University 117
Seale, William B. (25)
National Speakers Bureau, Inc. 135
Micali, Paul (44)
National Water Well Association 136
Tosi, Donald (6)
Pennsylvania State University 151
Elder, James T. (41)
Reynolds Tobacco Company, R.J. 165
Speakers Unlimited 177
Success Leaders Speakers Service 180
Adams, Bill (2)
Bobrow, Edwin E. (16)
Carter, Arnold (23)
Christianson, John N. (27)
Cimberg, Alan (28)
Dornoff, James (43)
Flarsheim, Henry (53)
Foster, Ray (55)
Gardner, Dick (60)
Giblin, Les (63)
Goodwin, Frank (64)
Hall, Woodie (72)
Hegarty, Christopher J. (81)
Herman, Fred (82)
Jansen, Robert H. (89)
Johnson, Mildred (92)
Koschel, Ed S. (101)
Lapp, Charles (103)
Letterese, Peter D. (106)
Marine, Jules A. (117)
Micali, Paul (120)
Norman, Thom (132)
Powell, Miles (139)
Saint-Laurent, Henri (147)
Staight, Robert (163)
Sturgeon, Paul (172)
Thomas, M. Donald (178)
Walters, Dorothy M. (186)
Wolfe, John (196)
Yoho, Dave (200)
Ziglar, Judge (201)
Ziglar, Zig (202)
Wilson Celebrities, Lola 225
Loder, H. Leith (25)

SCHOOL ADMINISTRATION

Auburn University 16
Duncan, J.W. (8)
East Carolina University 56
Jones, Douglas R. (48)
Eastern Illinois University 57
Matzner, Gerhard C. (55)
Marquette University 105
Kaiser, Jeffrey S. (42)
Tracy, William T. (51)
Murray State University 117
Fitch, Franklin G. (41)
Matarazzo, S.M. (46)
Noffsinger, Hugh A. (49)
National School Supply and Equipment Association 132
Bresnan, Don (2)
Girdler, R.J., Jr. (5)
Long, James W. (6)
Pace, John (7)
Payne, William J. (8)
Schmelzel, E.W. (10)
Northeastern Illinois University 142
Skvarla, Melvyn A. (79)
Vogel, Francis X. (91)
Pennsylvania State University 151
Milakofsky, Louis F. (106)
Saint Cloud State University 168
Farrah, George A. (14)
Temple University 181
Lebofsky, Dennis S. (112), (304)
Pavan, Barbara (118)
Walters, Donald L. (45), (130)
Villanova University 214
Niosi, Jerome J. (37)

SCIENCE
See also: ASTRONOMY; BIOLOGY; GEOGRAPHY; GEOLOGY; MATHEMATICS; METEOROLOGY; PHYSICS; ZOOLOGY

American Teilhard Association for the Future of Man 11
Kraft, R. Wayne (8)

SCIENCE (continued)

Auburn University 16
Jemian, Wartan A. (41)
California Polytechnic State University 28
California State University, Fullerton 29
Dittman, Roger R. (120), (255), (268)
Johnson, Fred M. (272)
McLaren, Robert B. (241), (275)
Walkington, David L. (32), (111), (278), (352)
Woodward, James F. (156), (184), (279)
Drew University 52
DeJong, Peter (23)
Ollom, John F. (65)
Phillips, Joy (68)
Siebert, Donald R. (86)
Eastern Illinois University 57
Buchanan, David (6)
Ferguson, Karen (20)
Leyden, Michael B. (50)
Intercollegiate Studies Institute, Inc. 85
Tonsor, Stephen J. (33)
Vivas, Eliseo (36)
Marquette University 105
Deshotels, Warren J. (117)
Newsweek, Inc. 139
Northeastern Illinois University 142
Dobbs, Frank W. (19)
Gilbert, R.L. (31)
Wiercinski, Floyd J. (96)
Pennsylvania State University 151
Furrow, Stanley D. (267)
Hagenbuch, Keith M. (258)
Heinsohn, Robert Jennings (269)
Henisch, Heinz K. (73)
Jennings, Robert (269)
Kujundzic, Zeljko (27)
Marsicano, Arthur J. (131)
Roy, Rustum (272)
Tomezsko, Edward S.J. (273)
Wallach, David L. (274)
Weed, Merwin L. (149)
Podium Management Associates, Inc. 154
Ordway, Frederick (17)
Puget Sound, University of 159
Berry, Keith O. (11)
Rousslang, Kenneth (55)
Rowland, Thomas V. (56)
Simon Fraser University 171
Curzon, Albert (33)
Funt, B.L. (34)
Huntley, Dave (36)
Schwarz, Abbey (54)
Southwestern Louisiana, University of 174
Keiser, Edmund D., Jr. (53)
Speaker's Bureau of Philadelphia 176
Bergman, Jules (8)
Temple University 181
Offenbacher, Elmer L. (279)
Villanova University 214
Scott, Thomas (22)
Virginia Polytechnic Institute and State University 216
Snizek, William E. (118)
Teates, Thomas G. (129)
Van Damme, Frans N. (136)
Washington, University of 218
Western Electric Company 222
Women's Classical Caucus 227
Sowa, Cora Angier (44)

SCIENCE FICTION

Auburn University 16
Lewis, W. David (51)
California State University, Fullerton 29
McNelly, Willis E. (206)
East Carolina University 56
Lawler, Donald (64)
Mid West Program Service, Inc. 112
Gunn, James (49)
Murray State University 117
Forrester, Kent (88)
Pennsylvania State University 151
Hopper, Paul T. (235)
Temple University 181
McCain, Roger A. (141), (231)
Villanova University 214
Esmonde, Margaret P. (46)
Virginia Polytechnic Institute and State University 216
Espley, John L. (34)
Women's Classical Caucus 227
Broege, Valerie (4)

SCULPTURE

Drew University 52
Dehoney, Martyvonne (22)
East Carolina University 56
Farnham, Emily (10)
Virginia Polytechnic Institute and State University 216
Carter, Dean (16)
Women's Classical Caucus 227
More, Judith de Luce (32)

SECRETARIES
See also: OFFICE MANAGEMENT

Murray State University 117
Wells, Faye C. (27)
Naremco Services, Inc. 119
Schiff, Robert A. (1)
Southwestern Louisiana, University of 174
Lacaze, Marie Louise (60)

SECURITY
See also: POLICE

American Polygraph Association 7
Atwood, Walter F. (1)
Weir, Raymond J., Jr. (2)
California State University, Fullerton 29
Gala, Basil E. (136)
Pinkerton's Inc. 153
Success Leaders Speakers Service 180
Humphries, Russell J. (86)
Temple University 181
Kutney, Andrew J. (58)

SELF IMPROVEMENT
See: PERSONAL DEVELOPMENT

SEX AND SEXUALITY

California State University, Fullerton 29
McCarthy, Miles D. (174), (274)
Russell, J. Michael (118), (245)
Webber, Arthur W. (250)
White, Geoffry D. (252)
Duquesne University 54
East Carolina University 56
Johnson, Thomas H. (3), (47)
Knox, David (5)
Eastern Illinois University 57

SEX AND SEXUALITY (continued)

Noland, Carol (64)
Intercollegiate Studies Institute, Inc. 85
Kuehnelt-Leddihin, Erik Von (18)
Van Den Haag, Ernest (35)
Marquette University 105
Doherty, Dennis J. (104)
McCall, Raymond J. (100)
Piacsek, Bela E. (3)
Morality in Media, Inc. 116
Chernus, Jack (1)
Douglas, John (2)
Gavrin, Irving (3)
Hill, Morton A. (4)
Murphy, Paul (5)
Shapiro, Stephen E. (6)
Volatis, Constantine (7)
Northeastern Illinois University 142
Hostetler, Frank C. (39)
Moorhead, Hugh S. (62)
Styer, Sandra (84)
Walker, Robert (92)
Pennsylvania State University 151
Zavodni, John J. (160)
Puget Sound, University of 159
Phillips, John W. (48)
Saint Cloud State University 168
Halton, Patrice Hoffman (23)
Schwerdtfeger, Dale (66)
Wise, Jeffrey (73)
Simon Fraser University 171
Hurst, Michael Eliot (48)
Wilden, Anthony (56)
Southwestern Louisiana, University of 174
MacNair, Wilmer (69)
Morella, John R. (76)
Spokespeople 178
McGlachlin, Kay (3)
Temple University 181
Glass, Dorothea D. (165)
Isard, Eleanore S. (221), (284)
Legos, Patricia M. (227), (286)
Rubini, Dennis A. (238)
University Speakers Bureau 211
Callahan, Sidney (2)
Francoeur, Robert T. (3)
Virginia Polytechnic Institute and State University 216
Fu, Victoria R. (40)
Washington, University of 218
Whittier College 224
Olson-Prather, Emelie (12)
Wilson Celebrities, Lola 225
Calvet, Corinne (5)
Canary (6)
Chagall, David (8)
Women's Classical Caucus 227
Hallett, Judith P. (18)

SOCIAL PROBLEMS
See also: SOCIAL RESPONSIBILITIES; SOCIAL WELFARE

California, Irvine, University 27
Binder, Arnold (37)
California State University, Fullerton 29
Brower, Jonathan J. (282)
Sims, Melvin D. (153), (350)
Drew University 52
O'Kane, James M. (63)
Varner, James (95)
Duquesne University 54
Intercollegiate Studies Institute, Inc. 85
Anderson, Martin (1)
Crane, Philip M. (3)
Demsetz, Harold (4)
Herberg, Will (12)
Kirk, Russell (16)
Kuehnelt-Leddihin, Erik Von (18)
Opitz, Edmund A. (25)
Van Den Haag, Ernest (35)
Wiggins, James W. (38)
Murray State University 117
Garfield, Gene J. (116)
Johnson, Jack B. (100)
National Speakers Bureau, Inc. 135
Gallup, George (21)
Pennsylvania State University 151
Harkness, William L. (262)
Puget Sound, University of 159
Moreland, Steve J. (43)
Saint Cloud State University 168
Andrzejewski, Julie (4)
Herbison, Priscilla J. (26)
Simon Fraser University 171
Hurst, Michael Eliot (48)
Southwestern Louisiana, University of 174
Harris, Patricia A. (42)
Speaker's Bureau of Philadelphia 176
Bernard, Clara (11)
Schwartz, Loretta (103)
Spokespeople 178
Spock, Benjamin (5)
Temple University 181
Batra, Gopal K. (333)
Villanova University 214
Betz, Joseph (83)

SOCIAL RESPONSIBILITIES
See also: ETHICS AND MORALS; SOCIAL PROBLEMS

Auburn University 16
Carroll, Chester C. (11)
White, J. Herbert (87)
Business Communication Council 23
California State University, Fullerton 29
Barish, Natalie (113)
Reckinger, Nancy R. (347)
Smythe, Ted C. (119), (312)
Intercollegiate Studies Institute, Inc. 85
Anderson, Martin (1)
Mid West Program Service, Inc. 112
Delaney, R.E. (30)
Pennsylvania State University 151
Gilmore, Harold L. (43)
Puget Sound, University of 159
Anton, Paul (3)
Saint Cloud State University 168
Lieberman, Harold (42)
Marmas, James G. (45)
Speaker's Bureau of Philadelphia 176
Ammond, Alene (3)

SOCIAL SCIENCES

California, Irvine, University of 27
DiMento, Joseph F. (38)
Price, Michael J. (45)
Carnegie-Mellon University 31
Moyer, Kenneth E. (7)
Duquesne University 54
Eastern Illinois University 57
Dow, Ruth (15)
Intercollegiate Studies Institute, Inc. 85
Herberg, Will (12)
Molnar, Thomas (23)
Leigh Bureau 102
Packard, Vance (22)
Tiger, Lionel (35)
Marquette University 105
Blascovich, James J. (99)
Metz, Donald L. (21)

SOCIAL SCIENCES (continued)

Williams, Don L. (31)
Maryland, University of 106
Mid West Program Service, Inc. 112
Ardrey, Robert (3)
Brothers, Joyce (16)
Murray State University 117
Johnson, Jack B. (100)
Muehleman, Tom (109)
Stranahan, Joan (110)
Northeastern Illinois University 142
Garrett, Philip R. (28)
Singleton, Gregory H. (78)
Uliassi, Edward C. (87)
Pennsylvania State University 151
Mandle, Joan D. (167)
Queen's University 160
Sinclair, Duncan (19)
Willett, Terry (21)
Saint Cloud State University 168
Andrzejewski, Julie (4)
Boltuck, Charles J. (7)
Mertens, Gerald C. (47)
Risberg, Douglas F. (63)
Rosenthal, Eugene (64)
Schwerdtfeger, Dale (66)
Wollin, Dorothy (74)
Simon Fraser University 171
Wilden, Anthony (56)
Southwestern Louisiana, University of 174
Gaudet, Irby J., Jr. (32)
Harris, Patricia A. (42)
Hotard, Stephen R. (50)
MacNair, Wilmer (69)
Spokespeople 178
Hudiburgh, Kayren (1)
Success Leaders Speakers Service 180
Furbay, John H. (59)
McGrane, William J. (113)
Smith, Leonard J. (159)
Stewart, Suzanne (165)
Uni, Miriam (182)
Temple University 181
Baenninger, Ronald (281)
Legos, Patricia M. (286)
Millison, Martin B. (290)
Smith, Rita (294)
Steisel, Ira M. (296)
Thurman, Ken (126)
Villanova University 214
Gallagher, Bernard J. (65), (86)
Heitzmann, William Ray (78)
Sheldon, Paul (79)
Virginia Polytechnic Institute and State University 216
Thye, Forrest W. (134)
Washington, University of 218
Western Washington University 223
Barnhart, Michael W. (22)

SOCIAL WELFARE

American Graduate School of International Management 3
Roessler, Helmut R. (6)
Carnegie-Mellon University 31
Kaplan, Robert S. (38)
Duquesne University 54
Murray State University 117
Garfield, Gene J. (116)
Johnson, Jack B. (100), (117)
Rose, Joseph L. (119)
Pennsylvania State University 151
Beck, Edward S. (161)
Saint Cloud State University 168
Herbison, Priscilla J. (26)
Simon Fraser University 171
Hutchinson, John (49)
Socialist Party, USA 172
Rosenhaft, Ann (10)
Temple University 181
Adams, Ernestyne James (308)
Galper, Jeffry (309)
Jaipual, Inderjit (56)
Myers, Robert J. (40)
Pittman, Audrey S. (311)
Transier, Lee (66), (248)
Vandivier, Frances (252), (313)
United States Department of Health, Education and Welfare 199

SOLAR ENERGY

See also: ENERGY

Auburn University 16
Brewer, Robert N. (8)
California State University, Fullerton 29
Sowell, Edward F. (110)
Marquette University 105
Deshotels, Warren J. (117)
Pennsylvania State University 151
Gilman, Stanley F. (126)
Houlihan, John F. (127)
Villanova University 214
Rice, William J. (43)
Virginia Polytechnic Institute and State University 216
Long, C. Hardy (71)
Vaughan, David H. (137)
Washington, University of 218
Western Electric Company 222

SOUTH AMERICA

Associated Film Artists 15
Francisco, Clay (2)
California, Irvine, University of 27
Guerra-Cunningham, Lucia (11)
California State University, Fullerton 29
Weightman, Barbara A. (167), (190), (325)
Drew University 52
Weiner, Joan S. (97)
East Carolina University 56
Leahy, Edward P. (120)
McGuire, Martin E. (6)
Eastern Illinois University 57
Anderson, Eulalee L. (1)
Fame Limited 59
Gerstle, Ralph (4)
Forrest, Martin A. 69
DuBois, Jean Louis (3)
Lange, George (7)
Memphis State University 110
Gerstle, Ralph (5)
Moore, William (8)
Murray State University 117
Koenecke, Alice (140)
O'Neil, Charles (102)
Northeastern Illinois University 142
Lopez, Jose E. (56)
Pennsylvania State University 151
Ameringer, Charles D. (213)
Virginia Polytechnic Institute and State University 216
Andrew, Loyd D. (2)
McMillion, Martin B. (78)

SOUTHEAST ASIA

Duquesne University 54
East Carolina University 56
Gowen, Robert J. (91)
Singh, Avtar (123)
Eastern Illinois University 57
Chen, Robert P. (9)
Moll, Edward O. (59)
Fame Limited 59
Armstrong, Ken (1)

SOUTHEAST ASIA (continued)

Intercollegiate Studies Institute, Inc. 85
  Possony, Stefan T. (29)
Memphis State University 110
  Parrott, Alton (10)
Northeastern Illinois University 142
  Feldman, Reynold (22)
  Husain, Asad (41)
Pennsylvania State University 151
  Albinski, Henry S. (189)
  Breckenridge, Jay (162)
Saint Cloud State University 168
  Levilain, Guy (41)
Southwestern Louisiana, University of 174
  Rense, William C. (82)
  Webb, Robert M. (91)
Villanova University 214
  Thanawala, Kishor (52)
Wilson Celebrities, Lola 225
  Sargent, Wyn (35)

SOUTHERN UNITED STATES

Auburn University 16
  Griessman, B. Eugene (24)
  Lewis, W. David (51)
Center for Southern Folklore 32
Drew University 52
  Ackerman, Robert K. (1)
East Carolina University 56
  Rodabaugh, Karl (8)
Eastern Illinois University 57
  Williams, Glenn D. (96)
Forrest, Martin A. 69
  Kern, Richard (6)
Murray State University 117
  Hammock, James W., Jr. (69)
Podium Management Associates, Inc. 154
  Deal, Borden (6)
  Dick, David (7)
Southwestern Louisiana, University of 174
  Conrad, Glenn R. (19)
  Cordes, Carroll (20)
Virginia Polytechnic Institute and State University 216
  Havard, William C. (50)

SPACE
  See also: ASTRONOMY

California State University, Fullerton 29
  Johnson, Fred M. (272)
  Ryan, John A. (152), (276)
East Carolina University 56
  Batten, J.W. (98)
Eastern Illinois University 57
  Taitt, Henry A. (87)
Hutaff, Charles 83
  Neff, Earl (15)
Johnson, Carl M. 94
  Phillips, Ted (3)
Mid West Program Service, Inc. 112
  Cook, Ron (25)
National Speakers Bureau, Inc. 135
  Hynek, J. Allen (30)
  Schirra, Walter (56)
Northeastern Illinois University 142
  Gilbert, R.C. (31)
Pennsylvania State University 151
  Smith, Hubert C. (34)
Podium Management Associates, Inc. 154
  Ordway, Frederick (17)
Simon Fraser University 171
  Bennett, Tom (31)
Temple University 181
  Dubeck, Leroy W. (213), (276)
Villanova University 214
  Sion, Edward M. (10)
Virginia Polytechnic Institute and State University 216
  Arndt, Richard (3)
  Marchman, James F., III (79)
  Schetz, Joseph A. (108)
Western Washington University 223
  Quigley, Robert J. (4)
Wilson Celebrities, Lola 225
  Carpenter, Scott (7)

SPAIN
  See also: EUROPE

California State University, Fullerton 29
  Prado, Marcial (125), (151), (323)
Drew University 52
  Cochran, Lillian T. (16)
Memphis State University 110
  Booth, John N. (1)
Viewpoint Speakers Bureau 213
  Jenness, Linda (6)
Virginia Polytechnic Institute and State University 216
  Aceves, Joseph B. (1)
Washington, University of 218

SPANISH-AMERICAN
  See: CHICANOS

SPEECH

Auburn University 16
  Phillips, Phyllis P. (67)
East Carolina University 56
  Lewis, Frederick C. (53)
  Muzzarelli, Robert A. (55)
Eastern Illinois University 57
  Nicely, James E. (63)
  Thurman, Wayne L. (90)
Marquette University 105
  Staudacher, Joseph M. (13)
Murray State University 117
  Hufnagle, Jon (133)
  Mayes, Jerry W. (135)
  Valentine, Robert (136)
Northeastern Illinois University 142
  Flory, Joyce Ann (25)
Pennsylvania State University 151
  Frank, Tom (96)
  Mester, Cathy S. (78)
  Sias, John D. (83)
Saint Cloud State University 168
  Grachek, Arthur F. (17)
  Kendall, Robert D. (34)
  Lease, A.A. (40)
Southwestern Louisiana, University of 174
  Billeaud, Frances P. (8)
  Hobbs, Brenda Castille (47)
  Lyle, Marguerite R. (66)
Success Leaders Speakers Service 180
  Bennett, Millard (14)
  Powell, J. Lewis (138)
Washington, University of 218

SPORTS
  See also: PHYSICAL EDUCATION; PHYSICAL FITNESS; RECREATION; WATER SPORTS

Associated Film Artists 15
  Jay, John (3)
Auburn University 16
  Howard, Milford Kenneth (38)

SPORTS (continued)

Jenkins, Stephen R. (42)
Simms, Jack (74)
Blackman and Raber Limited 21
Burns Sports Celebrity Service, Inc. 22
California State University, Fullerton 29
Bailey, C. Ian (130), (299)
Brower, Jonathan J. (282), (300)
Colletto, James M. (24), (301)
Qureshi, Naimuddin (303)
Sims, Melvin D. (153), (304)
Witchey, Ronald L. (305)
Yessis, Michael (296), (306)
Carnegie-Mellon University 31
Birdy, Earl J. (39)
Contemporary Forum 42
Duquesne University 54
East Carolina University 56
Compton, Rod (76)
Stasavich, Clarence (87)
Eastern Illinois University 57
McFarland, Gene (58)
Mullally, Mike (60)
Sanders, J.W. (74)
Shull, Carl (82)
Feminist Karate Union 62
Bateman, Py (1)
Fulton Inc., Richard 71
Hutaff, Charles 83
Cockroft, Don (2)
Jones, Harry (14)
Learning Exchange 99
Mahgo Enterprises, Inc. 104
Marquette University 105
Byrne, Kevin (112)
DeRoche, Robert J. (113)
Dunn, J. Michael (114)
Fitts, Robert H. (115)
Shiely, Catherine (126)
Mid West Program Service, Inc. 112
Gowdy, Curt (44)
McKay, Jim (86)
Podolak, Ed (101)
Rice, Bruce (107)
Miller Agency, Gilbert 113
Gowdy, Curt (1)
Piersall, Jimmy (2)
National Speakers Bureau, Inc. 135
Blanda, George (7)
Newsweek, Inc. 139
Northeastern Illinois University 142
Johnson, Violet (46)
Kasper, Raymond (49)
Meyer, Betty (60)
Riess, Steven A. (72)
Pennsylvania State University 151
Agate, Paul B. (275)
Caporali, John M. (204)
Costa, Joseph J. (93)
Denbow, Terry (69)
Harris, Dorothy V. (276)
Henry, Richard L. (277)
Lauffer, Herbert (278)
Lupton, Charles (187)
Miller, Sayers J., Jr. (279)
Morehouse, Chauncey A. (280)
Nelson, Richard C. (209)
Onorato, Ed (282)
Powell, John W. (283)
Stoner, Clarence H. (284)
Sweeting, Roger (285)
Tait, G. Thomas (286)
Podium Management Associates, Inc. 154
Gifford, Frank (9)
Puget Sound, University of 159
Bowman, Dawn (14)
Saint Cloud State University 168
Bartlett, Gary E. (5)
Kleiber, Douglas A. (36)
Waxlax, Robert (71)
Simon Fraser University 171
Banister, Eric (23)
Davies, W. Lorne (25)
Ross, William (28)
Savage, Margaret (29)
Werner, Hal (30)
Southwestern Louisiana, University of 174
Hennessey, Jefferson T. (45)
Speaker's Bureau of Philadelphia 176
Brenner, Glenn (18)
Gary, Steve (42)
Henderson, Don (48)
Leitner, Ted (63)
Levy, Steve (65)
Meltzer, Al (77)
Roberts, Robin (94)
Stevenson, Samantha (112)
Woodeshick, Tom (121)
Success Leaders Speakers Service 180
Jones, L. Bevel (93)
Temple University 181
Barone, Marian T. (2)
Lockhart, Barbara D. (6), (327)
Offenbacher, Elmer L. (7), (279)
University Speakers Bureau 211
Novak, Michael (6)
Villanova University 214
Heitzmann, William Ray (11)
Virginia Polytechnic Institute and State University 216
Gunsten, Paul H. (46)
Nachlas, Joel A. (87)
Thye, Forrest W. (134)
Washington, University of 218
Women's Classical Caucus 227
Hallett, Judith P. (18)
Women's Martial Arts Union 228

STATE AND LOCAL GOVERNMENT
See also: COMMUNITIES; GOVERNMENT; PUBLIC ADMINISTRATION; URBAN AFFAIRS

Auburn University 16
Johnson, Gerald W. (43)
McMillan, Malcolm C. (55)
California State University, Fullerton 29
Saltzstein, Alan L. (66), (262)
Carnegie-Mellon University 31
Schatzman, Dennis (27)
Drew University 52
Mastro, Julius (54)
Duquesne University 54
Eastern Illinois University 57
Leigh, Peter R., II (49)
Marquette University 105
Klitzke, Ramon A. (56)
National Water Well Association 136
Heiss, Harold W., Jr. (26)
Northeastern Illinois University 142
Pastors, Charles R. (67)
Pennsylvania State University 151
Hand, Irving (226)
Wolf, George D. (222)
Puget Sound, University of 159
Baarsma, William (4)
Saint Cloud State University 168
Williamson, Homer E. (72)
Socialist Party, USA 172
Hart, William (3)
Kissell, Rick (5)
Southwestern Louisiana, University of 174
Kurtz, Donn M., II (59)
Oliver, James R. (79)
Temple University 181
Weiler, Conrad (275)
Virginia Polytechnic Institute and State University 216
Sturm, Albert L. (124)
Western Washington University 223
Barnhart, Michael W. (22)

STATE AND LOCAL GOVERNMENT (continued)

Whittier College 224
Harvey, Richard B. (8)
Thomas, Larry (15)

STATISTICS

Pennsylvania State University 151
Harkness, William L. (262)
Murty, Vedula N. (251)
Salvia, Anthony A. (252)
Villanova University 214
Mason, Saul (33)
Washington, University of 218
Women's Classical Caucus 227
Villeneuve, Winnie Frohn (51)

STOCK MARKET

Auburn University 16
Davis, Robert D. (17)
Carnegie-Mellon University 31
Kaplan, Robert S. (1)
Commodity Exchange, Inc. 38
Intercollegiate Studies Institute, Inc. 85
Manne, Henry G. (19)
New York Mercantile Exchange 138
Falis, Melvin (2)
Gabler, Howard (3)
Levine, Richard (4)

T

TAXES

Americans United 12
Business Communication Council 23
California State University, Fullerton 29
Graubert, Burton L. (307)
Duquesne University 54
Eastern Illinois University 57
Matzner, Gerhard C. (55)
Florida Association of Realtors 65
Stemper, William H., Sr. (61)
Marquette University 105
Piasecki, Michael J. (7)
Massachusetts Bar Association 107
Pennsylvania State University 151
Hefferan, Colien (166)
Kelly, B. Wayne (44)
Monahan, Robert E. (50)
Puget Sound, University of 159
Bernstein, Jeffry A. (9)
Frankel, Sheldon S. (22)
Veseth, Michael (64)
Saint Cloud State University 168
Madsen, Russell D. (44)
Temple University 181
Lamont, Jay (37)
Virginia Polytechnic Institute and State University 216
Spann, Robert M. (119)
Washington, University of 218

TECHNOLOGY

Auburn University 16
Lewis, W. David (51)
Eastern Illinois University 57
Coleman, Wayne (11)
Lauda, Donald P. (46)
Intercollegiate Studies Institute, Inc. 85
Kintner, William R. (15)
Tonsor, Stephen J. (33)
Wiggins, James W. (38)
Leigh Bureau 102
Fadiman, Clifton (11)
Packard, Vance (22)
Marquette University 105
Deshotels, Warren J. (117)
Horgan, James D. (118)
Murray State University 117
Lilly, George T. (80)
Lynn, Paul K. (81)
Schanbacker, Eugene M. (82)
National Micrographics Association 128
National Speakers Bureau, Inc. 135
Schirra, Walter (56)
National Water Well Association 136
Gass, Tyler E. (25)
Heiss, Harold W., Jr. (26)
Lehr, Jay H. (27)
May, Judy (28)
Northeastern Illinois University 142
Nissim-Sabat, Charles (65)
Saiet, Ronald A. (75)
Pennsylvania State University 151
Bierderman, Edwin, Jr. (124)
Chapin, Jack (265)
Dandois, Joseph E. (53)
Elias, Edward M. (140)
Furrow, Stanley D. (267)
Gamble, Hays B. (225)
Heinsohn, Robert Jennings (269)
Johnson, John C. (141)
Kroger, Manfred (177)
McCormick, Robert H. (47)
Marsicano, Arthur J. (131)
Mullen, Sharman Stanic (79)
Queeney, Donna S. (288)
Reethof, Gerhard (145)
Roy, Rustum (272)
Santulli, Michael A. (157)
Schenck, George (134)
Shemick, John M. (118)
Steffy, Denton A. (146)
Walden, Daniel (245)
Weed, Merwin L. (149)
Podium Management Associates, Inc. 154
Ordway, Frederick (17)
Puget Sound, University of 159
Bland, Jeffrey (12)
Queen's University 160
de Pencier, Robert (8)
Saint Cloud State University 168
Bjorklund, L.R. (6)
Lease, A.A. (40)
Lieberman, Harold (42)
Simon Fraser University 171
Hurst, Michael Eliot (2)
Southwestern Louisiana, University of 174
Young, Robert L. (97)
Temple University 181
Wilson, Samuel M. (47)
Virginia Polytechnic Institute and State University 216
Pitt, Joseph C. (95)
Pusey, Robert H. (100)
Van Damme, Frans N. (136)
Washington, University of 218
Western Washington University 223
Hackler, Clyde (31)
Whittier College 224
Farmer, Malcolm F. (5)

TELEVISION
See also: MEDIA

American Radio Relay League 9
O'Dell, Peter (1)
Auburn University 16
Wegener, Ed (86)
California State University, Fullerton 29
Mewett, Jack H. (310)
Directors Guild of America 49

TELEVISION (continued)

Drew University 52
Nelson, Gregory (60)
Eastern Illinois University 57
Heumann, Joseph (32)
Hutaff, Charles 83
Adair, Doug (1)
Hickey, William (11)
International Industrial Television Association 87
Leigh Bureau 102
Johnson, Nicholas (15)
Marquette University 105
Allen, Craig G. (65)
Sheikh, Anees E. (103)
Siettmann, James P. (85)
Tiedge, James T. (69)
Mid West Program Service, Inc. 112
Beasley, Edward (9)
Morality in Media, Inc. 116
Chernus, Jack (1)
Douglas, John (2)
Shapiro, Stephen E. (6)
Murray State University 117
Howard, Robert (84)
Mofield, William Ray (86)
National Cable Television Association 124
Schmidt, Robert L. (1)
Wheeler, Thomas E. (2)
National Speakers Bureau, Inc. 135
Lower, Elmer W. (41)
Northeastern Illinois University 142
Flory, Joyce Ann (25)
Robinson, Edward A. (74)
Stevens, Humphrey (83)
Pennsylvania State University 151
Carter, Joe Douglas (66)
Haskin, Lynn Martin (72)
Waun, Roger J. (87)
Podium Management Associates, Inc. 154
Stuart, Mary (24)
Weston, Av (26)
Puget Sound, University of 159
Somerville, Thomas F. (62)
Saint Cloud State University 168
DeSanto, R. John (10)
Fields, Dennis C. (15)
Montgomery, Terry (50)
Pehler, Jim (59)
Speaker's Bureau of Philadelphia 176
Schreffler, Ken (102)
Toffel, Bill (115)
Zabrowsky, Marian (125)
Temple University 181
Galey, Minaruth (70), (98), (215)
Metallinos, Nikos (76), (232)
Virginia Polytechnic Institute and State University 216
Haines, Kenneth H. (47)
Steffen, Robert F. (123)
Washington, University of 218
Wilson Celebrities, Lola 225
Rickman, Peter Mark (30)

TEXTILES

Auburn University 16
Hardin, Ian R. (28)
Pancheri, Lillian Unger (64)
Handweavers Guild of America 79
Aaron-Taylor, Susan (1)
Adrosko, Rita J. (2)
Alexander, Marthann (3)
Anderson, Jeorgia (4)
Austin, Joan F. (5)
Baker, Mary (6)
Bank, Rose S. (7)
Barret, Clotilde (8)
Belfer, Nancy (9)
Berlin, Rosalind K. (10)
Best, Eleanor (11)
Blackburn, Edna (12)
Bringle, Edwina (13)
Brooks, Lois Ziff (14)
Brown, Janice C. (15)
Burhen, Jan (16)
Busse, Jane (17)
Cahlander, Adele (18)
Carson, Ted (19)
Carter, Grace (20)
Cawood, Robert (21)
Chapin, Doloria (22)
Chase, Eleanor (23)
Chetwynd, Hilary (24)
Clement, Doris and Ted (25)
Constandse, Martha E. (26)
Cope, Louise Todd (27)
Correll, Leslie (28)
Coutts, Lucille (29)
Crawford, Libby (30)
Creager, Clara H. (31)
Crockett, Candace (32)
Culbertson, Ruth Pearson (33)
Davidson, Mary Frances (34)
Dendel, Esther Warner (35)
Druding, Susan C. (36)
Eicher, Joan B. (37)
Elliott, Verda (38)
Ericson, Lois (39)
Friel, Jonda (40)
Frost, Gordon W. (41)
Fuhrmann, Brigita (42)
Gerber, Fred and Nita (43)
Ginsberg-Place, Ruth (44)
Goodman, Ronald (45)
Gordon, Beverly (46)
Gordon, Lida G. (47)
Gotthoffer, Esther (48)
Grandin-Nettles, Margareta (49)
Grant, Susan (50)
Grayson, Persis (51)
Gulick, Evelyn M. (52)
Guy, Sallie T. (53)
Hall, Joanne A. (54)
Hallman, Ted (55)
Hart, Arthur A. (56)
Hauptli, Ellen (57)
Henry, Kathleen M. (58)
Hicks, C. Norman (59)
Higgins, Mary Lou (60)
Hinman, Mary Bausch (61)
Hofstrom, Juanita (62)
Holroyd, Ruth (63)
Howard, Margaret F. (64)
Janeiro, Jan (65)
Janis, Phyllis M. (66)
Jones, Jeanetta L. (67)
Jupena, Urban (68)
Karlin, Edith (69)
Kaufman, Glen (70)
King, Bucky (71)
Klein, Sheila (72)
Kowalek, Jon W. (73)
Krasnoff, Julienne Hallen (74)
Krondahl, Hans (75)
La Lena, Connie (76)
Lenderman, Max L. (77)
Lester, Michelle (78)
Levinson, Mimi (79)
Livingston, Savetta L. (80)
Lyster, Patricia M. (81)
McBride, Lois and Walter (82)
Marks, Copeland H. (83)
Marvin, Grace (84)
Mattera, Joanne (85)
Meilach, Dona Z. (86)
Meltzer, Marilyn (87)
Moorman, Theo (88)
Morrow, Mable (89)
Nisbet, Jacquetta (90)
Noble, Judith G. (91)
Nottingham, Walter G. (92)
Nyquist, Janet (93)
O'Shaughnessy, Marjorie (94)
O'Sullivan, Sallie (95)
Painter, Hal (96)
Papish, Norma (97)
Paque, Joan Michaels (98)

TEXTILES (continued)

Handweavers Guild of America 79
Pauli, Karen (99)
Pendleton, Mary (100)
Pennington, Beth (101)
Piranian, Louise (102)
Platus, Libby (103)
Pocock, Sylvia (104)
Pohlmann, Marjorie F. (105)
Porcella, Yvonne (106)
Posner, Sally (107)
Proctor, Richard M. (108)
Rabinowe, Victoria (109)
Ray, Gale (110)
Reed, Mrs. Curtis (111)
Regensteiner, Else (112)
Reiss, Zenaide (113)
Riccardi, Mary Elinor (114)
Riis, Jon Eric (115)
Robinson, Irma F. (116)
Rodwell, Marianne S. (117)
Rushfelt, Joy M. (118)
Russell, Joan (119)
Sager, Cindy (120)
Saltzman, Joan Reid (121)
Schroeder, Philis Alvic (122)
Senungetuk, Joseph E. (123)
Shawley, Stephen D. (124)
Shimkunas, Susan L. (125)
Slickpoo, Allen P., Sr. (126)
Snow, Lee Erlin (127)
Someroski, Mel (128)
Sreenivasam, Elsa M. (129)
Stack, Lotus (130)
Stein, Judith (131)
Sykora, Merle H. (132)
Tacker, Sylvia and Harold (133)
Taylor, Janet Roush (134)
Temple, Mary (135)
Thomason, Roger K. (136)
Thompson, Margaret (137)
Thurston, Stephen (138)
Tonken, Winifred M. (139)
Towner, Naomi Whiting (140)
Trumble, Merta Sue (141)
Turner, Alta R. (142)
Van Dommelen, David B. (143)
Van Gelder, Lydia (144)
Voiers, Leslie C. (145)
Waller, Irene (146)
Walling, Marie (147)
Weaver, Ken (148)
Weigle, Palmy (149)
Weltge, Sigrid (150)
West, Virginia (151)
Westfall, Carol D. (152)
Wilson, Jean (153)
Wittenberg, Barbara (154)
Wollenberg, Jackie (155)
Yacopino, Phyllis (156)
Zien, Kathleen L. (157)
Znamierowski, Nell (158)
Zotto-Beltz, Mary Ann (159)
Maryland, University of 106
Pennsylvania State University 151
Schwartz, Alice M. (32)
Reid Interiors 164
Reid, Charlotte (2)
Saint Cloud State University 168
Sykora, Merle H. (69)
Southwestern Louisiana, University of 174
Kelly, Heather C. (54)

THEATER

Auburn University 16
Harrison, A. Cleveland (29)
California State University, Fullerton 29
McPherson, Michael L. (146), (309)
Odle, D. Richard (311)
Tait, Miriam C. (43), (313)
Contemporary Forum 42
Drew University 52
Barry, Paul (3)
Occhiogrosso, Frank V. (61)
Duquesne University 54
East Carolina University 56
Loessin, Edgar (12)
Eastern Illinois University 57
Gabbard, Lucina P. (23)
Free Southern Theater 70
O'Neal, John (1)
Keedick Lecture Bureau, Inc. 97
Eder, Richard (20)
Hawkens, Betty Jo (28)
Hayes, Peter Lind (29)
Wright, Bob (72)
Marquette University 105
Price, Michael J. (24)
Siettman, James P. (26)
Northeastern Illinois University 142
Hesler, Richard (37)
Robinson, Edward A. (74)
Walker, Robert (92)
Pennsylvania State University 151
Grove, Ellis (289)
Podium Management Associates, Inc. 154
Bullins, Ed (4)
Roth, Wolfgang (22)
Puget Sound, University of 159
Berry, J. Raymond (10)
Herlinger, Ilona (27)
Martin, Jacquie (40)
Roussin, Ramon (54)
Somerville, Thomas F. (62)
Queen's University 160
Robertson, Roderick (16)
Saint Cloud State University 168
Kendall, Robert D. (34)
Southwestern Louisiana, University of 174
Hoch, Stewart (48)
Speaker's Bureau of Philadelphia 176
Cunningham, Dennis (29)
Haynes, Trudy (46)
Horwitz, Murray (49)
Temple University 181
Drummond, Caroline (81), (139)
Villanova University 214
Helmetag, Charles H. (66)
Virginia Polytechnic Institute and State University 216
Distler, P.A. (32)
Siemoneit, Martin A. (112)
Washington, University of 218
Wilson Celebrities, Lola 225
Richman, Peter Mark (30)
Wallace, Paul (39)
Women's Classical Caucus 227
Clayman, Dee Lesser (7)
Gebhard, Elizabeth R. (14)
Hartigan, Karelisa (19)
Kohler, Frances Coulborn (25)
Rossi, Mary Ann (39)
Trachy, Carol Law (48)

TIME MANAGEMENT

East Carolina University 56
Carroll, Diane (95)
Eastern Illinois University 57
Dow, Ruth (15)
Florida Association of Realtors 65
Jacobson, Alan W. (32)
Moore, Steven A. (44)
Marquette University 105
Staudacher, Joseph M. (13)
Pennsylvania State University 151
Ambruster, David L. (35)
Calamidas, Alec (38)
Ciervo, Arthur (67)
De Wald, Samuel C. (39)
Mathews, H. Lee (48)
Success Leaders Speakers Service 180
Anderson, Howard M. (3)
Douglass, Merrill E. (46)

TIME MANAGEMENT (continued)

Time Life and Lee, Inc. 182
Virginia Polytechnic Institute and State University 216
Crump, Michael W. (27)
McCollum, Robert H. (76)

TRAFFIC SAFETY

Auburn University 16
Brown, David B. (9)
Champion Spark Plug Company 33
East Carolina University 56
King, Alfred (84)
Schlick, John (85)
Marquette University 105
Ishii, Thomas K. (119)
National Association of Fleet Administrators, Inc. 120
Pennsylvania State University 151
Suloff, Charles E. (263)
Southwestern Louisiana, University of 174
Bonnette, Richard M. (12)
Temple University 181
Snider, H. Wayne (243)
Union Electric Speakers Forum 189
United States National Transportation Safety Board 207
Villanova University 214
Schorr, David J. (88)
Virginia Polytechnic Institute and State University 216
Spray, Richard A. (121)

TRANSACTIONAL ANALYSIS

California, Irvine, University of 27
McCann, James K. (7)
Marquette University 105
Dotson, Virginia (77)
Pennsylvania State University 151
Lewis, Blake D., Jr. (46)
Success Leaders Speakers Service 180
Coats, Jeff (32)

TRANSPORTATION
See also: AUTOMOBILES; AVIATION; POSTAL SERVICE; RAILROADS; TRAFFIC SAFETY

Auburn University 16
Horton, George B. (36)
California, Irvine, University of 27
Hollinden, Al (39)
Carnegie-Mellon University 31
Baumann, Dwight M. (40)
Delta Nu Alpha Transportation Fraternity 46
Duquesne University 54
Marquette University 105
Bakr, Mamdouh (116)
Yoo, Chai Hong (121)
Murray State University 117
DeVine, John W. (17)
Pennsylvania State University 151
Abler, Ronald (183)
Chan, Y. (290)
Dahir, Sabir H. (291)
Larson, Thomas D. (292)
McCauley, Bert J. (293)
Weber, H.E. (295)
Saint Cloud State University 168
Hortis, Theophanis (29)
Johnson, James C. (31)
Southwestern Louisiana, University of 174
Moffat, Joseph F. (74)
Vodraska, Walter C. (90)
Success Leaders Speakers Service 180
Wilsman, Leo G. (192)
Temple University 181
Snider, H. Wayne (243)
Trans World Airlines 186
Union Electric Speakers Forum 189
United States Department of Transportation 203
United States National Transportation Safety Board 207
Villanova University 214
Schorr, David J. (88)
Schuster, James J. (89)
White, Theodore H. (90)
Virginia Polytechnic Institute and State University 216
Dickey, John W. (31)
Spray, Richard A. (121)
Whitelaw, Robert L. (143)
Washington, University of 218

TRAVEL
See also: TRAVEL FILMS

American Institute for Exploration 4
Allen, Ruthann (1)
Alley, John (2)
Bank, Ted P., II (3)
Kitchen, Herman (4)
Ransom, Jay Ellis (6)
Auburn University 16
Schroeder, Charles G. (72)
California State University, Fullerton 29
Earick, Arthur D. (135), (159), (314)
Fasheh, Issa I. (216), (225), (318)
Kalupa, Frank B. (4), (122), (318)
Kaye, Alan S. (5), (16), (38), (128), (163), (218), (228), (319)
McLaren, Robert B. (321)
Odle, D. Richard (11), (148), (322)
Weightman, Barbara A. (8), (22), (167), (325)
Weinzweig, Marjorie S. (326)
Zeltzer, Allen M. (327)
Forrest, Martin A. 69
Baker, Norman (1)
Bjerre, Jens (2)
DuBois, Jean Louis (3)
Jones, Dewitt (4)
Kefford, Michael (5)
Kern, Richard (6)
Lange, George (7)
Litton, Martin (8)
Muller, Kal (9)
Mundus, Frank (10)
Paling, John (11)
Payne, Roger (12)
Sterling, Tom (13)
Walker, Theodore (14)
Waterman, Stanton (15)
Hutaff, Charles 83
Doney, James (3)
Keedick Lecture Bureau, Inc. 97
Sullivan, Walter (62)
Thomas, Lowell (64)
Lecture Services, Inc. 100
Furbay, John H. (1)
Geary, Phillip (2)
Lewis Program Service, Ann 103
Robbins, Roland (6)
Marquette University 105
Pambookian, Hagop S. (23)
Maryland, University of 106
Murray State University 117
Jacks, Lloyd P. (137)
Keeslar, Suzanne M. (138)
Keller, Howard H. (139)
Koenecke, Alice (140)
Lubachko, Ivan S. (141)
Schanbacker, Eugene M. (142)
Northeastern Illinois University 142
Gonzalez, Rodrigo C. (34)

TRAVEL (continued)

Pennsylvania State University 151
Botdorf, Ruth (264)
Dickinson, Winifred (296)
Erwin, Stuart (297)
Lynch, Catherine M. (298)
Perry, William L. (299)
Pierucci, Francis (300)
Seward, D.M. (11)
Ward, Marjorie E. (301)
Puget Sound, University 159
Bauska, Barry (7)
Phillips, John W. (48)
Roesler, Ned 166
Roesler, Ned (1)
Saint Cloud State University 168
Hagen, Owen (21)
Phillips, Mary H. (61)
Southwestern Louisiana, University of 174
Rense, William C. (82)
Speaker's Bureau of Philadelphia 176
Cooper, Dolores (27)
Success Leaders Speakers Service 180
Frost, Ralph W. (58)
Trans World Airlines 186
Washington, University of 218
Western Washington University 223
Critchfield, Howard J. (32)
Harder, K. Peter (33)
Hildebrand, Francis (34)
Paulus, Ingeborg (36)
Schwartz, Maurice (37)
Wilson Celebrities, Lola 225
Linker, Halla Gudmundsdottir (24)
Sargent, Wyn (35)

TRAVEL FILMS

Associated Film Artists 15
Borden, Chris (1)
Francisco, Clay (2)
Jay, John (3)
Lark, Ed (4)
Wolfgang, Ken (5)
Douglas Management 51
Douglas, Neil (1)
Fame Limited 59
Armstrong, Ken (1)
Bjerre, Jens (2)
Butler, Willis (3)
Gerstle, Ralph (4)
Johnson, Irving M. (5)
Jones, Dewitt (6)
Jones, Doug (7)
Litton, Martin (8)
Madsen, Bill (9)
Mentes, Matthew and Sherilyn (10)
Nichols, Frank (11)
Pederson, Harry (12)
Reddy, Dick (13)
Roberts, John (14)
Roney, Bob (15)
Stockdale, Bill (16)
Taylor, Charles (17)
Walker, Theodore (18)
Iowa Mountaineers, Inc. 91
Memphis State University 110
Booth, John N. (1)
Bumiller, Ted (2)
Dodson, Sid (3)
Franklin, Ralph (4)
Gerstle, Ralph (5)
Hagar, Jonathan (6)
Meyers, Howard (7)
Moore, William (8)
Nichols, Frank (9)
Parrott, Alton (10)
Perrigo, Lucia (11)
Roberts, John (12)

U

UNITED NATIONS
See also: NATIONAL DEFENSE; PEACE

Auburn University 16
King, Nelson B. (45)
Nelson, Daniel J. (59)
California State University, Fullerton 29
Qureshi, Naimuddin (63), (330)
Drew University 52
Cowell, David A. (20)
Rhone, Richard S. (75)
Simon, Douglas W. (87)
Eastern Illinois University 57
Faust, John R. (19)
Keedick Lecture Bureau, Inc. 97
Melady, Thomas Patrick (42)
Leigh Bureau 102
Hottelet, Richard C. (14)
Scali, John (28)
Pennsylvania State University 151
Carr, Marion M. Odell (65)
Murty, Vedula N. (251)
Southwestern Louisiana, University of 174
Beckman, William C. (4)
Villanova University 214
Logue, John J. (54)

UNITED STATES
See also: ALASKA; EASTERN UNITED STATES; HAWAII; SOUTHERN UNITED STATES; UNITED STATES HISTORY; WESTERN UNITED STATES

American Party 6
Anderson, Tom (1)
Shackelford, Rufus (3)
Douglas Management 51
Douglas, Neil (1)
Drew University 52
Bicknell, John W. (7)
Simon, Douglas W. (87)
Duquesne University 54
Fame Limited 59
Jones, Doug (7)
Stockdale, Bill (16)
Taylor, Charles (17)
Glendale Federal Savings and Loan Association 75
Carlson, Kenneth A. (1)
Intercollegiate Studies Institute, Inc. 85
Herberg, Will (12)
Kuehnelt-Leddihin, Erik Von (18)
Pfaltzgraff, Robert L., Jr. (28)
Keedick Lecture Bureau, Inc. 97
Duke, Angier Biddle (18)
Duke, Mrs. Angier Biddle (19)
Magidoff, Nila (40)
Miles, Leland (43)
Leigh Bureau 102
Rumsfeld, Donald (26)
Salisbury, Harrison (27)
Lewis Program Service, Ann 103
Robbins, Roland (6)
Marquette University 105
Sokolnicki, Alfred J. (27)
Mid West Program Service, Inc. 112
McFarland, Kenneth (85)
Guyer, Tennyson (50)
Terzian, Carl (121)
Murray State University 117
Johnson, Jack B. (100)
National Committee for Responsible Patriotism 125

UNITED STATES (continued)

Wiley, Charles (1)
National Speakers Bureau, Inc. 135
Agronsky, Martin (1)
Bergsten, Fred (6)
Delaney, R.E. (14)
Janeway, Eliot (31)
McFarland, Kenneth (42)
Wilson, Heartsill (59)
Northeastern Illinois University 142
Singleton, Gregory H. (78)
Pennsylvania State University 151
Barton, Michael (214)
Zelinsky, Wilbur (184)
Podium Management Associates, Inc. 154
Edwards, Douglas (8)
Kuralt, Charles (15)
"Pride in America" Company 155
Cahill, George F. (1)
Saint Cloud State University 168
Johnson, David C. (30)
Lieberman, Harold (42)
Southwestern Louisiana, University of 174
Millet, Jeremy (72)
Speaker's Bureau of Philadelphia 176
Bierbauer, Charles (15)
Temple University 181
Adams, Ernestyne James (256)
Galper, Jeffry (263)
Keto, Clement T. (28)
Lapsansky, Emma (268)
Stivers, Eugene H. (146), (272)
Union Electric Speakers Forum 189
United States Department of Defense 193
University Speakers Bureau 211
Novak, Michael (6)
Villanova University 214
Betz, Joseph (73)
Losoncy, Thomas A. (6)
Regan, Daniel T. (75)
Virginia Polytechnic Institute and State University 216
Sherman, Arnold A. (111)

UNITED STATES HISTORY
See also: LOCAL HISTORY

American Institute for Exploration 4
Kitchen, Herman (4)
Auburn University 16
Davis, Neil O. (15)
California State University, Fullerton 29
Hansen, Arthur A. (139), (160), (333)
Namasaka, Boaz N. (82), (194), (261), (337)
Rietveld, Ronald D. (338)
Duquesne University 54
East Carolina University 56
Gowen, Robert J. (91)
Eastern Illinois University 57
Hamand, Lavern M. (28)
Hockman, Dan (35)
Maurer, David J. (56)
Titus, Charles (91)
Williams, Glenn D. (96)
Lewis Program Service, Ann 103
Owen, Lewis (5)
Marquette University 105
Berens, John F. (60)
Murray State University 117
Burke, Robert L. (66)
Elder, Harvey L. (67)
Hammock, James W., Jr. (69)
Lawson, Hughie G. (71)
Strohecker, Edwin C. (75)
Valentine, Robert (76)
Venza, J. Riley (77)
Northeastern Illinois University 142
Frederick, Duke (27)
Morton, Joseph C. (63)
Sochen, June (80)
Pearl Harbor Survivors Association, Inc. 149
Pennsylvania State University 151
Barton, Michael (214)
Franz, George W. (216)
Griffith, Cyril E. (217)
Hauser, Robert E. (218)
Price, J. Lorell (219)
Richman, Irwin (257)
Riforgiato, Leonard R. (221)
Wolf, George D. (222)
Podium Management Associates, Inc. 154
Brown, Robert (3)
Puget Sound, University of 159
Brubaker, David (16)
Roosevelt Association, Theodore 167
Gable, John A. (1)
Kraft, Mrs. Harold (2)
Southwestern Louisiana, University of 174
Brasseaux, Carl A. (14)
Conrad, Glenn R. (19)
Green, Joe L. (38)
Millet, Jeremy (72)
Rice, Lawrence (83)
Speaker's Bureau of Philadelphia 176
Katen, Tom (56)
Temple University 181
Bennett, Douglas (259)
Ershkowitz, Herbert (262)
Haller, Mark H. (264)
Heinrichs, Waldo (265)
Miller, Robert (269)
Viewpoint Speakers Bureau 213
Foner, Philip (3)
Heisler, Ed (4)
Novak, George (8)
Villanova University 214
Heitzmann, William Ray (57), (69)
Niosi, Jerome J. (58), (62)
Virginia Polytechnic Institute and State University 216
Sherman, Arnold A. (111)
Western Electric Company 222
Western Washington University 223
Brewster, Laurence W. (2)
Buckland, Roscoe L. (3), (26)

UNIVERSITIES
See: COLLEGES AND UNIVERSITIES

URBAN AFFAIRS
See also: COMMUNITIES; LAND USE

Auburn University 16
McCord, R. Warren (54)
California State University, Fullerton 29
Earick, Arthur D. (52), (135), (159)
Carnegie-Mellon University 31
Tarr, Joel A. (13)
Contemporary Forum 42
Duquesne University 54
East Carolina University 56
Hankins, W.W. (101)
Hooks, Edgar W. (80)
Wardrep, Bruce (22)
Intercollegiate Studies Institute, Inc. 85
Anderson, Martin (1)
National Speakers Bureau, Inc. 135
Gallup, George, Jr. (21)
Northeastern Illinois University 142

URBAN AFFAIRS (continued)

Gilpatric, C. Edward (33)
Kiang, Harry (50)
Pennsylvania State University 151
Hand, Irving (226)
Summers, Luis Henry (148)
Saint Cloud State University 168
Lofgreen, Harold A. (43)
Simon Fraser University 171
Hurst, Michael Eliot (48)
Socialist Party, USA 172
Zeidler, Frank P. (12)
Southwestern Louisiana, University of 174
Johnson, David C. (51)
Manuel, David P. (70)
Temple University 181
Claflen, George L., Jr. (78) (260), (335)
Ershkowitz, Herbert (262)
Haller, Mark H. (264)
Johnson, Lane J. (134), (222)
Schmidt, Arthur (240)
Transier, Lee (248)
Weiler, Conrad (254), (275)
Villanova University 214
Schorr, David J. (44)
Virginia Polytechnic Institute and State University 216
Dickey, John W. (31)
Garrett, J.C. (42)
Goldfield, David R. (43)
Washington, University of 218
Western Washington University 223
Monahan, Robert L. (14)
Women's Classical Caucus 227
More, Judith de Luce (32)

V

VALUES
See also: ETHICS AND MORALS; SOCIAL RESPONSIBILITIES

Auburn University 16
Foy, James F. (21)
California State University, Fullerton 29
McLaren, Robert B. (116), (241)
East Carolina University 56
Dunn, Patricia (43)
Eastern Illinois University 57
Lauda, Donald P. (46)
Intercollegiate Studies Institute, Inc. 85
Van Den Haag, Ernest (35)
Vivas, Eliseo (36)
Marquette University 105
Horgan, James D. (118)
Metz, Donald L. (21)
Mid West Program Service, Inc. 112
Haggai, Tom (52)
Murray State University 117
Taylor, John (58)
Northeastern Illinois University 142
Hostetler, Frank C. (39)
Pennsylvania State University 151
Beck, Edward S. (161)
Mathews, H. Lee (48)
Roy, Rustum (272)
Santulli, Michael A. (157)
Tomezsko, Edward S.J. (273)
Puget Sound, University of 159
Albertson, Robert G. (1)
Hoyt, Milton (32)
Saint Cloud State University 168
Montgomery, Terry (50)
Southwestern Louisiana, University of 174
Werner, Jan (94)
Success Leaders Speakers Service 180
Harrison, Lillian K. (78)
Temple University 181
Legos, Patricia M. (113)
Rappaport, Margaret M. (292)
Virginia Polytechnic Institute and State University 216
Andrew, Loyd D. (2)
Pitt, Joseph C. (95)
Whittier College 224
Beukema, Phil (2)

VETERINARY MEDICINE

Auburn University 16
Bailey, Wilford S. (4)
Robertson, B.T. (69)
Virginia Polytechnic Institute and State University 216
Bell, Wilson B. (7)
Cherry, Jerry A. (18)
Huff, Arden N. (57)
Oyler, J.M. (90)
Talbot, Richard B. (127)

VOCATIONS
See: CAREERS

W

WASTES AND REFUSE

Auburn University 16
Askew, Raymond S. (2)
Leppert, Alfred M. (50)
Food Processing Machinery and Supplies Association 67
Gilde, L. (13)
Manwaring, Robert T. (22)
Marquette University 105
Kipp, Raymond J. (120)
National Solid Waste Management Association 133
Hanneman, Richard L. (1)
Hill, Michael (2)
Johnson, Charles A. (3)
Nowers, Phil (4)
Wingerter, Eugene J. (5)
Pennsylvania Electric Company 150
Good, Cynthia D. (4)
Pennsylvania State University 151
Johnston, Richard G. (128)
Lieb, John A. (154)
McCarthy, Gregory J. (130)
Roy, Rustum (272)
United States Environmental Protection Agency 204

WATER SPORTS

California, Irvine, University of 27
Reinhart, Carl (13)
California State University, Fullerton 29
Hanauer, Eric S. (138), (302), (316)
East Carolina University 56
Sharf, Ray (86)
Eastern Illinois University 57
Hadwiger, Kenneth E. (27)
Fame Limited 59
Johnson, Irving M. (5)
Keedick Lecture Bureau, Inc. 97
Lindbergh, Jan Morrow (38)
Marquette University 105
DeRoche, Robert J. (113)
Miller Agency, Gilbert 113
Gowdy, Curt (1)

WATER SPORTS (continued)

National Water Well Association 136
Hunt, Joel (18)
Northeastern Illinois University 142
Braun, Vern (10)
Creely, Daniel (18)
Gilbert, R.L. (31)
Pennsylvania State University 151
Fletcher, Peter W. (304)
Southwestern Louisiana, University of 176
Wagner, Lou (117)
Temple University 181
Barone, Marian T. (2)
Leahy, Robert (5)
Offenbacher, Elmer L. (7), (279)
Slook, Thomas H. (10)
Virginia Polytechnic Institute and State University 216
Lee, John A.N. (68)
Prince, William (98)
Swift, George W. (126)
Telionis, D.P. (130)
Washington, University of 218
Western Washington University 223
Hildebrand, Francis (30), (34)

WEATHER

See: METEOROLOGY

WEIGHT REDUCTION

See: PHYSICAL FITNESS

WESTERN UNITED STATES

Associated Film Artists 15
Lark, Ed (4)
Eastern Illinois University 57
Atkins, Ferrel (3)
Krause, Paul (43)
Fame Limited 59
Jones, Dewitt (6)
Litton, Martin (8)
Mentes, Matthew and Sherilyn (10)
Nichols, Frank (11)
Roney, Bob (15)
Forrest, Martin A. 69
Jones, Dewitt (4)
Litton, Martin (8)
Walker, Theodore (14)
Memphis State University 110
Nichols, Frank (9)
Northwest Mining Association 143
Pattee, Eldon (10)
Weissenborn, Albert E. (14)
Pennsylvania State University 151
Zervanos, Stam M. (302)
Puget Sound, University of 159
Brubaker, David (16)
Roesler, Ned 166
Roesler, Ned (1)
Western Washington University 223
Buckland, Roscoe L. (3)

WILDERNESS

Auburn University 16
Schroeder, Charles G. (72)
Eastern Illinois University 57
Atkins, Ferrel (3)
Northwest Mining Association 143
Pattee, Eldon (10)
Pennsylvania State University 151
Masteller, Edward (308)
Roesler, Ned 166
Roesler, Ned (1)
Saint Cloud State University 168
Partch, Max (56)
Washington, University of 218
Western Washington University 223
Monahan, Robert L. (35)

WILDLIFE

American Institute for Exploration 4
Kitchen, Herman (4)
California State University, Fullerton 29
Thomas, Barry (75), (277), (324)
Eastern Illinois University 57
Moll, Edward O. (59)
Forrest, Martin A. 69
Paling, John (11)
Mid West Program Service, Inc. 112
Burch, Monte (18)
Murray State University 117
Schanbacker, Eugene M. (142)
Northeastern Illinois University 142
Beaver, Joseph C. (2)
Pennsylvania State University 151
Hunt, Edward E., Jr. (208)
Keiper, Ronald R. (305)
Lindzey, James S. (306)
McKinstry, Donald (307)
Masteller, Edward (308)
Ondik, Michael (309)
Zervanos, Stam M. (302)
Saint Cloud State University 168
Partch, Max (56)
Southwestern Louisiana, University of 174
Cordes, Carroll (20)
Keiser, Edmund D., Jr. (53)
Temple University 181
Baenninger, Ronald (281)
Virginia Polytechnic Institute and State University 216
Cross, Gerald H. (26)
Washington, University of 218

WOMEN

Ahmadiyya Movement in Islam, Inc. 1
Ahmad, Imam Masud (2)
American Teilhard Association for the Future of Man 11
Brennan, Anne (2)
Auburn University 16
Burkhart, Mary Quinn (10)
Vallarino, Lidia M. (81)
California, Irvine, University of 27
Curiel, Ramon (2)
Kloke, Eloise E. (41)
Wildman, Helen D. (47)
California State University, Fullerton 29
Hynes, Teresa M. (35), (142), (285), (308), (335)
Jaskowski, Helen M. (202), (336)
Lynn, Joanne M. (145)
McPherson, Michael L. (146), (309)
Namasaka, Boaz N. (6), (337)
Nyaggah, Mougo (7)
Schatz, Madeline F. (182), (222)
Weinzweig, Marjorie (251)
Wood, Corinne S. (168)
Childbirth Without Pain Education Association 36
Hommel, Flora (1)
Contemporary Forum 42
Booth, Heather (148)
Cobb, Gloria (149)
Eichelberger, Brenda (150)

WOMEN (continued)
Evans, Mari (151)
Janeway, Elizabeth (152)
Payne, Ethel (153)
Rosner, Charlotte (154)
Sanchez, Sonia (155)
Schrager, Joyce (156)
Sochen, June (157)
Drew University 52
Gillespie, Joanna Bowen (32)
Phillips, Joy (68)
Weimer, Joan S. (97)
Duquesne University 54
East Carolina University 56
Baker, Ira (61)
Faulkner, Janice Hardison (131)
Gross, Tennala A. (126)
Gulati, Usha T. (119)
Webber, Edith (132)
Eastern Illinois University 57
Anderson, Eulalee L. (1)
Butts, Bob (8)
Ferguson, Karen (20)
MacLaren, Fred (54)
Wild, Rebecca Smith (95)
Feminist Karate Union 62
Bateman, Py (1)
Mitten, Suzanne (2)
Reid, Kathy (3)
First Federal of Broward 63
Florida Association of Realtors 65
Frost, Robert J., III (20)
Intercollegiate Studies Institute, Inc. 85
Van Den Haag, Ernest (35)
International Wages for Housework Campaign - Canada 90
Ramirez, Judith (1)
Keedick Lecture Bureau, Inc. 97
Bergen, Polly (6)
Javits, Marion (32)
Martin, Leila (41)
Leigh Bureau 102
Ephron, Nora (9)
Marquette University 105
Asp, Carolyn (123)
Gabryshak, Betty J. (124)
Richards, Marva A. (125)
Schreier, James W. (84)
Shiely, Catherine (126)
Swan, Jane D. (86)
Massachusetts Bar Association 107
Mid West Program Service, Inc. 112
Bishop, Paula (11)
Dimond, Mary Clark (33)
Peale, Ruth Stafford (99)
Schlafly, Phyllis (113)
Murray State University 117
DeVine, John W. (17)
Kumar, Frederick L. (97)
Wells, Jane Freeman (28)
National Speakers Bureau, Inc. 135
Kleiman, Carol (37)
National Water Well Association 136
May, Judy (21)
Northeastern Illinois University 142
Caron, Josiane (14)
Crawford, Margo (17)
Flory, Joyce Ann (25)
Lucas, James A. (57)
Parker, Bettye J. (66)
Pedroso, Angelina (68)
Sochen, June (80)
Pennsylvania State University 151
Allison, Priscilla H. (61)
Beatty, John W. (88)
Caputo, Richard (205)
Frankforter, A. Daniel (215)
Graham, Robert J. (234)
Harris, Dorothy V. (276)
Haskin, Lynn Martin (72)
Kummer, Mary J. (142)
Labbauf, Abbas (153)
Mandle, Joan D. (167)
Raneri, Marietta (114)
Richman, Irwin (257)
Rocco, Emma S. (31)
Schlow, Marthamae C. (200)
Seward, D.M. (11)
Singh, Jane M. (241)
Smith, Mary (242)
Podium Management Associates, Inc. 154
Korda, Michael (14)
Puget Sound, University of 159
Bowman, Dawn (14)
Sloman, Carol L. (60)
Wagner, Esther (65)
Wilson, Roberta A. (69)
Rainier National Bank 162
Saint Cloud State University 168
Andrzejewski, Julie (4)
Craik, Mary B. (9)
Halton, Patrice Hoffman (23)
Medler, Meredith A. (46)
Reha, Rose K. (62)
Simon Fraser University 171
Savage, Margaret (29)
Schwarz, Abby (54)
Socialist Party, USA 172
Hermann, Beatrice (4)
Southwestern Louisiana, University of 174
Brabant, Sarah C. (13)
Cain, Joan A. (15)
Harris, Patricia A. (42)
Kelly, Heather C. (54)
Lebas, Sherry (64)
Werner, Jan (94)
Speaker's Bureau of Philadelphia 176
Cole, Charles C. (26)
Spokespeople 178
Hudiburgh, Kayren (1)
Lenaerts, Sue (2)
McGlachlin, Kay (3)
Stevens Model and Merchandising Agency, Patricia 179
Stevens, Patricia (2)
Success Leaders Speakers Service 180
Dorrance, Rose (44)
Walters, Dorothy M. (186)
Temple University 181
Brodey, Jean L. (49), (320)
Cote, Mary Louise (158), (321)
Gilpin, Nancy E. (52), (322)
Isard, Eleanore S. (221), (284), (323)
Kidder, Louise (324)
Kutney, Andrew J. (224), (325)
LaVallee-Williams, Marthe (109), (326)
Lockhart, Barbara D. (6), (327)
Morse, J. Mitchell (234), (305)
Smith, Rita (31), (328)
Yadav, Bibhuti S. (330)
University Speakers Bureau 211
Callahan, Sidney (2)
Viewpoint Speakers Bureau
Jaquith, Cindy (5)
Jenness, Linda (6)
Reed, Evelyn (11)
Wright, Pat (18)
Villanova University 214
Betz, Joseph (83), (92)
Bloom, Rosalind (8), (93)
Niosi, Jerome J. (85), (94)
Schorr, Beverly (95)
Virginia Polytechnic Institute and State University 216
Cheney, Anne (19)
Haines, Kenneth H. (47)
Harper, Laura J. (48)
Washington, University of 218
Western Washington University 223
Robinson, Mary (19), (38)
Whittier College 224
Olson-Prather, Emelie (12)

WOMEN (continued)

Wilson Celebrities, Lola 225
Calvet, Corinne (5)
Canary (6)
Chagall, David (8)
Linker, Halla Gudmundsdottir (24)
Manning, Patricia (27)
Women's Classical Caucus 227
Barnard, Sylvia (2)
Broege, Valerie (4)
Deagon, Ann (9)
Dickison, Sheila K. (10)
Fisher, Elizabeth A. (12)
Gordon, Diane R. (16)
Hallett, Judith P. (18)
Hartigan, Karelisa (19)
Katz, Phyllis B. (21)
Keuls, Eva C. (22)
King, Joy K. (24)
Kohler, Frances Coulborn (25)
Lefkowitz, Mary R. (28)
Loomis, Julia W. (29)
Morgan, Kathleen (33)
Pomeroy, Sarah B. (37)
Rossi, Mary Ann (39)
Trachy, Carol Law (48)
Wiggers, Nancy (54)
Women's Martial Arts Union 228
World Modeling Association 229
Tolman, Ruth (5)

WRITING

Auburn University 16
Hitchcock, Walter B., Jr. (34)
Drew University 52
Berke, Jacqueline (6)
Eastern Illinois University 57
Pearson, Sharon (66)
Shank, Kathlene (79)
Marquette University 105
Mitchell, Robin C. (46)
Pehowski, Marian (68)
Northeastern Illinois University 142
Husain, Asad (41)
Parker, Bettye J. (66)
Pennsylvania State University 151
Adams, James D. (231)
Curtis, Anthony R. (68)
Mullen, Sharman Stanic (79)
Raneri, Marietta (114)
Puget Sound, University of 159
Roussin, Ramon (54)
Saint Cloud State University 168
Lawson, Jonathan (39)
Otto, Don H. (53)
Southwestern Louisiana, University of 174
Fackler, Herbert V. (29)
Villanova University 214
Schwarz, John H. (47)
Virginia Polytechnic Institute and State University 216
McMillion, Martin B. (78)
Snipes, Wilson (117)

Y

YOGA
See also: PHYSICAL FITNESS

Eastern Illinois University 57
Sharaway, H.S. (80)
Pennsylvania State University 151
Beatty, John W. (88)
Speaker's Bureau of Philadelphia 176
Nelson, Alma (82)
Temple University 181
Yadav, Bibhuti S. (300), (307)

YOUTH
See also: CHILDREN; COLLEGE STUDENTS

California, Irvine, University of 27
Binder, Arnold (37)
Kent, Deryck R. (30)
California State University, Fullerton 29
Corey, Gerald F. (88), (231)
Nyaggah, Mougo (7)
Prinsky, Lorraine E. (62), (288), (346)
Sadovszky, Otto J. (102), (246), (349)
Contemporary Forum 42
Duquesne University 54
Intercollegiate Studies Institute, Inc. 85
Tonsor, Stephen J. (33)
National Speakers Bureau, Inc. 135
Linkletter, Art (40)
Pennsylvania State University 151
Bleiler, Mae D. (20)
Brown, Robert E. (163)
Mandle, Joan D. (167)
Ongiri, David O. (111)
Perrine, James L. (170)
Riforgiato, Leonard R. (221)
Puget Sound, University of 159
Wagner, Esther (65)
Wallrof, Paul (67)
Saint Cloud State University 168
Johnson, Milford (32)
Southwestern Louisiana, University of 174
Oliver, James R. (79)
Success Leaders Speakers Service 180
Luchs, Fred E. (110)
Qubein, Nido (141)
Temple University 181
Hetznecker, William (282)
Meyer, Harold (17), (181)
Villanova University 214
Bush, David F. (77)
Washington, University of 218
Youth Liberation Press, Inc. 231
Autin, Al (1)
Autin, Diana (2)
Hefner, Keith (3)

Z

ZOOLOGY
See also: ANIMALS; MARINE LIFE; WILDLIFE

Drew University 52
Rohrs, Harold Clark (80)
Mid West Program Service, Inc. 112
Clarke, Gary K. (24)
Virginia Polytechnic Institute and State University 216
Roberts, James E. (102)